THE
ENCYCLOPEDIA
OF
AMERICAN
MUSIC

ALSO BY EDWARD JABLONSKI

The Gershwin Years, with Lawrence D. Stewart
Harold Arlen: Happy with the Blues
George Gershwin
The Knighted Skies
The Great War
Flying Fortress
Warriors with Wings
Ladybirds: Women in Aviation
Airwar
Atlantic Fever
Seawings
Double Strike
Doolittle—A Biography, with Lowell Thomas
A Pictorial History of the World War II Years
A Pictorial History of the World War I Years
Man with Wings

'THE ENCYCLOPEDIA OF AMERICAN MUSIC'

Edward Jablonski

Doubleday & Company, Inc., Garden City, New York   1981

Library of Congress Cataloging in Publication Data

Jablonski, Edward.
The encyclopedia of American music.

Discography: p. 579
Includes index.
1. Music—United States—Dictionaries.   I. Title.
ML100.J28   781.773′03′21
ISBN: 0-385-08088-3
Library of Congress Catalog Card Number 77–16925

For
WANDA and JERRY SIMPSON—
1116½ and all that

Love's the only thing that matters.
IRA GERSHWIN, 1931

Foreword

This encyclopedia is, I must confess, a labor of love. Ever since I was a youngster in Michigan, where I was introduced to that special something we call American music through the discovery of the works of George Gershwin, I have been hearing, reading about, and studying our American music. In its more formal phase this study was done under two delightful teachers, Henry Cowell and John Tasker Howard. Both were pioneers in their unique ways. Cowell ranged through virtually the whole world of sound and produced compositions of stunning variety. John was truly the first historian-musician to attempt to set down a comprehensive history of American music. Some Johnny-come-latelies have criticized him for various reasons but never fail to follow the path he had prepared for them.

Since this is rather an individualistic, perhaps eccentric, compilation, some general description of its approach and format might prove useful. The book is broken down chronologically. I have divided the history of American music into seven, admittedly arbitrary, periods (although they work reasonably well, I think). Each section opens with a short historical introduction in which the general character of musical activity is indicated, certain key composers mentioned along with other pertinent social-cultural currents. This is followed by the individual entries, listing alphabetically the composers, organizations, certain works, publications, and terminology in use during the time. In this way the musicians active during a certain time, their works and, in some instances, their language, are grouped together, not unlike a standard history but more succinctly and, because the entries are alphabetized, with sometimes quite curious contiguity.

A word about dates of composition, especially since some of my dates may not correspond with those listed in other musical reference books. To a great extent—at least 90 percent of the time—the dates in this work are the dates of *completion* of the composition (and as often as possible checked with the composer). When all else has failed, the date of the *first performance* may have to serve. This is not always ideal, for some compositions by important composers had to wait years before a performance—and it was only then that the work was registered and dated. When there is a lag of a year or so from date of completion to public performance, there is no important problem, of course. But in the case of Charles Ives, for example, we have a composer who had stopped writing at about the beginning of the 1920s, only to enjoy many first performances in the '40s and after. If we are interested in a composer's development, it is often illuminating to learn that he may have composed, or completed, his *Symphony No. 3* after a well-received performance of a *Symphony No. 4*. So, wherever possible, to repeat: dates of works are dates of completion.

How did I decide in which section, say, a composer's entry belongs? Rather capriciously, I must admit. I added thirty to his birth year and that decided the section in which the entry appeared. This may not be very tidy, but neither is making it in the world of music. Most of our major composers were known, even recognized, by the time they reached thirty. In general, however, this method worked. For example, Aaron Copland arrived on the American musical scene indelibly during the '20s; his major biographical entry belongs in the section on that period. But he did not stop composing and continued to produce major works long after the '20s fizzled into the Depression. So Copland appears in later section introductions and in entries such as *Piano Variations, Appalachian Spring,* etc. The General Index in the appendix lists all entries alphabetically without regard to section.

I am not certain that everyone who should be entered, is. But I have tried. I consider this work a beginning, not the last word. Some composers enjoyed a moment of glory, performances, even recordings, then seemed to have simply vanished from histories, even from comprehensive reference works. Some I have been able to find through various means. Others are still missing (I have a pile of "undeliverable" letters). Perhaps we can fill these inadvertent gaps in (one hopes!) future printings. We can also remedy the no doubt countless errors—all mine—that we will be hearing about. The errors that have been eliminated must be credited to the copy editing of Elaine Chubb and Glenn Rounds. I would like to add my thanks to the indexer, David Beams.

Although the gamut of American music is encompassed in this single volume: "serious music" from "Adams and Liberty" to Ellen Taffee Zwillich, jazz, folk music, popular song, the lyric theatre, film music, rock, etc., some readers may detect a paucity of popular performers. Since the emphasis of this work is on the creative contributor, the pop singer, no matter how much an adored superstar, is a *re*-creator. It is true, the composer-lyricist needs the singer, but without the song, who needs the singer?

Many special people have helped me compile this encyclopedia over the past several years. Its most consistent champion has been my friend, and remarkably patient editor, Harold Kuebler; I thank him for his enthusiasm, encouragement, suggestions, and understanding. My late wife Edith shared all these same qualities with Harold and assisted me, as she had with all previous books, through about 3 quarters of this encyclopedia. Our children (in order of appearance), David Ira, Carla Leonore, and Emily Rose, were lovingly generous with ideas, suggestions, and research assistance. Without them I know I could never have completed this book.

A long-standing personal gratitude is owed to the dedicatees, Wanda and Jerry Simpson, of Saginaw, Mich., who took me under their cultured wing so long ago. I must thank Ira Gershwin, of Beverly Hills, Calif., who nurtured the dreams and talent of a high school boy who wrote long, scrawly letters on three-ring notebook paper. I treasure his letters, gifts, and warm friendship. Harold Arlen has been more than a close friend during the writing of this book; his counsel, wit, and affection have helped more than I can say. To Irving Berlin I owe thanks for his interest and concern while the book was being compiled and, not the least, for a most touching painting.

Kay Swift, Emily Paley, Mable Schirmer, and Frances Gershwin Godowsky, all of New York, were frequently present (at times in spirit, but present) while the work was in progress. Their interest and their illuminating questions were most helpful and I borrowed from them shamelessly. Their generous presence in a time of need will never be forgotten.

Warm friendship as well as musical assistance were tendered by pianist Kevin Cole, Bay City, Mich.; pianist-organist Eric Smith, Sydney, Australia; pianist-songwriter Lynn Lavner, Brooklyn, N.Y.; poet-writer Carol Sokoloff, Toronto, Canada; violinist-gadfly Amy Parrent, Bay City, Mich.; and writer-curator Lynn Shapiro.

Support and suggestions were given by my sister Mary Birdsall, Saginaw, Mich.; painter-sculptor the raffish Robert Bolles and the lovely Anne Kenny, New York, N.Y.; Dr. Norman and Shelly Dinhofer, Brooklyn, N.Y.; Jean and John Bartel, Bay City, Mich.; dear friends Kay and Stanley Green, Brooklyn, N.Y.; Diane and Art Hofmeister, Cockeysville, Md.; Alan Dashiell, Trenton, N.J.; my collaborator Lawrence D. Stewart, Beverly Hills, Calif.; longtime friends Milton A. Caine and his lovely Elaine who publish the fine *American Record Guide,* Melville, N.Y.; and James E. Murray, New York, N.Y.

Thanks also to Donna Bassi, American Society of Composers, Authors and Publishers (ASCAP), New York, N.Y.; Frank Campbell, Music Division, the New York Public Library, New York, N.Y.; Annemarie Franco, American Federation of Musicians, New York, N.Y.; Earl W. Gross, Department of Music, Vassar College, Poughkeepsie, N.Y.; Carter Harman, Composers Recordings, Inc., New York, N.Y.; Richard Jackson, Americana Collection, the New York Public Library, New York, N.Y.; Michael Kerker, (ASCAP), New York, N.Y.; Burt Korall, Broadcast Music, Inc., New York, N.Y.; Karl Kroeger, Moravian Music Foundation, Winston-Salem, N.C.; Elizabeth Lessard, Librarian, Manchester Historical Association, Manchester, N.H.; Gerald Marks, formerly of Saginaw, Mich., now ASCAP; Barbara Narendra, Yale University, New Haven, Conn.; Carol J. Oja, musicologist, Brooklyn, N.Y.;

Andrew Raeburn, consultant, New York, N.Y.; Don L. Roberts, Head Music Librarian, Northwestern University, Evanston, Ill.; and Karen Sherry, Executive Editor, *ASCAP in Action,* ASCAP, New York, N.Y.

Special mention must be made of new friends Steve Heisler, Jimmy Connelly, Wendy Bromley, and Amy Warner; they gave me *Shelter* through a most difficult time.

EDWARD JABLONSKI
New York, N.Y.
March 1980

Contents

THE
ENCYCLOPEDIA
OF
AMERICAN
MUSIC

I

In the Beginning
(ca. 1620–1750)

Early chroniclers of American music decried its paucity, ignoring the reality that our first ancestors did not voyage to the American continent to make music; they had other goals in mind.

Undoubtedly a number of musicians had signed aboard the various exploratory ships that initially touched the continent before actual colonization began. Perhaps sailors sang chanteys and, if the crews were accompanied by a clergyman, some form of religious music may have been sung on land and sea. Long before the English established any colony in America, it is possible that the very first settlers, the Indians, heard Spanish, French, as well as English music. It is possible, too, that those first seekers heard the Indians sing but would hardly have recognized what they heard as music. Before the Pilgrims, in short, no true musical exchange occurred, no roots were planted. The American musical heritage would have to begin, in a sense, from the beginning.

The Pilgrims (or Puritans—the terms being interchangeable: generally, however, the Pilgrims are those Puritans who settled at Plymouth and the more puritanical Puritans at Massachusetts Bay) have suffered a bad press. They have been stigmatized as either nonmusical or completely antimusical. The standard view was expressed by Rupert Hughes in *Famous American Composers* (1900). The Puritans, he claimed, "had a granite heart, and a suspicious eye" —not ear?—"for music." He also indicated that "we have had more hindrance than help from our heritage of English music, in which there has not been a master of the first rank, Purcell and the rest"—dismissing such as Byrd, Dowland, Weelkes, et al.—"being after all brilliants of lesser magnitude . . . The influences that finally made American music are chiefly German," he concluded, voicing yet another prevalent view (of which more later).

Hughes was not alone, nor was he the last, to set out on both wrong feet. On the other hand, he did not benefit from quite as much hindsight (and more diligent research) as those historian-musicologists who came after.

He makes no mention of the fact that a year before the Puritans arrived at Plymouth, 20 Negro "Indentured Servants" (unlike their white counterparts, they were indentured for life) were delivered at Jamestown, Virginia, which had been inhabited by Englishmen since 1607. The impact of the 2 musical cultures has not been recorded and Hughes did not deem it worth mentioning. But even in his time he conceded that the "folk-music of the negro slaves is most frequently mentioned as the right foundation for a strictly American school," a fallacy he placed at the door of "Dr. Antonín Dvořák."

"The vital objection, however," he goes on, "to the general adoption of negro music as a base for an American school of composition is that in no sense is it a national expression." (A few pages before he has not objected to "a national school" and "its necessary and complete submission to German influences.") Negro music, Hughes maintained, was not "even a sectional expression, for the white Southerners among whose slaves this music grew, as the people of the North, have always looked upon negro music as an exotic and curious thing. Familiar as it is to us, it is yet as foreign a music as any Tyrolean jodel or Hungarian czardas."

Another Establishment attitude was revealed as late as 1931 in Daniel Gregory Mason's *Tune In, America,* in which he warned against influence of another group of early arrivals that had come to the then New Amsterdam in 1654. "The insidiousness of the Jewish menace to our artistic integrity," he wrote, "is due to the speciousness, the superficial charm and persuasiveness of Hebrew art, its violently juxtaposed extremes of passion, its poignant eroticism and pessimism."

The curious examples of early standard authorities whose followers repeated their views merely dramatizes the fact that important influences upon what would emerge as "American" music 3 centuries or so later were present, if not recognized, from the earliest colonization. One of the Pilgrims, Edward Winslow, casually observed of the band that crossed the Atlantic in 1620, "we refreshed ourselves, after tears, with singing of psalms, making joyful melody in our hearts, as well as with voice, there being many of our congregation very expert in music . . ."

Having turned their backs on their native England over religious issues, they, after a stay in Holland, came to the New World bringing their music—and, as Winslow indicated, some musicians with them. It is unlikely that many, if any, instruments could be jammed into the tiny *Mayflower*. That left only the human voice.

The psalms they sang were carried in their memories or in their psalter, Ainsworth's *The Book of Psalms.* Another current collection was the older Sternhold and Hopkins Psalter, from which Ainsworth had lifted a few of the tunes for his psalm collection "Englished both in Prose and Metre." These were sung in the churches without instrumental accompaniment, the consensus being that such assistance smacked of popery.

That instruments were used in private homes and secular songs—many the classic folk songs of Britain—were sung is documented although not as thoroughly as the psalm tradition. Two early students of Harvard left records of music-making and ballad singing which date the practice to the middle of the 17th century and probably earlier. Researchers have found evidence of musical instruments from around the same time. The traditional view of the nonmusical Pilgrim/Puritan, even with such minimal evidence, must be revised.

Having established that our British musical ancestors were, indeed, music lovers, it is also true that their religiosity rather narrowed musical tastes; the bulk of the music consists of psalms and hymns. The music was appropriated from English, French, and German sources. Despite those members in the various congregations who were "very expert in music," there appears to be no record of a Puritan composer in New England ca. 1630 or so. There arose, however, dissatisfaction with the psalters they had brought with them among the Puritans of the Massachusetts Bay Colony, who believed that Sternhold and Hopkins had taken serious liberties with the translation of the psalms. So it was that some 30 "pious and learned Ministers" prepared a new psalter, *The Whole Booke of Psalmes Faithfully Translated into English Metre*. Printed at Cambridge, Mass., in 1640, it was the first book to be published in America and was popularly known as the *Bay Psalm Book*. In time the book would supplant the "foreign" psalters throughout New England.

As before, the settings were the old traditional tunes (although several editions of the *Bay Psalm Book* were published before music was included). It was found, too, that the original compilers were long on piety and short on poetry and that their metrical renderings of the psalms, however faithful to the Hebrew originals, were not always singable. Time, too, dimmed memories as the old tunes were forgotten or distorted. Musicianship, too, deteriorated and ministers complained, to use one example, of how "the tunes are now miserably tortured, and twisted, and quavered, in some churches, into a horrid Medly of confused and disorderly Noises."

The practice of "lining-out" (already in use in England) was introduced: assigning a precentor the task of singing a line or 2 of a psalm solo, to be followed by the congregation's attempting to repeat the melody as faithfully as possible. If the deacon knew music, or the various melodies, all would be reasonably well. Others, perhaps with better or worse musical memories or skills, might remember the tunes differently. However much the traditionalists, or musical reformers, attempted to reestablish the original tunes, congregations appeared to be inclined toward changing them—one reverend reformer despaired because of the "strange Metamorphoses" the original tunes had undergone when left to the "Mercy of every unskilful Throat." The tunes were passing through a phase that later folklorists would recognize: the introduction of unconscious variations. However, one man's variation was another's deterioration and New England clergymen initiated a movement to reform the presentation of music in churches which led to the publication of instruction books in music, the first being the Reverend John Tufts's *An Introduction to the Singing of Psalm-Tunes* (ca. 1721).

This, and the instruction books that followed, would form the base on which musical education in America would grow, particularly in New England. Esthetic battle lines were drawn between the Regular way (i.e., the traditional manner) and the "Common" way of singing psalms; the former being the preference of the clergy-led Gentry and the latter that of "the Country People," who disturbingly were introducing "Depravations and Debasements" into psalmody with their untutored improvisations.

So it may be stated roughly that in the century since the Pilgrims came ashore at Plymouth, music and music-making (but not the creation of original music) had come to the New World. In this period also music-making had declined (depending on the point of view: singing by note or rote); a book of psalms had been printed and, ultimately, a book of music instruction. While the Puritans were not quite as hard on music as certain early musicologists had drawn them, they could hardly have passed as patrons of the art—especially if it involved instruments (of the devil). The New World, ca. 1620–1720, inspired no New Music, especially in New England.

Less is known about the colonies to the south, particularly in reference to the colonization period. Although slaves had arrived at Jamestown as early as 1619, the musical influence, if any, has not been documented. Nor has that of the Dutch, who arrived in New Amsterdam in 1624, the Swedes at Fort Christian, now Wilmington, Del., in 1638, the German Mennonites in Pennsylvania, 1683, the French in Mississippi, 1699, as well as the Spanish, who came to Florida in 1565 and were in New Mexico in 1598. Where settlements of any permanence were established, it might be assumed that religions also flourished (how else rationalize the killing off of the "savage heathens"?) and, along with them, their music.

Pennsylvania, because of its German settlers, became a rich colonial musical center, although not as influential as the British colonies. Among the earliest of the Protestant sects that left a musical record were a group of Pietists that came to Pennsylvania in 1694 under the leadership of Johannes Kelpius. They sang psalms, hymns, and anthems, although, unlike the Puritans to the north, they did not reject the use of instruments in worship music. It is believed that Kelpius, in 1705, compiled a collection of sacred music, *The Lamenting Voice of the Hidden Love . . . ;* there have been claims, unsubstantiated, that he also composed some of the 10 tunes. If true, this would make Kelpius, although foreign-born, the first known composer on American soil, an academic distinction.

Another self-contained colony was established at Ephrata (Lancaster County), Pa., in 1732 by the German Seventh-Day Baptist, Conrad Beissel. Music was important in the worship services in what became known as the Ephrata Cloister and Beissel not only produced a set of musical principles, he also composed the music for the hymns, most of which was gathered in a collection entitled *Song of the Lonely and Forsaken Turtle Dove . . .* (1746). As a composer, Beissel appears to have been self-taught and his creativity was more functional and primitive than musically memorable. Because of this, Beissel, too, has been nominated by some as "the first composer in America."

The same year, 1732, that Beissel established the Ephrata Cloister, a group calling themselves "Unitas Fratem" had left their native Bohemia (more precisely Moravia) and sought refuge in Georgia; by 1741 the colony moved northward to Pennsylvania and founded, among others, the colony named Bethlehem. The Moravians were remarkably musical and their music-making was not confined to vocal and religious music. Within 3 years of the establishment of the settlement, the Collegium Musicum (a performance society) was formed and choral, orchestral, and chamber works were heard (many for the first time in America), among them compositions by several Bachs, Handel, Haydn, and Mozart.

The Moravians did not reject instruments, imported many, and encouraged the building of organs in another settlement, Lititz, Pa. This very musical community, in time, produced a number of fine musicians and native-born composers. One of the earliest Moravian composers was Jeremiah Dencke, a German emigrant who did not arrive in Bethlehem until 1760 (properly belonging to the following section); there he composed the first sacred music for voice and instruments (soprano, strings, and organ) in the United States. Although the music of the Moravians was known in colonial times (it made an impact on the young British minister John Wesley on a visit to America and therefore upon Methodist hymnology), the insularity of the colony precluded a wider American influence. Of interest is the fact that among the original settlers at Bethlehem was one Andreas der Mohr (Andrew the Negro). Within 6 years more free blacks had joined the community; their musical activities are not known, but considering the musical level of the Moravians, their musical skills were undoubtedly excellent.

This period is characterized by a number of "firsts," beginning with the publication of the *Bay Psalm Book*. There are records of the various first organs: the first imported into New England, owned by Thomas Brattle of Boston and which he procured some time in 1711. The Smithsonian Institution has an organ that may have arrived in Virginia as early as 1700; an organ was definitely used in the Gloria Dei Church (Swedish Lutheran), Philadelphia, in 1703. The pastor at Gloria Dei was the musically inclined, and German-born, Justus Falckner. The English painter–organ maker Christopher Witt emigrated to Philadelphia a year later and, besides painting a portrait of Johannes Kelpius, built the first organ in America. The first native American to build an organ was Boston-born and Harvard-educated Edward Bromfield, Jr., who built the instrument for the Reverend Thomas Prince of Boston in 1745.

The first known public concert was given by one Peter Pelham—a *"concert of Music* on Sundry instruments"—in Boston on Dec. 30, 1731. The following April the *South Carolina Gazette* announced a "Consort of Musick at the Council Chamber, for the Benefit of Mr. Salter" in what was then known as Charles-Town, for the first recorded public concert in that city (3 years later Charleston was also the scene of the first opera performance in America. The English ballad opera *Flora, or Hob in the Well* was presented at the Courtroom on Feb. 18, 1735). New York, which was backward musically as compared to New England, Charles-Town, and some of the Pennsylvania settlements, did not have its first public concert of record until 1736. On Jan. 21 there was a *"Consort* of Musick, Vocal and Instrumental, for the benefit of Mr. Pachelbel, the Harpsichord Part performed by himself. The songs, Violins and German Flutes by private Hands." Son of the more celebrated Johann (an early influence on Bach), Karl Theodor came to America ca. 1730. An organist, Pachelbel spent some time in Boston, Newport, R.I. (where he was organist at Trinity Church), then to New York City, and eventually to the musically richer Charles-Town, where he served as organist in St. Philip's Church (1738) until his death in 1750.

Following Pachelbel's initial "consort," musical life, or the keeping of its records, became more active in New York. A kind of musical theatre flourished also, the favorites generally being the imported English "ballad operas," often as not a collection of songs and dances. Among the various imports was John Gay's *The Beggar's Opera* (1728), with music added (i.e., borrowed) and arranged by Christopher Pepusch. A mocking social satire, Gay's opera was also a parody of Italian opera of the period, with special attention given to Handel. The first American performance of *The Beggar's Opera* is believed to have been given in New York on Dec. 3, 1750. It became extremely popular and played several American cities. The tone and structure of the ballad opera might easily cause it to qualify as the grandfather of musical comedy.

From the landing of the Pilgrims until the production of *The Beggar's Opera,* a period of little more than 100 years, music had been brought to the New World and nurtured. Though the new land had not encouraged the creation of original music, that which had come with the early settlers had undergone subtle permutations. A tradition of musical education had begun and, in time, the first American composers would arrive upon the scene.

"AINSWORTH PSALTER" The popular name for a collection compiled by the Reverend Henry Ainsworth (ca. 1570–1622) entitled *The Book of Psalms: Englished both in Prose and Metre. With Annotations, opening the words and sentences, by conference with other scriptures. By H. A.* The book was prepared by Ainsworth for the Puritans who had gone to Holland, where it was published in Amsterdam in 1612 and brought to Plymouth 8 years later.

The Ainsworth Psalter contains all 150 psalms metrically "Englished" to fit 39 different tunes. Ainsworth explained his selection of the melodies so: "The singing-notes . . . I have taken from our former Englished Psalms, when they will fit the measure of the verse. And for the other long verses I have taken (for the most part) the gravest and easiest tunes of the French and Dutch Psalms." In other words, some of the melodies were borrowed from an earlier English collection (which in turn had also borrowed from French sources) by Sternhold and Hopkins (1562) as well as from the French and German—an international collection.

The selection of tunes was exceptional. Some are still sung, although perhaps not in the original form, today—"Old 100th" and "Old 124th," for example. Ainsworth's tune selection, as well as his wide choice of meters, 15 in all, produced a freer, folk-like, collection as compared with the more staid, 4-square, conventional psalter style that favored the 4-line "common meter" (q.v.). The melodies, most of them cast in sturdy old modes, were endowed with a fresh rhythmic variety which undoubtedly made them more interesting to sing than the standard psalms.

The psalter was popular among the Pilgrims, went through several editions (the last in 1690), and was used at Plymouth until 1692 when the colony merged with the Massachusetts Bay Colony, which had depended on less influential psalters, the Ravenscroft as well as the Sternhold and Hopkins, until dissatisfied members of its clergy banded together to produce their own psalter in 1640.

BAY PSALM BOOK Published at Cambridge, Mass., in 1640 under the editorship of 30 "pious and learned Ministers," the *Bay Psalm Book* is notable as the first book to be published in the colonies. Although invariably referred to by its popular title, the book in its first edition was called *The Whole Booke of Psalmes Faithfully Translated into English Metre. Whereunto is prefixed a discourse declaring not only the lawfulness, but also the necessity of the Heavenly Ordinance of Singing Scripture Psalms in the Churches of God.*

Although a committee of 30 has been mentioned, it would appear that the bulk of the work was done by the Reverends Thomas Welde and John Eliot, of Roxbury, Mass., and the Reverend Richard Mather of Dorchester. Their translations, which attempted to adhere more closely to the original Hebrew of the Bible than the psalters then in use in Massachusetts Bay, and England as well, depended on the tunes from the Sternhold and Hopkins psalter and Thomas Ravenscroft's *The Whole Book of Psalms* (London, 1621). The "learned Ministers" chose to use only 6 meters to fit their rhymed translations, most of them (112 of the 150) in Common Meter (q.v.). Ainsworth had used 15 meters and Sternhold and Hopkins 17. Musical variety was sacrificed to textual fidelity. As Mather pointed out in the preface to the first edition, "If . . . the verses are not always so smooth and elegant as some may desire or expect, let them consider that God's Alter needs not our pollishings . . ." He explained that "we have respected a rather plaine translation, and so have attended Conscience rather than Elegance, fidelity rather than poetry, in translating the Hebrew words into English language, and David's poetry into English meetre: that so we may sing in Sion the Lord's songs of praise according to his own will; until hee take us hence, and wipe away all tears, and bid us entre our masters joye to sing eternall Halleluiahs."

No music was printed in the first edition of the *Bay Psalm Book*, the assumption being that the references to the old tunes of the previous psalters would suffice. Also, it was unlikely that there were facilities for engraving music at the time in America. Despite Mather's justifications, when a 3rd edition was published in 1651 (the 2nd was an English reprint of the first edition), the versification was, in fact, "pollished" by Henry Dunster (the first president of Harvard) and Richard Lyon, including the title, which was changed to *The Psalms Hymns and Spiritual Songs of the Old and New Testament faithfully translated into English metre for the use, edification, and comfort of the saints in publick and private, especially in New England*. Again, no printed music was included, but the revision of the texts rendered the psalms more singable and perhaps more poetic and became the standard form of the *Bay Psalm Book*.

Of the extant copies, the first edition in which music was included was the 9th (1698); it is probable that an earlier but still undiscovered edition with music may exist. The music, crudely printed in the back of the book, totaled a mere 13

melodies, 9 in common meter. These had been lifted from several editions of John Playford's *An Introduction to the Skill of Musick* (London, 1623–1686) and known by the popular titles "Oxford," "Litchfield," "Low Dutch," "York," "Windsor," "Cambridge," "St. David's," "Martyrs," "Hackney," "119th Psalm Tune," "100th Psalm Tune," "115th Psalm Tune," and "148th Psalm Tune." These were generally known melodies and could be applied to the words which fit their particular metrical structure.

The musical settings, in 2 parts, were for soprano and bass and occupied 5 pages of the *Bay Psalm Book*. The words were printed separately from the music, although each tone of the melodies was identified by the then standard "fasola" (q.v.) notation. The tunes were further identified by their popular names, i.e., "York," "Oxford," as above.

The *Bay Psalm Book* was widely used in the colonies and went through at least 27 printings (it being published in 1762) and even achieved popularity in Britain, where it prospered into 1754, when the 18th edition was published. In the New World, and particularly New England, it served as the basic source of music for over a century until supplanted by the more sophisticated Tate and Brady *New Version of the Psalms of David* (1696) of British origin (to America ca. 1713). The efforts of the New England reformers who complained about the degeneration of the singing in the churches forced the *Bay Psalm Book* out of circulation by the middle of the 18th century. By this time, however, the sturdy simplicities, as well as subconscious improvisational accretions to the original 13 tunes, had had an influence on a new generation of American-born incipient music makers.

BEISSEL, CONRAD (1690–1768) Born in Eberbach, Germany, Johann Conrad Beissel was 30 years old when he emigrated to America in 1720, settling first in Boston. Son of a baker, he was scantily trained in music and, although he played the violin, appears to have been self-taught. In 1732 Beissel moved to Pennsylvania, which had become the refuge of many religious sects from Central Europe, several of them German-speaking. Beissel founded a community in Lancaster County at Ephrata devoted to the beliefs of the Seventh-Day Baptists (Dunkards). Music was essential to worship in the community and, to a great extent, it was Beissel, self-taught as he was, who supplied much of it. He established the Ephrata Cloister (q.v.), formed a well-disciplined choir and provided them with strict rules (even touching on diet, depending on the type of voice, etc.) and with literally hundreds of hymns and other biblical musical settings.

Undaunted by his lack of a formal musical education, Beissel began composing around 1743, making up his own rules of harmony as he went along. He published a *Dissertation on Harmony* as well as collections of hymns, most notably the bulky (750 hymns) *Der Gesang der einsamen und verlassenen Turtel-Taube nämlich der Christlichen Kirche* ("The Song of the Solitary and deserted Turtle-Dove, namely, the Christian Church"). Compilation was completed in 1746 and the book was published the following year without music. In the Foreword, Beissel set forth his concepts of harmony—which were primitive. Beissel's methods, while serving the uses of the Ephrata Cloister, had little impact outside the colony. His work, however, was known by early distinguished Americans, among them Washington, the composer Francis Hopkinson, and Benjamin Franklin, whose beautifully printed copy of *Turtel-Taube* is in the Library of Congress.

COMMON METER In psalmody the arrangement of the 4 lines of a verse into 8 syllables in the first line, 6 in the 2nd, 8 in the 3rd, and 6 in the 4th. In turn, the melodies were structured accordingly and any verse set to Common Meter could be sung to appropriate melodies. Generally, each note in the tune of a psalm was set to a syllable of the text. For example, the 23rd Psalm, set to the Low Dutch Tune, is set in the 8/6/8/6 of Common Meter in the *Bay Psalm Book*:

> The Lord to me a shepheard is:
> Want therefore shall not I,
> Hee in the foulds of tender grass
> Doth make me down to ly.

Common Meter was so called because it was just that, the most frequently used, particularly in the Sternhold and Hopkins *Psalter* and the *Bay Psalm Book*. Other meters included "6/6/8/6" (Short Meter), "8/8/8/8" (Long Meter), doublings, i.e., 8-line stanzas of the Common and Long Meters and the more complex "6/6/6/6/4/4/4/4" (Hallelujah Meter). Irregular meters of various patterns and different stanza groups were designated by numbers, i.e., 6-8s meant 6 lines, 8 beats (or syllables) to the line. The *Bay Psalm Book* employed 6 meters for its 150 psalms: Common (112), Short (14), Long (15), Hallelujah (6), 6-8s (2) and 12-8s (1); this compares with the 17 different meters used in the earlier Sternhold and Hopkins *Psalter*—a decided dwindling of the repertory.

EPHRATA CLOISTER The religious community founded by Johann Conrad Beissel (q.v.) in 1732 in Lancaster County, Pa. Ephrata was settled by German-speaking émigrés. Beissel took over the musical life, which was most active, of Ephrata, creating a rich musical center and hundreds of homespun hymns. Beissel was succeeded by one Peter Miller. The primitive music of the Cloister had little influence beyond its own confines.

"FASOLA" NOTATION A system in which the tones of a melody are indicated by a letter: FSLM, fa, sol, la, and mi, used as a mnemonic teaching device replaced later by the more familiar do-re-mi system). The practice of using letters to indicate pitch and tones dates back to the ancient Greeks, although it was believed by some writers in the 18th century to have been "first contrived by Reverend Mr. [John] Tufts (q.v.)." Tufts is credited with producing the first American music textbook, but the system of indicating tones by letters was used in the 9th edition of the *Bay Psalm Book,* in Playford, and was widely used in England. The use of syllables to identify tones is also called solmization. Eventually in America fasola notation evolved into "shape notes," which will be covered in the next section.

FLORA, OR HOB IN THE WELL The first known "opera," actually a ballad opera, to be performed in America (Charleston, S.C., in 1735). The author and composer are unknown although the farce had been presented in its longer, original, form in England as *Country Wake, or Hob in the Well* and published in 1729 (it has been attributed to Colley Cibber). Contemporary descriptions give the impression that *Flora* was a rather loosely constructed vaudeville show, a one-acter with various "entertainments" interspersed. The advertisement for the first performance which appeared in the *South Carolina Gazette* for the week of Feb. 8, 1732, read in part: *On Tuesday the 18th inst. will be presented at the Courtroom the opera of "Flora, or Hob in the Well," with the Dance of the two Pierrots, and a new Pantomime entertainment, called the Adventures of Harlequin Scaramouch . . .* Although *Flora* might be historically important, marking as it did the opening of Charleston's first theatrical season, and the first recorded introduction of the ballad opera into America, its influence was minimal.

GYNECANDRICAL DANCING A form of dancing that aroused certain New England theologians to the publication of tracts condemning the practice as a "Scandalous Immorality." Increase Mather in his *An Arrow Against Profane and Promiscuous Dancing* (1684) denounced gynecandrical dancing as "sinful" and defined it as "that which is commonly called *Mixt* or *Promiscuous Dancing,* viz. of Men and Women . . . together."

HYMN A sung expression of praise or thanks to the Deity. Although hymns are popularly associated with Christian religions, some of the earliest known ones were sung to Apollo in Greece ca. 150 B.C. Early Christians applied the term to all their religious music, but eventually it referred to those sacred songs with man-made words as differentiated from the God-given (i.e., biblical) psalms and canticles. Fundamentalists rejected any but scriptural texts, restricting songs of worship generally to psalms. This persisted in England until the 18th century, affecting the musical bias in the British colonies. Among the rejects would have been the chorales written by, or attributed to, the Protestant reformer Martin Luther (1483–1546). Hymn singing gradually came to be tolerated, depending on the religious whims of the monarch, and hymnbooks began to appear early in the 18th century. An important hymnal was published by the Englishman John Wesley (q.v.) whose work was influenced by the Moravians (q.v.). It was entitled *A Collection of Psalms and Hymns* and was published in the then Charles-Town, S.C., in 1737. Wesley's hymnal was popular both in the colonies and in England.

INTRODUCTION TO THE SINGING OF PSALM TUNES The first musical textbook published in America; a response to the demand by New England's clergymen for an improvement in congregational singing and musicality in general. Musicologists have not always agreed on the date of the *Introduction's* first edition, but the most feasible is early January 1721, when "A Small Book containing 20 Psalm Tunes, with Directions how to Sing them, contrived in the most easy Method ever yet Invented, for the ease of Learners, whereby even Children, or People of the meanest Capacities, may come to Sing them by Rule . . ." was announced for publication by "Samuel Gerrish Bookseller; near the Brick Church in Cornhill, Price 6d." It was not until later, when the booklet went through several printings, that the advertisements credited the author, the Reverend John Tufts (q.v.) of Newbury, Mass. By the extant copy of the 5th edition, the number of tunes had grown to 37 (in 3 parts; the first edition contained a single line of music) and the author was acknowledged.

Tufts's modest text, its reprint in Irving Lowens' *Music and Musicians in Early America,* covers less than 3 pages and explains the rudiments of music—pitch, time, and other helps for singing the songs properly. Tufts borrowed his tunes from several of the standard sources, including Playford—the originality of the music, of course, was not the issue. In later editions Tufts appropriated from other sources, including yet another American textbook, Thomas Walter's (q.v.) *The Grounds and Rules of Musick Explained,* published in the same year as Tufts's pamphlet.

A notable feature of Tufts's *Introduction* was the use of the fasola system (q.v.) of notation for the melodies. Instead of the standard musical notation he placed the letters of the system on the appropriate line or space on the musical staff, thus setting the pitch; the time was indicated by what the author called "points," a period, a colon, or no "point" indicating the length of time any tone was held.

Tufts was often credited with devising the fasola notation system by early American musicologists. The system, however, had been in use since the mid-16th century as well as in one of his sources, Playford's *An Introduction to the Skill of Musick.*

Of no little importance was Tufts's tune selection (which included all 13 from the *Bay Psalm Book*), about half of which were still being sung in the 20th century. Not every source has been traced, and one melody, "100th Psalm Tune New," may have been composed by Tufts himself, making him yet another "first native American composer."

But Tufts was not to make his mark as a composer but as a compiler and pioneer in American musical education. His influence was felt in his time and beyond.

KELPIUS, JOHANNES (1673–1708) The leader of a group of German Pietists that settled in Pennsylvania, near Philadelphia, on the Wissahickon River. In time the group was known as the Mystics, or Hermits, of the Wissahickon. The original group, consisting of about 40, was known to have brought certain musical instruments from London. The Mystics enjoyed a reputation for musicality and Kelpius as a musician (clavichord and organ); the composition of no less than 19 hymns has been attributed to Kelpius, although with no definiteness. These are included in a manuscript collection entitled *The Lamenting Voice of the Hidden Love, at the time when She lay in Misery & Forsaken; and oprest by the multitude of Her Enemies.* Authorship is attributed to "one in Kumber" ("distress") and the date is 1705. Kelpius may have written the texts; many of the melodies have been traced to German sources. Kelpius was also associated with the Swedish Gloria Dei Church in Philadelphia, where he may have served as organist before his death.

LINING-OUT The practice in 18th-century New England churches (borrowed from Britain) of leading a congregation in psalm singing by having the tune sung first line by line by a minister, or member of the congregation, who could either read music or knew the correct melodies to the psalms. This was the practical solution to the twin problems of bad memory or musical illiteracy which tended to introduce yet another problem, depending upon the musical skill, if any, of the precentor. Interestingly, the custom of lining-out continued as a quasi-folk usage even after its original function no longer obtained.

The precentor, or deacon, who "set the tune" off pitch no doubt contributed to the congregational cacophony to which the ministers objected and which led to the reforms in music instruction, the publication of the early "how-to" books by such pioneers as Tufts and Walter and the New England singing schools that followed.

THE MORAVIANS A Protestant religious group founded by the reformer Jan Hus in 1457. Originally active in what was then known as Bohemia and Moravia, members of the sect began emigrating to the New World in 1732, when a small band arrived in Georgia. They were also known as Unitas Fratem (Unity of Brethren) but have become more generally identified as the Moravians. Although the settlement in Georgia failed, the Moravians established other settlements in the New World, the most famous being the one at Bethlehem, Pa., in 1741. Other settlements were established at other Pennsylvania sites and at Salem (now Winston-Salem), N.C. All Moravian settlements were characterized by a rich musical life, the

one at Bethlehem being especially notable.

Moravian musical activity was not confined to religious expression. Nor did they reject instruments in either sacred or secular music. Small and isolated, the community drew upon its European roots for its music and, while the Moravian musical life may have been the most sophisticated in Colonial America, its influence was necessarily confined. (However, the impression of Moravian music-making aboard a ship transporting the young minister, the Reverend John Wesley, to the colonies was profound and would have an effect on Methodist hymnology.)

Musical activity, particularly at Bethlehem, took many forms: chamber groups, orchestras, and choruses. In 1744 a musical society, *Collegium Musicum,* was founded and musical life flourished. Published music or manuscript copies were imported from Europe. Often the first American performances of music by such contemporary composers as Handel, Haydn, and Mozart, as well as lesser composers, were given in Bethlehem. One of the traditions of the colony was the performances by trombone choirs stationed on rooftops or the church tower.

Inevitably original compositions emanated from the Moravian settlements, although its creators belong properly to the section which follows. The earliest surviving Moravian music was composed by the German-born Jeremiah Dencke and dates from 1766. Other notable Moravian composers were the Dutch Johann Friedrich (later John Frederick) Peter and the American-born John Antes. To this day the Bach Choir of Bethlehem sustains the musical traditions of the Moravians.

PACHELBEL, CHARLES THEODORE (1690–1750) One of the sons of the organist-composer (and influence on J. S. Bach) Johann Pachelbel

(1653–1706). Carl Theodorus was born in Stuttgart, Germany, into a musical family; an older brother, Wilhelm, was also an organist-composer like their father and, after the latter's death, may have housed and taught Carl. He was already in his forties when he appeared on the American scene in Boston ca. 1732–33. (His one known surviving composition, *Magnificat in C Major* for Double Chorus and Continuo, was undoubtedly written before his coming to America.)

Soon after his arrival, Pachelbel was established as organist at Trinity Church, Newport, R.I., where he remained until 1735. In January of the following year he organized the first concert of which any documentation remains in New York; in 1737 Pachelbel appeared in Charleston, where he presented a concert, the first "of this kind in a publick manner in this Province . . ." At this time it was noted that there would be sung "a Cantata suitable to the occasion," although its identity remains a mystery; whether or not it was his own excellent *Magnificat* is not known. In time Pachelbel became the organist at St. Philip's Church and served in that capacity until his death in September 1750. While his American years do not appear to have inspired Pachelbel's creativity, his activities in musical life in both New York and Charleston represent the early recognition of good musicianship in the colonies.

PLAYFORD, JOHN (1623–1686) English music publisher who, though he never visited the New World nor probably ever composed a note of music, was a force in the music of Colonial America. Several of Playford's publications served as models or sources for early American music books; such collections as *The English Dancing Master* (1650, a classic compilation of secular music), *Breefe Introduction to the Skill of Musick*

(1654), and *The Whole Book of Psalms* . . . (1673), among others, were obviously used by several American writers on music, including the compilers of the *Bay Psalm Book* and Tufts's *Introduction to the Singing of Psalm-Tunes.*

PSALM Sacred song whose texts are drawn from the Book of Psalms, a practice dating back to very early Jewish and Christian ritual. The biblical texts, either newly translated from the original Hebrew or paraphrased, were set in meters (i.e., beats) and rhymed; the musical setting followed. Psalm texts invariably drew upon the Bible and were regarded as "inspired," as opposed to hymns (q.v.) with their man-made texts.

PSALTER A collection of metrical psalms in book form for use in congregational singing. The earliest known psalters date back to 16th-century France and Britain. Various editions of the latter influenced the evolution of American psalmody, among them the Ainsworth (1612), Sternhold and Hopkins (1624), Ravenscroft (1621), Allison (1599), and others.

"REGULAR SINGING" Singing by note rather than rote; a term used by the 18th-century New England reformers who hoped to improve congregational singing. Since the art of reading music had been all but lost in the 100 years or so since the first British colonies had been established in America. "Regular singing" was preferred by a group of young reformers (the most influential of whom were Harvard graduates), among them John Tufts (q.v.), Thomas Walter, and Thomas Symmes, who were joined by Cotton Mather (uncle of Walter) and Nathaniel Chauncey. In the 1720s all published attacks on "the usual" or "common" way of singing, although only Tufts managed to produce the first helpful instruction book. The clerical vituperation became rather heated in the rejection of what may well have been an incipient folk art and the writings contain pointed comments on the poor singing of "the Country People." In 1722 there was a notice of a sermon preached by the Reverend Thomas Walter in Boston on the subject "The Sweet Psalmist of Israel" under the auspices of the Society of Promoting Regular Singing, which was dedicated to "reforming the Depravations and Debasements our Psalmody labours under, In Order to introduce the proper and true Old Way of Singing."

The efforts of the true believers in "Regular Singing" did produce the first American music textbooks and, whatever can be said for untutored folk art, an improvement in American musical education; despite their efforts, of course, "the Country People" clung to their ways and preserved a rich musical counterculture.

TUFTS, JOHN (1689–1750) Born in Medford, Mass., Feb. 26, 1689, Tufts was graduated from Harvard in 1708 and became pastor at the Second Church at Newbury, Mass. Tufts was one of a group of ministers who believed that the singing in their churches had deteriorated and it was Tufts who produced an *Introduction to the Singing of Psalm-Tunes* (ca. 1721, perhaps earlier). This was the first attempt by an American to write a music instruction book. In it Tufts hoped to simplify the reading of music by adopting a system of solmization, designating the degrees of the musical scale by sounds rather than notes; in Tufts's system letters were used instead of notation but did not have much effect. Even so, Tufts's *Introduction* went through several editions, an 11th edition being published as late as 1744. Tufts appears to have resigned his ministry, after being "accused of immorality by some women in his parish," and moved to Amesbury, Mass., in 1738, became a

shopkeeper and so remained until his death there on Aug. 17, 1750.

TUNEBOOK General name for a collection of songs, originally psalms, though later collections contained also hymns, anthems, other forms, as well as music instruction. Early tunebooks were those of Tufts (q.v.) and Walter (q.v.) which were used by churches, singing societies, and the singing schools that followed in the wake of the reform movement in New England's church singing in the 1720s. The tunebooks served as a musical source for the church as well as for secular occasions in the home and field.

UNITAS FRATEM See The Moravians.

WALTER, THOMAS (1696–1725) Born in Boston, Walter was the scion of a distinguished New England family. His grandfather was the Reverend Increase Mather and his uncle, the Reverend Cotton Mather. Like them Walter was a graduate of Harvard (1713, at the age of 17); he was ordained in 1718 and became a minister at the Roxbury (Mass.) Church. A member of the New England musical reform group, Walter published his *Grounds and Rules of Musick Explained, or An Introduction to the Art of Singing by Note* in 1721, only 4 years before his death, in Roxbury, at the age of 29. Like his contemporary John Tufts, Thomas Walter was probably not a trained musician and borrowed the music for his book from other sources.

WESLEY, JOHN (1703–1791) British founder of Methodism, who, during a visit to America in 1735, discovered the music of the Moravians, which deeply impressed him. In 1737 Wesley published his *A Collection of Psalms and Hymns* (Charleston, S.C.), his first contribution to Methodist hymnology. Returning to England the following year, Wesley preached a fervent evangelism and recognized the importance of music to his cause: salvation. His influence on hymnody was profound; his brother Charles (1707–1788) was a prolific composer of hymns, among them the words of the still sung "Jesus, Lover of My Soul" and "Hark! The Herald Angels Sing." Although the Wesleys' great contribution was primarily theological, their musical efforts provide a fascinating link between the music of the Moravians and British and American Method-ist hymnology. Wesley's style of preaching attracted followers and disciples, notably George Whitefield (1714–1770), who visited America several times, drawing great throngs to hear his religious orations, and contributed to a wave of religious revivals of the latter 18th century in America known as "The Great Awakening." The movement had its beginnings in New England with the sermonizing of Jonathan Edwards, who set the scene for Whitefield's great success.

II

A Time of Revolution
(1750–1800)

The Colonies were not a musical oasis before the War of Independence, nor were they a desert. Urbanization, on a modest scale, and the eventual and gradual emergence of the wealthy merchant or landowner produced the setting in which culture could be pursued and nurtured.

There was a decided difference in the attitudes toward music, as well as the other arts, held by those whose forebears had come to the New World seeking religious asylum and those who had come in quest of wealth. Music as art, entertainment, or recreation was cultivated more readily in the South where the settlers practiced the Anglican faith; from, roughly, Philadelphia northward, the Quakers and the Puritans, while not completely antimusic, preferred their austere, unaccompanied psalms and generally condemned theatricals (which often featured music) as wicked, not worthy of the attention of good men, and wasteful of time. This was not purely a New World attitude, but one brought over by the colonists from England. The harder conditions of life in the Colonies, of course, would have underscored the Puritan's delight in much work and minimal play.

The Pilgrim proscription applied to their church music. It is now known, as it was not to some early musical historians, that members of the Puritan communities sang secular songs and even owned and performed on musical instruments. Dancing, however, mingling the sexes, continued to vex—although dancing masters had opened shop in New England before the middle of the 18th century. The clamor for the reform of crude church singing, the proliferation of tunebooks and the rise of the New England "singing school" under itinerate singing masters, both native and foreign born, served to improve the general music-making and also led to secularization of music. This evolution led to what could be called the first New England school of composers, most of them born in America. Among these American musical pioneers were William Billings, Justin Morgan, Samuel Holyoke, Lewis Edson, Supply Belcher, and Timothy Swan, to name a handful.

Perhaps the most fascinating of the first New England school was the primarily self-taught tanner-turned-composer William Billings. Not only did Billings create religious and secular songs, his work as a singing school master and author of several song collections undoubtedly had some influence on the musical scene in New England and the South. Although not the creator or only composer of the "fuging tune" (not to be confused with the classic fugue), Billings composed several "fuges" as well as choral pieces in other forms, including anthems, carols, and "Chester," one of the most popular of Revolutionary War songs.

The folkish, near primitive, compositions of the New England composers were eventually supplanted by the more elegant works of better trained composers—especially the European masters. The taste for "better" music and music-making was stimulated after the Revolution by the influx of immigrants. The homely canons and fuges of the likes of Billings were rejected and more genteel melodies, harmonies, and rhythms substituted.

The general attitude that would lead to changes in musical education, not to mention to a musical snobbery, is revealed in a New Hampshire newspaper reporting a concert commemorating the death of a local musician: "We are pleased to see a correct Musical taste growing out of the jargon which has been too long prevalent in our churches. We are glad to see the performances of Williams, of Handel, of Giardini preferred to the 'unmeaning and frivolous airs' of American authors who present nothing like 'concert of sweet sound'— nothing of the spirit of true devotion."

This attitude began spreading after the Revolution and would reach a deleterious peak by the mid 19th century. An advertisement for the final edition of *The Village Harmony* (first edition, 1795) intimated a purging of the earlier editions: "Those alterations have been made which correspond to the progressive improvement of the publick taste in Sacred Musick. A few Classical European tunes have been substituted for some of a less perfect character, and the valuable foreign musick which is retained, and which the publick has not ceased to venerate and admire, is still preserved in this collection, secure from the touch of American innovation."

This musical self-consciousness and inferiority complex set the scene for the coming of the 2nd New England School of composers/educators of the 19th century which all but obliterated the "innovative" and sturdily charming works of the first and Teutonized American music (this will be covered in the next 2 sections).

Farther south the social setting was more secular and less grim. Music, most of it if not all, was imported from Europe—nationalism was not an issue. Prerevolutionary Charleston, S.C., was regarded as a center of "social refinement" that approached that of the European capitals (by no less an observer than Edmund Burke); by 1783, when it was incorporated as a city, Charleston was the most populous (16,000) and wealthiest city in the South. Its merchants and professional men could afford the social refinements, among them music, a theatre, and dancing masters. Flourishing, it attracted professional musicians, who moved up and down the Atlantic seaboard from Charleston to Boston. Musicians found work in its theatres, playing in orchestras for concerts —and teaching the young of the wealthy.

Out of Charleston's concerts grew what would be the oldest musical organization in the United States, the St. Cecelia Society, in 1762. Instruments and singing of secular songs were not forbidden in sophisticated Charleston.

Moving northward, to Virginia, Philip Alexander Bruce, in *Social Life of Virginia in the Seventeenth Century,* provides a glimpse of the provisions for making music in certain well-appointed households: "For the amusement of guests in the house as well as of the members of the family, musical instruments were to be found in nearly all the planters' residences: there are frequent references in the inventories to the virginaal, the hand lyre, the fiddle, the violin, and also the recorder, flute and hautboy [the oboe], as part of personal estates."

Princeton graduate Philip Fithian, hired to tutor the children of Robert Carter in Westmoreland County, Va., wrote of the lively musical life in that plantation's manor. "Mr. Carter is practicing this evening on the guitar," he wrote in a letter (1774). "He has here at home a harpsichord, fortepiano, harmonica [or, rather, the armonica, a set of musical glasses], guitar, violin, and German flutes; and at Williamsburg, he has a good pipe organ. Mr. Christian, in the dancing room, teaches the children country dances and minuets . . ."

As a young law student in Williamsburg, Thomas Jefferson enjoyed the friendship of the musical governor Francis Fauquier, in whose home he met to participate "with two or three other amateurs in his weekly concerts." Jefferson, a violinist of some skill (he studied with Francis Alberti in Charlottesville and practiced "no less than three hours a day"), often joined in duets with another amateur, Patrick Henry.

"Music is invaluable," Jefferson wrote to a friend some years later, ". . . it furnishes a delightful recreation for the hours of respite from the cares of the day and lasts us through life." Our most musical president, Jefferson made his home, Monticello, a virtual music center, complete with various instruments (most imported from Britain) and a sizable collection of music as well as books on music. (George Washington enjoyed music and the theatre, though only as a listener.) No musical chauvinist, Jefferson imported the music of the time that was regarded as "good," including works of Haydn, Clementi, and Mozart. Among the collection are compositions by composers no longer heard, such as Johann Schobert, Daniel Purcell (brother of the great Henry), and Wenceslaus Wodizka. Jefferson's music library contained much chamber music for home performance, duos and solo pieces for instruments (he owned two harpsichords purchased for his daughters), and vocal music, ranging from popular airs to opera arias.

The sophisticated music lover in the Colonies, even before the Revolution, might very well be acquainted with the compositions of Handel, Haydn, and Bach (provided the latter's given names were Johann Christian or Carl Philipp

Emanuel; at the time, the father's reputation was confined to a small section of Thuringia, Germany).

Among Jefferson's extant correspondence there are many letters to and from Francis Hopkinson of Philadelphia. Like Jefferson, Hopkinson was a man of extraordinary interests and gifts and, in music, "a gentleman amateur" (in the phrase of musicologist O. G. Sonneck). Hopkinson could and did claim the distinction of being "the first Native of the United States who has produced a Musical Composition" (this in a letter to his friend George Washington). He was 22 when he composed the song "My Days Have Been So Wondrous Free," the earliest known secular song written in America, in 1759 (Billings published his first collection, *The New-England Psalm-Singer* in 1770). Another Philadelphia resident, the Reverend James Lyon (born in New Jersey), published his collection of psalms entitled *Urania* there in 1761. *Urania* was primarily a compilation of British tunes borrowed from several sources, although 6 of the 96 tunes have been attributed to Lyon. While he made no claims to precedence, Lyon, while a student at what is now Princeton University, was credited with the composition of an *Ode* 1759—the same year as Hopkinson's "My Days Have Been So Wondrous Free."

Hopkinson was a most versatile man, patriot, inventor, painter, poet as well as musician, our first Secretary of the Navy, among other official positions. In this he conjures up the figure of another music-loving Philadelphian, Benjamin Franklin, who played several musical instruments, wrote perceptively about music, refined the workings of a curious instrument called the glassychord, but better known as the armonica (Franklin's designation; but it eventually came to be known popularly as the harmonica). Franklin has even been credited with the composition of a suite for string quartet; unlikely but possible. As a printer Franklin turned out many collections of music by others. He admired the musical abilities of the Moravians, loved to sing, and often performed on his armonica for friends in his home.

Among the songs in Franklin's repertoire were such as "The Old Man's Wish" and "a little drinking song which I wrote thirty years ago" (he was in his seventies when he wrote this line) which opened with the words "Fair Venus calls: Her voice obey." It is more likely that Franklin provided new words to a known melody, a practice in which he believed and so advised his brother Peter when the latter sent Franklin a newly composed ballad.

Philadelphia's secular musical side was evident in a quite lively theatrical life, despite the general opposition by the Quakers. In April 1754 a "Company of Comedians from London" managed to obtain permission to present 24 performances provided the plays contained nothing "indecent or immoral." The group was led by Lewis Hallam and eventually became known as the Old American Company that flourished along the Atlantic seacoast cities—New York, Philadelphia, Baltimore—before settling in New York. The Old American Company's actors also doubled as singers and even tripled as dancers; music was an important factor and, if the play presented was not a musical, was performed during intermissions. Among the company's repertoire were such ballad operas as *Flora, or Hob in the Well* and the ubiquitous *Beggar's Opera*.

The Old American Company was ready to present the first American-made ballad opera in 1767, but the libretto, which satirized easily identifiable prominent Philadelphians of the time, caused pressure to be put on the author and forced a withdrawal of the work as "unfit for the stage." This "new American comic opera in two acts" was *The Disappointment: or the Force of credulity* by one Andrew Barton, Esq. (believed to be a pseudonym of Colonel Thomas Forrest, of Germantown, though there is no proof of this; no other literary or dramatic work by Andrew Barton seems to exist). Although the libretto was published, the opera was not produced and had no influence on the evolution of the American musical. Barton provided "the coarse but very witty and clever libretto," according to O. G. Sonneck, and borrowed 18 tunes for his songs which are numbered and called "airs." Of historical interest is Air IV to the tune of "Yankee Doodle." This places the "hit song" of the American Revolution in the public domain some years before the Boston Massacre and Tea Party as well as the Battle of Bunker Hill. Undoubtedly of British origin, "Yankee Doodle" was merely borrowed by the colonists in the War for Independence.

On Apr. 18, 1796, the Old American Company successfully produced what has been called the "first American opera" (O. G. Sonneck) or the first musical (Julian Mates)—the latter distinction has been generally reserved for *The Black Crook* (1866). This was *The Archers, or Mountaineers of Switzerland* with a libretto by William Dunlap and music by Benjamin Carr and it was presented at the John Street Theatre in New York City. The music was original, not appropriated "airs," but little of it has survived except an *Archer's March* and the song "Why, Huntress, Why?" English-born Carr was an important contributor to the musical life of Philadelphia, and to American music, as a publisher and as a composer.

The Carrs, including Benjamin's father Joseph and brother Thomas, were not the only foreign-born musicians to enhance the cultural life of Philadelphia after the Revolution. From Britain came Raynor Taylor, after a stay in Baltimore and Annapolis; also his student, Alexander Reinagle, a composer-musician who was also active in the music theatre in Philadelphia. What Charleston had been to music before the Revolution, Philadelphia became after. (The coming of war not only curtailed music-making in the colonies, it also discouraged the arrival of foreign-born music makers.)

War rarely inspires inspiring songs and invariably restricts musical activity. Concert life—as meager as it was—and theatrical productions were curtailed with the coming of the Revolution. British occupation of such cities as Boston, New York, Philadelphia, and Charleston reinforced the English influence on music in the colonies and, to some extent, emphasized the music of the military band. When war came, the colonist's creative energies were generally channeled into the writing of patriotic songs, the words of which were diffused throughout the Colonies via broadsides.

As in the beginning, the colonists freely borrowed from the mother country, the most famous being the tune to "Yankee Doodle," which the British troops sang derisively and which, in time, was turned on them. Incendiary pre-Revolution songs included "The Liberty Song" (to the popular British tune "Heart of Oak"), Francis Hopkinson's satirical words to the tune of "Maggie Lauder" entitled "The Battle of the Kegs," and Dr. Joseph Warren's "The New Massachusetts Liberty Song" (tune: "The British Grenadiers"). "Adams and Liberty," "The Boston Patriotic Song," with words by one Thomas Paine (not *the* Thomas Paine) appropriated the tune of "The Anacreontic Song" which, according to the original sheet music, was "Sung at the Crown and Anchor Tavern in the Strand." The original words were by Ralph Tomlinson, "late President of that Society." The song extolled the delights of "Bacchus's Vine" and "the myrtle of Venus"; in short, it was a drinking song of the Anacreontic Society. Paine adapted the tune to his revolutionary statement; within a generation Francis Scott Key would use the same tune for his "The Star-Spangled Banner," eventually the American national anthem (1931). Even "God Save the King" was permutated by the colonists, parodied to the discomfort of the British (even in 1795 setting the words to a song, "Rights of Woman") and best known today as "My Country, 'Tis of Thee." It also served as the tune to "Hail Godlike Washington," who was the subject of countless musical praises, odes, and marches.

Philip Phile, a Philadelphian of German birth, composed a *President's March* believed to have been written by the violinist-conductor for the first President's inaugural. Published in 1793, the march was popular as an instrumental piece but gained even greater popularity when words were added by Joseph Hopkinson (son of Francis) 5 years later under the title of "Hail! Columbia."

Other original songs, not dependent on earlier tunes, were composed during the period by Boston's Billings, among them 2 outstanding contributions, "Lamentation Over Boston" (the text an adaptation of the words to the 137th Psalm) and "Chester" (to which the composer set new words; the earlier version had words by Isaac Watts), perhaps the most popular patriotic song of the American Revolution. Another worthy original was Andrew Law's "attributed" musical setting of Nathaniel Niles's "The American Hero—commemorating the battle of Bunker-hill and the burning of Charlestown" entitled "Bunker-hill."

James Hewitt, a postwar immigrant from Britain, demonstrated his patriotism in "A Sonata," dedicated to Washington, entitled *The Battle of Trenton,* a characteristic descriptive period battle piece into which the composer wove such popular themes as *Washington's March* (attributed to Hopkinson) and "Yankee Doodle." Two years later (1794), Benjamin Carr, the Philadelphia publisher of *The Battle of Trenton,* arranged a number of popular airs, including *The President's March* (the one by Phile) and the ubiquitous "Yankee Doodle." Curiously, Hewitt produced *The New Federal Overture* (ca. 1797) employing practically the same tunes—a common practice at the time.

The Treaty of Paris (1783) officially ended the War of Independence, the United States of America was recognized as a nation free of British ties and dependence. While there may not have been a sudden flowering of native arts—it was the new President Washington himself who observed that "only arts of a *practical* nature would for a time be esteemed"—the once moribund theatrical life and concert activity quickened with the coming of peace. So did immigration, resulting in the arrival of numbers of foreign-born musicians who would influence the course of American musical life. They were predominantly English (William Selby, who flourished in Boston, had arrived even before the Revolution), Reinagle, Taylor, Hewitt, the Carrs, George K. Jackson; also the Dane, Hans Gram, John Christopher Moller, probably from Germany, Victor Pelissier from France, Gottlieb Graupner from Germany, et al.

On the opposite coast, in California, a musical influence of a different national coloring was established by the Spanish Franciscan missionary Junípero Serra. Serra came to California (from Mexico, where he had served since 1749) in 1769 with explorer Gaspar de Portolá. Once established at Carmel, Serra began founding a chain of missions—in time a total of 21—from San Diego north to San Francisco. In these paternalistic centers the Indians were introduced to Spanish music primarily through the ritual of the Roman Catholic Mass. The resultant music was a charming, at times naïve, blending of the traditional plainsong with simple Spanish airs. The bulk of California mission music currently known has come down to us in the hand of Father Juan Sancho, like Serra of Majorcan birth. Sancho served in the mission at San Antonio de Padua (founded in 1771) situated between Santa Barbara and San Francisco. Apparently skilled in music, Sancho was musical copyist for the mission, taught the Indians the Mass as well as the popular songs of his native Spain. Of the California Indians and their musical gifts Sancho wrote: "The neophytes sing Spanish airs to perfection and easily learn any song or hymn taught them in figured as well as plain song. They sing at Holy Mass, and at other occasions. In this they are aided by their clear and sonorous voices and sharp ear with which men and women are blessed."

It would be some time before East and West would meet musically as well as culturally during the great westward expansion yet in the future. The immediate future of the direction of American music lay in the latter 18th century in the East, particularly in New England and the burgeoning commercial centers to the immediate south.

The singing school movement of New England, which had spread widely during this period, encouraged a greater musical literacy and the demand for more music and tune books. With musical sophistication came the rejection of the relatively crude fuging tunes of Billings and his "school," if so it could be called. Andrew Law, "composer" of "Bunker-hill," minister and musician, contemporary of Billings, opposed what he regarded as the "inferior" products of such as Billings and propagandized in his writings for "better music," and cried out against "turning churches into theatres and ministers into comedians . . ."

Law's best-known surviving tune is entitled "Archdale" (he copyrighted but did not necessarily write "Bunker-hill"); his agitation for "good music" and for copyright protection of his publications may have left him little time for inspired original work. He also claimed credit for introducing a "new plan" of musical notation now known as "shape notes."

This he allegedly did in the 4th edition of *The Art of Singing* (1803); not only did Law eliminate the musical staff lines but also the standard shape of the musical notations. Instead of the egg-like form of the conventional notehead, he used a triangle, a circle, a square, and a diamond to indicate pitch and duration—an improvement over the "plain and easy" system used in Tufts's *An Introduction to the Singing of Psalm-Tunes* earlier in the 18th century.

However, in 1798, William Little and one Edward Stammers copyrighted *The Easy Instructor, or a New Method of teaching Sacred Harmony*. Precisely what Stammers contributed to this publication is not known, for later editions credit the *Easy Instructor* to Little and a William Smith. The rather mysterious authorship is not as interesting as the fact that the "new method" utilized shape notes—and certainly before Law. But Little and Smith did not abandon the staff, which enabled the eye to follow the flow of the melody much better than Law's later "new plan."

The idea of both plans was to teach the reading of music on sight. Law went a bit further and hoped that his method would bring on an era of "better music" producing a higher level of "correct taste" in church music, hoping to rid the earth of "the pitiful productions of numerous composuists, whom it would be doing too much honor to name." Ironically, Law's "new plan" (if indeed it was his plan) did not catch on, while Little's, which was also eventually rejected by the "better music" lovers as fit only for rural singers, went underground and was adopted by teachers and musicians of the West and the South (where it is still in use). The Southern and Western shape-note tunebooks served to preserve the songs of those "composuits" that Law could not bring himself to name, among them those of William Billings.

As the 18th century closed, music was an established fact of American life. While no neat patterning emerged, musical activities based on European models energized the cultural scene: a reasonably regular concert season in the urban centers along the Atlantic seaboard as well as concerts in the smaller towns, in conjunction, generally, with theatrical entertainments whose members were musical. The spread of singing schools and singing societies, particularly in New England, laid the groundwork for an American choral tradition which has gone generally unrecognized. The influx of foreign-born, well-trained musicians contributed to the raising of professional standards, which was at once salutary and harmful. The good is obvious, but American-made music, compared to that imported from Europe, was regarded as inferior, resulting in, to borrow a phrase from contemporary composer William Schuman, "inverse chauvinism." This thinking became predominant during the 19th century and greatly influenced the American composers of the period, who tended to seek their musical educations and models in Europe, especially Germany.

Europeans in the New World were also important in the field of music publishing, which began to flourish in New York, Philadelphia, Boston, and other towns and cities in Maryland, Connecticut, New Hampshire, and reaching as far north as Maine. Coupled with the American manufacture of musical instruments, both the music and the means of making music came within the reach of more Americans than ever before. The postwar emergence of a middle class with time for leisure supplied the purchaser, the student, and the audience.

As the United States expanded in the next century, music and the making of music spread with it. As the nation grew, it virtually split into 2 nations, urban and rural, and so did its music.

"ADAMS AND LIBERTY" A patriotic song with words by Thomas Paine (not the revolutionary writer-philosopher) to the tune of a British drinking song, "To Anacreon in Heav'n," known also as "The Anacreontic Song." The words to the original song were written by Ralph Tomlinson, but the composer's identity remains in dispute although 2 favorite choices remain: Samuel Arnold and John Stafford Smith (the current favorite). The song was addressed to the Grecian poet Anacreon (fl. ca. 520 B.C.), noted for his drinking and amours. In reply to the Society's petition Tomlinson has the "Jolly Old Grecian" sing:

"Voice, Fiddle and Flute, no longer be
   mute,
   I'll lend you my name and inspire you
    to boot,
   And, besides, I'll instruct you like me
    to intwine
   The myrtle of Venus with Bacchus's
    vine."

Thomas Robert Treat Paine was commissioned in 1798 by the Massachusetts Charitable Fire Society to write the song in commemoration of its 4th anniversary. Revolution being in the air, the old drinking song was rendered patriotic and, spread by broadside, became very popular. Paine's first stanza (of 9) runs:

Ye sons of Columbia, who bravely have
   fought,
For those rights, which unstained, from
   your sires had descended,
May you long taste the blessings your
   valour has bought,
And your sons reap the soil which your
   fathers defended.
   Mid the reign of mild peace,
   May your nation increase,

With the glory of Rome and the
   wisdom of Greece;
And ne'er shall the sons of Columbia be
   slaves,
While the earth bears a plant, or the sea
   rolls its waves.

The final couplet was common to all stanzas. "Adams and Liberty" was but one of dozens of American parodies of "The Anacreontic Song," which achieved a final canonization in an adaptation by Thomas Carr to the words of Francis Scott Key (in 1814) as "The Star-Spangled Banner."

THE AMERICAN MUSICAL MAGAZINE The first American music periodical founded by Daniel Read (q.v.) and Amos Doolittle and published in New Haven, Conn., from May 1786 to September 1787, a total of 12 issues.

"THE ANACREONTIC SONG" See entry under "Adams and Liberty."

ANTES, JOHN (1740–1811) Born in Montgomery County, Pennsylvania, into a German/Moravian/American family, Antes went to school in Bethlehem, where he was also apprenticed to a wheelwright. His Moravian background would have introduced him to music which he studied as a youth, revealing an early facility on various stringed instruments. Some even credit him with constructing the first violin in America. In 1764 Antes left the United States for Herrnhut, Saxony, a great Moravian center; 5 years later he was ordained as a Moravian minister. He was stationed from 1770 to 1781 in Cairo, Egypt, as the first American missionary. It was there, according to Sonneck, who got it from early musicologist Rufus A.

Grider's *Historical Notes on music in Bethlehem* (1873), that "the Turks punished him with the *bastinado,* from the effects of which he never entirely recovered. While laid up in that country, he amused himself by composing . . ." Antes apparently returned to Europe during his convalescence and eventually moved to Bristol, England, where he died, aged about 70. While in Vienna, again according to Grider, he was befriended by Haydn, who supposedly performed some of Antes' compositions. Antes' original works, obviously influenced by Haydn and other important European musicians of the time, are regarded as among the best written by an American-born composer during the closing years of the 18th century. Antes wrote more than 2 dozen religious works for chorus, several chorales, and 3 surviving *Trios for two violins and cello* published between 1783 and 1790 and composed in Cairo, dedicated to the Swedish ambassador, by "Giovanni A— T—S, Dilettante Americano."

ANTHEM In the Anglican Church, "anthem" originally designated a choral work, with text from the Scriptures or the Book of Common Prayer sung by a divided choir, or by soloists and choir. The word itself derives from the Greek *antiphona.* The later anthem employed the soloists and choir antiphonally and used not only scriptural texts but also poems of a religious character. In Colonial America the anthem, although Billings called it "a devine song, generally in prose," used texts of a secular nature as well as religious, i.e., Billings' "Modern Music." In general, American anthems were longer than psalms and hymns, and were written in several parts for mixed voices. Both Daniel Read and Billings produced anthems to the words of the Reverend Dr. Byles's "Down Steers the Bass" (Billings' title was "Consonance"), a most descriptive celebration of music.

THE ARCHERS: OR, THE MOUNTAINEERS OF SWITZERLAND Generally recognized as the first American ballad opera or, even, the first "musical." The libretto was a treatment of the story of William Tell by New Jersey-born author-playwright William Dunlap (q.v.). The music was by English-born Benjamin Carr (q.v.) and had its premiere at the John Street Theatre, New York City, on Apr. 18, 1796. The theme of the libretto is freedom and oppression, although the setting is not the Colonies but Switzerland under the Austrians. Following the *Overture* the question is asked by the Prologue: *Can liberty with base injustice dwell?/ As well seek virtue in the depths of hell."* What follows is a curious mixture of the comic and serious, the lighter touches being provided by a young and supposedly pretty basketseller, "Cecily," and a street vendor, "Conrad," who is eventually impressed into the Austrian Army. The serious aspect of the plot centers around the noble William Tell, the chosen leader of the revolution against the Austrians. He is joined by patriotic bowmen, pikemen, and other Swiss warriors —including "Rhodolpha," who offers the services of her 50 "virtuous Maidens" (huntresses all) to fight alongside the men. This introduces one of the surviving songs from the show, "Why Huntress Why?" sung by her true love, "Arnold." Carr's score abounds in various songs, choruses, marches, dances, etc., very little of which has been preserved. By the third act curtain the Swiss have defeated the Austrians, William Tell has successfully shot the apple off his son's head (he also slays the principal villain), and the 2 sets of lovers marry and the company ends the show in a song about the rights of the common man and the rightness of law, ending the evening's entertainment on a moral political/social note.

ARMONICA One of the names applied to Benjamin Franklin's improved design for an instrument consisting of tuned musical glasses (an instrument that had been around for a long time before Franklin "disposed [the glasses] in a more convenient form, and brought together in a narrower compass, so as to admit of a greater number of tones, and all within reach of hand to a person sitting before the instrument"). In 1761, when Franklin produced his improved instrument, it was called the "glassychord," though Franklin's own name was armonica, which eventually was aspirated into harmonica. Franklin disposed of the traditional glasses and water; he also eliminated the stems and used only the bowls of various sizes arranged horizontally like a keyboard instrument. The armonica, Franklin explained, "is played upon, by sitting before the middle of the set of glasses as before the keys of a harpsichord, turning them with the foot, and wetting them now and then with a sponge and clean water." The instrument produced an exquisite musical sound which led to widespread popularity and attracted several worthy contemporary composers, among them Mozart and Beethoven.

BARN DANCE Although more popularly associated with the Western pioneers, the barn dance was a feature of Colonial America's social life, especially in rural areas. Though some Puritans in New England denounced the "lascivious dancing to wanton ditties," barn dances were the ultimate climax to a harvesting, cornhusking, or the completion of some hard labor or other. The "wanton ditties" were generally of British origin, jigs and reels like "Yankee Doodle" and "Irish Washerwoman." Accompaniment was invariably by a country fiddler (or 2, maybe more). Performances were rough and ready and the dances were vigorous. The tunes were learned by ear and passed on by tradition. More refined dancing and dance tunes were encountered in the cities, where printed sheet music could be acquired: hornpipes, strathspeys, all forms imported from Britain. The square dance, also associated with the rural barn dance, was popular also in the cities during the latter 18th century. In the vernacular, barn dances were also called "knockdowns" and "kitchen whangs," even "hog wrasslin's."

BARTON, ANDREW Author of the book to "America's first ballad opera," *The Disappointment: or, the Force of Credulity* (q.v.). Probably a pseudonym (one "Sir Andrew Barton" is the subject of a 2-part ballad published in Thomas Percy's *Reliques of Ancient English Poetry*, 1765). Historian George O. Seilhamer in his *History of the American Theatre* (3 vols., 1888–89) suggested that "Andrew Barton" was really one Colonel Thomas Forrest of Germantown, Pa. Sonneck, among other early— and later—musicologists, did not accept Seilhamer's contention (the evidence, a copy of the libretto with the title page inscribed "by Col. Thomas Forrest of Germantown" in ink, is quite circumstantial). Andrew Barton appears never to have written any other extant works— nor do we know much about the literary output of Colonel Forrest, who died in 1828, aged 83.

THE BATTLE OF TRENTON "A sonata for the pianoforte," by James Hewitt (q.v.). "Dedicated to General Washington." Obviously influenced by the voguish *The Battle of Prague* by Franz Kočzwara (also Kotzwara), which surfaced ca. 1793. Hewitt, who had emigrated from England in 1792, wished to celebrate Washington's famed Christmas night crossing of the Delaware River to capture an entire Hessian garrison. The "sonata" (which it is not in the formal sense) lasts barely 10 minutes, carries a good deal of plot: *"Introduction—The*

Army in Motion—General Orders—Acclamation of the Americans—Drum Beat to Arms/Attack—cannons—bomb. Defeat of the Hessians—Flight of the Hessians—Begging Quarter—The Fight Renewed—General Confusion—The Hessians surrender themselves prisoners of War—Articles of Capitulation Signed —Grief of Americans for loss of companions killed in the engagement/Yankee Doodle—Drums and Fifes—Quick Step for the Band—Trumpets of Victory—General Rejoicing."

Besides working "Yankee Doodle" into his battle piece, Hewitt also used "Washington's March." Along with the bombast—with crashing chords to represent the sounds of battle—*The Battle of Trenton* reveals in its quieter passages a composer of considerable imagination and skill.

THE BEGGAR'S OPERA English ballad opera produced in 1728; written by John Gay, whose lyrics were designed to fit existing popular songs (ballads), arranged by a German musician, Johann Christoph Pepusch. *The Beggar's Opera* was at once a social and a musical satire, taking a jaundiced look at conditions in Britain of the 18th century and at Handelian, i.e., Italian, opera. The characters populating *The Beggar's Opera*—thieves, prostitutes, a "fence"-informer—were a far cry from the typical operatic roles of the period. The success of Gay's work is said to have ruined Handel's London career as a composer of opera. The success also encouraged the form of ballad opera and imitators. Introduced into the United States ca. 1750. Its influence, however, was evident in *Flora, or Hob in the Well* (London, 1729; Charleston, S.C., 1735) and, later, American produced and written ballad operas, the true antecedents of what would become the musical comedy of the 20th century. Musically, *The Beggar's Opera* consisted of an overture and 69 ballads borrowed by Pepusch (including some blatant cribs directly from Handel) for solos, choruses, and dances. The raffish characters, too, were harbingers of musical comedy, a break with the usual castings depicting royalty or mythological divinities. Gay's hard look at society would be reflected again in musicals 2 centuries later.

BELCHER, SUPPLY (1751–1836) Born in Stoughton, Mass., Belcher attended the singing classes of William Billings (q.v.) there and was influenced by him. On his own, Belcher was well educated in preparation for entering the business life of Boston; the coming of the Revolution canceled that plan and Belcher bought a farm in nearby Canton, where he established a tavern. Caught up in the war, Belcher served as a captain under a commission from Washington. After the war, Belcher moved his wife and family (he was the father of 10) to the District of Maine (then a part of Massachusetts), settling first at Hollowell (1785) and 6 years later at Farmington, County of Lincoln, where he remained until his death at the age of 85. Belcher was a remarkably active man. He was deeply involved not only in business, but also in the life of his community. He taught the first school in Farmington, he served as the first town clerk, justice of the peace, and as a representative in the State (Mass.) Legislature. Belcher was a singer, violinist, choir director, and composer. In 1794 he published his *The Harmony of Maine* (printed in Boston, "Being an original composition of psalm and hymn tunes of various metres suitable for divine worship. With a number of fuging pieces and anthems. Together with a concise introduction to the grounds of musick and rules for learners. For use of singing schools and musical societies." The collection includes a good number of secular songs, along with the psalm and hymn tunes—and many a fuging piece. Belcher's style ranged from the folk-simple to the ornate, the latter tendency earning him the honor of being called the "Handel of Maine" by his contemporaries. *The Harmony of Maine* is Belcher's only known publication and consists of his original compositions.

BELKNAP, DANIEL (1771–1815) A farmer, mechanic, and part-time singing master (self-taught), Belknap was born in Framingham, Mass. Little is known about him except that he married in 1800, had 5 children, and published 3 musical compilations: *The Harmonist's Companion* (1797), *The Evangelical Harmony* (1800), and *The Village Compilation of Sacred Music* (1806). Many of Belknap's original compositions were reprinted in the books of others. Among the most popular individual vocal pieces were "A View of the Temple—A Masonic Ode," "Spring," "Summer" (all 1797), "Funeral Ode," "Autumn," and "Winter" (all 1800). Other works: "Concord" and "Belknap's March" (1809). He died in Pawtucket, R.I., at the age of 44.

BILLINGS, WILLIAM (1746–1800) Born in Boston on Oct. 7, 1746, Billings was apprenticed to a tanner as a boy and worked at that trade for a time. He abandoned it to devote all of his time, considerable energies, and enthusiasms to music. The death of his father when Billings was 14 ended his formal schooling; as for music, it is likely that he was largely self-taught. Billings could hardly have been an impressive man physically, for, according to a now much quoted description by a contemporary, "He was a singular man, of moderate size, short of one leg, with one eye, without any address, and with uncommon negligence of person. Still he spake and sang and thought as a man above common abilities." He must have been, for, despite his rudimentary musical (technical) knowledge, Billings gave up

all else for a career in music. (He may well have been the first professional American composer; other composers of the period practiced composition as an avocation, earning a living in politics, tavern-keeping, horse-breeding, or some other useful line of work.) Billings died a pauper on Sept. 26, 1800, leaving a destitute wife and six children.

The Reverend William Bentley of Salem, whose description of Billings was quoted above, noted in his diary: "This self-taught man thirty years ago had the direction of all the music of our churches. He may be justly considered the father of our New England music."

Billings was about 24 when he published his first collection, *The New England Psalm Singer, or American Chorister* in 1770. The year before, in partnership with one John Barrey, he announced the establishment of "a Singing School . . . near the Old South Meeting-House, where any person inclining to learn to Sing may be attended upon at said School with Fidelity and Dispatch." Undeterred by his lack of a "scientific" mastery of music based on some study with a local master and whatever he could glean from the not always reliable British authority William Tans'ur, a copy of whose *The Royal Melody Complete: or, The New Harmony of Zion* (London, 1755; Boston, 1767) Billings owned. In his first book Billings rationalized his self-made musicianship by writing that "I don't think myself confined to any Rules for Composition laid down by any that went before me . . ." and suggested that those who followed him observe the same attitude "(were I to pretend to lay down rules)," and concluding that he thought it "best for every composer to be his own learner" and that "Nature is the best Dictator." Billings would not deny art— "for the more Art is displayed, the more Nature is decorated. And in some forms of Composition, there is dry Study required, and Art very requisite. For instance, in a *Fuge,* where the parts come in after each other, with the same notes . . ."

Billings is no longer regarded as the creator of the "fuge" (q.v.), nor was he the only composer to use the form, so characteristic of the early New England tunesmiths. Billings and his colleagues had merely adapted the English fuging psalm tune dating back at least to the late 16th century. Billings undoubtedly loved fuging tunes because they added excitement to the usually 4-square singing of psalms and presented the chorus with more to do than solemnly intone one grim chord after the other.

In his 2nd publication, *The Singing Master's Assistant* (1778), he apologized for some youthful crudities, reprinting those works he deemed worthy in the 2nd book and eliminating those pieces "never worth my printing or your inspection." His self-assurance did not desert Billings for he noted that he had "added several new peices [his spelling] which I think to be very good ones . . ."

The 2nd book contained the secular—patriotic—version of the famous "Chester" (q.v.) and a remarkable reply to his critics, "Jargon" (q.v.). Billings published a total of 6 tunebooks: the 2 already mentioned and *Music in Miniature* (so called because it was in a small, pocket-book, format; 1779), *The Psalm Singer's Amusement* (1781), *The Suffolk Harmony* (1786), and *The Continental Harmony* (1794). Despite this output and Billing's renown in his lifetime, he was not successful financially as a professional musician. The popularity of his works, frequently pirated by other tune book compilers, added nothing to his meager income.

The advent of the "scientific" music makers early in the 19th century eventually displaced the efforts of the first New England school and Billings and his music seemed to go into permanent eclipse. Driven out of his native New England and the cities of the East, the music of the first New England school, it was later learned, had been preserved by westward-moving pioneers in Southern folk hymnody.

Although dismissed by early American musicologists and historians, Billings has been rediscovered, and reevaluated, by their 20th-century counterparts and found to be one of the most original voices in American music. What he lacked in theoretical knowledge he more than compensated for in imagination and creativity. Such compositions as the canon "When Jesus Wept," the fuging tune "Kittery" (a setting of the Lord's Prayer), the Christmas carol "Judea" (or "A Virgin Unspotted"), the haunting "David's Lamentation," to mention but a few, and especially the apposite "Be Glad Then America," reveal him as a vital force in early American music. Had he been permitted to prevail, the sound of American music today might be quite different.

BREMNER, JAMES (d. 1780) Little is known about Bremner, who was probably born in Edinburgh, Scotland, before he arrived in Philadelphia in 1763. Teacher, organist, and composer, he opened a music school there in December of that year and was an important influence in the musical life of Philadelphia until his death. Bremner was also the organist in Christ Church. His music school was located at "Mr. Glover Hunt's near the Coffee House in Market Street." Bremner taught young ladies the harpsichord or guitar and "young gentlemen the violin, German flute, harpsichord, or guitar." Among these young gentlemen was probably Francis Hopkinson (q.v.). Bremner was related to British music publisher Robert Bremner, also a friend of Hopkinson.

BROADSIDE A sheet of paper printed on one side only and sold to circulate the texts of ballads, a practice dating back to early 16th-century England. Known folk songs were set to new lyrics, ranging from the patriotic to the bawdy. The broadside was introduced into the Colonies and there is a record of Cotton Mather complaining about their corrupting the "Minds and Manners" of people exposed to "foolish Songs and Ballads" as early as 1713. The term applied as much to the song as the original sheet and was interchangeable. Broadsides were used to circulate the fiery songs of the Revolution, beginning with the "liberty songs" set to popular British tunes such as "The American Hero" with music by Andrew Law (q.v.).

BROWN, WILLIAM Little is known about Brown, except that he gave a concert in New York in 1783, just before the British evacuated the city and soon after went to Philadelphia. A virtuoso flutist, Brown (whose name may have been Braun, according to Sonneck) remained, "having been prevailed upon by several gentlemen to continue his stay in Philadelphia, and being inclined to gratify them." Brown gave concerts and composed a *Flute Concerto* (ca. 1786) and *Three Rondos for the Pianoforte or Harpsichord,* "composed and humbly dedicated to the Honorable Francis Hopkinson, Esqr." Whether Brown was a native-born composer or one of the émigré musicians of the period is not certain; nor are his precise dates known.

"BUNKER HILL" ("The American Hero") One of the fine, memorable, songs of the Revolution, words by Nathaniel Niles and circulated as a broadside (q.v.) entitled "The American Hero" and copyrighted, if not necessarily composed, by Andrew Law (q.v.) 2 years later in his *Select Number of Plain Tunes Adapted to Congregational Worship* (1777).

CARR, BENJAMIN (1768–1831) Born in London on Sept. 12, 1768, Carr was the son of Joseph and brother of Thomas—all important contributors to American musical life in the latter 18th century. Of the 3, Benjamin was the most distinguished as composer, organist, pianist, vocalist; all 3 were important music publishers, with music stores in Baltimore, Philadelphia, and New York. Benjamin Carr was 24 when he arrived in New York in 1793; soon after, he was joined by his father (then about 50) and his brother. The Carrs established their successful music businesses and Benjamin Carr, besides, was active as a singer, in opera as well as recitals. He organized what was known as the City Concerts in Philadelphia and was one of the founders of the Musical Fund Society (1820) in that city. Carr also produced a good deal of music, arrangements as well as original pieces, including 5 operas, dozens of songs, several pantomimes, religious music, and a number of instrumental pieces. He has a place in the history of American music as the composer of the opera, *The Archers* (1796, q.v.), one of the earliest of American operas. Among his works for the keyboard is *The Federal Overture* (1794, q.v.). Carr's contribution to the sacred music of his time in Philadelphia was considerable; he served as organist, and music director, of St. Augustine's (Roman Catholic) Church from 1801 until his death on May 24, 1831. Carr also served as editor of the *Musical Journal,* founded by his father in 1799, and which was regularly published for several years. This was a weekly magazine, alternating the publication of vocal with instrumental music "selected and arranged by B. Carr of Philadelphia, who from extensive materials in his possession, a regular supply of new music from Europe and the assistance of Men of Genius in the Country hopes he will present the public with a work that for novelty and cheapness will be fully worthy of their patronage."

"CATGUT" CHURCH Pejorative term of ca. 1770–80 referring to those meetinghouses of New England into which the use of instruments was creeping. The conservatives deplored the introduction of the bass viol (today's cello) into church music. The instruments of the period were strung with the dried intestines of animals, thus the term.

CHAPIN, LUCIUS (1760–1842) Relatively obscure Massachusetts-born fifer and music master, who moved to Virginia ca. 1787. He was joined there by his brother, Amzi, also a music master, in 1791. Lucius Chapin is one of the Yankee tunesmiths whose work was preserved in Southern hymnbooks of the 19th century. Four of Chapin's tunes, "Ninety-third," "Ninety-fifth," "Rockbridge," and "Rockingham," were published in John Wyeth's *Repository of Sacred Music, Part Second* (1813). The Chapins were a musical family, which has caused musicological confusion concerning identity and authorship—not to mention typographical mishaps that transformed one or the other into "Chopin" and vice versa.

"CHESTER" Originally published as a religious song, with words by Dr. Isaac Watts, in Billings' *The New England Psalm Singer* (1770); for his second publication, *The Singing Master's Assistant* (1778), Billings composed his own patriotic text, producing what would become the most popular anthem of the Revolutionary War.

COTILLION A medley of dances that closed a ball. An elaborate set of dances, frequently drawing upon English and French musical sources—reels, hornpipes, minuets, gavottes, and later the waltz—the cotillion was not unlike the rural square dance in that it employed lead couples to precede the couples following through the "figures" of the cotillion. The cotillion of the late 18th century consisted of a number of dances and figures; eventually the term was applied to a single dance (also spelled "cotillion"), generally a fast waltz.

DEARBORN, BENJAMIN (1754–1838) Born ca. April 1754, in Portsmouth, N.H., Dearborn was an important singing master and educator there for several years —in addition to shopkeeping, printing, writing, and auctioneering. In 1781 Dearborn opened up "An Evening School for young People of both Sexes" where he taught not only music but also "Grammar, Reading, Writing, Spelling, [and] Arithmetic." Around 1785 Dearborn devised *A Scheme for reducing the Science of Music to a more simple state . . .* His scheme made possible the printing of music employing standard printing type instead of the staff and notes. Tones were indicated by letters and time by numbers; sharps, flats, and other nuances were also indicated by various extant types (daggers, asterisks, etc.), an ingenious idea that did not catch on. Dearborn moved to Boston, after the closing of his quite progressive Portsmouth Academy (for young ladies), in 1792, where he established another academy. Active as a schoolmaster, auctioneer, and inventor, Dearborn published his important musical statement in *The Vocal Instructor* (Boston, 1797). He died in Boston on Feb. 22, 1838.

DENCKE, JEREMIAH (1735–1795) After serving in several Moravian settlements in Europe, Silesian-born Dencke emigrated to America in 1761. He is credited with having composed the first sacred music in America with instrumental accompaniment. His works include several songs for soprano, strings, and organ. From 1772 to 1784 Dencke served as Warden of the Moravian congregation at Bethlehem, Pa.

THE DISAPPOINTMENT The first American ballad opera, credited to "Andrew Barton, Esq." (q.v.) and printed in New York in 1767. The "comic opera," as Barton called it, was intended to satirize certain prominent Philadelphians engaged in the "foolish and pernicious practice of searching after supposed hidden treasure." The new opera was to have been performed by the American Company in Philadelphia at the Southwark Theatre on Apr. 20, 1767, but was withdrawn before it opened, the author undoubtedly having second thoughts about affronting some powerful local figures. Like the traditional ballad opera, *The Disappointment* consisted of a number of borrowed "airs" with appropriate new words. It told the tale of the search for the treasure of Blackbeard the pirate. If nothing else, the unproduced but twice-published *The Disappointment* was the first to use the tune of "Yankee Doodle" (q.v.), leading musicologists to believe that it was undoubtedly of British, not home, origin as had been thought for so long.

DUNLAP, WILLIAM (1766–1839) Artist, dramatist, novelist, historian, and theatrical manager, Dunlap was born in Perth Amboy, N.J. His Tory father moved the family to New York during the British occupation, in 1777. In 1784 Dunlap, despite the loss of an eye as a child, went to Britain to study painting with American-born artist Benjamin West. Dunlap soon after began painting portraits and writing plays. He also joined his father in the family business, eventually leaving that to become manager of the Old American Company (q.v.) in 1796. Dunlap also wrote plays, poetry, criticism, and translations. He produced his *History of the American Theatre* in 1832 and was the author of several other histories and studies. In American music Dunlap's name is associated with the libretto to Benjamin Carr's *The Archers* (q.v.); he also collaborated on operas with James Hewitt

(q.v.), *The Spanish Castle* (1800) and *The Wild Goose Chase* (1800), as well as with Victor Pelissier (q.v.), *Sterne's Maria, or the Vintage* (1799). A founder and vice-president of the National Academy of Design, Dunlap produced around 70 librettos, plays, translations in addition to prose works before his death at the age of 73.

EDSON, LEWIS, SR. (1748–1820) Self-taught singing master and composer, Edson was born in Bridgewater, Mass., on Jan. 22, 1748. His father was a farmer; both father and son (the latter barely in his teens) served as soldiers in the British Army from 1761 to 1763. Upon being discharged, 15-year-old Edson set up a blacksmith shop in Bridgewater. Where Edson learned music is unknown, but by 1769 he was teaching music to the members of a church in Halifax, Mass. The Edson family, some of whom may have been Tories, moved to Lanesboro, Mass., in 1776 and did not participate in the Revolution. Edson continued in music, serving as chorister in the local church. He chose the psalms to be sung and also set the tune for the congregation. Edson was noted for his fine voice. He never compiled a tunebook, but 3 of his tunes were printed in *The Chorister's Companion* (1782) and were widely reprinted for years. These were "Bridgewater," "Greenfield," and "Lenox," the latter still in print (although cleansed of its fuging) in the 20th century. Little more is known of Edson, except that he died in Shady, N.Y., sometime in 1820.

EDSON, LEWIS, JR. (1771–1845) Only child of Edson, Sr. (q.v.), born also in Bridgewater on Jan. 23, 1771. Obviously influenced by his father's musical interests, the son was familiar with the art, if not well grounded in it. Edson, Jr., left little biographical data but was known to have been a postrider in Cooperstown, N.Y., in 1795.

He was also a singing master and a poet. In 1800 he published his compilation *The Social Harmonist;* after this he moved to New York, working as a schoolteacher and carpenter. He retired to a farm at Shady, N.Y., and died there on May 23, 1845.

EVENING AMUSEMENT A collection of "fifty airs, song's, duett's, dances, hornpipe's, reel's, marches, minuet's, &c., &c., for 1 and 2 German flutes or violins." It was available at the Carr's Musical Repositories in Philadelphia, New York, and Baltimore and published in 1796. Among the "airs, &c." were a couple of Haydn pieces (one the Minuet from Symphony No. 26), several hornpipes, an inevitable *General Washington's March,* "Yankee Doodle" (spelled "Yanke" in one printing), a song entitled "The new bow wow," Alexander Reinagle's (q.v.) song, "America, Commerce and Freedom," "The Kentucky Volunteer," written by a lady of Philadelphia, composed by R [Raynor] Taylor (q.v.). Also, "The Marseilles Hymn," "The Irish Washerwoman," and "O! Dear! What Can the Matter Be?" A number of these pieces had already been used by Benjamin Carr in his *The Federal Overture* (q.v.). *Evening Amusement* is a treasury of the secular musical activity of the period. Many of its pieces could serve as sets for the later cotillions (q.v.).

THE FEDERAL OVERTURE An arrangement by Benjamin Carr of 9 tunes of patriotic cast, inoffensive to Federalists and Anti-Federalists alike. Intended to serve as a curtain-raiser for theatre band, the overture was published by the Carrs in 1794, undoubtedly because of its good reception in Philadelphia (it was later done in New York). Original publication was for piano; it was arranged for 2 German flutes and printed in the 5th and 7th issues of Carr's periodical, *The Gentle-* *men's Amusement,* in 1796. The overture consists of "Yankee Doodle" (in its first American printing), the "Marseillaise," "Ça Ira" (another French patriotic song), "O! Dear! What Can the Matter Be?" "The Irish Washerwoman," "Rose Tree" (a song from "Washington's favorite opera," *Poor Soldier*), "La Carmagnole" (a song of the French Revolution), "The President's March" (Phile's version; later "Hail, Columbia"), and "Viva Tutti," an air from an old Italian opera.

FLAGG, JOSIAH (1738–1794) Born in Woburn, Mass., Flagg eventually moved to Boston, where he published *A Collection of the Best Psalm Tunes* (engraved by Paul Revere in 1764); 2 years later Flagg issued *A Collection of All Tans'ur's and a number of other Anthems* (revealing the obvious source of his influences). The first collection contained 116 psalm tunes and 2 anthems—"the greater part of them never before printed in America." Which, if any, were original with Flagg is not known. His first collection was patently based on Lyon's *Urania* (1760) and, like most compilers of the time, he borrowed with a free hand. It was, however, as a promoter of concerts in Boston that Flagg truly made his mark (he may also have earned a kind of living as a jeweler) and, according to Sonneck, he "founded and drilled the first real militia band of Boston." Flagg's was the 64th Regiment band and his announcement for one of its concerts in 1771 promised music by, among others, Handel and Bach. The tradition of the Colonial band, mingling British and American traits, flourished after the Revolution in the bands of Pryor and Sousa and the concerts in the park of 19th-century America. The popular notion of the instrumentation of the military band would not apply to the militia band of Colonial America. One of Flagg's advertisements mentioned

"French horns, hautboys, etc.," which would suggest a more mellow, less brassy sound. Such bands were used in churches. Flagg's career as a concert manager did not prosper and around 1773 he presented a final concert in Boston hoping to raise enough money to enable him to leave "in an independent manner." He then seems to have vanished from musical history; he died in 1794, but the place remains unknown. His wife and 2 daughters returned to Boston for a benefit concert on their behalf, as Flagg apparently died poor and his "vile miscreant son," Dr. Josiah Flagg, Jr., was of no help. Mrs. and the Misses Flagg received $102 and returned to "the business of riveting and mending China and glass, and needle work of all kinds."

FOLK MUSIC The term encompasses both folk song and instrumental music and in its most "scientific" form is the traditional music of a people, generally rural. Folk music is of unknown authorship, not written down, and thus is subject to countless variations and combinations via the oral transmission from generation to generation. The folk musics (for it should be plural) pertinent to this section would be primarily of British origin (English, Scottish, and Irish), with some touches of French (via Canada and Louisiana) and Spain (via California and Mexico). The impress of black culture in the Colonies has not been preserved, but it is obvious from various slave announcements of the time that black musicians, many of whom played the fiddle, were prized for their musicianship. These musicians would most likely have played the popular tunes of their white masters; how much of their indigenous music was preserved and performed for their own amusement was not recorded by early historians.

Widely distributed through New England and the South were the traditional ballads—folk songs that told a story. It was the ballad that attracted the early 19th-century scholars, led by Francis J. Child in *English and Scottish Popular Ballads* (1882–98); the approach was impeccably scholarly, but concentrated on ballads—ignoring folk songs that did not fit the category—and upon the texts. (See Section IV, for Child.)

Among the ballads brought to America by the earliest settlers are "Black Is the Color of My True Love's Hair," which has been traced back to Elizabethan times, "The Daemon Lover" (also known as "The House Carpenter"), "The Devil's Nine Questions," "Barbara Allen" in dozens of variants, "The Farmer's Curst Wife," and perhaps hundreds of others. To these could be added the nonstorytelling folk songs (which would include popular songs of the time whose authors slipped into oblivion; nursery songs—"Froggie Went a-Courtin'," "All the Pretty Little Horses"; humorous songs; chanteys, game songs).

Instrumental folk music was dance music brought from Britain—jigs, reels, and country dances that could be played on such portable instruments as the violin (or the fiddle), viols, Jew's harp, and such woodwinds as the flute, flageolet, hautboy (oboe); the drum and trumpet were also known in Colonial New England. Some such instrumentation was used to provide the music for the Maypole revels at Thomas Morton's settlement at Mount Wollaston (Braintree, Mass.) that shocked the nearby Puritans of Plymouth. William Bradford noted in his *Of Plimmouth Plantation* that the wanton residents of Mount Wollaston "set up a May-pole, drinking and dancing aboute it many days together, inviting the Indean women, for their consorts, dancing and frisking together (like so many fairies, or furies rather), and worse practices . . ."

The ballads, songs, and dance music were transmitted to the next generations, often with strict attention to precise transmission and others with inventive variations. In time, the colonists and their children began improvising their own songs, beginning an indigenous American folk music tradition. Among the first American ballads was "Springfield Mountain," dating from around the time of the American Revolution. With the post-Revolutionary expansion of the country the quantity and character of American folk music expanded and diversified (where it did not, in isolated pockets, it stood still). As the pioneers moved away from the Eastern seaboard, their experiences provided the subject matter for their songs. Freely borrowing from one another (a characteristic of folk music), enriched by the contributions of the new immigrants, the Americans fashioned a distinctive folk music.

FRANKLIN, BENJAMIN (1706–1790) Among his numerous attributes, Franklin —writer, scholar, statesman, inventor, scientist, womanizer—was a music lover. He could play several instruments, among them the harp and guitar, sang and wrote songs (probably the lyrics). Franklin is credited with inventing the "glassychord," better known as the glass "armonica" (q.v.), but undoubtedly applied his ingenuity to improving an already existing instrument. Franklin revealed an astute mind in musical matters in the area of criticism and theory. It is possible that he composed the "string quartet" attributed to him, although it appears to have been unknown until discovered in Paris in the 1940s. The manuscript bore the inscription *Quartetto a 3 Violini con Violoncello, del Sig^re Benjamin Francklin*. It is not a string quartet at all in instrumentation or form. It is a grouping of 5 charming little dance-like movements. One of the interesting features of the quartet is that the entire piece was designed to be played on the open strings of the instruments, eliminating the necessity for fingering by the left hand (and simpler to play).

FRENCH, JACOB (1754–1817) A little-known member of the first New England group of composer-compilers of religious vocal music. Born in Stoughton, Mass., French served as a singing master in the First Congregational Church, Providence, R.I. (1796–97). Not much else is known about him except that he published 3 collections of music containing a number of his own compositions (including a fuging tune): *The New American Melody* (1789), *The Psalmist's Companion* (1793), and *The Harmony of Harmony* (1802).

FUGING TUNE Also "fuguing," but never fugueing, for the fuge and the fugue were distinctively different. The fuge (so far as we know it was pronounced *fudge*) was a favorite device of the early New England composers, who had borrowed it from the fuging psalm tunes of 18th-century England. The earliest printed example of the latter appeared in James Lyon's *Urania* (1761). The most enthusiastic native fuger, although probably not the first nor the most prolific, was William Billings. He undoubtedly delighted in the vigor and excitement that fuging lent to a psalm. Fuging is another word for imitation. After the psalm is sung by the chorus, it is sung again in parts with each of the voices making successive entries in imitation of what had just been sung. Billings insisted that there was "more variety in one piece of fuging music, than in twenty pieces of plain song, for while the tones do most sweetly coincide and agree, the words are seemingly engaged in musical warfare; and excuse the paradox if I further add, that each part seems determined by dint of harmony and strength of accent, to drown his competitor in an ocean of harmony, and while each part is striving for mastery, and sweetly contending for victory, the audience are most luxuriously entertained, and exceedingly delighted . . ." It is obvious that when Billings fuged a psalm he had his listeners in mind as much as God. Fuging, he believed, stimulated the brain. He described the process of fuging with fervor: "Now the solemn bass favors their [the audience's] attention, now the manly tenor, now the lofty counter, now the volatile treble, now here, now there, now here again— O inchanting! O ecstatic! Push on, push on ye sons of harmony . . . !" That is probably as good a definition of the fuge as any.

GLASSYCHORD See "Armonica."

GRAM, HANS (dates unknown) Born in Denmark, educated in Stockholm, Gram arrived in Boston sometime before 1790. In 1793 he was organist in the Brattle Street Church. In July 1791 he published "a new march" entitled *America;* the same year Gram's *The Death Song of an Indian Chief* for tenor and orchestra was published in the *Massachusetts Magazine*. It was the first orchestral score published in America. Gram's most important work was his collaboration with Holden (q.v.) and Holyoke (q.v.) on *The Massachusetts Compiler* (1795).

THE HARMONY OF MAINE Supply Belcher's collection of "psalm and hymn tunes of various metres suitable for divine worship. With a number of fuging pieces and anthems. Together with a concise introduction to the grounds of musick and rules for learners. For the use of singing schools and musical societies," published in Boston, 1794. Belcher's only known publication. Especially interesting is the fact that the collection includes a number of secular compositions.

HERBST, JOHANNES (1735–1812) Moravian of German birth, Herbst settled in Lancaster, Pa., in 1787. A pastor in the church, he served also at Lititz. He later left the state and at the end of his life he was a bishop at Salem, N.C. A prolific composer, during his American years Herbst produced over a hundred works—sacred songs and anthems—for voice with orchestral accompaniment. Herbst's best-known religious song is "I Will Go in the Strength of the Lord."

HEWITT, JAMES (1770–1827) A trained professional musician, Hewitt was born in Dartmoor, England, on June 4, 1770, and emigrated to America in 1792, where he first settled in New York. He immediately established himself in New York's growing concert life (at the time of his arrival dominated by Peter Albrecht van (later von) Hagen (q.v.). Hewitt, who had arrived in the company of several other musicians (like him, veterans of several fine English orchestras, including Haydn's), began organizing ambitious concerts. He competed with van Hagen—and both suffered, there being at the time too small a New York population to support 2 elaborate series of concerts. Hewitt eventually concentrated on conducting and composing for the Old American Company (q.v.) at the John Street Theatre (he conducted the premiere of Carr's *The Archers*) as well as for the Vaux Hall Gardens summer concerts and was director of military bands in New York. Although he began in music publishing in 1794, Hewitt emerged as an important figure after he bought the New York branch of Benjamin Carr's Musical Repository in 1798. Although Hewitt moved to Boston in 1812, his name appears on musical programs of various cities from New York to Augusta, Ga. He was active in the concert life of Boston and served as organist at Trinity Church. Hewitt's final years were miserable; his 2nd marriage broke up (Hewitt's first wife died shortly before he came to America); Hewitt was ill and underwent surgery about a year before his death. Although a prolific composer, Hewitt was rather careless in the preservation of his manuscripts and consequently nothing (except perhaps a brief march) remains from what may have been his most important work for the theatre, the opera *Tammany* (1794), an Anti-Federalist political work with an Indian hero. Hewitt composed a number of published songs; he composed many other opera scores, including *Columbus* (1799) and *The Patriot, or Liberty Asserted* (1794—the story of William Tell, antedating Carr's *The Archers* by 2 years and Rossini by 35). Among Hewitt's keyboard works are *Overture in 9 Movements* ("expressive of a battle"; 1792), *Overture* "to conclude with the representation of a Storm at Sea" (1794), *Three Sonatas for the Piano Forte*, Op. 5 (1796), *The Battle of Trenton* ("A Sonata for piano forte. Dedicated to General Washington"; 1797), and *The 4th of July* ("A Grand Military Sonata for the Piano Forte"; 1801). Hewitt died in Boston on Aug. 1, 1827.

HOLDEN, OLIVER (1765–1844) Born in Shirley, Mass., Holden eventually settled in Charlestown (also Mass.), where initially he worked at carpentry until about 1792, when he became a singing master. He also served as Charlestown's Justice of the Peace and was elected to the Massachusetts House of Representatives. Holden's first musical publication was a slender booklet entitled *The American Harmony* (Boston, 1792); his 2nd work was a 2-volume *Union Harmony* (Boston, 1793), notable for "Coronation" ("All hail the power of Jesus' name . . ."), a hymn still being sung and printed in the 20th century. Other Holden publications: *Plain Psalmody* (1800), *Charlestown Collection* (1803). He also composed a *Dirge, or Sepulchral Service* (1800) on the death of Washington. In collaboration with Hans Gram (q.v.) and Samuel Holyoke (q.v.), Holden produced *The Massachusetts Compiler* (Boston, 1795), a valuable work not only containing the usual sacred vocal music but also a theoretical essay (favoring modern European music-making as against the New England fuging composers) and a musical dictionary. Holden died in Charlestown in 1844.

HOLYOKE, SAMUEL (1762–1820) Son of a clergyman, Holyoke was born in Boxford, Mass., Oct. 15, 1762. At the age of 20 he entered Phillips Academy (now called Phillips Andover). He graduated from Harvard in 1789. By the following year Holyoke set up musical shop in the Salem, Mass., area teaching singing and conducting concerts. He taught sacred music at Phillips Academy from 1809 to 1810. His first publication, *Harmonia Americana* (1791), represented the philosophy of the "better music" school. In his introduction to the collection Holyoke wrote: "Perhaps some may be disappointed that fuguing pieces are in general omitted. But the principal reason why few were inserted was the trifling effect produced by that sort of music; for the parts falling in, one after another, each conveying a different idea, confound the sense, and render the performance a mere jargon of words" (for a different view see "Fuging Tune"). Holyoke collaborated on *The Massachusetts Compiler* (1795) with Holden (q.v.) and Gram (q.v.) and published *The Columbian Repository* (1799) and *The Instrumental Assistant*, Vol. I (1800), Vol. II (1807). The *Repository* was not merely a compilation of psalms and hymns but also a musical instruction book—the last 2 contained instructions on how to perform on various instruments as well as a number of airs, marches, and quick steps, among other forms, for the adept instrumentalist to play. *The Columbian Repository* preserved Holyoke's first song,

"Arnheim," composed when he was 16, and it is one of his few original hymn tunes to survive. It was as a music teacher that Holyoke left his mark. He died, aged 57, of "lung fever" in Concord, N.H., where he had gone to teach, on Feb. 7, 1820.

HOPKINSON, FRANCIS (1737–1791) Born in Philadelphia (Sept. 21, 1737), Hopkinson came from a distinguished family and spent his early years in a comfortable, cultured household. He was graduated from the College of Philadelphia (now the University of Pennsylvania) in 1757. Although he revealed a deep love of music, it was in politics and law that Hopkinson flourished professionally. Little is known about his musical education; he may have studied with the British musician James Bremner. He was an accomplished harpsichordist and apparently knew music well enough to instruct children in psalmody in Philadelphia churches. Hopkinson was also a poet, satirist (especially in politics), and an amateur composer. Like Benjamin Franklin, Hopkinson was a kind of Renaissance man of wide ingenious interests from invention (an "improved candlestick"; a new method for quilling the harpsichord) to art—for he was also a painter.

Hopkinson held several official positions, resigning them in 1776 to align with the patriots. He was a delegate to the Continental Congress and a signer of the Declaration of Independence. He wrote pamphlets for the cause, among them one entitled "The History of a New Roof"; he was also the author of a satiric song (to the tune of "Maggie Lauder"), "The Battle of the Kegs" (1778).

Hopkinson began composing while still a student, contributing original music to college entertainments. Hopkinson also began collecting, by copying a variety of music by the popular composers of the period (Handel, Arne, Purcell, etc.). Scattered among these were 6 initialed "F.H.," from which it is assumed they were original Hopkinson compositions. One, "My Days Have Been So Wondrous Free," (q.v.), which dates from 1759, when Hopkinson was 22, has gone down in the history of American music as "the first known secular composition by a native American composer." Among Hopkinson's lost works is an "oratorical entertainment," *The Temple of Minerva* (of which only the libretto is preserved), performed in Philadelphia in 1781. His most famous work is the *Seven Songs for Harpsichord or Forte Piano*, dedicated to Washington (1788): "Come Fair Rosina, Come Away," "My Love Is Gone to Sea," "Beneath a Weeping Willows Shade," "Enraptur'd I Gaze," "See Down Maria's Blushing Cheek," "O'er the Hills Far Away," Rondo—"My Gen'rous Heart Disdains," and an 8th song, "The Trav'ler Benighted and Lost." Both words and music are by Hopkinson. The next year Hopkinson produced one more song, "The Words and Music of a New Song by F. H. Esq." ("Give me thy heart as I give mine"). Hopkinson is also credited with editing *A Collection of Psalm Tunes, with a few Anthems and Hymns . . .* (Philadelphia, 1763) and *A Collection of Psalm and Hymn Tunes . . .* (New York, 1774).

Hopkinson died of apoplexy in Philadelphia on May 9, 1791.

HOPKINSON, JOSEPH (1770–1842) Son of Francis Hopkinson, Joseph was also an eminent lawyer and jurist. He is remembered in American music as author of the lyrics to the patriotic song "Hail! Columbia" (1798). It was written for a special performance at the Chestnut Street Theatre, Philadelphia, at the request of actor Gilbert Fox, once a schoolmate of Hopkinson's. The melody selected was Philip Phile's instrumental piece, *President's March;* Hopkinson entitled the result "The New Federal Song," which begins with "Hail! Columbia, happy Land hail!" Sung by Fox, it became an instant patriotic favorite in Philadelphia and eventually the rest of the country. "Hail! Columbia" was not the younger Hopkinson's only artistic endeavor. At the age of 17, 2 years before, he wrote an essay, "On Dancing," tried his hand at writing a play, and edited the plays of Shakespeare for American publication.

"JARGON" Song, words, and music by William Billings, first published in *The Singing-Master's Assistant* (Boston, 1778), composed by Billings in answer to his critics complaining about the blandness of his music. His "manifesto" giving performance directions is longer than the piece itself: "Let an Ass bray the bass, let the filing saw carry the tenor, let a hog who is extremely weak squeal the counter, and let a cart-wheel, which is heavy-loaded, and that has long been without grease, squeak the treble . . . etc." The complete text is:

> *Let horrid Jargon split the Air*
> *And rive the nerves asunder;*
> *Let hateful Discord greet the Ear*
> *As terrible as Thunder.*

This satiric piece, because of Billings' prankishness, has a remarkably contemporary sound. Sonneck called it a "grotesque composition . . . Its closing cadence would cause the most rabid modernist to shudder."

KIMBALL, JACOB (1761–1826) Son of a blacksmith and born in Topsfield, Mass., Kimball was graduated from Harvard in 1780. For a time he practiced law but appears to have abandoned that for music. Kimball served as a fifer during the Revolution and was probably a student of Hans Gram. He taught music in New England towns to earn a living and produced 2 song collec-

tions, *The Rural Harmony* (Boston, 1793) and *The Essex Harmony* (Exeter, N.H., 1800). Kimball eventually became an alcoholic and died in a poorhouse in Topsfield.

LAW, ANDREW (1749–1821) One of the leaders in the "good music" crusade of the latter 18th century, Law was one of the best educated of the early American hymnodists. He earned a master's degree at Rhode Island College (now Brown University), studied for the ministry, and was ordained a Congregationalist minister at Hartford, Conn., in 1787. Born in Milford, Conn., Law was devoted to music and gave much time to composing, the compiling of hymnbooks, developed an innovational method of notating music (not unlike the shape-note system, but without staff lines), campaigned for copyright protection of musical works (although he appears to have borrowed from time to time), and viewed the works of such musicians as Billings as quite inferior. In his prose writings Law vigorously attacked such music, preferring European models of correctness and "taste." As a teacher Law was influential; he was probably the instructor of one of the first black music teachers, Newport Gardner (ca. 1746–1826). Law is credited with the music of "Bunker Hill" (q.v.) and published several music collections and instruction books: *Select Number of Plain Tunes* (Boston, 1767), *The Select Harmony* (New Haven, 1778–79), and *The Art of Music* (New Haven, 1780) in 3 parts. In the 4th edition (Cambridge, Mass., 1803), Law put forth his "new plan of printing music." As a propagandist for "good music," Law was influential during his lifetime, and later, when his ideas were furthered by New England music educators. Law died in Cheshire, Conn., in 1821.

"THE LIBERTY SONG" One of the first American resistance songs, published in 1768. The words were written by a Philadelphia lawyer-farmer, John Dickinson, to the tune of an old English popular song "Heart of Oak" (music by William Boyce). The song became enormously popular in the Colonies and was sung at rallies, protests, etc. The song's refrain went:

In Freedom we're born and in Freedom we'll live,
Our purses are ready,
Steady, Friends, Steady.
Not as Slaves, but as Freemen our money we'll give.

"The Liberty Song" was published throughout the colonies in newspapers, broadsides, and in sheet music form. The British responded with a parody (which, in turn, inspired a parody of the parody); the British version of the song's opening call, "Come, join hand in hand, brave Americans all," was "Come shake your dull noodles, ye bumpkins, and bawl . . ." No firebrand, Dickinson caught the American mood of incipient rebellion (though he preferred conciliation, even refused to sign the Declaration of Independence). Dickinson (1732–1808) was author of the influential *Letters from a Farmer in Pennsylvania* (1767–68).

LYON, JAMES (1735–1794) Clergyman-psalmodist Lyon is generally awarded the position of the 2nd native composer after Hopkinson, who made the claim for first position himself. Born in Newark (East New Jersey, then) on July 1, 1735, Lyon was orphaned at about the age of 15 and cared for by a relative—though little else is known about his childhood and youth. He first made his appearance as a composer while still a student at New Jersey College (now Princeton) with an *Ode* composed for the Commencement of 1759 (the year of Hopkinson's "My Days Have Been So Wondrous Free," q.v.).

Lyon later attended the College of Philadelphia, where he apparently was acquainted with Hopkinson. For a Commencement there he composed an *Anthem* performed along with an *Ode* ("to the Memory of our late Gracious Sovereign, George II") by Hopkinson. While living in Philadelphia, Lyon completed work on his *Urania, or A Choice Collection of Psalm-Tunes, Anthems and Hymns* (1761, q.v.). Soon after receiving his master's degree, Lyon began preaching in New Brunswick. He was ordained a Presbyterian minister in 1764 and the following year was serving in Nova Scotia. Unable to provide for his family there, Lyon took another parish, in Machias, Maine, in 1771. When war came Lyon provided Washington with a plan for the conquest of the province of Nova Scotia and, because of his familiarity with the geography and terrain, offered to lead the expedition. Washington rejected the idea, although granting its feasibility. A total of ten compositions by Lyon have been preserved; in addition to six of his tunes in *Urania,* there were also a *Marriage Hymn,* the *17th Psalm,* the *19th Psalm,* and *Friendship* ("the Words from Dr. Watts' Lyric Poems—set to Music by the Rev. James Lyon"). There is evidence that Lyon compiled another collection which contained more of his original compositions, but it was not published. Lyon's contribution to American music lies chiefly in his pioneering tunebook, *Urania.* He remained in Machias as a minister, except for a few brief absences, until his death on Christmas Day, 1794.

"MODERN MUSIC" A secular anthem for 4-part chorus by Billings published in *The Psalm-Singer's Amusement* (Boston, 1781). Billings' text is virtually a description of a New England songfest. The piece is characterized by a shifting meter, a touch of fuge, even a little jig-like conclusion in which Billings asks for applause from the listeners.

MORGAN, JUSTIN (1747–1798) Morgan was a farm boy who "took to learning," and his name has come down through history as much because he was the establisher of a breed of horses named for him, as for his musical output —of which only 9 works are known. Morgan was born in West Springfield, Mass., and lived his last decade in Randolph, Vt. It was there that Morgan was best known as a town clerk, singing master, teacher, and tavern keeper. Morgan's wife, Martha, died in childbirth in 1791 and Morgan, apparently not a wealthy man, had to place all 5 of their children with friends and neighbors. Unlike most New England tunesmiths, Morgan never published a songbook; his compositions were preserved in the collections compiled by others. Morgan's works are (all choral): "Sounding Joy," "Judgement Anthem," "Montgomery," "Pleasant Valley," "Amanda," "Symphony," "Despair," "Weathersfield," and "Huntington."

"MY DAYS HAVE BEEN SO WONDROUS FREE" Song composed by Francis Hopkinson (q.v.), ca. 1759, and which, according to Sonneck and most musicologists, is "probably the earliest secular composition of a native American extant." The song, written when Hopkinson was in his early twenties, reveals the influence of the popular-art song of the period, especially British. The lyrics were written by one Dr. Thomas Parnell (1679–1718). A "pretty song," Sonneck fittingly called it.

OLD AMERICAN COMPANY A British theatrical troupe, originally the American Company, which arrived in America before the Revolution and brought entertainment, including concerts and musical plays, as far north as Annapolis and to the South. The com-

pany flourished under the direction of Lewis Hallam and traveled during the next decade to the larger cities, such as Charleston, Philadelphia, and New York. The American Company waited out most of the Revolution in Jamaica, returning in 1782, and by 1785 was known as the Old American Company. It was the most important group in America during the last half of the 18th century. By 1796 the company's home base was New York—in the John Street Theatre —under the management of William Dunlap (q.v.). Actors were expected to sing and singers to act, making it possible to present musical entertainments, operettas, comic operas, etc. The birth of the American musical theatre is generally traced back to the influential Old American Company.

PASTICCIO A form of musical entertainment, very popular in the late 18th century, consisting of a medley of songs (not necessarily by a single composer). The songs, "compiled from the most eminent masters," were strung out along a plot not unlike the ballad operas that the pasticcio eventually supplanted. The term comes from the Italian, meaning a pastry or pie. The French form is, of course, pastiche, a medley or hodgepodge.

PELISSIER, VICTOR (ca. 1760–1820) French-born, Pelissier arrived in America in 1792, spent a year in Philadelphia, then moved to New York. A trained musician, he was active in the musical life of the city; he made many concert appearances and was first horn player in the orchestra of the Old American Company (q.v.). Composer and arranger, Pelissier produced original works for the company (a job he shared with James Hewitt, q.v.). Among Pelissier's theatre works are the ballad opera *Edwin and Edwina* (based on a story by Oliver Goldsmith), produced in 1796, and *Ariadne Abandoned by Theseus in the Isle of Naxos* (1797) in which "Between the different passages spoken by the actors, will be Full Orchestral Music, expressive of each situation and passion." Also *Sterne's Maria, or the Vintage* (1799, with a book by William Dunlap, q.v.), and, among other works, an "allegorical musical drama," *The Fourth of July; or Temple of American Independence* (1799). Pelissier adapted, arranged, or orchestrated compositions of many other composers. Before his death in Philadelphia, Pelissier published a collection of his songs and instrumental pieces entitled *Columbian Melodies* (Philadelphia, 1811).

PETER, JOHN FREDERIK (1746–1813) Johann Friedrich Peter was born in Holland on May 19, 1746, studied there and in Germany before leaving for America and the Moravian community at Bethlehem, Pa., in 1770. Peter served in several Moravian communities during his lifetime, in Pennsylvania, Maryland, New Jersey, and a decade in Salem, N.C., as director of the Collegium Musicum. Not the least of his contributions to American musical life was the collection of music, mainly by Italian and German composers, that he had copied and brought to America. Peter is regarded as the most gifted of the Moravian composers. He was also an organist and violinist (and it might be noted that he married a musician, Catherine Leinbach, leading soprano of the Salem Church Choir). Peter's works number well into 100, most of them religious songs and anthems. A cantata, *A Psalm of Joy,* was compiled and arranged by Peter for a Moravian lovefeast (a prayer and song festival) at Salem in 1783; this was the first known organized celebration of the 4th of July. Most notable among Peter's secular works are the fine *Six Quintets* (1789). He died in Bethlehem on July 19, 1813.

PLAIN TUNE A homophonic setting, not to be confused with the Gregorian plainchant, of a psalm or hymn (text from the British hymnodist, the Reverend Dr. Isaac Watts: 1674–1748), structurally simpler than the fuging tune, the more elaborate anthem, or set piece.

PLAY-PARTY GAME Really a dance accompanied by voice or voices rather than an instrument, i.e., a country dance without the fiddler. Play-party games were popular where dances were forbidden, and combined dancing with the singing games of children. Dance movements were borrowed from traditional square dances (although intimacies such as a man swinging his party with his arms around her waist were not permitted). Play-party games were, even so, disguised flirtation and courtship.

READ, DANIEL (1757–1836) Roughly the contemporary of Billings (q.v.), Read was born in Attleboro, Mass., on Nov. 16, 1757, and became one of the most distinguished of the early New England group of composers. He, in fact, composed more fuging tunes than Billings. A soldier during the Revolution, Read settled in New Haven, Conn., and formed a printing partnership with Amos Doolittle (1754–1832). Where Read obtained his musical knowledge is not known, but he was active as a music master and compiler of tunebooks as well as a composer. Read was also the proprietor of a general store, which was undoubtedly the major source of his income. In 1785 he began publishing his collections, the first being *The American Singing Book* (New Haven) and which went into several editions. With Doolittle he began *The American Musical Magazine* the following year, but it lasted for only 12 issues. Read's other books include *An Introduction to Psalmody* (New Haven, 1790), *The Columbian Harmonist* (New Haven, 1793), which was republished, revised, and supplemented several times, and the unpublished *Musica Ecclesia or Devotional Harmony* completed in the composer's 75th year (1832). Read's musical career traversed those years of American music from the early crude but powerful works of the New England school to the advent of the proponents of the "scientific" school that would hold sway in the 19th century. In his later years Read admitted to the errors of his youth and agreed with the new musical educators. His early music, however, had been remarkably popular, enjoyed good sales and the doubtful recognition of being widely reprinted by pirate tunebook editors. Read died in New Haven on Dec. 4, 1836.

REINAGLE, ALEXANDER (1756–1809)   Born in Portsmouth, England, in 1756 of Austrian parents, Reinagle was one of the most versatile and well rounded of the foreign-born "American" musicians. Arriving in New York early in 1786 Reinagle introduced himself as a member of "the Society of Musicians in London." He had been a friend of the "great Bach," Carl Philipp Emanuel, and a student of Raynor Taylor (q.v.). Apparently not sufficiently recognized in New York, where he presented concerts as instrumentalist and vocalist, Reinagle moved to Philadelphia, where he was active as a teacher (he instructed Washington's adopted granddaughter, Nellie Custis and the children of Francis Hopkinson), gave concerts (harpsichord, piano, violin) and, most importantly, composed and was an important figure in the musical theatre of Philadelphia. He was co-founder, with Thomas Wignell, of the Chestnut Street Theatre (1793), for which Reinagle arranged, composed, conducted, and officiated at the keyboard. Besides preparing arrangements of the works of others, Reinagle was a prolific composer of songs, instrumental pieces, and music for the theatre. His most important works for the musi-

cal stage include *La Forêt Noire* (1794), *Slaves in Algiers, or, A Struggle for Freedom* (1794; text by Susanna Haswell Rowson, 1762–1824), *The Volunteers* (1795, also with a text by the British novelist-playwright Mrs. Rowson), *The Savoyard, or The Repentant Seducer* (1797), and the Richard Brinsley Sheridan adaptation of a play by Augustus von Kotzebue, *Pizarro, or the Spaniards in Peru* (1800, in collaboration with Raynor Taylor). His compositions for instruments include *A Selection of the Most Favorite Scots Tunes* (1787), the *Federal March* (1788), *Miscellaneous Quartett* (1793), *Concerto on the improved Pianoforte* (1794), *Preludes* ("In three classes for the improvement of practitioners on the pianoforte," 1794) and *Sonatas for Pianoforte* (I–IV, ca. 1786–1800). Reinagle also composed a number of popular songs: "I Have a Silent Sorrow Here" (1799), "Rosa" (1800), and the patriotic "America, Commerce and Freedom" (1794). In later years Reinagle managed a theatre in Baltimore, where he died on Sept. 21, 1809.

ST. CECILIA SOCIETY   The first music society, named for the patron saint of music, established in America in Charleston, S.C., in 1762 (another was formed in New York in 1791, merged with the Harmonical Society in 1799, and by 1800 had become the Philharmonic Society of New York). The original St. Cecilia Society employed a fine professional orchestra, a concert hall (a "large, inelegant building," according to journalist Josiah Quincy), and presented impressive concerts. The Society existed until 1912.

SELBY, WILLIAM (1738–1798)   Organist, harpsichordist, and composer, Selby arrived in Boston about 1771, where he soon found work as organist of King's Chapel; he also appeared in concerts performing his own works. During the Revolution, when music-making lagged, Selby opened up a shop where he sold "Port, Teneriffe, Malaga Wines, Tea, Brown and Loaf sugar, logwood, English soap, etc." As the war drew to a close, Selby became more active again and was instrumental in the emergence of Boston as one of the important musical centers in the United States. In February of 1782 he announced the forthcoming publication of *The New Minstrel,* a monthly publication of essays on music—instrumental and vocal—and promised "a collection of original compositions in Music." Apparently subscriptions were meager, for it never appeared. But Selby continued to promote concerts, compose, and publish. He had begun composing before his arrival in America and, in about 1767, had published *Ten Voluntaries for the Organ or Harpsichord;* in 1789 several of his songs were published in *The Massachusetts Magazine* in Boston, among them "Ode for the New Year," "On Musick," and "The Rural Retreat." In 1790 he announced the publication of *Apollo, and the Muse's musical compositions* which, in 6 parts, was to have consisted of several of his original works: *Anthems in four parts, with symphonies for the organ; Voluntaries or fuges for the organ or harpsichord; Sonatas or lessons for the harpsichord or pianoforte, also, transposed for the German flute and guitar; A piece with variations for the harpsichord or pianoforte, in concert with the violin and guittar* (sic); *A concerto for organ or harpsichord, with instrumental parts; A Sonata for two violins and violoncello* and *Two anthems for three and four voices.* Unfortunately only a few of Selby's compositions have been preserved. Except for a short period as an organist in Newport, R.I., Selby lived in Boston until his death in 1789.

SET PIECE A composition, either sacred or secular, especially written to a selected text (i.e., not to a metered hymn or psalm). The music to set pieces, because of their irregular meters, could not be transferred to other lyrics as could the music of psalms and hymns of specified meters.

SHAPE NOTE The use of geometric forms to denote musical pitch, instead of the standard notation. A triangle represented "fa" in the old solmization system, a circle "sol," a square "la," and a diamond "mi." The idea was to simplify sight-reading of music and, in America, appeared in one form as early as the beginning of the 18th century (Tufts's *Introduction to the Singing of Psalm-Tunes*). The first true shape-note tunebook, however, was Smith and Little's *The Easy Instructor* (1798), which was adapted by Andrew Law (q.v.) for his *Art of Singing,* 4th ed., 1803). The method of learning to read music via the shape note spread in the rural areas of New England (and was considered "unscientific" by the defenders of Better Music), eventually giving way to more sophisticated teaching methods. The shape-note system, however, was kept alive in the West, to some extent, and also spread to the South, where it is practiced to this day. Shape notes have also been popularly called "buckwheats."

STONE, JOSEPH See Abraham Wood.

SWAN, TIMOTHY (1758–1842) Born in Worcester, Mass., the chiefly self-taught Swan was an admirer of William Billings. Fatherless by the age of 16 (Swan was one of 13 children), he was apprenticed several times before he was employed by a hatter in Northfield, Mass. Around this time Swan attended a singing school, which excited his musical interests, learned to play the fife, and began jotting down original tunes that were circulated in manuscript as well as printed in tunebook collections. One of his songs, "Poland," composed around his 18th year, became very popular during Swan's long lifetime and after. Upon the completion of his apprenticeship in 1779, Swan moved to Suffield, Conn., where he set up business as a hatter and a singing master. He also married the daughter of a local pastor, Mary Gay, who was a singer and eventually became the mother of 10 musical Swans. Swan composed both sacred and secular songs besides writing poetry. While still living in Suffield he began gathering his original compositions and publishing them (along with some works of others). *The New England Harmony* and *The Songster's Assistant* were published ca. 1800 and *The Songster's Museum* in 1803. Swan's style was folklike and direct, not unlike that of his idol, Billings. He seems not to have earned much from his publications, however. In 1807 Swan moved again, to Northfield, where he had been apprenticed to a hatter as a boy, and where he spent his time writing, worked as a librarian (his neighbors called him "poor, proud, and indolent") until his death, at 84, in 1842. Several of Swan's original songs were still being reprinted and sung in the early 20th century, among them, "China," "Ocean," and "Pownall."

TAMMANY: OR THE INDIAN CHIEF The earliest known American opera on the Indian, libretto by Ann Julia Hatton, music by James Hewitt. First performed under the auspices of the Tammany Society in New York on Mar. 3, 1794. Mrs. Hatton based her plot on the Society's namesake, a Delaware chief who was supposed to have welcomed William Penn. The opera, despite its Indian theme, was patently political and Anti-Federalist. The libretto, though printed, appears to have been lost and only one song, "Alknomook (The Death Song of the Cherokee Indian)," survived. Hewitt later published a *Tammany* quickstep, but it is not certain that that, too, is an excerpt from the opera. *Tammany* was performed several times in New York, twice in Philadelphia, and once in Boston. It was well received by the Anti-Federalists and denounced ("wretched thing") by the Federalists. No musical critique has come down to us.

TAYLOR, RAYNOR (1747–1825) Born in England, Taylor, as a boy, sang in the King's Chapel Royal singing school. In addition to singing he undoubtedly studied the keyboard and began his professional career as an organist and music teacher (one of his students was Alexander Reinagle, q.v.). Eventually he became music director and composer at the Sadlers Wells theatre. He had become, by this time, well known as a composer of ballads. But, when he was about 45, Taylor appeared in Baltimore advertising himself as a "music professor, organist and teacher of music in general," in October 1792. He was also appointed organist of St. Anne's Church at Annapolis. Concurrently Taylor teamed up with one of his pupils, a Miss Huntley, "late of the theatre Royal, Covent Garden," for the presentation of "a musical entertainment on a new plan." This was an "olio," a musical extravaganza of songs and recitation which could be regarded as an antecedent to the revue or vaudeville. Taylor not only composed the songs, but also sang duets with Miss Huntley and provided "a piece on the Grand Pianoforte, preceding each part . . ." His salary as organist was not paid him so Taylor moved to Philadelphia in 1793 and became one of the city's leading musical figures. He continued to play the organ (in St. Peter's Church) and composed, primarily for the musical theatre, as well as for various instrumental combinations. Taylor may have written his *Six Sonatas for cello and continuo* before he left England; in America he produced, among other works, *An Ode to the New Year*

(1794), a *New Overture* (1796), and, at a concert in 1796, presented a *Divertimento for orchestra* and a *Violin Concerto;* in 1797 Taylor announced the publication of a *Symphony* (probably an overture) and a *Sonata for the pianoforte with an accompaniment for a violin.* For the theatre Taylor wrote the music for numerous productions (most of this material has been lost), one of the first being announced for production in Annapolis, *Gray Mare's the Best Horse* (ca. 1792, before the composer left London); others: *Capocchio and Dorinna,* a "mock Italian opera" (1793), *La Petite Piedmontese, or The Travelers Preserved,* a "serious pantomimical ballet" (1795), a play with music, *The Iron Chest* (1797), and *The Shipwrecked, or La Bonne Petite Fille* (1797). In addition, Taylor composed many individual songs and piano pieces and collaborated on musical scores with his pupil Reinagle (q.v.). Taylor died in Philadelphia on Aug. 17, 1825.

TUCKEY, WILLIAM (1708–1781) The name of Tuckey, an émigré from Somersetshire, England, first appeared in New York newspapers in 1753. He was apparently already an established musician, having served in Britain as the Vicar Choral of the Cathedral in Bristol. Tuckey soon found work in America as organist of Trinity Church, and taught music in the Charity School of the church. Under Tuckey's direction the Trinity Church Choir earned a fine reputation. Tuckey also organized concerts (he performed Handel's *Messiah* in America 2 years before its first performance in Germany, which occurred in April 1772). Outside the church Tuckey gave concerts of secular music and composed both secular and sacred music. He was unsuccessful in achieving publication of his works, except for individual pieces in the collections of others, such as his "Knighton," which was printed in Sim-

eon Jocelin's (1746–1823) *The Chorister's Companion* (1782). Tuckey's other known compositions are *Thanksgiving Anthem* (1760), *An Hymn (by way of an anthem),* *Three Dirges (for chorus),* both 1771, and *Anthem from the 97th Psalm* (1787). Tuckey's compositions were popular in his time, but are little known in the 20th century. His greater influence was in the field of music education, particularly in choral singing, and in his contribution to the growth of New York concert life. Tuckey died in Philadelphia on Sept. 14, 1781.

URANIA Tunebook compiled by James Lyon (q.v.) and published in Philadelphia in 1761. Historically important because of Lyon's efforts at instruction in his "Plainest & most Necessary Rules of Psalmody." The bulk of *Urania* was taken from earlier English collections. (It marked the first publication in America of "God Save the King,"—"America," to most—entitled "Whitefield's" in *Urania*. George Whitefield—thus the title—was author of the text.) The collection contained 70 psalm-tune settings, 14 hymns, and 12 anthems; of the total of 96 compositions, 6 are ascribed to Lyon (there are no composer credits). These are settings of 8th, 18th, 23rd, 95th, and 104th psalms, and an Anthem on the 150th psalm. *Urania* also contained the first published example of a fuging tune.

THE VILLAGE HARMONY A tunebook compiled by printer Henry Ranlet and published by him in Exeter, N.H., in 1795. Although Ranlet was probably not a musician, he was not ignorant of some of its theory and technicalities. *The Village Harmony* enjoyed wide popularity in New England and went through some 17 editions. The early printings (i.e., the 5th, 1799) were notable for the great number of songs by native Americans— Billings, Kimball, Holden, Holyoke, Swan, and many others. Around the turn of the century, the printer, in compliance with the Good Music movement, began ridding *The Village Harmony* of its American works. The advertisement for the 17th edition promised that "Those alterations have been made which correspond to the progressive improvement of the publick taste in Sacred Musick. A few Classical European tunes have been substituted for some of less perfect character, and the valuable foreign musick which is retained, and which the publick has not ceased to venerate and admire, is still preserved in this collection, secure from the touch of American innovation."

VON HAGEN, PETER ALBRECHT (1750–1803) Von Hagen emigrated from Holland before the Revolution, arriving in Charleston, S.C., in 1774. He billed himself as an "organist and [former] director of the City's Concert in Rotterdam." Von Hagen remained in Charleston for 15 years earning a living as a music teacher and giving concerts. His was a musical family, for his wife was a pianist, vocalist, teacher, and the mother of 2 musical offspring, a daughter (who sang) and a child prodigy son, Peter Albrecht, Jr. (see Section III). The latter made his debut, aged 8, in New York in 1789, when the family moved from Charleston. The family name, by the way, was still van Hagen; and until his son's debut the father was known as van Hagen, Jr. The family was active in New York's musical life as performers and teachers. Von Hagen, Sr., conducted theatre orchestras and was involved in managing subscription concerts (no doubt employing members of his family). In 1796 the von Hagens moved to Boston where he established a music school and opened up a "Musical Magazine and Warrented Piano Forte Ware House." Von Hagen, Sr., was conductor at times at the Haymarket Theatre and, in 1800, organist at the Stone Chapel. He composed music for the theatre, much of it of an incidental nature, or arrangements. Among his original works are a *Federal Overture* (1797) and a *Funeral Dirge* (sung after the death of George Washington).

WOOD, ABRAHAM (1752–1804) By profession a fuller (one who "fulls" cloth by shrinking to make it bulkier), Wood spent his lifetime in his native Northboro, Mass., except for brief service as a drummer in the Revolution. Largely self-taught in music, Wood was a singer as well as composer. Little is known about Wood except for these few facts. He composed well over 2 dozen songs, anthems, etc., such as "A Hymn on Peace" (1784) and "Ode on Spring" (text by Daniel George, 1789). Wood published his first compilation, *Divine Songs,* in 1789 and collaborated with Joseph Stone (1758–1837) on *The Columbian Harmony* (1793). Both contributed to the collection (Stone gets little attention in studies of American music, less even than Wood). Among the Wood songs in *The Columbian Harmony,* (which mixes sacred with secular songs) are "Music Descending on a Silent Cloud," "Sweet Muse Descend and bless ye Shade," "Swift as ye sun Revolves ye Day," and "An Elegy on the Death of a Young Lady." Among Stone's contributions are "Our Term of Time is Seventy Years" and "Farewell Honour's Empty Pride." Wood's "Warren," inspired by the Revolutionary War hero Joseph Warren, who died in the Battle of Bunker Hill, was also included in *The Columbian Harmony.* The song reveals a composer of remarkable invention.

"YANKEE DOODLE" Undoubtedly the top "hit" of the War of Revolution and one whose origin has eluded scholars for years. The tune has been credited to several nationalities—English, Hungarian, Dutch, etc.; it certainly dates from a time and came from a place where authorship meant little—and its patent folk quality indicates that it merely happened spontaneously. Nor is there agreement on the 2 words of the title. Some say Yankee is of Dutch origin, others that it is an Indian corruption of "Anglais," etc. "Doodle" may, or may not, be a corruption of "do little." That "Yankee Doodle" was used by the British soldiers to mock the colonists before the Revolution is an undisputed fact. The tune, if not the specific words, dates much further back. As early as 1730 the Reverend James Pike of Somersworth, N.H., notated in a manuscript tunebook the air to "Yankey Doodle"; it is one of the airs in the comic opera of 1767, *The Disappointment* (q.v.). The first known publication occurred in Glasgow in 1782, and the first American publication in 1794 in Benjamin Carr's *The Federal Overture*. The British taunted the Americans with the song, performed it during the occupation of Boston, and then had it turned on them. The Americans adopted the song as their own and sang it back at the British. Legend has it that it was played by an American band at the surrender of Cornwallis at Yorktown (a British band had just fittingly rendered "The World Turned Upside Down"). Whatever the full and factual story of the origin of the tune and text, "Yankee Doodle" has enjoyed a long life in the form of parodies, as a thematic idea in various overtures, variations, and medleys.

III

From the Second Awakening to the Second New England School

(1800–1865)

The currents of American music in the 19th century flowed out of the post-Revolution attitudes of the final decade of the 18th century. The folk traditions of music-making were supplanted, particularly in urban centers, by diffusion of the "scientifick musick" proponents who had all but done in the folk composers of the first New England school. The influx of foreign-born musicians was even greater than in the previous century and, by the end of the 19th, American-born musicians were either European-educated or going there—primarily to Germany, the cradle of "good music"—to be polished Teutonically in the solid, and often stolid, elements of "scientific" music. This product was formally well wrought but lacking in imagination—inspiration being impossible to teach. The music for the concert or recital hall composed during the latter 19th century and the early 20th was the first to be widely recognized as "American" music, despite its underlying Germanic sound.

From the turn of the century to the end of the Civil War a consolidation of American musical life, especially in the Eastern seaboard cities of the North, occurred with the birth and growth of opera companies, orchestras, the expansion of the music publishing industry; by midcentury there were 3 piano manufacturers extant—Chickering, Knabe, and Steinway. Musical education was placed on a truly systematic basis.

Interestingly, the 2 outstanding composers of this period (perhaps *the* 2) were Stephen Foster and Louis M. Gottschalk, both of whom did not disdain popular traditions in music. Gottschalk, whose best work utilized folk and popular themes, was a virtuoso pianist—and the virtuoso, particularly of European origin, did very well in the United States around midcentury. Showmanship became an element in the arts.

Popular song bloomed in the minstrel show and the sentimental ballad became a staple of the several singing families that toured the States; ballad singers—the most successful imported from England—spread the banality. Parlor pianos proliferated and so did colorfully lithographed sheet music on every possible pianistic subject, in addition to the usual quicksteps, marches, waltzes, and polkas. There was *The Wind Demon* (originally entitled *The Cyclone*), numerous battle pieces, plus *The Dying Poet,* not to mention an *Atlantic Telegraph Polka, Horticultural March,* and the grand march entitled *Corliss Engine.*

An important social movement, with cultural overtones, swept through sections of the country, especially the South and West. This was the religious revival movement that became known as the Second Great Awakening which flowered at a camp meeting in Logan County, Kentucky, in July 1800. In effect, it was the popularization of religion. Literally thousands of people, male and female, white and black, gathered to live in tents at the chosen site for several days participating in the services and to praise God in song. The extraordinary popularity of this evangelistic revivalism encouraged its diffusion northward through Maryland, Delaware, and Pennsylvania, southward into Tennessee and farther, and eastward into Virginia and the Carolinas.

Religious impact (and it was important) aside, the Second Awakening was also musically important. The tunebooks that were published in the wake of it preserved much valuable musical Americana—the Yankee fuging tunes, folk hymns, religious ballads, "spiritual songs," and revival hymns. Many of the tunebooks even continued the shape-note system. Packet songsters were used also but provided only the texts to songs. Among the important collections of folk hymnody growing out of the Second Awakening were John Scott's *Hymns and Spiritual Songs for the Use of Christians* (1803), perhaps the first; John Wyeth's *Repository of Sacred Music, Part Second* (1813); Ananias Davisson's *Kentucky Harmony* (1816); Allen D. Carden's *The Missouri Harmony* (1820); and other Harmonies: *Columbian* (1825), *Union* (1837), and *Knoxville* (1838), culminating in *The Southern Harmony* of William Walker (1835) and White and King's *The Sacred Harp* (1844). The latter, with revisions, but with shape notes intact, was still being published in 1960.

In the previous paragraph the term "spiritual songs" was used; around 1933 the musicologist-scholar George Pullen Jackson coined another term: "white spiritual." This was to distinguish between those revival songs sung by whites and those sung by blacks and it suggested that the haunting Negro spiritual may originally have been inspired by white revivalist singing. Since little attention was paid to the songs of the slaves before the 19th century, the extent and direction of the influence would be difficult to measure. Since the camp meetings were frequently interracial, undoubtedly the influence worked both ways. The white spiritual and the black were communal folk inventions of great power and beauty.

Opposed to the folk, the shape note, and the first New England school of songwriters were the conservative admirers of "scientific" music. This was not new, for the movement had begun before the turn of the century. In the early decades of the 19th century important musical organizations were formed. As early as 1810 Boston had a Philo-Harmonic Society, formed by German-born Gottlieb Graupner; 5 years later Graupner joined with others in the important Handel and Haydn Society. While the first did not survive, the latter exists to this day. In 1821 the Musical Fund Society was founded in Philadelphia by British-born Benjamin Carr and others; Bethlehem, Pa., had its Philharmonic Society in 1820 (it lasted until 1839). The first permanent musical organization was the New York Philharmonic Society, which was formed in 1842. Under the direction of trained musicians these orchestras brought musical enrichment to the growing cities—and the self-consciously cultured became concerned with "good" music and music education.

Along with the growth of the symphony orchestra, opera too began to assume a greater importance in the lives of Americans with the time, the money, and the inclination. New Orleans, which had supported opera as early as 1796, established its first opera company at the Orleans Theatre in 1810. The tour by this company (1827–33) brought opera to the Northern cities of Baltimore, Philadelphia, New York, and Boston. They did not, of course, present American operas, since there were none.

The movement for good music reached a culmination in the works of Lowell Mason, who was virtually sponsored by the powerful Handel and Haydn Society. Mason, at the time a bank clerk, not an aspiring musician, had compiled and edited a collection of hymn tunes, many by European masters (Beethoven, Mozart, Gluck, and, of course, Handel and Haydn), and published as *The Boston Handel and Haydn Society Collection* (1822). Its success encouraged Mason to leave Savannah, Ga., give up banking and return to Massachusetts, where he was to conduct music in several churches at a guaranteed salary. By 1827 he was the president of the Society and revealed a genius for music education of the "scientific" persuasion, if not for composition.

Mason's objectives were to "improve" the quality of the American psalm tune and to bring "better music" to the masses. The first he accomplished (at least to his satisfaction) in a regular series of songbooks that sold in the hundreds of thousands. Mason's 2nd accomplishment was far-reaching and significant: he pioneered in the field of music education, first by introducing the study of music in public schools and in the instruction of teachers who, in turn, would teach. From modest beginnings in Boston (where, with others, Mason founded the Boston Academy of Music in 1832), the idea of teaching music in schools quickly spread and effected the direction of American music into the 20th century. Mason spread the word by appearances at what he called "conventions," and with the aid of several colleagues, among them William B. Bradbury, a Britisher, George J. Webb, Isaac Woodbury, and Thomas Hastings (next in influential importance only to Mason himself). Also assisting in the "good music" campaign was journalist-musician (and ex-minister) John S. Dwight, whose powerfully influential *Journal of Music,* established in 1852, spread the gospel to the detriment of the native American composer. Mason, his followers, plus Dwight's *Journal,* contributed to the Germanization of American music that reached a flowering in the last half of the 19th century.

The quasi-folk tradition of the first New England school was kept alive in the face of Mason and company in the works of such latter-day psalmists as Jeremiah Ingalls, Eliakim Doolittle, Hezekiah Moors, and Elkanah K. Dare. In turn, many of their songs were sustained by the folk-spiritual outpourings of the Second Awakening.

Linking the sacred with the secular and popular was the remarkable Hutchinson family, which initiated a long concert career in a Baptist meetinghouse in their native New Hampshire (Milford) singing "hymns, anthems and glees," according to John, one of a family of 13 children. This was in 1839. Their father disapproved of their singing so that eventually various members of the "tribe of Jesse" began leaving the farm for the cities. Feeling they required polish, 4 of the brothers went to Boston where they came under the influence of Lowell Mason and George Webb, but it was not until 1842 that the vocal group that would become the Hutchinson Family made its concert debut. The idea of a family group of singers was not new, there being numerous ones before the Hutchinsons of European origin. There was, for example, a celebrated Rainer family, Tyrolean singers who were successful in England and America. Their disciplined singing (generally of folk songs) impressed scientific music advocate Lowell Mason and was regarded as the model of fine choral singing. For a time the Hutchinsons were called the "New Hampshire Rainers." Their success, in turn, encouraged other family troupes: the Alleghanians, Father Kemp's Old Folks, the Peak and Berger Families of Bell Ringers, the Amphions, the Orpheans, et al.

These groups specialized in simple presentations of simple songs, sentimental ballads, frequently heartrending, that enjoyed tremendous popularity before— and after, for that matter—the Civil War. The Hutchinsons were an enlightened group and, while they sang the songs of others, provided themselves with those songs that touched on their various causes, abolition, temperance, and women's suffrage. The Hutchinsons toured, in 1859, through Ohio with yet another singing family, the Lucases, whose members were black. The reception in Fremont in February of that year was curious but typical: ". . . but to see respectable white persons (we presume they are such) travelling hand in hand with a party of negroes, and eating at the same table with them, is rather too strong a pill to be gulped down by a democratic community." The use of the word "democratic" is indeed strange. Whatever the limitations of their repertoire, the Hutchinsons were impressively advanced in their thinking and influential in the dissemination of the appreciation of vocal music.

One of the Hutchinsons' most popular renditions was of the elaborate song —it has been called a cantata—"The Maniac," composed by Londoner Henry Russell. He was one of several English singer-songwriters who prepared the way for the Hutchinsons and others who enlivened American mid-19th-century concert life with doleful, sentimental song. Russell and fellow countryman Charles E. Horn arrived in the United States in 1833; 6 years later they were joined by John Philip Knight. All were ballad composers as well as singers; Horn enjoyed the added attraction of his singing wife. Knight remained in the States for a year, leaving behind, if nothing else, "Rocked in the Cradle of the Deep." Horn moved between Britain and the United States in various capacities: composer, musical director, and conductor. His songs, like most of the period, were in the genteel vein and it was as a musical influence that he was most important. He was one of the founders of the New York Philharmonic and served as conductor of the Handel and Haydn Society in Boston, where he died.

Russell remained in America for nearly 9 years and had a profound influence on the direction of American song and concert life. Russell's songs were in the tradition of the widely popular "Home, Sweet Home," an "aria" from the opera *Clari,* with music by an Englishman and words by an American actor. The sentiment of that song persisted from its days (beginning in 1823) well into the late 19th century. Russell made a sizable contribution to that tradition before returning to England: "Woodman! Spare That Tree!" "The Old Arm Chair" (a mother song) and its sequel, "Oh! Weep Not." This was customary of the time—successful songs were followed by a companion song, or by an "answer," to a previous song. The reception of such songs was frequently the flow of tears as much as applause.

American-born songwriters created in the same vein. One of the most successful of the period was John Hill Hewitt, son of James Hewitt, and known for some time as the "Father of the American Ballad." Another successful songwriter was Septimus Winner, who often composed under the pen name of "Alice Hawthorne," and was best known for a song he/she never wrote, "Listen to the Mocking Bird." Winner attributed the tune to a black youth, Richard Milburn.

The most gifted songwriter of the pre-Civil War period and beyond was Stephen Collins Foster, one of the great melodists of American music. Foster's early interest in music was not encouraged by his merchant father, but by the time he was 16 or so he had produced his first song, "Open Thy Lattice, Love," to words by George P. Morris (author also of the words to "Woodman! Spare That Tree!"). Foster's early songs were in the genteel, nostalgic genre of the time, conventional, melodic, and not very distinctive. By the time he produced "Old Folks at Home" (1851) Foster had found his own voice and in, roughly, a decade created nearly 200 songs—ballads, comic songs, duets—and a handful of modest instrumental pieces. Such ballads as "Wilt Thou Be True," "Beautiful Dreamer," "Jeannie with the Light Brown Hair," and "Come Where My Love Lies Dreaming" are melodically distinguished, sentimental or not. The duet—to words adapted from *Romeo and Juliet*—"Wilt Thou Be Gone, Love?" would not be out of place in an early 20th-century operetta. Such rhythmic, often nonsense, songs as "Oh! Susanna," "De Camptown Races," and "If You've Only Got a Moustache" have not lost their vitality—and the first was a kind of theme song for Americans moving westward during the great gold rush of '49. The songs of Foster were absorbed into the fabric of American folk song.

A handful, but best known, portion of Stephen Foster's output was made up of what he called "Ethiopian songs," popularly known as "plantation melodies," i.e., the white man's imitation of, or borrowing from, the songs of blacks.

This practice coincided with the rise and flowering of a peculiarly American form of entertainment, the minstrel show. Its beginnings can be traced back to the 1820s, when white entertainers in blackface presented incipient stereotyped imitations of the Negro. Among the most successful of the early impersonators were George Washington Dixon, Bob Farrell, and Thomas Dartmouth Rice— the latter the creator of "Jim Crow." Rice also concocted what was called "Ethiopian Operas," a forerunner of the true minstrel show. All 3, and other entertainers not as well known, contributed bits of business, characterization, steps, and the free borrowing of Negro-like songs for their acts.

On the night of Feb. 6, 1843, the Virginia Minstrels, "being an exclusively musical entertainment combining the banjo, violin, bone castanets, and tambourine, and entirely exempt from the vulgarities and other objectionable features which have characterized negro extravaganzas," made their debut at the Bowery Amphitheatre. Of the 4 members, the fiddler was Daniel Decatur Emmett. Encouraged by their reception, the Virginia Minstrels increased their numbers as they toured, soon evolving into the classic minstrel organization.

Emmett's rival, Edwin P. Christy, is claimed to have organized his Virginia Serenaders in Buffalo 2 years before, but they did not make their New York City debut until 1844. No matter, for Christy made a fortune out of the minstrel show and gained wide fame. For a time his name was the generic term for the form; the minstrel show at home and abroad was known as a "Christy." Other troupes soon swelled the ranks as the Ethiopian Serenaders, White's Serenaders (which included the great black dancer, William Henry Lane, better known as "Juba"), and, among dozens of others, Bryant's Minstrels.

Chief composer-entertainer for the Bryant's Minstrels was ex-Virginia Minstrel, "Old Dan" Emmett, who composed or claimed to have composed such songs as "Old Dan Tucker," "Turkey in the Straw" (also known as "Zip Coon" and claimed by both Bob Farrell and G. W. Dixon), and, of course, "Dixie." Christy's Minstrels were musically provided for by Stephen Foster.

In the same year the Virginia Minstrels made their debut (1843), a Norwegian violinist, Ole Bull (1810–1880), began a highly successful concert tour (the first of 5) in the United States. A flashing virtuoso, Bull captivated large audiences for years, the first of foreign virtuosos to do that. No less a showman than P. T. Barnum imported soprano Jenny Lind (1820–1887), "The Swedish Nightingale." (It was Mendelssohn who said of her, "She sings bad music best.") Others followed in the wake of Barnum's press-agentry, such vocalists as Henriette Sontag, María Malibran, and dazzling keyboard artists Henri Herz, Sigismond Thalberg, and, in the same flamboyant imported tradition, the conductor Louis Antoine Jullien (1812–1860), master of the "monster concert for the masses."

Wearing white gloves and waving a jeweled baton, Jullien brought his spectacular music-making to New York in the summer of 1853. M. Jullien's forte was showmanship. He favored the colossal (he loved a swollen orchestra à la Berlioz) and he promoted music, from the symphonies of Beethoven to the most trivial polka. His musicianship was equal to his showmanship and he popularized symphonic concerts with ballyhoo that brought in the masses and presented them with stylishly performed music and his own histrionics (at the finish of a work he would cap "its climax by subsiding into his crimson gilded throne, overwhelmed by his exertions, a used up man . . . "). Newspapers openly referred to Jullien as a humbug but recognized the excellence of his orchestra, its discipline, and that, if Jullien wished, he could interpret the finest music splendidly. Jullien, however, loved to put on a show, such as his *Night, or the Firemen's Quadrille,* complete with an enlarged orchestra, 3 fire companies, real flames, water, and fainting ladies. Beyond such extramusical high jinks, Jullien did manage to whet American appetites for music and perhaps even brought many into the concert hall who had never been there before, as much to observe as to listen. More importantly, he was among the first to make a point of programming American music in his concerts, an innovation in itself in the middle of the 19th century.

America produced its own colorful composer-virtuoso in Louis Moreau Gottschalk, the first native-born musician to achieve an international reputation. By curious coincidence, Gottschalk returned from a stay in Europe the same year that Jullien arrived in the United States, 1853. Like the French conductor, Gottschalk, an extraordinary pianist—a student of Berlioz, a favorite of Chopin—was the ultimate musician as matinee idol. Young women, in the thousands, literally swooned when Gottschalk played, especially such heart-rending works as his own *The Dying Poet* or *The Last Hope.*

These were concessions to popular demand, in the granting of which Gottschalk was not alone. Other exceedingly romantic, programmatic piano pieces were churned out by other composer-pianists (or was it the other way around?) such as Richard Hoffman, George William Warren, Thomas Greene Bethune (more popularly known as "Blind Tom"), Charles Jerome Hopkins, and the unbelievably prolific Charles Grobe.

Gottschalk's importance as a musician lay not merely in his virtuosity at the keyboard. True, he was the first native-born American to convince Europeans that America was not "only a country of steam engines" (i.e., locomotives), as he was informed when first refused admission to the Paris Conservatoire. He was lionized and petted in Europe, in America, literally coast to coast, and in Latin America. As a composer Gottschalk anticipated later American composers in his use of native materials, the Creole melodies of his birthplace, New Orleans, and the exotic rhythms of the places he visited and the Negro. He also employed popular and folk songs, often borrowing freely and unashamedly from Foster. That Gottschalk did not inspire a school or creative followers may be attributed to the fact that his reputation as a virtuoso predominated and the direction his creative bent appeared to be going was not approved of by Lowell Mason and his arbiters of what was good and beautiful in music.

While Gottschalk was not particularly self-consciously American (though he expressed his patriotism during the Civil War in an elaborate piano piece, *The Union*), there were some voices raised in behalf of the "American" composer by the middle of the 19th century.

The most unabashed and perhaps most interesting "American" was the Bohemian-born Kentuckian, Anton Philipp Heinrich, once called, with breath-taking imprecision, the "Beethoven of America" by John Rowe Parker, editor of *The Euterpeiad*. Heinrich, however, preferred the more modest designation, "the log-house composer from Kentucky."

Enthusiasm being no substitute for genius, Heinrich has not gone down in the history of American music for his compositions. Despite a general rejection (or patronization) by recent historians and critics, the music of the Americanized Anthony Philip Heinrich is not without some merit and charm. All things American were grist for his musical mill: the Indian, "Yankee Doodle" (*The Wild Wood Spirit's Chant, or Scintillations of Yankee Doodle*), *The Dawning of Music in Kentucky, The New England Feast of Shells,* even Jenny Lind and the Negro banjo (the latter in a work entitled *Barbecue Divertimento* that, in turn, appeared in *The Sylviad; or Minstrelsy of Nature in the Wilds of N. America,* published between 1823 and 1826). It might be noted that Heinrich's banjo antedated Gottschalk's by nearly 3 decades.

But it was as a proponent of the American composer (it has been intimated that Heinrich had a specific American composer in mind) and a champion of American music that Heinrich was most influential. He did not remain in his Kentucky log cabin and eventually settled in New York where he became an important, if eccentric, figure in its expanding musical life. He knew all the musicians of the time and was even chairman of the committee that first met to form the Philharmonic Society in New York. He was affectionately called "Father" Heinrich by his musical friends and obviously influenced their thinking about the native composer and his music.

Following in Heinrich's chauvinistic musical footsteps, though perhaps even noisier, were William Henry Fry, credited with the composition of the first American grand opera, *Leonora,* and George Frederick Bristow, credited with composing the *second* American opera, but the first based on an American theme, *Rip Van Winkle*.

Of the 2, Fry was probably the more influential because, in addition to being a musician-composer, he was also a critic and lecturer. As editor of the New York *Tribune* in Europe and later music editor of the *Tribune* in New York, Fry could broadcast his views on the American composer and decry the indifference of American audiences and orchestras. The colorful Jullien performed several of Fry's orchestral works, which are not particularly "American" in sound, revealing European influence.

Bristow was a professional musician who played in the first violin section of the Philharmonic Society from its inception in 1842. He joined Fry in the attack on the musical establishment, which resulted in his resignation from the Philharmonic in 1845 (he later returned and remained for several decades). Bristow's resignation dramatized the position of the native-born composer and the chronic nonperformance of his works but had little effect. Still, his own opera, *Rip Van Winkle*, was performed in 1855 and revived in New York and Philadelphia in 1870. All of his symphonies were performed in his lifetime, not only by the novelty-seeking Jullien but also by the beleaguered Philharmonic.

The important musical organizations, in general, preferred playing the standard works, with emphasis on the Germanic. When he struck out on his own, Theodore Thomas (who had played in both Jullien's orchestra and the Philharmonic) continued the practice, although occasionally performing American works. A fine conductor and an astute programmer (i.e., audience pleaser), Thomas stated his position honestly when he said, "I do not believe in playing inferior works merely because they are American."

American works, inferior or superior, had a better chance of performance by the growing number of bands and popular band concerts. The tradition, dating back to before the Revolution, grew in the decades between so that by the end of the 19th century, few cities, and even small towns, did not support bands and concerts in the park.

The marching band was an imported idea (the so-called "concert band" was developed by a German, Wilhelm Wieprecht) and shaped to American needs. Initially the marching band served a military function, though by the 19th century, what with fluctuating instrumentation—easing out of the woodwinds and the ascendance of brass and then combining them—bands evolved into concert units of some size. Special arrangements were made of classic works, quicksteps, polkas, overtures, and song medleys and were performed along with marches. Of the known 19th-century bandmasters the most influential was Irish-born Patrick S. Gilmore, who formed his band in 1859. Among his contemporaries were the black leader Francis Johnson and members of the Dodworth family—Allen, Harvey, and their father Thomas, who not only led bands, but also composed and published their marches. Another contemporary was Claudio Grafulla (1810–1880), composer of *The Washington Greys*.

It was Gilmore, however, who set the tone of the American band—its instrumentation, repertoire, and even the practice of wearing the quasi-military uniform. (Upon his death, his position was filled by another Irish immigrant, Victor Herbert, whose story belongs in a later section.) Gilmore's penchant for showmanship recalled Jullien's monster concerts and employed a chorus of 5,000 and a band of more than 500. Once when he performed the "Anvil Chorus," he added an additional anvil part "performed by One Hundred Members of the Boston Fire Department."

Gilmore's love of musical giantism did not carry into the Victor Herbert leadership, nor into the golden era of the band that followed in the latter 19th century and the advent of the master bandmaster of all, John Philip Sousa, and his protégé, Arthur Pryor.

Gilmore, using the pseudonym "Louis Lambert," composed or adapted one of the outstanding songs of the Civil War, "When Johnny Comes Marching Home." Before that could happen the United States endured 4 shattering years of brutal war, the effects of which would last for generations. The warring factions not only shared the same language, they also shared the same songs. Those songs, as have none ever since, expressed the emotions of the peoples engulfed in the war, singing of their hopes, fears, joys, heroes, villains, and hatreds. Unlike the songs from future wars, the songs of the Civil War have lived, practically folklore, long after the devastating events that inspired them.

A good explanation for the quality of our Civil War songs may lie in the fact of their quantity: over 2,000 songs were published during the first year alone. By 1865 many thousands more were added to the outpouring. Out of this some were bound to be memorable, honest, and endowed with long life.

The surprising "hit" of the war was undoubtedly Dan Emmett's old minstrel-show "walk-around," "I Wish I Was in Dixie's Land"—"Dixie" to most— which was played at the inauguration of Jefferson Davis, President of the Confederacy (Feb. 18, 1861). The Union Army bands clung to the song also, but its Southern associations led to fewer performances, if not abandonment, by midwar. "Dixie," despite Northern authorship, remained the South's unofficial national anthem.

A satiric song, taunting one Sergeant John Brown, improvised by members of his company and adapted to a hymn tune, was initially known as "John Brown's Song." It served as a popular marching song for the volunteers at Fort Warren, Mass., and was sung in various versions, including "They will hang Jeff Davis to a sour apple tree, etc." Following the aborted raid on Harper's Ferry by abolitionist John Brown, the song, better known as "John Brown's Body," was revised to commemorate that event. This version was heard by Mrs. Julia Ward Howe, who composed new words and title: "The Battle Hymn of the Republic" ("Mine eyes have seen the Glory of the coming of the Lord, etc.").

Similar in title, but livelier, was George F. Root's "The Battle Cry of Free-dom," a rallying song and Root's answer to Lincoln's call for troops in 1861. Root, a prolific songwriter, also produced other songs of the period, among them "Just Before the Battle, Mother," "The Vacant Chair," and the classic "Tramp! Tramp! Tramp!"

Lincoln's call encouraged not only a poem by James Sloan Gibbons, but no less than 16 musical settings (one by Stephen Foster): "We Are Coming, Father Abraam, 300,000 more."

Sentimental songs abounded, of course, since the tradition was already established. The slaughter of young was a favorite subject and the mother of the soldier irresistible. Despite the national tragedy, humor was not altogether lost. The South produced a "comic song" reply to Gibbons' poem with the song, "We're Coming, Fodder Abraham," actually more caustic than comic in its references to "the new American citizens of African Descent." More characteristic was "Mother on the Brain" by Eugene T. Johnson, who had the last word on the glut of mother songs by utilizing their titles strung together with caustic commentary of remarkable wit.

The truth was that young men and even boys were being killed on the battlefield and the sight of a boy whose only contribution to the battle was playing a drum genuinely stirred poets and songwriters. "The Drummer Boy of Shiloh" by Kentuckian William Shakespear Hays was such a song; not in the same genre, but affecting, was "Tenting On the Old Camp Ground" by Walter Kittredge. There was also "All Quiet Along the Potomac Tonight," which New York-born Southerner John Hill Hewitt set to the words of another New Yorker (Goshen), Mrs. Ethel Lynn Eliot Beers (the words had originally been claimed, in a melodramatic tale, by one Major Lamar Fontaine, a Confederate Cavalry officer).

Mrs. Beers composed an astute comment on the typical official military bulletin: "All quiet along the Potomac," which separated the Confederate and Union armies, within shot of each other. Her point is made in the line, "Not an officer lost, only one of the men." Hewitt's simple setting was effective. Hewitt, it might be noted, served for a time as a drill master of Southern troops in Richmond.

The loyalties of several songwriters were questioned during the Civil War. After the occupation of New Orleans, in 1862, an overzealous General Benjamin Franklin Butler closed down the Blackmar music store for selling Confederate songs. He imprisoned Will S. Hays, who was at the time a war correspondent, for writing "seditious songs" (Butler was recalled from his post within a few months).

A more celebrated case was that of popular songwriter Septimus Winner, who penned the appeal, "Give Us Back Our Old Commander," after Lincoln fired General George B. McClellan in 1862. Edwin M. Stanton, the Secretary of War, had Winner imprisoned for his "seditious" song. He was pardoned by the President himself. Lincoln's death by assassination 3 years later inspired Winner's "A Nation Mourns Her Martyr'd Son."

By war's end the nation had more than 600,000 sons to mourn. Great sections of the South were devastated physically, economically, and culturally. Its lands had been the setting for the war's battlegrounds and the resting places for promising young men, North and South. The period of Reconstruction that ensued after Lincoln's death—vindictive, corrupt, inefficient—did not nurture the arts. The North had sacrificed good men too, but it did not suffer the direct consequences of defeat; its communications systems, industries, commerce, way of life, churches and schools did not lie in ruins. The North's urban centers prospered and would dominate all phases of music in the decades to come, primarily out of New York and New England and its Second School of musicians-composers.

ALLEN, RICHARD (1760–1831) Born a slave, Allen served the family of his master, Philadelphia lawyer Benjamin Chew, until he and his family were sold to the owners of a large plantation in Delaware when he was seven. Though poorly educated, Allen was intelligent and hard-working. At the age of 17 he converted to Methodism after attending nighttime secret religious services for blacks. Allen, still a slave, took on additional work to purchase his freedom. He then went into the ministry, eventually founding the African Methodist Episcopal Church in 1794, marking a break with the white Methodists. In time Allen was elected bishop of the A.M.E. Church, whose influence spread from Philadelphia to Baltimore, Charleston, and New York. Rather than depend on the current Methodist hymnal, Allen chose to compile his own, selecting those tunes he knew were favored by his congregations, and published *A Collection of Spiritual Songs and Hymns Selected from Various Authors by Richard Allen, African Minister* (Philadelphia, 1801). The first printing contained 54, and the 2nd, the same year, with Allen identified as "Minister of the African Methodist Church," 64—texts only. The music was known from the traditional Methodist hymnbooks (Wesley, Watts, et al.). The texts may have been edited by Allen and some of the tunes may have been folk songs or original compositions. One critic of the period complained of "a growing evil" in the singing of sacred songs, and specifically referred to "merry airs, adapted from old songs" adapted to traditional hymn texts. He also suggested that many of the hymns were "composed and first sung by the illiterate blacks of the society." Obviously the Negro congregations were enlivening the 4-square Methodist hymns—a practice which led to attracting white visitors to hear "a quicker and more animated style of singing . . . than prevailed in the slower heavier cadence of the other churches of the city [Phila.]" Allen's hymnbook, the first of its kind, was used by A.M.E. churches until 1818, when a revised edition was issued. The new edition eliminated most of the original hymns and replaced them with more sophisticated ones. Allen's influence, however, had been deep and hymns that he may have created were retained by the congregations.

"AMERICA" The tune of this non-belligerent patriotic song is of doubtful authorship and has been attributed to many, from Henry Carey to John Bull. Research over the years has not uncovered the name of its composer. It is known, however, that it was first printed in Britain in 1774. Under the title of "Whitefield's" it was first published in America in Lyon's *Urania* (1761), opening with the words "Come thou almighty King," and identifying the tune as "God Save the King," which was and is the British national anthem. After the Revolution the tune served for several songs: "Hail Godlike Washington," "God Save 'The Rights of Man,'" "Now Let Rich Musick Sound," and one, among many others, that began:

> *God save each female's right*
> *Show to her ravish'd sight*
> *Woman is free.*

That was in 1795, no less; a song whose time had not, alas, come. It was in 1831 that the most enduring text was written. Lowell Mason (q.v.) presented a young Boston clergyman, Samuel Francis Smith (1808–1895), with a collection of German music books, suggesting that Smith might come upon a suitable tune that might be adapted to a song for children. The one selected was entitled *"Heil dir im Siegerkranz,"* which apparently Smith did not recognize was sung to the tune of the British national anthem. He produced his version as "My Country, 'Tis of Thee," which was introduced at a children's celebration of the American independence at Boston's Park Street Church on July 4, 1831.

"THE BATTLE HYMN OF THE RE-PUBLIC" The melody to this song was probably written by a Charleston, S.C., organist-choirmaster William Steffe (ca. 1830–1890). A composer of Sunday school hymns, Steffe's original song was entitled "Say, Brothers, will you meet us?" which was popular at camp meetings in the late 1850s. It was also popular among glee clubs, and it was one such group from a Massachusetts Infantry Battalion ("The Tigers") that revised the words as a joke(?) on one of their members, Sergeant John Brown. The unsuccessful raid on Harper's Ferry (1859) and subsequent hanging of another John Brown apparently rendered the song timely and the new first line, "John Brown's body lies a-mouldering in the grave," and the final line of the verse, "His soul is marching on!" celebrated his martyrdom (as some abolitionists believed him to be; others thought that Brown was a hotheaded madman). Attempts were made to sing of a less questionable martyrdom by substituting the name of one of the war's first celebrated fatalities, a Colonel Elmer E. Ellsworth, murdered by a secessionist hotel owner in Alexandria, Va. Many songs commemorated the death (Ellsworth had torn a Confederate flag off the roof of the Marshal House and was shot for his gesture), but John Brown remained the hero of that song. As such it was widely sung by marching soldiers and performed by bands (some of the soldier-sung words were rather ribald). It was while she was visiting Washington, D.C., and saw a small battle, that author-lecturer Julia Ward Howe (1819–1910) heard troops going into battle singing "John Brown's Body," more correctly "Glory! Hallelujah!" One member of the party, the Reverend James Freeman Clark, suggested that Mrs. Howe write new words to the song. The text appeared in the *Atlantic Monthly* and was published early in 1862. The title page read: "Battle Hymn of the Republic/Adapted to the favorite Melody/of/ 'Glory Hallelujah,'/Written By/Mrs. Dr. S. G. Howe." The new, powerful words undoubtedly assured the song's longevity.

BETHUNE, THOMAS GREEN— "BLIND TOM" (1849–1908) Born a slave, May 25, 1849, and blind from birth, Thomas and his mother, Charity Wiggins, were eventually sold to a Colonel Bethune, who recognized the unique musical ability of the youngster and proceeded to make a fortune off his property. When Thomas Wiggins was about 7 he revealed a phenomenal musical memory and was capable of playing difficult exercises on the piano merely through having heard a single performance; he had no musical instruction. Bethune saw the value of this gift and, after bestowing his name on the young pianist, arranged for his first concert in Savannah, Ga., in 1858—"Blind Tom," as he was to be widely known, was 9. He was an instant success and Bethune arranged for extensive tours in the United States and Britain. Blind Tom's pianistic ability as well as his remarkable memory encouraged his exploitation as a kind of freak (some writers classify him as an idiot savant). His repertoire consisted of pieces by the usual masters—Bach, Chopin, Beethoven

—and contemporary flashy pieces by Richard Hoffman (q.v.), Gottschalk (q.v.), Sigismond Thalberg, et al. Operatic paraphrases were a staple of Blind Tom's programs also, revealing his ability to improvise variations on the various themes. His original works were often "imitations" or descriptions in sound of rainstorms, a battle, various instruments (bagpipe, harp, music box, etc.), a waterfall. It was claimed that he had committed some 700 pieces to memory and could perform them on demand. Blind Tom Bethune was unique—another feat: playing "Yankee Doodle" with one hand, a hornpipe in another key with the other, while singing, in a 3rd key, "Tramp! Tramp! Tramp!" Unfortunately, his exploitation by the Bethune family placed him more firmly in the category of vaudeville rather than in the American musical mainstream. His popularity continued even after he was no longer the "Negro Boy Pianist," for as late as 1904, just 4 years before his death, he was appearing on the concert stage. None of his original works were taken up by later pianists. He died sometime in 1908.

BRADBURY, WILLIAM BATCH-ELDER (1816–1868) One of the members of the group of musical reformers associated with Lowell Mason (q.v.), Bradbury was born in York, Maine, on Oct. 6, 1816. From a musical family, Bradbury had all the advantages of a solid musical education and by the time he was in his teens he had mastered several instruments. He went to Boston to study harmony and later became a pupil of Mason's. The latter helped Bradbury obtain a job as a music teacher in Machias, Maine, in 1836. Bradbury, who was then 20, divided his time between Machias and Boston, where he became a disciple of Mason and his teaching methods. He became the organist of the Baptist Tabernacle (1840) and, with

Mason, helped to found the New York Normal Institute. Bradbury was one of the first American musicians who studied in Germany (ca. 1847–49). He was also a successful businessman (he and a brother owned a piano manufacturing company) and a prolific, and again very successful, producer of music books for Sunday schools—more than 50 between 1841 and 1867. These books had such titles as *Bradbury's Golden Shower of Sunday School Melodies, The Golden Chain, The Golden Censer*—they sold in the hundreds of thousands. Bradbury collaborated with another Lowell disciple, Thomas Hastings (q.v.), on *The Mendelssohn Collection* (New York, 1849). Among his better known original songs are "Jesus Loves Me" (1859), "Sweet Hour of Prayer" (1860), and "He Leadeth Me" (1864). Overwork aggravated a lung condition and Bradbury died, aged 51, in Montclair, N.J., on Jan. 7, 1868.

BRISTOW, GEORGE FREDERICK (1825–1898) The son of an English conductor and singing teacher, Bristow was born in Brooklyn, N.Y., on Dec. 19, 1825. He studied piano with Henry C. Timm (1811–1892), a German-born pianist and organist and a future president of the New York Philharmonic. By the time he was 11, Bristow was playing the violin in a theatre orchestra. Upon the founding of the Philharmonic, he became a member of it and remained with it for about 40 years, except for one brief period of estrangement. The hiatus occurred when Bristow resigned after accusing the Philharmonic of neglecting the native composer. Bristow at one time studied composition with George A. MacFarren and, in fact, had had his own *Concert Overture*, Op. 3, performed by the Philharmonic in 1847. Besides being a vocal champion of the American composer, Bristow was a prolific contributor to the American music repertory. He composed 6 symphonies and was working on a 7th (*Niagara*) at the time of his death. His opera *Rip Van Winkle* was produced at Niblo's Garden, New York City, the 2nd opera composed by an American but the first based on a native theme. It was a success and was revived again in 1870. For all his avowed Americanism, Bristow obviously drew upon Italian opera for his inspiration. Another opera, *Columbus,* was never completed. Bristow was also active as conductor with the Harmonic Society, a choral group that performed American works, including one of Bristow's oratorios, *Praise to God* (1861); he also composed a cantata, *The Great Republic* (1879), 2 string quartets, and smaller pieces for organ, violin, or piano. He died in New York City on Dec. 13, 1898.

CAMP MEETING A revivalist religious gathering at which services were held in the open or in tents. Characterized by exhortations by folk preachers, congregational participation and singing, the camp meeting represented a democratization of American religion. In the 19th century the revival began in Logan County, Ky., and became known as the "Second Awakening" (the first "Great Awakening" occurred just before the middle of the 18th century and also affected religious music in America). Baptist primarily, the camp-meeting revival quickly spread to the frontiers, southward and westward. In the wake several hymnbooks were published; the camp meeting not only preserved some of the earliest American musical traditions (to the present) such as fuging tunes and the use of shape notes but also gave birth to the spiritual, black and white.

CARRELL, JAMES P. (1787–1854) A wealthy farm owner, the Reverend Carrell was also a compiler of hymnals and a composer. He was born in Lebanon, Va., on Feb. 13, 1787. Little is known about Carrell except that he was orphaned at an early age. He eventually became a Methodist minister and revealed his musical abilities with the publication of *Songs of Zion* (1821), "a small collection of tunes, principally original," and the larger *Virginia Harmony* (1831), containing 17 original tunes by the author and, among others, 2 by another pioneer in the Southern folk hymn tradition, Ananias Davisson (q.v.). Several of Carrell's most popular tunes—"Solemn Thought," "Ebenezer," "Sussex," "Melody," "Lebanon New," etc.—were republished in other Southern collections, including the classic *Sacred Harp* (q.v.). Carrell died in Lebanon on Oct. 28, 1854.

CHILD, EBENEZER (1770–1866) Connecticut-born, Child was a resident of Vermont from the age of 12, when his family moved to Leicester. He was a typical New England farmer-musician who worked at several jobs, including surveyor, town clerk, etc. Child's musical background is unknown, but in 1804 he published *The Sacred Musician,* consisting of the usual introduction to the rudiments of Psalmody and a "Variety of Psalm Tunes" as well as a "Large number of Anthems, Odes and Dirges," of which, the author indicated, a "Great Part" were "Never Before Published." Child, one of the pioneers of Vermont music makers, died at the age of 96 in Castleton, Vt.

CHRISTY, EDWIN P. (1815–1862) Showman, one of the early organizers of the minstrel show (q.v.), Christy began with his "Virginia Serenaders" in Buffalo, N.Y., in 1842 and, as the "Ethiopian Serenaders," at Palmo's Opera House, New York City, in 1846. A year later Christy's Minstrels took over Mechanic's Hall on Broadway and remained there for a decade. The show was as successful and popular in England as in the United States. Christy is equally known as the man who exploited Stephen Foster (q.v.), who provided the Christy Minstrels with numerous "Ethiopian Songs." Christy is credited with a number of songs, but since he frequently took credit for the work of others (i.e., Foster), they may be questionable. Christy retired in 1854, turning over the minstrels to his adopted son, George Harrington, who kept the troupe going until ca. 1868. Christy, in a fit of depression, killed himself by jumping out of a hotel window in New York.

A COLLECTION OF SPIRITUAL SONGS AND HYMNS SELECTED FROM VARIOUS AUTHORS BY RICHARD ALLEN, AFRICAN The first hymnal compiled for a black congregation, the African Methodist Episcopal Church of Philadelphia, by its founder and pastor, Richard Allen (q.v.). Published in 1801, with texts only, the *Collection* went through several editions to which eventually tunes were added, among them probably the earliest "spirituals" (q.v.).

CONNOR, A. J. R. (fl. 1844–1860) Not a great deal is known about this early Philadelphia Negro composer-musician except that he was a virtuoso on the ophiclcide (a large, bassoon-shaped bugle, eventually replaced by the tuba). Connor composed popular pieces for the period "social orchestra" (q.v.) and led an orchestra drafted from the famed Frank Johnson's Colored Band.

DA PONTE, LORENZO (1749–1838) Venetian-born poet. Though he tried to associate himself with American opera ventures in New York, Da Ponte failed, as he had in many other ventures. He moved from Italy to Vienna, to London, and then to New York, hounded by debtors. Unsuccessful as a grocer and liquor dealer, Da Ponte taught Italian at Columbia College in his later life. He is best remembered for having written the librettos to Mozart's *The Marriage of Figaro, Don Giovanni,* and *Così fan tutte* (during his Vienna stay).

DARE, ELKANAH KELSEY (1782–1826) A Methodist minister, musical theorist, and composer about whom little is known. Dare was dean of boys at Wilmington College, Del., and apparently contributed to John Wyeth's (q.v.) seminal *Repository of Sacred Music, Part Second* (q.v.), an important link between the first New England School and Southern folk hymnody. Dare published his own collection, *The Periodical Harmony,* in 1810; Wyeth included 13 tunes in the *Repository,* among them the excellent "Babylonian Captivity."

DAVISSON, ANANIAS (1780–1857) A singing-school master, composer and compiler of hymns, Davisson was born Feb. 2, 1780, somewhere "along the borderline of Maryland and Virginia" (according to early historian William Blake in *Musical Million,* published in 1884). When he was about 45, Davisson retired from teaching and lived out the rest of his life on a farm, where he died, aged 77, on Oct. 21, 1857, near Dayton, Va. His considerable contribution to American music was made in the compilation of *Kentucky Harmony* (q.v.) in 1816 or '17, the first of the Southern hymnbooks. In 1820 Davisson published the *Supplement to the Kentucky Harmony,* consisting of entirely different songs. Several tunes in book collections were composed by Davisson, one of which, "Idumea," was widely reprinted in later Southern tunebooks.

DIGNAM, WALTER (1827–1891) Manchester, N.H., musician, arranger for brass band, and composer. Dignam was born in Paddum, England, on Apr. 3, 1827. He came to America in 1844 and worked for a time in Rhode Island and New Hampshire in the fabric industry. He eventually joined the Manchester

Cornet Band in the 1850s, composing ("Spring Flower Polka" and "Wooden Spoon Lancers") and arranging. During the Civil War, Dignam was active with the 4th New Hampshire Regiment Band. He died in Manchester on Apr. 23, 1891.

"DIXIE" "I Wish I Was in Dixie's Land" was a minstrel show "walk-around" (q.v.) that, according to the first edition's cover, was "Written & composed expressly for Bryant's Minstrels by Dan D. Emmett" (q.v.) and published in 1860. The song was sung as early as April 1859 (which explains a pirated edition, claimed by one J. C. Vierick, which was published in New Orleans before Emmett's was issued in New York). The derivation of the title is not certain but is generally thought to be a reference to the Mason-Dixon Line (the 2 men were English surveyors and astronomers) —the settlement of a boundary dispute between Pennsylvania and Maryland— which divided the slave from the free states. "Dixie," as a popular name for the South, may have been used before Emmett used it in the song's title. The tune was adapted to the "Lincoln Grand March" by F. W. Rauch and served as one of Lincoln's campaign songs; it was also played as "Way Down South in Dixie" at his inauguration. It served a similar function at Jefferson Davis' inauguration. Already popular in the South, it became a Southern anthem with the eruption of the Civil War and new bellicose words by Albert Pike (1809–1891). The easygoing minstrel words were transformed into a call to arms. After Lee's surrender, Lincoln addressed a crowd that had come to serenade him at the White House. He then requested the band to play "Dixie," commenting that though "our adversaries over the way had attempted to appropriate it, I insisted yesterday that we had fairly captured it." On checking with the Attorney General, Lincoln informed the crowd, "he gave his opinion that it is our lawful prize. I ask the band to give a good turn upon it." "Dixie," despite appropriation and (jokingly) recapture as a spoil of war, remains a quintessential American song.

DODWORTH FAMILY A musical family specializing in composing, playing, arranging, and selling music for the brass band. The family patriarch was Thomas, but it was his son Harvey B. (ca. 1820–1890) who most contributed to family fame and fortune. Thomas was a cornetist and, during the Civil War, leader of the famous Dodworth's Band which was active in Washington during much of the early months of the war. Harvey B. Dodworth, who led the band from 1860–1890, also performed in New York's Central Park. He was composer of such works as "Hymn of Columbia," "The Raw Recruit Quadrille," and "Leap Year Polka." In 1853 his *Brass Band School* was published and sold at H. B. Dodworth & Co. at 493 Broadway and Dodworth is identified as Leader and Director of Cornet Band. A brother, Allen, was a violinist, a composer as well as the leader of the National Brass Band. As early as ca. 1825 Allen and his father, Thomas, were members of the Independent Band in New York. It later split into separate units, Allen Dodworth's National Brass Band, Harvey Dodworth's 13th Regiment Band, David L. Downing's 9th Regiment Band, and Claudio Grafulla's 7th Regiment Band (1834). While these early band musicians are biographically elusive, their band pieces and arrangements are extant, their creations being considered, in general, ephemeral. But they contributed to a lively American tradition; the Dodworths were especially influential and Harvey was known to have aided a young immigrant musician, Theodore Thomas (Sec. IV). And the Dodworths were members of the infant New York Philharmonic. According to John Tasker Howard, a "C. Dodworth was a virtuoso on the trombone, and C. R. played the concertina."

DOOLITTLE, ELIAKIM (1772–1850) Born in Cheshire, Conn., Doolittle was an itinerant singing master who attended Yale. He was also a regular teacher in schools and taught in New York and Vermont, traveling from his home in Hampton, N.Y. Doolittle's musical interest may have been influenced by his older brother, Amos (1754–1832), who owned a music shop and publishing house in New Haven, Conn. It was there that Eliakim's collection of original songs, *The Psalm Singer's Companion*, was published in 1806. One of Doolittle's most popular secular songs was inspired by an incident during the War of 1812—when the American ship, the *Hornet*, sank the British man-o'-war, *Peacock*, "The Hornet Stung the Peacock." As a composer he belonged to the early New England School employing a folkish approach to the fuging tune and innovative rhythmic and harmonic ideas. He died in Argyle, N.Y.

DWIGHT, JOHN SULLIVAN (1813–1893) A powerful voice in the "good music" crusade, Dwight was born in Boston on May 13, 1813. A Harvard graduate (1832), he became a Unitarian minister. He abandoned that to teach music and Latin at Brook Farm, the transcendentalist center of utopian socialism (1841–47; the experiment ended when a fire destroyed the main building). Dwight returned to Boston where, with the aid of the Harvard Musical Association (which he had helped to found), he began publication of one of the most important musical periodicals, *Dwight's Journal of Music*, in 1852. He was editor, critic, publisher, and owner for 6 years. When Dwight sold the magazine to the Oliver Ditson Co. in 1858,

he remained as editor. After several other changes of ownership, the magazine ceased publication in 1881. In those 29 years or so, the *Journal*, which Dwight subtitled "A Paper of Art and Literature," had a profound impact on music in America. For 20 years weekly, and for 9 fortnightly, *Dwight's Journal* crusaded for "better music" by publishing European critical essays, biographies of composers, assorted articles on music, poems, essays and articles not necessarily on music, as well as complete works by such Dwight favorites as Bach, Beethoven, and Gluck—even complete operas in piano reduction. Dwight stated his credo in the first issue: "A thousand specious fashions too successfully dispute the place of true art in the favor of the public . . . It [art] needs a faithful, severe, friendly voice to point out steadfastly the models of the TRUE, the *ever* Beautiful, the Divine." Dwight was prepared to provide that voice. His especial favorite was Beethoven in particular and German music in general (he had trouble with Wagner, however). He had his aversions, too, among them the songs of Stephen Foster (Dwight did not accept popular music at all), Louis M. Gottschalk (q.v.), primarily because he had studied in Frivolous France and not in Germany, and, for some reason, Brahms (because he was not Beethoven) and such monster concerts as the French conductor Jullien and bandmaster Patrick S. Gilmore perpetrated. Despite his prejudices and conservatism, Dwight disseminated the word on good music, insisting that listening to music was a worthwhile experience, not mere entertainment. It was not "a wandering away from the business of life, an amusement to idle away an hour." Dwight's advocation of the Germanic, while it propagandized for much excellent music, had a profound influence upon the direction of American music and the American composer in the latter 19th century. Dwight did not do all the writing for the *Journal*. He "borrowed" freely from foreign journals and had correspondents in the music centers of the country. George William Curtis reported from New York, W. S. B. Mathews, who was to write the second history of American music, from Chicago; likewise Frederick Lewis Ritter, who wrote the first. A. W. Thayer, American consul at Trieste, also contributed; later he would write one of the best biographies of Beethoven. Dwight also published, for the first time in America, almost all of J. N. Forkel's *Life of Bach* (1855). In his late sixties, after the *Journal* suspended publication, Dwight continued to write music criticism (for the Boston *Transcript*), contributed articles to *The Atlantic Monthly,* and served as president and librarian of the Harvard Musical Association. He spent his final 3 years in retirement and in the admiring company of the cultural elite of Boston (among Dwight's good friends over a long lifetime were Hawthorne, Longfellow, Emerson, Lowell, and Oliver Wendell Holmes). Dwight died on Sept. 5, 1893.

ECKHARD, JACOB, SR. (1757–1833) Born in Eschwege, Germany, Eckhard emigrated to America in 1776, arriving at Richmond, Va., where he was organist and music teacher at St. John's Episcopal Church. Ten years later Eckhard settled in Charleston, S.C., as organist and choir director of the German Lutheran Church and, in 1809, in the same capacities at St. Michael's Episcopal Church. Eckhard compiled a tunebook in manuscript which was used by his choir; in 1816 he published his *Choral Book,* also a compilation from English, German, and American sources. His "Naval Song (The Pillar of Glory)," celebrating American victories over the British Navy in the War of 1812, was a prizewinning song of 1813. Eckhard died in Charleston in 1833.

EMMETT, DANIEL DECATUR (1815–1904) Along with E. P. Christy (q.v.), Emmett is associated with the birth of blackface minstrelsy in the United States in the early 1840s. Emmett was born on a farm near Mt. Vernon, Ohio, on Oct. 29, 1815, one of 4 children, and had little schooling. In his early teens he worked for printers and then joined the Army at the age of 17. Even as a youngster Emmett had shown a gift for music and it was in the Army that he actually studied music, playing the drum and fife (he later mastered the banjo, flute, and violin). In 1835 he was discharged from the Army when his true age was learned and he joined a circus and played in the band. Under the influence of Negro singers and song, Emmett began composing his own (in the tradition of Dixon and Rice), according to his account, before he left Mt. Vernon. Although "Old Dan Tucker" was not published until 1843, Emmett claimed to have written it in 1830 or '31. It was in that same year that the Virginia Minstrels made their debut at the Bowery Amphitheatre on Feb. 6. This marked the true beginning of what would become the traditional minstrel show: its form, its songs, and its personnel (although that would expand as the form gained popularity). Emmett provided the songs for the minstrels. Some of these songs were original, some were borrowings or adaptations (i.e., "De Boatman's Dance," "Turkey in the Straw"). Emmett moved from minstrel troupe to troupe, joining Bryant's Minstrels in 1858, under the direction of showman Dan Bryant (born Daniel O'Brien; 1833–1875). For this group Emmett wrote his songs and "walkarounds" (q.v.) and, of course, his most celebrated song, "Dixie's Land" (1859). In 1888 Emmett retired to his home near Mt. Vernon, Ohio, but was persuaded to make a tour with Al Field's Minstrels in 1895—when he was truly

"Old Dan" (his early stage name was "Old Dan Emmit"). Emmett was 88, and living on a pension, when he died on June 28, 1904.

"FASOLA FOLK" General term for the rural people of the South and West who clung to the fa-sol-la system of designating the degrees of the scale by syllables instead of letters (solmization). Fasola folk also utilized the shape-note system and along with it many of the early songs by New England composers in disrepute because of the emphasis upon "scientific music" during the 19th century. The songs of the fasola folk were preserved in such collections as *The Repository of Sacred Music, Part Second* (q.v.) and *The Sacred Harp* (q.v.).

FOSTER, STEPHEN COLLINS (1826–1864) America's first great popular songwriter was born on July 4, 1826, at Lawrenceville (near Pittsburgh), Pa. The town, which would eventually be absorbed by Pittsburgh, had been established by his father, William Barclay Foster, landowner-businessman. Although Stephen evidenced an early interest in music, he was not encouraged. His father's comment: "His leisure hours are all devoted to musick, for which he possesses a strange talent." Foster was then 16 and had already written, 2 years before, *The Tioga Waltz*, while a student. His first published song, "Open Thy Lattice, Love," also belongs to Foster's 17th year (it was published, however, in 1844). It was a characteristic sentimental period piece, the first of many in Foster's output. (It might be kept in mind that the term "sentimental," as condescendingly applied to the songs of the mid and latter 19th century by musicologists and music historians, is a recent usage. The people who composed, sang, and loved those songs hardly regarded them as "sentimental" in the current, rather pejorative, sense.) Although Foster may have been a musical product of his time, had a scanty professional education and a weakness of character, he succeeded in transcending his faults with a natural gift. He quickly revealed no love for business, even considered a Navy career (his father was more inclined to West Point), but finally settled for a position with his brother in Cincinnati to learn bookkeeping. Despite the legends, Foster was good at his work —but better at songwriting. It was his success in getting his early songs published that decided Foster's future and fate. The popularity of "Oh! Susanna" (1848)—Foster was then 22—led to contract offers from publishers and to Foster's abandonment of the business and into a disastrous marriage to Jane McDowell, the daughter of a physician, in 1850. The newlyweds moved in with the senior Fosters in Allegheny, Pa. It is from the first 5 years of this unstable marriage that some of Foster's most enduring songs date: "Old Folks at Home," "Massa's in de Cold Ground," "My Old Kentucky Home, Good Night" "Old Dog Tray," "Jeannie with the Light Brown Hair," and "Come, Where My Love Lies Dreaming"—all produced from 1851 to 1855, along with several others. Foster's larger, and later, reputation has rested primarily on his "Ethiopian Songs" written for E. P. Christy (q.v.) and his Minstrels. Actually these songs form a small fraction of the songwriter's output, although they have proved to be the most durable. This could be attributed partly to Foster's gift as a songwriter and partly to his firsthand knowledge of his material, picked up on the rivers, riverboats, and loading wharves he knew as a child and young man. He borrowed themes he had heard in a Negro church (to which he had been taken by his nurse) for at least 2 of his songs, "Oh! Boys, Carry Me 'Long" and "Hard Times Come Again No More." It is notable that near the end of his life Foster abandoned the use of the crude minstrel show Negro dialect (for "Down Among the Cane Brakes" and "Old Black Joe," 1860). Foster, who only went into the production of Ethiopian melodies reluctantly (he permitted Christy to take full credit for "Old Folks at Home"), suffered attacks in the "better music" press for these creations, most notably at the hands of Thomas Hastings (q.v.), one of the members of the Mason group. Hastings regarded "Old Folks at Home" as belonging to "the lowest dregs of music" that filled the minds of the young with "poisonous trash." But the growing popularity of these songs led Foster to relent and he turned out songs for minstrel shows unashamedly in time (although he never saw his name on the sheet music of "Old Folks at Home" in his lifetime). A little-known aspect of Foster's work was his attempts at the composition of instrumental music, arranging and orchestration. In 1854 Firth, Pond & Co. published his *Social Orchestra* for "flute or violin—arranged as solos, duets, trios and quartets." The collection contained arrangements of many Foster melodies ("Old Folks" was attributed to E. P. Christy), various waltzes, polkas, and songs by numerous composers, including Mozart and Beethoven. New Foster compositions included *Village Festival Quadrilles, Jennie's Own Schottisch, Village Festival Jig, The Old Folks Quadrilles,* which is a charming arrangement of 4 earlier songs, and the *Cane Brake Jig.* Foster was reasonably successful; he was published, popular, and receiving royalties. He was not, however, as affluent as he should have been. There were money and personal problems. There were frequent separations and reconciliations. The Fosters had a daughter, Marion, born in 1851; she died in 1935. Foster drank; he desperately sold the rights to new songs outright for trivial sums. In 1860 the Fosters moved to New York, the major publishing center, and the composer attempted to straighten out his overdrawn royalty accounts by producing a stream of hackwork songs. In the summer of 1861, when Foster's drinking had worsened, Jane Foster left him again, fearing he would be unable to support her and their child. She eventually found work with a telegraph company in Pennsylvania, and the marriage, though not totally broken off, was virtually over. Foster deteriorated into a song-peddling drunkard, and yet he managed to compose such songs as the witty "Mr. and Mrs. Brown" and "Beautiful Dreamer" (one of several of Foster's "last songs"). That year Foster was living on the Bowery. In his hotel room, ill, he fell and gashed himself on a washbowl. Taken to Bellevue Hospital, he died there in his 38th year, on Jan. 13, 1864.

FRY, WILLIAM HENRY (1813–1864) Champion of the American composer, journalist and composer, Fry was born in Philadelphia on Aug. 10, 1813. From a publishing family, Fry was largely self-taught in music. He later studied theory with Leopold Meignen (1793–1873), a French-born teacher and arranger. He began composing early, an overture when he was 14, and by the age of 20 had succeeded in having one of his overtures performed by the Philadelphia Philharmonic Society. Opera was Fry's first love (especially Italian) and although his first attempt, *Aurelia,* was not produced, another one, *Leonora* (with a libretto by his brother, Joseph), was performed at the Chestnut Theatre on June 4, 1845. This is generally considered the first American opera. Fry, although his greater experience lay in the field of journalism (he covered music, art, and the theatre on his father's *National Gazette*), was graduated from the University of Philadelphia (1830) and was eventually admitted to the bar. However, he was first of all a music lover. The year after the production of

Leonora, Fry went to Europe as a correspondent, spending 6 years in London and Paris, where he met Berlioz, among other musicians. In 1852 he returned to the United States and became music critic and an editorial writer for the New York *Herald Tribune.* From this post, and via lectures, Fry expounded his favorite cause: the American composer and his plight. He also continued to compose. Among his works are a *Stabat Mater;* four of his symphonies—*Childe Harold, A Day in the Country, The Breaking Heart,* and *Santa Claus*—were performed by the eccentric Jullien in 1853. A 2nd opera, *Notre Dame de Paris,* was produced in Philadelphia in 1864; the *Overture to Macbeth* was composed 2 years before Fry's death of tuberculosis in Santa Cruz, West Indies, on Sept. 21, 1864.

GILMORE, PATRICK SARSFIELD (1829–1892) Irish-American bandmaster. Born at Ballyar, near Dublin, on Dec. 26, 1829, cornetist Gilmore, at 19, came to the United States, via Canada, as a member of a band. He began conducting a band in Salem, Mass., in 1848 and organized "Gilmore's Band" by 1859. During the Civil War, Gilmore's band was attached to the 24th Massachusetts Infantry; after the occupation of New Orleans, Gilmore was appointed Bandmaster of the Union Forces in the Department of the Gulf. It was while stationed there that Gilmore composed "When Johnny Comes Marching Home" (1863), dedicating it "To the Army and Navy of the Union" and using the name "Louis Lambert" as a pseudonym. There being a Roman Catholic priest who also wrote lyrics at the time, Father Louis Lambert, chaplain of the 18th Illinois Regiment, it is possible that Gilmore wrote only the music and Lambert the words—although the original printing of the song credits "Words and Music" to "Louis Lambert." The next year Gilmore staged a monster concert, in the spirit of Jullien, celebrating the inauguration of a federal governor of Louisiana. For the occasion Gilmore assembled a chorus of 5,000 and a massed band of about 500. Back in Boston after the war, Gilmore was to repeat a series of such massive concerts in his National Peace Jubilee (1869), a World's Peace Jubilee (celebrating the end of the Franco-Prussian War), and, finally, a Third World Peace Jubilee (1873), all employing musical forces in the thousands. In 1872 Gilmore became the Bandmaster of the 22nd Regiment, New York National Guard, which he led until the end of his life and with which he toured extensively. Except for "When Johnny Comes Marching Home," Gilmore's original compositions are little known today. He died, while on tour with the 22nd Regiment Band, on Sept. 24, 1892, in St. Louis while appearing at that city's Exposition.

GOTTSCHALK, LOUIS MOREAU (1829–1869) Pianist-composer, Gottschalk was born into an affluent New Orleans family on May 8, 1829. Revealing an early musical gift, he was given violin lessons at the age of 6. Later he switched to the piano. When he was 13 he left New Orleans for Paris for further piano study but was rejected by Pierre Zimmerman, the director of the Paris Conservatoire, without so much as a hearing, because he was an American and therefore incapable of art. Gottschalk then studied privately—piano and composition. Among his fellow students were such talents as Camille Saint-Saëns and Georges Bizet. His wealth and "connections" made it possible for Gottschalk to know all the right people; his true talent did the rest. Among his admirers were Hector Berlioz (also his teacher) and Frédéric Chopin, who, before Gottschalk was 16, predicted he would become a "king of pianists." Berlioz called him "a consummate pianist." In 1849 Gottschalk made his Paris debut, dazzling audiences with his playing and also presenting several of his own "Creole" compositions on the program, including *Bamboula* and *Le Bananier*. These were based on Afro-American songs and dances he had heard in New Orleans when he was a boy; they also represent the first use of native materials by an American composer. After concert tours through France, Switzerland, and Spain —leaving behind a trail of musical triumphs, adulation, amatory adventures— Gottschalk returned to the United States early in 1853. He made his American debut at Niblo's Salon on Feb. 11. Interestingly, Gottschalk's exotic Americana did not impress his countrymen as much as his pianistic extravaganzas, bravura arrangements of national airs such as his "Caprice Americaine," *Columbia,* or his more obvious tone paintings, such as *The Dying Poet* or *The Last Hope.* As in Europe, Gottschalk quickly became good box office—to the degree that he was able to reject, with some scorn, an offer from Barnum of $20,000 for a year's concert tour. He plunged into the concert world, giving 80 concerts in New York in the winter of 1855–56 alone. He made a tour of the West Indies; he returned to the United States in 1862 and made an extensive tour of the country, from great cities to tiny mining towns, covering 80,000 miles by rail and steamboat in, as Gottschalk noted, "less than two years, giving, on an average, three concerts every two days." His popularity was phenomenal, particularly among the young ladies—which led to problems, as, in addition to numerous satisfied music lovers, he left behind ex-virgins. A sensualist, Gottschalk loved his stay in the West Indies, where he went native—and also composed a good deal. His adaptation of the musics of the many lands he visited —from Spain to Cuba—is one of his

most enduring contributions to music. It was during what was to be his final tour of the United States that Gottschalk was involved in a scandal having to do with the daughter of a prominent San Francisco family who also happened to be a young student at the Oakland Female Seminary. The scandal got newspaper coverage nationwide. (Actually Gottschalk had taken 2 young ladies for an innocent but rather late-hour carriage ride. The public damage was done by an enemy of Gottschalk's, who also resented the pianist's favoring the Chickering piano.) On Sept. 18, 1865, Gottschalk boarded a ship and slipped out of San Francisco under cover of night. He spent his final years in South America, where he performed in concerts and became involved in the presentation of massive concerts of his works. He continued to be the musical matinee idol of the time in Peru, Argentina, Chile, and Uruguay. After settling in a suburb of Rio de Janeiro, he died, aged only 40, of peritonitis (complicated by overwork) on Dec. 18, 1869.

Despite a short life, a career devoted primarily to concertizing and romantic adventuring, Gottschalk managed to compose a good number of valuable works. Of his more than 150 pieces of various proportions, many are bravura piano compositions ranging from the showy, through the lachrymal, to the sublime. Among the latter would be Gottschalk's excellent treatment of folk themes: *Bamboula,* Op. 2, *La Savane,* Op. 3 (based on a Creole ballad), *Le Bananier* (The Banana Tree), *The Banjo,* Op. 15, *El Cocoye, Midnight in Seville, Souvenir of Porto Rico, Fantasy on the Brazilian National Anthem, Columbia,* Op. 34, and *Battle Cry of Freedom,* Op. 55. Also 2 "symphonies," No. 1, *"La Nuit de Tropiques,"* and No. 2, *"A Montevideo."* A one-act opera, *Escenes Campestres (Cuban Country Scenes),* a *Grand Tarantelle for Piano and Orchestra, Variations on the Portu-guese National Hymn for Piano and Orchestra,* several piano duets, and a handful of songs. Gottschalk, America's first musical celebrity, was also the first to suggest that there was a rich vein of musical Americana in its own backyard, an idea that the Bohemian Dvořák would act on nearly a quarter of a century after Gottschalk was buried in Brooklyn.

GRAUPNER, GOTTLIEB (1767–1836) Born in Hanover, Germany, on Oct. 6, 1767, Graupner, who was an oboist like his father, came to America in the early 1790s. In Charleston, S.C., Graupner married a celebrated singer, Mrs. Catherine Hillier. Teaming with his wife, Graupner concertized in Charleston, New York, and Boston, where they settled ca. 1798. It was here that Graupner opened a music store (he was also a publisher) and was prominent in Boston's musical development. He became an American citizen in 1808; 2 years later he gathered a number of musician friends together and formed the Philharmonic Society which performed classic works for their own pleasure. In 1815, Graupner was one of the founders of the Handel and Haydn Society (q.v.), which set high standards of music performance and taste in Boston. Graupner's book, *Rudiments of the art of playing the pianoforte,* was published in 1819. He was also a composer, but little of his work has survived. He performed works for the oboe in his early concertizing years which he may have composed; there is record of a song, "music by Mr. Graupner," performed in Salem in 1799 and entitled "Columbia's Bold Eagle." Dating from the same year is mention of "The Gay Negro Boy" sung by Graupner "accompanying himself on the banjo," an act that antedates the minstrel efforts of Dixon and Rice. Graupner had evidently become acquainted with Negro song and that char-acteristic minstrel instrument, the banjo, during his stay in Charleston. It was, however, as the "Father of American Orchestral Music" that he made his true mark in American music. His Philharmonic Society lasted for more than a decade; the Handel and Haydn Society remains active today. Graupner died in Boston on Apr. 16, 1836.

GREENFIELD, ELIZABETH TAYLOR (1809–1876) Born a slave in Natchez, Miss., Elizabeth Taylor was adopted, while still an infant, by a Mrs. Greenfield, a Quaker, in Philadelphia. The child evidently revealed a fine singing voice and, despite the Quaker's objections to music as a profession, she was given voice training. Initially singing at private gatherings, Elizabeth Taylor Greenfield made her public debut before the Buffalo Musical Association in 1851. "The Black Swan," as she quickly became known, toured the northern United States and Canada. By 1854 she was singing for Queen Victoria at Buckingham Palace. Famed for her "remarkably sweet tones and wide vocal compass," Elizabeth Greenfield enjoyed wide acclaim but only a short career on the concert stage; she retired, taught voice in Philadelphia, where she died in 1876.

GROBE, CHARLES (?1817–18??) Although he existed—there are portraits of him—very little, biographically, is known about Grobe. He was supposedly born in Weimar and came to the United States ca. 1839, was teaching music in Wesleyan Female College at Wilmington, Del., in 1841. By the following year he was known for "numerous" original pieces for the piano—a "stupefying output," in the phrase of author Robert Offergeld. Grobe's forte was mass-producing sheet music for America's burgeoning parlor piano. With the publication of his *Music of the Union* in 1861, Grobe's opus numbers reached 1,348. Before he died, whenever and however, his *opera* count was over 2,000. All was grist for Grobe's musical mill. Waltzes? *Amusement de Salon, Cologne Water, Snails, United States Grand Waltz,* and even *Sophie Waltz* (borrowed from Strauss). Polkas? *My Heart and Lute, Ne Plus Ultra,* etc., etc. And so on, through reams of gallops (*Banisher of Sadness, Ice Cream, Short and Sweet*), marches and quicksteps, rondos and dozens of variations (usually on popular themes by others), as well as piano duets. Grobe was also the author of *New Method for the Piano-Forte* (1859). Like his music, so lavishly circulated in his productive lifetime, Grobe appears to have vanished from the American musical scene.

GUIRAUD, ERNEST (1837–1892) Born in New Orleans on June 23, 1837, Guiraud studied music with his father Jean Baptiste, a musician and Grand Prix de Rome recipient. The son's first opera, *Le Roi David,* written while he was in Paris 1849–51, was produced in New Orleans when he was 15. Shortly after, he returned to Paris to study and remained to teach and compose. He wrote 7 operas, one of which, *Frédégonde,* was completed by Saint-Saëns after Guiraud's death. He also composed a successful ballet, *Gretna Green* (1873), and several well-wrought orchestral pieces. Guiraud was a most respected musician in France and was asked to do unusual work for others. It was Guiraud who completed and orchestrated Offenbach's *Tales of Hoffmann;* he also composed the recitatives for Bizet's *Carmen.* He was teacher of composition at the Paris Conservatoire when he died of a stroke in his 54th year on May 2, 1892.

HANBY, BENJAMIN RUSSELL (1833–1867) Son of a minister, Hanby was born in Rushville, Ohio, and was graduated from Otterbein University, Westerville, in 1858. He served for a time as minister in the United Brethren Church, New Paris, Ohio. His father, the Reverend William Hanby, ran an underground railroad in Westerville and the son was inspired by the story of one of the fugitive slaves who passed through to write his most famous song, "Darling Nelly Gray" (1856). Nelly Gray was the sweetheart of another slave, who watched her, in chains, sent back to slavery. The song became a popular antislavery rally cry. Although Hanby composed around 80 songs, none equaled the popularity of "Darling Nelly Gray" with its Foster-ish feeling. He had another popular song in "Ole Shady; the Song of the Contraband" (1861). "Contraband" was a term applied to escaped slaves who fled through the lines to the North. (The most famous "contraband song," though not by Hanby, was "O Let My People Go," also known as "Go Down, Moses," a spiritual.) Hanby eventually joined the staff of Root and Cady in Chicago; among his other song titles are "Adoration," "Lowliness," and "Santa Claus, or Up on the House Top" (*Up on the house top click, click, click,/Down thro' the chimney with good St. Nick*). Hanby died in Chicago in 1867.

HANDEL AND HAYDN SOCIETY Formed under the encouragement of Gottlieb Graupner (q.v.) in Boston on Mar. 30, 1815, the Handel and Haydn Society is the oldest such group still functioning in America. Its first president was Thomas Smith Webb and the Society presented its first public concert at Stone Chapel on Christmas Day, 1825. Handel's *Messiah* was given its first presentation in 1818. Among other early performances of great choral works were Haydn's *Creation,* Beethoven's *Ninth Symphony,* the Bach *B Minor Mass,* etc. The Handel and Haydn Society continues as an important force in Boston's musical life.

HARMON, JOEL, JR. (1773–1833) Though born in Suffield, Conn., Harmon is associated with the early Vermont hymnwriters. He moved to Pawlet, Vt., where he was known as a merchant, music teacher, and compiler of tunebooks. He published *The Columbian Sacred Minstrel* in 1809 and about 5 years later, *A Musical Primer*. Harmon served in the War of 1812, achieving the rank of major. He eventually settled in York, Pa., where he died in 1833.

HASTINGS, THOMAS (1784–1872) An important spokesman for the cultivation of "scientific music," Hastings was born in Washington, Conn., on Oct. 15, 1784. His early musical training was not extraordinary, his father being a curious combination of farmer and country doctor. The Hastings family moved to Clinton, N.Y., when Thomas was 12; 6 years later he is recorded as leading a local choir. He also began collecting hymn tunes, in addition to composing his own tunes and texts. By 1818 Hastings had moved and was teaching music in Geneva, N.Y. From 1823 to 1832 he was editor of the religious publication *Western Recorder*. Four years later, settled in New York City, he became choirmaster of the Bleecker Street Presbyterian Church and became acquainted with musical crusader Lowell Mason (q.v.) They saw eye to eye on the future direction of American music, especially that for the church. In his famous *Dissertation on Musical Taste* (1822), Hastings professed a decided preference for "*German* musick," proclaiming that the "science, genius, the taste, that every where pervade it, are truly captivating to those who have learned to appreciate it; but such, we presume, are not yet the *majority* of American or English auditors or executants." Hastings also anguished over the effect of Stephen Foster's Ethiopian melodies on the tender minds of the young. His association with

Mason resulted in the founding of the New York Normal Institute and the *Musical Magazine* (1836). Hastings' was a powerful voice, second only to Mason's, in setting musical standards. He was also a prolific writer with songs numbering over 1,000; his first collection, in collaboration with Solomon Warriner (1778–1860), was *Musica Sacra, or the Springfield and Utica Collections United* (1816). Hastings' best-known hymn tune is "Rock of Ages" (text by Augustus Toplady, 1740–1778), which appeared in his and Mason's *Spiritual Songs for Social Worship* (Utica, 1831). Hastings died, aged 88, in New York City on May 15, 1872.

HAUSER, WILLIAM (1812–1880) The remarkable Reverend William Hauser, M.D., was born on Dec. 23, 1812, near Bethania (Forsyth County), N.C. One of 11 children, Hauser lost his father when he was 2 so that, except for some help from his mother, he was largely self-taught (he acquired a command of English, Greek, Latin, and a smattering of German). The church occupied him first and in 1834 he was licensed to preach in the Methodist Church. In 1841, with wife and daughter, Hauser moved to Richmond County, Ga., where he taught school and began, aged 29, to study medicine. (Two years later he went into practice and by 1859 was teaching physiology and pathology in the Oglethorpe Medical College in Savannah.) Where Hauser learned music is unknown, but he did, once he retired from medical practice, devote his final years to music, teaching, composing and collecting tunes, including Southern folk melodies. Hauser published his first collection, *The Hesperian Harp*, employing shape notes, in 1848. In addition to 36 original songs by himself, he used songs of other contemporary "folk" hymnodists, among them Ananias Davisson (q.v.) and William Walker (q.v.), in some 550 pages of music. Most of the songs are religious, but also included are "The Last Rose of Summer" and some patriotic songs. Thirty years later Hauser issued *The Olive Leaf,* which served to preserve the spiritual folk song tradition. Among its songs is "Beautiful River" by Robert Lowry (1826–1899). Hauser died at Wadley, Ga., on Sept. 15, 1880, leaving a widow, a daughter, and 2 sons.

"HAWTHORNE, ALICE" See Septimus Winner.

HAYS, WILLIAM SHAKESPEAR (1837–1907) For a time Will Hays, as he was best known, was considered Stephen Foster's chief rival on the American popular music scene. In fact, Hays made a greater impact with his songs following the Civil War, and after Foster's death. His songs of self-pity and motherless children, and other tear-jerkers, would serve to set the tone of much popular song of the Gay (?) Nineties. He was born in Louisville, Ky., on July 19, 1837. He began studies in 3 different colleges but did not finish any. Around 1853 he started writing songs, many of which were extremely popular; his output totaled nearly 300. During the Civil War, Hays was a correspondent for a newspaper, traveled through Confederate lines to New Orleans, where he was arrested by the military commander, General Butler, for writing seditious songs. Hays's best-known war song was "The Drummer Boy of Shiloh" (1862). Other efforts included "My Southern Sunny Home" (1866), "Mollie Darling" (1871), and such patent minstrel songs as "Roll Out! Heave Dat Cotton" (1877), and "Early in de Mornin'" (1877). He also wrote what historian John Tasker Howard has called "one of the most maudlin self-pity songs," "Driven from Home." Few of Hays's songs are sung today (unlike Foster's), except as dated novelties from another time. One song, "She's the Sweetest of

Them All" (1869), contains a couple of interesting usages—the word "charmer" applied to a girl and the expression "you bet." Hays died in Louisville on July 22, 1907.

HEINRICH, ANTHONY PHILIP (1781–1861) The "Beethoven of America" was born Anton Philipp, in Schönbüchel, Bohemia, on Mar. 11, 1781, into a successful business family. Banking became his vocation, though he had studied the violin (he owned a Cremona). During his early affluent period, Heinrich traveled a good deal; on a visit to America he married a lady "abundantly rich in beauty, accomplishments and qualities of noble heart" from Boston. The Heinrichs had a daughter before the death of the wife in 1814; leaving the infant with a relative in Europe, Heinrich lost track of her for some 23 years. He came to America more or less permanently (for he moved back and forth over the Atlantic) in 1810, settling in Philadelphia as director of the Southwark Theatre. A concurrent business failure may have been the reason for his switching to music as a career. Soon after Heinrich moved to Kentucky (ca. 1817), where he earned a living in Louisville giving violin lessons. He then moved to Bardstown, where he lived among the Indians while convalescing from an illness. His obvious love of music and the land prompted friends to encourage Heinrich to try his hand at composition. Undaunted, and already nearly 40, Heinrich did: his *Dawning of Music in Kentucky, or the Pleasures of Harmony in the Solitudes of Nature* appeared in 1820. He became the first unabashed nationalist composer, the champion of the native American musician. In his preface Heinrich stated, "The many and severe animadversions, so long and repeatedly cast on the talent for Music in the Country, has been one of the chief motives of the Author, in the exercise of his abilities; and should he be able, by this effort, to create but one single *Star* in the *West,* no one would ever be more proud than himself, to be called an *American Musician*—He however is fully aware of the dangers which, at present day, attend talent on the crowded and difficult road of eminence; but fears of just criticism, by *Competent Masters,* should never retard enthusiasm of genius . . ." True to his own word, despite his rather small talent and equal command of musical technique, Heinrich let nothing retard the enthusiasm of his genius. He poured out his works, traveled around promoting them, and eventually acquired a reputation for eccentricity, but he was also affectionately regarded by the musical community, especially that of New York City, where he settled in 1837 and lived out the rest of his life. His expression took its most definitive form in grandiose orchestral compositions. His compilations following the publication of *The Dawning of Music in Kentucky* consisted, like that work, of a mixture of pieces for various combinations of instruments and/or voice. *The Western Minstrel,* a supplement to *Dawning,* was published in 1820 also and *The Sylviad; or Minstrelsy of Nature in the Wilds of N. America* (in 2 volumes) was issued in 1823 and 1824–26. Although an important figure in the founding of the New York Philharmonic Society, Heinrich, feeling he had been snubbed by the Society, would not permit it to perform his works. In 1853 the leading musicians of New York banded together to honor "Father Heinrich," and if possible to raise some needed money for him. They performed some of his big works, among them the autobiographical *The Wildwood Troubadour, National Memories* ("a Grand British Symphony" dedicated to Queen Victoria), *The Tower of Babel, or Language Confounded,* and other compositions of similar stamp. Though Heinrich

enjoyed performances in his time, he was not frequently published (both published and unpublished manuscripts are in the Library of Congress). As compositions, Heinrich's music may be more attractive than early writers have described it. He did not live long enough to see American composers drawing upon American musical resources (not until another Bohemian, Dvořák, arrived in America with the same message was Heinrich's view taken seriously). Ill, and apparently still trying (*"Hope on, hope ever,"* he wrote just before embarking on another musical promotion tour), he died in New York City on May 3, 1861.

HEWITT, JOHN HILL (1801–1890) Composer, playwright, poet, editor, and eldest son of James Hewitt (Section II), Hewitt has been called the "Father of the American Ballad," for reasons difficult to determine today. Hewitt also achieved a kind of dubious literary distinction by winning first prize in a poetry contest; in 2nd place was Edgar Allan Poe. (Poe had won first prize in the short story category so the judges decided to give Hewitt the first in poetry—for "The Song of the Wind"—and Poe the 2nd. By coincidence, Hewitt was also editor of the prize-giving *Visitor.*) The 2 were never friends again, even exchanged a few harmless blows in the street. Thereafter Hewitt rarely missed an opportunity to take a crack at Poe (even long after the poet was dead). Hewitt was born in New York on July 11, 1801. For a time he appeared to be destined for a military career and was admitted to West Point in 1818; there he studied music with Richard Willis (1795–1830), the Irish-born first music teacher and leader of the Academy Band. Hewitt left before graduation (1822) for the South, where he taught music and worked at journalism, spending his time in Georgia and South Carolina. Upon the death of his father in 1827, Hewitt returned to

Boston where he joined the staff of the *Massachusetts Journal*. He was already the composer of a popular song, "The Minstrel's Return from the War" (1825). He returned South again soon after and spent most of the rest of his life in Baltimore, although moving a good deal. It was in Baltimore that he had his "little unpleasantness" with Poe. Between 1841 and 1850 he taught music at the Chesapeake Female College in Hampton, Va. The Civil War prompted Hewitt to move South again and in Richmond, Va., he offered his services to the Confederacy (he was over 60) and was accorded the task of drillmaster of recruits. Meanwhile he continued composing, his eventual output adding up to about 300 songs. His 2nd song was published in 1835 and was entitled "The Knight of the Raven Black Plume" and one of his best, "All Quiet Along the Potomac Tonight" (*Dedicated to the Unknown Dead of the Present Revolution*), was published in 1864. The last was a favorite Confederate song. After the war Hewitt returned to Baltimore. Besides his vast song output, he also published a volume of poetry (1838), saw several of his plays produced—among them such pro-Southern works as *The Scouts; or, The Plains of Manassas* (1861) and his "musical burletta," *King Linkum the First* (1863). Hewitt's songs of the Civil War earned him the title of "Bard of the Stars and Bars" and were published in *The Musical Olio; or, Favorite Gems of That Popular Southern Composer, John H. Hewitt,* a collection of 8 "gems," among them "Rock Me to Sleep, Mother," "The Young Volunteer," and "Somebody's Darling." Hewitt ventured also into larger forms: oratorio (*Jephta*), cantata (*The Fairy Bridal, The Musical Enthusiast*), and opera (*Rip Van Winkle, The Artist's Wife*). He died in Baltimore on Oct. 7, 1890. His son, Horatio, one of 11 children by 2 wives, was also a

composer and critic and died only 4 years after Hewitt.

HILL, URELI CORELLI (ca. 1802–1875) Son of composer, compiler, violinist Uri K. Hill (q.v.), Hill was born in Northampton, Mass., sometime in 1802. (His brother, George Handel "Yankee" Hill, was a well-known actor.) Hill, too, studied the violin and, after work with Ludwig Spohr in Germany (1835–37), settled in New York to teach as well as conduct and perform on the violin. Hill was conductor of the New York Sacred Music Society and was the major force behind the founding of the Philharmonic Society (1842). Hill remained with the Philharmonic, as conductor and violinist, off and on until he retired in 1873. He was also a music publisher and sometime composer. After his retirement (at 70), Hill continued working in a theatre orchestra. Financial problems (he had dabbled in real estate) led to Hill's suicide in his home at Paterson, N.J., on Sept. 2, 1875.

HILL, URI K. (?1780–1844) Probably born in Rutland, Vt. (Connecticut is another possibility), Hill appears to have been, from what little we know of him, a full-time musician. He moved to Northampton around 1800, then to Boston in 1805 to serve as organist in the Brattle Street Church. He settled in New York 5 years later to teach music and, in 1815, went into the music publishing business with his father, Frederick. In 1822 he moved to Philadelphia where he was known as "U. K. Hill, Esq., professor of music." Hill's first compilation, *Vermont Harmony,* "A Collection of Sacred Vocal Music," was published in 1801. In it Hill brought together several of his original compositions as well as those of other Vermont psalmodists, Justin Morgan (Section II) and Joel Harmon (q.v.). Hill's musical sophistication led him to embrace European influences in later collections: *The Sacred Minstrel, No. 1* (1806), *The Handelian Repository* (1814), and *Solfeggio Americano* (1820). He was the father of the founder of the Philharmonic Society of New York, Urelli Corelli Hill (q.v.). He died in Philadelphia in 1844.

HOFFMAN, RICHARD (1831–1909) A lifelong British citizen, Hoffman, who was born in Manchester, England, on May 24, 1831, spent practically the whole of his adult life in the United States. A student of his father, plus others (but not Liszt as claimed), he was an excellent pianist. His family being rather crowded with virtuosos, Hoffman decided to seek a pianistic career in the United States and arrived in 1847. He made an impressive debut at the Broadway Tabernacle and later performed with the Philharmonic, with which he formed a long association. He also toured the United States giving piano recitals on the frontier as far west as Chicago. He also served as accompanist to Jenny Lind for her New York debut as well as her tour of the United States. When Gottschalk, then 23, made his New York debut, Hoffman, then 21, was asked to serve as assisting artist. Their friendship and mutual admiration lasted a lifetime (Gottschalk's *The Banjo* was dedicated to Hoffman). Hoffman enjoyed a long successful career as piano virtuoso—his debut was commemorated with a concert in 1897, a 50th anniversary—after which he devoted his time to teaching. He was also a composer of flashy piano pieces (i.e., *Dixiana*, "Caprice for the Pianoforte on the Popular Negro Minstrel's Melody 'Dixie's Land'"); also *La Gazelle* (which was often played by his friend Gottschalk) and the moving *In Memoriam L.M.G.* (1870). His autobiography was published a year after his death and was entitled *Some Musical Recollections of Fifty Years* (1910). Hoffman was the father of three sons and three daughters; the youngest of the latter, Malvina, became an important 20th-century sculptor. Hoffman died at Mt. Kisco, N.Y., Aug. 17, 1909.

"HOME, SWEET HOME" An American song primarily by adoption, although the text is by an American actor, John Howard Payne (1791–1852). Payne was also a singer and writer and closed out his career as American consul general in Tunis, North Africa. Payne collaborated with English composer Henry Rowley Bishop (1786–1855) on an adaptation of a French play into an opera (actually a ballad opera), *Clari, or, The Maid of Milan.* All that remains of that work is the song "Home, Sweet Home," music by Bishop, words by Payne; in his note to the song, Bishop indicates that the tune was "composed and partly founded on a Sicilian Air." *Clari* was presented in London on May 8, 1823, and its "hit song" was published in the same year.

HOPKINS, CHARLES JEROME (1836–1898) Self-taught composer, organist and teacher, Hopkins was born in Burlington, Vt., on Apr. 4, 1836. Upon graduation from the University of Vermont, Hopkins attended New York Medical College, but ca. 1856 he chose a career in music. That year he founded the American Music Association, adding his voice to those of Fry (q.v.) and Bristow (q.v.) in the cause of the native composer. Apparently teaching himself music, Hopkins became a church organist, spread the word on the American composer across the country in lecture-recitals, and taught music (in 1865 he established the Orpheon Free Schools). He founded and edited the New York *Philharmonic Journal* (1868–1885) and composed more than 700 works: a symphony, a *Fantasia* for 5 pianos, an *Easter Festival Vespers,* 2 operas—

Samuel and *Dumb Love*—numerous elaborate piano pieces with titles to match: *The Wind Demon* (*Rhapsodie Caractéristique pour Piano*), Op. 11. Among his works for voice were "Spirit of God" and "Calm on the Listening Ear of Night." Hopkins died in Athenia, N.J., Nov. 4, 1898.

HORN, CHARLES EDWARD (1786–1849) British-born (London, June 21, 1786), Horn was a singer-composer who came to the United States in 1833. He produced ballad operas in New York's Park Theatre. Following a return to England, Horn came back to the United States and served as conductor of the Handel and Haydn Society (q.v.) in Boston. Among his works are *The Remission of Sin,* later retitled *Satan,* an oratorio drawn from Milton's *Paradise Lost,* a cantata, *Christmas Bells,* 22 operettas, and dozens of songs, among them "Cherry Ripe," "Meeta," and "Near the Lake, Where Droop'd the Willow" (both supposedly based on Negro Airs). Horn was one of the group that, led by Urelli C. Hill (q.v.), founded the Philharmonic Society of New York. He died in Boston on Oct. 21, 1849.

HUBBARD, JOHN (1759–1810) Farmer, minister, judge, postmaster, professor of mathematics and natural philosophy (Dartmouth College), Hubbard was born in Townsend, Mass., on Aug. 8, 1759. He spent his early years farming. He entered Dartmouth at the age of 22, preparing for the ministry. A "vocal weakness" diverted Hubbard from theology to teaching in several Massachusetts towns and then he settled in Hanover, N.H., (1805) where he taught at Dartmouth until his death. Where Hubbard picked up his musical knowledge is not known, but considering his ability to master Greek and Latin at a relatively advanced age, music should have presented few problems to a man also skilled in mathematics. Although he was aware of and delighted in secular music, it was the music of the church that particularly engaged Hubbard. He was a pioneer in the good music crusade—even antedating Lowell Mason (q.v.), who picked up Hubbard's ideas. In his *Essay on Music* (1807), Hubbard criticized American hymn composers and lauded European music; he was especially hard on fuging. That same year Hubbard established a Handel Society at Dartmouth and served as its first president, aiming "to improve and cultivate the taste and promote true and genuine music and discountenance trifling unfinished pieces." Among his published collections were *Harmonica Selecta* (1789) and *Thirty Anthems* (1814). Hubbard was more powerful as an influence for "better music" than as an original composer. Out of his views came the germ of Mason's theories and the stifling of the work of Billings and the first New England school. Hubbard died in Hanover on Aug. 14, 1810, aged 51.

HUTCHINSON FAMILY The "tribe of Jesse," for that was the name of their disapproving father, was born on a farm near Milford, N.H., on numerous dates, there being ultimately 13 in all, not counting Jesse and his, no doubt, long-suffering wife. For the record, there were 11 sons and 2 daughters. Relaxation, after the hard work on the farm, came from music, although their father believed it "smacked of the devil." They sang to their own accompaniment of violins, cello, and guitar. In November 1839 all 13 of the Hutchinsons gave their first public concert at the Baptist Church in Milford and, according to one of them, John, were "enthusiastically received" as they raised their voices in "hymns, anthems, and glees." In time the older boys drifted away from the farm to the cities. Two, John and Asa, reached Boston and were invited to become members of the Handel and Haydn Society—quite an honor in Professor Lowell Mason's domain—but they decided to strike out on their own. In the summer of 1842, John, Judson, Asa, and 12-year-old Abigail (better known as Abby) formed the Aeolian Vocalists and began a concert tour; shortly after, they took the family name for their group and set out upon one of the most successful collective careers in American music. Their programs consisted of popular ballads of the period, sentimental songs, dramatic songs like Russell's "The Maniac," and songs with a religious flavor. They also presented what can only be termed songs of social significance, expressing their own views on slavery, alcohol, women's suffrage, quack doctors, even Congress (many of these songs were composed by one or the other of the Hutchinsons). Their big abolitionist song, "Get Off the Track," was written by Jesse, Jr. (to the tune of "Old Dan Tucker"). John, who served generally as family spokesman, composed the melodies to such message songs as "A Hundred Years Hence" to the words of feminist Frances Gage and a "dirge for a soldier," "Close His Eyes! His Work Is Done," to words by George H. Baker. The Hutchinsons made a successful tour of England in 1846. Abolitionism was a favorite topic and ex-slave Frederick Douglass accompanied the Family on their English tour. Back in America they took up "John Brown's Body" before the Civil War and, during it, "Tenting on the Old Camp Ground." Their sentiments were not always welcomed by their audiences, especially in states where abolitionists were regarded as villains (one of their free concerts in an army camp ended in a near riot; only Lincoln's intervention prevented the cancellation of their permit to sing in camps). It might be noted that the Hutchinsons appeared as a quartet so that when the original group was touring England, another formed around Zephaniah and included Caleb, Joshua, and Rhoda, to sing the songs associated with the Family. At times there were no less than three Hutchinson Families touring simultaneously, led by John, Asa, or Judson. Abby married in 1849 and retired from the group, rejoining it to serve in support of Lincoln. She died in 1892. Asa died in 1884 and John kept the family name alive well into the 1890s. The broadside for his recital in the Town Hall of his birthplace, Milford, claimed that he had given over 11,000 concerts. Also: "Mr. Hutchinson is the only surviving member of the world-renowned Hutchinson Family, who for fifty years or more thrilled the hearts of the American people with their songs of abolition, temperance, woman suffrage and human brotherhood. Though of such venerable age, Mr. Hutchinson has still a strong musical voice as of old." He was assisted by Miss Effie Mae Stevens, "the favorite soprano of East Lynn fame." John, the last of the Hutchinsons died, aged 87, in 1908.

INGALLS, JEREMIAH (1764–1828) A jack-of-many-trades, Ingalls was a tavern keeper, cooper, church deacon, choirmaster, and farmer. He was born in Andover, Mass., Mar. 1, 1764. He was orphaned by the age of 15 (his father, Abijah, died of exposure during the Revolution); his mother died in 1779. Ingalls was apprenticed to learn the cooper's trade (the making of wooden tubs and barrels). His musical education is unknown, but he has been reported as teaching in singing schools as a young man. In 1791 he moved to Newbury, Vt., was married, and settled down to several of his jobs. He operated a tavern out of his large house, was important in the Congregational church and apparently very musical, having a fine voice and skill on the bass viol. In 1805 Ingalls published *The Christian Harmony,* a collection of borrowed and original tunes, the latter of an appealing folk quality; included too were the fuging tunes despised by the "better music" faction. Ingalls often drew upon secular sources for his songs. His hymn tunes continued to live on in the shape-note tunebooks, particularly in the South, well into the 20th century. His fuge "Northfield" is one of his longest-lived creations. Ingalls might be said to form a link between the first New England School and Southern folk hymnody. Business reverses, possibly in connection with the publication of his one tunebook, led to Ingalls' expulsion from his church and other problems; in 1810, Ingalls moved his family to Rochester, Vt., where he became active in the church as choir director and bass viol player. He died in 1828 and was buried in nearby Hancock, Vt.

JACKSON, GEORGE K. (1745–1823) Born in Oxford, England, Jackson was a choirboy at the Chapel Royal, organist, as well as music teacher, and author of musical textbooks before coming to America in 1796. After arriving at Norfolk, Va., Jackson worked his way northward in several musical jobs—teaching and playing the organ—came to New York—where he composed, in 1804, *David's Psalms*—and finally settled in Boston in 1812. He served as one of the organists of the newly formed Handel and Haydn Society, played the organ in several churches and organized concerts. He was a prolific composer of sacred music and issued compilations of church music, including *A Choice Collection of Chants* (1816). He also composed a "Dirge for General Washington," an "Ode for General Hamilton's Funeral," as well as "songs, serenades, cantatas, canzonetts, canons, glees, &c. &c." Father of 11 children, Jackson died practically destitute in Boston in 1823.

JENKS, STEPHEN (1772–1856) Itinerant composer-compiler, Jenks was born in New Canaan, Conn., in 1772. He was living in Ridgefield, Conn., about the time he published the first of his several tune books, *New England Harmonist*. Stylistically, Jenks belongs to the pioneer first New England school, composed fuging tunes, and had his songs preserved in the compilations of others, including later Southern tunebooks. Other Jenks collections: *The Delights of Harmony; or, Norfolk Compiler* (1805), *The Hartford Collection of Sacred Harmony* (1807) and *Laus Deo, the Harmony of Zion* (1818). In 1829 Jenks moved to Thompson, Ohio, where he died in 1856.

"JOHN BROWN'S BODY" See "The Battle Hymn of the Republic."

JOHNSON, FRANCIS (1792–1844) Composer, master of several instruments, and bandleader, Johnson was probably America's first black musical celebrity. He was born in Philadelphia in 1792 and began building a musical reputation in the early years of the 19th century as a violinist (fiddler), bugler, and trumpeter. Ca. 1815 Johnson began in the concert band business. His organization was generally known as "Frank Johnson's Colored Band" and was made up principally of woodwinds, with augmented strings for society events. The Johnson Band was not only popular in Philadelphia, playing for such social organizations as the Philadelphia Grays and State Fencibles, but also in other parts of the country on successful tours. In 1838 Frank Johnson's Band played for Queen Victoria during a European tour; the leader was presented with a silver bugle. Not only did Johnson lead and play in the band, he also composed much of its program (he may even have arranged current popular songs into incipient jazz). His *Collections of Cotillions* was published in 1818; he produced a great number of piano arrangements—*Philadelphia Fireman's Cotillion, London Polka, Princeton Grand March*—87 of which were collected in 1821. He composed music for special occasions, such as a march honoring the visit of Lafayette, a *Recognition March on the Independence of Hayti;* one of his most popular pieces was a *Voice Quadrille.* Johnson died in Philadelphia in 1844.

"JUBA" A complex rhythmic pattern, characteristic of slave dances, accomplished by clapping of hands, tapping of feet, and slapping thighs, i.e., syncopation. Also called "pattin' juba." The word is of African origin. The nickname Juba was eventually given to a very skilled black dancer, William Henry Lane, who worked with white minstrel shows in the United States as well as Europe ca. 1840s. Others were nicknamed "Juba," but Lane was the first. The term has been associated with African-based dance music, rather than individuals and may be heard in Gottschalk, cakewalks and, of course, ragtime (Section IV).

JULLIEN, LOUIS ANTOINE (1812–1860) Though not an American, whether by birth or adoption, Jullien exerted much influence on the American musical scene during a single visit in 1853. This "splendid, bold, and dazzling humbug" (as one New York newspaperman viewed him) set New York on its ear, literally, with a series of spectacular "Monster Concerts for the Masses." Combining outrageous showmanship with splendid musicianship, Jullien stirred up the musical press as well as public interest in music. He went even further: he programmed music by living American composers. Arriving in New York with a 40-piece orchestra, Jullien expanded the number to 100 and even advertised an *American Quadrille* "which will contain all the NATIONAL AIRS and embrace no less than TWENTY SOLOS AND VARIATIONS." Having made his point, Jullien returned to Europe where, after losing most of his manuscripts in a fire and his money in

an unsuccessful opera investment, he died in an insane asylum in Paris, Mar. 14, 1860.

KITTREDGE, WALTER (ca. 1832–1905) A one-song composer (although he may have attempted more), Kittredge does not loom large biographically in American music. He may have been born in Merrimack, N.H., on Oct. 8, 1832 (some sources say 1834) and billed himself as a "concert ballad singer." He was rejected from service by the Union Army ("feebleness of constitution"), so spent the war singing for troops in army camps. In 1862 he composed, words and music, "Tenting on the Old Camp Ground," one of the great songs of the Civil War (sales of sheet music reached 100,000 by the end of the war). The Hutchinsons (q.v.), particularly the "tribe of Asa," were greatly responsible for the song's initial popularity and eventual publication. Kittredge recovered from the rheumatic fever that kept him out of the Army and continued writing songs and compiling songbooks long after the war. There is a mention of his singing "Tenting Tonight" at a Grand Army of the Republic convention in Washington in 1892. He died in Merrimack on July 8, 1905.

McCURRY, JOHN GORDON (1821–1886) Of pioneer stock, McCurry was born in Hart County, Ga., on Apr. 26, 1821, and lived there as a farmer, tailor, and musician (although a physical problem made it impossible for McCurry to sing for the last 40 years of his life). Contemporary accounts recall the singing activity in the McCurry home at Bio, Ga., where the music-making was spontaneous and a little primitive. In 1855 McCurry published *The Social Harp,* "A Collection of Tunes, Odes, Anthems, and Set Pieces, Selected from Various Authors: Together with Much New Music . . ." The title page also claimed ". . . a Full Exposition of the Rudiments of Music. And the Art of Musical

Composition so Simplified that the Most Unlearned Person Can Comprehend it with the Utmost Facility." *The Social Harp* is one of the most important collections of Southern folk hymnody, the songs ranging from the sacred ("Birth of Christ") to secular ("John Adkins' Farewell," the last words of a wife-murderer). The religious songs have a revivalist flavor; most songs have a folk quality— and all are set down in shape notes. Among the borrowed songs are 10 taken from the earlier White-King compilation, *The Sacred Harp* (q.v.); McCurry claimed authorship to 49 of the songs, although some appear to be his arrangements of folk songs. Although *The Social Harp* went out of print after only a few printings (undoubtedly a casualty of the Civil War), it has rightly been called "one of the richest storehouses of Southern indigenous music and text in all the fasola literature" (G. P. Jackson, *White Spirituals in the Southern Uplands*). McCurry died at Bio, Ga., on Dec. 4, 1886.

MASON, LOWELL (1792–1872) The high priest of the Boston-centered "good music" movement, Mason was born in Medfield, Mass., on Jan. 8, 1792. A lifelong music lover, Mason originally planned for a career in banking. He was primarily a self-taught musician. While his parents encouraged his taste for music, they did not wish to see him become a professional musician—thus, Mason "spent twenty years of his life doing nothing save playing on all manner of musical instruments," becoming proficient on the organ. At 20 he moved to Savannah, Ga., to work in a bank, but continued to study music—getting some real instruction from Frederick L. Abel (1794–1820), a German-born violinist, pianist, composer. Under Abel's direction, Mason began composing; at the same time he became a choir leader and organist in the Independent Presbyterian Church. During his 14 years in Savannah, Mason, with Abel's help, compiled a collection of hymns, drawing from an earlier book, Gardiner's *Sacred Melodies* (which, in turn, had adapted hymns from the melodies of Beethoven, Mozart, and Haydn). To these Mason added tunes of his own. Mason was not successful in having it published until it was placed in the hands of Dr. George K. Jackson (q.v.) of the Handel and Haydn Society. The work was issued as the *Boston Handel & Haydn Society's Collection of Sacred Music* in 1822 and was instantly popular and remained in print for some 35 years. Having accomplished this in Boston, Mason returned to Savannah and his wife, whom he had married in 1817, and initiated what would become a virtual musical dynasty. In 1827, with his songbook a success, Mason was asked to return to Boston to oversee the music in several churches. He remained to become a leading force in American musical education and the general "raising of American musical taste"—a not always flawless enterprise. This led to a suppression of indigenous music, particularly for the church, and to the Germanization of the "serious" American composer. It was in the popularization of musical education in American schools that Mason made his lasting contribution. He began by introducing the concept of teaching music in Boston's public schools; in 1832, in company with George J. Webb, Samuel A. Eliot, and others, he established the Boston Academy of Music. Children were taught free according to a method devised by a Swiss reformer, Johann Pestalozzi. The Academy, which eventually also taught adults, lasted 15 years. Mason began spreading his ideas more widely by holding "music conventions," the first in 1834. These conventions were attended by teachers (12 attended the first; 1,000 came in 1849), who were taught to sing by rote and then returned to their home areas to teach. The meetings generally lasted about 2 weeks, during which the nonmusicians among the teachers were taught quite a bit. Mason himself traveled to Europe to better understand the Pestalozzian system and, on returning from one of those trips, settled in New York (taking a home in Orange, N.J.). He founded, with George F. Root and William Bradbury, the New York Normal Institute for training teachers in 1853. As a proponent of "better music" Mason, in his own compilations (and they were numerous), favored "distinguished European Composers" as a source of tunes for his psalms and hymns—and himself, for he was a prolific composer also. Among his important publications were such "firsts" as *The Juvenile Psalmist; or, The Child's Introduction to Sacred Music* (1829), the first such collection for Sunday schools, and *The Juvenile Lyre* (1830), the first of Mason's books prepared for schools. These were followed by several other collections for the younger students. There were dozens of other assorted compilations, sacred and secular: *The Odeon* (with George J. Webb, 1837), *The Boston Glee Book* (1838), *The Gentleman's Glee Book* (1841), *The Psaltry* (with Webb, 1845), and *Carmina Sacra Enlarged: The American Tune Book* (1869), among others. Among the songs composed by Mason, the best known today are "From Greenland's Icy Mountains" (dating from his Savannah bank clerk days), "My Faith Looks Up to Thee," and "Nearer My God to Thee." Mason's son William (Section IV) became a fine pianist and a composer; sons Lowell, Jr., and Henry founded the firm of Mason and Hamlin. A grandson, Daniel Gregory (son of Henry), was an eminent composer in the early 20th century. Lowell Mason died in Orange, N.J., on Aug. 11, 1872.

MERRILL, DAVID (fl. 1799) Little is known about David Merrill except that

he was a resident of Exeter, N.H., and compiled the *Psalmodist's Best Companion* (1799), consisting of tunes by Billings, Holyoke, Kimball, and others. Six tunes were contributed by Merrill: "Alfred," "Anthem for Thanksgiving," "Vermont," "Unity," "Gilmanton," "Mount Vernon." Though obviously familiar with and influenced by the work of Billings, Merrill composed in a distinctive style of his own. In his introduction to his book, Merrill makes a point of "several years' study and practice in vocal Music," which might indicate more than a rudimentary knowledge of music and work as a singing master in Exeter.

MERRILL, RICHARD (fl. 1797) As with David Merrill (q.v.), very little is known about the life of Richard Merrill of Hopkinton, N.H., except that the 2 were probably not related and that Richard was a composer of decided originality. He published his *The Musical Practitioner; or, American Psalmody* early in 1797. Merrill was inspired by Billings' *New England Psalm-Singer* (1770) and from his preface it might be deduced that Merrill was a relatively young man when he published the collection (he requests that the "critical be tender, and rectify those errors which through inexperience may escape the notice of youth.") Included in the 50-odd-page tunebook is "An Explanation of the most Useful Terms that are used in Music . . ." The definition of "Syncopation" is a gem: "sounds driven through the bars."

MINSTREL SHOW A variety show entertainment based on the white man's imitation of the black, a concept that can be traced back to 18th-century Britain. White men, their faces blackened, caricatured the Negro's dialect, dress, dancing, and songs in the United States from around the 1820s, but as single acts, and were extremely popular. By the late 1820s such Negro impersonators as

George Washington Dixon and Thomas D. Rice (q.v.) had introduced their specialties, the former, "Zip Coon," and the latter, "Jim Crow." A lesser known contributor, Andrew Jackson Levitt, added a new term to the language with his song "The Hamfat Man." Grease paint was not introduced into the United States until ca. 1868 so that blackface comedians covered their faces with hamfat before applying the blacking, usually from a burned cork. In time "hamfat men" was applied to low-rated thespians (who had apparently appropriated the song) and was eventually abbreviated simply to "ham." The classic minstrel show, with borrowings from antecedents and additions by new exploiters, emerged just before the mid-1840s with the advent of Daniel D. Emmett's Virginia Minstrels (1843) and Edwin P. Christy's Minstrels (1844). The success of the minstrel show immediately led to the birth of rival troupes and to the evolution of the form of the show. There were generally 3 parts, the first consisting of the show proper employing a seated chorus in blackface, a white Interlocutor (a mix of master of ceremonies and straight man), who exchanged jibes and quips with the end men—i.e., at either end of the chorus line—Mr. Tambo, with his tambourine, and Mr. Bones, with his castanets. The 2nd part was called the "olio," a word borrowed from the Spanish and meaning mixture, or medley. The olio occurred between the 2 acts of the show and functioned as a showpiece for various artists, who performed their specialties—a precursor of what would eventually become vaudeville. The finale was called the "walk-around" and employed the full cast in various song-and-dance bits, with occasional and no-doubt-humorously-intended interruptions from the end men. Among the most important musical contributors to the minstrel show were Stephen Foster (q.v.), Daniel D. Emmett

(q.v.), and James A. Bland (Section IV). Toward the close of the minstrel show's run of popularity real Negroes—some in blackface!—came upon the scene: Lew Johnson's Plantation Minstrels. By 1882 whiteface acts—Ferguson and Mack, Irish comics—were interloping. The minstrel show, weakened, persisted into the early 20th century, supplanted by the variety show, vaudeville, burlesque—and good taste, perhaps. It faded out, as it began, with individual performers such as Eddie Cantor and Al Jolson, leaving behind little but a few stereotypes, some memorable songs, and the incipient ragtime band.

MICHAEL, DAVID MORITZ (1751–1825) Although he lived in the United States for only 20 of his 74 years, Michael was important in the Moravian centers of Nazareth and Bethlehem in Pennsylvania. He was born in Kuhnhausen (near Erfurt), Germany, in 1751. As a musician he served in a Hessian military regiment. In 1781 he joined the Moravian Church and came to America in 1795. He was a teacher, composer, and played several instruments (the violin and practically all wind instruments). He was first stationed at Nazareth and ca. 1804 was transferred to Bethlehem where apparently he reorganized the Collegium Musicum which became the Philharmonic Society. In 1811 the Philharmonic performed Haydn's *Creation* in Bethlehem and, not long after, *The Seasons*. Although he was more impressive as a music educator and conductor-performer, Michael composed 16 suites (*Parthien*) for assorted (quintet and sextet) wind combinations before coming to the United States. He wrote music in America intended to be performed near or on water: *Bey einer Quelle zu blasen* (1808) for 2 clarinets, 2 horns, and bassoon, "To be played by a spring." The following year came *Bestimmt zu einer Wasserfahrt auf der Lecha*, "intended for a water ride on the Lehigh," for the same instrumental grouping with an added bassoon. In November 1808, Michael's fine cantata, *Psalm 103*, was introduced at Bethlehem, Pa. His work completed in America, Michael returned to Germany in 1815 and died at Neuwied in 1825.

MOORS, HEZEKIAH (1775–1814) Son of a farmer and Revolutionary War veteran, Moors too was a farmer. He was born in 1775, in Shirley, Mass., and named for his maternal grandfather, the Deacon Hezekiah Sawtell. The elder Moors, after the war, moved his family to the new state of Vermont, first settling in Hartland and later in Mount Holly. Hezekiah was then about 20. If he had had any musical training during the first 20 years of his life it may have been in his birthplace, Shirley, where another Yankee tunesmith, Oliver Holden (Section II), had also been born and was 10 years Moors's senior. What is definite is that Moors owned a 45-acre farm near Mount Holly, raised a family, and served in several capacities in the town: petit juror, tax collector, surveyor, and constable. In 1812 Hezekiah and his 14-year-old son, Ransom, enlisted in the Vermont militia and served 2 months, 13 days. Shortly after, Moors moved to New York, settling in the Town of Union (near Binghamton). Sometime between early 1802 and 1809 Moors managed to publish his single songbook, *The Province Harmony* (Boston, ca. 1809). In it Moors collected 90 3- and 4-part "Airs," and 4 anthems, many ornamented with fuges. A good number were set to texts by Dr. Isaac Watts and titled after towns of Vermont (and one, "Shirley," Mass.) Moors's compositions reveal a remarkably well-educated musician of unusual sophistication for his time and place, "In a country where Musick has not yet become a regular calling," to quote from

his preface. In it he also hoped sales of *The Province Harmony* would encourage further editions, but that was not to be. Moors died, aged 39, at Mount Holly in 1814, only a year after moving to New York.

MORRIS, GEORGE POPE (1802–1864) Poet, journalist, lyricist, Morris, a Philadelphian transplanted to New York, was co-founder of the New York *Mirror* and other publications. He was also the author of the words of several of the most popular songs in what is generally called "the genteel tradition" of the mid-19th century. Stephen Foster's first song, "Open Thy Lattice, Love," was set to a Morris poem found in one of Morris' papers, the New York *Mirror*. He supplied the words to Henry Russell's (q.v.) "Woodman, Spare That Tree," the Hutchinsons' (q.v.) "My Mother's Bible," and Charles Edward Horn's (q.v.) "On the Lake Where Droop'd the Willow." Horn also set a cycle of Morris' poems to music, entitling it *National Melodies of America* (which included "On the Lake" and other songs based on indigenous themes, including a New York chimney sweep "carol," "Northern Refrain"). Morris and Horn also collaborated on an opera, *The Maid of Saxony* (1842). One of Morris' last lyrics, to music by William Plain, was the Civil War declamation, "The Union, Right or Wrong." Morris died in New York in 1864.

MOUNT, WILLIAM SIDNEY (1807–1868) Noted American landscape painter, born in Stony Brook, Long Island, N.Y., Mount was also a fiddler and sometime composer. His uncle was an eccentric grocer-musician from New York, Micah Hawkins (1777–1825) from whom Mount learned music. Art, however, was his major love and he studied at the National Academy of Design, New York City, began as a professional portraitist, and eventually began specializing in Long Island landscapes and scenes from everyday life, e.g., "Bargaining for a Horse." Mount also had a practical inventive bent and designed and built small sailing craft, a horse-drawn studio-on-wheels and a special violin (the most prominent feature was a curved back) which he called the "Cradle of Harmony." Mount collected a good deal of music and undoubtedly played it on his fiddle—typical dance tunes of the period. One of Mount's own fiddle tunes is *In the Cars on the Long Island Railroad* (1850). This colorful genre piece is Mount's only known surviving composition. His paintings, however, are preserved in several museums. He died in Stony Brook in 1868.

"MY COUNTRY, 'TIS OF THEE See "America."

OLIVER, HENRY KEMBLE (1800–1885) Born in Beverly, Mass., Oliver was a graduate of Dartmouth (1818). Though he was an organist and a choirmaster, music was his avocation and he made his living as a schoolmaster. He was also adjutant-general of Massachusetts and superintendent of the Atlantic Cotton Mills (Lawrence, Mass., where he lived for 10 years). Oliver was also treasurer of Massachusetts during the Civil War and chief of the state's Department of Labor for a decade. During these busy periods he was associated with musical organizations, some of which he founded and ran. These activities encouraged Oliver's original compositions. Esthetically he was allied with Lowell Mason's (q.v.) "better music" campaign in the Boston area. Among Oliver's published compilations were *Oliver's Collection of Hymn and Psalm Tunes* and a collaboration (with Samuel P. Tuckerman, 1819–1890, and Silas Atkins Bancroft, 1823–1886), *The National Lyre: a New Collection of Sacred Music* (1848). His best-known hymn tune is "Federal Street." Oliver died in Salem, Mass., in 1885.

"PATTING JUBA" See "Juba."

PHILHARMONIC SOCIETY OF NEW YORK See Hill, Urelli Corelli.

REPOSITORY OF SACRED MUSIC, PART SECOND A collection, one of the earliest and the most influential, of folk hymns, published at Harrisburg, Pa., in 1813. Compiler John Wyeth (1770–1858) was an editor and publisher, not a musician. His original *Repository,* published in 1810, had been very successful, which encouraged Wyeth to publish *Part Second.* Though both books were in the same oblong (end-opener) format, employed shape notes, their musical content was different. The first book was a conventional collection of popular psalms and fuging tunes of the day; *Part Second* consisted of a great number of folk hymns. Of the 149 tunes, 58 were claimed by Wyeth as being new (musicologist Irving Lowens found 44 a more accurate number—and a goodly one). Thirty of the tunes have no composer ascription, although one—that of Elkanah Kelsey Dare (q.v.)—has led to the supposition that he served as musical editor and arranger of *Part Second.* The book was published in time for the spread of camp meetings that came in the wake of the Second Awakening and the astute Wyeth profited. Copies of *Part Second* were carried southward and served as a model for the series of Southern folk hymn tunebooks that followed, beginning with Davisson's *Kentucky Harmony* through Walker's *The Southern Harmony* and White and King's *The Sacred Harp.* Not the least of Wyeth's contribution was in the preservation of examples of the tunes of members of the first New England school, then going into eclipse: Billings, Kimball, Holden, Holyoke, Morgan, and others.

RICE, THOMAS DARTMOUTH (1808–1860) Entertainer, showman, New York–born Rice has been called "the father of American minstrelsy." Of a poor background, Rice took to the theatre, eventually ending up in a stock company in Louisville, Ky. According to legend, it was there that Rice observed the shuffling dance of a crippled black stable hand as he worked singing. Rice adapted the song and dance and introduced it at the Louisville Theatre in his between-the-acts spot, calling it "Jim Crow": *Wheel about, turn about,/ Do jis so,/ And every time I wheel about/ I jump Jim Crow.* Rice imitated the original stable hand right down to worn shoes and clothing. Rice and the song were extremely successful in the United States and, eventually, England (1836). The character of Jim Crow was a precursor of the minstrel show black man. Rice was popularly known as "Jim Crow" Rice, or sometimes "Daddy," acknowledging his fathering of the minstrel show. Rice claimed, with others, another popular minstrel song, "Clare de Kitchen" in the 1830s. Stephen Foster apparently saw Rice during the "Jim Crow" phase and later submitted songs to the old minstrel; much later—1851— Rice commissioned Foster's "This Rose Will Remind You" (words by G. Mellon). Because of the song's slight antislavery sentiment, Rice was advised not to use it; "This Rose Will Remind You" was not published until 1931. Although Rice appeared in a few of the later minstrel shows, he was at his best as a single act and never again repeated the success of "Jim Crow," on which most of his theatrical career was founded. He died in New York in 1860.

ROOT, GEORGE FREDERICK (1820–1895) Composer, organist, teacher; born in Sheffield, Mass., Aug. 30, 1820. When Root was 6 the family moved to North Reading, Mass. He studied music in nearby Boston with Benjamin Franklin Baker (1811–1889) and George James Webb (q.v.). Root eventually began teaching music himself and was associated with Lowell Mason (q.v.), helped him in teaching music in Boston's public schools and in the Boston Academy of Music. Root's initial compositional efforts were in Mason's good music hymn genre ("The Shining Shore"). Ca. 1844 Root moved to New York City to teach voice at Abbott's School for Young Ladies and other schools. He was also organist for the Mercer Street Presbyterian Church. In 1850 he began a year of study in Europe. Upon his return he noted the minstrel show craze, the popularity of Foster's Ethiopian songs (so detested by his Boston mentor Mason and good music's mouthpiece John S. Dwight). Using the name "G. Fredrich Wurzel," Root submitted songs to the Christy Minstrels; their success prompted Root to devote his time to composition. In collaboration with a former pupil, the blind Fanny Crosby (1820–1915)—Root had taught at the New York Institute for the Blind—he produced such songs as "Hazel Dell" (1853), "There's Music in the Air" (1854), and "Rosalie, the Prairie Flower" (1855). These were in the period's sentimental, genteel genre. Sometime after this successful collaboration, Root joined, as a partner, the music publishing firm of Root and Cady (established by his brother, E. Towner Root, and C. M. Cady) in Chicago. Thanks in part to George Root, the firm became one of the most prosperous producers of Civil War songs. (Besides Root, Root and Cady published the songs of Henry Clay Work, q.v.) Beginning modestly and early, Root wrote "The First Gun Is Fired," sometime before April 1861; this was followed by 3 of the most popular songs of the war: "The Battle Cry of Freedom (Rally 'Round the Flag, Boys)," "Just Before the Battle, Mother," and "Tramp! Tramp! Tramp!" A bad fire in 1871 ended Root and Cady, though not Root's writing. He published some 70 song collections; he published his autobiography, *The Story* *of a Musical Life* (1891). His cantatas, *The Flower Queen, Daniel* (both 1853), *The Pilgrim Fathers* (1854), *The Haymakers* (1857), and *Belshazzar's Feast* (1860), etc., have not proved to be very enduring. Root's son, Frederick Woodman (1846–1916) was an eminent organist, teacher, and a composer also. The elder Root died on Bailey's Island, Maine, Aug. 6, 1895.

RUSSELL, HENRY (1812–1900) An Englishman who spent a mere 6 years in the United States, Russell had a great influence on the popular music of the time. He had already gained a reputation as a vocalist in Britain before coming to America in 1836, eventually finding work as organist and choirmaster of the First Presbyterian Church, Rochester, N.Y. Inspired by the speaking style of Henry Clay, Russell began writing of what he called "descriptive songs" through which he hoped to "make music the vehicle of grand thoughts and noble sentiments, to speak to the world through the power of poetry and song!" Before he finished, Russell turned out some 800 songs which he shared with the world, beginning in New York City and touring the rest of the country. Russell was successful as a performer and a number of his songs were popular and lucrative. Among the best known were "A Life on the Ocean Wave," "The Old Arm Chair," "The Gambler's Wife," "The Maniac," and "Woodman, Spare that Tree," the last with words by George Pope Morris (q.v.). Russell's success and recital stage style influenced other songwriters and performers in the United States. Back in England in 1841, Russell continued to enjoy his successful composer-singer career; Dwight's *Journal*, in 1853, referred to him as "a great charlatan," because of his continuing love of showmanship and publicity-seeking. One son, Henry, Jr., became an opera impressario in Britain and another,

Landon Ronald, a composer-conductor. Russell died in London in 1900.

THE SACRED HARP One of the most important of the Southern folk-spiritual compilations, the original being edited by Georgians Benjamin F. White (1800–1879) and the rather mysterious E. J. King, whose precise dates are unknown. King either withdrew from the project or died before the revised and enlarged edition of 1850. The first edition was issued in 1844, was 262 pages in length (26 of which were taken up by a Preface, Rudiments of Music, and a Dictionary of Musical Terms). A notable inclusion was the first printing of the folksong "Poor Wayfaring Stranger," it being the practice in the Southern folk hymnody to adapt secular tunes to spiritual usage. Between 1844 and 1869 *The Sacred Harp* was revised 3 times; a 4th (planned for 1879) was not accomplished because of the death of its committee chairman, B. F. White. Revisions led to adding more songs to the book. The sales of *The Sacred Harp*, and its popularity, lessened in the latter 19th century, there being other tunebooks competing with it. The livelier 7-noters (that is, using the 7 shape-note system; *The Sacred Harp* employed the 4-shape system) were especially competitive. In 1911 no less than 2 editions appeared, one under the chairmanship of B. F. White (son of the first editor) and the other under the supervision of Joe S. James and the musical editorship of Alabaman S. M. Denson (1854–1936). The latter edition was entitled *The Original Sacred Harp* and contained over 600 songs, drawing upon all previous editions. The 4-shape system was again used and Denson added an alto part to more than 300 of the 3-part songs. As indicated in its curious, quite statistical, "Summary Statement," a high percentage of the texts and tunes were contributed by local poets and composers, making the book a treasure trove of folklore. (Other statistics: 10,643 lines of poetry, 4,295 sharps and 2,241 flats.) The Preface criticized other sacred songbooks (undoubtedly the 7-shapers with their newer, more ornate songs) because they were "badly tainted with operatic, secular and rag-time strains of music." Added to the 1911 revision were 71 songs, most of which had been dropped from the 1869 edition. Most were contributed by S. M. Denson. Denson's revision is still in use today, kept alive by the vigorous singing of the Sacred Harp Singers of Alabama.

SHAKERS A religious sect, originating in England in 1747, which called itself "The United Society of Believers in Christ's Second Appearance." In 1774 the illiterate mystic Ann Lee led a small band of Shakers to America and toured New England, establishing Shaker colonies and gathering followers. She was variously known as "Mother Ann" or "Ann the Word." The Shakers did not, as commonly believed, reject music and lively musical expression. The term "Shaker" was applied to them because of their rituals in which they literally did shake and performed other physical displays to drive out the devil: jerking, stamping, etc. In tune with the Second Awakening, the Shakers experienced a great revival in the late 1830s lasting a decade. Songs were important to the Shaker meetings which were enlivened with dancing. There were "shaking" songs ("Shake Off the Flesh"), "action" songs ("I Will Bow and Be Simple," "Hop Up and Jump Up," "Bow Down Low," "Sweep, Sweep and Cleanse your Floor," "Drink Ye of Mother's Wine," a reference to Mother Ann). The best-known Shaker song is, of course, "Simple Gifts," because of its sensitive and ingenious handling by 20th-century composer Aaron Copland in his ballet score, *Appalachian Spring* (1944). The song,

although the authorship is unknown, was written ca. 1848. Because of their uninhibited ritual, the Shakers produced a vigorous body of folk songs and dances. As a group, the Shakers were farmers and craftsmen. A belief in celibacy and recruitment only by conversion assured their eventual extinction.

SHAW, OLIVER (1779–1848) Born in Middleboro, Mass., Shaw was to have followed his father in the sea-faring trade, but by the age of 21 that was changed by Shaw's total blindness. As a boy he accidentally stabbed himself in the right eye with a penknife. Later, after a siege of yellow fever, he took nautical observations of the sun with his remaining eye. He was not fully recovered and the strain led to the loss of the sight of his left eye. Shaw then began taking music lessons from organist John L. Berkenhead, also blind; later he went to Boston to study with Gottlieb Graupner (q.v.). In 1807, Shaw, settled in Providence, R.I., where he set up shop as a music teacher and served as organist of the First Congregationalist Church. One of his pupils was Lowell Mason (q.v.), on whom he had much influence. Shaw was one of the founders of the Psallonian Society "for the purpose of improving themselves in the knowledge and practice of sacred music and inculcating a more correct taste in the choice and performance of it." Shaw's own compositions were predominantly for the church (his secular output was limited to a handful of marches and songs), among them a *Thanksgiving Anthem* for voices and small orchestra (1809). His most important compilations include *For the Gentlemen,* a collection of instrumental pieces "in four parts" (1807), *Melodia Sacra* (1819), and *The Social Sacred Melodist* (1835). Shaw died in Providence in 1848.

SHOUT Slave dance of religious significance, usually danced in a circle ("ring shout"). Characteristic of the shout was a shuffling step, with feet barely off the floor, accompanied by clapping of hands or slapping of thighs. Could be accompanied by the singing of a spiritual, although, as a rule, the shouters did not sing. White observers first became aware of the shout when watching the slave dances in New Orleans' Place Congo and later at camp meetings. The term was later applied by 20th-century jazz pianists James P. Johnson, Lucky Roberts, and others to quite complex instrumental pieces.

THE SOCIAL HARP A valuable collection of folk hymns and folk songs edited by John G. McCurry (q.v.) of Hart County, Georgia. Besides contributing nearly 50 tunes himself, McCurry gathered others from relatives and friends in Georgia and South Carolina. He also borrowed a few from the earlier *Sacred Harp* (q.v.). *The Social Harp* was probably published initially in 1855, although no copy of the first edition has been found. The title's word "Social," in contemporary usage, was understood to mean "congregational" as, for example, in Mason and Hastings' *Spiritual Songs for Social Worship* (1831). Among the titles collected in *The Social Harp* (and all attributed to McCurry) are "The Beggar," "Navigation," "Memphis," "River of Jordan," "The Cross," "Dove of Peace," "Hail, Ye Sons," "Morning Star," and "Slabtown." In style, the Social Harp songs preserve some of the musical traditions brought by the Scotch-Irish immigrants to the section of the United States in which McCurry was active.

SOCIAL ORCHESTRA The dance band of the mid and late 19th century (also called a Quadrille band), consisting of 2 violins, cello, clarinet, flute, cornet, piano (or harp). The number of instruments varied with the size of the hall. A full band in a good-sized hall would carry more brass instruments. The social orchestra's repertory consisted of popular songs of the period, waltzes, quicksteps, marches, polkas, quadrilles, etc. Dancing to the social orchestra became quite formalized, as evidenced by Elias Howe's (1820–1895) *Complete Ball-Room Hand Book* (1858). Balls frequently went on for hours, beginning at 8 in the evening and ending around 4, with the playing of "Home, Sweet Home." The evening would begin with a march and got livelier as it went on. There were rules for dress and dancing and deportment, as well as in the selection of the musical numbers. The dancers were often treated to a concert by the social orchestra before the dancing began. Stephen Foster published a work entitled *Social Orchestra* (1854) consisting of arrangements for "solos, duets, trios and quartets" of his own songs and favorites by other composers.

THE SOUTHERN HARMONY One of the most important of the Southern folk hymn collections compiled by William Walker of Spartanburg, S.C., and published in 1835. "Singin' Billy," as he was popularly known, was born near the village of Cross Keys, S.C., in 1809 and died in Spartanburg in 1875. The nickname was not only a recognition of Walker's vocal abilities, but was also to distinguish him from 2 other William Walkers living in the small town of Spartanburg; in honor of their respective occupations they were known as "Hog Billy" and "Pig Billy" (the distinction is beyond the scope of this encyclopedia). Of a poor family and sketchily educated, Walker became an ardent Baptist early in life and believed in praising the Lord in song. Collecting various tunes from several sources, many of them folk hymns, he issued a compilation of 209 "Tunes, Hymns, Psalms, Odes, and Anthems" entitled *The Southern Harmony*. The work became popular and lucrative and went through several editions. The last edition of 1854 contained 40 original Walker tunes. Walker spread the word and melody with his book and established informal singing schools in the South and the West. Other songbooks followed, *Southern and Western Harmony* (1845), *The Christian Harmony* (1866), and a children's collection, *Fruits and Flowers* (1869). None surpassed *The Southern Harmony* in its exemplification of certain elements of the Southern shape-note tradition—the adaptation of popular tunes—e.g., "Auld Lang Syne"—to spiritual song, or borrowing a melody and adding shape-note harmonization and a characteristic sonority. Walker took pleasure in adding the initials "A.S.H." after his name; they stood for "Author, *Southern Harmony*." He died in Spartanburg in 1875.

SPIRITUAL SONG Songs of a religious nature, the original sense as stated in Colossians 3:16: "Let the word of Christ dwell in you richly in all wisdom; teaching and admonishing one another in psalms and hymns and spiritual songs, singing with grace in your hearts to the Lord." During the Great Awakening the camp meeting brought a more specific meaning to the term: a folk-inspired expression of religious feeling, rather than the more staid psalms and hymns of the established church. The newer usage was applied by John Scott in his *Hymns and Spiritual Songs for the Use of Christians* (1803), following in the footsteps of "African Minister" Richard Allen (q.v.) whose *A Collection of Spiritual Songs and Hymns* . . . had been published 2 years before. Although slaves had sung spiritual songs long before the Civil War, little notice was made of it until after the war. The first published collection was issued in 1867: *Slave Songs of the United States* (Section IV). Negro spirituals were often adaptations of the spiritual songs of their masters (leading to the

theory that all spirituals were of white origin); in light of the mingling of black and white at camp meetings it is more likely that each borrowed from the other. Also, the Negro with a rich African musical heritage contributed many original, even unique, elements to the form and content of the "spiritual": complex, sophisticated rhythms (including syncopation), melodic patterns, harmony and polyphony, etc. Whether these can be defined as African survivals or adaptations is irrelevant, for all folk cultures —black and white—are shameless borrowers and unselfish sharers. White and black spirituals share some elements and each has its own unique sound.

"THE STAR-SPANGLED BANNER" Francis Scott Key (1779–1843), familiar with the old English drinking song "Anacreon in Heaven" (Section II), had it in mind when he composed a stirring poem the night of Sept. 13/14, 1814. His poem, "Defence of Fort McHenry," was published as a broadside within days after and bore this introduction: "The annexed song was composed under the following circumstances—A gentleman (*Francis S. Key, Esq. of Georgetown, District of Columbia*) had left Baltimore, in a flag of truce for the purpose of getting released from the British fleet a friend of his [Dr. William Beanes] who had been captured at Marlborough.—He went as far south as the mouth of the Patuxent and was not permitted to return lest the intended attack on Baltimore should be disclosed. He was therefore brought up the Bay to the mouth of the Patapsco, where the flag vessel was kept under the guns of a frigate, and he was compelled to witness the bombardment of Fort McHenry, which the Admiral [Sir Alexander Cochrane] boasted that he would carry in a few hours, and that the city must fall. He watched the flag at the Fort through the whole day with anxiety that can be better felt than described, until the night prevented him from seeing it. In the night he watched the bomb shells, and at early dawn his eye was again greeted by the proudly waving flag of his country." Newspapers picked up the poem from the broadside and, "Adapted and Arranged" by Thomas Carr, it was soon published as a song by Joseph Carr of Baltimore. (Two years later, James Hewitt set the same words to a different melody, but the song in that form did not catch on.) "The Star-Spangled Banner" was widely printed and reprinted and was the most popular song of the War of 1812. It rose again in popularity during the Spanish-American War (1898) and after, was commended to service bands by President Woodrow Wilson in 1916 and, finally, in 1931, was designated by Congress as the official American national anthem.

THE VIRGINIA MINSTRELS The first organized minstrel show troupe, which made its debut in New York's Bowery Amphitheatre on Feb. 6, 1843. The members were Frank Brower (castanets —"bones"), Dick Pelham (tambourine —"tambo"), Billy Whitlock (banjo), and the most important member, Daniel Decatur Emmett (q.v.). Each man was costumed rather outlandishly, projected a specific character, had blackened his face, and had his own specialty. Out of this idea the minstrel show grew into one of the most popular entertainments of the time. It was refined and enlarged from the original quartet, but the general idea was retained by the minstrels that followed.

VON HAGEN, PETER A., JR. (1781–1837) Violinist, pianist, vocalist, son of Von (or Van) Hagen, Sr. (Section II). A prodigy, the younger Von Hagen made his New York debut performing 2 violin concertos and a piano concert at the age of 8. Von Hagen was probably born in Charleston, S.C., where his parents lived after emigrating from the Netherlands. The Von Hagens moved to New York and eventually to Boston, where they all participated in concerts (Mrs. Von Hagen was also a musician and music teacher). The Von Hagens established a Musical Magazine and Warranted Piano Forte Warehouse in Boston (1796) and began publishing music the next year. Eventually the father withdrew from the business and the son carried on. He was also organist at Trinity Church and composed a few songs— "Adams and Washington" (1798), "To Arms, Columbia" (1799), "Anna" (1802), "Gentle Zypher" (1802), etc. Von Hagen, an alcoholic, died in Boston in 1837.

"WALK-AROUND" The minstrel show's finale in which the entire company participated. Initially it was danced, but later it was expanded into bits of business, patter, song and dance, and clapping of hands in time to the music. It was most effectively introduced ca. 1858 by the Bryant's Minstrels and taken over by others.

WALKER, WILLIAM ("SINGIN' BILLY") See *The Southern Harmony*.

WARREN, GEORGE WILLIAM (1828–1902) Composer-organist, largely self-taught in music, George Warren was born in Albany, N.Y., Aug. 17, 1828. After several years as an organist in Albany, he moved to Brooklyn, where he remained for 10 years as organist at Holy Trinity Church and came to Manhattan (1870) as organist at St. Thomas Church. Warren edited *Warren's Hymns and Tunes, as Sung at St. Thomas Church* (1888). He composed the music for many hymns, among them "Behold the Lamb of God," "God of Our Fathers," "National Hymn," as well as 2 Easter cantatas and a number of piano pieces, e.g., the Gottschalk-inspired *The Andes, Marche di Bravura*. Warren's primary interest, however, was in church music. He was still St. Thomas' organist when he died on Mar. 17, 1902.

WEBB, GEORGE JAMES (1803–1887) Composer, organist, teacher, and organizer, Webb was born near Salisbury, England, June 24, 1803. He began the study of music at 7, learning both the piano and the violin. He settled in Boston in 1830; became organist in Old South Church and met Lowell Mason (q.v.), with whom he helped to found the Boston Academy of Music. Webb was in charge of secular music (Mason attended to sacred music), also promoted the study of instrumental music at the Academy and organized an orchestra for presentation of concerts. When Mason moved to New York City to expand his music teaching operations, Webb followed, taking up residence in New Jersey (1871). Of personal interest: Webb's daughter, Mary, married Mason's son, William (Section IV). Webb's musical output was predominantly in the field of church music, though he published such songs as "Art Thou Happy, Lovely Lady?" "Oh, Go Not to the Field of War," "Homeward Bound" soon after his arrival in Boston. He also composed a set of *Boston Cotillions* for piano. With Mason he compiled *The Massachusetts Collection of Psalmody* (1840; published by the Handel and Haydn Society). His *The Odeon,* a song collection, was published in 1837; his *Ode to the 4th July, 1832* for soloists and chorus remains unpublished. The tune known as "Webb" —to the opening words: "Stand Up, Stand Up for Jesus"—is Webb's most enduring song. Webb died in Orange, N.J., Oct. 7, 1887.

WEST, ELISHA (1756–18??) Born in Yarmouth, Maine, earned his living as a carpenter-builder ("housewright" was the contemporary term). Little else is known about him except that he moved to Vermont ca. 1790, where he was a singing master and choir leader in the area of Woodstock-Pomfret. West's style, quite primitive and folkish in character, would suggest that he was a self-taught, typical Yankee composer of the first New England persuasion. In 1802 he published his compilation, with tunes by Jeremiah Ingalls (q.v.), one J. West, and himself, *The Musical Concert.* A 2nd edition followed 5 years later. Sometime in 1810, plagued by financial as well as other problems, West left the Woodstock area and disappeared from view.

WILLIAMS, HENRY F. (1813–1889) Boston-born Negro composer-arranger, teacher, and violinist. After music study in Boston, Williams went to Philadelphia, where he joined the famous Frank (Francis) Johnson (q.v.) band. Williams later returned to Boston to teach, play in various local bands, and to arrange, specifically for the celebrated Gilmore band. In 1872, when Gilmore conducted an orchestra of 2,000 at the World's Peace Jubilee, Williams was one of the 2 black violinists who played in that mammoth congregation (the other violinist was one F. E. Lewis). Williams composed a few songs: "Lauriette," "Come, Love, and List Awhile," "It Was by Chance We Met," and "I Would I'd Never Met Thee" (the first in 1840, the last in 1876). He also composed an instrumental suite, *Parisien Waltzes* (1854). He died, presumably in Boston, in 1889.

WILLIS, RICHARD STORRS (1819– 1900) Editor, writer, critic, and composer, Willis was born in Boston, Feb. 10, 1819. A graduate of Yale, he studied also in Germany. He returned to the United States and became editor of the New York *Musical World and Times;* was an early Gottschalk champion and a not always kind critic of Americanist William Henry Fry (q.v.). Willis' creative interests were mainly in music for the church; he was author of *Our Church Music* (1856) and published numerous choral pieces and songs. His best-known song, words by Edmund H. Sears (1810–1876), is the Christmas carol "It Came Upon a Midnight Clear." Willis died in Detroit, Mich., May 7, 1900.

WINNER, SEPTIMUS (1827–1902) Composer, teacher, publisher; born in Philadelphia, Pa., where he began his professional career as a teacher of violin, guitar, banjo, etc. In 1847 Winner went into the music publishing business (Winner & Shuster) and composed many of the songs the firm published. Winner's greatest song hit was "Listen to the Mocking Bird," based on a tune he heard whistled by a Negro barber-guitarist in Philadelphia, Richard Milburn (ca. 1845–1900). Winner arranged the melody and composed a lyric and published it using as his pseudonym "Alice Hawthorne." The first printing of this wildly popular song carried the name of Milburn but it disappeared in later printings. Winner went on to write a great number of songs under the name of Alice Hawthorne. Among his other better-known efforts: "Oh, Where Has My Little Dog Gone?" (also an adaptation, from a German folk song, "Lauterbach"), the jingly "Ten Little Indians," and the duet for soprano and alto "Whispering Hope." Winner was also the author of musical instruction books, including a standard method for the banjo, made literally thousands of arrangements for piano and violin, and also published a *Collection of Music for the Violin: Cotillions, Polkas, Quadrilles, Waltzes, Hornpipes, Reels, Jigs, Schottiches, Mazourkas, Marches, Fancy Dances, and Other Popular Airs* . . . Winner died in Philadelphia on Nov. 22, 1902.

WOODBURY, ISAAC BAKER (1819–1858) Born in Beverly, Mass., Woodbury was as a youngster a music-loving blacksmith's apprentice. At 13 he went to Boston to study music; in 1838, aged 19, he went to Europe to study in London and Paris. After a year, he returned to Boston where he taught music and became a member of the Bay State Glee Club which gave concerts throughout New England. During a tour Woodbury, who "had a beautiful voice and sang various styles, but excelled in the ballad and descriptive music," was persuaded by a storekeeper in Bellow Falls, Vt., to remain. Woodbury did and organized the New Hampshire and Vermont Musical Association of which he was also conductor. In 1851 he left for New York City where he was choirmaster of the Rutgers Street Church and eventually editor of the *New York Musical Review*. Ill health curbed Woodbury's activities, but he managed to compose great numbers of secular and church songs as well as compile song collections and instruction books. Among his publications: *The Dulcimer* (1850), *The Cythera* (1854), *The Lute of Zion* (1856). Woodbury was also author of *Woodbury's Self-Instructor in Musical Composition and Thorough Bass*. Woodbury's hymn tunes were widely popular in his lifetime although only 2 are remembered today: "Sweet Hour of Prayer" and "He Leadeth Me." His collection of songs, *The Song Crown* (1856), contained such songs as "The Farmer's Daughter" and the glee "Stars of the Summer Night," with words by Henry Wadsworth Longfellow (1807–1882). Because of his frail health Woodbury spent winters in the South; on one of these trips he died en route, in Columbia, S.C., in 1858, in his 39th year.

WORK, HENRY CLAY (1832–1884) A printer by trade, Work was encouraged to take up composing as a profession by another great songwriter, George F. Root (q.v.). Born in Middletown, Conn., Oct. 1, 1832, Work was still a boy when his family moved to Illinois, where his father Alanson Work, a dedicated abolitionist, was active in the Underground Railroad which assisted escaped slaves. The father was imprisoned in 1841 for his efforts, and when he was released 4 years later, he returned to Connecticut, leaving his son with friends. Work learned the printing trade and ca. 1855 went to Chicago, eventually finding his way to the publishing firm of Root and Cady. Upon seeing one of Work's early songs, "Kingdom Coming" (1862) Root suggested that Work give up printing and take up songwriting. He also appointed Work editor of the house publication *The Song Messenger of the Northwest*. In the July 1863 issue Work criticized, though not by name, the Great Arbiter of Music, Lowell Mason (q.v.). Work, a deeply religious man and a naturally gifted musician, questioned Mason's right to "improve" the old hymn tunes. Root defended Mason and soon after Work departed Root and Cady. However, he continued to provide the company with his songs. Imbued with his father's attitude toward slavery, Work found an outlet in song, some in dialect, some amusing, some sad. "Grafted in the Army" (1862) is a humorous yet touching play on malapropisms; "Uncle Joe's 'Hail Columbia!'" is an exhilarating freedom song of an old slave who will "Fling de chains in de ribber." Work's most notorious Civil War song was "Marching Through Georgia" (1865), celebrating Sherman's destructive march to the sea. Its unpopularity in the South has never waned. Work's pro-North sentiments were further revealed in "Who Shall Rule This American Nation?" a criticism of the failure of Reconstruction. This was in 1866; in the same year Work's wife suffered a mental breakdown and he composed only sporadically, even returned to his trade of printing and proofreading. He also fell in love with an 18-year-old girl (he was then about twice her age), only to see her marry another man. Between bouts of despair and frustration, Work managed to write a song, among these "Grandfather's Clock" (1876) and the superb "The Silver Horn," composed in 1883, the year of his wife's death in an insane asylum. Another of Work's causes was temperance and he wrote several songs in that vein, the most "classic" being "Come Home, Father!" (1864: *Father, dear father, come home with me now!/The clock in the steeple strikes one . . .*) Only a year after his wife's death, Work died of a heart attack in Hartford, Conn., June 8, 1884.

WYETH, JOHN See *Repository of Sacred Music, Part Second.*

IV

The Romantic Classicists

(1865–1919)

The efforts of Lowell Mason and the good music militancy of John Sullivan Dwight came to fruition in what could be called the "Second New England School." They have also been labeled the "Boston Classicists," and the "New England Academics" which, if nothing else, implies their geographic grouping, a solid musical education, and musical conservatism. Their leader-teacher was John Knowles Paine who was awarded the first music professorship at Harvard in 1875. Paine, as did most of the composers he taught or who followed him, finished off his musical education in Germany. Paine was the first American symphonist to be taken seriously in Europe—a high honor that brought him recognition at home. He, his students, and their students were the first accepted "American" composers.

"Coddling is no longer the chief need of the American composer," Rupert Hughes stated in his *Contemporary American Composers* (1900). "While he still wants encouragement in his good tendencies,—much more encouragement than he gets, too,—he is now strong enough to profit by the discouragement of his evil tendencies." Hughes suggested that the "first and most vital flaw of which his work will be accused is the lack of nationalism." Hughes did not agree. He then described the product of the Second New England school succinctly: "The influences that finally made American music are chiefly German. Almost all of our composers have studied in Germany, or from teachers trained there; very few of them turning aside to Paris, and almost none to Italy. The prominent teachers, too, that have come from abroad have been trained in the German school, whatever their nationality. The growth of a national school has been necessarily slow, therefore, for its necessary and complete submission to German influences."

Paine, and those composers of ability that followed, Arthur Foote, George Chadwick, George Templeton Strong, Arthur Whiting, and Horatio Parker, to name but a few—good musicians all—have much in common, including their

Germanic musical point of view. Hughes could not have predicted their rapid eclipse when he said in 1900 that "practically every American composer of even the faintest importance is now living." They are rarely heard in the 20th-century concert hall, and this, culturally speaking, is unfortunate.

One of the great burdens of the American composer has, of course, been the comparison with European composers and those Americans who enjoyed a good press in the latter 19th century produced rather pale imitations of the music of their models. They sublimated personal expression in the name of "good" music. There were exceptions, the most original and important being Charles Ives, who was barely known during his active creative life and, alas, founded no Third New England School. Had he, the evolution of American music would have been very different.

The American composer of this period was Edward MacDowell, who was not a member of the New England group. Born a New Yorker, he even studied briefly in Paris, but felt more at home in Germany, where he hoped to study the piano but, under the urging of his teacher, Joachim Raff, a composer of some distinction, switched to composition. It prepared MacDowell for a stellar place among the American Romantics.

An interesting aspect of the period was the appearance of the woman composer on the "serious" music scene. (When the *Rosebud Quickstep* was published in the 1840s the composer was identified simply as "Mary." Writing music was regarded as a man's game obviously though there were those who looked upon composing music as unmanly.) One of the most interesting composers of the period was Amy Marcy Cheney, who preferred signing her works Mrs. H. H. A. Beach. Amy Beach's works for solo piano, chamber groups, and a splendid piano concerto make good listening today. Margaret Ruthven Lang composed for orchestra and chorus and was especially skilled at writing songs. Irene Baumgrass, who married a Boston music critic, Philip Hale, was a pianist and composer of little piano pieces and songs rarely, it ever, heard after her lifetime. It seemed to be woman's lot to specialize in miniatures. Other women songwriters of the period were Mary Turner Salter, Gina Branscombe, and Harriet Ware. None achieved the success of Carrie Jacobs Bond, an invalid after a fall on an icy sidewalk, who produced such songs as "I Love You Truly" and "A Perfect Day."

The Germanic esthetic was challenged by a 2nd generation of composers who were influenced by the impressionism of the new French composers or the nationalism of the Russians. By the turn of the century a new breed of Americanists came forward with works in which American musical themes—from the Indian to the Negro—figured. The leader of this group was Arthur Farwell, who was joined by such gifted men as Henry F. B. Gilbert, Arthur Shepherd, Edgar Stillman Kelley, Edward Burlingame Hill (all of whose works were published by Farwell's Wa-Wan Press). Even Boston conservative Daniel Gregory Mason employed Negro and English folk songs in his compositions, as did the aristocratic Virginian, John Powell. The nationalist movement in

American music had received great stimulus from the visit of the Bohemian composer Antonín Dvořák, who spent the years 1892–95 as director of the National Conservatory of Music in New York.

Dvořák not only spoke in favor of using American folk themes, he employed them himself in his own work, most notably in his *New World Symphony*. His handling of folkish themes of his native country was also stimulating to the younger Americans who wished to do the same. His influence helped to lead the way toward breaking the hold of German music on the American composer.

Other musicians of foreign birth who later influenced American musicians (if not necessarily American music) were Charles Martin Loeffler, an Alsatian, and Ernest Bloch, a Swiss. Both composed a good deal of fine music in America and taught many distinguished students. Loeffler's musical vocabulary was decidedly French and Bloch drew often on Jewish themes.

The American music lover, if not necessarily the American composer, benefited from the founding of great orchestras: the Boston Symphony (1881), the Chicago Symphony (1891), the Philadelphia Orchestra (1900); by 1903 Minneapolis had its symphony orchestra (now the Minnesota Orchestra). The formation of the orchestras encouraged the construction of great halls to house them.

An interesting, offbeat, orchestra was organized in New York in 1903, the Russian Symphony Orchestra, which introduced New Yorkers to the exotic music of the Russian nationalists as well as the ultra exotic sounds of Scriabin. It was a change from the usual German diet served up by the Philharmonic.

Opera flourished also. By 1906 New York had 2 great opera houses, the Metropolitan and Oscar Hammerstein's Manhattan Opera House. Boston opened its new Opera House in 1909, and Chicago its Auditorium in 1910. While few American operas were presented and virtually every opera star was of foreign birth, Americans with time and money in the larger urban areas (and smaller, too, when opera companies toured) could enjoy the great operas of the past as well as works of contemporaries Richard Strauss and Claude Debussy.

Lowell Mason's concept of musical education for all came to full fruition with the introduction of music courses in colleges (the first full professorship was established at Harvard in 1875) and the founding of conservatories. One of the most interesting was the National Conservatory of Music of America (1885), the brainchildren—there was a school in New York and in Washington—of Mrs. Jeanette M. Thurber (1851–1946). Tuition was free until 1915. The National Conservatory employed a most distinguished faculty, among whom were numbered such disparate musicians as Victor Herbert and Horatio Parker. Dvořák was director for a time, as has been mentioned.

The discovery that it was possible to preserve musical performances phonographically was made during the late 19th century. Thomas Edison developed a method of recording sounds onto a cylinder coated with tinfoil in 1877; a decade later Emile Berliner contributed the idea of issuing recordings on discs, making mass production and commercialization possible. By the turn of the century several record manufacturers in the United States and Europe were in business. The impact upon the dissemination of music by the phonograph's centennial was undreamed of by Edison when he tinkered with his "talking machine."

While the music produced by American composers during this period was predominantly secular, religious music was not abandoned. Dudley Buck, a contemporary of Paine, was the leader in music for the church in the post-Civil War period. His pupils, Frederick Grant Gleason, Charles Beach Hawley, John Hyatt Brewer, and others, achieved distinction in the field of music for the church. Folk hymnody flourished as before in the South, and the gospel hymn, which many regarded as a commercialization and cheapening of religious music, came into vogue. This hymn style, marked by popular song chromatic harmonies, first came to light in William Hauser's *The Olive Leaf* (1878). The musical style and the texts might have originated in Tin Pan Alley had there been one at the time. The fasola folk ruralized the hymn and the gospel hymnists urbanized it. Most successful in this were such composers as Philip P. Bliss and Ira D. Sankey.

The Negro spiritual gained wide popularity and new stature with the tour, financially and esthetically profitable, of the Fisk Jubilee Singers beginning in 1871. While the original spirituals may have been rearranged and smoothed out for the trained voices, the Fisk choral group brought the spiritual to white America as well as Europe.

The minstrel show by the 1880s was gradually being supplanted by vaudeville and burlesque. The last great minstrel composer, who happened to be black, was James A. Bland. Vaudeville and burlesque would provide a platform for comics, songwriters, and singers and dancers—Harrigan and Hart, Weber and Fields, Edward E. Rice, George M. Cohan, David Braham. *The Black Crook* (1866), frequently called the "first musical comedy," fits the description because it did combine several elements that are associated with musical comedy: song, dance, and girls—plus spectacular scenic effects, flamboyant costumes, even a ballet company, and a quite negligible plot. *The Black Crook* was, in fact, a mishmash of an "extravaganza." The term "musical comedy" came into general use around the end of the 1890s; it was a blend of influences—borrowings from Viennese operetta, French *opera comique,* English music hall, and of greater importance musically and lyrically, the comic operas of Gilbert and Sullivan. The themes, techniques, form, songs, and dances evolved from the ponderous extravagance of *The Black Crook* to the light elegance of the operettas of Victor Herbert—even the march king John Philip Sousa wrote popular operettas—Gustave Kerker, Reginald De Koven, Jean Schwartz, and finally emerged into the indigenous musicals of George M. Cohan, Irving Berlin, and Jerome Kern. When a new generation of American songwriters arrived on the scene, it was set for the blossoming of the American lyric theatre in the 1920s.

Popular music flourished in the decades following the Civil War and, by the coming of the First World War, was big business indeed. Exploiting such outlets as vaudeville and related entertainments requiring music, sheet music sales, phonograph records, the publishing of popular music expanded. The major cluster of music publishing houses was strung along New York's 28th Street, mostly between Broadway and Sixth Avenue. This was in close proximity to the William Morris booking agency and the vaudeville-popular music trade journal, the *New York Clipper*. With the windows of the publishing houses open and the pianos pounding out the latest tune, an aspiring vaudeville singer or dancer could hear his next hit. Legend has it that the sounds along 28th Street on a warm day, with dozens of pianos tinkling and clattering, inspired writer Monroe H. Rosenfeld to call it "Tin Pan Alley" (supposedly as the title of an article he had written for a newspaper; the story is generally considered apocryphal).

The sentimental songs so popular before and after the Civil War continued as a staple in Tin Pan Alley, some of the most bathetic emerging during the misnamed "Gay Nineties," e.g., Gussie L. Davis' "In the Baggage Coach Ahead" or "The Little Lost Child," or Rosenfeld's preachy "Those Wedding Bells Shall Not Ring Out!" There were more cheerful effusions: "After the Ball" (Charles K. Harris), "My Sweetheart's the Man in the Moon" (James Thornton), "On the Banks of the Wabash" (Paul Dresser), and "At a Georgia Camp Meeting" by a prescient Kerry Mills, in one of the first successful Tin Pan Alley manipulations of ragtime. The general pepping-up of American society was reflected after the turn of the century in songs like "Good Bye, My Lady Love" (Joseph E. Howard), "I've Got Rings on My Fingers" (Maurice Scott; lyrics by Weston and Barnes), "Meet Me in St. Louis, Louis" (Kerry Mills; lyrics by Andrew B. Sterling), "Wait 'Til the Sun Shines, Nellie" (Harry Von Tilzer; lyrics by Andrew B. Sterling), and dozens of others. The quickening of the American pace was also reflected in the popular dances that reached craze proportions around the beginning of the First World War. The old-fashioned waltzes, though never completely abandoned, the polkas, and schottische of social dancing were supplanted by the faster two-step and given such names as fox-trot, turkey trot, grizzly bear, and the bunny hug. The most popular dance team of the period, one of many, was Vernon and Irene Castle who swept the country with their appearances in clubs and the theatre. They inspired a number of "Castle" steps, the most popular being "The Castle Walk" as well as "The Castle House Rag" by black bandleader Jim Europe.

The style of piano music eventually named ragtime reached its peak before the turn of the century, enjoyed popularity for a time, and waned before the end of the First World War. Although the first rags were published in 1897, the style of playing is much older and grew out of syncopated banjo performances by slaves. Pianists took up the style and since they often as not could neither read nor write music their music was not preserved. Instrumental and vocal styles intermingled and even before the term ragtime was used syncopated "coon songs" were popular ("All Coons Look Alike to Me," written by a black performer-songwriter Ernest Hogan in 1896 was extremely popular). The more complex piano rags evolved independently and grew out of what was called "jig music," the jig being the dance; ragtime playing was associated also with the competitive cakewalks.

A Negro invention, ragtime ironically was publically introduced by white men to the New York public. In 1896 Kentuckian Ben R. Harney introduced his "You've Been a Good Old Wagon" and initiated a general interest in the lilting yet powerful style. In January 1897 white bandleader William H. Krell published his *Mississippi Rag* for piano solo; in December Tom Turpin, a black composer, published *Harlem Rag*. The ragtime craze swept the country and ragtime pianists did their stuff in New Orleans, Chicago, New York, Detroit, Kansas City, St. Louis, and Sedelia, Mo. It was in Sedelia that the publishing company of John Stark (a white man) issued in March 1899 the *Original Rags* and in September, *Maple Leaf Rag* by Scott Joplin. Because of his training as a musician Joplin was capable of notating the intricately syncopated music; he also proved to be a remarkably gifted composer. It was *Maple Leaf Rag* that made the country truly rag conscious—with Europe following soon after. European "serious" composers, from Debussy to Stravinsky, in fact, adapted touches of ragtime into their own compositions.

It is interesting to contrast the work of the American "serious" composer and his piano miniatures that appeared on parlor pianos alongside ragtime sheet music. About this same time, William Mason, son of reformer Lowell, composed some attractive little piano pieces, but he preferred teaching as a profession. MacDowell's miniatures numbered the charming *Woodland Sketches* among them, with *To a Wild Rose* almost as ubiquitous as *Maple Leaf Rag*. Consider the perfumed delicacies of Ethelbert Nevin and his popular *Narcissus* (from *Water Scenes*), or the perfectly conventional effusions of the prolific W. F. Sudds. That these 2 musics existed side by side—the one dreamy and pallid, the other lively and vital—is intriguing. (At least 2 exceptions come to mind: the mystical tone painting of Charles Tomlinson Griffes and the surprising experimentalism of Charles Ives, who discovered the fun of ragtime long before the rest of his countrymen.)

The success of Joplin inspired imitators, some of whom were excellent themselves, and exploiters in Tin Pan Alley who distorted ragtime into a cheap parody. Among the followers of Joplin were Arthur Marshall, James Scott, Artie Matthews, such Easterners as Eubie Blake and James P. Johnson and two outstanding white ragtime composers, Percy Wenrich and Joseph F. Lamb. The Tin Pan Alley products tended toward showiness, fast tempos, flashy, meaningless keyboard runs, all of which destroyed the delicate beauty of the true rag. The decline in popularity began about mid-First World War, partly because of a flooding of the market and partly because of a new sound

Ferdinand Jelly Roll Morton, a master ragtime pianist out of New Orleans, once claimed that he invented jazz, overlooking the historical fact that as early as 1894, when Morton was 9, it was also claimed that trumpeter Buddy Bolden "invented the hot blues" and was the inventor of jazz. Unlikely stories, as is the one that New Orleans was the cradle of jazz (although it was certainly an important hotbed). The blues too are of uncertain origin, but no one can argue the black folk-origin. Primarily a vocal style, when taken up by a brass band and ragged the result was incipient jazz. The characteristics of jazz derived from the playing style (often improvised) of the musicians, the instrumentation, and the manner of performance, balancing solos and ensemble.

The most legendary assemblage of pioneer jazz musicians was to be found in New Orleans. The more successful bands began touring in the early 1900s, influencing the musicians in other parts of the country as well as the white listeners (and musicians also). There were the bands of Freddie Keppard and King Oliver (who employed a young Louis Armstrong) before the First World War. Oliver carried his own style from New Orleans up to Chicago and eventually to New York. But, ironically again, it was a white group, the 5-member Dixieland Jass (*sic*) Band, that initiated the Jazz Age in New York. Originally from New Orleans, the band opened at a cafe in mid-January 1917, made their first recording in February, and by March jazz was here to stay. Calling themselves eventually the Original Dixieland Jazz Band, the group literally brought jazz to the world. Their best-selling recordings and personal appearances prepared the way for the great jazz masters who were only waiting to be heard. Their impact on American music was profound and lasting.

"ALEXANDER'S RAGTIME BAND" In the words of its creator, "Alexander's Ragtime Band" is "a song *about* ragtime," and not an attempt at re-creating a ragtime song. The song, words and music, was conceived by Irving Berlin (q.v.) in 1911; it was his biggest song hit up to that time and while it certainly did not lead to the ragtime craze, as some Tin Pan Alley legends have it, it stimulated the popularity of ragtime, black and white.

AMERICAN SOCIETY OF COMPOSERS, AUTHORS AND PUBLISHERS See ASCAP.

ASCAP Acronym for American Society of Composers, Authors and Publishers founded in 1914 by composers Victor Herbert, Louis A. Hirsch, Raymond Hubbell, Silvio Hein, and Gustave Kerker, lyricist Glen MacDonough, publishers George Maxwell and Jay Witmark, and copyright attorney Nathan Burkan. The Society grew out of a lawsuit Victor Herbert brought against a New York restaurateur. Upon entering the restaurant Herbert heard its small orchestra performing one of his songs. Since the music was obviously performed to please the customers, Herbert considered what he heard was a public performance for profit. The restaurant owner (and others), hotel owners, and cabaret proprietors insisted that since they did not charge admission they were not using Herbert's work for gain. The suit went as high as the Supreme Court and Herbert won. Supreme Court Justice Oliver Wendell Holmes stated, in part, the Court's unanimous opinion: "If the music did not pay, it would be given up. If it pays, it pays out of the public pocketbook. Whether it pays or not, the purpose of employing it is profit, and that is enough." The copyright owners of songs were to be compensated for the use of their works in public performances. To oversee this, the Society was formed on Feb. 13, 1914, with Herbert as vice-president and Maxwell as president. ASCAP collected performance fees from the various sources using the works of their members. When radio and television were introduced ASCAP scrutinized and licensed these outlets also. In 1914 the membership stood at 182 (of these 22 were publishers, the rest were songwriters); by the 1970s the total was something like 12,000. ASCAP's function has been as a monitoring and collection agency for its members, whose works are performed in public for profit (license without fee is granted to certain nonprofit organizations such as churches, veteran organizations, the armed services, noncommercial radio and television). The ASCAP membership roster reads like a Who's Who of American Music in all fields of music, from songwriting to symphonic. The organization was unique in the field until the organization of Broadcast Music, Inc. (BMI) in 1940 (Section VI). Since its founding the presidents of the Society have been George Maxwell (1914–24), Gene Buck (1924–42), Deems Taylor (1942–48), Fred E. Ahlert (1948–50), Otto A. Harbach (1950–53), Stanley Adams (1953–1980) and Hal David (1980–). ASCAP is governed by a 24-member board of directors (half of which is made up of publishers and the other half of songwriters/composers). The membership governs the organization, supervises policy, etc. A nonprofit organization, ASCAP distributes its licensing fee profits among its members.

AYER, NAT D. (1887–1952) Composer, vocalist. Little is known about Nathaniel Davis Ayer, except that he was born in Boston, Mass., in 1887 and went to England with a singing group called the American Ragtime Quartet. When the others returned to the United States, Ayer decided to remain in London where he soon established himself as a successful songwriter. Before the trip, Ayer had written a fairly popular song, "Moving Day in Jungle Town" (a satiric comment on Theodore Roosevelt's big game hunting habit; the lyrics were by A. Seymour Brown, 1909). Ayer wrote the songs for a revue, *The Bing Boys Are Here,* the first in the popular series about the Bing family. The show was very popular during its 1916 run and was followed the next year by a sequel, *The Bing Girls Are Here.* Among Ayer's best songs are "Oh, You Beautiful Doll" (lyrics by Brown, 1911) and "If You Were the Only Girl" which was introduced in *The Bing Boys Are Here;* it became popular in the United States in 1925 and was later used in the film *The Vagabond Lover* in 1929. The words were by the English lyricist Clifford Grey (1887–1941). Another Ayer song is the mildly naughty "If You Talk in Your Sleep, Don't Mention My Name" (lyrics by Brown, 1911). One of Ayer's last show scores was *Somewhere in England* (1939). He died in Bath, Somersetshire, England, in 1952.

AYRES, FREDERICK (1876–1926) Composer, teacher. Born Frederick Ayres Johnson in Binghamton, N.Y., Mar. 17, 1876, Ayres, as he preferred to be known professionally, finished Cornell before he began to study music seriously with Edgar Stillman Kelley (q.v.) and Arthur Foote (q.v.). Ayres eventually settled in Colorado Springs, where he taught theory and composition and produced original compositions. He was, during his lifetime, especially noted for his songs, several of which were issued by the Wa-Wan Press (q.v.). Among Ayres's instrumental compositions are *Two Fugues for Piano, Op. 9* (1910), *Trio for Piano, Violin and Cello, Op. 13* (1914), *Overture for Orchestra, "From the Plains," Op. 14* (ca. 1914), *Sonata for Violin and Piano, Op. 15* (1914), and *String Quartet, Op. 16* (rev. 1916). A *Second Sonata for Violin and Piano,* a *Sonata for Cello and Piano,* and an uncompleted *Second String Quartet* date from Ayres's final year. He died in Colorado Springs, Nov. 26, 1926.

BALL, ERNEST R. (1878–1927) Songwriter, performer, born in Cleveland, Ohio, July 21, 1878, Ball revealed an early musical aptitude and studied at the Cleveland Conservatory. While still a young man, he moved to New York City, where he began as a relief pianist at Keith's Union Square Theatre before joining the publishing firm of M. Witmark & Sons as staff pianist and composer in 1907. A born songwriter, Ball provided the firm with a steady stream of hits. Even before joining Witmark, Ball had produced "Will You Love Me in December as You Do in May?" (1905, words by one James J. Walker, who would one day be Mayor of New York); the next year brought the popular "Love Me and the World Is Mine" (lyrics by Dave Reed, Jr., 1872–1946). Ball had an affinity for the Irish ballad and supplied the American tenor Chauncey Olcott (1858–1932) with such songs as "Mother Machree" (1910, written with Olcott; words by Rida Johnson Young, q.v.), "When Irish Eyes Are Smiling" (1912, lyrics by George Graff, Jr., 1886–1973), and "A Little Bit of Heaven, Sure They Call It Ireland" (1914, words by J. Keirn Brennan, 1873–1948). Brennan also supplied the lyrics to another long-lasting Ball melody in 1919, "Let the Rest of the World Go By." Besides songwriting, Ball toured in vaudeville. On tour, after completing his act on stage in a Santa Ana, Calif., theatre, he suffered a heart attack in his dressing room and died, aged 49, on May 3, 1927.

BARTLETT, HOMER NEWTON (1846–1920) Organist, pianist, and composer. Bartlett was born in Olive, N.Y., Dec. 28, 1846. American educated (organ, piano, composition), he began on the violin as a youngster, making his public debut at the age of 8; he began composing 2 years later. At 14 he became organist at the Madison Avenue Baptist Church, a post held for almost 35 years; Bartlett was one of the founders of the American Guild of Organists (1896). He not only wrote for the organ but was a prolific composer for the piano, as well as music for diverse instrumental combinations for orchestra and voice. An early work, *Grande Polka de Concert* (1867), was called by historian Rupert Hughes "one of the most outrageously popular piano pieces ever published in America . . ." Much of Bartlett's piano composition was clearly influenced by Chopin. Among his 250 works are an opera, *La Vallière*, an oratorio, *Samuell*, a cantata, *The Last Chieftain*, a *Concerto for Violin and Orchestra*, and about 80 songs and other small works for various instrumental combinations. Bartlett died in Hoboken, N.J., Apr. 3, 1920.

BEACH, AMY, MRS. (1867–1944) Composer, pianist. Amy Marcy Cheney was born in Henniker, N.H., Sept. 5, 1867, and was musical practically from birth. She revealed a good musical memory before she was 2 and began the study of the piano with her mother at the age of 6, though she had been playing the instrument for 2 years. The family moved to Boston when Amy was 8 and it was there she began to study in earnest, apparently with the career of concert pianist in mind. Except for some study of harmony, she was generally self-taught in composition and orchestration. She made her debut at the age of 16 playing the Moscheles *Piano Concerto in G Minor.* In 1885 she married an eminent physician-surgeon, Dr. Henry Harris Aubrey Beach, which led to less activity in the concert hall and more concentration on composition. These works were invariably signed Mrs. H. H. A. Beach (the marriage lasted until the death of her husband in 1910). Mrs. Beach was one of the rare composers of the period, one whose musical training was accomplished in America. Amy Beach was greatly admired in her lifetime and highly regarded even in the company of her male contemporaries, Foote, Chadwick, Parker, et al., no small achievement. She was, however, best known for her songs, church music, and small piano pieces—and her ability as a concert pianist. Among her works are a *Mass in E-flat,* Op. 5 (1892); in the same year she was commissioned to write a work for the dedication of the Woman's Building at the Chicago World's Fair, resulting in *Festival Jubilate,* an impressive composition. Her *Gaelic Symphony* was published in 1897, though its writing dates from the previous year when she also composed a *Sonata for Violin and Piano,* Op. 34. A *Piano Concerto,* Op. 45 dates from 1900 and was widely performed in the United States and Europe (its scintillating *Scherzo* is remarkably inventive and carried off with a sure touch). Other compositions include a *Piano Quintet,* Op. 67 (1909), and numerous piano pieces; one of the last was *Five Improvisations for Piano,* Op. 148. After her husband's death in 1910, Mrs. Beach spent 4 years in Europe playing in concerts in Hamburg, Leipzig, and Berlin, where her performances and works were enthusiastically received by the critics and public alike. Upon her return she spent the rest of her life composing—she was 65 when she completed a one-act opera, *Cabildo*—and was active in New York's musical life until her death there on Dec. 27, 1944.

"BEAUTIFUL OHIO" A popular song, published in 1918, lyrics by Ballard Macdonald (1882–1935) and music by "Mary Earl" (one of the pseudonyms of Robert King, who was born Robert Keiser, 1862–1932). One of the best songs (in waltz time) of the period, and still sung. Macdonald later collaborated with B. G. DeSylva and George Gershwin (Section V) on "Somebody Loves Me" as well as King (who also used the names "R. A. Wilson" and "Mrs. Ravenhall").

BERLIN, IRVING (b. 1888) Songwriter. The most influential, most prolific and most successful American songwriter of the 20th century was born Israel Baline in Temun, Russia, on May 11, 1888. The family left Russia in an era of pogroms and settled in New York's Lower East Side ca. 1892. Cantor Moses Baline died in 1896, leaving his wife Leah and 8 children; Israel was then about 8. With only 2 years of public schooling, he quit to work as a newsboy to contribute to the family income. His only musical experience had come through his cantor father; he never has learned to read music. He began his professional career, still in his teens, as a singing waiter in a Bowery cafe. Songs were in great demand so Berlin began, at first, producing lyrics; he taught himself to play the piano. He also worked as a song plugger (q.v.) for the publishing firm owned by Harry Von Tilzer (q.v.). His first song, "Marie from Sunny Italy," with music by one M. Nicholson and lyric by "I. Berlin," a printer's error on the sheet music which suggested his professional name. The song, written for performance in the Pelham Cafe—a rival to a nearby Chinatown saloon—

enjoyed mild popularity. Two years later, in 1909, Berlin was hired as a staff lyricist by the Ted Snyder Co., which published the 2nd all-Berlin song (the first, "Best of Friends Must Part," was never published), words and music by the ex-singing waiter "Dorando." It too was successful. In 1910 Berlin began vaudeville appearances and in a Broadway musical with Snyder, *Up and Down Broadway*. In 1911 Berlin produced "Alexander's Ragtime Band," which made his an international name. By 1913 he was a partner in Waterson, Berlin & Snyder Co. In 1914 he wrote his first full score for a Broadway musical, *Watch Your Step;* before, Berlin had contributed incidental songs that were interpolated into revues and musicals. Serving in the U. S. Army during the First World War, Sergeant Irving Berlin scored the soldier musical *Yip! Yip! Yaphank,* for which he wrote "Mandy" and "Oh! How I Hate to Get Up in the Morning" (1918) and a patriotic song that was not used but which was revived in 1939: "God Bless America." After the war, Berlin formed his own publishing company and in 1921, in partnership with producer Sam H. Harris (1872–1941), became a proprietor of his own theatre, The Music Box. With an uncanny ear tuned to the public heart and mind Irving Berlin proceeded to become the most successful songwriter in history. Whether anticipating a rhythmic pattern, a new dance craze, a sentiment, or a public emotion, Berlin was the popular songwriter who most consistently produced the song that met that public demand. The songs ranged from those of disarming simplicity ("Easter Parade," 1933) to the patently sentimental ("All Alone," 1924), the musically complex ("Let's Face the Music and Dance," 1936), to the comic ("I Say It's Spinach —the Hell With It," 1932) and sociological ("Supper Time," 1933, a comment on lynching). A sophisticated folk artist, Berlin, though he plays the piano (in the key of F-sharp only), has employed musical secretaries to notate his melodies. He has a sharp ear for harmonies and knows precisely what should be set down. An instinctive songwriter, his output has encompassed the gamut of national, even international, songs and dances for more than half a century. His "hits," which he loves, have included individual published songs, plus show and film music. Among the nonproduction successes, i.e., songs not written for a show or film (only a fraction can be listed): "What'll I Do" (1924), "Always" (1925), "Remember" (1925), "Blue Skies" (1927), and "Marie" (1928). The shows/revues include several *Ziegfeld Follies*, the *Music Box Revues* (1921–24), *Face the Music* (1932), *As Thousands Cheer* (1933), *Louisiana Purchase* (1940), *This Is the Army* (1942), *Annie Get Your Gun* (1946), *Miss Liberty* (1949), *Call Me Madam* (1950), and *Mr. President* (1961). Film scores: *Top Hat* (1935), *Follow the Fleet* (1936), *On the Avenue* (1937), and *Holiday Inn* (out of which came "White Christmas"; 1941). In 1965 Berlin wrote new songs for a proposed film, *Say It with Music,* which has not been produced. Berlin's wife, the former Ellin Mackay, is a successful novelist and active in the Girl Scouts of America. They have been married since 1926 and are the parents of 3 daughters. Since the change of musical scene on Broadway and in Hollywood, Berlin has kept busy with an occasional song and with his painting. He is the recipient of numerous awards (the Academy Award for "White Christmas"; a special Congressional Medal of Honor for "God Bless America" whose earnings are contributed to the Boy Scouts and Girl Scouts) and honorary degrees and was among the first to be elected to the Songwriters' Hall of Fame.

BIRD, ARTHUR (1856–1923) Composer, pianist. A pre-1920s expatriate, Massachusetts-born (Cambridge, July 23, 1856), Bird spent most of his adult life in Germany. As a child he revealed early pianistic ability and a gift for improvisation. At 19 he went to Berlin to study piano and theory; at Weimar he studied with Liszt, who thought highly of the "young American composer." Bird returned to America in 1877 to serve as a church organist and choirmaster in Halifax, Nova Scotia; he also taught piano. He returned to Berlin for further study with Heinrich Urban (1837–1901) in composition and orchestration. He made his successful debut as a pianist in Berlin in 1866; the same year, under the sponsorship of Liszt, his *Carnival Scene* for orchestra was very well received. Bird then came to his native land for the last time to serve as the director of the Milwaukee Music Festival; following a brief stay he returned to Berlin, where he was prominent in its musical life. His works were regularly performed and published in Europe (many thought of him as European). He composed works for the piano and organ, a comic opera, *Daphne* (produced in New York in 1897), a ballet, *Rubezahl,* and several suites for orchestra. His *Serenade for Wind Instruments,* Op. 40, was awarded the Paderewski Prize in 1891. Bird died in Berlin on Dec. 22, 1923.

THE BLACK CROOK The alleged first American musical which opened at New York's Niblo's Garden on Sept. 12, 1866, and ran for 474 performances. While it is true that *The Black Crook* combined the elements of song, settings, and dance, it had originally been intended by author Charles M. Barras as a girl-free melodrama. The girls were introduced, along with a number of other elements, because the Academy of Music, which was to have provided the showcase for the French ballet, burned.

The respective managements struck a deal and the girls from the Academy were worked into the melodrama in rehearsal at Niblo's. Barras objected but management's money prevailed. The result was a mélange of Faustish plot, extravagant scenic effects, popular songs, and scantily clad French ballerinas, some of whom were still in their teens. Some of the costumes were quite fantastic. The choreography was the work of David Costa, ballet master of the original company. The story had something to do with an evil sorcerer called "The Black Crook" (because of a deformation) and how he beguiled and nearly won over the hero, a painter, in love with the lovely Amina. Hertzog, the sorcerer, provided the excuse for spectacular hurricanes, flying angels, and other impressive technical innovations. The opening night performance began at 7:45 and ended at 1:15 or so in the morning, to no one's dismay. Word of mouth was excellent, with special mention of the scenics and the girls. Business was not hurt when the New York *Tribune* editorialized against their "daring" costumes. *The Black Crook* was the show to see, enjoyed a very long run, toured extensively and was frequently revived, most recently as late as 1929. A London production ran for more than 200 performances and a sequel, *The White Fawn,* opened in New York in 1868; its story about a princess who is transformed into a white fawn did not have *The Black Crook*'s staying power. Most of the music was written by the musical director of Niblo's Garden, Giuseppe Operti. One of his efforts was *The Amazon March.* The best-known song, "You Naughty, Naughty Men," "composed for and sung by Miss Millie Cavendish," was produced by G. Bickwell (music) and T. Kennick ("poetry"); all 3 were British. The distinguishing musical comedy feature of *The Black Crook* was not the music but the extravagant blend of many elements.

The preposterous story would count for something, however, considering the "books" of the later musical comedies.

BLAND, JAMES A. (1854–1911) Songwriter, entertainer. The son of Allen Bland, the first Negro to be appointed examiner in the U. S. Patent Office, James Bland was born in Flushing, N.Y., Oct. 22, 1854. Upon his father's appointment, the family moved to Washington, D.C., where the son completed high school and enrolled in Howard University (where his father had earned a degree in law). Though not an exceptional student, young Bland was popular because of a pleasant personality and his musical abilities. He had taught himself to play the banjo and, influenced by the singing of the ex-slaves who worked at Howard, composed his own songs. He was in demand as an entertainer at various Washington social events, black and white. For these gatherings Bland often wrote new songs, among them "Carry Me Back to Old Virginny" (1878). The minstrel show was still in its heyday (though there was scant room for a real black man in their troupes). Bland, to his father's disgust, left Howard to join one of the early all-black minstrel shows, appearing in New York with Haverly's Genuine Colored Minstrels ca. 1879; after a tour the troupe went to Europe in 1881. When the Minstrels returned to the United States, Bland chose to remain and was successful in Britain's music halls and on the Continent (especially in Germany, where he was grouped with Foster and Sousa as one of the three American songwriters most admired by the Germans). Notably, Bland dispensed with the obligatory blackface makeup for his European stay. But time had run out on the minstrel show, which was being supplanted by vaudeville, and by 1901 Bland decided to return to the United States. He lived in Washington for a brief time, hoping to begin anew, composing the score for an unsuccessful musical entitled *The Sporting Girl*. Bland was not able to equal his earlier output: "Oh! Dem Golden Slippers" (1879), "In the Evening by the Moonlight" (1879), and "Hand Me Down My Walking Cane" (1880). "Carry Me Back to Old Virginny" was adopted as the official state song of Virginia in 1940. Bland, who evidently spent his money as he earned it during his better days, which lasted for some 20 years, died penniless in Philadelphia on May 5, 1911.

BLUES A form of Negro folk song, originally spontaneous, improvised and characterized by a melancholy feeling, which dates at least to pre-Civil War days. The term itself in its nonmusical meaning, indicating sadness, defeat, or depression, was used as early as 1807 by Washington Irving (*Salmagundi*) and by Thoreau in *Walden* (1854). Songs expressing sadness, loss, or disappointment are common to all races and nationalities, but the form sung by the American Negro, an accretion of African, Caribbean, and Anglo-American elements has proved the most memorable. The origin of the blues is lost, since masters, or their visitors, had no interest in the songs of the slaves. The early blues were unaccompanied plaints or commentaries by field hands or other workers, and often a form of communication between blacks that the whites did not understand. Adding instrumental accompaniment introduced harmonization; the banjo, guitar, and eventually the piano or even a small band carried the blues out of the South northward and westward (which undoubtedly had their own forms) until it was discovered by white music publishers and commercialized. Among the earliest black blues singers was Gertrude "Ma" Rainey (Section V), who claimed she coined the word "blues" as descriptive of the sad songs she sang. She popularized the form and encouraged followers. In 1912 the great Negro musician W. C. Handy (q.v.) published "The Memphis Blues." For the first time the blues were set down on paper, formalizing the structure. The published blues, as contrasted with the sung blues, generally took the form of 12 bars (or sometimes 8 or 16; the former was probably the earliest or "primitive" form). While influenced by European harmony, the blues singer (or performer) tended to flatten the 3rd and 7th notes of the scale ("blue notes"). Certain vocal tricks—grace note inflections, slurring, swooping—were reproduced on instruments, particularly the trumpet and clarinet. The piano was a favored solo as well as accompaniment instrument; the blues piano masters, from Ferdinand "Jelly Roll" Morton (q.v.) to the primitive-sophisticated practitioners of "boogie-woogie" (Section VI) of the 1930s, reveal the infinite possibilities of invention of relatively simple form. The lyric of the sung blues, at least in its earliest original form, consisted of a 3-line stanza, the 2nd line being a repetition of the first and the 3rd a commentary on the initial statement. The 12-bar blues generally followed a chord progression of I-IV-I-V-I; the first line was set in the tonic (i.e., I), the 2nd in the subdominant, and the 3rd in the dominant, then resolving back to the tonic at the end. Such analysis is ex post facto and does not cover all instances where a vocalist or instrumentalist improvised on the spur of the moment. The original blues performers expressed themselves spontaneously—"like I feel"—and not according to the formulas that came later. The impact of the blues on all of American music was deep; the blues are the basis of jazz as well as various commercial forms, including the stylized "torch songs" (Section VI) of popular music, attempts to use certain characteristics in music for the concert hall (Gershwin's

Rhapsody in Blue, Section V), white folk music, and music for films and Broadway. Contemporary European composers, among them Milhaud, Weill, Hindemith (all of whom eventually emigrated to the United States), Martinů, and Krenek, attempted to use blues touches in their works. A Negro folk creation, ignored initially, the blues have become part of the universal musical language.

BOLDEN, CHARLES "BUDDY" (ca. 1868–1931) Cornetist, trumpeter, bandleader. One of the legendary figures of early jazz (q.v.), Bolden was born ca. 1868 in New Orleans. Little is known about him except that he was also a barber. Sometime in 1895 he formed a band which played in street parades and club dances. Bolden's trumpet technique earned him the nickname of "King" and a following of younger black musicians, among them Joseph Oliver (who was also known as "King"), Willie G. "Bunk" Johnson, and an even younger Louis Armstrong. Bolden made his mark on the musical scene in New Orleans before the turn of the century; what few details are known about his early life depended primarily on the recollections of other early jazzmen. Although a "reader," Bolden was known for his improvisations and for his powerful horn. He made no recordings, so even his playing style lived on only in the memories of the musicians who played with, and were influenced by, him. A poor businessman, an unstable personality, Bolden was eventually moved out of his own band. In 1907 while marching and playing in a Labor Day Parade in New Orleans in yet another band, Bolden went berserk and was committed to the East Louisiana State Hospital for the insane. He died in Jackson, La., Nov. 4, 1931.

BOND, CARRIE JACOBS (1862–1946) Songwriter, pianist. Indomitable, courageous, and industrious, Carrie Bond was born into a musically gifted family in Janesville, Wis., Aug. 11, 1862. As a child she played by ear, a talent lost when she began studying the piano at 10. Her father's death, after losing all of his money in a grain panic, when she was 12 was but the beginning of her misfortunes. She moved into her grandfather's home where she first began writing songs. At 25 she married a local physician, Dr. Frank L. Bond, soon after moving to Chicago where her first song, "Is My Dolly Dead?" was published. This was a children's song, written at the publisher's request because he considered the other songs she submitted as "too artistic." Two additional blows followed: the death of her husband and her own fall on an icy sidewalk, leaving her penniless and an invalid with a young son. With her gift for songwriting to draw upon, she formed "The Bond Shop," to serve as an outlet for her wares. In this she was helped by the singer Jessie Bartlett Davis (1860–1905) with money and in the promotion of songs. The first publication of The Bond Shop was entitled *Seven Songs* which contained 2 songs whose success encouraged her to publish them separately, "I Love You Truly" (1906) and "Just A-Wearyin' for You" (1901). Carrie Jacobs Bond not only wrote the words and music, but also designed and illustrated the sheet music covers. Despite her handicap she also appeared in vaudeville singing her songs, sang in the White House for President Theodore Roosevelt, and during the First World War toured the army camps entertaining the troops. Her songs enormously successful, Mrs. Bond was eventually able to settle down in comfort in her own home in Hollywood, Calif. A California sunset inspired the last of her big 3: "A Perfect Day" (1910). Her autobiography, *The Roads of Melody,* was published in 1927. She died in Hollywood, Dec. 28, 1946.

BRAHAM, DAVID (1838–1905) Songwriter. London-born, Braham emigrated to the United States at the age of 18 before the Civil War. He quickly found work in the orchestra of Pony Moore's Minstrels and eventually in most theatre orchestras in New York City. Eventually he graduated to music director and conductor (at Tony Pastor's, q.v.) and began composing about the time he met Edward Harrigan. It was as the chief composer for the musical comedy team of Harrigan and Hart (q.v.) that Braham was best known; he introduced some elements of the English music hall style into the American theatrical scene. Braham was most successful during the 1870s and '80s supplying music to the lyrics of Harrigan (who eventually married Braham's oldest daughter, Annie). The collaborators hit their stride in the ethnically (Irish) flavored *The Mulligan Guard Ball* (1879), expanded from an earlier comic skit into a farcical playlet; the "Mulligan" series was popular into the 1880s. Among the songs Braham wrote for the Harrigan and Hart shows (he was also the conductor) were the march "The Mulligan Guard," "The Babies on Our Block," "The Widow Nolan's Goat" (from *Squatter Sovereignty*, 1881), and "Maggie Murphy's Home" (*Reilly and the 400*, 1890). Braham, who signed his Harrigan lyrics with the shortened "Dave," collaborated with other lyricists, including Gregory K. Hyde ("You're the Idol of My Heart," 1874), precursor by 30 years of "Sweet Adeline!" In 1876 he set a lyric of George Cooper (1840–1927), "To Rest Let Him Gently Be Laid." His best work, however, was that done with Harrigan. Braham died in New York City, Apr. 11, 1905.

BRANSCOMBE, GENA (1881–1977) Composer, pianist, conductor. Although Canadian-born (Picton, Ont., Nov. 4, 1881), Gena Branscombe received much of her musical education in the United States. Among her teachers were Felix Borowski (Chicago Musical College) and Rudolph Ganz (also CMC). European studies with Engelbert Humperdinck followed. In 1907–9 Branscombe headed the piano department at Whitman College, Wash. She was active as a choral conductor in New York and New Jersey: the Branscombe Choral, the State Chorus of New Jersey, Contemporary Club Choral (Newark), and MacDowell Chorale (New Jersey). Branscombe was known before the First World War as a song composer and later for her choral compositions. A popular *Festival Prelude* for orchestra dates from 1913 and a *Sonata for Violin and Piano* from 1920. A symphonic suite, *Quebec,* was introduced by the Women's Symphony in Chicago, the composer conducting, in 1928. *Pilgrims of Destiny*, a long work for soloists, chorus, and orchestra was widely performed and was awarded a prize by the National League of American Pen Women in 1928. Gena Branscombe was married to John Ferguson Tenney. She died in New York City, July 26, 1977.

BROCKWAY, HOWARD (1870–1951) Composer, pianist, teacher. Brockway was born in Brooklyn, N.Y., Nov. 22, 1870. He was devoted to music from childhood, when he was taken to concerts conducted by Theodore Thomas and to chamber music recitals. He began the study of the piano in the United States then went to Berlin at the age of 19 to study piano with Karl H. Barth (1847–1922) and composition with an expatriate American, Otis B. Boise (1844–1912). In February 1895, before he returned to the United States, Brockway, then 24, was honored with a concert of his works at Berlin's Sing-Akademie; among these was the highly praised *Symphony in D major, Op. 12,* a work that was not heard in the United States until 1907. Brockway established himself in New York City upon his return to the United States in 1895 as a teacher at the Institute of Musical Art and the Mannes School (for a time he was associated with the Peabody Institute, Baltimore). Many of Brockway's early works were issued by German publishers, who apparently regarded him more seriously than his own countrymen. In addition to his symphony, Brockway also composed a *Sonata for Violin and Piano,* Op. 9, 2 other works dating from the period of the symphony, a *Cavatina and Rommanza for violin and orchestra* and a *Ballade in G minor,* Op. 11. A skillfully orchestrated *Sylvan Suite* was published in 1903. Brockway also composed a handful of works for chamber groups and piano, among the latter 4 pieces grouped under the title *Fantasiestück,* Op. 21; in 1916 he published 2 collections of Kentucky mountain tunes. Conservative and gifted, Brockway published very little during the later years of his life. He died in New York City, Feb. 20, 1951.

BROOKS, SHELTON (b. 1886) Composer, pianist, vaudeville entertainer. Brooks was born in Amesbury, Ontario, May 4, 1886. When he was very young, his family moved to Detroit, Mich., where he became known as a child prodigy and pianist. He began playing professionally in Detroit cafes and eventually broke into vaudeville. In 1910 Brooks, inspired by a snatch of overheard conversation, wrote "Some of These Days," which he introduced into his vaudeville act. The song was later taken up by Sophie Tucker (1884–1966) and was associated with her until her death. Five years later Brooks wrote another long-lived song, "The Darktown Strutters' Ball." Brooks also wrote special songs for vaudevillians Nora Bayes (1880–1928) and Al Jolson (1886–1950).

Brooks was active himself in vaudeville for some 45 years; he appeared in the all-black *Plantation Revue* with which he traveled to Europe (and a command performance in Britain).

BUCK, DUDLEY (1839–1909) Organist, composer. Buck was to American church music what J. K. Paine (q.v.) was to secular music for orchestra. Buck was especially known for his compositions for the organ and choral groups. Born into a Puritan family in Hartford, Conn., Mar. 10, 1839, Buck overcame parental objections to a career in music by sheer force of devotion to the art. He began studies in his native Hartford, then left, at 19, for further polishing in Europe. After 4 years spent in Leipzig and Dresden, Buck returned to take a job as organist in a Hartford church. In the same year (1862) he moved to Chicago to become organist at St. James Church, where he remained for 10 years. An association with conductor Theodore Thomas (q.v.) and the Cincinnati May Festival (1872) eventually led to Buck's position as assistant conductor of Thomas' Central Park Garden Concerts in New York City and to that of organist in various churches in Brooklyn. During this period, which closed in 1903 when Buck resigned, he was active as a composer producing many works for church performance, secular choral pieces, as well as organ and orchestral compositions. He was also author of several books, among them *The Influence of the Organ in History, A Dictionary of Musical Terms* and, most notably, *Illustrations in Choir Accompaniment* (1877). His choral works were most successful during Buck's lifetime, among them *The Centennial Meditation of Columbus* (composed for the Philadelphia Centennial Exposition, 1876); the cantata, *The Golden Legend* (text by Longfellow, 1880); *Light of Asia,* premiered in London, 1885; also popular were 3 short cantatas for church performance, *The Coming of the King, The Story of the Cross,* and *Christ the Victor.* In 1886 Buck published a *Grand Sonata in E Flat,* Op. 22, for solo organ; a 2nd followed in 1877. Among his works for orchestra are a symphonic overture, *Marmion,* and a *Festival Overture* (on "The Star-Spangled Banner," 1887). To round out the output, Buck even composed a comic opera, *Deseret* (libretto by W. A. Croffut), in 1880 which suffered a very short run in Brooklyn, where Buck was living at the time. He was more influential in the field of Episcopal church music and through the work of several talented students, Frederick Grant Gleason (q.v.), Charles Beach Hawley (1858–1915), and John Hyatt Brewer (1851–1931)—all of whom helped to revive the American organ tradition, then all but swamped by the rise in popularity of the symphony orchestra. Buck died in Orange, N.J., Oct. 6, 1909.

BURLEIGH, HARRY THACKER (1866–1949) Vocalist, arranger, and composer. Burleigh was born in Erie, Pa., Dec. 2, 1866 (he was christened Henry). He was a pioneer in American music in that he was one of the first of his race to be recognized as an important musician-composer and one of the first black nationalists to work with Negro folk music. Although Burleigh was interested in music as a boy, the family situation made it impossible for him to study formally. The early death of his father forced his well-educated mother to find work as a domestic. Burleigh was 26 before he was able to study music, although he had done a good deal of listening and much singing in Erie. In 1892 he was awarded a scholarship at the National Conservatory of Music, New York City, where he came under the influence of Dvořák (q.v.) and studied with Rubin Goldmark (q.v.) and Max

Spicker (1858–1912). Not only did Burleigh study singing, he also played in the conservatory orchestra: double bass and timpani. He later taught voice there. In 1894 he became baritone soloist at St. George's Church, New York, a position he held until 1946; he also, in 1900, began singing in Temple Emanu-El, remaining there until 1920. Simultaneously, Burleigh enjoyed a successful concert singing career. He began composing just before the turn of the century, although he is best known for his arrangements of Negro folk melodies. His works include *Six Plantation Melodies for Violin and Piano* (1901), *From the Southland,* for piano (1914), the song "I Love My Jean" (text by Robert Burns, 1914), *Southland Sketches for Violin and Piano* (1916), and *Five Songs* (text: Laurence Hope, 1919). In 1916 Burleigh published his collection *Jubilee Songs of the United States of America* containing his masterly arrangements of Negro folk songs. A simpler collection, *Old Songs Hymnal,* followed in 1929. Burleigh is undoubtedly best remembered for his classic arrangements of "Heav'n, Heav'n," "Deep River," and "Go Down, Moses" ("Let My People Go"). Active well into his 80th year, Burleigh died in Stamford, Conn., Sept. 12, 1949.

BUSCH, CARL (1862–1943) Conductor, composer. Born in Bjerre, Denmark, Mar. 29, 1862, Busch entered the University of Copenhagen to study law but soon switched to music: violin, piano, and theory. After a year in Paris he emigrated to the United States, settling in Kansas City, Mo., in 1887. Busch contributed much to the musical life of Kansas City, not the least being the formation of an Orchestral Society that eventually evolved into the Kansas City Philharmonic. In 1912 he became conductor of the Kansas City Symphony; he was guest conductor with orchestras throughout the United States and abroad, frequently performing his own compositions. Besides such nonprogrammatic works as two symphonies, a string quartet, and an *Elegy* for string orchestra, Busch produced much in the Americana vein: *Chant from the Great Plains, Ozarka, Minnehaha's Vision,* frequently drawing upon Indian themes. Among his works are more than 40 songs, several cantatas and choruses, and smaller works for the violin. Although an American citizen, Busch was knighted by the Danish Government in 1912. He died in Kansas City, Dec. 19, 1943.

BUTTERFIELD, JAMES AUSTIN (1837–1891) Singer, violinist, teacher, and editor. Butterfield was born in England and came to the United States at 19. He settled in Chicago and earned a living as a music teacher. For a time he edited and published *The Musical Visitor* in Indianapolis, Ind. He later returned to Chicago where he was leader of the Mendelssohn Society. Butterfield also produced the melodies to more than a hundred songs but is remembered by one: "When You and I Were Young, Maggie." After finding the text in a collection of poems, *Maple Leaf,* by Canadian poet-scholar George W. Johnson (1839–1917), Butterfield set it to music. The poem was in fact written to and about Johnson's wife, Maggie Clark; the two were married in 1865, moved to Cleveland, Ohio, where Johnson, a graduate of the University of Toronto, taught school. Maggie Johnson died shortly after; they had been married less than a year. Butterfield's melody captured the nostalgic integrity of Johnson's poem and the song has been around ever since.

CADMAN, CHARLES WAKEFIELD (1881–1946) Composer, organist, lecturer. Cadman was born in Johnstown, Pa., Dec. 24, 1881. Unlike most composers of the period he received all of his musical education in the United States, specifically in Pittsburgh. His family was not musical (his father was a metallurgist) and he did not begin piano lessons until he was 13. Although trained in orchestration and the organ also, Cadman initially intended to become a writer and for a time wrote music criticism for the Pittsburgh *Dispatch* (1908–10). Cadman's earliest efforts were unsuccessful comic operas and operettas. Around 1909 he rekindled a boyhood interest in the American Indian after a visit to the Omaha Indian Reservation. One of the first results was his Opus 45, *Four American Indian Songs* (1909), with words by an ex-school teacher from Nebraska (though Detroit-born), Mrs. Nelle Richmond Eberhart (1871–1944). One of the songs, "From the Land of the Sky-Blue Water," was taken up by the popular singer of the time (who had appreciated one of Cadman's reviews of her recital), Lillian Nordica (1857–1914), and it became widely known, sung, and purchased. An earlier (1906) collaboration of Cadman and Eberhart, "At Dawning," was also sung to impressive popularity by Irish tenor John McCormack (1884–1945). Cadman's fascination with Indian lore led him to work with ethnologist Francis LaFlesche, to lecture on the subject of Indian music in the United States, Britain, and France (1910). Upon his return to the United States he settled for a while in Denver, composing and serving as a church organist. Eventually Cadman settled in Los Angeles, where he was associated with the University of California. Cadman produced an Indian opera, *Shanewis* (Metropolitan Opera, 1918) and a choral work, *The Sunset Trail* (Denver, 1922). Much of his instrumental music also reveals the Indian influence: *Thunderbird Suite* (for solo piano, also orchestrated, 1914); *To a Vanishing Race,* for strings (1925). Cadman eventually abandoned the Red Man as a subject. *A Witch of Salem* was produced in Chicago in 1926; a *Suite on American Folktunes* was premiered in Saratoga in 1937; a fantasy for piano and orchestra, *Dark Dancers of the Mardi Gras,* was composed in 1933. Among Cadman's other works are a *Piano Sonata* (1915) and a *Sonata for Violin and Piano* (1930); a lone *Symphony* dates from 1939. Cadman even composed a *Hollywood Suite* ("Mary Pickford," "Charlie Chaplin," "To My Mother," and "Hollywood Bowl") which was performed by the New York Orchestra in 1932. These works are rarely performed today and Cadman is best remembered for his rather watered-down Indian-inspired songs. He died in Los Angeles, Dec. 30, 1946.

CAKEWALK A late 19th-century dance of Southern black origin. Very lively and characterized by fancy high-stepping. Winning couples were awarded the prize, generally a cake, hence the name. Originally a social slave dance, cakewalking was taken up by various minstrels, most notably Bert Williams and George Walker. The musical backing for the early cakewalk was undoubtedly the banjo, which led to ragtime (q.v.). Dancing the cakewalk reached craze proportions in the 1890s.

CARPENTER, JOHN ALDEN (1876–1951) Composer, pianist, and businessman. Carpenter was born in Park Ridge, Ill., Feb. 28, 1876. His family was in the railway, shipping, and mill supplies business which he joined upon graduation from Harvard in 1897. He became vice-president of George B. Carpenter & Co. in 1909 and remained with the firm until 1936. Despite his training and preparation for the family business, Carpenter also had a rich musical background. He began the study of music as a child with his mother, who was a talented amateur singer. Unlike most of his contemporaries, Carpenter was musically educated in the United States (except for a

short period in 1906 when he studied with the English composer Edward Elgar in Rome). He studied piano with Amy Fay (1844–1928), a student of Liszt, and William Seeboeck (1859–1907), a student of Brahms. At Harvard he took theory under John Knowles Paine. Back in Chicago he continued with Bernhard Ziehn (1845–1912), to whom he dedicated one of his earliest extended compositions, the *Sonata* for violin and piano (1911). As a composer Carpenter began modestly composing songs, with lyrics by his first wife, Rue Winterbotham: *When Little Boys Sing* (1904) and *Improving Songs for Anxious Children* (1907). The publication in 1914 of his *Gitanjali,* 6 songs to the poems of Rabindranath Tagore, established Carpenter as a composer of stature; the same year he also composed a popular orchestral suite, *Adventures in a Perambulator* (first performed by the Chicago Symphony in March 1915). While his style was distinctly his own, Carpenter revealed a leaning toward the French Impressionists rather than the Germans, who were more popular among his contemporaries. Elegance and wit plus mastery of the orchestra were characteristic of Carpenter's music. He rejected the label "American composer," believing that deliberate striving in that direction "must inevitably result in the impression that we have a greater concern for affixing the national label than for the contents of the package—it must inevitably result, for the composer who allows himself to be influenced by it, in a self-consciousness which is death to the real creative impulse . . . You may lead your creative impulse to our very best American folkmusic material, but you can't make it drink . . ." Carpenter followed his *Adventures* with a trio of ballets, *The Birthday of the Infanta* (after Oscar Wilde, 1919), *Krazy Kat* (based on the popular cartoon character, 1922), and the very American *Skyscrapers* (1926). Other orchestral works include 2 symphonies (1917, 1941), *Patterns* (for the 50th anniversary of the Boston Symphony, 1931), a tone poem, *Sea-Drift* (after Whitman, 1933), *Danza* (1935), and *The Seven Ages,* symphonic suite (1945). Also a *Concertino for Piano and Orchestra* (1917), a *Concerto for Violin* (1937), and *Carmel Concerto* (1948). Besides a good number of songs, Carpenter's works for voice include *Water Colors,* 4 Chinese songs (1918), *Song of Faith,* for chorus and orchestra (1931), and *Song of Freedom* for chorus and orchestra (1941). His chamber music, in addition to the early *Violin Sonata,* includes a *String Quartet* (1928) and a *Piano Quintet* (1934). Carpenter, like his contemporary Charles Ives (q.v.), combined a successful business career with a creative life; he was also active as director of the Illinois Children's Home and Aid Society. He died in Chicago, Apr. 26, 1951.

THE CASTLES Popular dance team ca. 1914–17, during the great American dance craze of the period: Vernon and Irene Castle. Castle, whose real name was Vernon Blythe, teamed up with Irene Foote (1893–1969) in 1911. The next year, after appearing in a number of musical shows, they became the dancing Castles and, in time, the most popular ballroom dance team in the world. They introduced such dances as the Castle Walk, and popularized others: the tango, maxixe, turkey trot, etc. The couple appeared for the last time on Broadway in Irving Berlin's (q.v.) *Watch Your Step* (1914). With the coming of the First World War, Vernon Castle, who was born in England (1887), died in an aircraft training crash in 1918. Following this, Irene Castle virtually stopped dancing.

CHADWICK, GEORGE WHITE-FIELD (1854–1931) Composer, choral conductor, organist, and teacher.

Chadwick was born in Lowell, Mass., Nov. 13, 1854. He had his first piano lessons from his older brother, Fitz Henry. Although their father was musical, taught singing, organized and conducted a neighborhood chorus and orchestra, he was primarily a businessman (fire and life insurance) and hoped his sons would follow him. Young George played the church organ. Upon graduation from high school, he traveled into Boston regularly for piano lessons and studied harmony at the New England Conservatory. He worked for his father until he reached the age of 21 and quit to become a music teacher at Olivet (Mich.) College (1876–77). In the fall of 1877, against his father's wishes, Chadwick set out for Germany to study music. Among his teachers was Karl A. Haupt (1810–1891), who had also been the teacher of John Knowles Paine (q.v.). Another important teacher was Joseph Rheinberger (1839–1901). When Chadwick returned from Germany in 1880, he brought back with him 3 original works, 2 string quartets, and a *Rip Van Winkle* overture. He set up shop as a teacher in Boston; like Paine he would influence a new generation of New England composers. In 1882 he joined the faculty of the New England Conservatory as an instructor and was named director in 1897, a post he held until his death. Among Chadwick's distinguished students were Horatio Parker, Arthur Whiting, Edward Burlingame Hill, Henry Hadley, Frederick Converse, Daniel Gregory Mason (all q.v.), and William Grant Still and Leroy Robertson (Section V). Described as "a traditionalist in style who was independent in spirit," Chadwick produced works with an academic touch but with flashes of humor. He composed 3 symphonies, the first in 1882 and the 3rd in 1893; a *Symphonietta* dates from 1901 and a prize-winning *Suite Symphonique* from 1910. Chadwick turned out a number of popular concert overtures with literary allusions: *Thalia* (1883), *Melpomene* (1887), *The Miller's Daughter* (1888), *Adonais* (1900), *Euterpe* (1903), and *Cleopatra* (1906). He composed a few pieces for piano, including his Op. 7, *Six Characteristic Pieces.* Two caprices and 3 waltzes for solo piano were much performed in his lifetime. Chadwick's chamber music included 5 string quartets and a *Quintet for Piano and Strings.* The *Theme, Variations and Fugue for Organ and Orchestra* (1909) is rarely heard today. Choral works include *Dedication Ode* (1886), *Phoenix Expirans* (1882), *Columbian Ode* (text by Harriet Monroe, 1893), and *Noel* for soloists, chorus, and orchestra (1908), among others. Chadwick composed about 100 songs, several drawing upon folk sources of several countries. One of his outstanding songs, to lyrics by Sidney Lanier (q.v.), is "Ballad of Trees and the Master." Chadwick also produced several stage works, including a comic opera, *Tabasco* (1894); also *Judith* (1900), a "lyric drama," and an operetta, *Love's Sacrifice* (1915). Of Chadwick's orchestral works the most performed remains the well-wrought suite for orchestra, *Symphonic Sketches:* "Jubilee" (1895), "Noël" (1895), "Hobgoblin" (1907), and "A Vagrom Ballad" (1896). Chadwick's textbook, *Harmony,* was published in 1898. He died in Boston, Apr. 7, 1931.

CHILD, FRANCIS JAMES (1825–1896) Philologist, scholar, and teacher. Child was born in Boston, educated at Harvard and in Germany. Upon returning to the United States, Child became a professor of English at Harvard. While Child's interest was primarily literary, he deserves a mention at least in American music as the collector-author of *English and Scottish Popular Ballads* (Boston, 1883–98), a multivolumed set which preserved the words (no music) of hundreds of American folk songs of British origin, and variants. Child's work in the field was influential and inspired other studies by musically oriented collectors, including Cecil Sharp (with Olive Dame Campbell), who compiled the monumental *English Folk-Songs from the Southern Appalachians* (1917), and various regional studies covering the South, West, Northeast, etc., by others such as Phillips Barry, Reed Smith, and Arthur Kyle Davis, Jr. Unfortunately Child's preoccupation with literary quality may have caused him to overlook the tune of many a fine ballad, but his work was seminal.

COERNE, LOUIS ADOLPHE (1870–1922) Composer, organist, and teacher. Coerne was born in Newark, N.J., Feb. 27, 1870. His musical aptitude was evident early for he began studying music at the age of 6 in Paris, then went on to Stuttgart. Upon returning to the United States he entered Boston Latin School and Harvard (in 1888); at Harvard he studied theory under John Knowles Paine (q.v.) and, independently, the violin under Franz Kneisel (1865–1926). In 1890, Coerne returned to Germany for further study with Joseph Rheinberger (organ and composition) and took courses in conducting and violin at the Munich Royal Academy; he was graduated with highest honors in 1893. While in Munich his symphonic poem *Hiawatha* was performed and Coerne conducted his *Organ Concerto in E Major* (1892). Coerne again returned to the United States and took a number of teaching jobs (he apparently abandoned the idea of becoming a concert violinist). He composed during his lifetime some 500 works of which about 300 were published. His first opera, *A Woman of Marblehead,* was produced and warmly received in 1897; his next, *Zenobia,* Op. 66 (1905), was written during yet another stay in Germany and was performed in Bremen, the first opera by an

American to be so honored. In 1905 also Coerne was awarded the first American Ph.D. in music from Harvard. His thesis, *The Evolution of Modern Orchestration,* was published in 1908. From 1910 to 1915 Coerne was head of the music department, University of Wisconsin at Madison. From 1915 until his death he served as professor of music at the Connecticut College for Women, New London. Among his other, now neglected, compositions are a *String Quartet in C Minor,* Op. 19 (1893), a *Violin Concerto* ("Romantic"), Op. 51, a *Dedication Ode,* Op. 82, for orchestra (1915), and Incidental Music to *The Trojan Women,* Op. 113 (1917). Also *Swedish Sonata for Violin and Piano,* Op. 60 (1904), and other chamber, vocal, and piano pieces. Coerne died in Boston, Sept. 11, 1922.

COHAN, GEORGE MICHAEL (1878–1942) Actor, dancer, librettist, songwriter (words and music), and producer. Cohan was born in Providence, R.I., July 4, 1878. He was literally born in a trunk and received his earliest stage training as a member of the family vaudeville act, eventually known as the Four Cohans (including his parents, Jerry and Nellie, and sister, Josie). The youngest Cohan picked up musical skills in vaudeville houses and was forced to take violin lessons by his father; his formal schooling was even more sparse. By the time he was 7 he made his vaudeville debut. Cohan revealed an early aptitude for rhyme, dramatic writing, and a genius for entertainment. His unique talent was best described by another actor, William Collier, who said, "George is not the best actor or author or composer or dancer or playwright. But he can dance better than any author, write better than any actor, compose better than any manager, and manage better than any playwright. That makes him a very great man." Cohan's gift to the Ameri-

can musical theatre was in his contribution to its transition from vaudeville to the brash, incipient musical comedy. This he did with a blatant waving of the American flag, songs of colloquial native flavor and snappy pacing. By the time he was sixteen Cohan was writing vaudeville sketches for the Four Cohans; several of these sketches were later expanded into full-length plays or musicals. His first musical comedy, *The Governor's Son,* an expanded skit, was produced in 1901; Cohan hit his stride in *Little Johnny Jones* (1904) in which he starred. Among its songs were his personal theme song, "The Yankee Doodle Boy," and "Give My Regards to Broadway." His last starring, Cohan-written, musical was *The Merry Malones* (1927); his final score was for *Billie,* the next year. In more than 20 musicals and revues Cohan had a number of characteristic songs: "Mary's a Grand Old Name" (*Forty-five Minutes from Broadway,* 1906), "You're a Grand Old Flag" (*George Washington, Jr.,* 1906), "Harrigan" (*Fifty Miles from Boston,* 1907), and "Nellie Kelly, I Love You" (*Little Nellie Kelly,* 1922). His best-known song, "Over There," was written the day that the United States declared war on Germany, Apr. 6, 1917. Cohan in 1940 was awarded a special Medal of Honor by Congress for the song and its morale-lifting value; his writing of "You're a Grand Old Flag" was noted at the same time. The Medal was presented to Cohan by President Franklin D. Roosevelt. Among Cohan's nonmusical comedy-dramas were *Get-Rich-Quick Wallingford* (1910), *Seven Keys to Baldpate* (1913), *The Tavern* (1920), and *The Song and Dance Man* (1923). Cohan also appeared in the film *The Phantom President* (songs by Rodgers and Hart, Section V) in 1932 and as F.D.R. in Rodgers and Hart's *I'd Rather Be Right* (1937). Cohan proved himself an actor (in his own productions he generally appeared as himself) in Eugene O'Neill's *Ah, Wilderness!* (1933). Cohan's influence on the American musical occurred in the first decade of the 20th century, when he exercised his breezy, fast-moving style in songs of immediate appeal, unabashed patriotism, and hard-boiled sentimentality. Cohan's approach to the musical marked a turning away from the popular, European-rooted operettas of the period. Although he produced less and less during the 1920s, his impact was felt in the sparkling toughness of the great musicals of that time. Cohan, who referred to himself as a "song and dance man," wrote about 500 songs, about 40 plays, many of which he produced (sometimes in partnership with Sam H. Harris), and was an important figure in the American theatre for nearly a half century. He died in New York, Nov. 5, 1942.

COLE, ROBERT A. "BOB" (1863–1911) Songwriter, entertainer, and playwright. Bob Cole, as he was known professionally, was born in Athens, Ga., and attended Atlanta University, after which he came to New York City. Though not a trained musician, Cole was a student of drama and for a time was resident playwright and manager of the All-Star Company, the first Negro stock company. In 1898 Cole produced the first Negro full-length musical, *A Trip to Coontown.* Ca. 1901 Cole formed a songwriting partnership with two brothers, James Weldon Johnson and J. Rosamond Johnson (q.v.), the former a great black poet and the latter a distinguished musician. Their first successful collaboration was "My Castle on the Nile," music by J. Rosamond and lyrics by James Weldon and Cole. The trio also wrote musical comedy scores for all-black musicals that broke with the minstrel show approach. Among these were *The Shoo-Fly Regiment* (1907) and *The Red Moon* (1909), both with books by

Cole. In 1903 they published an interesting collection, *The Evolution of Ragtime,* "a musical suite of six songs tracing and illustrating Negro music." The team wrote songs for several of the popular entertainers of the day. Anna Held (1865–1918) sang their "Maiden with the Dreamy Eyes" and Marie Cahill (1870–1930) interpolated their best-known song, "Under the Bamboo Tree," into the musical *Sally in Our Alley* (1902). The song, of curious origin, was written at the suggestion of Cole, who liked the spiritual "Nobody Knows the Trouble I've Seen" so much that he suggested that J. Rosamond Johnson adapt it as a popular song for their vaudeville act. Johnson, a student of Negro music, was shocked and called the idea "desecration." Cole chided him: a graduate of the New England Conservatory and he "couldn't change a little old tune around?" Challenged, Johnson did alter the melody by simple inversion and Cole wrote words fitting the syncopated new tune, resulting in one of their most long-lived songs. The team began to dissolve in 1906 when James Weldon Johnson was appointed U.S. consul at Puerto Cabello, Venezuela. Another Cole-Johnson collaboration is "Oh, Didn't He Ramble (1902), a favorite of brass and jazz bands. Cole died, probably in New York, in 1911.

COLE,   ROSSETTER   GLEASON (1866–1952) Teacher, organist, composer. Cole was born in Clyde, Mich., Feb. 5, 1866. His family moved to Ann Arbor when Cole was about 8; he received his schooling there and was graduated from the University of Michigan in 1888. His own composition, a cantata entitled *The Passing of Summer,* Op. 14, was presented at the graduation ceremonies. Cole taught Latin and German in high schools for 2 years. Awarded a scholarship at Berlin's Royal Master School, he spent 3 years studying; among his instructors was Max Bruch (1838–1920). Upon his return to the United States in 1892 Cole began a lifetime of teaching music: Ripon College (Wis.), Grinnell College (Iowa), and the University of Wisconsin. From 1908 to 1939 Cole was head of the Columbia University Music Department Summer Sessions (one of his students in the summer of 1922 was young composer George Gershwin, Section V). A Chicagoan, Cole was head of the Theory Department and dean at the Cosmopolitan School of Music. Cole's original works were regularly performed during his lifetime, although they were generally forgotten by the middle of the century. He composed for various combinations of voices and instruments: *Marche Celeste,* Op. 6 for organ (1888); *Eight Children's Songs,* Op. 7; *Sonata in D for Violin and Piano,* Op. 8 (1892); *Overture "Pioneer,"* Op. 35 (1918); his choral work for soloists, women's voices, and orchestra, *The Rock of Liberty,* Op. 36 (1920), was widely performed and an opera, *The Maypole Lovers* (1931), was awarded the David Bispham Memorial Medal. From this work Cole arranged 2 orchestral suites, one in 1934, the other in 1942. Cole's instrument was the organ for which he composed several solo pieces as well as the *Heroic Piece,* Op. 39, for organ and orchestra (1924). Cole died in Lake Bluff, Ill., May 18, 1952.

CONVERSE, FREDERICK SHEPHERD (1871–1940) Composer, teacher. Converse was born in Newton, Mass., Jan. 5, 1871. At Harvard he studied under John Knowles Paine (q.v.), graduated with high honors, and then tried his hand in the business world. This lasted for 6 months, after which Converse abandoned business for a lifetime in music. He studied with George W. Chadwick (q.v.) for a while before going to Germany to work with Josef Gabriel Rheinberger (1839–1901), who had also been Chadwick's teacher, at the Munich Royal Academy. He was graduated in 1898; for the event he composed his early *Symphony in D Minor.* Upon his return to the United States in 1899, Converse taught harmony for a year at the New England Conservatory, then left to teach composition at Harvard. He was appointed assistant professor in 1904 and resigned 3 years later to devote all of his time to composition. Eventually Converse returned to musical education, taught theory at the New England Conservatory and served as the dean of the faculty (1931–38). During the period in which he concentrated on his own work he produced symphonic poems, "orchestral romances," based on the poems of Keats: *The Festival of Pan,* Op. 9 (1900); *Endymion's Narrative,* Op. 10 (1901); *The Mystic Trumpeter* (1905) was inspired by Whitman. For chamber groups Converse composed 3 string quartets, a *Trio for Violin, Cello and Piano* (1931) and a *Sonata for Violin and Piano* plus a number of solo piano pieces, *Suite,* Op. 2, *Waltzes,* Op. 4, etc. Converse's choral compositions include a cantata, *The Peace Pipe* (1914), the oratorio *Job* (1907), and 2 additional cantatas, *The Answers of the Stars* (1920) and *The Flight of the Eagle.* A *Symphony in F Major,* his 3rd, dates from 1936. A humorous tone poem, *Flivver Ten Million* (1927), was inspired by the Model-T Ford (the score utilized the sound of the flivver's horn). Converse made his first impression on the American musical scene with the production of his one-act opera, *The Pipe of Desire,* Op. 21, the first opera composed by a native American to be produced by the Metropolitan (Mar. 18, 1910). *Sacrifice,* a full-length opera, was presented in Boston in 1910. In 1937 converse was elected to the American Academy of Arts and Letters; he died in Westwood, Mass., June 8, 1940.

COOK, WILL MARION (1869–1944) Composer, conductor, violinist. Born in Washington, D.C., Jan. 27, 1869. Revealing an early talent for music, Cook at 13 entered Oberlin Conservatory in Ohio to study the violin; at 16 he went to Berlin to study with Joseph Joachim (1831–1907). Back in the United States, Cook settled in New York City, where he studied with Dvořák at the National Conservatory of Music. Inspired by the then current ragtime craze, Cook composed his first score, *Clorindy, the Origin of the Cakewalk,* with libretto and lyrics by Negro poet Paul Laurence Dunbar (1872–1906). Although most of the libretto was eliminated by the time the show opened in 1898 at the Casino Roof, the songs created a sensation, particularly "Emancipation Day" and "That's How the Cakewalk Is Done." Although no longer a full evening's show, *Clorindy* was historic in that it presented an all-black cast ("twenty-six of the finest Negro voices in America," according to Cook) in a well-constructed musical evening. It was superior to Bob Cole's (q.v.) *A Trip to Coontown,* which was a full-length show of the same year. As Cook put it, "Negroes were at last on Broadway, and there to stay. Gone was the uff-dah of the minstrel! Gone the Massa Linkum stuff. We were artists and we were going a long, long way." In demand after the success of *Clorindy,* Cook wrote several scores achieving another high point in the satirical *In Dahomey* (Book by Jesse A. Shipp with lyrics by Dunbar and Alex Rogers). The show opened, after a tour, at the Grand Theatre, Oct. 20, 1902, and moved to Broadway's New York Theatre in February of the next year. Among its stars were the popular team of Bert Williams and George Walker; they also starred in *In Abyssinia* (1906) and *In Bandana Land* (1907). One of his last scores for Broadway was entitled *In Darkeydom* (1914); Another,

The Cannibal King, was never produced. In 1929 Cook composed *St. Louis Woman* in collaboration with his son, W. Mercer Cook (b. 1903); it could be classified as a true folk opera. Cook's *Collection of Negro Songs* was published in 1912. Although he was not very active as a songwriter after ca. 1914, Cook was busy as a conductor, arranger, and vocal coach. Among his best-known individual songs are "A Little Bit of Heaven Called Home," "I May Be Crazy But I Ain't No Fool," "Darktown Is Out Tonight" (from *Clorindy*), and "I'm Comin', Virginia." In 1918 Cook organized the all-Negro New York Syncopated Orchestra—later the American Syncopated Orchestra, which successfully toured the United States and Europe (one important member was the jazz clarinetist Sidney Bechet). Cook was married to soprano Abbie Mitchell (1884–1960), who introduced "Summertime" in Gershwin's *Porgy and Bess* (1935). Cook was helpful and encouraging to a number of younger musicians, among them Duke Ellington (Section V) and Harold Arlen (Section VI). He died in New York City, July 19, 1944.

"COON SONG" A genre of popular song associated with a black or, more likely, blackface performer. Coon songs were a staple of the minstrel show and generally parodied the Negro race. (The term "coon" is short for raccoon in the South and other parts of the country.) A revival of coon songs was sparked at the close of the 19th century with the publication of "All Coons Look Alike to Me" by Ernest Hogan (1865–ca. 1910), a Negro actor-songwriter. Its infectious ragtime rhythms made it one of the most popular songs of the period and inspired numerous imitations (a fact that Hogan later regretted). His was, of course, not the first of the coon songs. "The Coon from the Moon" was issued in 1894, 2 years before; "The Coon with the Big

White Spot" was published the same year as Hogan's song, 1896. Then came "Coon Hollow Capers" (1899) and "The Most Successful Song Hit of 1901," the ultimate expression of the form: "Coon! Coon! Coon!" The demand waned and the songs were eventually replaced by other ethnic affronts—to the Chinese, Jews, and Irish.

DAMROSCH, WALTER (1862–1950) Conductor, educator, and composer. Damrosch was born in Breslau (now Wrocław, Poland), Jan. 30, 1862. His father Leopold (1832–1885) was a physician-turned-musician and an eminent conductor. Damrosch's older brother, Frank (1859–1937), was also active in music. Walter Damrosch began studying music with his father and continued with others. The family came to the United States in 1871, when Damrosch was about 9. By the time he was 20 he was appointed conductor of the Newark Harmonic Society; in 1885 he succeeded Leopold Damrosch as conductor of the Oratorio Society and the Symphony Society of New York (both of which the elder Damrosch had founded). In 1894 he founded the Damrosch Grand Opera Company which specialized in presenting Wagnerian operas throughout the United States. One of the works done by the company was Damrosch's own *The Scarlet Letter* (1894). Damrosch's greater contribution to American music was in the field of conducting (he even abandoned composition for a time in the early 1930s) and helped to found what is now the New York Philharmonic (which resulted from a fusion of Damrosch's Symphony Society of New York with the Philharmonic Society in 1927). Damrosch was an early radio pioneer, beginning as musical counsel to NBC in 1927. For years he conducted the famous weekly NBC Music Appreciation Hour designed for schoolchildren

and broadcast on Friday afternoons in the 1930s. As conductor, Damrosch introduced many new works to American audiences, among them compositions by Tchaikovsky, Brahms, as well as operas by Wagner and Saint-Saëns. He also encouraged the American composer with performances and commissions. As a composer himself, Damrosch is probably best remembered for his setting of the Kipling poem "Danny Deever," Op. 2, No. 7 (1897). His first operatic effort, *The Scarlet Letter*, was not well received; his 2nd *Cyrano de Bergerac*, staged by the Metropolitan Opera in 1913, did better. Damrosch composed little while he concentrated on broadcasting, but in the late 1930s he began writing quite regularly. *Abraham Lincoln Song* for baritone, chorus, and orchestra was completed in 1936; in 1937 he composed another opera, based on *The Man Without a Country*. A one-act fantasy, *The Opera Cloak*, was produced in New York in 1942; one of his last efforts, *Dunkirk* (words by Robert Nathan), was inspired by the Second World War battle and was broadcast by NBC on May 2, 1943. Damrosch's autobiography, *My Musical Life*, was published in 1923. He died in New York City, Dec. 22, 1950.

DANCE IN THE PLACE CONGO Orchestral composition by Henry F. B. Gilbert (q.v.) based on Louisiana Creole tunes. Place Congo was an open square (now Beauregard Square) in New Orleans where slaves were permitted to assemble on Sunday afternoons to dance. The practice was noted as early as the late 18th century. Gilbert selected his Creole melodies from an article by George W. Cable published in *The Century Magazine* in April 1886. After completing the score, Gilbert recognized its dramatic potential and devised a ballet scenario for it; in this form *Dance in the*

Place Congo was performed for the first time at the Metropolitan Opera House on Mar. 23, 1918.

DANIELS, MABEL WHEELER (1878–1971) Composer, teacher. Daniels was born in Swampscott, Mass., Nov. 27, 1878. Of a musical family (her father, George F. Daniels, was a president of the Handel and Haydn Society), Daniels was educated at Girls Latin School and was graduated from Radcliffe. A student first of George W. Chadwick (q.v.), she also studied composition with Ludwig Thuille (1861–1907) in Munich. At Radcliffe, Daniels was director and soloist of the Glee Club and composed 3 operettas for women's voices before she began to study with Chadwick. Upon her return to the United States she taught as well as composed, much of her work being for voice. As early as 1911, when she was teaching at Bradford Academy, she was awarded prizes from the National Federation of Music Clubs for songs: "Villa of Dreams," "Voice of My Beloved," and "Eastern Song." From 1913 to 1918 she was music director at Simmons College, Boston. Daniels' output was predominantly vocal; among her works are *The Desolate City* for baritone and orchestra (1913), *Peace with a Sword,* chorus and orchestra (1917), *Songs of Elfland,* soprano soloists, women's chorus, chamber orchestra (1924), *The Holy Star,* chorus and orchestra (1928), *Exultate Deo,* chorus and orchestra (composed for the 50th anniversary of Radcliffe College, 1929) and, among others, *Song of Jael,* soprano, chorus, orchestra (1937). Her best-known work for orchestra is *Deep Forest* (1931); her chamber works include a *Violin Sonata, Three Observations for Three Woodwinds* (1943), and *Four Observations for Four Strings* (1945). Daniels served as a trustee of Radcliffe College

(1945–51), produced a book about her student days, *An American Girl in Munich,* and was active as a composer into her nineties. She died in Boston, Mass., Mar. 10, 1971.

DAVIS, GUSSIE L. (1863–1899) Songwriter. One of the first successful black composers of Tin Pan Alley, Davis was born in Dayton, Ohio, worked for a time as a Pullman porter and later as a janitor in the Cincinnati Conservatory of Music, where he managed to pick up the rudiments of the craft by listening in on lectures. His first songs were published by a Cincinnati publisher in the late 1880s ("The Lighthouse by the Sea," "Wait Till the Tide Comes In," and "The Hermit") after which Davis moved to New York City. He hit his stride in "The Fatal Wedding" (words by singer W. H. Windom, 1893), one of the first of the composer's essays into the typical sad song of the "Gay" '90s. Davis' musical gifts were superior generally to the lyrical talents of his collaborators and the songs, in later years, were easily parodied. Among such songs were "Picture 84," (words by Charles B. Ward, 1894), "Down in Poverty Row" (lyrics by Davis, music by one Arthur Trevelyan, 1895), "Parted at the Altar" (1895), and "Beyond Pardon, Beyond Recall" and "If I could Only Blot Out the Past" (both 1896). That same year he composed, words and music, a song based on an actual incident, "The Baggage Coach Ahead," his most successful song (sheet music sales exceeded 1,000,000 copies). The idea for the song dated from Davis' Pullman period. The "plot" told of a bereaved father, with a young child, mourning the death of his wife "in the baggage coach ahead." Davis, who composed some 300 songs in a brief lifetime, also wrote more cheerful numbers, such as "When I Do de Hoochy Koochy in de Sky" (which still reveals a preoccupation with death, but was associated with the Chicago World's Fair, 1896) and "My Creole Sue" (1898). Davis died the following year, aged 36.

DE KOVEN, REGINALD (1859–1920) Composer, Henry Louis Reginald, the son of a clergyman, was born in Middletown, Conn., Apr. 3, 1859. In 1872 the family moved to England and De Koven completed his education there, graduating from St. John's College, Oxford, in 1879. He studied piano, harmony, singing, and composition in various European music centers: Stuttgart, Vienna, Florence, and Paris; among his most distinguished teachers were Franz von Suppé (1819–1895) and Léo Delibes (1836–1891). De Koven's first job, however, was in a brokerage firm, and for a time in 1882 he owned a dry-goods business. He returned to the United States to become the music critic for the Chicago *Evening Post;* later he also reviewed music for *Harper's Weekly,* the New York *World* and the New York *Herald.* In 1902 he organized the Philharmonic Orchestra (Washington, D.C.) and was its conductor until 1905. At the same time De Koven was a prolific composer: hundreds of songs, several ballets, solo piano pieces, a piano sonata, and 2 operas, *The Canterbury Pilgrims* (Metropolitan Opera, 1917) and *Rip Van Winkle* (1920). It was as a composer of operetta that De Koven was best known; between 1887 (*The Begum*) and 1913 (*Her Little Highness*) he composed the scores for 24 operettas. De Koven's most popular score was for *Robin Hood* (1890), "A Comic Opera," with book and lyrics by De Koven's chief collaborator, Harry B. Smith (1860–1936). Among its best-known songs are "Song of Brown October Ale" and "Oh, Promise Me." De Koven was a contemporary of Victor Herbert (q.v.) with whom he shared a gift for melody

and orchestration. He died in Chicago, Jan. 16, 1920.

DETT, ROBERT NATHANIEL (1882–1943) Composer, educator, pianist, choral director. Dett was Canadian-born: Drummondville, Ont., Oct. 11, 1882. In his birthplace Dett heard Negro spirituals and folk songs, for the community had been founded by ex-slaves who had made their way into Canada via the Underground Railroad. His family returned to the United States and Dett received musical training at the Halstead Conservatory, Lockport, N.Y., and at Oberlin (Ohio) Conservatory, where he was awarded his Mus. B. in 1908. Dett later also studied with Rossetter G. Cole (q.v.) at Columbia University. He also toured as a concert pianist and taught at Lane College (Jackson, Miss., 1908–11) and Lincoln Institute (Jefferson City, Mo., 1911–13) before becoming director of music at Hampton Institute (Virginia, 1913–35). Dett meanwhile continued to study; in 1920 he took leave of absence to study piano with Arthur Foote (q.v.) at Harvard and, in 1929, studied composition in France with Nadia Boulanger (Section V). Dett also taught music privately for a time in the 1930s in Rochester, N.Y. He contributed greatly to the rise in importance of the Hampton Institute Choir, which toured the United States and Europe in the '30s. Dett's work with Negro folk song was published in *Religious Folk Songs of the Negro* (1926) and the 4-volume *The Dett Collection of Negro Spirituals* (1936). Dett drew upon the music of the Negro for his own original work, his best single composition being the solo piano suite *In the Bottoms* (1913) with its famous "Juba Dance." Other piano suites are *Magnolia* ("Magnolias," "The Deserted Cabin," "To My Lady Love," "Mammy," "The Place Where the Rainbow Ends," 1912), *Enchantment* ("Incantation," "Song of the Shrine," "Dance of Desire," "Beyond the Dream," 1922), *Cinnamon Grove* ("Dear Love for Nothing Less than Thee," "When Thou Commandest Me to Sing," "Was it Real?" "Winter'll Soon Be Over," 1928), and *Tropic Winter* ("The Daybreak Charioteer," "A Bayou Garden," "Pompons and Fans," "Legend of the Atoll," "To a Closed Casement," "Noon Siesta," "Parade of the Jasmine Banners," 1938). For orchestra Dett composed a *Symphony in E Minor* and a suite, *An American Sampler,* but made his greatest contribution in the field of choral music, which included 2 oratorios, *The Chariot Jubilee* for tenor, chorus, and orchestra (1921) and *The Ordering of Moses* for soprano, contralto, tenor, baritone, chorus, and orchestra (1937), one of his most performed works. Dett died in Battle Creek, Mich., Oct. 2, 1943.

DRESSER, PAUL (1857–1906) Songwriter, vaudeville performer, music publisher. Dresser was born in Terre Haute, Ind., Apr. 21, 1857. The family name was Dreiser and included a younger brother, Theodore, who would become a novelist. Dresser was in training for the priesthood at Saint Meinrad College, Switz City, Ind., when he ran away at 16 to join a medicine show. He toured in vaudeville as a singer and monologist, wrote a humor column for a newspaper and his own vaudeville sketches. In 1885 he was an end man in Billy Rice's Minstrels; the next year he produced his first successful song, "The Letter That Never Came." Largely self-educated in music, Dresser became a master of the characteristic sentimental ballad of the so-called Gay '90s. As his brother recalled, "He seemed to have a peculiar fondness for the twilight hour, at which time he might be found thrumming over one or another strain, until at last some particular one might capture his fancy

and presently he might be in tears. The sighings over home and mother and lost sweethearts and dead heroes that were there! Yet with something in the completed song or mood which gave it the wide appeal which most of his songs enjoyed." In that vein Dresser wrote his next great success, "The Pardon Came Too Late" (1891). Dresser, a large, gregarious, generous man, believed in the songs he composed. When he sang one of his most popular songs, "Just Tell Them That You Saw Me" (1895), "tears stood in his eyes and he wiped them away." He continued to produce songs, not all of them successful but popular enough to provide the songwriter with a sizable income and a partnership in a publishing company—which went bankrupt within 4 years because of disagreements and poor management. Dresser wrote his best-known song, "On the Banks of the Wabash Far Away," in 1897 (Theodore Dreiser claimed that he suggested the idea for the song to his brother; friends denied this). Another song of the same year was "The Curse of the Dreamer," an elaborate song in 6 sections, about a wife's desertion of her husband and their baby (Dresser's wife, May Howard, had done just that). By 1903 Dresser had lost his touch; his marriage had failed, his partnership with Howley, Haviland & Dresser broke up and he formed his own publishing company. In 1905, as he lived in near obscurity with a sister in Brooklyn, the Paul Dresser Publishing Co. issued his last great hit, "My Gal Sal." Dresser did not live to enjoy its popularity and the money it provided; he died, as most writers have noted, of a "broken heart" on Jan. 30, 1906.

DVOŘÁK, ANTONÍN (1841–1904) Great Bohemian composer who came to the United States in October 1892 to serve as director of the National Conservatory of Music in New York. He remained there until May 1894 (and in the United States until April 1895). During his American stay Dvořák influenced and was influenced; his students included Rubin Goldmark (q.v.) and Harry Thacker Burleigh (q.v.) and he himself was impressed with American folk song (particularly that of the Negro) and the American landscape, for during his stay Dvořák traveled a good deal. He also composed; his *Symphony in E Minor* ("From the New World") was completed and performed for the first time in the United States in 1893. He also composed a *String Quartet*, Op. 96 ("American Quartet"), a *Quintet*, Op. 97, and a cantata, *The American Flag*, Op. 102 (1893). Dvořák's message to the American composer was: "Look around you for your inspiration," implying, "Why go to Berlin?" He did not advocate the mere adaptation of American Indian and Negro melodies, but the assimilation of native musical culture as a basis for a homegrown art. His influence at the time was minimal, the idea was even attacked (MacDowell was quite hostile), but time has proved Dvořák the wiser prophet in a land not his own. He was not, of course, profoundly informed or familiar with the folk music he loved, but his views and opinions based on that love were salutary.

EDWARDS, GUS (1879–1945) Songwriter, entertainer, publisher. Edwards was born in Hohensalza, Germany, Aug. 18, 1879; his family came to the United States when Edwards was 9, settling in Brooklyn. A boy soprano, he gave up a job in a cigar factory at 13 to go into show business. Eventually he became a vaudeville headliner and began writing his own songs. His first successful song was "All I Want Is My Black Baby Back" (1898; words by Tom Daly). Although he eventually taught himself to play the piano, Edwards employed

trained musicians to transcribe his tunes for him; one of the first was Charles Previn, who later became a noted film conductor. This was followed by other successes (though now little known) such as "I Can't Tell Why I Love You, But I Do" (1900; words by Will Cobb) and—hitting his stride—"In My Merry Oldsmobile" (1905; words by Vincent Bryan), "Tammany" (1905; Vincent Bryan), "I Just Can't Make My Eyes Behave," written for Anna Held (1906; Will Cobb), and "School Days" (1907; Will Cobb), in the same year Edwards contributed a couple of songs to the first *Ziegfeld Follies*. In 1908 he and Cobb wrote "Sunbonnet Sue" and the following year, in collaboration with lyricist Edward Madden, produced "By the Light of the Silvery Moon." The fictional safecracker, the invention of O. Henry, was immortalized in the Edwards-Madden song of 1911, "Jimmy Valentine." Beginning in 1905 Edwards wrote scores for Broadway musicals, though with little success. In that year he did *When We Were Forty-One*. *Hip-Hip-Hooray* followed in 1907, *The Merry-Go-Round* and *School Days* in 1908. *Breaking into Society* (1909), *Ziegfeld Follies of 1910*, and *Sunbonnet Sue* (1923) rounded out Edwards' Broadway shows. Edwards contributed songs to one of the earliest film musicals, *Hollywood Revue of 1919*. A revue, *Broadway Show-Window* (1936), utilized 3 Edwards songs, but Broadway was not Edwards' domain; he was most comfortable in Tin Pan Alley and vaudeville. Not the least of his gifts was the ability to spot talent, and some of his best songs were written for vaudeville acts starring youngsters discovered by Edwards. The standard Tin Pan Alley joke of the period was "Better hide your kids or Gus Edwards will get 'em," or "Gus is hanging around the maternity wards looking for new talent." Among the young performers given their first important opportunity to sing, dance, and clown in the Big Time (some were rescued from mediocre acts by Edwards) were George Jessel, Eddie Cantor, Groucho Marx, Walter Winchell (who turned to newspapering when his voice changed), Ray Bolger, the Duncan Sisters, Elsie Janis, dancer Paul Haakon —and Sally Rand. About 1938 Edwards' health failed and he spent most of the rest of his life confined to bed; he died in Los Angeles, Nov. 7, 1945.

EICHHEIM, HENRY (1870–1942) Composer, violinist. Eichheim was born in Chicago, Jan. 3, 1870, and received his musical education at Chicago Musical College. For a time he was a violinist in the Theodore Thomas Orchestra (in which his father was cellist). In 1890 Eichheim joined the Boston Symphony as violinist and remained with it for more than 2 decades. He resigned in 1912 to devote his time to composition and an occasional recital. Eichheim had a deep interest in the music of the Orient, through which he traveled extensively collecting indigenous instruments and musical themes (including street cries of Korea and Thailand, then known as Siam). These studies resulted in such compositions as *Oriental Impressions* for orchestra (1922) which received an award from the Society for the Publication of American Music. Other orchestral works, often employing the instruments Eichheim had collected, were *Chinese Legend* (also a ballet, 1924), *Burma* (1927), *Java* (1929), and *Bali* (1933). Other ballets: *A Burmese Pwe* (1926) and *The Moon, My Shadow and I* (1926). On commission from music patron Elizabeth Sprague Coolidge he composed a *Japanese Nocturne* (1930); a *Sonata for Violin and Piano* was introduced in 1934 at the Pittsfield Festival (Mass.). Eichheim's works were widely performed and well received during his lifetime, but have been little heard since.

He died in Santa Barbara, Calif., Aug. 22, 1942.

ENGLISH FOLK-SONGS FROM THE SOUTHERN APPALACHIANS Collection by Olive Dame Campbell and Cecil James Sharp, published by G. P. Putnam's Sons in 1917. Mrs. Campbell began collecting tunes in 1907 and Sharp in 1916; the texts were taken down by Maud Karpeles, another English folklorist. The collection contains 122 songs and ballads and a total of 323 tunes, 37 of which appear also in the text-only collection of Child (q.v.). Sharp was an experienced collector of folk song and made a practice of preserving both music and text as well as noting other data: dates, locations, identification of singer, etc. Sharp (1859–1924) later expanded the work and it was published, edited by Karpeles, in 2 volumes by Oxford University Press, London, in 1932. An important work of its kind, it has been called by Bertrand H. Bronson (writing in the *Journal of American Folklore*, 1954) "the best *regional* collection we shall ever get, but (also) the most representative of the whole British tradition in the United States."

EUROPE, JAMES REESE (1881–1919) Bandleader, composer. Europe was born in Mobile, Ala., and brought to Washington, D.C., at the age of 10. He studied the violin with Enrico Hurlei, then assistant director of the U. S. Marine Band, and also studied piano. In 1904 Europe went to New York City where he found work eventually in an experimental all-Negro band, the Nashville Students. Numbering about 20 of the finest black musicians in New York, the band made its debut at Proctor's (on 23rd Street) in the spring of 1905. The band was unique in that it performed in theatres rather than dancehalls, onstage rather than in the pit. The sound of the band would best be described as prejazzy, for syncopation was important to its effect—the conductor, Will Dixon, literally danced the beat before the orchestra. The instrumentation of the band was also unusual in that it emphasized the guitar, mandolin, and banjo and the saxophone over the strings and woodwinds that dominated dance bands of the period. The band's sound made an impression on Europe, who left to take a job as musical director of the all-Negro musical *The Shoo-Fly Regiment*. He was director also of another J. Rosamond Johnson (q.v.) musical, *Mr. Lode of Kole,* before he decided, in 1910, to form a black musician's organization he called the Clef Club. It served as a kind of booking agency, providing musicians for various functions and occasions on order. The "Clef Club Symphony Orchestra" made its official debut at the Manhattan Casino, in Harlem, on Oct. 20, 1910; in 1912 it made an appearance in Carnegie Hall. The Clef Club Orchestra's instrumentation was obviously inspired by that of the earlier Nashville Students and made a great impression on the audience. Europe's own "Clef Club March" opened the program, which also featured music by Will Marion Cook (q.v.) and other Negro musicians. Europe eventually left the Clef Club and formed a similar group, the Tempo Club Orchestra. Around 1914 Europe joined forces with the popular dance team, Vernon and Irene Castle (q.v.), conducting and composing special dances for them. With the coming of the First World War, Europe enlisted, hoping to form a first-class band. In time, and with the help of private funding, the 369th Infantry Band was formed and eventually went to France. As did all military bands, Europe's organization played for the troops and entertained in rest camps and hospitals. But what made the "Hell Fighters," as they were popularly known, unique was their extraordinary popularity among the French, for they were permitted by the Army to play also for ci-

vilians. In August 1918, Europe's band played at the Théâtre des Champs-Élysées and remained for a month. Europe's syncopated arrangements for a well-disciplined band (something approaching but not quite jazz) captivated the French. After the war, Europe kept the band, numbering 65, intact for a worldwide tour. One reviewer, after a New York concert in March 1919, noted the band's "gorgeous racket of syncopation and jazzing." During the tour Europe's life came to a sudden violent end in Boston on May 10, 1919. Backstage, in Symphony Hall, he was stabbed by a member of the band and died of a wound in the neck.

FARWELL, ARTHUR (1872–1952) Composer, teacher, lecturer. Farwell was born in St. Paul, Minn., Apr. 23, 1872. Although he studied the violin as a child, he was a graduate of the Massachusetts Institute of Technology (1893), where he majored in electrical engineering. Practically on graduation he began to study composition with Homer Norris (1850–1920) in Boston until 1897; he then went to Germany where he studied with Engelbert Humperdinck and Hans Pfitzner and later to Paris to study with Alexandre Guilmant. Farwell returned to the United States in 1899 to lecture on the history of music at Cornell. Around the turn of the century, partially influenced by Dvořák (q.v.), he developed a deep interest in the music of the American Indian. In 1901 he founded the Wa-Wan Press (q.v.), Newton Center, Mass., for the publication of American music, stating at the time, "We shall ask of the composer, not that he submit to us work which is likely to be in demand, but that he express himself." The press was not dedicated to the commercialization of music or the American composer, so Farwell continued to earn a living by writing and teaching. He joined the staff of the publication *Musi-*

cal America as a critic in January 1909 and remained until 1915; he also supervised New York's Municipal Concerts (1910–13), was director of Music School Settlement, New York (1915–18); from 1918–19 he was acting head of the music department, University of California; he was awarded a composer's fellowship by the Pasadena Music and Art Association (1921–25) and from 1927 until his retirement in 1939, Farwell taught theory at Michigan State College. Musicologists categorize him as an "Indianist," with some reason, although his works include many not based on Indian themes. The earliest of his Indian pieces was *Dawn,* for orchestra, which was premiered at the St. Louis Exposition in 1904; it appeared in other guises—for chamber orchestra, solo piano—later. Farwell drew upon the research of musical ethnologist Alice C. Fletcher, as well as his own experiences among the Indians of the Southwest. His Op. 2 is entitled *Impressions of a Wa-Wan Ceremony* (1906). Borrowing from Omaha melodies collected by Fletcher, Farwell composed *American Indian Melodies* for solo piano in 1900. In 1908 he arranged 3 for voice and piano, *Three Indian Songs, Op. 32,* the last of which, "The Old Man's Love Song," he arranged for unaccompanied chorus. This piece is No. 2 (of 4) of his Op. 102 (*Four Choruses on Indian Themes,* 1937). Farwell was unquestionably the most gifted of the so-called "Indianists." Among his other major works are: for orchestra, *Symbolistic Study No. 3* (after Walt Whitman; 1922), *The Gods of the Mountain* (1917, orchestrated 1928), *Symbolistic Study No. 6, "Mountain Vision,"* (a one-movement piano concerto, 1931), and the *Rudolph Gott Symphony* (1934). For chorus Farwell composed a *Gloria* (1920), *Mountain Song* (1931), and the *Four Choruses,* already mentioned. His chamber music includes *The Hako*

(string quartet, 1922), *Sonata for Violin and Piano* (1927), *Sonata for Solo Violin* (1934), and a *Quintet* for strings and piano (1937). Among his works for the theatre are *Caliban* (Shakespeare Tercentenary Masque, 1916), *The Evergreen Tree* (Christmas Masque, 1917), *La Primavera* (Santa Barbara Community Music Drama, 1920), *The Pilgrimage Play* (The Story of Christ, 1921), and *Grail Song,* for chorus, orchestra, and dancers, 1925. Farwell's best-known "Indianist" pieces appeared in the Wa-Wan publication *From Mesa and Plain* (1905): *Navajo War Dance* and *Pawnee Horses* (the collection also included pieces based on Negro and cowboy songs). Another work is a *Symphonic Song on "Old Black Joe"* for orchestra and audience (1924). Near the end of his life Farwell completed an arrangement of the American folk tune *Sourwood Mountain* for piano solo. He died in New York City, Jan. 20, 1952.

FILLMORE, HENRY (1881–1956) Bandleader, composer, arranger, and trombonist. Born in Cincinnati Dec. 2, 1881, Fillmore began his professional career as a trombonist in a circus band. He formed his own band in 1916, composed and arranged for his band, and also became a successful music publisher. Fillmore's band was one of the first to be heard regularly on the radio. He composed dozens of marches, among them "Footlifter," "Miss Trombone," "His Excellency," "Men of Ohio," "Miami," and a *Gypsy Festival* and *Determination*—both overtures. Fillmore died in Miami, Fla., Dec. 7, 1956.

FISK JUBILEE SINGERS Singing group formed at Fisk University, Nashville, Tenn., in 1867. Fisk was established in 1865 as an institution of higher learning for Negroes. George L. White formed a singing group at the request of John Ogden, head of the university. White, who incidentally was white, taught music to promising students and formed a singing group of 11 with a pianist to accompany. The group gave its first concert in Nashville in 1867 and was well received. White then decided to take his troupe on tour, hoping to raise funds for Fisk's building program. The tour began on Oct. 6, 1871, and, although not initially a success, eventually raised $150,000 for Fisk. Because the end of Negro slavery heralded the "year of jubilee," White decided to call his group the Fisk Jubilee Singers. Their appearance at the Boston World Peace Jubilee 1872 earned them the attention that eventually brought them worldwide fame and tours. White early elected to let his group sing the music of their own people, in addition to standard concert fare. The Fisk Jubilee Singers, therefore, contributed to the diffusion of spirituals and plantation songs (in genteel adaptations). In 1885 a Music Department was founded at Fisk and the Jubilee Singers became a permanent organization. Two Fisk graduates, father and son, continued the work of White, John Wesley Work, Sr. (1873–1925) (q.v.) and John Wesley Work, Jr. (1901–68). The father took the Jubilee Singers on tours for 16 years; he also compiled the *New Jubilee Songs* and *Folk Songs of the American Negro* with his brother, Frederick, in 1907. John W. Work, Jr., was chairman of Fisk's Music Department and directed the Jubilee Singers from 1948 to 1957. He was the composer of several songs, the cantata *The Singers, Yenvalou* for string orchestra, and a choral cycle, *Isaac Watts Contemplates the Cross.*

FOOTE, ARTHUR (1853–1937) Composer, organist, pianist, and teacher. Foote was born in Salem, Mass., on Mar. 5, 1853. He exhibited only a slight musical interest as a boy (Foote's father was editor and part-owner of the local newspaper, the Salem *Gazette*). At 14

Foote studied piano with a Miss Fanny Paine; he later studied harmony privately with Stephen A. Emery. He entered Harvard College, where he began preparing for a career in business and kept his hand in music as conductor of the Harvard Glee Club. He also took courses in music with John Knowles Paine (q.v.); following his graduation in 1874, Foote returned to Harvard and further music study with Paine. His was the first master's degree in music given by Harvard (1875). Foote followed that with piano and organ lessons with B. J. Lang in Boston. Foote was unique among his New England contemporaries in that he acquired all of his musical training in the United States, except for some study with Stephen Heller during a European trip. Having finally chosen music as his profession, Foote remained in Boston to teach; in 1878 he became the organist of the First Unitarian Church, a position he held for 32 years. Foote's first published work, 3 pieces for cello and piano, came out in 1882. In the larger forms Foote produced *Francesca da Rimini,* Op. 24 (1893), a symphonic prologue inspired by Dante and probably his best-known work; Foote also composed several works for string orchestra, among them the *Serenade in E,* Op. 25 (1886), *Suite in D Minor,* Op. 36 (1896), and the *Suite in E,* Op. 63 (1910). Music for voices forms a large part of Foote's output, both secular and for church performance. Among his best-known choral works are *The Farewell of Hiawatha,* Op. 11 (1886), *The Wreck of the Hesperus,* Op. 17 (1888), and *In the Gateway of Ispahan* for women's voices (1914). Foote also left a large number of songs (ca. 150), but few entered the standard song repertory. His works for piano solo and organ solo seem to have suffered the same fate. Foote's chamber pieces have fared better; among his works in this genre are the early *String Quartet,* Op. 4 (1885), the *Sonata in G Minor* for violin and piano, Op. 20 (1890), *Piano Quartet,* Op. 23 (1898), *Piano Quintet,* Op. 38 (1898), and *String Quartet in D,* Op. 70 (1911). Among Foote's important organ works is the *Toccata and Suite in D,* Op. 54. Among his published books are *Modern Harmony* (1905) and *Modulation and Related Harmonic Questions* (1912). Although primarily American-trained, Foote was obviously highly influenced by Brahms; his own works are well wrought, gentlemanly, and refined. Foote died in Boston, aged 84, on Apr. 8, 1937.

GILBERT, HENRY FRANKLIN BELKNAP (1868–1928) Composer, violinist, and rugged musical individualist (although not so much as Charles Ives). Gilbert was largely self-taught. Even so, he is also remembered as the first American pupil of Edward MacDowell. Born in Somerville, Mass., Sept. 26, 1868, Gilbert studied violin with Emil Mollenhauer (1855–1927) and harmony at the New England Conservatory. While studying with MacDowell for about 3 years (1889–92), Gilbert made a living playing the violin in dance and theatre orchestras. Upon completion of his musical studies he was forced to take odd jobs and eventually worked in a relative's printing plant. In 1900 he boarded a cattle boat to attend one of the premiere performances in Paris of Charpentier's *Louise,* after which he decided he would devote himself to music. Rejecting the conventional influences of his time, Gilbert, an individualist, chose to turn to folk music for his inspiration, particularly the music of the Americas. This predilection eventually brought him into the sphere of Arthur Farwell (q.v.) whose Wa-Wan Press (q.v.) published several of Gilbert's compositions. Among his earliest works was *Two Episodes* (1896), composed before the trip to Paris; the 2nd was later (1902) transcribed for piano as *Negro*

Episode. His setting of R. L. Stevenson's "Pirate Song" enjoyed great popularity, but it was not until 1911 that Gilbert's *Comedy Overture on Negro Themes* performed by the Boston Symphony brought him to general attention. Its blatant Americanism contributed to Gilbert's notoriety, if not to wider popularity. His best-known work is *Dance in the Place Congo* (q.v.), originally completed in 1908 as a symphonic poem and revised in 1916. It was finally performed as a ballet at the Metropolitan Opera, New York, Mar. 23, 1918. Other works: *Americanesque* for orchestra (1903), *Celtic Studies* for voice and piano (1905), *The Fish Wharf Rhapsody* for voice and piano (1909), *Humoresque on Negro Minstrel Tunes* (1910), *Three American Dances in Ragtime Rhythm* (1911) and *Negro Rhapsody* (1913) —both for orchestra, and *Riders to the Sea,* symphonic prelude (1904, rev. 1915). Among Gilbert's last works is an impressive *Nocturne* for orchestra (1926). His one-act opera, *Fantasy in Delft,* has yet to be performed. Besides composing, Gilbert also lectured at Columbia and Harvard universities. Gilbert was unique as a composer and as an individual; born with a heart defect, he managed to work, lecture, and write despite the fact that even the slightest exertion brought on breathing problems. When he died in Cambridge, Mass., on May 19, 1928, in his 60th year, Gilbert had managed to live longer by more than 20 years than any other victim of this disease—and he was the subject of an article in the *Journal of the American Medical Association,* an unusual distinction for a musician.

GILCHRIST, WILLIAM WALLACE (1846–1916) Composer, organist, choirmaster. Gilchrist was born in Jersey City, N.J., Jan. 8, 1846. Although both his parents were musical (though not professionally), Gilchrist initially attempted to make a career in law. His family moved to Philadelphia in 1857, where Gilchrist was to become a major musical figure. His fine baritone voice led him to join singing societies and to become active in church work as vocalist and conductor. Gilchrist studied voice, organ, and composition with Dr. Hugh A. Clarke at the University of Pennsylvania. He organized and for a time (1874–1914) led the Mendelssohn Glee Club; he also served as Choirmaster at the Church of New Jerusalem. Gilchrist also taught voice at the Music Academy. In 1882 he attracted notice when he won the $1,000 prize offered by the Cincinnati Festival for his setting of the 46th Psalm for soprano, chorus, and orchestra. Other choral works include *A Christmas Idyl, The Rose, Song of Thanksgiving, The Lamb of God,* and *Easter Idyl.* Gilchrist produced a good number of songs, among them "A Song of Doubt and a Song of Faith," "A Dirge for Summer," *Eight Songs* (1885), and "Southern Lullaby." Other compositions include 2 symphonies, a *Nonet in G Minor,* a *Piano Quintet,* a string quartet, and a *Rhapsody, Perpetual Motion,* and *Fantasie* for violin. Gilchrist died in Easton, Pa., Dec. 20, 1916.

GLEASON, FREDERICK GRANT (1848–1903)   Composer, organist. Gleason was born in Middletown, Conn., Dec. 17, 1848. Gleason, whose father was an amateur musician, had no real musical instruction until he was 16 and had already composed a *Christmas Oratorio.* Having moved to Hartford, Gleason began to study with Dudley Buck (q.v.) and later continued work in the musical centers of Leipzig and Berlin. In 1875 Gleason was appointed organist of the Asylum Hill Congregational Church in Hartford; he transferred the following year to the First Congregational Church, New Britain. In 1877 Gleason moved to Chicago, where he taught organ, piano, composition, and orchestration at the Hershey School of Music. From 1884 to 1889 Gleason served as music critic for the Chicago *Tribune.* Gleason's compositions exhibit a Wagnerian coloration, but his work was impressive enough to be performed by Theodore Thomas and the Chicago Orchestra. His symphonic poem, *Edris,* was played by that orchestra in 1896, and his *Song of Life* in 1900. Gleason composed several operas, few of which were performed in his lifetime. His *Otho Visconti* (ca. 1892) was presented in 1907. Another opera, *Montezuma,* was never performed, although one of its arias was widely sung. Among Gleason's other works are a choral work, *The Culprit Fay,* such orchestral compositions as a *Processional of the Holy Grail* and *Auditorium Festival Ode* and a piano concerto. From 1900 until his death, Gleason was director of the Chicago Auditorium Conservatory. He died in Chicago, Dec. 6, 1903.

"GOD BLESS AMERICA" Song, words and music by Irving Berlin, originally written for an all-soldier show while the songwriter served in the U. S. Army during the First World War. When the show, *Yip! Yip! Yaphank,* opened in 1918, Berlin had eliminated "God Bless America." Sergeant Berlin himself appeared to sing "Oh! How I Hate to Get Up in the Morning." In 1939, with war raging in Europe, a concerned Berlin revived the patriotic song and it was introduced by popular singer Kate Smith on her radio show on Armistice Day. Since then "God Bless America" has virtually become the second national anthem.

GOETSCHIUS, PERCY (1853–1943) Teacher. Born in Paterson, N.J., Aug. 30, 1853, Goetschius received his training in Europe at the Stuttgart Conservatory of Music. Upon graduation he remained there as instructor in harmony

(1876–85) and professor of history of music and theory (1885–90). Goetschius returned to his homeland in 1890 to become a professor at the College of Fine Arts at Syracuse University; he then moved to Boston where he taught composition, history, and theory at the New England Conservatory (1892–96) and privately from 1896 to 1905. Goetschius came to New York in 1905 and spent the next 20 years teaching at the Institute of Musical Art (absorbed into the Juilliard School of Music in 1926). Although Goetschius composed some piano and vocal pieces he was most important as a teacher. His students range from conservatives—Daniel Gregory Mason (q.v.)—to moderate moderns—Bernard Rogers (Section V)—and experimentalists—Wallingford Riegger (Section VI). He was also a prolific writer for magazines and journals. His published books include several important standard texts: *The Material Used in Musical Composition* (1882, revised editions 1889, 1914), *The Theory and Practice of Tone Relations* (1892, 1916), *Exercises in Melody Writing* (1900), *Applied Counterpoint* (1902), *Masters of the Symphony* (1929), *The Structure of Music* (1933), and others. Goetschius died in Manchester, N.H., Oct. 29, 1943.

GOLDMAN, EDWIN FRANKO (1878–1956) Composer, conductor, cornetist, and teacher. Born in Louisville, Ky., Jan. 1, 1878, Goldman received early exposure to music. His mother (whose family name was Franko) was a child prodigy pianist and 2 of her brothers were violinist/conductors. Goldman won a scholarship at the National Conservatory of Music in New York, where he studied with Dvořák; he also studied cornet with Jules Levy. In 1895 Goldman joined the orchestra of the Metropolitan Opera as cornetist, a position he held until 1905. He then became a teacher of band instruments, and later a member of the faculty at Columbia University (1919–26). In 1911 he founded the famous Goldman Band which began presenting free concerts in New York's Central Park and later (1934) in Brooklyn's Prospect Park. In 1911 also, Goldman published one of his most popular marches, "The Pride of America." He had published his first march in 1909 and published his last in the year of his death. Among his most popular marches (of which he composed more than 100) are "Central Park," "On Parade," "Chimes of Liberty," and "On the Mall" (composed in 1923). Goldman also produced several valuable books on the subject of bands, among them *The Amateur Band Guide and Aid to Leaders* (1916) and *The Goldman Band System for Developing Tone, Intonation and Phrasing* (1935). Goldman's son, Richard Franko (Section VI) followed his father in the field of band music, composition, and writing. Edwin F. Goldman founded the American Bandmasters Association in 1929 and was its first president and later honorary lifetime president; he died in the Bronx, N.Y., Feb. 21, 1956.

GOLDMARK, RUBIN (1872–1936) Teacher and composer. Goldmark was born in New York City, Aug. 15, 1872. He attended the College of the City of New York and the University of Vienna. His musical studies were accomplished at the Vienna Conservatory (1889–91) where he studied piano and theory; he also taught these subjects there for a time. Upon returning to New York he continued studies at the National Conservatory with Dvořák (composition) and Rafael Joseffy (piano). Goldmark, after graduation, became a teacher himself at the Conservatory until poor health forced him to move to Colorado, where he became director of the Colorado College Conservatory. In 1902 he was able to return to New York and became a private teacher of piano and theory. Among his pupils were Aaron Copland (Section V), George Gershwin (very briefly; Section V), Vittorio Giannini (Section VI), Frederick Jacobi (Section V), and Paul Nordoff (Section VI). In 1924 Goldmark joined the staff of the Juilliard School of Music as director of the Department of Composition. Goldmark enjoyed some success as a composer, although he was best known as a teacher. His *Hiawatha Overture* (1900) was first performed by the Boston Symphony; the tone poem, *Samson,* was also introduced by the same orchestra in 1919. His most popular work was the *Requiem* (inspired by Lincoln's Gettysburg Address), premiered by the New York Philharmonic in 1919. Other works include a *Negro Rhapsody, The Call of the Plains,* both for orchestra, a *Piano Trio* (which impressed Dvořák), a string quartet, a violin and piano sonata, and some songs. Goldmark was the nephew of Hungarian composer Karl Goldmark (1830–1915). He died in New York, Mar. 6, 1936.

GRIFFES, CHARLES TOMLINSON (1884–1920) Composer, pianist. Born in Elmira, N.Y., Sept. 17, 1884, Griffes began the study of music at the Elmira Academy with Mary Broughton and George McKnight. Griffes originally intended to become a pianist but during a period of study in Berlin he was persuaded to concentrate on composition by one of his teachers, Engelbert Humperdinck (1854–1921). Griffes spent 4 years studying in Berlin (1903–7) and then returned to take the position of music director at the Hackley School, Tarrytown, N.Y., a private school for boys. As a composer, Griffes initially exhibited the influence of his training in Germany; later he turned to Impressionism, but shortly before his early death he had evolved a strong and prom-

ising personal style. Griffes' earliest known compositions were written for piano—his Op. 2 is entitled *Six Variations in B flat,* produced when Griffes was 18. During his German stay Griffes composed a good number of songs to German texts; he also left an even greater number of songs to English texts, among them the outstanding "The Lament of Ian the Proud" (1918), the early "By a Lonely Forest Pathway" (ca. 1908), *Four Impressions* (1912–16), and *Three Poems of Fiona MacLeod,* Op. 11 (1918). Griffes composed many piano pieces, not all of which have yet been published; among his outstanding works for the piano are *Three Tone Pictures,* Op. 5 (1911), *Fantasy Pieces,* Op. 6 (ca. 1911–13), *Roman Sketches,* Op. 7 (q.v., 1915–17), and the remarkable *Piano Sonata* (1918). As early as 1903 Griffes attempted to compose for the string quartet but his only published work in this genre is the *Two Sketches for String Quartet on Indian Themes* (1918–19). Griffes arranged several of his piano pieces for orchestra; among his other orchestral works are the *Kairn of Koridwen* (1916) and *Sho-Jo* (1917), both for chamber groups. His major orchestral work, *The Pleasure-Dome of Kubla Khan,* completed in 1917, was introduced to great acclaim by the Boston Symphony in 1919. He composed a fine *Poem for Flute and Orchestra* in 1918. Toward the end of his short life, although he was getting the recognition he deserved, Griffes suffered some frustration in having to earn a living as a teacher and in exhausting himself in the laborious copying of the scores and parts of his orchestral works for performance. He also published piano study pieces under the pseudonym "Arthur Tomlinson." Griffes was an accomplished artist, gifted with the pencil and watercolors. Never in robust health, he died, aged 35, of empyema in New York, Apr. 8, 1920.

HADLEY, HENRY KIMBALL (1871–1937) Composer, conductor. Born on Dec. 20, 1871, in Somerville, Mass., Hadley began the study of music, piano and composition, with his father. He studied also with Chadwick (q.v.) and Stephen Emery (1841–91) at the New England Conservatory and earned his degree in music at Tufts College. At 22 Hadley toured the United States as the conductor of the Mapelson Opera Company; in 1893 he went to Vienna to study composition with Eusebius Mandyczewski (1857–1929). Upon his return to the United States he became music instructor at the St. Paul's Episcopal School for Boys, Garden City, N.Y. (1896). In 1904 Hadley again went to Europe where he studied with Ludwig Thuille (1861–1907) in Munich in addition to conducting in Warsaw and Mainz. After a 5-year stay Hadley returned to the United States to conduct the Seattle Symphony Orchestra (1909–11). He later also led the San Francisco Symphony (1911–15) and became associate conductor of the New York Philharmonic in 1920. In 1929 Hadley founded the Manhattan Symphony Orchestra which, under his leadership, made a point of presenting the works of American composers on each program. He was also the founder of the National Association for American Composers and Conductors (NAACC) in 1933. Although a prolific composer, Hadley is best remembered as the conductor-champion of the American composer. Even so, during his lifetime he was the recipient of several prizes in composition, and his works were played abroad. His *First Symphony* ("Youth and Life") was conducted by Anton Seidl in 1897. His first opera, *Safie*, was presented in Mainz in 1909. His *Second Symphony*, "The Four Seasons," took no less than 2 prizes in 1901. A symphonic poem, *Salome*, was popular and played by major orchestras in Boston, Monte Carlo

(1907), Warsaw, and Kassel (1908). His opera *Cleopatra's Night* (1920) was performed for 2 seasons at the Metropolitan. In his lifetime Hadley received commissions for occasional works, many for chorus. Opera and works for orchestra were his principal interests. Hadley composed more than 100 songs and several chamber works. His *String Quartet No. 2* was written in 1934; he completed his *Fifth Symphony*, without descriptive title, the following year. Hadley died in New York, Sept. 6, 1937.

HAMPTON, ROBERT (18??–1944) Ragtime pianist-composer. Little is known about Rob Hampton, who was probably born in Little Rock, Ark., and who flourished as a pianist-composer in St. Louis in that generation of gifted black musicians that followed Joplin. Although not a trained musician, Hampton composed some 40 rags, three of which were published by John Stark. His best-known work, revealing certain classical leanings, is *Cataract Rag* (1914); it was set down by his friend and colleague Artie Matthews (q.v.). After the ragtime interest waned Hampton remained in St. Louis eking out a poor living; he later went to California, where he died in 1944.

HANDY, WILLIAM CHRISTOPHER (1873–1958) Composer, publisher, cornetist, bandleader. Born in Florence, Ala., Nov. 16, 1873, Handy was given music lessons early in life. His first instrument was the organ; his father being a minister in a local church, the instrument seemed appropriate. Surreptitiously, however, young Handy studied the cornet with a local white bandmaster. The purchase of a secular guitar (with his own hard-earned money) resulted in family displeasure and the return of the guitar, the money then being used for something "useful," a dictionary. After that young Handy bided his time, working in the fields around

Florence and as an apprentice to a printer. When a traveling minstrel show came to town, Handy, the cornetist, left with it, only to be stranded when the show went bankrupt. Handy returned to Florence to complete his formal schooling, to work for the McNabb Iron works, and to teach school for a short time. Meanwhile, he continued to be musically active, organizing bands and singing groups and writing arrangements for them. In 1893 Handy left home again, in company with a vocal quartet; their goal was the impending World's Fair at Chicago. Handy and troupe learned upon arrival that the Fair had been postponed for a year. Heading homeward, penniless, Handy (then about 20) got as far as St. Louis, where he spent a miserable time; he was even forced to sleep in vacant lots and on the cobblestoned levees. But it was also in St. Louis that Handy first became aware of Negro folk forms, the "sorrow songs," known as the blues. In those Depression years Handy drifted from one job to another, playing in small bands. By 1896 he was playing cornet with the Mahara Minstrels; in 1900 he became music director at the Alabama Agricultural and Mechanical College, Huntsville. He moved to Clarksville, Miss., to lead a Knights of Pythias band and to teach music. Handy, married to a childhood sweetheart in 1898, prospered in Clarksville as bandleader-teacher; he had also begun composing under the influence of the black music he had heard along the Mississippi River, and had acquired a solid reputation. In 1909 Handy was leader of a band hired to enliven the Memphis mayoral campaign of one Edward H. Crump, later known as "Boss" Crump. Handy composed an instrumental piece for the occasion entitled *Mr. Crump*, which became immediately popular among blacks and whites alike. (Crump, incidentally, was elected.) Although embarrassed by the words that were eventually

set to the tune. Handy was certain that in the blues melody (in the 12-bar form) he had the possibility of a popular song. With new, nonpolitical lyrics, the song was finally published (not without adversity) as "The Memphis Blues" (q.v.) in 1912. Although not the first published blues, as Handy believed throughout his lifetime (Artie Matthews' "Baby Seal Blues" and Hart Wand's "Dallas Blues" were published earlier in the same year), the point is academic, for "The Memphis Blues" was the first authentic blues to achieve worldwide popularity and, in the music business, the status of a "standard." In short, Handy is to the blues what Joplin is to the rag. Handy's experiences in getting the song published, his eventual mistake of selling it outright and then seeing it become popular and profitable, encouraged him to go into the music publishing business, which he did with Harry A. Pace, forming Pace and Handy Music Co. in 1913 (eventually the firm went bankrupt and Handy reformed it as Handy Brothers Music Co.). The firm's first publication was the instrumental *Jogo Blues*, which was followed by other Handy compositions, among them "The St. Louis Blues" (1914), "Joe Turner Blues," "In the Land Where Cotton Is King" (words by Pace, 1916), "Beale Street Blues" (1917), "The Kaiser's Got the Blues" (words by Dorner C. Brown, 1918), "Aunt Hagar's Children Blues" (words by J. Tim Brymn, 1922), "Atlanta Blues" (words by Dave Elman, 1924), "Wall Street Blues" (words by Margaret Gregory, 1929), and "Chantez Les Bas," among many others. Handy also arranged dozens of spirituals for various combinations of voice and instruments. Author of several books and anthologies, Handy produced at least 2 important volumes, *Blues: An Anthology*, with introduction and notes by Abbe Niles (1926), and his autobiography, *Father of the Blues* (1941). Blindness in his later years did not dim Handy's optimism. During the last 3 years of his life a stroke confined him to a wheelchair but did not confine him to his home, in Yonkers, N.Y., when a special occasion called for his appearance. He died, aged 84, in New York, Mar. 28, 1958.

HARNEY, BENJAMIN R. (1871–1938) Ragtime pianist-composer. Born near Middleboro, Ky., Mar. 6, 1871, Harney enjoyed a career in vaudeville billed as "The Inventor of Ragtime." Not much is known about him except that he was white, was in a military school in his teens, married early, played piano in saloons in Louisville, Ky., and other Southern towns, eventually ending up in New York, where he created a sensation at Keith's and Tony Pastor's (1896). Although unable to write down his music, Harney composed complete musical scores. In the early 1890s he and his wife, Jessie Boyce, toured in a minstrel-like show, *South Before the War,* for which he composed the songs. The sensation Harney had created in his New York debut resulted from his piano playing, which was syncopated and based on black music styles. Initially called "jig piano" (q.v.), it soon came to be called ragtime as soon as that term became common in the popular press. Although Harney did not "invent" ragtime, he was the first white man to play it authentically and to encourage its popularity and diffusion. This was at a time when ragtime was little known except in black communities; Harney apparently got along well with blacks (he teamed up with a famous black vaudevillian, "Strap" Hill), who shared their music with him. Although he never composed an instrumental rag, Harney's ragsongs reveal early traces of the real thing; some are undoubtedly based on folk materials he heard in his travels. In 1896 he published two such songs, "Mister Johnson, Turn Me Loose" and "You've Been a Good Old Wagon, But You've Done Broke Down." The first was interpolated in the musical revue *Courted in Court* and sung by the great black entertainer May Irwin (1862–1938). The popularity of Harney's songs led to the publication of his *Rag Time Instructor* (1897). He took his music, in his words, "three trips around the big globe," spreading his syncopated style into such unlikely corners as China and the Fiji Islands; he was very popular in Britain. Among his other songs: "I Love My Honey" (1897), "You May Go But This Will Bring You Back" (1898), "Draw That Color Line" (1898), "The Cake-Walk in the Sky" (1899), "The Only Way to Keep Her Is in a Cage" (1901), and "Cannon Ball Catcher" (1914). A heart attack in 1923 slowed down Ben Harney's career and he finally retired in 1930, his wife and he moving into a slum neighborhood in Philadelphia. The Harneys then lived off his Actors' Fund and welfare checks. Harney died on Mar. 1, 1938. It took his wife 3 years to raise the money for his tombstone, on which she had inscribed his epitaph: "Creator of Ragtime."

HARRIGAN AND HART Edward "Ned" Harrigan (1844–1911) and Tony Hart (pseudonym of Anthony J. Cannon, 1855–91) were a famed comic stage team, whose specialty was dialect farces with music. Harrigan, born on New York's Lower East Side, and Cannon, born in Worcester, Mass., formed their partnership in Chicago in 1871. One of their early popular variety sketches was entitled "The Mulligan Guard" which satirized the fondness for quasi-military organizations among immigrant groups (in this instance, the Irish). The music was by David Braham (q.v.) and the sketch, and probably the words to the song, was by Harrigan Six years later, in 1879, the sketch was expanded into a playlet with added plot (a Negro marching unit which rents the same hall for the same night) as *The Mulligan Guards' Ball*. The comedy and the characters proved to be popular and a series of Mulligan musical farces ensued: *The Mulligan Guards' Chowder* (1879), *The Mulligan Guards' Surprise* (1880), *Cordelia's Aspirations* (1883), etc. In these comedies Harrigan appeared as "Dan Mulligan" and Hart frequently in a female role—in *The Mulligan Guards' Nominee* (1880) he appeared as "Rebecca Allup." The Harrigan and Hart farces, though not strictly musicals, were very popular in New York and spawned a number of popular songs of the period. Their dialect-laden (Irish, Negro, Jewish, Italian) sketches were broadly satirical, the songs topical, the general tone of their shows earthy and rowdy, reflecting the life of New York at that time. Their success was great enough to pay for their own Theatre Comique on Broadway and Spring Street. In 1884 the theatre burned and a few months later the partners had a falling out and split up, each then going his own way. Neither prospered, although Harrigan built a theatre named for himself in 1890 and presented one of his last and most successful shows, *Reilly and the Four Hundred*. By the late 1890s Harrigan was in retirement. The demand for his kind of musical farce was replaced by one for the livelier vaudeville and incipient musical comedy.

HARRIS, CHARLES K. (1865–1930) Composer, lyricist, publisher. Charles Kassel Harris was born in Poughkeepsie, N.Y., May 1, 1865, and began his professional career as a banjoist in vaudeville. He added to his income by writing special songs for special occasions. A self-taught musician, Harris specialized in sentimental "song-stories," long narrative songs designed to bring on the tears. His one major success, "After the Ball," was written for an amateur minstrel show production in Milwaukee, where Harris was living in 1892 (the sign on his home read: "Prof. Charles K. Harris/Banjoist & Song Writer"). Initially the song made no impact—the first night the vocalist forgot the words (there being so many of them), but it was interpolated into the score of *A Trip to Chinatown*. Sung by one J. Aldrich Libby, it became tremendously popular and was taken up by John Philip Sousa and later introduced at the Chicago World's Fair. The song is still played today (Jerome Kern even interpolated it into his *Show Boat* score in 1927, for period flavor) but free of the several stanzas telling the tale of a foolish old man who caught his girlfriend kissing another man—at a ball, of course—rejected her and after a long lonely life, learned, after the girl's death, that the "other" man had been her brother. For years Harris attempted to mine a similar lachrymose vein but without further success. Some of his other efforts include "Break the News to Mother" (1897—just in time for the Spanish-American War), "Hello, Central, Give Me Heaven" (1901—a child calling her dead father) and, among more of the same, "For Sale: A Baby" (1903). Harris luckily was also his own publisher; he was one of the charter members of the American Society for Composers, Authors and Publishers (1914). He died in New York City, Dec. 22, 1930.

HERBERT, VICTOR (1859–1924) Composer, cellist, conductor. Herbert was born in Dublin, Ireland, Feb. 1, 1859. His father died while Herbert was still an infant and his mother remarried, a Dr. Wilhelm Schmid. The new family settled in Stuttgart, where Schmid had his practice and where Herbert, who had evidenced an early musical aptitude, began to study music. He was trained as a cellist and was employed in several German and Austrian orchestras. In 1886 he was engaged to the soprano

Therese Förster, who was asked by Walter Damrosch to sing with the Metropolitan Opera Company. Förster agreed on the condition that Herbert become a member of the opera's orchestra. Damrosch agreed, the couple were married, and the young virtuoso cellist arrived in the United States in October 1886. That arrival would have a great and lasting effect on American popular music. Herbert initially played in the pit orchestra of the Metropolitan and later in orchestras under Theodore Thomas (q.v.) and Anton Seidl before setting out on his own as a conductor. He also appeared as soloist in performances of his cello concertos; the *Concerto No. 2 for Cello and Orchestra,* Op. 30, he performed with the New York Philharmonic, to which it is dedicated, in 1898. The first *Cello Concerto* dates from 1894, the year of Herbert's first operetta, *Prince Ananias.* The commission for this operetta, or light opera, had come from the Bostonians (originally the Boston Ideal Opera Company), which had been formed in 1879, drawing mainly on the ranks of Boston's church choirs, to present Gilbert and Sullivan's *Pinafore.* Herbert's contribution intensified the influence of Viennese operetta's impact on the evolving American musical. In 1895, Herbert, encouraged by the success of *Prince Ananias,* composed the music for *The Wizard of the Nile* (libretto and words by Harry B. Smith), which was even more successful. Herbert went on to compose the music to more than 40 operettas and became one of the most prolific, successful, and influential figures in the American lyric theatre. Among his enduring scores are: *Babes in Toyland* (1903; "Toyland," "The March of the Toys," "I Can't Do the Sum"), *Mlle. Modiste* (1905; "Kiss Me Again"), *The Red Mill* (1906; "The Streets of New York," "Because You're You"), *Naughty Marietta* (1910; "Tramp! Tramp! Tramp!" "I'm Falling in Love

with Someone," "Italian Street Song," "Ah! Sweet Mystery of Life"), *Sweethearts* (1913; "Sweethearts," "Pretty as a Picture"), *Eileen* (1917; "Thine Alone"), *Orange Blossoms* (1922; "A Kiss in the Dark"); Herbert's final score, *The Dream Girl,* was produced in the last year of his life, 1924. Besides his operetta scores Herbert composed dozens of instrumental pieces and arrangements; his 2 operas, *Natoma* (1911) and *Madeleine* (1913), were not successful. After conducting the Pittsburgh Symphony (1898–1904) and serving as guest conductor of the New York Philharmonic, Herbert founded his own orchestra, which specialized in light music and recorded extensively—his own works and those of others. Among his extended orchestral works are a *Serenade for String Orchestra,* Op. 12 (1889), the *Irish Rhapsody* (1892), the symphonic poem, *Hero and Leander,* Op. 33 (1900), and *A Suite of Serenades* composed for the Paul Whiteman Orchestra in 1924. Herbert's piano piece, *Indian Summer* (1919), set to a lyric by Al Dubin, was very popular in the late 1930s and early '40s. Herbert's musicianship produced dozens of well-wrought songs; his longer works are rarely performed. He was also an astute businessman and was a moving force in protecting the works of songwriters which were performed in public without compensation. His suit against Shanley's Restaurant, New York City, whose orchestra was performing some of his songs without permission, resulted in a Supreme Court decision in 1917 protecting the rights of songwriters. Herbert was also one of the founders of the American Society of Composers, Authors and Publishers in 1914. A popular figure on Broadway and its environs in the early years of the 20th century, Herbert enjoyed living the good life, was generous with money and indulged himself as well as his friends. Ignoring medical advice that he curb his appetite, Herbert loved to dine well and voraciously at such restaurants as Lüchow's. Celebrating the completion of *The Dream Girl* at the Lambs Club on May 26, 1924, Herbert consumed an elaborate lunch of several courses, suffered a heart attack, and died.

HILL, EDWARD BURLINGAME (1872–1960) Composer, teacher, author. Son of a Harvard chemistry professor, and grandson of an early president of the university, Hill was born in Cambridge, Mass., Sept. 9, 1872. He continued in the family tradition scholastically, except that he majored in music and was a student of Frederick F. Bullard (1864–1904) (composer of the timeless "A Stein Song") and, at Harvard, of J. K. Paine (q.v.). Other teachers included A. B. Whiting (q.v.), G. Chadwick (q.v.) and, in Paris, C. M. J. A. Widor (1884–1937). Hill graduated from Harvard in 1894 with highest honors in music; in 1908 he joined the faculty as an instructor. In 1918 he was made professor of music and 10 years later was appointed chairman of the Music Division. He retired from Harvard in 1940. Hill was an authority on French music, lectured on the subject, and published his *Modern French Music* in 1924. As a composer he has generally been categorized as a conservative who leaned a bit toward French Impressionism. His creative output was predominantly orchestral and includes 4 symphonies, several orchestra suites, including the 2, based on the poems of R. L. Stevenson, entitled *Stevensoniana* (No. 1, 1917 and No. 2, 1922). His symphonic poems include *Lancelot and Guinevere,* Op. 21 (1915), *The Fall of the House of Usher,* Op. 26 (1920), and *Lilacs* (inspired by Amy Lowell, 1927). His ballet scores include *Jack Frost in Midsummer* (1908) and *Pan and the Star,* Op. 19 (1914). Although his graduation piece was a

highly regarded piano sonata, Hill did not produce a great deal for that instrument; a number of his early pieces for the piano include *Four Sketches,* Op. 7, *Three Poetical Sketches,* Op. 8, and *Country Idyls,* Op. 10. During the 1920s he produced 4 *Jazz Studies* for 2 pianos and a *Piano Concertino* (1931). His chamber works include a *String Quartet,* Op. 40 (expanded as *Sinfonietta for String Orchestra,* Op. 40A), a *Sonata for Clarinet and Piano* (1927), a *Sextet for Winds and Piano* (1934), and a *Quintet for String Quartet and Clarinet* (1945). Many of Hill's orchestral works were introduced by the Boston Symphony, including a *Violin Concerto* (1933–34, rev. 1937) and a *Concertino for Strings* (1940). Hill was also an influential teacher whose students included Walter Piston, Randall Thompson, Virgil Thomson, Arthur Berger, and Elliott Carter. Hill died in Francestown, N.H., July 9, 1960.

HOWARD, JOSEPH EDGAR (1878–1961) Songwriter, singer, actor, producer. Son of a saloonkeeper, Joe Howard, born in New York City, Feb. 12, 1878, ran away from home at the age of 8, shortly after his mother's death. He traveled westward, out of his father's reach, by hopping freight trains and earned a living selling newspapers or singing in saloons. Howard eventually made his vaudeville debut at the age of 11 as "Master Joseph, the Boy Soprano." He toured with a stock company production of *Uncle Tom's Cabin* (in which he played Little Eva). He formed a song-and-dance team with singer Ida Emerson (who would be the second of his several wives) which by 1885 was a hit in Chicago's Olympic Theatre. The team was also successful at Tony Pastor's in New York City. Toward the close of the century Howard began writing his own songs, producing "Hello! Ma Baby" (with Ida Emerson) in 1899 and "Good

Bye, My Lady Love" in 1904. Beginning in 1905 Howard composed the songs for the first of 20 musicals, produced in Chicago and New York. His last was done in 1915. These musicals, which often starred Howard, were not very successful in New York. *The Prince of Tonight* (1909) contained another of Howard's long-lived songs, "I Wonder Who's Kissing Her Now" (written in collaboration with Harold Orlob—who had to sue to get co-composer credit in 1948). With the death of vaudeville, Howard continued to be active in nightclubs, radio and television, billing himself as the Gay Nineties Troubadour and zestfully singing his most popular songs. Howard continued to work for the rest of his life, his money having been used up on, in his own words (paraphrasing, as he pointed out, a Strauss waltz), "wine, women and alimony," a rueful reference to no less than 7 unsuccessful marriages. Fittingly, perhaps, Howard died in Chicago while making a curtain call in a theatre on May 19, 1961.

HUNTER, CHARLES (1878–?1906) Composer, pianist. Born blind in Columbia, Tenn., sometime in 1878, Hunter learned the trade of piano tuning at the School for the Blind in Nashville. On leaving the school, he began working as a tuner for the Jesse French Piano Co. in Nashville, where he taught himself to play the piano. Interestingly the white blind pianist became one of the early ragtime pioneers. His first composition, *Tickled to Death—Ragtime March and Two Step*, published in 1899, became very popular; his 2nd, *A Tennessee Tantalizer*, was issued in 1900. In 1902 Hunter moved to St. Louis where he worked in the French store for a while and then gave up his job to spend his time in the St. Louis tenderloin playing ragtime piano. Hunter produced only a handful of (published) works among them the delicate *'Possum and 'Taters*

(1901), *Cotton Bolls* (1901), *Just Ask Me* (1902), *Why We Smile* (1903) and, his last piece, *Seraphine Waltzes* (1905). Hunter died when he was about 28, in St. Louis, only a few weeks after he had married; the cause of death was tuberculosis.

HUSS, HENRY HOLDEN (1862–1953) Composer, pianist, teacher. Huss was born June 21, 1862, in Newark, N.J., and began the study of music with his father; later he studied theory under Otis Bardwell Boise (1844–1912). Huss rounded out his musical education in Munich, where he spent 3 years, beginning in 1883, to study with Joseph Rheinberger (counterpoint). His graduation composition was a *Rhapsody for Piano and Orchestra in C* (1885), with Huss at the piano. His *Piano Concerto in B* (1894) was well received and Huss performed it with major orchestras throughout the country. After settling in New York City, he taught piano, theory, and lectured at Hunter College. He also gave joint recitals in the United States and Europe with his wife, the soprano Hildegard Hoffmann. The compositions of Huss were praised and performed in his lifetime but, lacking staying power, have rarely been performed since his death. Huss composed several piano works, including the poetic *La Nuit* (orch. 1939), several chamber works, including 2 string quartets and songs as well as choral compositions, including *The Ride of Paul Revere,* for soprano, women's chorus, and orchestra (1920), *Winged Messengers of Peace* for mixed chorus (1937), and *The Mystery of Night* (1938). Huss died in New York City, Sept. 17, 1953.

"I DON'T CARE" Lively popular song, words by Jean Lenox, music by Harry O. Sutton, written in 1905. Popularized by vaudeville star Eva Tanguay (1878–1948), who became known thereafter as the "I Don't Care Girl."

"IN THE BAGGAGE COACH AHEAD" Sentimental song, words and music by Gussie L. Davis (q.v.) about a child, a father, and a "mother . . . in a casket in the baggage coach ahead"; published in 1896.

IVES, CHARLES EDWARD (1874–1954) Composer, businessman. Son of a bandmaster, musician, and music teacher, Charles Edward Ives was born in Danbury, Conn., Oct. 20, 1874. His father, George E. Ives, was of an experimental bent and was fascinated by strange sound combinations and the science of acoustics; his influence on his son was profound. At 14 Charles Ives was Sunday organist in Danbury's Second Congregational Church and had already begun composing. In 1894, the year of his father's death, Ives was a student at Yale and organist at Centre Church in New Haven. At Yale, Ives studied composition with Horatio Parker (q.v.); teacher and student were not musically compatible. He also studied the organ with Dudley Buck (q.v.). To keep the peace, Ives practiced his musical experiments privately (polytonality engaged him long before European avant-garde composers discovered it). After graduation from Yale in 1898 Ives moved to New York City to work in the insurance business. Although he continued to compose prodigiously, music to Ives was an avocation. He was innovative, creative, and most successful in insurance and was one of the founders of one of the most prosperous firms in the country, Ives & Myrick. Ives confined his composing to weekends, or to off moments while commuting between New York and the Ives home in Redding, Conn. Because he did not depend upon his music for his livelihood, Ives, following in his father's eccentric footsteps, created a remarkable body of extraordinarily original and "advanced" music. Unfortunately, it was original, difficult, and rarely performed so that Ives's innovations and experiments were not recognized until years after he had used them. Because he chose to remain out of the strife and politics of the musical scene, Ives was not recognized as the genius and original that he was (except by a few) until he had become inactive as a composer. Ives was a pioneer in the stretching and breaking of the rules of proper music-making; his use of American themes—ragtime, jazz, popular song, hymns, fiddle tunes—was, and is, unparalleled and inventive. Unfortunately he heard very little of his music performed in his lifetime, although toward the end of his life more of his compositions were programmed. In 1947 Ives was awarded the Pulitzer Prize for his *Third Symphony*, which had been completed in 1904! Although he began composing early (ca. age 13, in 1887), his productive period was confined roughly to the years 1902 (the year of his *Symphony No. 2*) to 1918, when he became seriously ill. Although his illness did not end Ives's musical activities, it did slow him down considerably. Ives's health problems (a heart condition plus other weaknesses) led him to resign from Ives & Myrick in 1930. Despite the limited hours he devoted to composition, Ives turned out a large body of work: 4 numbered symphonies, a *Holidays* symphony (1904–13), and an unfinished *Universe Symphony* (begun in 1911 and worked on for years). His first *String Quartet*, subtitled "A Revival Service," dates from 1896 and the *String Quartet No. 2* from 1913 (begun 1907). Ives composed 2 stunning piano sonatas. No. 1 was written 1902–9. The *Sonata No. 2*, known as the "Concord Sonata," was begun in 1909 and completed (if any work of Ives can be considered completed, since he continued to revise them even after publication) in 1915. Ives published the work himself in 1919. In addition there are several solo piano pieces among them, *Three Quarter Tone Pieces, Three-Page Sonata, Some Southpaw Pitching,* and *Anti-Abolitionist Riots.* There are also 4 piano and violin sonatas, the first dating from ca. 1908 and the 4th, "Children's Day at the Camp Meeting," from 1915. Ives composed a great number of works for orchestra, sometimes combining them into suites which he called "Sets." The *Theatre Orchestra Set* ("In the Cage," "In the Inn," "In the Night") was completed in 1911, as was *Three Outdoor Scenes* ("Hallowe'en," "The Pond," "Central Park in the Dark"). *Orchestral Set No. 1* is better known as *Three Places in New England* ("The 'St. Gaudens' in Boston Common," "Putnam's Camp, Redding, Connecticut," "The Housatonic at Stockbridge") and was completed in 1914. Ives also composed well over a hundred songs and pieces for his own instrument, the organ. One of his earliest compositions is the *Variations on a National Hymn* in which Ives takes "America" through a number of rather irreverent polytonal variations; this work was composed in 1891. Several choral pieces round out Ives's output: *The Celestial Country* (1899), *Three Harvest Home Chorales* (1898–1902), *General William Booth Enters into Heaven* (1914); there are also many psalm settings of uncommon beauty. Ives was a musical and social thinker of originality and independence; he published his views on insurance, on politics ("A Suggestion for a 20th Amendment," 1920), and music, *Essays Before a Sonata* (1920). His *Memos* on people and music was published in 1972. Charles Ives died, aged 79, in New York, May 19, 1954. He was survived by his wife, the appositely named Harmony Twichell, and an adopted daughter, Edith (Mrs. George Grayson). Unfortunately Ives, because of his indifference to recognition and the rarity of the performances of his music, had little influence upon the musicians of his own generation. He was

not the leader of any school, such as formed around Arnold Schoenberg and Igor Stravinsky. The music of Charles Ives was widely appreciated only after others had independently discovered similar devices and techniques. Not that Ives lived in a musical vacuum (although he preferred not hearing the music of others since he felt it muddled his own musical thinking); he formed lifelong friendships with composers of pretty much the same adventuresome attitudes as he held—Henry Cowell, Carl Ruggles, and John Becker. Unselfishly Ives encouraged performances and publication of their works and that of others; he assisted struggling musicians financially (when he won the Pulitzer Prize, he immediately sent the money that came with it to Becker). Charles Ives was unique in the history of anyone's music.

JACKSON, TONY (1876–1921) Pianist, vocalist, composer. Anthony Jackson was born sometime in 1876 in New Orleans. His family was poor and he was raised by an older sister. He was given the standard schooling but taught himself the piano in the backroom of a local bar. Jackson began his professional career as pianist and singer in New Orleans' Storyville, playing in the fancy establishment of Antonia P. Gonzalez, "Female Cornetist," whose advertisement in the *Blue Book* (the directory of the joys of Storyville) promised "fun among a lot of pretty Creole damsels . . ." Jackson's playing earned him a great reputation among musicians in New Orleans; even Ferdinand "Jelly Roll" Morton (q.v.) admitted coming under the influence of Jackson's piano style. Jackson left New Orleans in 1904 with the Whitman Sisters' New Orleans Troubadours, a traveling theatrical group. Jackson was signed as featured vocalist. He left the troupe in Louisville, Ky., which had a flourishing musical life in the tenderloin. He played for a time in one of the bars and heard variants of ragtime played by now little-known masters like "Piano Price" Davis and Glover Compton. By 1905 Jackson moved to Chicago, where he spent the rest of his life performing in cafes and bars. Many of the piano pieces he played were original Jackson compositions, few of which ever saw publication because he refused to "give them away for $5 apiece," as was the practice then among publishers. A few of Jackson's rags were recalled later by Jelly Roll Morton; these include *The Naked Dance* and *Michigan Water*. Jackson's first known song, "The Clock of Time," was written in collaboration with Glover Compton in Louisville in 1904. Among his dozen or so known songs, the most enduring is "Pretty Baby" (1916), written in collaboration with Egbert Van Alstyne (1882–1951) with words by Gus Kahn (Section V). Jazz historians tend to suggest that the melody was all Jackson's and that Van Alstyne's name was added to assure publication. However, Jackson did not publish any other song that achieved so much popularity, nor did he take advantage of this hit and go on to produce other songs in its wake. Jackson preferred to reserve his creations for his own presentation, limiting his influence to pianists who were impressed with his performances. His was a form of ragtime rather more elaborate than the more genteel Joplin style. Jackson also had a tremendous repertoire of popular songs which he played with imaginative natural skill. Jackson died, aged only 45, after an 8-week-long attack of hiccups, in Chicago, Apr. 21, 1921.

JAZZ Although that form of folk music called jazz flowered in the 1920s, its true beginnings belong to the late 19th, early 20th centuries. Jazz is the creation of the American Negro. It was an outlet for self-expression. The music was a blend of African, European, and personally created elements. The music, not yet called jazz, was untutored (and sounded crude to the overly sensitive ear) and improvisational. Its beginnings, lost because few whites paid attention to it, certainly occurred even before the slave jubilees in New Orleans' Place Congo in the early 19th century. After the Civil War the publication of *Slave Songs in the United States* (q.v.) brought attention to and stimulated interest in the music (spirituals) of the Negro, as did the later tour of the Fisk Jubilee Singers (q.v.). While this music was hardly jazz, it prepared the way for the Negro musician. What became known as jazz in the 1920s grew out of the music improvised by black musicians for their own pleasure; black musicians also entertained whites, as they had before the Civil War. There was a difference in the music's sound for the 2 audiences—that which the black musician played for a black audience was undoubtedly more lively, more jazzy, than that played for whites (this practice continued well into the 1930s). Instruments played a role in the evolution of jazz and at first the most basic were used: the voice, a guitar, even a fiddle (although a violin as a jazz instrument is just not right), the piano (although it could not be carried like so many other instruments associated with jazz) and the clarinet, trumpet or cornet, the saxophone. The first improvisational style of jazzy music was ragtime (q.v.), which began to get wide notice and publication toward the end of the 19th century; the blues (q.v.) came to notice just before the First World War with the publication of W. C. Handy's (q.v.) "Memphis Blues." In 1915 Ferdinand Morton (q.v.) published his arrangement of "Jelly Roll Blues." In 1918 James Reese Europe was presenting jazz concerts in Paris and was followed the next year by Will Marion Cook (q.v.) and his Southern Syncopated Orchestra. The noun "jazz" first came into general use in 1917–18, when the Dixieland Jass [*sic*] Band (q.v.) introduced to white audiences in Chicago and New York a kind of music they had learned from black musicians in New Orleans. The etymology of the word is obscure and subject to various guesses. It is claimed by some to be of West African origin and, as a verb, is just another 4-letter word pertaining to sex. In its musical context it generally meant that the music was to be played at a fast tempo, i.e., to "jazz up." Other theories trace its derivations to black musicians with such names as "Chas." (for Charles of course), or "Jas." (for James), or one Jazbo Brown. One theory is as good as another, but it was the advent of the Original Dixieland Jazz Band, as they called themselves later, that gave the noun currency and, to some extent, definition. It was the beginning of new, though not so young, American musical expression that flowered in the 1920s and had a great influence on the evolution of all American music.

JIG BAND A small orchestra, usually all black, that played for white dances, cotillions, etc. The programs consisted of lively waltzes, schottisches, and jigs (whence the name) performed in a vivacious, rhythmic style which evolved into the cakewalk (q.v.) craze of the 1890s in the United States. The term jig eventually lost its dance connotation and was absorbed into the vocabulary of the bigot.

JIG PIANO Dance music, characterized by a strong percussive bass, performed by a soloist. The term was eventually supplanted by "ragtime" (q.v.).

JOHNSON, J. ROSAMOND (1873–1954) Composer, conductor, actor. Son of a minister, Johnson was born in Jacksonville, Fla., Aug. 11, 1873. He received his musical training in Boston, at the New England Conservatory. Although trained as a "serious" musician, Johnson initially made his way in vaudeville as an entertainer. For a time, after finishing work at the Conservatory, he was supervisor of music in the public schools in Jacksonville. He then traveled in vaudeville (United States and Europe), making his New York stage debut in *Oriental America* in 1896. Johnson also began collaborating on songs with his brother, James (q.v.), and Bob Cole (q.v.) and presenting their songs in their acts. An early effort by the team (James Weldon Johnson and Cole provided the lyrics), *Toloso,* unsuccessfully made the rounds of producers in New York in 1901. Though the songs were admired, the Johnson-Cole book satirizing U.S. imperialism so soon after the Spanish-American War was regarded as too hot to handle. Eventually the book was abandoned and the songs interpolated into other musicals, including the very popular "My Castle on the Nile" (published in 1901) and "Under the Bamboo Tree" (lyrics by Cole, 1902). Johnson composed songs for the recital stage such as "Lift Every Voice and Sing" (lyrics by James W. Johnson, 1900), "Li'l Gal" (lyrics by Paul Laurence Dunbar, 1901), and "Since You Went Away" (lyrics by James W. Johnson, 1913). The 2 Johnsons and Cole formed a musical comedy collaboration out of which several popular musicals resulted, among them *In Newport* (1904), *Humpty Dumpty* (1904), *The Shoo-Fly Regiment* (1907), and *The Red Moon* (1909). The team began dissolving when James Weldon Johnson left to join the U.S. diplomatic service in 1906; Cole's death in 1909 ended the successful collaboration. In 1909 Johnson collaborated with comedian Bert Williams (q.v.) on the songs for *Mr. Lode of Kole.* Johnson moved to New York City in 1901 and was connected with the

Henry Street Settlement Music School. During the First World War he served with the 15th Infantry of the New York National Guard. He published several song collections: *The Book of American Negro Spirituals* (1925), *The Second Book of Negro Spirituals* (1926), both in collaboration with his brother James; also: *Shout Songs* (1936) and *Rolling Along in Song* (1937). He also formed the Rosamond Johnson Quintet, and he appeared in the stage productions *Porgy and Bess, Mamba's Daughters,* and *Cabin in the Sky.* Johnson was one of the first Americans of his race to adapt Negro idioms without resorting to stereotype (as did some black composers of the period); in this sense he is an important pioneer in our music. He died in New York, Nov. 11, 1954.

JOHNSON, JAMES WELDON (1871–1938) Poet, lyricist, author, actor, singer, diplomat. The brother of composer J. Rosamond Johnson (q.v.), Johnson was born in Jacksonville, Fla., June 17, 1871. Educated in Jacksonville and Atlanta University, Johnson earned a master's degree in 1904. He served briefly as principal of a black school in his hometown; he also founded and edited a newspaper, the *Daily American.* Studying law in his spare time, he was admitted to the bar in 1897. He abandoned the law for the stage when he joined his brother in New York in 1901, eventually teaming up with Bob Cole as a touring vaudeville act. Cole (q.v.) and James supplied the lyrics for Rosamond's songs. James quit vaudeville to become U.S. consul in Venezuela (1906–8) and Nicaragua (1909–12); he resigned the diplomatic service to devote himself to writing and to the black movement. In 1912 he published his book *The Autobiography of an Ex-Colored Man.* He became a field secretary of the National Association for the Advancement of Colored People in 1916; he published *Fifty*

Years and Other Poems in 1917 and was editor of the New York *Age* during this same period. His best-known work is *God's Trombones* (1927) in which he drew upon Negro folk poetry. Among his other books are *Black Manhattan* (1930), *Along This Way,* an autobiography (1933), and *Negro Americans, What Now?* (1934). His best-loved songs were those written with his brother, J. Rosamond Johnson. The literary Johnson was probably better known for his moderate but militant approach to the plight of the American Negro during the years before and after the First World War through the Depression. He was also a teacher, and was professor of creative literature at Fisk University (1930–34) and visiting professor at New York University (1934–38). Johnson died in Wiscasset, Maine, June 26, 1938.

JOPLIN, SCOTT (1868–1917) Composer, pianist. Son of an ex-slave, Joplin was born in Texarkana, Texas, Nov. 25, 1868. His father, Giles, was a violinist and his mother, Florence Givens, sang and played the guitar. Joplin's 2 brothers and sisters were also musical. Joplin revealed an early musical talent; his father was encouraged by this and acquired an old piano out of his salary as a railroad worker. Florence Joplin took in washing. Joplin was self-taught on the family piano, but his musical gift was talked about and a local teacher, of German birth, offered to teach the gifted youngster. Thus was Joplin's natural ability given a solid groundwork in the fundamentals of music; undoubtedly the teacher (whose name sadly seems lost to history) introduced him to the music of the masters. Despite this background the opportunities for a black concert pianist were slim and, what with the near-poverty level of his family, Joplin set out in his early teens to make his own way as a pianist. At the age of 14 he began playing piano in sporting houses in Mississippi, Texas, and Louisiana. He spent several years in St. Louis; in 1893 he was heard (with his own little band) at the exposition in Chicago. In his travels Joplin heard and absorbed a good deal of music and heard several "professors" in the tenderloins of various cities play jig piano (q.v.) and early ragtime (q.v.). He had also begun composing such early pieces as "A Picture of Her Face" and "Please Say You Will," both described on the sheet music as a "waltz song." They are in the Victorian mold, sentimental, conventional, well-wrought. So is Joplin's early instrumental, *The Great Crush Collision March,* a typical period piece—a descriptive work (about a train wreck) that so pleased the audiences of the time. Though not indicated in the published music, the *March* reveals intimations of the syncopations of ragtime. After a tour with his Texas Medley Quartette, Joplin decided to settle for a time in Sedalia, Mo., in 1896. It was here that the man who came to be called the "King of Ragtime" came into his own. In Sedalia, still a frontier town, but a bustling one with a large black population (who worked on the railroads, farms, and in other industries) and a celebrated "district," Joplin found an outlet for his pianistics; he also studied theory, harmony, and counterpoint at the George R. Smith College for Negroes. Out of Sedalia came his *Original Rags,* the first composition by Joplin to use the term, published in March 1899 [making it the 3rd rag published in the United States, after Krell's *Mississippi Rag* (January 1897) and Turpin's *Harlem Rag* (December 1897)]. In Sedalia, too, Joplin met music publisher John Stark (1841–1927) q.v., who recognized Joplin's gifts and published his 2nd rag, *The Maple Leaf Rag,* in September 1899. The title memorialized the club in which the 2 men met—and the piece itself became very popular and remains one of the most played of all ragtime compo-

sitions. It made both publisher Stark and composer Joplin. Stark was a unique individual: he did not dismiss ragtime as mere "whorehouse music," was astute enough to publish it and dealt honestly, via contract, with Joplin. Joplin was unique too, in that he was musically sophisticated and able to read and write music so skillfully that he could capture on paper many elusive nuances of folk music. While not the creator of ragtime, he was its most influential and creative composer. The tremendous success of *Maple Leaf Rag* encouraged Stark to move to St. Louis to expand his music publishing business in 1900 and Joplin soon followed. There he established himself in business (he owned a boardinghouse), taught music, and continued to compose. Joplin was ambitious musically and, though he continued to produce profitable rags, in 1903 saw production in St. Louis of his opera *A Guest of Honor.* Joplin also entered into an unsuccessful marriage whose dissolution deeply affected him. But he also continued to write exquisite and inventive rags, most of them published by a now prosperous John Stark: *Peacherine Rag* (1901), *Elite Syncopations* and *The Entertainer* (1902), *Palm Leaf Rag* (1903), *The Chrysanthemum—An Afro-American Intermezzo* (1904), *The Ragtime Dance* (1906, an abridged version of a ballet, with narrator, written in 1902), and dozens of others. In 1908 Joplin prepared his book on the proper performance of ragtime entitled *School of Ragtime,* which Stark published. Emboldened by success, Stark decided to move to New York in 1905. His marriage dissolved, Joplin followed in 1907. Stark remained in New York for only a few years, returning to St. Louis in 1911; Joplin, however, remained. In New York, Joplin married for the 2nd time. His wife, Lottie Stokes, managed the boardinghouse Joplin acquired, while he taught and composed such rags as

Wall Street Rag, Solace, Euphonic Sounds (all 1909). Around the time that Stark returned to St. Louis, Joplin had become preoccupied with a new serious work, *Treemonisha,* an opera; he gave up teaching to spend all of his time on it and even underwrote its publication. This was a composition beyond the reach of Stark, who turned it down, thus causing a break between the 2 friends. *Treemonisha* was published in 1911 but Joplin could not arrange for a production of it until 1915, and then it was little more than a run-through without scenery or orchestra (Joplin played the single piano for this one performance). The failure of *Treemonisha* crushed the obsessed Joplin, who had all but worn himself out in his dedication to the opera. A breakdown revealed an even more serious illness: syphilis contracted in his days as an itinerant musician. By late 1916 Joplin had to be confined to Manhattan State Hospital suffering from dementia paralytica. Though his mind failed, Joplin had occasional moments of lucidity when he continued to write bits of music. He did not know, when the United States entered the First World War, that his world had come to an end. The ragtime craze that he had contributed so much to was over; there was no longer any demand for his kind of music (it would come back even stronger in the 1970s, when the genius of Scott Joplin was rediscovered). He died in New York City on Apr. 1, 1917.

JORDAN, JOE (1882–1971) Composer, conductor, pianist, teacher, arranger. Born in Cincinnati, Ohio, Feb. 11, 1882, Jordan grew up in St. Louis and attended the Lincoln Institute in Jefferson City, Mo. He also studied music privately and learned to play several instruments, including piano, violin, and drums. He was a member of the Taborin (Brass) Band with which he traveled to Chicago in 1903. By this time Jordan had begun composing and had published early piano rag compositions. In 1904 he went to New York City and formed his own band. In 1905 he wrote and orchestrated the music for "the first public concert of syncopated music in America" performed by the Memphis Students Orchestra at Proctor's Theatre. Jordan toured with his own orchestra, appeared in vaudeville, and made arrangements of the music for several Ziegfeld shows. In 1906 he returned to Chicago to become music director of the Pekin Theatre and remained there, with some excursions, until 1913. Jordan traveled to New York now and then to appear in musicals—he was in Will Marion Cook's (q.v.) *In Bandana Land* in 1908; the next year he worked with Bob Cole (q.v.) and J. Rosamond Johnson (q.v.) on their *The Red Moon;* he collaborated with Will Marion Cook on a song, "Lovie Joe," for Fanny Brice in 1910. His "That Teasin' Rag" was the theme song of vaudeville star Ada Overton. Jordan composed the full scores for the mildly successful Broadway musicals *Deep Harlem* (1929) and *Brown Buddies* (1930). Although he wrote several fine early rags, Jordan's special affinity was with show music. He was also a wise investor in Chicago real estate. During the Depression in New York, Jordan conducted and composed the background music for the Federal Theatre Project's *Macbeth* (the Orson Welles production) and *Haiti.* During the Second World War, Jordan reached the rank of captain in the U. S. Army. He later joined the faculty of the Modern Institute of Music, Tacoma, Wash. He died in Tacoma, Sept. 11, 1971.

KELLEY, EDGAR STILLMAN (1857–1944) Composer, teacher. According to historian Rupert Hughes, Kelley was diverted from a career in painting to music after hearing "Blind Tom" Bethune (q.v.) play Liszt's transcription of Mendelssohn's *A Midsummer Night's Dream.* By this time Kelley, however, had had much music training. Born in Sparta, Wis., Apr. 14, 1857, he studied the piano with his musician mother from his 8th to 17th year. He then went to Chicago (1874–76) to study harmony, counterpoint, and piano. He completed his musical education in the traditional way, in Germany. Kelley studied at the Stuttgart Conservatory from 1876 to 1880 and, upon returning to the United States, settled in San Francisco where he taught piano, organ, and composition; he also conducted and toured with a light opera company. In addition he was a professional organist in San Francisco and Oakland. From 1893 to 1895 he was music critic for the San Francisco *Examiner.* In Hughes's *American Composers* (1900) Kelley appears in the section entitled "The Innovators," a classification obviously based on an early work, *Aladdin,* in which the composer drew upon Chinese musical devices he had heard in San Francisco's Chinatown. Composed before the turn of the century, it was finally published in 1915. Kelley's creativity flourished in the field of program music; an early symphony begun in San Francisco, but not completed until Kelley's 80th birthday celebration in 1937, was inspired by *Gulliver's Travels.* His 2 symphonic poems, *Macbeth* and *Ben Hur,* were written before 1900. In 1892 he composed the music for a comic opera, *Puritania,* which was successful in San Francisco but not in New York. Other early works are a piano suite, *The Flower Seekers,* Op. 2, and a song cycle, *The Phases of Love,* Op. 6, from which one song, "The Lady Picking Mulberries," enjoyed popularity. Kelley was active as a teacher in New York and at Yale in New Haven. From 1902 to 1910 he taught composition in Berlin, where he also composed such works as a *Piano Quintet,* Op. 20, a *String Quartet,* Op. 25, and his *New England Symphony* in which Kelley drew upon the log of the *Mayflower* for inspiration and used early hymn tunes, bird calls, and quotations from Indian music. He returned to the United States to take the post of Dean of Music at the Cincinnati Conservatory of Music which he held from 1910 until his death. Kelley's best-known work was the oratorio *The Pilgrim's Progress* (1918); among his other popular works at the time were a symphonic suite, *Alice in Wonderland* (1919), and *The Pit and the Pendulum* (1925). Two of his most popular songs, "Eldorado" and "Israfel," were set to texts by Edgar Allan Poe. Kelley died, aged 87, in New York, Nov. 12, 1944.

KERN, JEROME (1885–1945) Composer. One of the major figures in American popular song, Kern was born in New York City on Jan. 27, 1885. His father was a successful businessman and his mother a musician; it was with his mother, Fanny, that Kern began taking piano lessons. He later studied piano and harmony at the New York College of Music. (A short time spent in his father's business proved Kern was no businessman: he was sent to order 2 pianos from a piano factory and instead ordered 200.) By this time, 1902, Kern had begun writing little tunes, his first published piece, *At the Casino,* for solo piano was published that year. The next year Kern was sent to Europe by his father (possibly to keep him away from the family business), where he continued to study music (theory and harmony) in Heidelberg. He also spent some time in England becoming acquainted with the musical theatre and contributing occasional songs to London musicals. His early songs revealed Kern's gift for melody and form, unusual in popular song at the time. In 1904 he returned to the United States to make his way in Tin Pan Alley and the musical theatre. He worked as a staff pianist in a music publishing house, as a sheet music salesman in a New York department store, as an accompanist, and as an interpolater of songs into several musicals. These musicals were often of foreign origin; Kern's job was to Americanize them. In 1912 he composed the music (to lyrics by Rida Johnson Young, q.v.) for *The Red Petticoat*, his first full-scale score. A song interpolated into the score of *The Girl from Utah* (songs mostly by Paul Rubens and Sidney Jones), "They Didn't Believe Me" (lyrics by Herbert Reynolds), brought serious attention to Kern from Broadway producers in 1914—although his first hit song, "How'd You Like to Spoon with Me?" (lyrics by Edward Laska) dates from 1905, an interpolation into *The Earl and the Girl*. From 1915 to 1918 Kern established himself as an important theatre composer with a series of unpretentious musicals—small cast, small orchestra, and small theatre, The Princess. Among Kern's Princess Theatre shows were *Very Good Eddie* (1915; for which Kern, with lyricist Schuyler Greene, wrote "Babes in the Wood"), *Oh, Boy!* (1917; " 'Til the Clouds Roll By," lyrics by Kern, P. G. Wodehouse, q.v., and Guy Bolton), and *Oh, Lady! Lady!* During the same period Kern composed songs for other shows in New York and London. In 1910, on one of his English visits, Kern married Eva Leale; they had one child, a daughter, Elizabeth. By the beginning of the 1920s Kern was an established figure in the musical theatre, composer of dozens of show scores, and a great influence on a rising generation of young songwriters, among them George Gershwin (who served as a rehearsal pianist for one of Kern's musicals, *Miss 1917*) and Richard Rodgers. During the great musical outpouring during the 1920s and '30s Kern composed the scores for such shows as *The Night Boat* (1920), *Sunny* (1925), *Show Boat* (1927) (q.v.), *Sweet Adeline* (1929), *The Cat and the Fiddle*

(1931), *Music in the Air* (1932), *Roberta* (1933), and *Very Warm for May* (1939). In 1934 Kern moved to Beverly Hills, Calif., which had, through the rise of the film musical, become the musical center of the country. Several of Kern's stage musicals had been filmed (with generally unhappy results). His first original film score, *I Dream too Much* (1935), was followed by *Swing Time* (1936), *High, Wide and Handsome* (1937), *You Were Never Lovelier* (1942), *Can't Help Singing* (1944), *Cover Girl* (1944), and *Centennial Summer* (1946). From these films came a great number of distinguished songs with lyrics by such lyricists as Dorothy Fields, Oscar Hammerstein II, Johnny Mercer, E. Y. Harburg, Ira Gershwin, and Leo Robin. Despite a solid musical background Kern did not attempt to compose in the larger forms; he did arrange a *Scenario for Orchestra* on themes from *Show Boat* and a *Mark Twain Suite*. Never really contented in Hollywood, Kern returned to New York to work on a new Broadway musical late in 1945. Before he could begin, Kern suffered a cerebral hemorrhage and died on Nov. 11, 1945, at the age of 60. The show he was to have written was then set to words and music by his good friend Irving Berlin (q.v.) and was produced as *Annie Get Your Gun*. Kern and Berlin were undoubtedly the 2 most important influences on the development of American popular song in this century. Among Kern's most distinguished melodies are: "The Siren's Song," "Good Night Boat," "Look for the Silver Lining," "Who?" "Make Believe," "Ol' Man River," "Why Do I Love You?" "Bill," "Why Was I Born?" "Don't Ever Leave Me," "The Night Was Made for Love," "Smoke Gets in Your Eyes," "In the Heart of the Dark," "All in Fun," "All the Things You Are," "The Way You Look Tonight," "Can I Forget You?" "The Last Time I Saw Paris," "You Were Never

Lovelier," "More and More," "Long Ago and Far Away," and many, many others.

LAMB, JOSEPH F. (1887–1960) Composer, pianist. Regarded by ragtime historian-enthusiasts as the 3rd in the Ragtime Triumvirate (along with Joplin and James Scott), Lamb is unique in that he was white. He was born in Montclair, N.J., Dec. 6, 1887. Lamb was not trained in music, although 2 of his sisters were. His mother hoped he would enter the priesthood, but Lamb had electrical engineering in mind. At 14 he entered a Canadian college. He eventually dropped out and found a job in a New York fabric house (a job he held for the rest of his life). A self-taught pianist, Lamb was greatly attracted to ragtime music as a youngster, particularly the compositions of Scott Joplin (q.v.). Lamb dropped in regularly at the New York offices of Joplin's publisher, Stark Music Co., to pick up the latest rags. He had, ever since his interrupted college days, been composing songs and waltzes; his *Celestine Waltzes* was published by the Harry H. Sparks Co., Toronto. A meeting with Joplin in the Stark office led to the publication of Lamb's first rag, *Sensation.* To assure publication Joplin had the legend, "Arranged by Scott Joplin," printed on the sheet music cover. From 1908 to 1919, when the ragtime craze petered out, Lamb published 12 rags under the Stark aegis (an even greater number of rags remained unpublished). Since Lamb was not a public performer, nor a recording pianist, he remained relatively unknown although his works sold well and were recorded by others on piano rolls. Though influenced by Joplin, Lamb had a distinct style of his own, characterized by ragtime scholar Rudi Blesh as having a "poignant lyricism, [a] wayward serpentine *art nouveau* melodic line [and a] rich, brooding harmony." After Lamb's rediscovery in 1949 by Blesh and the late Harriet Janis (while researching their classic, *They All Played Ragtime*), the composer, who had continued to work in a fabric house and lived quietly with his family in Brooklyn, began composing again and brought out his many unpublished pieces. Among the lovely Lamb rags are *American Beauty Rag* (1913), *The Ragtime Nightingale* (1915), *Top Liner Rag* (1916), *Bohemia Rag* (1919), *Alaskan Rag* (1959), and several published after his death, *Hot Cinders, Blue Grass Rag, Ragtime Bobolink,* and *Arctic Sunset.* Lamb died in his Brooklyn home on Sept. 30, 1960, at the age of 72.

LANG, MARGARET RUTHVEN (1867–1972) Composer. Daughter of distinguished teacher-musician Benjamin J. Lang (1837–1909), Margaret R. Lang was born in Boston, Nov. 27, 1867. A contemporary of Amy Beach, she studied first with her father and later with MacDowell (q.v.) and Chadwick (q.v.); in Munich with Victor Gluth (1852–1917). Her subjects were piano, violin, voice, orchestration, and composition. Most of her output consists of songs, although some early orchestra overtures, *Witichis* and *Dramatic* (both 1893), were performed by the Theodore Thomas and Boston Symphony orchestras. She also composed a few piano pieces, among them a *Revery* and a *Spring Idyl,* Op. 33 (both before 1900). Her *The Jumblies* (to a text by Edward Lear) was set for male chorus with 2-piano accompaniment. Other works for voice and orchestra are *Sappho's Prayer to Aphrodite* (1895) and *Armida* (1896); an orchestral *Ballade* dates from 1901. Lang composed hundreds of songs and frequently performed them herself at meetings of music clubs, etc. A carol for mixed voices, *In Praesepio,* was frequently performed in her long lifetime. She died in Boston, May 29, 1972.

LANIER, SIDNEY (1842–1881) Poet, composer, flutist. Born in Macon, Ga., Feb. 3, 1842, Lanier revealed an early gift for music. As a child he taught himself to play several instruments, among them the violin and the flute. Although he was not discouraged in this pastime, it was expected that eventually Lanier would join his father's law firm. Lanier was 18 when he was graduated from Oglethorpe College and, instead of going to Europe to study music as he had hoped, he enlisted in the Confederate Army a year later, in 1861. He was captured in 1864 and imprisoned for several months. In prison he entertained fellow inmates with his flute; he was also stricken with a fever. Released from this prison at Point Lookout, Md., Lanier returned to Macon, after walking painfully through the Carolinas, in March 1865. He immediately fell ill and remained so for 2 months. Although his father hoped to have him join his law practice, Lanier expressed a wish to devote his life to poetry and music. He worked at odd jobs and traveled in search of a climate that might be kinder to his health. He married in 1867. In 1873, explaining to his father that he could not settle down to become a "third-rate struggling lawyer," Lanier moved his family to Baltimore. Around this time Lanier was obviously suffering from tuberculosis (a trip to San Antonio, Tex., led to some improvement; while there Lanier composed his *Fieldlarks and Blackbirds* for solo flute). A return to Baltimore resulted in Lanier's appointment as first flutist of the Peabody Symphony Orchestra. In 1879 he was named lecturer in English literature at Johns Hopkins University. Simultaneously producing poems and musical compositions, Lanier frequently wrote poetry on the subject of music, e.g., *The Symphony, To Wagner,* and *To Beethoven* (all completed in 1877). His theoretical volume, explaining his conception of the relationship between poetry and music, *The Science of English Verse,* was published in 1880; another book, *Music and Poetry,* was published posthumously. Lanier produced very little music, a handful of songs and pieces for his own instrument, the flute, among them, *Swamp Robin, Danse des Moucherons* for flute and piano (both 1873), and *Longing* and *Wind-song* (both 1874). Despite debilitating tuberculosis, Lanier continued to write, teach, and compose, observing that "Pretty much the whole of my life has been merely not dying." This occurred, at the age of 39, in Lynn, N.C., on Sept. 7, 1881.

LOEFFLER, CHARLES MARTIN (1861–1935) Composer, violinist. When he arrived in the United States in 1881, aged 20, Loeffler was fully formed musically and could only be claimed as an "American composer" because he lived the rest of his life in the United States and composed the bulk of his music as a resident. He was born in Alsace (when it was then in French possession) on Jan. 30, 1861, of French-German parentage. His father was an agriculturist-scientist so that young Loeffler's early life was cosmopolitan, as his father's work took the family to Russia, Hungary, and Switzerland. Loeffler began to study the violin when he was about 8 and living in Kiev. Because he evidenced a talent for the violin he later studied with Joseph Joachim (1831–1907), Lambert Joseph Massart (1811–92), and composition with Ernest Guiraud (1837–92). Loeffler found work in private orchestras of European noblemen and with string groups before deciding to come to the United States. He joined the Damrosch Orchestra in New York City and then, in 1883, was hired to play in the first violin section of the Boston Symphony—a post he held for 20 years until his resignation in

1903. Although Loeffler had composed a number of works which were performed, if not necessarily published, he left the Boston Symphony to devote himself to composition and to teaching the violin to a select number of students. Loeffler's work at the time was described as "modernistic" and even "decadent" in the sense that it was so finely wrought that too much time was devoted to details rather than content. In sound, today, Loeffler's music reveals touches of French Impressionism (he very rarely drew upon Americanisms) and an interest in Medieval music. He found inspiration in the poems of Maeterlinck, Baudelaire, and Verlaine which for many solidified the decadent label. Loeffler was indifferent to labels and remained out of the mainstream of American music, creating a music of his own; he left no disciples. His best-known composition is *A Pagan Poem*, Op. 14, for orchestra, piano, and English horn, originally composed in 1901 and revised for a Boston Symphony performance in 1907. Other works: a *Suite for Violin and Orchestra* (1891), *Divertimento for Violin and Orchestra* (1895), poem for orchestra, "La Bonne Chanson" (1901), *Four Melodies for Voice and Piano*, Op. 10 (1903), *Four Poems for Voice and Piano*, Op. 15 (1906), *Hora Mystica* for orchestra and male voices (1916), *Music for Four Stringed Instruments* (1917), *Memories of My Childhood—Life in a Russian Village* (1923), *The Canticle of the Sun*, for voice and chamber orchestra (1925), *Clowns, Intermezzo for Orchestra* (written for the Leo Reisman dance band, 1928), *Evocation* for chorus, orchestra, and speaker (1930), and a *Partita for Flute, Violin and Piano*—one of Loeffler's last works, commissioned by Elizabeth Sprague Coolidge. In its third movement there are allusions to "jazz" and the "blues." When Loeffler retired from the Boston Symphony, he moved to a farm at nearby Medfield; he died there in his 74th year, on May 19, 1935.

MACDOWELL, EDWARD (1860–1908) Composer, pianist, teacher. During his short lifetime MacDowell enjoyed extraordinary fame, even in Europe, and heard himself called "the greatest musical genius America has produced." He was certainly the most appreciated American composer of the late 19th century. MacDowell was born into a comfortable mercantile family in New York City, Dec. 18, 1860. He was the sole member of the family who showed an interest in music and began taking informal piano lessons from a family friend when he was 8. He continued to study at home until he was 16, systematically with Paul Desvernine, and on occasion with concert pianist Teresa Carreño (1853–1917), onetime student of Gottschalk (q.v.). In April 1876, accompanied by his mother, MacDowell went to France to study at the Paris Conservatoire. Unhappy with the French method of teaching and with French musical mannerisms (one of his fellow students was a young Achille—as he was known then—Debussy), the MacDowells moved on to Wiesbaden in 1878 for study with Ludwig Ehlert (1825–1884). The next year MacDowell moved on again, this time to the Hoch Conservatory in Frankfurt, where he found congenial teachers in Carl Heymann (1854–1922), with whom he studied piano, and Joachim Raff (1822–1882), composition. In the beginning MacDowell had hoped to train as a concert pianist, but it was Raff who convinced him that composition was his forte. That same year, Mrs. MacDowell, certain that her by then 18-year-old son had found himself musically in Germany, left him in the hands of Heymann and Raff and returned to the United States. MacDowell was to remain in Germany for 12 years (with one exception: when he returned to the United States to marry one of his ex-students, Marian Nevins, in 1884), from 1876 to 1888. During his long stay in Germany MacDowell taught piano and, in 1881, headed the piano department at the Darmstadt Conservatory; he also composed several of his major works, including the 2 piano concertos, suites, and piano pieces. One of MacDowell's admirers was Franz Liszt, who arranged for the publication (in Germany) of some of MacDowell's compositions, including the *First Modern Suite,* Op. 10, for piano and *Piano Concerto No. 1.* The MacDowells lived for a time in Wiesbaden, where the composer continued to teach, and then in 1888 returned to the United States and settled in Boston. By this time both his good European friends Raff and Liszt were dead, which may have contributed to MacDowell's decision to move to Boston. There he continued to compose, teach, and make concert appearances. He was piano soloist when his *Piano Concerto No. 2* was performed for the first time in New York on Mar. 5, 1889, with the Theodore Thomas Orchestra. During his Boston period MacDowell gained a reputation as a virtuoso pianist, a role he cared little for. In 1896, when he was approached by Columbia University to become head of the newly formed Music Department, MacDowell accepted and moved to New York. The composer began his work at Columbia in September of that year; around the same time the MacDowells acquired a small farm at Peterborough, N.H., which served as a summer retreat. MacDowell did not fit into the academic world and had very individual ideas about teaching and the makeup of a Fine Arts department. (His lectures were collected posthumously; entitled *Critical and Historical Essays,* they were published in 1911.) During a period when MacDowell was on sabbatical—much of which was spent as a

piano soloist in the United States and abroad—the newly appointed president of Columbia, Nicholas Murray Butler, reorganized the Department of Fine Arts. Soon after he returned from his sabbatical in October 1903, MacDowell resigned from his post at Columbia. A period of public recrimination ensued; Butler gave as the reason for MacDowell's resignation the wish to devote more time to composition. MacDowell publicly denied this; he even made it known that Columbia's Division of Fine Arts was little more than "a co-educational department store" dedicated to "materialism rather than idealism." The trustees of Columbia replied in kind. In 1904, the year he was elected to the American Academy of Arts and Letters, MacDowell officially cut all ties with Columbia University (which continues to have an Edward MacDowell Chair of Music, despite the break). During this unpleasant time MacDowell was also hit by a cab and injured; whether this or the disagreement with Butler led to his mental breakdown in the spring of 1905 is debatable. (Butler is generally, and rather romantically, painted as the villain.) After leaving the university, MacDowell continued to compose and accepted a few private piano students, but early in 1905 he showed signs of exhaustion and suffered from insomnia; even a summer at Peterborough did little good. The medical opinion of the time diagnosed his illness as "cerebral collapse." Whatever the precise medical name for his illness, MacDowell spent the final 2 years of his life in a state of near vegetation; he died in his hotel, tended by his remarkable wife, in New York on Jan. 23, 1908. He was only 48. (Marian MacDowell lived to be 99—she died in 1956—and devoted the rest of her long life to perpetuating the memory and music of her husband. She lectured on, and performed, MacDowell's piano pieces and founded the MacDowell Colony of the Edward MacDowell Association at Peterborough, N.H., which continues to serve as a retreat for composers, painters, writers, poets, sculptors, etc., where they may work in pleasant surroundings.) MacDowell's works have suffered a rather bad press in recent years, perhaps, in part, as a reaction to the lionization he received during his lifetime. His work is a product of his time—romantic, at times sentimental, created to evoke pictures or moods rather than to explore form. MacDowell, for example, composed no symphony; his piano sonatas have descriptive titles. Nor did MacDowell profess to be an "American" composer; he preferred no performances to being heard merely because he was an "American" composer. He has frequently been dismissed as a "miniaturist" and is best known for his small piano pieces, such as "To a Wild Rose" from the *Woodland Sketches,* Op. 51 (1896). His solo piano output comprises most of MacDowell's work, beginning with his Op. 1, *Amourette* (1896, published under the pseudonym of Edgar Thorn), and ending with the *New England Idyls,* Op. 62 (1902). The 4 piano sonatas span a period from 1893, the year of the *Sonata Tragica,* to 1901, when the *Keltic* Sonata was completed and dedicated to Norwegian composer Edvard Gricg. The piano concertos were relatively early works (the 2nd, Op. 23, 1890, is an obvious nod to Grieg) and reveal MacDowell as a skillful orchestrator. Besides these 2 works, he composed 6 more for orchestra alone, beginning with *Hamlet and Ophelia,* Op. 22 (1885); in 1897 MacDowell took a rare excursion into self-conscious Americana in his *Second Suite,* Op. 48, subtitled the "Indian Suite." MacDowell borrowed Indian themes as a starting point and made no attempt at re-creating the real thing. The *Second Suite* is a work of much substance and the section entitled "Dirge" is especially fine. MacDowell produced

more than 40 songs (providing the words for many), many of which deserve continued hearing. Several songs for various combination of voices round out MacDowell's vocal compositions.

MARSHALL, ARTHUR OWEN (1881–1956) Pianist, composer. A protégé of Scott Joplin (q.v.), Marshall was born on a farm in Saline County, Mo., on Nov. 20, 1881. About 1885 the family moved to Sedalia, Mo., where Marshall attended school. He undoubtedly had piano lessons as a boy. When Joplin came to Sedalia in 1896, he lived for several months in the Marshall home and was an obvious influence on the young Marshall. Four years later, when Marshall was 19, his *Swipsey Cakewalk* was published, with Joplin's name on the cover as co-composer (the trio section was composed by Joplin; his name on the cover could only have been helpful to sales). Marshall, with Joplin's help, played the piano in the Maple Leaf Club and other centers of entertainment. Marshall made the tour of the "parlors" and clubs as a pianist in Chicago and St. Louis. The death of his 2nd wife, Julia Jackson, affected him deeply and, after recovering from an illness, he moved to Kansas City in 1917. Because of a spasm of his left hand, Marshall retired from his career as a pianist. He composed only a handful of rags; his best-known, besides his first Joplin collaboration, is *Kinklets* (1906). The next year he collaborated again with Joplin, producing their *The Lily Queen.* Other Marshall compositions: *Ham and* (1908), *The Peach* (1908), and *The Pippin Rag* (1908). Three additional rags were copyrighted by Marshall in 1950: *Silver Arrow, National Prize,* and *Missouri Romp.* Marshall died in Kansas City, Mo., 1956.

MASON, DANIEL GREGORY (1873–1953) Composer, teacher, author, lecturer. Born in Brookline, Mass., on Nov. 20, 1873, Mason was predestined for a career in music. His grandfather, Lowell (1792–1872) (q.v.), had been a great musical power in Boston; his father, Henry (1831–1890), was the Mason of the Mason and Hamlin Piano Co., and his uncle, William (1829–1908) (q.v.), was a noted pianist and teacher. Daniel Gregory Mason started playing the piano and composing at the age of 7. At Harvard he studied music with John Knowles Paine (q.v.) but found Paine unsatisfactory as a teacher; after graduation from Harvard in 1895 he took up music again with Chadwick (q.v.) in Boston and Percy Goetschius (q.v.) and Arthur Whiting (q.v.) in New York. Mason's Opus 1, *Birthday Waltzes* for piano solo, dates from around this time (1894). His first book (of more than 15), *From Grieg to Brahms*, was published in 1902. Because he suffered from lameness in one arm Mason was unable to perform and earned a living lecturing and writing. In 1909 he became a member of the musical faculty of Columbia University, where he remained until 1942 (in 1929 he was appointed MacDowell professor). Throughout this period Mason continued to compose, lecture, and write. In 1913 Mason spent the summer in France studying with Vincent d'Indy (1851–1931). Mason was most prolific in the field of chamber music; his *Sonata for Violin and Piano,* Op. 5, dates from 1913. In 1918 he composed a *Quartet on Negro Themes,* Op. 19. Opus 40, *Variations on a Quiet Theme* for string quartet, was completed in 1939. Mason heard his works frequently performed by the more important orchestras of his time; his music was also broadcast. A few of his orchestral pieces were widely performed, especially his Festival Overture, *Chanticleer,* Op. 27 (1926); "A Lincoln Symphony," his 3rd symphony, completed in 1936, was popular for a time. A musical conservative, Mason was probably more influential as a writer of prose and a proponent of the balanced, "classical" approach to music-making than as a composer. Among his books of interest are *The Dilemma of American Music* (1928), *Tune In, America* (1931), and the autobiographical *Music in My Time, and Other Reminiscences* (1938). After his retirement from Columbia, he moved to Greenwich, Conn., where he died on Dec. 4, 1953.

MASON, WILLIAM (1829–1908) Pianist, teacher. Son of the great Boston musical arbiter-pedagogue, Lowell Mason (q.v.), Mason was born in Boston, Jan. 24, 1829. A career in music being inevitable, he began to study piano as a boy in Boston; he was 17 when he gave his first piano recital there. In 1849, when he was 20, Mason went to Europe to complete his studies. He remained for 6 years and studied with Moritz Hauptmann (1792–1868) and Ignaz Moscheles (1794–1870) in Leipzig, and with Alexander Dreyschock (1818–1869) and with Franz Liszt (1811–1886) in Weimar. During his European stay, Mason gave piano recitals in Weimar, Prague, Frankfurt, and London. He apparently made a great impression on Liszt; one of Mason's piano pieces, *Les Perles de Rosée,* is dedicated to Liszt. Upon his return to the United States in 1854, Mason set off on a cross-country tour, going as far west as Chicago; the unique feature of Mason's tour was that it consisted only of his solo piano recitals (in the smaller towns in those days, a "serious" pianist would be but one item in an evening of culture). After the tour, Mason settled in New York, where he became an important personage in the musical life of the city. He was one of the founders of the Mason and (Theodore) Thomas Soirees of Chamber Music; he taught (and was recognized as one of the finest piano teachers in the country) and, to a lesser extent, composed. Mason produced about 40 pieces for the piano, many obviously designed to display a well-developed technique so popular in the age of musical romanticism—and they are quite attractive. One little composition, *Silver Spring*, Op. 6, named after his father's home, was very popular; Liszt was known to have admired and performed *Amitié pour Amitié*, Op. 4. Mason was the author of the influential *A System for Beginners* (1871) and *Pianoforte Technics* (1878); his autobiography, *Memories of a Musical Life*, was published in 1901. He died in New York City, July 14, 1908.

MATTHEWS, ARTIE (1888–1959) Composer, pianist, teacher. Born in Minonk, Ill., Nov. 15, 1888, Matthews spent most of his boyhood in Springfield, where he received a conventional— as opposed to a ragtime-jazz—musical training. According to his own account, Matthews was not exposed to the music of Scott Joplin (q.v.) until 1904, when as a 16-year-old pianist he visited the St. Louis Exposition and heard some of the best ragtime pianists of the day. Returning to Springfield, he explored the intricacies of syncopation. He eventually returned to St. Louis, where he worked for John Stark (q.v.) transcribing compositions for ragtime composers who could not notate the music and writing songs for the variety shows presented at the Booker T. Washington Theatre. As early as 1912, Matthews transcribed and arranged "Baby Seals Blues" (Seals was a vaudeville personality at the time on the all-black Theatre Owner's Booking Association, known as TOBA); this blues was published even before Handy's "Memphis Blues" (q.v.). Many of Matthews' songs have been lost though about 9 have survived because they were published; the earliest is "Give Me, Dear, Just One More Chance" (1908 and the latest, "Everything He Does Just Pleases Me" (1916). In 1915, because Stark wanted a blues to compete with

Handy's popular "St. Louis Blues" of the year before, he encouraged his writers to produce such a selection. Matthews produced "Weary Blues," which became a popular and long-lasting jazz band standard. While still with Stark, Matthews composed a suite of *Pastime Rags* (numbered 1 through 5, although 8 supposedly were projected). These are among the most remarkable of all ragtime compositions in the tradition of Joplin: graceful, beautifully formed, inventive—and yet completely original. *Pastime Rag No. 4* is an extraordinary composition and, although composed in 1913, was not published until 1920, after the ragtime craze had ended. After completing his *Pastime Rags*, Matthews decided to get out of the popular music business and St. Louis and he moved to Chicago, where he worked as the organist at the Berea Presbyterian Church. In 1918 he moved to Cincinnati, Ohio, and established the Cosmopolitan Conservatory of Music. In the Conservatory Matthews taught theory (his ragtime days were over); the school prospered until Matthews' death. Before founding the conservatory devoted to teaching the classics and the classic approach, Matthews took courses at the Cincinnati College of Music and at Columbia University in New York. The rest of his life was spent in running the school, arranging and serving as secretary of the (no longer existent) black branch of the Cincinnati American Federation of Musicians. Matthews died in Cincinnati, Oct. 25, 1959.

"THE MEMPHIS BLUES" Composition by W. C. Handy (q.v.) originally entitled *Mr. Crump*, an instrumental written for the 1909 political campaign of Edward H. "Boss" Crump. The popularity of the tune led to its publication in 1912 as "The Memphis Blues"; eventually lyrics were added by George A. Norton. Although "The Memphis Blues" was not the first to use the word "blues" in the title, it was the first to achieve widespread popularity, which led to a proliferation of similar folklike songs. Handy undoubtedly based his blues on authentic folk blues he heard during his travels. It was, indeed, the first of his now classic blues, but not, as he believed, the first published blues. For the record: "Baby Seals Blues," by Baby F. Seals, "Arr. by Artie Matthews" (q.v.), was published in St. Louis on Aug. 3, 1912; "Dallas Blues," music by Hart A. Wand, words by Lloyd Garrett, was published in Oklahoma City, Sept. 6, 1912. "The Memphis Blues" was published in Memphis, Sept. 28, 1912. Who got there first with the word, at this date, seems overwhelmingly unimportant—especially if Handy's total contribution to the evolution of the folk-popular blues form is considered.

MILLS, KERRY (1869–1948) Composer, violinist, publisher. Frederick Allen "Kerry" Mills was born in Philadelphia, Feb. 1, 1869. He studied the violin; he proved proficient enough to head the violin department at the University of Michigan's School of Music in Ann Arbor (1892–93). Mills also taught privately during his Ann Arbor residence. Tired of the academic life, Mills left Ann Arbor for New York, where he went into the music business as F. A. Mills—and signed his songs Kerry Mills. His arrival in New York coincided with the beginning of the ragtime craze and his first published song was "Rastus on Parade" (1895), a syncopated piece in the cakewalk genre. In 1897 Mills composed another cakewalk rag, "At a Georgia Camp Meeting," which he claimed was written in protest against the racist "coon" songs of the period. Mills did not specialize in creating a white man's version (though excellent) of Negro songs and dances; in recognition of the great event of the year, the St. Louis Exposi-

tion (1904), he wrote the music to the words of Andrew B. Sterling (1874–1955), the classic "Meet Me in St. Louis, Louis." Mills turned to the Indian for the inspiration of his popular "Red Wing" (1907), described on the sheet music as "An Indian Intermezzo." The words were by Thurland Chattaway (1872–1947). Mills returned to his early inspiration and published *Kerry Mills Cake Walk* in 1915. He produced little after that. Mills contributed some songs, notably "Love Is the Theme of My Dream," to the Broadway musical, *The Fascinating Widow* (1911). He spent his final years in retirement in Hawthorn, Calif., where he died Dec. 5, 1948.

"MISSISSIPPI RAG" The first published rag, written by white bandleader-pianist William H. Krell. *Mississippi Rag* was printed by the S. Brainard's Sons company in Chicago, January 1897. The sheet music cover announces that the piece was the "First Rag-Time Two Step Ever Written and First Played by Krell's Orchestra, Chicago." Little else is known about Krell although the same cover identifies him as the composer of *The Cakewalk Patrol, Arbutus Waltz,* and *Strolling on the Beach Waltz.* The first ragtime piece composed by a Negro was published in December 1897: Tom Turpin's (1873–1922) *Harlem Rag,* issued by Robert De Yong & Co., St. Louis. But, of course, the real flowering of ragtime began in 1899 with the publication of 2 rags by Scott Joplin (q.v.).

MORTON, FERDINAND "JELLY ROLL" (1885–1941) Composer, pianist, arranger, bandleader. One of the most colorful figures in American music, Jelly Roll (as he preferred being called) Morton was born in New Orleans, Sept. 20, 1885. Morton claimed French ancestry and was actually born Ferdinand Joseph La Menthe. His father, a Creole, was F. P. La Menthe, a contractor who left his wife, who then married a man named Morton (Jelly Roll Morton claimed he had invented the name for "business reasons"). Morton also provided biographers with several birthdates —1885, 1886, 1890—and claimed to have "invented jazz" in "the year 1902"! Indubitably, Morton studied music as a youngster; he began on the guitar at around the age of 7. At 10 he switched to the piano, of which he quickly revealed himself to be a master. On the subject of education, Morton was also vague (members of his family were uncertain as to whether he dropped out of school in the 4th or 8th grades), but he did claim he took lessons in music theory at St. Joseph's University and further studies with a "Professor Nickerson" (or Nicholson). As a youngster growing up in New Orleans, Morton would have heard examples of early jazz and, in New Orleans' famed red-light district, Storyville, the sounds of the "Professors" playing the pianos in the parlors. When he was about 16 or 17, in 1902, when he "invented jazz," Morton himself went to work in Storyville. Because he was playing "cheap music" in the District, Morton was drummed out of the family by his grandmother, who informed him that a "musician is nothing but a bum and a scalawag" and ordered him to leave (Morton's mother had died when he was about 14 and he was taken in by relatives). Jelly Roll (the nickname has nothing to do with the art of baking; it has a sexual connotation) soon became one of the best-known Professors in Storyville (named, incidentally, for Sidney Story, a New Orleans alderman, who established and demarcated a legal prostitution district in 1896; he thus achieved a kind of immortality). Morton also proved to be a sharp pool player, was noted for his splendid dress, his sharp tongue, and a decided way with the ladies. Restless and a loner, Morton left New Orleans (ca. 1907) and moved around playing his piano and

taking "suckers" in pool games. He toured several Southern states and went as far afield as Chicago, New York, and Los Angeles, where he remained from 1917 to 1922. Morton returned to Chicago at a time when the Jazz Age (q.v.) dawned and formed his own band, the Red Hot Peppers; around the same time he began recording solo piano renditions of his own works. Fame and fortune smiled upon Morton during this period and, besides his music, he was known for his expensive clothes, a gold front tooth into which a diamond was set and, later, a very large banknote (generally reported as a thousand-dollar bill) which he flashed in good times and bad as verification of his place in life. By the 1930s, and the waning of the Jazz Age with the advent of swing (he claimed he had "originated" that too), Morton found little work and eventually surfaced in Washington, D.C., where he managed and was part owner of a nightclub, The Jungle, in 1937. A small musical storm occurred when the outspoken Morton, in announcing his creation of both "blues and jazz" via the Ripley "Believe It or Not" radio show, managed to make several unkind remarks about the venerable W. C. Handy (q.v.), whom he accused of publishing folk music and claiming it as his own. He added also that Handy was incapable of playing jazz. An acrimonious debate ensued in the letter columns of the musical publication Downbeat. The flurry led to his being asked by Alan Lomax of the Library of Congress to record his recollections which, in turn, resulted in no less than 12 albums of biography, folklore, reminiscences, lies, fabrications, inventions, and keyboard ramblings of remarkable value. This led to a brief revival of Morton's recording career in New York City in 1939. Aging (though only in his early fifties), recovering from a knife wound from his Washington stint, and generally ill, Morton decided to return to California after his final record sessions. In November 1940 he formed a unique caravan for the California trip: he drove his ancient Lincoln (from better days) and towed his superannuated Cadillac. After an epic, miserable trip Morton eventually ended up in Los Angeles, in search of a kind climate, for he was ill. His last letters to his 2nd wife, Mabel, tell of his lack of money, work, and of deteriorating health. Morton's best-known compositions (some, in fact, arrangements or adaptations of works of others) are: "King Porter Stomp," "Wolverine Blues," "The Pearls," "I Thought I Heard Buddy Bolden Say," "Winin' Boy Blues," "The Naked Dance," and "Milenberg Joys." Morton's earliest known original composition, *The Jelly Roll Blues,* dates from around 1905 and was not published until 1915. Fortunately Morton recorded the bulk of his own compositions, many of which he also arranged for his various orchestras. He died of asthma and heart failure in Los Angeles Hospital, July 10, 1941.

THE MUSICAL QUARTERLY A publication devoted to generally scholarly, musicological articles on music and musicians. Founded in 1915, the first issue was published in January of that year. Sponsored by the G. Schirmer publishing house, *The Musical Quarterly* was edited by musicologist and historian O. G. Sonneck; he was succeeded after his death by Carl Engel, who was followed by Paul Henry Lang, who was succeeded by Joan Peyser. *The Musical Quarterly* has published a variety of articles and has even devoted entire issues to American music (i.e., the January 1932 issue) and regularly published a book list encompassing publications in English and other languages. Recordings, too, are reviewed from time to time. *The Musical Quarterly* is issued in January, April, July, and October in New York City.

NEVIN, ARTHUR (1871–1943) Composer, conductor, teacher, lecturer. Younger brother of famed songwriter Ethelbert (q.v.), Arthur Nevin was born in Edgeworth, Pa., Apr. 27, 1871. Nevin expressed no interest in music until he was 18, after which he studied at the New England Conservatory (1891–93): voice, piano, and theory. Four years in Europe put the customary Germanic polish to his art (one of his composition teachers was Engelbert Humperdinck, 1854–1921). In 1897 he returned to the United States to teach and to write. Sometime in 1903 he became interested in the music of the American Indian and spent about a year among the Blackfoot Indians in Montana. Drawing on this material, Nevin began to lecture on Indian culture and music—the first was given in the White House, in 1907, at the invitation of President Theodore Roosevelt. Nevin's first opera, *Poia,* was based on his Indian studies and was first performed at the Royal Opera, Berlin, Apr. 23, 1910 (the first American opera performed there). Nevin was appointed Professor of Music at the University of Kansas (1915–20) and later was director of municipal music in Memphis, Tenn. During World War I he served as music director at Camp Grant, Ill. Nevin's compositions are few and little known; among his earliest works are the 4 piano pieces entitled *May Sketches,* a piano trio, and some songs, "Were I a Tone" and "In Dreams." Nevin followed *Poia* with another opera, *Twilight* (1911), which went unproduced by the Metropolitan Opera because of a misunderstanding; in 1918 it was done in Chicago retitled *A Daughter of the Forest.* Among Nevin's other works: *Lorna Doone Suite,* for orchestra (1897), *Miniature Suite,* for orchestra (1902), *Springs of Saratoga,* for orchestra (1911), *String Quartet* (1919), *Symphonic Poem* (1930), *Arizona* (1935);

also *Southern Sketches* for solo piano and a rhapsody and a concerto for piano. Nevin died in Sewickley, Pa., July 10, 1943.

NEVIN, ETHELBERT (1862–1901) Composer, pianist, teacher. Born in Edgeworth, Pa., Nov. 25, 1862, Nevin revealed his musical precocity at 5 by improvising on his mother's piano (itself famous for being the first grand piano to cross the Allegheny Mountains). Nevin's father, a poet, writer, and musician (his income was derived from writing for magazines and newspapers), encouraged his son's boyish musical interests (Nevin began piano lessons at 8), even underwrote further study at the Williams Conservatory in Pittsburgh and, during a year the family spent in Europe, more piano lessons with Franz Bohme (1827–1898) in Dresden. Nevin proved to be a hapless student in his more conventional studies and dropped out of Western University, Pittsburgh, after only a year. He then spent several unhappy months in the Pittsburgh office of the Pennsylvania Railroad (his father's idea). Nevin finally confronted his father and convinced him that he wished to devote himself to music, not commerce. In the winter of 1880 he concentrated on piano practice and began studying counterpoint with a Dr. Austin Pearce in New York City—by mail. He plunged into intensive study the next year when he went to Boston to study with Benjamin J. Lang (1837–1909) and Stephen A. Emery (1841–1891), piano and harmony, respectively. He followed this with a trip to Berlin in 1884 to study with Karl Klindworth (1830–1916), a pupil of Liszt, and graduated from the Klindworth School with highest honors. He also studied theory with Carl Bial, who convinced Nevin that he should do more composing. Upon his return to Pittsburgh, in 1886, he made his official

debut there as a pianist in December and was highly praised; on the program he included one of his own compositions, a theme and variations for piano. In January he moved to Boston, which he regarded as a livelier music center than Pittsburgh. Nevin settled in and earned a living as a piano teacher and composed songs and miniatures for the piano. In 1891 a suite of piano pieces entitled *Water Scenes,* Op. 13, was published; one, "Narcissus," became extremely popular and haunted Nevin for the rest of his brief life. Another suite, *A Day in Venice,* Op. 25, was inspired by a visit to Europe (1891–97), a trip that also resulted in *In Arcady* and *May in Tuscany,* all attractive little piano compositions. Meanwhile Nevin composed dozens of songs (his Op. 2 was entitled *Sketch Book,* appeared in 1888, and contained his famous "Oh That We Two Were Maying!"). In the autumn of 1897 Nevin returned to New York and the next year, inspired by a poem by Robert C. Rogers, composed one of his most popular songs, "The Rosary." Never a robust man, Nevin suffered from poor health during much of the last years of his life; he became exhausted easily and had frequent nervous breakdowns. He contended with these problems by taking what was euphemistically called "stimulants" in the late 19th century. Despite health and financial problems, Nevin married a Pittsburgh sweetheart, Anne Paul; they had 2 children. After a year of recuperation from a breakdown at the family farm in Pennsylvania, Nevin and his family moved to New Haven, Conn., in 1900. There he composed another favorite song, "Mighty Lak' a Rose" (lyrics by Frank L. Stanton) and, fittingly, "To Anne" and "At Rest"—all in what was to be the final year of his life. In his diary Nevin once wrote, "I have a horror of being 'a successful drawing-room songwriter' with nothing to back it up." Despite this, Nevin never attempted (or did not have the need, energy, or technical equipment) to compose in the larger forms. The greater portion of his output is in the song genre. Nevin died suddenly of "a stroke of apoplexy" in New Haven, Feb. 17, 1901, after one day's illness.

OLDBERG, ARNE (1874–1962) Composer, pianist, teacher. Born in Youngstown, Ohio, July 12, 1874, Oldberg began playing the piano at the age of 5. He is reported to have joined his father, a pharmacist, in performing duo piano renditions of Haydn symphonies when Arne was 6. He began to study the piano with the Swedish pianist-composer August Hyllested (1856–1946) in Chicago; further piano study was completed under Theodor Leschetizky (1830–1915) in Vienna. He studied composition in Munich with Joseph Rheinberger (1839–1901). In 1899 Oldberg was appointed head of the piano department at Northwestern University, Evanston, Ill. Oldberg was a prolific composer, although he eventually rejected his first 14 numbered works; his Op. 15 was a *String Quartet in C Minor* (1900), one of several compositions for chamber group. His orchestral output includes overtures, (*Paola and Francesca*, Op. 21, 1899, was very popular) and symphonic poems— *The Sea* was composed in 1937. He completed 2 piano concertos, the first, Op. 17, dates to ca. 1904; the 2nd was completed in 1931 and won first prize ($1,000) in a Hollywood Bowl competition. Two symphonies, the F Minor, Op. 23 (ca. 1910), and the C Minor, were also prizewinners. Oldberg's *Fourth Symphony* (1939), was premiered by the Chicago Symphony in December 1942. His *Sixth Symphony*, Op. 58, was completed in 1956. He also produced a number of solo piano compositions, among them a *Piano Sonata*, Op. 28, (1909), a *Theme and Variations*, 3 *Miniatures*, an *Improvisation*, etc. Old-

berg left little vocal music, although an early Op. 22 is entitled *Four Songs for Contralto and Orchestra*. He died in Evanston, Ill., Feb. 17, 1962.

THE OLIVE LEAF Published in Wadley, Ga., in 1878, *The Olive Leaf* was one of the last of the shape-note tunebooks, edited by the veteran compiler-composer William Hauser (q.v.), who had produced the earlier *Hesperian Harp* (1848), and a younger collaborator, Benjamin Turner. It contained Hauser's own contributions, some adaptations of folk hymns, number 56, with other tunes by William Walker (q.v.), Ananias Davisson (q.v.), and others, including Aldine Kieffer, T. W. Dennington, and Charles H., Gabriel, of the younger school of sacred song composers. Hauser-Turner employed the 7 shape-note system for their collection.

ORIGINAL DIXIELAND JASS BAND Five-member band formed by native New Orleans musicians sometime in 1916. The band opened at Reisenweber's Restaurant, New York City, on Jan. 26, 1917, as The Original Dixieland Jass (*sic*) Band and not only introduced the sound of New Orleans music to the metropolis but also the word Jass, which eventually evolved into Jazz. Dixieland, too, served as a term for jazzy, improvisational music. The original members of the band (all born in New Orleans) were Dominic "Nick" LaRocca (1889–1961), cornet; Larry Shields (1893–1953), clarinet; Edward Branford "Eddie" Edwards (1891–1963), trombone; Henry Ragas (ca. 1890–1919), piano— later replaced by J. Russel Robinson (1892–1963), who came from Indianapolis, Ind.; and Anthony "Tony" Sbarbaro —later Spargo—(1897–1969), drums. The immediate popularity of the band led to a recording session on Feb. 26, 1917, out of which came their first Victor recording, "Dixie Jass Band One-Step"/"Livery Stable Blues," which became a best-selling disc. The novelty of the instrumental animal imitations (rooster, horse, and donkey) undoubtedly made for much of the popularity. The sound of the band and the instrumentation were based on the sound and bands that the 5 white musicians had heard in their native New Orleans. The sound, it has been reported, mystified the customers at Reisenweber's who initially sat and stared at the musicians until the manager informed them that it was music for dancing. Once introduced, "jass" in a rather watered-down white man's version swept New York and soon imitators sprang up and the Jazz Age in popular music began and flowered soon after in the 1920s. The Dixieland Jazz Band, as it came to be called, made several recordings, toured, and did well until 1925, when internal bickering led to a breakup of the band. A brief reunion in 1936 produced additional recordings (the sound of the band and the playing was even better than in 1919). This lasted for only 2 years before the final dissolution of the unit. Certain songs and instrumental numbers are still associated with the Original Dixieland Jazz Band (with the members sharing collective credits for composition). Other numbers played by the band include "Tiger Rag," "Fidgety Feet" (not the Gershwin song of the same name), "Barnyard Blues" (same tune as "Livery Stable Blues")—all of these are credited to LaRocca. "Margie" and "Singin' the Blues" are credited to J. Russel Robinson, as composer, with others collaborating on the lyrics. While the Original Dixieland Jazz Band was hardly a true "hot jazz" band such as its members heard in New Orleans, it introduced a vital American music to a wide audience and set the scene for others, white and black. The idea that 5 musicians could play independently and yet together was unusual; solos were often improvised during performance. It was, for most Americans, an entirely new kind of music.

"OVER THERE" Warlike, patriotic song, words and music by George M. Cohan (q.v.), written in April 1917, shortly after President Woodrow Wilson signed a Declaration of War against Germany. Based on a simple bugle-call-like theme (which Cohan readily and frequently pointed out), "Over There" was without question the single most popular song written by an American during the First World War. Cohan wrote the song in a single evening—Saturday, Apr. 7, 1917.

PAINE, JOHN KNOWLES (1839–1906) Composer, organist, teacher. Born into a Yankee musical family, Jan. 9, 1839, in Portland, Maine, Paine began to study with a German musician, Hermann Kotzschmar (1829–1909) in Portland. Like most aspiring American musicians at the time, Paine went to Germany to complete his education. In 1858 he went to Berlin to study at the Hochschule für Musik (principally organ with Carl Haupt, 1810–1891). He also studied composition and orchestration. A gifted organist, Paine soon earned an impressive reputation in Germany, where he toured giving recitals. (Paine actually made his organ debut in Portland at the age of 18; he later gave a series of subscription concerts to help raise some of the money for his stay in Europe.) He returned to the United States in 1861 and a year later joined the staff of Harvard as chapel organist and choirmaster; Paine also took on the position of instructor in music (without salary), feeling that the students should be acquainted with the fundamentals of music. The course earned the students no credits toward a degree and some members of the faculty saw no point to it. When Charles W. Eliot became president of Harvard in 1870, the attitude toward music by the administration was changed and Paine was officially appointed assistant professor of music in 1873; he became full professor in 1875. Harvard then could boast a full-fledged music department, the first university in the United States to have one. Among Paine's students were some of the next generation's most celebrated names in music: John Alden Carpenter, Frederick Converse, Arthur Foote, and Daniel Gregory Mason (all q.v.) as well as critics Richard Aldrich and Henry T. Finck. As a composer Paine was honored in his lifetime, recognized as the first American to handle the symphony in the same league with European composers. His works were well received (even published) in Europe and at home and were quite regularly performed in Boston. Although he composed his first string quartet at the age of 16, Paine's mature works exemplified the teachings of his German masters. His reputation as America's first major symphonist rests on his output of 2 symphonies, one in C Minor (1876) and one in A, subtitled "In Spring" (1880). His *First Symphony* was the first American work in that form to be published (in Germany!); his *Second Symphony* was published by Arthur P. Schmidt in Boston. Other orchestral compositions include the symphonic poems *Island Fantasy* and *The Tempest,* the overture *As You Like It,* and a *Duo Concertante for Violin, Cello and Orchestra.* Paine also composed several grand works for chorus, including a *Mass in D* (1867), which he conducted in Berlin; his oratorio, *St. Peter,* was given its first performance in Paine's birthplace, Portland, in 1873. Paine also composed incidental music for Sophocles' *Oedipus Tyrannus* (1881) and for *The Birds* of Aristophanes. The Prelude to *Oedipus Tyrannus* was awarded a gold medal in Berlin and performed at the unveiling of a statue to Wagner. Paine completed his only opera, for which he also wrote the libretto, in 1903. Entitled *Azara,* it was never performed except in concert. Paine

left an uncompleted symphonic poem based on the life of Lincoln. He resigned from his Harvard professorship in 1905. After a brief illness, he died in Cambridge, Mass., Apr. 25, 1906.

PARKER, HORATIO W. (1863–1919) Composer, organist, teacher. Born in Auburndale, Mass., Sept. 15, 1863, Parker was the son of a successful architect and cultured mother, an organist in the village church. Parker's initial schooling was wholly conventional (except that he attended a private school in nearby Newton) and he evidenced no interest in music until his 14th year. His mother Isabella Jennings Parker was his first teacher in piano and organ; within a year Parker had begun to compose (setting poems by Kate Greenaway). At 16 he was playing the organ in a Dedham church. His first formal study was begun in Boston where he worked under George W. Chadwick (q.v.) in composition, Stephen A. Emery (1841–1891) in harmony, and John Orth (1850–1932) in piano. As was the Bostonian tradition at this time, he went to Germany for further study—to Munich where he made a deep impression, and vice versa, on Joseph Rheinberger (1839–1901). In 1885 Parker returned to the United States, settling in New York, where he taught music at the Cathedral School of St. Paul, Garden City, for 2 years and then, from 1888 to 1893 was organist at Holy Trinity Church. He also taught at the National Conservatory of Music. In 1893 Parker returned to his native Boston area to be organist at Trinity Church (until 1901). He became head of Yale's Music Department, a position he held for the rest of his life. What Paine (q.v.) had been to Harvard, Parker was to Yale, where he taught counterpoint, composition, and orchestration besides lecturing on the history of music, in addition to conducting choral and orchestral concerts at Yale (and other points in

Philadelphia and New York). It was an active life and Parker managed also to compose, during his "spare time" as well as during his summer vacations and sabbaticals. The bulk of his original work lies in the realm of choral music, sacred and secular. His Op. 1, *The Shepherd Boy* for men's voices, dates from 1882 when he was a student in Munich. He produced more than 40 works for various vocal/orchestral combinations. There are also a handful of chamber works, piano and organ pieces, several song collections, 2 operas and 10 orchestral works, among them his only *Symphony in C Minor* (1885) and *A Northern Ballad*, Op. 46 (1899). Parker's oratorio, *Hora Novissima*, Op. 30, is generally regarded as his "masterpiece." Completed in 1892, the work was inspired by 12th-century Latin verses of one Bernard de Morlaix (the translation was done by Parker's mother) and employs soprano, alto, tenor, and bass soloists, a chorus and orchestra. *Hora Novissima* was well received in New York (where it was first performed in 1893), Boston, and Cincinnati. When it was performed at the Three Choirs Festival (1899) at Worcester, England, its success with the choral-loving English led to commissions for other works (*A Wanderer's Psalm*, Op. 50, 1900, and *A Star Song*, Op. 54, 1901) to be presented by British choral societies. Another large choral composition, *The Legend of St. Christopher*, Op. 43 (1898), was sung at Bristol and led to his degree, Doctor of Music (1902) from Cambridge University. As historian John Tasker Howard indicated, Parker's "fame in England was almost greater than in America." This was, of course, based on his choral compositions, which to the ears of the listener of the late 20th century may sound ponderous, not to say suggestive of the influence of Wagner, Mendelssohn, and others. Parker achieved distinction in the field of American opera. His first, *Mona* (1911), won

a $10,000 prize from the Metropolitan Opera and was performed there a few times in the 1912 season. The libretto was by a Yale colleague, Brian Hooker (1880–1946); the plot had to do with the Roman invasion of Britain and the problems of a British princess in love with the son of a Roman governor. Parker's 2nd opera, also with a text by Hooker, *Fairyland*, won a $10,000 prize from National Federation of Women's Clubs and was given its premiere in Los Angeles in 1915. It was one of his last works. Parker died in Cedarhurst, N.Y., Dec. 18, 1919, at the age of 56. His relatively early death is generally attributed to the heavy workload he so willingly carried.

PASTOR, TONY (1837–1908) Vaudeville impresario, singer. Antonio Pastor was born in New York City on May 28, 1837—when he was willing to admit it, for he became sensitive about his age. As an entertainer, Pastor was a kind of prodigy and began singing in public as early as age 6; at 10 he was a member of Raymond and Waring's Menagerie and participated in the minstrel show. For years Pastor toured with such circus-like entertainments; in later life he was billed as "America's Own Comic Vocalist." But it was not as an entertainer that Pastor made his contribution to the evolution of the American musical theatre. He abandoned circus life in Chicago in his 24th year and returned to New York to open up his first "theatre," in fact, a bar at 444 Broadway, known to all simply as "444." The year was 1861 and Pastor, as star vocalist, treated his customers to patriotic and topical songs. In 1865 Pastor moved his enterprise to the Bowery where he opened Tony Pastor's Opera House in the building that had once housed the rather notorious Volk's Garden, a cheap bar. As he prospered, Pastor moved his theatres farther uptown, finally settling into

"Tony Pastor's New Fourteenth Street Theatre," which opened with a burlesque entitled *The Pie-Rats of Pen-Yan,* an obvious takeoff on Gilbert and Sullivan. Pastor by this time had come into competition with the more gifted Harrigan and Hart (q.v.) and was not doing well. He ultimately junked the burlesque–topical satire format (wisely leaving that to Harrigan and Hart) and introduced a new concept into the popular American theatre on Oct. 21, 1881: a variety show suitable for both ladies and gentlemen. Gentlewomen did not attend variety shows in those days, for they purveyed low comics, roughhouse, and vulgarity. Pastor changed all that. His shows featured acrobats, songs and dances, blackface comics, impersonators (male and female), and, as the billing read, "Tony Pastor at every performance." The portly impresario sang. Pastor's "clean" show became popular and he prospered until variety evolved into a more businesslike vaudeville (q.v.) in the early 20th century. Although not known for his generosity with wages, Pastor was willing to feature new, young talent (which was never in a position to demand a high salary). Among the stellar names that appeared at Pastor's Fourteenth Street Theatre were ragtime pioneer Ben Harney (q.v.), May Irwin, Sophie Tucker, and Irving Berlin (q.v.). Pastor's little theatre (which was actually a part of Tammany Hall) could not compete with the vaudeville houses and their traveling acts. Borrowing Pastor's concept of shows for ladies and gentlemen, the big vaudeville chains brought an end to Pastor's variety shows. Pastor himself died in Elmhurst, N.Y., of a stroke, Aug. 26, 1908.

PETRIE, HENRY W. (1857–1925) Songwriter, singer. Born in Bloomington, Ill., Mar. 4, 1857, Petrie was a performer in minstrel shows before he became a successful songwriter. He is best remembered for his 2 great song hits: "I Don't Want to Play in Your Yard" (1894; lyrics by Philip Wingate) and the basso favorite, "Asleep in the Deep" (1897; lyrics by Arthur J. Lamb). Though he tried to compose sequels to these songs ("You Can't Play in Our Yard Any More" and "At the Bottom of the Deep Blue Sea"), his niche in the history of our popular song depends on the 2 big hits. He died in Paw Paw, Mich., May 25, 1925.

PLAYER PIANO An instrument that plays mechanically (either by foot-pedal or electric motor) via a perforated roll of paper. These piano rolls were precut by the musician and designed for playing in the home by nonmusicans. The player piano, as we know it today, originated in France in 1863; the so-called "Pianista" was exhibited at the Philadelphia Centennial Exposition in 1876. This pneumatic player piano was a crank-operated artificial finger device (wooden "fingers" applied the pressure to the keyboard) actuated by a bellows that forced air through perforations in a paper roll. Once the idea had been planted—and it could be traced back to the barrel organs and musical snuffboxes of the 18th and 19th centuries, respectively—other inventive minds contributed to the evolution of the true player piano. In the United States the Aeolian Co. patented a pedal-operated player piano with all its reproducing mechanism inside the cabinet (this was the brainchild of the company's E. S. Votey), calling the result a "Pianola." Although registered by Aeolian, Pianola (with a lower case "p") was interchangeable in the public mind with player piano. Player pianos proliferated during the first decade of the 20th century; by 1919 they outnumbered conventional pianos in American homes. With proliferation came improvement— the introduction of electrical power, even a method to capture the pianists' expression, the shadings of loudness and softness, pedaling, that distinguished one pianist's touch from another's (this development was pioneered by the M. Welte firm in Germany ca. 1904; it was introduced to the American public by Aeolian and dubbed "Duo-Art." Others eventually followed). It was then possible to record on paper the performances of notable pianists and composers in a reasonable facsimile of their actual playing. Along with "serious" music by the likes of Grieg, Debussy, Ravel, and Stravinsky (as well as the pianistic giants: Godowsky, Paderewski, Levitzki), popular songs were punched into rolls (often with the words printed alongside for those who wished to sing along). The products of Tin Pan Alley clattered through American parlors, amusement parks, and nickelodeons. Bright young pianists earned extra money in the early years of the 20th century cutting piano rolls, among them George Gershwin, Vincent Youmans, and Roy Bargy, all of whom came into their own during the 1920s. Many black pianists made piano rolls also, setting down ragtime, blues, and improvisations on original or popular tunes. Younger aspiring black pianists, unable to afford teachers, taught themselves to play by fingering the keys while a master's performance unrolled (among these would be Eubie Blake, James P. Johnson, Scott Joplin, and Jelly Roll Morton). The rise of the phonograph record in the '20s eventually led to the falling off of the player piano by the end of that decade; the Depression did the rest. The Nostalgia Craze (which coincided with the rediscovery of Scott Joplin in the 1970s) has brought about a small renaissance of the player piano and the reissuance of early historic rolls as well as the cutting of new ones. But the Golden Age of the player piano in the United States was roughly 1916–25.

POWELL, JOHN (1882–1963) Composer, pianist. Born into a cultured Virginia family in Richmond, Sept. 6, 1882, Powell traced his ancestors on his father's side to the Britain of King Alfred and, on his mother's, to an early court musician in England named Laniere. His father ran a girl's school in Richmond and his mother was musical. Powell began at the piano early by studying with his sister and then with a pupil of Liszt, F. C. Hahr, who had settled in Richmond. After graduating from the University of Virginia in 1901, Powell went to Vienna to study piano with Theodor Leschetizky (1830–1915) and composition with Karel Navrátil (1867–1936). He made his debut as a pianist in Berlin and then toured Europe for 4 years before returning to the United States. He made his American debut in Richmond in May 1912, and his New York debut at Carnegie Hall the next year. He presented his own compositions, along with standard fare, in his recitals during the U.S. and European tours. In his original work, Powell could be described as an Americanist who adapted Negro themes; his greater interest lay in the Anglo-Saxon song of his ancestors. Among his first works are 3 piano sonatas, all with such romantic names as *Psychologique, Noble,* and *Teutonica,* Op. 24 (1913). His *Rapsodie Nègre* for piano and orchestra (1918) established Powell as a composer of some popularity and the rhapsody was frequently performed well into the 1920s, often with the composer at the piano. Other works for orchestra include an overture, *In Old Virginia* (1921), *At the Fair* (1925; also for solo piano), *Natchez on the Hill* (1931), *A Set of Three,* based on folk tunes of Virginia (1935), *Symphony in A* (Virginia Symphony, 1937). Powell's chamber music includes a *Sonata Virginianesque* for piano and violin (1919), a *Sonata for*

Violin and Piano (1928), and a *String Quartet*. He also composed 2 piano concertos and a violin concerto; among his choral works are *The Babe of Bethelehem* for mixed chorus (1934), *Folk Hymns* (1934), and *Soldier, Soldier* for soprano, baritone, and chorus (1936). Powell remained active as a pianist (he played a benefit recital in Carnegie Hall celebrating his 25th anniversary in 1938); his *Symphony on Virginia Folk Themes and in the Folk Modes* was given its premiere on "John Powell Day" (Nov. 15, 1951) when he was honored by his fellow Virginians. By this time Powell had retired from public life (which he did in 1936) and was living quietly with his wife, Louisa Burleigh, in Charlottesville, Va. The Powells had musical gatherings for students and faculty of the University of Virginia (where Powell's manuscripts are deposited). He died in Charlottesville on Aug. 15, 1963.

PRATT, SILAS GAMALIEL (1846–1916) Composer, teacher. Although born in Addison, Vt., Aug. 4, 1846, Pratt grew up in Chicago, where he first encountered music working as a boy in a music store. Pratt was financially on his own by the time he was 12. Self-educated, self-supporting, Pratt worked in the music business until he was 22 and had saved enough money to go to Germany to study. There he majored in the piano with Theodor Kullak (1818–1882) and Franz Bendel (1833–74) at the Kullak Academy of Music in Berlin; he also studied composition with Friedrich Kiel (1821–1885). Originally Pratt intended to become a pianist but practiced with such zeal that he injured his wrists and was forced to devote himself to composition. Before this occurred he did, for a time, serve as organist at the Church of the Messiah, Chicago, in 1872 (this was just after the great Chicago fire and he had returned to a city virtually without concert halls).

That same year he helped to found the Apollo Musical Club, which still exists. Pratt moved between the United States and Europe, where his works were frequently performed—and well received. In 1875, present at the Wagner opera presentations at Bayreuth, he met Liszt. The next year he conducted his own *Centennial Overture* in Berlin and London (former President U. S. Grant, to whom the work was dedicated, was present at the Crystal Palace reading in London). Back in Chicago in 1878, Pratt was active in the musical life of the city, where he conducted performances of his own works. He then moved to New York in 1888, where he spent the next 14 years teaching, some of it at the Metropolitan School of Music. Pratt left New York for Pittsburgh, where in 1906 he founded his own Pratt Institute of Music. As a composer, Pratt thought in grand terms and patriotically. John Tasker Howard categorized him as a kind of latter-day Father Heinrich (except that Pratt had more musical training). His orchestral works include *Paul Revere's Ride,* a *Fantasy* on the Civil War, a *Lincoln* symphony, *The Battle of Manila, A Tragedy of the Deep* (on the sinking of the *Titanic*). Pratt's *Second Symphony* ("The Prodigal Son," 1885) he conducted himself at London's Crystal Palace. He also produced cantatas and operas on large themes: the operas *Zenobia, Queen of Palmyra* (1882), *Lucille* (originally *Antonio,* 1887), and the work he expected would be his greatest, *The Triumph of Columbus* (1892). He also composed a symphonic suite inspired by Shakespeare's *The Tempest,* and a cantata entitled *The Last Inca.* A lecturer also, Pratt published such books as *Lincoln in Story* (1901) and *The Pianist's Mental Velocity* (1903). He died in Pittsburgh, Oct. 30, 1916.

PRYOR, ARTHUR (1870–1942) Composer, conductor, trombonist. Born in St. Joseph, Mo., Sept. 22, 1870, Pryor had his first music lessons from his father, Samuel, who was leader of the Silver Cornet Band. At the age of 12 young Pryor was playing the slide trombone in his father's band. On his own, and without professional training, Pryor became a virtuoso trombonist, obtaining sounds and effects out of his instrument simply because no one told him they couldn't (or shouldn't) be done. He began his real professional career as first trombonist in the traveling band of Alessandro Liberati; he soon came to the attention of Patrick Gilmore (q.v.), but did not join that band because of an illness. In 1892, widely known as a virtuoso of the trombone, he joined the John Philip Sousa (q.v.) Band in New York; 3 years later he was assistant leader. In the United States and Europe, Pryor's solos with the Sousa Band earned him the reputation as the greatest trombonist in the world. He was featured as soloist and began composing pieces that highlighted his instrument. After 11 years with Sousa, Pryor broke away and formed his own band in 1903. Unlike Sousa, who consistently made world tours, Pryor stayed home. He made cross-country tours and his band played regularly at Asbury Park, N.J. (no less than 25 summers), Willow Grove, Pa., and Royal Palm Park, near Miami, Fla. (11 winters). Unlike Sousa, also, Pryor did not detest the phonograph record and began making records for the Victor Talking Machine Co., ca. 1910 (it might be noted that he often conducted the recordings made by the Sousa Band, since Sousa did not trust the talking machine). Pryor's recording career extended into the electrical recording era and the Pryor Band was often heard on early radio, but band dates and recording sessions were curtailed by the Depression. Pryor went into virtual retirement shortly after 1930. Pryor's Band rivaled that of Sousa's in the heyday of the concert band. It may be of some musicological interest to mention that it was Pryor's Band that was performing at the Capitol Theatre, New York, in October 1919 and introduced the song that a year later would become George Gershwin's first great hit: "Swanee." Primarily a trombonist-conductor, Pryor produced but a handful of original compositions, not all of them marches. A early work reveals his interest in ragtime: *Southern Hospitality* (1899). Another, *The March King*, was a bow to Sousa; several— *Trombonium, 'Lasses Trombone, Trombone Sneeze*, and *Razzazza Mazzazza*— were showpieces for himself during his Sousa years. (These pieces reveal not only a virtuoso trombonist, but a folkish instrumentalist of a jazzy bent.) Pryor's best-known instrumental is "The Whistler and His Dog" (1905). He died in West Long Branch, N.J., June 18, 1942.

RAGTIME Originally a piano style, with the melody syncopated in the right hand (treble) and with a steady, accented rhythm in the left (bass). A style invented and developed by black musicians sometime during the late 19th century, it was undoubtedly played earlier but not identified and named until later. The generally agreed upon dates for ragtime's heyday are ca. 1897–1917. An amalgam of Afro-American and European musical styles, with roots in song, dance, and the march, ragtime evolved into its classic form in the works of Scott Joplin (q.v.) and his followers. Because it was a kind of music played in the parlors of bordellos, ragtime was rejected for a long time by genteel folk, black and white. The stigma had worn away by 1897, when William Krell's *Mississippi Rag* was published, and with the publication of Joplin's *Maple Leaf Rag* in September 1899 it grew into a craze and was accepted worldwide. In form, the classic rag is related to the march—depending on the composer's desires. The time signature for the classic rags is invariably 2/4 with the marking "Slow March Time" or "Slow March Tempo." Joplin, especially, objected to a fast performance of his rags. His rags were printed with a warning: *"NOTE: Do not play this piece fast. It is never right to play Ragtime fast."* He was almost as strict in adherence to form: an introduction was followed by the first strain, which was repeated; then came the 2nd strain, also repeated; then came the "Trio," so called because it was a contrasting 3rd theme in the subdominant (also repeated), the 4th strain returned to the tonic (i.e., the original key) and was repeated. In other words: Introduction, AA, BB, CC (the trio), and AA. This structure was not always the basis of rags, but it was the most frequently used, particularly by Joplin. Ragtime was not jazz; in its classic form it was a notated and printed music, not improvisation. As its popularity spread, ragtime was easily taken up by bands, especially those led by Sousa (who introduced ragtime to Europe on one of his tours in 1900) and Pryor. Rag orchestrations were eventually issued by publishers such as Stark Music Co., the pioneer publishing firm in ragtime. Stark sometime in late 1914 or early 1915 issued a folio of rags orchestrated for the standard (or nearly so) theatre band of the time. Its official title was *Standard High-Class Rags,* but it has become best known by the name under which it was called by musicians, "The Red Back Book" (q.v.). The classic rags of such fine rag composers as Joplin, James Scott (q.v.), and Joseph F. Lamb (q.v.), to name only the Big Three of early ragtime, are hauntingly sensitive, often delicate, compositions well within the ken of the pianist who plays Chopin. The Tin Pan Alley exploitations and exaggerations that came later destroyed the poetry of these fragile pieces. These were fre-

quently bravura keyboard gyrations performed in the fast tempo that Joplin abhorred. With the death of Joplin in 1917—and the rise of popular jazz (q.v.)—the ragtime craze petered out. Its works were kept alive by pianists and small jazz bands through the years, until the 1970s, when another resurgence grew around the work of Joplin. This led not only to the rediscovery of Joplin's music, but also to that of Scott, Lamb, and others. Though that peaking of interest from musicologists, filmmakers, and record companies has waned, the renaissance served to remind us that ragtime, the background music for houses of ill repute, is a music of great beauty and charm.

RED BACK BOOK A folio of 15 rags, with orchestrations, published by John Stark (q.v.) ca. 1915. The title was *Standard High-Class Rags* and contained 15 rags (including Stark's best-seller, *Maple Leaf*) and came to be known among the musicians of New Orleans as "The Red Back Book" because of its distinctive cover. The arrangements were made by Stark's son, Etilmon Justus Stark, D. S. DeLisle, and others (not identified), for an orchestra of 11 instruments (and any combination thereof, depending on availability). This group contained such unjazzy instruments as the violin, flute, piccolo, viola, and cello; the sound was characteristic of the theatre pit band of the period. Of the 15 rags included in "The Red Back Book," 11 were by Joplin.

ROMAN SKETCHES A suite of Impressionistic, and original, piano pieces by Charles Tomlinson Griffes (q.v.). The 4 sections of the work, Griffes' Opus 7, are: 1. *The White Peacock* (1915), 2. *Nightfall,* 3. *The Fountain of the Acqua Paola,* and 4. *Clouds* (the final 3 were completed in 1916). The pieces were inspired by the poetry of William Sharp—the collection entitled

Sospiri di Roma (1891). Sharp (1855–1905), a Scot, also wrote poetry under the name of "Fiona Macleod." Griffes also set some of these poems. The *Roman Sketches,* especially *The White Peacock,* was Griffes' most-played work in his lifetime. Griffes also made an orchestration of this section for the Adolph Bolm dance company in 1919.

THE ROSARY Sentimental but well-wrought song, music by Ethelbert Nevin (q.v.) and words by Robert C. Rogers (1862–1912). Early in 1898 someone sent Nevin a copy of the poem "The Rosary" by Rogers which he set to music and presented to a singer friend, Francis Rogers (1870–1951), to be introduced at his next recital. This occurred the following week, on Feb. 15, 1898, when Rogers (not related to the poet) introduced the song at the Madison Square Concert Hall. As Rogers later wrote, "The Rosary" was "the hit of the afternoon." The song's popularity quickly grew and Rogers took it to England, where it was also most successfully introduced. Since 1898 "The Rosary" has been widely sung (and often abused, even satirized). It remains an inspired creation despite its sentimentality. Sheet music sales from its publication in 1898 to 1928 totaled 2,500,000 copies, the best year being 1913, when nearly 300,000 copies were sold. This did Nevin little good for he had by then been dead for 12 years. He had been haunted in his last years by the extreme popularity of his piano piece *Narcissus* and "The Rosary."

ROSENFELD, MONROE H. (1861–1918) Songwriter, columnist, editor. A colorful, rather mysterious, character, Rosenfeld was born in Richmond, Va., in 1861. At some time in his life he was living in Cincinnati and apparently writing songs, for music publisher Frank Harding invited him to come to New York. Another publisher, E. B. Marks

described Rosenfeld as a persuasive talker with a "hypnotic line" and as "a melodic kleptomaniac." As a songwriter, Rosenfeld made his first important impression with the song "Her Golden Hair Was Hanging Down Her Back" (1884) and his most important contribution—an example of his melodic kleptomania—with "Johnny Get Your Gun" (1886). His true specialty, fulfilling the demand of the period, was the tear-jerking sentimental ballad, such as "With All Her Faults I Love Her Still" (1888) and "Take Back Your Gold" (1897). Using several pseudonyms—"F. Heiser," "F. Belasco," even "Monroe Rosevelt"—Rosenfeld published several popular songs toward the end of the 19th century. He even collaborated with songwriter Theodore A. Metz (1848–1936), composer of "A Hot Time in the Old Town," on an operetta about the Indian, *Poketa.* Rosenfeld wrote the libretto and Metz the music. The fact that Metz insisted that Rosenfeld had lifted one of his tunes for the melody of "With All Her Faults" did not complicate the collaboration; the result, however, was an instant failure. Rosenfeld became an almost mythical figure in New York's musical world—he was a notorious womanizer, gambler, and horse player. Besides songs, words and music, he also wrote articles and columns for newspapers and magazines. He wrote regularly for the New York *Clipper* (predecessor of today's *Variety*) and for the New York *Herald,* usually about songs and songwriting. His early (1903) article praising the works of Scott Joplin, published in the St. Louis *Globe-Democrat,* revealed a sensitive ear and taste in music. Toward the end of his life, the sentimental song era long gone, Rosenfeld worked as editor of the Boston-based music magazine, *The Tuneful Yankee* (1917). Perhaps Rosenfeld's lasting claim to fame is based on the apocryphal tale, told by music publisher Harry Von Tilzer. Sometime in the early

1900s, according to Von Tilzer, Rosenfeld was visiting the music publisher in his office on New York's 28th Street; he was working on an article about the music business, which was then centered there. Hearing Von Tilzer's specially prepared piano (paper strips were woven through the wires), Rosenfeld is supposed to have said, "It sounds like a tin pan." That, mingled with the other pianos heard in the building and along the street, inspired Rosenfeld to entitle his article "Tin Pan Alley" (q.v.). This supposedly was the first time the name was applied to the street and to the popular music business in general. Whether true or not, and there are doubters, Rosenfeld was capable of coining the term. He died in New York City in 1918.

"ST. LOUIS BLUES" Popular blues song, music and words by W. C. Handy (q.v.), published in 1914. The composition, based on the folk blues form, is actually an arrangement of blues themes (this includes the words) that Handy had heard during his years as an itinerant musician. Its chorus was based on a preacher's exhortation Handy heard in Florence, Ala. Whether wholly original or not, "St. Louis Blues" exemplifies the form in a sophisticated manner, preserving both the music and its characteristic harmonies as well as the folk poetry of the genuine blues. Since its publication it has proved to be the most successful song in this genre. It has been performed by jazz groups, lush large orchestras, and was used as the theme in a jazz symphony (1925) by Alberte Chiaffarelli (1884–1945). Handy used a modified version of the traditional 12-bar blues structure, and in the verse of the text the 3-line (with the 2nd a repeat of the first) stanza typical of the folk blues.

SALTER, MARY TURNER (1856–1938) Composer, vocalist, teacher. Born Mary Turner in Peoria, Ill., Mar. 15, 1856, she became Mary T. Salter in 1881 when she married her composition teacher, Sumner Salter (1856–1944), himself an organist and composer. Mary Salter initially planned to be a singer and began her studies with Alfred Arthur and Max Schilling in Burlington, Iowa. She continued vocal studies in Boston with John O'Neil and later in New York with Hermine Rudersdorff. From 1875 she had a successful career of about 20 years as soprano soloist in concerts, with choral societies, and in churches from Boston to Atlanta. In 1877 she was soprano soloist at the Broadway Tabernacle, New York, and 2 years later held the same position in New Haven's Trinity Church. From 1879 until 1881 (when she married) she taught singing at Wellesley College. She retired from singing around 1893 to devote her time to composing and teaching. Most of her output consists of songs for solo voice, grouped in cycles with such titles as *Three Spring Songs,* Op. 4 (1904), *Outdoor Sketches* (a set of 6 songs, 1908), or even a simple title like *Five Songs,* Op. 34 (1916). Her best-known song, "The Cry of Rachel," was featured by the eminent contralto Ernestine Schumann-Heink (1861–1936). In her 80th year Salter composed the lovely "A Christmas Song" (1936). She died in Orangeburg, N.Y., Sept. 13, 1938.

SANKEY, IRA DAVID (1840–1908) Singer, composer, author. Born in Edinburg, Pa., Aug. 28, 1840, Sankey became known as a gospel singer when he joined forces with evangelist Dwight L. Moody. From 1871 to 1899 they toured the United States and Britain singing what became popularly known as Moody and Sankey songs, gospel hymns, most of which were composed by Sankey. Among them, "There Were Ninety and Nine" (1868), "I Am Praying for You," "A Soldier of the Cross," "He Is Coming," and "Shine On, O Star!" These were very popular Sunday school songs for generations despite their, in the words of John Tasker Howard, "obvious banality and sentimentality." In 1873 Sankey compiled a number of these popular hymns and published them as *Sacred Songs and Solos;* this was followed by other such compilations. When Sankey left Moody in 1899, he settled in Newcastle, Pa., for a time, where he was president of the local YMCA. He was writing a book telling the stories behind gospel songs when he went blind—and then lost the manuscript to his book in a fire. He dictated a new version of his book to a friend and it was published as *My Life and Sacred Songs* in 1906. Sankey died in Brooklyn, N.Y., Aug. 13, 1908.

SCHELLING, ERNEST (1876–1939) Composer, pianist, conductor. Born in Belvidere, N.J., July 26, 1876, Schelling was a musical prodigy who made his debut at the Academy of Music, Philadelphia, at the age of 4. He first began to study the piano with his father Felix; by the time he was 7 he was enrolled at the Paris Conservatory. Among his celebrated teachers in Paris and other points were Georges Mathias (1826–1910), Moritz Moszkowski (1854–1925), Theodor Leschetizky (1830–1915), and Ignace Paderewski (1860–1941). Schelling then began a brilliant career as a concert pianist; this was interrupted, at the age of 16, when he was afflicted with neuritis. It was after this that he was invited by Paderewski to Switzerland, where Schelling remained for 4 years and, apparently cured, took up his pianistic career again, achieving international fame. Another interruption occurred when he served in the infantry (with a final rank of major) during the First World War. An automobile accident in Switzerland after the war, in 1919, ended his career as a pianist, and Schelling turned to conducting and composition. He was guest conductor with sev-

eral major American orchestras and organized and led the New York Philharmonic-Symphony's children's concerts for several years, beginning in January 1924, and continued until his death. In 1935 he was appointed conductor of the Baltimore Symphony, where he remained until 1938. Schelling's early compositions were written as vehicles for himself. These include the *Fantastic Suite* for piano and orchestra (1905) in which the songs "Dixie" and "Old Folks at Home" are the subjects of variations. Another such work is *Impressions from an Artist's Life* for piano and orchestra (1913). Other orchestral works include *Légendes Symphoniques* (1904), a *Concerto for Violin and Piano* (1916), *A Victory Ball,* "dedicated to an American soldier" (1923), the symphonic tableau *Morocco* (1927), and a *Symphony in C Minor.* Schelling's chamber works include an early *Sonata for Violin and Piano* and a *Divertimento* for string quartet and piano (1925). He also composed a *Tarentelle* for string quartet and several solo piano pieces, among them a *Gavotte,* a *Romance, Valse Gracieuse, Theme et Variations,* etc. Schelling died in New York City, Dec. 8, 1939.

SCOTT, JAMES (1886–1938) Composer, pianist. Born in Neosho, Mo., in 1886, Scott was largely self-taught, except for a few piano lessons from a friend named John Coleman. Scott was also gifted with absolute pitch. His family moved a good deal, seeking work, and at around the time he was 14, Scott was living in Ottawa, Kans., where he practiced on a cousin's small organ. The family moved again to Carthage, Mo., where his father bought a piano. To help the family Scott took a job in a shoeshine stand; at 16 he began working in a local music store, where he washed windows and began learning the trade of picture framing (an extra service of Dumars' Music Store). One day he was heard playing one of the pianos and was hired by the owner to work in the sheet music department since Scott could read music. Undoubtedly Scott was familiar with the rags of Scott Joplin (q.v.) and, inspired by him, began composing. His first published work (written when he was about 17) was *A Summer Breeze— March and Two Step,* issued by Dumars' Music. Scott remained with Dumars' for about 12 years—although Dumars' did not succeed as a publisher. It was in 1906 that Scott's first rag, *Frog Legs Rag,* was published by the pioneer rag publisher John Stark (q.v.). In 1914 Scott moved to Kansas City where he married and earned his living by teaching, playing the organ, and arranging music for Kansas City theatres. He also composed a steady stream of rags, which has earned him a place among the Big Three of ragtime, in company with Joplin and Joseph Lamb (q.v.). While Scott's early pieces reveal Joplin's influence, he quickly developed his own style and produced such works as *Grace and Beauty* (1910), *Quality—A High Class Rag* (1911), *The Ragtime Oriole* (1911), *Climax Rag* (1914), *Pegasus— A Classic Rag* (1920), *Modesty Rag—A Classic* (1920), *Don't Jazz Me (I'm Music)* (1921); his last published work was the *Broadway Rag—A Classic* (1922). It might be noted that Scott rarely, if ever, provided titles for his pieces; these were generally concocted by Stark—whose attitude toward the new music threatening classic ragtime is revealed in the title of Scott's 1921 composition. Scott also collaborated on a few songs and composed 3 waltzes: *Hearts Longing Waltzes* (1910), *Suffragette,* and *Springtime of Love* (1914 and 1919). When the rag heyday ended, Scott continued to compose but did not publish. He taught, was active in the local theatres (until sound film came in), and formed a small band which played in theatres in Kansas City. Scott's last

years were painful, for he suffered from dropsy, which made it difficult for him to play. He died in Kansas City, aged only 52, on Aug. 30, 1938.

SHEPHERD, ARTHUR (1880–1958) Composer, teacher, pianist, conductor. Born in Paris, Idaho, Feb. 19, 1880, Shepherd was enrolled in the New England Conservatory of Music, Boston, when he was 12. Among his important teachers in composition were Percy Goetschius (q.v.) and George W. Chadwick (q.v.). Shepherd then began a career divided between teaching and composition (with some conducting added). He won the first of a series of prizes with an orchestral work, *Ouverture Joyeuse* (1902); the National Federation of Music Clubs awarded Shepherd no less than 3 prizes, 2 for his *Piano Sonata* and the song "The Lost Child" in 1909, the year in which he joined the faculty of the New England Conservatory. An interruption occurred in 1917, when Shepherd went to France as a Field Artillery bandleader. After the war, he moved to Cleveland, where he was assistant conductor of the Cleveland Symphony, in charge of the children's program and as program annotator. Shepherd eventually reviewed music for the Cleveland *Press* and joined the faculty of Western Reserve University (he was chairman of the Music Department from 1927 to 1948). Stylistically Shepherd was attracted to French Impressionism, despite the Germanic training he had received at the New England Conservatory; he was also a student of American folk song. His first symphony, *Horizons* (1927), is based on several cowboy songs. In 1946 he completed a *Fantasia on Down East Spirituals.* Other orchestral works include the overture *Festival of Youth* (1915), a *Fantasy for Piano and Orchestra* (1916), an *Overture to a Drama* (1919), *Choreographic Suite* (1931), *Symphony No. 2 in D* (1938),

Fantasia Concertante (1943), and a *Concerto for Violin and Orchestra* (1946). Shepherd composed more than a dozen choral works including *Song of the Sea Wind* for women's voices and orchestra (1915), the cantata *Song of the Pilgrims* for tenor, chorus, and orchestra (1937), and *Psalm 42* for chorus and orchestra (1944). There are smaller piano pieces as well as 2 piano sonatas, the 2nd dating from 1929. Chamber works include 3 string quartets (1928, 1935, 1936), a *Sonata for Violin and Piano* (1927), the *Quintet for Piano and Strings* (1940), *Praeludium for Winds and Strings* (1942), a *Divertissement for Winds* (1943); and his best-known work in this medium, the *Triptych* for soprano and string quartet (1926). Shepherd's compositions were frequently performed during his lifetime (with himself often conducting) and were given radio performances via the large networks. He died in Cleveland, Jan. 12, 1958.

"SHINE ON, HARVEST MOON"

Very popular song, words and music by the vaudeville man-and-wife (temporarily) team of Nora Bayes (ca. 1880–1928) and Jack Norworth (1879–1959). Bayes interpolated the song into the score of the *Ziegfeld Follies of 1908*. Norworth was also known for his lyrics for "Take Me Out to the Ball Game" (1908) to the music of Albert Von Tilzer (q.v.). Although the marriage did not last (Norworth was the second of Bayes's 5 husbands), the song has endured as a souvenir of a simpler America.

SKILTON, CHARLES SANFORD

(1868–1941) Composer, teacher, organist. A New Englander, Skilton was born Aug. 16, 1868, in Northampton, Mass., but was best known for his treatment of American Indian music. A graduate of Yale (B.A. in literature, 1889), he taught languages at Sigler's Preparatory School, Newburgh, N.Y. (1899–91) and then left for Berlin to study music. He returned in 1893 to take up the first of several teaching positions and, for a year (1897–98), studied in New York with Harry Rowe Shelley (1858–1947) and Dudley Buck (q.v.). In 1903 Skilton joined the staff of the University of Kansas, where he remained for the rest of his life. He began as professor of organ and lecturer in music theory and history; from 1903 to 1915 he was also dean of the School of Fine Arts. Skilton's interest in authentic Indian music was started by one of his students, an Indian, who offered to exchange tribal songs for lessons in harmony. Skilton pursued his studies further by visiting the nearby Haskell Institute (a government-run school for Indians). In 1915 he composed a *Deer Dance* and a *War Dance* for string quartet; in 1920 he orchestrated these pieces and added more Indian material, calling the expanded work *Suite Primeval*. This work, especially the 2 early dances, was widely performed in concert and broadcast. Other orchestral works in this genre are *American Indian Fantasie*, with cello (1932), and *Sioux Flute Serenade* (1920). For the theatre Skilton wrote music for Sophocles' *Electra* (1918) and 2 operas using Indian themes and background, *Kalopin* (1927) and *The Sun Bride* (1930). Non-Indian works include music to Barrie's *Mary Rose* (1933) and *The Day of the Gayomair* (1936), both operas; the choral pieces *The Witch's Daughter* (1918), *The Guardian Angel* (1925), *Song Folio: From Forest and Stream* (1930), *Midnight* and *The Fountain* for women's voices, and a cantata, *Ticonderoga,* for male chorus and orchestra (1933). A *Sonatina for Violin and Piano,* a *String Quartet in B Minor,* and a *Sarabande for Wind Instruments* plus the 2 early Indian Dances round out Skilton's works for chamber groups. Skilton was also the author of *Modern Symphonic Forms*. He died in Lawrence, Kans., Mar. 12, 1941.

SLAVE SONGS OF THE UNITED STATES The first collection of slave songs published in the United States, compiled and edited by William F. Allen, Charles Ware, and Lucy McKim Garrison. Published by A. Simpson & Co., New York, 1867. Allen wrote an analytical preface, describing the social setting and the performances. The songs were collected, with the aid of the Freedmen's Commission, in South Carolina and the Gulf States. Many of the songs printed in the collection came to be called spirituals (q.v.). While hardly a work of scientific musicology, *Slave Songs of the United States* remains a valuable compilation.

SMITH, DAVID STANLEY (1877–1949) Teacher, composer, conductor, organist. The son of an amateur organist and composer-businessman father and a mother who sang, Smith was born in Toledo, Ohio, July 6, 1877. Despite this musical background, Smith did not reveal a serious interest in music until he was a student at Yale and came under the influence of Horatio Parker (q.v.). Smith graduated from Yale in 1900, then returned to study music with Parker, receiving his Mus.B in 1903. He then, at Parker's suggestion, went to Europe where he studied with the great French organist-composer Charles-Marie Widor (1844–1937). Upon his return to the United States he joined the Yale faculty, where he eventually was appointed assistant to Parker; in 1920 he succeeded his teacher as dean of the School of Music. Smith was also the conductor of the New Haven Symphony Orchestra, led the Horatio Parker Choir, and was guest conductor of several leading orchestras in the United States. He retired from Yale in 1940, although he continued teaching composition. As a composer, Smith first came to public attention when he won the Paderewski Prize in 1909 with *The Fallen Star* for chorus

and orchestra. In 1912 he produced the first of 4 symphonies. The last, Op. 78, dates from 1937. Smith's chamber music output was extensive—no less than 10 string quartets, plus sonatas for oboe and piano (Op. 43, 1918), violin and piano (Op. 51, 1921), cello and piano (Op. 69, 1928), and a quintet, Op. 56, for piano and strings (1927). For chamber orchestra Smith composed a suite of 4 pieces entitled *Flowers,* Op. 52 (1924), a *Sinfonietta* for strings (1931), and a *Sonatina* for junior string orchestra (1932). Besides the 4 symphonies, Smith composed several orchestral works, among them *Impressions,* Op. 40 (1916), *Fête Galante* for flute and orchestra (1920), *Cathedral Prelude* for organ and orchestra (1926), *1929—A Satire,* Op. 66 (1932), and its sequel, *Overture—Tomorrow* (1933); also a *Requiem for Violin and Orchestra,* Op. 81 (1939), *Credo,* Op. 83 (1941), *Four Pieces for String Orchestra,* Op. 89 (1943), and *The Apostle,* Op. 92 (1944). Among Smith's later choral works were a *Rhapsody of St. Bernard,* Op. 38 (1915), *Vision of Isaiah,* Op. 58 (1927), *The Ocean,* Op. 94 (1945), and *Daybreak* (1945). Smith also composed a few songs and piano pieces, including a *Piano Sonata in A Flat,* Op. 61 (1929). An early, unproduced opera, *Merrymount,* dates from 1914. Smith died in New Haven, Conn., Dec. 17, 1949.

SONG PLUGGER A Tin Pan Alley (q.v.) term, popular during the early 20th century, applied to vocalists employed by popular music publishers to publicize the latest songs of the firm. Pluggers frequently stood up in the audience and suddenly appeared to burst into song spontaneously in a theatre (arrangements with the management, orchestra, or accompanist having been made earlier), to introduce the new song. Pluggers traveled from town to town doing this. (In the late 19th century they were called "boomers.") They also approached vaudeville singers, dancers, and others—anyone who could use the company's wares. Irving Berlin (q.v.) was an early plugger. A pianist who demonstrated a publisher's songs (the company usually had several tiny demonstration rooms for this) was called a "piano pounder." Early pounders, before they switched to songwriting, were Jerome Kern, George Gershwin, and Richard Rodgers. A song's popularity in the early days of the 20th century was believed to depend a good deal on the amount of plugging the publisher gave it. Quality appears to have been a remote consideration. This was before radio, whose "disc jockeys" eventually supplanted the plugger, in all ways, including the publisher's payoff. Another form of plugging a song was to get a very popular entertainer to sing it constantly; often the singer's photo adorned the song sheet and even his name was added to those of the composer and lyricist, thus cutting him in on the song's royalties. Popular "Mammy" singer Al Jolson was a noted practitioner of this "art."

SOUSA, JOHN PHILIP (1854–1932) Composer, bandleader. Born in Washington, D.C., Nov. 6, 1854, of immigrant parents (his father was Portuguese and his mother Bavarian), Sousa began to study the violin at the age of 7 with John Esputa. Sousa's father, Antonio, played trombone in the Marine Band (though he also worked as a cabinetmaker). Even as he studied the violin, Sousa picked up the rudiments of various brass instruments, for he evinced an early liking for band music. At 14 he was an apprentice boy in the Marine Band in which, besides menial chores, he played the cymbals. He later joined the Washington Orchestral Union as first violinist and studied composition and harmony with its leader, George Benkert. It was Benkert who encouraged Sousa in

composition. His first published work, *Moonlight on the Potomac* (1872), was issued when he was about 18 and consisted of a group of waltzes; several other pieces followed, none of them marches. In 1877 he produced a *Te Deum*, which may be Sousa's sole attempt at a "serious" composition. Besides composing, Sousa gained experience in theatre orchestras, some of which he conducted. He served as first violinist under the great French operetta composer, Jacques Offenbach, who conducted at the Philadelphia Centennial Exposition (1876). At the Exposition, Sousa heard and was deeply impressed by the Patrick Gilmore (q.v.) Band. Under the influence of Offenbach and, later, Gilbert and Sullivan, Sousa composed his first operetta score, *Our Flirtation* (1880). The operetta was mildly successful, although that was not to be Sousa's avenue of fame. On Oct. 1, 1880, he became the leader of the Marine Band. Under his leadership (Sousa remained with the band for the next 12 years), the Marine Band became one of the finest in existence. He reorganized the band, its repertoire, its blend of instruments (especially the balance between brass and woodwinds), and transformed it into a virtuoso instrument. Sousa continued to compose all those years, both operetta scores and, for the band (and often for special occasions), marches. John Tasker Howard has written that Sousa "was to the march what Johann Strauss was to the waltz." His marches earned him the undisputed title of "The March King." After a series of early attempts, Sousa hit his stride, shall we say, with *The Gladiators* (1886) and composed his first "classic," *The Washington Post* (1889), for the newspaper of that name. Many of Sousa's marches were sold to publishers outright (sometimes for as little as $35), but he eventually learned about the advantages of the royalty arrangement. Sousa's success with the Marine Band led him to resign from that organization and to form his own band, which gave its first concert in Plainfield, N.J., on Sept. 26, 1892. This remarkable group was to survive for 40 years (except for a brief breakup during World War I). The Sousa Band toured the United States, playing at expositions, fairs, in town band shells, to become the best-known band of the time. There were no less than 4 European tours and a world tour (1910–11). On these tours not only did Sousa perform his own marches, but also those of others as well as nonmarch fare. He is credited with introducing Europe to ragtime in 1900. Although his marches became very popular and were played throughout the world, Sousa continued to compose operetta scores, some of which were reasonably successful and which contained a march or two. Among Sousa's operetta efforts are *Désirée* (1884), *El Capitan* (1896), *The Bride Elect* (1897), *The Charlatan* (1898), *The Free Lance* (1906), and *The American Maid* (1913; actually a revival-revision of *The Glass Blowers*, 1893). Sousa also contributed incidental music to *Everything* (1918), a musical spectacle staged at New York's Hippodrome. Sousa is, of course, best remembered for his march output—to name a few, *Semper Fideles* (1888), *High School Cadets* (1891), *El Capitan* (which combines 2 tunes from the operetta, 1896), *Stars and Stripes Forever* (1897), and *U. S. Field Artillery March* (1918). Sousa was also a writer, published 2 novels, *The Fifth String* and *Transit of Venus*, a children's book, *Pipetown Sandy*, a compilation, *National Patriotic and Typical Airs of All Countries* (1890), a miscellany entitled *Through the Years with Sousa* (1910), and an autobiography, *Marching Along* (1918). Although the Sousa Band recorded extensively, Sousa rarely led it during its recording sessions (he presented his reasons in an article, "The

Menace of Mechanical Music," 1906). He did not, however, object to radio and he broadcast frequently until the advent of jazz brought an end to the marching band era. Sousa's most ambitious efforts, which belong to the tone poem and suite genre, are little known; these have such titles as *The Chariot Race* (inspired by *Ben-Hur*), *Sheridan's Ride, Three Quotations, The Last Days of Pompeii*, and *Impressions at the Movies*. Sousa died, following a heart attack, in Reading, Pa., where he had gone to serve as guest conductor of a high school band, Mar. 6, 1932.

STARK, JOHN (1841–1927) John Stillwell Stark was born on a farm in Shelby County, Ky., Apr. 11, 1841, one of 11 children of Adin and Eleanor Stillwell Stark. After the death of his mother in childbirth, Stark went to live with his brother, who had a farm in Indiana. Stark remained there until he was about 22, when he enlisted in the Indiana Heavy Artillery Volunteers, spending the years 1864–66 in the Union Army. Most of Stark's military service was devoted to participation in the occupation of New Orleans; he was listed on the roster as bugler. Stark met, and married, Sarah Ann Casey (then barely out of her teens) during his New Orleans stay. After his release from the Army, the Starks returned to Indiana, where John Stark worked one of his brother's farms. Restless, Stark took his small family (now consisting of his wife and a son, Etilmon) and in 1869 moved by covered wagon to Maysville, Mo. Setting up a homestead, Stark established a farm which prospered until he decided to sell it and move into the town of Cameron, Mo., where he went into the recently inaugurated business of dispensing ice cream. Stark became a peddler, with a cart taking the new product to outlying farmlands; he expanded his inventory by adding an organ, later a piano, and so on. This led eventually to his giving up peddling to establish a music store; in 1885 or so, he had set up John Stark & Son in the bustling rail center town of Sedalia, Mo. (The "Son" was 15-year-old William; elder son Etilmon was already a violinist-to-be and daughter Eleanor also showed musical promise and would one day study with Moritz Moszkowski in Berlin.) Stark's store became a music center in Sedalia and prospered. The even greater upward turn in its prosperity began in the summer of 1899, when John Stark happened to hear a young black pianist, Scott Joplin (q.v.), performing in the Maple Leaf Club. The compositions of Joplin prompted Stark to go into the music publishing business and, unlike most music publishers of the time (and later, for that matter), Stark actually paid Joplin an advance and royalties on their first joint effort, *Maple Leaf Rag*. The piano piece proved to be the making of both Joplin and Stark, besides rendering the too often disdained rag popular and respectable. Stark was able to expand his business to St. Louis and New York and published rags by all of the great ragtime composers: James Scott (q.v.), Joseph Lamb (q.v.), Arthur Marshall (q.v.), and Artie Matthews (q.v.). Stark's honorable treatment of his composers is one of the brighter aspects of the often savage music publishing business. While ragtime was popular and profitable Stark did well, but the waning of the rag and the rising of jazz brought an end to Stark's prosperity. In 1912 he left New York and moved back to Missouri, taking up residence with his son Etilmon, in Maplewood, a suburb of St. Louis. From there Stark managed his shrinking business and even (in 1913) collaborated on an operetta, *The Vital Question,* with his son. Despite the decline of ragtime, Stark continued to publish rags, waltzes, and whatever music caught his fancy. By 1923 the company published a mere 2 rags; its greater output consisted of reprints of earlier publications. The ragtime era had ended. He spent his final years reading classics and hoping for another *Maple Leaf Rag*. As late as November 1926, he was preoccupied with the copyrights of his best-selling publication. The next year, aged 86, John Stark died in Maplewood, Mo., Nov. 20, 1927.

STROMBERG, JOHN (1853–1902) Composer, conductor. Stromberg, born in New York City in 1853, was working as an arranger for a publishing house with a single song, "My Best Girl's a Corker" (1895) to his credit, when he encountered the burlesque team of Weber and Fields (q.v.). The team had decided to stop touring and to open up their own music hall in New York to present their own kind of humor, consisting of sketches parodying currently popular shows or books. The virtually unknown Stromberg was to compose the songs sung between the Weber and Fields comedy skits and to conduct the orchestra. The first show, *The Art of Maryland* (1896), was quite successful. The team's popularity grew and their form of comedy attracted audiences and Stromberg prospered with them. He provided them with songs for a series of burlesques between 1896 and 1902. A few of the individual songs achieved some popularity: "Ma Blushin' Rosie" from *Fiddle-Dee-Dee* (1900; lyrics by Edgar Smith) and "Come Down Ma Evenin' Star" (1902; lyrics by Robert B. Smith) introduced by Lillian Russell in *Twirly Whirly*. Stromberg was doing well with the Weber and Fields shows but lost money in a Long Island real estate venture; he was also in poor health. After a mere 7 years as composer in residence for Weber and Fields, Stromberg died, a possible suicide, in 1902, in New York City. He had just written "Come Down Ma Evenin' Star" but had not completed the score of *Twirly Whirly*. Legend has it that Lillian Russell broke down during the show's opening while attempting to sing Stromberg's last song; she later included in her repertoire, along with another Stromberg song written for her, "When Chloe Sings a Song" from *Whirl-I-Gig* (1899).

STRONG, GEORGE TEMPLETON (1856–1948) Composer, painter. One of the earliest of American expatriates, Strong was born in New York City, May 26, 1856. His family was musical; his mother was an accomplished pianist and his father an amateur organist who, for a time, was president of the New York Philharmonic Society. Strong began the study of music on the piano and violin, later switched to oboe (and, even later, to the viola). He began composing at around age 13 and had begun to play the oboe professionally. A family quarrel about Strong's future prompted him to leave the United States at the age of 23 to study in Leipzig (1879–86). Later he moved to Wiesbaden where he saw much of another American, Edward MacDowell (q.v.), and the latter's teacher, Joseph Raff. Strong was also on excellent terms with Liszt. In 1891 he returned to the United States and spent a year at the New England Conservatory, Boston, as a teacher, but despite MacDowell's urging he returned to Europe the following year and settled in Vevey, Switzerland. Strong believed that the composer had no chance in the United States—most, if not all, of his published music was issued in Germany. A product of his time and education, Strong produced well-wrought music in the Germanic mold; several have German titles. He composed 3 symphonies, the 2nd of which is subtitled *Sintram* (based on a German romance), Op. 50 (1895), and is dedicated to Mac-Dowell. Much of Strong's output can be categorized as program music, as might be gleaned from his titles: the first symphony is entitled *In den Bergen* (In the

Mountains) and the 3rd, *An der See* (At Sea); his orchestral suite *Die Nacht* consists of 4 sections, *At Sunset, Peasants' March, In Deep Woods,* and *Awakening of the Forest Spirits.* Strong also composed the suite *Une Vie d'Artiste* for violin and orchestra, 2 large choral works, the symphonic poem *Le Roi Arthur,* the 2 *American Sketches for Violin and Orchestra,* an *Elegie* for cello and orchestra, *Songs of an American Peddler* for baritone and orchestra, several piano pieces and chamber works. In 1935 the Philadelphia Orchestra performed one of Strong's most effective works, *Chorale on a Theme by Hassler* for strings. Besides music, Strong was also devoted to painting and was a master of watercolor. He died in Geneva, Switzerland, June 27, 1948.

THOMAS, THEODORE (1835–1905) Conductor. The son of a town musician, Thomas was born in Esens, Hanover (Germany), Oct. 11, 1835. The family moved to New York City when Theodore was 10; he helped support the family by playing the violin in theatres, saloons, and private homes. Thomas was largely self-taught and embarked on a career as "Master T.T., The Prodigy." After a tour of the South, Thomas returned to New York to become part of the burgeoning musical scene. He was first violinist in the orchestra of histrionic conductor Louis Antoine Jullien. Other orchestral work followed and Thomas joined the New York Philharmonic (1854), formed a music-making partnership with William Mason (q.v.) in 1855 for the performance of chamber music, and was concertmaster of the orchestra at the Academy of Music. This eventually led Thomas into a career of conducting and educating Americans in music. In 1862 Thomas formed his own orchestra which toured the country bringing symphonic music to towns and cities from coast to coast. These annual tours introduced many Americans to the music of Mozart, Beethoven, Haydn, et al. along what became known as the "Thomas Highway." By 1867 the orchestra had become an established institution and continued to tour and, after 1872, to give concerts regularly in New York's Steinway Hall. This assured employment for musicians enabled Thomas to build an excellent orchestra. He branched out to become conductor also of the Brooklyn Philharmonic and, with his own orchestra, gave summer concerts in Central Park. In 1873, his fame spreading, Thomas was asked to organize and conduct the Cincinnati May Festival; 3 years later he did the same for the Philadelphia Centennial Concerts—which failed financially and Thomas himself paid off the debts. There was at least one artistic failure, in Thomas' view: the *Centennial March* he had commissioned from Richard Wagner he considered an "insult." In 1877 Thomas became conductor of the New York Philharmonic, although he did not relinquish his own orchestra. He took time out to head the Cincinnati College of Music for a year, hoping to spread his musical gospel as an educator, but after a year he resigned because of the patent commercialism of the enterprise; he returned to New York to the Thomas Orchestra and the Philharmonic, which he proceeded to whip into shape. In 1885 Thomas formed an unfortunate affiliation with the American Opera Company, which went bankrupt when abandoned by its backers (because it was not an immediate money-maker). By this time a rival conductor and orchestra had come upon the scene— Walter Damrosch (q.v.) and his New York Symphony. In 1891, unhappy with conditions in New York, Thomas moved to Chicago, where a group of businessmen guaranteed substantial backing for a symphony orchestra. The result was the Chicago Symphony, which

Thomas conducted until his death. He made it into one of the finest such orchestras in the country, and characterized by exceptional programming. Thomas was often accused of performing too much "advanced" music—i.e., contemporary, or little known older compositions. Despite this, Thomas' backers kept their word and continued to finance the Chicago Symphony and to pay its deficits. Thomas headed the orchestra until his death in Chicago, Jan. 4, 1905.

THORNTON, JAMES (1861–1938) Songwriter, vaudeville performer. Born in Liverpool, England, Dec. 4, 1861, Thornton was brought to the United States when he was about 9. He had a long career—about 50 years—in vaudeville and for a time was teamed with Charles Lawlor (1852–1925), with whom he also collaborated on some of his earliest songs. (Lawlor is best known for the tune of "The Sidewalks of New York.") In 1892 he wrote one of his 2 great successes, "My Sweetheart's the Man in the Moon," which was popularized by his wife, Bonnie Thornton. Besides plugging her husband's songs, it was Bonnie Thornton's chore to intercept Thornton's salary checks before he got them. An alcoholic, Thornton frequently sold his songs outright to publishers and then drank up the money. This may have occurred with his best-known song, "When You Were Sweet Sixteen" (1898), inspired by his wife and made popular by her. Thornton sold the song for $15. By the turn of the century Thornton's kind of music-making had seen its day and he faded from the musical scene, particularly as a songwriter. He often provided lyrics for other songwriters, although in the cases of his 2 most popular creations he wrote both words and music. As late as 1929, when his songs had been all but forgotten, Thornton appeared on Broadway in the Jerome Kern musical *Sweet Adeline.* He died in Astoria, N.Y., July 27, 1938.

TIN PAN ALLEY Popular name for the onetime center of the popular music business attributed to Monroe H. Rosenfeld (q.v.). At the time (ca. 1900) the music business was concentrated on New York's West 28th Street, near Fifth Avenue. Not all publishing houses were there, but most of the more successful ones were; so were, at one time, the William Morris Talent Agency and the trade paper of vaudeville, the New York *Clipper.* By the 1920s Tin Pan Alley had scattered and moved uptown. Its much later counterpart was the Brill Building, 1619 Broadway. In the 1970s it might be said that it had shifted to Nashville, Tenn., the country and western mecca.

TREEMONISHA Opera "in Three Acts/Words and Music/By Scott Joplin," to quote the cover of the libretto. That the great ragtime composer Scott Joplin, newly arrived in New York, was at work on a "grand opera" was announced in the New York *Age* in March 1908. Joplin, who also wrote the libretto, completed the work ca. 1910–11; he published a vocal-piano score in 1911 at his own expense. The plot of *Treemonisha* pits the forces of enlightenment and education against those of superstition and ignorance. The setting is a plantation "somewhere in the State of Arkansas" after the Civil War. A childless couple, "Ned" and "Monisha," pray for a child —and their prayers are answered "in a remarkable manner." One day Monisha finds an infant girl under a tree near their cabin. Thus "Treemonisha." Monisha and Ned work hard to earn an education for the daughter they claim to be their own. The opera opens when Treemonisha, now 18, returns to begin "her career as a teacher and leader." Despite a certain naïveté in book and lyrics, the idea of a black woman leader was remarkable for 1911; and perhaps Joplin's

view that education was the answer to ignorance was equally obvious, but worthy. *Treemonisha* is not an opera in the conventional sense, nor is it a "ragtime" opera. It has charming musical moments, among them "Aunt Dinah Has Blowed de Horn" and the brilliant finale, "A Real Slow Drag." Joplin did not live to see a production of the work that obsessed him during his last years. A performance was announced for 1913 but it never came off; a single run-through (with Joplin at the piano, no scenery or costumes) took place in Harlem sometime in 1915. This attracted no backers for the opera and Joplin never quite recovered from the rejection and he died 2 years later. During the 1970s Joplin resurgence *Treemonisha* was "rediscovered" and performed first in Atlanta in January 1972. Since the orchestrations were lost (except for one fragment), the opera was given a new orchestration by Thomas J. Anderson. A 2nd revival was staged by the Houston Opera, with another set of orchestrations by Gunther Schuller, in May 1975. This version was also recorded.

TURPIN, TOM (ca. 1873–1922) Composer, pianist. Thomas Million Turpin was born in Savannah, Ga., ca. 1873. By the 1880s the family had settled in St. Louis where the father, "Honest John" Turpin, ran a saloon and a livery stable. Turpin was a self-taught pianist with scant musical ambitions. When he was 18 he and a brother bought an interest in a Nevada gold mine which produced very little gold. After traveling in the West for a while Turpin returned to St. Louis where he opened the Rosebud saloon in "the district." It was a meeting place for black musicians, particularly ragtime pianists, in St. Louis. Turpin himself was an accomplished pianist and has gone down in the history of ragtime as the first black composer to publish a rag; this was *Harlem Rag,* published in December 1897. Although known as the "Father of St. Louis Ragtime," Turpin composed comparatively little and it is likely that much of his incidental music for the theatre and his brother's tent show is lost. Other Turpin rags include *Bowery Buck* (1899), *A Ragtime Nightmare* (1900), *St. Louis Rag*, and *The Buffalo Rag*. Stylistically, Turpin was less polished than his friend Joplin and was more active as saloon proprietor and entrepreneur than as a composer. Despite his meager output, he was a major musical influence on the younger ragtime pianists of St. Louis. One of his last works, inspired by World War I, was *When Sambo Goes to France*, an instrumental. Turpin died in St. Louis, Aug. 13, 1922.

VAN DER STUCKEN, FRANK (1858–1929) Composer, conductor. Van der Stucken was born in Fredericksburg, Tex., Oct. 15, 1858; his father was Belgian and his mother German. His father attained the rank of captain in the Texas Cavalry of the Confederate Army during the Civil War. Shortly after the war, the family returned to Belgium, where Van der Stucken received his musical training as a boy, beginning on the violin. He later moved on to Leipzig, where he studied with, among others, Edvard Grieg. He began earning a living by conducting, from time to time programming his own works. In 1883 he was invited to Weimar by Liszt to present a concert of his compositions. The next year Van der Stucken returned to the land of his birth; he was then about 25. In New York he succeeded Leopold Damrosch as conductor of the all-male chorus, the Arion Society. During the season of 1885–86 he presented a series of "novelty concerts," at one of which he performed the Brahms *Third Symphony* for the first time in the United States. He was also the champion of the American composer at these concerts. While on

tour of Europe, Van der Stucken continued bringing the music of the American composer to audiences that had never, or rarely, heard it. In 1895 he became conductor of the Cincinnati Symphony (where he remained until 1907) and was director of the Cincinnati College of Music. He also conducted the Cincinnati May Festivals (1906–12), succeeding Theodore Thomas (q.v.). He was also conductor of festivals in Europe, where, after 1908, he spent most of his time. It was in July 1889 that Van der Stucken presented a historic All American concert at the Paris International; among the works presented on that program was MacDowell's (q.v.) *Second Piano Concerto* with the composer at the piano. Other Americans on the program were Chadwick, Foote, Paine, Lang, and Van der Stucken. Among his works are the incidental music to *The Tempest* (1862), *Prologue to William Ratcliff* (after Heine, 1883)—both of which made very good impressions in Europe. While in the United States, Van der Stucken composed an orchestral *Pax Triumphans* and an overture entitled *Louisiana*. He also composed several solo piano pieces and songs. He died in Hamburg, Germany, after surgery on Aug. 18, 1929.

VAUDEVILLE A form of popular entertainment, combining comedians, vocalists, dancers—undoubtedly inspired by the earlier minstrel show, and the circus. The beginnings have been traced back to about the early 1850s, though the term itself did not come into general use until the 1880s. Its first known use as applied to a variety type of show is attributed to showman John W. Ransone, whose specialty was playing the stereotype Dutch comic ("Vas you effer in Zinzinatti?"). "Vaudeville" is an Americanization (if that's the word) of the French Val (or Vau) de Vire—a river valley in Normandy, noted for its songs.

Vaudeville began to flourish in the 1880s and there were few cities that did not have a theatre that booked variety acts. As early as 1882 there was a Vaudeville Theatre in San Antonio, Tex. Whether Ransone borrowed his term from the marquee or vice versa is unknown. The great vaudeville impresario Tony Pastor (q.v.) preferred the less fancy, more direct term, "variety." The vaudeville/variety vogue began to lessen by the 1920s and was virtually dead by the '30s, the victim of the movies, radio, and the Depression. It provided an outlet and training ground for legendary entertainers: Lillian Russell (1861–1922), May Irwin (1862–1938), Harrigan and Hart (q.v.), Elsie Janis (1889–1956), George M. Cohan (q.v.), Anna Held (1865–1918), W. C. Fields (1879–1946), Bert Williams (q.v.), Nora Bayes (1880–1928), Weber and Fields (q.v.), and Fred and Adele Astaire (b. 1899; 1898–1981); among many others. (Harry Gabler, "glass eater," is not included since he contributed little to the evolution of the American musical theatre.) Vaudeville is believed to have died at the Palace Theatre, New York, sometime in 1932.

VON TILZER, ALBERT (1878–1956) Songwriter, publisher. Born Albert Gumm in Indianapolis, Ind., Mar. 29, 1878, Von Tilzer followed his older brother, Harry (q.v.), into show business and borrowed the name his sibling was already using. The "Tilzer" portion was their mother's maiden name, the "Von" was pure fabrication. Von Tilzer was a self-taught pianist who came to New York around the turn of the century and worked for a time as a shoe salesman while studying harmony. He joined the staff of his brother's publishing company. Soon he began writing songs, one of his earliest being the (then) popular "That's What the Daisy Said" (1903) with words by yet another

brother, Wilbur Gumm. Although Von Tilzer wrote the scores for several musicals between 1911 and 1927, he was more successful in Tin Pan Alley where he produced such long-lasting songs as "Take Me Out to the Ball Game" (1908; lyrics by Jack Norworth, 1879–1959), "Put Your Arms Around Me, Honey" (1910; lyrics by Junie McCree, 1865–1939), and "I'll Be with You in Apple Blossom Time" (1920; lyrics by Neville Fleeson, 1887–1945). Albert Von Tilzer died in Los Angeles, Calif., Oct. 1, 1956.

VON TILZER, HARRY (1872–1946) Songwriter, entertainer, publisher. Born in Detroit, Mich., July 8, 1872, Harry Gumm grew up in Indianapolis, which he left in the summer of 1886, aged 14, to join a circus. He eventually joined a traveling vaudeville company as a juvenile and vocalist, often singing his own songs. It was about then that he adopted his mother's premarriage name and became Harry Von Tilzer (a name his brother Albert, q.v., also used professionally). After touring the Midwest vaudeville circuit, Von Tilzer arrived in New York in 1892, without money or a job. He approached Tony Pastor (q.v.) and began turning out songs. Like his younger brother, he was a self-taught pianist. By the turn of the century he was one of Tin Pan Alley's most successful songwriters and, eventually, a publisher. In the latter role he is notable for having been the publisher of the youthful Irving Berlin and George Gershwin. The earliest of his best-known songs is "A Bird in a Gilded Cage" (1900; lyrics by Arthur J. Lamb, 1870–1928). Other songs include "Down Where the Wurzburger Flows" (1902; lyrics by Vincent P. Bryan, 1883–1937), "Wait 'Til the Sun Shines, Nellie" (1905; lyrics by Andrew B. Sterling, 1874–1955), "I Want a Girl—Just Like the Girl That Married Dear Old Dad" (1911; lyrics by William

Dillon, 1887–1966), and "When My Baby Smiles at Me" (1920; lyrics by Sterling). A couple of attempts at writing show scores was not successful. Harry Von Tilzer died in New York City, Jan. 10, 1946.

WALKER, JAMES J. (1881–1946) Songwriter, attorney, politician. Born in New York City, June 19, 1881, Walker is best remembered as the Mayor of New York from 1925 to 1932, when he resigned after being charged with "several counts of financial impropriety." Walker studied law, became involved in politics in 1909, when he was elected assemblyman and later (1914) state senator. During his period as Mayor of New York, Walker was known as the "night Mayor," because of his love of night life, the theatre, and show girls. Before all this occurred he had written the lyrics to several songs, including one which earned him this entry: "Will You Love Me in December as You Do in May?" (1905) with music by Ernest R. Ball (q.v.). Other Walker titles: "Kiss All the Girls for Me," "Good Bye, Eyes of Blue," and "There's Music in the Rustle of a Skirt." Following his resignation, Walker spent several years in Europe and returned to find himself, despite the scandals, as popular as ever. He served for a time as a labor arbitrator (1940–44) and, after that, as an executive of a record company. He died in New York City, Nov. 18, 1946.

WARE, HARRIET (1877–1962) Composer, pianist. Born in Waupun, Wis., Aug. 26, 1878. She was graduated from the Pillsbury Conservatory, Owatonna, Minn., and then came to New York to study with William Mason (q.v.). In Paris she studied piano and composition with Sigismund Stojowski (1870–1946), after which she returned to the United States and settled in New York in 1906. Ware made her earliest impressions on the musical scene as a pianist and as a

songwriter. Her song "The Cross," to a poem by Edwin Markham, was especially well received. Other works include a piano concerto which she performed with orchestras, a song cycle, *A Day in Arcady,* a cantata, *Sir Oluf,* the *Women's Triumphal March* (1927), a tone poem, *The Artisan,* premiered by the New York Symphony in 1929. Several songs and solo piano pieces round out Ware's compositional output. She died in New York City, Feb. 9, 1962.

WA-WAN PRESS Nonprofit music publishing company, founded in 1901 by composer Arthur Farwell (q.v.) and dedicated to the publication of music by American composers. Unsuccessful in placing one of his compositions, based on Indian themes, Farwell decided to do it himself. The Press's publications were printed in Newton Center, Mass., the cost of which was taken care of by Farwell himself with some help from financier George F. Peabody. For 11 years Farwell published his own music as well as works by such composers as Frederick Ayres (q.v.), Gena Branscombe (q.v.), Henry F. Gilbert (q.v.), Edward Burlingame Hill (q.v.), Edgar S. Kelley (q.v.), Arne Oldberg (q.v.), and Arthur Shepherd (q.v.) and about 30 others. Although the works tended toward the folk-inflected, Farwell did not make that a stipulation for publication. In addition to Farwell's Indian-inspired compositions, the Wa-Wan Press (named for an Omaha Indian ceremony) published the more scientific studies of Indian music by Natalie Curtis Burlin and Carlos Troyer, who were more interested in authenticity than art. Other Wa-Wan Press composers drew upon Negro materials, while others produced purely abstract music. Having provided an outlet for the ignored American composer of the nontraditional bent and having made his point (as well as, no doubt, losing some of his money), Farwell sold the publications of Wa-Wan Press to G. Schirmer Inc., New York, in 1912.

WEBER AND FIELDS Joseph Weber (1867–1942) and Lew Fields (1867–1941) formed a comedy team in 1885 in burlesque (they portrayed wildly dressed, bewhiskered Dutch comics with thick dialects) and eventually graduated into the musical theatre. Their Weber and Fields Broadway Music Hall presented a series of musicals, most with music by John Stromberg (q.v.), featuring the antics of the comedians. The act broke up in 1902, although after a decade the team reunited now and then. Fields (born Lewis Schanfield) and Weber gave up performing for producing; the former helped to launch the musical theatre songwriting team of Rodgers and Hart (of whom more in Section V) and Weber produced several musicals by Victor Herbert (q.v.). Fields was additionally known as the father of librettists Herbert and Joseph Fields and lyricist Dorothy Fields (q.v., Section V). The musical productions associated with the names of Weber and Fields were transitional between burlesque (low comedy, not the stripper type of show) and the "classic" musical comedy of the 1920s.

WENRICH, PERCY (1887–1952) Composer, pianist. Born in Joplin, Mo., Jan. 23, 1887, Wenrich was known for a time as the "Joplin Kid," because of his birthplace, not because he was regarded as a Scott Joplin (q.v.) disciple, although he composed several early and excellent rags. Son of the town postmaster and given early musical training by his mother, Wenrich first began composing while in his teens. His father provided the lyrics for those early political songs singing the praises of such as William Jennings Bryan and Grover Cleveland. As a youngster Wenrich also frequented the sporting section of Joplin, listening to black pianists. When he was

17, Wenrich paid for the publication of his first instrumental effort, *L'Inconnu,* which he himself sold door-to-door. When he was 21, Wenrich was sent to Chicago, where he studied briefly at the Chicago Musical College. He drifted away from formal education and into playing the piano in saloons and composing. He was doing well as a pianist in Freddie Train's, a saloon, when he placed his first professional song with the Chicago firm of Buck and Carney. (It may be a musicological curiosity to point out that the Buck of that firm eventually became Frank "Bring 'Em Back Alive" Buck, ex-lyricist, explorer, and wild animal collector.) The year was 1902 and the song was entitled "Wabash Avenue After Dark" with lyrics by Jim O'Dea; it was not published, but Buck and Carney did issue Wenrich's first rag, *Ashy Africa.* Wenrich worked at other jobs in publishing, even as a song plugger before coming to New York in 1908. He also toured vaudeville for several years with Dorothy "Dolly" Connelly. Wenrich composed rags and songs through this period. He regarded *Noodles* (1906) as his first rag and when the publisher issued *The Smiler* (1907), it was subtitled "A Joplin Rag." This term was rather misleading, though stylistically it was Joplinesque. However, the nickname, the "Joplin Kid," stuck. Between 1903 and 1916, Wenrich published 18 rags, but it was in the field of popular song that he was to enjoy his greatest success. Like so many successful Tin Pan Alley composers, he was not very lucky on Broadway. He composed scores for 4 musicals, *Crinoline Girl* (1914), *The Right Girl* (1921), *Castles in the Air* (1926; his greatest success, with a mildly good run of 120 performances), and *Who Cares?* (1930; his least successful show, which ran for 32 performances). In the popular field, Wenrich made his greatest impression as the composer of the tunes to "Put On Your Old Gray Bonnet" (1909;

lyrics by Stanley Murphy, 1875–1919), "Moonlight Bay" (1912; lyrics by Edward Madden, 1878–1952), and "When You Wore a Tulip and I Wore a Big Red Rose" (1914; lyrics by Jack Mahoney, 1882–1945). Although confined to a wheelchair during the last years of his life, Wenrich lived comfortably on the royalties brought in by these 3 songs. He died in New York City, Mar. 17, 1952.

"WHEN YOU AND I WERE YOUNG, MAGGIE" Popular, sentimental song, published in 1866; words by George W. Johnson and melody by James Austin Butterfield (q.v.).

WHITING, ARTHUR B. (1861–1936) Composer, pianist. Born in Cambridge, Mass., June 20, 1861, Whiting was the nephew of the distinguished organist-composer George E. Whiting (1840–1923). He studied at the New England Conservatory, piano with William Hall Sherwood (1854–1911) and composition with Chadwick (q.v.). He made his debut as a pianist in Boston at the age of 19. He then went to Europe for further study (1883–85) with Joseph Rheinberger in Munich. Whiting then returned to Boston, where he composed, organized concerts, and served as organist for the New England Conservatory. In 1895 he moved to New York, where he played in concerts and recitals; he also taught piano and composition. Whiting became an authority on ancient instruments and gave lecture recitals and performed the music written for those instruments. As a composer, Whiting was not prolific; he made his first impression on the national music scene in the first decade of the century with such works as a *Fantasy for Piano and Orchestra,* Op. 11, the *Six Bagatelles,* and (3) *Characteristic Waltzes* for piano, a *Sonata for Violin, Piano Quintette, Suite for Strings;* later works include a song cycle, *Floriana,* a *Concert Overture* for orchestra, a *String Quartet* (1929), a

dance pageant score for chamber orchestra, *The Golden Cage,* and other solo piano pieces and songs. Whiting died in Beverly, Mass., July 20, 1936.

WILLIAMS, BERT (1874–1922) Comedian, vocalist, songwriter. Born Egbert Austin Williams, Nov. 12, 1874, in the British West Indies of Afro-Spanish parentage, Williams was brought to the United States when the family settled in Riverside, Calif. At 19 Williams joined the Mastadon Minstrels, coaxing another song-and-dance man, George Walker (ca. 1872–1911), to join him. They eventually formed the vaudeville team of Williams and Walker and were discovered by producer Thomas Canary in French Lick Springs, Ind., in 1896. Canary saw their performance in a hotel and immediately signed them to appear in *The Gold Bug,* a farce then running in New York. The team was a tremendous hit and appeared after that in a number of musicals. Walker and Williams were among the first to attack the stereotyped minstrel show Negro. After Walker died in 1911, Williams continued on as a single—in blackface!—and became the most celebrated black actor on Broadway. His walk, his costume, his timing were unique and assured his appearance in 8 editions of the *Ziegfeld Follies* (1910–19; he missed the *Follies* of '13). Williams' comic routines consisted of monologues, pantomime, and songs, many of which he composed himself (with lyrics frequently by Walker). His own songs included "Mammy's Little Pickaninny Boy" (1896), "Snap Shot Sal," (1899), "The Voodoo Man" (1900), "Nobody," his most famous song (1905), and "That's a-Plenty" (1909; the words were by Harry Creamer, 1879–1930). Williams' last Broadway appearance was in *Broadway Brevities* (1920). He died, after contracting pneumonia during a vaudeville tour, in New York City, Mar. 4, 1922.

"WILL YOU LOVE ME IN DECEMBER AS YOU DO IN MAY?" Popular song, published 1905, with music by Ernest R. Ball and words by James John Walker (q.v.).

WILSON, MORTIMER (1876–1932) Composer, teacher. Born in Chariton, Iowa, Aug. 6, 1876, Wilson received his musical education at the Chicago Conservatory of Music. One of his teachers was Frederick Gleason (q.v.). Wilson then spent 6 years teaching theory at the University School of Music, Lincoln, Neb., after which he went to Leipzig for 3 years to study with Max Reger (1873–1916), who made a deep impression on the young American. In 1911 Wilson returned to the United States to teach at the Atlanta (Ga.) Conservatory, where he taught harmony and composition. Wilson was also conductor of the Atlanta Philharmonic and taught at Brenau College in Gainesville. He went to New York in 1918 and remained there for the rest of his life. He taught at the Malkin School and also accepted private students. As a composer Wilson was a pioneer of sorts, for he composed music for films in the silent era (most large city film houses had orchestras then). Among his works in that vein were the *Overture "1849,"* written for the 1923 film *The Covered Wagon;* Wilson composed background music for a number of Douglas Fairbanks films, among them *The Thief of Bagdad* (1924). Among his other works are several orchestral suites: *New Orleans, Country Wedding, In Georgia* (originally for piano); a *Mardi Gras* overture, *From My Youth* (a trio expanded into an orchestra work which was performed by the New York Philharmonic), an *Organ Sonata,* 2 sonatas for violin and piano, a "scenic fantasy," *"My Coun-*

try," many piano and vocal pieces, plus 5 (unpublished) symphonies. Wilson published the book *The Rhetoric of Music* in 1907. He died in New York City, Jan. 27, 1932.

WODEHOUSE, P. G. (1881–1975) Author, lyricist. Pelham Grenville Wodehouse was born in Guildford, England, Oct. 15, 1881, and came to the United States in 1909. Primarily a writer, he started out as a columnist in Britain and began writing short stories for the *Saturday Evening Post* in 1914. He eventually produced a great number of whimsical novels featuring an unflappable and wise butler named "Jeeves." Wodehouse was also an influential lyricist and librettist. His early work was studied by such younger men as Ira Gershwin and Lorenz Hart (q.v., Section V). Wodehouse furnished both lyrics and books for several shows by Jerome Kern (q.v.) and collaborated also on songs with Rudolf Friml (Section V), Louis A. Hirsch (Section V), Sigmund Romberg (Section V), and Victor Herbert (q.v.). Among his best-known songs: "Bill," "Leave It to Jane," "The Siren's Song," and "You Never Knew About Me," all to melodies of Kern. Wodehouse's chief collaborator on musical books was Guy Bolton (b. 1884), with whom he wrote the books to many of the early Kern Princess Theatre shows and the 1927 Gershwin musical *Oh, Kay!* Wodehouse's last Broadway collaboration was Cole Porter's *Anything Goes,* written with Bolton, and which was then rewritten by Howard Lindsay and Russel Crouse. Wodehouse devoted his later years to writing his delightful, slightly dotty, novels. He became an American citizen in 1955 (he had spent several years abroad and was in France, where he was more or less trapped, during the Second World War). He was knighted in 1975, after he had reached the venerable age of 93; he died at Southampton, N.Y., Feb. 14, 1975.

WOODLAND SKETCHES, OP. 51 A collection of piano pieces by Edward MacDowell (q.v.) composed in 1896. The 10 pieces are entitled: 1) "To a Wild Rose," 2) "Will o' the Wisp," 3) "At an Old Trysting Place," 4) "In Autumn," 5) "From an Indian Lodge," 6) "To a Water-Lily," 7) "From Uncle Remus," 8) "A Deserted Farm," 9) "By a Meadow Brook," and 10) "Told at Sunset."

WORK, JOHN WESLEY, SR. See Fisk Jubilee Singers.

YOUNG, RIDA JOHNSON (1869–1926) Lyricist, librettist. Born in Baltimore, Md., Feb. 28, 1869, Rida Johnson, after finishing college, entered show business via the E. H. Sothern and Viola Allen acting companies. She drifted into the music business and worked for music publishers; she also revealed a talent for writing. Among her straight plays are *Brown of Harvard* (1906), *The Boys of Company B* (1907), and *The Girl and the Pennant* (1913), among others. She wrote book and lyrics for *Barry of Ballymore* (1910) which contained a song with music by Ernest R. Ball (q.v.) and Chauncey Olcott (1858–1932), who made his debut in this show. The song was "Mother Machree." That same year Mrs. Young provided both book and lyrics for the Victor Herbert (q.v.) operetta, *Naughty Marietta,* which introduced such songs as "Ah! Sweet Mystery of Life," "Italian Street Song," "I'm Falling in Love with Someone," and "Tramp, Tramp, Tramp." Other composer collaborators included Sigmund Romberg (*Maytime,* 1917) and Rudolf Friml (*Sometime,* 1919); her last musical, *The Dream Girl,* reunited her with Victor Herbert in 1924 (it was also Herbert's last score). Rida Johnson Young died in Stamford, Conn., May 8, 1926.

V

The Twenties

(1920–1929)

Neatly enclosed historical periods are created by historians; they have no objective existence except in the human mind. Still, the 1920s do form a specific, definable period in our history that began with the ending of a Great War and closed with the beginning of a Great Depression. In this brief time, as histories go, American business and industry flourished; so did the arts, and American music came of age in what is frequently called the Jazz Age.

And it might be noted that what was consistently called "jazz" during the Jazz Age wasn't jazz at all, but rather popular music or dance music spiced with mangled jazzisms borrowed from the Negro. The appropriation from folk and popular sources is a long and honorable practice—consider a Haydn minuet or a Chopin waltz—but when a "serious" composer lifted from jazz for rhythmic spice, or a bluesy harmonic touch, or even for the unusual sonorities provided by a true jazz band, or from a dance band for that matter, he succeeded in raising many a critical hackle and prided himself in being quite "radical" and daring. But to the extent of his seriousness, it was possible that he was merely slumming musically and had only a minimal idea of what he was doing and what jazz really was. Transforming the Philharmonic into a bloated theatre pitband and hoping to get its 100 men to break into a feverish fox-trot, let alone an authentic blues, may have titillated—or outraged—the Philharmonic audience but, as we know now, it produced very little music that survived. Nothing ages quite so quickly as the latest thing. Of the supposed jazzy creations that came out of the '20s only a handful of works by George Gershwin have proved to be perennially transcendent of the period; and that has nothing to do with minimal (if any) jazz content.

Compositions that the composer claimed were rooted in jazz, or what he believed was jazz, are not without charm. Consider Aaron Copland's *Music for the Theatre* and *Piano Concerto;* or Carpenter's *Skyscrapers,* Cole Porter's *Within the Quota,* George Antheil's *A Jazz Symphony*—all delightful to hear. So are several European attempts based on firsthand knowledge gleaned in

New York (especially Harlem) speakeasies or from listening to dance band recordings. Among these are Milhaud's *La Création du Monde,* Stravinsky's *Ragtime for 11 Instruments,* Kurt Weill's *Three Penny Opera,* Martinů's *Le Jazz,* and Krenek's *Jonny Spielt Auf* (Johnny Strikes Up the Band), an opera with a black bandleader as the protagonist. These are but a few works by Europeans that were influenced by American popular music.

The preoccupation with jazz, the true and the false, was a minor characteristic of the American musical ferment during the '20s. Even more important and lasting was the break with the tradition that sent the young American musician to Germany to be polished into professionalism. This represented an esthetic severance with the Second New England School. The younger composers chose to go to France to study with a remarkable teacher, Nadia Boulanger. In Paris the young American was exposed to the music of the "modernists," Stravinsky, Bartók, and Schoenberg, as well as to the wild young Frenchmen and one woman known as *Les Six.* Stimulated, the young American returned home to set his music-loving countrymen on their figurative ear.

Postwar America was bubbling economically so there was money for the arts, not just music. Artistic self-consciousness resulted in a flowering of poetry, literature, dance, theatre, and painting as writers and artists attempted to interpret their America. Musicians banded together, with the help of patrons, to assure hearings of the "New Music." An ex-Parisian, Edgard Varèse founded the International Composers' Guild in 1922; his aim was to perform the music of the more experimental composers, not necessarily American. A splinter group the following year broke away from the Guild to form the League of Composers, whose emphasis, while still international, leaned toward the American composer.

Of no little importance to the modern American composer was the arrival of the Russian-born Serge Koussevitzky in 1924 and Polish-born Leopold Stokowski in 1909. Koussevitzky became conductor of the Boston Symphony and was a powerful champion of the contemporary composer, American and European. Stokowski, who headed the Philadelphia Orchestra by 1912, was also open to the new musical ideas of the younger composer.

If he did not want to go to Paris (or could not afford it) the aspiring American composer of the '20s could turn to 3 new important institutions, the Eastman School of Music, Rochester, N.Y. (1921), the Juilliard School of Music, New York City (1923), and the Curtis Institute, Philadelphia (1924). The Eastman School, under the leadership of composer-conductor Howard Hanson, provided a training ground and outlet for numerous composers and performing musicians. Opera continued to flourish, especially in the larger cities, although there was little interest in opera by the American composer. When Deems Taylor's *The King's Henchman* was produced at the Metropolitan Opera in 1927, the very fact that it was by an American was noted as much as the opera itself.

It was in the field of light opera and the musical theatre that a great flowering occurred in the '20s. This was because a new generation of songwriters had come upon the scene. Inspired by the well-crafted songs of Victor Herbert and especially Jerome Kern as well as the earthy quasi-folk-like creations of Irving Berlin, the younger songwriters initiated a redefinition of American popular song. Composers were actually musicians, and lyricists were masters of light verse; popular songs, especially those originating in the musical theatre, were, at their best, literate and musicianly. Tin Pan Alley still remained, generally to produce the quick hit and imitations thereof.

The musical theatre in its musical comedies and revues provided an outlet for the more sophisticated talents (the operetta genre co-existed alongside these more brittle products in the work of Sigmund Romberg and Rudolf Friml). During the '20s the musical theatre brought forth musicals with songs by George and Ira Gershwin, Richard Rodgers and Lorenz Hart, Cole Porter, Vincent Youmans, Oscar Hammerstein, DeSylva, Brown and Henderson, Harry Tierney and Walter Donaldson. The quality of the work of most of these songwriters would influence several generations of songwriters, besides many in their own time. And when the Depression curtailed Broadway productions and the sound film became practicable, most of these same creators would contribute to the flowering, in turn, of the film musical of the '30s.

The popular misconception that jazz was to be equated with dance bands, i.e., Paul Whiteman's, Isham Jones, Ted Lewis, et al., was proliferated by many "serious" music critics, among them the *Musical Courier*'s Henry O. Osgood and Carl Van Vechten; one important critic, Paul Rosenfeld, refused to accept jazz (he too really meant popular music aping jazz). Whiteman's was a remarkable band which did indeed employ true jazz musicians from time to time, but it was really one of the first of the big bands—an industry that would flourish in the '30s and early '40s. Whiteman's activities during the Jazz Age would earn him a bad press from the professional jazz critics who surfaced in such books as *Jazzmen* and little magazines as *Jazz Information* and *The Jazz Record* in the late '30s and '40s.

These esoteric publications, while sometimes shrill, did succeed in bringing attention to the true jazzmen of the period, King Oliver, Louis Armstrong, Bessie Smith, Kid Ory, Fletcher Henderson, and the white musicians they had influenced: Bix Beiderbecke, Jimmy McPartland, the Wolverines, Frank Teschemacher, and the New Orleans Rhythm Kings. Duke Ellington organized one of the first true jazz bands. The performances of many of these jazz musicians were recorded on what came to be called "race records," which were pressed primarily for the Negro market.

These were the 3 major currents in American music in the '20s: the traditionalists of the Second New England School (which, though fading, was not finished), the iconoclasts who broke with them, and the writers of popular music, especially as it flowered in the theatre and jazz. Parenthetically, a more conservative school of young traditionalists thrived also. They were centered mostly around Howard Hanson and the Eastman School. These elements were fused and given wide dissemination by the technical developments of the age: the phonograph, which went electronic (as opposed to acoustic) by the mid

'20s, radio, which arrived in the first year of the decade, and the sound film, which began its life toward the close of the period in the appropriately titled *The Jazz Singer* (1927). Within 2 years the Hollywood film musical would emerge.

It was a time rich in musics (the noun is plural intentionally and that plurality contributed to the period's confusion, productivity, and charm). It did not really define American music or the American composer, although there was much self-conscious discussion on the subject. There was even some self-conscious writing, but as William Schuman has observed, only "a chauvinist would claim there is a qualitative factor related to Americanism in music—that is, that the degree of identifiable 'Americanism' in a work directly affects or indicates its value. Whether or not a piece is 'Americana' has nothing to do with its being a better or less good musical work."

AGER, MILTON (1893–1979) Composer, pianist. Born in Chicago, Ill., Oct. 6, 1893, Ager was a self-taught pianist who got his start, after dropping out of high school, as a pianist in the Chicago branch of Waterson, Berlin and Snyder. He also played in film houses and in vaudeville. Arriving in New York in 1913, he found work again with Waterson, Berlin and Snyder as pianist and musical secretary (he notated songs for the writers who could not, or didn't want to, write down the piano copies of their songs, among them Berlin, Walter Donaldson, and Jean Schwartz). He later joined the William Jerome Co., where he was affiliated with George M. Cohan. He enlisted in the U. S. Army during World War I and was stationed at Fort Greenleaf, Ga.; it was there he began composing songs, including his first published song, "Everything Is Peaches in Georgia" (written with George Meyer, lyrics by Grant Clarke). It became a hit after Al Jolson introduced it at the Winter Garden in 1918. He had another success in "A Young Man's Fancy," written for his first Broadway show, *What's in a Name?* (1920; the lyrics were by Jack Yellen). Ager did songs for 4 more shows but did best with his single Tin Pan Alley songs: "I Wonder What's Become of Sally?" (1924; lyrics by Yellen); "Hard Hearted Hannah, the Vamp of Savannah" (1924; lyrics by Yellen, Bob Bigelow, and Charles Bates). "Ain't She Sweet?" (lyrics by Yellen) was a great hit in 1927 and after; "Auf Weidersehn, My Dear" (with Al Goodman, lyrics by Ed Nelson and Al Hoffman) was written in 1932, by which time Ager had settled in Hollywood. He contributed songs to *Honky Tonk* (1929), *The King of Jazz* (1930), and to *Chasing Rainbows* (1930), from which came "Happy Days Are Here Again" (lyrics by Yellen) whose popularity became even greater than it originally was when the song was adopted by the Democrats in the campaign that made Franklin D. Roosevelt President; the song literally became his theme song. Although he continued to compose songs until about 1939, Ager was not very productive after his early successes. He died in Inglewood, Calif., Apr. 6, 1979.

ALTER, LOUIS (1902–1980) Composer, pianist. Born in Haverhill, Mass., June 18, 1902, Alter began studying music at the age of 9; at 13 he was a pianist in a local theatre providing the background music for silent movies. Alter studied piano with Frank Stuart Mason (1833–1929)—not one of *the* Masons, but an eminent teacher. After completion of study at the New England Conservatory, Alter moved to New York in 1922, where he was hired as accompanist by vaudeville star Nora Bayes for whom he worked for 5 years touring the United States and Europe. Although Bayes was the star, Alter was permitted to introduce his own compositions during the tours. After Bayes, he was accompanist for Irene Bordoni, Beatrice Lillie, and Helen Morgan. He earned additional money between jobs as an arranger. In 1928, in the wake of the "symphonic jazz" that Paul Whiteman and others had nurtured, Alter composed an instrumental piece entitled *Manhattan Serenade* (q.v.). Its popularity led to an entire suite of such pieces: *Manhattan Moonlight* (1929), *Manhattan Masquerade* (1932), *Metropolitan Nocturne* (1936; winner of the Venice Film Festival Gold Medal, 1936), and *Side Street in Gotham* (1938). Other Alter instrumental compositions include *American*

Serenade, Tribute, Ivory Lace, and *Candle in the Wind.* In 1938, "Manhattan Serenade" emerged as a popular song with lyrics by Harold Adamson. In 1925 Alter began contributing interpolated songs to musicals, beginning with the *Earl Carroll Vanities* of that year. With the advent of the film musical, Alter moved on to Hollywood where he contributed songs to several films; his most popular songs were written for films of the 1930s. He created the melody to "Rainbow on the River" (lyrics by Paul Francis Webster) for the film of the same title; and for *The Trail of the Lonesome Pine* (1936), he wrote "A Melody from the Sky" and "Twilight on the Trail" (both with lyrics by Sidney D. Mitchell [1888–1942]). "Twilight on the Trail" was known to have been one of President Franklin D. Roosevelt's favorite songs. Alter produced another popular song in "Dolores" for the film *Las Vegas Nights* (1941), with lyrics by Frank Loesser. During World War II he served with the U. S. Army Air Forces, Special Services; during this period he appeared with the Los Angeles Philharmonic in performances of his own work. After the war Alter continued moving between Hollywood and Broadway. He composed his *Jewels from Cartier* suite in 1956 and several unpublished piano pieces and songs. Alter died in New York City, Nov. 3, 1980.

"AMERICA" An orchestral work by the Swiss-American composer Ernest Bloch (q.v.). Completed in 1926, its subtitle is "An Epic Rhapsody in Three Parts for Orchestra." The 3 movements traverse a long stretch of American history, although the composition was not intended to be program, or storytelling, music. The first movement is entitled "1620" and makes musical reference to the Indians and Pilgrims. The second movement, "1861–1865," invokes the mood of the Civil War, and the final movement, "1926," touches on the then present and the future, concluding with a sung anthem, "America! America!" In *America* Bloch uses Indian and other folk themes, including quotations from Stephen Foster and songs popular at the time of the Civil War. His final movement is properly jazzy. It is a work written with honest emotion; in the score Bloch noted that "This Symphony has been written in love for this country, in Reverence to its Past, in Faith in its Future. It is dedicated to the memory of Abraham Lincoln and Walt Whitman whose vision has upheld its inspiration." *America* won the *Musical America* prize in 1928 and was performed for the first time by the New York Philharmonic, Dec. 20, 1928.

"AMÉRIQUES" Orchestral composition by the French-American composer Edgard Varèse (q.v.). "A purely sentimental title," the composer once said. "When I wrote *'Amériques'* I was still under the spell of my first impression of New York—not only New York seen, but most especially heard." Varèse chose the plural for his title because he wished to symbolize in sound the various meanings of the New World. Completed in 1922, *Amériques* was extremely avant-garde in its time and remains so a half century later. Utilizing an orchestra of percussion instruments, Varèse created a musical medium entirely his own. The composition was performed by the Philadelphia Orchestra under Stokowski for the first time on Apr. 9, 1926.

"AN AMERICAN IN PARIS" Tone poem for orchestra by George Gershwin (q.v.). The initial idea for *An American in Paris* occurred to Gershwin during a brief visit in 1926. In the spring of 1928 he returned for a longer stay and did most of the work there, although he had a 2-piano sketch ready as early as January. Accompanied by a friend, Mabel Schirmer, Gershwin found a set of taxi horns which he intended to use in the orchestration. After Gershwin's return to the United States, he worked on the composition and completed the orchestration on Nov. 18, 1928. Unlike his 2 earlier concert works, *Rhapsody in Blue* (q.v.) and *Concerto in F,* there was no solo piano part. *An American in Paris* was given its world premiere by the New York Philharmonic, which had commissioned it, on Dec. 13, 1928, Walter Damrosch conducting.

ANTHEIL, GEORGE (1900–1959) Composer, pianist, author. Born in Trenton, N.J., July 8, 1900, Antheil, a prodigy, was playing the piano at 6 and composing at 12. He studied with Constantin von Sternberg (1852–1924) at the Sternberg Music School in Philadelphia and later with Ernest Bloch (q.v.). He began his professional career in Europe, where (1921–23) he gave piano recitals in Britain, Austria, and Hungary, performing works from the standard repertory and his own modernistic shockers, such as the *Sonata Sauvage.* In 1923 Antheil settled in Paris with his wife and remained for 10 years. A self-styled "bad boy of music," he was a member of the group of Paris intellectuals, among them James Joyce, Ezra Pound, and others, who were determined to enliven the arts through radical change, and a sharp break with tradition. Antheil made his first strike in his *Ballet Mécanique* (q.v.), completed in 1925, premiered in Paris the next year, and performed in New York in 1927, to the consternation of all. The instrumentation, a battery of pianos, xylophones, bells, even an aircraft engine— and the sounds that issued therefrom— immediately typed Antheil as a musical troublemaker. Antheil contributed further to that appraisal with his *A Jazz Symphony* during the same period. He returned to Europe to compose and in 1928 became Assistant Music Director of the Stadtheatre, Berlin. The Depression put a crimp on the money supply that Parisian (and American) society

supplied for experimental music; in 1933 Antheil returned to the United States, settling in New York City. Three years later, in poor health, he moved to the gentler climate of California, settling in Hollywood, where he produced film scores and wrote newspaper and magazine articles (one of his subjects was criminal endocrinology!); he also wrote an advice-to-the-lovelorn column. Despite these other interests Antheil managed to produce a considerable body of music: 6 symphonies—the first, *Zingreska,* composed in 1921 and the last in 1948. He also wrote a piano concerto (1926) and a violin concerto (1946). His chamber works include 3 string quartets (1924, '28, '46), 3 violin and piano sonatas (1923–24), and a *Sonatina for Violin and Piano* (1946). For the stage Antheil composed some incidental music for *Oedipus* (1928), several ballets, among them *Fighting the Waves* (1929), *Dreams* (1935), and *Capital of the World* (1953). His operas include *Transatlantic* (1929), *Helen Retitires* (1932), and *Volpone* (1950). His film scores: *The Scoundrel, The Plainsman, Make Way for Tomorrow,* and *Specter of the Rose.* Antheil's autobiography, *Bad Boy of Music,* was published in 1945. He died in New York City, Feb. 12, 1959.

"APRIL SHOWERS" Popular song, words by B. G. "Buddy" DeSylva (see DeSylva, Brown, and Henderson) and music by Louis Silvers (1889–1954). The song was interpolated into the score of the Broadway show *Bombo* (1921), starring Al Jolson, who popularized it and was associated with the song for several decades.

ARMSTRONG, LOUIS (1900–1971) Trumpeter, bandleader. One of the great figures in American jazz, Armstrong was born in New Orleans, July 4, 1900. Poor, he grew up in what was to be called Storyville, or the District, and earned his first money performing in the streets. Inadvertence gained Armstrong his first formal musical training. On New Year's Eve 1914 he borrowed his stepfather's gun which he proceeded to fire off in the street in celebration. This earned him some time in the Colored Waif's Home for Boys where he studied music with a black instructor named Peter Davis. Armstrong worked his way through several instruments and eventually became lead cornetist in the Waif's brass band; before he was released from the home he had become leader of that band (which incidentally played at picnics and joined in the traditional New Orleans parades). After his release, Armstrong worked at several jobs, one as a driver of a coal cart days and another as cornetist evenings and weekends in the District. The young cornetist came to the attention of and was influenced by King Oliver, the reigning musical monarch of the District. During these formative years, while he was still in his teens, Armstrong played in the established bands of Kid Ory (q.v.) and Fate Marable, a legendary leader whose band provided music on a Mississippi River steamboat. It was King Oliver who, in 1922, called for Armstrong to join him in Chicago. He was soon recognized as an extraordinarily inventive artist, with a gift for improvisation and, primarily through recordings, influenced generations of jazz musicians, black and white. Inevitably he left Oliver to strike out on his own (although joining other bands, notably Fletcher Henderson's and Erskine Tate's on his way), forming such groups as his Hot Five (q.v.) and Seven as well as larger orchestras. Armstrong's early "race records" (q.v.) spread his mastery of the trumpet from Chicago to other cities as well as Europe, where he was probably more appreciated than in his own country during the 1920s and '30s. He formed his own big band in 1927

and performed in clubs and theatres. In 1932 he appeared at the Palladium in London with great success. A born showman, Armstrong developed a public personality not unlike his private personality: lovable, clowning, warmly humorous, satirical. This, plus his success in show business, earned him criticism in the serious jazz lover circles. Despite changing musical tastes, from the real jazz of the 1920s through "bop" and so-called "progressive jazz" of the '50s, Armstrong remained constant. He appeared in films, on Broadway, and in dance halls all over the world; in the '50s he toured Europe, Japan, Africa, and the British West Indies as a musical goodwill ambassador for the United States. He was called Ambassador Satch by the press (from his nickname "Satchmo," a shortened version of Satchel-mouth, which was bestowed upon him by fellow musicians). Armstrong's recording career began in 1925 and continued practically until his death. His Hot Five recordings are regarded as among the greatest treasures of jazz; some of his big bands, however, employed 2nd-rate musicians and have not been always welcomed by the jazz fraternity. His gravelly singing style produced unique renditions of popular songs ("Mack the Knife," "Hello Dolly") and imitators, but his singing trumpet style was inimitable. In the '60s Armstrong's health began to decline and he curtailed his travels but made concert, film, and television appearances. Among his last classic recordings are an album devoted to the songs of W. C. Handy and a *Porgy and Bess* collection shared with Ella Fitzgerald. Among Armstrong's own compositions are "Satchel Mouth Swing," "Sugar Foot Stomp," "Struttin' with Some Barbecue," "Ol' Man Mose," and "Someday." Armstrong died 2 days after his 71st birthday, July 6, 1971, at his home in Queens, N.Y.

LOUIS ARMSTRONG'S HOT FIVE
See Hot Five.

BACON, ERNST (b. 1898) Composer, pianist, conductor. Born in Chicago, Ill., May 26, 1898, Bacon received his musical education both in the United States and Europe. Among his teachers, besides his mother, were Alexander Raab (piano), Karl Weigl (theory), Ernest Bloch (composition), and Eugene Goosens (conducting). For a time Bacon performed as a piano soloist in Europe and the United States. He was active as a conductor in the San Francisco area (1934–37); he was also a director of the Federal Music Project there. Bacon taught in several schools: the Eastman School of Music, Converse College (S.C.), and Syracuse University, N.Y. (1945–63). He was the recipient of several fellowships, including the Pulitzer and Guggenheim; he was one of the founders and the first conductor of the Bach Festival, Carmel, Calif. In much of his original work, Bacon drew upon the American scene for his subject matter: *Ford's Theatre* and *From These States* (both 1943); his 3rd (of 4) symphony is subtitled "Great River." His *Symphony* No. 4 was completed in 1963. For the theatre he has written *Take Your Choice* (1936), a musical comedy, *A Tree on the Plains* to a libretto by poet Paul Horgan (1940, rev. 1962), and *A Drumlin Legend* (1949). Other orchestra works, besides the symphonies, include *Prelude and Fugue, The Enchanted Island,* and a concerto for piano and orchestra, *Riolama* (1964). His chamber works include a *Piano Quintet,* a *Cello Sonata,* and a *String Quintet.* There is also a solo piano work entitled *The Hootnanny.* Bacon has also composed several songs, frequently to the lyrics of Emily Dickinson and Walt Whitman. There are also several works for chorus and orchestra: *Ecclesiastes* (1936), *From Emily's Diary* for soprano, alto, and chorus (1944), *The Lord Star* for bass solo and chorus (1950), *By Blue Ontario,* and *The Last Invocation* (1971). Bacon is also the author of 2 books, *Words on Music* (1960) and *Notes on the Piano* (1963).

"BALLET MÉCANIQUE" Notorious composition by the American composer George Antheil (q.v.). Originally composed as background music for a film made by the French painter Fernand Léger in 1924–25, the work's first title was *Message to Mars.* It was given its first concert performance in the home of a wealthy American, Mrs. Christian Gross (whose husband was First Secretary at the American Embassy), and conducted by Vladimir Golschmann. The orchestration, often the cause of disturbances, consisted of 8 grand pianos, one pianola, 2 aircraft engines, and assorted percussion instruments. The first public performance took place in Carnegie Hall, New York City, on Apr. 10, 1927, with the composer conducting. It made him instantly famous and controversial. His scoring for the concert was virtually the same, but with added pianos and no pianola. The New York *Times* reported: "First Performance of Ballet Mécanique in This Country Draws Varied Response—Hisses, Cheers Greet Him—Concatenation of Anvils, Bells, Horns, Buzzsaws Deafens Some, Pleases Others." This spectacular reaction made Antheil an instant musical celebrity in his own land but he never repeated this "success." In later life he came to regard *Ballet Mécanique* as his "C-sharp minor Prelude" (the piece that haunted Rachmaninoff throughout his life). In 1954 the work was presented on Feb. 20 in New York at Columbia University in a revised version. (Playing time was cut nearly in half, i.e., to about 18 minutes, and only 4 pianos employed. Instead of actual engines, a recording of a jet plane was used, along with a battery of percussion instruments. With Antheil in the audience, *Ballet Mécanique* was very well received and later recorded by Columbia. The conductor on both occasions was Carlos Surinach. It might be said that *Ballet Mécanique* echoes the Stravinsky of *Les Noces* and anticipates the Bartók of *Sonata for 2 Pianos and Percussion.*

BARGY, ROY (1894–1974) Pianist, bandleader, composer. Born in Newaygo, Mich., July 31, 1894, Bargy grew up in Toledo, Ohio, where he began taking piano lessons at age 5. Bargy aspired to a career as a concert pianist but could not afford the requisite trip to Europe and so, despite 12 years of study, he began earning his living as a popular and band pianist. He also played the piano and organ in Toledo movie houses. His professional career began in 1919, when he was hired by the Imperial Player Roll Co. to make piano rolls (he was signed by Imperial to compete with another white rag composer-pianist, Zez Confrey, q.v.). For these roll-cutting sessions Bargy created several original rags, among them *Knice and Knifty, Jim Jams, Pianoflage, Behave Yourself,* and others written in the early 1920s. Bargy switched to disc recordings in 1920, when he became arranger, pianist, and director of the Benson Orchestra (named for its organizer, booking agent Edgar Benson) which recorded for RCA Victor. He moved on to other bands, among them that of Isham Jones (q.v.), and then in 1928 joined the enormously successful Paul Whiteman (q.v.) Orchestra as pianist-arranger. He remained active with Whiteman for 12 years, made numerous recordings and radio appearances before striking out on his own in 1940 as a radio bandleader for the shows of Lanny Ross, Garry Moore, and Jimmy Durante (1943). Bargy retired from active conducting in 1963; he died in Vista, Calif., Jan. 16, 1974.

BARLOW, SAMUEL L. M. (b. 1892) Composer, pianist, author. Born in New York City, June 1, 1892, Samuel Latham Mitchill Barlow was the son of a judge who showed early musical promise. He began composing and publishing while still a schoolboy; he received his first commission at 19, which resulted in incidental music to Ángel Guimerá's play *María Rosa.* After Harvard, where he majored in music, Barlow went on to Paris to study piano with Isidor Philipp and to Rome to study orchestration with Ottorino Respighi (1923). During World War I he served in France with the rank of lieutenant. Before and after that service, besides composing, Barlow was active in the musical life of New York, where he lectured, taught, and attempted to improve the teaching of music in the city's schools. Although politically and socially progressive, Barlow was conservative in his music. His first major work for orchestra, the symphonic poem *Alba* (1927), was premiered by the Cincinnati Orchestra under Fritz Reiner in 1928. He was piano soloist in the first performance of his *Piano Concerto* by the Rochester Philharmonic, under Eugene Goosens, in 1931. Other works for orchestra include *Ballo Sordo* (1928), a ballet from which, in 1950, Barlow extracted the finale, *Cortège.* Also: the *Mon Ami Pierrot Overture* (1934) from the opera of the same title—the first American opera presented at the Opéra-Comique in Paris. Barlow also composed a symphonic poem based on the *Babar* tales; a *Circus Overture* dates from 1960. His chamber works include a quartet, *Ballad* (1933), a *Scherzo,* for string quartet (1933), and *Conversation with Chekhov* for piano, violin, and cello (1940). For solo piano Barlow composed the suites *Spanish Quarter* and *Jardin de le Nôtre.* For chamber orchestra he has written *Three Songs from the Chinese* for tenor and septet (1924), *Vocalise* (1926), *Biedermeier Waltzes* and *For Strings* (both 1935). Barlow's work for the theatre includes the scores for *Mon Ami Pierrot* (1934), *Amanda* (1936), and *Amphitryon '38* for the Theatre Guild production starring Alfred Lunt and Lynn Fontanne (1937). During World War II Barlow traveled, lecturing on music; he wrote for *Modern Music* on various topics and is the author of *The Astonished Muse* (1961).

BARRELHOUSE A style of blues piano playing characterized by a rough-and-ready technique—a generally rural version of the Harlem stride piano (q.v.). A generic term for the kind of piano music heard in brothels and gin mills (i.e., bars). The term derives from the setting where the music was heard—a bar that served beer (usually, but sometimes hard liquor) directly from the barrel.

BARTH, HANS (1897–1956) Pianist, composer, teacher. Born in Leipzig, Germany, June 25, 1897, Barth was brought to the United States in 1903, when he was about 6. He made his New York debut as a pianist at the age of 11. He continued his studies both in the United States and abroad (a scholarship at the Leipzig Conservatory). He taught piano at Mannes School of Music (New York) and was director of the Yonkers Institute and, later, director of the National School for Musical Culture (New York). During this time Barth performed his own compositions in recitals and concerts. In the late 1920s he made a study of microtones—sound divisions smaller than those between the tones on the piano keyboard. In 1931 Barth constructed a quarter-tone piano on which he could play his own compositions. The instrument consisted of 2 keyboards, the standard 88-note piano keyboard with the black and white key arrangement; a 2nd keyboard, below the first, had red and blue keys pitched between the tones of the upper keyboard. As Barth ex-

plained: "The music written for this instrument at first sounds weird to the average listener, but after a while it gives one a new feeling of tone color never experienced before." He composed several works for this instrument, including a *Piano Concerto with Strings*, Op. 15 (1930), and a *Quintet* (also with strings, 1930). There is also a Suite for quarter-tone strings, brass, and kettledrums (1930). Other compositions include 2 piano sonatas (1929; 1932) and 2 symphonies (1938; 1948). Barth composed 2 works for the theatre: an operetta, *Miragia* (1916, rev. 1931) and *Save Me the Waltz*, incidental music for a play (1939). His book, *Technic* (1949), is a widely used text. Barth joined the faculty of the Miami Conservatory (Fla.) in 1948, where he taught piano for several years. He died in Jacksonville, Fla., Dec. 8, 1956.

BAUER, MARION (1887–1955) Composer, teacher. Born in Walla Walla, Wash., Aug. 15, 1887, Bauer first studied music with her sister, Emilie. Their father was a musician and their mother a professor of languages. Among her other teachers were Henry H. Huss, Eugene Heffley, and Nadia Boulanger (q.v.). Bauer joined the staff of New York University in 1926; she also taught music at the Juilliard School, Mills College, Carnegie Institute of Technology, and the Cincinnati Conservatory. She was also active in such organizations as the League of Composers, American Composers Alliance, and the National Federation of Music Clubs. Bauer was especially known as an understanding and helpful teacher who went out of her way to aid young composers and musicians. Though her own music is of decided conservative cast, she was tolerant of and interested in the more "advanced" music of her day and unselfishly helped to promote it. Her compositions include a *Violin Sonata*, Op. 14 (1922), a *Fan-*

tasia Quasi una Sonata for violin and piano (1928), a *String Quartet* (1928), *Sun Splendor* for 2 pianos (1930), *Symphonic Suite for Strings* (1940), *Concerto for Piano and Orchestra,* Op. 36 (1940), *A Lament on African Themes* (the slow movement from the *String Quartet,* for string orchestra, 1928), *Faun Song* for soprano and chamber orchestra (1934), *Concertino for Oboe, Clarinet, and String Quartet* (or optional string orchestra, 1943), *Prelude and Fugue for Flute and Strings,* incidental music for *Prometheus Bound* for 2 pianos and flutes (1930), and *Pan,* a choreographic sketch for a film for flute, oboe, clarinet, piano, and string quartet (1937). Bauer was also the New York editor of *Musical Leader* and was the author of *How Music Grew* and *Music Through the Ages* (in collaboration with Ethel Peyser) and *Musical Questions and Quizzes* and *Twentieth Century Music* (1933, rev. 1947). She died in South Hadley, Mass., Aug. 9, 1955.

BEACH, JOHN PARSONS (1877–1953) Composer, pianist, teacher. Born in Gloversville, N.Y., Oct. 11, 1877, Beach was trained at the New England Conservatory of Music. His principal teachers there were Chadwick and Loeffler. He later studied with André Gédalge in France and Gian Francesco Malipiero in Italy. Beach taught piano at Northwestern Conservatory, Minneapolis, Minn., and piano and theory at the University of Minnesota; he also taught in New Orleans and Boston. Beach was regarded as one of the first American "modernists" by the conservatives (the more modernist musicians regarded him as a conservative). After World War I, in which Beach saw action on the Italian Front, he settled in New York for several years where he produced some of his early "radical" works such as *Asolani* for orchestra (1920), *Phantom Satyr* for orchestra (1924), and *New Orleans*

Street Cries (1925). For chamber orchestra Beach composed *Angelo's Letter* for tenor or baritone and 17 instruments and *Enter Buffoon* for 11 instruments; his chamber music includes *Naïve Landscape* for piano, flute, oboe, and clarinet (1917), *Poem for String Quartet* (1920), and *Concert for Six Instruments* (1929). Besides *Phantom Satyr,* which was also performed as a ballet, Beach composed *Pippa's Holiday* for soprano and orchestra (1916) and *Mardi Gras,* a ballet (1925) for the theatre; an opera, *Jorinda and Jorindel* was based on a Grimm fairy tale. Beach also composed several songs and piano pieces. He died in Pasadena, Calif., Nov. 6, 1953.

BECKER, JOHN J. (1886–1961) Composer, teacher. Born in Henderson, Ky., Jan. 22, 1886, Becker became a member in good standing of American composers of experimental bent (all of whom were friends and assisted one another): Charles Ives, Henry Cowell, Carl Ruggles, and Wallingford Riegger. His musical training, encouraged by his parents, was solidly Germanic though completely done in the United States. His principal teachers were Alexander von Fielitz, Carl Busch and, most importantly, Wilhelm Middelschulte, with whom he studied composition and counterpoint. Shortly after his graduation from the Kreuger Conservatory, Cincinnati, Ohio, Becker embarked on a career that combined teaching, composing, and fighting for contemporary music. He taught at North Texas College, was director of music at Notre Dame, was chairman of the Fine Arts Department at the College of St. Thomas, St. Paul, was Minnesota state director of the Federal Music Project and, from 1943 until his retirement in 1957, was composer in residence at Barat College, Lake Forest, Ill. Unlike most Midwesterners with artistic aspirations, Becker did not leave the Midwest for the big cities—not even

Chicago. He chose to remain in the smaller university towns where he became a champion of advanced music. His own music was initially conventional, influenced by his study with Middelschulte and his own interest in early polyphony. In the late 1920s Becker's music became markedly experimental and personal, making him one of the most fascinating, if little known, of all American composers. His works include 7 symphonies, the first dating from 1915 and the last from 1953–54 (not completed). The 3rd, *Symphonia Brevis* (1929), has been performed and even recorded. Becker also composed 2 piano concertos, a horn concerto (1933), a *Concerto Pastorale* for 2 flutes and orchestra (1933), a *Viola Concerto* (1937), and a *Violin Concerto* (1948). He produced several *Soundpieces* for various instruments, i.e., *Soundpiece No. 4* (1937) is for string quartet and No. 5 is a piano sonata. Becker composed several works for solo voice and chorus: *Rouge Bouquet* for a cappella male chorus, trumpet, and piano (1917), *Four Songs for Soprano and String Quartet* (1919), *A Heine Song Cycle* (8 songs for high voice; 1924), *Missa Symphonica* (a cappella male chorus; 1933), *Moments from the Passion* for soloists, mixed voices a cappella (1945). There are a great number of stage works also, including *Dance Figure* for a singer, dancers, and large orchestra (1933); *Obongo,* a ballet, calls for an orchestra of 29 percussion instruments (1933). Becker composed music for several one-act plays *Rain Down Death* (1939), *When the Willow Nods* (1939), *Privilege and Privation* (1940), and the longer *Madeleine et Judas* (1958). Other Becker works include *The Snow Goose: A Legend of World War II* (1944), the film score *Julius Caesar* (1949), and the 4 songs entitled *At Dieppe* for soprano and piano (1959). Becker was also active as a conductor of contemporary music, lecturer, and writer and editor. His most quoted statement, which comes from his article "Imitative Versus Creative Music in America" (1933), defines the man: "Laws [i.e., "the rules of music" as are conventionally taught] are made for imitators. Creators make laws." Becker taught composition at the Chicago Musical College (1949–50) and retired from his post at Barat College in 1957. He died in Wilmette, Ill., Jan. 21, 1961.

BEIDERBECKE, LEON BIX (1903–1931) Cornetist, pianist. Born in Davenport, Iowa, Mar. 10, 1903, Beiderbecke was a self-taught pianist who later took up the cornet. Gifted with perfect pitch and a remarkable musical memory, he found formal music study tedious. During his later high school years Beiderbecke played the piano in a local dance band; at around the age of 14 he switched to the cornet. He developed a singing golden tone and became one of the first great white jazz musicians; though influenced by such black trumpeters as Louis Armstrong (q.v.), Beiderbecke quickly revealed a unique style that won him followers and imitators among jazz musicians, black and white. In 1921 he was enrolled in the Lake Forest Military Academy (near Chicago) but in May 1922 was asked to leave by the faculty because of his musical activities, which kept him out after hours (he was caught one night slipping down the dormitory fire escape after lights out). Beiderbecke quickly found work with bands, the first important one being the Wolverines (q.v.), with which he made his first recordings (1924); he later joined the Charlie Straight Band in Chicago. Other bands included those of Jean Goldkette, Paul Whiteman (q.v.), Frankie Trumbauer, Hoagy Carmichael, and several pickup bands with such names as Sioux City Six, the Goofus Five, and Bix Beiderbecke and his

Rhythm Jugglers, among others. Most of Beiderbecke's best recorded cornet solos were made with the Goldkette and Whiteman orchestras. Though some jazz authorities insist the great jazz man was smothered in the massive Whiteman organization, the records reveal that the arrangements (most by William Challis) featured Beiderbecke's horn. Whiteman even kept Beiderbecke on the payroll when the cornetist was unable to play. The tragedy of Bix Beiderbecke was that he had a serious drinking problem and much drink that he consumed during Prohibition was not of the best. There were periods during which he could not play, although musicians such as Whiteman, Carmichael, others, tried to look after him. It was Beiderbecke's drinking that forced him eventually out of the Whiteman band, but he managed to keep working, often with broadcast bands in New York, and with the early Benny Goodman and the Dorsey Brothers orchestras. Beiderbecke, however, could not control his drinking and worked less and less. His recorded work had become a legend among musicians. Besides his distinctive cornet improvisations (which were copied by others), he also composed *Davenport Blues* and a suite for piano, *In a Mist, Flashes, Candlelight,* and *In the Dark.* These impressionistic compositions are not jazz but are Beiderbecke's tribute to such composers as MacDowell and Nevin (with a touch of the more modern Debussy). Early in August 1931, Beiderbecke began drinking heavily and by Aug. 4 appeared to be ill; on Aug. 6 he suffered an attack of delirium tremens (which he had had before) and died in his Queens, N.Y., apartment. The official cause of death was given as "lobar pneumonia." He died on Aug. 6, 1931; Beiderbecke was then only 28.

BENNETT, ROBERT RUSSELL (b. 1894) Composer, orchestrator-arranger, pianist, conductor. Born in Kansas City, Mo., June 15, 1894, Bennett began the study of music with his parents, both of whom were musical. He continued with the Danish-American composer-conductor Carl Busch. Awarded a Guggenheim Fellowship, he went to Paris in 1926 to study with Nadia Boulanger. By this time Bennett had been active as an arranger for a music publisher and, during World War I, had served as a bandleader. He was also an accomplished organist, violinist, and violist. In the mid 1920s Bennett began to establish himself as a composer with such works as the *Charleston Rhapsody* (1926), *Paysage for Orchestra* (1928), *Sights and Sounds* (1929), *Abraham Lincoln Symphony* (1929), *March for Two Pianos and Orchestra* (1930), *Concerto Grosso for Small Dance Band and Orchestra* (1933), *Eight Etudes for Symphony Orchestra* (1938), *Symphony in D for the Dodgers* (1941), *Concerto for Violin and Orchestra* (1941), and *Four Freedoms Symphony* (1943); another *Symphony* dates from 1946. Bennett has also composed for small units: *Song Sonata for Violin and Piano, Hexapoda (Five Studies in Jitteroptera)* for violin and piano, *Sonatina* for harp, flute, and cello. He has composed 2 one-act operas, *Endymion* (1927) and *The Enchanted Kiss* (1935) and a 3-act opera, *Maria Malibran* (1944). *Four Nocturnes* were composed in 1960. Bennett is best known as an orchestrator of Broadway shows (estimates place the number at about 300). He has orchestrated the music of Kern (*Show Boat, The Cat and the Fiddle*), Gershwin (*Of Thee I Sing*), Rodgers (*Oklahoma, South Pacific,* etc.), Porter (*Kiss Me Kate*), Loewe (*My Fair Lady*), to name a few. Bennett was also responsible for the arrangements and orchestrations of Rodgers themes that comprised the score of the television series *Victory at Sea* (1952–53). He has also arranged a "symphonic picture" based on Gershwin's *Porgy and Bess* and a *Symphonic Story of Jerome Kern.* Bennett also provided arrangements and orchestrations for several classic musical films of the 1930s. His greater reputation rests on his Broadway musical activities and his own original compositions, many of them rooted in American popular song and dance.

BINDER, ABRAHAM WOLFE (1895–1966). Composer, conductor. Born in New York City, Jan. 13, 1895, Binder received his musical education at the New York College of Music and Columbia University, where he studied with Daniel Gregory Mason and Cornelius Rybner. Binder was awarded his degree in music in 1926. He became interested in Jewish music and made several trips to Palestine to collect songs, many of which he arranged and published. Binder was active as a choir leader with several Jewish organizations and schools. He taught liturgical music at the Jewish Institute of Religion and was musical director of the Free Synagogue, New York City. Binder's original compositions were greatly influenced by his musical interests. His works include 3 symphonic suites for orchestra; the first is entitled *Holy Land Impressions* (1927; the others appeared in 1929 and 1934). His overture, *He Chalutsim* (The Pioneers), was composed in 1927. Other orchestral works: *Concertino and Night Music for String Orchestra, Concertante, Israeli Suite, Rhapsody for Piano and Orchestra,* and *Lament—In Memory of the Defenders of the Warsaw Ghetto* (1944). Several choral works, among them *Hibbath Shabbath* (1927), *Rinnath Shabbath* (1932), and *Kabbalath Shabbath* (1940), were conceived for synagogue services; there are also a cantata, *Amos on Times Square* (1940), *Six American Folk Songs* for mixed choir (1941), and 4 volumes of Palestinian folk songs published in 1945. Binder

composed his *String Quartet* in 1935; other chamber works: *Trio for Violin, Piano and Cello* (1926), *Trio for Oboe, Cello and Piano* (1935), as well as 2 piano sonatinas and a *Sonata for Violin and Piano* (1937). Binder was also the music editor of the *Union Hymnal* (3rd ed.). His *Sabbath in Israel* was published in 1956. Binder died in New York City, Oct. 10, 1966.

BINGHAM, SETH (1882–1972) Composer, organist, teacher. Born in Bloomfield, N.J., Apr. 16, 1882, Bingham studied with Horatio Parker at Yale and then spent the years 1906–7 in Paris, where he studied composition with Vincent d'Indy and the organ with Charles Widor. Shortly after his return to the United States, Bingham was appointed professor of organ at Yale (1908–19). He then settled in New York, where he was organist in several churches and was appointed associate professor of music at Columbia. Bingham composed a great deal for the organ: *First Suite* (1923), *Harmonies of Florence* (1928), *Pastoral Psalms* (1937), and a *Concerto for Organ and Orchestra* (1946). Other orchestral works include a *Passacaglia* (1918), *Memories of France* (1920), *Pioneer America* (1925), and *The Breton Cadence* (1928). There are also several choral works, one of which, *Wilderness Stone* for narrator, soloists, chorus, and orchestra (1933), was popular for a time. One opera, *La Charelzenn* (1917), remains in manuscript. So does a string quartet from about the same period. Bingham was active as an official in the American Guild of Organists. He died in New York City, June 21, 1972.

BLACK BOTTOM A popular dance of the late 1920s. The title is an obvious double-entendre, although in the lyrics the reference is to the mud flats of a Southern river. The song/dance by DeSylva, Brown and Henderson (q.v.) was introduced in the *George White's Scan-*

dals of 1926 where it was the finale of the first act. Associated popularly with the diminutive Ann Pennington, it was also performed by the McCarthy Sisters, Tom Patricola, and Frances Williams. It was a regular feature of the *Scandals* to introduce somewhat risqué, eccentric dances. It did not catch on.

"THE BLACK MASKERS" Incidental music to the play by Leonid Andreyev composed by Roger Sessions (q.v.) in 1923 on commission from Professor S. A. Eliot and the senior class of Smith College, Northampton, Mass. Andreyev's play dealt symbolically with Man, his Soul, and the strange Black Maskers who "are the powers whose field of action is the soul of man . . ." according to the author. In 1928 Sessions arranged a 4-section suite based on *The Black Maskers* score for large orchestra; it was his first major composition and has become his most frequently played. Sessions' description of scenes follows:

I. Dance: *Stridente—Sarcastico.* The Dance from Scene I: a wild melody in which are heard malicious laughter, cries of agony and despair, and someone's sad plaining.

II. Scene: *Agitato molto.* This movement contains the music originally written for Scene III of the play, in which the festive gathering is gradually overwhelmed by the increasing hordes of Black Maskers. It has a middle section representing (the protagonist) Lorenzo's song, given to the bass flute, with solo viola obbligato. At the end the victorious trumpetings of the Black Maskers are heard.

III. *Dirge: Larghissimo.* This movement served as an introduction to Scene IV of the play. The music is interspersed with reminiscences of the wild trumpetings of the Black Maskers, and later by trumpet calls announcing from the turrets of the castle the death of Lorenzo.

IV. Finale: *Andante moderato—Un poco agitato.* The music of the final scene: as his castle is overwhelmed by the conflageration, Lorenzo finds redemption in the symbolic purity of the flames.

The Black Maskers is dedicated to Sessions' teacher Ernest Bloch (q.v.).

BLAKE, JAMES HUBERT "EUBIE" (b. 1883) Composer, pianist. The son of former slaves, Blake was born in Baltimore, Md., Feb. 7, 1883. He began to study music at 6, when his family acquired an organ. This was a great sacrifice, for at the time his father worked as a stevedore and his mother took in laundry. Blake studied with a church organist, Margaret Marshall, and with the conductor of the Baltimore Colored Symphony, Llewellyn Wilson. He soon revealed an aptitude for improvisation, and his tendency to rag the hymns he was supposed to study disturbed his very religious mother. Blake's ear was attuned to popular rags and marches and not to the stately hymns of Miss Marshall. Before the turn of the century he had evolved a distinctive piano style and began playing in Baltimore's district in Agnes Shelton's "house of ill repute," in Blake's phrasing. Then barely 16, Blake earned his way also playing for parties, in cafes and the local stage. Around this time (1899) Blake composed his first piano piece, *Charleston Rag.* From 1905 to 1914 Blake also appeared in Atlantic City, where his reputation spread and he became acquainted with other important pianists of the period, James P. Johnson and Willie "The Lion" Smith. Blake's ragtime style was unlike Joplin's Midwestern style, but more tricky and faster.

In the spring of 1915 Blake's professional career took a new turn; in Baltimore he met Noble Sissle, an Indianapolis-born vocalist who was singing in a touring band. The 2 men decided to team up as songwriters (their first song was "It's All Your Fault," 1915, introduced by vaudeville star Sophie Tucker). They also formed a vaudeville team. Their collaboration was interrupted when Sissle became a member of Lieutenant James Reese Europe's Infantry Band. After the war Blake himself joined the band which toured the United States. Sissle and Blake (Blake especially) aspired to Broadway and it was Europe who helped to bring this about by introducing the songwriting team to the writing-performing team of Flournoy Miller and Aubrey Lyles. The result was *Shuffle Along* (q.v.), the first all-Negro show on Broadway since the Walker and Williams productions of a decade before. Opening in May 1921, it became a success and ran for more than 500 performances, a record for any show of whatever ethnic origin and backing. Sissle and Blake collaborated on 3 more shows (ignoring an unfortunate revival of *Shuffle Along* in 1952): *Elsie* (for an all-white cast, incidentally, 1923), *The Chocolate Dandies* (1924), and *Shuffle Along of 1933* (1932). In addition Blake collaborated with Andy Razaf on *Lew Leslie's Blackbirds of 1930,* from which came the song "Memories of You," and *Swing It* (1938), in collaboration with Milton Reddie and Cecil Mack. The team of Sissle and Blake broke up temporarily in 1927, when Sissle formed his own band to tour Europe, after their successful appearances in London and Ireland. Blake returned to the United States to work in vaudeville and Broadway. During World War II, Blake was conductor of a United Services Organization (USO) band which entertained hospitalized soldiers. After retiring from active musical activity, Blake enrolled at New York University where he took up music again and studied the Schillinger System (he was then 66). Despite his "retirement" Blake remained active, appearing in concerts, television, and other events. A successful musical, *Eubie!* opened on Broadway in 1978. In December 1978 Blake, age 95, was awarded an honorary doctorate at the University of Maryland. It was but one of the many honors bestowed on him in his very active later years. His best-known song, written with Sissle (who died in December 1975), is "I'm Just Wild About Harry" (1921).

BLOCH, ERNEST (1880–1959) Composer, teacher. Born in Geneva, Switzerland, July 24, 1880, Bloch came to the United States in 1916, already a respected and established composer. A composer by the age of 11, Bloch, in his mature works, exhibited a deep affinity for Jewish music. While he could hardly be classified as an American composer he, during a long residence in the United States, not only produced a large body of music but was a most influential teacher of several important American composers, among them Isadore Freed, Frederick Jacobi, Quincy Porter, Bernard Rogers, and Roger Sessions. Before his arrival in the United States, Bloch was already known as the composer of several outstanding works: the opera *Macbeth* (produced in Paris, 1910), *Trois Poèmes Juifs* (1913), *Schelomo Rhapsody* for cello and orchestra and the *Israel Symphony* (both completed in 1915). Bloch settled in New York in 1917 to teach composition at the David Mannes School; in 1920 he left to become director of the Cleveland Institute of Music and in 1925 became director of the San Francisco Conservatory of Music. He became an American citizen in 1924; 2 years later he completed his rhapsodic symphony, *America* (q.v.). He retired from teaching in 1930 and returned to Europe to concentrate on composition and conducting, dividing his time between residence in France and Switzerland. Bloch returned to the United States in 1939 and in 1941 settled at Agate Beach, Ore. He was appointed professor of music at the University of California, Berkeley, where he taught until his retirement in 1952. Bloch composed a great deal of chamber music during his American years (4 of his 5 string quartets), his *Concerto Grosso No. 1* for piano obbligato and orchestra (1925) is considered to be one of his finest works. But Bloch was no more self-consciously "American" than he was "Jewish" (except, of course when he drew upon traditional materials); he was an original and it was this quality that he impressed on his many students. Other works by Bloch include *Voice in the Wilderness* for cello obbligato and orchestra (1936), a *Concerto for Violin* (1938), *Suite Symphonique* (1944), *Sinfonia Breve* (1952), *Symphony for Trombone and Orchestra* (1954); his *Sacred Service* (*Avodath Hakodesh,* 1934) is his most important choral work. After his retirement in 1952, Bloch spent his final year composing. Ill with cancer, he died in Portland, Ore., July 15, 1959.

"BLUE MONDAY" George Gershwin's (q.v.) "one act" opera, with libretto and lyrics by B. G. DeSylva. Subtitled "Opera Ala Afro-American," *Blue Monday* was thrown together in 5 days and nights for presentation in the *George White's Scandals of 1922*, during a period of Broadway Negrophilia. It was the youthful Gershwin's earliest public attempt at a "serious" work. Running a bit longer than 20 minutes, *Blue Monday* is, in fact, a small opera consisting of integrated songs interspersed with musical passages. Of the songs, the titular "Blue Monday Blues" and "Has Anyone Seen Joe?" are good Gershwin—the last is based on the theme of an early study for a string quartet. The original

orchestration to *Blue Monday* was done by Gershwin's friend Will Vodery (1885–1951), a black bandleader, arranger, orchestrator. It was performed by a white cast in black face accompanied by the Paul Whiteman (q.v.) band. Its single performance in the *Scandals* occurred on opening night, Aug. 28, 1922; the critical—and audience—reception was so unfavorable that White cut it from the revue. Whiteman revived the "opera" in 1925. Reorchestrated by Ferde Grofé (q.v.) and retitled *135th Street,* it was presented at Carnegie Hall on Dec. 29. Following this performance, Gershwin chose to forget *Blue Monday*. In recent years it has been revived on television by George Bassman, in concert halls by Skitch Henderson and the Gregg Smith Singers in Smith's own effective orchestration.

BLUE NOTE A flatted note, most usually on the 3rd or 7th tones of the scale. Favored by blues singers and instrumentalists. Characteristic of the blues and jazz; often adapted by white popular composers, such as Gershwin, for harmonic effects. Blue notes undoubtedly arose from the singing style of blues singers who did not sing according to the rules of the musical scale. A true-sung blue note often came somewhere between the staff line and the space in pitch. The vocal inflection was adapted by jazz instrumentalists, especially trumpeters and clarinetists. When used by a blues pianist, the blue note, no longer vocal in nature, is then musicologically defined as the flatted 3rd or 7th (or 5th); a true blue note, however, is really sung, not written.

BONNER, EUGENE MACDONALD (b. 1889) Composer, conductor, critic. Born in Jacksonville, N.C., July 24, 1889, Bonner was trained at the Peabody Conservatory of Music, Baltimore, where he studied piano, organ, and composition. In 1911 he went to England for further study in composition and orchestration. He returned to the United States in 1917 to enlist in the Field Artillery; when the war ended he remained in Paris where he continued to study music. Bonner returned again to the United States in 1927 to become music editor of *Outlook* magazine; he later wrote music criticism for different newspapers, among them the Brooklyn *Eagle*, the *Daily Mirror*, and the New York *Herald Tribune*, as well as for magazines. Bonner's works include several operas: *Barbara Fritchie* (1921), *Celui Qui Epousa une Femme Muette* (1923), *The Venetian Glass Nephew* (1927), *The Gods of the Mountain* (1936), and a comic opera, *Frankie and Johnny* (1945). For orchestra he composed *Whispers of Heavenly Death*, 3 Whitman poems for voice and orchestra (1922), *White Nights* (1925), and *Taormina* (1939); also *Incidental Music for "The Young Alexander"* for chamber orchestra and a *Concertino for Piano and Strings*. Other works include *Flutes* for voice and 4 instruments (1923), a *Piano Quintet* (1925), and a *Suite Sicilienne* for violin and piano (1926).

BORNSCHEIN, FRANZ CARL (1879–1948) Composer, conductor, violinist, teacher. Born in Baltimore, Md., Feb. 10, 1879, Bornschein first studied music with his father and then at the Peabody Conservatory, Baltimore (1896–1902). While still a student Bornschein composed a prizewinning string quartet (1900). In 1905 he joined the staff of the Peabody Conservatory where he taught violin, harmony, and composition. He also was director of orchestras at the Baltimore Music School, organized a choral society at Smithsburg, Md., conducted the Myrtle Club women's chorus and was choir director for the First Unitarian Church, Baltimore. Bornschein composed much for chorus and many of his compositions were awarded prizes and were regularly performed in his life-

time. He composed one operetta, *The Willow Plate* (1932) and a *Piano Quintet* (1942). There are several large choral works: *Vision of Sir Launfal* (1928), *Enchanted Isle,* for women's voices (1933), *Conqueror Worm* for women's voices and piano (1936), *Joy* (1944), etc. For orchestra Bornschein wrote *Cape Cod Impressions* (1935), *Southern Nights* (1936), *Moon over Taos* for flute, strings, harp, timpani, and Indian drum, (1943), *The Earth Sings* (1944), and in 1945 Bornschein produced 3 works, *Ode to the Brave, Lament,* and *Phantasy.* He died in Baltimore, June 8, 1948.

BOROWSKI, FELIX (1872–1956) Composer, teacher, writer. Born in Burton, England, Mar. 10, 1872, Borowski began the study of music with his parents. He was graduated from the Cologne Conservatory of Music, after which he taught violin for 5 years before coming to the United States in 1897. He joined the staff of the Chicago Musical College, where he taught composition and lectured on the history of music; from 1916 to 1925 he was president of the College. Borowski after that became prominent in the musical life of Chicago, serving as president of the Civic Music Association and editing the program annotations for the Chicago Symphony concerts. Borowski also wrote on music for several newspapers, including the Chicago *Herald* and the *Christian Science Monitor.* He lectured on music at Northwestern University, Evanston, Ill. Borowski's compositions include a *Concerto for Piano* (1913), an *Allegro de Concert for Organ and Orchestra* (1915), *Peintures* (1917), *Le Printemps Passionné* (1920), *Youth* (1922), 2 tone poems, *Ecce Homo* (1923) and *Semiramis* (1925), and 3 symphonies (1932, 1933, 1937). Borowski also composed 3 string quartets and several stage works: *Boudoir,* a ballet pantomime produced by the Chicago Opera Company

(1918); a *Century of the Dance* (1934) was commissioned by the Ford Motor Company for production at the Chicago World's Fair. Borowski was also co-author of *The Standard Concert Guide* and *The Standard Opera Guide*. As a composer Borowski was best known for his popular piano and violin piece *Adoration*. He died in Chicago, July 6, 1956.

BOOGIE-WOOGIE A blues-based piano style characterized by a reiterative figure in the bass (*basso ostinato*); variously called 8-to-the-bar (fast boogie being performed 8 beats to a measure) or "rent party piano," an allusion to the practice of hiring a pianist to entertain guests at a party, where a collection was taken in order to raise rent money. This was also known as "pitchin' boogie," particularly in Chicago. Some jazz historians claim that the playing style originated in Texas work camps in the late 19th century; but there is no arguing that it flourished in Chicago in the 1920s. Such pianists as Pine Top Smith (q.v.), Jimmy Yancey (q.v.), Meade Lux Lewis (q.v.), and Albert Ammons (q.v.) performed at rent parties and in nightclubs before they were discovered in the late '30s, which led to a proliferation of imitation and such popular approximations as "Beat Me, Daddy, Eight to the Bar" by the big bands. Kansas City, too, produced a boogie-woogie style, best exemplified by the work of Pete Johnson (q.v.). Although boogie-woogie is generally described as a crude style, in the hands of Yancey, Lewis, Ammons, and Johnson it produced several pieces of exceptional and inventive beauty.

BOULANGER, NADIA (1887–1979) Teacher, composer, conductor. Paris-born (Sept. 16, 1887), Boulanger came from a family with a long musical history. She was a graduate of the Paris Conservatory, where she excelled in organ, fugue, harmony, and counter-point. In 1908 she won a Prix de Rome with her composition *La Sirène*. But it was as a remarkable teacher that Boulanger earned a place in works on American music. In 1921 she began teaching at the American Conservatory at Fontainebleau, where her first American pupil was Aaron Copland (q.v.). Boulanger's dedication to music and her wide-ranging knowledge of musical history and performance, her dynamic zeal, made a great impression on her students, whose enthusiasm was transferred to others, among them Virgil Thomson (q.v.), Walter Piston (q.v.), Roy Harris (q.v.), Douglas Moore (q.v.), Howard Swanson (q.v.), David Diamond (q.v.), Roger Goeb (q.v.), Arthur V. Berger (q.v.), Richard Franko Goldman (q.v.), and numerous others. The influence of Nadia Boulanger on American music is considerable. She taught in the United States at Wellesley and Radcliffe colleges as well as the Juilliard School of Music. She also conducted such orchestras as the Boston Symphony and the New York Philharmonic. Although Boulanger taught many American composers who came to be regarded rather avant-garde, she herself preferred the older, conservative approach, as she revealed in her teachings and in her own composition. She died at the age of 92 in Paris, Oct. 22, 1979.

BREAK In jazz performance, a brief, improvised (maybe) solo passage by an instrumentalist or vocalist. Often worked-out, or written-out, arrangements provided for jazz breaks to feature a soloist of the ensemble.

BUCK, GENE (1885–1957) Songwriter, artist, executive. Born in Detroit, Mich., Aug. 8, 1885, Edward Eugene Buck started in the music business as a designer of sheet music covers (he was a graduate of the Detroit Art School). He moved to New York in 1907 where he began working in the theatre as a designer-director, eventually becoming associated with showman Florenz Ziegfeld. Buck wrote the lyrics to the songs for several Ziegfeld productions beginning in 1912. Among his best-known songs are the perennial "Hello, Frisco!" (music by Louis Hirsch) and "Have a Heart" (from *Ziegfeld Follies* of 1916; music by Jerome Kern, q.v.). Buck was a charter member of the American Society of Composers, Authors and Publishers (ASCAP, q.v.) and served as a director from 1920 to 1957 and was president 1924 to 1941. He died in Great Neck, N.Y., Feb. 25, 1957.

BURLEIGH, CECIL (b. 1885) Violinist, composer, teacher. Born in Wyoming, N.Y., Apr. 17, 1885, Burleigh was about 9 when his family moved to Omaha, Neb. He began to study the violin in his teens, although he preferred improvising on the piano. He also began composing while in high school—incidental music to his assigned reading in literature classes. Burleigh then went to Berlin (1903–5), where he studied violin (Anton Witek, Max Grunberg) and composition with Hugo Leichtentritt. Upon his return to the United States he spent an additional 2 years at Chicago Musical College studying with Emile Sauret and Felix Borowski. Shortly after, Burleigh began a career devoted to composition, concert work, and teaching—all more or less concurrently. He taught at Morningside College, Sioux City, Iowa, the Denver Institute of Music and Dramatic Art, Montana State University (Missoula) and, following a period of further study of the violin, joined the faculty of the University of Wisconsin, where he taught violin and devoted much time to composition. Burleigh's works include 3 violin concertos (1915; 1919; 1928), a tone poem, *Evangeline* (1929), *Mountain Pictures* for orchestra (1930), and an unpublished *Trilogy of Symphonies:* "Creation," "Prophecy,"

"Revelation." His chamber compositions include 2 string quartets, 2 sonatas for violin, a *Hymn for Ancients* for string quartet and piano, *American Processional* and *Mountain Scenes,* both for violin and piano and both completed in 1945. Burleigh also composed many teaching pieces for the violin.

CAESAR, IRVING (b. 1895) Songwriter. Born in New York, N.Y., July 4, 1895, Caesar is a graduate of the City College of New York. Although as a child he had musical ambitions (he studied piano at the Third Street Music Settlement House), he began professionally in the business world. One of his earliest jobs was as a stenographer aboard Henry Ford's Peace Ship whose mission was designed to bring an end to World War I. Like many New Yorkers of the period interested in writing, Caesar eventually found his way into Tin Pan Alley and revealed a knack for writing lyrics for popular songs. He scored in 1919 when he and George Gershwin (q.v.) collaborated on "Swanee" which became a tremendous hit after being sung by Al Jolson. There were other Caesar-Gershwin songs, but none equaled the popularity of "Swanee." Other Caesar collaborators include Vincent Youmans (q.v.), Victor Herbert (q.v.), Rudolf Friml (q.v.), Oscar Levant (q.v.), and Gerald Marks (q.v.). Caesar's best-known songs include "I Want to Be Happy" and "Tea for Two" (all with Youmans, from *No, No, Nanette,* 1924), "Crazy Rhythm" (with Joseph Meyer and Roger Wolfe Kahn, 1928), "Lady Play Your Mandolin" (with Oscar Levant, 1930), "Just a Gigolo" (with Leonello Casucci, 1930), "If I Forget You" (words and music, 1933), and "Is It True What They Say About Dixie?" (with Sammy Lerner and Gerald Marks, 1936). With Marks, Caeser collaborated on the collection of teaching songs for use in classrooms, *Sing a Song of*

Safety, and wrote words and music to *Sing a Song of Friendship, Songs of Health,* and *Songs of Manners* (1979). Caesar has also written the suite *Pilgrim of 1940* for piano, orchestra, and chorus.

CALDWELL, ANNE (1867–1936) Songwriter, librettist, singer. Born in Boston, Mass., Aug. 30, 1867, Caldwell, after completing her education, set out as a singer in the Juvenile Opera Co. Her Broadway career began when she contributed sketches to revues such as *Top o' the World* (1907) or as co-librettist of musicals. Caldwell was a pioneer in a field dominated by men and by 1914 was writing lyrics for shows, with such proficiency that she was admitted as one of the charter members of ASCAP that same year. Although Caldwell collaborated with several composers, the most distinguished were Jerome Kern and Vincent Youmans. For Kern she wrote the lyrics to "Whose Baby Are You?" "Left All Alone Again Blues," and "Good Night Boat" (all from *The Night Boat,* 1920), "Ka-lu-a" (from *Good Morning, Dearie,* 1921); in collaboration with Youmans she wrote "I Know That You Know" (from *Oh, Please!* 1926). Her last Broadway show was *Three Cheers,* in collaboration with Raymond Hubbell in 1928. She was married to James O'Dea, also a songwriter. She died in Beverly Hills, Calif., Oct. 22, 1936.

CHARLESTON A very popular dance of the early 1920s, whose origin can be traced to the song of the same title, words by Cecil Mack (pen name of Richard C. McPherson; 1883–1944) and music by James P. Johnson (q.v.), identified on the sheet music as Jimmy Johnson. The song was written for the musical comedy *Runnin' Wild* in 1923 and makes reference to the South Carolina city. The characteristic feature of the song is the complex polyrhythmic structure in the accompaniment and the pattern of the tune on the word "Charleston": a quarter note—half rest—and an 8th note tied to a half, which results in a syncopated, eccentric effect—as was the dance itself, until the "Black Bottom" (q.v.) came along about a year later. Both Gershwin (q.v.) and Copland (q.v.) used the Charleston motif in their piano concertos.

CHICAGO STYLE A style of small band jazz associated with a group of white musicians, influenced by black Chicago musicians and the white New Orleans Rhythm Kings (q.v.). Formed while its members were still in Austin High School (accounting for their also being called the "Austin High Gang"), the original group consisted of Frank Teschemacher (1906–32), one of jazz's most original clarinetists (he also played saxophone), Jim Lannigan (piano, but later played bass), Jimmy McPartland (trumpet), Dick McPartland (banjo), and Lawrence "Bud" Freeman (saxophone). Mostly self-taught, the Austin High Gang learned by listening to recordings by the New Orleans Rhythm Kings, or slipping into (for they were barely in their teens) night spots where they could hear jazz. They began professionally playing for school dances and at parties and eventually took the name Blue Friars (after the Friars Inn, where the NORK band played). In time, with experience, the band evolved a characteristic style, hard-driving, polyphonic, ensemble and solo, all shaped by the instrumentation and the musicianship of the members of the band. The at times unbridled playing made for muddled listening, but when it went well, the band produced an exciting sound which eventually came to be called a "jam session" (the musicians jammed together, that is). The Austin Gang flourished in the late '20s and began recording in 1927, but the style itself continued into the

'40s, when it could be heard in New York at Nick's, a Greenwich Village nightclub, and Eddie Condon's and other spots. Other musicians associated with the Chicago Style: Joe Sullivan (piano), Dave Tough (drums), Jess Stacy (piano), George Wettling (drums), Muggsy Spanier (cornet), Pee Wee Russell (clarinet), and Eddie Condon (guitar).

CLAFLIN, AVERY (1898–1979) Composer, banker. Born in Keene, N.H., June 21, 1898, Claflin began to study music at 7 and produced his first compositions between the ages of 10 and 15. At Harvard he studied with Archibald T. Davison but dropped out and volunteered to serve as an ambulance driver in France during World War I. Claflin was wounded on the Verdun Front, which ended his ambitions as a concert pianist (he was awarded the Croix de Guerre at the time and in 1948 received the Légion d'Honneur). After the war Claflin returned to Harvard and was graduated in 1920. Claflin had hoped to devote himself to music (while in France he moved in a circle numbering Francis Poulenc, Darius Milhaud [q.v.], Georges Auric, and Erik Satie, with whom he occasionally studied) but found that not always financially rewarding. Claflin then found work as a messenger for the French-American Banking Corporation. When he retired 35 years later he was the firm's president. "I think my banking career has helped me as a musician and vice versa," he once said, paraphrasing composer-insurance man Charles Ives. "A banker's orderliness helps in composing, and my composer's imagination may have given me a bit of a jump on other bankers." Fresh out of Harvard, Claflin composed an opera based on Poe's *The Fall of the House of Usher* (1921); around the same time he wrote a *Trio for Piano, Violin and Cello*. His first opera was followed by 2 more,

Hester Prynne (inspired by *The Scarlet Letter,* 1932) and *La Grande Bretèche* (after Balzac, 1947). Following his retirement from the business world in 1954, Claflin devoted much time to music and began work on an opera based on *Uncle Tom's Cabin,* completed in 1966. Other works include 3 symphonies, a *Moby Dick Suite,* a *String Quartet* (1937), *Teen Scenes* for string orchestra, a *Piano Concerto* ("Concerto giocoso," completed in 1957). Claflin's best-known work is a madrigal, a setting of the income tax form entitled *Lament for April 15* (1955). He died in Greenwich, Conn., Jan. 10, 1979.

CONFREY, EDWARD "ZEZ" (1895–1971) Composer, pianist, bandleader. Edward Elzear Confrey was born in Peru, Ill., Apr. 3, 1895, the youngest of 5 children. He began to study the piano at about the age of 4, revealing at that age an aptitude for music by listening while his older brother took a piano lesson and then climbing onto the piano bench to play the study piece by ear. While still in high school Confrey had his own small band. He continued his studies at Chicago Musical College (which had been founded in 1867 by Florenz Ziegfeld, Sr., father of the great showman). During his college years Confrey earned his way as pianist in his and his brother's orchestra. After enlisting in the U. S. Navy at the onset of World War I, Confrey was based in Chicago, where he also began cutting piano rolls for the QRS Company there. Among his early pieces was the "novelty rag" (not really a rag, but obviously inspired by the form—and pianistically tricky; in short, a showpiece for the soloist), *My Pet.* The QRS roll was released in July 1918 and marked the beginning of Zez Confrey's active career as a novelty pianist. After the war Confrey moved to New York to continue making piano rolls as well as conventional records as soloist and with orchestra. He produced his greatest hit in 1921, when he published *Kitten on the Keys;* this was followed by *Stumbling* (1922) and *Dizzy Fingers* (1923). Other typical titles include *Jack in the Box, Charleston Chuckles, Humorestless, Pickle Pepper Polka,* and *Poor Butter-milk.* At the height of his success Confrey published a method book, *Modern Novelty Piano Solos* (1923), which remained in print for decades. In 1924 he and George Gershwin (q.v.) appeared as soloists at Paul Whiteman's (q.v.) famous "Experiment in Modern Music" (q.v.). Following this, Confrey formed a band, toured the vaudeville circuit, and was heard on radio. The vogue for novelty piano pieces eventually waned and Confrey retired from active band work to compose various types of piano pieces, including study pieces for students. He died in Lakewood, N.J., Nov. 22, 1971.

COOTS, J. FRED (b. 1897) Composer, pianist. Born in Brooklyn, N.Y., May 2, 1897, Coots first studied the piano with his mother. After finishing high school he found a job in Wall Street in a bank. His musical interests were reawakened when he heard a professional pianist in a music store "plugging" songs of 1914. Coots left Wall Street to work as a pianist and a stock boy in a music shop. His first song, "Mr. Ford You've Got the Right Idea," lyrics by Ray Sherwood, was published in 1917. (The song applauded Henry Ford's Peace Ship, launched—unsuccessfully—to end World War I.) Coots then spent some time in vaudeville as accompanist and as a writer of special songs for performers. In 1922 he composed his first Broadway score, *Sally, Irene and Mary* (lyrics by Raymond Klages), which proved to be very successful. This success led to a contract with the Shubert organization and an active career as a composer for Broadway shows and revues, among them *Artists and Models* of 1924 and 1925 and his last full Broadway score (and a success), *Sons o' Guns* in 1929. He then went to Hollywood briefly during the first film musical cycle and wrote one song, lyrics by Lou Davis, that gained popularity, "Precious Little Thing Called Love," from the 1929 film *The Shopworn Angel.* Coots actually was most successful in composing popular, nonshow, or film songs: "I Still Get a Thrill" (lyrics by Benny Davis, 1930), "Love Letters in the Sand" (lyrics by Nick and Charles Kenny, 1931), "Santa Claus Is Coming to Town" (lyrics by Haven Gillespie, 1934), "Beautiful Lady in Blue" (lyrics by Sam Lewis, 1935), and "You Go to My Head" with fine lyrics by Gillespie, published in 1938.

COPLAND, AARON (b. 1900) Composer, conductor, pianist, author. Born in Brooklyn, N.Y., Nov. 14, 1900, Copland initially studied music with his sister, Laurine. He was then about 11. He later studied more formally with Leopold Wolfsohn, Victor Wittgenstein, and Clarence Adler (all piano). After graduating from high school in 1918, Copland studied theory with Rubin Goldmark (q.v.). He decided that instead of going to college he would prefer to study music in Europe; in 1921 he enrolled in the Fontainebleau School of Music. By this time Copland had begun to compose and already had a reputation among Goldmark's students—and with Goldmark—as a most "radical" young composer. At Fontainbleau he studied under the conservative Paul Vidal for about 3 months before he was introduced to Nadia Boulanger (q.v.) and became her first American student. After 3 years Copland returned to the United States in 1924, to begin one of the most productive careers in American music. It began rather discouragingly: playing piano in a hotel trio in Milford, Pa., setting up shop as a piano teacher and getting no pupils —but at the same time working on an orchestral work with organ for his teacher, Boulanger. A friend-musician, Marion Bauer (q.v.), introduced Copland to the League of Composers (q.v.) which accepted him as a member and arranged for the first performance in the United States of works by Aaron Copland, two piano pieces: *Scherzo humoristique* (also known as "The Cat and the Mouse," written during his period with Goldmark in 1920) and the *Passacaglia* (written while he studied with Boulanger, completed in 1922). The former was Copland's first published composition. He completed his *Symphony for Organ and Orchestra* which was premiered in New York by the New York Symphony, Walter Damrosch (q.v.) conducting and Boulanger at the organ, on Jan. 11, 1925. This work launched the public Copland, for after the performance, Damrosch turned to the audience and said, "If a young man of twenty-three can write a symphony like that, in five years he will be ready to commit murder." His prediction, Copland later noted, "luckily came to nothing." Not long after this Copland came to the attention of Serge Koussevitzky, newly appointed conductor of the Boston Symphony, beginning a long and fruitful association-friendship. Hoping to shed some of his French accent, audible here and there in the organ symphony, Copland turned to the Americanisms of jazz, so much in the air at the time. The result was *Music for the Theatre* (q.v.), the *Concerto for Piano and Orchestra* (1926), and a set of blues (4) for piano (1926–1948), to which can also be added *Sentimental Melody* (1926), for solo piano. Copland soon became the leader of the more advanced group of young American composers and affiliated himself with organizations devoted to the cause of contemporary music: the International Society for Contemporary

Music, the League of Composers (q.v.), American Composers Alliance and others, including his own Copland-Sessions (q.v.) Concerts. He has also lectured widely in colleges (the New School in New York City, Harvard, etc.), preserving some of his talks in the several books he has written. A prolific composer, Copland has written music of extraordinary diversity, from the abstract, powerful *Piano Variations* (1930) and *Short Symphony* (1932–33) to the immediately accessible *El Salón México* (completed in 1936) and *Lincoln Portrait* (1942). Copland's musical materials—always identifiable as his whatever the means—range from the folksy (*Rodeo*, ballet, 1942) to the dodecaphonic (*Connotations*, 1962, and *Inscape*, 1967). He had composed for films (*Of Mice and Men*, 1939; *Our Town*, 1940; *The Red Pony*, 1948; *The Heiress*, 1948; and *Something Wild*, 1961, which score was the source for *Music for a Great City*, 1964). Copland's ballets include *Billy the Kid*, 1938; *Rodeo;* the classic *Appalachian Spring* (1944); and *Dance Panels* (1959). There are 2 Copland operas, *The Second Hurricane* (for a high school cast, 1936) and *The Tender Land* (1954). Besides the piano concerto, Copland had written a *Concerto for Clarinet* (1948). Important orchestral works include the *Symphonic Ode* (1929), *Statements* (1935), and *Third Symphony* (1946). His chamber works include *Two Pieces for String Quartet* (1923, 1928), *Two Pieces for Violin and Piano* (1926), *Vitebsk* for piano, violin, and cello (1928), *Sonata for Violin and Piano* (1943), *Quartet for Piano and Strings* (1950), *Nonet for Strings* (1960), *Duo for Flute and Piano* (1971), and *Threnody II,* for string trio and flute (1974). Major solo piano works, besides the *Piano Variations* (q.v.), are the *Piano Sonata* (1941), *Piano Fantasy* (1955–57), and *Night Thoughts* (1973). There are several song settings, including *Twelve Poems of Emily Dickinson* (1950) and *Old American Songs* (2 sets: 1950; 1954). Most of Copland's music has been recorded under the composer's direction and participation. His published books are *What to Listen for in Music* (1939), *Our New Music* (1941), *Music and Imagination* (1952), and *Copland on Music* (1963).

COPLAND-SESSIONS CONCERTS A series of 8 concerts presented in New York during 1928–31 organized by Aaron Copland (q.v.) and Roger Sessions (q.v.) to present works by contemporary composers, European as well as American. The emphasis was on presenting compositions by young, generally unknown composers, preferably of the avant-garde. Throughout the series 47 contemporary works were presented, 29 of them by American composers. The Copland-Sessions Concerts were terminated in 1931 because Sessions had moved to Europe and felt he could not actively participate from abroad. Copland ever since has worked in behalf of the younger composer in his efforts to get them a hearing or publication. Among the new generation of American composers whose works were performed at the Copland-Sessions Concerts were Roy Harris (q.v.), Virgil Thomson (q.v.), and Walter Piston (q.v.). Others included Carlos Chávez (Mexico), Nino Rota (Italy), and Bernard Wagenaar (the Netherlands, later to the United States).

COS COB PRESS A small publishing company formed in February 1929 to publish the compositions, "regardless of their commercial value," of American composers. The president, and founder, was Alma M. Wertheim, who furnished the funds (the M. in her name stood for Morganthau): vice-president Edwin F. Kalmus attended to business matters and handled distribution of the press's publications in the United States and Europe.

Among the first works to be issued were compositions by Aaron Copland (q.v.), Louis Gruenberg (q.v.), and Emerson Whithorne (q.v.). In time practically every major American composer (before he was recognized as major) was published by Cos Cob Press. Besides those mentioned there were also Charles Ives (q.v.), Virgil Thomson (q.v.), Roger Sessions (q.v.), and Walter Piston (q.v.), among others. Cos Cob Press was eventually absorbed by another nonprofit organization, Arrow Music Press, Inc., which had been formed by Copland, Thomson, Marc Blitzstein (q.v.), and Lehman Engel (q.v.). The publications of both presses are now distributed by Boosey & Hawkes, New York City.

COTTON CLUB A Harlem nightclub at 142nd Street and Lenox Avenue, one flight up over the Douglas Theatre. The club was owned by mobster Owney Madden, whose aide, George "Big Frenchy" DeMange, managed the place. The legitimate front for the organization was Walter Brooks, the supposed manager. The Cotton Club flourished during the late 1920s and early '30s as an outlet for Madden's product, Madden's No. 1 Beer (this was during Prohibition), and some of the finest entertainment in New York. The Cotton Club became the smart in place of the time, attracting celebrities, the wealthy, even slumming royalty. No Negroes were permitted in unless they performed in the elaborate, often bawdy, shows—or were celebrated representatives of their race—Paul Robeson, Ethel Waters, or Bill "Bojangles" Robinson, for example. Over the years the Cotton Club employed such bands as Duke Ellington's, Cab Calloway's, and Jimmie Lunceford's. Great songs were provided by such songwriting teams as Jimmy McHugh (q.v.) and Dorothy Fields (q.v.) and Harold Arlen (q.v.) and Ted Koehler (q.v.). McHugh-Fields eventually moved on to Broadway and the Arlen-Koehler team took over to write some of the finest songs of the period, including "Between the Devil and the Deep Blue Sea," "I Love a Parade," "I've Got the World on a String," the classic "Stormy Weather" (1933), and "Ill Wind." They then went on to Hollywood and Broadway. The end of Prohibition, and the Great Depression, ended the heyday of the Cotton Club, which had served as settings for such talents as Ethel Waters, Aida Ward, Avon Long, and a very young Lena Horne. The Club closed in February 1936. Another Cotton Club opened in Times Square later in the year starring Bill Robinson and Cab Calloway which proved most successful; Ellington returned in 1938, but the formula had worn thin and the new Cotton Club closed in June 1940.

COWELL, HENRY (1897–1965) Composer, pianist, teacher, musical theorist. Born in Menlo Park, Calif., Mar. 11, 1897, Cowell was a precocious youngster—and remained so all his life. He began to study the violin at the age of 5, appeared in public performing on it and then 2 years later gave the instrument away. Cowell was determined to know music thoroughly, without the crutch of an instrument. Since his boyhood was spent in parts of California, Iowa, Kansas, and Oklahoma, Cowell absorbed the music of these various locales. He made his debut as composer-pianist in San Francisco on Mar. 12, 1912; many in the audience were shocked by his strange compositions. Up to this time Cowell was self-taught, although he had already revealed himself as an experimentalist who was highly suspicious of the standard "rules" of music. As early as 1912 he was using what he called "tone clusters," extended chords of adjacent notes produced by striking the keys of a piano with the entire palm of the hand or the forearm.

Cowell eventually took a course of systematic studies with Charles Seeger (q.v.), at the University of California, Berkeley. Seeger was the right teacher for so free a spirit and a certain basic groundwork in musical techniques was acquired by Cowell, if only to ignore them. His studies were interrupted by a stretch in the U. S. Army during World War I. That over, he came to New York for further study with Raymond Huntington Woodman and Percy Goetschius (q.v.). In 1923 he traveled through Europe giving recitals of his works based on tone clusters, as well as playing the piano in an unorthodox manner: plucking and strumming directly on the strings. In 1928 he was invited to Moscow to perform his by then notorious compositions; in the early '30s, on Guggenheim Fellowships, he went to Berlin to study comparative musicology. Cowell was fascinated by the musics of other cultures and was not only familiar with the range of Western art and folk music, but also with the musics of the East, from Iran to Japan. He composed pieces, blending East and West, using indigenous Eastern instruments with the Western orchestra. He also spent nearly a lifetime teaching, beginning at the New School, New York City, in 1928; he taught also at Stanford, Mills College (Calif.), the University of California, and Columbia University. As an innovator, Cowell attracted other innovators (some of whom were also his pupils): Charles Ives (q.v.), Carl Ruggles (q.v.), John Becker (q.v.), Wallingford Riegger (q.v.), as well as, at the time, such younger musical explorers as his students Lou Harrison (q.v.) and John Cage (q.v.). To give these experimentalists a platform, Cowell in 1927 founded the New Music Society and began publishing the quarterly *New Music* (q.v.) to encourage "advanced" music; he also organized concerts and even backed recordings of these works. His career was disrupted in 1937 when he was sentenced to prison on an alleged morals charge, an experience that should have proved shattering but which did not disconcert the ebullient and resilient Cowell. He kept busy with musical matters, taught, and was occupied until he was pardoned (at the request of the prosecuting attorney) in 1941. Besides taking up an active musical life again in 1941, Cowell also married musicologist-author Sidney Robertson, with whom years later he collaborated on *Charles Ives and His Music* (1955). Cowell was one of the most prolific of American composers—he composed no less than 20 symphonies, the last in the final year of his life. Stylistically his output ranged from the simplest to the most complex. He drew upon Celtic themes (influenced by an Irish ancestry), American folk songs, and more exotic musics for such works as *Irish Suite in Three Movements* (1933), *Tales of Our Countryside* for piano and orchestra (1939), a series of *Hymn and Fuguing Tunes* for various instrumental combinations (there are 18 of these, written between 1944 and 1964), *Ancient Desert Drone* (1940), 5 string quartets (1916–65), and dozens of piano pieces ranging from the early *The Tides of Manaunaun* (1912) to *Tiger* (1928). Cowell produced concertos for the conventional piano as well as for the rhythmicon (which he helped to develop in association with Professor Leon Theremin), thundersticks, *tar* (a Persian —or Iranian—instrument), *koto* (Japan) *tablatarang* (India), as well as the harp, harmonica, percussion, and accordion. There is also a large catalog of vocal and chamber music. His book *New Musical Resources* was published in 1930; Cowell, in addition, edited a valuable collection, *American Composers on American Music* (1933, republished 1962). He also contributed many articles to various musical publications, 1925–58. The wide range and large output of Cowell, in whatever vein, Occidental, experimental, or Oriental, is invariably purely Cowell. As he once observed, "If a man has a personality of his own, I don't see how he can keep it out of his music." Then he added: "And if he hasn't, how can he put it in?" Cowell's music is inventive, the product of an always youthful, inquisitive, and active mind. Ill in his last years, he continued to work despite it; he died of cancer in Shady, N.Y., Dec. 10, 1965.

"LA CRÉATION DU MONDE" The score for a ballet composed by French composer Darius Milhaud (q.v.) in 1923. With a libretto by Blaise Cendrars and settings and costumes by Fernand Léger, *La Création du monde* was performed for the first time by the Ballets Suédois (Swedish Ballet) on Oct. 25, 1923, in Paris (on the same program: Cole Porter's ballet *Within the Quota*, q.v.). The ballet's story depicted the Creation as it might be visualized in African mythology according to the imagination of a white Frenchman. Milhaud drew upon his experience with jazz, some of which he picked up during a visit to the United States the year before when he spent much time listening to musicians in Harlem hot spots and to such popular bands as that of Leo Reisman. While hardly jazz, *La Création du monde* is one of Milhaud's most charming and popular compositions, replete with the sound of the saxophone, much percussion, and an ingenious fugal climax that sounds much like a jam session: all of which invariably wrings the withers of the jazz purist. The work is a fine period piece and exemplification of what the trained musician saw (heard) as the essence of jazz. Not that Milhaud was the first—there were attempts at jazz touches in such disparate works as Debussy's *Golliwog's Cakewalk*, Ravel's *L'Enfant et les sortilèges*, and Stravinsky's *L'Histoire du soldat* and *Rag-*

time. In the United States, John Alden Carpenter (q.v.) attempted the same in his *Krazy Kat* ballet in 1922, a year before Milhaud wrote *La Création du monde;* George Gershwin made his first excursion in 1922 in the one-act opera *Blue Monday* (q.v.). He would find his real voice in yet another jazz-inspired work, *Rhapsody in Blue* (q.v.), in 1924, a year after Milhaud's fling with jazz—a fact some musicologists use to suggest that Gershwin may have borrowed the idea from Milhaud. Since Gershwin had not heard the Milhaud work before he began his rhapsody in January 1924, the innuendo is nonsense.

CREOLE JAZZ BAND Many jazz bands that originated in New Orleans (and some that did not) were called or took the name Creole; it was a generic term. In 1912 the great jazz trumpeter Freddie Keppard (1883–1932) was a member of the Original Creole Orchestra; but it was the King Oliver Creole Jazz Band of the early '20s that is most associated with the name. Formed in Chicago in 1929, the band consisted of Oliver on trumpet, Lil Hardin, of Memphis, on piano, Honoré Dutrey on trombone, Ed Garland on bass, (later replaced by Bill Johnson), Johnny Dodds clarinetist, and Minor Hall on drums, later replaced by Warren "Baby" Dodds. The band's personnel fluctuated sometimes because of friction, sometimes because one of its members received a better offer. It was eventually joined by the young Louis Armstrong, whose cornet was 2nd to Oliver's trumpet. The band played around Chicago and went as far west as Los Angeles and made some of the earliest jazz recordings for Gennct Record, Richmond, Ind., in April 1923 with the following: Oliver, Armstrong, Dutrey, Johnny Dodds, Lil Hardin, Bill Johnson, and Baby Dodds.

CRIST, BAINBRIDGE (1883–1969) Composer, teacher. Born in Lawrenceburg, Ind., Feb. 13, 1883, Crist studied the piano at the age of 5 with his mother. He later studied the flute with Theodore Hahn. Music, however, was not originally regarded as his profession-to-be. When Crist was 13, the family resettled in Washington, D.C., and he eventually enrolled in George Washington University, where he received a degree in law. He then moved to Boston. He practiced law—and joined the Boston Orchestral Club in which he played the flute. He also wrote original works for the Club. After 6 years Crist abandoned the legal profession and left for Europe to study theory, orchestration, and voice in Berlin with Paul Juon and Claude Landi. Returning to the United States in 1915, he began teaching singing in Boston and Washington. In his composition Crist concentrated on vocal music, although he also produced a good deal of works for orchestra, many of which employ voices. He was interested in exotic music, as will be seen from some of the titles. His theatre works include *Le Pied de la Momie* (1915), *Pregiwa's Marriage,* a Javanese ballet (1926), and *The Sorceress* (1926). Crist's orchestral compositions include: *Egyptian Impressions* (1914), *A Bag of Whistles* (1915), *Abisharika,* for violin and orchestra (1921), *Chinese, Arabian and Nautch Dances* (1922), *Vienna—1913* and *Chinese Procession* (both 1933); the *Hymn to Nefertiti* was written in 1936, the *American Epic—1620,* a tone poem, in 1941. Among Crist's works for voice and orchestra are *Drolleries from an Oriental Doll's House* (6 songs, 1920), *Coloured Stars* (4 songs translated by E. Powys Mathers, 1921), also *Chinese Mother Goose Rhymes, America My Blessed Land,* for chorus and orchestra (1942), and *Howdy, Folks,* memorial poem to Will Rogers for voice and orchestra

(1943). He was the author of *The Art of Setting Words to Music.* He died in Barnstable, Mass., Feb. 7, 1969.

DANCE BAND During the 1920s what should properly have been designated as popular dance bands—Paul Whiteman, Vincent Lopez, Ted Lewis, Isham Jones, et al.—were called jazz bands, primarily because of the sudden and wide popularity of true jazz bands. In general dance bands were larger, ranging from 6 musicians (who often doubled on other instruments) to 12 or so. Trumpets or cornets were important to the instrumentation, as were saxophones, a trombone, perhaps a tuba, a banjo, piano, and drums. The fancier society bands frequently had a small string section. The music performed was generally written out in special arrangements, which on occasion gave the band's star a solo. This was true of the Paul Whiteman Orchestra whose arrangements frequently gave the nonreader Bix Beiderbecke an opportunity to solo. Jazz bands were generally built around a trumpet or cornet and went from there with other instruments: piano, drums, clarinet, trombone, etc. Instrumentations varied from band to band. Dance music was often discreetly provided in the "better" hotel dining rooms for tea dancing. Sometimes only a trio—violin, piano, sax —or sometimes 12 or more, the band seemed to be hidden behind some potted palms. The characteristic sound of these orchestras and their setting earned their product the name of "potted palm music." They were more properly called salon orchestras. All 3 types of bands flourished during the '20s: jazz bands in the racier clubs and speakeasies, the dance band in the more respectable clubs and country club dances and the potted palm orchestras in the more genteel settings of hotels, country clubs, and the homes of the wealthy.

DANIELS, CHARLES N. See Neil Moret.

DAWSON, WILLIAM LEVI (b. 1898) Composer, choral conductor. Born in Anniston, Ala., Sept. 26, 1898, Dawson was the son of a poor black field laborer. He left home at the age of 13 to attend Tuskegee Institute where he was first introduced to music. After graduation Dawson continued in music, first at the Horner Institute for Fine Arts (Kansas City, Kans.) and later at the Chicago Musical College and the American Conservatory of Music (M.A., Music, 1927). While he studied he supported himself by playing trombone in the Chicago Civic Orchestra. In 1931 he returned to Alabama to become director of music and choir director at Tuskegee, a post he held until his retirement in 1955. Dawson was then sent by the U. S. State Department to Spain to work there with choral groups. Dawson's original composition was done primarily for voice (for which he was awarded the Rodman Wanamaker Prize, 1930, 1931). His choral pieces include *Out in the Fields* (1928), *Break, Break, Break* (1929), and *Ain'-a That Good News* (1937). In 1925 Dawson composed a *Trio in A* for violin, cello, and piano and his *Sonata in A* for violin and piano in 1928. His best-known composition is the *Negro Folk Symphony, No. 1* (1931, revised 1952 after a trip to West Africa). The well-received work, which combines original as well as Negro folk themes, was premiered by the Philadelphia Orchestra under Stokowski on Nov. 16, 1934. Since his retirement Dawson, a resident of Tuskegee, devotes his time to composition, the study of Negro music, and guest-conducting orchestras in performances of his works.

DE SYLVA, BROWN, AND HENDERSON Very successful songwriting team of the 1920s and '30s. B. G.

"Buddy" DeSylva (1895–1950) and Lew Brown (1893–1958) were the lyricist-librettists and Ray Henderson (q.v.) the composer of the combination, although the collaboration was close and interchangeable. Their first song collaboration was the song popularized by Al Jolson, "It All Depends on You" (1926); their first show, the *George White's Scandals of 1925*. The next year's production of the *Scandals* resulted in such popular songs as "Black Bottom" and "The Birth of the Blues"; *Good News* (1927) was one of the team's most successful shows, out of which came several very popular songs: "The Best Things in Life Are Free," "The Varsity Drag," and "Lucky in Love." Other songs by DeSylva, Brown, and Henderson include "You're the Cream in My Coffee" (*Hold Everything!* 1928) and "Button Up Your Overcoat" (*Follow Through*, 1928). All of the members of the trio worked before and after with other songwriters. DeSylva, who eventually quit songwriting to become a Hollywood producer, wrote songs with George Gershwin (q.v.), Victor Herbert (q.v.), Jerome Kern (q.v.), and Vincent Youmans (q.v.). Lew Brown also moved on to Hollywood where he collaborated on film scores with such composers as Harold Arlen (q.v.), Louis Alter (q.v.), and Harry Warren (q.v.). Ray Henderson collaborated with lyricists Ted Koehler (q.v.), Irving Caesar (q.v.), and Jack Yellen. DeSylva, Brown, and Henderson provided the songs for one of the earliest film musicals, Al Jolson's *The Singing Fool* (1928), from which came "Sonny Boy."

DIXIELAND A kind of jazz music performed by a white band influenced by the black jazz bands of New Orleans. Such a group was the Original Dixieland Jass Band (q.v.). The music was more or less improvised with solos alternating with ensemble work. The characteristic sound of Dixieland jazz resulted from the instrumentation: trumpet, trombone, clarinet, piano, bass, and drums. The route most often taken by the Dixieland jazz bands was New Orleans to Chicago to New York, not necessarily physically. The black bands, such as King Oliver's (q.v.), transported the style to Chicago where, like the Original Dixieland Jass Band (whose members had also come from New Orleans), it influenced Chicago musicians who had never gotten closer to New Orleans than South Chicago. Dixieland, or simply Dixie, has stood for this type of improvised small-band jazz and enjoyed long popularity, even into the modern jazz era. In New York it could be heard in such clubs as Cafe Society (Downtown and Up), Eddie Condon's, and Nick's in Greenwich Village. The association with the last was so long-standing that the style was often simply called "Nicksieland."

DONALDSON, WALTER (1893–1947) Songwriter. Born in Brooklyn, N.Y., Feb. 15, 1893, Donaldson was not interested in music as a boy, despite the fact that his mother was a pianist-teacher. He was in high school when he decided he would teach himself how to play the piano in order to write songs for school musicals. His schooling concluded, Donaldson went to work in Wall Street, then quit to begin his musical career as a pianist with a publishing company. He was fired for writing songs on the company's time. He soon began turning out very popular songs. One of his first to be published, "Back Home in Tennessee" (lyrics by William Jerome, 1915), sold over a million copies. When the United States entered World War I, Donaldson became an entertainer of soldiers at Camp Upton on Long Island, N.Y. He spent 19 months there—and met another songwriter, Irving Berlin (q.v.), then a sergeant. After the war,

Donaldson joined Berlin's publishing company as a staff composer for a long stay of 10 years, during which he composed the tunes for such songs as "How Ya Gonna Keep 'Em Down on the Farm?" (lyrics by Sam M. Lewis and Joe Young, 1919), "My Mammy" (Lewis and Young, 1920), "My Buddy" (lyrics by Gus Kahn, q.v., 1922), "Carolina in the Morning" (lyrics by Kahn, 1922), "Yes Sir, That's My Baby" (Kahn, 1925), "My Blue Heaven" (lyrics by George Whiting, 1927), and "At Sundown" (lyrics by Donaldson, 1927). Donaldson, before he left for Hollywood, composed 2 show scores, *Sweetheart Time* (lyrics by Ballard MacDonald and Irving Caesar, 1926) and the outstanding *Whoopee* (lyrics by Kahn, 1928) from which came "I'm Bringing a Red, Red Rose," "Makin' Whoopee!," and "Love Me or Leave Me." Although he was not as prolific in Hollywood as he had been in Tin Pan Alley, Donaldson produced a number of very successful songs: "You're Driving Me Crazy!"; "Little White Lies" (both with Donaldson lyrics and both 1930); for Eddie Cantor's *Kid Millions* (1934) he and Gus Kahn composed "An Earful of Music," "Okay, Toots," and "When My Ship Comes In." For the 1936 Jean Harlow film *Suzy* he and Harold Adamson wrote "Did I Remember?" which was sung by Cary Grant. One of Donaldson's last great song hits was "Mister Meadowlark" (lyrics by Johnny Mercer, q.v., 1940). By the mid 1940s, Donaldson's health had begun to fail and he retired from active composing in 1946; he died in Santa Monica, Calif., July 15, 1947.

DONOVAN, RICHARD (1891–1970) Composer, organist, teacher. Born in New Haven, Conn., Nov. 29, 1891, Donovan studied music at Yale (1912–14) and later in New York City at the Institute of Musical Art

(1914–18). He later went to Paris to study organ with the great French composer-organist Charles Widor. Upon his return from Europe, Donovan began a long career in teaching, with incidental work as choral director and organist. In New York he taught at the Institute of Musical Art and Finch College. In 1928 he returned to Yale, where he taught for several years; from 1947 to 1960 he was professor of theory. Donovan was also active in the musical life of New Haven: he conducted the Bach Cantata Club (1933–44), was associate conductor of the New Haven Symphony (1936–51), and organist and choir director at Christ Church (1928–65). He was also active in the promulgation of contemporary music and served on the committee for the Yaddo Festivals of Contemporary Music at Saratoga Springs, N.Y., a member of the board of New Music publishers, and was president of the American Composers Alliance (1961–62). Donovan's original work covers a wide range, with a large output of choral works and some for organ. There are a good number of pieces for orchestra: *Wood-Notes,* for small orchestra (1925), a symphonic poem, *Smoke and Steel* (1932), *Symphony for Chamber Orchestra* (1937), *Passacaglia on Vermont Folk Tunes* (1949), and *Epos* (1963). For chamber orchestra: *Ricercare for Oboe and Strings* (1938), *Suite for Oboe and Strings* (1943), *Design for Radio* (1944). For chamber groups: *Sextet for Winds and Piano* (1932), *Four Songs for Soprano and String Quartet* (1933), *Trio* for violin, cello, and piano (1937), *Serenade for Oboe, Violin, Viola and Cello* (1941), *Terzetto* for 2 violins and viola (1950), and *Music for Six* (1961). There are also 2 piano suites (1933 and 1953) and several choral pieces: *How Far Is It to Bethlehem?* 1927), *Chanson of the Bells of Oseney* (1930), *Fantasy on American Folk Ballads* (1940), *Hymn to the Night* (1947),

Mass (1955), *Five Elizabethan Lyrics* (1957), and *Magnificat* (1961). Donovan died in New Haven, Aug. 22, 1970.

DORSEY, THOMAS A. "GEORGIA TOM" (b. 1899) Composer, pianist. The son of a black country teacher, Dorsey was born near Atlanta, Ga., sometime in 1899. He began to study the piano while still a youngster and, although there was no piano in the Dorsey home, young Thomas learned quickly and began earning money playing for local dances. When he was about 20 Dorsey decided he would move northward and settled for a time in Gary, Ind., where he worked in a steel mill. He eventually organized his own small band and began playing for dances in Gary and Chicago; some of his earning went into music lessons. At the same time Dorsey had already begun writing the arrangements for his 5-piece band and to compose original songs. Dorsey's band, with the leader at the piano, was a popular jazz band in the Gary-Chicago area. Dorsey's membership in Chicago's Pilgrim Baptist Church kindled his interest in gospel songs and he began, ca. 1921, to write songs in the mode. Dorsey, about this time, began working with a band and was active as a blues pianist for such singers as Madlyn Davis, Ma Rainey, Bertha "Chippie" Hill, and Stovepipe Johnson. He formed a fruitful partnership with another singer-pianist, "Tampa Red" (Hudson Whittaker). On these dates Dorsey was identified as "Georgia Tom." One of their song collaborations was the popular jazz standard "It's Tight Like That." Among the Dorsey-Whittaker bands were the State Street Stompers and Tampa Red's Hokum Jug Band. In the early 1930s Dorsey left the jazz field to concentrate on gospel songs in which he combined elements of jazz and blues and, once he hit his stride, composed hundreds of such sacred songs, among them "There'll

Be Peace in the Valley," "He Knows How Much You Can Bear," and "Precious Lord, Take My Hand." Dorsey is also the founder of the National Convention of Gospel Singers.

DUKE, JOHN WOODS (b. 1899) Composer, pianist, teacher. Born in Cumberland, Md., July 30, 1899, Duke studied composition with Gustave Strube at the Peabody Conservatory, Baltimore. At the age of 20 Duke moved to New York City where he studied piano with Franklin Cannon and counterpoint with Howard Brockway (q.v.). Following this, in 1923, Duke joined the staff of Smith College, Northampton, Mass., as associate professor of music, eventually reaching full professorship. He spent a year (1929–30) in Europe, where he studied piano under Artur Schnabel and composition with Nadia Boulanger (q.v.). Among Duke's compositions are the *Overture in D Minor* (1928) and *Carnival Overture* (1941), both for orchestra; a *Concerto for Piano and Strings* (1938); 2 operas, *Captain Lovelock* (1953) and *The Sire de Maletroit;* and an operetta, *The Yankee Pedlar* (1962). For chamber groupings Duke has composed a *Suite for Solo Cello* (1934), *Fantasie in A Minor* for violin and piano (1937), a *Trio for Violin, Viola and Cello* (1937), a *Trio in D Major* for violin, cello, and piano (1943), and 2 string quartets (1941 and 1947). Duke has written many songs, most of them to words by American poets (Archibald MacLeish, Elinor Wylie, and Edwin Arlington Robinson), among them "A Piper," "Here in This Spot with You," "In the Fields," "Richard Cory," and "Miniver Cheevy."

ELLINGTON, EDWARD "DUKE" (1899–1974) Composer, arranger, pianist, bandleader. Edward Kennedy Ellington was born in Washington, D.C., Apr. 29, 1899. The nickname "Duke" was bestowed on him by a boyhood friend, not because of Ellington's regal manner (even then) or his position in jazz, which he earned and maintained for decades, but because it seemed fitting. Ellington's biography does not fit the classic jazz myth: he grew up in a wholesome family setting, he was not crippled by poverty, and it would seem that he was not deeply affected by the racial prejudices endemic in the Washington of his youth. Although his mother was a pianist, young Ellington showed little musical interest. Even so, he began to study the piano at about the age of 7. In high school he studied music but seemed directed toward a career in art. He studied music privately with Henry Grant; he also began to absorb the music played by jazz pianists who performed in Washington, among them James P. Johnson and Willie "The Lion" Smith. When Ellington received a scholarship from the Pratt Institute of Fine Arts, Brooklyn, N.Y., he had already been earning a living with his own small band, so he rejected the offer and stayed with music. In the early 1920s Ellington brought his band to New York, with little initial success, but by 1923 the Washingtonians and, later, Duke Ellington's Kentucky Club Orchestra began to attract attention. In his band Ellington had such men as Sonny Greer (drums), Otto Hardwicke (alto sax), Elmer Snowden (banjo), Arthur Whetsol (trumpet)— who remained with him for years—to which were added such other great instrumentalists as Johnny Hodges (alto sax), Barney Bigard (clarinet), Cootie Williams (trumpet), Bubber Miley (trumpet), Tricky Sam Nanton (trombone), and many others. The characteristic style of the Ellington sound evolved out of the improvisational ideas of the various instrumentalists and Ellington based his arrangements on their remarkable capabilities. The band first attracted national attention when it went into the Cotton Club (q.v.) in December 1927. Radio broadcasts from the club introduced the orchestra to a wider audience; so did a film appearance in the Amos 'n' Andy film, *Check and Double Check* (1930). Ellington the composer was noticed around this time also, as evidenced by the popularity of a recording of "Dreamy Blues," better known later as "Mood Indigo." The band's unique sound, the blend of instruments, the use of advanced chord structures and progressions, plus the star solos, contributed to its success. The insistent beat and the growling of Miley's trumpet and Nanton's trombone earned the band its then renown for playing "jungle music." Its reputation spread and the band made its first successful European tour in 1933. By the mid 1930s the Ellington band was considered the outstanding jazz orchestra in the world, reaching its peak in 1940–43, shortly after the band was joined by Billy Strayhorn (1915–1967). Ellington did not let up for the rest of his life and produced, often in collaboration, thousands of arrangements, songs, and concert works. Among his most popular songs are "Sophisticated Lady" (lyrics by I. Mills and Mitchell Parish), "Solitude" (lyrics by I. Mills and Eddie De Lange), "I Let a Song Go Out of My Heart," "I Got It Bad and That Ain't Good" (from the musical *Jump for Joy*, lyrics by Paul Webster, 1941), "Do Nothin' Till You Hear from Me" (lyrics by Bob Russell), and "Don't Get Around Much Anymore" (lyrics by Russell). On Jan. 23, 1943, Ellington presented his orchestra in Carnegie Hall for the first time (several more concerts followed this event) and introduced a new extended work, *Black, Brown and Beige*—"a tone parallel to the history of the American Negro." As early as 1927 Ellington had composed *Black and Tan Fantasy*, which was followed by several extended works, among them *Creole Rhapsody, Reminiscing in Tempo, New World A'Coming* for piano and orchestra, *Harlem, Liberian Suite, New Orleans Suite, The River* (a ballet), *Togo Brava Suite,* and the *Sacred Concerts,* the 3rd of which was presented in Westminster Abbey, London, Oct. 24, 1973. The bulk of Ellington's work remains preserved, in his own interpretation, on recordings. Six months after the Westminster Abbey concert, Ellington died in New York City, May 24, 1974, of cancer, complicated by pneumonia. An autobiography, *Music Is My Mistress,* was published in 1973. His son, Mercer (b. 1919), took his father's place at the head of the Ellington Orchestra.

ELWELL, HERBERT (1898–1977) Composer, teacher, critic. Born in Minneapolis, Minn., May 10, 1898, Elwell attended the University of Minnesota and then, in 1919, came to New York City to study with Ernest Bloch (q.v.) and later went on to Paris to study with Nadia Boulanger (q.v.). A recipient of a fellowship at the American Academy in Rome in 1926, he remained there for 2 years and returned to the United States to join the staff of the Cleveland Institute of Music. In 1932 he became music critic for the Cleveland *Plain Dealer.* He later taught at the Oberlin (Ohio) Conservatory of Music. One of his outstanding students was Howard Swanson (q.v.). Elwell as a composer made his first impression with an early work, the ballet *The Happy Hypocrite* (1925), which he arranged into a suite that was often performed. Elwell composed many chamber works: *Quintet for Piano and Strings* (1923), a *Piano Sonata* (1926), *Divertimento for String Quartet* (1929), *String Quartet in E Minor* (1938), *Sonata for Violin and Piano* (1939), and *Blue Symphony* for medium voice and string quartet (1943). His *Introduction and Allegro* (1941) received the Juilliard Publication Award, and *Lincoln* for baritone, mixed chorus, and orchestra (1945) the Paderewski Fund Award. El-

well's output included pieces for piano and songs. He died in Oberlin, Ohio, Apr. 17, 1977.

"AN EXPERIMENT IN MODERN MUSIC" The title of a concert presented by Paul Whiteman (q.v.) at Aeolian Hall, New York City, Feb. 12, 1924. Whiteman's stated purpose was to feature his Palais Royal Orchestra (the Palais Royal was a Times Square nightclub) in a concert hall to prove that jazz, or rather what he thought was jazz, was acceptable music. According to a program note, written by Hugh C. Ernst, "The experiment is to be purely educational. Mr. Whiteman intends to point out, with the assistance of his orchestra and associates, the tremendous strides which have been made in popular music from the day of the discordant Jazz, which sprang into existence about ten years ago from nowhere in particular, to the really melodious music of today, which—for no good reason—is still called Jazz." This educational experiment is now best remembered because it marked the first performance of George Gershwin's *Rhapsody in Blue* (q.v.). The rest of the program consisted of Whiteman band specialties—"Mama Loves Papa," "Limehouse Blues," an Irving Berlin medley in "Semi-Symphonic" arrangements, "Whispering," etc.—plus an appearance of the very popular Zez Confrey (q.v.) to perform 3 of his piano novelties, including "Kitten on the Keys," and the premiere of Victor Herbert's (q.v.) *Suite of Serenades,* written, like the *Rhapsody in Blue,* especially for Whiteman's "Experiment." The great success of the concert, attributable to the impression made by the Gershwin rhapsody, led to a repeat in Aeolian Hall on Mar. 7 and another, a benefit for the American Academy in Rome, at Carnegie Hall on Apr. 21, 1924. The "Experiment" made both Whiteman and Gershwin.

FIELDS, DOROTHY (1905–1974) Lyricist, librettist. The daughter of co-median-producer Lew Fields (1867–1941) of the comedy team Weber and Fields (q.v.), Dorothy Fields was born in Allenhurst, N.J., July 15, 1905. Her brothers, Herbert (1897–1958) and Joseph (1895–1966) were successful librettists; the former especially, who wrote or collaborated on the books of such musicals as *Hit the Deck, Something for the Boys,* and *Annie Get Your Gun* (written with his sister, whose idea it was). Family objections, particularly by her father, tended to keep Dorothy Fields out of show business. She finally, and defiantly, struck out on her own when she teamed up with a successful song-writer, Jimmy McHugh (q.v.), to write songs for the Cotton Club (q.v.) in Harlem (ca. 1927–30). They also collaborated on songs for other revues and shows, which eventually led to a Broadway show, the all-black *Blackbirds of 1928,* which was undoubtedly inspired by the Cotton Club shows. For this production Fields and McHugh wrote several songs of great popularity, among them "Diga Diga Do" and "I Can't Give You Anything But Love" (originally written the year before as "I Can't Give You Anything But Love, Lindy" in honor of Charles A. Lindbergh's flight across the Atlantic); the song was dropped from *Harry Delmar's Revels* and rewritten for *Blackbirds.* Fields and McHugh collaborated on *Lew Leslie's International Revue* (1930) from which came "Exactly Like You" and "On the Sunny Side of the Street." They then went to Hollywood, where they wrote several good songs: "Cuban Love Song" (*The Cuban Love Song,* 1931), "Don't Blame Me," (*Dinner at Eight,* 1933), "Lost in a Fog" (*Have a Heart,* 1934), "I Feel a Song Comin' On" (with George Oppenheimer) and "I'm in the Mood for Love" (*Every Night at Eight,* 1935). Fields also teamed with Jerome Kern (q.v.) with whom she did the scores for *I Dream Too Much* (1935), *Swing Time* ("The Way You Look Tonight," which won an Academy Award, and "A Fine Romance," 1936), *Joy of Living* (1938), and *One Night in the Tropics* (1940). She returned to Broadway to collaborate with Arthur Schwartz on *Stars in Your Eyes* (1939) and, later, *A Tree Grows in Brooklyn* (1951) and *By the Beautiful Sea* (1954). On the last she also collaborated on the book with Herbert Fields—as she did on several musicals from 1941 (*Let's Face It*) through 1959 (*Redhead,* with music by Albert Hague). She also collaborated with composers Sigmund Romberg (q.v.) on *Up in Central Park* ("Close as Pages in a Book," 1945), Morton Gould (q.v.) on *Arms and the Girl* (1950), and Cy Coleman on *Sweet Charity* ("Where Am I Going?") and *Seesaw,* her final 2 shows in 1966 and 1973, respectively. She also collaborated with Harold Arlen (q.v.) on 2 films and with Burton Lane (q.v.) on the TV production of *Junior Miss* (1957). Dorothy Fields devoted nearly a half century to writing lyrics, as well as to other theatre activities, and in a restricted field she proved to be one of the finest wordsmiths of American popular song. She died in New York City, Mar. 28, 1974.

FILM MUSICAL I The film musical, or films with songs, came into being in the late 1920s, specifically in 1927 with the opening of Al Jolson's *The Jazz Singer* at the Warner Theatre, New York City, on Oct. 6. While it was not the first of the early films to bring music, speech, and sound to the screen (that was John Barrymore's *Don Juan* with attached musical sequences in August 1926), *The Jazz Singer* was the first to integrate songs into the film (the high—or low—point was Jolson's rendition on his knees of "My Mammy") and it was also, more importantly, most successful financially. The success of *The Jazz Singer* ended the silent film era and ushered in the first cluster of film musicals. By 1929 several songwriters left Broadway for Hollywood, as did many of Broadway's popular performers—Helen Morgan, Eddie Cantor, Fanny Brice, et al.—and, to assure a supply of song, the film studios began buying up the New York publishing houses. The first film musicals were very Broadway-oriented with titles like *The Broadway Melody, Gold Diggers of Broadway, Broadway Babies* and, simply, *Broadway*, all released in 1929; further Broadway borrowings included the filming of former Broadway shows: *The Desert Song, Little Johnny Jones, Rio Rita, Sally,* and a strangely adapted *Show Boat* that retained but one of the original songs, "Ol' Man River." Another typical form of 1929 film musical was one in which the top stars of the various studios were tossed into a production for name value, if not much else: *Fox Movietone Follies, Hollywood Revue* (MGM), and Warner Brothers' *Show of Shows.* Interestingly, *The Broadway Melody,* a typical backstage musical drama, was chosen as the Best Picture of the year; its score was mostly by Nacio Herb Brown and Arthur Freed (q.v.). Dozens of musical films were released in 1929, some with more or less original stories—often as not constructed around a Broadway name, e.g., Fanny Brice was seen in *My Man* doing several of her specialties, including the title song. The early film musicals, generally, were quite static; much had to be learned about flexible camera work, how to use sound, how to direct—an exception was *The Love Parade* directed by Ernst Lubitsch and starring Jeanette MacDonald and Maurice Chevalier. But no real formula and no style were evident; the film musicals of 1930 followed the same ruts as the year before. By 1931 film musicals were no longer box office and the flow of musical films practically dried up until 1933, when Hollywood found its voice, style, and skills and began producing some of the best-scored, most delightful musical films ever released. (See Film Musicals II, Section VI.)

FIRST LITTLE SHOW (1929) The correct title for this special revue is *The Little Show,* but because it initiated a series of unpretentious, sharp-witted, musically and lyrically superior shows, it is popularly known as the *First Little Show* (and was followed by a *Second,* 1930, and a *Third,* 1931). *The Little Show* opened at the Music Box Theatre on Apr. 20, 1929, and starred Clifton Webb, Fred Allen, and Libby Holman. The sketches were written by George S. Kaufman, Newman Levy, and Howard Dietz, who also wrote the lyrics to the music of Arthur Schwartz (q.v.). Their outstanding song was "I Guess I'll Have to Change My Plan." Dietz also collaborated on "Moanin' Low" (music by Ralph Rainger, q.v.). *The Little Show* marked the debut of a new songwriting team: Kay Swift (q.v.) and "Paul James" (the banker James Warburg and Swift's husband); their contribution was the distinguished "Can't We Be Friends?" The revue ran for more than 300 performances, which was remarkable for those Depression days.

FOX-TROT Name for a popular dance of the 1920s, in 2/4 or 4/4 time, alternating slow with fast movements or steps. The 2/4 or alla breve duple time was also known as the two-step. The bulk of popular songs is written in 4/4 or "common" time. The many other dances named for animals—bunny hug, turkey trot, grizzly bear—however danced, were danced to either of these tempos.

FREED, ISADORE (1900–1960) Composer, teacher. Born in Brest-Litovsk, Russia, Mar. 26, 1900, Freed was brought to the United States at the age of 3, when his family emigrated to Philadelphia. He was educated at the University of Pennsylvania and the Philadelphia Conservatory. He was a student of piano and composition, and his major teachers were Ernest Bloch (q.v.), with whom he studied from 1918 to 1921, and Vincent d'Indy (composition, 1929–30). Freed also studied the organ at the Schola Cantorum, Paris. While there he organized and conducted the Concerts Spirituels for 3 years. He taught at the Curtis Institute and at Temple University, Philadelphia, and was visiting professor of composition at Hartt College, Hartford, Conn., beginning in 1944. Freed was also conductor-founder of the Philadelphia Chamber Orchestra. He composed in virtually every musical genre. For chamber groups he wrote the *Suite for Viola and Piano* (1923), 3 string quartets (1925, 1930, 1936), a *Sonata for Violin and Piano* (1926), *Quintet for Piano and Strings* (1937), *Trio for Flute, Harp, and Viola* (1940), and *Triptych for Violin, Viola, Cello and Piano* (1943). For solo piano Freed produced a *Fantastic Holiday* suite (1926), *Sonorités Rhythmiques* (1931), *Five Pieces for Piano* (1933), *Sonata* (1933), and *Lyrical Sonorities* (1934). His orchestral compositions include *Pygmalion*, a symphonic rhapsody (1926), *Jeux de timbres* (1931), *Music for Strings* (1937), a *Viola Rhapsody* (1939), *Violin Concerto* (1939), 2 symphonies (1942; 1951) and a *Cello Concerto* (1954). Among his choral works are the *Sacred Service for the Sabbath* (1937), *Postscripts* (1942), and *Micah,* written for the 10th anniversary of the state of Israel (1958). For the theatre Freed composed the ballet *Vibrations* (1928), from which he abstracted a suite (1929), and 2 operas, *Homo Sum* (1930) and *The Princess and the Vaga-*

bond (1948). Freed died in Rockville Center, N.Y., Nov. 10, 1960.

FRIML, RUDOLF (1879–1972)
Born in Prague, Czechoslovakia, Dec. 7, 1879, Friml studied at the Prague Conservatory with Dvořák (q.v.) and Josef Jiránek and received a thoroughly classical training. Friml graduated at the age of 17 and formed a partnership with a classmate, the violin virtuoso Jan Kubelik. They toured the musical capitals of 'Europe and came to the United States twice. On the 2nd visit, in 1906, Friml decided to remain and made appearances with major orchestras as a piano soloist. His *Concerto in B Major* was performed in Carnegie Hall in 1906 by the New York Symphony under Walter Damrosch (q.v.), with the composer at the piano. For the next 6 years Friml made concert appearances and composed piano pieces and art songs. Friml made his entrance upon the operetta scene in an unusual manner. Victor Herbert (q.v.) had been commissioned to write the music for an operetta for Emma Trentini, who had scored a great success in Herbert's *Naughty Marietta* in 1910. At the time Herbert was in Philadelphia and Trentini in New York; neither would leave their respective cities to meet and discuss the songs. Producer William Hammerstein, who had a book and lyrics, but no score, took his troubles to music publisher Rudolph Schirmer—who suggested that Hammerstein approach Friml, whose instrumental pieces and songs Schirmer published. The result was *The Firefly,* which opened on Dec. 2, 1912. It proved to be reasonably successful and 2 of its songs even more so: "Giannina Mia" and "Sympathy." For the next quarter century Friml turned out traditional operetta scores, whatever the Broadway fashion during the jazz age (as did Sigmund Romberg, q.v.), and enjoyed several successes and produced dozens of enduring songs. He hit his

stride with *Rose-Marie* (1924), his 14th musical. From this enduring chestnut came such songs as "Totem Tom-Tom," "Rose-Marie," and "Indian Love Call" (all with lyrics by Otto Harbach and Oscar Hammerstein II). Another success followed the next year, *The Vagabond King* (lyrics by Brian Hooker): "Waltz Huguette" and "Only a Rose." Friml's last major Broadway success was the popular *The Three Musketeers* (1928) with lyrics by Clifford Grey and P. G. Wodehouse (q.v.). His 3 most successful shows were converted into film musicals that were most successful in the 1930s; *Rose-Marie* starred Jeanette MacDonald and Nelson Eddy (1936) and *The Firefly* (1937), MacDonald and Allan Jones. For *The Firefly,* Friml and Herbert Stothart polished up an old instrumental, *Chansonette,* which, with lyrics by Bob Wright and Chet Forrest, became the popular "The Donkey Serenade." Friml's last film score was written for a Nelson Eddy flop, *Northwest Outpost.* Friml spent the rest of his long life traveling; he had a special affection for the Orient. He composed, recorded, and made concert appearances well into his eighties. He died in Hollywood, Nov. 12, 1972.

GAUTHIER, EVA (1885–1958) Mezzo-soprano. Born in Ottawa, Canada, Sept. 20, 1885, Gauthier was educated in a convent where she began the study of music: piano and voice. She sang in church choirs in Ottawa, often taking the solos. She continued her studies in Paris, London, and Rome and made her operatic debut in the role of "Micaëla" in *Carmen.* For about 5 years, beginning in 1910, she made a tour of the Orient studying the music of the Far East. Settling in New York, she became the vocal champion of the ultramoderns: Stravinsky (q.v.), Bartók (q.v.), and Schoenberg (q.v.). She pro-

grammed the Oriental-inflected songs of Charles Tomlinson Griffes (q.v.), John Alden Carpenter (q.v.), Leo Ornstein (q.v.), and other little-known young American composers. She created a musical stir when, on Nov. 1, 1923, she presented her "Recital of Ancient and Modern Music for Voice" and at the suggestion of Carl Van Vechten (q.v.) included a set of American popular songs in her program. Gauthier agreed and asked a young composer-pianist to be her accompanist; he was George Gershwin (q.v.). The American song portion of the recital opened with Berlin's "Alexander's Ragtime Band" and continued through Kern's "The Siren's Song," Donaldson's "Carolina in the Morning," and closed with a group of Gershwin: "I'll Build a Stairway to Paradise," "Innocent Ingenue Baby," and "Swanee." Other composers represented on the program were Hindemith, Purcell, Byrd, Schoenberg, Milhaud, Bartók, Bellini, Bliss, and Delage. The recital marked the first time that a "serious" singer dared to present popular songs on the recital stage of Aeolian Hall. The recital was very successful, generating much heat in the next day's musical columns, and was repeated in January 1924 in Boston, where it was also well received, with Gershwin getting much attention; he was already preparing for an even greater debut at Aeolian Hall (see *Rhapsody in Blue*). Needless to say, the critics called his inventive accompaniment "jazz." The recital was Gauthier's career highpoint and she eventually retired from active concert life to lecture and teach voice. She died in New York City, Dec. 26, 1958.

"GEORGIA TOM" See Thomas A. Dorsey.

GERSHWIN, GEORGE (1898–1937) Composer, songwriter, pianist. Born in Brooklyn, N.Y., Sept. 26, 1898, Gershwin came to music rather late in life for one who wished to become a concert pianist. He was about 12 when a piano arrived in the Gershwin household for older brother Ira (q.v.), who was to take lessons. But it was George who immediately demonstrated that he already had a rudimentary piano technique, self-taught on a neighbor's piano. It was not until George found Charles Hambitzer (1878–1918) that his musical education took the right turn. Hambitzer was impressed with Gershwin's learning powers and his pianistics. He encouraged him to study theory, harmony, and orchestration with Edward Kilenyi (1884–1968), for whom Gershwin produced one of his first "serious" pieces, the *Lullaby* for string quartet (ca. 1919). Gershwin also revealed an interest in popular music, especially the songs of Irving Berlin and Jerome Kern. He lost interest in school and withdrew from the High School of Commerce to work as a pianist in a music publishing house. The death of Hambitzer ended Gershwin's ambitions for a career as a recitalist and he concentrated on popular music, although continuing to study with Kilenyi and others whenever possible. His early songs were published and one, "Swanee" (1919), became very popular and led to commissions for Gershwin show scores. A series of *George White's Scandals* (1920–24) established Gershwin as a Broadway composer, a position underscored by his first major success, *Lady, Be Good!* (1924), which was also the first all-Gershwin Broadway show, with lyrics by his brother Ira. That same year, in February, Gershwin made his first impression in the "serious" field with the *Rhapsody in Blue* (q.v.). He followed that with the *Concerto in F* (1925), *Preludes for Piano* (1926), *An American in Paris* (1928, q.v.), *Second Rhapsody* (1931), *Cuban Overture*

(1932), *Piano Transcriptions of 18 Songs* ("George Gershwin's Song Book," 1932), and the *"I Got Rhythm" Variations* (1934). Fourteen additional show scores followed *Lady, Be Good!*, among them *Tip-Toes* (1925: "Looking for a Boy," "That Certain Feeling," "Sweet and Low-Down"), *"Oh, Kay!* (1926: "Someone to Watch Over Me," "Maybe," "Do-Do-Do," "Clap Yo' Hands"), *Funny Face* (1927: "'S Wonderful," "My One and Only," "He Loves and She Loves," "Let's Kiss and Make Up"), *Treasure Girl* (1928: "I've Got a Crush on You," "Oh, So Nice," "I Don't Think I'll Fall in Love Today," "Where's the Boy? Here's the Girl!"), *Show Girl* (1929: "Liza," "Do What You Do," "So Are You!"), *Strike Up the Band* (1927, revised 1930: "Soon," "I Mean to Say," "Strike Up the Band"), *Girl Crazy* (1930: "Bidin' My Time," "Embraceable You," "I Got Rhythm," "But Not for Me"), *Of Thee I Sing* (1931; the first Pulitzer Prize musical) and its unsuccessful but brilliant sequel, *Let 'Em Eat Cake* (1933). The Gershwins, collaborating with poet-playwright DuBose Heyward, completed the opera *Porgy and Bess* in 1935. Although not too successful then, it has since been recognized as Gershwin's masterpiece and has been sung virtually all over the world. The Gershwins wrote the songs for 4 films (although their songs have been used in several): *Delicious* (1931: "Blah-Blah-Blah," "Somebody from Somewhere"), *Shall We Dance* (1937: "They Can't Take That Away From Me," "Slap That Bass," "They All Laughed"), *A Damsel in Distress* (1937: "A Foggy Day," "Nice Work If You Can Get It," "Things Are Looking Up"), and *The Goldwyn Follies* (1937: "Love Is Here to Stay," "Love Walked In," "I Was Doing All Right"), which George Gershwin did not live to complete; he died of a brain tumor (after an unsuccessful operation) in Hollywood, July 11, 1937, at the age of 38.

GERSHWIN, IRA (b. 1896) Lyricist, writer. Born in New York City, Dec. 6, 1896, Gershwin was educated in New York schools and appeared to be headed for some profession, like teaching. Bookish, he read a good deal and, impressed with the work of Gilbert, began writing light verse for high school and college papers as well as for newspaper columns that published unknown writers. Since his younger brother George (q.v.) had entered the popular musical world, Ira Gershwin was exposed to lyrics and lyricists. He dabbled in the form while working at various jobs in his father's various establishments, including a Russian bath. So it was that the Gershwins began to exchange song ideas and rather casually began their collaboration. Since George had already arrived in Tin Pan Alley and had had several songs published, Ira took a pen name borrowed from his other siblings (his youngest brother and their sister): "Arthur Francis." Their first joint effort that was sung in a show and published was "The Real American Folk Song (Is a Rag)" from *Ladies First* (1918; it was published years later). Their first published song was "Waiting for the Sun to Come Out" (from *The Sweetheart Shop*, 1920) and their first sizable score was written for *A Dangerous Maid*, 1921, although it never opened in New York. Ira Gershwin also collaborated with other composers at this time, including Vincent Youmans (q.v., *Two Little Girls in Blue*, 1921) and Lewis Gensler. It was in 1924, when the Gershwins did the songs for *Lady, Be Good!* that "Arthur Francis" was abandoned and Ira Gershwin emerged. He was soon recognized as one of the outstanding Broadway lyricists with a wry point of view and polished craftsmanship. Besides his brother he worked with other

songwriters during the 1920s and '30s: Phil Charig (*That's a Good Girl*, 1928), Harold Arlen (q.v., *Life Begins at 8:40*, 1934), and Vernon Duke (q.v., *Ziegfeld Follies*, 1936). After George Gershwin's death Ira Gershwin worked with Duke to fill out the score for the film *The Goldwyn Follies*, rested for a time, and then began writing individual songs with Jerome Kern (q.v.). He successfully returned to Broadway with *Lady in the Dark* (1941) with music by Kurt Weill (q.v.). In 1945 they collaborated on the interesting but unsuccessful *The Firebrand of Florence*. Ira Gershwin's last Broadway effort was *Park Avenue* (1946) with music by Arthur Schwartz (q.v.). Gershwin, in fact, preferred working in California and collaborated on several film musicals: *North Star* (score by Aaron Copland, q.v., 1943), *Cover Girl* (Kern, q.v., 1944), *Where Do We Go from Here?* (Weill, 1945), *The Barkleys of Broadway* (Harry Warren, q.v., 1949), *Give a Girl a Break* (Burton Lane, q.v., 1953), *A Star Is Born* (Harold Arlen, q.v., 1954), and *The Country Girl* (Arlen, 1954). Gershwin has devoted several years to the formation of a Gershwin Archive at the Library of Congress where he has been depositing manuscripts, documents, etc. (mostly associated with his brother George); all materials are carefully annotated. Gershwin has also been working on the unpublished materials his brother left (some was used in the films *The Shocking Miss Pilgrim* (1946) and *Kiss Me, Stupid* (1964); he has also prepared songs and instrumental pieces for publication. Among the songs written with composers other than his brother are: "Sunny Disposish" (Phil Charig, 1926), "Cheerful Little Earful" (Harry Warren, 1930), "You're a Builder Upper," "Fun to Be Fooled," and "What Can You Say in a Love Song?" (Arlen, in collaboration with E. Y. Harburg, q.v., 1934), "I Can't Get Started" (Vernon Duke,

1936), "My Ship," "Jenny," "Tschaikowsky" (all with Kurt Weill, 1941), "Long Ago and Far Away" and "Sure Thing" (Kern, 1944), "You're Far Too Near Me," "A Rhyme for Angela," "Sing Me Not a Ballad" (all: Weill, 1945), "Don't Be a Woman If You Can" (Arthur Schwartz, 1946), "You'd Be Hard to Replace" and "Shoes with Wings On" (Harry Warren, 1946), "In Our United State" and "It Happens Every Time" (Burton Lane, 1953), "The Man That Got Away," "It's a New World," "The Search Is Through," "Dissertation on the State of Bliss (or Love and Learn)" (Harold Arlen, 1954). His book, *Lyrics on Several Occasions,* was published by Alfred A. Knopf in 1959.

GRIFFIS, ELLIOT (1893–1967) Composer, pianist, teacher. Born in Boston, Mass., Jan. 28, 1893, Griffis was a student of painting as well as music. He studied at Ithaca College; he later studied at Yale with Horatio Parker (q.v.) and at the New England Conservatory with Stuart Mason. He was also awarded a Juilliard Fellowship. Griffis first attracted attention with his *Piano Sonata* (1919). He taught music at Grinnell College (Iowa), Brooklyn Settlement School, the St. Louis Institute of Music, and privately in New York, Vienna, and Paris. Besides several songs, Griffis' work includes the *String Variations* for orchestra (1924), *A Persian Fable* for English horn and orchestra (1925), the symphonic poem *Colossus* (1928), *First Symphony* (1932) and a symphony for strings, *Fantastic Pursuit* (1941), the orchestral suite *Yon Green Mountain* (1943), 3 string quartets (1926; 1930; 1937), a *Sonata for Violin and Piano* (1931), a *Suite* for violin, cello, and piano (1941), *The Aztec Flute* for flute, violin, cello, and piano (1942), and *Variations for Violin and Viola* (1946). Griffis' works for stage include an operetta, *The Blue Scarab,* and a one-act

opera, *Port of Pleasure.* His *Prayers to the Sun and the Wind,* 2 songs for soprano and orchestra, was completed in 1939. Besides composing and painting, Griffis published several volumes of verse. He died in Los Angeles, Calif., June 8, 1967.

GRISELLE, THOMAS (1891–1955) Composer, pianist, arranger, conductor. Born in Sandusky, Ohio, Jan. 10, 1891, Griselle attended the Cincinnati College of Music, where he studied with Albino Gorno and Louis Sarr. He also studied with Nadia Boulanger (q.v.) and Arnold Schoenberg (q.v.). Griselle initially earned his living as accompanist for vaudeville stars such as Nora Bayes and with more "serious" singers, Alice Nielsen and Clarence Whitehill. Griselle was one of the earliest to use popular music elements in extended works. His *Cubist* for pit band was heard in the *Cohan Revue of 1918,* which incidentally starred Bayes. Griselle also composed *Two Pieces from Olden Times* (1921), *Two American Sketches*: "Nocturne" and "March" which won the Victor Talking Machine Award of $10,000, and a Victor Recording, in 1928. Other works include the satirical *Program Music* (1937), a *Keyboard Symphony* for 6 pianos, a *Dance Suite,* and other works for orchestra and chamber groupings. Griselle eventually settled in California where he worked in radio as an arranger-conductor. He died in Hollywood, Dec. 27, 1955.

GROFÉ, FERDE (1892–1972) Arranger, composer, pianist, violist, teacher. Born in New York City, Mar. 27, 1892, Grofé studied piano, violin, and harmony with his mother and the viola with his grandfather, Bernhard Bierlich, who played the cello in the orchestra at the Metropolitan Opera. The family eventually moved to California and after a brief period of itinerant musicianship as a pianist in mining towns, Grofé settled in Los Angeles and spent 10 years in the Los Angeles Symphony as violist. He also found extra work as a pianist in local dance bands and eventually found his way into an early Paul Whiteman (q.v.) band, then playing in Los Angeles, in 1920. Soon Grofé, whose musicianship Whiteman noted, began writing special arrangements and orchestrations for the band. In his orchestrations Grofé left room for solo breaks and utilized what he called a "harmony chorus," a solo instrument, usually the saxophone, quietly backed by sustained chords in the brass and a genteel rhythm accompaniment by piano (Grofé), banjo, and bass. This performance of popular dance music and the instrumentation, roughly that of the standard jazz band, soon earned the Whiteman band the reputation as being a jazz orchestra and led to its great success and eventual triumphs in New York. This reached a peak with Whiteman's "Experiment in Modern Music" (q.v.) when Gershwin's *Rhapsody in Blue* (q.v.) was introduced. The scoring was done by Grofé and immediately led to a successful career as orchestrator, arranger, and composer. Grofé left Whiteman in 1924 to devote his time to this work. He also began composing and arranging his own original compositions: *Broadway at Night* (1924), *Mississippi Suite* (1925), *Metropolis* (based on themes by Matty Malneck and Harry Barris, 1927), *Three Shades of Blue* (1928), *Grand Canyon Suite* (1931), *Tabloid Suite* (1933), *Hollywood Suite* (1935), *Aviation Suite* (1945), etc. Grofé also composed a *Piano Concerto* (1960) and a (New York) *World's Fair Suite* (1964). He also scored several motion pictures including the Whiteman opus *King of Jazz* (1930) and *Minstrel Man* (songs by Paul Francis Webster and Harry Revel, 1944), for which Grofé won an Academy Award. Grofé made a final break with Whiteman in 1933 to conduct (he did much radio work) and make guest appearances in concerts. He also taught orchestration and composition at the Juilliard School of Music (1939–43). He is best remembered as the orchestrator of the *Rhapsody in Blue* and the composer of 2 popular themes, "On the Trail" from *Grand Canyon Suite* which was used as the radio theme of the "Philip Morris Playhouse" and the popular song "Daybreak" adapted from the "Mardi Gras" section of *Mississippi Suite,* with words by Harold Adamson, in 1942. Grofé died in Santa Monica, Calif., Apr. 3, 1972.

GRUENBERG, LOUIS (1884–1964) Composer, pianist, teacher. Born in Brest-Litovsk, Russia, Aug. 3, 1884, Gruenberg was brought to the United States at the age of 2. He studied piano with Adele Margulies in New York and went to Berlin in 1903 to study with Ferruccio Busoni. He spent the years 1912–19 in a master class in the Vienna Conservatory. Gruenberg made his debut as a pianist with the Berlin Philharmonic in 1912; he toured Europe extensively and also the United States, giving concerts, but eventually gave up the pianist's career to concentrate on composition. In 1930 he was appointed the head of the Department of Composition, Chicago College of Music. He later moved to New York and settled in Brooklyn; he was active in the League of Composers (q.v.) and the International Society for Contemporary Music. He first came to the attention of the musical world in 1919 when his symphonic poem *Hill of Dreams* was awarded the Flagler Prize and a performance by the New York Symphony. He followed that with *Vagabondia* for orchestra in 1920. Gruenberg was an early "jazz" aficionado and produced a number of works in that vein, his earliest being *Indiscretions* for string quartet (1922) followed by *The Daniel Jazz* for tenor and octet (1923), *Jazz*

Suite for orchestra (1925), *The Creation* for baritone and octet (1924), and *Jazzettes* for violin and piano (1937). Gruenberg eventually turned to more conventional methods and composed a large body of works: 4 symphonies (1930; 1941; 1941; 1946), 2 piano concertos (1914; 1938), a *Violin Concerto* (1944), *Music to an Imaginary Ballet* and *Music to an Imaginary Legend,* both for orchestra and both composed in 1945. These were followed by *Americana* for orchestra and *Dance Rhapsody,* both also completed in 1945. Gruenberg produced a good deal of chamber music: 3 violin sonatas (1912; 1924; 1950), 2 string quartets (1937; 1941), 2 piano quintets (1929; 1937), and *Five Variations on a Popular Theme* for string quartet (1942). His operas include *Jack and the Beanstalk* (1930), *The Emperor Jones,* his best-known work (1932), *Queen Helena* (1936), *Green Mansions,* a "nonvisual opera" written for radio (1937), and *Antony and Cleopatra* (completed in 1962). Gruenberg composed several film scores, among them *Fight for Life* (1940), *Commandos Strike at Dawn* (1942), *So Ends Our Night* (1943), and *Counterattack* (1945). He died in Beverly Hills, Calif., June 9, 1964.

GUION, DAVID W. (b. 1895) Composer, pianist, teacher. Born in Ballinger, Tex., Dec. 15, 1895, Guion began to study the piano at Polyclinic College, Fort Worth, and completed his studies at the Vienna Conservatory with Leopold Godowsky, Sr. He taught music in several Texas schools and colleges and later joined the staff of the Chicago College of Music. Guion developed a deep interest in Americana and lectured on Southern and Western folk music besides using it as a springboard for his own compositions. He set many folk songs in various vocal arrangements: "Ride Cowboy Ride" for men and boys' voices (1918),

"Hopi Indian Cradle Song" for mixed voices (1918), "What Shall We Do with a Drunken Sailor?" for men and boys' voices (1924), and "Home on the Range" for the same voices and mixed chorus (1931). Guion's orchestral works include *Southern Nights Suite* (1922), *Sheep and Goat Walking to the Pasture* (1922), *Alley Tunes* (1926), *Mother Goose Suite* (1930), *Shingandi* on African themes (1932), *Suite for Orchestra* (1937), plus *Texas* and *Prairie Suites* commissioned in the 1950s. Guion's best-known transcription is a piano arrangement of *Turkey in the Straw* (which exists also in a bravura orchestral setting, a favorite of the various "Pops" orchestras).

HAMMERSTEIN, OSCAR, II (1895–1960) Lyricist, librettist. Born in New York City, July 12, 1895, Hammerstein was raised in a musical-theatrical setting. His grandfather, after whom he was named, was an opera impresario who also composed and wrote lyrics. His uncle, Arthur, was a producer of musicals in the 1910s and '20s. Hammerstein was a student at Columbia University studying law; during this time he wrote and appeared in the famous varsity shows at Columbia. Deciding to abandon law, Hammerstein went to work for his uncle as a stage manager. In 1920 he began collaborating with composer Herbert Stothart (1885–1949) on a series of musicals (no less than 3 in a single year) and came of lyrical age in the 1923 musical *Wildflower* with music by Stothart and Vincent Youmans (q.v.). In 1925 he collaborated with Jerome Kern (q.v.) on the popular *Sunny;* their collaboration reached a high point with *Show Boat* (1927) and a (financial) low with Kern's last Broadway show, the beautifully scored *Very Warm For May* (1939) for which they wrote such songs as "All the Things You Are," "In the Heart of the Dark," and "All in Fun."

Hammerstein, who had a gift for the romantic operetta-like musical, also wrote with Rudolf Friml (q.v.) and Sigmund Romberg (q.v.). Hammerstein not only wrote the lyrics to the songs, he frequently wrote, or collaborated on, the books to the musicals; he was also active in films (Kern's *High, Wide and Handsome*, 1937; their song "The Last Time I Saw Paris" interpolated into the score of the film *Lady Be Good*—which was not related to the Gershwin musical—won the Academy Award for best film song in 1941). After a period of Broadway successes in the 1920s, and little success in the '30s, Hammerstein formed a partnership with Richard Rodgers (q.v.) to write the songs for an unlikely musical with a Western setting and the title of *Away We Go!* Based on Lynn Riggs's folksy *Green Grow the Lilacs*, the musical came to Broadway as *Oklahoma!* (1943) and proved to be a landmark of the American musical theatre. Hammerstein's poetic lyrics and Rodgers' fine melodies were smoothly and seamlessly woven into the plot (what little there was of it) to begin the new era of the "integrated musical," in which all the music (sometimes ballet) and songs advanced the plot or somehow delineated character. The next Rodgers and Hammerstein musical was equally successful, both aesthetically and financially. This was *Carousel*, based on Ferenc Molnár's *Liliom*, but transported from Hungary to New England. The collaboration produced 7 more musicals, 3 of which were moderately successful, but 4 were smash hits: *South Pacific* (1949), *The King and I* (1951), *Flower Drum Song* (1958), and their last, *The Sound of Music* (1959). Hammerstein was often criticized for sentimentality in his lyrics, of seeing life through rose-colored glasses (he was often compared unfavorably to Rodgers' earlier lyricist, the acerb, tricky, and often mildly cynical Lorenz Hart). But Hammerstein, who

was himself optimistic, content, hopeful, and romantic, continued until the end to produce singable, well-crafted lyrics. Among the songs for which he wrote the words (and the list but scratches the surface of his output) are: "Bambalina," (Youmans), "Rose-Marie" and "Indian Love Call" (Friml, in collaboration with Otto Harbach), "Who?" (Kern), "One Alone" (Romberg), "Ol' Man River" and "Why Do I Love You?" (Kern), "Lover, Come Back to Me" (Romberg), "Why Was I Born?" (Kern), "I've Told Every Little Star" (Kern), "I'll Take Romance" (Ben Oakland), "Can I Forget You?" (Kern), "People Will Say We're in Love," "Oh, What a Beautiful Mornin'," "It Might as Well Be Spring," "If I Loved You," "Soliloquy," "You'll Never Walk Alone," "The Gentleman Is a Dope," "Some Enchanted Evening," "Younger Than Springtime," "Hello, Young Lovers," "Getting to Know You," "No Other Love," "Love, Look Away," "Climb Ev'ry Mountain," and "The Sound of Music" (all with Rodgers). In 1943, the year of *Oklahoma!*, Hammerstein reworked the Bizet score to *Carmen*, set the plot in a Southern factory town in wartime, and employed an all-black cast. The result was *Carmen Jones*, which ran for more than 500 performances before embarking on a long tour. Hammerstein also published a book, *Lyrics by Hammerstein* (Simon & Schuster, 1949). After finishing the lyrics to *The Sound of Music*, Hammerstein retired to his farm in Pennsylvania, terminally ill with cancer. He died in Doylestown, Pa., Aug. 23, 1960.

HAMMOND, RICHARD (b. 1896) Composer. Born in the county of Kent, England, Aug. 26, 1896, Hammond was educated at Yale. His musical studies were interrupted when he served in the U. S. Navy during World War I, after which he studied in the United States with Emerson Whithorne and Mortimer

Wilson and in Paris with Nadia Boulanger (q.v.). Hammond made his earliest impression in the concert world with his *A Voyage to the East,* to poems by Amy Lowell, for voice and chamber orchestra (1926), and the ballet *Fiesta* for medium orchestra and "two voices backstage" (1929). Founder and vice-president of the Composer's Music Corporation which was dedicated to the publication of contemporary music, Hammond was also a member of the board of the League of Composers (q.v.); he frequently wrote articles for the League's publication, *Modern Music* (q.v.), on ballet and dance music during the late 1920s and early '30s. A member of the Franco-American Music Society, Hammond spent much time in France but eventually moved to California, where he was a member of the board of the Hollywood Bowl Association. Besides *Fiesta* he produced 2 more ballet scores, *Carnival* (1931) and *Ballet* (1935). He composed many works for orchestra: *Five Chinese Fairy Tales* (1921), *The Sea of Heaven* (1929), *West Indian Dances* (1930), *Suite After Reading "The Woman of Andros"* (1930), *Sinfonietta* (1931), *Dance Music* (1937), a suite, *Unto the Hills* (1939), *Excursion* (1940), and 2 *Partitas* (1940; 1942). For voice Hammond wrote the *Suite for Five Prières Arabes, Cinq Chansons Grecques, Six Women's Choruses* (all 1928), and *Five Madrigals* (1930). A *Sonata for Oboe and Piano* dates from 1924. Hammond also composed many songs and solo piano pieces.

HANSON, HOWARD (1896–1981) Composer, conductor, educator. Born in Wahoo, Neb., Oct. 28, 1896, Hanson began to study music with his mother. He continued at Luther College, Wahoo, and at the Institute of Musical Art, New York City, with Percy Goetschius (q.v.) and with Arne Oldberg (q.v.) at Northwestern University, Evanston, Ill. He

was just 20 when he was appointed professor of theory at the College of the Pacific, Stockton, Calif. (1916); 3 years later he was named dean. The years 1921–24 were spent in Rome at the American Academy under a Prix de Rome fellowship. Upon his return in 1924, Hanson was appointed director of the Eastman School of Music, Rochester, N.Y., where he remained active—and important—for several decades (he retired in 1964). In that post, besides teaching countless American composers, Hanson provided a valuable outlet for their compositions in festivals of American music held regularly in Rochester. Hanson conducted the Eastman School orchestra in the first performances of virtually hundreds of works by young (and not so young) American composers. He often conducted at the National Music Camp, Interlochen, Mich. He also managed to squeeze in time for his own composition. He was a prolific composer of large orchestral works of romantic dimension and sound. Of his 7 symphonies, whose production spans the years 1923–68, the 2nd is unabashedly entitled "Romantic" (1930); the first, "Nordic" (1923), is Hanson's tribute to his Scandinavian ancestry. His 4th, "Requiem" (1943), dedicated to the memory of the composer's father, was awarded the Pulitzer Prize. Hanson's 7th, "A Sea Symphony," was composed in 1977. Other orchestral works include the symphonic poems *North and West* (1923), *Lux Aeterna* (1923), and *Pan and Priest* (1926); also: *Serenade* for flute, strings, and harp (1946), *Elegy* (1956), *For the First Time* (1962), and *Rhythmic Variations on Two Ancient Themes* (1977). His chamber compositions include the *Quintet,* Op. 6 (1916), *Concerto da Camera* for piano and string quartet (1917), and a *String Quartet,* Op. 23 (1923). Hanson's concertos include the *Organ Concerto* (1926), *Concerto for*

Organ, Strings and Harp (1943), *Piano Concerto* (1948), and *Fantasy Variations on a Theme of Youth* for piano and orchestra (1951). For the stage Hanson composed *California Forest Play of 1920* (1919) and *Merry Mount* (1932; a *Merry Mount Suite* was extracted in 1937). Besides many songs Hanson also wrote large works for voices and orchestra: *Lament for Beowulf* (1925), *Songs from "Drum Taps"* (text by Walt Whitman, 1935), *Hymn for the Pioneers* (1938), *Song of Democracy* (1957), and the cantata *Song of Human Rights* (1963). There are also several early solo piano pieces, most of them composed between 1915 and 1920. Hanson is best known for his large romantic orchestral or choral works—and not least for his promotion of the works of American composers, whether he agreed with their musical aesthetics or not. Hanson also recorded a wide range of American music, including definitive performances of his own work. He died in Rochester, N.Y., Feb. 19, 1981.

HARBACH, OTTO (1873–1963) Lyricist, librettist. Born in Salt Lake City, Utah, Aug. 18, 1873, Harbach began professional life as an English professor, before moving on to newspaper work in New York City. From 1903 to 1910 he worked in an advertising agency. He began in the musical theatre writing lyrics to the music of the Bohemian composer Karl Hoschna (1877–1911). Two of their songs became immediate hits: "Cuddle Up a Little Closer" (from *The Three Twins*, 1908) and "Every Little Movement" (from *Madame Sherry*, 1910). After Hoschna's death Harbach continued as either lyricist or librettist (or both) with such composers as Rudolf Friml (q.v.), with whom he did several musicals, including *Rose-Marie* (1924); Louis A. Hirsch (1887–1924), with whom he did the songs for *Mary* (1920) from which came "The Love Nest"; Vincent You-

mans (q.v.), with whom he did, among other scores, *No, No, Nanette* (1925); Harbach's most important collaboration with Sigmund Romberg (q.v.) resulted in the songs for *The Desert Song*. His most fruitful work was undoubtedly done with Jerome Kern (q.v.), with whom he worked on *Sunny* (1925), *The Cat and the Fiddle* (1931), and *Roberta* (1932). Among the songs for which Harbach wrote the lyrics are "Indian Love Call" (in collaboration with Oscar Hammerstein II, q.v.), "Who?" (in collaboration with Hammerstein), "One Alone" (in collaboration with Hammerstein), "She Didn't Say 'Yes,'" "The Night Was Made for Love," "Try to Forget," "You're Devastating," "Smoke Gets in Your Eyes," "Yesterdays," and "I Won't Dance" (in collaboration with Hammerstein). In addition to collaborating on the book and lyrics of many musicals, Harbach wrote several shows for which he did no lyrics at all; he was also co-author of the very successful nonmusical farce *Up in Mabel's Room*. Harbach enjoyed a long career in the musical theatre and devoted much of his later years to ASCAP (q.v.). He died in New York City, Jan. 24, 1963.

HARLEM STRIDE PIANO A postragtime style of piano performance in which the left hand provided a powerful rhythmic drive, alternating a chord near the middle of the keyboard with a tenth chord, or even a single note or an octave, in the lower keyboard. The right hand played, or played around with, the tune. The variations on this tune could be very intricate (this showmanship no doubt inspired Tin Pan Alley's novelty piano pieces which displayed the soloist's dexterity and musical imagination). The figure of great importance in the transition between ragtime and stride piano was Eubie Blake (q.v.). The most gifted of all Harlem stride pianists was James P. Johnson (q.v.) who was undoubtedly also influenced by Charles Luckeyeth "Lucky" Roberts (1895–1968) and Abba Labba, whose original name was Richard McLean. Johnson's star pupil was Thomas "Fats" Waller. Another fine stride pianist was William Henry Joseph Berthol Bonaparte Bertholoff (1897–1973), who was better known as "Willie the Lion" Smith. Stride piano was heard at rent parties in Harlem (as boogie-woogie, q.v., was heard in Chicago), at monthly gatherings where the flashiest pianists performed in "cutting contests" (that is, each tried to outdo the other in their improvisations and invention). James P. Johnson was generally regarded as the master of these Saturday night events.

HARRIS, ROY (1898–1979) Composer, teacher. Born in Lincoln County, Neb., Feb. 12, 1898, Harris was taken by his family in 1903 to a farm near Los Angeles, where he grew up. His mother, a guitarist, gave him his first music lessons and also acquired a piano for the Harris farmhouse. Harris was barely out of Covina High School when he enlisted during World War I to serve in the Army. Later he enrolled in the University of California to study economics and philosophy; he attended classes at night and drove a truck by day to earn a living. A latecomer to music, Harris became a student of Arthur Farwell (q.v.) around 1923—he was then about 25. He also studied with the Russian cellist-conductor Modest Altschuler and English composer Arthur Bliss, who was then living in Santa Barbara. The early compositions of Harris soon attracted notice for their rugged, honest awkwardness. His *Andante* for orchestra was performed in New York in the summer of 1926; this undoubtedly led to the first of 2 Guggenheim Fellowships awarded to Harris. He then spent the years 1927–29 in Paris studying with Nadia Boulanger (q.v.). While in France Harris composed the *Concerto for Piano, Clarinet and String Quartet,* a *Piano Quintet,* and the *Piano Sonata*—all works that brought him more attention. A broken spine forced Harris to return to New York for surgery in 1929 and while convalescing he wrote his first *String Quartet,* the first work he composed without the aid of the piano keyboard. Harris' increasing popularity led to more fellowships and teaching positions. He also enjoyed the unfettered role of composer-in-residence at such universities as Cornell, Colorado, and California (Los Angeles). During World War II, Harris took a leave of absence from Colorado College to serve as chief in the music section of the Office of War Information. In later years he traveled under the auspices of the State Department promoting American music. Harris was fortunate in another area: he was commissioned to write more than 100 works. He is known primarily as a symphonist, although he also composed fine chamber works and for voice. Harris was fortunate in that he had acquired 2 powerful champions, Howard Hanson (q.v.) and Serge Koussevitzky. It was Koussevitzky who commissioned Harris' first large work, *Symphony 1933.* Koussevitzky and the Boston Symphony also introduced the Harris *Third Symphony* (1938), generally regarded as his major symphonic composition. There are, however, several other fine works in the symphonic form: the *Fourth (Folk Song) Symphony* (1940), *Fifth Symphony* (1943), the *Seventh Symphony* (1952) and so on through more than a dozen. For orchestra he also wrote: *When Johnny Comes Marching Home* (1934; originally *Overture from the Gayety and Sadness of the American Scene* and revised), *Time Suite* (written for CBS radio, 1936), *Four Minutes* for orchestra (written for Paul Whiteman, 1937), *American Creed* (1940), *Folk Rhythms of Today* (1942), *Ode to Friendship* (1942),

Memories of a Child's Sunday (1945), *Celebration* (variations on a theme from Hanson's *Third Symphony*, 1946) *Quest* (1948), *Kentucky Spring* (1949), *Cumberland Concerto* (1951), *Epilogue to Profiles in Courage: JFK* (1963), *Horn of Plenty* (1964), etc., etc. Harris composed several pieces for piano and orchestra: *Concerto for Piano and Orchestra* (1945), *Concerto for Two Pianos and Orchestra* (1946), *Piano Concerto No. 2* (1953), *Fantasy for Piano and Orchestra* (1954) and *Concerto for Amplified Piano, Percussion and Brasses* (1968). Harris also wrote much chamber music, several works (especially the early ones) of which are outstanding: *Three Variations on a Theme* (String Quartet No. 2, 1933), *Trio for Violin, Cello and Piano* (1934), *Quintet for Piano and Strings* (1936), *Sonata for Violin and Piano* (1942), and the later *Piano Sextet* (1968). Harris composed much choral music, including *A Song for Occupations* (1934), a *Symphony for Voices,* a cappella (1935), a *Mass* for men's voices and organ (1948), *Abraham Lincoln Walks at Midnight* (1953), *Give Me the Splendid Silent Sun* (1961), and *Canticle to the Sun* (1961). There are also several songs. Although Harris wrote for the stage (2 ballets: *From This Earth,* 1941, and *What So Proudly We Hail,* 1942) and films (a documentary score), he never attempted opera. Harris died in Santa Monica, Calif., Oct. 1, 1979.

HART, LORENZ (1895–1943) Lyricist, librettist. Born in New York City, May 2, 1895, Hart began writing shows while still a student at Columbia University. He left Columbia in his sophomore year to translate plays from the German for the Shuberts. Hart also wrote light verse and, though he had left Columbia officially, continued to contribute to the annual Varsity Shows. In 1919 he was introduced to hopeful composer Richard Rodgers (q.v.) who needed a lyricist. Hart was then about 25 and Rodgers 19. They were almost complete opposites as personalities: Rodgers was dependable, Hart unpredictable; Rodgers was hardworking while Hart procrastinated (he once had Rodgers' daughter hide him in her tree house to escape work). Both men, however, shared a respect for craftsmanship; Hart was one of the half dozen or so master lyricists. His wit, his skillful rhyming, and his hard-boiled (almost cynical) poetry resulted in some superb, unsentimental songs. The first Rodgers and Hart (q.v.) show was *Poor Little Ritz Girl* (1920) in which songs by Sigmund Romberg were also heard; it was not very successful and Hart considered going back to doing translations for the Shuberts and Rodgers took a job as a salesman. But in 1925 they collaborated on the songs for *The Garrick Gaieties,* which was intended to be a short-run fund-raising show for the Theatre Guild. It proved successful and so did some of the Rodgers and Hart songs: "Romantic You and Sentimental Me" and "Manhattan." The team went on to write songs and films, a total of 28 shows (3 in London) and 4 film scores. Among their show scores are *A Connecticut Yankee* (1927), *Jumbo* (1935), *On Your Toes* (1936), *I'd Rather Be Right* and *Babes in Arms* (1937), *The Boys from Syracuse* (1938), *Too Many Girls* (1939), *Pal Joey* (1940), and *By Jupiter* (1941). Hart, who drank heavily, became a serious problem for Rodgers when contracts were signed and work had to be done. With Hart's blessing Rodgers formed a partnership with Oscar Hammerstein II (q.v.) to make a musical of Riggs's *Green Grow the Lilacs*—a story that did not interest Hart. The result was *Oklahoma!* (1943), which Hart saw and praised. Rodgers and Hart collaborated one final time on the 1943 revival of *A Connecticut Yankee* to which they added 6 songs, among them one of Hart's most brilliant lyrics, the mordant "To Keep My Love Alive." To list but a few of Hart's song titles gives a small idea of his inventiveness but none of the finely polished rhymes and poignant wit: "My Heart Stood Still," "With a Song in My Heart," "A Ship Without a Sail," "Ten Cents a Dance," "Dancing on the Ceiling," "Isn't it Romantic?" "You Are Too Beautiful," "Blue Moon," "Easy to Remember," "The Most Beautiful Girl in the World," "My Romance," "There's a Small Hotel," "Glad to Be Unhappy," "Where or When," "My Funny Valentine," "The Lady Is a Tramp," "Falling in Love with Love," "This Can't Be Love," "I Didn't Know What Time it Was," "I Could Write a Book," "Bewitched, Bothered and Bewildered," "Wait Till You See Her," and "Nobody's Heart." After the Philadelphia opening of the revised *A Connecticut Yankee*, Hart overdrank at a party and was hospitalized. He left the hospital for the New York opening (Nov. 17, 1943), disappeared for 2 days, and was found unconscious in his apartment. He was suffering from an advanced case of pneumonia. Hart died in New York City, Nov. 22, 1943.

HAUBIEL, CHARLES (b. 1892) Composer, teacher. Born in Delta, Ohio, Jan. 30, 1892, Haubiel began his musical career as an aspiring pianist. He studied with Rudolph Ganz in Berlin and with Rosina and Josef Lhévinne in New York City. He also studied composition at the Mannes College with Rosario Scalero (1919–24); much later he studied orchestration with Modest Altschuler (1948–52). He toured with violinist Jaroslav Kocián as piano accompanist and then took a position as a teacher of piano in Oklahoma; from 1915 to 1917 he was at the Musical Art Institute in Oklahoma City. During World War I he was a bandmaster with the rank of second lieutenant. In 1921 he returned to New York to teach at the Institute of Musical Art; he also taught music history at New York University (1922–47). As a composer, Haubiel first attracted attention with his *Karma: Symphonic Variations* for orchestra (1928), which won first prize in the Schubert Centennial Contest. Other prizewinning works—*Ritratti* (1935) and *Passacaglia* (1938)—gained Haubiel performances by first-rate orchestras such as the Chicago Symphony and the New York Philharmonic. Other orchestral works include *Pastoral* (1930), *Suite Passecaille* (1932), *Vox Cathedralis* (1934), *Symphony No. 1* (1937), *Miniatures for Strings* (1938), *Nuances* for flute and string orchestra (1944), the "symphonic saga" *Pioneers* (1946), *American Rhapsody* (1948, rev. 1962), and *Heroic Elegy* (1967). Among Haubiel's chamber compositions are *Gothic Variations* for violin and piano (1919), *Echi Classici* for string quartet (1936), *Duo-Forms* for cello and piano (1929–33), *Cello Sonata* (1941), *In the French Manner* for oboe, violin, cello, and piano (1942), *Violin Sonata* (1945), *Pastoral Trio* for flute, cello, and piano (1949) and *Epochs* for violin and piano (1954–55). His stage works include *Brigands Preferred* (1932), incidental music to *The Passionate Pilgrim* (1932), and *Sunday Costs 5 Pesos* (1949). There are also many choral works, including *The Cosmic Christ* (1937), *Vision of St. Joan* (1939), *Both Brave and Gay* (1944), and *What Wondrous Sacrifice Is This?* (1945). Haubiel also contributed to the cause of American music as a lecturer and as the founder (and for many years, president) of the Composers Press (1935) for the purpose of publishing the compositions of contemporary American composers; Haubiel retired from the presidency of the Composers Press in 1967.

HAYES, ROLAND (1887–1977) Concert singer. Born on his family's small farm near Curryville, Ga., June 3, 1887, Hayes grew up in near poverty. He was barely in his teens when the death of his father led to the family's moving to Chattanooga, Tenn., where the boy got work in a foundry. His only early musical experience was as a member of a church choir. A visiting student, A. Arthur Calhoun, hearing Hayes sing, was impressed with his voice and suggested he study. Calhoun, via recordings, introduced Hayes to some of the great vocalists and the songs they sang. Determined to become a singer, Hayes entered Fisk University, Nashville, Tenn., where he earned his way "working for a family" and singing whenever possible; his final 3 years were a little easier because he was given scholarships. Upon graduation he went to Louisville, where he worked as a waiter and sang. He then received an offer to join the Fisk Jubilee Singers in Boston. At the bidding of a white benefactor, Henry Putnam, Hayes remained in Boston and studied voice privately (he was also offered a scholarship at the New England Conservatory) with Arthur Hubbard. He supported himself by singing in local churches and working as a messenger for an insurance company. Six years later, in 1917, Hayes felt he was ready for his formal debut, which he made in Boston's Symphony Hall in 1917. After a successful tour of the United States, Hayes went to Europe for further study in 1920. He also made a deep impression on European audiences, so that when he returned to the United States 3 years later he was virtually a celebrity. On Dec. 2, 1923, Hayes made his true triumphant debut at Symphony Hall, in which he impressed the audience as well as critics. Soon after, he became the first black singer to appear at New York's Carnegie Hall. Hayes's tenor voice was described as "silken smooth in mezzo forte, ringingly vibrant in fortes and trained to perfect evenness of production in all its registers." Thus began one of the most illustrious careers in American music. Hayes not only sang the classic repertoire, he also included Negro folk songs in his recitals. He opened the door for the black artist who was not a vaudeville figure or popular entertainer and through it passed other great musicians of his race: Marian Anderson, Paul Robeson, Dorothy Maynor, Adele Addison, Todd Duncan, William Warfield, and Leontyne Price, among others. Confronted with the race problem, they transcended it with their artistry and professionalism. Hayes enjoyed a long and fruitful career. As late as his 75th birthday (1962) he sang at Carnegie Hall for the benefit of the Negro Scholarship Fund. From 1950 he taught at Boston University. He died in Boston, Jan. 1, 1977.

HENDERSON, FLETCHER (1897–1952) Arranger, bandleader, pianist, composer. Born in Cuthbert, Ga., Dec. 18, 1897, Henderson began to study the piano at 6 and continued for several years; his subject was the classics, for his father, an educator, did not approve of jazz or popular music. When Henderson went to Morehouse College in Atlanta, he majored in chemistry. In 1920 he came to New York City, where he worked as a laboratory assistant and simultaneously as a song demonstrator in the Pace Handy Music Co. When Pace left the firm to form his own recording company, Black Swan Records, Henderson joined him as the official piano accompanist. One of his earliest records, in which he accompanied Ethel Waters, was most successful and Henderson was encouraged to accompany Waters on tour. This marked the end of Henderson's career as a chemist. By 1923 he had acquired a reputation as accompanist and bandleader for such popular blues singers as Bessie Smith (q.v.) and Ma Rainey. In 1924 Henderson formed his first band and settled in at the Club Alabam near New York's Times Square. Henderson's first successes could be attributed to the band's musicianship and to the skill of his arrangements. Among the musicians who played in Henderson's various orchestras were Louis Armstrong (q.v.), Tommy Ladnier, Benny Carter, Buster Bailey, Coleman Hawkins, Red Allen, Roy Eldridge, J. C. Higginbotham, Edgar Sampson, John Kirby, and Sid Catlett. The band's arrangements were written by Henderson, or Don Redman (1900–1964), one of the outstanding arrangers of popular-jazz music, Benny Carter, and Henderson's brother, Horace (b. 1904). The effect of the Henderson band on other bands of the 1920s was tremendous, although the fortunes of the band fluctuated, especially after Henderson was seriously injured in an automobile accident in August 1928. The Depression also contributed to fewer jobs and recordings. The band's personnel changed. Some of its members left to form their own bands or to join bands that met the payroll more regularly. Carter, for example, and Redman joined McKinney's Cotton Pickers. The Henderson band, thanks to radio, enjoyed some prominence in the mid 1930s, but by the end of the decade that had begun to fade. Henderson around this time began making arrangements for others, most notably the new "King of Swing," Benny Goodman (q.v.). Jazz historians attribute Goodman's impact on the jazz scene to Henderson's arrangements. He also arranged for such bands as those of Will Bradley, Isham Jones, the Dorsey Brothers, Glen Gray, and Jack Hylton. Although he attempted to form new bands in the '40s, Henderson was not able to revive his early position as a pi-

oneer in scoring for popular orchestras. He even briefly teamed up with Ethel Waters, touring the club circuits. In 1950 he attempted to get a new Henderson band started and had barely begun when he suffered a stroke in December. In April 1951 he had a 2nd, which left him partially paralyzed. In New York City on Dec. 29, 1952, a 3rd attack killed him.

HENDERSON, RAY (1896–1970) Composer, pianist. Born in Buffalo, N.Y., Dec. 1, 1896, Henderson first learned music from a musical father. As a youngster he played the organ and sang in a church choir; during his high school years he played the piano in local bands. Because his talent was evident early—Henderson was composing at the age of 8—he was enrolled, after finishing high school, in the Chicago Conservatory of Music. Instead of embarking on a concert career when he finished at the Conservatory, Henderson headed for New York, where he got work as a professional pianist with music publishers or as an accompanist for vaudeville performers. In 1922 he teamed with lyricists B. G. DeSylva (1895–1950) and Lew Brown (1893–1958) to produce a song, "Georgette," which was interpolated into the score of the *Greenwich Follies of 1922*. The 3 songwriters were not quite yet the famous team of DeSylva, Brown, and Henderson (q.v.)—this would not come until 1925, when they began writing songs for the *George White's Scandals*. In the meantime, Henderson collaborated with other lyricists on such popular songs as "That Old Gang of Mine" (Billy Rose and Mort Dixon, 1923), "Alabamy Bound" (DeSylva and Bud Green, 1925), "Five Foot Two, Eyes of Blue" (Sam Lewis and Joe Young, 1925), "Don't Bring Lulu" (Billy Rose and Brown, 1925), "Bye Bye Blackbird" (Mort Dixon, 1926), and others. Beginning with the *Scandals* of 1925, Henderson did 8 Broadway scores with DeSylva and Brown, plus several original film scores and adaptations of their stage successes. When De-Sylva left the team in 1931 Henderson continued collaborating with Brown and others, including Ted Koehler (q.v.), Irving Caesar (q.v.), and Jack Yellen (b. 1892). Among Henderson's most popular melodies are (all with DeSylva-Brown lyrics unless noted): "Black Bottom" and "The Birth of the Blues" (from *Scandals* of 1926), "The Best Things in Life Are Free," "The Varsity Drag," and "Lucky in Love" (from *Good News*, 1927), "You're the Cream in My Coffee" (from *Hold Everything!* 1928), "Button Up Your Overcoat" (from *Follow Thru*, 1928), "Without Love" (from *Flying High*, 1930), "Life Is Just a Bowl of Cherries" and "That's Why Darkies Were Born" (from the *Scandals* of 1931, with Lew Brown), "Sonny Boy" (also with Al Jolson; from the film *The Singing Fool*, 1928), "I'm a Dreamer (Aren't We All?)", "If I Had a Talking Picture of You" (from the film *Sunny Side Up*, 1929), "Animal Crackers in My Soup," "When I Grow Up" (from the film *Curly Top*, lyrics by Koehler and Caesar, 1935). Except for some work in television in the 1950s, Henderson produced little after the mid-1940s. He died in Greenwich, Conn., Dec. 31, 1970.

HIER, ETHEL GLENN (1889–1971) Composer, pianist, teacher. Born in Cincinnati, Ohio, June 25, 1889, Hier was graduated from the Cincinnati Conservatory of Music and the Institute of Musical Art, New York City. Her composition teachers included Edgar Stillman Kelley (q.v.), Hugo Kaun (in Berlin), and Ernest Bloch (q.v.). She studied piano with Richard Thalberg and Carl Rudolf Friedberg and theory with Percy Goetschius (q.v.). Among Hier's works are *Suite for Sextet* (1925), *Suite for*

String Quartet (1926), the ballet *Choréographe* (1931), a *Rhapsody* for violin and piano (1933), a *Suite for Voice and Strings* (1935), *Asolo Bells* for orchestra (1938), *Carolina Suite* (1939), *Mountain Preacher* for solo, chorus, and orchestra (1940), and *Then Shall I Know* for baritone, mixed chorus, and organ (1945). She has also set "America the Beautiful" for chorus and orchestra. Her play in 7 scenes, *Boyhood and Youth of Edward MacDowell*, was often performed by Junior Music Clubs in the United States. Hier memorialized a stay at the MacDowell Colony with *A Day in the Peterboro Woods*, a suite for piano. She died in New York City, Jan. 14, 1971.

HILL, MABEL WOOD (1870–1954) Composer, teacher. Born in Brooklyn, N.Y., Mar. 12, 1870 (not 1891 as usually given), Hill studied with Walter Rothwell (1872–1927) and Peter Martin Rybner (1855–1929), both of whom were composer-pianists. She first attracted general attention with her songs in 1920 and began winning various prizes from such organizations as the National League of American Pen Women and the Associated Glee Clubs of America and Canada. The Canadian Government commissioned her operetta, *The Jolly Beggars* (1929; completed in 1931). Active also as an educator, Hill was associated with the New York Music School Settlement, and she helped found the Brooklyn Music School Settlement and the Hudson River Music School. Hill's earliest known works were orchestral transcriptions of compositions by Bach and Couperin. For the theatre, after *The Jolly Beggars*, she did a ballet, *The Adventures of Pinocchio* (1934), an *Interpretive Solo Dance* for piano and percussion (1937), and a musical play, *The Rose and the Ring* (1941). For orchestra she composed *Impressions*, "After Yeats" (1936), *The Wind in the*

Willows (1936), *Courage,* a symphonic march (1940), and *Scottish Overture* (1943). Works employing voice include the suite *Fables of Aesop* for solo voice and orchestra (1939), *French Canadian Folksongs* for women's voices (1939), *Gaelic Rune of Hospitality* for mixed chorus (1941), and *Song for Courage* (1944). For chamber orchestra Hill wrote a *Quintet* and *Voice Reciting* (1936), *Old English Suite* (1938), *Reactions to Prose Rhythms* (1942), and others. By 1933 she had composed 4 string quartets, a 5th entitled *From a Far Country* (of only 4 minutes' duration, 1937). Other chamber music includes a *Trio* for piano, horn, and clarinet (1937) and an *Out-of-Door Suite* (1943). Mabel Hill (the name is sometimes given as Wood-Hill) died in Stamford, Conn., Mar. 1, 1954.

HONKY-TONK Popular designation, origin in doubt, of a saloon, gin mill, or dance hall. The music in honky-tonks was supplied by an out-of-tune piano playing a ragtime-like music characterized by a heavy bass and syncopated melodic line. This style of piano music came to be called honky-tonk also. The instrument itself was muted at times with strips of paper inserted into the strings, producing a jangly, tinny sound.

"HONKY TONK TRAIN BLUES" A boogie-woogie (q.v.) piano piece by Meade Lux Lewis (q.v.). Lewis originally recorded this descriptive blues for Paramount Records ca. December 1927. It was the discovery of this recording that led jazz impresario John Hammond to seek out Lewis years later; this revived Lewis' career and began the popular proliferation of the boogie-woogie craze in the late 1930s. Lewis recorded *Honky Tonk Train Blues* again in 1937 (and many times after), retaining the original rhythmic drive of the railroad train (a favorite device in many blues) and the rolling bass. It is one of the most

famous of all boogie-woogie pieces; another is *Pine Top's Boogie Woogie,* recorded in Chicago in 1928, by Clarence Pine Top Smith (q.v.).

HOT FIVE The term jazz aficionados use when referring to what should properly be called Louis Armstrong and his Hot Five. With this group Armstrong began making his own way via recordings beginning on Nov. 12, 1925, when the first recording sessions for the Okeh label took place in Chicago. Besides Armstrong on cornet and vocals the members of this group were Edward "Kid" Ory (1886–1973) on trombone, Johnny Dodds (1892–1940), clarinet and alto saxophone, Lillian Hardin Armstrong (1902–1971), piano, and Johnny St. Cyr (1890–1966), banjo. The Hot Five was formed specifically for recording; the records were intended for the "race" (q.v.) market but attained a great popularity among whites also, especially the growing band of jazz collectors. Later, in the 1930s and '40s, the Armstrong Okeh Hot Five records were sold at high prices among collectors. Most have been brought back into general release (often sounding better than the original 78-rpm shellacs) by record companies. Armstrong also formed a Hot Seven unit for later recordings; in it John Thomas replaced Ory on trombone, Warren "Baby" Dodds (1898–1959) was on drums, and Pete Briggs on tuba.

HOWE, MARY (1882–1964) Composer, pianist. Born in Richmond, Va., Apr. 4, 1882, Howe studied piano with Ernest Hutcheson and composition with Gustav Strube; she later studied with Boulanger (q.v.) in Paris. From 1920 to 1935 she toured with pianist Anne Hull as a duo piano team and as a soloist. She eventually settled in Washington, D.C., and was active there in the Friends of Music, Library of Congress. Her compositions, which reveal the influence of Impressionism, include *Chain Gang Song* for male or mixed chorus and piano, or orchestra (1925); other choral works: *Fiddler's Reel* (1936) and *Prophecy, 1792* (1943). Her orchestral works include *Dirge* (1931), *Sand* (1932), *American Piece* (1933), *Castellana* for 2 pianos and orchestra (1935), *Paean* (1940), and *Potomac* (1940). For smaller orchestral combinations Howe wrote a *Poema* for soprano, mezzo, and 11 instruments (1924), *Spring Pastoral* for violin and chamber orchestra (1936), *Coulennes* (1936), and *Stars and Whimsy* (1937). Her chamber compositions include a *Sonata for Violin and Piano* (1923), a *Suite* for piano and string quartet (1923), *Quatuor* for string quartet (1939), and *Three Pieces after Emily Dickinson* (1941). In 1936 Howe composed a ballet score for 2 pianos and drums entitled *Cards*. The same year she produced a *Scherzo and Fugue* for string quartet. There are also several piano pieces which were written for her tour performances. Howe died in Washington, D.C., Sept. 14, 1964.

INTERNATIONAL COMPOSERS' GUILD An organization of musicians, founded by Edgard Varèse (q.v.), devoted to the performances of contemporary music. Other original members of the group were French-born composer-harpist Carlos Salzedo (1885–1961), American composer Emerson Whitehorne (q.v.), musicologist Julius Mattfeld, among others. In his Manifesto issued when the Guild was formed in May 1921, Varèse stated that "the composer is the only one of the creators of today who is denied direct contact with the public." So it was the aim of the Guild to present performances of new works "in programs intelligently and organically constructed, and, with the disinterested help of singers and instrumentalists, to present these works in such a way as to reveal their fundamental spirit." The Guild, he further an-

nounced, "disapproves of all 'isms'; denies the existence of schools; recognizes only the individual." The ICG presented its first concert on Dec. 17, 1922, a program of short works by Arthur Honegger, Dane Rudhyar (q.v.), Lazare Saminsky (q.v.), François Gaillard, Maurice Ravel, Carl Ruggles (q.v.), and Arthur Lourié. During its brief existence the Guild presented authentically performed works by such composers as Alban Berg, Stravinsky (q.v.), Carlos Chávez, Arnold Schoenberg (q.v.), Paul Hindemith, and William Grant Still (q.v.). The "individualism" of which Varèse wrote in 1921 eventually led to factionalism. Certain members of the Guild came to believe that the American composer was being given short shrift by the Guild and that the Guild was musically "inflexible," so they broke away from it in April 1923 to form the League of Composers (q.v.). The 2 organizations continued independently for several years until November 1927, when Varése announced the dissolution of the International Composers' Guild in a letter to the New York *Times,* stating that, having succeeded in awakening an interest in contemporary music, the work of the Guild was completed.

JACOBI, FREDERICK (1891–1952) Composer, teacher. Born in San Francisco, Calif., May 4, 1891, Jacobi studied piano with Paolo Gallico and Rafael Joseffy and composition with Rubin Goldmark (q.v.) and Ernest Bloch (q.v.). At the Berlin Hochschule für Musik he also studied composition with Paul Juon. He returned to New York where he was an assistant conductor at the Metropolitan Opera from 1914 to 1917. In the early 1920s Jacobi, deeply interested in the music of the American Indian, went to New Mexico and Arizona to study Pueblo Indian music, which influenced much of his early work. Later in his life Jacobi developed a similar interest in Jewish music. In 1936 he joined the staff of the Juilliard School of Music, where he taught composition for 15 years. He also lectured or taught at the University of California, Berkeley, Mills College, Oakland, Calif., and at the Hartt Musical Foundation, Hartford, Conn. Among Jacobi's pupils were Alexei Haieff (q.v.), Robert Starer (q.v.), and Robert Ward (q.v.). The first work by Jacobi that brought him recognition was the *String Quartet on Indian Themes* (1924); other chamber music includes 2 more string quartets (1933; 1945), a *Scherzo* for winds (1936), *Three Biblical Narratives* for string quartet and piano (1938), *Hagiographa* for piano and string quartet (1939), *Fantasy for Viola and Piano* (1941), *Ballade for Violin and Piano* (1942), and *Music for Monticello* for flute, cello, and piano (1945). Jacobi's orchestral works consist of 2 symphonies (1922; 1948), *The Eve of St. Agnes* (1919), *Indian Dances* (1928), a *Cello Concerto* (1932), a *Piano Concerto* (1935), *Violin Concerto* (1941), *Ode* (1941), and *Concertino for Piano and String Orchestra* (1948). His works for voice include *Two Assyrian Prayers* for soprano or tenor and small orchestra (1923), *From the Prophet Nehemiah* (1942), a *Friday Evening Service* (1930), *Hymn* (1942), and *Ahavas Olom* for tenor, mixed chorus, and organ (1945). For chamber groups Jacobi composed a *Rhapsody* for harp and string orchestra (1940) and *Night Piece* for flute and small orchestra (1942). In 1944 Jacobi completed his only opera, *The Prodigal Son* (libretto by Herman Voaden); a year later he extracted an orchestral *Four Dances* from the opera. Jacobi was a frequent contributor to the League of Composers' publication, *Modern Music* (q.v.). He died in New York City, Oct. 24, 1952.

JAMES, PHILIP (1890–1975) Composer, conductor, teacher. Born in Jersey City, N.J., May 17, 1890, James studied music at New York University and Trinity College, London. His teachers included Homer Norris, Elliot Schenck, Rosario Scalero, and Rubin Goldmark (q.v.). For several years (1911–16) he was a conductor of musicals and operettas, including some by Victor Herbert (q.v.). During World War I, James was an infantry bandmaster, eventually leading the American Expeditionary Force General Headquarters Band (known as "General Pershing's Band"). In 1922 he helped to found and conducted the New Jersey Symphony; in 1927 he was appointed conductor of the Brooklyn Orchestra Society. In the early days of radio broadcasting James was conductor of the Bamberger Little Symphony Orchestra for New York's station WOR (1929–36). He was also guest conductor of many leading orchestras. In 1927, also, James joined the staff of the music department of New York University; he was appointed chairman of the department in 1933 and professor emeritus in 1955. James also taught music at Columbia University. His best-known work for orchestra is the satirical, prizewinning ($5,000) piece *Station WGZBX* (1931); other orchestral works include the *Bret Harte Overture* (1925), the *Overture in Olden Style on French Noels* (1926), a *Sea Symphony* (1928), *Songs of the Night* (1930), the rhapsody *Gwallia* (1936), *Brennan on the Moor* (1940), and *First Symphony* (1943). For smaller orchestral forces James wrote a *Suite for Chamber Orchestra* (1924), 2 suites for string orchestra (1934; 1943); also a *Kammersymphonie* for 11 instruments (1926) and a *Sinfonietta* for 17 instruments (1943). Of his many choral compositions, the best-known is *General William Booth Enters into Heaven* (to the poem by Vachel

Lindsay, 1932). Among others is the *Skyscraper Romance (The Typist and the Mailman)* for soprano, women's chorus, and piano (text by Amy Bonner, 1949). His chamber works include 2 string quartets, an organ sonata, a woodwind quintet, and a piano quartet. His ballet with narrator, *Judith,* was completed in 1927; he also composed some incidental music for the stage. James's masque, *Founded for Freedom,* was written in 1942; there are also a few piano pieces, including a *Concert Variations in A-Flat* and a *Passacaglia in F.* An organist also, James composed several works for the organ. He died in Southampton, Long Island, N.Y., Nov. 1, 1975.

JAZZ II During the 1920s 2 types of jazz flourished, the true jazz of the black bands and the "jazz" of white imitators, some of which might be included under the true jazz grouping. The performances of the most talented white jazz musicians were highly influenced by the black creators of classic improvised jazz of the period. To most Americans of the '20s jazz was represented by Paul Whiteman's band and, it is true, he did employ many fine jazz musicians in his time, most notably Bix Beiderbecke (q.v.), Jack Teagarden, Frankie Trumbauer, the Dorsey brothers, and others. But his orchestra was essentially a large band designed to provide dance music for white social functions. Closer to the real thing but still filtered through the white musical-social experience was the quasi-jazz of such groups as the Original Dixieland Jazz Band (q.v.), the New Orleans Rhythm Kings (q.v.), Mound City Blue Blowers (q.v.), and the Wolverines (q.v.), among others. Pure jazz, if such exists, in the '20s originated in the black communities and often as not remained there in the dance halls and on race records (q.v.). The seminal band of King Oliver (q.v.) produced Louis

Armstrong (q.v.), one of the greatest jazz musicians. The Fletcher Henderson (q.v.) orchestra pointed in the direction of "swing" (q.v.), which would become the sound most representative of the '30s. Jelly Roll Morton (q.v.) produced good jazz recordings, using arrangements which he devised. Duke Ellington (q.v.) initiated a long successful sophisticated jazz career in the '20s. From the west came the band of Walter Page, out of which came Count Basie; from the same center—Kansas City—came the band of Andy Kirk featuring Mary Lou Williams. By the end of the decade, while many bands continued to play pretty much in the same style as they had at its beginning, the trend was away from improvisation and toward arrangements that allowed for individual improvisational breaks. The time was ripe for the advent of swing. Some of the best jazz of the '20s was heard on race records featuring such blues singers as Bessie Smith (q.v.), Mamie Smith, Gertrude "Ma" Rainey, and Bertha "Chippie" Hill. They were sometimes accompanied by small groups, bands, or solo pianos (or guitars). Blues piano in the '20s evolved out of ragtime into sophisticated Harlem "stride piano" (q.v.), boogie-woogie (q.v.), and other more personal expressions, depending on the pianist and his experience, there being a difference between the piano styles of the New Orleans, Chicago, New York, and Kansas City based musicians. But, in general, jazz performances by black musicians were hardly heard by the mass of the American population that listened to Paul Whiteman, Isham Jones, George Olsen, Ted Lewis, and the other popular bands of the time that supposedly dispensed jazz. It took a new generation of scholars and critics (often as not white) to make definitions and distinctions between what was real and what was not real jazz. This often meant more to them than it did to the public and the musician of whatever color; they continued to play as they preferred and left categorization and the arguments to the "critics."

"THE JAZZ SINGER" Film, produced by Warner Brothers, which is considered to be the one that ended the era of the silent movie. It opened at the Warner Theatre in New York City on Oct. 6, 1927 and starred Al Jolson. Although it would hardly qualify as the first film musical, *The Jazz Singer* was the first to combine song and dialogue. During the early phases of the filming Jolson's speaking voice was accidentally recorded immediately after he had finished a singing sequence (the original plan was to use no dialogue—only songs; the remainder of the film was to have been silent). The effect of Jolson's "Wait a minute! You ain't heard nothin' yet!" on the soundtrack had such an effect on the extras in the scene and on others on the sound stage that it was decided to work some dialogue into the film. A short monologue—to his "Mammy"—was written for Jolson to interject between choruses of the song "Blue Skies." *The Jazz Singer* proved to be a tremendous success, apparently because people wished to hear Jolson speak as well as sing. This marked the end of the silents and the beginning of the "talkies" and the incipient musical film.

JESSYE, EVA (b. 1895) Choral conductor, arranger. Born in Coffeyville, Kans., Jan. 20, 1895, Jessye was musical from an early age. She organized her own singing group when she was 12 and, although her parents were not trained, they were musical and encouraged her interests. She received encouragement also from the great black conductor Will Marion Cook (q.v.), for whom she did emergency music copying when his orchestra played in Coffeyville—at the time Jessye was 12. She studied music at Western University, (Kansas) and Lang-

ston University (Oklahoma). Upon graduation in 1916 she began a long teaching career, first in Oklahoma public schools and later at Morgan College, Md. She moved to New York City in 1922 and studied with Cook and Goetschius (q.v.). She established herself in New York, which was not easy considering that she was both black and a woman. Within 4 years she founded her Original Dixie Jubilee Singers which eventually evolved into the Eva Jessye Choir. She and her group appeared frequently on radio in New York and London. One of her first professional assignments was as choir director in the famous all-black film *Hallelujah*. In 1934 she was choral director of the Thomson-Stein opera *Four Saints in Three Acts* (q.v.); the next year she began a long association with Gershwin's *Porgy and Bess* (q.v.). She was choral director of the original production as well as several of the later revivals. Between such assignments the Eva Jessye Choir toured the country; Jessye has also taught in various colleges, often as composer-in-residence. Her published collections include *My Spirituals* (1927), *The Life of Christ in Negro Spirituals* (1931), *Paradise Lost and Regained* (after Milton, 1934), *The Chronicle of Job* (1936), and arrangements of many other spirituals.

JOHNSON, HALL (1888–1970) Choir director, arranger, composer. Born in Athens, Ga., Mar. 12, 1888, Johnson studied piano with his sister. His mother, who had been a slave as a child, was an accomplished singer and his father was associated with the town's Methodist church. Johnson acquired his more advanced musical training in several schools before coming to New York City in 1914; he continued after graduation and studied at the Institute of Musical Art with Goetschius (q.v.). A trained violinist, Johnson found work in James Europe's Clef Club Band; he later played in the pit band of the musical *Shuffle Along* (q.v.). In 1925 Johnson, whose major interest lay in vocal music, formed a small group, later enlarged to 20, which became the Hall Johnson Choir. The Choir toured widely, giving concerts, sang on radio and, as early as 1928, made recordings. Johnson was arranger and choral director for the Marc Connelly play *The Green Pastures* (1930). Three years later Johnson saw his own folk play, *Run Little Children,* produced. It proved to be quite successful and had the distinction of being the only opera-like work of the time composed by a Negro. Other Johnson compositions include an Easter cantata, *Son of Man,* an operetta *Fi-Yer,* and a great number of arrangements of spirituals. Johnson was active for several years in Los Angeles with the Negro Festival Chorus, and in New York later with the Festival Chorus (beginning in 1946). His own Choir represented the United States at Berlin's International Festival of Fine Arts (1951). He died in New York City, Apr. 30, 1970.

JOHNSON, JAMES P. (1891–1955) Pianist, composer. Born in New Brunswick, N.J., Feb. 1, 1891, Johnson began to study the piano with his mother. Later, after the family moved to New York City in 1908, he studied more formally with Bruno Giannini. By this time Johnson had been playing professionally for 4 years. His earliest musical experiences included church music, popular songs, ragtime (in Jersey City, where the family lived in 1902), and the more rugged ragtime of New York as performed by Luckeyeth Roberts and Abba Labba McLean. He began playing the piano in New York clubs and was soon known as one of the most talented "stride" (q.v.) pianists in New York. Johnson was a great influence on the young Thomas "Fats" Waller (q.v.) and the already

formed Duke Ellington (q.v.). Johnson was also a popular accompanist and played for several leading vocalists of the time including Bessie Smith (q.v.), Mamie Smith, and Ethel Waters. He was a prolific cutter of piano rolls and recordings on disc, both as soloist and accompanist. In the 1920s he had his own band which played at Harlem's Clef Club. During this period Johnson was active as a composer and wrote solo piano pieces—rags, stride works, blues—and songs. Johnson also contributed to the musical theatre—an early taste for which he acquired when he toured during the early '20s with the show *Plantation Days* in Europe. His first Broadway score was written for the successful *Runnin' Wild* (1923) out of which came "Old-Fashioned Love" and "Charleston" (q.v.), both with lyrics by Cecil Mack (pen name of Richard C. McPherson: 1883–1944). Johnson composed scores also for *Messin' Around* (1929), *Change Your Luck* (1930), and *Sugar Hill* (1931). A popular nonproduction song was "If I Could Be with You One Hour Tonight" (with Henry Creamer, 1926). Although he made many recordings with several famous jazz bands, white and black, Johnson became inactive as a performer during the early 1930s to concentrate on composition. His earliest works were solo piano pieces that highlighted his playing style; these include *Caprice Rag* (1914), *Harlem Strut* (1917), *After Hours* (1923), *Carolina Shout* (1925), *Eccentricity Waltz* (1926), *Snowy Morning Blues* (1927), *You've Got to Be Modernistic* (1930), *Steeple Chase* (1936), and *Just Before Daybreak* (1942). Besides his rather ambitious arrangements—Johnson produced a *Symphonic Suite on "St. Louis Blues"*— he composed several works of symphonic scope: the Negro rhapsody *Yamekraw* (orchestrated by William Grant Still, q.v.), written in 1928; a *Harlem Symphony* was written in 1932, the *Jas-*

mine Concerto in 1935, and *Old Time Suite* in 1942. During this same period, primarily during the Depression, Johnson composed other lesser-known works: *African Dreams, Piano Concerto in A Flat, Mississippi Moon, City of Steel, Sonata in F Major*, and 2 ballets, *Manhattan Street Scene* and *Sefronia's Dream*. Ca. 1939 Johnson resumed his active nightclub and recording career, although in 1940 a slight stroke curtailed that activity. A severe stroke in 1951 left Johnson virtually helpless; he died in New York City, Nov. 17, 1955.

JOLSON, AL (1886–1950) Entertainer, singer. Born Asa Yoelson in St. Petersburg, Russia, Mar. 26, 1886, Jolson was about 4 when his family moved to the United States. He grew up in Washington, D.C., where his father was a rabbi. He was expected to follow his father in the synagogue but instead joined a traveling burlesque troupe and worked his way into vaudeville. For a time he was a member of Dockstader's Minstrels. He made his Broadway debut around the turn of the century and by 1911 was featured in the musical *La Belle Paree*. Jolson's trademark was blackface makeup and white gloves— and getting down on his knees when he addressed a song to his "Mammy." He was a dynamic tireless entertainer and enjoyed a long career in vaudeville especially; his most successful Broadway shows, *Sinbad* (1918) and *Bombo* (1921), were more notable for their interpolated songs than their orginal scores; Gershwin and Caesar's "Swanee" was sung in the former. Jolson was known as a performer who "could put over a song." Among the songs he popularized are "April Showers" (B. G. DeSylva, Louis Silvers, 1921), "California, Here I Come" (Jolson, B. G. DeSylva, Joseph Meyer, 1924), "Toot, Toot, Tootsie!" (Gus Kahn, Ernie Erdman, Dan Russo, 1922), "I'm Sitting on Top of the World" (Sam M. Lewis, Joe Young, Ray Henderson, 1925), "My Mammy" (Joe Young, Sam Lewis, Walter Donaldson, 1920), "Sonny Boy" (Jolson, DeSylva, Brown, and Henderson, 1928), and "There's a Rainbow Round My Shoulder" (Jolson, Billy Rose, Dave Dreyer, 1928). Jolson's last Broadway show was *Hold On to Your Hats* (1940). He appeared in what is generally recognized as the first "talkie," *The Jazz Singer* (q.v.). His film career did not flourish. One of his best was the biographical *The Jolson Story* (1946) which starred Larry Parks as Jolson and with Jolson singing on the sound track. Jolson was popular as a radio personality in the 1930s and '40s, one being the "Kraft Music Hall" (1947–49). In 1950 Jolson went to Korea to entertain American troops stationed there during that war. As usual Jolson gave his all and returned exhausted and died within a month in San Francisco, Calif., Oct. 23, 1950.

JONES, ISHAM (1894–1956) Composer, bandleader. Born in Coalton, Ohio, Jan. 31, 1894, Jones learned to play both the saxophone and the piano; by the time he was 20 he led his own band, which became one of the most popular in the Midwest during the late 1920s. By 1924 the Isham Jones Orchestra was known across the nation as well as in Britain. In the early 1930s, with arrangements by Gordon Jenkins and others, the band achieved a reputation for musicianship and good musical taste under Jones's quite authoritarian leadership. It appeared in the country's best hotels and on radio. Its recording in 1931 of the Mitchell Parish–Hoagy Carmichael (q.v.) song "Star Dust" was a best-seller of the time—in a time when the recording industry was dwindling. Jones himself wrote a number of standard popular songs; one of his best years was 1924 during which, in collaboration with lyricist Gus Kahn (q.v.), he wrote "It Had to Be You," "I'll See You in My Dreams," "Spain," and "The One I Love Belongs to Somebody Else." The Depression curtailed the dance band business and Jones eventually disbanded his orchestra in 1936 (and in 1942, after trying again). Out of his first band came the group around which the Woody Herman band was formed. Jones retired to a California ranch where he continued to write songs and, on occasion, emerged to conduct and make recordings. He died in Hollywood, Oct. 19, 1956.

JOSTEN, WERNER (1885–1963) Composer, conductor, teacher. Born in Elberfeld, Germany, June 12, 1885, Josten had already reached his musical maturity before moving to the United States in 1921. He rejected a business career (planned for him by his father) and studied music in Munich with Rudolf Siegel (harmony and counterpoint) and in Switzerland with Émile Jaques-Dalcroze, who devised the "Eurhythmic" teaching method. Before coming to the United States, Josten conducted in Paris and Munich, where he was assistant conductor at the Munich Opera. Two years after his arrival in America, Josten joined the music staff of Smith College, Northampton, Mass., where he remained until 1949. Josten's interest in the music of the Baroque period led him to initiate a series of regular concerts of the music of the 17th and 18th centuries as well as performances of operas of the same period. Josten also conducted these works at Smith. He appeared at the Metropolitan Opera and as a guest conductor at Lewisohn Stadium in New York. Over the 26 years spent at Smith, Josten continued to compose. His major works include *Crucifixion* for bass and chorus (1915), *Hymnus to the Quene of Paradys* for alto, women's chorus, organ, and strings (1921), *Indian Serenade* for tenor and orchestra (1922), *Ode for St.*

Cecilia's Day for soprano, baritone, chorus, and orchestra (1925), *Concerto Sacro I*: "The Annunciation" and "The Miracle" (1925), *Concerto Sacro II*: "Lament" and "Sepulchre and Resurrection" (1925), *Jungle* (1928), *Joseph and His Brethren*, a ballet (1932), *Endymion*, a ballet (1933), *Serenade for Orchestra* (1934), *Symphony for Strings* (1935), *Symphony in F* (1936), *Canzona Seria* for strings (1940), and *Rhapsody for Orchestra* (1957). Josten's compositions for chamber groups include a *String Quartet* (1934), 2 sonatas for violin and piano (1936; 1945), a *Piano Sonata* (1937), a *Sonata for Cello and Piano* (1938), and several trios in various instrumental combinations. Josten also composed a ballet, *Batoula*, for chorus and orchestra (1931). He died in New York City, Feb. 6, 1963.

KAHN, GUS (1886–1941) Song lyricist. Born in Coblenz, Germany, Nov. 6, 1886, Kahn was brought to the United States when he was about 5. His family settled in Chicago. Kahn went to school there and began trying his hand at writing lyrics while still in high school. His first professional assignments consisted of writing special songs for vaudeville performers. Primarily a popular-song writer, Kahn enjoyed his first success in a collaboration with Egbert Van Alstyne (1882–1951), also a Chicagoan. Their song "Memories" was one of the great hits of 1915. Kahn came to New York, the heart of the music business, and began contributing lyrics to songs that were interpolated into show scores. In the early 1920s he formed a productive partnership with composer Walter Donaldson (q.v.) which resulted in the popular songs "My Buddy" and "Carolina in the Morning" (both 1922) and "Yes Sir, That's My Baby" (1925). Their collaboration culminated in the hit show *Whoopee* (1928) out of which came such songs as "Love Me or Leave

Me," "I'm Bringing a Red, Red Rose," "Makin' Whoopee!" and "My Baby Just Cares for Me." Kahn did the lyrics to 4 show scores, the last being *Show Girl* (1929) for which he was co-lyricist with Ira Gershwin; the music was by George Gershwin. Among *Show Girl*'s songs: "Liza," "Do What You Do," and "I Must be Home by Twelve O'Clock." During the 1920s Kahn also collaborated on individual popular songs with Isham Jones (q.v.). (Another collaborator was his wife, Grace LeBoy.) In the early 1930s, like so many other Tin Pan Alley songwriters, Kahn moved to Hollywood. There he wrote the lyrics—with Edward Eliscu—for the film that enhanced the flowering of the movie musical. This was *Flying Down to Rio* (1933). Vincent Youmans set to music the words for "Carioca" "Orchids in the Moonlight," and "Flying Down to Rio." This film was also notable because it introduced a graceful, wisecracking song-and-dance team, Fred Astaire and Ginger Rogers. Other films for which Kahn wrote the lyrics: *Kid Millions* (1934), music by Donaldson: "Okay, Toots," "An Earful of Music," "When My Ship Comes In," and "Your Head on My Shoulder"; *Thanks a Million* (1935), music by Arthur Johnston: "Thanks a Million" and "I'm Sittin' High on a Hilltop"; *A Day at the Races* (1937), music by Walter Jurmann and Bronislaw Kaper: "Blue Venetian Waters" and "All God's Chillun Got Rhythm." Kahn also wrote single songs that were interpolated into film scores; among them: "Shadows on the Moon" and "Who Are We to Say?" (*The Girl of the Golden West*, 1938; music by Sigmund Romberg), "Blue Lovebird" (*Lillian Russell*, 1940; music by Bronislaw Kaper), and "You Stepped Out of a Dream" (*Ziegfeld Girl*, 1941; music by Nacio Herb Brown). Kahn also wrote the lyrics to the famous "Chloe," music by "Neil Moret" (Charles N. Daniels: (1878–1943). One

of Kahn's last efforts was the poetic "Day Dreaming" written in 1941 with Jerome Kern (q.v.). Kahn died in Beverly Hills, Calif., Oct. 8, 1941.

KÁLMÁN, EMMERICH (1882–1953) Composer. Although he could hardly be classified as an "American" composer, Kálmán, who was born in Siófok, Hungary, Oct. 24, 1882, was an influence on the American musical as operetta. He shares this position with other European composers, Franz Lehár (1870–1948), Rudolf Friml (q.v.), and Sigmund Romberg (q.v.). Kálmán did not arrive in the United States until 1940, but several of his operettas since *The Gay Hussars* (1909) had been produced on Broadway. His operettas were frequently Americanized with the interpolation of songs by native-born songwriters, especially Jerome Kern. Kálmán's best-known song is "Play Gypsies—Dance Gypsies" from *Countess Maritza* (1926), lyrics by Harry B. Smith. Kálmán's last Broadway production was *Marinka* (1945). He also composed concert music and conducted Toscanini's NBC Symphony in a concert of his works. After the end of World War II, Kálmán moved to Paris where he died on Oct. 30, 1953.

KALMAR, BERT (1884–1947) Lyricist, librettist. Born in New York City, Feb. 16, 1884, Kalmar left home at the age of 10 to join a traveling tent show as a boy magician. He eventually became a burlesque and vaudeville comedian and writer. He drifted into lyric writing and one of his earliest songs, with music by Ted Snyder (1881–1965), "In the Land of Harmony," achieved popularity in 1911. Kalmar was a partner in a music publishing firm when he formed a songwriting team with one of the firm's staff pianists, Harry Ruby (q.v.). Kalmar's partner in the business, Harry Puck (1890–1964), suggested that the 2 men collaborate on songs for vaudeville star Belle Baker. Kalmar had suffered an injury while doing a comic dance in Boston and was forced to retire from vaudeville. The first Kalmar-Ruby song was entitled "He Sits Around." Their first real success, however, was "So Long! oo-Long" (1920). Other nonproduction successes were "Who's Sorry Now?" (1923), with Ted Snyder collaborating on the tune, and "Nevertheless" (1931). Their first musical was entitled *Helen of Troy, New York* (1923), the first of 8 Broadway shows. The more notable: *The Ramblers* (1926), from which came "All Alone Monday"; *Five O'Clock Girl* (1927): "Thinking of You"; *Good Boy* (1928): "I Wanna Be Loved by You"; *Animal Crackers* (1928) which starred the Marx Brothers and introduced the song "Hooray for Captain Spalding." The last Broadway production was *The High Kickers* (1941). In the early 1930s Kalmar and Ruby moved to Hollywood where they not only wrote songs but Kalmar also wrote the screenplays for several of their films. Their first, which starred the blackface radio team of "Amos 'n' Andy" (Freeman F. Gosden and Charles F. Correll), was *Check and Double Check*; it produced one memorable item, the song "Three Little Words." After 1930 Kalmar and Ruby composed songs for several comedies starring the Marx Brothers, Wheeler and Woolsey, Eddie Cantor, and Joe E. Brown. Few lasting songs resulted except "I Love You So Much" from *The Cuckoos* (1930). While the songs were not very important, the screenplay of the Marx Brothers' antiwar film *Duck Soup* (1933), on which Kalmar collaborated, was. He also did the screenplay to *Look for the Silver Lining* (1949), a film biography of musical comedy star Marilyn Miller. A dual film biography of Kalmar and Ruby, *Three Little Words*, was released after the lyricist's death. He died in Los Angeles, Calif., Sept. 18, 1947.

KANSAS CITY STYLE A term coined by writers on jazz to differentiate the musical "sound" of the jazz musicians from New Orleans, Chicago, New York, and Kansas City. The characteristic sound depended upon the instrumentation and the individual playing of the musicians. Kansas City bands were generous in brass and featured a driving ensemble performance. Kansas City musicians were undoubtedly influenced by the riverboat musicians who traveled up the Mississippi and the Missouri rivers from New Orleans. One of the earliest of the well-known Kansas City bands was Bennie Moten's (1894–1935), who formed his band ca. 1922. Out of his band came such important musicians as trumpeter Oran "Hot Lips" Page (1908–1954), saxophonist Ben Webster (1909–1973), and pianist William "Count" Basie (b. 1904). Basie eventually, after Moten's death, formed his own band featuring the same powerful ensemble style. Another Kansas City band organized by Andy Kirk (b. 1898) came to great prominence in the 1930s. Known as the Twelve Clouds of Joy, the star was pianist Mary Lou Williams (b. 1910). Some critics argue that there was no "Kansas City Style," only a transitional series of bands moving from New Orleans to Swing, but when the term is used it generally applies to the bands of Moten, Kirk, and Basie.

"THE KING'S HENCHMAN" Opera with libretto by Edna St. Vincent Millay and music by Deems Taylor (q.v.). Commissioned by the Metropolitan Opera, *The King's Henchman* was completed by Taylor in Paris on Sept. 3, 1926, and given its first performance at the Metropolitan on Feb. 17, 1927. The setting is Saxon England in the 10th century and tells the story of King Eadgar, who wishes to marry Aelfrida, daughter of the Thane of Devon. Eadgar sends his henchman, the woman-hater Aethelwold, to present his case to Aelfrida. Under a spell Aethelwold and Aelfrida fall in love. They marry, and the King is informed that Aelfrida is not suitable for royalty. The following spring, when the King comes to Devon, Aethelwold confesses to Aelfrida that, because of his love for her, he has betrayed his King. Aethelwold tries to persuade the shocked Aelfrida to make herself ugly for the King but she decides the King must see her as she is. When the King sees her beauty he is saddened by his friend's betrayal. Aethelwold, unable to explain, stabs himself. Musically, as with all of Taylor's work, the opera was conventional and conservative (some critics found it Wagnerian). It was Taylor's first full-length opera and was, in fact, remarkably successful. In the 3 seasons it was in the Metropolitan Opera repertory it was performed 14 times—unusual for a contemporary American work.

"KITTEN ON THE KEYS" Popular novelty solo piano piece by Zez Confrey (q.v.). Written early in 1921, *Kitten on the Keys* was recorded on a piano roll by Confrey in February; the piece was published in July 1921. The ragtime-like little piece has been recorded many times and has never gone out of print.

KRAMER, A. WALTER (1890–1969) Editor, composer. Born in New York City, Sept. 23, 1890, Kramer began music study on the violin with his father, Maximilian, a Moravian musician and teacher at the Horace Mann High School. Kramer studied further with Carl Hauser and Richard Arnold; he also played the viola and the piano. He was largely self-taught in composition. On graduation from the College of the City of New York, Kramer joined the staff of the magazine *Musical America* in 1910, writing articles and criticism. From 1929 to 1936 he was editor-in-

chief. He left *Musical America* to become managing director and vice-president of Galaxy Music Corporation, a publishing house. He was also founder of the Society for the Publication of American Music; from 1934 to '40 he was the Society's president. Although prolific, Kramer was best known for his vocal works (he composed no opera, however). Two early orchestral works, *Two Symphonic Sketches* (1914) and a *Symphonic Rhapsody* for violin and orchestra (1915), were regularly performed in his lifetime. Among his choral works is the "Rococo Romance" *In Normandy* for soprano, women's voices, and orchestra (1924). His songs include "The Last Hour," text by Jessie C. Brown (1914), "Joy" and "Swans," words by Sara Teasdale (1917), and "The Faltering Dusk," words by Louis Untermeyer (1919). *His Interlude for a Drama* for wordless medium voice, oboe, viola, cello, and piano was composed in 1921. Kramer also wrote great numbers of short piano pieces, chamber works, organ compositions, and songs. He died in New York City, Apr. 8, 1969.

KRAZY KAT A "jazz pantomime," i.e., ballet, composed by John Alden Carpenter (q.v.) and based on the very popular comic strip by George Harriman. The cartoon had a wide following among intellectuals during the early 1920s. Carpenter's music, while not jazz, is jazzy in the studied manner of the trained musician. The small orchestra evokes the theatre pit band and is charming with its bluesy dance inflections. Carpenter completed the score "early" in 1921 and it was performed as an orchestral work by the Chicago Symphony under Frederick Stock, Dec. 23, 1921. The ballet was given its first full performance in New York at Town Hall, Jan. 20, 1922. Krazy Kat was danced by choreographer Adolph Bolm and the orchestra was conducted by George Barrère. The backdrop was designed by Harriman; it moved scenes across the stage on rollers, as in the comic strip. The story was simple, and it involved Krazy, eternally optimistic, loving, and trusting, with Ignatz Mouse and Offisa Pup. *Krazy Kat* excited much discussion and attention in its day. Gilbert Seldes in his *The 7 Lively Arts* (1924) devotes an entire chapter to the comic strip and concludes with Carpenter's detailed description of the ballet's action. Incidentally, musical indications were lettered on Harriman's moving backdrop—such characteristic tempo markings as *Jazzando, Kantando, Kurioso* and, of course, *Pizzi-kat-to.*

LADY, BE GOOD! Musical comedy with music by George Gershwin (q.v.) and lyrics by Ira Gershwin (q.v.); the show was the Gershwins' first full-fledged collaboration. Originally entitled *Black-Eyed Susan, Lady, Be Good!* opened at the Liberty Theatre, New York, Dec. 1, 1924, and ran for more than 300 performances. The book was devised around the talents of the brother-sister song-and-dance team, Fred and Adele Astaire; secondary roles were filled by the comedian Walter Catlett and singer-comedian Cliff "Ukulele Ike" Edwards. The Gershwins' score consisted of such songs as "Fascinating Rhythm," "Oh, Lady Be Good!" "So Am I," "The Half of It, Dearie, Blues," "We're Here Because," and several fine but neglected choruses. "The Man I Love" was eliminated from *Lady, Be Good*'s score during the Philadelphia tryout (where it was sung by Adele Astaire) because its slow tempo was felt to interfere with the pacing of the show. *Lady, Be Good!* with the Astaires opened in London at the Empire Theatre, Apr. 14, 1926, and again ran for over 300 performances. A new song was concocted for the Astaires entitled "I'd Rather Charleston" with words by English lyricist Desmond Carter.

LANE, EASTWOOD (1879–1951) Composer. Born in Brewerton, N.Y., May 22, 1879, Lane was self-taught in music—a fact in which he prided himself; throughout his life he maintained that too much musical education would ruin his natural talents. He dropped out of Syracuse (N.Y.) University. His output consists primarily of groups of piano pieces with such titles as *Adirondack Sketches, 4th of July, Five American Dances,* and *Sold Down the River.* His larger works include a ballet, *Boston Fancy,* and a tone poem, *Sea Burial.* Lane's works enjoyed a vogue during the early 1920s and some were often programmed by Paul Whiteman (q.v.). Whiteman's chief arranger at the time, Ferde Grofé (q.v.), orchestrated *Minuet for Betty Schuyler, Persimmon Pucker,* and *Sea Burial* for the concert orchestra. One of Lane's most popular early pieces was the jazzy *Crap Shooters.* Lane also composed a *Central Park Suite* and a *Children's Suite* for orchestra and many songs. From 1914 to 1935 he served as assistant concert director of the Wanamaker Auditorium Concerts in New York. He died in Central Square, N.Y., Jan. 22, 1951.

LA VIOLETTE, WESLEY (b. 1894) Composer, teacher. Born in St. James, Minn., Jan. 4, 1894, La Violette grew up in Spokane, Wash., and was graduated from Northwestern University's School of Music in 1917. During World War I he served in the U. S. Army in France. He completed his musical education at the Chicago Musical College, whose faculty he joined as head of the theory department. He later became dean of the College. Eventually La Violette left to head the theory department of the De-Paul University School of Music; he also served as director of the University's press established to publish works by

American composers. La Violette was also a popular lecturer on the subject of contemporary music and traversed the United States. One of his early works, *The Broken Vine* for tenor, chorus, and organ (1921), earned him recognition as a composer (it was performed at the 2nd Pacific Festival of American Music, San Jose, Calif.). His *Requiem* (1925) and *Penetrella* for string orchestra (1928) were also frequently performed during the 1920s and early '30s. Between 1936 and 1942, La Violette composed 4 symphonies. The first was entitled simply *Symphony*. The 3rd, *Song of Angels*, was for chorus and the 4th was for band. There are also 2 violin concertos (1929; 1939) and a *Piano Concerto* (1937). Among his more important chamber works are 3 string quartets (1926; 1933; 1936), *Piano Quintet* (1927), *Octet* for oboe, clarinet, bassoon, horn, violin, cello, and bass (1934), 2 violin-piano sonatas (1934; 1937), a *Flute Sonata* (1942), *Flute Quintet* (1943), and *Serenade* for flute and string quartet (1945). La Violette's later compositions include a *San Francisco Overture: Music from the High Sierras* (commissioned by conductor Pierre Monteux), a cantata, *The Road to Calvary*, and an opera, *The Enlightened One*. La Violette's first opera, *Shylock* (1929), based on Shakespeare's *The Merchant of Venice*, was awarded the David Bispham Medal.

LEAGUE OF COMPOSERS An organization of musicians, most of them composers, formed in 1923 as an offshoot of the International Composers' Guild (q.v.). The League was dedicated to the performance of contemporary compositions with special emphasis on music by Americans. It was a happy blending of art and money, for many involved in the League of Composers and its work—commissions, performances, financial aid—not only were devoted to

contemporary music but also had access to funds. The executive director from the League's founding was Claire R. Reis (Mrs. Arthur M. Reis, of Robert Reis and Co.). Mrs. Otto Kahn, wife of the banker who was also a music devotee, was on the Auxiliary Board. The League of Composers assisted American, European, and Latin American composers and arranged for performances of literally thousands of premieres of new as well as ancient works. Stravinsky's *Les Noces* was presented in the United States for the first time (April 1929) under the League's sponsorship; so was Schoenberg's *Die Glückliche Hand* (1930); complete programs were devoted to such visiting composers as Kurt Weill (1935), Béla Bartók (1940), and others. The League also sponsored the first radio performances of many new works during the 1940s. The names of American composers whose compositions were first performed at League concerts—which ranged from chamber works to operas—go into the hundreds; so would a list of those composers who received League of Composer commissions. Among these, to name a few, are Aaron Copland, Ernst Bacon, Roy Harris, Virgil Thomson, William Grant Still, Walter Piston, Roger Sessions, Randall Thompson, Douglas Moore, William Schuman, Marion Bauer, Harold Shapero, Conlon Nancarrow, and hundreds of others. In the 19th season of its existence the League announced in its publication, *Modern Music* (q.v.), that it would sponsor a program of new works by "Young Americans" (Edward T. Cone, Lionel Nowak, Charles Mills, Vincent Persichetti, and Paul Schwartz) at the Music Room of the New York Public Library; it had arranged for programs of contemporary orchestral music to be broadcast "coast-to-coast" via the Columbia Broadcasting System; it was issuing a recording of Ives's *Children's Day at the Camp Meeting* featuring violinist

Josef Szigeti and pianist Andor Foldes; and promised the broadcast premiere of Randall Thompson's opera *Solomon and Balkis* (text by Rudyard Kipling), the premieres of Ernst Bacon and Paul Horgan's *A Tree on the Plains* and *The New York Opera* by Marc Blitzstein, which did not materialize (possibly because Blitzstein went into the U. S. Army Air Forces). During World War II members of the League served in the armed forces and composed special pieces related to the war; the League also arranged for musical events for hospitals. After the war the League of Composers continued to be active in American and international musical life. By the late 1940s many of these activities were curtailed; the old guard had virtually become the Establishment and the younger musicians took over the reins of the organization. Its important work, accomplished during the 1920s, '30s, and '40s, made the League of Composers one of the most influential musical organizations in the United States as well as Europe. Eventually the League of Composers was absorbed into the International Society for Contemporary Music, American Section (the ISCM was originally a Viennese group with member units throughout the world).

THE LINDY A strenuous popular dance that came into vogue in the late 1920s, some time after 1927 when Charles Lindbergh, one of whose nicknames was "Lindy," crossed the Atlantic alone in a single engined aircraft. After the Jazz Age and popular music blended with "Swing" (q.v.) as disseminated by the Big Band (q.v.), the Lindy was readily transformed into the even more energetic dances of the jitterbug (q.v.) of the late 1930s and early '40s.

LUENING, OTTO (b. 1900) Composer, teacher, theoretician. Born in Milwaukee, Wis., June 15, 1900, Luening received his musical training in Europe.

He studied at the State Academy, Munich, Germany (1914–17), and at the Municipal Conservatory, Zürich, Switzerland (1917–20). He also studied privately with Ferruccio Busoni. Luening remained in Europe for several years and gave concerts as a flutist, an accompanist touring Germany, Switzerland and, later, the United States. He was also conductor of light opera for 5 years (1915–20) in Zürich and Munich. He also conducted concerts and opera. He returned to the United States ca. 1920 and settled in Chicago, where he was one of the founders of the American Grand Opera Company; in 1922 he conducted one of the first All-American opera performances there. In 1925 he moved on to Rochester, N.Y., to become executive director of the Opera Department of the Eastman School of Music (1925–28); he was also conductor of the American Opera Company in Rochester during the same period. Luening taught at the University of Arizona, Bennington College (where he was chairman of the Music Department), Barnard College, and Columbia University. Since 1959 he has been a co-director of the Columbia-Princeton Electronic Music Center. Luening's original works cover a wide range of expression, from the traditional to the contemporary utilization of tape and electronic devices. His Opus 1 was a *Sonata for Violin and Piano* (1918), the first of 3 in this genre—Op. 9 (1922) and the 3rd (1945). A *Sonata No. 3 for Solo Violin* dates from 1970–71. His first large orchestral work was the *Symphonic Poem*, Op. 5 (1921). Other compositions for orchestra include *Concertino for flute, harp, celeste, and strings* (1923), *Symphonic Poem* (1924), *Americana* (1936), *Divertimento* (1936), *Dirge* (1936), *Two Symphonic Interludes* (1936), *Suite for String Orchestra* (1937), *Two Fantasias* (1945–46), *Kentucky Concerto* (1951), *Music for Orchestra* (1952). Other chamber works include 3 string quartets (1919; 1922; 1928), *Coal Scuttle Blues* for 2 pianos (composed in collaboration with Ernst Bacon, 1921), *Trio for Piano, Violin and Cello* (1922), *The Soundless Song* for soprano, string quartet, piano, flute, and clarinet (1922), *Trio for Flute, Violin and Soprano* (1923), *Piano Sonata* (1929), *Fantasia Brevis* for string trio (1936), *Short Sonata for Flute and Piano* (1939), *Suite for Soprano and Flute* (1939), *Fuguing Tune for Flute, Oboe, Clarinet, Bassoon and Horn* (1941), *Suite* for cello and piano (1946), *Three Nocturnes* for oboe and piano (1951), *Trio* for violin, flute, and piano (1952). For the stage Luening composed a setting for Maeterlinck's *Sister Beatrice* (1925) and the opera *Evangeline* (1932). In the early 1950s Luening began composing with a magnetic recording tape, producing such works as *Fantasy in Space* (flute on tape, 1952), *Low Speed* (flute on tape, 1952), *Invention* (flute on tape, 1952), *Incantation* (on tape, in collaboration with Vladimir Ussachevsky, 1952), *Poem in Cycles and Bells* (on tape, with Ussachevsky, 1954), *Theatre Piece No. 2* (tape, voice, brass, percussion, and narrator, 1956), *Synthesis* for orchestra, electronic sounds (1960), *Concerted Piece* (for tape orchestra, with Ussachevsky, 1960), *Gargoyles* (for violin and electronic sounds, 1961), *Diffusion of Bells* and *Electronic Fanfare* (tape, in collaboration with Halim El Dabh, 1962) and *Moonflight* (flute on tape, 1967). In addition to composing, teaching, and co-directing the Columbia-Princeton Electronic Music Center, Luening has also been active in the work of the American Music Center, American Composers Alliance (q.v.), and Composers Recordings Inc. (CRI), of which he has served as chairman of the board since 1970.

MACCOLL, HUGH FREDERICK (1885–1953) Composer, organist, businessman. Born in Pawtucket, R.I., Feb. 22, 1885, MacColl studied the violin, piano, and organ as a youngster. He studied further at St. Paul's School, Concord, N.H., where he also served as unofficial organist. He attended Harvard (1903–7), studying under Walter Raymond Spalding and Frederick S. Converse (q.v.). Upon graduation, MacColl settled in Providence, joined a firm of investment bankers which eventually became MacColl, Fraser and Co., while continuing his dedication to music. He was a charter member of and accompanist for the University Glee Club of Providence, formed in 1911; MacColl was also a trustee of the New England Conservatory of Music and a member of the visiting committee in the Department of Music, Brown University, R.I. His compositions were performed by such orchestras as the Providence Symphony, the Rochester Civic Symphony, and the Boston Symphony. MacColl's works include *Arabs*, a "symphonic illustration" (1932), *Ballad* for piano and orchestra (1934), *Romantic Suite in the Form of Variations* (1935), and *Noel* (1940). There are also several choral compositions, songs, and chamber works. Among the latter: *Sahara Suite* for 2 pianos (1927), 2 string quartets (1928; 1945), *Martha*, a suite for 2 pianos (1930), *Variations on an Original Theme in F* for solo piano (1934), *Trio in E Minor* for piano, violin, and cello (1935), and a *Sonata for Violin, Cello and Piano* (1938). MacColl died in Providence, R.I., Oct. 17, 1953.

MCCOLLIN, FRANCES (1872–1960) Composer, conductor. Born in Philadelphia, Pa., Oct. 24, 1892, McCollin grew up in musical surroundings; her father was a singer associated with musical groups in Philadelphia. Despite blindness, McCollin studied music with William Wallace Gilchrist (q.v.) and H. Alexander Matthews. After graduation from Bryn Mawr, she was active as a lecturer, choral conductor, and composer. Although she wrote many orchestral works, McCollin produced a great number of compositions for the voice, beginning with the early prizewinning "O Sing Unto the Lord" (1916). Other works for voice or voices include the cantata *The Singing Leaves* for soprano, tenor, bass, women's chorus, and piano (1917), *Night Before Christmas* for mezzo-soprano, women's chorus, and piano (1922), *Spring in Heaven* for women's voices and piano (1929), *Going Up to London* for women's chorus, flute, and piano (1931), *The True God* for mixed chorus a cappella (1938), *How Firm a Foundation* for soprano, alto, mixed chorus, and organ (1941), and others. She also composed a number of works for string orchestra: *Adagio* (1927), *Scherzo, "Heavenly Children at Play"* (1929), *Prayer* (1930), and *Suite for Strings* (1941). For larger orchestra McCollin wrote a *Pavane* (1932), a *Suite in F* (1934), *Suburban Sketches* (1936), *Christmas Fantasia* (1938), *Nocturne* (1940), *Madrigal for Flute and Orchestra* (1941), and *Variations on an Original Theme* for piano and orchestra (1942). She also composed a *String Quartet in F* (1920) and a *Fantasia* for string quartet (1936) as well as a *Quintet for Piano and Strings* (1927), a *Sextet* for strings (1932), and a *Diversion for Five Wind Instruments* (1943). McCollin wrote a children's opera, *King Christmas* (1926), as well as many songs and solo organ pieces. She died in Philadelphia, Feb. 26, 1960.

MCDONALD, HARL (1899–1955) Composer, pianist, organist, teacher. Born on a ranch near Boulder, Colorado, July 27, 1899, McDonald received his earliest lessons in music from his mother. He began composing around the age of 7. He studied further with other teachers, including Vernon Spencer and Ernest Douglas, in the United States and in Leipzig, at the Conservatory, with Robert Fichmuller. He studied (orchestration) at the Académie Tournefort in Paris, where he also taught piano. While in Europe, McDonald heard one of his earliest compositions, *Mojave,* performed by the Berlin Philharmonic in 1922. The next year he embarked on a career of recitalist, accompanist, and teacher. In 1925–26 he taught at the Philadelphia Academy of Music and then joined the faculty of the University of Pennsylvania, where he taught from 1926 to 1946; in 1939 he was appointed manager of the Philadelphia Orchestra. McDonald's orchestral works include 4 symphonies: *Santa Fé Trail* (1934), No. 2 (*Rhumba,* 1935), No. 3, for soprano, chorus, and orchestra (1936), and No. 4 (1937). Other works include a *Festival of the Workers* suite (1932), *Three Poems on Traditional Aramaic and Hebrew Themes* (1935), *Concerto for Two Pianos and Orchestra* (1936), 2 nocturnes, *San Juan Capistrano* (1938), *Chameleon Variations* (1940), *From Childhood,* suite for harp and orchestra (1940), *Bataan* (1942), *My Country at War* (1943), and *Concerto for Violin and Orchestra* (1943). McDonald's choral works include a *Lament for the Stolen* (inspired by the Lindbergh kidnapping, 1938), *The Sea* (1939), *Dirge for Two Veterans* for women's chorus and orchestra (1940), *Pioneers, O Pioneers* (1941), *Day Break* (1941), and *Song of Free Nations* (1945). For small groups, McDonald wrote a *Trio in G Minor* for piano, violin, and cello (1931), a *Fantasy* for string quartet (1932), a 2nd trio (1932), and a *Quartet on Negro Themes* (1933). His *Saga of the Mississippi* was given its premiere by the Philadelphia Orchestra under Eugene Ormandy in 1948. McDonald died in Princeton, N.J., Mar. 30, 1955.

MCHUGH, JIMMY (1894–1969) Songwriter. Born James Francis in Boston, Mass., July 10, 1894, McHugh was taught to play the piano by his mother. A graduate of St. John's Preparatory School and Holy Cross College, McHugh for a time considered going into his father's business and worked as a plumber's apprentice. Offered a scholarship in the New England Conservatory of Music, McHugh chose instead to work as a rehearsal pianist at the newly opened Boston Opera House. He then worked as a song plugger in the Boston branch of the Irving Berlin publishing firm. McHugh covered his territory on a bicycle supplied by Berlin, about 3 theatres a night, to demonstrate new Berlin songs. In the early 1920s McHugh decided to move on to New York, where he began turning out his own songs. In 1924 he produced his first hit song, "When My Sugar Walks Down the Street" (lyrics by Irving Mills and Gene Austin) and soon after began writing songs for Harlem's popular Cotton Club (q.v.). It was during this period that McHugh teamed up with his first major lyricist, Dorothy Fields (q.v.). They made their first major impression with their songs for the Broadway production *Blackbirds of 1928*: "Diga Diga Doo" and "I Can't Give You Anything But Love." McHugh wrote the songs for 5 more Broadway shows; the last was *As the Girls Go* (1948, with lyrics by Harold Adamson). McHugh moved to California during the first film musical cycle, which began for him and Fields with *Love in the Rough* (1930) and resulted in many film scores and some fine songs: "Cuban Love Song" (from *The Cuban Love Song*, with Herbert Stothart, 1931), "Don't Blame Me" (*Dinner at Eight*, 1933), "Lost in a Fog" (*Have a Heart*, 1934), "I Feel a Song Comin' On" and "I'm in the Mood for Love" (*Every Night at Eight*, 1935).

Fields eventually worked on film scores with Jerome Kern (q.v.) and, later, returned to New York to collaborate on stage musicals, so McHugh teamed up with other lyricists—chiefly Harold Adamson, Frank Loesser, and Johnny Mercer. Out of these collaborations came "A Lovely Way to Spend an Evening" (lyrics by Adamson, from *Higher and Higher*, 1943), "Murder He Says" (lyrics by Loesser, from *Jam Session*, 1944), and "It's a Most Unusual Day" (lyrics by Adamson, from *A Date with Judy*, 1948). During World War II, McHugh and Adamson produced the patriotic and popular "Coming In on a Wing and a Prayer" (1943). McHugh was active in charity work, in business (he founded his own publishing firm in 1959), and was associated with the Beverly Hills Chamber of Commerce, of which he was president from 1950 to 1952. He died in Beverly Hills, Calif., May 23, 1969.

MCKAY, GEORGE FREDERICK (1899–1970) Composer, teacher. Born in Harrington, Wash., June 11, 1899, McKay received musical training at the University of Washington, Seattle, and at the Eastman School of Music, Rochester, N.Y., where he studied with Christian Sinding and Selim Palmgren. He was graduated in 1923. His *Sinfonietta No. 1* was selected for performance at the first American Composers' Concert at Rochester in 1925. He joined the faculty of the University of Washington, where he was eventually appointed professor of music. He retired in 1968. McKay composed for virtually every combination of instruments and voice. He composed 3 more *Sinfoniettas* for orchestra (1929; 1933; 1942), a *Prairie Portrait* (1932), a *Symphony*, "Evocation" (1935–45), *Symphonie Miniature* (1937), *Concerto for Violin* (1940), *To a Liberator* (1940), *Cello Concerto* (1942), *Suite of*

Fiddler's Tunes (1943), *Variations* on "There's a Great Day Coming" (1943), and a *Suite on Northwest Indian Song and Dance* (1945). For smaller orchestras McKay wrote *Three Lyric Soliloquies* (1928), a *Sonatine* for clarinet and string orchestra (1929), a *Fantasy on a Western Folksong* (1936), *Variants on a Western Tune* (1937), *Port Royal, 1861* (suite based on Negro folk songs, 1939), *Pastoral Soliloquy* for oboe and small orchestra (1941), and *Suite on Children's Themes* for string orchestra (1942). His chamber music includes 4 string quartets, 2 organ sonatas, and several quintets, including *American Street Scenes* for clarinet, trumpet, saxophone, bassoon, and piano (1935). There are also several choral works of which the cantata *Lincoln Lyrics,* to a text by Edwin Markham (1945), is outstanding. McKay also composed study pieces such as his *Suite for the Bass Clef Instruments* and works for young people's orchestras such as *The Big Sky.* His solo piano works include a *Sonata,* a *Caricature Suite,* and an *April Suite,* among other works. His major stage work is the dance drama in "four American phases," *Epoch,* which was given its first performance and was conducted by the composer at the University of Washington in 1935. McKay died in Stateline, Nev., Oct. 4, 1970.

MCKINLEY, CARL (1895–1966) Composer, organist, teacher. Born in Yarmouth, Maine, Oct. 9, 1895, he studied music at Knox College, Galesburg, Ill., and at Harvard. While at Harvard he won the Francis Boott Prize for his *The Man of Galilee,* for chorus and organ (1917), and upon graduation won a Naumberg Fellowship, which enabled him to spend the winter of 1917–18 in New York City, where he studied with several teachers, among them Rubin Goldmark (q.v.), composition, and Gaston M. Déthier, organ.

McKinley then worked as a church organist, choirmaster, and teacher and was organist of the Capitol Theatre (1923). In the later '20s he received 2 Guggenheim Fellowships, making it possible for him to study with Nadia Boulanger (q.v.) in France, after which he worked for a time as vocal coach and stage assistant at the Munich Opera. Returning to the United States in 1929, McKinley joined the staff of the New England Conservatory. Besides many works written for the organ, including the popular *Cantilena,* McKinley has composed songs, solo piano pieces, and a *Suite for Five Wind Instruments* (1935), a *String Quartet in One Movement* (1942), *Indian Summer Idyl* for orchestra (1917), a symphonic poem *The Blue Flower* (1920; won the Flagler Prize in '21), *Masquerade,* an American rhapsody (1925), and *Chorale, Variations and Fugue* (1941). McKinley died in Boston, Mass., July 24, 1966.

MAGANINI, QUINTO (1897–1974) Composer, conductor, flutist. Born in Fairfield, Calif., Nov. 30, 1897, Maganini attended the University of California and later studied with Georges Barrère (flute) and, in France, with Nadia Boulanger (q.v.). In 1919 Maganini joined the San Francisco Symphony as flutist; 2 years later he was hired by the New York Symphony, and remained with it until 1928. He received a Guggenheim Fellowship (1928–29) and in 1930 became conductor of the New York Sinfonietta. He formed his own chamber orchestra in 1932. He also taught orchestration and counterpoint at Columbia University. Maganini was also a successful businessman and frequently helped his fellow composers by publishing their works through his own company, Edition Musicus, and by performing their compositions at concerts given by his orchestra. He composed several works especially for his group, among them a *Concerto in D Minor* for strings (1929), *Nocturne* for strings (1929), *An Ornithological Suite* (1930), *Genevieve,* a "rhapsody for orchestra" (1930), and *Ladies of the Ballet* (1938). For larger orchestras Magnini wrote *Tuolumne,* a California rhapsody (1920), *South Wind,* an orchestral fancy (1922), *Cuban Rhapsody* (1925), *Napoleon I* (1931), *Symphony in G Minor* (1932), *A Night in the Tropics* (1933), *Sahara Suite* (1937), *The Royal Ladies Suite* (1938), *At the Setting of the Sun* (1939), *Americanese,* suite on 3 early American pieces (1940), *France Forever* (1943), *Moonlight on the Painted Desert,* from *Western Sketches* (1944), *An Ancient Greek Melody* (1945), and *Peaceful Land* (1945). Of Maganini's choral works, *Songs of the Chinese* for women's voices, 2 pianos, and percussion (1925) and *Cathedral at Sens* for cello, mixed choir, and orchestra (1935) were frequently performed. There are also a few works for chamber groups, which include an extended *Sonata da Camera* for violin and piano (1935). Of Maganini's 4 operas, *The Argonauts* (completed 1934), was the most ambitious. A tetralogy, the opera deals with no less than the history of California and took the composer more than a decade to complete. *The Argonauts* won him the Bispham Medal. An engineer also, Maganini eventually became president of the Kingsbury Machine Works. He died in Greenwich, Conn., Mar. 10, 1974.

"MAH LINDY LOU" Song, words and music by Lily Strickland (q.v.). Described as "A Banjo Song," "Mah Lindy Lou" is written in a kind of black dialect, musically as well as lyrically. Published in 1920, it was one of Strickland's most popular creations and was sung by such concert artists as Paul Robeson and John Charles Thomas.

"MANHATTAN SERENADE" An instrumental composition for piano and or-

chestra composed by Louis Alter (q.v.) for the Paul Whiteman (q.v.) Orchestra. This version was first presented in 1928. Its popularity encouraged Alter to compose several other metropolitan-inspired pieces: *Manhattan Moonlight* (1929), *Manhattan Masquerade* (1932), *Metropolitan Nocturne* (originally a film score, 1936), and *Side Street in Gotham* (1938). In 1942, with words added by Harold Adamson, "Manhattan Serenade" also achieved popularity as a song.

"THE MAN I LOVE" Song, words by Ira Gershwin (q.v.), music by George Gershwin (q.v.), written in 1924 for the score of their first major Broadway show, *Lady, Be Good!* (q.v.). Regarded by many as the Gershwins' finest creation (by what process is difficult to discern considering Gershwin's output), "The Man I Love" has an interesting if oft-told history. Originally intended to be sung by Adele Astaire, "The Man I Love" was cut from the show during the Philadelphia tryout run by one of the producers, Vinton Freedley, who thought the slow ballad interfered with the pace of the show. The show became successful without the song, but some people remembered it. A friend of George Gershwin's, Lady Mountbatten, took it back to London with her, gave a copy to a favorite band, and soon made the song a hit there. Assured that the song had potential, Gershwin put it into the score of the first version of *Strike Up the Band* (1927)—but it was ejected again. He tried again with *Rosalie* (1928), with the same result. He finally decided that it was simply not a production number. The song was eventually published and has done well ever since. It is one of the earliest of the collaborations by the Gershwin brothers that revealed their artistry.

MANNES, LEOPOLD DAMROSCH (1899–1964) Composer, pianist, teacher. Born in New York City, Dec. 26,

1899, Mannes came from a musical family. His mother was Clara Damrosch (daughter of Leopold Damrosch); she was also a fine pianist. His father, David Mannes, was a violinist and teacher. Mannes graduated from Harvard University and had been trained in the piano and composition. He won several scholarships, one of which enabled him to study in Paris with the pianist Alfred Cortot. Mannes made an impressive beginning as a composer, was given the Pulitzer Prize for composition in 1925, eventually taught composition at his parents' school, the David Mannes School. Another interest was research, into both chemistry and photography. Mannes abandoned music to join the research staff of Eastman Kodak Co., Rochester, N.Y. In collaboration with another musician, Leopold Godowsky, Jr. (son of the great pianist), Mannes was the co-inventor of the Kodachrome color photography process. Before this event Mannes had composed a *Suite* for orchestra (1924) and *Two Madrigals for Chorus* (1926); his chamber works include a *Suite for Two Pianos* (1922) and a *String Quartet* (1927). He also composed incidental music for a children's production of Shakespeare's *The Tempest* (1930). Mannes died in Martha's Vineyard, Mass., Aug. 11, 1964.

MARKS, GERALD (b. 1900) Composer, pianist, bandleader. Born in Saginaw, Mich., Oct. 13, 1900, Marks was self-taught in music and began playing the piano around the time he was 8 years old. In high school he accompanied the glee club and began working in dance bands, forming his own, which was popular and busy in the Saginaw Valley during the late 1920s. He began writing songs around this time; the first to achieve some popularity was entitled "I Can't Write the Words" (lyrics by Arthur "Buddy" Fields), followed by

"You're the One (You Beautiful Son-of-a-Gun)" (lyrics by Fields) and "The Night Shall Be Filled with Music" (lyrics by Fields and Will Collins). In 1931 Marks collaborated with Detroit lyricist Seymour Simons to produce one of his several standards, "All of Me." An established composer and hit songwriter, Marks concentrated on writing songs for Broadway and Hollywood, with an occasional pop song published from time to time. His songs were heard in such productions as *Earl Carroll's Sketch Book* (1935), *White Horse Inn* (1936), *My Dear Public* (1943), and *Hold It!* (1948). One of his best-known film songs is "That's What I Want for Christmas" (lyrics by Irving Caesar), written for a Shirley Temple film, *Stowaway* (1936). Other songs include "Mount'n Gal" (lyrics by Marks), "Oh, Susannah, Dust Off That Old Pianna" (lyrics by Caesar and Sammy Lerner), and "Is It True What They Say About Dixie?" (lyrics by Caesar and Lerner). With Caesar, Marks collaborated on a series of songs for children entitled *Sing a Song of Safety,* which were widely used in schools. His other collections include *The Ten Jewish Holidays, Ten Catholic Holy Days, The Ten Protestant Days, The A-B-C Stories of Jesus,* and *Nine Days for Americans.* Active in the promotion of the songwriter and of popular song, Marks was one of 5 ASCAP members who, in 1954, toured U. S. Army bases in Europe and Africa. (He himself served in the Merchant Marine during World War II.) Since 1970 Marks has been a member of ASCAP's board of directors and also serves as chairman of its public relations committee. He is also on the board of the Songwriter's Hall of Fame.

MICROTONE   See Hans Barth.

MODERN MUSIC A quarterly magazine published by the League of Composers (q.v.). Edited by Minna Lederman, a Barnard and Vassar graduate, who specialized in writing on music, *Modern Music* was first published in February 1924 and lasted through 23 volumes, with the final issue published in the fall of 1946. *Modern Music* was unique in its coverage of the currents of contemporary music, including dance, film, radio, and recordings. Reviews of concerts appeared along with critical articles on music and biographies of contemporary composers. Coverage was not limited to the United States, and correspondents from Germany, Britain, Italy, Mexico, and other parts of the world reported on musical activity. Among the authors who published articles in *Modern Music* were Béla Bartók (q.v.), Alban Berg, Carlos Chávez, Darius Milhaud, Arnold Schoenberg (q.v.), Edwin Denby, Alfred Einstein, and Albert Roussel. Active League members also contributed, among them Marc Blitzstein, John Cage, Elliott Carter, Aaron Copland, Henry Cowell, and Roger Sessions (all q.v.). After *Modern Music* ceased publication, some of the vacuum it left was filled by an 8-page small newspaperlike publication, *The Composer's News-Record*.

MOORE, DOUGLAS (1893–1969) Composer, teacher, author. Born in Cutchogue, Long Island, N.Y., on Aug. 10, 1893, Moore studied at Yale, where he received a B.A. in liberal arts (1915) and his Mus.B. in 1917. At Yale, Moore studied with Horatio Parker. In Paris he studied with Vincent d'Indy at the Schola Cantorum (1921) and with Ernest Bloch (q.v.) at the Cleveland Institute of Music in 1924. Two years later he joined the staff of the Music Department of Columbia University, New York; from 1940 to 1962 Moore served as chairman of the Music Department, succeeding Daniel Gregory

Mason (q.v.). A meeting with poet Vachel Lindsay while still a student in Cleveland awakened Moore's interest in American themes, which determined the general direction of his compositions. His works for orchestra include *Four Museum Pieces* (1922), *Pageant of P. T. Barnum* (1924), *Moby Dick* (1928), *A Symphony of Autumn* (1930), *Overture on an American Tune* (1931), Suite from *The Power and the Land* (film, 1941), Suite from *Youth Gets a Break* (film, 1941), *Village Music* (1942), *In Memoriam* (1943), *Symphony No. 2 in A* (1945), *Farm Journal* (1947), and *Cotillion Suite* (1952). Moore's chamber compositions include a *Sonata for Violin and Piano* (1929), a *String Quartet* (1933), a *Quintet* for woodwinds and horn (1942), the *Down East Suite* for violin and piano (or orchestra, 1944), and *Quintet* for clarinet and strings (1946). Moore is probably best known for his operas: *The Devil and Daniel Webster* (libretto by Stephen Vincent Benét, 1938), *The Emperor's New Clothes*, one-act children's opera (1948), the Pulitzer Prize–winning *Giants in the Earth*, based on the novel by O. E. Rølvaag (libretto by Arnold Sundgaard, 1950), *The Ballad of Baby Doe* (libretto by John Latouche, 1956), *Gallantry*, a "soap opera" (libretto by Sundgaard, 1957), *Wings of the Dove*, based on the Henry James novel (libretto by Ethan Ayer, 1961), and *Carry Nation* (libretto by William N. Jayme, 1966). Moore composed several choral works, including *God Rest You Merry, Gentlemen*, a cappella (1932), *Perhaps to Dream* for a cappella women's chorus (1938), and *Prayer for the United Nations* for alto, chorus, and orchestra (1943). Moore was the author of *Listening to Music* (1932, rev. 1937) and *From Madrigal to Modern Music* (1942), as well as several articles in newspapers and periodicals. He died in

Greenport, Long Island, N.Y., July 25, 1969.

MORET, NEIL (1878–1943) Composer, lyricist. Born Charles N. Daniels in Leavenworth, Kans., Apr. 12, 1878. The pseudonym "Neil Moret" appeared for the first time on a piano piece entitled *Hiawatha—a Summer Idyl* in 1900. It later achieved popularity with words by Jim O'Dea. Daniels apparently had studied music as a youngster and had a natural talent. In 1904 he was co-founder of the publishing company of Daniels and Russell in St. Louis. He later joined the Detroit firm of Whitney-Warren (later known as Remick) as an arranger. He became an executive at Remick in New York and later founded his own publishing house, Villa Moret, in San Francisco. Although "Moret's" output was small, he produced several very popular, very profitable songs: "You Tell Me Your Dream, I'll Tell You Mine" (lyrics by Seymour A. Rice and Al H. Brown, 1908), "Moonlight and Roses" (based on Edwin H. Lemare's *Andantino* for organ, with words by Moret and Ben Black, 1925), "Chloe" (lyrics by Gus Kahn, 1927), and "She's Funny That Way" (with composer-lyricist Richard A. Whiting q.v., 1928). Moret also composed an instrumental collection, *Cavalcade of Marches.* He died in Los Angeles, Calif., Jan. 21, 1943.

MORRIS, HAROLD CECIL (1890–1964) Composer, pianist, teacher. Born in San Antonio, Tex., Mar. 17, 1890, Morris was educated at the University of Texas, Austin, and completed his musical education at the Cincinnati Conservatory of Music. He also studied piano with Leopold Godowsky. Morris made his first mark on the American musical scene with his *Piano Concerto,* which he performed as soloist with the Boston Symphony under Koussevitzky in 1931 (the work was completed in 1927). Morris toured the United States and Canada as soloist, performing his own compositions. He also lectured on music at the Rice Institute, Houston, Tex.; in 1921 he joined the staff of the Juilliard School of Music, New York. For orchestra, Morris composed 3 symphonies (1936, 1943, and 1946), also *Poem* after Tagore's *Gitanjali* (1915), *Passacaglia and Fugue* (1936), *Suite for Orchestra* (1937), *Concerto for Violin* (1938), *American Epic* (1942), and *Overture Heroic* (1943). For chamber orchestra there are *Dum-A-Lum,* variations on a Negro spiritual (1915), a *Suite for Piano and Strings* (1940), and *Suite for Strings* (1941). Morris also composed 4 piano sonatas, 2 string quartets, 2 sonatas for piano and violin, and several works of smaller dimension, many of which were awarded prizes. Morris himself was given the Award of Merit from the National Association of American Composers and Conductors for his services to American music, in 1938–39. He died in New York City, May 6, 1964.

MOUND CITY BLUE BLOWERS Small Chicago-based white group of jazz musicians led by William "Red" McKenzie (1907–48), who performed on the "blue blower" (a comb wrapped in tissue paper). Originally formed ca. 1923, the group was made up of McKenzie, Dick Slevin (kazoo), Jack Bland (banjo), and Eddie Lang (guitar). The name of the group was used for other McKenzie bands, including one that recorded in the late '20s and early '30s whose members included Glenn Miller (q.v.), Pee Wee Russell, Coleman Hawkins, Jack Bland, Eddie Condon (q.v.), Al Morgan, and Gene Krupa. The name was taken up again in 1935 by a group of musicians from the Bob Crosby Band: Yank Lawson (trumpet), Eddie Miller (clarinet and tenor sax), Nappy Lamare (guitar), Pete Peterson (bass), and Ray Bauduc (drums). The name is most closely associated with the 1929–31 band and such recordings as *One Hour* and *Hello Lola,* recorded on the Bluebird label, a subsidiary of RCA Victor.

MUSIC BOX REVUE The title of musical productions designed to be presented in the Music Box Theatre, New York, which, in turn, was designed as a showplace for musicals with songs by Irving Berlin (q.v.). The theatre was a joint venture by Berlin and producer Sam H. Harris (1872–1941). There were 4 annual editions, 1921, 1922, 1923, and 1924. Lavishly presented, they featured big-name stars of the period and employed skilled directors, choreographers, and designers. The first *Music Box Revue* was the most successful (it ran for 440 performances), although all of the revues were popular and had very good runs. The best-known song from the 1921 edition was "Say It with Music," which became the theme song for the others; another interesting song from the same production was "Everybody Step." The 1922 production had such songs as "Crinoline Days," "Lady of the Evening," and "Pack Up Your Sins and Go to the Devil." "An Orange Grove in California" was the hit song of the 1923 edition, and an extraordinary lullaby, "Rock-A-Bye Baby," was an outstanding creation for the *Music Box Revue* of 1924. Among the performers who appeared in these shows were Berlin himself (in the '21 revue), William Collier, Emma Haig, Charlotte Greenwood, John Steel, William Gaxton, Robert Benchley (reading his famous "Treasurer's Report"), Frank Tinney, Phil Baker, Grace Moore, Clark and McCullough, Oscar Shaw, Fanny Brice, and the Brox Sisters.

"MUSIC FOR THE THEATRE" Suite for small orchestra composed by Aaron Copland (q.v.) during May–September 1925. Written in Copland's "jazz" (with a slight French accent) style, the suite is in 5 sections: I: *Prologue;* II: *Dance;* III: *Interlude;* IV: *Burlesque,* and V: *Epilogue. Music for the Theatre* was commissioned by the League of Composers (q.v.) at the suggestion of Serge Koussevitzky, to whom it is dedicated. Koussevitzky conducted members of the Boston Symphony in the work's premiere performance in Boston, Nov. 20, 1925. He also conducted the first New York performance at a League concert at Town Hall, Nov. 28. *Music for the Theatre* has been one of the most popular of Copland's early works. Koussevitzky was so impressed with it that he immediately commissioned Copland's next jazz-inflected work, the *Concerto for Piano and Orchestra.*

NEW MUSIC A quarterly publication, founded by Henry Cowell (q.v.) in 1930 and published initially by his New Music Society of California, which he had organized 3 years before. *New Music's* function was to disseminate "serious new compositions which might not have a chance of distribution through ordinary channels" (i.e., conservative, commercial publishing houses). Vol. 1, No. 1, for example, contained Carl Ruggles' (q.v.) *Men and Mountains* for orchestra, a work of considerable modernity. *New Music Edition,* as the publication was also called, was a true music magazine, in that it contained music. Among the composers whose works appeared in *New Music* were George Antheil, John J. Becker, Aaron Copland, Cowell himself (after years of not publishing his own music), Ruth Crawford, Charles Ives, Oscar Levant, Walter Piston, Wallingford Riegger, William Grant Still, Virgil Thomson, Edgard Varèse, and Ben Weber (all q.v.). Works by non-American composers were also included in *New Music:* compositions by Julián Carrillo (Mexico), Carlos Chávez (Mexico), Oscar Lorenzo Fernandez (Brazil),

Aram Khachaturian (Armenia-Russia), Arnold Schoenberg (Austria; q.v.), and Heitor Villa-Lobos (Brazil). The first director and managing editor of *New Music* was composer Gerald Strang (q.v.); associate editors were Wallingford Riegger, John J. Becker, and Nicolas Slonimsky (all q.v.). Despite the fact that *New Music* was a nonprofit activity, it persisted through various changes of editors and boards. Its catalog was acquired by the Theodore Presser Co., Bryn Mawr, Pa., in 1959.

NEW ORLEANS RHYTHM KINGS A group of white musicians whose performance style was greatly influenced by black jazz musicians and who, in turn, greatly influenced other white jazz musicians. The group formed in 1921 as the Friars' Society Orchestra, which played in Chicago's Friars' Inn. The leader was New Orleans–born Paul Mares, whose instrument was the trumpet; other members were George Brunies (trombone), also from New Orleans, and Leon Rappolo (clarinet) from Lutheran, La. Future bandleader Ben Pollack, a Chicagoan, was on drums. When the band made its first recordings for Gennett in 1922, the name was changed to New Orleans Rhythm Kings, and it was under that name that it was an influence on other musicians who heard the recordings. The band's personnel changed frequently, but for its early discs, *Tin Roof Blues, Maple Leaf Rag,* and *That's A-Plenty,* it consisted of Mares (trumpet), Brunies (trombone), Rappolo (clarinet), Mel Stitzel (piano), Lou Black (banjo), and Frank Snyder (drums). By 1925 the original New Orleans Rhythm Kings had disbanded. The name was revived in 1934–35, first with Wingy Manone on trumpet and later with Muggsy Spanier. The only element common to all 3 groups was the trombone of George Brunies. The NORK coexisted with the slightly older Original

Dixieland Jazz Band (q.v.), but was not considered by jazz historians and aficionados as quite so "hot."

OLIVER, JOSEPH "KING" (1885–1938) Cornetist, trumpeter, bandleader. Born in New Orleans(?), La., May 11, 1885, Oliver was raised by a half sister after the death of his mother ca. 1900. About this time he joined a neighborhood brass band for children in which he learned to play the cornet. As a teenager he played in various New Orleans bands, and by 1914 or so he was a member of the famous band of Kid Ory (q.v.); it is often said that it was Ory who bestowed the title "King" on Oliver. His playing style, technique, and personality made him the idol of the younger New Orleans musicians, among them a youngster named Louis Armstrong (q.v.). Legend has it that Oliver gave Armstrong his first trumpet. In 1915 Oliver formed his own band to play in and around New Orleans, both for white college dances and in such black night spots as Pete Lala's Cafe. He was summoned to Chicago by bandleader-bassist Bill Johnson to play in his band at the Royal Garden Cafe. Within 2 years (i.e., 1920) Oliver was leading his own band, the Creole Jazz Band, which made a deep impression on the Chicago musical community, white and black. He spread his musical gospel with a tour to the West Coast (1920–21). Oliver then settled in Chicago again and sent for his young protégé Louis Armstrong to join him (both he and Armstrong played cornets), Honoré Dutrey (trombone), Johnny Dodds (clarinet), Lil Hardin (piano), Charlie Jackson (bass saxophone), and Baby Dodds (drums). Oliver began recording with this band in 1923 and made some of the earliest recordings of classic jazz. The personnel, as usual, changed for the usual reasons: disagreements, other job offers—even Armstrong left in 1924.

Misfortune plagued Oliver; the Lincoln Gardens, his home base in Chicago, burned in 1924, and Oliver broke up the band and took a job with Peyton's Syncopators at the Plantation Cafe. He eventually formed another band, toured the Midwest in 1927, and, then, another misfortune: he rejected an offer to be leader of the house band at New York's Cotton Club (q.v.); this refusal paved the way for the youthful Duke Ellington (q.v.). Oliver remained active until 1930, touring and making his last recordings for RCA Victor. Tooth problems made it difficult for Oliver to play as once he had (although his 1930 Victors reveal a still-solid, imaginative talent). An attempt to form another band in 1931 did not last beyond a brief tour of the South and Southwest. Oliver gave up and settled in Savannah, nearly penniless, dispirited, and in poor health. His teeth gone, Oliver was unable to play his cornet, and he took menial jobs to keep going; he became a poolroom janitor and spent his final days suffering from high blood pressure and on relief. He was virtually forgotten as a new era of music, called swing, emerged. But Oliver's playing, arrangements, and original jazz compositions continued to be heard even in the new age. Such numbers as *Chimes Blues*, *Snag It*, *West End Blues*, *Doctor Jazz*, and *Sugar Foot Stomp* (written with Armstrong), were taken up by the younger generations that came after. He died in Savannah, Ga., Apr. 8, 1938.

"OL' MAN RIVER" Song, music by Jerome Kern, lyrics by Oscar Hammerstein II, from the 1927 musical production *Show Boat* (q.v.). It was introduced in Act I by baritone Jules Bledsoe (1898–1943). It was later sung by Paul Robeson in the 1928 London production and in the 1936 Universal Productions film version. Oscar Hammerstein has written that it was "a song sung by a character who is a rugged and untutored philosopher. It is a song of resignation with a protest implied." It is one of the outstanding creations of American song, popular or "serious."

"135TH STREET" See *Blue Monday*, one-act opera by Gershwin.

ORIGINAL MEMPHIS FIVE A band made up of white musicians that recorded frequently ca. 1923–28. It was formed by trumpeter Phil Napoleon and trombonist Irving Milfred "Miff" Mole. Other members were Frank Signorelli (piano), Jimmy Lytell (clarinet), and Jack Roth (drums). This New York–based group, influenced by the Original Dixieland Jazz Band (q.v.), and King Oliver (q.v.), played a kind of Dixieland music, although only Mole could be honestly described as a jazz musician. The performances were partly arranged, so that much of the improvisational spontaneity of the black jazz bands was missing. The recordings made by the Original Memphis Five, however, were influential (specifically on such young musicians as Harold Arlen, q.v.), and Mole and Signorelli went on to enjoy successful years in jazz and popular music. In 1931 Napoleon revived the group and recorded under the original name. For these sessions he assembled such musicians as Jimmy and Tommy Dorsey, Signorelli on piano again, and Ted Napoleon on drums.

ORNSTEIN, LEO (b. 1892) Composer, pianist. Born in Kremenchug, Russia, Dec. 11, 1892, Ornstein was brought to the United States in 1907. He began to study music in Russia at the age of 7. His father was his first teacher; later, aged 10, Ornstein entered the St. Petersburg Conservatory, where he studied with Alexander Glazunov. By this time Ornstein was regarded as a child piano prodigy. But the family decided to leave Russia, driven out by the Cossack pogroms. They settled in New York's

Lower East Side. Ornstein came to the attention of Percy Goetschius (q.v.), who arranged for the boy to study with an eminent piano teacher, Bertha Feiring Tapper, at the Institute of Musical Art. Ornstein made his debut as a pianist in 1911, after which he toured as a piano soloist and performed with several of the important orchestras in the United States. In 1913 he made a tour of Europe, where he also lectured at the Sorbonne in France and at Oxford University in England. He returned to the United States in 1915 and gave a series of modern piano music recitals at the Band Box Theatre, New York, introducing new works by such composers as Schoenberg, Ravel, Bartók, Stravinsky, and Scriabin. Although his training had been traditional, Ornstein revealed a taste for the "futurist," as it and he were called at the time. Besides the modern Europeans, Ornstein programmed his own works, which startled, alienated, or delighted his audiences. He was typed as an *enfant terrible* and classed with such upstarts as Henry Cowell (q.v.) and the later George Antheil (q.v.). An early biographer described his effect on audiences, writing that many regarded Ornstein as "an evil musical genius wandering without the utmost pale of tonal orthodoxy, in a weird no-man's-land haunted with torturous sound, with wails of futuristic despair, with cubistic shrieks and post-impressionistic cries and crashes." From ca. 1911 until ca. 1933 Ornstein visited such music upon his recital audiences with the expected reactions, depending on individual tastes. In 1935 Ornstein suddenly retired from the concert world to devote his time to teaching and composing. He became head of the piano department of Zeckwar Hahn School in Philadelphia, where eventually he established the Ornstein School of Music, of which he was director and head of the piano department until his retirement in 1955. Ornstein

also taught at the Philadelphia Musical Academy and served on the faculty of Temple University, Philadelphia. As a composer, Ornstein made his greatest impression with his early piano pieces, the content and form of which were undoubtedly determined by emotional dictates rather than by what he had learned in his orthodox schooling. His very earliest pieces were innocuous, but by 1911 he began attracting attention with such piano pieces as *À la Chinoise,* and he achieved notoriety with *Danse Sauvage* ("Wild Man's Dance") in 1913 and solidified his reputation as the then bad boy of music with his *Three Moods: Anger, Grief, Joy* (ca. 1914). Once Ornstein dropped from public view, however, the interest in his music waned to a great extent. His *Nocturne and Dance of the Fates* (1936) was well received when performed by the St. Louis Symphony in February 1937. Among Ornstein's works are the symphonic poem *The Fog* (1915), a *Piano Concerto* (1923), *Two Nocturnes* (1924), *Lysistrata Suite* (1930), and a *Symphony* (1936). Ornstein also composed 2 string quartets (1929, 1940); other chamber works include 2 sonatas for violin and piano of uncertain dates, Op. 26 and Op. 31, and *Quintette* for piano and strings, Op. 92 (1927). Ornstein also composed numerous piano works: *Deux Impressions de Notre-Dame* (1914), 10 *Poems of 1917* (1918), *A la Mexicana* (3 pieces, 1920), *Arabesques* (1921), 6 *Water Colors* (1935), *Suicide in an Airplane* (1940), and *Twenty Waltzes* (1955–68). Ornstein, with his wife, whom he married in 1918, chose to keep out of the musical mainstream and left the musical centers to live in the solitudes of New Hampshire, Arizona, Florida, and finally Texas, where they settled into a mobile home in Brownsville. In his 84th year Ornstein completed a 2nd *Piano Sonata* and a 2nd *String Quartet.* In 1975 he was presented with the Marjorie Peabody Waite Award from the National Institute of Art and Letters.

ORY, EDWARD "KID" (1886–1973) Trombonist, bandleader. Born in Laplace, La., Dec. 25, 1886, Ory learned to play several instruments but was a master of the New Orleans "tailgate" trombone. (The name derives from the New Orleans practice of carrying small bands through the streets on festive occasions in wagons; the trombone, with its slide, was placed on the wagon's tailgate.) As a boy, Ory organized his own small band, which played on homemade instruments. According to his ASCAP biographical entry, Ory studied music privately, although it is likely he picked up a good deal of knowledge by listening to early jazz bands. His musical experience dated back to the heyday of the legendary Buddy Bolden before the turn of the century, when he is supposed to have sat in with Bolden's band. He formed his own band ca. 1911 and began performing in New Orleans; this band at one time or another employed King Oliver (q.v.), Louis Armstrong (q.v.), Johnny Dodds, Sidney Bechet (q.v.), and other great musicians of the New Orleans "school." In 1919 Ory moved to California, where he formed another band, and then, after turning over the band to Mutt Carey, the trumpeter, went to Chicago, where he played in various bands including King Oliver's; he also recorded with Louis Armstrong and various blues singers. Ory returned to Los Angeles, where he retired from music and spent about a decade as a chicken rancher. He returned to music in the '40s and formed his own Creole Jazz Band made up of veteran New Orleans musicians; the band played concerts, touring the United States and Europe (in 1956 and 1959). In 1954 Ory settled in San Francisco and opened up his own club, On the Levee, where he was active until 1961. In 1966 he retired

to Honolulu, where he died Jan. 23, 1973. As a composer, Ory was best known for the jazz compositions *Savoy Blues* and *Muskrat Ramble*.

PIMSLEUR, SOLOMON (1900–1962) Composer, pianist, teacher. Born in Paris, France, Sept. 19, 1900, Pimsleur was brought to the United States at the age of 3. He received his musical education at Columbia University, New York, where he studied composition with Daniel Gregory Mason (q.v.); awarded a Juilliard Scholarship, Pimsleur also studied with Rubin Goldmark (q.v.). In 1929 he went to Salzburg, Austria, to study orchestration and conducting. Pimsleur then returned to New York, where he devoted his time to composition and teaching (piano, harmony, theory, and composition). His works include a *Symphonic Ballad* (1924), *Meditative Nocturne* (1924), the *Neo-Classic Overture* (1927), *Symphony of Disillusionment* (1928), a tone poem, *Miracle of Life and the Mystery of Death* (1932), *Symphonic Suite* (1935), *Symphonic Ode and Peroration* (1936), *Four Dramas in a Cycle of Symphonies* (an entire evening of music, composed 1931–45), and *Symphony of Terror and Despair* (1947). Pimsleur also composed 5 string quartets, several choral works, and songs and solo piano works. He died in New York City, Apr. 22, 1962.

"PINE TOP'S BOOGIE WOOGIE" A solo piano blues in boogie-woogie (q.v.) style composed by Clarence "Pine Top" Smith (q.v.) and recorded by him in Chicago, Dec. 29, 1928. This became one of the most popular and most imitated of boogie-woogie pieces and undoubtedly gave currency to the term. Although Smith's recording was known in black communities, the piece did not achieve wide sales and popularity until ca. 1935, when a new recording was made by Cleo Brown. Virtually every blues pianist learned "Pine Top's Boogie Woogie." It was orchestrated and played by such big bands as Bob Crosby's and Glenn Miller's (q.v.). In Pine Top Smith's original version a spoken monologue describes the dance that was to be done to the music. He admonishes the "girl with the red dress" to "shake that thing" as he performs variations on his simple, but effective, theme while his left hand sustains the primitive beat.

PISTON, WALTER (1894–1976) Composer, teacher. Born in Rockland, Maine, Jan. 20, 1894, Piston moved with his family to Boston when he was about 10. He began to study music there, although not with a musical career in mind, after his father presented him with a violin. Piston graduated from the Mechanical Arts High School in 1912 and took a job as a draftsman. He later studied painting and drawing at the Massachusetts Normal Art School, from which he was graduated in 1916. While in art school he continued to study music and earned extra money playing in restaurants, dance halls, and theatres. Piston enlisted in the U. S. Navy during World War I and played saxophone in a navy band. After the war, at the suggestion of Dr. Archibald T. Davison of the Harvard Music Department, Piston, then already married to painter Kathryn Nason, and 26 years of age, enrolled as a freshman at Harvard to study music. He was graduated, summa cum laude, in 1924. Awarded a John Knowles Paine Fellowship, Piston went to Paris, where he studied with Nadia Boulanger (q.v.). In 1926 he returned to the United States, joined the Harvard faculty, and taught there until his retirement in 1959. (Among Piston's students were Leonard Bernstein, Elliott Carter, Irving Fine, and Harold Shapero; all q.v.). One of the most distinguished of American composers, Piston is usually described as a

neoclassicist, primarily because he chose to reject the modernisms of the more trendy composers of his time. He sometimes referred to his compositions as "mid-Victorian," which hardly describes his output either. Piston's mastery of technique, counterpoint, and orchestration and his keen harmonic sense resulted in clear, strong, well-wrought musical statements. His most popular work is his single ballet score, *The Incredible Flutist* (1938). He also composed 8 symphonies (1937, 1943, 1947, 1950, 1954, 1955, 1960, and 1965), of which the *Third* and *Seventh* won the Pulitzer Prize. Other orchestral works: *Symphonic Piece* (1927), *Suite for Orchestra* (1928), *Concerto for Orchestra* (1933), *Prelude and Fugue* (1934), *Sinfonietta* (1941), *Prelude and Allegro* for organ and strings (1943), *Fugue on a Victory Tune* (1944), *Toccata* (1948), *Serenata* (1956), *Ricercare* (1968), and *Concerto for String Quartet, Wind Instruments and Percussion* (1976). Piston also composed 2 violin concertos (1939, 1960), *Tunbridge Fair* for band (1950), a *Viola Concerto* (1957), a *Concerto for Two Pianos and Orchestra* (1959), *Variations for Cello and Orchestra* (1966), and a *Clarinet Concerto* (1967). His works for chamber groups include the *Concertino for Piano and Chamber Orchestra* (1937), 5 string quartets (1933, 1935, 1947, 1951, and 1962), 2 piano trios (1935, 1966), a *Sonata for Flute and Piano* (1930), *Piano Quintet* (1949), *Wind Quintet* (1956), and a *String Sextet* (1964). Piston was also the author of such standard texts as *Principles of Harmonic Analysis* (1933), *Harmony* (1941), *Counterpoint* (1947), and *Orchestration* (1955). He died in Belmont, Mass., Nov. 12, 1976.

PORTER, COLE (1891–1964) Composer, lyricist. Born in Peru, Ind., June 9, 1891, Porter grew up on his father's 750-acre farm in comfortable surroundings. However, the bulk of Porter's expected wealth came from his maternal grandfather, J. O. Cole, who had become a millionaire by investing in timber and coal. Porter's mother saw to it that he had violin lessons at 6 and piano lessons at 8. One of his earliest compositions, *Bobolink Waltz* for solo piano, was published (at family expense) in 1902, when Porter was about 11. But Grandfather Cole could not visualize his grandson as an impractical musician and threatened to deny him his inheritance, which at the time amounted to more than $1 million. Porter began preparing for a career in the law. Although he did not give up music, Porter attended Worcester Academy (Mass.) and, in 1913, graduated from Yale with a B.A. in law and planned to do graduate work at Harvard. At Worcester Academy and at Yale, Porter was active in dramatics and in musical affairs; he was a member of the Whiffenpoofs and the Yale Glee Club. At Yale he wrote 2 songs still sung there: "Bingo Eli Yale" (1910) and "Bull Dog" (1911). After a year of law at Harvard, Porter, at the urging of the school's dean, transferred to the School of Music; precisely what Porter studied there is questionable, for he was busy writing songs and performing at the piano (he had acquired a reputation for writing very witty, often risqué, lyrics and for partying). With a fellow student, Porter wrote his first Broadway score, *See America First,* which opened in March 1916. Described by one newspaper critic as "the newest and worst musical in town," the show closed after 15 performances. Discouraged, Porter left for Europe the next year and settled in Paris. There being a war on, Porter attached himself to a relief organization; later he was with the American Aviation Headquarters and then, in April 1918, he joined the French Foreign Legion. A year later he was "stricken from Controls" and moved to Paris. He enrolled

in the Schola Cantorum and studied (composition, counterpoint, harmony, and orchestration) with Vincent d'Indy. For nearly a decade Porter lived in Europe; he had money and he spent the time amusing himself and his friends. He wrote witty, well-proportioned, and unusual songs. He married "the most beautiful woman in the world," a divorcée, Mrs. Linda Lee Thomas, in December 1919. She was even more wealthy than Porter. His way of life—travel to exotic places with friends; grand homes, including a palazzo in Venice; parties—did not commend Porter to producers looking for a songwriter to write a show score. But by chance Porter met producer Raymond Hitchcock on a ship and played some of his songs. Hitchcock signed Porter to do the songs for a show entitled *Hitchy-Koo of 1919,* in which Hitchcock also starred. The show was a success and one of the songs, "An Old-fashioned Garden," was popular. Porter then returned to his Paris-Riviera-Venice partying, although he continued to contribute songs to revues. In 1923 he composed a ballet, *Within the Quota* (q.v.), and even supplied a few songs to the Yale Dramatic Society's 1925 production *Out o' Luck.* He hit his stride in 1928 with a score for a Paris nightclub revue (which starred Frances Gershwin, sister of George and Ira, whose songs, at Porter's request, she sang). He then wrote the score for a New York show, *Paris,* whose score and success finally convinced the producers that Cole Porter was not a playboy dilettante. Porter left Paris for New York and began to write the scores for a series of successful (and, now and then, not successful) shows. Porter's words and music were exceptional, literate and musically polished, and though the word "sophisticated" (a term he eventually detested) was applied to his songs, they enjoyed great popularity among the not so sophisticated. Porter wrote the scores to more than 20 shows (plus several in London), 6 film scores, and one television musical. Among his outstanding scores were *Fifty Million Frenchmen* ("You've Got That Thing," "You Do Something to Me," 1929), *Wake Up and Dream,* in London and New York ("What Is This Thing Called Love?," "I'm a Gigolo," 1929), *The New Yorkers* ("Where Have You Been?," "Love for Sale," "I Happen to Like New York," 1930), *Gay Divorcee* ("After You, Who?," "Night and Day," 1932), *Nymph Errant,* in London ("Experiment," "The Physician," "It's Bad For Me," "How Could We Be Wrong?" 1933), *Anything Goes* ("I Get a Kick Out of You," "All Through the Night," "You're the Top," "Blow, Gabriel, Blow," "Anything Goes," 1934), *Jubilee* ("Begin the Beguine," "Why Shouldn't I?," "Just One of Those Things," 1935), *Red, Hot and Blue!* ("Down in the Depths, on the Ninetieth Floor," "It's De-Lovely," "Ridin' High," 1936), *Leave It to Me* ("Get Out of Town," "My Heart Belongs to Daddy," 1938), *DuBarry Was a Lady* ("Do I Love You, Do I?," "Well, Did You Evah!," "Friendship," 1939), *Panama Hattie* ("Let's Be Buddies," "Make It Another Old-Fashioned, Please," 1940), *Let's Face It* ("Ev'rything I Love," "You Irritate Me So," "Let's Not Talk About Love," 1941), *Something for the Boys* ("Could It Be You?," 1943), *Mexican Hayride* ("I Love You," 1944), *Seven Lively Arts* ("Ev'ry Time We Say Goodbye," "Only Another Boy and Girl," 1944), *Kiss Me, Kate* ("Why Can't You Behave?," "So in Love," "Wunderbar," "I Hate Men," "Brush Up Your Shakespeare," 1948), *Out of This World* ("Use Your Imagination," "Where, Oh, Where?," "No Lover for Me," 1950), *Can-Can* ("Never Give Anything Away," "C'est Magnifique," "I Am in Love," "It's All Right with Me," "I Love Paris," 1953), and *Silk Stockings* ("Paris Loves Lovers," "All of You,"

"Without Love," 1955). Porter's screen scores include, besides adaptations of his Broadway musicals, *Born to Dance* ("Easy to Love," "I've Got You Under My Skin," 1936), *Rosalie* ("Rosalie," "In the Still of the Night," 1937), *Broadway Melody of 1940* ("I Concentrate on You," "I've Got My Eyes on You," 1940), *You'll Never Get Rich* ("So Near and Yet So Far," "Dream Dancing," 1941), *Something to Shout About* ("You'd Be So Nice to Come Home To," 1942), *The Pirate* ("Love of My Life," "Be a Clown," 1948), *High Society* ("You're Sensational," "True Love," "I Love You, Samantha," "Now You Has Jazz," 1956), and *Les Girls* ("You're Just Too, Too!," "Ca, C'est l'Amour," 1957). Porter composed a score for television in 1958, *Aladdin,* with such songs as "I Adore You" and "Come to the Supermarket in Old Peking." It was his last effort. Porter's last years were marked by pain and misery— and the miracle that he accomplished anything at all. In the summer of 1937 he suffered a riding accident in which his horse fell, crushing both of Porter's legs and damaging his nervous system. This was further complicated by chronic osteomyelitis (a bone infection) that necessitated some 30 operations over a period of 20 years. In 1958 his right leg was amputated, after which he no longer wrote songs, saw only a few close friends, and suffered greatly from depression and deteriorating health. His alma mater Yale conferred a doctor of humane letters degree upon Porter in 1960 in a precedent-breaking ceremony; the Yale committee came to Porter, then living in the Waldorf Towers, New York, to present the degree. From that time on, Porter spent his time in and out of hospitals or in near-seclusion in his various homes in New York, in the Berkshires, or, finally, in California. He died after surgery for the removal of a kidney stone; his weakened condition and a bladder infection were the causes of death. Porter died in Santa Monica, Calif., Oct. 15, 1964.

PORTER, QUINCY (1897–1966) Composer, teacher. Born in New Haven, Conn., Feb. 7, 1897, Porter came from old New England stock. His father was a minister and a professor at the Yale Divinity School. Porter, however, chose the School of Music and, after study with Horatio Parker (q.v.) and David Stanley Smith (q.v.), graduated in 1921. He then went to Paris, where he studied with Vincent d'Indy. Back in the United States, he earned his way as a violinist in a theatre orchestra and studied with Ernest Bloch (q.v.). When his teacher moved on to the Cleveland Institute of Music, Porter accompanied him (along with another student, Roger Sessions, q.v.) to serve as an assistant. He left for a period of about 3 years (1928–31) to return to Paris for further study on a Guggenheim grant. He returned to Cleveland in 1931 and taught again; he also played the viola in the De Ribaupierre Quartet. Porter moved on to Poughkeepsie, N.Y., where he began teaching at Vassar in 1932; in 1938 he joined the staff of the New England Conservatory, Boston. He became professor of music at Yale in 1946 and remained there until his retirement in 1965. As a composer Porter is generally grouped with the traditionalists, with a special skill in writing for strings —he composed no less than 10 string quartets. His orchestral output includes 2 symphonies (1934, 1962), a *Ukrainian Suite* for strings (1925), *Suite in C Minor* (1926), *Poem and Dance* (1932), *Two Dances for Radio* (1938), *Music for Strings* (1941), *A Moving Tide* (1944), a *Viola Concerto* (1948), *Concerto Concertante* for 2 pianos and orchestra (1953), *New England Episodes* (1958), *Concerto for Harpsichord and Orchestra* (1959), and *Concerto for*

Wind Instruments (1959). Porter composed a *Piano Sonata* in 1930, 2 sonatas for violin and piano (1926, 1929), a *Quintet in One Movement* on a theme from childhood for flute and strings (1940), a *Duo* for violin and viola (1954), a *Divertimento* for woodwind quintet, and a *Quintet for Oboe and Strings,* "Elegiac," Porter's last-completed major work (1966). He died in Bethany, Conn., Nov. 12, 1966.

"POTTED PALM" ORCHESTRA A small band, often only a string trio, that provided music in the better hotels and restaurants during the early years of the 20th century and the '20s. The name derives from the standard lobby decorations, small palms in pots, which often discreetly hid the musicians. The musical fare was generally made up of genteel popular period songs, waltzes, etc., performed in a nonobtrusive manner. Potted palm music was dominated by the lead violin and was quite bland and unexciting. The term was applied to this type of music. See also Dance Band.

POUND, EZRA See *Le Testament de Villon.*

RACE RECORD A phonograph recording manufactured specifically for the black market. The first, according to historians, was Mamie Smith's "Crazy Blues," recorded by the Okeh Recording Company in August 1920. The financial success of the recording encouraged the birth of other recording companies, some of which specialized in race records. Many of the great blues singers and jazz musicians made these records, several of which became collector's items. Among the early race record stars were Bessie Smith (q.v.), Ma Rainey, Chippie Hill, Louis Armstrong (q.v.), James P. Johnson (q.v.), and Fletcher Henderson (q.v.). Although the practice of separate black and white catalogs continued into the '30s, many vocalists and musicians who began on race records—for example, Ethel Waters and such bands as Duke Ellington's (q.v.) and Cab Calloway's—easily made the transition from race to standard popular records.

"RAMONA" Popular song, music by Mabel Wayne (q.v.), lyrics by L. Wolfe Gilbert, published in 1927. One of the year's most popular songs, "Ramona" was the movie "theme song" associated with the silent film of the same title. During this early period of the talkies it was common practice to provide new films, whether musicals or not, with a theme song. "Ramona" was contrived by a publicity man who thought a theme song based on the name of the film's heroine would help promote a generally not well-received film. The song's popularity contributed to the eventual success of the film. "Ramona" remained popular for several years after the film was forgotten. The song was also associated with *Ramona*'s star, Dolores Del Rio.

REVUE A variety show that had evolved out of burlesque and vaudeville and which reached a peak in the 1920s and '30s. A nonbook show, a revue was basically a collection of assorted "acts" that might range from a beauty pageant to rough-and-tumble comics. Music and songs were not always the major components of the revue; when the form assumed its classic form and its pinnacle with the Ziegfeld Follies (q.v.) in the middle '20s, the songwriter, however important his contribution to the total effect, was superseded in importance by beautiful, rather undraped show girls, lavish settings and costumes, comedians, and dancers—even the vocalists who sang their songs. Without plot, the revue had to entertain with fast-moving skits, spectacle, and the exposure, or, as Ziegfeld put it, "glorification" of the American girl. Although the *Follies* had been around since 1907, it wasn't until the 1919 production that the latency of the

form was recognized and its potential for lavish moneymaking was appreciated. With the 1930 edition, the *Follies* became, by a press agent's admission, "A National Institution." It had songs by Irving Berlin and Victor Herbert; two great comics, Fanny Brice and W. C. Fields; and, for a touch of art, dancer Mary Eaton. Imitations, not so lavish perhaps, but with the same ingredients of girls, comedians, skits, songs, and dances, soon followed with the *George White's Scandals* in 1919, and the *Earl Carroll Vanities* in 1923. More modest, and often more pointed in their social point of view, were the *Greenwich Village Follies,* which began in 1919, and the *Grand Street Follies,* which began production in 1924. These more politically oriented shows reached a high point in the *First Little Show* (q.v.) of 1929, by which time, with the coming of the Great Depression, the lavish era of the revue was ended. Revue writers then tended more toward commenting on the social scene and not depending upon the scenery and girls. The tone was set for the political operettas that materialized in the '30s and for the left-wing revues of the same period.

"RHAPSODY IN BLUE" Musical composition for piano and "jazz band" (i.e., Paul Whiteman's, q.v., augmented orchestra) by George Gershwin (q.v.), performed for the first time at New York's Aeolian Hall, Feb. 12, 1924. The work was "commissioned" by Whiteman by newspaper announcement. Whiteman had been impressed with Gershwin since he performed in the pit of a *George White's Scandals* (1922) and conducted Gershwin's one-act opera *Blue Monday* (q.v.). Gershwin and Whiteman had spoken about writing a piece employing the popular features that were considered as jazz, but the subject was dropped until late in 1923, when Whiteman planned a concert of "jazz" in a concert hall. Word then came to him that another "jazz" bandleader was planning the same thing. Whiteman quickly announced in the papers that he was advancing the date of his concert to Feb. 12, 1924, and that Gershwin was at work composing "a jazz concerto" for the concert. Gershwin read of this in a newspaper dated Jan. 4. He was not at that moment working on such a composition. Whiteman ultimately convinced Gershwin that he could produce something in the little over a month remaining and, after they compromised on a rhapsodic piece rather than the more formal concerto, Gershwin began working on his 2-piano version on Jan. 7. The work was then orchestrated for the Whiteman band by his arranger-orchestrator Ferde Grofé (q.v.); the score contains some suggestions by Gershwin. The *Rhapsody in Blue*—the title was the suggestion of brother Ira Gershwin (Gershwin's original was *American Rhapsody*)—was completed in time for the Aeolian Hall concert except for a few pages in the solo piano score, which Gershwin improvised during the concert. The work was the hit of the concert and launched Gershwin, despite critical carpings, as a "serious" composer. Its success led to a repeat of the concert at Carnegie Hall (Whiteman's original choice for the concert) in March, with the composer again at the piano. The *Rhapsody*, which combines popular jazzisms with Lisztian pianistics and a touch of Tchaikovskian melody, has proved to be one of Gershwin's most enduring compositions. Although he orchestrated all of his later concert works, he did not interfere with Grofé's orchestration. When it was prepared for a full symphonic orchestra in 1926, it was Grofé who did the work. This is the version most heard today.

RIEGGER, WALLINGFORD (1885–1961) Composer, cellist, conductor, teacher. Born in Albany, Ga., Apr. 29, 1885, Riegger grew up in a musical family; his mother was a pianist and his father a violinist as well as conductor of their church choir. Riegger began studying the violin and later the cello before going on to Cornell, from which he switched to the Institute of Musical Art (later Juilliard), New York, in 1905. He studied composition with Goetschius (q.v.) and, after graduation in 1907, went to Berlin, where he studied further with Edgar Stillman Kelley (q.v.), Max Bruch, and Anton Hekking. He returned to the United States in 1910 and found work as a cellist in the St. Paul Symphony, but returned again to Germany in 1913 to conduct opera in Würzburg and Königsberg and an orchestra in Berlin; he left in 1917, just before the United States declared war on Germany. Riegger, who had not yet decided to make his way as a composer, took teaching positions at Drake University, Iowa, and at the Ithaca Conservatory, New York. In the late '20s he returned to New York City, where he taught in several institutions: Teachers College, Columbia University, New School for Social Research, Metropolitan Music School. Riegger began composing ca. 1918, while he was teaching at Drake, and the work reflected the solid, conventional, musical background of his early training. But some time after the mid-'20s, after he had met such musical pioneers as Varèse (q.v.) and especially his own countrymen Cowell, Ives, and Ruggles (all q.v.), Riegger's original work took an adventurous turn. In his *Study in Sonority* (1927) for 10 violins (or any multiple of 10), Riegger hit his stride. During the '30s he allied himself with leading contemporary choreographers and produced several striking modern dance scores for such dancers as Martha Graham, Hanya Holm, Charles Weidman, and Doris Humphrey. Besides teaching and composing on commission (whenever possible), Riegger augmented his income by working for several music publishers as editor and arranger. This work was done under various pseudonyms, among them John H. McCurdy (his mother's family name), Gerald Wilfring Gore, Edgar Long and Leonard Gregg. Under these and several other pen names, Riegger produced hundreds of arrangements for various instrumental combinations and chorus. In his own work he began to adapt the Schoenbergian principles of the 12-tone technique. The compositions in this style are not mere imitations of the great Austrian theorist but Riegger's masterly manipulation of the techniques. Unassuming, soft-spoken, witty, and blessed with a delightful sense of humor, Riegger, despite his stature as composer (his worth was generally recognized by fellow composers) remained little known in his lifetime. He genuinely avoided the limelight, refused to seek publicity, and remained aloof from the political contentions of the musical world. Nonetheless, he was awarded with commissions and prizes: Paderewski (1922), Coolidge (1924), and the Brandeis Creative Arts Award (1961). His *Third Symphony* (1947) won the New York Music Critics' Circle Award in 1948. Riegger completed his *Fourth Symphony* in 1957. His other works include a *Trio in B Minor* for violin, cello, and piano (1920), *La Belle Dame sans Merci* (1923), *American Polonaise,* "Triple Jazz" for orchestra (1923), *Rhapsody* for orchestra (1925), *Fantasy and Fugue* for organ and orchestra (1931), *Dance Suite* for orchestra or band (1937), *Canon and Fugue* for strings (1939), *Passacaglia and Fugue* for strings (1942), *Music for Brass Choir* (1949), *Piano Quintet* (1951), *Nonet for Brass* (1952), *Woodwind Quintet* (1952), *Concerto for Piano and Woodwind Quintet* (1952), *Variations for Piano and Orchestra* (1953), *Dance Rhythms* for orchestra (1955), *Movement* for 2 trumpets,

trombone, and piano (1957), *Festival Overture* (1957), *Variations for Violin and Orchestra* (1959), and *Duo for Piano and Orchestra* (1960). Among Riegger's most important chamber works are *Dichotomy* for 14 instruments (1932) and the ballet score *New Dance* (1935) for piano and 12 instruments; also for full orchestra (1944). There are also 3 string quartets (1939, 1947, 1948), several choral works, and numerous study pieces. Riegger died, just a month short of his 76th birthday, after a street accident (he was tripped by a dog's leash, fell, and struck his head); his death occurred in New York City, Apr. 2, 1961.

ROBERTS, CHARLES LUCKEYETH "LUCKY"   (1893?–1968) Pianist, composer, entertainer. Born in Philadelphia, Pa., Aug. 7, 1893 (or 1887, or 1895), Roberts became an actor around the age of 3, when he became a member of an *Uncle Tom's Cabin* company. He toured in vaudeville as a boy tumbler, traveling to Europe 3 times in his childhood. He took up the piano when he was around 5 and began playing professionally in vaudeville, even while teaching himself the instrument. He quickly developed a distinctive playing style— many regard him as one of the pioneers of Harlem stride piano (q.v.), who influenced James P. Johnson, "Willie the Lion" Smith and the other great Harlem pianists who followed him. After traveling the vaudeville circuits of Newark, Baltimore, and Philadelphia, Roberts settled in New York City around 1910. He then studied music formally with black teachers Eloise Smith and Melville Charlton. His first popular composition was the *Junk Man Rag* (1913), which was followed by *Pork and Beans,* another rag, in the same year. Others include *Music Box Rag* (1914), *Palm Beach* (1914), *Shy and Sly* (1915), *Helter Skelter* (1915), and the intricate *Ripples* *of the Nile,* which, in slower tempo and with words by Kim Gannon, was transformed into the popular "Moonlight Cocktail" in 1941. Roberts collaborated on several songs and, in the '20s, the scores for Broadway musicals: *Go! Go!* (1923), *Charlie* (1923), and *My Magnolia* (1928), none of which achieved much success. It was as a pianist-performer that Roberts was most successful; during the '20s he became the darling of society and frequently led his band at "exclusive" parties in Newport or Palm Beach or on Park Avenue. (In 1949, it might be noted, Roberts wrote a *Park Avenue Polka.*) Roberts was a prodigious pianist who composed many brilliant piano pieces, including such concert works as *Whistlin' Pete,* a "Miniature Syncopated Rhapsody for Piano and Orchestra" (ca. 1939), and a *Spanish Suite* ("Spanish Venus," "Spanish Fandango," "Porto Rico Maid") also for piano and orchestra, composed in the late '30s. Despite an auto accident that crushed his hands, Roberts continued to play in his own Rendezvous Bar in Harlem well into the '50s. He died in New York City, Feb. 5, 1968.

ROBERTSON, LEROY (1896–1971) Composer, teacher. Born in Fountain Green, Utah, Dec. 21, 1896, Robertson first made music on a home made violin and taught himself to play the family's parlor organ. He took music lessons later and, while still in grammar school, formed a small band to play his own early compositions. He heard much traditional Mormon music while spending some of his high school years living with his grandparents in Pleasant Grove, Utah. A graduate of Brigham Young University, Provo, Utah, Robertson took further music study at the New England Conservatory in 1923, where one of his teachers was George W. Chadwick (q.v.). He later studied with Ernest Bloch (q.v.) in San Francisco and with Ernst Toch in Los Angeles. His studies in Europe were done with Roveredo Capriasca (Switzerland) and Hugo Leichtentritt (Berlin). In 1925 Robertson returned to join the music staff of Brigham Young University, where he remained until 1948 as professor of music and finally chairman of the Music Department. He then moved to the University of Utah, Salt Lake City, where he was also professor, then chairman and composer-in-residence. An authority on the music of the Mormons, Robertson drew upon their music for his original compositions; he was also familiar with the music of the American Indians, notably in his *Violin Concerto.* Robertson's work was first recognized when his *Overture in E Minor* (1923) was awarded the Endicott Prize. His chamber music includes a *Quintet in A Minor* (1933), *Quartet in E Minor* (1940), and *American Serenade* for string quartet (1944). For orchestra he composed the prizewinning ($25,000) *Trilogy* (1948) as well as *Prelude, Scherzo and Ricercare* (1941), *Rhapsody* for piano and orchestra (1944), the *Punch and Judy Overture* (1945), and the *Violin Concerto* (1949). His choral setting of the *Lord's Prayer* (1939) was widely performed. Robertson's major achievement is the oratorio from *The Book of Mormon* (1953). He died in Salt Lake City, July 25, 1971.

RODGERS AND HART Outstanding songwriting team of Richard Rodgers (q.v.) and Lorenz Hart (q.v.), whose show songs were characterized by literate, witty, and often tricky poetic lyrics and suave, well-fashioned melodies and sprightly rhythms. Rodgers and Hart first collaborated in 1919 and worked on their first full-scale musical in 1920 (*Poor Little Ritz Girl*). Their last collaboration was on the revival of *A Connecticut Yankee* in 1943 (when Rodgers had begun his collaboration with Oscar Hammerstein II). Rodgers and Hart collaborated on more than 30 musicals and films (mostly musicals, produced in New York and London). Their collaboration resulted in what is generally called a "Rodgers and Hart" song, invoking such efforts as "Manhattan," "Dancing on the Ceiling," "Glad to Be Unhappy," "Thou Swell," "My Funny Valentine," "Bewitched, Bothered, and Bewildered," etc., etc.

RODGERS, RICHARD (1902–1979) Composer. Born in New York City, June 28, 1902, Rodgers grew up in comfortable surroundings (his father was a physician) which afforded him music lessons and the opportunity to go to the theatre and opera. He attended public schools in New York City and later Columbia University and the Institute of Musical Art (1921–23), which is now the Juilliard School. Rodgers was a student at Columbia when he was introduced by librettist Herbert Fields to a Columbia dropout, Lorenz "Larry" Hart (q.v.). Rodgers had written songs for several amateur productions, including one, *Up Stage and Down* (1919), some of whose songs had lyrics by Oscar Hammerstein II (q.v.), also a Columbia student. In 1920, with *You'd Be Surprised,* "An Atrocious Musical," and *Fly with Me,* a Columbia Varsity show, Rodgers and Hart began their long, fruitful collaboration. Their first Broadway production, done in the same year, was a mildly successful *Poor Little Ritz Girl.* Typical of Hart's way with words was the title of the song "Love's Intense in Tents." The team then had a lean period, ca. 1920–24, when they had little luck in placing their songs; Rodgers contemplated leaving the business for a career as a salesman. They agreed to do the songs for a fund-raising show for the Theatre Guild entitled *The Garrick Gaieties,* which opened for a limited run on May 17, 1925—and ran for a total of 211 performances. A revue, it was made up of sketches, songs, and dances. The song that attracted the most attention was Rodgers and Hart's "Manhattan." Even while *The Garrick Gaieties* was still running a second show, *Dearest Enemy* opened and enjoyed an even longer run (286 performances). Its most interesting song was "Here in My Arms." A 2nd *Garrick Gaieties* followed the next year (out of which came "Mountain Greenery"), as did 3 other shows and one London production. From then until Hart's death in 1943, the team of Rodgers and Hart was one of the most prolific, successful, and admired songwriting combinations in the musical theatre and film. Among their later, most significant, often groundbreaking shows were *A Connecticut Yankee* ("My Heart Stood Still," "Thou Swell," 1927), the London production of *Ever Green* ("Dancing on the Ceiling," 1930), *Jumbo* ("The Most Beautiful Girl in the World," "My Romance, "Little Girl Blue," 1935), *On Your Toes* ("It's Got to Be Love," "There's a Small Hotel," "Quiet Night," "Glad to Be Unhappy," the ballet *Slaughter on Tenth Avenue,* 1936), *Babes in Arms* ("Where or When," "My Funny Valentine," "Johnny One Note," 1937), *I'd Rather Be Right* ("Have You Met Miss Jones?" 1937), *I Married an Angel* ("Did You Ever Get Stung?," "I Married an Angel," "Spring Is Here," 1938), *The Boys from Syracuse* ("Falling in Love with Love," "This Can't Be Love," "The Shortest Day of the Year," "You Have Cast Your Shadow on the Sea," 1938), *Too Many Girls* ("I Like to Recognize the Tune," "I Didn't Know What Time It Was," 1939), *Pal Joey* ("I Could Write a Book," "Bewitched," "Zip," 1940), and *By Jupiter* ("Nobody's Heart," "Ev'rything I've Got," "Wait Till You See Her," 1942). Many of these musicals were transformed into films of varying success. Rodgers and Hart composed songs for several original films: *Love Me*

Tonight ("Mimi," "Lover," "Isn't It Romantic?," 1932), *The Phantom President* (1932), *Hallelujah, I'm a Bum* ("You Are Too Beautiful," 1933), and *Mississippi* ("Soon," "Easy to Remember," 1935). Hart was still alive when Rodgers, forced by Hart's unwillingness to work, formed a collaboration with Oscar Hammerstein II. Beginning with *Oklahoma!* (1943), Rodgers and Hammerstein turned out the scores for 9 musicals, the bulk of them highly successful financially and artistically. Outstanding were *Oklahoma!*, which initiated a new trend in musicals, skillfully blending song, dance, plot, and ballet; *Carousel* (1945), *South Pacific* (1949), *The King and I* (1951), and *The Sound of Music* (1959). During their partnership Rodgers and Hammerstein also produced plays and musicals (notably Irving Berlin's *Annie Get Your Gun*) by others. They also collaborated on the songs for the film *State Fair* ("It's a Grand Night for Singing," "It Might as Well Be Spring," 1945) and a television musical, *Cinderella* ("In My Own Little Corner," "Ten Minutes Ago," 1957). After Hammerstein's death in 1960 Rodgers did words and music for the musical *No Strings* (1962) and collaborated on *Do I Hear a Waltz?* (Stephen Sondheim, 1965), *Two by Two* (Martin Charnin, 1970), *Rex* (Sheldon Harnick, 1976), and *I Remember Mama* (Charnin, 1979). Rodgers has written for orchestra also: the ballet *Ghost Town* (1939) was presented at the Metropolitan Opera; *Victory at Sea* (notably orchestrated by Robert Russell Bennett) was written for a 26-episode television series that ran in 1952–53. *Winston Churchill: The Valiant Years,* also a 26-episode series, with background scoring by Rodgers, was orginally shown in 1960. Rodgers' autobiography (written with the aid of Stanley Green), *Musical Stages,* was published in 1975. Rodgers died in New York City, Dec. 30, 1979.

ROMBERG, SIGMUND (1887–1951) Composer, conductor. Born in Nagykanizsa, Hungary, July 29, 1887, Romberg, though he studied music as a youngster, was a graduate engineer when he arrived in the United States in 1909. Unable to find work as an engineer, Romberg took jobs as a pianist in a Hungarian restaurant; in this way he drifted out of engineering and into the musical theatre. In 1913, having acquired a kind of musical reputation in New York, he was hired as staff composer by the Shubert organization. Romberg's first scores for the Shuberts were the revues *The Whirl of the World, Dancing Around,* and *The Passing Show of 1914* (all produced in 1914). Romberg composed some 40 scores for the Shuberts, many of them revues, but the most successful were in the genre in which Romberg was a master: operetta. He hit his stride with *Maytime* (one of the 3 shows he did in 1917), with lyrics by Rida Johnson Young; the score is best remembered for the song "Will You Remember?" *Blossom Time* (lyrics by Dorothy Donnelly, 1921) was based on the life—and the music—of Franz Schubert (a theme from the *Unfinished Symphony* is heard as "Song of Love"). *The Student Prince* (lyrics by Donnelly, 1924) had such songs as "Deep in My Heart, Dear," "The Drinking Song," and "Serenade." Other successful Romberg operettas include *The Desert Song* (lyrics by Otto Harbach and Oscar Hammerstein II, 1926), for which they collaborated on "The Desert Song," "The Riff Song," and "One Alone"; *The New Moon* (lyrics by Hammerstein, 1928), whose songs included "Softly, As in a Morning Sunrise," "Stout Hearted Men," "One Kiss," "Wanting You," and "Lover, Come Back to Me"; *Up in Central Park* (lyrics by Dorothy Fields, 1945), from which came "The Big Back Yard," "It Doesn't Cost You Anything to Dream," and "Close As Pages in a

Book." Romberg's last complete Broadway score (lyrics by Rowland Leigh) was *My Romance* (1948); it was not very successful. A posthumous score, with lyrics by Leo Robin, was produced in 1954. This was *The Girl in Pink Tights* (based on the story of how *The Black Crook*, q.v., was produced); it was not a success either, although it had some excellent music and a very good, typical Romberg melody in "Lost in Loveliness." In his later years, after the demand for the operetta type of musical had waned, Romberg conducted a large orchestra on his radio show "An Evening with Romberg." Although his type of musical had gone out of style, his songs remained popular, and his early operettas are frequently revived. Romberg also toured with his orchestra, presenting concerts of his songs as well as the songs of other theatre and operetta songwriters. He composed a few songs for films while he was a resident of Beverly Hills. His most notable original film score was composed for *The Girl of the Golden West* (1938), with lyrics by Gus Kahn, and such songs as "Senorita," "Soldiers of Fortune," "Who Are We to Say?" and "Shadows on the Moon." Romberg died in New York City, Nov. 9, 1951.

"ROSE-MARIE" An operettalike musical with music by Rudolf Friml and Herbert Stothart and book and lyrics by Otto Harbach and Oscar Hammerstein II. Opening on Sept. 2, 1924, *Rose-Marie* ran for 557 performances, was filmed several times (notably in 1936 and 1954), and has had countless revivals. With a Canadian setting, *Rose-Marie*'s 2nd hero is a Mountie who is out to capture a murderer (an unusual character in a musical at the time). The suspect is the hero, a trapper, who is in love with the heroine of the title. The secondary complication is the Mountie's infatuation with Rose-Marie. But all

works out and the real murderer is captured by the Mountie and the lovers are united for the finale. The score was finely integrated with the plot, although some songs became popular on their own: "Rose-Marie" (music by Friml), "Indian Love Call" (Friml), and "Totem Tom Tom" (music by Friml and Stothart). The original stars were Mary Ellis as Rose-Marie, Dennis King as the trapper, Jim, and Arthur Deagon as the Mountie.

ROSENFELD, PAUL (1890–1946) Music critic, writer. Born in New York City, May 4, 1890, he was brought up by his maternal grandmother after the death of his mother in 1900. His father was successful as a small manufacturer who collected books; Rosenfeld's mother had been a fine pianist. At 13, Rosenfeld entered the Riverview Military Academy, Poughkeepsie, N.Y., after which he went to Yale, where he began writing criticism for a local paper and the *Yale Lit.* He then did graduate work at the Columbia School of Journalism. Graduation led to newspaper work, which, after 6 months, Rosenfeld gave up to take a trip to Europe. He had decided not to work at anything he did not enjoy. Upon returning to New York City, Rosenfeld started to write a novel and to immerse himself in the cultural ferment then beginning to flourish in the city. This was the new art of John Marin and Georgia O'Keeffe and, especially, the new music of such new composers as Leo Ornstein, Ernest Bloch, and Stravinsky (all q.v.). Rosenfeld wrote about Arnold Schoenberg (q.v.) as early as 1916. Rosenfeld made himself an important figure in the arts by the beginning of the '20s. He discovered young composers and wrote about them in such publications as *Seven Arts, The New Republic,* and *The Dial,* as well as more popular magazines, *Vanity Fair* and *Arts & Decoration.* He also wrote for *Modern Music* and *Musical Quarterly.* He himself first came to gen-

eral attention with the publication of a collection of essays entitled *Musical Portraits* in 1920. This was followed by *Musical Chronicle* (*1917–23*), *Port of New York: Essays on Fourteen American Moderns* (1924), *Men Seen* (1925), *Modern Tendencies in Music* (1927), *By Way of Art* (1928), *Boy in the Sun* (1928), *An Hour with American Music* (1929), and *Discoveries of a Music Critic* (1936). It might be noted that Rosenfeld did not confine his views to music; he also wrote on literature and art (including sculpture and photography). Opinionated, even prejudiced, Rosenfeld made no claim of objectivity. He was a powerful advocate in print for those whose works he admired and disparaged those he did not favor. He was a faithful friend and often, through his connections with the wealthy, obtained commissions or financial assistance for young struggling artists. Unfortunately, after the Depression had ruined Rosenfeld, he spent his last years struggling himself. He did not lose his enthusiasm, however, for modern American music and was planning 2 books, one of them a critical biography of Charles Ives, when he was stricken by a heart attack. Rosenfeld died in New York City, July 21, 1946.

RUBY, HARRY (1895–1974) Composer. Born in New York City, Jan. 27, 1895, Ruby was largely self-taught as a pianist, although he had a few lessons as a boy. After graduating from high school he worked for a while in the business world (his real ambition was to play professional baseball). He found work as a pianist in the publishing houses of Gus Edwards and Harry Von Tilzer. He also played the piano in vaudeville as a member of the Messenger Boys Trio and the Bootblack Trio. It was during this vaudeville period that Ruby met another vaudevillian, Bert Kalmar (q.v.), with whom he formed one of the most suc-

cessful songwriting teams. Both had written songs with other collaborators before their meeting, Ruby as early as 1917 (with Edgar Leslie) and Kalmar even earlier. But it was as a team that Kalmar and Ruby did their best on Broadway and, from 1930, in Hollywood. Their most popular songs were "Who's Sorry Now?," "All Alone Monday," "Thinking of You," "I Wanna Be Loved by You," "Three Little Words," "Nevertheless," "Hooray for Captain Spaulding," and "I Love You So Much." After the death of Kalmar, Ruby produced very little, although he wrote an occasional film song and the lyrics for the songs in *Carnival in Costa Rica* (music by Ernesto Lecuona, 1947) and the song "Blue (With You or Without You)," music by Alfred Newman, for the film *Pinky* (1949). Ruby also composed the theme music for the television show "The Real McCoys." He died in Los Angeles, Calif., Feb. 23, 1974.

RUDHYAR, DANE (b. 1895) Composer, author, poet, painter. Born Daniel Chennevière-Rudyard, in Paris, France Mar. 23, 1895, Rudhyar graduated from the Sorbonne (1911) with a degree in philosophy. Although he also studied at the Paris Conservatory, Rudhyar was largely self-taught in music. An essay on the music of Debussy brought him to the attention of a French music publisher, who issued some of Rudhyar's early piano compositions. In 1916 Rudhyar came to New York to oversee the performance of 2 of his ballet scores at the Metropolitan in 1917; he then decided to remain in the United States and eventually became a citizen. He became a leading figure in the avant-garde music of the American '20s. Rejecting the rules of Western music, Rudhyar produced compositions of rather vague tonality and form. Besides composing, Rudhyar has written on philosophical subjects and writes poetry and lectures; he has pro-

duced several books outlining the "humanistic approach to astro-psychology." As a composer he was most active during the '20s, when his works were frequently performed, especially by the groups associated with Henry Cowell (q.v.) and Charles Ives (q.v.—it was Ives who helped toward the publication of Rudhyar's music in the New Music, q.v., Editions). His works include *Three Melodies for Flute, Cello, and Piano* (1919), several *Tetragrams* for solo piano (1920–67), 5 *Syntonies* for orchestra (1920–54), *Paeans* for piano (1927), and *Granites* for piano (1932). His major orchestral works include *The Surge of Fire* (1921), *To the Real* (1923), *Ouranos* (1924), *First Symphony* (1928), *Five Stanzas* (1928), *Two Tripthongs* (1919), *Hero Chants* (1930), and *Sinfonietta* (1931). After a long period of giving up music for writing and painting, Rudhyar again turned to composition late in the '70s. In 1978 he was the recipient of the Marjorie Peabody Waite Award, presented by the American Academy and Institute of Arts and Letters.

RUGGLES, CARL (1876–1971) Composer, conductor, teacher. Born in Marion, Mass., Mar. 11, 1876, Ruggles began the study of music on a home-made violin. In his teens he went to Boston, where he earned a living playing in a theatre orchestra and studied with Josef Claus, Walter Spalding, and, at Harvard, with John Knowles Paine (q.v.). He then moved on to Winona, Minn., where he founded a symphony orchestra which he led from 1912 to 1917. In 1922 he joined forces with Edgard Varèse (q.v.) and was active in the International Composers' Guild and the Pan-American Association of Composers. For 10 years, beginning in 1937, Ruggles taught at the University of Miami. He eventually moved to Ver-

mont, where he lived and worked in a converted schoolhouse. Flinty, crusty, and totally independent as artist and man, Ruggles literally spent years on the handful of compositions he finally completed (and some of these were worked and reworked until he was fully satisfied). Ruggles was fortunate in that a patron, Harriette Miller, made it possible for him and his wife to live comfortably while he slowly wrote or painted. His *Men and Angels*, originally dating from ca. 1920, was eventually scrapped and portions salvaged for 3 other works, among them *Men and Mountains* (1924) and *Angels* (1921). His other compositions include *Toys* for voice and orchestra (1919), *Vox Clamans in Deserto* for voice and orchestra (1925), *Portals* for string orchestra (1927), *Suntreader* (1927–28), *Polyphonic Composition for Three Pianos* (1940), *Evocations: Four Chants for Piano* (1945), and *Organum* for orchestra (1947). In 1963 Ruggles was elected to the National Institute of Arts and Letters. Three years later he entered a nursing home (his wife had died in 1957) in Bennington, Vt.; he died there Oct. 24, 1971.

SAMINSKY, LAZARE (1882–1959) Composer, conductor, author, lecturer. Born near Odessa, Russia, Oct. 27, 1882, Saminsky studied philosophy and mathematics at the University of St. Petersburg, while studying music at the St. Petersburg Conservatory. One of his instructors in composition and orchestration was Nikolai Rimski-Korsakov. In Russia, Saminsky also made studies of folk song, conducted, and was director of the Tiflis Conservatory. He came to the United States in 1920, settling in New York, where he was most active in the city's musical life for several years. Saminsky was one of the founders of the League of Composers (q.v.). Beginning

in 1924, he was music director for Temple Emanu-El, New York City, where, in 1936, he began the annual Three Choirs Festival. An authority on Eastern music, Saminsky composed much liturgical music, some of it based on Jewish themes. His works include 5 symphonies (1914, 1918, 1924, 1926, 1930), *Ausonia: Italian Pages* (1930), *To a New World* (1932), *Three Shadows* (1935), *Pueblo, a Moon Rhapsody* (1936), *Stilled Pageant* (1937), *The Vow*, concerto for piano and orchestra (1943), *East and West*, suite for violin and orchestra (1943). For chamber orchestras Saminsky wrote *Venice* for 10 instruments (1927), a *Chassidic Suite* for violin or cello and orchestra (1937), and a *Rye Septet* with voice. Saminsky's choral compositions include *By the Rivers of Babylon* for soprano, baritone, chorus, and 4 instruments (1926), *Psalm 93* for soprano, chorus, clarinet, piano, and percussionist (1933), *Newfoundland Air* for chorus and piano (1935), *Requiem* for soloists, chorus, and orchestra (1945), and *A Song Treasury of Old Israel* for voice and piano (1951). Saminsky's books include *Jewish Music, Past and Present* (1914), *Music of Our Day* (1932, rev. 1939), *Music of the Ghetto and the Bible* (1934), *Living Music of the Americas* (1949), and *Physics and Metaphysics of Music and Essays on the Philosophy of Mathematics* (1957). Saminsky died in Port Chester, N.Y., June 30, 1959.

SEEGER, CHARLES (1886–1979) Musicologist, composer, teacher. Born in Mexico City, Mexico, Dec. 14, 1886, Seeger majored in music at Harvard, from which he graduated in 1908. He went to Germany for further study and settled briefly in Cologne, where he served on the conducting staff of the Cologne Opera. While he wished to compose, Seeger was also deeply interested in musicology and became a pioneer in American scientific music study. A hearing problem caused him eventually to give up composition and to concentrate on musicology. Upon his return from Germany he joined the staff of the University of California at Berkeley (1912–19), where he taught the first course in musicology given in the United States. He later lectured at the Institute of Musical Art and its successor, the Juilliard School of Music (1921–33), and at the New School for Social Research, New York (1931–35). During the Depression, Seeger served as a technical adviser in the Farm Security Administration and, in 1938, was the assistant to the director of the Federal Music Project, which amassed a large collection of American folk song and music for the National Archives. In 1935 he was one of the founders of the American Musicological Society and was also associated with the American Library of Musicology and the American Society for Comparative Musicology. Seeger was an important influence on Henry Cowell (q.v.), who studied theory and composition with him; he was also an influence on the work of his wife, Ruth Crawford Seeger (q.v.). Before he turned to musicology, Seeger composed a few pieces, among them *Twenty-five Songs* (1906–11), *The Shadowy Waters*, an overture for orchestra (1908), *String Quartet* (1913), *Sonata for Violin and Piano* (1913), *Studies* in single, unaccompanied melody and in 2-line dissonant counterpoint (1915–32), *Derdra*, pageant for orchestra and chorus (1914), and *Parthenia* for orchestra (1915). His books include *An Outline of a Course in Harmonic Structure and Musical Invention* (with E. G. Stricklen, 1913), *Harmonic Structure and Elementary Composition* (1916), *The American Ballad Book* (with Duncan B. Emrich, 1946), and *Studies in Musicology*

(1977). Seeger died in Bridgewater, Conn., Feb. 7, 1979.

SEEGER, RUTH CRAWFORD (1901–1953) Composer, pianist, teacher. Born in East Liverpool, Ohio, July 3, 1901, Crawford (as she was generally known professionally) studied, and later taught piano, at the School of Musical Arts, Jacksonville, Fla., in 1918. She then moved to Chicago, where she studied at the American Conservatory; from 1925 to 1929 she also taught there. In 1929 she came to New York City, where she studied with Charles Seeger (q.v.); they were married in 1931. Before that, Crawford, on a Guggenheim Fellowship, studied in Berlin (1930–31). The bulk of her original work was done during this period; as a mother of 4 children, Crawford had little time for composition. She also assisted her husband in his folk music research, after they settled in Washington, D.C., in 1935. She also collaborated with John A. Lomax and Alan Lomax (as music editor) on *Our Singing Country* (1941). Her original compositions include *Nine Preludes for Piano* (1926–28), *Two Movements for Chamber Orchestra* (1926), *Sonata for Violin and Piano* (1927), *Suite for Four Strings and Piano* (1927), *Suite for Flute, Oboe, Clarinet, Horn, Bassoon, and Piano* (1927), *Three Movements for Winds and Piano* (1928). *Four Diaphonic Suites* (2 cellos, 2 clarinets, oboe, and flute, 1931), *String Quartet* (1931), *Three Songs*, words by Carl Sandburg, for voice and chamber orchestra (1933), *Rissolty Rossolty* for 10 wind instruments, timpani, and strings (1941), *Suite for Wind Quintet* (1952); there are also several volumes of folk song collections: *American Folk Songs for Children* (1948), *Animal Folk Songs for Children* (1950), *American Folk Songs for Christmas* (1953), and *Let's Build a Railroad* (published 1954). She died of cancer in Chevy Chase, Md., Nov. 18, 1953.

SESSIONS, ROGER (b. 1896) Composer, teacher. Born in Brooklyn, N.Y., Dec. 28, 1896, Sessions, at age 4, began to study the piano under his mother's teaching. He began composing at 12; a year later he produced his first opera, *Lancelot and Elaine*. At 14 he was a student at Harvard, where he studied with Edward Burlingame Hill (q.v.) and Archibald Davison; he also studied with Horatio Parker (q.v.) at Yale. He graduated from Harvard in 1917 and was awarded his doctorate in music from Yale in 1917. From 1917 to 1921 Sessions taught at Smith College, Northampton, Mass. (where he had grown up, after the family moved from Brooklyn). He studied privately with Ernest Bloch (q.v.), when Bloch moved on to the Cleveland Institute of Music in 1921, Sessions accompanied him. Sessions was head of the Theory Department when he received one of his many fellowships to live abroad to study and work. He returned to the United States briefly during this period: for example, when he was involved with the Copland-Sessions Concerts (q.v.) in the late '20s. In 1933 Sessions returned again to take a teaching position at Boston University, beginning a long, and important, teaching career in various important music teaching centers —the University of California at Berkeley, Princeton, and Harvard—and, after his retirement, continued to teach at the Juilliard School of Music. Several of his students have themselves contributed much to music: Leon Kirchner, David Diamond, Milton Babbitt, Vivian Fine, David Del Tredici, Andrew Imbrie, and Hugo Weisgall (all q.v.), to name a few. As a composer, Sessions is highly regarded as one of the major voices in American music, although he does not try to sound self-consciously American.

His music is generally abstract, chromatic, personal, and well crafted. He has composed 9 symphonies (1927, 1946, 1957, 1958, 1964, 1966, 1967, 1968, 1975) and 3 works for the stage, *The Black Maskers* (1923 and its suite, 1928), the one-act opera *The Trial of Lucullus* (1947), and an opera in 3 acts, *Montezuma* (completed 1962). There are 2 string quartets (1936, 1951) and 3 piano sonatas (1930, 1946, 1965). Sessions composed his *Violin Concerto* in 1935, a *Piano Concerto* in 1956, and a *Concerto for Violin, Cello, and Orchestra* in 1971. Between 1937 and 1939 he worked on a small suite for solo piano entitled *Pages from a Diary* and published as *From My Diary*. Other works include *Duo for Violin and Piano* (1942), the *Sonata* for solo violin (1953), *String Quintet* (1958), and *Six Pieces* for cello (1966). Sessions' works for voice include *Turn O Libertad* for chorus and piano, 4 hands (1944), *Idyll of Theocritus* for soprano and orchestra (1954), *Mass* for male choir and organ (1955), *Psalm 140* (1963), and the cantata for soloists, chorus, and orchestra *When Lilacs Last in the Dooryard Bloom'd* (text by Walt Whitman, 1970). And finally, some smaller works for orchestra: the *Divertimento* (1960), *Rhapsody* (1970), and *Concertino* for chamber orchestra (1971). Sessions is also the author of *The Musical Experience of Composer, Performer and Listener* (1950), *Harmonic Practice* (1951), *Reflections on the Musical Life in the United States* (1956), and *Questions About Music* (1970).

SHILKRET, NATHANIEL "NAT" (b. 1895) Composer, conductor. Born in New York City, Dec. 25, 1895, Shilkret studied music with Charles Hambitzer (who also taught George Gershwin) and was a musical prodigy; he was playing in orchestras as early as the age of 13 and was clarinetist in the Russian Symphony, the New York Philharmonic, and the Metropolitan Opera Orchestra. He also played in the bands of John Philip Sousa and Arthur Pryor. Shilkret received his degree in music from Bethany College, Lindsborg, Kans. His all-around experience in music, in orchestras, and in instruments led to Shilkret's position as director of light music for the RCA-Victor Record Company, beginning in 1915 and lasting until 1945. He was most active in this capacity during the 1920s and early '30s. Shilkret assembled some of the finest orchestras in New York for his recording sessions and often served as conductor. He was an active radio conductor also, especially in the '30s. Shilkret went to Hollywood in 1935 to participate in the 2nd flowering of the musical film and worked as musical director and arranger for many of the now classic film musicals of the period and, later, of film background scores. His earliest successful efforts were written for films: the theme song for the film *Lilac Time*, "Jeannine, I Dream of Lilac Time" (lyrics by L. Wolfe Gilbert, 1928), and "The Lonesome Road" (lyrics by Gene Austin), which was written for the first film version of *Show Boat* in the same year. Shilkret's more ambitious compositions include *Four Poems, "The Seasons,"* for violin and orchestra (1924–38), a tone poem *Skyward* (1928), *Quintet* for clarinet and strings (1936), *Sextet* for clarinet, piano, and strings (1938), *Ode to Victory* (1942), *Concerto for Trombone* (1942), *Serenade Rhapsodie* (1942), *Creation* from the *Genesis Suite* (to which other composers, including Stravinsky, q.v., and Schoenberg, q.v., contributed movements, 1943), a ballet, *New York Ballet* (1937), and several film scores: *Winterset* (1936), *Mary, Queen of Scots* (1936), *Hoodlum Saint* (1945), *Faithful in My Fashion* (1946), and *Tenth Avenue Angel* (1946). There are also some small pieces for violin, such as *Southern Humoresque* and *Jealous Ballerina*. Shilkret made hundreds of recordings with the Victor Orchestra, the Victor Concert Orchestra, and the Victor Salon Orchestra.

"SHORT'NIN' BREAD" Popular art song, adapted by composer Jacques Wolfe (b. 1896) from a song attributed to a black composer, Reese D'Pree, who is said to have written it originally in 1905. Wolfe's version was published in 1928 and became a standard song for concert singers ever since.

"SHOW BOAT" Musical with music by Jerome Kern and lyrics by Oscar Hammerstein II, based on the novel of the same title by Edna Ferber. Opened at the Ziegfeld Theatre, New York, Dec. 27, 1927. The original production ran for 572 performances; there have been several revivals ever since and 3 film versions, the best being the one produced by Universal in 1936. *Show Boat* tells the story of Magnolia, the daughter of a show boat captain, and a handsome but weak river gambler, Gaylord Ravenal. The music, or operetta as some might suggest, was outstanding in its well-worked-out plot (a secondary story touched on miscegenation—a white man married to a woman with black ancestry —which was daring in 1927), the use of song and dance ("integration"), and characterization. Its score was one of Kern's finest and one of "the outstanding achievements" (in George Gershwin's phrase) of the American musical theatre. Among its songs: "Make Believe," "You Are Love," "Can't Help Lovin' Dat Man," "Why Do I Love You," "Life upon the Wicked Stage," the classic "Ol' Man River," and "Bill," which Hammerstein adapted from an earlier (1918) Kern song with a lyrics by P. G. Wodehouse. In the new "Bill," Hammerstein shared the lyrics credit with Wodehouse. When the second film version was produced in 1936, Kern and Hammerstein wrote additional songs: "I Have the Room Above Her," "Gallivantin' Around," and "Ah Still Suits Me." For the 1946 stage revival Kern composed his last song, "Nobody Else but Me" (he died of a cerebral hemorrhage before the revival opened). Outstanding members of the original 1927 cast were Norma Terris, who portrayed Magnolia, Howard Marsh who was Gaylord, Charles Winninger (Cap'n Andy), Helen Morgan (the mulatto, Julie), Jules Bledsoe (Joe), and Edna May Oliver (Parthy, wife of Cap'n Andy). Paul Robeson, who was to have been the original Joe, was unavailable when *Show Boat* opened, but sang the role in the London production as well as in the fine 1936 film version. Irene Dunne, who replaced Terris for the show's tour, portrayed Julie in the film version also. Winninger did Cap'n Andy many times, in the original, the 1936 film, and several revivals. The original orchestrations for *Show Boat* were the work of Robert Russell Bennett. For period flavors certain non-Kern-Hammerstein songs were woven into the score, notably "After the Ball," by Charles K. Harris. The longest run ever achieved by *Show Boat* was its London production, which began on July 29, 1971, and ran for 910 performances (until Sept. 29, 1973).

"SHUFFLE ALONG" The most successful all-black musical of its time, with music by Eubie Blake, lyrics by Noble Sissle, and book by Flournoy Miller and Aubrey Lyles (all of whom, incidentally, appeared in the show). *Shuffle Along* opened at the Sixty-third Street Music Hall, New York, on May 23, 1921, and ran for 504 performances. The book was an expansion of a Miller-Lyles vaudeville skit, "The Mayor of

Dixie," which had something to do with a mayoral election, and which served as a vehicle for the comic talents of the book's authors, both of whom portrayed sharp-dealing politicians as opposed to the honest Harry (Roger Matthews). After its successful Broadway run, *Shuffle Along* enjoyed a long life on the road well into 1923. Its significance lay primarily in the fact that it had been produced, written, and performed by blacks —with so much success; the earlier all-black shows had not proved so successful. The best-remembered Sissle and Blake songs from *Shuffle Along* are "Bandana Days," "Love Will Find a Way," and, of course, "I'm Just Wild About Harry."

"SKYSCRAPERS" Ballet, composed by John Alden Carpenter (q.v.) on commission from the Russian impresario Sergei Diaghilev and presented for the first time in Monte Carlo in 1925. Billed as "a ballet of modern American life," *Skyscrapers* was performed for the first time in the United States at the Metropolitan Opera, New York, February 1926. Written for full symphony orchestra, the ballet consists of 6 scenes: (1) *Symbols of restlessness;* (2) *An abstraction of the skyscraper and the work that produces it—and the interminable crowd that passes by;* (3) *The transition from work to play;* (4) *Any "Coney Island," and a reflection of a few of its manifold activities—interrupted presently by a flash-back, in the movie sense, and reverting with equal suddenness to play;* (5) *The return from play to work;* (6) *Skyscrapers.* Although any expression of modern American life during the '20s evoked the musical imagery of jazz, *Skyscrapers,* while rhythmically busy (especially in the opening) and drawing upon jazzy sounds, is not jazz, nor was it intended to be. There are references to folk themes, the blues, even the sound of

a theatre pit band—all refined through the trained musical sensibilities and wit of Carpenter. A work of much charm and a worthy period piece.

SLONIMSKY, NICOLAS (b. 1894) Composer, pianist, author, encyclopedist. Born in St. Petersburg, Russia, Apr. 27, 1894, Slonimsky began the study of music by taking piano lessons from his aunt, Isabelle Vengerova; further study in theory and orchestration was done at the St. Petersburg Conservatory. From 1920 to 1923 Slonimsky toured Europe as an accompanist and piano soloist; he came to the United States in 1923 and remained to become an important figure in contemporary—as well as contemporary American—music. Upon his arrival in the country he joined the staff of the Eastman School of Music, Rochester, N.Y. (1923–25), and left to become secretary to conductor Serge Koussevitzky; he also conducted the Boston Chamber Orchestra as well as other orchestras, including his own carefully selected group, which specialized in the performance of modern American music. During the early '30s and into the '40s Slonimsky brought the music of such composers as Ives, Varèse, Ruggles, and Cowell (all q.v.) to Europe, South America, and various music centers in the United States for the first time. Slonimsky was also a pioneer in getting some of these "difficult" composers recorded for the first time. In his own original work Slonimsky tended toward the experimental, as were the works of those composers he championed. His early compositions reveal his educational origin— e.g., *Russian Prelude*—but his later work, written after the mid 1920s, was experimental: *Five Advertising Songs* for voice and piano (1927), *I Owe a Debt to a Monkey* for voice and piano (1927), a suite for piano, *Studies in Black and White,* excursions into polytonal atonality (1928). His fragment *Orestes* is for strings, trumpet, suspended cymbal, tambourine, and tam-tam, and is written in the Greek enharmonic, quarter-tone, scale (1933). Slonimsky's variations on a Brazilian tune, *My Toy Balloon* (1942), employs an orchestra and 100 balloons, which burst at the close of the piece. One composition, *Little Piece* (1941), calls for a flute, oboe, percussion—and a typewriter and the sound of a cat meowing. His *Möbius Strip Tease* (1965) calls for a soprano and tenor who presumably sing the "Perpetual rondo" which is written in "linearly dodecaphonic, vertically consonant counterpoint." Slonimsky is also author of *Music Since 1900* (1937, rev. ed. 1971), *Music of Latin America* (1945), *Thesaurus of Scales and Melodic Patterns* (1947), *The Road to Music* (1947), *Lexicon of Musical Invective* (1953, rev. ed. 1969); he has also edited the *International Cyclopedia of Music and Musicians* (1946–58) and *Baker's Biographical Dictionary of Musicians* (5th and 6th eds., 1958, 1978).

SMITH, BESSIE (1894–1937) Blues singer. Born in Chattanooga, Tenn., Apr. 15, 1895, Elizabeth Smith was reared in extreme poverty. While still in her teens she joined a touring show, Ma Rainey's Rabbit Foot Minstrels—Ma Rainey was herself a popular black singer and coached the young vocalist. Smith toured in tent shows, clubs, and carnivals, developing an earthy singing style. She was singing in a nightclub in Selma, Alabama, when a Columbia Records executive, Frank Walker, heard her and decided he wanted to record her. In February 1923 Smith began recording with composer-pianist Clarence Williams and rapidly became a best-selling recording star and a vaudeville headliner. She was most active in recording studios ca. 1924–28, when, popular with black audiences and white jazz enthusiasts, she was known as "the Empress of the Blues." She worked with some of the most gifted jazz musicians of the time: Louis Armstrong (q.v.), James P. Johnson (q.v.), Don Redman, and Fletcher Henderson (q.v.). Her last recordings in November 1933 were with a band with a mixed personnel, 2 of whom, Jack Teagarden and Benny Goodman, were white. As her fortunes grew, Smith developed problems, including heavy drinking and the expectation of several members of her family that she would support them. Her husband, Jack Gee, a former policeman, became her manager, and between them they once went through $16,000 in 6 months. By the beginning of the Depression, what with drinking and financial problems, Bessie Smith's career took a downward turn. She fought with her employers and by 1930 had divorced Gee and had been virtually dropped by Frank Walker at Columbia Records. Smith was forced to take work that was uncongenial and not worthy of her gifts; she eventually returned to touring the vaudeville circuit, chiefly in the South. Her jazz recordings, among them "Back Water Blues" (1927), "St. Louis Blues" (1925), "Young Woman's Blues" (1926), the autobiographical "Me and My Gin" (1928), "Nobody Knows You When You're Down and Out" (1929), and "Empty Bed Blues" (1928), are still available on records today. In 1929 Smith made a film appearance in a short subject entitled *St. Louis Blues*. In September 1937 she was traveling with Winsted's *Broadway Rastus* in Mississippi and, while driving toward Memphis, was in an automobile wreck. She suffered internal injuries and a nearly severed arm. A physician who came upon the scene of the accident realized she was bleeding profusely and attempted to put her into his car to drive her to the hospital; his car was then struck and wrecked. Some minutes later the ambulance arrived and Smith was taken to a hospital in Clarksdale, Miss., where she was treated and her arm amputated. The legend that she was repeatedly turned away from several hospitals because she was black, and as a result bled to death, is just that, a legend. She died later that day, Sept. 26, 1937, in the G. T. Thomas Hospital, Clarksdale, Miss.

SMITH, CLARENCE "PINE TOP" (1904–1929) Composer, pianist, vocalist. Born in Troy, Ala., June 11, 1904, Smith lived in Birmingham, Ala., for a while, apparently playing the piano and entertaining. At 16 he was in Pittsburgh, where he played in nightclubs and theatres. He played in vaudeville with Ma Rainey, and with the team of Butterbeans and Susie, and eventually settled in Chicago, where he was popular as a singer, pianist, and entertainer in black clubs. It is possible that he heard the pianist Jimmy Yancey, an early boogie-woogie exponent. Who influenced whom is impossible to answer today, but it is more probable that the older man, Yancey, influenced Smith, as he did Albert Ammons and Meade "Lux" Lewis. But Smith was an original on his own and luckily, between Dec. 29, 1928, and Jan. 15, 1929, he made several recordings in Chicago, including two takes of the celebrated "Pine Top's Boogie Woogie" (q.v.). Smith was scheduled to make additional recordings, but one day failed to arrive for the sessions. His wife arrived at the studio and told recording director Mayo Williams that the night before, Mar. 14, 1929, Smith had been killed in a nightclub argument. As with so many jazz personalities, the story of Smith's death has 2 versions (at least): some say that he was shot as the classic innocent bystander; Mayo Williams told jazz historian William Russell that Smith was shot in a fight over "some ol' gal in a cheap West Side dance hall."

SOWERBY, LEO (1895–1968) Composer, organist, teacher. Born in Grand Rapids, Mich., May 1, 1895, Sowerby received most of his musical education in Chicago, where his family lived from about the time he was 14. Sowerby studied at the American Conservatory; his teachers were Calvin Lampert (piano) and Arthur Olaf Andersen (composition). He also studied piano for a while with the Australian-American composer pianist Percy Grainger. Sowerby was self-taught on the organ. During World War I he was a bandmaster in the field artillery in the United States, England, and France. He was the first American to be awarded the Prix de Rome (1921) and spent 3 years in Rome composing such works as *King Estmere* for 2 pianos and orchestra and one of his best-known compositions, *From the Northland,* for orchestra (originally for piano). In 1925, back in the United States, Sowerby joined the faculty of the American Conservatory, Chicago, to teach composition, where he remained until 1962. A year later he became organist and choirmaster at the St. James Episcopal Cathedral, Chicago, a post he also relinquished in 1962, when he founded the College of Church Musicians at the National Cathedral, Washington, D.C. He served as dean of the college until his death. Sowerby's works for organ are numerous, many composed for performances in churches. His first impressions upon the musical scene were made with his chamber and especially his orchestral compositions. Sowerby's overture *Comes Autumn Time* and witty (and very popular) arrangement of the folk tune *The Irish Washerwoman* date from 1916. He produced 5 symphonies (1921, 1928, 1940, 1947, 1964), a symphonic poem *Prairie* (1929), *Synconata* and *Monotony* for "jazz" orchestra (1924 and 1925—written for the Paul Whiteman, q.v., orchestra), *Passacaglia, Interlude, and Fugue* (1931), 2 organ concertos (1936, 1967), *Theme in Yellow* (1938), *Fantasy on Hymn Tunes*

(1943), *"Classic" Concerto for Organ and Strings* (1944), *Portrait,* a "fantasy in triptych" (1946), *All on a Summer's Day* (1954), *Rhapsody for Chamber Orchestra* (1923), and *Sinfonietta for String Orchestra* (1934). Sowerby also composed 2 piano concertos (1919, 1932) and a *Cello Concerto* (1933); he also wrote important choral works: *Vision of Sir Launfal* (1926), *Great Is the Lord* (1934); *Forsaken of Men* (1942), *The Canticle of the Sun* (1943, Pulitzer Prize 1946), *Christ Reborn* (1950), *The Throne of God* (1957), *The Ark of the Covenant* (1959), and *Solomon's Garden* (1965). Besides the early *Serenade* for string quartet (1916), Sowerby wrote 2 numbered string quartets (1923, 1935) and 2 sonatas for violin and piano (1921, 1944); also the *Symphony for Organ* solo (1930), *Suite* for organ (1933), *Canon, Chacony, and Fugue* for organ (1949), *Whimsical Variations* for organ 1950), *Bright, Blithe, and Brisk* for organ (1962), *Symphonia Brevis* for organ (1966), and *Passacaglia* for organ (1967). Sowerby's chamber compositions include a *Suite for Violin and Piano* (1916), *Quintet* for flute, oboe, clarinet, bassoon, and horn (1916), *Pop Goes the Weasel* for the same instruments as the *Quintet* (1927), a *Sonata for Clarinet and Piano* (1938), *Poem for Viola and Organ* (1942), *Sonata for Trumpet and Piano* (1945), *Ballade* for English horn and organ (1949), *Trio* for violin, viola, and cello (1952), *Fantasy for trumpet and organ* (1954), *Piano Sonata* (1964), and *Dialogue* for organ and piano (1967). Sowerby also composed a large number of songs and made many arrangements of American folk songs. Among his better-known songs are "With Strawberries," "Prayer of the Singer," and "Three Psalms." Sowerby died in Port Clinton, Ohio, July 7, 1968.

SPELMAN, TIMOTHY MATHER (1891–1970) Composer. Born in Brooklyn, N.Y., Jan. 21, 1891, Spelman studied music with Harry R. Shelley in New York and with Edward B. Hill and W. R. Spalding at Harvard (1909–13). Upon winning a Naumberg Fellowship he went to Munich, Germany, for further study with Walter Courvoisier (1913–15). Spelman returned to the United States to lecture on opera in a series of lecture recitals. In 1920 he settled in Florence, Italy, where he remained for about 15 years until the coming into power of Mussolini. This long residence abroad undoubtedly contributed to Spelman's relative obscurity in American music. His works, however, accumulated some performances during the late 1920s and '30s. Spelman's early interest was in writing for the voice and one of his first works was the one-act drama *La Magnifica* (1920); a 3-act opera, *The Sea Rovers,* followed in 1928; his "fantastic comedy" *Babakan* was produced in 1935. He also composed the music for a 4-act pantomime, *Snowdrop* (before 1920) and another opera, *The Sunken City* (1930). For orchestra, Spelman wrote a suite entitled *Barbaresques* (1923), *Saint's Days* (1925), the *Symphony in G Minor* (1935), the "rhapsody" *Homesick Yankee in North Africa* (1945), and the "pocket ballet" *Jamboree* (1945). Of his choral works the *Litany of the Middle Ages* for soprano and women's chorus (1928) and *Pervigilium Veneris* for soprano, baritone, chorus, and orchestra (1929) were frequently performed. Spelman also produced *Five Whimsical Serenades* for string quartet (1924) and a *Piano Sonata* (1929). He died in Florence, Italy, Aug. 21, 1970.

STEINERT, ALEXANDER LANG (b. 1900) Composer, conductor, pianist. Born in Boston, Mass., Sept. 21, 1900, Steinert, before graduation from Harvard (1922), studied with Charles Martin Loeffler (q.v.) in Boston, then went to Paris where he studied with Vincent d'Indy, Charles Koechlin, and André Gédalge at the Conservatory. He also worked informally, with Maurice Ravel. In 1927 he was awarded the Prix de Rome and spent the next 3 years at the American Academy in Rome. He made his American debut in 1925 as piano soloist with the Boston Symphony. He also found work as a conductor of musical comedies and opera. He later conducted at the Fine Arts Center, Colorado Springs, and in 1941 was appointed conductor of the Los Angeles Youth Orchestra. Steinert also did orchestrations for films, among them the Walt Disney production *Bambi*. In 1942 he enlisted in the U. S. Army Air Forces and composed scores for documentaries and training films. Steinert remained in Hollywood scoring films—*Blondie Knows Best, The Unknown,* and *The Strangler of the Swamp*—and then went to New York. Before his Hollywood sojourn he had served as musical coach and alternate conductor of the original (1935) production of Gershwin's *Porgy and Bess* (q.v.). Steinert also scored television and radio shows. Besides his film, television, and radio scores, Steinert has written several orchestral works: *Nuit Méridionale* (1926), *Leggenda Sinfonica* (1931), *Concerto Sinfonica* for piano and orchestra (1935), *Air Corps Suite* (1942), *Flight Cycle* (1944), *Rhapsody for Clarinet and Orchestra* (1945), and *The Nightingale and the Rose* for orchestra and narrator (1950). Steinert's smaller works include *Three Poems by Shelley* for soprano (1932), a *Sonata for Violin and Piano* (1925), *Trio for Violin, Cello, and Piano,* and a *Piano Sonata.* He has also written several songs and instrumental pieces.

STILL, WILLIAM GRANT (1893–1978) Composer, arranger. Born in Woodville, Miss., May 11, 1895, Still was an infant when his father died and his mother moved to Little Rock, Ark., where she remarried and Still grew up. Still's stepfather, a teacher and an opera lover, introduced the boy to music and to music lessons; in time he was to learn to play the violin, cello, and oboe. Still began his college studies, however, as a premed student, although at the same time he formed a string quartet and maintained an interest in music. Sometime in 1916 he began working for W. C. Handy (q.v.) in Memphis, work that kindled Still's interest in the music of Africa and the music it inspired and influenced. He began his music study in earnest at Oberlin Conservatory, Ohio, working with George W. Andrews (composition), F. J. Lehmann (theory), and Maurice Kessler (violin). Between sessions at Oberlin, Still served in the U. S. Navy during World War I. He then joined W. C. Handy, who by this time had moved his publishing company to New York City. In 1921 Still was playing oboe in the pit band of the production *Shuffle Along* (q.v.). While the show was in Boston, Still studied privately with George Chadwick, president of the New England Conservatory (Chadwick was so impressed with Still's musicianship that he refused payment for the lessons). When he returned to New York, Still also studied, and without fee, from 1923 to 1925 with Edgard Varèse (q.v.). During this period Still not only worked on his original compositions but also did orchestrations for various radio shows and for such popular orchestras as those of Paul Whiteman (q.v.), Donald Voorhees, and Artie Shaw (q.v.); he later worked in Hollywood and television in the same capacity. Still revealed his aesthetic intent with one of his early orchestral works, *Darker America* (1924), with its four movements entitled "The American Negro," "Sorrow," "Hope," and "Prayer." This was followed by *From the Black Belt* (1926), *Africa* (1930), and his first and most famous *Afro-American Symphony* (q.v. 1931). His work in this genre also includes the *Symphony in G Minor* (1937), *Symphony No. 3,* "Western Hemisphere" (1945), *Symphony No. 4,* "Autochthonous" (1947), and *Symphony No. 5* (1954). Other Still orchestral compositions are the suite *A Deserted Plantation* (1933), *Ebon Chronicle,* poem for orchestra (1934), *Kaintuck!* for piano and orchestra (1935), *The Black Man Dances* (1935), *Dismal Swamp* (1936), *Beyond Tomorrow* (1936), *Song of a City* for chorus and orchestra (1939), *Plain-Chant for America* for baritone, organ, and orchestra (1941), *Old California* (1941), *In Memoriam: The Colored Soldiers Who Died for Democracy* (1943), *Pages from Negro History* for school orchestra (1943), *Festive Overture* (1944), *Poem for Orchestra* (1944), *Archaic Ritual* (1946), *Danzas de Panama* (1948), *The Little Song That Wanted to Be a Symphony* for speaker, women's trio, and orchestra (1955), and *The Peaceful Land* (1960). Of Still's choral works, the best known is *And They Lynched Him on a Tree* for contralto, chorus, narrator, and orchestra (1940). He produced 7 operas, of which the best received were *Troubled Island* (1938) and *Highway 1, U.S.A.* (1960). Still also composed the music for stage works that included ballet and sometimes vocalists. *La Guiablesse* is a ballet (1927); *Sahdji* calls for a corps de ballet, solo dancers, soloists, chorus, and orchestra (1930); *Lenox Avenue* employs a chorus, a corps de ballet, and an orchestra (1937); a similar grouping of artists, without chorus, is used in *Miss Sally's Party* (1940). Still composed music specifically for young people: *The Prince and the Mermaid* (1968) and *The American Scene: Five Suites for Young Americans* (1968). He wrote a few works for chamber groups: *Suite for Violin and Piano* (1943), *Pastorella* for violin and piano (1946),

Seven Traceries for solo piano (1940), *Three Visions* for piano (1935), and *Ennanga* for harp, piano, and strings (1956). While Still drew upon black folk materials, primarily spirituals, he did not indulge in self-conscious ethnicity and his compositions are free of forced exotica; his harmonic and melodic materials are in the Western mode. Still died in Los Angeles, Calif., Dec. 3, 1978.

STOESSEL, ALBERT (1894–1943) Composer, conductor, violinist. Born in St. Louis, Mo., Oct. 11, 1894, Stoessel received his initial musical education there and then went to Berlin, Germany, to study at the royal *Hochschule* (composition and violin). He made his debut as a violinist in Berlin in 1915; he returned to the United States, where he appeared as a soloist with the St. Louis Symphony and toured with Enrico Caruso as accompanist. During World War I he served as a bandmaster of an infantry band and later was head of the Bandmaster School at Chaumont, France. In 1923 Stoessel was appointed head of the music department of New York University, a position he held until 1930, when he resigned to join the staff of the Juilliard School of Music. In addition, Stoessel conducted the Bach Cantata Club and the Oratorio Society, as well as the Worcester, Mass., Music Festival, and was musical director of the Chautauqua Institution. His works include *Hispania Suite* (1921), an *Early Americana Suite* (1935), a *Concerto Grosso* for piano and strings (1936), and the opera *Garrick,* with libretto by Robert A. Simon (1936). There are also a *Suite Antique* for chamber orchestra (1922) and a *Sonata for Violin and Piano.* Stoessel died of a heart attack while conducting, New York, May 12, 1943.

STOTHART, HERBERT (1885–1949) Composer, conductor, pianist. Born in Milwaukee, Wis., Sept. 11, 1885, Stothart was musically educated in Milwaukee, graduated from Milwaukee Teachers College, and for several years taught in schools there; he later served as instructor of musical dramatics at the University of Wisconsin. This faculty eventually brought Stothart to New York City, where, from 1917 to 1928, he was involved with the producer Arthur Hammerstein as conductor and composer. His first full score was for the musical *Always You* (with lyrics by Oscar Hammerstein II, q.v.), which was produced in 1920; that same year saw the production of *Tickle Me* (lyrics by Hammerstein and Otto Harbach) and *Jimmie* (lyrics by Hammerstein and Harback). In most of his later shows Stothart shared composer credits with others: Youmans (q.v.) (*Wildflower,* 1923), Friml (*Rose-Marie,* 1924), Gershwin (q.v.) (*Song of the Flame,* 1925), and Ruby (*Good Boy,* 1928). In 1929 he went to Hollywood to score the Lawrence Tibbett film *The Rogue Song* and remained there for the rest of his career. Stothart became general music director of Metro-Goldwyn-Mayer and composed many film background scores, besides overseeing the scoring and conducting of the music for several film musicals. His scores can be heard in the backgrounds of *Viva Villa* (1933), *David Copperfield* (1934), *Mutiny on the Bounty* (1935), *Dragon Seed* (1944), *National Velvet* (1945), and *The Yearling,* among others. Although he did not write the songs, Stothart scored the music for *The Wizard of Oz* (songs by Harold Arlen and E. Y. Harburg, both q.v.), for which he won an Academy Award in 1939. Although during World War II Stothart composed a musical pageant, *China,* and a cantata, *Voices of Liberation,* the bulk of his work consists of his few songs—e.g., "Song of the Flame," (with George Gershwin, q.v., 1925) and "Cuban Love Song" (with Jimmie McHugh

1931)—and his output of film background scores. Stothart died in Los Angeles, Calif., Feb. 1, 1949.

STRICKLAND, LILY (1887–1958) Composer, pianist. Born in Anderson, S.C., Jan. 28, 1887, Strickland graduated from Converse College, Spartanburg, S.C., with a degree in literature. In 1910 she came to New York to study piano and theory privately. She then received a scholarship to study at the Institute of Musical Art (later Juilliard), where she studied with William Humiston and Percy Goetschius, q.v. (1909–11). After her marriage to J. Courtney Anderson she settled in New York for a time, but later traveled a good deal from ca. 1920 to 1930. Her music, primarily songs, reflects the influence of her travels: *Moon of Iraq, Himalayan Sketches, Songs of India,* and the African song cycle *Oubangi.* Although she composed instrumental works such as the symphonic suite *Carolina,* a *Piano Concerto,* and *Dance Moods,* Strickland is best remembered as a fine songwriter. Her collections of Southern-inspired songs are among her best: Bayou Songs, and individual songs such as "Here in the High Hills," "Dreamin' Time," "Jes' My Song," "My Love Is a Fisherman," "At Eve I Hear a Flute," and "My Arcady." Her best-known, enduring song is "Mah Lindy Lou" (q.v.), published in 1920. Strickland died in Hendersonville, N.C., June 6, 1958.

STRIDE See Harlem Stride Piano.

STRINGFIELD, LAMAR (1897–1959) Composer, flutist, collector of American folk music. Born in Raleigh, N.C., Oct. 10, 1897, Stringfield initially planned to go into medicine, but his love for music diverted him. He enlisted in the U. S. Army before World War I and served for 3 years as a bandsman; after the war he began to study the flute; he eventually came to New York to study with the great French flutist George Barrère at the Institute of Musical Art (later Juilliard). He also studied composition with Percy Goetschius (q.v.), among others, and conducting with Henry Hadley (q.v.). Thereafter he was active as a flutist and conductor as well as composer. Returning to his native South, Stringfield formed the Institute of Folk Music at the University of North Carolina, Chapel Hill, (1930) and became the conductor of North Carolina State Symphony (1932–38). He returned to New York in 1938 and was associate conductor at Radio City Music Hall and lecturer in American Music at the Juilliard School of Music (1939–41). He then moved on to California, where he taught theory and composition at Claremont College besides working in an aircraft factory during World War II. In 1946 he became director of the Knoxville Symphony (1946–47), after which he moved to Charlotte, N.C., where he headed the Symphonette and the Symphony until 1949. Stringfield's major works are rooted in Anglo-American folk music; one of his early pieces, the orchestral suite *From the Southern Mountains* (1927), won the Pulitzer Prize. His other works for orchestra include the symphonic poem *Indian Legend* (1925), a symphonic ballet, *The Seventh Queue* (1928), a symphonic fantasy, *At the Factory* (1929), *A Negro Parade* (1931), *The Legend of John Henry* (1932), *Moods of a Moonshiner* (1934), *From the Blue Ridge Mountain* (1936), and *Mountain Dew*, a serenade for string orchestra (1937). Among Stringfield's best-known works is *The Lost Colony*, a historical music drama, with a libretto by Paul Green; Stringfield also composed an opera, *The Mountain Song*, in 1931. There is a good deal of chamber music dating from the early '20s: *Mountain Sketches*, *Indian Sketches*, *The Ole Swimmin' Hole*, *A*

Mountain Episode (for string quartet, 1933), *Chipmunks* for flute, clarinet, and bassoon (1940), and *Mountain Dawn* (1945), all representative of the composer's interest in folk music. Stringfield's more abstract chamber music includes a *Prelude and Fugue* for flute and string quartet (1924), *Concert Fugue* for string quartet (1924), *Introduction and Scherzo* for small orchestra (1926), and *Impromptu* for flute and cello (1927). *From a Negro Melody* (1928) is composed for an orchestra of 12 instruments. Stringfield died in Asheville, N.C. Jan. 21, 1959.

STRINGHAM, EDWIN JOHN (1890–1974) Composer, teacher, author. Born in Kenosha, Wis., July 11, 1890, Stringham took his degrees in music at Northwestern University, Evanston, Ill., where he studied with Arne Oldberg (q.v.) and Peter C. Lutkin. At the Cincinnati Conservatory he studied with Edgar Stillman Kelley (q.v.). Until he went to Rome in 1929, at the invitation of the Italian Government, to study at the Royal Academy of Music, Stringham held several teaching positions in Chicago; Grand Forks, N. Dak.; and Colorado; he eventually became dean of the College of Music, Denver. From 1919 to 1929 he was a music critic for the Denver *News* and the *Post*. In Italy Stringham studied composition and orchestration with Ottorino Respighi. Upon his return to the United States, Stringham settled in New York and taught at the Union Theological Seminary and Teachers College, Columbia University. In 1938 he founded and was chairman of the Music Department, Queens College, New York (1938–45). During World War II, Stringham was head of the music department of the U. S. Army University Study Center, Biarritz, France. Besides composing and teaching, Stringham did much writing, including one of the standard "music appreciation" books,

Listening to Music Creatively, and articles for various magazines. His works include the symphonic poem *The Phantom* for orchestra (1916), *Three Pastels* (1917), *Visions* (1924), *The Ancient Mariner,* a symphonic poem (1926), *Springtime* overture (1927), *Danses Exotiques* (1928), *Symphony No. 1* (1929), *Nocturne* (1932), *Symphonic Suite* (1937), *Nocturne No. 2* (1938), and *Fantasy on American Folk Tunes* for violin and orchestra (1942). For chamber orchestra Stringham composed a *Notturno* (1936); there is also a *String Quartet* (1935). His choral works include a cantata, *Pilgrim Fathers* (1931), *Dream Song* for soprano, 2 altos, and piano (1937), *Ave Maria* for mixed chorus, a cappella (1937), and *Longing* for women's voices (1944). Stringham's teaching and his editorial work—he was music editor for the music publishing house Carl Fischer, Inc., and general music editor for the American Book Company—impinged upon his time for original composition. He produced several volumes of teaching pieces for use in schools and colleges. He died in Chapel Hill, N.C., July 1, 1974.

"SUNNY" Successful musical comedy, music by Jerome Kern (q.v.), with book and lyrics by Otto Harbach and Oscar Hammerstein II (q.v.). *Sunny* opened at the New Amsterdam Theatre, Sept. 22, 1925, and ran for 517 performances (the 1926 London production ran for 363 performances). The stars were Marilyn Miller (as Sunny), Jack Donahue (Jim), and Clifton Webb (Harold Wendell-Wendell), with the George Olsen Orchestra. *Sunny* represents the first collaboration of Kern and Hammerstein. Some of its songs: "Two Little Blue Birds," "Sunny," and "Who?"

"SWEET SUE (JUST YOU)" Popular song, published in 1928, with words by Will J. Harris (b. 1900) and music by Victor Young (q.v.). "Sweet Sue" was popular with the bands and singers of the late 1920s and early '30s. Its melody and chord sequence have also proved useful to jazz musicians. Young composed few popular songs (his real specialty was film music), but "Sweet Sue" proved to be one of his perennials.

TAYLOR, DEEMS (1885–1966) Composer, author, commentator. Born in New York City, Dec. 22, 1885, Taylor was self-taught in music—and revealed a musical bent as a youngster when he wrote what he called "musical shows." Upon graduation from New York University (1906), Taylor worked as an editor for Nelson's Encyclopedia and later for the Encyclopaedia Britannica. Between 1908 and 1911 he studied music systematically for the first time with Oscar Coon, and then took a job as assistant editor of *Western Electric News.* For a time it appeared that Taylor was destined for a journalistic career: he joined the staff of the New York *Tribune* and from 1916 to 1917 was its French correspondent; he was an associate editor of the famous weekly *Colliers* and then, at last, was made music critic of the New York *World* (1921–29); he edited *Musical America* (1927–29) and for a time was music critic of the New York *American.* In the '30s Taylor drifted into radio and became widely known as the intermission commentator of the New York Philharmonic broadcasts (1937–44). Taylor's no-nonsense, often anecdotal remarks about music and musicians made him a popular speaker on those subjects. Many of his talks were gathered into very popular books: *Of Men and Music* (1937) and *The Well-Tempered Listener* (1940); he also wrote on other subjects—his *Pictorial History of the Movies* was published in 1943 and *Some Enchanted Evenings,* a dual biography of Rodgers and Hammerstein, in 1953. His other books include *Music to My Ears* (1949) and

The One-Track Mind (1953). As a composer, Taylor is generally classified with the traditionalists, the conservatives. His critics invariably found traces of Wagner or Puccini (or both) in his ambitious compositions. His early theatrical works, operas in fact, brought him the most success. As early as 1910 Taylor succeeded in getting a musical comedy, *The Echo,* produced on Broadway. An orchestral composition, *The Siren Song* (1913), won him a National Federation of Music Clubs prize. This was followed by a cantata, *The Highwayman,* for chorus and orchestra (1914). Taylor's most successful work for orchestra was *Through the Looking Glass* (composed 1917–19; rescored 1922), a suite based on the Lewis Carroll stories. A less ambitious but most attractive work is *The Portrait of a Lady* for strings, woodwinds, and piano (1924). Other works for orchestra include the symphonic poem *Jurgen* (1924), *Circus Day,* composed for the Paul Whiteman (q.v.) Orchestra and scored by Ferde Grofé (q.v.; 1925), ballet from incidental music to *Casanova* (1937), *Processional* (1941), *Fantasy on Two Themes* (1943), *Marco Takes a Walk* (1943), *Elegy* for orchestra (1944), *Restoration* suite (1950), and *The Dragon* (1954). Taylor's opera *The King's Henchman* (q.v.) was presented at the Metropolitan Opera (1927) and was regarded as one of the American musical events of the '20s, although the work has had few performances since. A 2nd opera, *Peter Ibbetson* (1931), was even more successful (16 performances in 4 seasons). A 3rd opera, *Ramuntcho,* was presented in 1942 in Philadelphia (it had been completed in 1937). Taylor also composed incidental music for productions of *Liliom, The Adding Machine,* and *Rita Coventry.* His suite for string quartet, *Lucrece,* was written in 1936. Taylor appeared as the commentator in the Walt Disney musical extravaganza *Fantasia*

(1940). He also served as musical adviser to the Columbia Broadcasting System (1936–43) and was an active member of the American Society of Composers, Authors and Publishers (director 1933–66; president 1942–48). Taylor died in New York City, July 3, 1966.

LE TESTAMENT DE VILLON A musical curiosity: an opera based on texts by 15th-century French poet François Villon, in translations and with music by the American renegade poet Ezra Pound (1885–1972). Although he had little musical training as a child, Pound was an amateur in the art; he did, however, write a good deal on music as well as musical criticism, produced concerts in Rapallo, Italy, and played the bassoon. He composed a number of small violin pieces for a friend, Olga Rudge, and began 2 more but never completed operas. *Le Testament de Villon* was written sometime during 1920–21 to demonstrate certain theories Pound held about the relationship between music and poetry. The instrumentation has a decided period sound— 15th century, not the 1920s. Pound's friend George Antheil (q.v.) assisted with the orchestration, which was completed in 1923. The action, set in Paris, 1462, revolves around Villon's death sentence; he sits in an alehouse writing his last will and testament. Various others come by to sing about life, death, love, beauty. Production of *Le Testament de Villon* was long in coming, confirming Pound's prediction of 1922: "It will be twenty years before they can stand it." There were presentations of individual songs, beginning in 1924, but the more or less complete (i.e., reconstructed) opera was not staged until November 1971, when it was done at the University of California, Berkeley.

THEME SONG A song concocted, initially in the era of silent films, to advertise the film. One of the earliest successful such creations was "Mickey," for the 1918 film of the same title. The music was by Neil Moret (Charles L. Daniels) and words by Harry Williams. Although it did not plug the film's title, an even earlier, more enduring theme was written to accompany the love scenes in *The Birth of a Nation*, "The Perfect Song," by Clarence Lucas (words) and Joseph Carl Breil (music). Originally written in 1915, "The Perfect Song" became even better known after 1928, when it became the theme of the "Amos 'n' Andy" radio show. Three early popular songs written to promote silent films were "Charmaine," by Lew Pollack and Erno Rapee, for the film *What Price Glory?* (1926), "Ramona" (q.v.), by Mabel Wayne and L. Wolfe Gilbert (1927), and "Jeannine, I Dream of Lilac Time," by L. Wolfe Gilbert and Nat Shilkret, for the film *Lilac Time* (1928). The advent of sound did not end the theory and practice of the theme song. Many songs "from the picture of the same name" became popular and contributed to the success of the film, especially during the '30s: "Flying Down to Rio" (1933), "Forty-second Street" (1933), "Top Hat" (1935), and "Pennies from Heaven" (1936), to name a few. The old practice continued as feature films were provided with theme songs, though they were by no means musicals. "Angel," for example, by Leo Robin and Frederick Hollander, was written for the 1937 Marlene Dietrich film; there was also "Eternally Yours" (L. Wolfe Gilbert and Werner Janssen, 1939). When the film musical stream dried up in the 1950s and '60s there was a return to the old theme song idea—the *James Bond Theme*, for example, used as a signature for the 007 melodramas. The theme song had come full circle.

THOMPSON, RANDALL (b. 1899) Composer, teacher, organist. Born in New York City, Apr. 21, 1899, Thompson was graduated from Harvard in 1920 after study with Walter Spalding and Edward Burlingame Hill (q.v.); he later studied privately with Ernest Bloch (q.v.). He was first noticed while still a fellow at the American Academy in Rome (1922–25), where some of his early works were performed: the orchestral prelude *Pierrot and Cothurnus* and *The Piper at the Gates of Dawn*. Thompson was also the recipient of 2 Guggenheim Fellowships (1929 and 1930). His teaching career began at Wellesley College in 1927; since, he has lectured at Harvard (1929), as well as serving in various capacities at the University of California, Berkeley; the Curtis Institute of Music, Philadelphia; University of Virginia, Charlottesville; Princeton; and Harvard again, where he was professor of music 1948–67. Besides teaching in one or the other of these universities, Thompson often led the chorus and played the organ. Although he has written substantial works for orchestra, his choral works are among his most performed: *Americana* (1932), *The Peaceable Kingdom* (1936), *Alleluia* (1940), *The Testament of Freedom*, to words by Thomas Jefferson (1943), *Mass of the Holy Spirit* (1956), *Frostiana* (1959), *A Concord Cantata* (1975), and *Five Love Songs* (1978). Thompson even composed songs for an early revue, *The Grand Street Follies* of 1926; his songs included such titles as "Fixed for Life," "The Booster's Song of the Far North," "Taxi Driver's Lament," "My Icy Flow," and "Ice Mazurka"; the lyrics were by Agnes Morgan and additional songs were contributed by Arthur Schwartz. For orchestra, Thompson has written a *Jazz Poem* for piano and orchestra (1928) and 3 symphonies (1929, 1931, and 1948). For string quartet he has written *The Wind in the Willows* (1924) and *String Quartet No. 1* (1941); for piano, a *Piano Sonata*

(1923) and a *Suite* for piano (1924). Thompson has composed a *Suite* for oboe, clarinet, and viola (1940), incidental music for *The Straw Hat* (1926), and a one-act opera, *Solomon and Balkis* (1942).

THOMSON, VIRGIL (b. 1896) Composer, critic, author. Born in Kansas City, Mo., Nov. 25, 1896, Thomson began the study of music around the age of 5. By the age of 12 he played the organ in the Calvary Baptist Church. In high school he contributed to student magazines, revealing a flair for writing. When the United States went to war in 1917, Thomson enlisted in the Aviation Section, A.E.F., and was commissioned a lieutenant in time for the armistice. He resigned and entered Harvard, where he studied with Edward Burlingame Hill (q.v.) and Archibald T. Davison. Even before receiving his degree Thomson was an assistant instructor at Harvard (1920–25); he also conducted the Harvard Glee Club. On a tour with the group in 1921, Thomson decided to remain in Paris to study with Nadia Boulanger (q.v.) and to absorb French culture. In France he came under the influence of the iconoclastic composer Erik Satie and his group, popularly known as Les Six, all determined to break the yoke of Romanticism in music. In Paris, Thomson also met the American expatriate Gertrude Stein (1874–1946), with whom he wrote one of his most famous works, the opera *Four Saints in Three Acts* (1928, produced 1934). Thomson remained in Paris from about 1925 until 1932, making occasional trips back to the United States, and finally settled in New York City in 1940, where he joined the staff of the *Tribune* as a critic. Fellowships, commissions, conducting, and other musical assignments enabled Thomson to live in Paris during the exciting days of the '20s. Much of his earliest music was

composed there, among the first being a song, "Vernal Equinox," to words by Amy Lowell, dated July 1920. Thomson's first major work was the *Sonata da Chiesa* for clarinet, trumpet, viola, horn, and trombone (1926). Other important chamber works include *Captials, Capitals* to a text by Gertrude Stein for 4 men's voices and piano (1927); 4 piano sonatas (2 in 1929; 1930, 1940), 2 string quartets (1931, 1932), *Stabat Mater* for soprano and string quartet (1931), *Serenade* for flute and violin (1931); there are also dozens of musical portraits of Thomson's friends for piano solo and various other instrumentation, a practice begun by Thomson in the late '20s. His *Ten Etudes* for piano were composed in 1943–44; the *Nine Etudes* in 1940 and 1951. Aside from his film and ballet scores, Thomson has written several substantial orchestra works: *Symphony on a Hymn Tune* (1928), *Symphony No. 2* (an orchestration of *Piano Sonata No. 1*, 1931), *Portraits for Orchestra* (1937–44), *The Seine at Night* (1947), *Wheat Field at Noon* (1948), *Sea Piece with Birds* (1952), and *Symphony No. 3* (1972). The solo/orchestra compositions number a *Concerto for Cello and Orchestra* (1950), *Concerto for Flute, Strings, Harp, and Percussion* (1954), and *Autumn,* a concertino for harp, strings, and percussion (1964). Thomson was a pioneer in the composition of music for films: *The Plow That Broke the Plains* (1936), *The River* (1937), *The Spanish Earth* (in collaboration with Marc Blitzstein, 1937), *Tuesday in November* (1945), *Louisiana Story* (1948), and *The Goddess* (1957). His ballet *Filling Station* (choreographed by Lew Christensen, 1937) was one of the first that drew upon Americana for its choreography and musical themes. Thomson has also written incidental music for more than a dozen plays ranging from Shakespeare to Truman Capote. He has also composed a great deal for the voice—for soloists and choral groups, notably *Five Songs from William Blake* for baritone and orchestra (1951), *Praises and Prayers* for soprano and piano (1963), and *The Feast of Love* for baritone and orchestra (1964). In collaboration with Stein he completed 2 operas, *Four Saints in Three Acts* (1928) and *The Mother of Us All* (1947), the last centered on the character of the activist Susan B. Anthony. Although often regarded as controversial, Thomson does not write "difficult" music. Often drawing upon the hymn tunes of his boyhood and folk material, which he handles with deceptive simplicity, Thomson writes with clarity and tasteful ease. He has also written on music with the same wit and clarity. His books are *The State of Music* (1939, rev. 1961), *The Musical Scene* (1945), *The Art of Judging Music* (1948), *Music Right and Left* (1951), his autobiography, succinctly entitled *Virgil Thomson* (1966), *Music Reviewed 1940-1954* (covering his years at the New York *Herald Tribune*, 1967), and *American Music Since 1910* (1971).

TIERNEY, HARRY (1890-1965) Songwriter. Born in Perth Amboy, N.J., May 21, 1890, Tierney had his first piano lessons from his mother and his uncle, Nicholas Morrissey, a trumpeter who played in several leading orchestras. After high school, Tierney took further study at the Virgil School of Music, New York. He then toured the United States as a concert pianist, although he had already begun writing melodies for popular songs. He joined the staff of the London publishing house Francis, Day and Hunter in 1915, and it was there that his first songs were heard in revues that same year. Returning to the United States in 1918, Tierney joined the staff of Remick in New York City and began interpolating songs into revues and musicals. He also worked for a time on the staff of Waterson, Berlin and Snyder, while continuing to interpolate songs into shows. His first Broadway score was written for *Irene* (1919), which was most successful (670 performances). The lyricist was Joseph McCarthy (1885–1943), with whom Tierney had begun working the year before. Their songs for *Irene* included the title song and "Alice Blue Gown." The collaborators produced the songs for an additional 6 shows, of which 2 were especially successful: *Kid Boots* (1923) and *Rio Rita* (1927). The score of the first was not notable and the show ran on the strength of the popularity of the star, Eddie Cantor; *Rio Rita*, which opened the newly designed Ziegfeld Theatre, was more successful in its songs: the title song, "The Rangers' Song," and "If You're in Love, You'll Waltz." Tierney and McCarthy did one more show, *Cross My Heart* (1928), with no success and virtually dried up. Tierney wrote the songs for a St. Louis production of *Beau Brummell*, with lyrics by Edward Eliscu and Raymond Egan, but the show never came to New York. Tierney did very little after *Rio Rita*: the films *Dixiana* and *Half Shot at Sunrise* (both 1930) and little else. He died in New York, Mar. 22, 1965.

TUTHILL, BURNET C. (b. 1888) Composer, teacher. Born in New York City, Nov. 16, 1888, Tuthill was the son of an organist (his mother, Henrietta Corwin) and an architect, W. B. Tuthill (who had designed Carnegie Hall). Music, initially, was an avocation, for Tuthill went into the world of business after his graduation from Columbia in 1909. While at Columbia he was first clarinetist in the student orchestra, which later—1908-9—he conducted. He continued to conduct the orchestra even after graduation; he was also associated with the Bronx People's Choral Union, the New York Oratorio Society, and the Young Men's Symphony. In 1919, with his father, Tuthill founded the Society for the Publication of American Music (the specialty was chamber music). In 1922 he joined the staff of the Cincinnati Conservatory of Music as general manager; he earned a master's degree in music there in 1935. Tuthill moved on to Memphis, where he was music director at Southwestern College; this was followed by his assignment as director of the Memphis College of Music (1937–59). During this period Tuthill often conducted the Memphis Symphony. In 1945 Tuthill served as chief, Fine Arts Section, at the U. S. Army University, Shrivenham, England. Tuthill's Op. 1 was a *Scherzo* for 2 clarinets and basset horn (1927); other chamber works include *Fantasy Sonata* for clarinet and piano (1932), *Nocturne* for flute and string quartet (1933), *Sonatine* for flute and clarinet (1933), *Trio* for piano, violin, and cello (1933), *Variations* for woodwind quintet and piano on "When Johnny Comes Marching Home" (1934), *Sailors' Hornpipe*, Op. 10, No. 1 (1935), *Divertimento*, Op. 10, No. 2 (1936), *Quintet* for clarinet and strings (1936), *Sonata* for violin and piano (1937), and *Sonata* for oboe and piano (1946). Among Tuthill's orchestral works are a pastorale, *Bethlehem* (1934), a rhapsody, *Come Seven* (1935), a symphonic poem *Laurentia* (1936), and *Symphony in C* (1940). There are also a *String Quartet* and a *Festival Prelude* for organ and 7 brass instruments.

TWEEDY, DONALD NICHOLS (1890–1948) Composer, teacher. Born in Danbury, Conn., Apr. 23, 1890, Tweedy received his musical education at Harvard under Edward Burlingame Hill (q.v.), Walter R. Spalding, and William Clifford Heilman. He also studied briefly in Europe and then, in New York, at the Institute of Musical Art (later Juilliard) with Percy Goetschius (q.v.). Tweedy served in the military

during World War I and reached the rank of first lieutenant. Returning to music, he taught at Vassar College (Poughkeepsie, N.Y., the University of California (Los Angeles), the Eastman School of Music, (Rochester, N.Y.), Hamilton College (Clinton, N.Y.), and Texas Christian University (Fort Worth). Tweedy composed a handful of music, beginning with a *Sonata for Viola and Piano* (1916); also a *Sonata for Violin and Piano* (1920), a *Sonata for Cello and Piano* (1930) and a *Suite* for piano (1935). For the theatre he composed incidental music for the play *Swords* (by Sidney Howard) and a ballet, *Alice in Wonderland* (1935). For orchestra, Tweedy wrote a symphonic study, *L'Allegro* (1925), *Three Dances for Orchestra* (1934), *March* in B-flat for student orchestra (1940), and a suite for orchestra, *Williamsburg* (1941). Tweedy died in Danbury, Conn., July 21, 1948.

VAN VECHTEN, CARL (1880–1964) Author, critic, advocate, gadfly of the arts. Born in Cedar Rapids, Iowa, June 17, 1880, Van Vechten came from a family with money, grew up in a cultured atmosphere, and, as a youngster, was interested in the theatre. His earliest writing was done for the Cedar Rapids High School paper. He left for the University of Chicago and, upon graduation in 1903, became a cub reporter for the Chicago *American*. The next year he published *Five Old English Ditties with Music by Carl Van Vechten*. He left Chicago in 1906 to join the staff of the New York *Times* as assistant music critic, the beginning of a long, active, and many-faceted career in the arts. Van Vechten was to be a music and dance critic, author, novelist, and photographer. By the '20s Van Vechten was one of the most important voices in the arts in New York. He was one of the first American critics to write favorably of Stravinsky (q.v.)—Van Vechten, in fact, was present at the Paris premiere of *Le Sacre du Printemps* and wrote a colorful article about the near-riot that ensued. He was the first to write about a young George Gershwin (q.v.); he was fascinated by American popular music and jazz. Whatever, or whomever—musician, dancer, writer, cats—excited him, Van Vechten aided with his articles, advice, or support. He gave up criticism at 40, explaining that at that time "intellectual hardening of the arteries" set in. (This was not true, certainly, in his case, for during the later years of his long life he was interested in the latest in music, dancing, and the other arts; he must have been one of the first to have a kind word to say about Elvis Presley, q.v.) Having collected most of his writings on music in several books, Van Vechten began writing novels; the first, with the hero patterned on himself, was *Peter Whiffle, His Life and Works* (1922). *Nigger Heaven* (1926) was unusual for its time not only because of the title but also because it presented a picture of black life little known to people in the '20s. (Van Vechten was a lifelong friend of the black race, perhaps one of the earliest of the civil rights proponents, as was pointed out in his New York *Times* obituary.) His last novel, *Parties* (1930), presented a sympathetic portrait of his friends Zelda and Scott Fitzgerald. One of his important books was a study of the cat, from folklore to fact, entitled *The Tiger in the House* (1920). Upon concluding his career as a novelist, although he continued writing occasional articles, prefaces, and introductions to books, Van Vechten took up photography and with his 35 mm Leica proceeded to photograph virtually everyone in the art world from the '30s until the '60s. Over those last years he deposited copies of these historic photographs in various institutions: the Museum of the City of New York, Yale, the Schomberg Collection of the New York Public Library, the George Gershwin Memorial Collection of Music and Musical Literature (Fisk University, Nashville, Tenn.), and other archives and libraries. His correspondence was voluminous—this, too, has been deposited in libraries. His books on music include *Music After the Great War* (1915), *Music and Bad Manners* (1916), *Interpreters and Interpretations* (1917), *The Merry-Go-Round* (1918), *The Music of Spain* (1918), and *Red: Papers on Musical Subjects* (1925). Van Vechten died in New York City, Dec. 21, 1964.

VARDELL, CHARLES G., JR. (1893–1962) Composer, teacher. Born in Salisbury, N.C., Aug. 19, 1893, Vardell was a graduate of Princeton University before he changed to music and attended the Eastman School, Rochester, N.Y., where he earned a master's and a doctorate in music. He also studied composition with Percy Goetschius (q.v.) at the Institute of Musical Art (later Juilliard), New York. He taught at the Flora MacDowell College, Red Springs, N.C., and eventually was appointed dean of the Music Department; he later, in 1928, moved to Winston-Salem, N.C., to become dean of the School of Music at Salem College. Vardell's most-played original work was one of his earliest compositional efforts, an orchestral arrangement of a folk song entitled *Joe Clark Steps Out* (1933); his other works include a *Symphony in G Minor* ("Folk Symphony from the Carolina Hills," 1938), *Nocturne Picaresque* (1939), *The Shelf Behind the Door* (1941), and *Exit the Axis* (1944); also *The Inimitable Lovers* for soloists and chorus (1928), *Christmas Prayer for a Nation at War* (1944), and the cantata, *Song in the Wilderness* (1948). A later orchestral work is entitled *Saturday Night*. Vardell died in Winston-Salem, N.C., Oct. 19, 1962.

VARÈSE, EDGARD (1883–1965) Composer, conductor. Born in Paris, Dec. 22, 1883, Varèse seemed destined for a career in engineering (had he complied with his engineer father's wishes) or mathematics, in which he majored as a youngster. He was about 17 when his family moved to Turin, Italy, and Varèse studied harmony and counterpoint at the Turin Conservatory. In 1903 Varèse returned to Paris determined to study music, which he did with Vincent d'Indy and Albert Roussel at the Schola Cantorum and with Charles Widor at the Paris Conservatory. Between 1908 and 1915 Varèse was active in both Paris and Berlin as a choral and orchestra conductor. In France at the time of the outbreak of World War I, he was conscripted into the Army, but then released because of poor health. In December 1915 Varèse arrived in New York City and almost immediately became extraordinarily active in its cultural life. He founded the New Symphony Orchestra (1919) and presented concerts of new music (he resigned when asked to program more accessible music); he also helped to found the International Composers' Guild (q.v.) and the Pan-American Association of Composers (1928). Varèse, best described as an experimentalist, aligned himself with the innovators of American music: Cowell, Ives, Ruggles, et al. (all q.v.). He broke with the musical conventions of the past, introducing new concepts of instrumentation, compositional techniques, and the very function of music itself; Varèse was admired by the avant-garde and detested by traditionalists. He was among the first to experiment with electronic music. By the mid to late 1930s the excitement over experimental music subsided and Varèse virtually stopped composing; he moved westward, where he taught in Santa Fe, N.Mex., and in Los Angeles. He returned to New York in 1940 and founded a choral group that specialized in early music. After World War II a new interest in "modern" music brought Varèse again into the limelight. Some of his "advanced" music, more read about than heard, was recorded, and a new generation discovered him. In the early '50s Varèse began composing on tape. Although many of his early compositions were lost, his most influential were composed after his move to the United States. These include *Amériques* (completed 1922, q.v.), *Offrandes* for soprano and orchestra (1922), *Hyperprism* for woodwinds, brass, and percussion (1923), *Octandre* (1924), *Intégrales* for woodwinds, brass, and percussion (1925), *Arcana* (1927), *Ionisation* for percussion (1933), *Ecuatorial* for bass piano, organ, theremins, brass, and percussion (1934); *Density 21.5* for flute (1936), *Symphony with Chorus* (1937), *Étude pour espace* for chorus, pianos, and percussion (1947), *Déserts* for winds, brass, percussion, and tape (1954), *Good Friday Procession in Verges* for taped sounds (film background score, 1956), *Poème électronique* for 3 tapes (1958), and *Nocturnal* for soprano, bass chorus, and orchestra (begun 1960; completed by Chou Wen-chung, q.v., 1968). Varèse died in New York City, Nov. 6, 1965.

VICTROLA The trademark of the phonograph produced by the Victor Talking Machine Co. (later RCA Victor), introduced in 1906. The word eventually entered the language as the generic term for all phonographs (around the same time that the Edison Home Phonograph, the Columbia Gramophone Company's Grafonola, and others existed). Its pervasiveness was demonstrated in the 1940s, when the President's wife, Eleanor Roosevelt, appeared on CBS radio to accept an album of Columbia Records in celebration of a Columbia anniversary. Upon receiving the records, she graciously thanked the donor and spoke into the microphone, promising to "go right home and play them [the records] on my victrola."

WAGENAAR, BERNARD (1894–1971) Composer, conductor, teacher. Born in Arnhem, The Netherlands, July 18, 1894, Wagenaar studied music with his father, Johan, and with Gerard Veerman and Mme. Veerman Bekker at the Utrecht Conservatory. From 1914 to 1920 he taught the violin and conducted in Holland; he came to the United States in 1920 and, the next year, joined the New York Philharmonic as a violinist. He also performed on harpsichord, piano, organ, and celeste. He branched out as a teacher and joined the staff of the Institute of Musical Art in 1925 and remained there, after it became the Juilliard School of Music, until 1968. He also taught privately, conducted, and lectured on music. Although his works had been performed in the United States in the '20s—the *Divertissements for Orchestra* (1927) won the Eastman School Publication Award and his *Violin Sonata* (1928) the Society for the Publication of American Music Award—Wagenaar won wider attention when Toscanini conducted the New York Philharmonic's performance of the *Second Symphony* in Nov. 1932. In all, he completed 4 symphonies (1926, 1931, 1935, 1949). Other works for orchestra include a *Sinfonietta* (1929), *Triple Concerto* for flute, harp, cello, and orchestra (1935), *Concerto for Violin and Orchestra* (1940), *Fanfare for Airmen* for brass (1942), *Feuilleton* (1942), *Song of Mourning* (1944), *Divertimento No. 2* (1953), *Concert Overture* (1954), and *Preamble* (1965). Wagenaar's works for chamber orchestra are *Fantasietta on British-American Ballads* (1940), *Arrangement of Two Spanish Folksongs* (1942), and *Concertino for Eight Instruments* (1942). For even smaller groupings there are *Three Songs from the Chi-*

nese for voice, flute, harp, and piano (1921); 4 string quartets (although the first was withdrawn; the others: 1931, 1936, 1960); *Sonatina for Cello and Piano* (1934), and *Four Vignettes for Harp* (1965). A *Piano Sonata* dates from 1927. Wagenaar produced one work for the stage, *Pieces of Eight*, "an operatic comedy," presented at Columbia University in May 1944. Other compositions for voice include *From a Very Little Sphinx* (text by Edna St. Vincent Millay, 1925), *El Trillo* for chorus, 2 guitars, drum, and castanets (1942), and *No quierotus Avellanas* for alto, women's chorus, and chamber orchestra (1942). Wagenaar died in Kennebunkport, Maine, May 18, 1971.

WAGNER, JOSEPH FREDERICK (1900–1974) Composer, conductor, teacher. Born in Springfield, Mass., Jan. 9, 1900, Wagner studied with Frederick Converse (q.v.) at the New England Conservatory (1921–23) and with Italian composer Alfredo Casella (during a visit by Casella to the United States, 1928) and in Paris with Nadia Boulanger (q.v.); in Europe he also studied conducting with Pierre Monteux and Felix Weingartner. He settled in the Boston area and for years was associated with the Boston public schools (1923–44); he taught music at Boston University, Rutgers University (New Brunswick, N.J.), Brooklyn College and Hunter College (New York City), the University of Oklahoma, and other institutions. In 1963 he was appointed composer in residence at Pepperdine University, Los Angeles, Calif. Wagner had also been active as a conductor. He founded the Boston Civic Symphony in 1925 and served as conductor until 1944; he conducted the Buffalo Philharmonic, the Duluth Symphony, the Orquesta Sinfónica de Costa Rica, and others. His works include a *Divertissement* (1928), a *Concerto for Piano and Orchestra*

(1929), 3 symphonies (1934, 1945, 1951), *Variations on an old Form* (1939), the overture *American Jubilee* (1945), *Concertino for Harp and Orchestra* (1947), *Concerto Grosso* for band (1949), *Northland Evocation* (1949), *Violin Concerto* (1956), *Concerto for Organ, Brass, and Percussion* (1963), and the ballets *The Birthday of the Infanta* (1935), *Dance Divertissement* (1937), and *Hudson River Legend* (1941). Works for smaller orchestras or chamber groups include a *Rhapsody for Clarinet, Piano, and Strings* (1928), *Sinfonietta Americana* (1931), *Sinfonietta No. 2* (1941), *Two Moments Musical* for string quartet or string orchestra (1927), *Quintet* for piano, flute, clarinet, viola, and cello (1933), *Serenade* for oboe, violin, and cello (1934), *Quartet in C Minor* (1940), *Sonata for Violin and Piano* (1941), *Sonata for Cello and Piano* (1943), *Piano Sonata* (1946), *Fantasy and Fugue* for wind quintet (1963), *Fantasy Sonata* for harp (1963), *Sonata with Differences* for 2 pianos (1963), *Preludes and Toccata* (1964), and *Twelve Concert Preludes* (1970). Wagner's one-act opera, *New England Sampler,* was completed in 1967. There are also several choral works. He died in Los Angeles, Calif., Oct. 12, 1974.

WALD, MAX (1889–1954) Composer, teacher. Born in Litchfield, Ill., July 14, 1889, Wald taught himself to play the piano, studied theory on his own for several years, and wrote songs, a musical comedy, and an operetta before he took formal music studies. This began when he studied harmony in Chicago with Walter Keller in 1904. After a year or so of conducting a touring theatre orchestra, Wald again returned to music study, this time in counterpoint, orchestration and composition with Arthur O. Anderson. Upon completion of these courses Wald himself began teaching at the American Conservatory, Chicago, in 1921. He went to Paris for further study with Vincent d'Indy (1922–23). For the next several years Wald remained in Europe, composing and lecturing in Florence, London, and Vienna. He eventually returned to Chicago, where he again taught at the American Conservatory and became chairman of the Theory Department at the Chicago Musical College in 1936. Wald's compositions include *Sentimental Promenades* for orchestra (1922), *Retrospectives* (1925), *The Dancer Dead* (1931; winner of NBC Award, 1932), *Comedy Overture* (1937), *The Streets of Spring* (1942), *In Praise of Pageantry* (1945), and *Symphony in F* (1947). For chamber orchestra, Wald wrote *Three Serenades* (1937) and *Rhapsody* for small orchestra (1938). His chamber music includes 2 piano sonatas and a sonata for violin and piano. For the theatre, Wald produced *Mirandolina* (1933), *The Country of the Young* (1938), and *Gay Little World* (1942). He also completed an opera in the Americana vein, *A Provincial Episode.* There are also several songs, including some early (1922) ones written under the pseudonym of Paul Ardayne. His *Cycle for Soprano and String Quartet* was completed ca. 1946. He died in Dowagiac, Mich., Aug. 14, 1954.

WARREN, HARRY (b. 1893) Composer. Born Salvatore Guaragna in Brooklyn, N.Y., Dec. 24, 1893, Warren taught himself to play several instruments before dropping out of high school to play the drum in a brass band and traveling with it on the carnival circuit. He had his only formal musical training from the organist of his church (Warren sang in the choir), Pauline Schneider. For years Warren worked at odd jobs, even as an extra, and later assistant director, in early silent movies. He first began playing the piano—to provide mood music for actress Corinne

Griffith—when he worked at the Vitagraph Studios in Brooklyn before World War I; he also began dabbling in songwriting. When war came he enlisted in the Navy, in which he continued playing the piano and composing tunes that no one wanted. After his release from the Navy in 1918, Warren returned to Vitagraph, then drifted to other jobs, from insurance investigator to playing the piano in Healey's Saloon in Brooklyn. One night he was heard by a couple of song pluggers, who liked one of Warren's original tunes and brought him into the publishing firm Stark & Cowan. Two years later, in 1922, Warren published his first successful song, "Rose of the Rio Grande," with Ross Gorman and lyrics by Edgar Leslie; the next year he joined the staff of the major publishers Shapiro, Bernstein & Co. as staff composer. During the '20s Warren collaborated with several lyricists, turning out popular songs, although a song, now and then, might be interpolated into a revue. In 1926 he did "Where Do You Work-a John?" (lyrics by Mortimer Weinberg and Charley Marks); 2 years later he wrote "Nagasaki" with Mort Dixon; it has proved to be one of Warren's most enduring tunes, an especial favorite with jazz musicians. In 1930 he contributed songs to the revue *Sweet and Low*, out of which came "Cheerful Little Earful" (lyrics by Ira Gershwin and Billy Rose) and "Would You Like to Take a Walk?" (lyrics by Dixon and Rose). Warren would return to Broadway again, but he truly found his voice in a place he detested: Hollywood. As were so many New York–based composers, Warren was summoned to California at the beginning of the Depression to work for films. Teamed with Al Dubin (1891–1945) at Warner Brothers, Warren hit his stride in *42nd Street* (1932), one of the best of the backstage musical films—and one that initiated the second cycle of the genre. For it Warren and

Dubin produced the evocative title song and "Shuffle Off to Buffalo," among others; they continued in good form with their next film, *Gold Diggers of 1933*, with its Gold Diggers' Song, "We're in the Money," a Depression lament "Remember My Forgotten Man" (at the time, the unemployed veteran of World War I), and the beautiful "Shadow Waltz" (almost equally famous for the choreography and camera direction by Busby Berkeley). For nearly a decade Warren dominated the musicals at Warner Brothers (although other writers worked there also) and composed some of the most popular songs of the Depression: "Boulevard of Broken Dreams" (*Moulin Rouge,* 1934), "I'll String Along With You" (*Twenty Million Sweethearts,* 1934), "I Only Have Eyes for You" (*Dames,* 1934), "Lullaby of Broadway" (*Gold Diggers of 1935,* 1934), "About a Quarter to Nine" (*Go into Your Dance,* 1935), "Don't Give Up the Ship" (*Shipmates Forever,* 1935), "With Plenty of Money and You" (*Gold Diggers of 1937,* 1936), "Remember Me?" (*Mr. Dodd Takes the Air,* 1937), "September in the Rain" (*Melody for Two,* 1937), "You Must Have Been a Beautiful Baby" (*Hard to Get,* lyrics by Johnny Mercer, 1938), "Jeepers Creepers" (*Going Places,* lyrics by Mercer, 1938), and "Down Argentine Way" (*Down Argentine Way,* lyrics by Mack Gordon, 1940). By this time Warren had moved over to other studios, eventually doing most of his later work for 20th Century-Fox. The second phase of musical film resurgence was unexpectedly followed by a third, which reflected the change from Depression to war. Warren very skillfully made the transition from the music of one era to another and composed some of the best-known film songs made popular by the big bands. One of the first was "Chattanooga Choo Choo" from *Sun Valley Serenade* (lyrics by

Gordon, 1941), which featured the Glenn Miller band; this was followed by "I've Got a Gal in Kalamazoo" and "Serenade in Blue" (*Orchestra Wives*, lyrics by Gordon, 1942), "You'll Never Know" (*Hello, Frisco, Hello*, lyrics by Gordon, 1943), and "The More I See You" (*Diamond Horseshoe*, lyrics by Gordon, 1945). Warren then moved to MGM, where he collaborated with Johnny Mercer on the songs for *The Harvey Girls* (1946), out of which came "On the Atchison, Topeka and the Santa Fe." With Ralph Blane he did the songs for *Summer Holiday* (based on O'Neill's *Ah, Wilderness*) in 1948. Although its best-known song was "The Stanley Steamer," the entire score was one of his best. With Ira Gershwin he collaborated on *The Barkleys of Broadway* (1949) with excellent results: "You'd Be Hard to Replace," "Shoes with Wings On," and "My One and Only Highland Fling." But the film cycle had run its course again, and after a few more film scores, including *Summer Stock* (1950) and *The Belle of New York* (1952), an unsuccessful return to Broadway with *Shangri-La* (a musical version of *Lost Horizon*, 1956), and a number of individual songs, Warren went into involuntary retirement. Flexible, he returned to the theme song for the television age and wrote the musical signatures for Wyatt Earp ("The Legend of Wyatt Earp," lyrics by Harold Adamson, 1954), "The Californians" (lyrics by Adamson), plus several film titles, among them "The Rose Tattoo" (lyrics by Jack Brooks, 1955), "Hey, Marty" (lyrics by Paddy Chayefsky, 1955), and "Separate Tables" (lyrics by Adamson, 1958). In 1970 Warren wrote several songs with lyricist Richard O. Kraemer and published later (ca. 1975) a dozen of his *Piano Vignettes*. Warren is unique in that he is the only composer to receive 3 Academy Awards ("Lullaby of Broad-way," "You'll Never Know," "On the Atchison, Topeka and the Santa Fe").

WAYNE, MABEL (b. 1904) Composer, pianist, vocalist. Born in Brooklyn, N.Y., July 16, 1904, Wayne grew up in a family of music makers. She began piano lessons as a girl in Brooklyn, took private lessons while visiting an aunt in Switzerland, and upon returning enrolled in the New York School of Music. In 1920, her schooling completed, she went into vaudeville as a singer and dancer who also played the piano. Drawn to popular songs, she spent her free time during her vaudeville career composing tunes. The first published song, "Don't Wake Me Up, Let Me Dream" written with Abel Baer and L. Wolfe Gilbert (1925) was successful enough to enable Wayne to take a California vacation. Inspired by her Southern California surroundings, or the climate, she composed the tune that became "In a Little Spanish Town," which was given lyrics by Sam Lewis and Joe Young. Published in 1926, it became Wayne's first million-copy song; in the same vein, the next year she and L. Wolfe Gilbert collaborated on "Ramona" (q.v.). This song, too, sold a million copies of sheet music and was very popular; it also typed Wayne as a composer with an American-Hispanic accent. In keeping with this, she composed the melody to "It Happened in Monterey" (lyrics by Billy Rose) for the film *The King of Jazz* (1930). She broke out of the Spanish mold with the popular "Little Man, You've Had a Busy Day" (lyrics by Al Hoffman and Maurice Sigler) in 1934. Besides traveling widely, she continued to compose songs, but has not been prolific. She had some success with "A Dreamer's Holiday" (lyrics by Kim Gannon) in 1949 and wrote "Guessing" (lyrics by Sammy Gallop) in 1954. In the '30s she made frequent radio appearances and toured with her own orchestra.

WEAVER, POWELL (1890–1951) Composer, organist, pianist. Born in Clearfield, Pa., June 10, 1890, Weaver studied at the Institute of Musical Art (later Juilliard School of Music), New York, with Goetschius (q.v.; composition) and Gaston Dethier (organ); he later went to Italy, where he studied with Ottorino Respighi and Pietro Yon. Weaver gave organ recitals in Italy, e.g., at St. Peter's in Rome. He settled, after his return to the United States, in Kansas City, Kans. He eventually became head of the Music Department at Ottawa University, Kans.; he was also organist and choir director at the First Baptist Church, as well as music director at the Grand Avenue Temple and the B'nai Jehudah Temple in Kansas City. He was also, for a time, piano accompanist for such singers as Johanna Gadski and Richard Crooks. Weaver produced a great deal of choral music and some chamber works and orchestra compositions. Of the latter, his best known is the symphonic poem *The Vagabond* (1930); other works for orchestra include *Plantation Overture* (1925), *An Imaginary Ballet* (1925), *The Faun,* a suite in 3 movements (1927), *Symphonic Poem* (1937), *Dance of the Sand-Dune Cranes* for piano and orchestra (1941), and *Fugue for String Orchestra* (ca. 1946). His chamber works include *Exultation* for organ and piano (1933), *An Ode* for piano and string quartet (1936), a *String Quartet* (1937), and a *Sonata for Violin and Piano* (1945). Weaver's vocal pieces include *Ho! For Windy Weather, Boating Song,* 2 *Sabbath Evening Services,* and the songs "Moon-Marketing," "The Abbot of Derry," and "The Night Will Never Stay." Before his death Weaver completed *Copper Country Sketches* for organ. He died in Oakland, Calif., Dec. 22, 1951.

WEISS, ADOLPH (1891–1971) Composer, conductor, bassoonist. Born in Baltimore, Md., Sept. 12, 1891, Weiss studied with Adolf Weidig at the Chicago Conservatory and with Cornelius Rybner and Abraham Lilienthal in New York. From 1907 to 1924 Weiss played the bassoon in various orchestras: the Russian Symphony (at the age of 16), the New York Philharmonic, and the New York and Chicago symphonies. He went to Berlin in 1924, enrolled in the Akademie der Künste, and became the first American-born musician to study with Arnold Schoenberg (q.v.), with whom he worked until 1927. Some of his works were composed under the influence of Schoenberg's 12-tone system. His works include a piano *Fantasie* (1918), *I Segreti* for orchestra (1924), 4 string quartets (1923, 1926, 1929, 1932), *Chamber Symphony* (1928), *Twelve Preludes* for piano (1927), *American Life,* a "Scherzoso Jazzoso" (1929), *Seven Songs* for soprano and string quartet (text by Emily Dickinson, 1928), *Sonata da Camera* for flute and viola (1930), *Wind Quintet* (1932), *Piano Sonata* (1932), *Theme and Variations* for orchestra (1931), *Suite* for orchestra (1941), *Petite Suite* for flute, clarinet, and bassoon (1939), *Violin Sonata* (1941), *Concerto for Bassoon and String Quartet* (1949), *Trumpet Concerto* (1952), *Tone Poem* for brass and percussion (1957), and *Rhapsody* for 4 French horns (1957). Weiss's major choral work is entitled *The Libation Bearers* (after Aeschylus) for soloists, chorus and orchestra (1930). He also composed a ballet for 2 pianos (1945). There are other, smaller, works for instruments and voice. Weiss died in Van Nuys, Calif., Feb. 20, 1971.

WESSEL, MARK (1894–1973) Composer, pianist, teacher. Born in Coldwater, Mich., Mar. 26, 1894, Wessel was a graduate of Northwestern University, Evanston, Ill.; he also studied with Schoenberg (q.v.). He later taught—theory and piano—at Northwestern and, after that, was appointed professor of piano and composition at the University of Colorado. Wessel frequently appeared in concerts and recitals as piano soloist. The bulk of his output consists of chamber music, which includes a *Sextet* for flute, oboe, horn, bassoon, clarinet, and piano (1928), *Sonata for Violin and Piano* (1930), *Trio* for violin, cello, and piano (1931), *Prelude and Fugue* for string quartet (1931), *String Quartet* (1931), *Sonatine* for piano (1935), *Ballade* for 2 pianos (also for violin and piano, 1936), *Plains and Mountains* for piano and string quartet (1937), *Sonatine* for trumpet and piano (1942), and *Sonata* for cello and piano (1943). For orchestra, Wessel composed a *Symphonie Concertante* for piano, horn, and orchestra (1929), a *Symphony* (1932), *Holiday* (1933), *Song and Dance* (1934), a *Concerto for Piano and Orchestra* (1942); a *Concertino* for flute and chamber orchestra (1928), and a *Ballade* for violin, oboe, and string orchestra (1932). Wessel's *Scherzo Burlesque* for piano and strings was presented with the composer at the piano and Howard Hanson conducting at the Eastman School Festival (1926). Wessel was awarded 2 Guggenheim Fellowships and a Pulitzer Scholarship. Wessel died in Beverly Hills, Mich., May 2, 1973.

WHITE, CLARENCE CAMERON (1880–1960) Composer, violinist, teacher. Born in Clarksville, Tenn., Aug. 10, 1880, White grew up in Oberlin, Ohio, where his father was a doctor. After his father's death, White's mother remarried and the family moved to Washington, D.C., where White attended public schools and Howard University. He studied the violin and enrolled at the Oberlin Conservatory for further work, hoping to become a concert violinist.

After graduation in 1901, White returned to Washington, where he taught violin at the Washington Conservatory of Music. In 1906 he went to London to study with the eminent Russian violinist Michael Zacharewitsch; he returned again in 1908 and worked with (and possibly also studied with) the great black English composer Samuel Coleridge-Taylor. Upon returning to the United States, White settled in Boston, where he taught for several years, between concert tours as a recitalist. In 1924 he became head of the Music Department at West Virginia State College; later he was appointed director of music at Hampton Institute, Va. For much of his original work, White drew upon black themes; his compositions include *Bandana Sketches* for violin (1920), *Cabin Memories* (1921), *From the Cotton Fields* (1921), and a handful of orchestra works: *Piece for Strings and Timpani, Katamba Rhapsody, Symphony in D Minor,* and 2 violin concertos. White also published collections based on black music: *Forty Negro Spirituals* (1927) and *Traditional Negro Spirituals* (1940). His *String Quartet* (1932) is based on black themes. For the stage, White composed incidental music to the play *Tambour* (by John F. Matheus; 1928), which includes also the ballet *Meringue*. White and Matheus also collaborated on the opera *Ouanga* (1932), based on the life of the Haitian liberator Jean Jacques Dessalines. The opera has been presented several times, e.g., at the Metropolitan in 1956. White's orchestral *Elegy* won the (Edward B.) Benjamin Award in 1954. He died in New York City, June 30, 1960.

WHITE, PAUL (1895–1973) Composer, violinist, teacher. Born in Bangor, Maine, Aug. 22, 1895, White began studying the violin in his hometown and completed his musical education at the New England Conservatory, Boston,

with George W. Chadwick (q.v.), Felix
Winternitz, and Daniel Gregory Mason
(q.v.). He also studied the violin with
Eugène Ysaÿe and conducting with Eugene Goossens. He was first violinist
with the Cincinnati Symphony for several years. He returned to the New England Conservatory to teach and to serve
as concertmaster (1921–23). He later
joined the staff of the Eastman School of
Music, Rochester, N.Y., where he taught
conducting, and where several of his
works were first performed. His most
performed compositions were the *Five
Miniatures* for orchestra (1933) and *Sea
Chanty* for harp and strings (1942).
Other works include *Lyric Overture*
(1919), *Feuilles Symphoniques* (1920),
Poem for Violin (1922), the overture
Pagan Festival (1927), *Voyage of the
Mayflower* for chorus and orchestra
(1928), *Symphony in E Minor* (1932),
Lake Spray (1938), *Boston Sketches*
(1938), *Lake Placid Scenes* (1943), *Idyl*
(1944), and *Andante and Rondo* for
cello and orchestra (1945). For chamber
orchestra, White produced an *Old Fashioned Suite* (1921), *Fantastic Dance*
for woodwinds (1922), and *Sinfonietta*
for strings (1936); he also composed a
String Quartet (1925) and a *Sonata for
Violin and Piano* (1926). White died in
Rochester, N.Y., May 31, 1973.

WHITEMAN, PAUL (1890–1967)
Bandleader, violinist. Born in Denver,
Colo., Mar. 28, 1890, Whiteman came
from a musical family and was an accomplished violinist and violist. He was
a member of the Denver Symphony's
string section and, later, of the People's
Symphony, San Francisco, Calif. He
spent some time in the U. S. Navy as a
bandsman during World War I. In 1919
he formed a band that became quite
popular on the West Coast. One of the
members of that band was pianist-
arranger Ferde Grofé (q.v.). In 1920
Whiteman brought the band to New

York and began his reign as the alleged
"King of Jazz." Employing such arrangers as Grofé and, later, Bill Challis,
Whiteman featured spiced-up dance
music that was highly arranged and
flavored with jazzy touches (some of
which were supplied by the true jazzmen
Whiteman employed in the late '20s).
The Whiteman band, then consisting of
8 men and Whiteman, began recording
for Victor Records in 1920 and quickly
became a popular recording orchestra,
concentrating on deftly arranged popular
and show tunes. The band was also successful in clubs and theatres and, following a successful tour, became very popular in Europe. It was in 1924 that Whiteman made his greatest impression with
an "Experiment in Modern Music"
(q.v.) in Aeolian Hall; the concert introduced a new work, the *Rhapsody in Blue*
(q.v.), by George Gershwin (q.v.).
Although not a jazz work, the *Rhapsody
in Blue* (which almost everyone claimed
was a study in jazz) ensured Whiteman
his crown as king. By 1928 his band
boasted such membership as Bix Beiderbecke (q.v.), Frankie Trumbauer, Red
Nichols, Jimmy and Tommy Dorsey
(q.v.), Joe Venuti, and Eddie Lang.
Whiteman also employed such vocalists
as Bing Crosby (q.v.; as one of the 3
Rhythm Boys), Ramona Davies, Johnny
Mercer (q.v.), and Joan Edwards.
Whiteman's band appeared on the stage
and in films and, especially during the
'30s, was busy with radio work. Essentially, Whiteman's was one of the earliest
of the big bands. After the sensational
success of the Gershwin *Rhapsody*,
Whiteman sought to duplicate it by com-
missioning various American popular
composers to write specifically for his
band. Although he never achieved this,
a few of these are worth mentioning:
Rube Bloom's *Soliloquy* (1926), *Metropolis*, a "fantasy of themes by Matt
Malneck and Harry Barris" arranged

and orchestrated by Ferde Grofé (q.v.; 1927), *Three Shades of Blue* (Grofé, 1928), *Blue Moonlight* by Dana Suesse (q.v.; 1934), and *Deep Purple* by Peter De Rose (q.v.; 1934). Others who composed for the Whiteman band include Eastwood Lane, John Alden Carpenter, Leo Sowerby, Deems Taylor, and Richard Rodgers (all q.v.). The rise of the big bands led to a waning of Whiteman's popularity, though he frequently conducted on radio or appeared in pops concerts, invariably programming the *Rhapsody in Blue* (its middle theme was his signature music). In 1955 he was the summer replacement show for Jackie Gleason on television, but did not remain consistently active. Whiteman died in Doylestown, Pa., Dec. 29, 1967.

WHITHORNE, EMERSON (1884–1958) Composer, pianist, teacher, writer. Born in Cleveland, Ohio, Sept. 6, 1884, Whithorne studied music in Cleveland with James H. Rogers, who encouraged him to stay with music despite the objections of Whithorne senior. By the time he was 15, Whithorne played the piano professionally on the Chautauqua circuit. He went to Vienna for further study with Robert Fuchs and Theodor Leschetizky. Whithorne then moved to London (1907–14), where he taught, wrote music, and was a music critic for the *Pall Mall Gazette*. He returned to the United States in 1915 and settled in St. Louis, where he was executive editor for the Art Publication Society. He left in 1920 to take a position as vice-president in the Composers' Music Corporation. Whithorne decided in 1922 to drop his executive activities to concentrate on composition. His suite for piano *New York Days and Nights* (which he later orchestrated) was selected as the representative American composition at the International Festival of Contemporary Music at Salzburg in 1923. He also composed 2 symphonies

(1929, 1935). Other works for orchestra include *La Nuit* (1917), *Adventures of a Samurai* (1919), *The Aeroplane* (1920), *Fata Morgana* (1927), *The Dream Pedlar* (1930), *Fandango* (1931), a *Violin Concerto* (1931), and *Moon Trail* (1933). His vocal compositions include 2 settings of poems by the black poet Countee Cullen: *Saturday's Child* for soprano, tenor, and chamber orchestra (1926) and *The Grim Troubadour* for baritone and string quartet (1927). Whithorne's *Stroller's Serenade* was completed in 1943. His chamber works include 2 string quartets (the first subtitled "Greek Impressions," 1917; 1930), a *Piano Quintet* (1928), and a *Violin Sonata* (1932). There is also a suite for solo piano, *El Camino Real* (1937). His ballet, *Sooner or Later* (1925), was staged in 1925 and is scored for chorus and chamber orchestra. Whithorne also composed incidental music for the Theatre Guild's production of O'Neill's *Marco Millions* (1928). He composed one work for piano and orchestra, *Poem*, in 1926. Incidental information: Whithorne's *New York Days and Nights* was presented in its jazzy orchestral version by a Paul Whiteman rival in the "symphonic jazz" field, Vincent Lopez, at the Metropolitan Opera in November 1924. Whithorne died in New York City, Mar. 25, 1958.

WHITING, RICHARD A. (1891–1938) Composer. Born in Peoria, Ill., Nov. 12, 1891, Whiting was completely self-taught in music, although both his parents were musical. His formal schooling was acquired at the Harvard Military School, Los Angeles (there was yet no Hollywood, as such). Back in Peoria, Whiting began writing songs, even inducing his parents (his father was a successful real estate man) to finance the publication of some of his early efforts. A trip with a musician friend to Detroit led to a meeting between Whiting and music publisher Jerome Remick, who not only took 3 of Whiting's songs for publication, but also offered him a job as the professional manager of the Remick office in Detroit. Whiting began work at Remick in 1912 (at $25 a week) and earned extra money playing the piano with a hotel band. As a songwriter, Whiting hit his stride in 1915, with the publication of the very successful "It's Tulip Time in Holland" (lyrics by Dave Radford). Several other popular hits followed and he had yet another great-selling song, "Till We Meet Again" (lyrics by Ray Egan, 1918). By 1920 Whiting was one of the most successful composers in Tin Pan Alley. He moved into Broadway briefly in 1919 to provide the music for two revues: *Toot Sweet* (lyrics by Ray Egan) and *George White's Scandals of 1919* (lyrics by Arthur Jackson). Neither score produced any song as popular as Whiting's Tin Pan Alley songs: "The Japanese Sandman" (lyrics by Egan, 1920), "Ain't We Got Fun?" (lyrics by Egan and Gus Kahn, 1921), "Sleepy Time Gal" (with Ange Lorenzo; lyrics by Egan and Joseph R. Alden, 1925), the novelty hit "Horses" (lyrics by Byron Gay, 1926), and, among others, "She's Funny That Way" (with Neil Moret, 1928). Most of these songs were written in Detroit, where Whiting lived through the bulk of his so-called Tin Pan Alley years; his daughter, Margaret, who became a fine popular singer, was born there in 1924. In 1929 Whiting, like so many writers of popular song, went to Hollywood. His first assignment was to write the music for a Maurice Chevalier movie, *Innocents of Paris* (1929), out of which came the popular "Louise" (lyrics by Leo Robin). Except for another brief Broadway outing—*Free for All* (1931) and *Take a Chance* (1932) to which he contributed "You're an Old Smoothie" (with Nacio Herb Brown, lyrics by B. G. DeSylva)—Whiting remained pretty much a Hollywood composer for the rest of his life. Some of his more enduring songs from films were "Beyond the Blue Horizon" (from *Monte Carlo;* with W. Franke Harling, lyrics by Robin, 1930), "My Ideal" (from *Playboy of Paris;* with Newell Chase, lyrics by Robin, 1930), "One Hour with You" (from *One Hour with You;* lyrics by Robin, 1932), "On the Good Ship Lollipop" (from *Bright Eyes;* lyrics by Sidney Clare, 1934), "When Did You Leave Heaven?" (from *Sing, Baby, Sing;* lyrics by Walter Bullock, 1936), "I Can't Escape from You" (from *Rhythm on the Range;* lyrics by Robin), "Have You Got Any Castles, Baby?" (from *Varsity Show;* lyrics by Johnny Mercer, 1937), "Too Marvelous for Words" (from *Ready, Willing and Able;* lyrics by Mercer, 1937), and "Hooray for Hollywood" (from *Hollywood Hotel;* lyrics by Mercer, 1937). Whiting died in Beverly Hills, Calif., Feb. 10, 1938.

"WITHIN THE QUOTA" Ballet, music by Cole Porter (q.v.) and "libretto" by an old Yale friend, Gerald Murphy. The ballet spoofed the American Way of Life of the jazzy '20s and featured such identifiable types as a cowboy, a movie star (obviously patterned after Mary Pickford), the moneyed—all as seen through the innocent eyes of a newly arrived immigrant. Murphy's backdrops, on which the front pages of newspapers were projected ("Unknown Banker Buys Atlantic"), underscored the satire. Porter's well-wrought music complemented the tone of the piece. This marked one of the earliest attempts at using jazz elements in what was substantially a concert composition. *Within the Quota* was premiered at the Théâtre des Champs-Élysées, Paris, by the Ballets Suédois, Oct. 23, 1923, and presented in New York at the Century Theater in November. Presented on the same program at the Paris premiere was Milhaud's *La Création du Monde* (q.v.), another early jazz-inflected work.

THE WOLVERINES A band of white musicians formed in Chicago in 1923 to play in the jazz manner of Joseph "King" Oliver (q.v.). The notable fact about this group was the presence of Bix Beiderbecke (q.v.) on cornet; other members included Al Gande (trombone), Jimmy Hartwell (clarinet), George Johnson (tenor saxophone), Dick Voynow (piano), Bob Gillette (guitar), Min Leibrook (tuba), and Vic Moore (drums). The Wolverines made their first recordings for Gennett Records in February 1924. Later in the year, Beiderbecke left the band to join the Charley Straight band for a while before moving on to New York. Without Beiderbecke, the Wolverines broke up. Their recordings on which Beiderbecke is heard have become collector's items among jazz enthusiasts.

WOOD-HILL, MABEL See Mabel Wood Hill.

YANCEY, JIMMY (1894–1951) Composer, pianist. Born in Chicago, Ill., sometime in 1894, Yancey was a boy singer (at 6) and dancer with the Bert Earl Company in vaudeville. He toured the United States and Europe before World War I (and is said to have appeared before King George V and Queen Mary of Britain). He settled back in Chicago ca. 1913 after retiring from vaudeville; his only piano lessons he had from his brother Alonzo. Yancey was popular as a pianist in clubs and rent parties and an influence on such younger pianists as Meade "Lux" Lewis, Albert Ammons, and Pine Top Smith. His was a poetic, gentle style of performing 8-to-the-bar boogie-woogie. Around 1925 Yancey, tired of playing in gin mills, took a job as grounds keeper at the Chicago White Sox' Comiskey Park. He continued to play in private, but no longer appeared in clubs and virtually dropped out of sight, just as some of his "students" came to prominence. A Decca recording by "Lux" Lewis, *Yancey Special*, brought attention to Yancey, and the later boogie-woogie craze brought even more until he was coaxed out of retirement in 1939 to record. He made dozens of recordings, including many with his wife, Estelle "Mama" Yancey. He made his last recordings in 1950. He died in Chicago, of diabetes, Sept. 17, 1951.

"YES! WE HAVE NO BANANAS" An extremely, some would say revoltingly, popular nonsense song published in 1923. The collaboration of Irving Conn (1898–1961) and Frank Silver (1896–1960), "Yes! We Have No Bananas" supposedly memorialized the saying of a Greek fruit dealer whose sentences combined the positive with the negative. It was a phrase difficult to avoid for some time in the '20s. According to tune detective Sigmund Spaeth, the melody was constructed from phrases borrowed from several songs, plus a quotation from Handel's *Hallelujah Chorus* and "My Bonnie Lies Over the Ocean." To the many who made it one of the best-selling songs of the era, this intelligence meant very little. Conn and Silver produced only a few other songs, none of which struck the public fancy like "Yes! We Have No Bananas."

YOUMANS, VINCENT (1898–1946) Composer. Born in New York City, Sept. 27, 1898, Youmans, though he took the customary childhood piano lessons, prepared originally for a career in engineering. (He apparently had little urge to go into the family business: Youmans Hats.) On completion of his schooling, Youmans took a job in Wall Street, and with the coming of World War I enlisted in the U. S. Navy, which stationed him at the Great Lakes Naval Training Station. There he assisted in the production of entertainment and began writing music. One of his efforts pleased John Philip Sousa and was widely played as a march (this was later used by Youmans as "Hallelujah" in the stage musical *Hit the Deck* in 1927). Out of the Navy, Youmans abandoned the idea of an engineering career and went to work as a pianist for the T. B. Harms company; he also worked as a rehearsal pianist for Victor Herbert shows. Youmans was signed as a staff composer at Harms by the astute Max Dreyfus and was given his first show assignment in 1921. The result was *Two Little Girls in Blue,* with music also by Paul Lanin and lyrics by "Arthur Francis" (pseudonym of Ira Gershwin, q.v.). While the show was not especially successful, some of its songs were popular: "Oh, Me! Oh, My! (Oh You!)," "Dolly," and Who's Who with You?" In 1923 Youmans had 2 shows on Broadway, *Wildflower* and *Mary Jane McKane;* for the former he wrote a characteristic rhythm number, "Bambalina" (lyrics by Otto Harbach and Oscar Hammerstein II). His first long-running hit show was *No, No, Nanette* (1925), for which Youmans wrote such songs as "Tea for Two," "I Want to Be Happy," and "Where Has My Hubby Gone Blues." He was coproducer of his next success, *Hit the Deck* (1927), from which came "Sometimes I'm Happy" (lyrics by Irving Caesar) and "Hallelujah" (lyrics by Clifford Grey and Leo Robin). Encouraged by the experience of *Hit the Deck,* Youmans, who wished to control all aspects of his shows, decided to be sole producer of his next show, which, after a long time aborning, turned out to be *Great Day!* (1929), a dismal failure. Not musically, however, for it was graced with such songs as "Great Day," "More Than You Know," and "Without a Song" (all with lyrics by Edward Eliscu and Billy Rose). The following year, 1930, was no more successful, except that from *Smiles* came

"Time on My Hands" (lyrics by Harold Adamson and Mack Gordon). Youmans' final attempt at the dual role of composer-producer resulted in *Through the Years* (1932), another failure. Three of its songs were excellent: "Through the Years," "Drums in My Heart," and "You're Everywhere" (lyrics by Edward Heyman). After this series of failures, Youmans left for California, where several of his earlier shows had already been filmed. His first full-fledged effort was the highly successful *Flying Down to Rio* (1933)—and it was also his last. The film was notable for several reasons: it introduced the new dance team of Fred Astaire and Ginger Rogers, and Youmans and lyricists Gus Kahn and Edward Eliscu provided such songs as "Music Makes Me," "Orchids in the Moonlight," "The Carioca," and the title song. *Flying Down to Rio* was important in that its success spurred on the then new phase of the film musical. But Youmans gained little from this; afflicted with tuberculosis, he was hospitalized in a Denver sanatorium. He left after a while and announced that he intended to move to New Orleans to work on "serious" music, none of which appears to have been written. He also spoke of a trunkful of songs, but few of those have materialized. In 1944 he felt strong enough (or ambitious enough) to mount a new production, *The Vincent Youmans Ballet Revue,* which suffered 2 disastrous openings in Baltimore and Boston. Youmans was hospitalized again and, shortly after, returned to Denver, where he died on Apr. 5, 1946.

THE ZIEGFELD FOLLIES A series of opulent revues produced by Florenz Ziegfeld, Jr. (1867–1932), the first in 1907 and his last in 1932 (the tradition, complete with his name, was carried into the '40s). Ziegfeld, whose showmanship overshadowed his musicianship, put his money on girls, costumes (and the lack thereof; he was "glorifying the American girl"), and elaborate sets designed by the great Joseph Urban (beginning with the 1915 edition). Although such songwriters as Irving Berlin (q.v.), Victor Herbert (q.v.), Rudolf Friml (q.v.), Louis Hirsch, and Harry Tierney (q.v.) contributed songs to the *Follies*, the revues were best remembered for its stars, among them Anna Held (who was Mrs. Ziegfeld for a time), Fanny Brice, Bert Williams, Ann Pennington, Ed Wynn, W. C. Fields, Eddie Cantor, Will Rogers, Gilda Gray (known for her "shimmy"), Vivienne Segal, Ruth Etting, Marilyn Miller, and Helen Morgan. The success of the *Follies* resulted in imitations such as *George White's Scandals* and *Earl Carroll's Vanities*. Many of the *Follies* stars also appeared in other Ziegfeld productions of note: Marilyn Miller and Leon Errol in *Sally* (1920), Helen Morgan in *Show Boat* (1927), and Ruth Etting and Eddie Cantor in *Whoopee* (1928). Perhaps the best-known song identified with the *Follies* is Irving Berlin's "A Pretty Girl Is Like a Melody" from the 1919 edition; for this production Berlin also wrote "You'd Be Surprised." After Ziegfeld's death the Shubert brothers bought the rights to the name and produced a *Follies* in 1934, 1936, and 1943. But without Ziegfeld the day of the *Follies* was over.

VI

Time of Trouble:
Depression and War
(1930–1950)

The social-political-economic disasters that enclosed the period to be covered in this section affected musicians and music as they did other professions and arts. In the concert world a general conservatism set in (with the usual expected exceptions); avant-garde and experimental music were not welcomed as they had been during the Jazz Age. Even the earthy and lively jazz submerged and sweet bands became popular; melancholy torch songs—such as the classic "Stormy Weather" and "Brother, Can You Spare a Dime"—set the theme of much popular music of the Depression of the 1930s. The musical theatre concentrated on the less expensive revue, although a few classic musicals emerged even in those tight-money days. Hollywood enjoyed one of its golden ages in the Depression, musically; some of the most enduring songs of the '30s were written for films.

Even the old masters of Broadway went West: Irving Berlin, Jerome Kern, the Gershwin brothers, Cole Porter, Vincent Youmans, others; they were eventually joined by the younger masters who came of professional age during the early '30s, such as Harold Arlen, Arthur Schwartz, Hoagy Carmichael, and Frank Loesser. There they worked side by side with the established Hollywood songwriters, Harry Warren, Nacio Herb Brown, Richard Whiting, Harry Revel, Ralph Rainger, and Arthur Johnston, to name only a few. The background scoring for feature films (as opposed to musicals) developed into an important form of its own, with scores ranging from Max Steiner's *King Kong* to Virgil Thomson's music for the documentary film *The Plow That Broke the Plains*. A good deal of Hollywood's film scores during the '30s, '40s, and '50s were composed by European-born and -trained musicians: Steiner, Miklós Rózsa, Franz Waxman, Dmitri Tiomkin, and Erich Wolfgang Korngold, among others. Native-born composers also wrote for films with often impressive results: Alfred

Newman, (*Street Scene, The Song of Bernadette*), Bernard Herrmann (*Citizen Kane, Psycho*), Victor Young (*For Whom the Bell Tolls, Around the World in 80 Days*), Aaron Copland (*Of Mice and Men, Our Town*), Thomson (primarily documentaries), and the younger Leonard Bernstein (*On the Waterfront*).

During this same period, despite the Depression and its pinch, there was a flowering of the American symphony, a flurry of opera, and the birth of ballet. Fittingly, early in 1930 Randall Thompson's *Symphony No. 1* was heard for the first time and, near the close of the year, Howard Hanson's "Romantic" (his 2nd) was premiered. These well-wrought, rather conservative works seemed to set the general mood of the time, which, Virgil Thomson observed, "was not for novelty." His own *Symphony No. 2* was completed the next year, as were Thompson's splendid *Symphony No. 2* and William Grant Still's impressive, evocative *Afro-American Symphony*. And so it continued through the '40s: Bernard Wagenaar's *Symphony No. 2* (1932), Copland's prickly, superb *Short Symphony* (1932–33, his 2nd), Roy Harris' *Symphony 1933* (1934), and William Levi Dawson's *Negro Folk Symphony* (1934). Samuel Barber, of the new generation, completed his *Symphony in One Movement* in 1936, the same year in which Daniel Gregory Mason, of an older generation, produced *A Lincoln Symphony*. Roy Harris composed a masterwork in his *Third Symphony* (1938) and a charming compilation in the *Folk Song Symphony* (1941). Two members of the younger generation were heard in 1941, William Schuman (with his 3rd) and Paul Creston (his first); Leonard Bernstein also completed a first symphony in 1942—the *Jeremiah*. The following year Schuman's fine *Symphony for Strings* (his 5th) was performed in Boston for the first time; that same year brought 2 exceptional compositions from what the younger men regarded as the Establishment: Howard Hanson's *Fourth Symphony* and Walter Piston's *Second*. By this time the United States was embroiled in the Second World War and the music mirrored that, either in mood or directly, as in Marc Blitzstein's *Airborne Symphony*, written while he was serving in the U. S. Air Force (1944). Creston scored a hit with his well-received *Symphony No. 2*, with its remarkable, rhythmic, and at times big band sound, finale (1945). As the '40s came to a close, the symphonic outpouring reached a peak in 1946 with Copland's *Third Symphony*, Howard Swanson's *Short Symphony*, Roger Sessions' *Symphony No. 2*, and Peter Mennin's *Symphony No. 3*.

As if to underscore such fruitful activity, the Pulitzer Prize committee saw fit to recognize the American symphony by awarding its prize in 1947 to Charles Ives! This was for his *Third Symphony* which dated from 1911.

Wallingford Riegger's *Third Symphony*, also an award winner (New York Music Critics Circle Award), employing a modified (i.e., personal) 12-tone technique, marked the end of the primarily conservative trend and suggested another period of experimentation that the '50s would bring; a great deal of the New Music that would come was not written in the symphonic form at all.

Although opera suffered during the Depression years (there was a "Save the

Metropolitan" campaign in 1933), the '30s were a time of productivity in American opera. Deems Taylor's *Peter Ibbetson* was produced at the Metropolitan with great fanfare in 1931; Louis Gruenberg's *The Emperor Jones,* starring the American baritone Lawrence Tibbett, opened there early in 1933. Howard Hanson's *Merry Mount,* which drew upon American themes of an earlier time, was first seen in 1933; the next year brought, with appropriate consternation, Thomson's musical setting of Gertrude Stein's *Four Saints in Three Acts.* One of the most impressive of all American operas, George Gershwin's *Porgy and Bess,* was presented in a Broadway theatre, not an opera house (it eventually played at La Scala, Milan, one of Italy's finest opera houses, in the 1950s)—and proved unpopular with critics as well as unprofitable as a theatrical venture. It took some American musicologists, critics, and even musicians, some 40 years to admit that *Porgy and Bess* is really an opera and not a collection of hit songs.

Copland's *The Second Hurricane* exemplified his aim, as expressed in his *Our New Music* in 1941, to "say what I had to say in the simplest possible terms." Written for the students of New York's High School of Music and Art, the little opera is charmingly melodious and direct. Melody and charm were notable that same year, 1937, in a work by the Italian-born Gian Carlo Menotti, *Amelia Goes to the Ball* (it was presented the following year at the Metropolitan Opera). The American accent was more evident in Douglas Moore's *The Devil and Daniel Webster* (1939), based on the folkish short story by Stephen Vincent Benét. Near the close of the '40s Virgil Thomson again collaborated with Gertrude Stein on yet another offbeat opera, *The Mother of Us All.*

Many of the same names figure in the birth of American ballet which virtually came to life with Thomson's *Filling Station* (1937). However, one of the first ballets with an American setting and theme was composed by Nicolas Nabokov (who was Russian-born) and entitled *Union Pacific;* it was first presented in Philadelphia in 1934. Copland followed Thomson with a series of splendid ballets, beginning with *Billy the Kid* (1938) and reaching a peak in *Appalachian Spring* (1944). The younger men also composed for the ballet: Schuman, *Undertow, Judith;* Morton Gould, *Interplay, Fall River Legend;* Bernstein, *Fancy Free, Facsimile;* Menotti, *Sebastian;* Barber, *The Serpent Heart* (later called *Cave of the Heart*); and Elliott Carter, *The Minotaur.* Collaborating with these composers were the American choreographers Martha Graham, Agnes de Mille, Jerome Robbins, and Michael Kidd. Interestingly, many of these scores hold up on their own, without the dancing, and some have continued in the repertory since their introduction in the '30s and '40s.

The impact of the Depression in Europe produced social unrest, disturbances and, eventually, the rise of antidemocratic political parties. In Germany, Hitler's Nazis rose on a platform of militarism, the theory of a "master race" and its concomitant anti-Semitism. Scholars, scientists, and artists left, or were made to leave, for various reasons. Among those who fled an uncertain Europe before, or during, the Second World War were such important composers as Arnold Schoenberg (fired from a teaching post in Berlin because he was a Jew in 1933). Ernst Toch arrived in 1935, as did Kurt Weill; Ernst Krenek left Vienna in 1937. That great cosmopolitan, Igor Stravinsky, left France in 1939, the first year of the war; the next year Darius Milhaud also left France. The same year, 1940, Béla Bartók left his native Hungary in protest of its alliance with Hitler. With musicians such as these, and others, America became the haven of some of the best musical minds of the century. Either because they taught or merely because of their presence, or both, they would have a significant influence on the evolution of American music. While it would be vain to suggest that a Bartók or a Stravinsky or a Hindemith (1940) composed American music, they represented potent forces in American musical creativity.

They influenced many of a new generation of composers, including those already mentioned and David Diamond, Norman Dello Joio, William Bergsma, Robert Ward, Marc Blitzstein, and others. Such innovators as John Cage and Harry Partch went their separate ways (in the path of Varèse), while others, as had the generation before them, turned to Boulanger, who taught in the United States during most of the war. Among her students were Diamond, Elliott Carter, Elie Siegmeister, Arthur Berger, Irving Fine (although not necessarily during her sojourn in the United States).

Jazz, during the Depression and war years, evolved into swing, which employed larger bands and often written-out arrangements. This was the time, too, of the big bands, the commercial version of the jazzy swing band. Traditional jazz, improvised, spontaneous, was kept alive by the older musicians and purists who collected old recordings. A turning back occurred with the advent of an all-white band using the old instrumentation of the New Orleans bands in the '40s; this was the Yerba Buena Jazz Band led by Lu Watters of San Francisco. A real old-timer, Bunk Johnson, who had played with many of the early New Orleans jazz masters, came out of retirement and enjoyed a satisfying career in his old age. Small record companies, Blue Note, Commodore, Hot Record Society, Solo Art, United Hot Clubs of America, either reissued the long-deleted classic jazz records or recorded new performances by jazzmen who otherwise earned a regular living playing in a "commercial" swing or big band. Commodore, for example, specialized in recording the men who had formed around Eddie Condon and played at Nick's, a nightclub in New York's Greenwich Village. The larger companies, too, recorded jazz from time to time (although the real money was in popular music as performed by the big bands). It was RCA-Victor that made the first commercially released recordings by the boogie-woogie master Jimmy Yancey.

The noncommercial companies recorded free and easy "jam sessions," the after-hours coming together of musicians to play for their own pleasure. The old jazz was transformed into the new as younger musicians, seeking different means of expression, introduced virtuoso thematic and rhythmic variations. These, melodically, often were built on short, repeated, phrases; the style was variously called rebop, bebop, or simply bop. It was just the beginning in a revolution in jazz, one that the old-timers would have trouble assimilating. So would a perplexed audience. But such musicians as Charles Parker, known as "Yardbird" or "Bird," and John Gillespie, who earned the nickname "Dizzy," attracted a large following. What was "hot" jazz became "cool" in studied, detached, rambling improvisations; a fascinating exponent of cool is trumpeter Miles Davis.

Popular music, as usual, both reflected and ignored the social issues; the public taste in song was monitored and reported at times rather breathlessly on "Your Hit Parade," a radio show that began airing in 1935. Many of the songs that made "Your Hit Parade" originated in films or Broadway shows. The number one song on the first broadcast of Apr. 20, 1935, was Rodgers and Hart's "Soon," from the film *Mississippi;* number 2 was Al Dubin and Harry Warren's "Lullaby of Broadway," from the *Gold Diggers* film of that year; number 3 was yet another film song, "Lovely to Look At" by Dorothy Fields, Jimmy McHugh, and Jerome Kern from *Roberta.* Duke Ellington's "Solitude" (lyrics by Eddie DeLange and Irving Mills) was in 15th place. Songs taking notice of the economic problems of the early part of this period generally were not "Your Hit Parade" material, E. Y. Harburg and Jay Gorney's "Brother, Can You Spare a Dime" for example. More popular were the uplift songs that promised better times, like Jack Yellen and Milton Ager's "Happy Days Are Here Again," which was not related to the Depression but became popular during it. Another song was "Who's Afraid of the Big, Bad Wolf?" by Frank E. Churchill and Ann Ronell which was used in a Walt Disney cartoon, *The Three Little Pigs* (1933). The cartoon villain symbolized the "wolf at the door" of a great number of American families. Only the more brutal catastrophe, the Second World War, ended the American Depression.

Radio was responsible, to a great extent, for the dissemination of what its detractors chose to call "hillbilly" music. By the '60s and '70s it would be more respectfully known as "country music." It was not a new phenomenon and in its rural (i.e., most pristine) form had been here from the beginning, in the fiddle music of the early settlers. The country music of the late '20s and early '30s was, in a sense, the citification of what had been a rural music. The city was Nashville, Tenn., and the vehicle of diffusion was the radio show known by 1927 as "The Grand Ole Opry." Many of the early country music stars were heard on the program broadcast by Nashville's WSM, including such popular vocalists as Ernest Tubb and Roy Acuff. Recordings, too, played a part in preserving some of the first Big Names, among them the Carter Family and Jimmie Rodgers. During World War II their recordings could be heard on virtually every Army post jukebox in the South and West. Regional variations were often homogenized by radio and recordings, but there were differences. Bluegrass music, which began coming into its own around the mid '40s, has a sound distinct from that of the country music of, say, Texas or Mississippi. Commercialization of these folk forms would place country music, by the '60s, in the field of popular music.

The Broadway theatre, though it too felt the economic pinch of the Depression, responded with the more economical revues satirizing political figures and commenting on the condition of the nation; some were even outspokenly critical and considered by many as subversive, such as Harold Rome's mild labor revue, *Pins and Needles* (1937), and Marc Blitzstein's biting *The Cradle Will Rock* (1937).

The '30s decade opened for Broadway with a Gershwin musical, *Strike Up the Band,* lampooning war; the Gershwins followed with 2 extraordinary political operettas, *Of Thee I Sing* (1931) and its unsuccessful but brilliantly scored sequel, *Let 'Em Eat Cake* (1933). The revues mingled social commentary with pure entertainment: *The Band Wagon* (1932), *As Thousands Cheer* (1933), *Life Begins at 8:40* (1934), and *Sing Out the News* (1938). There were the usual *Follies, Scandals,* and *Vanities* out of which came fine songs: "I Gotta Right to Sing the Blues" (Ted Koehler, Harold Arlen), "Suddenly" (E. Y. Harburg, Vernon Duke), "I Can't Get Started with You" (Ira Gershwin, Vernon Duke), and "Are You Havin' Any Fun?" (Jack Yellen, Sammy Fain). One of the greatest successes of the decade was the zany, plotless *Hellzapoppin* (1938), whose perpetrators chose to ignore the Depression and the gathering war clouds of Europe.

Much the same might be said of one of the most seminal of American musicals, *Oklahoma!* Though produced in wartime (1943), it was an excursion into Americana, set in a simpler America of an earlier day. The plot was minimal but the songs were so beautifully intertwined with story, as were the ballets by Agnes de Mille, that it has come to be called the first "integrated" musical. While this is not true (even the nearly mindless musicals of the '20s had songs integrated with plot and attempted to delineate character), *Oklahoma!* was, and is, one of the most skillfully conceived musicals of all time. It also has a splendid score by Richard Rodgers and Oscar Hammerstein II, who continued in the popular Americana vein, with the successful *Carousel* and other shows, to become one of the most successful songwriting teams in the American theatre. Another popular Americana musical was Harold Arlen and E. Y. Harburg's *Bloomer Girl* (1944), which touched on such delicate subjects as slavery, women's suffrage, and war, in this case the Civil War.

Incidentally, speaking of integrated musicals, *Lady in the Dark,* which was produced 2 years before *Oklahoma!,* presented, in song and dance, a story of a young woman undergoing psychoanalysis. The superior songs were written by a German refugee, Kurt Weill, and Ira Gershwin, in his first Broadway musical since the sudden death of his brother.

Wartime prosperity enabled Broadway to recover from its '30s slump and lavish musicals appeared again written by Cole Porter (*Kiss Me, Kate,* 1948) and Berlin (*Annie Get Your Gun,* 1946). The success of *Oklahoma!* initiated a new era on Broadway.

In August 1935 the Government, in a sense, went into the music business. With unemployment at its highest in years, unemployed musicians were forced to go on relief. President Franklin D. Roosevelt's Works Progress Administration set up a Federal Music Project to provide work for musicians. With community help, the Government helped to sponsor musical programs in various institutions (hospitals, schools, etc.). Although American composers were not commissioned for new works, the performance of American music was encouraged and many a community heard American music regularly during the Federal Music Project's existence (the coming of war in 1941 ended it).

One of the most valuable of the Project's works was in the collection of American folk music in the field. It is preserved in the Archive of American Folk-Song, Library of Congress. Much of this authentic material is available today on long-playing records. It is interesting that this effort virtually coincided with the work of so many American composers, Copland, Thomson, Harris, Thompson, who chose to work with Americana.

As for the effect of the Second World War on music, it was slight and short-lived. Musicians served in various branches of the military, many in bands or with Special Services. Many a march or overture or fanfare was composed by serviceman and civilian alike, but that music for a special occasion is rarely heard today. Nor was popular song of a warlike nature any more than fleetingly popular: "Praise the Lord and Pass the Ammuntion," "There's a Star-Spangled Banner Waving Somewhere," "Remember Pearl Harbor"—and worse. Perhaps the best-remembered song of the war was Irving Berlin's "White Christmas," whose link with the war was in Berlin's genius for expressing the emotion of so many who were far from home for several Christmases.

The period encompassing the Depression and the Second World War was one of general musical conservatism and consolidation. The composers who came to the front in the '20s proved themselves, and their younger colleagues —often their students—found their own voices by the close of the '50s. As the was burned itself out, a new, cold war loomed, as new, strange currents began to greet—some would insist, assault—the American ear.

"AFRO-AMERICAN SYMPHONY" Symphony in 4 movements completed by black composer William Grant Still (q.v.) in 1930. The first performance was given in Rochester, N.Y., Oct. 29, 1931. The movements were given extramusical titles later: "Longings" (Moderato assai), "Sorrows" (Adagio), "Humor" (Scherzo), and "Aspirations" (Lento con risoluzione). The major theme of the work is a bluesy melody. The lively *Scherzo* was often performed separately from the work as a self-contained piece of jocular Americana. The last movement is an eloquent statement; the harmonies, as Still himself pointed out, are generally conventional and the *Afro-American Symphony* is a thoroughly "American" work in the manner of the period which, while it employs Negro themes, is ethnic without being exotic. Still revised the symphony in 1969 but made no drastic changes. It is one of his important contributions.

"ALL THE THINGS YOU ARE" Song, words by Oscar Hammerstein II and music by Jerome Kern, written for the musical *Very Warm for May* (1939). The show was unsuccessful, ran for only 59 performances, and was Kern's last Broadway score. Some of Kern's finest songs were written for *Very Warm for May:* "In the Heart of the Dark," "That Lucky Fellow," and "All in Fun." "All the Things You Are" is one of Kern and Hammerstein's most impressive creations; melodically it ranks in a class with Kern's "Ol' Man River" which also has Hammerstein lyrics.

AMMONS, ALBERT (1907–1949) Pianist, composer. Born in Chicago, Ill., Sept. 23, 1907, Ammons was a member of a musical family; both his parents were pianists. Ammons, however, began as a drummer. He was a drummer in the 8th Illinois Home Guards for a time during World War I. In his twenties he began to play the piano and was a disciple of Jimmy Yancey (q.v.) and friend of Pine Top Smith (q.v.), Meade Lux Lewis (q.v.), and Hersal Thomas. Lewis and Ammons in the early '20s drove cabs for the Silver Taxicab Co., where they met and exchanged musical ideas on the piano that the owner of the company had installed in the clubroom. They soon formed a piano duo to play at rent parties and neighborhood clubs. Besides being a fine soloist and especially powerful as a boogie-woogie pianist, Ammons played in several bands in the early '30s and between 1934 and 1938 had his own band, the Rhythm Kings. Ammons was playing with his band in the Club De Lisa when John Hammond, a white jazz aficionado, heard him play. Hammond was searching for Lewis whose *Honky Tonk Train* he had heard and admired. When Hammond's now historic *Spirituals to Swing* concert was first presented in 1938, Lewis and Ammons were present; so was another boogie-woogie master, Pete Johnson (q.v.). This marked the beginning of the boogie-woogie popularity and, for the so-called Boogie Woogie Trio, a career in concerts, clubs, and on recordings. Ammons made his first recordings in 1939 with such original pieces as *Shout for Joy, Boogie Woogie Stomp* (a variation on *Pine Top's Boogie Woogie*), *Suitcase Blues* (by his lesser known friend, Hersal Thomas), *Bass Goin' Crazy,* and *Chicago in Mind.* Ammons recorded many piano solos but he also recorded with small groups and accompanied such blues singers ("shouters" they were often called) as Big Bill Broonzy, Joe Turner, and Bumble Bee Slim. Ammons suffered misfortune in the '40s: he sliced off a fingertip while making a sandwich and later suffered paralysis of both hands. In February 1944 he resumed his career with a newly formed Ammons Rhythm Kings and played in Chicago nightclubs; he also began recording again, often with a band which included his son, saxophonist Gene Ammons. But illness interfered and, after a period of little activity, Ammons died in Chicago, Dec. 5, 1949.

ANDERSON, LEROY (1908–1975) Composer, conductor. Born in Cambridge, Mass., June 29, 1908, Anderson had his first lessons in music from his mother, an organist. At 11 he studied piano at the New England Conservatory; he then went to Harvard, where he studied with Edward Ballantine, Walter Piston, and Walter Spalding. He was graduated in 1929, then remained another year to earn an M.A. For several years Anderson was active in the Cambridge area as organist, conductor, arranger. In the mid '30s he became a staff arranger for the Boston Pops Orchestra. His own *Jazz Pizzicato* was introduced in 1935 and was an immediate success, prompting conductor Arthur Fiedler to suggest a companion piece, which was named *Jazz Legato*. Anderson was recognized as a master of brilliant, light orchestral pieces of satisfying intellectual content which were readily accessible. Anderson was also an inventive orchestrator. His career as composer of descriptive pieces was interrupted by World War II, during which Anderson served in military intelligence (he served also during the Korean War, 1951–52). Upon resumption of his musical career, Anderson enjoyed a rich period of productivity and popularity. Such pieces as *The Syncopated Clock* (1945, which be-

came a television theme for "The Late Show"), *Fiddle Faddle* (1947), *Serenata,* (1947), *Sandpaper Ballet* (1954), *Forgotten Dreams* (1954), and *The Typewriter* (1950) were widely played and recorded (often in composer-conducted performances). One of his best and most popular pieces was *Blue Tango* (1952). Anderson wrote the score to one Broadway musical, *Goldilocks* (lyrics by Joan Ford, Walter and Jean Kerr) in 1958. One of his last works was *A Harvard Festival,* completed in 1969 (a revision of the earlier *Harvard Fantasy*). Anderson died of cancer in Woodbury, Conn., May 18, 1975.

"ANNIE GET YOUR GUN" Musical with songs by Irving Berlin (q.v.). Originally conceived as *Annie Oakley* by Dorothy Fields (q.v.) as a vehicle for musical comedy star Ethel Merman; the music was to be done by Jerome Kern (q.v.), who died before he could begin work. Producers Rodgers and Hammerstein then assigned the project to Berlin; Fields remained as collaborator on the book with her brother Herbert. The plot was woven round the hillbilly character of Annie Oakley, who became a circus sharpshooter, and her rivalry with "Frank Butler," a sharpshooter with Buffalo Bill's Wild West Show. *Annie Get Your Gun* continued in the Americana tradition so successfully begun with *Oklahoma!* and *Bloomer Girl.* The show opened at the Imperial Theatre, New York City, May 16, 1946, starring Ethel Merman in the title role and Ray Middleton as her male rival for marksman honors. The show was colorful, rich in character, and replete with great Berlin songs: "There's No Business Like Show Business," "Doin' What Comes Natur'lly," "The Girl That I Marry," "I Got the Sun in the Morning," "I Got Lost in his Arms," "Anything You Can Do (I Can do Better)," "You Can't Get a Man with a Gun," and "They Say It's

Wonderful." *Annie Get Your Gun* ran for 1,147 performances in its original production and had an even longer run in London in 1947; the London "Annie" was Dolores Gray. Mary Martin starred in a year-long tour in 1947. A film version was released by MGM in 1950; its stars were Betty Hutton and Howard Keel. *Annie Get Your Gun* was revived, starring Merman, in 1966 at Lincoln Center; for this revival Berlin wrote a new song, "An Old-Fashioned Wedding."

"APPALACHIAN SPRING" Ballet score composed by Aaron Copland (q.v.) for Martha Graham on commission from the Elizabeth Sprague Coolidge Foundation. *Appalachian Spring* is Copland's 4th, the earlier 3 being *Hear Ye! Hear Ye!* (1934), *Billy the Kid* (1938, q.v.), and *Rodeo* (1942). Copland began work on what he called "Ballet for Martha" in June 1943, while in Hollywood writing the score, in collaboration with Ira Gershwin, for the film *North Star*. He completed it in Cambridge, Mass., in June 1944. The final title was Graham's and was taken from a poem by Hart Crane. Her ballet tells the story of a young bride and her husband settling in their new farmhouse ca. 1800 in Quaker Pennsylvania. To underscore the folkish elements Copland conceived original folk-like themes and used the Shaker hymn "Simple Gifts" in the penultimate section of the work. He scored the ballet for a small orchestra of 13 instruments because that was all the pit of the new Coolidge Auditorium at the Library of Congress would hold. *Appalachian Spring* was performed there, in Washington, D.C., for the first time on Oct. 30, 1944, with Graham dancing the role of the bride; the conductor was Louis Horst. It was immediately recognized as a brilliant work and the music was especially noticed; it won the New York Music Critics Circle Award as the outstanding theatrical work of the season. In the spring of 1945 Copland extracted a suite from the ballet, scoring it for a larger orchestra; this version was performed for the first time by the New York Philharmonic on Oct. 4, 1945; the conductor was Artur Rodzinski. In this form *Appalachian Spring* was awarded the Pulitzer Prize that year. Serge Koussevitzky became one of the leading exponents of the suite and performed it frequently with the Boston Symphony and was the first to record it in October 1945. The suite exists in a 2nd form— the original 13 instrumentation. *Appalachian Spring* is one of the great achievements in American music.

"APRIL IN PARIS" Popular song, words by E. Y. Harburg (q.v.) and music by Vernon Duke (q.v.). It was introduced by Evelyn Hoey in the revue *Walk a Little Faster* (1932). According to lyricist Harburg, the song was written to utilize a Parisian set that had been left over from an earlier Shubert show. Duke's distinguished melody is poetically set by Harburg (who at that time had not yet visited Paris) with literate imagery: "Chestnuts in blossom/Holiday tables under the trees," and the very grammatical, "Whom can I run to?" *Walk a Little Faster* marked Duke's debut on the Broadway scene with a full-length score; the popularity of "April in Paris" established him as a distinguished composer of superior songs. Harburg by 1932 was quite a veteran. They collaborated again in 1934 on a *Ziegfeld Follies* and again produced a fine score—among the songs were "I Like the Likes of You," "What Is There to Say?," and "Suddenly" (with Billy Rose as co-lyricist, a doubtful claim. It was his practice, and others in Tin Pan Alley, to make a minimal contribution to a song and then claim co-authorship. "Suddenly" sounds all-Harburg).

ARLEN, HAROLD (b. 1905) Composer, pianist, singer. Born in Buffalo, N.Y., Feb. 15, 1905, Hyman Arluck was the son of a cantor noted for his fine singing voice. His mother was a gentle, cultured lady who started her son on piano lessons when he was 9; his teacher was the distinguished Buffalo musician Arnold Cornelissen. Arluck also sang in the synagogue choir directed by his father. But young Hyman revealed an early preference for popular music and jazz; before he was out of high school he had formed his own little bands and played in some of Buffalo's more unwholesome night spots. In true jazz tradition he even played on the lake boats that made excursions from Buffalo to Canadian ports. Arluck's musicianship was such—he played the piano, arranged and sang—that he was asked to join a successful local band, the Buffalodians. In 1925, with this band, Harold— as he was then known—Arluck arrived in New York City. Another bandleader, Arnold Johnson, enticed him away from the Buffalodians and soon Harold Arlen, as he was finally known, was singing with the Johnson band in the *George White's Scandals* (1928). He then set out as a single in vaudeville for a time singing the songs of others; he then landed a role singing-acting in the Vincent Youmans show *Great Day*. Sitting in one day for an ailing rehearsal pianist, he began improvising on the traditional piano "pickup" (the signal to the dancers to get ready) and so changed it that it became a new tune. Song-plugger, composer Harry Warren (q.v.) heard the new tune and introduced Arlen to a lyricist, Ted Koehler (q.v.), whom he believed would be the ideal lyricist for the tune. He was. The song turned out to be "Get Happy," was interpolated into the score of the short-lived *Nine-Fifteen Revue* (1930) and became very popular. This closed Arlen's professional life as performer and he became one of the greatest of American popular songwriters. He and Koehler went on to create several remarkable songs for Harlem's Cotton Club (q.v.): "I Love a Parade" and "Between the Devil and the Deep Blue Sea" (1931), "I've Got the World on a String" (1932), "Stormy Weather" (1933), and "As Long as I Live" and "Ill Wind" (1934). They did their first film score in 1933, *Let's Fall in Love* (released the following year). Besides the title song, there were also "This Is Only the Beginning" and "Love Is Love Anywhere." Arlen wrote his first Broadway score with another ex-native of Buffalo, Jack Yellen. The show was *You Said It* (1931) from which came such songs as "Learn to Croon," "Sweet and Hot," and "You'll Do." During this period Arlen interpolated several songs in different revues: "I Gotta Right to Sing the Blues" (Koehler, from *Earl Carroll's Vanities,* 1932); "Satan's Li'l Lamb" (E. Y. Harburg and John Mercer, *Americana,* 1932; his first collaboration with 2 of his most important lyricists); he and Harburg, plus Billy Rose, did a song for the unsuccessful *The Great Magoo:* "It's Only a Paper Moon." Before heading for Hollywood, where he settled for a long stay, Arlen collaborated with Harburg again on a great song, "Last Night When We Were Young" (1935), and with Harburg and Ira Gershwin on the revue *Life Begins at 8:40* (1934), from which came "You're a Builder Upper," "Fun to Be Fooled," "What Can You Say in a Love Song?," and "Let's Take a Walk Around the Block." Although he contributed songs to several films in the mid and late 1930s, the films were not memorable until *The Wizard of Oz* (lyrics by Harburg) was released in 1939; its "Over the Rainbow" won the Academy Award for best song. Some of those film musicals produced during this period are remembered more for their songs than plot or stars: *Blues in the Night* (lyrics by Mercer) produced the title song and "This Time the Dream's on Me" (1941); from *Star Spangled Rhythm* (Mercer) came "Hit the Road to Dreamland" and "That Old Black Magic" (1942); *Cabin in the Sky,* an excellent musical film, had songs by Harburg and Arlen as well as some of the original songs from the Broadway show by Vernon Duke (q.v.), Ted Fetter, and John Latouche. The Arlen–Harburg contribution included "Life's Full of Consequences" and "Happiness Is a Thing Called Joe" (1943); *The Sky's the Limit* (Mercer) had fine songs—"My Shining Hour" and "One for My Baby (and One More for the Road)." Arlen's Broadway shows have been few: *Hooray For What!* (1937), *Bloomer Girl,* his most successful show (1944), *St. Louis Woman,* one of his outstanding scores (1946), *House of Flowers,* another superior score (1954), *Jamaica* (1957), *Saratoga* (1959), *Blues Opera* (also known as *Free and Easy,* 1959), and the one-act television musical *Clippity Clop and Clementine,* with the lovely "I Had a Love Once," (unproduced, written with Leonard Melfi, with Arlen lyrics and music, 1973). Arlen's last film scores were done with Ira Gershwin, *A Star Is Born* (1954) and *The Country Girl* (1954), and E. Y. Harburg, the cartoon musical *Gay Purr-ee* (1961). His wife's death in 1970 led to Arlen's virtual retirement. Besides songs he has written such instrumental pieces as *Mood in Six Minutes* (1935, orchestrated by Robert Russell Bennett) and *American Minuet* (1939). In 1939 Arlen collaborated with Ted Koehler on a collection of songs for solo voices and chorus entitled *Americanegro Suite.* His *Hero Ballet,* composed for the antiwar musical *Hooray for What!,* is a unique work for a Broadway show (the choreography was by Agnes de Mille).

"AS THOUSANDS CHEER" A revue with sketches written by Moss Hart (1904–1961) and songs by Irving Berlin (q.v.). Starring Marilyn Miller, Clifton Webb, Helen Broderick, and Ethel Waters, *As Thousands Cheer* presented its sketches based on a newspaper format, with headlines announcing the point of the sketch. For example, when Waters sang "Suppertime," Berlin's poignant song about lynching, it was introduced by a headline projected on a screen reading: "Unknown Negro Lynched by Frenzied Mob." Lighter moments spoofed celebrities of the day, politicians, and other subjects. The "Advice to the Lovelorn" column inspired one of Berlin's most interesting songs, "Lonely Heart." Others include: "Heat Wave," "How's Chances?," and "Easter Parade." *As Thousands Cheer* opened at the Music Box, Sept. 30, 1933, and ran for 400 performances. A sequel, *More Cheers,* was planned for the next year but was never produced.

"AS TIME GOES BY" Popular song, words and music by Herman Hupfeld (1894–1951), introduced in the musical *Everybody's Welcome* (1931). The song languished until 1943, when it was revived in the movie *Casablanca* and became tremendously successful. Hupfeld also wrote such songs as "Sing Something Simple" (1930), "When Yuba Plays the Rumba on the Tuba" (1931), and "Let's Put Out the Lights" (1932).

"BALLAD FOR AMERICANS" Cantata for solo voice, chorus, and orchestra, text by John Latouche (1917–1956) and music by Earl Robinson (q.v.). Originally written as the *Ballad of Uncle Sam* for a Works Progress Administration production of the show *Sing for Your Supper* in 1939 as part of the Federal Theatre project. Later in the year Norman Corwin, who retitled the work, introduced *Ballad for Americans,* slightly revised by the composers, on his Sunday afternoon CBS radio show, "Pursuit of Happiness." The vocalist was the great black bass-baritone, Paul Robeson (1898–1976), with the American People's Chorus and an orchestra backing him. The cantata, fervently patriotic in a time when war raged in Europe, was an immediate success. It was reported that the CBS studio audience applauded for 15 minutes after the program went off the air. Robeson and the Chorus sang *Ballad for Americans* more than 100 times after its premiere in November 1939 and there was a performance at New York City's Lewisohn Stadium in July 1942, by which time the United States was at war. They also made a successful recording in 1940, with Robinson leading the chorus and Nathaniel Shilkret (q.v.) conducting. *Ballad for Americans* celebrated American democracy and national diversity in a troubled time; its viewpoint now seems rather naïve, but its sincerity makes up for that, if not for the line "And Czech and double Czech American."

"THE BAND WAGON" A revue with sketches by George S. Kaufman (1889–1961) and Howard Dietz; songs by Arthur Schwartz (music) and Dietz. *The Band Wagon* was most notable for its excellent songs and the dancing of Fred and Adele Astaire (she retired from the theatre after completing her run in this show). Among the songs: "New Sun in the Sky," "I Love Louisa," "Where Can He Be?," and "Dancing in the Dark." The revue opened at the New Amsterdam Theatre, New York City, June 3, 1931, and ran for 260 performances. A film of the same title, starring Fred Astaire, was released in 1953; it was not related to the original stage production except for Astaire and a few songs.

BARBER, SAMUEL (1910–1981) Composer. Born in West Chester, Pa.,

Mar. 9, 1910, Barber began to study music at the age of 6 and composition a year later. He was only 13 when he entered the Curtis Institute, Philadelphia, where he studied piano (Isabelle Vengerova), composition (Rosario Scalero), and voice (Emilio de Gogorza). Barber's early compositions soon attracted attention—his Opus 1 was a *Serenade* for string quartet; an early Sonata for violin won a prize and his Overture to *The School for Scandal* was premiered in Philadelphia in 1933 (it too was a prize winner). Opus 3 was *Dover Beach* for baritone and string quartet (1931) which the composer himself recorded commercially. Barber's numerous prizes and fellowships enabled him to study at the American Academy in Rome, where he remained from 1935 to 1937. While in Italy Barber composed several of his most popular works, among them the *String Quartet No. 1* (1936), one movement of which was to be the oft-played *Adagio for Strings*. In Rome, Barber composed his (first) *Symphony in One Movement*, which was performed there in December 1936. After his return to the United States, Barber taught at the Curtis Institute, continued to write, and conducted a choral group. In 1942 he enlisted in the U. S. Army Air Forces, which commissioned his *Second Symphony* (1944; it has since been withdrawn, except for one movement entitled *Night Flight*). While in uniform Barber also composed a *Commando March* for band (1943). Upon his discharge Barber resumed his musical career, one of the most impressive in American music. Although he is generally labeled a "neo-conservative," Barber has not hesitated to employ "modern" devices—dissonance, even dodecaphony—in his composition. Much of his work is characterized by a fine lyricism. Besides the works for orchestra already mentioned he has composed *Music for a Scene for Shelley* (1933),

3 *Essays* for orchestra (1937, 1942, and 1979), *Violin Concerto* (1939), *Capricorn Concerto* for flute, oboe, trumpet, and strings (1944), *Cello Concerto* (1945; New York Music Critics Circle Award, '46), *Piano Concerto* (1962; Pulitzer Prize, '63; New York Music Critics Circle Award, '64), *Concertino* for oboe (1979), and *Third Essay* for orchestra (1980). Barber composed the music for the Martha Graham ballet *The Serpent Heart* (1946; it was later called *Cave of the Heart*) out of which Barber extracted the suite *Medea* (1947). His choral works include *The Virgin Martyrs* for women's chorus a cappella (1935), *Let Down the Bars, O Death* for mixed chorus a cappella (1936), *A Stopwatch and an Ordnance Map* for men's voices, percussion, and brass (1940), *Prayers of Kierkegaard* for chorus and orchestra (1954), and *The Lovers* for baritone, chorus, and orchestra (1971). Other works for voice include *Knoxville: Summer of 1915* for soprano and orchestra, text by James Agee (1948), *Andromache's Farewell* for voice and orchestra (1962), *Mélodies passagères* (1951), *Hermit Songs* for voice and piano (1953), and the song cycle *Despite and Still* (1969). Barber's works for solo piano include *Excursions* (1944) and the celebrated *Piano Sonata* (1949). His operas include *Vanessa* (1958, libretto by Gian Carlo Menotti), *A Hand of Bridge,* one-act opera (1959, libretto by Menotti), and *Antony and Cleopatra* (1966, revised 1975). Barber died in New York City, Jan. 23, 1981.

BARLOW, WAYNE (b. 1912) Composer, teacher. Born in Elyria, Ohio, Sept. 6, 1912, Barlow was educated primarily at the Eastman School, Rochester, N.Y., where, since 1937, he has taught. His teachers were Bernard Rogers, Howard Hanson, and Edward Royce. Barlow also studied with Arnold Schoenberg at the University of California (1935). He is best known for his lyrical *The Winter's Passed* for oboe and strings (1938) based on 2 American folk songs. He is also the composer of an important ballet score, *The Black Madonna* (1941), and a *Mass in G* for chorus and orchestra (1951). Other Barlow compositions include *Three Moods for Dancing* for orchestra (1940), *Lyrical Piece* for clarinet and strings (1945), *Nocturne* for chamber orchestra (1946), *Night Song* for orchestra (1957), *Sinfonia da camera* (1962), and *Saxophone Concerto* (1970). There are several choral works and compositions for the organ. Barlow is also the author of *Foundations of Music* (1953).

BARROWS, JOHN, JR. (1913–1974) Composer, horn player, teacher. Born in Glendale, Calif., Feb. 12, 1913, Barrows was initially trained as an instrumentalist. He studied the horn at the Eastman School, Rochester, N.Y., and later studied composition at Yale with Richard F. Donovan (q.v.) and David S. Smith (q.v.). At Yale he also became proficient on the cello. From 1938 to 1942 he played the horn in the Minneapolis Symphony and later in the orchestras of the New York City Opera and the New York City Ballet. Barrows was associated with several performing groups, among them the New York Woodwind Quintet and the Marlboro Festival Orchestra. He taught horn at Yale, New York University, and the University of Wisconsin. Barrows composed a number of chamber works: 2 string quartets (1936, 1937), a *Woodwind Quartet* (1936), a *Divertimento* for string trio (1937), a *Sonata* for French horn and piano (1937), a *Sonata* for cello and piano (1937), a *Piano Sonatina* (1937), a *Trio* for flute, horn, and bassoon (1937), and other works. His chamber orchestra compositions include *Variations* for French horn and strings (1935), a *Nocturne* for English horn (1935), a *Concertino* for piano and chamber orchestra (1937), and a *Suite* for string orchestra (1937). During his service with the Army Air Forces during World War II, Barrows composed *Three Marches* for band. He died in Madison, Wis., Jan. 11, 1974.

BARTÓK, BÉLA (1881–1945) Composer, pianist. Born in Nagyszentmiklós, Hungary, Mar. 25, 1881, Bartók was already recognized as one of the century's major composers when he came to the United States in 1940. This move was made as a protest against the Nazification of his native Hungary. By this time he had written classic papers on folk music and had composed several extraordinary works, including his 6 string quartets, the remarkable *Music for Strings, Percussion and Celesta*. Bartók and his wife, Ditta, arrived in the United States and were soon joined by their son, Peter (who served in the U. S. Navy during the war). Bartók did not have an easy time during his American years; never in good health, he began showing symptoms of the leukemia that would take his life. Fiercely proud, he refused to accept money unless he earned it and suffered financially. He did work in folk music at Columbia University, planned lectures (none of which he was able to make), and accepted a few commissions. Because he did not believe that composition could be taught, Bartók did not accept students in that discipline; he did, however, have a few piano students. His compositions, once regarded as most difficult, were not frequently performed in his later years (the flood came after his death), so royalties were meager and his European royalties were tied up in a warring Europe. (Bartók forbade performances of his works in Fascist or Nazi-held countries, a further depletion of his income.) But there were a few performances of his works. He made some recordings and friends conspired to get him commissions and extra money.

The first of his commissions, from the Boston Symphony and Serge Koussevitzky, resulted in the *Concerto for Orchestra* (1944); Yehudi Menuhin commissioned the *Sonata for Solo Violin* (1944). Bartók did not live to complete his *Third Piano Concerto* which he had planned as a gift to his wife. The final 17 bars were orchestrated by his friend and colleague, Tibor Serly (q.v.). Serly also reconstructed Bartók's *Viola Concerto* (a commission from William Primrose) from a mass of manuscript paper; this work was performed for the first time about 4 years after Bartók's death. Although Bartók cannot be claimed as an American composer, his influence on American composers has been strong. In the years after his death, his compositions have been widely played throughout the world. He died of leukemia—not starvation as has often been implied—in New York City, Sept. 26, 1945.

BASIE, WILLIAM "COUNT" (b. 1904) Pianist, bandleader. Born in Red Bank, N.J., Aug. 21, 1904, Basie began studying the piano with his mother as a child. He picked up ragtime and jazz in New York, listening to such musicians as James P. Johnson and especially Fats Waller (q.v.), from whom he also learned to play the organ. For a time Basie performed in New York clubs and eventually joined the orchestra of a touring musical which ran out of funds when the show was playing in Kansas City, Mo., in 1927. Stranded, Basie took odd jobs, including playing the organ for silent films; he joined Walter Page's Blue Devils in 1928 and then switched to Bennie Moten's Band a year later. Absorbing what has since come to be called Kansas City Style, Basie remained the pianist in Moten's band until the latter's death in 1935. Basie and Moten's brother, Buster, then took over the band, out of which, eventually, grew Count

Basie's famous orchestra. Basie's spare piano style was backed by a strong rhythm section (originally: Freddie Green, guitar; Walter Page, bass; and Jo Jones, drums) and such instrumentalists as Lester Young and Herschel Evans on saxes and Buck Clayton on trumpet. By the summer of 1935 there were 10 men in the band, including vocalists Helen Humes and the blues singer Jimmy Rushing. Jazz enthusiast John Hammond happened to hear a radio broadcast by the band and was instrumental in getting the band bookings in Chicago and New York. In 1937 the band began making its first recordings, which led to even wider popularity. By 1938 the Count Basie Band played the famed Savoy Ballroom in New York City. The 1940s saw the establishment of the band as one of the major jazz groups in the country and it has remained active into the 1980s, making recordings, playing hotels, theatres, and clubs in the United States and Europe and in several films. During this long period the early nucleus of Basie, Green, Page, and Jones has remained constant through several changes of personnel. The band's arrangements were worked out by Eddie Durham, Ernie Wilkins, Neal Hefti, and others. Much of what they played was improvisational: "head arrangements." The band's theme was composed by Basie and became a jazz standard: "One O'Clock Jump." Basie's band is regarded by jazz historians as the quintessential example of Kansas City Style, employing riffs (short repeated figures), balancing the brasses against the reeds, percussive drive, and featuring virtuoso soloists backed by the band. The size of the group fluctuated and at times qualified as a "big band." In 1957 Basie's band played a Command Performance at Buckingham Palace.

"BEAT ME, DADDY (EIGHT TO THE BAR)" Popular big band instru-mental, with vocal, exploiting the popularity of the boogie-woogie style. The song grew out of an instrumental idea by pianist Freddy Slack and drummer Ray McKinley of the Will Bradley band. The number emphasized the eight-to-the-bar boogie beat, extended piano passages and breaks for soloists. One evening 2 songwriters, Don Raye and Hughie Prince, heard the Bradley band at the Famous Door and at one point during a performance of the piece, McKinley interjected the phrase "Oh, beat me, daddy, eight to the bar!" instead of taking his drum break. Raye and Prince approached him and asked for permission to compose a musical number from the piece and offered McKinley a percentage of the royalties. Because of contractual technicalities, McKinley's wife's name was used instead of his; "Beat Me, Daddy . . ." is credited to Don Raye, Elinor Sheehy, and Hughie Prince and was published in 1940. Recorded by the Will Bradley band, in an unusual 2-sided (10-inch, 78-rpm) format, the song became the Bradley band's best-selling disc. The reference to a Texan "who plays the best piano by far," was thought to have been a reference to Peck Kelley, but McKinley later refuted that legend. The success of "Beat Me, Daddy . . ." encouraged a spate of similar big-band boogie songs, "Scrub, Me, Mamma, with a Boogie Beat," "Rock-a-Bye the Boogie," "Rhumboogie," and others. On the original "Beat Me, Daddy . . ." recording Freddy Slack provided the piano background and McKinley sang the vocal; other solos were by Joe Wiedman (trumpet) and Bradley (trombone).

"BEBOP" A revolutionary jazz style that surfaced in the early '40s, near the end of the big band era. In sound, bebop (or rebop, as it was called in the beginning; the final term is bop), is distinct from traditional jazz and swing. Melodic fragments—to which "rebop" or "bebop" could be sung—were repeated and rhythms were broken up. Harmonies sounded sour even to musicians. Bop was not jazz as anyone had known it before. Jazz master Louis Armstrong found that in bop "you got no melody to remember and no beat to dance to . . . you get all them weird chords which don't mean nothing . . ." Two great leaders in bop dominated the style: trumpeter John Birks "Dizzy" Gillespie (q.v.) and Charles "Yardbird" Parker (q.v.). Trumpeter Gillespie and saxophonist Parker met at Minton's Playhouse in Harlem; this was a club where black musicians met to exchange musical ideas and to experiment with new techniques. Characteristic of both men was a remarkable mastery of their instruments (the "wrong notes" they played were the result of a complex harmonic sense), melodic and harmonic inventiveness, and an affinity for the Afro-Cuban rhythms (one scholar, Maurice Crane, attributes the origin of "rebop" to the Spanish exclamation, " 'Riba!" from "Arriba," a call for "Up!" roughly equivalent to, "Go, man, go!"). Both Gillespie and, especially, Parker inspired many imitators and followers in the field of bop or, as it later became, "cool" jazz (q.v.) in the '50s. This was as opposed to the standard hot jazz of the past. Cool jazz does have a detached quality in some performances. Larger white—or predominantly white—bands also took up bop, most importantly those of Woody Herman and Stan Kenton, whose style was often termed "progressive" (q.v.). Certain white musicians also emerged as respected exponents of bop: pianist Lennie Tristano (b. 1919), saxophonist Gerry Mulligan (b. 1927), and the Danish trombonist Kai Winding (b. 1922). The postwar bop era, experimental, controversial, evolved into the "cool" period toward the end of the '40s and early '50s.

BECHET, SIDNEY (1897–1959) Clarinetist, saxophonist, composer. Born in New Orleans, La., May 14, 1897, Bechet taught himself music on his brother's clarinet. At 8 he became the protégé of clarinetist George Baquet (1883–1949), who had played in several of the early New Orleans jazz bands. Bechet followed in his footsteps and, even as a youngster, played in the bands of Freddie Keppard, the Eagle Band (to which he was brought by Bunk Johnson, q.v.), and the King Oliver Band. Bechet followed the traditional New Orleans to Chicago to New York route. In 1919 he joined Will Marion Cook's Southern Syncopated Orchestra; during its European tour Bechet deeply impressed Swiss conductor Ernest Ansermet, who publicly praised him. In the 1920s Bechet switched to the soprano sax and developed a style characterized by a heavy vibrato. He made some early recordings with the Clarence Williams Blue Five and was busy with several jazz or theatre bands in the United States and Europe until 1938, when he retired temporarily to run a tailor shop in New York City. In the 1940s Bechet began playing with the Eddie Condon groups at the famous jazz club, Nicks, in Greenwich Village. He made countless recordings, many for the Blue Note label. Bechet settled in Paris in 1947 and, although he traveled between France and the United States, he remained in France for the rest of his life. Not only was Bechet recognized as a jazz saxophonist in France, he also enjoyed a career in the music halls; he composed several works with such titles as *Petite Fleur, Delta Mood,* and *As-tu la Cafard.* Bechet died in Paris, May 14, 1959, on his 62nd birthday.

BERGER, ARTHUR V. (b. 1912) Composer, critic, teacher, author. Born in New York City, May 15, 1912, Berger received a B.S. in music, after study with Vincent Jones, in 1934.

He moved on to Harvard (1934–37), where he studied with Walter Piston (q.v.). Berger's other teachers include Boulanger (q.v.) and Milhaud (q.v.). Berger's initial compositions were written under the influence of the Schoenbergian school; these works he eventually abandoned. His study with Boulanger (1937–39) was devoted to Stravinsky and his works. Upon returning to the United States, Berger taught at Mills College, Oakland, Calif., and resumed a career as music critic-writer as well as composer. He has also taught at Brooklyn College, Juilliard and, since 1953, Brandeis University, Waltham, Mass. He was a music critic for the New York *Sun* (1945–48) and the New York *Herald Tribune* (1948–53); Berger has also written for a number of publications, including the *Saturday Review*. In 1962 he was cofounder of *Perspectives in New Music,* serving as editor in its first year. His compositions include *Two Episodes* for piano (1933), *Three Songs of Yeats: "Words for Music Perhaps"* (1940), *Entertainment piece,* ballet for 3 dancers and piano (1940), *Woodwind Quartet* (1941), *Serenade for Orchestra* (1944), *Three Pieces for Strings* (1944), *Three Pieces* for string quartet (1944), *Duos* for violin and pianos (1948, 1950), *Duo* for cello and piano (1951), *Ideas of Order* for orchestra (1952), *Polyphony* for orchestra (1956), *Chamber Music for 13 Players* (1956), *String Quartet* (1958), *Chamber Concerto* (1960), *Three Pieces* for 2 pianos (1961), *Five Pieces* for piano (1968), and *Septet* for flute, clarinet, bassoon, violin, viola, cello, and piano (1966). Berger is the author of *Aaron Copland* (1953).

BERGSMA, WILLIAM (b. 1921) Composer, teacher. Born in Oakland, Calif., Apr. 1, 1921, Bergsma left Stanford University in his 2nd year and, from 1940 to 1944 was a student at the Eastman School, Rochester, N.Y., where he studied with Howard Hanson (composition) and Bernard Rogers (orchestration). In 1946 Bergsma joined the staff of the Juilliard School, New York City, where he remained until 1963, when he left to become director of the School of Music, University of Washington, Seattle. Known for his beautifully constructed, lyrical works, Bergsma has been the recipient of many commissions and awards. His works include the ballets *Paul Bunyan* (1937) and *Gold and The Señor Commandante* (1941), *Symphony for Chamber Orchestra* (1942), 4 string quartets (1942, 1944, 1953, 1970, rev. 1974), *Music on a Quiet Theme* (1943), *Suite from a Children's Film* (1945), *Six Songs* to texts by E. E. Cummings (1945), *Symphony No. 1* (1949), *Tangents* for piano (1951), the opera *The Wife of Martin Guerre* (1956), *Concerto for Wind Quintet* (1958), *Fantastic Variations on a Theme from Tristan and Isolde* for viola and piano (1961), *Confrontation from the Book of Job* for chorus and orchestra (1963), *Violin Concerto* (1965), *Serenade to Await the Moon* for chamber orchestra (1965), *Illegible Canons* for clarinet and percussion (1969), *Clandestine Dialogues* for cello and percussion (1972), the opera *The Murder of Comrade Sharik* (1973), *Wishes, Wonders, Portents, Charms* for chorus and small orchestra (1975), and *In Space* for soprano and small orchestra (1975).

BERNSTEIN, LEONARD (b. 1918) Composer, conductor, pianist. Born in Lawrence, Mass., Aug. 25, 1918, Bernstein began in music on the piano; his first teachers were Helen Coates and Heinrich Gebhard. Bernstein entered Harvard to study with Walter Piston, Tillman Merritt, and Edward Burlingame Hill; he was graduated in 1939. This was followed by study at the Curtis Institute, Philadelphia, where he studied with Randall Thompson (orchestration), Isabelle Vengerova (piano), and Fritz Reiner (conducting). After graduation, in 1941, Bernstein returned to the Boston area, where he studied conducting with Koussevitzky; a year later he became his assistant. In 1943 he was appointed assistant (to Artur Rodzinski) conductor of the New York Philharmonic and, that same year, on Nov. 14, made a remarkable impression on the musical world when he substituted on short notice as the conductor of a difficult program when guest conductor Bruno Walter became ill. This was the start of an extraordinary career as a man of many talents, for Bernstein, multi-faceted in his gifts, was to prove to be a brilliant conductor, a fine pianist, and a composer for the concert hall, Broadway, films, and ballet. As a conductor, particularly in his early years, Bernstein was a champion of contemporary music, with added emphasis on American music. In time he commanded a wide repertory and, besides becoming the conductor of the New York Philharmonic (1959–69) after years as assistant, Bernstein has led virtually every major orchestra in the world. In 1969 he became "Laureate conductor" of the Philharmonic in order to have more time for composing. His compositions include *Clarinet Sonata* (1942); 3 symphonies: *Jeremiah* (1942), *"The Age of Anxiety,"* with piano (1949), and *Kaddish,* for narrator, chorus, and orchestra (1963); the song cycle *I Hate Music* (1943); *Seven Anniversaries* for piano (1943); 3 ballets: *Fancy Free* (1944), *Facsimile* (1946), and *Dybbuk* (1974). Other concert works include: *La Bonne Cuisine* for voice and piano (1945), *Hashkivenu,* solo voice, chorus, and orchestra (1945), *Four Anniversaries* for piano (1948), *Prelude, Fugue and Riffs* (1949), *Serenade* for violin, strings, and percussion (1960), *Chichester Psalms* (1965), *Mass* ("Theatre Piece, for

Singers, Players and Dancers," 1971), *Songfest* ("A Cycle of American Poems for Six Singers and Orchestra," 1977), *Slava!* (A Political Overture, 1977), *Divertimento for Orchestra* (1980), *A Musical Toast in Memory of André Kostelanetz* for orchestra (1980), *Touches* for piano (1981) and *"Halil"* for flute and orchestra (1981). Bernstein's music for the theatre includes the musicals *On the Town* (1944), *Trouble in Tahiti* (1952), *Wonderful Town* (1953), *Candide* (1956), *West Side Story* (1957), and *1600 Pennsylvania Avenue* (1976); also incidental music (5 songs) to a stage production of *Peter Pan* (1950) and the film score to *On the Waterfront* (1954). Bernstein has taught conducting at the Berkshire Music Center and has been professor of music, Brandeis University, Waltham, Mass. (1951–56). He also has presented music appreciation courses on television. He is the author of *The Joy of Music* (1959), *Leonard Bernstein's Young People's Concerts for Reading and Listening* (1962), and *The Infinite Variety of Music* (1966). Bernstein's *The Unanswered Question,* the Norton lectures given at Harvard University (1973), have been recorded on 17 long-playing records.

"THE BIG APPLE" Popular 1930s designation for New York City; if you played New York you were in the Big Time. During the late '30s, in the swing era, the Big Apple was a popular dance. The dance was described in a 1937 song by Lee David and John Redmond as a group effort, with the dancers formed in a circle and a caller (as in the old-fashioned square dance) calling the movements. According to David and Redmond you "Do that stomp with lots of pomp and romance/Big Apple, big apple!" *Variety* reported that dancing the Big Apple required "a lot of floating power and fannying." Actually the Big Apple combined steps from several earlier dances: the shag, Black Bottom, truckin', etc. The dance, as did the song, often ended with the shouting of the words "Praise Allah!" The dance has faded but New York continues as the Big Apple. Upstate (mostly rural) New Yorkers are called Apple Knockers, fittingly.

BIG BAND General name applied to the bands that flourished from the late 1930s until World War II. Some bands were holdovers from the '20s, the heyday of the dance bands; some were formed by musicians who had played in these bands, theatre orchestras, or the radio bands. Some big bands fused jazz performances with dance and were called "swing" bands; those bands that continued the traditional styles were called "sweet" or—in the pejorative— "straight" or "square." The most successful of the big bands evolved a definite style or sound, developed popular instrumental soloists (most of the bands were formed around a soloist) and vocalist. The arranger for these bands was supremely important. The beginning of the swing band is popularly dated from the debut of the Benny Goodman Orchestra on Aug. 21, 1935—as good a date as any. Other bands in the swing category were those of Jimmie Lunceford, the Dorsey Brothers (eventually to split into two: Jimmy and Tommy), Bob Crosby, Duke Ellington, Chick Webb, Count Basie, and Woody Herman, to scratch the surface. The "commercial" swing bands were those of Glenn Miller, Artie Shaw, Harry James, Larry Clinton, Freddy Martin, and the veteran Paul Whiteman. The sweeter bands were led by Glen Gray (the Casa Loma Orchestra), Leo Reisman, Eddie Duchin, Isham Jones (another veteran), Kay Kayser, and Les Brown. The out-and-out confectionary dispensers were the very popular, successful, and maligned (by jazz and swing aficionados)

bands of Guy Lombardo, Lawrence Welk, and Wayne King. Some of the vocalists who came out of the big band era were Ella Fitzgerald (Chick Webb), Jo Stafford (Tommy Dorsey), Dick Haymes (Harry James), Frank Sinatra (Tommy Dorsey), Peggy Lee (Benny Goodman), Ivy Anderson (Duke Ellington), Helen O'Connell (Jimmy Dorsey), Helen Forrest (Shaw, Goodman, James), Frances Wayne (Woody Herman), and Mildred Bailey (Whiteman and Red Norvo). Among the most important arrangers of the period (other than the leader himself): Fletcher Henderson, Sy Oliver, Billy Strayhorn, Eddie Sauter, Bill Finegan, Johnny Mandel, Paul Weston, and Ralph Burns. The big bands flourished via grueling one-night stands on the road, in hotels and theatres (the New York Paramount was famous for its big bands), radio and recordings. After the Depression slump, the making of popular records picked up ca. 1938— and were further disseminated by the ubiquitous coin machines that came to be called "jukeboxes." The coming of World War II brought an end to the big band era; bands were broken up as musicians were drafted or enlisted in the various services. Artie Shaw was a chief petty officer in the U. S. Navy. Glenn Miller was a captain in the U. S. Army Air Forces and led its band; Miller was killed when his plane fell into the English Channel. Postwar conditions were inimical to the big band. Expenses, salaries, other costs made one-night stands impractical; booking agencies tended to take large percentages of the income. Although many of the successful big bands of the '30s and '40s attempted to come back in the '50s, most eventually disbanded. Some, like those of Glenn Miller and the Dorseys, were kept alive by the leader's name, the old, nostalgic arrangements, and some of the original members of the bands. Benny Goodman has remained active on a lim-

ited scale, forming bands for special occasions or recordings. Ellington remained active and after his death his son took over the direction of the band. The consensus is that the rich era—the late '30s and roughly half of the '40s—was the golden age of the big band.

"BILLY THE KID" Ballet by Aaron Copland (q.v.)—his 2nd, and first in the Americana vein—with choreography by Eugene Loring, who also danced the title role. Copland began composing the music, based on traditional cowboy songs, in Paris, June 1938, and completed the score in Peterborough, N.H., in September. The world premiere by the Ballet Caravan took place in Chicago on Oct. 16; the New York premiere at the Martin Beck Theatre occurred on May 24, 1939. *Billy the Kid* tells the story of the mythical American gunman in his last days. The complete ballet takes a little more than half an hour to perform; from this Copland extracted a suite of about 20 minutes' duration. The suite is divided into 7 sections: *The Open Prairie, Street in a Frontier Town, Card Game at Night, Gun Battle, Celebration after Billy's Capture, Billy's Demise,* and *The Open Prairie Again.* Some of the traditional songs Copland skillfully worked into his score are "The Old Chisholm Trail," "The Dying Cowboy," "Old Paint," and "Git Along Little Dogie." Other arrangements of *Billy the Kid* include a solo piano compilation by Lukas Foss (q.v.) and the composer's own 2-piano version, of around 8 and 12 minutes in length, respectively. Copland also arranged a *Waltz* and *Celebration* for violin and piano. The premiere of the suite was presented by the Boston Symphony, Jan. 30, 1942.

"BLACK, BROWN AND BEIGE" Instrumental suite for his orchestra composed by Duke Ellington (q.v.) and presented for the first time at Carnegie Hall, in the first of a series of concerts by Ellington there, on Jan. 23, 1943. In 3 movements (as in the title), the work is subtitled "A Tone Parallel to the History of the American Negro." In its original presentation *Black, Brown and Beige* took nearly 50 minutes to perform. It was Ellington's first really extended composition, although he had written longer than average instrumentals for his orchestra (*Reminiscing in Tempo* and *Black and Tan Fantasy*) before. While the work may not conform to the classical concept of sonata form, etc., it is an important statement by a major American composer. Some of the effect of *Black, Brown and Beige* depended upon the great Ellington soloists who performed it: saxophonist Johnny Hodges, Sam Nanton's trombone, the vocal in the "Blues" section by Betty Roche, and Ellington himself, since, as usual, Ellington left room for improvisation. Reception of the work ranged from incompetent (New York *Daily News*) to perplexed (New York *Post*) to surprisingly hostile, from someone who should have known better. Composer Paul Bowles in the New York *Herald Tribune* stated: "The whole attempt to fuse jazz as a form with art music should be discouraged." Possibly discouraged by the reviews (although the music magazines praised the work), Ellington revised *Black, Brown and Beige* when he recorded it in 1944, cutting it by more than half. After the advent of the long-playing record he made a more complete but revised again version with Mahalia Jackson in 1958. Luckily the original broadcast is preserved on recordings. The suite consists of the following sections: "Work Song," "Come Sunday," "The Blues," "West Indian Dance," "Emancipation Celebration," and "Sugar Hill Penthouse." Later in 1943 Ellington produced another longer composition entitled *New World A'Coming* for piano and orchestra which is in more conventional form and most attractive; the or-

chestration (for full symphony) is filled with Ellingtonisms. Other Ellington concert works include the *Liberian Suite* (1947), *Harlem* (1950), and the *Sacred Concerts,* written near the end of his life.

BLANE, RALPH (b. 1914) Lyricist, composer, vocalist. Born in Broken Arrow, Okla., July 26, 1914, Blane was educated at Northwestern University, Evanston, Ill. His principal music teacher was Estelle Liebling. He began his musical theatre career in the 1937 Harold Arlen musical *Hooray for What!* as a vocalist. Also singing in the show was composer-to-be Hugh Martin (q.v.). Blane and Martin joined forces to form a singing quartet known as The Martins in 1940 which sang in clubs and on the radio. Individually Martin and Blane also did vocal arrangements for several Broadway shows—Blane, for example, worked on Rodgers and Hart's *Too Many Girls* (1939), Cole Porter's *DuBarry Was a Lady* (1939), and Irving Berlin's *Louisiana Purchase* (1940). In 1941 Blane and Martin teamed up to do the score for the lively hit show *Best Foot Forward* from which came such songs as "Ev'ry Time," "Shady Lady Bird," "Buckle Down, Winsocki," and "What Do You Think I Am?" When the successful film version was made in 1943 Martin and Blane wrote a new song, "Wish I May, Wish I Might." They then did their first and most successful film score, *Meet Me in St. Louis:* "The Boy Next Door," "Have Yourself a Merry Little Christmas," and "The Trolley Song." The song "Love" was written by Martin and Blane for the film *Ziegfeld Follies* (1945). A break in the team's continuity occurred during World War II, when Martin served in the Army. Blane worked with other songwriters, Johnny Green (*Easy to Wed,* 1946), Harry Warren (*Summer Holiday,* 1948), (*My Dream is Yours,* 1949), Harold Arlen (*My Blue Heaven,* 1950). Martin

and Blane joined again to produce songs for 2 films in the '50s: *Athena* and *The Girl Most Likely.* They also wrote the score for a Broadway show, *Three Tigers for Tessie* (1956), which was never produced. In 1952 Blane did both words and music for the successful *Three Wishes for Jamie.*

BLITZSTEIN, MARC (1905–1964) Composer, lyricist, librettist. Born in Philadelphia, Pa., Mar. 2, 1905, Blitzstein revealed his gifts very early; his parents started him on the piano at the age of 3. His first public recital was given when Blitzstein was 6; at 16 he made his concert debut as a soloist with the Philadelphia Symphony. He continued musical studies at the University of Pennsylvania and at the Curtis Institute, where he studied composition with Rosario Scalero. In New York he studied piano with Alexander Siloti. In 1926 Blitzstein went to Europe, where he studied with Nadia Boulanger in Paris and Arnold Schoenberg in Berlin. In this last city Blitzstein was impressed with the politically motivated musicals of Bertolt Brecht and Kurt Weill (q.v.). Upon his return to the United States in 1927 Blitzstein lectured on "modern" music in Brooklyn and Manhattan. Blitzstein's earliest compositions reflect his initial classical training, but it was in his works for the theatre and voice in which Blitzstein expressed what was called "social consciousness." (During the Depression, this kind of thinking was branded Left Wing and in the McCarthy era Pinko.) His compositions include *Gods* for mezzo-soprano, cello, and string orchestra (1926), *Jig-Saw,* a ballet (1927), *Piano Sonata* (1927), the opera-farce *Triple Sec* (1928), *Percussion Music* for piano (1929), *Serenade* for string quartet (1930), *Is 5,* songs to texts by E. E. Cummings (1929), *Parabola and Circula,* one-act opera (1929), *Romantic Piece* for orchestra (1930), *String Quar-*

tet (1930), the ballet *Cain* (1930), *Piano Concerto* (1931), *Harpies,* one-act opera (1931), *The Condemned,* oratorio inspired by the Sacco-Vanzetti case (1932), *Variations for Orchestra* (1934), *Children's Cantata* (1935), *I've Got the Tune,* radio play (1937), *Spanish Earth,* film score in collaboration with Virgil Thomson (1937), *Freedom Morning,* symphonic poem for chorus and orchestra (1943), *The Airborne,* symphony for narrator, chorus, and orchestra (1944), *The True Glory,* film score (1945), and *The Guests,* a ballet (1948). Blitzstein's most important work for the theatre began with the 1936 production of *The Cradle Will Rock,* a musical play about unionization, strikes, and workers vs. management set in a steel mill town. Originally sponsored by the Works Progress Administration's Federal Theatre Project, the first performance was canceled by the WPA because of the incendiary nature of the play. So on June 15, 1937, instead of opening at the Maxine Elliott Theatre, the cast and some of the audience moved to the Venice Theatre (a last-minute acquisition), where with Blitzstein at the piano (there was no room for the orchestra), and some of the cast seated in the audience, *The Cradle Will Rock* was presented for the first time. In 1940 Blitzstein produced a similar work, with words and music by himself: *No for an Answer.* From 1942 until 1945 Blitzstein was in the U. S. Army Air Forces and served with the 8th Air Force in England. His *Airborne* symphony is a musical warning against the great potential for destruction by air power. In 1946, out of the Air Force, Blitzstein composed incidental music for the Lillian Hellman play *Another Part of the Forest,* a sequel to her successful *The Little Foxes.* Blitzstein converted it, retitled *Regina,* in 1949. He also translated, adapted, and wrote the lyrics for a revival of the Brecht-Weill *The Three-penny Opera* in 1952; it became a long-running hit after its 1954 production. Other Blitzstein theatre works: *Reuben, Reuben,* a musical which closed in Boston in 1955; *Juno,* based on Sean O'Casey's *Juno and the Paycock* (1959). Blitzstein did not live to fulfill his commission from the Metropolitan Opera for an opera based on the Sacco and Vanzetti case (1964). Blitzstein died in Fortde-France, Martinique, Jan. 22, 1964, after suffering a brain injury in a bar brawl with 3 merchant mariners.

BLUEGRASS A kind of country music (q.v.) that evolved out of the traditional folk music and performance styles from the southern Appalachians. The name derives from the Kentucky origin of bandleader-mandolinist Bill Monroe and his Blue Grass Boys, who became popular, chiefly via radio and recordings, in the 1930s. Monroe established the "old-timey" characteristic sound of bluegrass with a typical rural instrumentation: acoustic (not electric) guitar, mandolin, fiddle (bluegrassers rarely use the term "violin"), and bass. A banjo might also figure in the instrumentation. Vocals in the Monroe group were handled by the Monroe brothers, Bill and Charlie; the presentation was characteristic of the earlier rural, mountain style, with one voice singing above the melody, almost falsetto. Although Monroe was active long before the mid '40s, when bluegrass attracted attention beyond the confines of the South, the style has since become associated with 2 of his group's alumni, Lester Flatt and Earl Scruggs, who left Monroe to form their own band. Monroe became noted for a unique style of playing the 5-string banjo with a 3-finger technique (which had been used as early as the '20s by such country recording artists as Dock Walsh and in the '40s by Snuffy Jenkins). By the '60s, under the disseminating possibilities of recordings, television, and widespread

bluegrass festivals, bluegrass music had become big business and one of the staple products of country music's Tin Pan Alley, Nashville, Tenn.

BOP See "Bebop."

BOWLES, PAUL (b. 1910) Composer, writer. Born in New York City, Dec. 30, 1910, Bowles left the University of Virginia upon completing his freshman year (never to return) with plans to visit Gertrude Stein in Paris. This was in 1931; he had begun studying with Aaron Copland (q.v.). In Paris he later studied with Stein's friend Virgil Thomson. Stein was a great influence upon Bowles as a writer; she also suggested that he visit North Africa, which made a lasting impression on the young writer-composer. As a composer Bowles turned out a good deal of incidental music for contemporary plays, such as William Saroyan's *My Heart's in the Highlands,* Tennessee Williams' *Summer and Smoke,* and many others. He wrote 3 operas: *Denmark Vesey* (1937), *The Wind Remains* (1943), and *Yerma* (1958). There are also 4 ballets, *Yankee Clipper* (1937), *The Ballroom Guide* (1937), *Sentimental Colloquy* (1944), and *Pastorela* (1947). Bowles composed a *Suite* for small orchestra (1933), the *Melodia* for 9 instruments (1937), *Danza Mexicana* (1941), *Sonata for Two Pianos* and *Concerto for Two Pianos, Winds and Percussion* (1947). He has also written some distinguished songs, among them "They Can't Stop Death," "Night Without Sleep," "Song for My Sister," and "When Rain or Love Began." Bowles's study of Latin-American and African music greatly influenced his musical output, although after the rise of his literary reputation, he spent less time on composition. His first major book was *The Sheltering Sky* (1949) which was followed by *The Delicate Prey,* other novels and short stories, most set in North Africa, where Bowles settled after the Second World War.

BRANT, HENRY (b. 1913) Composer, teacher. Born in Montreal, Canada, Sept. 15, 1913, Brant began to study music with his father, an American violinist who taught at McGill University, Montreal. The family moved to New York City in 1929 and Brant continued his studies with James Friskin (piano) and Leonard Mannes (composition); he later studied with Rubin Goldmark at Juilliard and privately with George Antheil, Aaron Copland, and Wallingford Riegger. Brant also had a period of study in conducting with Fritz Mahler. In the 1930s Brant made arrangements for such diverse orchestras as those of Benny Goodman and André Kostelanetz; he also composed film scores. In 1945 he began teaching (orchestration, composition, arranging) at Columbia University; he has also taught at Juilliard and Bennington College, Vermont. Brant's hobby is collecting unusual musical instruments, many of which he plays (he also plays several more or less standard instruments in the percussion family plus organ, flute, etc.). A creative innovator, particularly since ca. 1950, Brant has produced works that express his theoretical views on music, how it is made and its place in society. His earliest compositions, most now withdrawn, drew upon jazz and popular music—e.g., *Variations* (1930), *Symphony in B* (1931), and *Five and Ten Cent Store Music* (1932), which is performed on piano and pots, pans, tin cans, and other kitchen paraphernalia. His later works (the post 1950 pieces alluded to) are written in a highly experimental manner, what Brant calls "spatial music in temporal polyphony." Groups of musicians are deployed in different parts of the concert hall and play different kinds of music simultaneously. This, Brant be-

lieves, represents the "multidirectional assaults of contemporary life on the spirit." Other compositions include: the ballet *The Great American Goof* (1940), *Symphony in C Minor* (1937), *Good Weather Overture* (1940), *Fantasy and Caprice* for violin and orchestra (1941), *Concerto for Saxophone* (1942), *Symphony in F* (1942), *Symphony in B-flat* (1945), *Clarinet Concerto* (1946), *Promised Land Symphony* (1947), *Millennium I* (1950), *Percussion Symphony* (1952), *Stresses* for 2 orchestras (1953), *Signs and Alarms* (1953), *Antiphony I* for 5 orchestral groupings (1953), *Galaxies* (1954), *Encephalograms* (1954), *Ceremony* (1954), *Grand Universal Circus* (1956), *Hieroglyphics III* (1957), *Dialogue in the Jungle* for soprano, tenor, chorus, winds, and percussion (1959), *Violin Concerto* with lights (1961), *Verticals Ascending* for 2 instrumental groups (1968), *Immortal Combat* for spatial band (1972), *Sixty* (1974), *Grand Pianos Bash Plus Friends* (1974), *Nomads* for voices (wordless text) and percussion (1974), *A Plan of the Air* for voices, brass, and percussion (1975), *Spatial Concerto* for piano and voices (1976), and *American Weather* for voices (1976).

BRITAIN, RADIE (b. 1903) Composer, teacher. Born in Amarillo, Tex., Mar. 17, 1903, Britain began to study music at Clarendon College, in Texas, at the age of 7; at 14 she was graduated with high honors. She then went to Chicago to study at the American Conservatory, taking piano with Heniot Lévy and also studied the organ with Marcel Dupré in Paris. She studied composition with A. Albert Noelte. Although best known for her many prizewinning choral compositions, Britain has composed a good number of orchestral works. Among them are: *Heroic Poem,* inspired

by the Lindbergh transatlantic flight (1929), *Rhapsodie Phantasie* for piano and orchestra (1931), *Light* (1935), *Southern Symphony* (1937), *Cactus Rhapsody* (1945), *Radiation* (1955), *Cowboy Rhapsody* (1956), and *Chipmunks* for harp, woodwinds, and percussion (1964). Her chamber compositions include a *String Quartet* (1929), *Epic Poem* for string quartet (1934), and *Western Suite* for piano (1940). Her works for voice include *Drums of Africa* for mixed chorus (1934), *Noontide* for 2 sopranos and 2 altos (1940), the chamber opera *Kuthara* (1960), and the *Translunar Cycle* of songs (1970).

"BROTHER, CAN YOU SPARE A DIME." Depression theme song, words by E. Y. Harburg (q.v.) and music by Jay Gorney (b. 1896). "Brother, Can You Spare a Dime" was written for the topical revue, *New Americana,* which opened at the Shubert Theatre in October 1932. Harburg's lyrics caught the spirit of the time and the plight of the unemployed veteran of World War I. In the show it was sung by Rex Weber but became very popular as a recording by Bing Crosby. Ever since it has been the quintessential Depression song. It nearly was not used, however. When the composers sang and played it for producer Lee Shubert, he rejected it on the grounds that it was "too sorbid." But Harburg and Gorney persisted and it became the major song hit of the show.

BROWN, NACIO HERB (1896–1964) Composer. Born in Deming, N.Mex., Feb. 22, 1896, Brown began to study music with his mother at the age of 5; he later also studied the violin. The entire family was musical, including Brown's father, who was also the sheriff of Deming. In 1904 Brown senior became a deputy sheriff of Los Angeles, to which the family moved and where Brown junior was educated. He was diverted from college when he took the job as accompanist for a vaudeville singer, Alice Doll. Discouraged by one-night stands, Brown returned to Los Angeles where he opened a successful tailor shop; he also dabbled in profitable Beverly Hills real estate. Success afforded Brown the time to dabble also in music; in 1920 his first song, "Coral Sea," was published and performed by the popular Paul Whiteman band. "When Buddha Smiles" was published the next year but Brown returned again to real estate. An instrumental, *Doll Dance*, was published in 1927 and taken up by several bands. The piece was used in a Hollywood Music Box Revue (not to be confused with the Irving Berlin revues in New York) and attracted the attention of producer Irving Thalberg, who asked Brown to compose the music for Metro-Goldwyn-Mayer's impending first musical, *Broadway Melody*. A 3-month contract joined Brown with lyricist Arthur Freed (q.v.), resulting in 2 popular 1929 film scores and a series of successful songs. From *Broadway Melody* came "The Wedding of the Painted Doll" and "You Were Meant for Me." From *Hollywood Revue* "Singin' in the Rain" was to begin a long life as a popular song and as an interpolated song in several films. Brown gave up real estate to collaborate with Freed on film scores and interpolated numbers: "Pagan Love Song" (*The Pagan*, 1929), "Should I" (*Lord Byron of Broadway*, 1930), "Paradise" (*A Woman Commands*, 1932), "Temptation" (*Going Hollywood*, 1933); "All I Do Is Dream of You" (*Sadie McKee*, 1934), "Alone" (*A Night at the Opera*, 1935), "You Are My Lucky Star," "I've Got a Feelin' You're Foolin'," and "Broadway Rhythm" (*Broadway Melody of 1936*), and "Good Morning" (*Babes in Arms*, 1939). Other Brown songs with other lyricists: "You Stepped Out of a Dream," lyrics by Gus Kahn (*Ziegfeld Girl*, 1941) and "Love Is Where You

Find It," lyrics by Edward Heyman and Earl Brent (*The Kissing Bandit*, 1948). Brown wrote the music to one Broadway song of consequence, "You're an Old Smoothie," lyrics by B. G. DeSylva and Richard Whiting (*Take a Chance*, 1932). Brown composed a 2nd instrumental, *American Bolero*, dedicated to his mother. When the production of Hollywood musicals waned, Brown would frequently take extended vacations; in 1943, for example, he left California for Mexico, where he remained for 5 years before returning to Hollywood to do what turned out to be his last full film score, *The Kissing Bandit*. The last Freed-Brown song was written for the film *Singin' in the Rain* (1952), "Make 'Em Laugh" (which tune Freed freely borrowed from Cole Porter's "Be a Clown"). Brown died in San Francisco, Sept. 28, 1964.

BROWN, RAYNOR (b. 1912) Composer, organist. Born in Des Moines, Iowa, Feb. 23, 1912, Brown received his degree in music from the University of Southern California. He settled in the Los Angeles area where he became active as a church organist and with a group of California musicians banded together to publish and record the works of like-minded creators, Western International Music. Brown's compositions include a *Piano Quartet* (1947), 3 symphonies (1952, 1957, 1958), *String Quartet* (1953), *Brass Quintet* (1957), *Concertino for Piano and Band* (1966), *Sonata For Flute and Organ* (1970), and *Fantasy-Fugue for Brass* (1971).

BRUNSWICK, MARK (1902–1971) Composer, teacher. Born in New York City, Jan. 6, 1902, Brunswick began studying with Rubin Goldmark at the age of 16. In 1923 he went to Cleveland to study composition, fugue, and counterpoint with Ernest Bloch (he also came under the influence of Bloch's pupil-colleague Roger Sessions). Brunswick then went to Paris where he studied with Nadia Boulanger from 1925 to 1929. After several years in Vienna (1929–37), Brunswick returned to New York where he began teaching at the Greenwich House Music School; he later taught at Kenyon College, Gambier, Ohio, and returned to teach at Brooklyn College and, in 1946, joined the music teaching staff of the City College of New York. He also served for several years as chairman of the Music Department there. Brunswick's compositions include *Two Movements* for string quartet (1926), *Fantasia* for solo viola (1932), the motet *Fragment of Sappho* for 4 mixed voices, a cappella (1932), a ballet, *Lysistrata,* for mezzo, women's chorus, and orchestra (1936), *Symphony* for chorus and orchestra (1937), *Symphony in B-flat* (1945), *Eros and Death* for mezzo, chorus, and orchestra (completed 1954), *Quartet* for viola, violin, cello, and double bass (1957), *Septet* for winds, viola, and cello (1958), *Five Madrigals* for chorus, viola, cello, and double bass (1966), and *Air with Toccato* for string orchestra (1967). An opera, *The Master Builder,* was left uncompleted when the composer died of a heart attack in London, May 26, 1971.

CAGE, JOHN (b. 1912) Composer, teacher, theoretician. Born in Los Angeles, Calif., Sept. 5, 1912, Cage is one of the most colorful, controversial, and adventurous figures in American music. He began conventionally, studying piano with Richard Buhlig and Fannie Dillon in Los Angeles. A period in Paris brought him into the piano classes of Lazare Lévy. Cage then came under the sway of such experimenters as Henry Cowell, Adolph Weiss, and Arnold Schoenberg. From Cowell, Cage picked up the idea of tampering with the piano's interior workings ("prepared piano") to achieve certain curious sounds. Before embarking on a performer-composer's

career, Cage served on the faculties of the Cornish School, Seattle, Wash., Mills College, Oakland, Calif., the School of Design, Chicago, Ill., and the New School for Social Research, New York City. In New York, Cage became associated with the dancer Merce Cunningham, for whom he composed several ballet scores. Cage established himself as a leader of the avant-garde by the late 1930s; his "prepared piano" recitals were hailed and damned. The woodscrews, pieces of metal, rubber bands, and strips of paper that Cage placed inside the standard piano produced exotic sounds. His fascination with rhythms and percussion instruments also greatly influenced Cage's original work. Another important influence was the music of the East, especially that of India. What others might describe as noise, as well as silence, are ingredients of the music of Cage. Because of his determination to break completely with music's past, Cage's music defies categorization. He rarely uses conventional musical forms, such as a quartet or a concerto, and when he does the form is quite unconventional. His earliest compositions drew upon the 12-tone method of his teacher Schoenberg; he then discovered the "prepared piano." Later came aleatory—or random—composition. There have been gigantic mixed-media works for standard instruments, taped sounds, films, slides, and lights. The next step in a Cage composition may depend on an imperfection in the music paper, the throw of the dice, or a tossed coin. Among the works of Cage are *Two Pieces* (1935), *Metamorphosis* (1938), *Bacchanale,* the first prepared piano piece (1938), *Imaginary Landscapes* (1939), *Amores* for piano and percussion (1943), *Root of an Unfocus* (1944), *Suite for Toy Piano* (1948), *Dream* (1948), *Sonatas and Interludes* (1948), *String Quartet in Four Parts* (1950), *Concerto for Prepared Piano and Orchestra* (1951), *Imaginary*

Landscape No. 4 for Twelve Radios, Twenty-four Players (1952), *4'33"* for piano in 3 movements (1954; the pianist sits at the keyboard for the designated time but does not play a note), and so on. Cage's "masterpiece," no doubt, is his 1962 work, *0'00"*, a silent piece in which anyone can perform anything, ad lib. Cage is the author of *Silence* (1961), *A Year from Monday* (1967), and *Notations* (1969).

CAHN, SAMMY (b. 1913) Lyricist. Born on New York's Lower East Side, June 18, 1913, Cahn took violin lessons as a youngster but had few if any musical ambitions. At 14 he worked in a meat packing plant, amusing himself by concocting parodies of popular songs. Falling back on his early musical training, he began to play the violin in local bands, in vaudeville, in the Catskill Mountains resort area, and finally in his own band formed with Sol Kaplan (now composer-producer Saul Chaplin). Although no music publisher showed interest in Cahn's song parodies or several of his early attempts at lyrics writing, he finally produced a popular song, with music by Chaplin, "Rhythm Is Our Business," in 1935. He and Chaplin collaborated on several highly popular songs, among them, "Bei Mir Bist du Schön" (with music by Sholom Secunda) in 1937. The next year they did a sequel (both recorded by the Andrews Sisters), "Joseph! Joseph!" as well as a fine ballad, "Please Be Kind." In the '40s Cahn moved to Hollywood where he began collaborating with Jule Styne (q.v.) and turned out a remarkable series of very popular songs: "I've Heard That Song Before" (from a film short, *Youth on Parade*, 1943), "I'll Walk Alone" (from *Follow the Boys*, 1944), "It's Been a Long, Long, Time" (1944), "I Should Care" (1945), "Let It Snow, Let It Snow" (1945), "The Things We Did Last Summer" (1946), and "Love Is a Merry-Go-Round" (from *Tars and Spars*, 1946). In 1947 Cahn and Styne composed the songs for a very successful Broadway musical, *High Button Shoes*. Cahn returned to California and began mining the Hit Parade again with composer Jimmy Van Heusen, primarily with individual songs, or film title songs —most of which were popularized by Frank Sinatra (q.v.). Some of their most popular songs have been: "The Tender Trap" (1955), "Love and Marriage" (1955), "All the Way" (1957), "High Hopes" (1959), "The Second Time Around" (1960), and "Call Me Irresponsible" (1963). Cahn and Van Heusen collaborated on a most unsuccessful Broadway musical, *Skyscraper* (1965); they had the same poor luck with *Walking Happy* the next year. Cahn was much more successful in his autobiographical show, *Words and Music* (1963), in which he related the story of his career and sang his songs. Popular on broadway (the show originated from New York's famous center of music and art, the 92nd Street Y), the show was also successful in London and on the road. His autobiography, *I Should Care*, was published in 1974.

CARMICHAEL,   HOAGLAND "HOAGY" (b. 1899) Composer, pianist, vocalist. Born in Bloomington, Ind., Nov. 22, 1899, Carmichael was largely self-taught as a pianist. His mother was a professional pianist, however, and played for local dances and for silent films, often taking her son with her on these dates. The family moved to Indianapolis in 1915, when Carmichael dropped out of high school to work as a cement mixer operator. Four years later Carmichael returned to Bloomington to live with his grandparents and to complete his education. He helped to pay the way by playing the piano for dances; in 1922 he decided to enter college to study law. He continued to play solo and in small bands and soon came under the influence of the jazz bands that moved up from New Orleans into the Midwest. In 1926, a graduated attorney, Carmichael planned to go into a law practice with a friend, but on the way to Miami he detoured to New York where he talked publisher Irving Mills into publishing one of the songs he had written while a student at the University of Indiana, "Washboard Blues" (published in 1925). Hearing a recording of his tune by the Red Nichols band led Carmichael to give up law and return to music-making. He played in several popular bands of the period—Jean Goldkette's, Paul Whiteman's, and eventually his own. Carmichael had a great affinity with jazz musicians and played in bands that included such jazzmen as Benny Goodman, the Dorsey brothers, Jack Teagarden, and Bix Beiderbecke. As a songwriter, Carmichael made his big breakthrough with the 1931 publication of a song based on an instrumental piece he had composed at Indiana's campus hangout, The Book Nook. The composition was "Star Dust," with lyrics by Mitchell Parish (q.v.). Other popular hits followed: "Georgia on My Mind" (lyrics by Stuart Gorrell, 1930), "Rockin' Chair" (lyrics by Carmichael, 1930), "Lazy River" (lyrics by Sidney Arodin, 1931), "Lazybones" (lyrics by Johnny Mercer, 1933), "One Morning in May" (lyrics by Parish, 1933), "Little Old Lady" (lyrics by Stanley Adams, from the revue The Show Is On, 1937), "Two Sleepy People" (lyrics by Frank Loesser, from the film Thanks for the Memory, 1938), "I Get Along Without You Very Well" (lyrics by a "Mrs. Thompson," who mailed her song to Carmichael for a musical setting, 1939), "Hong Kong Blues" (lyrics by Carmichael, 1939), "Can't Get Indiana Off My Mind" (lyrics by Robert De Leon, 1940), "Skylark" (lyrics by Johnny Mercer, 1942), "How Little We Know" (lyrics by Johnny Mercer, from the film

To Have and Have Not, 1944), "Memphis in June" (lyrics by Carmichael, from the film Johnny Angel, 1945), "In the Cool, Cool, Cool of the Evening" (lyrics by Mercer, from the film Here Comes the Groom, 1951; this song won the year's Academy Award). Besides the interpolations into The Show Is On (1936), Carmichael composed but one Broadway score, Walk with Music (1940), with lyrics by Johnny Mercer; the show was not very successful, although a couple of its songs enjoyed popularity: "Ooh, What You Said" and "The Rhumba Jumps." Carmichael also managed to work in a modest film career, beginning with an appearance in Topper (1937), with meatier roles in To Have and Have Not (1944), The Best Years of Our Lives (1946), and Young Man with a Horn (1950). Carmichael generally portrayed himself: a relaxed pianist singing in an engagingly gritty voice. Many of the films were graced with Carmichael songs. In 1979 Carmichael was the subject of a tribute by the Newport Jazz Festival in Carnegie Hall. For this event he composed a new piece entitled Piano Pedal Rag.

"CAROUSEL" A "musical play," music by Richard Rodgers (q.v.) with lyrics and book by Oscar Hammerstein II (q.v.); based on Ferenc Molnar's Liliom. Hammerstein took the original out of its Hungarian setting and placed it in New England. The story of the ill-fated ne'er-do-well "Billy Bigelow" and his unfortunate marriage to "Julie Jordan," who works in the town's factory, comes to a tragic end when Billy is killed during a robbery attempt. The Molnar fantasy, to which Hammerstein added some of his own, permits Billy to return to earth to see and comfort his daughter (who was born after he had been killed). Thus having done his good work, Billy goes to heaven and daughter "Louise" is ready to face the world. Car-

ousel was Rodgers and Hammerstein's 2nd musical (the first since their initial triumph, *Oklahoma!*); it too was extraordinarily successful. Among its songs: "If I Loved You," "June Is Bustin' Out All Over," "What's the Use of Wond'rin'?," "Soliloquy," and "You'll Never Walk Alone." *Carousel* opened at the Majestic Theatre. Apr. 19, 1945, and had a run of 890 performances; it also had a successful run in London in 1950, and was made into a film in 1956. In the original production John Raitt portrayed "Billy," Jan Clayton, "Julie," Jean Darling, "Carrie Pepperide," Eric Mattson was "Enoch Snow," and Bambi Linn, the daughter of Billy and Julie. Dancing was important to the plot of *Carousel* and Agnes de Mille provided the choreography.

CARTER, ELLIOTT (b. 1908) Composer, teacher. Born in New York City, Dec. 11, 1908, Carter entered Harvard in 1926 as a student of literature and languages; simultaneously he studied piano at the Longy School, Cambridge, Mass. Four years later he decided to concentrate on music and studied with Walter Piston (counterpoint, harmony) and Edward Burlingame Hill (orchestration); he also studied briefly with Gustav Holst and then moved on to Paris where he studied with Nadia Boulanger (1932–35). After he returned to the United States he became musical director of Ballet Caravan, for which he composed the "Ballet Legend in One Act," *Pocahontas* (1939). After leaving Ballet Caravan, Carter taught at St. John's College, Annapolis (physics, classical Greek, and mathematics!). He later turned to teaching music at the Peabody Conservatory, Baltimore, Md., Columbia University, New York City, Yale, New Haven, Conn., and others, including Juilliard, New York City. Although he composed several works before and after *Pocahontas*, Carter first excited musical

attention with his *String Quartet* in 1951, a work that won first prize at Liège; his *String Quartet No. 2* (1959) was awarded the Pulitzer Prize and the New York Music Critics Circle Award; the *String Quartet No. 3* (1971) also won the Pulitzer Prize. By this time Carter was regarded as the outstanding American composer, widely respected by his colleagues—even singled out and praised by Stravinsky. Carter's mature works are highly intellectualized, tightly packed with musical ideas, skillfully fashioned, complex and, for many, difficult. His works include: incidental music and choruses for Sophocles' *Philoctetes* (1933), *Flute Sonata* (1934), *Tarantella* for male chorus and orchestra (1936), incidental music and choruses for Plautus' *Mostellaria* (1936), *To Music* for chorus, a cappella (1938), Suite from *Pocahontas* (1939), *The Defense of Corinth* for male voices and piano, 4 hands (1941), *Symphony No. 1* (1942), *Adagio* for viola and piano (1943), *Warble for Lilac Time* for soprano and orchestra (1943), *Elegy for Strings* (1943), *Holiday Overture* (1944), *Piano Sonata* (1945), the ballet *The Minotaur* (1946), *Sonata for Cello and Piano* (1948), *Eight Etudes and Fantasy* for woodwind quartet (1950), *Sonata for Flute, Oboe, Cello and Harpsichord* (1952), *Variations for Orchestra* (1955), *Double Concerto* for harpsichord, piano with 2 chamber orchestras (1961), *Piano Concerto* (1965), *Concerto for Orchestra* (1970), *Symphony for Three Orchestras* (1976), *Syringa* (1979), and *Night Fantasies* for piano (1980).

CASTELNUOVO-TEDESCO, MARIO (1895–1968) Composer, teacher. Born in Florence, Italy, Apr. 3, 1895, Castelnuovo-Tedesco was already an established composer by the time he arrived in the United States in 1939, driven out of Italy by the Fascist regime. Before this event he was known for his compositions; his opera *La Mandragola* won the Italian Prize for Opera in 1926. He had composed several operas, chamber music, orchestral works, and songs. Castelnuovo-Tedesco settled in Beverly Hills, Calif., where he continued to compose, became a prolific film composer, and taught at the Los Angeles Conservatory. Among his early "American" works were *Indian Songs and Dances* and *An American Rhapsody*. Among his most popular works are the *Concertino for Harp and Chamber Orchestra* (1937), *Concerto in D* for guitar (1939), and the *Concerto for Two Guitars and Orchestra* (1967). His film scores include *And Then There Were None, Down to Earth, The Loves of Carmen,* and *Everybody Does It.* His pupils are among the most successful in films: Henry Mancini, Jerry Goldsmith, George Duning, Nelson Riddle, John Williams, and André Previn. Castelnuovo-Tedesco died in Hollywood, Mar. 16, 1968.

CAZDEN, NORMAN (1914–1980) Composer, pianist, teacher. Born in New York City, Sept. 23, 1914, Cazden studied piano at the Institute of Musical Art, New York, and, later, when its name had been changed to the Juilliard School of Music, undertook graduate piano study with Ernest Hutcheson and composition with Bernard Wagenaar. At Harvard he studied with Walter Piston and Aaron Copland. He began to teach piano at Juilliard in 1934; he also taught at Vassar, the Peabody Institute, the University of Illinois, the New School in New York City, and the University of Maine at Orono. Cazden was also the recipient of several fellowships and awards, among them 2 Juilliard Fellowships (1927, 1939), Harvard (1943–45), Westminster Choir Award (1936), the George A. Knight Prize (1945), and the John Knowles Paine Traveling Fellowship (1945–46). His compositions include *Sonatina* for piano

(1935), *String Quartet* (1936), *Concerto for Ten Instruments* (1937), *Five American Dances* for piano (1938), *Piano Sonata* (1938), *Three Chamber Sonatas* for clarinet and viola (1938), *Preamble* for orchestra (1938), *On the Death of a Spanish Child* (1939), *Quartet* for violin, clarinet, viola, and cello (1939), *Six Definitions* for chamber orchestra (1939), *Three Dances* for orchestra (1940), *American Suite* for piano and cello (1940), *Quintet* for 2 violins, 2 cellos, and viola (1941), *Sonata* for horn and piano (1941), *Etcetera* for piano, reciter, and dancer (1941), *Suite* for violin and piano (1943), *The Lonely Ones* for piano, dancers, and cartoons by William Steig (1944), *Symphony* (1948), *Three Ballads* for orchestra (1949), *Three New Sonatas* for piano (1950), *Suite* for brass sextet (1951), *Dingle Hill,* a play with music (1958), *Quintet* for oboe and strings (1960), *Woodland Sketches* for orchestra (1960), *Adventure* for orchestra (1963), *Chamber Concerto* (1965), *Woodwind Quintet* (1966), *Piano Trio* (1969), and *Six Preludes and Fugues* for piano (1974). He died in Bangor, Maine, Aug. 18, 1980.

CHANLER, THEODORE (1902–1961) Composer. Born in Newport, R.I., Apr. 29, 1902, Chanler began to study the piano at the age of 6; he later studied, in Boston, with Hans Ebell (piano and composition) and Arthur Shepherd (harmony). He continued at the Institute of Musical Art (later the Juilliard School), New York City, where he worked under Percy Goetschius (counterpoint) and Richard Buhlig (piano). Chanler also studied with Ernest Bloch, Nadia Boulanger in Paris, and at Oxford University (1923–25). He remained in Paris for several years, returning to the United States in 1934. He eventually joined the staff of the Boston *Herald* as music editor; he also wrote for the League of

Composers' *Modern Music*. In 1945 Chanler joined the staff of the Peabody Conservatory, Baltimore, Md. Chanler's forte was the small form and he was highly regarded as a composer of songs. Among his instrumental works: *Sonata for Violin and Piano* (1927), *Five Short Colloquies* for piano (1936), *Second Joyful Mystery* for piano (1943), and the ballet *Pas de Trois* (1942). His compositions for voice: "Memory," text by William Blake (1919), "The Shepherd," text by Blake (1919), "These, My Ophelia," text by Archibald MacLeish (1925, rev. ed. 1937), "Agnus Dei" from *Mass for Two Women's Voices and Organ* (1930), "The Doves," text by Leonard Feeney (1935), "O Mistress Mine!" text by Shakespeare (1936), *Eight Epitaphs*, texts by Walter De La Mare (1937), "Pianissimo," text by Feeney (1938), *Three Epitaphs*, texts by De La Mare (1940), *Four Rhymes from "Peacock Pie,"* texts by De La Mare (1940), "The Lamb," text by Blake (1941), "I Rise When You Enter," text by Feeney (1942), "The Flight," text by Feeney (1944), and *The Children*, 9 songs with texts by Feeney (1945). Chanler's chamber opera, *The Pot of Fat*, was produced in 1955. The composer died in Boston, July 27, 1961.

CHASINS, ABRAM (b. 1903) Pianist, composer, author. Born in New York City, Aug. 17, 1903, Chasins was a piano student of Ernest Hutcheson and a composition student of Rubin Goldmark; he later studied with Josef Hofmann at the Curtis Institute, Philadelphia. Chasins then spent several years teaching piano at the Institute. He also spent many of his early professional years, beginning ca. 1926, as a concert pianist giving recitals and concerts in the United States and abroad. In the early 1930s he went into radio as commentator on music and as a pianist; in 1941 he joined the staff of the New York City "good music" station WQXR and remained there for several years, until 1965. He moved to California in 1972 to join the faculty of the University of Southern California, Los Angeles; he was also the director of the university's radio station. As a composer Chasins was most active in the late-1920s and '30s. His original works include the *Blue Danube Waltzes* for 2 pianos (1925), *Twenty-four Preludes* for piano (1928), *Piano Concerto in F-minor* (1929), *Three Chinese Pieces* for orchestra, or solo piano (1929), *Parade* for orchestra (1930), *Piano Concerto No. 2* (1932), *Three Violin Preludes* for violin and piano (1935), *Carmen Fantasy* for 2 pianos (1937), and *Melody* for piano (1938). Chasins is the author of *Speaking of Pianists* (1958), *The Van Cliburn Legend* (1959), *The Appreciation of Music* (1966), and *Music at the Crossroads* (1972). He also made many transcriptions for piano of compositions by Bach, Bizet, Gluck, and Rimsky-Korsakov.

CITKOWITZ, ISRAEL (1909–1974) Composer, teacher, poet. Born in Russia, Feb. 6, 1909, Citkowitz was brought to the United States as an infant and grew up in New York City. He studied with Aaron Copland and Roger Sessions in New York and with Nadia Boulanger in Paris. He joined the faculty of the Dalcroze School of Music, New York, where he taught composition. He wrote about music for *Modern Music* and *Musical Mercury* and poetry for *Poetry*. The bulk of his work is in the chamber music genre or for voice. His works include a *Passacaglia* for piano (1927), *Sonatine* for piano (1929), *Song Cycle to Words of Joyce* from "Chamber Music" (1930), *String Quartet* (1932), *Andante Tranquillo* for string quartet (1932), *Song Cycle* to poems by William Blake (1934), *Song Cycle* to words of Robert Frost (1936), *The Lamb* (Blake) for a cappella chorus (1936), and *Songs of Protest* for a cappella chorus (1936). Citkowitz died in London, May 4, 1974.

COHN, ARTHUR (b. 1910) Composer, conductor, author. Born in Philadelphia, Pa., Nov. 6, 1910, Cohn began the study of violin, theory, and pedagogy at the Combs Conservatory of Music in 1920; he later studied privately with William Happich (composition) and Sascha Jacobinoff (violin) and did graduate work at the Juilliard School, New York City, with Rubin Goldmark (composition) and George Volkel. At the University of Pennsylvania he also studied the art of chamber music performance which eventually led to his organizing of the Dorian and Stringart Quartets, which specialized in contemporary music. His Opus 1 is a string quartet entitled *Four Preludes* (1928). In addition to being a musician Cohn has also been an administrator and music publishing executive. From 1934 until 1952 he was curator and director of the Edwin A. Fleisher Collection, the Free Library of Philadelphia. Cohn has also been associated with several local symphony orchestras in the Philadelphia area in the role of conductor. He has also held important positions with the firms of Mills Music, MCA Music, and Carl Fischer, where he serves as director of serious music. His works include an additional 5 string quartets (1930, 1932, 1935, 1935, 1945), *Suite* for viola and piano (1930), *Sonata for Violin and Piano* (1932), *The Pot Bellied Gods,* for baritone and string quartet (1933), *Music for Brass Instruments* (1933), *Transcriptions* for string quartet (1934), *Paraphrase on a Folk Tune* for string quartet (1935), *Machine Music* for 2 pianos (1937), *Music for Ancient Instruments* (1938),

Quintuple Concerto for Five Ancient Instruments (1940), *Music for Bassoon and Piano* (1944), and *Music for Bassoon,* solo (1947). Cohn's orchestral compositions include the *Suite for Orchestra* (1931), *Five Nature Studies* (1932), *Retrospections* for string orchestra (1933), *Four Preludes* for string orchestra (1937), *Suite for Viola and Orchestra* (1937), *Four Symphonic Documents* (1939), *Histrionics* for string orchestra (1940), *Concerto for Flute and Orchestra* (1941), *Variations for Clarinet* (or saxophone) and orchestra (1945), *Quotations in Percussion* (1958), and *Kaddish* for orchestra (1964). Cohn is the author of *The Collector's Twentieth-Century Music in the Western Hemisphere* (1961), *Twentieth-Century Music in Western Europe* (1965), and *Musical Quizzical* (1970).

COLE, ULRIC (b. 1905) Composer, pianist, teacher. Born in New York City, Sept. 9, 1905, Cole began to study piano at 5 and composing at 8. Among her teachers were Rubin Goldmark (composition), Percy Goetschius, and Josef Lhévinne (piano) at the Juilliard School of Music. She also studied with Nadia Boulanger in Paris. As a child prodigy she toured the Chautauqua circuit in the Midwest; she also performed her own compositions with several orchestras. She has served as a copy editor on *Time* magazine for several years. She taught music at Masters School, Dobbs Ferry, N.Y., and has also taught composition and piano privately. Her works include 2 piano concertos (1930, 1942), *Two Sketches for String Orchestra* (1937), and a *Divertimento* for strings and piano (1942). Her chamber works include 2 sonatas for violin and piano (1927, 1929), *Suite for Trio:* piano, violin, cello (1931), *Quartet,* 2 violins, viola, cello (1932), *Fantasy Sonata* for piano (1933), *Suite for String Quartet* (1936),

Quintet for piano and strings (1936), and *Round Dance for Strings* (1940).

COMDEN AND GREEN Songwriting and performing team: Betty Comden (b. 1915) and Adolph Green (b. 1915). Began professionally as a nightclub act called The Revuers, another member of which was Judy Holiday. The Revuers made their debut in Greenwich Village at the Village Vanguard and eventually worked their way uptown to the Blue Angel and the Rainbow Room. Comden and Green wrote most of their sketches. In 1945 they wrote the book and lyrics for—and appeared in—*On the Town* (music by Leonard Bernstein, q.v.), based on the Bernstein ballet *Fancy Free.* This began an extraordinarily long career on Broadway and in Hollywood during which they wrote the books and scripts and fashioned the lyrics. Their Broadway shows include *Billion Dollar Baby* for which they did the book and lyrics, music by Morton Gould (1945), *Two on the Aisle,* libretto and lyrics, music by Jule Styne (1951), *Wonderful Town,* lyrics, music by Bernstein (1953), *Bells Are Ringing,* book and lyrics, music by Styne (1956), *Say Darling,* lyrics, music by Styne (1958), *Do Re Me,* lyrics, music by Styne (1960), *Subways Are for Sleeping,* book and lyrics, music by Styne (1961), *Fade Out —Fade In,* book and lyrics, music by Styne (1964), *Hallelujah, Baby!,* lyrics, music by Styne (1967), *Applause,* book only, lyrics by Lee Adams, music by Charles Strouse (1970), and *On the Twentieth Century,* book and lyrics, music by Cy Coleman (1978). Comden and Green worked on the screenplays of several film musicals; among the best are *Good News,* songs mostly by DeSylva, Brown, and Henderson; Comden and Green contributed "The French Lesson," music by Roger Edens (1947), *On the Town,* with additional songs by Comden, Green, and Edens (1949), *Singin' in the Rain,* with songs mostly by Arthur Freed and Nacio Herb Brown (1952), *The Band Wagon,* songs by Arthur Schwartz and Howard Dietz (1953), and *It's Always Fair Weather,* screenplay and lyrics, music by André Previn (1955). They have also appeared as themselves, singing their various songs, in *An Evening with Comden and Green.*

COMDEN, BETTY (b. 1915) Librettist, lyricist, vocalist. Born in New York City, May 3, 1915. See Comden and Green.

CONDON, EDDIE (1906–1973) Bandleader, guitarist. Born in Goodland, Ind., Nov. 16, 1906, Condon grew up in Momence and Chicago Heights, Ill. His family was musical in an amateur way, but his sisters did learn the piano and Condon listened to their lessons. He was self-taught on the ukulele and banjo— and it was as a banjoist that he began playing in local bands when he was about 15. He moved into Chicago in the 1920s and became associated with the young jazz musicians there: Frank Teschemacher, Gene Krupa, Joe Sullivan, Bud Freeman, and others. In 1927 Condon joined with Red McKenzie, a jockey turned vocalist, to form a classic recording group, the McKenzie-Condon Chicagoans; the following year, in New York they recorded with a unit known as the Mound City Blue Blowers. During the late-1920s and the '30s Condon played with various groups, from small pickup jazz groups to such commercial bands as that of Riley-Farley (whose most famous recording was the notorious "The Music Goes Round and Round") and became associated with what came to be called Chicago Jazz and, with less precision, Dixieland Jazz. Condon proved to be a good organizer and promoter. He was most frequently associated with the jazzmen who played at a Greenwich Village nightclub, Nick's (the owner was an aspiring nonjazz pianist, Nick Rongetti).

Condon used many of these musicians for recordings, broadcasts, and for a series of jazz concerts in Town Hall. Among the musicians were trumpeters Muggsy Spanier, Bobby Hackett, Wild Bill Davison, and Max Kaminsky; clarinetists Pee Wee Russell, Rod Cless, Edmond Hall, and Ernie Caceres; pianists Jess Stacy, Joe Bushkin, Joe Sullivan, and Mel Powell; trombonists Lou McGarrity and Miff Mole; saxophonist Bud Freeman and drummers George Wettling and Dave Tough. In 1942 Condon produced, in association with a friend, Ernie Anderson, his first jazz concert at Carnegie Hall; the star was pianist Fats Waller and Condon led an intermission band made up of Bud Freeman, Pee Wee Russell, Gene Krupa, Max Kaminsky, bassist John Kirby, and Condon on guitar. Anderson and Condon then took their concerts to Town Hall for a series of successful Saturday afternoon jazz sessions. Condon also toured with his jazz groups, bringing his brand of jazz to cities that only knew the music through recordings. Most of these musicians gathered for recording sessions at the Commodore Music Shop and even for the more commercial labels such as Decca and Columbia. In 1945 Condon opened up his own club (he was undoubtedly tired of being fired and rehired by Nick) at 47 West 3rd Street, where he employed the musicians not working at Nick's. In 1958 the club moved to East 56th Street. In the interim Condon became a celebrity, produced jazz shows for television, wrote articles and reviews, and was widely quoted. He once dismissed a French jazz critic and writer with, "We don't tell him how to jump on a grape." When asked why a concert had fallen through, Condon attributed to the absence of an impresario —explaining it thus, "He got cold on us, we had to throw dirt on him" (meaning the man had died, of course). "For a hangover," he once advised, "take the juice of two quarts of whisky." The new definitions of jazz that came after the end of World War II rendered Condon's type of jazz old hat—it was dismissed as "moldy fig" by the new breed. But Condon prevailed and, besides his television shows, took his bands on tour. In 1964 "Eddie Condon and his All-Stars" performed in Japan, Australia, and New Zealand; in 1969 he led his band at the Inaugural Ball in Washington, D.C. One of his last appearances was at Alice Tully Hall, leading a "Stars of Jazz" concert in September 1971. He was co-author of We Called It Music, with Tom Sugrue (1947), and Eddie Condon's Scrapbook of Jazz, with Hank O'Neal (1973). He died of cancer, Aug. 4, 1973.

CONE, EDWARD TONER (b. 1917) Composer, teacher. Born in Greensboro, N.C., May 4, 1917, Cone was a student of Roger Sessions at Princeton University, from which he graduated in 1939. He also studied at Columbia University (musicology) and piano with Karl Ulrich Schnabel. He had just begun teaching at Princeton when he entered the U. S. Army in 1942 (he was discharged in 1945). After studying on a Guggenheim Fellowship in 1947, Cone returned to Princeton to teach. His works include a String Quartet (1939), The Lotus Eaters for male chorus and orchestra (1939), Sonata for Violin and Piano (1940), Clarinet Quintet (1941), Divertimento for Woodwinds (1946), Prelude and Variations for piano, 4 hands (1946), Symphony (1952), Elegy (1953), Prelude, Passacaglia and Fugue for piano (1957), Violin Concerto (1958), Music for Strings (1965), String Sextet (1966), and Variations for Orchestra (1969). Cone is the author of Musical Form and Musical Performance (1968).

COUNTRY MUSIC All-embracing term for quasi-folk, popular folk music of the peoples of the American South and West (it is often called country and western, or "C&W," in commercial music circles). The pejorative among "sophisticates" is "hillbilly music." Some of the first recordings of rural music date back to the early '20s and were made by Texans such as A. C. (Eck) Robertson, who recorded a country dance, *Ragtime Annie,* playing a solo fiddle. This kind of music dated back many years and was kept alive by rural barn dances. Such performers as Jimmie Rodgers and the Carter family enjoyed considerable success in the late '20s; the advent of the weekly radio show "The Grand Ole Opry," from Nashville's WSM, in 1927 spread the popularity of country music. The popularity, however, was generally limited to the rural areas of the Southwest. Recordings on Army post jukeboxes served to bring the music to service men and women from other parts of the country. This, in turn, led to the great surge in interest and popularity of country music, as well as one of its branches, Bluegrass (q.v.), in the late-1950s and the '60s. (The subject will be covered in more detail in the final section of this book, for it was in this period that country music truly came into its own.)

"THE CRADLE WILL ROCK" A "play in music" by Marc Blitzstein (q.v.). Also described in one of its early flyers as "A Worker's Opera," *The Cradle Will Rock* was set in Steeltown, U.S.A., a town entirely in the grip of factory owner "Mr. Mister." He also "owns" the town's leading citizens— businessmen, the newspaper owner, et al. —and has formed them into a so-called "Liberty Committee," which he uses to thwart the rights of the workers in his steel mill. The leader of the workers is named "Larry Foreman." The action of the work centers around Mr. Mister's attempts, with conniving help from his

committee, to frame and jail Foreman. Characters are patently good or evil: the clergy, the press, a doctor, educators, are all under the thumb of Mr. Mister, as opposed to Foreman and the workers and simple folk. Originally sponsored by the Federal Theatre branch of the WPA (Works Progress Administration), *The Cradle Will Rock* was scheduled to open at the Maxine Elliott Theatre "about June 1" (1937). The theme of Blitzstein's opera apparently made someone in Washington nervous and word came down that there would be no new WPA productions until after July 1. By this time an actual date, June 16, had already been set. With the Elliott Theatre denied them (that also included the sets designed for use there), the cast, director Orson Welles, and composer Blitzstein hastily arranged for the use of the Venice Theatre and put on a primitive, but effective performance under less than ideal conditions. Many of the cast performed from the audience and, instead of an orchestra, only Blitzstein provided accompaniment on an old piano. Later in the year *The Cradle Will Rock* ran on Sunday nights at the Mercury Theatre, with which Welles was associated. It finally had its true Broadway opening at the Windsor Theatre on Jan. 3, 1938. It had a good run of 108 performances and several revivals. Of the original cast, only one member became a professional: Howard Da Silva, who portrayed "Larry Foreman." The songs, none of which ever became popular, are truly integrated with the plot and characters. The songs have such titles as "The Freedom of the Press," "Art for Art's Sake" (sung by 2 artists who have sold out to Mrs. Mister), "The Rich," "Nickel Under the Foot," "Leaflets," and the title song in which Foreman predicts a victory over Mr. Mister and his Committee. Blitzstein would return to the subject of the plight of the working man with *No for an Answer* (1940).

CRESTON, PAUL (b. 1906) Composer, organist, teacher. Born—as Guttoveggio—in New York City, Oct. 10, 1906, Creston began in music by studying the piano and, later, organ. Although he had made tentative compositional attempts as early as his 8th year, he did not begin seriously composing until he was in his mid-twenties. As a composer he is self-taught. He was a film theatre organist for several years during the 1920s and organist at St. Malachy's Church, New York, for more than 3 decades, beginning in 1934. Creston—a name he adapted from a nickname he had during his school days—has taught at the New York College of Music, Swarthmore College, Pa., and the Central Washington State College, Ellensburg, Wash., where he is also composer-in-residence. He has written 5 symphonies (1941, 1945, 1950, 1952, 1956); his Opus 1 is a piano work entitled *Five Dances*. Creston's other compositions include *Iron Flowers*, incidental music for a ballet for piano (1933), *Out of the Cradle Endlessly Rocking* for chamber orchestra (1934), *Suite* for alto saxophone and piano (1935), *String Quartet* (1936), *Partita* for flute, violin, and strings (1937), *Two Choric Dances*, for orchestra or chamber orchestra (1938), *Threnody* for orchestra (1938), *Concertino* for marimba and orchestra (1940), *Prelude and Dance* (1941), *Concerto* for saxophone and orchestra (1941), *Dance Variations* for soprano and orchestra (1942), *Fantasy* for piano and orchestra (1942), *Chant of 1942* for orchestra (1943), *Frontiers* for orchestra (1943), *Dawn Mood* for orchestra (1944), *Poem* for harp and orchestra (1945), *Brought to Action,* score for U. S. Navy film (1945), *Fantasy* for trombone and orchestra (1948), *Piano Concerto* (1949), *Concerto* for 2 pianos and orchestra (1951), *Invocation and Dance* (1954), *Dance Overture* (1954), *Violin Concerto No. 1* (1956), *Toccata*

for orchestra (1957), *Accordion Concerto* (1958), *Janus* for orchestra (1959), *Violin Concerto No. 2* (1960), *Corinthians XIII,* symphonic poem for orchestra (1964), *Metamorphoses* for piano (1964), *Choreografic Suite* for piano and orchestra (1966), *Pavane Variations* for orchestra (1966), *Chthonic Ode* for piano and orchestra (1967), *The Psalmist* for contralto and orchestra (1967), *Anatolia* for band (1967), *The Northwest* for chorus and orchestra (1969), *Thanatopsis* for orchestra (1971), and *Hyas Illahee* for chorus and orchestra (1976). It might be noted that in his symphonies Creston reveals a fine skill in manipulating the elements of popular song and, especially, dance with remarkable skill and imagination. This is demonstrated especially well in his *Symphony No. 2* of 1945. Creston is the author of *Principles of Rhythm* (1964) and *Creative Harmony* (1970).

CROSBY, HARRY L. "BING" (1903–1977) Crooner, actor, comedian. Born in Tacoma, Wash., May 3, 1903 (dates vary), Crosby had begun to prepare for a law career at Gonzaga University, Spokane, but formed a vaudeville singing team with vocalist Al Rinker (b. 1907) and headed for California. By 1926 they were members of the Paul Whiteman band as vocalists; a 3rd member was added, Harry Barris (1905–1962), to form the popular Rhythm Boys. Crosby spent about 3 years with Whiteman, made several recordings, and appeared in the film *The King of Jazz* (1930), after which the Rhythm Boys left to join the band of Gus Arnheim at the Cocoanut Grove, Los Angeles. Crosby ventured on a career as a single in 1931, began making radio appearances and film shorts, singing in a relaxed, deep-voiced, distinctive style that came to be called crooning. Crosby's offhand manner, plus his way with a song, led to immediate popularity after a few film appearances and his first starring role in *College Humor* (1933). Scores of musical films were made by Crosby, most of them with excellent songs tailored to his singing style; he also began making recordings on his own which sold even in the 1930s, when the recording industry was in a slump. He became a fixture on radio in the late '30s, beginning with the Kraft Music Hall, for which he served as permanent host, in 1936. His gift for casual comedy was often evident and led to a teaming of Crosby and Bob Hope (plus Dorothy Lamour) in *The Road to Singapore* (1940), the first in a series of zany "Road" pictures. One of Crosby's outstanding musical films was *Holiday Inn* (1942), with songs by Irving Berlin. Crosby's recording of "White Christmas" from this movie has become one of the best-selling recordings of all time. As he matured, Crosby also revealed himself as a fine actor, a fact first noted when he won the "Best Actor" Academy Award in 1944 for his role as a priest in *Going My Way*. He was outstanding as an alcoholic in *Country Girl* (1954) but received no special recognition for that. His last film appearance was in the remake of the classic western, *Stagecoach* (1966). Although not as active as most entertainers in television, Crosby appeared as a guest on several shows and, from time to time, in his own specials—frequently around Christmas time. Crosby's informal, insouciant singing style influenced at least a generation of imitators. In later years he made a few concert appearances in the United States and Europe. Affectionately known as the "Groaner," Crosby was an active performer for troops during World War II; he was also popular with the enemy, the German troops, who called him "Der Bingle." Crosby was on a European concert tour when, while golfing near Madrid, Spain, he suffered a heart attack and died, Oct. 14, 1977.

DAHL, INGOLF (1912–1970) Composer, teacher. Born in Hamburg, Germany, June 9, 1912, Dahl was thoroughly formed as a musician before he arrived in the United States in 1935. His parents were Swedish and Dahl received his musical training in Sweden and Switzerland. For a time he gave piano recitals in Europe and was conductor at the Municipal Opera House, Zürich. In the United States, Dahl found work as an arranger-orchestrator for radio orchestras in New York City and eventually (in 1938) settled in California. He became active in the musical life in the Hollywood area and was associated with the famous "Evenings on the Roof" concerts which presented concerts of contemporary music. Dahl also joined the staff of the University of Southern California as an assistant professor, beginning in 1945. He later taught at the Berkshire Music Center, Tanglewood, Mass. (1952–55). Dahl was a trusted associate of Stravinsky and made some arrangements of Stravinsky's works. Dahl's original compositions include *Rondo for Piano*, 4 hands (1938), *Suite* for piano (1941), *Allegro and Arioso* for flute, oboe, clarinet, horn, and bassoon (1942), *Music for Brass Instruments* (1944), *Variations on a Swedish Folktune* for flute (1945), *Concertino in One Movement* for clarinet, violin, and cello (1946), *The Deep Blue Devil's Breakdown* for 2 pianos, 8 hands (1946), *Duo for Cello and Piano* (1946), *Concerto for Saxophone and Winds* (1949), *Sonata Seria* for piano (1953), *The Tower of St. Barbara* for orchestra (1954), *Piano Quartet* (1957), *Sonata pastorale* for piano (1959), *Serenade* for 4 flutes (1960), *Sinfonietta* for concert band (1961), *Piano Trio* (1962), *Elegy Concerto* for violin and chamber orchestra (1963), *Aria sinfonica* for orchestra (1965), *Duo Concertante* for flute and percussion (1966), and *Intervals* for strings (1970). Dahl died at Frutigen, Switzerland, Aug. 7, 1970.

DELANEY, ROBERT MILLS (1903–1956) Composer, teacher. Born in Baltimore, Md., July 24, 1903, Delaney began to study the violin at the age of 5; after the family moved to Wenonah, N.J., he entered the Military Academy there and continued his studies. Upon completion of his schooling, Delaney traveled a good deal and settled in Italy, where he took up music again. He returned to the United States in 1921 and enrolled in the College of Music, University of Southern California. He then returned, the next year, to Europe to study with Nadia Boulanger, Lucien Capet (violin), and Arthur Honegger. He remained in France for about 5 years. He was awarded a Guggenheim Fellowship (1929–30). Delaney returned to the United States again and took a teaching post at the School of Music, Concord, Mass.; later he taught at Northwestern University, Evanston, Ill., and the Santa Barbara School in California. During World War II Delaney worked in a defense plant and at a Naval Air Station in California. His works include *The Constant Couple* for orchestra (1926), *Don Quixote Symphony* (1927), a tone poem, *Pastoral Movement* (1930), 2 symphonic pieces (1935, 1937), *Work 22* (1939), *Symphony No. 1* (1942), and a choral symphony, *John Brown's Song* to a text by Stephen Vincent Benét (1931), which was awarded the Pulitzer Prize. Among Delaney's choral works is an ambitious work for 5-part chorus and orchestra entitled *Western Star* (1944). A *Violin Sonata* dates from 1927; there are also 3 early string quartets and an *Adagio* for violin and string orchestra (1935). Delaney died in Santa Barbara Sept. 21, 1956.

DELLO JOIO, NORMAN (b. 1913) Composer, teacher, organist. Born in New York City, Jan. 24, 1913, Dello Joio began the study of music with his father, an organist; he also studied with Pietro Yon, his godfather, organist at St. Patrick's Cathedral, New York. Dello Joio's first practical work in music began when he was 12 assisting his father at the organ. His experience in liturgical music has influenced Dello Joio's original composition; his *New York Profiles* (1949), for example, draws upon Gregorian chant for its motives. He completed his musical training under Bernard Wagenaar (Juilliard School, 1939–41) and Paul Hindemith (Yale University, 1941–43). Dello Joio has taught at Sarah Lawrence College, Bronxville, N.Y., and at the Mannes College of Music, New York City. Since 1972, Dello Joio has been dean of Fine Arts, Boston University. He has been awarded many prizes and fellowships, among them 2 Guggenheims, a Juilliard Fellowship, and the Elizabeth Sprague Coolidge Award. Among Dello Joio's most significant works are *Concertino for Piano and Chamber Orchestra* (1939), *Sinfonietta* for orchestra (1941), *Sonata No. 1 for Piano* (1942), *Magnificat* (1943), *American Landscape* (1944), *On Stage!* a ballet (1945), *Ricercari* for piano and orchestra (1946), *Harp Concerto* (1947), *Variations, Chaconne and Finale* for orchestra (1948), *Two Nocturnes* for piano (1949), the opera *The Triumph of St. Joan* (1950), *Epigraph* for orchestra (1954), *Lamentation of Saul* for baritone and orchestra (1954), *Meditations on Ecclesiastes* for strings (1956), ballet, *There is a Time* for strings (1956), the cantata *To St. Cecelia* (1957), *Fantasy and Variations* for piano and orchestra (1961), the opera *Blood Moon* (1961), *Songs of Walt Whitman* for chorus and orchestra (1967), *Mass* for chorus, brass instruments, and organ (1968), *Homage to Haydn* for orchestra (1969), *Evocations* for chorus and orchestra (1970), *Lyric Fantasies* for viola and strings (1973), *Notes from Tom Paine* for chorus and piano (1975), *Mass* for chorus, soloist, organ, and brass (1976), and *Colonial Variations* for orchestra (1976).

DEPAUL, GENE (b. 1919) Composer, pianist, arranger, vocalist. Born in New York City, June 17, 1919, DePaul studied the piano as a youngster then began playing in dance orchestras. He also had a career as a singer, made arrangements for vocal groups, and ca. 1940 began writing songs with Don Raye (b. 1909), chiefly for films. Among their songs: "Mr. Five by Five" (from *Behind the Eight Ball,* 1942), "I'll Remember April" with Pat Johnson (from *Ride 'Em Cowboy,* 1942), "Cow Cow Boogie" (1943), and "Milkman, Keep Those Bottles Quiet" (from *Broadway Rhythm,* 1944). In 1954 DePaul collaborated with Johnny Mercer (q.v.) on the songs for an outstanding film musical, *Seven Brides for Seven Brothers.* They teamed again to produce the songs for *Li'l Abner* (1956), a Broadway show based on the Al Capp comic strip. Very successful, it ran for nearly 700 performances and was made into a film in 1959.

DEROSE, PETER (1900–1953) Composer, pianist. Born in New York City, Mar. 10, 1900, DeRose came from a large musical family. His only music lessons, on the piano, he took from his sister at the age of 12. After 4 lessons DeRose decided that he would be a self-taught pianist. After graduation from high school he worked as a stock room clerk for the music publisher G. Schirmer in 1920, when he began seriously to consider writing popular songs. His first published effort, "When You're Gone I Won't Forget" with lyrics by Ivan Reid (1920), proved successful and led to work with yet another publishing house, the Ricordi Co. In 1923 DeRose formed a radio partnership with a young woman known as "The Ukulele Lady," May Singhi Breen. Their radio show ran for 16 years (1923–39) during which time they were known as "The Sweethearts of the Air" (they were, in fact, eventually married) and their show served as an outlet for DeRose's songs. Although he contributed songs to Broadway shows and a film or 2, the bulk of DeRose's output consisted of single songs that achieved remarkable popularity. His songs include "When Your Hair Has Turned to Silver" (lyrics by Charles Tobias, 1930), "Wagon Wheels" (lyrics by Billy Hill, 1931, interpolated into *Ziegfeld Follies of 1934*), "Have You Ever Been Lonely?" (lyrics by Hill, 1933), "Deep Purple" (lyrics by Mitchell Parish; originally an instrumental composed in 1933 and introduced by Paul Whiteman. Parish wrote the lyrics in 1939 after which "Deep Purple" enjoyed great popularity), "Lilacs in the Rain" (lyrics by Parish; this was a 2nd theme from the original *Deep Purple,* 1939), and *American Waltz* (which was composed as an instrumental in 1940; Parish wrote lyrics 5 years later, but it never equaled the success of "Deep Purple"). DeRose remained active until his death, which occurred in New York City, Apr. 23, 1953.

"THE DEVIL AND DANIEL WEBSTER" "Folk opera in one Act" by Douglas Moore (q.v.), based on the story by American poet Stephen Vincent Benét (1898–1943). The opera tells the story of a New Hampshire farmer, Jabez Stone, who has sold his soul to the Devil in return for material prosperity and success. On Stone's wedding day the devil arrives to claim payment. One of the wedding guests, the famous orator Daniel Webster, offers to defend Stone and to break the contract. However, the devil —"Mr. Scratch, a Boston lawyer"—fills the jury box with several scoundrels from the American past. Webster manages to appeal to their humanity and patriotism and defeats the devil. Produced by the American Lyric Theatre at the Martin Beck Theatre, *The Devil and Daniel Webster* opened on May 18, 1939, and had a successful run. Moore's lyricism made for attractive songs and stirring pronouncements about freedom and democracy. The opera was broadcast in 1953 and later was produced at Sturbridge, Mass., in July–August 1953.

DIAMOND, DAVID (b. 1915) Composer, teacher. Born in Rochester, N.Y., July 9, 1915, Diamond began on the violin at around the age of 8; he began systematic study of violin and harmony at the Cleveland Institute (family finances had forced the Diamonds to leave Rochester to live with relatives in Cleveland). In 1929 they returned to Rochester and Diamond enrolled in the School of Music, where he studied composition with Bernard Rogers and violin with Effie Knauss. Unhappy with the general conservatism at Rochester, Diamond left for New York, where he studied with Roger Sessions (1934–35). He had been awarded a modest scholarship and supplemented his small income by mopping floors and other menial labor. He also began to move easily among the artists, writers, and intellectuals in Greenwich Village. Working with E. E. Cummings, the poet, Diamond composed a ballet score, *Tom*, based on *Uncle Tom's Cabin*, in 1936. This led to Diamond's going to Europe to discuss the ballet with choreographer Leonide Massine—and meeting with other notables in Paris at the time: Milhaud, Roussel, Ravel and, of course, Gertrude Stein. Two years later Diamond returned to Paris on his first Guggenheim Fellowship and studied with Nadia Boulanger. The coming of World War II in 1939 forced Diamond to return to the United States. The recipient of many fellowships,

awards, and publications, Diamond often was forced to make his way as a performing musician—for example, for several years he was a violinist in the "Your Hit Parade" orchestra on radio; he also played in theatre pit bands. After the war Diamond settled in Florence, Italy (1953–65), and then returned to chair the composition department of the Manhattan School of Music; he has also taught at the Juilliard School of Music. His works include a *Psalm* for orchestra (1936), 3 violin concertos (1936, 1947, 1967), *Variations for Small Orchestra* (1937), *Elegy in Memory of Ravel* (1937), *Heroic Piece for Small Orchestra* (1938), *Cello Concerto* (1938), *Music for Double String Orchestra, Brass and Timpani* (1938), 8 symphonies (1940, 1942, 1945, 1945, 1951, 1959, 1960, 1964), *Concerto for Two Pianos* (1942), *Music for Shakespeare's "The Tempest"* (1944), *Rounds* for string orchestra (1944), *Piano Sonata* (1947), *Romeo and Juliet* (1947), *Piano Concerto* (1950), *Quintet* for 2 violas, 2 cellos, and clarinet (1950), *Mizmor L'David* for tenor, chorus, and orchestra (1951), *Sinfonia Concertante* (1954), *The World of Paul Klee* for orchestra (1957), *Choral Symphony* (1967), and *Music for Chamber Orchestra* (1969). Diamond's song output includes "Lift Not the Painted Veil," "Love Is More," and "David Mourns for Absalom."

DIETZ, HOWARD (b. 1896) Lyricist, writer, public relations director. Born in New York City, Sept. 8, 1896, Dietz prepared for a career in journalism at Columbia University, where he wrote for the college paper and contributed little pieces to newspapers of the period. He found work as a copywriter in an advertising agency after graduation. He served in the U. S. Navy during World War I. He eventually became associated with advertising and promotion in the motion picture business, which led to collaboration with popular songwriters. His first published song, "Alibi Baby," with music by Arthur Samuels, was interpolated into the score of the W. C. Fields hit, *Poppy* (1923). The next year Dietz collaborated with Jerome Kern (q.v.) on the songs of the unsuccessful *Dear Sir*. Dietz was co-librettist (with Morris "Morrie" Ryskind) on his next show, *Merry-Go-Round* (1927), which ran for a reasonable length of time. It was not until he received a collaboration request (which he initially turned down, for he *had* written with Kern and had a show that ran for more than 100 performances) from a stagestruck attorney, Arthur Schwartz (q.v.), that Dietz found his perfect collaborator. It was 1929 when Dietz began his partnership with Arthur Schwartz with their successful *The Little Show,* one of the brightest revues ever produced. From then until their last collaboration, *Jennie* (1963), the songwriting team of Schwartz and Dietz produced a great number of outstanding songs— music and lyrics. Some of the best remembered are "Something to Remember You By" from *Three's a Crowd* (1930), "New Sun in the Sky" and "Dancing in the Dark" from *The Band Wagon* (1931), "A Shine on Your Shoes" and "Alone Together" from *Flying Colors* (1932), "If There Is Someone Lovelier Than You" and "You and the Night and the Music" from *Revenge with Music* (1934), "Love Is a Dancing Thing" from *At Home Abroad* (1935), "By Myself" and "I See Your Face Before Me" from *Between the Devil* (1937), "Haunted Heart" from *Inside U.S.A.* (1948). "You're Not the Type" and "Magic Moment" from *The Gay Life* (1961), "I Still Look at You That Way" and "Where You Are" from *Jennie* (1963). Dietz also collaborated with Vernon Duke (q.v.) in 1944 on 2 not very successful Broadway shows, *Jack Pot* and *Sadie Thompson;* out of the last

came a very fine song, "The Love I Long For." Dietz also prepared English-language versions of *Die Fledermaus* (1950) and *La Bohème* for the Metropolitan Opera. During this productive period Dietz continued to hold down a job in the promotion of films for MGM, served as a director for ASCAP since 1959, and eventually became a vice-president in Loew's Inc. until his retirement. His autobiography, *Dancing in the Dark,* was published in 1974.

DORSEY, JIMMY (1904–1957) Clarinetist, alto-saxophonist, bandleader. Born in Shenandoah, Pa., Feb. 29, 1904, Dorsey studied with his father, a music teacher. Beginning on the cornet, Dorsey learned several instruments and was a proficient saxophonist (both tenor and alto) but switched to the clarinet. His first work was playing, when he was 8 or so, in his father's brass band. By his teens he was playing in professional bands, including those of Jean Goldkette and Paul Whiteman. Around 1928 Dorsey formed a recording band with his younger brother Tommy (q.v.). By 1934 the Dorsey Brothers Orchestra employed several important sidemen: Glenn Miller (who also did the arrangements), Charlie Spivak (trumpet), and Ray McKinley (drums). The band broke up the next year after a typical argument between the brothers; each then formed his own orchestra. The Jimmy Dorsey Orchestra became one of the most successful of the big band era, recorded prolifically, and enjoyed several hit records (among them "Green Eyes" with vocals by singers Bob Eberly and Helen O'Connell). Dorsey himself was featured on the band's instrumentals, such as *John Silver* and *Dusk in Upper Sandusky.* The band appeared in several movies in the forties. One, *The Fabulous Dorseys* (1947), reunited the Dorsey brothers after years of virtual estrangement. Despite the general dissolution of big bands after World War II, the Dorseys, individually, managed to keep going. When Tommy Dorsey tragically died in 1956, Jimmy Dorsey took over the band. This lasted for less than a year. Jimmy Dorsey died of cancer in New York City, June 12, 1957.

DORSEY, TOMMY (1905–1956) Trombonist, bandleader. Born in Shenandoah, Pa., Nov. 19, 1905, Dorsey, like his brother Jimmy (q.v.), learned music from their father, music teacher Thomas Dorsey, Sr. He was an excellent trumpeter (and, like his brother, considered a fine jazz soloist during the 1920s) but is best known as a trombonist. His professional career roughly paralleled his brother's—they were, in fact, often members of the same bands, including the Goldkette and Whiteman bands. Tommy Dorsey also played in the bands of Rudy Vallee, André Kostelanetz, Victor Young, and Nat Shilkret. The Dorsey Brothers Orchestra was formed in 1928 and lasted until 1935, when differences between the brothers led to a split. Jimmy Dorsey formed a new band around their band and Tommy Dorsey formed one around what once had been the Joe Haymes Band. During its long tenure the Tommy Dorsey Orchestra employed many fine musicians, among them Bud Freeman, Bunny Berigan, Max Kaminsky, Yank Lawson, Joe Bushkin, and others. Among his star vocalists were Dick Haymes, Frank Sinatra, Stuart Foster, Jo Stafford, and the Pied Pipers. The band recorded extensively. Among the most popular of their recordings were: "I'm Getting Sentimental Over You" (the band's theme song), "Marie," "Boogie Woogie," "I'll Never Smile Again," and "This Love of Mine." The band was active on radio and in films. After the war, and after the fading of the big bands, Jimmy Dorsey reunited with his brother and joined the Tommy Dorsey Orchestra in 1953. Tommy Dorsey's

troubled home life (in 1956 he was being divorced) often led him to depend upon sleeping pills. One night in his home in Greenwich, Conn., after a supposed heavy meal, he took several sleeping pills. During that night, Nov. 26, 1956, he became ill, threw up in his sleep and choked to death.

DUKE, VERNON (1903–1969) Composer, pianist. Born in Parfianovka, Russia, Oct. 10, 1903, Vladimir Dukelsky began attending the Kiev Conservatory at the age of 13; one of his teachers was Reinhold Glière. Dukelsky proved to be a precocious student and a great future in "serious" music seemed to be in the offing. But his family fled Russia in the wake of the Revolution in 1920. The next year Dukelsky himself arrived in the United States, hoping to break into the music business. He went to Paris in 1924, where he was more successful, especially in the field of ballet. His *Zéphyr et Flore* was presented by the great impresario Diaghilev in Paris in 1925. He returned to the United States in 1929 and began a dual career as a serious composer and a popular songwriter. The name Vernon Duke was suggested by his friend George Gershwin. For a long time he signed his serious works Dukelsky and his popular songs Duke; eventually he abandoned Dukelsky altogether. The popular Duke is the much better known. Through Gershwin, Duke met Gershwin's lyricist brother Ira and E. Y. Harburg, both of whom collaborated on the first song Duke wrote for a show, "I'm Only Human After All" for *Garrick Gaieties* (1930). He and Harburg did several songs for the revue *Walk a Little Faster* (1932), one of which was the outstanding "April in Paris" (q.v.). The 1934 production of the *Ziegfeld Follies* resulted in at least 3 fine Harburg-Duke songs: "I Like the Likes of You," "Suddenly," and "What Is There to Say?" Ira Gershwin then joined Duke in the *Fol-*

lies of the 1936–37 season and for it they produced a song that eventually became very popular, "I Can't Get Started." Other songs were "He Hasn't a Thing Except Me" and "Words Without Music." Duke's greatest Broadway success was *Cabin in the Sky* (1940) with an all-black cast headed by Ethel Waters. Duke joined with another lyricist, John Latouche, and produced such songs as "Taking a Chance on Love" (co-lyricist: Ted Fetter), "Love Turned the Light Out," the title song, and "Honey in the Honeycomb." This was to be Duke's last Broadway success, for after it he wrote songs for a series of flops. Unfortunately the failure of the shows often took some excellent songs down with them. Duke's losing streak began with the almost successful *Banjo Eyes* (1941), with lyrics by Latouche and Harold Adamson (one song, "We're Having a Baby," was interpolated in a 1944 movie); then came the very ill-fated *The Lady Comes Across* (lyrics by Latouche, 1942) from which came at least 2 excellent Duke melodies, "Summer Is A-Comin' In" and "Lady" (one of his most distinguished creations). In 1943 he joined Howard Dietz in *Dancing in the Streets* but the show never made it to Broadway. They tried again with *Jack Pot* and *Sadie Thompson* (both 1944). Both shows had short runs. Duke left Broadway for a time (he spent a year in France), then returned to do 2 shows with Ogden Nash as lyricist, *Two's Company* (with its outstanding "Roundabout") and *The Littlest Revue,* in 1952 and 1956, respectively. Duke also composed the incidental music and songs for the Helen Hayes stage production *Time Remembered* (1957). Among his concert works are a *Piano Concerto* (1924), 3 symphonies (1928, 1929, 1947), a *Violin Concerto* (1942), a *Cello Concerto* (1943), and *Ode to the Milky Way* (1945). There are also numerous songs, chamber works, solo

piano pieces, an opera (*Demoiselle Paysanne,* 1928), and several ballets, *Public Gardens* (1935), *Entr'acte* (1945), and *Souvenir de Monte Carlo* (1956). Duke was the author of an autobiography, *Passport to Paris* (1955), and *Listen Here! A Critical Essay on Music Depreciation* (1963). He died in Santa Monica, Calif., Jan. 16, 1969.

DUKELSKY, VLADIMIR See Vernon Duke.

EBONY CONCERTO A delightful work for clarinet and "jazz band" by Igor Stravinsky (q.v.). The idea originated with a music publisher, Aaron Goldmark, who talked with Stravinsky and jazz clarinetist Woody Herman. Both men agreed and Stravinsky familiarized himself with Herman's orchestra by listening to recordings, but Stravinsky, as usual, went his own way. The scoring is hardly that of a jazz band, calling as it does for a French horn and a harp. The story at the time was that Stravinsky had heard Herman play and was so taken with him and his band that he felt compelled to write a piece for him, thus eliminating the work of Mr. Goldmark. Stravinsky began working on the *Ebony Concerto* late in October or early November 1945 (certain problems had to be worked out: i.e., Herman's publicity announcement suggested that he and Stravinsky would "collaborate" on the composition). The first 2 movements were completed by Nov. 22 and the last movement was completed, in Hollywood, Calif., on Dec. 1, 1945. The first performance was given by Herman and his band at Carnegie Hall, New York City, Mar. 25, 1946; the conductor was Walter Hendl (Stravinsky had led the rehearsal at the Paramount Theatre, New York, before the premiere). Stravinsky conducted the nation-wide broadcast on Aug. 18 and recorded it the first time the next day in Hollywood. He later made a new recording with Benny Goodman as soloist. In 1960 the music was used as a ballet score by the New York City Ballet with choreography by John Taras.

"THE EMPEROR JONES" Opera, based on the Eugene O'Neill play, by Louis Gruenberg (q.v.). The libretto was by Kathleen de Jaffa and tells the story of a former Pullman porter, Brutus Jones, who had fled the United States after committing murder. He finds his way to an island in the West Indies and eventually sets himself up as the island's "emperor." His dictatorial reign comes to an end when the islanders revolt. Jones flees in the jungle in the night and, after firing his few bullets at shadows, is overtaken by his pursuers. He kills himself with his last—a silver—bullet. *The Emperor Jones* opened at the Metropolitan Opera House, New York City, Jan. 7, 1933, starring Lawrence Tibbett (1896–1960); the conductor was Tullio Serafin. Gruenberg's opera shared the bill with Leoncavallo's *Pagliacci.* Gruenberg, who had made a study of Negro folk music, composed a rich, apposite score. The opera's best-known aria, "Standin' in the Need of Prayer," was an actual folk song that Gruenberg worked into his score. *The Emperor Jones* was well received and was one of the first of the popular American operas. It had several performances at the Metropolitan as well as in Boston, Chicago, Los Angeles, and San Francisco. It was also performed in Amsterdam and, after World War II, in Milan, at La Scala.

ENGEL, LEHMAN (b. 1910) Conductor, composer, author. Born in Jackson, Miss., Sept. 14, 1910, Engel studied at the Cincinnati Conservatory and the Cincinnati College of Music before coming to New York to study with Rubin Goldmark (q.v.) on a scholarship at the Juilliard School. Engel also studied privately with Roger Sessions (q.v.). His schooling completed (in 1934), Engel became active in New York as composer and conductor, especially in the theatre. He founded and led the Madrigal Singers in the late 1930s and, with them, initiated a long recording career. He began in the theatre working with choreographer-dancer Martha Graham. In 1934 Engel was asked to write incidental music for a play, *Within the Gates,* the first of dozens of such scores. Engel was active in the Federal Theatre Project during the Depression. In 1937 he conducted the Kurt Weill musical *Johnny Johnson,* the first of literally hundreds of musicals Engel was to conduct over the years. He served in the U. S. Navy during World War II, conducting and writing scores for Navy films (*Fury in the Pacific, The Fleet That Came to Stay,* etc.). After the war Engel returned to what had become his primary occupation, conducting Broadway shows. He was also conductor of a series of show albums—in revivals chiefly of classic Broadway shows, such as *Pal Joey, Oh, Kay!, Anything Goes,* etc.—produced for Columbia Records by Goddard Lieberson (q.v.). Since 1959 Engel has been associated with the musical theatre workshops sponsored by Broadcast Music Inc. which provide an outlet for young songwriters. Among Engel's original compositions are *Jungle Dance* for orchestra (1930), 2 symphonies (1939, 1945), a *Concerto for Viola and Orchestra* (1945), *Overture for the End of the War* (1946), and *Dialogue* for violin and viola (1950). Other chamber works include a string quartet (1934), a piano sonata (1936), and a set of variations for piano, *The Gates of Paradise* (1940). There are several choral works, plus many (mostly early) compositions for dance, several of them written for Martha Graham: *Ceremonials* (1932), *Ekstasis* (1932), and *Imperial Gesture* (1934). Engel is author of an autobiography, *This Bright Day* (1956), *Planning and Producing the Musical Show*

(1957), *The American Musical Theatre* (1967), *Their Words Are Music* (1975), and others.

ETLER, ALVIN (1913–1973) Composer, oboist, teacher. Born in Battle Creek, Iowa, Feb. 19, 1913, studied at Western Reserve University, Cleveland, Ohio, with Arthur Shepherd (q.v.) and at Yale University, New Haven, Conn., with Paul Hindemith. He also studied the oboe with Philip Kirchner and Bert Gassman. After graduation he played the oboe in the Indianapolis Symphony (1938–40) and taught privately. He later taught at Yale, Cornell, the University of Illinois, Mt. Holyoke College, and Smith College. He was awarded Guggenheim Fellowships in 1940 and 1941. His works include a *Trio* for strings (1934), *Five Songs for Five People* (1935), *Six from Ohio,* suite for oboe, violin, viola, and cello (1936), *Music for Chamber Orchestra* (1938), *Five Speeds Forward* (1939), *Music for Brass* (1939), *Symphonietta I* (1940), *Symphonietta II* (1941), *Sonata* for oboe, clarinet, and viola (1944), *Quartet for Strings* (1945), *Sonata for Bassoon and Piano* (1951), *Sonata for Clarinet and Piano* (1952), *Sonatina* for piano (1955), *Concerto in One Movement* for orchestra (1957), *Concerto for Violin and Wind Quintet* (1958), *Elegy* for orchestra (1959), *Triptych* for orchestra (1961), *Brass Quintet* (1963), *String Quartet No. 1* (1963), *String Quartet No. 2* (1965), *Concerto for Brass Quintet, String Orchestra and Percussion* (1967), *Sonic Sequence* for brass quintet (1967), *Convivialities* for orchestra (1968), *Concerto for String Quartet and Orchestra* (1968), and *Clarinet Sonata No. 2* (1969). Etler died in Northampton, Mass., June 13, 1973.

"FACE THE MUSIC" A "musical comedy revue," one of the first to use the Depression as a satirical springboard, with a book by Moss Hart and songs by Irving Berlin (q.v.). The special targets were corrupt politicians, the wealthy, Do-Good crusaders, the Ziegfeld show, the Palace Theatre (for 5 cents one could see Albert Einstein, Ethel Barrymore, Tony the Talking Horse, and also: lunch). The slender plot—about a wealthy woman, whose husband is a corrupt policeman, who invests in a musical —provided the line along which the songs could be presented. Berlin composed several of his finest, most sophisticated songs for *Face the Music:* "Let's Have Another Cup of Coffee," "Soft Lights and Sweet Music," "On a Roof in Manhattan," and "I Say It's Spinach (and the Hell with It!)." The stars were Mary Boland, J. Harold Murray, and Andrew Tombes. *Face the Music* opened at the New Amsterdam Theatre, Feb. 17, 1932, and ran for 165 performances. A revival in 1933 ran for only 32.

"FANCY FREE" Ballet with music by Leonard Bernstein (q.v.) and choreography by Jerome Robbins. *Fancy Free* was produced by the Ballet Theatre, premiere: Apr. 18, 1944. The "plot" traced the adventures of 3 sailors on pass in wartime New York; they find 2 rather willing young ladies—not enough to go around, obviously. The 3 sailors take turns in a solo dance to win a girl. But near the end of the ballet they begin fighting and the girls run off. Friends again, the sailors continue their search. Bernstein's brash, jazzy music evoked the spirit of the young sailors and the feel of New York City at that time. The *Three Dances* ("Galop," "Waltz," "Danzon") are often performed as a unit in concert. Bernstein's first musical, *On the Town,* which opened later in the year, was based on Robbins' idea for *Fancy Free.*

FIEDLER, ARTHUR (1894–1979) Conductor, violist. Born in Boston, Mass., Dec. 17, 1894, Fiedler began to study music with his father, Emanuel, who was a violinist in the Boston Symphony. Fiedler completed his musical education in Berlin and returned to the United States to become a violist in the Boston Symphony. In 1929 he organized the outdoor Esplanade Concerts in Boston; this led to the formation of the Boston Pops Orchestra the next year, with Fiedler as conductor. Fiedler led the Pops for a half century, making it one of the most popular of all orchestras and an annual summer fixture in Boston. Fiedler specialized in presenting what was generally called "light" music, the "semiclassics" (as they were also termed) by Offenbach, Gilbert and Sullivan, Tchaikovsky, Gershwin, et al. The Pops was a well-disciplined orchestra and performed with sparkle and élan. Not only did it perform the light classics, it frequently, thanks to the Fiedler touch, ventured into out-and-out popular music—such as that of the Beatles (q.v.), Glenn Miller arrangements, Sousa marches, film scores, etc. Fiedler also arranged for commissions from such composers as Leroy Anderson (q.v.), Robert McBride (q.v.), and others, who were capable of treading the ground between the popular and the serious. Fiedler was also a showman (the annual 4th of July concert ended with an elaborate performance of the Tchaikovsky *1812 Overture*, complete with fireworks and a battery of real cannons). Fiedler and the Boston Pops were also hugely successful on radio, television, recordings (spanning in time the era from early shellac 78-rpms to long-playing discs), and worldwide tours. Fiedler was the force behind the success of the Pops, in its imaginative, nonsnob programming, even in fund-raising. Besides the Pops, Fiedler also conducted the Boston Sinfonietta, which specialized in offbeat "serious" chamber works, and the Cecelia Society (1926–49), but his major contribution was made through his long association with the Boston Pops. He died in Boston, July 10, 1979.

"FILLING STATION" Ballet, music by Virgil Thomson (q.v.) and choreography by Lew Christensen. Commissioned by Ballet Caravan, *Filling Station* was composed in 1937 and presented for the first time—with Christensen dancing the lead as filling station attendant—at Hartford, Conn., Jan. 6, 1938. The score consists of 12 quite brief sections—the longest, a *Tango* ("Rich Girl and Boy"), lasts about 4 minutes, the shortest, *Holdup,* about 40 seconds. *Filling Station* was one of the first American ballets to treat an American subject and was aimed, as Thomson has written, "to evoke roadside America as pop art." The music conjures up the popular song of the period, waltzes, a tango, even the Big Apple (the title of one of the sections). Thomson also prepared a *Filling Station Suite,* consisting of 7 sections and playing around 15 minutes (the complete ballet runs about 24).

FILM MUSICAL-II After the initial flurry following the release of *The Jazz Singer* and the films with music that followed, a decided slump was caused by the early Depression. Few worthwhile film musicals were made in 1930–32. Failure at the box office led to no interest on the part of management. And film makers had yet to evolve a style undominated by stage technique—one that exploited the possibilities of the camera. Intimations of a cinematic style for the film musical were visible in Ernst Lubitsch's direction of *The Love Parade* (1929), but most films of the period were little more than static revues (the "Star-studded" musicals that employed nearly everyone on the lot) or inept blending of story and artiness, as was attempted in David Butler's *Delicious* (1931), which wasted the lyrics of Ira Gershwin and the music of George Gershwin. Few musicals were made in 1932, a year that might be remembered for *The Big Broadcast,* which featured

Bing Crosby. Then, unexpectedly, a musical film renaissance began in 1933 with the release of 2 films, *42nd Street* and *Flying Down to Rio.* The first was another, but good, variation on the tried and true backstage musical—an easy way to explain where the songs are coming from. The 2nd introduced the wisecracking dancing team of Fred Astaire and Ginger Rogers (they were the second leads). Both musicals had exceptional songs; *42nd Street* was scored by Harry Warren (q.v.) and Al Dubin and *Flying Down to Rio* by Vincent Youmans (q.v.), Gus Kahn (q.v.), and Edward Eliscu.

Each musical had been made by different studios and set the style for their future productions. Warner Brothers had released *42nd Street* and RKO *Flying Down to Rio.* Warners would continue in the lavish pattern approach (eventually calling on the imagination of Busby Berkeley to conceive geometric human designs set to music, usually by Warren) and RKO exploited the instant success of Astaire and Rogers with less lavish, sophisticated comedies and scores by the finest composers to come to Hollywood: Jerome Kern, Irving Berlin, and the Gershwins. It might be noted, too, that Warners had a popular, though not as sparkling, team in Ruby Keeler and Dick Powell. At Paramount the best musicals were constructed around the star Bing Crosby, Fox had its Shirley Temple, Universal its Deanna Durbin, and MGM its box office team, Jeanette MacDonald and Nelson Eddy. They were provided with original screenplays and specially created songs, generally.

The classic (or profitable) Broadway musicals were regularly transcribed to the screen; one of the best was the 1936 version of Jerome Kern's *Showboat.* One of the finest original film musicals of the period was *The Wizard of Oz* (1939), with songs by Harold Arlen (q.v.) and

E. Y. Harburg (q.v.)—which made a star of 17-year-old Judy Garland (who had been in films since 1936). That same year saw the production of what appeared to be the final Astaire-Rogers musical, *The Story of Vernon and Irene Castle* (they were reunited a decade later in *The Barkleys of Broadway,* with songs by Harry Warren and Ira Gershwin). By 1939 the RKO and Warner Brothers domination had slipped and Metro-Goldwyn-Mayer was in the ascendance, thanks to the astuteness of producer-songwriter Arthur Freed (q.v.) and his musical right hand, Roger Edens (1905–1970). MGM's specialty was the Technicolor large-scaled film musical, many of which starred Judy Garland and Mickey Rooney. Astaire moved over to MGM also and continued with other dancing partners, among them Eleanor Powell, Jane Powell, Vera-Ellen, Cyd Charisse, and Judy Garland. Twentieth Century-Fox depended upon its blond stars Alice Faye and Betty Grable, with entertaining but not very memorable results. MGM led the field during the 1940s and '50s with such films as *For Me and My Gal* (1942), *Best Foot Forward* (1943), *Cabin in the Sky* (1943), *Meet Me in St. Louis* (1944), *The Harvey Girls* (1946), *Easter Parade* (1948), *Summer Holiday* (1948), *Annie Get Your Gun* (1950), and *Three Little Words* (1950). During this period other studios turned out some good musicals, although not with the regularity of the leading musical makers. In *Blues in the Night* (1941) Warner Brothers had a fine Harold Arlen–Johnny Mercer score, but not a very good movie; Paramount attempted to touch the same subject—jazz and jazz musicians—in *Birth of the Blues,* which starred their most reliable musical asset, Bing Crosby, and had a hodgepodge score. Twentieth Century-Fox released one of its formula pictures, only the blonde was an ice-skater who skated to music, Sonja Henie, in *Sun*

Valley Serenade. The film also featured the popular Glenn Miller orchestra and the songs of Harry Warren and Mack Gordon. In 1942 Paramount struck it rich with *Holiday Inn* with Crosby and songs by Berlin.

The coming of war inspired a number of service-centered pictures, *The Fleet's In, Johnny Doughboy, Private Buckaroo,* and, in a step backward, the old star-studded revue, *Ziegfeld Girl* (1941) and *Star-Spangled Rhythm* (1942). The best musical of that year was *Yankee Doodle Dandy,* a biographical musical based on the life of George M. Cohan, starring James Cagney; this too hit a sound patriotic note. The war provided a demand for the musical film. Escape and pure entertainment were dispensed in such efforts as *Stage Door Canteen* (1943), *Thank Your Lucky Stars* (1943), and the Irving Berlin Army show, *This Is the Army* (1943). Not all musicals reflected the fact of war and by 1945 the service cycle petered out. There were a small number of bloated musical biographies, with the composer generally the victim of Hollywoodization. *Rhapsody in Blue* (1945) purported to tell the story of George Gershwin but only succeeded in a fine presentation of his music. Jerome Kern got it in *Till the Clouds Roll By* (1946) and Cole Porter in *Night and Day* (1946). Al Jolson did much better, although biographically no better, in the popular *The Jolson Story,* which worked as entertainment where the composer biographies failed. No great musical upsurge followed the end of the war; the numbers of releases dwindled, as did the quality. Television had come along by the late '40s and Hollywood, an apprehensive eye on the dwindling European market, began to cut back (although feature films could be dubbed for foreign viewing, song lyrics suffered in translation—if they were sung in English the audience did not understand them). One of the great hit musicals at the end of the period was a sequel, *Jolson Sings Again* (1949), which featured the songs of the 1920s and '30s. The next decade would see fewer musical films, some that could even be regarded as classics, but economics (the loss of the European market), new technology (especially television), and a revolution in popular music styles, new musical personalities (who really could not replace the old) literally brought an end to what was called the "Hollywood musical."

"FINE AND DANDY" Musical comedy with music by Kay Swift (q.v.) and lyrics by Paul James (her husband, a banker-diplomat, James Paul Warburg). With a book by Donald Ogden Stewart, *Fine and Dandy* starred a zany comedian, Joe Cook (1890–1959), whose routines called for skill in juggling and acrobatics (alone, Cook did an imitation of a team of acrobats) as well as a talent for concocting wild, Rube Goldberg-like inventions. Although Cook was the star around which the show spun, *Fine and Dandy* is notable for its fine score, the first major musical composed by Swift. From it came the long-lasting "Fine and Dandy" as well as 2 other fine but rather neglected songs, "Can This Be Love?" and "Nobody Breaks My Heart." Not to be overlooked is the rueful "Let's Go Eat Worms in the Garden." *Fine and Dandy* opened at the Erlanger Theatre on Sept. 23, 1930, and enjoyed a run of 255 performances. Besides Cook the cast included Alice Boulden, Nell O'Day, and Eleanor Powell.

FINE, IRVING (1914–1962) Composer, teacher. Born in Boston, Mass., Dec. 3, 1914, Fine was a graduate of Harvard (1937), where he studied with Walter Piston (q.v.); he later studied with Nadia Boulanger, in both the United States, while she was visiting in 1939, and Paris, the next year. Other teachers included Edward Burlingame Hill (composition), Archibald Davison (choral conducting), and Serge Koussevitzky (conducting). Fine joined the faculty of Harvard University as assistant professor of music in 1939; he directed the Harvard Glee Club (1939–46). He also served on the faculty of the Berkshire Music Center, Tanglewood, Mass. In 1950 he joined the staff of Brandeis University, Waltham, Mass., where he was eventually appointed chairman of the School of Creative Arts. Fine did not compose a great deal, but his few works reveal a major creative talent. He first attracted attention with an early work, *The Choral New Yorker,* in which he set pieces selected from New York publications. His other works include: *Alice in Wonderland,* First Series (1942), Second Series (1949), *Music for Piano* (1947), *Partita* for wind quintet (1948), *Toccata Concertante* for orchestra (1948), *The Hour-Glass Suite* for chorus, text by Ben Jonson (1949), *String Quartet* (1950), *Notturno* for harp and strings (1951), *Mutability,* a cycle of 6 songs for contralto and piano (1952), *Serious Song: Lament for String Orchestra* (1955), *Fantasia* for string trio (1956), *Romanza* for wind quintet (1958), *McCord's Menagerie* for chorus (1959), and *Symphony* (1962). Fine died of a heart attack in Natick, Mass., Aug. 23, 1962.

FINE, VIVIAN (b. 1913) Composer, pianist, teacher. Born in Chicago, Ill., Sept. 28, 1913, Fine began the study of the piano in 1919 at the Chicago Musical College. Beginning in 1925, she studied composition at the American Conservatory, Chicago, where she was a student of Ruth Crawford (q.v.). Further study was done with Roger Sessions (q.v.) in composition and Abbey Whiteside (piano) in New York City in the late 1930s and early '40s. Fine began professionally in music as a pianist, spe-

cializing in contemporary music. She also taught privately and at New York University, the Juilliard School, and, among others, Bennington College, Bennington, Vt., since 1964. She has been active in the American Composers Alliance. She has also been the recipient of several prizes and foundation grants. Her works include *Solo for Oboe* (1929), *Four Pieces* for 2 flutes (1930), *Four Songs* for voice and strings (1933), *Prelude and Elegiac Song* for strings (1937), *Dance Suite* for orchestra (1938), *Sonatina* for oboe and piano (1939), *Concertino for Piano and Orchestra* (1944), *Capriccio* for oboe and string trio (1946), *The Great Wall of China* for voice, flute, cello, and piano (1947), *Divertimento* for cello and percussion (1951), *Sonata for Violin and Piano* (1952), *A Guide to the Life Expectancy of a Rose* for soprano, tenor, and chamber group (1956), *String Quartet* (1957), *Valedictions* for soprano, tenor, chorus, and chamber orchestra (1958), *Alcestis,* ballet (1960), *Fantasy* for cello and piano (1962), *Morning* for narrator, chorus, and organ (1962), *The Song of Persephone* for viola (1964), *Dreamscope* for piano, flute trio, cello, and percussion (1964), *Concertino* for piano and percussion (1965), *Chamber Concerto* for cello and sextet (1966), *Quintet* (1967), *Paean* for narrator, chorus, and brass (1969), and *Meeting for Equal Rights: 1866* (1976).

"FINIAN'S RAINBOW" A musical fantasy involving a leprechaun and a purloined pot of gold, with music by Burton Lane (q.v.) and lyrics by E. Y. Harburg (q.v.). Harburg also collaborated on the fanciful book with Fred Saidy (b. 1907). The musical's story concentrates on a wily Irishman, Finian, who has stolen the crock of gold from a leprechaun, Og. Finian believes if he buries the pot in U.S. soil (as at Fort

Knox), he will become rich. With him is his daughter, Sharon, who provides the love interest for union organizer, Woody. The setting is the American South in the state of "Missitucky." *Finian's Rainbow,* while entertaining, also provided Harburg and Saidy with a sounding board for their enlightened views on wealth, bigotry, and race. This was an unusual statement to make in what was supposed to be simple entertainment in 1947. One Southern senator is turned black (he is standing over the magic crock and someone wishes he would turn black so that he can experience a little bigotry himself). He learns his lesson, Woody and Sharon are joined, Og, falling in love with a mortal, turns mortal—and Finian moves on in pursuit of his rainbow. Among the Lane-Harburg songs were "How Are Things in Glocca Morra?" "Old Devil Moon," "The Begat," "When the Idle Poor Become the Idle Rich," "Something Sort of Grandish," and "When I'm Not Near the Girl I Love," to name but a few from a very rich score. *Finian's Rainbow* opened at the 46th Street Theatre, Jan. 10, 1947, and ran for 725 performances. It has been revived regularly and was made into a not very exceptional film in 1968. The original Finian was portrayed by Albert Sharpe, Sharon by Ella Logan, Og by David Wayne, and Woody by Donald Richards.

FINNEY, ROSS LEE (b. 1906) Composer, teacher. Born in Wells, Minn., Dec. 23, 1906, Finney learned to play the piano and cello as a child and began to study composition with Donald Ferguson at the University of Minnesota; his other teachers include Nadia Boulanger (q.v.), Edward Burlingame Hill (q.v.) at Harvard, Roger Sessions (q.v.) over an extended period of time, Alban Berg (in Vienna, 1931–32), and Francesco Malipiero in Venice. Finney received several aids in his career, among them 2 Guggenheim Fellowships and a Pulitzer Traveling Fellowship. He also combined his work with a long teaching career, beginning at Smith College, Northampton, Mass., in 1929; he taught also at the Hartt School of Music, Hartford, Conn., at Amherst, Amherst, Mass., and, in 1948, was appointed composer-in-residence at the University of Michigan, Ann Arbor, where he remained until his retirement in 1976. During World War II, Finney served with the OSS (Office of Strategic Services) for a year, earning a Certificate of Merit and a Purple Heart. During his tenure at the University of Michigan, Finney set up an electronics music laboratory. Much of his original work employs the 12-tone technique. His compositions include *Trio* for piano, violin, and cello (1931), *Piano Sonata No. 1* (1932), *Piano Sonata in D minor* (1932), *Sonata* for violin and piano (1934), *String Quartet in F Minor* (1934), *Concerto for Piano and Orchestra* (1934), *Eight Poems by Archibald MacLeish* (1937), *String Quartet in D Minor* (1937), *Overture for a Drama* for orchestra (1937), *Symphony for Strings* (1937), *Sonata for Viola and Piano* (1937), *Trio in D minor* for piano, violin, and cello (1938), *Barber Shop Ballad* for small orchestra (1939), *Slow Piece* for strings (1940), *String Quartet in G minor* (1940), *Sonata for Cello and Piano* (1941), *Piano Sonata No. 3* (1942), *Symphony No. 1,* "Communiqué" (1943), *Concerto for Violin and Orchestra* (1944), *Piano Sonata No. 4* (1945), *Pilgrim Psalms* (1945), *Poor Richard* (1946), *Spherical Madrigals* for chorus (1947), *Music to Be Danced* (1947), *Solemn Music* (1948), *Piano Quartet* (1948), *String Quartet No. 6* (1950), *Immortal Autumn* (1952), *Variations for Piano* (1952), *Quintet* for piano and strings (1953),

Violin Sonata No. 3 (1955), *Symphony No. 2* (1960), *Still Are New Worlds* for narrator, chorus, and orchestra (1962), *Symphony No. 3* (1964), *Percussion Concerto* (1965), *Nun's Priest's Tale* for narrator, soloists, folk singer, chorus, electric guitar, and chamber orchestra (1965), *Symphony Concertante* (1967), *Piano Concerto No. 2* (1968), *Symphony No. 4* (1970), *Violin Concerto No. 2* (1976), a *Concerto for Strings* (1977), and *Concerto for Strings* (1978). Finney is also the author of *The Game of Harmony* (1947).

FITZGERALD, ELLA (b. 1918) Vocalist. Born in Newport News, Va., Apr. 25, 1918, Fitzgerald was orphaned while still very young and went north, to New York City, to live with an aunt. She began singing in Harlem clubs in the early 1930s. She came to wider attention when, as a teenager, she won a Harlem Amateur singing contest. In 1934, at the age of 16, she joined the Chick Webb Band. Her smooth, clear, jazz-inflected style led to a popularity that was greatly generated after she recorded with the Webb band her version of the nursery song "A-Tisket, A-Tasket" in 1938. Upon the death of Webb in June 1939, she took over until ca. 1942, when she struck out as a soloist. A favorite of jazz musicians, she appeared with or recorded with Teddy Wilson, Benny Goodman, Ellis Larkins, Louis Armstrong, and others. She toured extensively with the Jazz at the Philharmonic concerts through the United States and Europe in the late 1940s and '50s. She appeared in several films, and on television, but was more successful in clubs and on the concert stage. In the '50s she began recording a series of *Song Books* devoted to the work of great American songwriters Arlen, Berlin, Gershwin, Porter, Rodgers and Hart. Despite serious eye problems, Fitzgerald continued singing in clubs and concerts in the '70s, proving herself as a remarkable interpreter of popular ballads as well as a singer of jazz, often using her voice as another instrument in the band.

"FLYING DOWN TO RIO" The first of the Fred Astaire–Ginger Rogers film musicals released by RKO in 1933. The excellent songs were by Gus Kahn (q.v.), Edward Eliscu, and Vincent Youmans (q.v.). These were "The Carioca," "Music Makes Me," "Orchids in the Moonlight," and the title song. The stars of the film were Dolores Del Rio and Gene Raymond, but the wise-cracking song-and-dance team of Astaire and Rogers stole the movie and RKO immediately began exploiting their popularity in a series of musical films that achieved high standards of brisk comedy, stylish dance routines, and songs by such composers as Berlin, Kern, Gershwin, and Porter, among others.

"42ND STREET" Musical film released by Warner Brothers in 1933. The songs were by Harry Warren and Al Dubin: "Shuffle Off to Buffalo," "Young and Healthy," "You're Getting to Be a Habit with Me," and the title song. The film *42nd Street* remains one of the best of the backstage formula musicals. It starred Warner Baxter, who was excellent in the role of the harried producer of a Broadway show in its pre-opening throes. This is the classic tale in which the understudy (Ruby Keeler, making her film debut) goes on for the star (Bebe Daniels), who has suffered a leg injury. Needless to say, the understudy is an immediate smash success after her big number dancing atop a taxicab to the strains of "42nd Street." Contributing greatly to the film's success were the direction of Lloyd Bacon and the camera choreography of Busby Berkeley. Ginger Rogers appeared in an amusing small role as a chorus girl; she had not yet been seen in *Flying Down to Rio* (q.v.).

FOSS, LUKAS (b. 1922) Composer, conductor, pianist, teacher. Born in Berlin, Germany, Aug. 15, 1922, Foss studied there, and in Paris, following his family's move to France in 1935. He also studied in the United States, to which the Fosses came in 1937. Foss, when he was about 18, enrolled at the Curtis Institute, Philadelphia, Pa., where he studied composition with Rosario Scalero, piano with Isabelle Vengerova, and conducting with Fritz Reiner. He later studied with Serge Koussevitzky (conducting) at the Berkshire Music Center, Mass., and with Paul Hindemith (composition) at Yale, New Haven, Conn. Although he had been composing from an early age, Foss was known initially as a brilliant pianist, and from 1944 to 1950 was the pianist for the Boston Symphony. His early works were composed for piano, among them the *Four Two-Part Inventions* (1937) and *Set of Three Pieces for Two Pianos* (1940). His early *Suite to The Tempest of Shakespeare* (1940) brought him attention and a Pulitzer scholarship; in 1945 he was the youngest composer awarded a Guggenheim Fellowship. Foss's compositions include the choral work *The Prairie* to a text by Carl Sandburg (1942), *Piano Concerto No. 1* (1943), *Symphony in G* (1944), the ballet *Gift of the Magi* (1945), *Ode* for orchestra (1945), *Song of Anguish* for baritone and orchestra (1945), *The Song of Songs,* cantata for soprano and orchestra (1946), *String Quartet* (1947), *Oboe Concerto* (1948), *The Jumping Frog of Calaveras County,* chamber opera after Mark Twain (1949), *Piano Concerto No. 2* (1951), a cantata, *A Parable of Death* (1952), an opera, *Griffelkin* (1955), *Psalms* for chorus and orchestra (1956), *Symphony of Chorales* (1958), *Time Cycle* for soprano and orchestra or "improvisation ensemble" (1959; about this time Foss's

work took on an experimental bent), *Echoi* for piano, clarinet, cello, and percussion (1963), *Elytres* for flute, strings, harp, piano, and percussion (1964), *Fragments of Archilochos* for speakers, chorus, countertenor, mandolin, guitar, and percussion (1965), *Cello Concert* (1966), *Phorion,* based on Bach Partita for solo violin in E major, for orchestra (1967), *Baroque Variations,* borrowing from Handel, Scarlatti, and Bach (i.e., Phorion) for orchestra (1967), *Geod* for "a musical action" for orchestra (1969), *Paradigm* for guitar, 3 other instruments, and percussion (1970), *Quintet for Winds* (1972), *Orpheus* for cello or violin or viola and orchestra (1972), *Divertissement* for string quartet (1972), *Ni Bruit Ni Vitesse* for 2 pianos, with 2 percussionists performing on the strings of the piano (1973), *Lamdeni Suite* for orchestra (1973), *Concerto for Percussion and Orchestra* (1974), *Folksong for Orchestra* (1975), *String Quartet No. 3* (1975), *Solomon Rossi Suite* for orchestra (1975), *Curriculum Vitae* for accordion and orchestra (1977), *Brass Quintet* (1978), *And the Rocks Began to Shoot* for chorus (1979), *Music for Six* (1979), *Thirteen Ways of Looking at a Blackbird* (1979), and *Quintets for Orchestra* (1979). Foss has also been a conductor with various orchestras; he was conductor of the Buffalo Philharmonic (1963–70), the Brooklyn Philharmonic (beginning in 1971), and the Jerusalem Symphony (since 1972).

"FOUR SAINTS IN THREE ACTS" Opera with music by Virgil Thomson (q.v.) and text by Gertrude Stein (1874–1946). Sometime early in 1927 Stein and Thomson decided to collaborate on an opera; Thomson wished to compose a work on the lives of saints, to which Stein concurred but added that they should be Spanish saints—and Thomson agreed. In June 1927 Stein completed the libretto; Thomson finished the score in July 1928. The libretto, to say the least, was quite unusual; without Thomson's deceptively simple music, the words make no sense (one famous line is: "Pigeons on the grass, alas."). The cast calls for 2 singers in the role of St. Teresa, "St. Teresa I" and "St. Teresa II." In fact, counting the Teresas, there are actually 7 saints—and there are 4 acts. *Four Saints* is a remarkable study in abstraction and yet a satisfying experience. Thomson's music is direct, beautifully fashioned with characteristic use of hymn-like tunes, dances (there is a delightful tango), all discreetly orchestrated. There is little real action, although there is some movement (choreography by Frederick Ashton and director John Houseman). The cast formed into groups against a setting of cellophane. Considering its unorthodoxies, *Four Saints* was produced within a reasonable time after completion. This was accomplished by the Friends and Enemies of Modern Music and took place at the Avery Memorial Theatre, Hartford, Conn., Feb. 7, 1934. (It later played New York City and Chicago.) Yet another unusual feature was the all-black cast; the leading roles of "St. Teresa I" and "St. Ignatius" were sung by Beatrice Robinson-Wayne and Edward Matthews (who later sang "Jake" in Gershwin's *Porgy and Bess,* q.v.). Although *Four Saints in Three Acts* confused a great number of people, especially the lovers of conventional opera, it was successful and ran a total of 60 performances in one year in its various cities. The opera was revived in New York City in 1952 with some success, but a production in Paris later in the year was not well received. It remains one of Thomson's most charmingly characteristic works.

FREED, ARTHUR (1894–1973) Lyricist, film producer. Born in Charleston, S.C., Sept. 9, 1894, Freed grew up in Seattle, Wash., and was schooled at the Phillips Exeter Academy, Exeter, N.H. His father, Max Freed, was an art dealer. Although members of the family were musical, Freed expressed himself in words (as a student he wrote poetry). He began his professional career in vaudeville with Gus Edwards (q.v.). He later formed a team with composer-performer Louis Silvers (1889–1954). During World War I, Freed served in the U. S. Army, reaching the rank of sergeant. After the war he teamed up again with Silvers to write sketches for vaudeville and as early as 1921 had begun writing songs in Los Angeles, to which he had moved and where he had become the manager of the Orange Grove Theatre. The song "When Buddha Smiles," with lyrics by Nacio Herb Brown (q.v.), was quite successful. Even more successful was "I Cried for You" (1923), with music by Gus Arnheim and Abe Lyman. It was during the film musical flurry following the birth of the Hollywood musical that Freed gave up theatre management and began concentrating on writing lyrics; he and Brown wrote the songs for the historic *The Broadway Melody* (1929). Besides the popular title song, the score also contained "You Were Meant for Me." That same year Freed and Brown wrote "Singin' in the Rain" for *Hollywood Revue.* Among their best-remembered songs are "Temptation" (1934, from *Going Hollywood*), "All I Do Is Dream of You" (1934, from *Sadie McKee*), "Alone" (1935, from *A Night at the Opera*), "You Are My Lucky Star" and "Broadway Rhythm" (1936, from *Broadway Melody of 1936*) and "Good Morning" (1939, from *Babes in Arms*). Freed collaborated with other songwriters also (he, in fact, also composed melodies). He wrote the popular "Fit as a Fiddle" with Al Hoffman and Al Goodhart and "This Heart of Mine" with Harry Warren (q.v.). It was as a producer that Freed made his greater mark, specializing in big musicals. He began as an associate producer for *The Wizard of Oz*. Among his most impressive productions were *Cabin in the Sky* (1943), *Best Foot Forward* (1943), *Meet Me in St. Louis* (1944), *Ziegfeld Follies* (1946), *Good News* (1947), *The Pirate* (1948), *The Barkleys of Broadway* (1948), *Annie Get Your Gun* (1950), *An American in Paris* (1951), *Singin' in the Rain* (1952), *The Band Wagon* (1953), *Brigadoon* (1954), and *Gigi* (1958). Freed had a genius for bringing together the right songwriters, writers, cast, directors, et al., and the prestige to shield them from the customary depredations from the Front Office, the businessmen-accountants who ran the studios but knew little about how a musical film was put together. Freed's most valuable aide was composer-arranger-pianist Roger Edens (1905–1970). Freed died in Los Angeles, Apr. 12, 1973.

FULEIHAN, ANIS (1900–1970) Composer, pianist, teacher. Born in Kyrenia, Cyprus, Apr. 2, 1900, Fuleihan came to the United States in 1915. He studied piano with Alberto Jonas. After some study of theory and composition with Harold V. Milligan (1888–1951), Fuleihan began a career as concert pianist in 1919. He settled in Cairo in 1925, to spend 3 years making a study of Mediterranean music. Upon returning to New York City he concentrated on composition, teaching the piano privately, and lecturing. Fuleihan also taught at Indiana University and lectured at the University of Illinois. Under the sponsorship of the U. S. State Department he founded and conducted the Orchestra Classique in Tunis. From 1953 to 1960 he was director of the Beirut Conservatory, Lebanon. His works include *Unsophisticated Preludes for String Quartet* (1921), *To the Young Prince* for voice and piano (1925), *Mediterranean* for or-

chestra (1930), *Preface to a Child's Story Book* for orchestra (1931), *Music for Puppets* for flute, oboe, clarinet, and bassoon (1931), *Symphony No. 1* (1936), *Concerto No. 1 for Piano and Orchestra* (1937), *Concerto No. 2 for Piano and Orchestra* (1937), *Fantasy* for viola and orchestra (1938), *Fiesta* for orchestra (1940), *Symphonie Concertante* for string quartet and orchestra (1940), *Concerto for Two Pianos and Orchestra* (1940), *Invocation* for orchestra (1941), *Epithalamium*, variations for piano and strings (1941), *Six Etudes* for orchestra (1942), *Suite* for cello and piano (1942), *Three Cyprus Serenades* for orchestra (1943), *Cypriana*, 5 pieces for piano (1943), *Comedy Overture* for orchestra (1944), *Concerto for Violin and Orchestra* (1944), *Toccata for Two Pianos* (1944), *Concerto for Theremin and Orchestra* (1944), *Sonorities* for piano (1945), *Rhapsody* for cello and strings (1945), *Overture for Five Winds* (1947), *The Pyramids of Giza* for orchestra (1952), *Toccata* for piano and orchestra (1959), *Islands* for orchestra (1961), *Concerto No. 3 for Piano and Orchestra* (1963), *Cello Concerto* (1963), *Violin Concerto No. 2* (1965), *Symphony No. 2* (1967), *Piano Trio* (1968), also 11 piano sonatas, 5 string quartets, and the opera *Vasco* (1960). Fuleihan died in Stanford, Calif., Oct. 11, 1970.

GARLAND, JUDY (1922–1969) Singer, actress. Born in Grand Rapids, Minn., June 10, 1922, Frances Gumm grew up to be Judy Garland. Her parents were in vaudeville and, while very young, Frances was one of the singing Gumm Sisters. Their professionalism eventually got them into the larger vaudeville circuits. While playing in Chicago the Gumms met another vaudeville performer, George Jessel, who suggested that Frances Gumm change her name to Judy Garland. The family and the

Gumm Sisters eventually separated (the former by divorce and the latter by marriages) and Judy Garland and her mother settled in California when she was about 13. Judy Garland was stage-mothered into screen tests and, thanks to a mature singing voice locked in a young girl's body, was given small parts in early film musicals and in musical shorts. Her first full-scale film was *Pigskin Parade* (1936); she first attracted wide attention with her performance of "You Made Me Love You" in *Broadway Melody of 1938,* in which she affectingly sang to a photograph of star Clark Gable (the song, arranged by Roger Edens, with additional spoken words, is also known as "Dear Mr. Gable"). Garland became an immediate star, after a number of intermediate films, with the release of *The Wizard of Oz* in 1939. She was cast after MGM failed to get the better known Shirley Temple. She appeared in several of MGM's most costly musical films, notably *For Me and My Gal,* which introduced Gene Kelly to films (1942), *Girl Crazy* (1943), *Meet Me in St. Louis* (1944), *The Harvey Girls* (1946), *The Pirate* (1948), *Easter Parade* (1948), *A Star Is Born* (not an MGM film, 1954). Her voice was heard in the cartoon musical *Gay Purr-ee* (1962). In 1945 Garland appeared in a nonsinging role in *The Clock;* her final film, *I Could Go On Singing* (1963), was also a drama. Her personal life, broken marriages, and drinking led to an end to Garland's film career. Often ill, she missed shooting sessions or was forced to withdraw from a film; her role in *Annie Get Your Gun* was taken over by Betty Hutton, and Ginger Rogers replaced her in *The Barkleys of Broadway.* She made numerous recordings, sang on early radio, and made many television appearances. Most of her later career was devoted to concert appearances in the great remaining vaudeville houses: the Palace

in New York, the Palladium in London. She was associated with 2 songs with music by Harold Arlen: "Over the Rainbow" (lyrics by E. Y. Harburg) and "The Man That Got Away" (lyrics by Ira Gershwin). Garland died of a drug overdose in London, Jan. 22, 1969.

GERSCHEFSKI, EDWIN (b. 1909) Composer, pianist, teacher. Born in Meriden, Conn., June 10, 1909, Gerschefski studied piano at Yale and at the Matthay Pianoforte School, London (1931–32). In 1935 he studied with Artur Schnabel in Italy. He studied composition under Richard Frank Donovan and Joseph Schillinger. He taught in several schools in and around New York; he was also on the faculty of Converse College, S.C., taught at the University of New Mexico, Albuquerque, and since 1960 has taught at the University of Georgia. His works include *Classic Symphony* (1931), *Concertino for Piano and Orchestra* (1932), *Piano Sonatina* (1933), *Piano Quintet* (1935), *Streamline* for symphonic band (1936), *Symphony for Band* (1937), *Movements in Three Speeds* for trumpets, trombones, horns, and tuba (1938), *American Tarantella* for piano (1939), *Little Symphony for Violins and Violas* (1941), *Introduction, Fugato and Finale* for chamber orchestra (1942), *Guadalcanal Fantasy* (1943), *March for Orchestra* (1945), *Half Moon Mountain* for baritone, women's chorus, and orchestra (1948), *The Lord's Controversy with His People* for baritone, women's chorus, and chamber orchestra (1949), *100 Variations for Solo Violin* (1952), *Toccata and Fugue* for orchestra (1954), *Piano Trio* (1956), *Rhapsody* for violin, cello, and piano (1963), *Celebration* for violin and orchestra (1964), *Psalm 100* for chorus (1965), *Twelve Etudes* for piano (1966), *Workout* for 2 violins and 2 violas (1970), and *Suite* for solo horn (1976).

GIANNINI, VITTORIO (1903–1966) Composer, teacher. Born in Philadelphia, Pa., Oct. 19, 1903, Giannini began the study of the violin with his mother. His father was the tenor Ferruccio Giannini (1869–1948). At the age of 10 Giannini went to Italy to study at the Royal Conservatory of Milan. He returned to the United States and studied for 5 years (1925–30) at the Juilliard School of Music with Rubin Goldmark (q.v.) and with Hans Letz (violin). In 1932 he went to Rome on a Prix de Rome for further study for 4 years. On his return he joined the faculty of the Juilliard School of Music, New York City, where he taught composition and orchestration. He also taught at the Curtis Institute, Philadelphia. Giannini composed in just about every genre. He was respected for his vocal writing, especially his operas. Among these were *Lucedia* (1932), *The Scarlet Letter,* in which his sister, the soprano Dusolina Giannini, sang the role of "Hester" (1935), *Flora* (1937), *Beauty and the Beast,* composed for radio presentation (1938), *The Taming of the Shrew* (1953), and others. His instrumental works include the *Prelude and Fugue* for string orchestra (1926), *Sonata for Violin and Piano* (1926), *Madrigal for Voice and String Quartet* (1929), *Suite in Four Movements* for orchestra (1931), *Springtime* for soprano, tenor, chorus, and orchestra (1933), *Concerto for Piano and Orchestra* (1935), *Requiem* for soloists, chorus, and orchestra (1936), *Concerto for Organ and Orchestra* (1937), *Prelude Chorale and Fugue* for orchestra (1939), *Concerto for Two Pianos and Orchestra* (1940), *Violin Concerto* (1944), *Concerto for Trumpet and Orchestra* (1945), *Concerto Grosso* for strings (1946), *Frescobaldinia* for orchestra (1948), *Canticle of Christmas* for baritone, chorus, and orchestra (1951), *Divertimento* (1953), *Prelude and Fugue* for strings (1955), *Canticle of the Martyrs* for chorus and orchestra (1957), *Symphony No. 4* (1960), *Psalm 130,* concerto for double bass and orchestra (1963), and *The Servant of Two Masters,* an opera presented after the composer's death. Giannini died in New York City, Nov. 28, 1966.

GIDEON, MIRIAM (b. 1906) Composer, teacher. Born in Greeley, Colo., Oct. 23, 1906, Gideon studied at Boston University, graduating when she was 20. (Twenty years later she attended Columbia University to study musicology.) She studied piano with Hans Barth and Felix Fox; her composition teachers included Lazare Saminsky and Roger Sessions. She has been on the music faculties of Brooklyn College and the City College of New York. She has also taught at the Jewish Theological Seminary, New York, and at the Manhattan School of Music since 1967. Her works include *Epigrams* for chamber orchestra (1941), *Lyric Piece* for strings, or string quartet (1942), *Four Madrigals* for mixed chorus a cappella (1943), *Sonata for Flute and Piano* (1943), *Hound of Heaven* for baritone, oboe, and string trio (1945), *Dances for Two Pianos* (1945), *String Quartet* (1946), *Sonata* for viola and piano (1948), *Fantasy on a Javanese Motive* for cello and piano (1948), *Sonnets from Shakespeare* for voice, trumpet, and string quartet (1950), *Symphonia Brevis* (1950), the opera *Fortunato* (1956), *The Adorable Mouse* for narrator and chamber orchestra (1960), *Sonata for Cello and Piano* (1961), *The Condemned Playground* for soprano, tenor, flute, bassoon, and string quartet (1963), *Questions on Nature* for voice, oboe, piano, tam-tam, and glockenspiel (1964), the cantata *The Habitable Earth* for soloists, chorus, oboe, and piano (1965), *Rhymes from the Hill* for voice, clarinet, cello, and marimba (1968), *The Seasons of Time* for voice, flute, cello, celeste, and piano (1970), Sabbath Morning Service for soloists, chorus, and organ (1971), *Sonata for Clarinet and Piano* (1973), *Nocturnes* for voice, flute, oboe, violin, cello, and vibraphone (1976), and many solo piano pieces and songs.

GILLESPIE, JOHN "DIZZY" (b. 1917) Trumpeter, arranger, composer. Born in Cheraw, S.C., Oct. 21, 1917, Gillespie learned to play several instruments when he was a youngster from his father, an amateur musician. He began on the trombone and later switched to trumpet. He studied harmony and theory at the Laurinburg Institute, N.C. Gillespie moved to Philadelphia in 1935, where he played in the Frank Fairfax Orchestra; he joined the band of Teddy Hill in 1937 in New York City and toured Europe. On returning Gillespie freelanced in New York, began writing arrangements, and spent 2 years in the Cab Calloway Orchestra (1939–41), when he began evolving an innovative style of trumpet performance that would come to be called "bebop" (q.v.). In 1943 he joined the band of Earl Hines, along with saxophonist Charlie "Yardbird" Parker (1920–1955); these 2 joined in the promulgation of the modern school of jazz. Gillespie worked in several bands—Charlie Barnet, Billy Eckstine, Duke Ellington, others—and eventually formed his own group ca. 1945. He formed a big band in the late 1940s and toured with it and was very popular in the United States and Europe; in 1956 the U. S. State Department sponsored 2 foreign tours. By this time the interest in bop had worn off and Gillespie turned to show business with comedy routines; he also sang a vocal now and then. His critics accused him of commercialization and detected less originality in his playing. Gillespie developed a trumpet whose bell inclined 45 degrees upward from the rest of the instrument;

whether this improved the sound or was yet another touch of showmanship is debatable. Gillespie composed or collaborated on some of the famous early bop instrumentals: *A Night in Tunisia, Swing Low Sweet Cadillac,* and *Anthropology.*

GILLIS, DON (1912–1978) Composer, teacher. Born in Cameron, Mo., June 17, 1912, Gillis was a trumpeter and trombonist in his high school band. Later he studied composition at Texas Christian University and North Texas State University, graduating in 1943. Gillis later was band director and taught theory at Texas Christian; he was also associated with an NBC affiliate radio station in Fort Worth, Tex., where he performed and wrote arrangements. In 1944 he joined the staff of NBC in New York as a music production director and was responsible for, among other broadcasts, the Toscanini NBC Symphony programs. After leaving NBC, Gillis was appointed vice-president of the Interlochen Music Camp, Mich., and later was chairman of the Arts Division, Dallas Baptist College, and composer-in-residence at the University of South Carolina, Columbia. Gillis' compositions are very accessible, witty, and skillfully orchestrated. He liked to work within a narrative framework and composed several tone poems, such as his symphonic poem *The Raven* (1937), *The Alamo* (1947), and *Tulsa* (1950). Most of his 10 symphonies have descriptive subtitles; there is also a *Symphony No. 5½* (1947), subtitled "Symphony for Fun," which was given its radio premiere under Toscanini. Among his other works are *Willy the Woolyworm* for narrator and orchestra (1937), *Thoughts Provoked on Becoming a Prospective Papa* (1939), *Prairie Poem* (1941), *Intermission—Ten Minutes* (1942), *Cowtown* for orchestra (1943), *The Man Who Invented Music* for narrator and orchestra (1949), *Rhapsody* for harp and orchestra (1952), *Piano Concerto No. 2* (1967), *Toscanini: Portrait of a Century* (1967), *Rhapsody* for trumpet and orchestra (1969), and *The Secret History of the Birth of the Nation* for narrator, chorus, and orchestra (1976). There are also several one-act operas written for children, cantatas, and chamber works. Gillis died in Columbia, S.C., Jan. 10, 1978.

GLANVILLE-HICKS, PEGGY (b. 1912) Composer, author. Born in Melbourne, Australia, Dec. 29, 1912, Glanville-Hicks began to study music at the Melbourne Conservatory and continued at the Royal College of Music, London, where she studied with Ralph Vaughan Williams (composition), Arthur Benjamin (piano), and Malcolm Sargent (conducting). She also studied with Nadia Boulanger in Paris and Egon Wellesz in Vienna. By the time she came to the United States, in 1939, her musical personality was already formed and she can hardly be claimed as an "American" composer, although during her 20-year residence (she moved to Athens, Greece, in 1959), she was an important figure on the American musical scene as a director of the Composers Forums (1948–59) at Columbia University and as a music critic for the New York *Herald Tribune*. Her own work was influenced by her interest in the music of India, North Africa, and Greece; she has written several operas and ballets. Among her works are the *Three Gymnopedies* for orchestra (1953), *Letters from Morocco,* settings for voice and orchestra of passages from letters to her by Paul Bowles (1953), *Etruscan Concerto* for piano and chamber orchestra (1956), and *Concerto romantico* for viola and orchestra (1957). Her opera, *Nausicaa,* with a libretto by Robert Graves, was premiered in Athens in 1961.

GOEB, ROGER (b. 1914) Composer, teacher. Born in Cherokee, Iowa, Oct. 9, 1914, Goeb, although he played several instruments as a youngster, was awarded a degree in agriculture by the University of Wisconsin. In the late 1930s he went to Paris to study music with Nadia Boulanger (q.v.) and, after his return to the United States in 1939, studied with Otto Luening (q.v.) in New York City. Goeb was awarded a Ph.D. in music from the State University of Iowa in 1945. He taught there as well as at the University of Oklahoma, the Juilliard School of Music, and at Stanford University (1954–55). From 1956 to 1962 Goeb was director of the American Composers Alliance. His compositions include *Symphony No. 1* (1942), *Symphony No. 2* (1945), *Prairie Songs* for woodwind quintet (1947), *Concertino for Trombone and Strings* (1950), *Symphony No. 3* (1952), *Five American Dances* for strings (1952), *Violin Concerto* (1953), *Piano Concerto* (1954), *Symphony No. 4* (1954), *Concertino II* for orchestra (1956), *Sinfonia No. 1* (1957), *Iowa Concerto* for chamber orchestra (1959), *Woodwind Quintet No. 2* (1956), and *Symphonia No. 2* (1962).

GOLDMAN, RICHARD FRANKO (1910–1980) Conductor, composer, author. Born in New York, N.Y., Dec. 7, 1910, Goldman followed in his father's footsteps as bandmaster. His father was Edwin Franko Goldman (q.v.) who sustained the line from Sousa (q.v.). The younger Goldman was graduated from Columbia University; he studied piano with Clarence Adler and Ralph Leopold and composition with Pietro Floridia, Nadia Boulanger (q.v.), and Wallingford Riegger (q.v.). He became assistant conductor of the Goldman Band and served in various other musical capacities in the American Bandmasters Association, the American Musicological Society, the League of Composers and the American Composers Alliance. During World War II he served with the Office of Strategic

Services. Upon the death of his father in 1956, he took over the leadership of the Goldman Band. In 1968 Goldman became the director of the Peabody Conservatory of Music, Baltimore, Md. His works include *Two Songs* to texts by R. L. Stevenson (1933), *Divertimento for Flute and Piano* (1937), *Hymn for Brass Choir* (1939), *A Sentimental Journey* for band (1941), *A Curtain-Raiser and Country Dance* for band (1941), *The Lee Rigg* for orchestra (1942), *Sonatina* for piano (1942), *Le Bobino,* suite for orchestra (1942), *Three Duets* for clarinets (1944), *Care-Charming Sleep* for a cappella mixed chorus (1944), *Sonatina* for 2 clarinets (1945), *Duo* for tubas (1948), and *Sonata for Violin and Piano* (1952). Goldman also composed 2 operas: *Athalia* and *The Mandarin.* He is the author of *The Band's Music* (1938), *The Concert Band* (1946), and *Harmony of Western Music* (1965). He died in Baltimore, Md., Jan. 19, 1980.

GOODMAN, BENNY (b. 1909) Clarinetist, bandleader. Born in Chicago, Ill., May 30, 1909, Benjamin David Goodman was born into a large, poor family. He began studying the clarinet at Hull House, founded by the social reformer Jane Addams (1860–1935). By age 10 he was playing quite well and, at 12, attracted notice with an imitation of popular clarinetist Ted Lewis in a Chicago theatre. This led to jobs with local bands by the time he was 13. In the early 1920s Goodman was a member of such bands as those of Arnold Johnson and Art Kassel. He joined the even more famed Ben Pollack band in the summer of 1925. When he left the band in 1929, Goodman had already begun to acquire a reputation as a soloist—many of his early solos are preserved on the recordings made with the Pollack band. Goodman moved to New York City after leaving Pollack and worked as a freelance in various local, radio, and theatre pitbands. In 1934 he organized the first nominal Benny Goodman band, which appeared at the Billy Rose Music Hall; that same year he led the band on the weekly radio show "Let's Dance." Goodman's arrangements and jazz-oriented band members led to their discovery by jazz enthusiast-impresario John Hammond and to recording contracts. Goodman established small groups within the band, such as the Trio consisting of Goodman, pianist Teddy Wilson, and drummer Gene Krupa. Goodman was an innovator socially as well as musically, for by employing the black Teddy Wilson (and later Lionel Hampton and Charlie Christian) to play alongside the predominantly white musicians, he took the chance of not being able to appear in several states—not necessarily in the South—where such mixing was unacceptable. The Goodman band recordings, broadcasts, and other appearances made it one of the most popular of the time. The band's style, evolving out of jazz, featured ensemble arrangements (by Fletcher Henderson, Benny Carter, Edgar Sampson, and others) that afforded opportunities for solo spots for Goodman, pianist Jess Stacy, trumpeter Bunny Berigan, saxophonist Bud Freeman, and Krupa, whose powerful drumming moved the band along. The smooth, yet hot, quality of the band's performance was described as swinging (the beat was freer and not as "square" as that of much traditional jazz) and was soon called "swing." By 1937, Goodman was hailed as the King of Swing. On Jan. 16, 1938, Goodman gave his first—and now historic—Carnegie Hall Jazz Concert. Throughout the 1930s the Goodman band, with various changes in personnel, enjoyed success, but by the early '50s with the advent of bop the big band swing era petered out and the regular Goodman group disbanded. Goodman himself kept busy, appeared on television a good deal, formed temporary bands for special occasions. In the '50s and '60s he toured as featured soloist throughout most of the world— from the Orient to the Soviet Union, Britain, Belgium, and Canada. By the '70s, in semiretirement, Goodman confined his appearances to television and occasional small band dates. In addition to radio, television, theatre, and dance hall dates, Goodman and his band were seen and heard in several films beginning with *Hollywood Hotel* (1938) and ending with *A Song Is Born* (1948). He was the subject of the film *The Benny Goodman Story* (1955) and provided all the clarinet work for the soundtrack. Goodman is also a fine "classical" clarinetist and has recorded works by Mozart, Stravinsky, Bernstein, Bartók, and Copland (he commissioned special composition from the last 2 composers). Goodman composed or collaborated on several important instrumentals of the swing era; among them: *Stompin' at the Savoy, Lullaby in Rhythm, Don't Be That Way, Flying Home,* and *Two O'clock Jump.* His autobiography, *Kingdom of Swing* (written with Irving Kolodin), was published in 1939.

GOULD, MORTON (b. 1913) Composer, pianist, conductor, arranger. Born in Richmond Hill, N.Y., Dec. 10, 1913, Gould was a prodigy whose first piano composition, *Just Six,* was published when he was 6 years old. He also appeared as a boy pianist in concerts, on radio and in theatres—a career he abandoned upon reaching the age of 17. Gould studied piano with the eminent teacher Abbey Whiteside and composition with Vincent Jones. At 17 he was hired as staff arranger at the Radio City Music Hall, later was appointed to the musical staff of NBC. He was conductor-pianist of his own radio shows in the late 1930s and early '40s. Gould has enjoyed

a long career as a conductor of his own works and the compositions of other (primarily contemporary and American) composers. In his work Gould draws upon American themes—including popular music and jazz—all handled with a facile orchestral skill. Gould has also been active as a recording artist, both as pianist and conductor. His works include *Chorale and Fugue in Jazz* for 2 pianos and orchestra (1932), *Piano Sonata No. 2* (1933), *Piano Concerto* (1937), *Violin Concerto* (1938), *A Foster Gallery* (1940), *Spirituals for Orchestra* (1941), 4 symphonies (1943, 1944, 1947, 1952), *Viola Concerto* (1943), the ballet *Interplay* (1943), *Concerto for Orchestra* (1944), *Harvest* for vibraphone, harp, and strings (1945), *Minstrel Show* (1946), the ballet *Fall River Legend* (1947), *Concerto for Tap Dancer and Orchestra* (1952), *Inventions* for 4 pianos and orchestra (1953), *Dance Variations* for 2 pianos and orchestra (1953), *Jekyll and Hyde Variations* for orchestra (1955), *Dialogues* for piano and strings (1956), the ballet *Fiesta* (1957), *Declaration Suite* (1957), *Rhythm Gallery* for narrator and orchestra (1958), *St. Lawrence Suite* for band (1958), *Prisms* (1962), *World War I,* background music for a television documentary series (1964), *Vivaldi Gallery* (1967), *Troubadour Music* for 4 guitars and orchestra (1968), *Symphony of Spirituals* (1976), *American Ballads* (1976), and the score to the television production *Holocaust* (1978). Gould has composed numerous pieces for piano, a series of "symphonettes," which includes the sophisticated *Symphonette No. 2* and the popular *Latin-American Symphonette* (1940). He has also scored several films and composed the music for the Broadway musicals *Billion Dollar Baby* (1944) and *Arms and the Girl* (1948).

"GRAND CANYON SUITE" Orchestral composition by Ferde Grofé (q.v.), who composed it especially for the Paul Whiteman (q.v.) orchestra in 1931. Unabashedly descriptive, the suite is composed of 5 sections: *Sunrise, Painted Desert, On the Trail* (whose main theme gained currency in the heyday of radio as the signature of the "Philip Morris Playhouse"), *Sunset,* and *Cloudburst. Grand Canyon Suite* was given its first performance by the Paul Whiteman Orchestra at the Studebaker Theatre, Chicago, Ill., Nov. 22, 1931. It achieved the distinction of being one of the few works by American composers performed and recorded by Arturo Toscanini.

GRANT, PARKS (b. 1910) Composer, teacher, author. Born in Cleveland, Ohio, Jan. 4, 1910, Grant revealed an early interest in music and began to study theory and composition, as well as organ, with teachers in Columbus, Ohio. He received his master's degree from Ohio State University and later studied with Herbert Elwell (q.v.) at the Eastman School of Music, Rochester, N.Y. Grant then earned a living teaching music in public schools and later taught at John Tarleton Agricultural College, Texas, Northeast Junior College of Louisiana State University, and the University of Mississippi, Oxford. His works include *Minuet in D* for orchestra (1928), *Poème Élégiaque* (1928), *Overture to Shakespeare's Macbeth* (1930), *Symphonic Fantasia* (1931), *Song of the Monks,* text by Schiller, for male voices a cappella (1931), *Benedictus* for male voices, a cappella (1933), the ballet *Dream of the Ballet-Master* for string quartet and piano (1934), *Symphony in D Minor* (1938), *A Shropshire Lad* (1939), *Piano Sonata* (1940), *The Masque of Red Death* for orchestra (1940), *Horn Concerto* (1940), *Symphony No. 2 in A Minor* (1941), 3 *Night Poems* for string quartet (1942), *Clarinet Concerto* (1945), *Poem for Strings* (1945), *Poem*

for Horn and Organ (1945), *Excursions* for 2 trumpets, horn, and trombone (1951), *Brevities* for brass quintet (1952), *Percussion Concert Piece* (1969), *Anoche cuando dormía* (1970), and *Varied Obstinacies* for saxophone and tape recorder (1971). There are other works for chamber groups. Grant has written on musical subjects and is an authority and editor of the music of Mahler.

GREEN, ADOLPH Lyricist. See Comden and Green.

GREEN, JOHN (b. 1908) Composer, pianist, arranger, conductor. Born in New York City, Oct. 10, 1908, Green took the usual music-piano lessons but was graduated from Harvard with a degree in economics. While at Harvard he began writing and arranging music. Green worked for a time in Wall Street but continued studying with Herman Wasserman, Ignace Hilsberg, and Walter Spalding. His first professional work was done for Guy Lombardo, for whom Green made arrangements. His first popular success was "Coquette" (1928) with lyrics by Carmen Lombardo (1903–1971). Green enjoyed an even greater success with "Body and Soul" (lyrics by Edward Heyman, Robert Sour, and Frank Eyton) interpolated into the revue *Three's a Crowd* (1930). Green—known as Johnny Green then— combined a career of song writing with that of accompanist (Ethel Merman, Gertrude Lawrence, James Melton), band pianist (Leo Reisman, Buddy Rogers), and the leader of his own bands, chiefly on radio. Green also moved between New York and Hollywood, the former for his radio work and the latter for film work. He settled in California around 1942 and began scoring musicals at MGM—*Broadway Rhythm* (1943) and *Bathing Beauty* (1944). From 1949 until the early '60s, when the musical film slumped, Green was musical director at MGM. Among his best-known productions were *An American in Paris* (1951) and *West Side Story* (1961). In 1957 Green provided the score and songs for *Raintree County*. As a songwriter Green was most productive in the '30s; among his enduring songs are "Out of Nowhere" (lyrics by Heyman, 1931), "I Cover the Waterfront" (lyrics by Heyman, 1933), "You're Mine, You" (lyrics by Heyman, 1933), and "Easy Come, Easy Go" (lyrics by Heyman, 1934). Green has also written several "serious" works: *Night Club, Six Impressions* for 3 pianos and orchestra (written for Paul Whiteman's Orchestra), and *Music for Elizabeth* for piano and orchestra (1942). Green was a frequent conductor at the Hollywood Bowl, the San Francisco Symphony, and the Los Angeles Philharmonic. For several years Green was conductor of the televised Academy Award shows.

GREEN, RAY (b. 1909) Composer, pianist, teacher. Born in Cavendish, Mo., Sept. 13, 1909, Green was a farm boy who, virtually from birth, heard his family singing hymns, an experience that influenced his composition. He was about 12 when the family moved to California, where he began taking piano lessons and, upon graduation from high school, took a few courses (those he could afford) at the San Francisco Conservatory. A scholarship enabled Green to study composition there with Ernest Bloch (q.v.); he also studied with Albert Elkus at the University of California, Berkeley. The young composer received encouragement from musical pioneer Henry Cowell (q.v.), who devoted an issue of *New Music* (q.v.) to his works. Although he was awarded the George Ladd Prix de Paris (1935), Green did not study with Milhaud or Boulanger, as the award entitled him to, but chose to

work on his own. Soon after his return to San Francisco 2 years later Green became associated with the May O'Donnell Dance Co., for which he was music director and composer (he and O'Donnell married later). Green was active in music in the San Francisco area for several years; from 1939 to 1941 he was supervisor and director of the Northern California Federal Music Project Chorus. In 1943 Green went into the U. S. Army and organized concerts and trained a soldier chorus. He also served as music instructor at Convalescent Hospital, Fort Logan, Colo. After the war Green stayed in uniform as chief of the Music Division, Veterans Administration, Washington, D.C. (1946–48). His duties entailed the formulation of a musical therapy program for convalescent veterans. This work completed, Green came to New York City, where he was active as executive secretary, American Music Center. Green has been a prolific composer; some of his works are: *Suite for Violin and Piano* (1929), *Some Pieces for String Quartet* (1932), *Two Madrigals* to texts by Walt Whitman (1933), *Sonata Brevis* for piano (1934), *Holiday for Four* for clarinet, bassoon, viola, and piano (1935), *Festival Fugues* for piano (1936), *Three Inventories on a Texas Tune* for piano and percussion (1936), *Concertino for Piano and Orchestra* (1937), *Of Pioneer Women*, ballet score (1937), *American Document*, ballet scored for 2 pianos and drums (1938), *Lullay Myn Lyking* for mixed chorus, a cappella (1939), *Three Inventions of Casey Jones* for percussion (1939), *So Proudly We Hail*, ballet (1940), *On American Themes*, ballet (1941), *Dance Theme and Variations* for piano (1943), *Hymn Tunes* for string quartet (1944), *Symphony No. 2* (1945), *Sunday Sing Symphony* (1946), *12 Short Sonatas* for piano (1949–70), *Folksong Fantasies* for trumpet and band (1949), *Lonesome Valley* for harp and orchestra (1950), *Violin Concerto* (1952), *Dance Sonata* for 2 pianos (1953), *Dance Sonata No. 2* (1957), and *Hymn Tune Set* for 2 pianos (1960). Green has also prepared a 6-volume set, *Piano Books for Young People* (1961).

GUTHRIE, WOODY (1912–1967) Folks singer, songwriter. Born Woodrow Wilson Guthrie in Okemah, Okla., July 14, 1912, into a troubled, generally insolvent, family. Both his parents sang and his father played the guitar, but Guthrie received no formal music study. He could play the harmonica and later taught himself to play the fiddle and mandolin. By the time he was 14, having dropped out of school when he was in the 10th grade, Guthrie left home and became a migrant worker during the Depression. He also performed and sang, picking up songs among his fellow workers, composing his own and, in the manner of the folk artist, devising variants on existing songs and fashioning them to his own taste. Guthrie was one of the first, and most influential, of what has come to be called a protest singer. He raised his voice against injustice, poverty, the Establishment in true folkloristic tradition. During the 1930s he gained attention as the composer-adapter of Dust Bowl ballads inspired by the dust storms that devastated the American West in this period (he later composed a song, "Tom Joad," inspired in turn by John Steinbeck's *The Grapes of Wrath*, which treated the same topic). Guthrie's songs inspired many younger singers of protest songs, among them Pete Seeger, Tom Paxton, and Bob Dylan. Among his best-known songs are "So Long, It's Been Good to Know You," "This Land Is Your Land," and "Reuben James" (the first was based on the folk tune "The Ballad of Billy the Kid" and the 3rd on "Wildwood Flower"). During the 1930s and '40s Guthrie sang in concert, made several recordings for commercial companies as well as for the Library of Congress. He served in the military during World War II, which earned him the right to a GI Bill education. He attended classes for a while at Brooklyn College, N.Y., but left with "degrees absent." His professional career closed when he contracted Huntington's chorea, for which there is no known cure, in the late 1950s. His autobiography, *Bound for Glory*, was published in 1943; his *American Folksong* was published in 1947. His son, Arlo Davy (b. 1947), also became a protest folk singer and is best known for the storytelling "Alice's Restaurant." Guthrie senior died in the Creedmore State Hospital, N.Y., Oct. 3, 1967.

"GUYS AND DOLLS" A "Musical Fable" based on a Damon Runyon short story (adapted by Abe Burrows and Jo Swerling) with songs by Frank Loesser (q.v.). The main plot centers on the unlikely romance of a professional gambler ("Sky Masterson") and a Times Square missionary, "Miss Sarah Brown." The subplot treats the more comic and long-running engagement (14 years) of 2 Runyonesque characters "Nathan Detroit," a crap game organizer, and "Miss Adelaide," a nightclub performer. Other characters have such names as "Nicely-Nicely," "Liver Lips Louie," "Harry the Horse," and "Big Jule." A metropolitan folktale, *Guys and Dolls* owed much of its considerable success to the score by Loesser. From its opening "Fugue for Tinhorns" through several lovely ballads ("I'll Know," "I've Never Been in Love Before") and comedy songs ("Adelaide's Lament," "Take Back Your Mink," "Sue Me," and "Sit Down, You're Rockin' the Boat"), as well as such rhythmic songs as "Luck Be a Lady," *Guys and Dolls* unfolds, opera-like, with great musico-lyrical inventiveness. Loesser's command of the Runyon patois is masterly (though it is unlikely that even Times Square denizens of the period spoke this kind of dialect). *Guys and Dolls* opened at the 46th Street Theatre on Nov. 24, 1950, and ran for 1,200 performances; it also enjoyed a long London run, a long tour, and was made into a mediocre film by Goldwyn in 1955. In the original the role of *Sky Masterson* was played by Robert Alda, *Miss Adelaide* by Vivian Blaine, *Nathan Detroit* by Sam Levene, *Miss Sarah Brown* by Lizbeth Webb, and *Nicely-Nicely* by Stubby Kaye.

HAIEFF, ALEXEI (b. 1914) Composer, teacher. Born in Blagoveshchensk, Russia, Aug. 25, 1914, Haieff moved to the United States when he was about 18. He attended the Juilliard School of Music where he studied with Frederick Jacobi (q.v.) and Rubin Goldmark (q.v.). He also studied during the same period with Constantin Shvedoff privately (1933–34). Upon completing his work at Juilliard, Haieff went to Paris to study with Nadia Boulanger, with whom he had worked earlier when she taught at Cambridge, Mass. He also studied the piano with Alexander Siloti. Haieff's work, much of it Stravinsky-influenced, won him several awards, among them Guggenheim Fellowships; he was also a Fellow at the American Academy, Rome (1947–48). Haieff has taught at the University of Buffalo, the Carnegie-Mellon Institute, and the University of Utah, Salt Lake City, where he was composer-in-residence (1968–71). His works include *A Short Cantata on a Russian Folk Text* for 4 solo voices and 4 string instruments (ca. 1939), *Serenade* for oboe, clarinet, bassoon, and piano (1940), *Suite for Violin and Piano* (1941), *Symphony No. 1* (1942), *Divertimento* for small orchestra (1944), *Sonata* for 2 pianos (1945), the ballet *Princess Zondilda and Her Entourage* (1946), *Violin Concerto* (1948), *Piano Concerto* (1950), *String Quartet No. 1*

(1951), *Eclogue* for harp and strings (1954), *Piano Sonata* (1955), *Symphony No. 2* (1957), *Saints' Wheel* for piano (1960), *Symphony No. 3* (1961), *Cello Sonata* (1963), *Éloge* for chamber group (1967), *Holy Week Liturgy* for chorus (1969), and *Caligula* for baritone and orchestra (1970).

HAINES, EDMUND (1914–1974) Composer, teacher. Born in Ottumwa, Iowa, Haines switched to music after beginning in mathematics. Upon graduating with a degree in music from the Conservatory of Kansas City, Haines continued at the Eastman School, Rochester, N.Y., where he studied under Howard Hanson (q.v.). His other teachers include Aaron Copland (q.v.), Otto Luening (q.v.), and Roy Harris (q.v.). He taught at the Conservatory, Kansas City, the Eastman School, the University of Michigan, Bard College, N.Y., and Sarah Lawrence College, Bronxville, N.Y., where he was chairman of the Music Department. He was composer-in-residence at La Napoule Art Foundation, France (1957–58). Haines was the recipient of a Guggenheim Fellowship, Pulitzer Prize, and the American Guild of Organists award. He served in the U. S. Army from 1943 to 1945. His works include a *Sonata* for violin and piano (1936), *Landscape* for orchestra (1936), *Poem* for viola and orchestra (1938), *Three Dances* for orchestra (1939), *Pastorale* for flute and strings (1939), *Symphony in Miniature* (1940), the Pulitzer Prize–winning *Symphony No. 1* (1941), *Two Sonatinas* for piano (1942), *Interlude* for strings (1943), *Sonatina* for piano (1945), *Coronach* for strings, brass, and timpani (1946), *Quartet* for 2 violins, viola, and cello (1946), *Piano Sonata* (1946), *Eclogue* for 2 violins, flute, and cello (1946), *Toccata* for brass quartet (1948), *Informal Overture* for orchestra (1948), *Promenade, Air and Toccata* for organ (1948), *Fallen Wing* for solo dancer (1951), *Prelude and Scherzo* for clarinet and piano (1951), *Mary Saw Her Son* for women's chorus (1952), *Piano Sonata No. 2* (1953), *Three Choral Pieces: The Moon's the North Wind's Cooky, The Mirror,* and *The Day the World Began* (1954), *Soliloquy in Seven Parts* for piano (1955), *Set of Five* for 2 pianos (1956), *Rondino and Variations* for orchestra (1957), *String Quartet No. 4* (1957), and *Concertino for Seven Instruments and Orchestra* (1959). Haines died in New York City, July 5, 1974.

"HAPPY DAYS ARE HERE AGAIN" Popular song during the Depression, words by Jack Yellen and music by Milton Ager (q.v.). Written in 1929 for the musical film *Chasing Rainbows,* it became a kind of Depression theme song, along with "Brother, Can You Spare a Dime" (q.v.), after the film was released in 1930. The optimism of the song, which originally was not intended to be a reaction to the Depression, led to its being adopted by the Democrats as a theme song for Presidential candidate Franklin D. Roosevelt.

HARBURG, E. Y. "YIP" (1896–1981) Lyricist, librettist. Born on New York's Lower East Side, Apr. 8, 1896, Harburg revealed an early gift for light, humorous verse as a high school student at Townsend Harris Hall, a school for exceptional students. It was there he joined with a boyhood friend, Ira Gershwin (q.v.), in publishing the school paper to which each contributed snappy poems. As a youth Harburg also had acting aspirations, but after leaving the City College of New York he began an electrical appliance business, which failed in 1929 with the coming of the Depression. Forced to fall back on his rhyming skill, Harburg decided to emulate his friend Gershwin and became a lyricist. He wrote his first professional songs with an already established songwriter, Jay Gor-

ney (b. 1896), with whom he collaborated on songs for the 1929 revue *Earl Carroll's Sketch Book.* This was followed by the assignment for the next year's show. Harburg continued to write lyrics for revues with Gorney as well as other composers with whom he would do fine work, Harold Arlen (q.v.), Vernon Duke (q.v.), and Burton Lane (q.v.). In 1932, for the show *Americana,* Gorney and Harburg wrote their Depression song, "Brother, Can You Spare a Dime" (q.v.). Harburg wrote for revues in the early '30s, producing lyrics of great polish, wit and, often, an undertone of social awareness unique in popular song. With Duke he wrote "April in Paris" (from *Walk a Little Faster,* 1932) and "What Is There to Say?" (from *Ziegfeld Follies,* 1934). Another revue united him with Arlen and, as co-lyricist, Ira Gershwin. *Life Begins at 8:40* (1934) resulted in such songs as "You're a Builder-Upper," "What Can You Say in a Love Song?" "Let's Take a Walk Around the Block," the satirical "Life Begins at City Hall," and the delightfully inarticulate "Things." Harburg and Arlen moved to Hollywood, where they wrote songs for some not-so-memorable films; one of their finest efforts, "Last Night When We Were Young" (1935), was to have been sung by Lawrence Tibbett but was cut from the movie. Harburg and Arlen left Beverly Hills in 1937 to work on their first joint book show, the antiwar musical *Hooray for What!* (1937). They returned to Hollywood, where they created the songs for the outstanding musical *The Wizard of Oz* (1938); their song "Over the Rainbow" won them the Academy Award for best song of the year. Arlen and Harburg did the songs for 2 more successful Broadway shows, *Bloomer Girl* (1944) and *Jamaica* (1957). Harburg went on to collaborate with another outstanding composer, Burton Lane (both in films and on Broadway), producing the songs for *Hold On to Your Hats* (1940) and one of the most successful of all musicals, *Finian's Rainbow* (q.v.), in 1947. As co-librettist with Fred Saidy (b. 1907), Harburg touched upon some unusual subjects in the plot: racism, capitalism, and greed—all carried off gracefully through fantasy and humor. Harburg's other Broadway shows include *Ballyhoo of 1932,* music by Lewis Gensler, *Flahooley* (music by Sammy Fain, 1951), *The Happiest Girl in the World* (music adapted from Offenbach by Henry Myers, 1961), and *Darling of the Day* (music by Jule Styne, 1968). Harburg's film experience was not as fruitful as his Broadway work—primarily because fine songwriters were rarely appreciated in Hollywood. Also, outspoken on social issues and injustice, Harburg was a bit too abrasive for conservative studio executives. Besides *The Wizard of Oz,* Harburg managed to write a few more songs for good film musicals: *Cabin in the Sky* (1943), for which he and Arlen wrote additional songs added to the original Vernon Duke Broadway score, *Can't Help Singing* (1944) with Jerome Kern (q.v.), and *Gay Purr-ee* (1962), a feature-length cartoon which used the voice of Judy Garland (q.v.), with music by Harold Arlen. Some of the songs with Harburg lyrics are: "I'm Only Human After All" (music by Duke, co-lyricist Ira Gershwin, 1930), "How Do You Do It?" (music by Lewis Gensler, 1932), "Satan's Li'l Lamb" (music by Arlen, co-lyricist, Johnny Mercer, 1932), "It's Only a Paper Moon" (music by Arlen, co-lyricist Billy Rose, 1933), "I Like the Likes of You" (music by Duke, 1934), "Moanin' in the Mornin'," "Down with Love," and "God's Country" (music by Arlen, 1937), "We're Off to See the Wizard," "Ding Dong, the Witch Is Dead" (music by Arlen, 1939), "Lydia, the Tattooed Lady" (music by Arlen, 1939), "Happiness Is Just a Thing Called Joe" (music by Arlen, 1943),

"Right as the Rain," "Evelina," "The Eagle and Me," and "I Got a Song" (music by Arlen, 1944), "More and More," "Any Moment Now," and "Can't Help Singing" (music by Kern, 1944), "How Are Things in Glocca Morra?" "Old Devil Moon," "When I'm Not Near the Girl I Love (I Love the Girl I'm Near)," "The Begat," and "Something Sort of Grandish" (music by Lane, 1947), "Here's to Your Illusions" and "The World Is Your Balloon" (music by Sammy Fain, 1951), "Leave the Atom Alone," "Cocoanut Sweet," and "Take it Slow, Joe" (music by Arlen, 1957), "Adrift on a Star" (music by Offenbach, 1961), and "Little Drops of Rain" and "Paris Is a Lonely Town" (music by Arlen, 1962). Harburg has published 2 volumes of light, trenchant verse: *Rhymes for the Irreverent* (1965) and *At This Point in Rhyme* (1976). He died in Los Angeles, Calif., March 5, 1981.

HARRISON, LOU (b. 1917) Composer, teacher, writer. Born in Portland, Oreg., May 14, 1917, Harrison came under the influence of Henry Cowell (q.v.) with whom he studied at San Francisco State College. He later (1941) studied at the University of California, Los Angeles, with Arnold Schoenberg. Harrison soon revealed an affinity with advanced, percussion-flavored music— and a taste for the musics of the East. He was associated at this time with another composer of the same philosophy: John Cage (q.v.). In 1941 he came to New York City, where he composed music for dance, earned some money as a copyist, and wrote music criticism for the New York *Herald Tribune* (1945–48). He wrote on music and dance also for various publications, including *Listen* and *Modern Music* (q.v.). Harrison also danced professionally, has conducted and, as an editor, has prepared several works of Charles Ives (q.v.) for publication; he conducted the first performance of Ive's *Symphony*

No. 3 in 1947. In his own compositions Harrison uses instruments from other cultures (Africa, Asia) along with traditional Western instruments plus such homemade soundmakers as cans, pots, and brake drums. Harrison has taught at Mills College, Oakland, Calif., Greenwich House Music School, New York City, and San Jose State College, Calif., since 1967. Harrison's works (many entitled in the international language of Esperanto, which he prefers) include *Canticle No. 1* for percussion (1940), *Fugue* for percussion (1941), *Canticle No. 3* for percussion (1941), *Suite* for piano (1943), *Three Sonatas* for harpsichord (1946), *Suite No. 2* for string quartet (1948), *Marriage at the Eiffel Tower,* ballet (1948), *Perilous Chapel,* ballet (1949), *Solstice* for chamber orchestra (1950), *Suite* for violin, piano, and small orchestra (1951), *Symphony on G* (1953), *Rapunzel,* opera (1954), *Recording Piece* for percussion (1955), *Five Strict Songs* for 8 baritones and orchestra (1955), *Koncherto Por La Violino Kun Perkuta Orkestro* (Esperanto for Concerto for violin and percussion orchestra, 1959), *Suite for Simfoniaj Kordoj* (Suite for strings, 1960), *Concerto in Slendro* for violin, celesta, and percussion (1961), *Moo gung kwa, Se tang ak* for Korean court orchestra (1961), *Pacifika Rondo* for an orchestra of Western and Oriental instruments (1963), *Jepthah's Daughter* (1963), *Nova Odo* for orchestra (1963), *Music for Violin* (ca. 1967), *Peace Piece One* for chorus (1968), *Young Caesar,* puppet opera (1970), and *Elegiac Symphony* (1975). Also songs, many instrumental works for exotic instruments, several additional ballets and sacred works, masses, motets, etc.

HELM, EVERETT (b. 1913) Composer, teacher, writer. Born in Minneapolis, Minn., July 17, 1913, Helm was a graduate of Harvard, where he studied with Walter Piston (q.v.); he also studied musicology with Hugo Leichtentritt. Further study, on a Paine Traveling Fellowship, was done under Gian Francesco Malipiero, Ralph Vaughan Williams, and Alfred Einstein. After his return Helm taught at the Longy School of Music, Cambridge, Mass., Mills College, Oakland, Calif., and Western College, Oxford, Ohio. Helm has also taught at the University of Ljubljana, Yugoslavia (1966–68). Since 1963 he has lived in Asolo, Italy. He has written widely in several languages; from 1961 to 1963 he was editor of *Musical America.* His works include *Sonata for Violin and Piano* (1936), *Three Pastorals* for soprano and cello (1940), *A Set of Carols* for mixed chorus, a cappella (1940), *Five Movements for Flute and Strings* (1940), *Three Gospel Hymns* for orchestra (1942), *Requiem* for mixed chorus and orchestra (1942), *Sonata Brevis* for piano (1942), *Sonata for Violin and Piano No. 2* (1943), *For You, O Democracy* for mixed chorus and chamber orchestra (1943), *Kentucky Sonata* for violin and orchestra (1944), *First String Quartet* (1938–44), *1865 Quartet* (1945), *Trio* for violin, cello, and piano (1945), *Sonata for Flute and Piano* (1945), *Brasiliana* for orchestra (1946), *Suite for Small Orchestra* (1946), *Symphony No. 1* (1946), *Concerto for Strings* (1950), *Piano Concerto No. 1* (1951), *Adam and Eve* for actors, chorus, and chamber orchestra (1952), *Concerto for Flute, oboe, bassoon, trumpet, violin, strings, and percussion* (1954), *Symphony for Strings* (1955), *The Seige of Tottenberg,* opera (1956), *Le Roy Fait Battre Tambour,* ballet (1956), *Piano Concerto No. 2* (1956), *Divertimento for Flutes* (1957), *Sinfonia da Camera* (1961), *String Quartet No. 2* (1962), *Woodwind Quartet* (1966), and *Concerto for Double Bass and Strings* (1968).

HERMAN, WOODROW "WOODY"
(b. 1913) Bandleader, clarinetist, vocalist. Born in Milwaukee, Wis., May 16, 1913, Herman began singing and dancing in local vaudeville theatres when he was about 6 years old. He was often billed as "The Boy Wonder of the Clarinet." He played the saxophone from about age 9 and played in local dance bands while still in high school. By the early 1930s he was playing in the Tom Gerun Band on the West Coast and gradually worked through the Harry Sosnik, Gus Arnheim, and Isham Jones bands. It was out of the Jones band that Herman's first band was formed, when Jones temporarily retired in 1936. Known as "The Band That Plays the Blues," it first came to wider notice because of a best-selling recording, "Woodchopper's Ball" (1939). Although the band did, indeed, play the blues, it also played the popular show and film songs of the period; a smaller group within the band, The Woodchoppers, played an updated Dixieland. As the band evolved it evidenced the influence of Duke Ellington and Jimmy Lunceford, especially in the arrangements by Neal Hefti and Ralph Burns. It was one of the finest bands of the '40s. Herman was innovative in a social sense, for he also hired women—not just as the traditional "girl singer" but as instrumentalists. Among these pioneers were Billie Rogers, who played trumpet, and Marge Hyams, a vibraphonist. The band went through changes, partly owing to the effects of the Second World War, and by the mid '40s was making sounds that sounded less like traditional jazz than the music of the classical modernists and was soon dubbed "Progressive Jazz." The band was called the Herman Herd and featured such "progressive" musicians as Flip Phillips (tenor sax), Bill Harris (trombone), Pete Candoli (trumpet), and Chubby Jackson (bass). Such instrumentals as *Bijou, Apple Honey,* and *Caldonia* were popular among record collectors and encouraged Herman to present his Carnegie Hall concert in March 1946, at which he introduced a work composed for him by Stravinsky, *Ebony Concerto* (q.v.). Several Herds followed the first, some formed for special appearances; in the 1970s Herman appeared with his current Herd on European and American tours. Herman's various bands made numerous recordings from the 78-rpm era into the long-playing record age. He and his band appeared in several films, beginning with 1942's "What's Cookin'?" Herman was credited, with collaborators Ralph Burns, Chubby Jackson, and other of his arrangers, with several instrumental band pieces, among them *Goosey Gander, Blues on Parade, Early Autumn, Your Father's Moustache,* and *Misty Morning.*

HERRMANN, BERNARD (1911–1975) Composer, conductor. Born in New York City, June 29, 1911, Herrmann studied music at New York University with Philip James (q.v.) and Percy Grainger; at the Juilliard Graduate School he worked under Bernard Wagenaar (q.v.) in composition and Albert Stoessel in conducting. At 20 he founded the New Chamber Orchestra and led it until he joined the staff of the Columbia Broadcasting System as conductor-arranger. His program, "Invitation to Music," was noteworthy for its presentation of neglected and contemporary compositions. As conductor of the background scores for CBS Symphony, Herrmann worked with the young actor-director Orson Welles on "The Mercury Theatre on the Air." When Welles moved on to Hollywood in 1940 to produce his first film, *Citizen Kane,* he asked Herrmann to accompany him and to compose the score. The result was one of the most praised film scores ever written. Herrmann was one of the most respected of all film composers and divided his time between composing for films, conducting and writing music for the concert hall as well. Although he chose to live in England from about 1965, Herrmann frequently returned to the United States to work on films. In England he made recordings of several of his own works as well as those of others, among them Charles Ives, whom Herrmann championed before Ives was "discovered." While known primarily as a composer of outstanding film scores, Herrmann created several works of quality, among them the *Currier and Ives Suite* for orchestra (1935), *Sinfonietta* for strings (1935), *Nocturne and Scherzo* (1936), *Moby Dick*, cantata for male chorus, soloists, and orchestra (1938), *Symphony* (1940), *Fantasticks* for mixed chorus and orchestra (1942), *For the Fallen* (1943), the opera *Wuthering Heights* (1950), *A Christmas Carol*, television opera (1954), *Echoes* for string quartet (1966), and *Souvenirs de Voyage* for clarinet quintet (1967). After his success with the *Citizen Kane* score, Herrmann was commissioned to write dozens of others; to name a few: *All That Money Can Buy* (1941; the suite, *The Devil and Daniel Webster* was done in 1944), *Jane Eyre* (1944), *Hangover Square,* from which came the *Concerto Macabre* for piano and orchestra (1945), *Anna and the King of Siam* (1946), *The Day the Earth Stood Still* (1951), and *The Trouble with Harry* (1955), *Vertigo* (1958), and *Psycho* (1960), 3 of the many scores composed for films directed by Alfred Hitchcock. Herrmann also scored *Fahrenheit 451* (1966) and *The Bride Wore Black* (1968). He had completed the music for *Taxi Driver* while in California; shortly after, on Dec. 24, 1975, Herrmann died of a heart attack in Los Angeles.

HILL, BILLY See "The Last Round-Up."

HILLBILLY MUSIC Condescending term used by urbanites as a pejorative synonym for country (q.v.) and bluegrass (q.v.) music. "Corn" is a related term but was generally applied by lovers of jazz and swing to the kind of music played by such orchestras as Guy Lombardo, Wayne King, and Lawrence Welk.

HINES, EARL "FATHA" (b. 1905) Pianist, composer, bandleader. Born in Duquesne, Pa., Dec. 28, 1905, Hines studied piano privately in Pittsburgh. He came from a musical family; his father was trumpeter in the Eureka Brass Band of Duquesne and his mother an organist. In his early teens Hines began playing in bands around Pittsburgh and, in 1922, became accompanist for the singer Lois Deppe. Hines toured for a time with the Carroll Dickerson band after leaving Deppe; he also performed as a soloist in clubs and had begun to conduct a bit. In 1927, in Chicago, he joined with Louis Armstrong (q.v.) to make a series of historic recordings. By this time Hines was noted for a so-called "trumpet style" of playing the piano—while his right hand played the melody in octaves, his left provided an orchestral-like bass accompaniment. Rhythmically complex, Hines's style was imitated by dozens of jazz pianists. Hines truly came into his own when he formed his own band in December 1928 and established himself in the Grand Terrace, a club on Chicago's South Side, where he remained for more than a decade. When the band broke up, Hines joined Louis Armstrong again (1948–51). He left to form his own little group to play in the Hangover Club, San Francisco. He teamed up with white trombonist Jack Teagarden, as co-leader of a band that toured Europe in 1957. Under U.S. auspices Hines himself took a small group of jazz musicians for a tour of the Soviet Union in 1966. He has remained active as a pianist and recording artist well into the '70s. Hines has enjoyed a long recording career which began in December 1928, when he cut his first discs for the Q.R.S. company (which specialized in piano rolls). His historic 1928 recordings made with Louis Armstrong are still available. He served as pianist in the bands of Jimmie Noone, Johnny Dodds, Clifford Hayes, and Sidney Bechet as well as in his own Grand Terrace Band for recordings. Hines has also recorded extensively as a soloist well into the '70s to much critical acclaim. As a composer Hines has written several works popular among other jazz pianists. These include *Rosetta, My Monday Date, Piano Man,* and *57 Varieties,* as well as a fascinating arrangement of a W. C. Handy classic, "Boogie Woogie on St. Louis Blues."

HOLIDAY, BILLIE (1915–1959) Vocalist. Born in Baltimore, Md., Apr. 7, 1915, Eleanor Gough was the illegitimate daughter of Clarence Holiday, guitarist in the Fletcher Henderson band. Although her parents married some 3 years later, they soon separated and her mother brought her to New York in 1928. The teenaged Holiday had a frightful time, including early experiences with drugs, drink, and prostitution. Hearing recordings by Bessie Smith and Louis Armstrong in some of the joints in which she worked awakened a wish to emulate them, to sing. During a low period in her life (both she and her mother were out of work and near starvation), Holiday applied for a job as a dancer in a Harlem nightclub, the Log Cabin. Manager Jerry Preston did not hire her; she then offered to sing—and her small, wistful blues and jazz inflected voice immediately attracted the attention of the patrons. When she sang "Body and Soul," she was definitely hired. (Since "Body and Soul" was published in 1930, Holiday would have been about 15 or 16 at the time.) John Hammond, the white jazz devotee and impresario who kept an alert ear on the Harlem night spots, sent others to hear Holiday, among them Benny Goodman. In November 1933, Holiday cut her first recording with the Goodman band, "Your Mother's Son-in-Law" for Columbia Records. Later she recorded with the Teddy Wilson band with great success, often singing popular songs in her special "instrumental" style. She recorded with Paul Whiteman and under her own name with a special pickup band. She sang in the orchestras of Count Basie (1937) and Artie Shaw (1938). She branched out as a single and appeared at Cafe Society in New York City as well as clubs in Chicago. Her private life, and singing, deteriorated in the late '40s. She was jailed in 1947 for taking drugs but began working her way back (although her voice revealed a coarse quality) in the '50s. She toured Europe with an entertainment called "Jazz Club U.S.A." in 1954 and as a soloist in 1958. By this time she was revealing signs of total breakdown owing to excessive dependence on alcohol and drugs. Although Holiday was classified as a "blues" singer, most of her recordings consist of popular songs. Among her best-known songs are "Strange Fruit" (Lewis Allan and E. B. Marks), a song about lynching; her own "Fine and Mellow" and the traditional "God Bless This Child." Her nickname, "Lady Day," was bestowed upon her by saxophonist Lester Young when Holiday objected to some coarse language used by members of the Basie band. Her autobiography (written with the help of Bill Dufty), *Lady Sings the Blues,* was published in 1956. Holiday died in New York City, July 17, 1959.

HOVHANESS, ALAN (b. 1911) Composer, conductor, teacher. Born Alan Vaness Chakmakjian in Somerville, Mass., Mar. 8, 1911, Hovhaness could read music by age 7. He began to study the piano at 9 with Adelaide Proctor; later with Heinrich Gebhard. He studied composition under Frederick Converse (q.v.) at the New England Conservatory, Boston. He also studied composition with Czech composer Bohuslav Martinů at Tanglewood, Mass. By the time he reached his twenties Hovhaness had composed a large amount of well-received music; in the Boston area he was referred to as "the American Sibelius." But some time before 1940 Hovhaness became interested in the music of the East, most particularly that of Armenia (his father, a chemistry professor at Tufts College, Boston, was of Armenian descent; his mother was of Scotch descent). For a period Hovhaness was organist in the Armenian church in Boston and was exposed to ancient modal music. Hovhaness also made profound studies of various musics of the Orient as well as early Christian music. He worked these materials into his compositions after 1940. He also destroyed a large body of work already composed, including several symphonies, chamber music, and operas. In his work Hovhaness blends Eastern and Western music and instruments; the sound is hypnotic, exotic, and often exquisitely beautiful. Besides composing Hovhaness has taught at the Boston Conservatory (1948–52) and has been the recipent of grants from the Rockefeller, Guggenheim, and Fulbright Foundations. His works number well over 300; he has completed—at last count—36 symphonies. Among Hovhaness' most important compositions are *Lousadzak* (Concerto No. 1 for piano and orchestra: the Armenian title means "The Coming of Light," 1944), *Two Armenian Rhapsodies for Strings* (1945), *Tzaikerk* for chamber orchestra (1945), *Flute Player of the Armenian Mountains* (1946), Symphony No. 8, *Arjuna* (1947), *Zartik Parkim* (Piano Concerto No. 2, 1948), *Saint Vartan Symphony* (Symphony No.

9, 1950), *Concerto No. 2 for Violin and String Orchestra* (1951, rev. 1957), *Khaldis* (Concerto for piano, 4 trumpets and percussion, 1951, rev. 1954), *Arevakal* for orchestra (1952), *Concerto for Orchestra* (1954), *Mysterious Mountain* for orchestra (1955), *Magnificat* for chorus, soloists, and chamber orchestra (1958), *Symphony No. 4* (sic., 1959), *The Burning House*, one-act opera (1960), *Madras Sonata* for piano (1960), *Symphony No. 11* ("All Men Are Brothers," 1960, rev. 1969), *Symphony No. 12* (Chorale, 1960), *Symphony No. 15* ("Silver Pilgrimage," 1962), *Symphony No. 16* for strings and Korean percussion instruments (1962), *Meditation on Zeami*, symphonic poem (1964), *Ukiyo* ("Floating World," symphonic poem, 1965), *The Holy City* for orchestra (1967), *Fra Angelico* for orchestra (1967), *Mountains and Rivers Without End* for chamber orchestra (1968), *And God Created Great Whales* for orchestra and the "songs" of the humpback whale on tape (1970), *Firdausi* for clarinet, harp, and percussion (1972), Symphonies Nos. 27, 28, 29, 30 (1976), Symphonies Nos. 31, 32, 33, 34 (1977), *Rubaiyat* for narrator and orchestra (1977), *Symphonies No. 35, No. 36* (1978), and *Revelations of St. Paul* for soloists, chorus, and orchestra (1981). Hovhaness has also written many songs and piano pieces.

HOWARD, JOHN TASKER (1890–1964) Author, composer, lecturer. Born in Brooklyn, N.Y., Nov. 30, 1890, Howard was a graduate of Williams College, Williamstown, Mass. He started out on a career in music by studying composition with Paul Tidden, Howard Brockway (q.v.), and Mortimer Wilson (q.v.). Howard chose to earn a living in writing and served as managing editor of *The Musician*, worked for the Ampico Corporation, was music editor of *McCall's* magazine (1928–30) and *Cue* (1937–38). In 1931 Howard published his monumental *Our American Music,* the first truly comprehensive attempt to trace the evolution of the American musical character. The book has gone through several revisions and printings, the most recent (after the author's death) in 1965. Although criticized by later musicologists for its conservative bias, *Our American Music* remains a pioneering work, invaluable in its coverage and for its bibliography. Howard was also the biographer of Foster in *Stephen Foster, America's Troubadour* (1934, rev. 1953). His other books include *Ethelbert Nevin* (1935), *Our Contemporary Composers, American Music in the 20th Century* (1941), *This Modern Music* (1942; revised edition by James Lyons, entitled *Modern Music,* 1957), *The World's Great Operas* (1948), and *A Short History of Music,* with George K. Bellows (1957). Howard also served as curator, American Division, New York Public Library (1940–56), and was active with the American Society of Composers, Authors and Publishers as director (1945–58) and as secretary (1953–57). Howard's original compositions were not performed often; those he himself mentioned in *Our American Music* include *Fantasy on a Choral Theme* for piano and orchestra (1929); he composed several works based on Foster themes, piano pieces, choral pieces, and songs. He died in West Orange, N.J., Nov. 20, 1964.

HUPFELD, HERMAN (1894–1951) Songwriter, vocalist, pianist. Born in Montclair, N.J., Feb. 1, 1894, Hupfeld, a lesser known songwriter of small output, wrote one of the most popular songs ever published, "As Time Goes By" (q.v.). Hupfeld studied the violin in Germany at the age of 9, received a high school education, and served in the U. S. Navy during World War I. His name first appeared on Broadway as a contributor to the score of *Ziegfeld's Midnight Frolic* (1912). During the 1930s Hupfeld contributed a few songs to Broadway shows and a couple of films. During World War II he visited Army camps in the United States and Europe entertaining troops; this would have coincided with the great popularity of "As Time Goes By." Hupfeld wrote some songs for a Broadway revue, *Dance Me a Song* (1950); it was his last try, and the show was a failure. He died in Montclair, June 8, 1951.

"I GOT RHYTHM" Popular song, words by Ira Gershwin (q.v.) and music by George Gershwin (q.v.). "I Got Rhythm" was introduced in the show *Girl Crazy* (1930) by Ethel Merman, making her Broadway debut. It was one of the composer's personal favorites among his songs and he played it at the drop of a hint. When he was contracted to make a tour of the United States and Canada in 1934, Gershwin prepared a new showpiece for himself entitled *"I Got Rhythm" Variations* for piano and orchestra. He completed the work (composed while he was also working on *Porgy and Bess,* q.v.) on Jan. 6, 1934, just in time for the first concert in Boston on Jan. 14. The *Variations* is dedicated to Ira Gershwin.

INCH, HERBERT (b. 1904) Composer, teacher. Born in Missoula, Mont., Nov. 25, 1904, Inch studied music at the State University of Montana and at the Eastman School of Music, Rochester, N.Y., where he worked under Edward Royce and Howard Hanson (q.v.). He taught theory at Eastman (1930–31), then left to compose under a Fellowship at the American Academy, Rome (1931–34). In 1937 he joined the faculty of Hunter College, New York City, and remained there until his retirement in 1965. Inch's works include *Variations on a Modal Theme* for orchestra (1927), *Suite for Small Orchestra* (1929), *Dirge for the Year* for mixed chorus, a cappella (1930), *Quintet* for piano and strings (1930), *Symphony* (1932), *Mediterranean Sketches* for string quartet (1933), *To Silvanus* for orchestra (1933), *Divertimento* for brass (1934), *Homily* for piano, violin, and cello (1934), *Piano Sonata No. 1* (1935), *String Quartet* (1936), *Serenade* for chamber orchestra (1936), *Piano Concerto* (1940), *Sonata* for violin and cello (1941), *Answers to a Questionnaire* for orchestra (1942), *Song of Liberation* for women's chorus and piano (1943), *Northwest Overture* (1943), *Three Conversations* for string quartet (1944), *Return to Zion* for women's chorus (1945), *Piano Sonata No. 2* (1946), *Violin Concerto* (1947), *Symphonietta No. 1* (1948), *Symphonietta No. 2* (1950), *Piano Trio* (1963), and *Piano Sonata No. 3* (1966).

"IT AIN'T NECESSARILY SO" Song, music by George Gershwin (q.v.) and lyrics by Ira Gershwin (q.v.) written for the opera *Porgy and Bess* (q.v.). The song began as a 16-bar notion by George Gershwin, who suggested it as a possible tune for the character of "Sportin' Life" (portrayed by vaudevillian John W. Bubbles in the original 1935 production). Sportin' Life was the city slicker from up North, who sold liquor and Happy Dust (cocaine) to the hardworking residents of the opera's locale, Catfish Row. His view of life was paganistic, rather cynical, and opportunistic. Ira Gershwin conceived a dummy title, "It Ain't Necessarily So," to denote the rhythm of the song (with accents on the 2nd, 5th, and 8th syllables) as a guide in writing the lyrics. After 2 days of struggle he realized he not only had the title but the general idea for the song. It contains some of the most ingenious of Gershwin rhymes. Incidentally, the scat singing interjections between stanzas were the contribution of George Gershwin.

"IT DON'T MEAN A THING (IF IT AIN'T GOT THAT SWING)" Song, music by Duke Ellington (q.v.) and words by publisher-songwriter Irving Mills. Recorded on Feb. 2, 1932, with a vocal by Ivy Anderson (1904–1949), it is claimed to be the first song that used the term "swing." This was 2 years before the debut of Benny Goodman's "swing" band. Exactly who coined the term originally is not known; undoubtedly it originated among black musicians in Harlem in the late 1920s or early '30s.

JAMES, DOROTHY (b. 1901) Composer, teacher. Born in Chicago, Ill., Dec. 1, 1901, James studied composition under Adolf Weidig at the Chicago Musical College under 2 scholarships. She also studied with Louis Gruenberg (q.v.), Ernst Krenek, and Eric De Lamarter. At the American Conservatory, Chicago, she also studied piano and theory. Upon graduation from the Conservatory, James joined the music faculty of Eastern Michigan University, Ypsilanti, in 1927 and remained there teaching theory until her retirement in 1968. Her works include *Four Preludes from the Chinese* for contralto and string quartet (1924), incidental music for *As You Like It* (1927), *Rhapsody* for violin, cello, and piano (1930), *Symphonic Fragments* for orchestra (1931), *Paolo and Francesca*, opera in 3 acts (1932), *String Quartet in One Movement* (1932), *Christmas Night* for mixed chorus, a cappella (1933), *The Jumblies* for youth chorus and orchestra (1934), *Elegy for the Lately Dead* for orchestra (1938), *Three Pastorales* for clarinet, harp, and strings (1938), *Paul Bunyan* for baritone, young people's chorus, and orchestra (1938), *Suite* for small orchestra (1940), *Niobe* for women's chorus, flute, strings, piano, and orchestra (1941), *Recitative* for viola, 2 violins, and 2 cellos (1943), *The Golden Year* for chorus and orchestra (1953), *Tone*

historic "From Spirituals to Swing" Concert, held at Carnegie Hall, Dec. 23, 1938. It was probably at this event that Johnson met 2 Chicagoans, Albert Ammons (q.v.) and Meade Lux Lewis (q.v.), with whom he would eventually join as a member of what came to be called the Boogie Woogie Trio. Although a master of the boogie-woogie piano style, Johnson was less bluesy than Ammons, and played in a somewhat more sophisticated jazz style, which might be attributed to his Kansas City beginnings. The Boogie Woogie Trio, however, presented a formidable array of powerhouse pianistics and recorded as a group and solo, besides appearing in concert, at New York's famous Cafe Society Downtown and Chicago's Sherman Hotel. Although boogie-woogie was primarily improvisation Johnson has been credited with several original compositions: *Roll 'Em, Pete, Cherry Red, Pine Creek, Basement Boogie, Death Ray Boogie, G Flat Blues, Pete's Blues,* and *Mama's Blues.* Although the boogie-woogie phase ended by the mid 1940s, Johnson remained active in clubs into the '50s. He toured with the "Jazz at the Philharmonic" concerts, with Joe Turner, in 1958. A heart attack late that same year ended his concert career. Johnson died in Buffalo, N.Y., Mar. 23, 1967.

JONES, CHARLES (b. 1910) Composer, teacher. Born in Tamworth, Ontario, Canada, June 21, 1910, Jones moved to New York City in 1928 and entered the Institute of Musical Art, from which he was graduated in 1932. He continued studying composition with Bernard Wagenaar at the Juilliard School (1935–39). He also worked under Aaron Copland (q.v.) at the Berkshire School, Mass. He taught at Mills College, Oakland, Calif., (1939–44) at Bryanston Summer Music School, England, and from 1951 at the Aspen Summer Music School, Aspen, Colo. Jones was a lecturer on American music in Germany and directed the music sessions at the Salzburg Seminar in American Studies (1950). His compositions include *String Quartet No. 1* (1936), *Suite for Strings* (1937), *Suite for Small Orchestra* (1937), *Symphony No. 1* (1939), *Galup* for orchestra (1940), *Cowboy Song* for oboe, percussion, and strings (1941), *Overture* for orchestra (1942), *Sonatina for Violin and Piano* (1942), *Down with Drink* for women's voices, piano, and percussion (1943), *String Quartet No. 2* (1944), *Five Melodies* for orchestra (1945), *Suite for Violin and Piano* (1946), *Piano Sonata No. 1* (1946), *Cassation* for orchestra (1948), *Piano Sonata No. 2* (1950), *String Quartet No. 3* (1951), *Sonata a Tre* for pianos (1952), *String Quartet No. 4* (1954), *Symphony No. 2* (1957), *Violin Sonata* (1958), *The Seasons,* cantata for soprano, baritone, and chamber group (1959), *Ballade* for piano (1961), *String Quartet No. 5* (1961), *Symphony No. 3* (1962), *Concerto for Four Violins and Orchestra* (1963), *Piers the Plowman* for tenor, chorus, and orchestra (1963), *Symphony No. 4* (1965), *I am a Mynstral,* cantata (1967), *Masque* for speaker, based on a text by Pope (1968), *Anima* for soprano, piano, and viola (1968), and *Symphony No. 6* (1969).

KAY, HERSHY (b. 1919) Composer, arranger. Born in Philadelphia, Pa., Nov. 17, 1919, Kay studied at the Curtis Institute of Music on a scholarship (1936–40). He came to New York City and soon became known as a fine orchestrator of Broadway shows, one of the first being Leonard Bernstein's (q.v.) *On the Town* (1944). Kay orchestrated others, including Bernstein's *Candide* (1956), Blitzstein's *Juno* (1958), and

Jerry Herman's *Milk and Honey* (1961); also several film scores, among them *Man with a Gun* (1955) and *Drat! The Cat!,* and television background scores. Kay is best known for his ballet scores based on musical themes written by others: *Cakewalk* (Gottschalk, 1951), *Western Symphony* (cowboy songs, 1954), *Concert* (Chopin, 1956), and *Stars and Stripes* (Sousa, 1957). Kay reconstructed and orchestrated Gottschalk's *Grand Tarantelle* (1957) for pianist Eugene List.

KAY, ULYSSES (b. 1917) Composer, teacher. Born in Tucson, Ariz., Jan. 7, 1917, Kay was related to the great jazz trumpeter Joe "King" Oliver (q.v.), who suggested that the youngster take up the piano. Later Kay studied at the University of Arizona, Tucson, then went on to do further work at the Eastman School of Music, Rochester, N.Y., where he studied composition with Howard Hanson (q.v.) and orchestration with Bernard Rogers (q.v.). He also studied with Paul Hindemith at the Berkshire Music Center, Tanglewood, Mass. From 1942 to 1945 Kay served in the U. S. Navy. After the war he won 2 awards, the Fulbright Fellowship and the Prix de Rome, which enabled him to live in Italy for several years (1949–52) to concentrate on composition. Upon his return to the United States, Kay became associated with Broadcast Music, Inc. (BMI) as consultant and, later, began teaching: Boston University (1965), University of California, Los Angeles, and (since 1968) at Lehman College of the City University of New York. Kay's works include a *Sinfonietta* for orchestra (1939), *Piano Sonata* (1940), *Five Mosaics* for chamber orchestra (1940), *Oboe Concerto* (1940), *Danse Calinda,* ballet (1941), *Four Pieces for Male Chorus* (1941), *Flute Quintet* for flute and string quartet (1942), *Suite in B* for oboe and piano (1942), *Suite for Brass*

Choir (1942), *As Joseph Was A-Walking* for chorus (1943), *Of New Horizons* for orchestra (1944), *Evocation* for band (1944), *A Short Overture* (1946), *Four Inventions* for piano (1946), *Suite for Strings* (1947), score for the film *The Quiet One* (1948), *Concerto* for orchestra (1948), *Sinfonia in E* (1951), *Three Pieces after Blake* for soprano and orchestra (1952), *Serenade for Orchestra* (1954), *Six Dances* for string orchestra (1954), *Song of Jeremiah,* cantata (1954), *The Boor,* opera based on a Chekov story (1955), *The Juggler of Our Lady,* one-act opera (1956), *Triptich* for chorus and strings (1962), *Fantasy Variations* for orchestra (1963), *Umbrian Scene* for orchestra (1964), *Emily Dickinson Set* for women's chorus and piano (1964), *Markings* for orchestra, dedicated to Dag Hammarskjöld (1966), *Stephen Crane Set* for chorus and chamber orchestra (1967), *Symphony in E* (1967), *Theater Set* for orchestra (1968), *The Capitolane Venus,* one-act opera (1970), *Scherzi musicali* for chamber orchestra (1971), *Quintet Concerto* for solo brass and orchestra (1976), and *Jubilee,* opera (1976).

KELLER, HOMER (b. 1915) Composer, teacher. Born in Oxnard, Calif., Feb. 17, 1915, Keller received his major musical training at the Eastman School, Rochester, N.Y. (1934–38), where he studied with Howard Hanson (q.v.) and Bernard Rogers (q.v.). Upon graduation Keller joined the teaching staff of Fort Hays Kansas State College (1938–41) after which he taught at Indiana University, Bloomington. From 1942 until 1946 he served with the U. S. Army Air Forces as band director in the South Pacific. He was music instructor at the Philippine Institute. Upon his return to the United States, Keller joined the staff of the Eastman School. In 1958 he moved to the University of Oregon, Eugene, where he was professor of composition and the director of the University Electronic Studio. Since 1977 he has been professor emeritus at the School of Music. His works include *String Quartet in One Movement* (1935), *Sonatina* for piano (1937), *String Quartet No. 2* (1937), *Serenade for Clarinet and Strings* (1937), *Symphony No. 1* (1939), *Chamber Symphony* (1941), *Sonata* for bassoon and piano (1941), *The Raider* for men's chorus and brass (1943), *Piano Sonata No. 2* (1946), *Symphony No. 2* (1948), *Piano Concerto* (1949), *Symphony No. 3* (1954), *Duo for Violin and Harpsichord* (1961), *Two Studies* for trumpet and piano (1963), *Three Constructs* for piano (1963), *Declaration* for violin, cello, and piano (1966), *Interplay* for flute, horn, and percussion (1969), *Sonorities for Orchestra* (1970), *Anthem: For Behold, I Create New Heavens and a New Earth* for chorus and organ (1971), *Piano Sonata* (1972), *Salutation of the Dawn* for chorus, a cappella (1974), and *Sonata for Cello and Piano* (1977).

KENNAN, KENT (b. 1913) Composer, teacher. Born in Milwaukee, Wis., Apr. 18, 1913, Kennan studied composition with Hunter Johnson (q.v.) at the University of Michigan, Ann Arbor (1930–32), then switched to the Eastman School, Rochester, N.Y., where he studied with Howard Hanson (q.v.) and Bernard Rogers (q.v.), composition and orchestration respectively. In 1936 he was awarded a Prix de Rome and moved to Europe for 3 years; while there he studied for a short time with Ildebrando Pizzetti. He returned to the United States and joined the music faculty of Kent State, Ohio; he also taught at the University of Texas (since 1964 he has served as chairman of the Music Department), Ohio State University, Columbus, and held summer courses at the Eastman School in 1954 and 1956. From 1942 to 1945 Kennan served in the U. S. Army

Air Forces. His works include a *Quintet for Piano and Strings* (1936), *Night Soliloquy* for flute and orchestra (1936), *Il Campo dei Fiori* for trumpet and orchestra (1937), *Nocturne* for viola and orchestra (1937), *Dance Divertimento* for orchestra (1938), *Symphony* (1938), *Promenade* for orchestra (1938), *Three Piano Preludes* (1938), *Andante* for oboe and orchestra (1939), *Blessed Are They That Mourn* for chorus and orchestra (1939), *Piano Sonata* (1942), *Concertino* for piano and orchestra (1942), *The Unknown Warrior Speaks* (1944), *Sonatina* for piano (1946), *Two Preludes* for piano (1951), *Theme with Variations* for organ (1952), and *Sonata* for trumpet and piano (1956). Kennan is the author of *Orchestration Workbook* (1952), *The Technique of Orchestration* (1952), and *Counterpoint* (1959). There are also a *Sea Sonata* for violin and piano and songs: "I Shall Not Care," "I Saw the White Daisies," and "A Clear Midnight."

KENTON, STAN (1912–1979) Pianist, bandleader, composer-arranger. Born in Wichita, Kans., Feb. 19, 1912, Kenton grew up in Los Angeles and studied with Charles Dalmorès there. After graduating from Bell High School, Kenton began as a pianist playing in local clubs. During the early 1930s he joined the band of Everett Hoagland, then moved over to Gus Arnheim (1936–38); later he joined Vido Musso. Ca. 1939 Kenton quit band work to study music theory, which awakened an interest in composing and arranging. In 1941 Kenton formed his own band and, using his own arrangements, made his debut as bandleader-arranger at Balboa Beach, Calif. The band was very successful in California, but when it opened at the Roseland Ballroom, New York City, in 1942, it was criticized for loudness and for playing undanceable music by the patrons and savaged by the "jazz"

396

critics. Kenton's arrangements were characterized by a heavy driving beat, staccato saxophone punctuations, and "walls of brass." Kenton called it "progressive jazz" and his critics called it noise. Slowly Kenton built a following among the young, who found the band's driving, screaming style exciting. Late in 1943 the Kenton Band made recordings, "Artistry in Rhythm" (the band's theme)/"Eager Beaver," which became a best-selling record and truly established Kenton. In 1944 he began featuring vocalists, beginning with Anita O'Day (who made a hit recording with Kenton, "And Her Tears Flowed Like Wine"), followed by June Christy and Chris Conner. Kenton, who also played the piano in the band, began sharing his arranger assignments with Pete Rugolo and others. During the final years of World War II the Kenton Band was very popular, especially on the college circuit. Illness, however, in 1947 forced Kenton to give up music for a time. After toying with the idea of taking up psychiatry, Kenton returned to the band business in 1950 and from then until his death remained active in music. He formed bands virtually annually for tours and concerts. He founded the Stan Kenton Clinic, which offered summer courses in music; in 1965 he was one of the founders of the Los Angeles Neophonic Orchestra, whose function was to perform the jazz-infused concert works that Kenton favored—such as City of Glass by Robert Graettinger. The Neophonic Orchestra was abandoned in 1968. In 1970 Kenton formed his own recording company (Capitol Records had let most of his recordings of the 1940s and '50s go out of print), Creative World Records. Kenton's was a controversial, experimental band, noted for some important jazz musicians: Kai Winding (trombone), Eddie Safranski (bass), Maynard Ferguson (trumpet), Shorty Rogers (trumpet), and Shelly Manne (drums),

among others. Kenton was the composer of such pieces as Artistry in Rhythm, Eager Beaver, Painted Rhythm, Concerto for Doghouse, Concerto to End All Concertos, and Artistry Jumps. In 1977 Kenton suffered a skull fracture from which he never fully recovered; he died following a stroke in Hollywood, Aug. 25, 1979.

KERR, HARRISON (b. 1897) Composer, teacher, author. Born in Cleveland, Ohio, Oct. 13, 1897, Kerr began in music with piano lessons with James Hotchkiss Rogers. In 1921 he was among the first American students to study composition with Nadia Boulanger in France; he also studied piano with Isidor Philipp. Upon returning to the United States, Kerr began teaching, and he was also editor of Trend, a bimonthly magazine devoted to the arts. He taught at Greenbriar College, Lewisburg, W.Va., the Chase School, Brooklyn, and, beginning in 1949, the University of Oklahoma, Norman, where he eventually became dean of the College of Fine Arts, and professor emeritus of music. He was active, mostly during the 1940s, with the American Composers Alliance and its allied American Music Center. His early works were written in a more or less conventional style; in his later compositions Kerr has adapted the 12-tone technique. His works include Three Songs with Chamber Orchestra (1928), Six Songs to Poems by Adelaide Crapsey (1928), Sonata No. 1 for Piano (1929), Symphony No. 1 (1929), Notations on a Sensitized Plate for voice, string quartet, clarinet, and piano (1935), Contrapuntal Suite for orchestra (1936), Trio for clarinet, cello, and piano (1936), Symphony No. 2 (1937), Wink of Eternity for chorus and orchestra (1937), String Quartet (1937), Dance Suite for orchestra (1938), Trio for violin, cello, and piano (1938), Dance Sonata for 2 pianos and percussion, or large orchestra, ballet (1938), *Suite for Flute and Piano* (1941), *Sonata No. 2 for Piano* (1943), *Symphony No. 3* (1945), *Overture, Arioso and Finale* for cello and orchestra (1944–51), *Violin Concerto* (1951), *Sonata for Violin and Piano* (1955), *The Tower of Kel,* opera (1960), and *Sinfonietta da Camera* (1968).

"KISS ME, KATE" Musical comedy, with songs by Cole Porter (q.v.) and book by Bella and Sam Spewack, with a little help from Shakespeare. The plot of *Kiss Me, Kate* revolves around an acting company preparing a production of *The Taming of the Shrew.* The principals, once man and wife, squabble offstage in real life as they do onstage as "Kate" and "Petruchio." There is a secondary romance between 2 other cast members, one of whom is a compulsive gambler (thus introducing further characters with comic possibilities—bill-collecting gangsters). The literate book provided Porter with excellent song cues and *Kiss Me, Kate* turned out to be his most successful musical. It inspired such songs as "Why Can't You Behave?" "Wunderbar," "I Hate Men," "Were Thine That Special Face," "So in Love," "Brush Up Your Shakespeare," "Too Darn Hot," "I'm Ashamed That Women Are So Simple," and "Always True to You (in My Fashion)." *Kiss Me, Kate* opened at the New Century Theatre, New York City, Dec. 30, 1948, and ran for 1,077 performances. It opened in London in March 1951; the run was a less spectacular 501. Since, there have been touring companies and revivals. A film version was released by MGM in 1953. In the original production Alfred Drake appeared as "Fred Graham," the co-star, producer, and director of *The Taming of the Shrew* (portions of which Porter set to words and music); Patricia Morison appeared as "Lili Vanessi," Graham's ex-wife and co-star; Lisa Kirk was "Lois

Lane" and Harold Lang the dancer-gambler "Bill Calhoun."

KIRCHNER, LEON (b. 1919) Composer, teacher, pianist. Born in Brooklyn, N.Y., Jan. 24, 1919, Kirchner began taking piano lessons at an early age. When he was 9 the family moved to Los Angeles, where Kirchner continued his piano study with Richard Buhlig; by the time he was 14 he was presenting piano recitals in public. Around 1938 he began to study music at the University of California, Berkeley, with Edward Strickland and Albert Elkus (theory) and with Ernest Bloch (composition). In 1942 Kirchner came to New York, where he studied with Roger Sessions (q.v.). From 1943 until 1946 he was in the U. S. Army. Almost immediately after leaving the Army, Kirchner joined the faculty of the San Francisco Conservatory; he has also taught at the University of California, Berkeley, the University of Southern California, L.A., Mills College, Oakland, Calif., and, since 1961, Harvard University. Kirchner has been the recipient of 2 Guggenheim Fellowships, a Pulitzer Award, and 2 New York Music Critics Awards. As a conductor Kirchner has led the Boston Symphony, the San Francisco Symphony, the New York Philharmonic, and the Boston Philharmonic. Kirchner's original work is contemporary in the sense that he utilizes "modern" musical language and, although it has been suggested that his compositions disclose a close affinity with his teacher Sessions and with Schoenberg, he does not fall back on the 12-tone system. The "sound" of his work is of today but the roots are nourished from the past, as expressed by an interesting musical intellect. Kirchner's works include *Duo* for violin and piano (1947), *Piano Sonata* (1948), *String Quartet No. 1* (1948), *Little Suite* (1949), *Of Obedience and the Runner* for soprano and piano (1950), *Sinfonia*

(1952), *Piano Concerto No. 1* (1953), *Piano Trio* (1953), *Toccata* for strings, winds, and percussion (1956), *String Quartet No. 2* (1958), *Concerto* for violin, cello, winds, and percussion (1960), *Piano Concerto No. 2* (1963), *Quartet No. 3 for Strings and Electronic Tape* (1966; Pulitzer Prize, 1967), *Music for Orchestra* (1969), *Lily*, for soprano and chamber orchestra, operatic segment based on *Henderson, the Rain King* by Saul Bellow (1973); the expanded opera was presented in New York City in 1977.

KLEINSINGER, GEORGE (b. 1914) Composer, pianist. Born in San Bernardino, Calif., Feb. 13, 1914, Kleinsinger came to New York City at an early age and had begun to prepare for a career in dentistry then switched to music. He studied at New York University with Philip James (q.v.) and at the Juilliard School of Music, New York, with Frederick Jacobi (q.v.) and Bernard Wagenaar (q.v.). He did further work with Marion Bauer (q.v.) and Charles Haubiel (q.v.). During the Depression, Kleinsinger worked in Civilian Conservation Corps camps and during World War II was music supervisor of Army bands of the 2nd Service Command. He is best known for his little work for children, *Tubby the Tuba* (1943). His other works include *Life in the Day of a Secretary*, one-act opera (1939), *String Quartet* (1940), *I Hear America Singing* for baritone, chorus, and orchestra (1940), *Victory Against Heaven* for 8 vocalists, 2 pianos (1941), *Farewell to a Hero* for baritone, chorus, and orchestra (1941), *Song for Pioneers* for chorus and piano (1941), *A Western Rhapsody* for orchestra (1942), *Brooklyn Baseball Cantata* (1942), *Jack and Homer the Horse* for narrator and chamber orchestra (1942), *Scherzo* for orchestra (1944), *Overture on American Folk Themes* (1945), *Fantasy* for violin and orchestra (1945), *Pee Wee the Piccolo* for narrator and chamber orchestra (1945), *Symphony No. 1* (1946), *Concerto for Cello and Orchestra* (1946), *Street Corner Concerto* for harmonica and orchestra (1947), *Violin Concerto* (1953), *Shinbone Alley*, chamber opera based on Don Marquis' *archy and mehitabel* (1954).

"KNOXVILLE: SUMMER OF 1915" Composition for soprano and orchestra by Samuel Barber (q.v.). The work was commissioned by opera star and recitalist Eleanor Steber (b. 1916) for performance by the Boston Symphony to be conducted by Serge Koussevitzky. The original concept was for a "concerto for voice and orchestra," i.e., a 3-movement work. This scheme was abandoned when Barber eventually chose a poem by author–film critic James Agee (1909–1955), "Knoxville: Summer of 1915," an evocative recollection of boyhood, of family, of an America in a simpler time than 1948, when Barber set the poem to beautifully apposite music. The first performance was sung in Boston by Steber, with Koussevitzky conducting the Boston Symphony, Apr. 9, 1948. Agee, incidentally, used the poem as the prologue to his Pulitzer Prize novel, *A Death in the Family. Knoxville: Summer of 1915* has proved to be one of Barber's most enduring works; a recording by Steber, accompanied by the Dumbarton Oaks Chamber Orchestra under William Strickland, is one of the classic recordings of American music. Steber, incidentally, sang the title role in the Metropolitan Opera's production of Barber's *Vanessa* (1958).

KOEHLER, TED (1894–1973) Song lyricist. Born in Washington, D.C., July 14, 1894, Koehler grew up in Newark, N.J., and New York City. He took piano as a youngster but seemed destined to a career in his father's photo engraving shop in New York. During the day,

Koehler worked in the shop and at night played piano in Newark hot spots. When ordered to be in bed by midnight, or go, Koehler went. He found work as a pianist in movie houses (it was still the silent film era) in New York and as far west as Chicago. He worked for music publishers as a "plugger," accompanied vaudeville performers and even wrote their "act" material as well as special songs. He was working for a New York publisher when in 1929 he was introduced by Harry Warren (q.v.), a songwriter-plugger himself, to a young singer-pianist, Harold Arlen (q.v.), who had just improvised a song based on the standard pickup musical signal the rehearsal pianist uses to alert the dancers that the routine is about to begin. Koehler provided the former pickup with a lyric and a title: "Get Happy." The song was used in an unsuccessful production, *9:15 Revue* (1930). This led to a long, fruitful collaboration with Arlen, resulting in such songs as "Between the Devil and the Deep Blue Sea" (1931), "I Gotta Right to Sing the Blues" (1932), "I've Got the World on a String" (1932), "Stormy Weather" (1933), "Let's Fall in Love" (1934), "Ill Wind" (1934), "Sing My Heart" (1938), and *Americanegro Suite* for soloists, chorus, and piano. While Arlen worked with other collaborators, Koehler remained in Hollywood (where he lived from the mid 1930s) writing lyrics for Shirley Temple songs: "Animal Crackers in My Soup" (from *Curly Top*, 1935, with collaborators Ray Henderson and Irving Caesar) and songs for the film *Dimples* (1936, with Jimmy McHugh). Also with McHugh, Koehler collaborated on songs for the film *King of Burlesque* (1935), from which came the song "I'm Shooting High." In 1939 Koehler wrote a nonproduction song with Rube Bloom, "Don't Worry 'Bout Me." His last work with Arlen was done for a Danny Kaye film, *Up in Arms*

(1944), which produced 2 fine songs, "Tess's Torch Song," and "Now I Know." Although Koehler worked with several fine songwriters—McHugh, Harry Warren, Jay Gorney—he never repeated the success he had had with Arlen. He contributed lyrics (to the music of M. K. Jerome) to the film score of *My Wild Irish Rose* (1947), his final sizable effort, and then lived in near retirement, painting and puttering around the house. Koehler suffered a stroke in the 1960s, then almost miraculously recovered. This was but a temporary remission; he died in Santa Monica, Calif., Jan. 17, 1973.

KOHS, ELLIS (b. 1916) Composer, teacher. Born in Chicago, Ill., May 12, 1916, Kohs studied composition with Carl Bricken (University of Chicago, 1933–38), with Bernard Wagenaar (q.v.) at the Juilliard School, New York City (1938–39), and with Walter Piston (q.v.) at Harvard (1939–41). From 1941 to 1946 Kohs served in the U. S. Army (in 1943 he was made bandleader). Upon being discharged, Kohs began teaching at Wesleyan University, Middletown, Conn. (1946–48), Conservatory of Kansas City (1948–50), and in 1950 became chairman of the Theory Department, University of Southern California, L.A. His works include a *String Quartet* (1941), *Concerto for Orchestra* (1941), *Life with Uncle* (*Sam*) (1943), *The Automatic Pistol* for men's voices (1943), *Night Watch* for flute, horn, and timpani (1944), *Concerto for Piano and Orchestra* (1945), *Sonatina* for bassoon and piano (1945), *Passacaglia* for organ and strings (1946), *25th Psalm* (1947), *Cello Concerto* (1947), *Variations on "L'Homme Arme"* for piano (1947), *Capriccio* for organ (1948), *String Quartet No. 2* (1948), *Chamber Concerto* for viola and string nonet (1949), *Symphony No. 1* (1950), *Fatal Interview, 5* songs to words by Edna St. Vincent Millay for voice and piano (1951), *Clar-*

inet Sonata (1951), Three Chorale Variations on Hebrew Hymns for organ (1952), Lord of the Ascendent for dancers, soloists, chorus, and orchestra (1955), Symphony No. 2 (1956), 23rd Psalm for soloists and chorus (1957), Studies in Variations for various instrumental combinations (1963), Sonata for snare drum and piano (1966), and the opera Amerika, after Kafka (1969). Kohs is the author of Musical Theory, a Syllabus for Teacher and Student (1961) and Musical Form: Studies in Analysis and Synthesis (1976).

KOUTZEN, BORIS (1901–1966) Composer, violinist, teacher. Born in Uman, Russia, Apr. 1, 1901, Koutzen started in music as a violin student of his father; he later studied the violin with Leo Zetlin. At 17 he played in the violin section of the State Opera House and later in the Moscow Symphony. Around this time he was also a student of composition under Reinhold Glière at the Moscow Conservatory. Koutzen came to the United States in 1923, joined the Philadelphia Orchestra and later the NBC Symphony. Koutzen taught at the Philadelphia Conservatory and at Vassar College, Poughkeepsie, N.Y. (1944–66). His works include String Quartet No. 1 (1922), Solitude, "poem-nocturne" for orchestra (1927), Sonata for Piano and Violin (1928), Symphonic Movement for violin and orchestra (1929), Sonatina for piano (1931), Valley Forge for orchestra (1931), Trio for Flute, Cello and Harp (1933), Concerto for Five Solo Instruments and Strings (1934), String Quartet No. 2 (1936), Symphony (1937), Music for Saxophone, Bassoon and Cello (1940), Concert Piece for cello and string quartet (1940), Duo Concertante for violin and piano (1943), From the American Folklore for orchestra (1943), String Quartet No. 3 (1944), Sonatina for 2 pianos

(1944), Violin Concerto (1946), Piano Trio (1948), Morning Music for flute and strings (1950), Eidolons for piano (1953), The Fatal Oath, one-act opera (1954), Divertimento for orchestra (1956), Rhapsody for band (1959), Concertino for piano and strings (1959), Fanfare, Prayer and March for orchestra (1961), Elegiac Rhapsody for orchestra (1961), You Never Know, one-act opera (1962), Poem for violin and string quartet (1963), Pastorale and Dance for violin and piano (1964), and Music for Violin Alone (1966). Koutzen died in Pleasantville, N.Y., Dec. 10, 1966.

KREUTZ, ARTHUR (b. 1906) Composer, violinist, teacher. Born in La Cross, Wis., July 25, 1906, Kreutz began his music studies at the University of Wisconsin, Madison, and finished at Columbia University, New York City. He also studied violin at the Royal Conservatory, Ghent, Belgium, where he won the Premier Prix. Among his teachers were Roy Harris (q.v.) and Cecil Burleigh (q.v.). Kreutz joined the faculty of Teachers College, Columbia University, in 1938; he moved to the University of Texas, Austin, in 1942 and, since 1952, has been with the Music Department, University of Mississippi. His works include Music for Symphony Orchestra (1940), Paul Bunyan for orchestra (1940), American Dances for chamber orchestra (1941), Violin Concerto (1942), Land Be Bright, ballet for chamber orchestra (1942), Salvage, score for film released by the Office of War Information (1942), Three Shakespearian Love Lyrics for soprano and chamber group (1943), Triumphal Overture for orchestra (1944), Four Poems, text by Robert Burns, for soprano and chamber group (1944), Symphonic Blues (1945), Symphony No. 1 (1945), Concertino for oboe, French horn, and strings (1946), Symphony No.

2 (1946), *Mosquito Serenade* for orchestra (1948), *New England Folksing* for chorus and orchestra (1948), *Incidental Music for Hamlet* (the famous "G.I. *Hamlet*," starring Robert Breen and presented at Elsinore, Denmark, *Hamlet*'s original setting, with the cooperation of the U. S. Department of State and the U. S. Army Air Forces; Kreutz also conducted, 1949), *Acres of Sky,* a ballad opera (1951), *The University Greys,* opera (1954), *Sourwood Mountain,* a folk musical (1959), also *Quartet Venuti* for string quartet, *Dixieland Concerto* for orchestra, and *Jazzonata.*

KUBIK, GAIL (b. 1914) Composer, violinist, conductor, teacher. Born in South Coffeyville, Okla., Sept. 5, 1914, Kubik started his study of music with his mother, a respected vocalist. He studied later (at the age of 14 on a scholarship) at the Eastman School, Rochester, N.Y., with Bernard Rogers (q.v.), Edward Royce (composition), Irvine McHose (theory), and violin with Samuel Belov. At the American Conservatory, Chicago, Kubik continued in composition with Leo Sowerby (q.v.) and at Harvard University with Walter Piston (q.v.) and Nadia Boulanger (1937–38; q.v.). Kubik then began to teach at Monmouth College and at Teachers College, Columbia University, while serving as staff composer and musical adviser to NBC in New York. From 1943 until 1946 Kubik served in the U. S. Army, for which he composed and conducted background scores for several films, including the award-winning *Memphis Belle* (1943), a filmed record of the final combat flight of a bomber of that name and its crew. After the war Kubik continued composing and teaching as well as lecturing in Europe, under a Prix de Rome, and the auspices of the United Nations (UNESCO). In 1970 Kubik was appointed composer-in-residence, Scripps College, Claremont, Calif. His composi-

tions include *Two Sketches* for string quartet (1932), *Trio* for violin, cello, and piano (1934), *Trivialities* for string quartet, flute, and horn (1934), *Variations on a 13th Century Troubadour Song* for orchestra (1935), *In Praise of Johnny Appleseed* for baritone, chorus, and orchestra (1937), *Daniel Drew* for soprano, alto, tenor, and bass with cello and string bass accompaniment (1938), *Men and Ships,* U. S. Maritime film (1940), *Scherzo* for orchestra (1940), *Puck,* for speaker, string quartet, woodwind quartet, horn, and trumpet (1940), *Violin Concerto* (1940), *Stewball* for band (1941), *Sonatina* for piano (1941), *Dance Suite* for piano (1941), *Sonatina* for violin and piano (1942), *Gavotte* for strings (1942), *The World at War,* score for Office of War Information (1942), *A Wartime Litany* for men's chorus, brass, and percussion (1943), *The Erie Canal* for orchestra (1944), *Three American Folk Songs* for chamber orchestra (1945), *Thunderbolt,* score for U. S. Army Air Forces film (1945), *Toccata* for organ and strings (1946), *Overture* for band (1946), *Frankie and Johnnie,* ballet with vocalist and dance band (1946), *A Mirror for the Sky,* folk opera (1946), *Piano Sonata* (1947), *Soliloquy and Dance* for violin and piano (1948), *Symphony No. 1* (1949), *Symphony* for 2 pianos (1949), film score for *Gerald McBoing-Boing* (1950), *Symphony Concertante* for piano, viola, trumpet, and orchestra (Pulitzer Prize, 1952), *Symphony No. 2* (1955), *Symphony No. 3* (1956), *Sonatina* for clarinet and piano (1959), *Divertimento No. 1* for chamber orchestra (1959), *Divertimento No. 2* (1960), *Scenes* for orchestra (1962), *Intermezzo: Music for Cleveland* for piano (1967), *A Christmas Set* for small chorus, chamber orchestra (1968), *Prayer and Toccata* for organ and chamber orchestra (1969), *A Record of Our Time* for narrator, chorus, singer, and orches-

tra (1970), and *A New Texas Gri-
morium,* for chorus and orchestra
(1976).

"LADY IN THE DARK" Musical
with a book by Moss Hart (1904–1961)
and score by Ira Gershwin (lyrics) and
Kurt Weill (music). Hart, after having
undergone psychoanalysis, decided to
write a play on the subject for Katharine
Cornell. As the work progressed Hart realized it was evolving into a play with
music. He then approached Ira Gershwin (q.v.), who had not written a full
score since the death of his brother
George in 1937. German expatriate Kurt
Weill (q.v.) was asked to do the music.
Hart's plot tells the story of a headstrong
but insecure editor of a fashion magazine, "Liza Elliott" (who was portrayed
by English actress–musical comedy star,
Gertrude Lawrence, b. 1898, d. 1952).
She is having an unsatisfactory affair
with the magazine's publisher, "Kendall
Nesbitt," who is not quite prepared to
leave his wife. She is also attracted to a
film actor, "Randy Curtis," and feuds
with her advertising manager, "Charley
Johnson." To resolve her problems she
goes into analysis; it is during these sessions that the music carries the plot,
revealing Liza's dreams, doubts, and
hopes. One song, "My Ship," weaves
leitmotiv-like through *Lady in the Dark,*
and Liza associates it with her unhappy
childhood. The major dream sequences
portray Liza seeing herself as a very
glamorous woman, then at her wedding,
and finally at a mad circus. The score
contains such songs as "This Is New,"
the ballad-like (i.e., storytelling) "The
Princess of Pure Delight," the famous
"The Saga of Jenny," who, unlike Liza,
continually "makes up her mind," to the
distress or destruction of all around her,
and the tongue-twisting Ira Gershwin
tour-de-force "Tschaikowsky." A notable
aspect of *Lady in the Dark* was the fact
that composer Weill, unlike most Broadway composers, provided his own orchestrations for the musical sequences.
Hart's book was sophisticated, literate,
and intelligent and, though *Oklahoma!* is
generally credited with being the first
fully "integrated" musical, it was produced about 2 years after *Lady in the
Dark.* The musical opened at the Alvin
Theatre, Jan. 23, 1941, and ran for 467
performances. It starred Gertrude Lawrence as "Liza," Bert Lytell as "Kendall Nesbitt," the publisher, and Macdonald Carey as "Charley," whom Liza
eventually chooses to the strains of "My
Ship." In the cast too were Victor Mature, typecast as the movie star "Randy
Curtis," and Danny Kaye, making a
great Broadway debut as a rather hyster-
ical photographer. A less successful film
version of *Lady in the Dark,* starring
Ginger Rogers, was released by Paramount in 1944.

LANE, BURTON (b. 1912) Composer, pianist. Born in New York City,
Feb. 2, 1912, Lane took early piano lessons, but after 3 lessons his parents decided he should not combine music lessons with kindergarten. At 11 Lane was
back at the keyboard, with a remarkable
aptitude that consumed teachers and
textbooks; it was even suggested that he
be sent to Europe to study music
seriously. His father, a practical real estate man, could not visualize a career in
music, so his son continued to struggle
through the New York High School of
Commerce and, later, the Dwight Academy. He was 14 when, after being overheard playing the piano by one of the
Shuberts' scouts, he was brought before
J. J. Shubert to demonstrate his own
songs. Shubert actually assigned him the
job of writing songs for a Shubert show
then in preparation. The show did not
come off because of the illness of the
star, but Lane gained much practice in
songwriting. Discouraged, he took a job
with the publishing house of Remick's,
where he accumulated more experience

and formed a friendship with his hero, George Gershwin (q.v.), who greatly encouraged him. At Remick's, Lane met another songwriter, lyricist Howard Dietz (q.v.), who happened to be working on a new revue, *Three's a Crowd* (most songs had music by Arthur Schwartz, q.v.). When the show opened in October 1930, its score contained 2 songs with music by Lane, "Forget All Your Books" and "Out in the Open Air." The next year he composed for 2 revues, the *Third Little Show* and *Earl Carroll's Vanities*, with a new lyricist, Harold Adamson (b. 1906). With the onset of the Depression, Lane found little work besides that as an arranger or accompanist, except for a couple of songs written with Adamson in 1933. Then came the call from Hollywood; something he and Adamson had done had impressed someone at MGM and they were sent for. Their first assignment was a Joan Crawford film, *Dancing Lady* (1933), which is now best remembered for the song "Everything I Have Is Yours" and the film debut of Fred Astaire (q.v.). Lane, it might be noted, was all of 21 at this time. He remained a resident of the Beverly Hills area for some 2 decades, writing individual songs for films, full scores, with an occasional excursion to New York to do a musical. Some of his songs from films include "Your Head on My Shoulder" (lyrics by Adamson, from *Kid Millions,* 1934), "You Took the Words Right Out of My Heart" (lyrics by Adamson, from *Follies Bergere,* 1935), "The Lady's in Love with You" (lyrics by Loesser, from *Some Like It Hot,* 1939), "How About You?" (lyrics by Freed, from *Babes on Broadway,* 1941), "Poor You" (lyrics by E. Y. Harburg, q.v., from *Ship Ahoy,* 1942), "Too Late Now" and "I Left My Hat in Haiti" (lyrics by Alan Jay Lerner, q.v., from *Royal Wedding,* 1951), "In Our United State," "Applause, Applause," "Dream World," and

"It Happens Every Time" (lyrics by Ira Gershwin, q.v., from *Give a Girl a Break,* 1952). Lane returned to Broadway in 1940 to work with E. Y. Harburg on the songs for an Al Jolson musical, *Hold On to Your Hats.* From it came such songs as "Don't Let It Get You Down," "The World Is in My Arms," and the great success "There's a Great Day Coming Manana." He collaborated on the lyrics with Al Dubin (1891–1945) on *Laffing Room Only* (1944). One song caught fire from that show, but only after a 3-year hiatus. (The Shuberts were at war with ASCAP and refused to permit the song to be broadcast.) Lane, angry with the Shuberts—most songwriters had trouble with the Shuberts—released the song, "Feudin' and Fightin'," himself to the so-called "Broadway Hillbilly" Dorothy Shay, and it became a tremendous hit after she finally introduced it on "The Bing Crosby Show" on the radio in 1947. That same year Lane produced one of his finest scores, *Finian's Rainbow* (q.v.), in collaboration with Harburg. A long wait resulted in yet another well-fashioned score, for *On a Clear Day You Can See Forever* (1965), written in collaboration with Alan Jay Lerner (q.v.). Among its songs: "What Did I Have That I Don't Have?" "Melinda," "Come Back to Me," and the title song. Lane and Lerner reunited in 1979 to compose the songs for *Carmelina*—good songs, but the show, burdened by its book, closed prematurely. Lane wrote the music, to Dorothy Fields' (q.v.) lyrics, for a television production of *Junior Miss* (1957).

"THE LAST ROUND-UP" Very popular quasi-cowboy song written by William J. "Billy" Hill (1889–1940) in 1931 and interpolated into the otherwise sophisticated score of the *Ziegfeld Follies* of 1934. "Wagon Wheels," written also by Hill, with music by Peter

DeRose (q.v.), was used in the same show and also enjoyed great popularity as what many believed to be a real western folk song. Hill was a curious figure in American popular song. Born in Boston, he seriously studied music at the Boston Conservatory and intended to become a violinist. At 17 he headed West and held several jobs as a cowpuncher, payroll keeper for a mining company, and eventually as a musician in Salt Lake City. He may have assimilated his musical western dialect that way. He also wrote the words and music to another rurally inflected song, "The Old Spinning Wheel" (1933), another western, "Empty Saddles," and the sentimental "In the Chapel in the Moonlight." These, like "The Last Round-Up," were written in New York City.

LATHAM, WILLIAM P. (b. 1917) Composer, teacher. Born in Shreveport, La., Jan. 14, 1917, Latham was educated at the University of Cincinnati, Ohio, and continued in music at Cincinnati Conservatory and the Eastman School, Rochester, N.Y. Among his teachers were Eugene Goosens and Howard Hanson (q.v.). During World War II, Latham served as a U. S. Army bandleader and as an infantry platoon leader. He has taught at Eastern Illinois State Teachers College and Iowa State Teachers College; since 1959 he has been a professor on the music staff at North State Texas University. His works include a *Fantasy Concerto* for flute and strings (1941), *The Lady of Shalott* for orchestra (1941), *Peace* for chorus and orchestra (1943), *Prayer after World War* for chorus (1945), *Fantasy* for violin and orchestra (1946), *Sonata for Oboe and Piano* (1947), *Symphony No. 1* (1950), *Suite* for trumpet and strings (1951), *Symphony No. 2* (1953), *Proud Heritage* for concert band (1955), *Three Chorale Preludes* for band (1956), *Court Festival* for band (1957), *Ply-*

mouth Variations for band (1962), *Escapades* for orchestra (1965), *Dodecaphonic Set* for orchestra (1966), *Prayers in Space* (1971), *The Music Makers* for chorus, rock group, and orchestra (1972), and *Fusion* for orchestra (1975). Latham has also written several piano pieces, including a *Sonatina* and *Improvisation on Salve Festa Dies*. There are many songs ("Nocturne," "Piper Play On," "Mad Nite"), band works (*Te Deum, Three by Four*), and chamber works, including 3 string quartets.

LAUFER, BEATRICE (b. 1922) Composer. Born in New York City, Apr. 27, 1922, Laufer attended the Chatham Square Music School and the Juilliard School where she studied under Marion Bauer (q.v.), Roger Sessions (q.v.), and Vittorio Giannini (q.v.). Her works include *Evolution* for mixed chorus (1943), *People of Unrest* for mixed chorus (1943), *Do You Fear the Wind?* for mixed chorus (1943), *Sergeant's Prayer* for baritone, chorus, and orchestra (1943), *Symphony No. 1* (1944), *Dance Festival* for orchestra (1945), *Dance Frolic* for orchestra (1945), *New Orleans* for women's voices a cappella (1945), *What Is to Come We Know Not* for women's voices a cappella (1945), *Rhapsody for Orchestra* (1946), *Ile,* one-act opera based on a play by Eugene O'Neill (1957), *Concerto* for flute, oboe, trumpet, and strings (1962), *Second Symphony* (1962), *Concerto for Violin* (one movement, 1963), *Fugue for Orchestra* (1963), *Trio* for violin, viola, and cello (1964), *Prelude and Fugue* for orchestra (1964), *Cry, An Orchestral Prelude* (1966), *The Great God Brown,* ballet (1966), *Lyric* for string trio (1966), *Dialogues* for orchestra (1968), and *Eight Orchestral Vignettes* (1969).

"LAURA" The theme music for the film *Laura* (1944), composed by David

Raksin (b. 1912) to underscore a key scene in which the hero, a detective seeking Laura's presumed murderer, falls in love with her portrait as he searches her apartment. Originally it had been intended to use Gershwin's "Summertime" for this scene, then Ellington's "Sophisticated Lady." Raksin was assigned as music director for the film (both Alfred Newman, q.v., considered the studio's top composer, and Bernard Herrmann, q.v., had turned down the job because word had gotten around that *Laura* was a hard-luck picture). Raksin wrote his theme over a miserable weekend (his wife had just left him) and won his small battle with director Otto Preminger vis-à-vis "Sophisticated Lady." His theme went in and set the mood beautifully and was heard, hauntingly, throughout the film, which starred Gene Tierney in the title role, Dana Andrews as the detective, and Clifton Webb in a waspish character based on writer Alexander Woollcott. *Laura* was very well received; it is still regarded as one of the best mysteries on film. The *Laura* theme became popular and was released on a recording. It was published in song form with lyrics by Johnny Mercer (q.v.) and spent several weeks on "Your Hit Parade" (q.v.) in the spring of 1945.

LEE, DAI-KEONG (b. 1915) Composer, conductor. Born in Honolulu, Hawaii, Sept. 2, 1915, Lee, though musically educated, initially studied medicine at the University of Hawaii. After hearing a local performance of one of his early original works, *Valse Pensieroso*, Lee decided to switch to music. He came to the United States in 1937 to study on a scholarship with Roger Sessions (q.v.) at Princeton University, N.J., with Frederick Jacobi (q.v.) at the Juilliard School, and with Aaron Copland (q.v.). From 1942 until 1945 Lee was in the U. S. Army, spending several months in the Southwest Pacific with the 5th Air Force. Lee composed special music for

the concerts he conducted and broadcasts from Australia. His works include *Prelude and Hula* for orchestra (1939), *Hawaiian Festival Overture* for orchestra (1940), *Introduction and Allegro* for strings (1941), *Golden Gate Overture* for chamber orchestra (1942), *The Return* for soprano, alto, tenor, and piano (1942), *North Labrador* for soprano, alto, tenor, bass, and piano (1942), *Pacific Prayer* (1943), *Overture in C* (1945), *Renascence* for orchestra (1945), *Symphony No. 1* (1946), *East and West* for chorus (1946), *Concerto for Violin and Orchestra* (1947), *Open the Gates*, opera (1951), *Symphony No. 2* (1952), *Speakeasy* (1957), *Polynesian Suite* for orchestra (1958), *Mele Ololi* for solo singer, chorus, and orchestra (1960), *The Golden Lotus* (1961), *The Gold of Their Bodies* (1963), and *Canticle of the Pacific* for chorus and orchestra (1968). Lee has also written background music for the film *Letter from Australia* (1945) and the play *Teahouse of the August Moon* (1954). His compositions also include chamber works and ballets.

LERNER, ALAN JAY (b. 1918) Lyricist, librettist. Lerner was born in New York City, Aug. 31, 1918, into a well-to-do clothing store family. He took music lessons as a youngster and went to good schools in the United States and England. Lerner graduated from Harvard with a Bachelor of Science degree in 1940; while there he also wrote scripts for shows. In the early 1940s he wrote scripts for radio shows (the loss of an eye in a college boxing match kept him out of the military during World War II). A chance meeting with composer-pianist Frederick Loewe (q.v.) in a New York club, where Loewe suggested that they collaborate on songs, led to a remarkable series of musicals. Their first show, a revue entitled *What's Up?* (1943), was not very successful, but their 2nd, *The Day Before Spring*

(1945), did somewhat better. The team of Lerner and Loewe hit its stride in the songs for the fantasy *Brigadoon* (1947), for which Lerner also wrote the book. Several fine songs came from this musical: "Almost Like Being in Love," "The Heather on the Hill," "My Mother's Wedding Day." This show was followed by *Paint Your Wagon* (1951: "I Talk to the Trees," "They Call the Wind Maria," and "I Still See Elisa"). *My Fair Lady* (1956), their greatest success, ran in its original production to 2,717 performances and was made into a popular motion picture. They produced an excellent film score for Colette's *Gigi* (1958: "Thank Heaven for Little Girls," "Gigi," "I Remember It Well," and "The Night They Invented Champagne"). Their final full-scale Broadway score was for *Camelot* (1960: "Follow Me," "If Ever I Would Leave You," "How to Handle a Woman," and "Camelot"). Lerner has written with other composers. With Kurt Weill (q.v.) he did the songs for the Broadway show *Love Life* (1948: "Greenup Time," "Love Song," and "Here I'll Stay"). He joined composer Burton Lane (q.v.) for the first time to do songs for the film *Royal Wedding* (1951: "I Left My Hat in Haiti," "Too Late Now," "Open Your Eyes," and "Every Night at Seven"). They then did a most successful Broadway musical, *On a Clear Day You Can See Forever* (1965: "On a Clear Day," "Come Back to Me," "What Did I Have That I Don't Have?"). Their *Carmelina* (1979) did not last long on Broadway. Lerner also worked with André Previn on the songs for *Coco* (1969) and with Leonard Bernstein (q.v.) on the disastrous *1600 Pennsylvania Avenue* (1976), which purported to present the hired-help's view of life in the White House over the years; it did not work. Lerner was also responsible for several of these librettos, including the adaptation of Shaw's *Pygmalion* (*My Fair Lady*) and the un-

fortunate *Carmelina*. He has also written several screenplays, among them his own *Royal Wedding* and *An American in Paris,* with music and songs by the Gershwins, which won Lerner an Academy Award for best screenplay in 1951. *The Street Where I Live,* his charming autobiographical account of the making of *My Fair Lady, Gigi,* and *Camelot,* was published in 1978.

LEVANT, OSCAR (1906–1972) Pianist, composer. Born in Pittsburgh, Pa., Dec. 27, 1906, Levant studied piano with Sigismund Stojowski and some composition with Arnold Schoenberg (q.v.) and Joseph Schillinger. Levant played the piano in dance bands, notably those of Rudy Wiedoeft and Ben Bernie. He was also employed in his early years in radio bands. He even appeared in the role of a pianist in the play *Burlesque* (1927) and its filmed version, *The Dance of Life,* 2 years later. A meeting with George Gershwin (q.v.) ca. 1925 was to have a great impact on Levant's professional, as well as personal, life. It stimulated Levant's desire to compose and his amazing pianistic facility led to his becoming a leading Gershwin interpreter, often at the composer's request. Although Levant later exaggerated their relationship (his famous wit at the expense of Gershwin's friends often annoyed Gershwin), they remained friends and colleagues until Gershwin's death in 1937. By this time Levant had written a number of good songs: "Keep Sweeping the Cobwebs Off the Moon" (lyrics by Sam Lewis and Joe Young, 1927), "Loveable and Sweet" (lyrics by Sidney Clare, from the film *The Street Girl,* 1929), "Lady, Play Your Mandolin" (lyrics by Irving Caesar, 1930), "Don't Mention Love to Me" and "Out of Sight, Out of Mind" (lyrics by Dorothy Fields, from the film *In Person,* 1935). In 1938 Levant became a national intellectual celebrity when he began appearing on the radio quiz show, *Information Please;* he was popular as a guest on radio shows as a pianist and a wise-cracking wit. He appeared in several films, among the best being *Rhapsody in Blue* (1945), in which he portrayed himself in a purported biography of Gershwin, *The Barkleys of Broadway* (1949), *An American in Paris* (1951), and *The Bandwagon* (1953). Emotional and physical problems led to Levant's retirement in the mid 1950s, although he often appeared on TV's "The Jack Paar Show" to air his problems and exploit his wit. He produced 3 books (generally with the help of others), the first, *A Smattering of Ignorance* (1941), being the best; then came *The Memoirs of an Amnesiac* (1965) and *The Unimportance of Being Oscar* (1968). Although best known as a pianist with a flair for the moderns, Levant was saddled with being typed as "the foremost interpreter of Gershwin" for most of his career. He also composed "serious" music which is little known and rarely played. Besides the film scores for *Charlie Chan at the Opera* (1936) and *Nothing Sacred* (1937), Levant also composed a *Piano Sonatina* (1931), *Sinfonietta* for chamber orchestra (1934), *Piano Concerto* (1936), *Nocturne* for orchestra (1936), *String Quartet No. 1* (1937), and *Sonatina* for piano, No. 2 (1937). There are also a 2nd string quartet, a *Suite* for orchestra, an *Overture 1912,* and a *Dirge* dedicated to Gershwin. Levant died in Beverly Hills, Calif., Aug. 14, 1972.

LEWIS, MEADE LUX (1905–1964) Pianist, composer. Born in Chicago, Ill., Sept. 4, 1905, Lewis studied the violin as a youngster. When he was about 16 he came under the influence of pianist Jimmy Yancey (q.v.) and eventually became acquainted with Albert Ammons (q.v.) and "Pine Top" Smith (q.v.), so it was natural that Lewis' style of playing would reflect the blues-boogie-woogie sound of Chicago in the 1920s. He recorded his own piece, *Honky Tonk Train* in 1929, but the recording did not sell. Lewis earned his living playing in Chicago clubs and, with the coming of the Depression, he and Ammons worked for a cab company. When John Hammond, the white jazz enthusiast, searching for the pianist who had recorded *Honky Tonk Train,* found Lewis he was working in a garage washing cars. Hammond brought Lewis and Ammons to New York City for his 1938 Jazz Concert at Carnegie Hall and helped launch the boogie-woogie renaissance. When Pete Johnson (q.v.) joined Lewis and Ammons to perform in clubs and concert, they were known as the Boogie Woogie Trio. The boogie-woogie craze petered out by the mid 1940s, but Lewis managed to keep going with a flexible style, only occasionally falling back on his 8-to-the-bar boogie style. He performed in clubs and on the radio well into the '50s, although his name had faded. Besides his classic *Honky Tonk Train,* Lewis is credited with *Yancey Special, Whistlin' Blues, Six Wheel Chaser, Chicago Flyer,* and *Celeste Blues.* Lewis died of injuries suffered in an auto accident in Minneapolis, Minn., June 7, 1964.

LIEBERSON, GODDARD (1911–1977) Recording executive, composer. Born in Hanley, Staffordshire, England, Apr. 5, 1911, Lieberson was brought to the United States when he was 4 or so. He began studying music with George McKay at the University of Washington, Seattle, and continued, under a scholarship, with Bernard Rogers at the Eastman School, Rochester, N.Y. While in school he earned a little extra money contributing reviews of music and drawing caricatures for a Rochester newspaper. In 1936 Lieberson settled in New York City, continued to do odd writing jobs, and in 1939 joined Columbia Records as a musical director. He quickly moved up the corporate ladder—director of Columbia Masterworks, executive vice-president, and, in 1955, president. While his work as an executive left Lieberson little time for original composition, he contributed greatly to the cause of contemporary—and American—music through his position at Columbia. Lieberson produced the original cast albums of Broadway musicals with a touch that no one else matched. He initiated a series of recordings of the classic shows for which no original cast albums existed (i.e., Rodgers and Hart's *On Your Toes* and *Pal Joey*, the Gershwins' *Oh, Kay!* and *Girl Crazy*, Kern's *Roberta*, Porter's *Anything Goes*, etc.). Lieberson also encouraged the recording of works conducted by their creators—Stravinsky, Copland, others. In the 1960s he began a Modern American Music series of recordings, resulting in the recording of several works by young or neglected composers; these were but a few of the projects carried out under Lieberson at Columbia Records. His original works include *Five Modern Painters* for orchestra (1929), *Sonata* for oboe, bassoon, viola, cello, and piano (1934), *Tango* for piano and orchestra (1935), *Three Chinese Poems* for mixed chorus (1936), *Alice in Wonderland*, incidental music for a puppet show (1936), *Sonata for String Quartet* (1937), *Homage to Handel* for strings (1937), *Symphony* (1937), and *String Quartet* (1938). There are also a number of songs and piano pieces. Lieberson also published a novel entitled *Three for Bedroom C*. He died in New York City, May 29, 1977.

LLOYD, NORMAN (1909–1980) Composer, educator, author. Born in Pottsville, Pa., Nov. 8, 1909, Lloyd studied at New York University and received his Doctorate of Music from the Philadelphia Conservatory of Music in 1963. Among his teachers were Vincent Jones, Aaron Copland (composition, q.v.), and Abbey Whiteside (piano). Lloyd, in turn, taught at New York University (1936–45), Sarah Lawrence College, Bronxville, N.Y. (1936–46), the Juilliard School of Music, New York City (1946–63), and Oberlin College, Oberlin, Ohio, where he was dean of the Conservatory of Music (1963–65). He served as the director for arts, Rockefeller Foundation, New York City, from 1965 to 1972. Always interested in the dance, Lloyd worked during the '30s with dancers at Bennington College, Vt. In 1970 he helped to found the North Carolina Dance Theatre at the University of North Carolina, Chapel Hill. His compositions include the *Lament for Ignacio Sánchez Mejías* for dancers, speaker, and orchestra (1946), the choral ballet *Restless Land* (1950), *Piano Sonata* (1958), *A Walt Whitman Overture* for band (1960), *Five Episodes* for piano (1960), and the score for the film *The Ancient Egyptian* (1962). Lloyd's books include *The Fireside Book of Folk Songs*, for which he did the piano arrangements (1947), and *The Golden Encyclopedia of Music* (1968). He died in Greenwich, Conn., July 31, 1980.

LOCKWOOD, NORMAND (b. 1906) Composer, teacher. Born in New York City, Mar. 19, 1906, Lockwood began in music at the University of Michigan, Ann Arbor, and completed his studies with Ottorino Respighi in Rome and Nadia Boulanger in Paris. Upon completion of his work with Boulanger in 1929, Lockwood was awarded a Prix de Rome (1929–32). He returned to the United States to take a teaching post at Oberlin College, Ohio; he also taught at Columbia University and Union Theological Seminary in New York City, Trinity University, San Antonio, Tex., and, beginning in 1961, the University of Denver, Colo., where he was named professor emeritus in 1974. His works include *Drum Taps* for chorus and orchestra (1930), *When Lilacs Last in the Dooryard Bloom'd* for tenor, chorus, and orchestra (1931), *Fragments from Sappho* for girl's voices (1933), *Sonata for Three Cellos* (1934), *Dirge for Two Veterans* for chorus (1934), *Dichromatic Variations* for piano (1935), *Sweet and Low* for mixed chorus (1935), *Six String Quartets* (1937), *Three Capri Songs* (1937), *Monotone* for mixed chorus (1937), *Gifts of the First Christmas* for women's chorus and piano (1939), *Out of the Cradle Endlessly Rocking* for chorus (1939), *Quintet* for piano and strings (1940), *Trio* for flute, viola, and harp (1940), *Symphony* (1941), *Sonata* for piano (1944), *Serenades* for string quartet (1945), *The Scarecrow*, a chamber opera (1945), *Stabat Mater: Mary, Who Stood in Sorrow* for soprano and orchestra (1946), *Moby Dick* for chamber orchestra (1946), *Four Songs from Joyce's "Chamber Music"* for voice and string quartet (1948), *Concerto for Organ and Brass No. 1* (1950), *Carol Fantasy* for chorus and orchestra (1952), *The Prairie* for chorus and orchestra (1953), *Light Out of Darkness* for baritone, chorus, and orchestra (1956), *Children of God* (1957), *Clarinet Quintet* (1960), *Early Dawn*, opera (1961), *The Wizards of Balizar*, opera (1962), *The Hanging Judge*, opera (1964), *Requiem for a Rich Young Man*, one-act opera (1964), *Oboe Concerto* (1966), *Symphonic Sequences* (1966), *From an Opening to a Close* for winds and percussion (1967), *Choreographic Cantata* for dancers, chorus, organ, and percussion (1968), *Shine, Perishing Republic* for chorus and chamber orchestra (1968), and *Concerto for Organ and Brass, No. 2* (1970).

LOESSER, FRANK (1910–1969) Composer, lyricist, librettist. Born in New York City, June 29, 1910, Loesser

came from a talented, intellectual family —and was the family noncomformist. He dropped out of the City College, New York, at 16; he refused to bother with piano lessons (his brother, Arthur, 1894–1969, was a fine pianist). Out of school, Loesser worked at odd jobs, as an office boy, and as a reporter for a small-town newspaper. It was during this phase of his career that he began writing song parodies, satirical lyrics to well-known melodies. In 1931 he published his first song, "In Love with a Memory of You"; the music was by an aspiring young composer, William Schuman (q.v.). The fact of publication led to his being hired by RKO Radio Pictures as a staff lyricist, although the songs Loesser wrote then have not been heard since. He began providing words to songs by Otto Motzan ("Sunday at Sundown," 1935), Joseph Meyer ("The Old Oak Tree," 1934), and J. Fred Coots ("Oh! What a Beautiful Baby," 1934). It was not until the mid 1930s that Loesser hit his stride writing film songs with composers Burton Lane (q.v.), Hoagy Carmichael (q.v.), Frederick Hollander, and Victor Schertzinger (q.v.). Among these songs were "Says My Heart" (music by Lane, from the film *Cocoanut Grove*, 1938), "Moments Like This" (music by Lane, from the film *College Swing*, 1938), "Small Fry" (music by Carmichael, from the film *Sing You Sinners*, 1938), "Two Sleepy People" (music by Carmichael, from the film *Thanks for the Memory*, 1938), "Heart and Soul" (music by Carmichael, from the film *A Song Is Born*, 1938), "See What the Boys in the Backroom Will Have" (music by Hollander, from the film *Destry Rides Again*, 1938), "Sand in My Shoes" (music by Schertzinger, from the film *Kiss the Boys Goodbye*, 1941), "I Don't Want to Walk Without You" (music by Jule Styne, 1941), "Jingle Jangle Jingle" (music by Joseph J.

Lilley, from the film *The Forest Rangers*, 1942), and "Praise the Lord and Pass the Ammunition" (words and music by Loesser, 1942). This last song marked Loesser's debut as a words and music man. His tenure with the U. S. Army Special Services resulted in some of the very few worthy war songs of this period: "The Road to Victory," "What Do You Do in the Infantry," "First Class Private Mary Brown," and "The Ballad of Rodger Young." Though he was in uniform Loesser managed to continue producing lyrics for films released during the war: "Let's Get Lost" (music by Jimmy McHugh, from the film *Happy-Go-Lucky*, 1943), "Can't Get Out of This Mood" (music by McHugh, from the film *Seven Days Leave*, 1943), "They're Either Too Young or Too Old" (music by Arthur Schwartz, from the film *Thank Your Lucky Stars*, 1943), "Spring Will Be a Little Late This Year" (words and music by Loesser, from the film *Christmas Holiday*, 1944), and "On a Slow Boat to China" (words and music by Loesser, 1948). After the war, sure of himself as the complete songwriter, Loesser moved to Broadway where he did both words and music for *Where's Charley?* an adaptation of the old farce *Charley's Aunt*, in 1948. A great success, *Where's Charley?* contained several good songs: "My Darling, My Darling," "Make a Miracle," "Lovelier than Ever," and "Once in Love with Amy." An even greater success followed 2 years later with the production of *Guys and Dolls* (q.v.), "A Musical Fable of Broadway," based on Damon Runyon characters. Loesser's next Broadway project was an ambitious quasi-opera, *The Most Happy Fella* (1956), based on the Sidney Howard play *They Knew What They Wanted*. Inspired by the story of the middle-aged California farmer who sends for a young mail-order bride—enticing her with a photograph of his young foreman—

Loesser not only wrote words and music, he also adapted the book. *The Most Happy Fella* was his most ambitious score (most of the evening is sung, there being less than 15 minutes of pure dialogue); its songs ranged from the operatic ("Rosabella") to popular ("Standing on the Corner"). Other good songs include "How Beautiful the Days" and "Joey, Joey, Joey." This unique operatic musical racked up a healthy 676 performances in New York City before setting out on a six-months' tour. *Greenwillow* (1960) was adapted by Loesser and Lester Samuels from the B. J. Chute novel. For the composer-lyricist it was yet another change of scene, and, like *Guys and Dolls* and *The Most Happy Fella*, was imbued with a folkish quality. It certainly proved Loesser's versatility— but *Greenwillow* was not a commercial success (it closed after 95 performances), though its score was worthy of Loesser and contains one of his most interesting creations, "Summertime Love." His final Broadway show was the successful, cynical look at the world of commerce, *How to Succeed in Business Without Really Trying* (1961). One of its best songs was "I Believe in You," sung by the upward-clawing "hero" to his image in a mirror. During the period when he was busy on Broadway, Loesser produced a fine film score for *Hans Christian Andersen* (1952), out of which came such songs as "Wonderful Copenhagen" and the contrapuntal "Inchworm." He died in New York City, July 26, 1969.

LOEWE, FREDERICK (b. 1901) Composer, pianist. Born in Berlin, June 10, 1901, of Austrian parents, Loewe received his early musical education in Germany. His teachers were Ferruccio Busoni, Eugen D'Albert, and Nikolaus von Reznicek. His father, Edmund, was a vocalist and Loewe himself was a child prodigy on the piano. He made his debut with the Berlin Philharmonic at the age of 14. The Loewes came to the United States in 1923 so that Loewe senior could sing in an operetta, but he died during rehearsals, leaving his wife and son penniless. Loewe took various odd jobs. He played the piano in German beer gardens in New York's Yorkville; for a while he was a professional boxer and, moving westward, worked on ranches and could be classified as a former cowboy. He finally went back to playing the piano in New York by the '30s (in 1933, for example, he was rehearsal pianist for the operetta *Champagne Sec*). One of his earliest song attempts was the mildly popular "A Waltz Was Born in Vienna" (lyrics by Earle Crooker). In 1938 Loewe and Crooker collaborated on the songs for the short-lived (20 performances) *Great Lady*. A chance meeting with another not very successful songwriter, lyricist Alan Jay Lerner (q.v.), in the Lambs Club led to one of the most successful collaborations of the American musical theatre. Their first Broadway attempt, *What's Up?* (1943), lasted a mere 8 weeks. Their next, *The Day Before Spring* (1945), revealed that Lerner the librettist had more to learn about that art, but that as songwriters Lerner and Loewe were first-rate. The successful proof of that came with *Brigadoon* (1947), a fantasy musical about a village in Scotland that materializes only once every 100 years and the effect upon it and its people when 2 American hunters stumble into it. The score was excellent and Loewe matched Lerner's atmospheric lyrics with such melodies as "Come to Me, Bend to Me," "The Heather on the Hill," "There But for You Go I," and "Almost Like Being in Love." Loewe then collaborated with Lerner on a series of successes: *Paint Your Wagon* ("I Talk to the Trees," "They Call the Wind Maria," "I Still See Elisa," 1951), *My Fair Lady* (q.v., 1956), and *Camelot* ("Follow Me,"

"How to Handle a Woman," "If Ever I Would Leave You," 1960). Loewe, tired of the tribulations of turning out one success after another and in fluctuating health (he suffered from a heart condition), decided to retire and to enjoy his substantial income. During their Broadway heyday, Loewe and Lerner wrote the songs for a fine film based on Colette's *Gigi* (1951): "I Remember It Well," "The Night They Invented Champagne," "Thank Heaven for Little Girls," and "Gigi." Eleven years after his retirement Loewe, impressed with Lerner's screen adaptation of Antoine de Saint-Exupéry's *The Little Prince,* decided that he would compose the music for the film, released in 1971. The film was poorly made, the songs were wasted, and Loewe returned to retirement.

"THE LORD'S PRAYER" A phenomenally popular "art song," with a musical setting from the New Testament by Philadelphia-born composer Albert Hay Malotte (1895–1964). Published in 1935, "The Lord's Prayer" was taken up by nearly every aspiring vocal recitalist and not a few popular singers who hoped to inject a serious moment into their acts. The sheet music sold in the millions. Malotte was a Hollywood-based composer and, as fate would have it, his other most popular song was "Ferdinand the Bull" (lyrics by Larry Morey) from the Walt Disney cartoon released in 1938.

"LOUISIANA STORY" Outstanding film score by Virgil Thomson (q.v.) for a "semidocumentary" film made by the great American filmmaker Robert Flaherty (1884–1951). The film tells the story of the effect of an oil-drilling crew on a family living in a Louisiana bayou, especially as seen through the eyes of a boy. Thomson drew upon Acadian themes in addition to composing original music and his score proved to be one of his finest (it was awarded the Pulitzer

Prize in 1949). From the score Thomson fashioned 2 separate works: *Suite from Louisiana Story,* consisting of 4 sections, "Pastoral," "Chorale," "Passacaglia," and "Fugue"; the 2nd suite, entitled *Acadian Songs and Dances,* is divided into 7 sections: "Sadness," "Papa's Tune," "A Narrative," "The Alligator and the Coon," "Super-Sadness," "Walking Song," and "The Squeeze-Box."

MCBRIDE, ROBERT (b. 1911) Composer, arranger, teacher. Born in Tucson, Ariz., Feb. 20, 1911, McBride learned music via the clarinet at the age of 10. By the time he was in high school he had also mastered the oboe, saxophone, and piano which he played in the school band, pit bands in a local theatre, and jazz bands. He wrote his earliest composition, *March for a Band,* while still in high school. In 1928 McBride enrolled in the University of Arizona, Tucson, where he studied composition with Otto Luening (q.v.). He received his master's in music in 1935. During the period at the university McBride also served as oboist and clarinetist in the Tucson Symphony. He began teaching wind instruments and theory at Bennington College, Vt., in 1935 and remained there until 1946, when he left to work as composer-arranger for Triumph Films, New York City. Since 1957 he has been on the music staff of the University of Arizona. McBride's expressive style is characterized by an affinity with big band jazz and a sophisticated mastery of the orchestra. His works include a *Mexican Rhapsody* for orchestra (1934), *Depression,* a sonata for violin and piano (1934), *Dance Suite* for piano (1935), *Prelude to a Tragedy* for orchestra (1935), *Fugato on a Well Known Theme* for chamber orchestra (1935), *Workout* for oboe and piano (1936), *Prelude and Fugue* for string quartet (1936), *Show Piece,* a ballet (1937), *Oboe Quintet* for oboe and string quartet

(1937), *Swing Stuff* for clarinet and orchestra (1938), *Hot Stuff, We Hope* for men's voices, clarinet, and piano (1938), *Wise Apple Five* for clarinet and 4 strings (1940), *Strawberry Jam* for orchestra (1941), *Jam Session* for flute, oboe, clarinet, horn, and bassoon (1941), *Turandot,* incidental music for stage production (1941), *Punch and Judy,* ballet for one or 2 pianos, also orchestral suite (1941), *Stuff in G* for orchestra (1942), *Side Show* for orchestra (1944), *Lonely Landscape* for band (1944), *Furlough,* ballet with solo piano accompaniment (1945), *Popover* for clarinet and orchestra (1945), *Sherlock Holmes Suite* for band (1945), *Aria and Toccata* for violin and piano (1946), *Concerto for Doubles* for saxophone and orchestra (1947), *Concerto for Violin* (1947), *Pumpkin Eater's Little Fugue* (1952), *Jazz Symphony,* a ballet (1953), *Fantasy on a Mexican Christmas Carol* for orchestra (1955), *Pioneer Spiritual* for orchestra (1956), *String Foursome* for string quartet (1957), *Five Winds Blowing* for wind quintet (1957), *Memorial* for organ (1958), *Vocalise* for chorus and piano (1959), *Panorama of Mexico* (1960), *Sunday in Mexico* for orchestra (1963), *Hill Country Symphony* (1964), *Country Music Fantasy* for orchestra (1965), *Symphonic Melody* for orchestra (1968), *Lament for the Parking Problem* for trumpet, horn, and trombone (1968), and *Way Out, But Not Too Far* for euphonium and piano (1970).

MCPHEE, COLIN (1901–1964) Composer, teacher, author. Born in Montreal, Canada, Mar. 15, 1901, studied composition with Gustav Strube at the Peabody Conservatory, Baltimore, Md. After completing his work there in 1921, he returned to Canada, where he studied piano with Arthur Friedheim. He also studied with Isidor Philipp in Paris and, after his return to New York City in

1926, with Edgard Varèse (q.v.). McPhee was active in New York musical circles until 1934, when he went to the island of Bali to study the music there. He remained, except for occasional side trips (he was in Mexico in 1936), until 1939. McPhee was regarded as an authority on Balinese music. After his return to New York he wrote a column regularly for *Modern Music*. In 1958 he was on the staff of the University of California's Institute of Ethnomusicology, Los Angeles. McPhee's works include a *Concerto for Piano and Orchestra* (1923), *Sonatina* for 2 flutes, clarinet, trumpet, and piano (1925), *Sarabande* for orchestra (1927), *Sea Shanty Suite* for baritone, men's chorus, 2 pianos, and timpani (1929), *Concerto for Piano and Wind Octet* (1929), *Symphony in One Movement* (1930), *H_2O*, film score (1931), *Bali* for orchestra (1936), *Tabuh-Tabuhan* for 2 pianos and orchestra (1936), *Balinese Ceremonial Music* for 2 pianos (1942), *Iroquois Eclogue* for orchestra (1944), *Four Iroquois Dances* for orchestra (1944), *Transitions* for orchestra (1951), *Symphony No. 2*, "Pastoral" (1957), *Nocturne* for orchestra (1958), *Concerto for Wind Orchestra* (1959), and *Symphony No. 3* (1962). McPhee was also the author of *A House in Bali* (1946), *A Club of Small Men* (1948), and *Music in Bali* (published in 1966). McPhee died in Los Angeles, Jan. 7, 1964.

MARTIN, HUGH (b. 1914) Composer, lyricist, vocalist, pianist. Born in Birmingham, Ala., Aug. 11, 1914, Martin was educated at Birmingham Southern College; he studied with Edna Ussen and Dorsey Whittington. Initially Martin had planned on a career as a concert pianist but after coming to New York in the late 1930s he became more interested in the musical theatre. He appeared as a vocalist in the Harold Arlen –E. Y. Harburg musical *Hooray for*

What! for which he also did some of the vocal arrangements. Also in the show was another singer, Ralph Blane (q.v.). They eventually formed a songwriting partnership as well as a singing group called the Martins. Their first show collaboration resulted in *Best Foot Forward* (1941). The successful show was made into an equally successful film a couple of years later and Martin and Blane joined to write the songs for *Meet Me in St. Louis*. They continued to write film songs for *Ziegfeld Follies* ("Love," 1946), *Good News* ("Pass the Peacepipe," 1947), *Athena* ("Venezia," 1954), *The Girl Rush* ("An Occasional Man," 1955), and *The Girl Most Likely* ("I Like the Feeling," 1958). The Martin-Blane songs from their first show and first film, namely "Ev'ry Time," "Buckle Down, Winsocki," "The Boy Next Door," and "The Trolley Song," are outstanding and although Martin was mostly the composer and Blane mostly the lyricist, the collaboration was so close that the division of labor was never defined. Each, however, worked with others and did complete scores on their own. Martin did words and music for *Look Ma, I'm Dancin'* (1948), with its popular "Shauny O'Shay," and for *Make a Wish* (1951). He and Timothy Gray collaborated on the successful London show *Love from Judy* (1952), based on *Daddy-Long-Legs*, and the Broadway success *High Spirits* (1964), based on Noël Coward's *Blithe Spirit*. Martin did both words and music for a television production of *Hans Brinker, or the Silver Skates* (1958). He also composed the background music for a documentary film about painter Grandma Moses in 1950. The *Grandma Moses Suite* was extracted, arranged, and orchestrated by Alec Wilder (q.v.). Although Martin has composed songs since *High Spirits* (including the Horatio Alger–based *Tattered Tom* with Blane), he has been virtually inactive on Broadway and in Hollywood since that last musical.

MENNIN, PETER (b. 1923) Composer, teacher. Born in Erie, Pa., May 17, 1923, Mennin (the family name was Mennini), studied composition with Normand Lockwood (q.v.) at the Oberlin Conservatory, Ohio, in 1941. After service in the U. S. Army Air Forces during World War II he returned to music studies at the Eastman School, Rochester, N.Y., where he studied with Howard Hanson (q.v.) and Bernard Rogers (q.v.). Upon graduation from Eastman in 1947, Mennin taught composition at the Juilliard School, New York City. He remained there until 1958 when he was appointed director of the Peabody Conservatory, Baltimore, Md. In 1962 he returned to Juilliard as president. Despite the demands on his time as a teacher and administrator, Mennin has been a prolific composer of large-scale symphonic works as well as smaller pieces. His compositions include a *Piano Sonata* (1941), *String Quartet No. 1* (1941), *Symphony No. 1* (1942), *Symphony No. 2* (1944; the *Allegro* movement of this work won the first George Gershwin Memorial Award, 1945), *Folk Overture* for orchestra (1945), *Concertino* for flute, strings, and percussion (1945), *Symphony No. 3* (1946), *Sinfonia* for chamber orchestra (1946), *Fantasia* for strings (1947), *Divertimento* (1947), *Partita* (1949), *Symphony No. 4* (1949), the cantata *The Christmas Story* for soprano, tenor, chorus, brass, timpani, and strings (1949), *Violin Concerto* (1950), *String Quartet No. 2* (1950), *Canzona* for band (1951), *Symphony No. 5* (1951), *Concertato for Orchestra*, "Moby Dick" (1952), *Symphony No. 6* (1953), *Sonata Concertante* for violin and piano (1956), *Cello Concerto* (1956), *Piano Concerto* (1958), *Canto* for orchestra (1963), *Symphony No. 7* (1964), *Piano Sonata*

(1967), *Cantata de virtute* for narrator, tenor, baritone, children's chorus, and orchestra (1969), and *Symphony No. 8* (1974).

MENOTTI, GIAN CARLO (b. 1911) Composer, teacher, librettist. Born in Cadigliano, Italy, July 7, 1911, Menotti, who began to study music with his mother at an early age, began writing operas before he enrolled in the Verdi Conservatory, Milan, at the age of 12. He came to the United States in 1927 and studied at the Curtis Institute, Philadelphia, with Rosario Scalero; he also studied piano with Vera Resnikoff. He was graduated in 1933. He later (ca. 1946) returned to Curtis as a teacher of composition. Menotti is noted for his work in opera, although he has written a number of instrumental compositions. As an opera composer he is unique in that he writes his own librettos and has written for other composers. He has been the recipient of 2 Guggenheim Fellowships (1946, 1947) and numerous opera commissions. His works include *Variations on a theme by Robert Schumann* for piano (1931), *Pastorale* for piano and strings (1933), *Trio for a House Warming Party* for piano, cello, and flute (1936), *Amelia Goes to the Ball*, one-act opera (1937), *Poemetti per Maria Rosa* for piano (1937), *The Old Maid and the Thief*, opera originally written for radio performance (1939), *The Island God*, 2-act opera (1942), *Sebastian*, a ballet (1944), *Piano Concerto in F* (1945), *The Medium*, one-act opera (1946), *The Telephone*, one-act opera (1947), *Errand into the Maze*, ballet (1947), *The Consul*, 3-act opera (1950), *Amahl and the Night Visitors*, one-act opera composed for television (1951), *Apocalypse* for orchestra (1951), *Concerto for Violin* (1952), *Ricercare and Toccata* for piano (1953), *The Saint of Bleecker Street*, 3-act opera (1954), *The Unicorn, the Gorgon and the Manticore,* ballet with voices (1956), *Maria Golovin,* 3-act opera (1958), *Labyrinth,* one-act television opera (1963), *The Death of the Bishop of Brindisi,* cantata for mezzo-soprano, bass, chorus, and orchestra (1963), *The Last Savage,* 3-act opera (1963), *Martin's Lie,* one-act opera (1964), *Canti della Lontananza,* songs for soprano and piano (1967), *Help, Help, the Globolinks!,* one-act opera for children (1968), *The Most Important Man in the World,* 3-act opera (1970), *The Hero,* comic opera (1976), *Symphony No. 1* (1976), *The Egg,* one-act opera (1976), *The Trial of the Gypsy* for high voices and piano (1978), *La Loca,* 3-act opera (1979), and *Mass: Missa O Pulchritudo* (1979). Menotti has written the librettos to Samuel Barber's *Vanessa* (1959) and *A Hand of Bridge,* one-act opera (1959). Menotti founded the Festival of Two Worlds, Spoleto, Italy, in 1958, and has staged operas, concerts, and other cultural events there; an American offshoot was established in 1977 at Charleston, S.C. Specifically characterizing Menotti as an "American" composer is difficult; although he spent many years in the United States, he remains an Italian citizen but lives in Scotland. His contribution to contemporary opera (in the tradition of the great 18th-century opera composers) has helped to keep the art alive and popular. Menotti's theatrical sense and melodic richness have won him performances throughout the world.

MERCER, JOHNNY (1909–1976) Lyricist, vocalist, sometime composer. Born in Savannah, Ga., Nov. 18, 1909, Mercer had scant musical training as a youngster. He was active in dramatics while attending prep school in Virginia. The Depression led to the ruin of his father's real estate business and Mercer, never an attentive student, quit school and set out for New York to become an actor. He brought with him a love for song and language and little experience. John H. Mercer arrived in New York City in 1929 and spent nearly a year trying to break into show business. When he was informed by one assistant director that "We only need girls and songs," Mercer produced his first song, written with that director, Everett Miller. It was "Out of Breath and Scared to Death of You" and was used in the *Garrick Gaieties* of 1930. (Mercer, incidentally, also married one of the "girls" in the show, which led to his abandoning songwriting for a time while the budding lyricist worked at a 9-to-5 job "misplacing stocks and bonds in Wall Street.") He returned to Broadway in 1932, when he collaborated with E. Y. Harburg (whom he had met when he did the *Garrick Gaieties*) and Harold Arlen to do "Satan's Li'l Lamb" for the revue *Americana.* Mercer quickly drifted away from Wall Street and settled into the music business. He sang with Paul Whiteman and was master of ceremonies of Whiteman's radio show in the mid 1930s. He also sang with Benny Goodman. His first really big song hit, "Lazybones" (1933), was written with Hoagy Carmichael (q.v.). The popularity of that song led to a call from Hollywood where Mercer eventually settled and wrote the lyrics for some of the most popular songs of the '30s and '40s. His Hollywood output included "I'm an Old Cowhand" (words and music by Mercer, from *Rhythm on the Range,* 1936), "Too Marvelous for Words" (music by Richard Whiting, from *Ready, Willing and Able,* 1937), "Have You Got Any Castles, Baby?" (music by Whiting, from *Varsity Show,* 1937), "Hooray for Hollywood" (music by Whiting, from *Hollywood Hotel,* 1937), "Ride, Tenderfoot, Ride" (music by Whiting, from *Cowboy from Brooklyn,* 1938), "Jeepers Creepers" (music by Harry Warren, from *Going Places,* 1938), "Girl Friend of the Whirling

Dervish" (music by Warren, from *Garden of the Moon*, 1938), "Blues in the Night," and "This Time the Dream's on Me" (music by Harold Arlen, from *Blues in the Night*, 1941), "Arthur Murray Taught Me Dancing in a Hurry," "I Remember You," and "Tangerine" (music by Victor Schertzinger, 1942), "Dearly Beloved," "You Were Never Lovelier," and "I'm Old Fashioned" (music by Jerome Kern, from *You Were Never Lovelier*, 1942), "Hit the Road to Dreamland" and "That Old Black Magic" (music by Arlen, from *Star Spangled Rhythm*, 1942), "My Shining Hour" and "One for My Baby" (music by Arlen, from *The Sky's the Limit*, 1943), "I Promise You" and "Ac-cent-tchu-ate the Positive" (music by Arlen, from *Here Come the Waves*, 1944), "How Little We Know" (music by Hoagy Carmichael, from *To Have and Have Not*, 1944), "Out of This World" and "June Comes Around Every Year" (music by Arlen, from *Out of This World*, 1945), "It's a Great Big World" and "On the Atchison, Topeka and Santa Fe" (music by Warren, from *The Harvey Girls*, 1946), "Fancy Free" (music by Arlen, from *The Petty Girl*, 1950), "In the Cool, Cool, Cool of the Evening" (music by Carmichael, from *Here Comes the Groom*, 1951), "Seeing's Believing" and "Baby Doll" (music by Warren, from *The Belle of New York*, 1952), "Wonderful, Wonderful Day" and "Lonesome Polecat" (music by Gene DePaul, from *Seven Brides for Seven Brothers*, 1954), "Something's Gotta Give" (music and lyrics by Mercer, from *Daddy Long Legs*, 1955). The production of big film musicals dropped off in the 1950s but Mercer kept his hand in by writing lyrics for movie title songs. Among the most notable of these were "The Days of Wine and Roses" (music by Henry Mancini, 1962; the year before they had contributed a popular song to *Breakfast at Tiffany's:* "Moon River") and "Charade" (music by Mancini, 1963). Mercer was not very active on Broadway, where his career there began with *Walk with Music*, music by Carmichael, in 1940. One song, "Ooh, What You Said," gained some popularity, but the show itself closed after a brief run. Mercer then collaborated with Harold Arlen on the superior score for *St. Louis Woman* (1946), another short-run show. Several songs enjoyed popularity— among them "Come Rain or Come Shine," "Anyplace I Hang My Hat Is Home," "Legalize My Name," "A Woman's Prerogative," and "I Had Myself a True Love." Mercer's first substantial Broadway hit was *Texas Li'l Darlin'* (1949) with a score by Robert Emmett Dolan. He did both words and music for *Top Banana*, another success; so was *Li'l Abner* (1956) with music by DePaul. He joined Arlen again in the short-lived *Saratoga* (1959) and Dolan in *Foxy* (1964), also a short-runner. Both scores had fine songs but the ponderous "books" were too much for all concerned. So such songs as "A Game of Poker," "Goose Never Be a Peacock," "Love Held Lightly," and "The Man in My Life" (from *Saratoga*) and "Bon Vivant" and "Run Cinderella" (*Foxy*) were stifled. Mercer did his last show lyrics for a London production, *The Good Companions*, music by André Previn, in 1974. He also wrote a number of fine nonproduction songs that should be noted: "Pardon My Southern Accent" (music by Matty Malneck, 1934), "Goody Goody" (music by Malneck, 1936), "Bob White" (music by Bernie Hanighen, 1937), "And the Angels Sing" (music by Ziggy Elman, 1939), "Day In—Day Out" (music by Rube Bloom, 1939), "Fools Rush In" (music by Bloom, 1940), "Skylark" (music by Carmichael, 1942), "The Strip Polka" (music and lyrics by Mercer, 1942), "G.I. Jive" (all Mercer, 1944), "Dream" (all Mercer, 1945), "Laura" (music by David Raksin, adapted from film theme music, 1945), "Autumn Leaves" (English words by Mercer, French words by Jacques Prévert, music by Joseph Kosma, 1950). Mercer died in Bel Air, Calif., several months after undergoing surgery for a brain tumor, on June 25, 1976.

"MERRY MOUNT" Opera in 3 acts by Howard Hanson (q.v.), with a libretto by Richard L. Stokes based on the story by Nathaniel Hawthorne, "The Maypole of Merry Mount." The opera was commissioned by the Metropolitan Opera Company in 1930. Hanson completed it in 1933 and conducted a concert performance in Ann Arbor, Mich., on May 20. The official opening at the Metropolitan in New York City took place on Feb. 10, 1934, and was generally hailed in the press. One paper reported 50 curtain calls on opening night. *Merry Mount* is set in 17th-century New England, where there is a conflict between the strict Puritans and the pleasure-loving Cavaliers. The effect is especially strong upon the pastor, "Wrestling (that's his name!) Bradford" who has been suffering by dreaming of Ashtoreth, goddess of fertility and sexual love. He falls hopelessly in love with one of the royalists, Lady Marigold Sandys—who, in turn, is engaged to marry one of the Cavaliers, Sir Gower Lackland. Bradford refuses to marry them, but an Anglican priest does. The Cavaliers celebrate the marriage with wild Maypole dances on Merry Mount. The Puritans, upset by such godlessness—and led by the envious Bradford—break up the dancing. About the same time the Indians raid the settlement so Bradford rescues Marigold by taking her deep into the forest. There he confesses his love for her. Sir Gower appears (having followed them into the forest) and the 2 men fight. Sir Gower is killed. Bradford then falls into a deep sleep and dreams that Marigold is Ashtoreth. When they return to the village they find it aflame after the Indian attack. The Puritans blame Marigold for their misfortune. Bradford takes Marigold in his arms and carries her into the church, where they perish in the flames "while the Puritans sing the Lord's Prayer." The score is typical Hanson, with strong melodic lines, rich choruses, and fine orchestral sequences. The song texts are in a quite clumsy quasi-17th-century dialect ("Bestead me now, ye furies of the pit"). Hanson's settings, however, make them sing. *Merry Mount,* one of the most successful of American operas of the 1930s, was produced 7 times at the Metropolitan and toured: Brooklyn, Philadelphia, and Rochester. It has had many revivals and concert performances. In the original production Lawrence Tibbett starred as the tortured Wrestling Bradford and Swedish soprano Göta Ljungberg as Lady Marigold Sandys. In 1938 Hanson extracted portions of the score to form a *Merry Mount Suite:* "Overture," "Maypole Dances," "Love Duet," and "Children's Dance."

MILLER, GLENN (1904–1944) Bandleader, arranger, trombonist. Born Mar. 1, 1904, in Clarinda, Iowa. Miller learned to play the trombone as a youngster. He grew up in the West, as his not wealthy parents moved frequently: North Platte, Neb., Grant City, Okla., and Fort Morgan, Colo. He left the University of Colorado to work as a trombonist and to write arrangements for the Boyd Senter band in Denver. In 1926 Miller joined the excellent Ben Pollack band in Chicago. By mid 1928 he had worked his way to New York City, where he free-lanced as an instrumentalist-arranger. He found work in such bands as those led by Red Nichols, Victor Young, Freddy Rich, and the Dorsey brothers, and he played in the pit bands for musicals, including Gershwin's *Strike Up the Band* and *Girl Crazy*. Miller was approached by British bandleader Ray Noble to organize an American band for him in 1935; it was one of the best bands of the period and, although not a jazz band, employed many of Miller's colleagues, which made it a good pop band. Miller himself continued arranging for the bands of Ozzie Nelson, Glen Gray, and others and then organized his own band in 1937. Although the band made recordings and toured, it was a financial failure and broke up by the end of the year. Miller, meanwhile, had studied with musical theoretician Joseph Schillinger and had begun to apply some of Schillinger's ideas to his own work. He also evolved a definite "sound" for an orchestra by a blend of reeds—the clarinet lead against the tenor sax and combinations thereof. The Miller sound, once recognized, was one of the most characteristic of the big band era. Miller formed a new band in 1938 and it was with this group that, by 1939, he made his mark. The smooth, controlled performance of the well-rehearsed, disciplined musicians (Miller was an exacting taskmaster and a no-nonsense businessman) soon began making appearances on the radio, in ballrooms, and on recordings. One of their first hit records was Miller's own composition and arrangement "Moonlight Serenade," which had been composed (as an instrumental) during his study with Schillinger. "Moonlight Serenade" with lyrics by Mitchell Parish, became a popular song. Miller's band featured such sidemen as Tex Beneke (tenor sax and vocals), Billy May (trumpet), Hal McIntyre (alto sax), Al Klink (tenor sax), and such vocalists as Marion Hutton, Paula Kelly, Ray Eberle, and the Modernaires. As the band's success grew, Miller assigned many of the arranging duties to Jerry Gray, Bill Finegan, and Billy May. The

Glenn Miller Orchestra made dozens of popular recordings ("In the Mood," "Tuxedo Junction," "Pennsylvania 6-5000," "Elmer's Tune," "A String of Pearls," "Moonlight Cocktail," etc.) and was in demand for personal appearances. Miller and the band appeared in several movies in the early 1940s out of which came more popular recordings: "Chattanooga Choo Choo," "I Got a Gal in Kalamazoo," "Serenade in Blue," and "At Last," among others. Miller broke up the band in September 1942 and enlisted in the U. S. Army Air Forces and organized a large band, drawing upon the best musicians in the Air Forces: pianist Mel Powell, drummer Ray McKinley, vocalist Johnny Desmond, and his own arranger, Jerry Gray. The band was popular in England with civilians as well as the military, made V-Discs for Allied Radio that were broadcast to all parts of the world. Following the Normandy D-Day landings, Miller made plans to move the band to France. By this time he had been promoted to major. On Dec. 15, 1944, he took off in a small plane accompanied by another officer and was never seen again; obviously the plane fell into the English Channel. After the war the Miller sound was kept alive by various ex-members of the band—Benckc, Gray, McKinley, others; the original Miller Orchestra recordings were reissued and attained great popularity. Although the Miller Orchestra was active for about 8 years, its musicianship and unique sound made it one of the most popular big bands of all time. Its later renaissance, postwar and into the '70s, might be attributed partly to a generation's nostalgia but mostly to Miller's driving ambition and musicianship.

MILLS, CHARLES (b. 1914) Composer. Born in Asheville, N.C., Jan. 8, 1914, Mills was largely self-taught until he came to New York City in 1933 and studied with Aaron Copland, Roy Harris, and Roger Sessions (all q.v.). He was active in the League of Composers and often wrote articles on radio performances of contemporary music for *Modern Music* (q.v.) in the 1940s. He taught composition and theory privately, received several commissions and the Roth String Quartet Prize for his *Third String Quartet* (1943). His other works include *Slow Movement for String Orchestra* (1935), *Concertino* for flute and orchestra (1939), *Chamber Symphony* (1939), *Ars Poetica* for chorus a cappella (1940), *Festival Overture* for chorus and orchestra (1940), *Symphony No. 1* (1940), *Piano Trio* (1941), *Chamber Concertante* for wind quintet (1941), *Symphony No. 2* (1942), *Chamber Concerto* for 10 instruments (1942), *John Brown,* ballet for piano, wind quintet, and drum (1945), *The Dark Night* for women's chorus and strings (1945), *Fourth Suite* for piano (1946), *Duo Piccolo* for violins (1946), *Serenade* for flute, horn, and piano (1946), *Piano Concerto* (1948), *The True Beauty* for chorus (1950), *Prelude and Dithyramb* (1951, rev. 1954), *Theme and Variations* for orchestra (1952), *Crazy Horse Symphony* (1958), and *Symphonic Ode* for string orchestra (1976).

MOROSS, JEROME (b. 1913) Composer, pianist. Born in Brooklyn, N.Y., Aug. 1, 1913, Moross was graduated from New York University in 1932; during his final year he also held a Juilliard School of Music fellowship. As an accomplished pianist Moross managed to keep working while composing; he also did orchestrations. He was the pit pianist when Gershwin's opera *Porgy and Bess* (q.v.) toured in 1936 and in its West Coast revival in 1938. In 1940 Moross settled in California where he earned his frustrating way orchestrating the film scores of others—and composing his own works. (It was not until the 1950s that Moross was given the opportunity to write complete film scores, among which was the outstanding *The Big Country* in 1958.) Much of his earlier work was written for ballet. His works include *Paeans* for orchestra (1931), *Those Everlasting Blues* for voice and chamber orchestra (1932), *Biguine* for orchestra (1934), *Suite* for chamber orchestra (1934), *American Pattern,* a ballet (1936), *A Tall Story* for orchestra (1938), *Frankie and Johnny,* ballet for women's trio and orchestra (1938), *Susanna and the Elders,* ballet for soprano, baritone, chorus, and orchestra (1940), *Symphony* (1942), *Willie the Weeper,* ballet for tenor, chorus, and orchestra (1945), *The Eccentricities of Davy Crockett,* ballet for soprano, alto, baritone, chorus, and orchestra (1945), *Riding Hood,* ballet for mezzo, tenor, chorus, and orchestra (1946), *Variations on a Waltz* for orchestra (1946), *The Last Judgement,* ballet (1953), *Sonatina* for clarinet choir (1966), *Sonatina* for contrabass and piano (1967), *Sonatina* for brass quintet (1968), *Sonatina* for woodwind quintet (1970) (the sonatinas have the combined title of *Sonatinas for Divers Instruments*), and *Music for Flicks,* a suite drawn from several of Moross' film scores composed between 1952 and 1965. His *Sonata for Piano Duet and String Quartet* was completed in 1975 and the *Concerto for Flute and String Quartet* in 1978. Moross' works for the theatre include the musical revue *Parade* (1935), the musical comedy-opera *The Golden Apple* with lyrics by John Latouche (1952) from which came a fine song, "Lazy Afternoon." *Gentlemen, Be Seated,* a 2-act opera with libretto by Edward Eager, was completed in 1957 and presented in New York City in 1963.

NABOKOV, NICOLAS (1903–1978) Composer, teacher. Born in Lubcha,

Russia, Apr. 17, 1903, Nabokov studied composition with Vladimir Rebikov in Russia, with Paul Juon and Ferrucio Busoni in Berlin. Because of the Revolution in Russia (Nabokov came from a wealthy background), he divided his time from the mid 1920s to the early '30s between the musical worlds of Berlin and Paris. It was in Paris that Nabokov's first major work was performed, a ballet commissioned by Diaghilev's Ballets Russes, *Ode, or Meditation at Night on the Majesty of God, as Revealed by the Aurora Borealis* (1928). Nabokov came to the United States in 1933. He taught at Wells College, Aurora, N.Y., St. John's College, Annapolis, the Peabody Conservatory, Baltimore, the American Academy, Rome, City University of New York, and State University of New York, Buffalo. After World War II, Nabokov served with the American Military Government in Berlin; he was also cultural advisor to the U. S. Ambassador and helped to establish a Russian branch of the Voice of America for the U. S. State Department. Nabokov was active on several worldwide committees devoted to holding music festivals: Paris, Tokyo, West Berlin. His works include: *Piano Sonata No. 1* (1926), *Symphony No. 1* (1930), *Piano Concerto* (1932), *Collectionneur d'échos* for soprano, bass, and percussion (1933), *Job* for soloists, chorus, and orchestra (1933), *Union Pacific*, a ballet (1934), *Vie de Polichinelle* for orchestra (1934), *Le Fiancé* for orchestra (1934), *String Quartet* (1937), *Piano Sonata No. 2* (1940), *Symphony No. 2* (1940), *America Was Promises*, cantata with text by Archibald MacLeish (1940), *The Last Flower*, a ballet (1941), *Symphonic Suite of Marches* (1945), *The Return of Pushkin* for voice and orchestra (1948), *La Vita Nuova* for soprano, tenor, and orchestra (1951), *Symboli Chrestiani* for bass-baritone and orchestra (1953), *Cello Concerto,* "Les Hommages" (1953), *The*

Holy Devil, an opera about Rasputin (1958), *Four Poems,* to texts by Boris Pasternak, for baritone and orchestra (1959), *Studies in Solitude* for orchestra (1964), *Don Quichotte,* ballet (1965), *The Wanderer,* ballet (1966), *Symphony No. 3* (1967), *Variations on a Theme by Tschaikovsky* for cello and orchestra (1968), and *Love's Labour Lost,* opera (1970). Nabokov was the author of *Old Friends and New Music* (1951) and *Igor Stravinsky* (1964). He died in New York, Apr. 6, 1978.

NEWMAN, ALFRED (1901–1970) Composer, conductor, arranger. Born in New Haven, Conn., Mar. 17, 1901, Newman began to study piano at the age of 7; a year later he made his public debut playing a Beethoven sonata. He was about 10 when he moved to New York City where he studied piano with Sigismund Stojowski and Ignace Paderewski and composition with Rubin Goldmark (q.v.). Later, after he moved to Hollywood, Newman studied also with Arnold Schoenberg (q.v.). He gave early piano recitals in Boston, New York, and Philadelphia and was piano soloist with the New Haven Symphony conducted by Horatio Parker (q.v.). Newman moved into show business as an accompanist in vaudeville; he was about 18 when he became conductor of a *George White's Scandals.* Newman was much sought after to conduct Broadway shows, including several with scores by Gershwin. In 1930 he went to Hollywood where he became a prolific composer of film scores after abandoning composition (his early work includes a piano sonata, a piano quintet, and several orchestra works) of "serious" music. One of his best-known scores is his first, *Street Scene* (1931). Newman provided the background scoring for nearly 300 films between 1931 and 1966 (some were based on the music of others and several won Academy Awards). Newman's own scores that won the Award were *The Song of Bernadette* (1943) and *Love Is a Many-Splendored Thing* (1955). He also received the Award for scoring the songs of Irving Berlin in *Alexander's Ragtime Band* (1938) and *Call Me Madam* (1953) and Rodgers and Hammerstein's *The King and I* (1956). Newman composed several film theme songs "How Green Was My Valley" (1941), "Anastasia" (1956), and "The Best of Everything" (1959). Two of his single songs became quite popular: "The Moon of Manakoora," with lyrics by Frank Loesser (q.v.), from *The Hurricane* (1937) and "Through a Long and Sleepless Night," lyrics by Mack Gordon, from *Come to the Stable* (1949). Newman was active as a conductor (most often at the Hollywood Bowl) and made several recordings of film music. He died in Hollywood, Calif., Feb. 17, 1970.

"NIGHT AND DAY" Song, words and music by Cole Porter (q.v.), written for the Broadway musical *Gay Divorce* (1932). Introduced by Fred Astaire in his first musical without his sister Adele, who had retired, "Night and Day" was more responsible for the show's popularity than its trivial book. Astaire sang, then danced to the music with his new partner, Claire Luce. Porter claimed that the verse of "Night and Day" had been inspired by Mrs. Vincent Astor who, exasperated by the sound of water dripping, exclaimed, "That drip, drip, drip is driving me mad!" The chorus, Porter further claimed, was inspired by a Moroccan religious chant. "Night and Day" is a characteristic Porter song in its unusual structure—it is not a typical 32-bar popular song; in fact, the chorus runs to 50 measures and Porter's use of chromatics throughout the song's chorus was quite daring for 1932.

NORDOFF, PAUL (1909–1977) Composer, teacher. Born in Philadelphia,

Pa., June 4, 1909, Nordoff was a music student by the time he was 8. At 14 he was enrolled in the Philadelphia Conservatory of Music where he studied piano with D. H. Ezerman and, later, with Olga Samaroff. He continued with Samaroff at the Juilliard School, New York City, and studied composition with Rubin Goldmark (q.v.) from 1928 to 1933. He began teaching at the Philadelphia Conservatory in 1937, where he was head of the Department of Composition. Nordoff also taught at Michigan State College (1945–49) and Bard College (1949–59). In the late 1950s he became interested in musical therapy, especially as related to handicapped children, and did much work in that field. He was appointed senior music therapy consultant and supervisor of music therapy research at the Child Study Center, Philadelphia. He worked in this field in the United States, Britain, Finland, and West Germany. Nordoff's works include *Prelude and Three Fugues* for orchestra (1932), *String Quartet No. 1* (1932), *Piano Concerto No. 1* (1934), *Secular Mass* for chorus and orchestra (1934), *Romeo and Juliet*, incidental music for flute, violin, harp, and cello (1935), *String Quartet No. 2* (1935), *Piano Quintet* (1936), *Piano Concerto No. 2* (1936), *Mr. Fortune*, opera in 2 acts (1937), *Every Soul Is a Circus*, ballet (1938), *Suite* for orchestra (1939), *Violin Concerto* (1940), *The Masterpiece*, opera in one act (1941), *Salem Shore*, ballet (1944), *The Sun*, for speaker, chorus, soprano, contralto, eurhythmists, and orchestra (1945), *Concerto for Violin, Piano and Orchestra* (ca. 1946), *Little Concerto* for violin, viola, cello, double bass, and orchestra (1950), *Gospel of Eve*, ballet (1950), *Winter Symphony* (1954), and *The Frog Prince* for narrator and orchestra (1955). Nordoff was the author of *Music Therapy for Handicapped Children* with Clive Robbins (1965) and, also in collaboration with

Robbins, *Music Therapy in Special Education* (1971). Nordoff died in Herdecke, West Germany, Jan. 18, 1977.

NORTH, ALEX (b. 1910) Composer, teacher, conductor. Born in Chester, Pa., Dec. 4, 1910, North began as a piano student. He won a scholarship to study at the Institute of Musical Art, New York City (1929–32), where he studied composition with Bernard Wagenaar (q.v.). In 1933 he went to Moscow to study further with Anton Weprik and became quite active there as music director of the German Theatre Group, the Latvian State Theatre, and was a member of the Union of Soviet Composers. Upon returning to the United States in 1937 North continued his studies with Aaron Copland (q.v.) and Ernst Toch. His association with the Anna Sokolow Dancers led to many compositions for the ballet. During World War II, North served with the U. S. Army, attained the rank of captain, and composed several scores for documentary films. After the war he became active as an outstanding film composer. In between, he taught at Sarah Lawrence College, Bronxville, N.Y., and other schools. North's compositions include *Slaughter of the Innocents* for guitar and chamber orchestra (1937), *Dog Beneath the Skin,* play with music (1937), *Quest* for orchestra (1938), *American Lyric,* ballet, for small orchestra (1938), *Suite* for flute, clarinet, and bassoon (1938), *Rhapsody* for orchestra and piano (1939), *Suite* for string quartet (1939), *Life and Death of an American,* incidental music (1939), *Negro Mother* for contralto and chorus (1940), *Golden Fleece* for chamber orchestra (1940), *Ballad of Valley Forge* for baritone and chorus (1941), *Yank and Christopher Columbus* for orchestra (1942), *Rhapsody, U.S.A.* for chorus (1942), *Woodwind Quintet* (1942), *Hither and Thither for Danny Dither,* children's opera

(1942), *A Better Tomorrow,* score for an Office of War Information film (1944), *Concert Suite* for clarinet and orchestra (1945), *Morning Star,* cantata for chorus, 2 pianos, and percussion (1946), *Revue* for clarinet and orchestra (1947), *Rhapsody* for piano and orchestra (1953), *Mal de Siècle,* ballet (1958), *Symphony No. 2* (1968), and *Symphony No. 3* (1971). In 1949 North composed the incidental music for the Arthur Miller play *The Death of a Salesman* which led to his first major film assignment, the jazz-inflected score for *A Streetcar Named Desire* (1951). Since that highly praised score North has composed for dozens of films of which several were outstanding: *Viva Zapata!* (1952), *The Member of the Wedding* (1952), *Unchained* (from which came the popular song "Unchained Melody," 1955), *The Wonderful Country* (1959), *The Sound and the Fury* (1959), *Spartacus* (1960), *The Misfits* (1961), *Cleopatra* (1963), *The Agony and the Ecstasy* (1965), *Who's Afraid of Virginia Woolf?* (1966), etc.

NOWAK, LIONEL (b. 1911) Composer, pianist, teacher. Born in Cleveland, Ohio, Sept. 25, 1911, Nowak studied piano, composition, harmony, and counterpoint at the Cleveland Institute of Music (1929–36); among his teachers were Herbert Elwell (q.v.), Quincy Porter (q.v.), and Roger Sessions (q.v.). After completion of his work at the Institute, Nowak joined the Humphrey-Weidman Dance Company as director and pianist. In addition to touring as a concert pianist, Nowak has taught at Converse College, S.C., Syracuse University, N.Y., and Bennington College, Vt. Much of his early output was written for the ballet. His works include *Suite in C* for orchestra (1936), *String Quartet* (1938), *Square Dances,* ballet for piano (1939), *On My Mother's Side,* ballet for piano (1939),

Danzas mexicanas, ballet for piano (1939), *Sonata* for solo violin (1940), *Mexican Suite* for piano (1940), *The Green Land,* ballet for piano (1941), *Suite* for flute and piano (1941), *String Trio* (1942), *Land of Ing* for voice, piano, and percussion (1942), *Flickers,* ballet for piano (1942), *Heritage for Tomorrow* for voice, piano, and percussion (1943), *Quartet for Winds* (1944), *Concertino* for piano and orchestra (1944), *Sonatina* for violin and piano (1944), *House Divided,* ballet for piano (1945), *Dancing Feet* for voice, piano, and percussion (1945), *Story of Mankind,* ballet for orchestra (1946), *Sonata* for oboe (1949), *Cello Sonata No. 1* (1950), *Diptych* for string quartet (1951), *Cello Sonata No. 2* (1951), *Trio* for clarinet, violin, and cello (1951), *Quartet* for oboe and strings (1952), *Wisdom Exalteth Her Children* for chorus (1952), *Fantasia* for piano (1954), *Trio* for violin, cello, and piano (1954), *Cello Sonata No. 3* (1960), *Concert Piece for Kettledrums* (1961), and *Soundscape* for 3 woodwinds (also for solo piano, 1964).

"OF THEE I SING" Political operetta with lyrics and music by George and Ira Gershwin (q.v.) and book by George S. Kaufman (1889–1961) and Morrie Ryskind (b. 1895). One of a trio of musical satires which began with Kaufman's libretto for an antiwar musical, *Strike Up the Band,* which was produced in 1927 and closed in Philadelphia. Revised in 1929 by Kaufman and Ryskind (who appears to have taken some of the bite out of the book), *Strike Up the Band* opened again in 1930 and enjoyed a healthy run of 191 performances. *Of Thee I Sing* opened at the Music Box, Dec. 26, 1931, and was most successful (441 performances). The book satirized American politics and introduced the bumbling, wistful Vice-President "Alexander Throttlebottom,"

portrayed by comedian Victor Moore. The candidate and later President "John P. Wintergreen" was portrayed by William Gaxton. Wintergreen and his corrupt gang of politicians manage to get in the White House by running on the Love Ticket, with the promise that Wintergreen, if elected, will marry the winner of a national beauty contest. Fittingly the campaign song is "Of Thee I Sing" and another song proclaims that "Love Is Sweeping the Country." The songs were woven into the plot and integrated by several musical passages and dances. Although one "Diana Devereaux" (Grace Brinkley), "The Illegitimate Daughter of an Illegitimate Son of an Illegitimate Nephew of Napoleon," wins the beauty contest, Wintergreen, upon winning the election, decides instead to marry his true love, "Mary Turner" (Lois Moran). His reason: because she "can really make corn muffins." The French Ambassador (Florenz Ames) protests and forces an impeachment proceeding against Wintergreen. He is saved at the last moment when Mary arrives at the Senate to announce, "I'm about to be a Mother (He's about to be a father)." Since the Senate had never in history impeached an expectant father, the final vote is Not Guilty. *Of Thee I Sing* was the first musical to get the Pulitzer Prize (although, since the Pulitzers were awarded to plays only in 1931, George Gershwin received nothing for his contribution to the show's success). That success encouraged the same quartet of writers and composer to produce a sequel with the same characters. This was *Let 'Em Eat Cake,* which opened in October 1933. Despite Gershwin's remarkable score, the tenor of the show—it savaged politicians again as well as radicals, motherhood, the military, etc.—did not capture the theatregoing public as had *Of Thee I Sing.* Its best-known song, the contrapuntal "Mine," is about all that remains of that superior and imaginative score. A revival of the reconstructed score (this work was done by composer-conductor Gregg Smith) was staged at the Berkshire Theatre, Stockbridge, Mass., in July 1978. The critics, as usual, found much fault with the book. So only *Of Thee I Sing* remains of the trio of Gershwin political operettas—and its book does not hold up too well. Considering the recent history of American politics, it is quite tame, if prescient (and *Let 'Em Eat Cake* more so). The songs written for *Of Thee I Sing* were closely integrated with the plot and were not designed for "Your Hit Parade" (q.v.), although a few are still known: the title song, "Wintergreen for President," "Love Is Sweeping the Country," and "Who Cares?" The operetta was revived in 1952 starring Jack Carson and Paul Hartman and had a short run of 72 performances.

"OKLAHOMA!" History-making musical, music by Richard Rodgers (q.v.) and lyrics and book by Oscar Hammerstein II (q.v.). Hammerstein based his book on the play *Green Grow the Lilacs* (1931) by Lynn Riggs. The setting is the Oklahoma Territory around the turn of the century and the story is about 2 ranch hands, "Curly" and "Jud," who court "Laurey," niece of the owner of the ranch. Curly and Laurey quarrel and she goes to a dance with Jud. Curly proves his love by bidding on the basket Laurey has prepared for the traditional auction at the dance. When he gives everything he has for the basket, true love triumphs. Laurey marries Curly and Jud smolders. He attacks Curly and in the ensuing fight stabs himself with his own knife. Curly is accused of murder but is exonerated. Almost at the same moment word comes in that Oklahoma has been admitted into the Union as a state. There is a great finale built around

the title song. *Oklahoma!* was the first collaboration by Rodgers and Hammerstein and its songs are outstanding. *Oklahoma!* was also notable for the storytelling choreography by Agnes de Mille, an innovational touch for the musical theatre—although not quite as new as claimed. (De Mille herself created an antiwar *Hero Ballet* to Harold Arlen's music in *Hooray for What!* in 1937 and George Balanchine choreographed the "Slaughter on Tenth Avenue" ballet, also related to the plot, for Rodgers and Hart's *On Your Toes* in 1936.) This does not, of course, detract from the value and importance of *Oklahoma!* with such songs as "Oh, What a Beautiful Mornin'," "People Will Say We're in Love," "Out of My Dreams," "The Surrey with the Fringe on Top," "Kansas City," "I Cain't Say No." *Oklahoma!* opened at the St. James Theatre on Mar. 31, 1943, and ran for 2,212 performances (in London it ran for more than 1,500). It has been revived several times and was made into a film in 1955. In the original production the leads were Alfred Drake (Curly), Joan Roberts (Laurey), and Howard Da Silva (Jud). Celeste Holm made a good comic impression in the role of "Ado Annie," the girl who couldn't say no. Because of the importance of the ballets to the plot *Oklahoma!* featured several dancers, among them Diana Adams, Bambi Linn, and Marc Platt.

"ON THE TOWN" Musical comedy, music by Leonard Bernstein (q.v.), and lyrics and book by Betty Comden and Adolph Green (q.v.). The book was an expansion of a ballet, *Fancy Free,* conceived by Jerome Robbins with music by Bernstein. The story concerns 3 young sailors on a 24-hour shore leave in New York, their adventures in the city, and the 3 girls they meet. The most serious of the romances is that of "Ivy Smith" and "Gabey," the more wistful of the sailors.

Ivy is a dancer who happens to be the subway's "Miss Turnstiles" of the month. The other romances involve "Chip" with a lady cab driver, "Brunhilde Esterhazy," and "Ozzie" with an anthropologist, "Claire de Loon." The plot of the musical, besides moving through various New York settings, is woven around Gabey's attempts to be reunited with Ivy before the 24 hours are up. He is aided by his friends and their girl friends. In addition to several fine songs, *On the Town* was notable for its ballet sequences. Among the songs: "New York, New York," "I Can Cook, Too," "Lonely Town," "Lucky to Be Me," "Carried Away," "Come Up to My Place," and "Ya Got Me." *On the Town* opened at Adelphi Theatre, New York City, Dec. 28, 1944, and ran for 463 performances (it was Bernstein's first musical). A London production (1963) did not run for long; neither did the 2 New York revivals in 1959 and 1971. A film version, which for reasons known only to Hollywood omitted much of the Bernstein music, was made in 1949. In the original production "Ivy" was portrayed by Sono Osato, "Gabey" by John Battles, "Chip" by Cris Alexander, "Brunhilde" by Nancy Walker, "Ozzie" by Adolph Green, and "Claire" by Betty Comden.

"PAL JOEY" Musical by Rodgers and Hart based on short stories by John O'Hara that appeared as letters in *The New Yorker*. O'Hara adapted some of these letters written by a shrewd, conniving dancer, "Joey," for the musical's book. (The letters were signed "Pal Joey," which explains the title.) *Pal Joey* was one of the few musicals in which the lead is a heel. Joey works in a nightclub in Chicago and manages, through his charm, to get his own club, Chez Joey, through a romance with the wealthy "Vera." She eventually tires of the crafty dancer and Joey ends up with nothing but his charm, which, as the musical

ends, he is turning on yet another ingenuous young woman. Originally there was some objection to *Pal Joey* and its callous protagonist—some critics objected that he was not a fit hero for a musical. The score is one of the best by Rodgers and Hart (q.v.). Among the songs: "Bewitched, Bothered and Bewildered," "Den of Iniquity," "Zip," "Take Him," and "I Could Write a Book." In the original production Gene Kelly, in his first important role, portrayed "Joey" and Vivienne Segal "Vera." *Pal Joey* opened at the Ethel Barrymore Theatre, Dec. 25, 1940, and ran for 374 performances (the 1952 revival ran for 542). A film version, with Frank Sinatra in the lead, was released in 1957.

PALMER, ROBERT (b. 1915) Composer, teacher. Born in Syracuse, N.Y., June 2, 1915, Palmer studied at the Eastman School of Music, Rochester, N.Y., with Bernard Rogers and Howard Hanson. He also studied with Roy Harris and Aaron Copland. He himself began teaching theory and composition in 1940 at the University of Kansas, Lawrence, and has taught at Cornell University, Ithaca, N.Y., since 1943. His works include *String Trio No. 1* for violin, viola, and cello (1937), *Poem* for violin and chamber orchestra (1938), *Piano Sonata No. 1* (1938), *String Quartet No. 1* (1939), *Concerto for Small Orchestra* (1940), *Three Preludes* for piano (1941), *String Trio No. 2* (1942), *Sonata for Violin and Piano* (1942), *Concerto for Orchestra* (1943); *Concerto for Five Instruments* (1943), *String Quartet No. 2* (1943), *Sonata for Two Pianos* (1944), *Irish Legend,* ballet (1944), *Quartet for Piano and Strings* (1945), *"K. 19," elegy for Thomas Wolfe,* for orchestra (1945), *Toccata Ostinato* for piano (1945), *Abraham Lincoln Walks at Midnight* for chorus and orchestra, text by Vachel Lindsay (1945), *Symphonic Variations* for orchestra (1946), *Variations, Chorale and Fugue* for orchestra (1947), *String Quartet No. 2* (1947), *Chamber Concerto* for violin, oboe, and strings (1949), *Piano Quintet* (1950), *Viola Sonata* (1951), *Wind Quintet* (1951), *Sonata* for piano, 4 hands (1952), *Slow, Slow Fresh Fount* for chorus (1953), *String Quartet No. 3* (1954), *The Trojan Women* for women's chorus, winds, and percussion (1955), *Memorial Music* for small orchestra (1957), *String Quartet No. 4* (1959), *Nabuchodonosor*, oratorio for tenor, baritone, men's chorus, brass, and percussion (1964), *A Centennial Overture* for orchestra (1965), *Symphony No. 2* (1966), *Choric Song and Toccata* for winds (1969), and *Concerto for Piano and Strings* (1970).

PARISH, MITCHELL (b. 1900) Popular song lyricist. Born in Shreveport, La., July 10, 1900, Parish grew up and was educated in New York City, at New York University and Columbia. At Columbia he edited the college magazine. Later he worked as a staff writer for music publishers. Parish had his first major hit in 1931, when he wrote the lyrics for a Hoagy Carmichael (q.v.) instrumental, "Star Dust." Although he contributed lyrics to shows and revues, Parish has been most successful with individual songs, or in transforming instrumental pieces into songs. His most popular songs: "Sophisticated Lady," music by Duke Ellington (1933), "Stars Fell on Alabama," music by Frank Perkins (1934), "Don't Be That Way," music by Benny Goodman and Edgar Sampson (1938), "The Lamp Is Low," adapted from Ravel's *Pavane pour une Infante Défunte* by Peter DeRose and Bert Shefter (1939), "Deep Purple" and "Lilacs in the Rain," 2 themes from Peter DeRose's *Deep Purple* (1939), "Moonlight Serenade," music by Glenn Miller (1939), and "Stairway to the Stars," based on a theme from *Park Avenue Fantasy* by Matty Malneck and Frank Signorelli (1939). Parish set words to several of Leroy Anderson's (q.v.) instrumentals, among them "Sleigh Ride," "Fiddle Faddle," "Serenata," "Belle of the Ball," and "Blue Tango." His lyricized adaptation of an Italian song, "Volare," was very popular in 1958. Parish is the author of a collection of verse, *For Those in Love*.

PARKER, CHARLES "YARDBIRD" (1920–1955) Alto saxophonist, bandleader, composer. Born in Kansas City, Mo., Aug. 29, 1920, Parker was largely self-taught, though he played in the brass section of the high school band. He dropped out of school to play in the brass section of the Jay McShann band in Kansas City at the age of 15. Parker arrived, a member of the McShann band, in New York City in 1941. Around this time he met trumpeter "Dizzy" Gillespie; the two would often meet with other band and jazz musicians at Minton's, a Harlem nightclub, where they began experimenting with new approaches to jazz. This new phase of jazz performance, by ca. 1943, came to be called "bop" (q.v.). Parker, Gillespie, and others (Thelonious Monk, Charlie Christian, Kenny Clark, et al.) are credited with the development of bop, with Parker generally heading the list. Parker played in several bands during the period that followed—Noble Sissle, Earl Hines, Andy Kirk, and Billy Eckstine. He also recorded with Dizzy Gillespie's band and one formed around him. By the mid 1940s Parker showed emotional problems; he drank a great deal and was heavily dependent on drugs. In 1946 he suffered a breakdown. He lost his performer's license to play in New York City because of drug addiction. Despite these problems, Parker made several recoveries and played in jazz groups that toured Europe in 1949 and 1950; he made many recordings, although these activities were interrupted by poor health. During these low periods (in 1954) Parker attempted suicide. He died at the age of 34 of a heart attack in New York City, Mar. 12, 1955. Parker influenced an entire generation of jazz musicians through his innovative musical ideas. He often constructed an original composition by borrowing the chord progressions from a composition of another composer. Among his "compositions" (actually improvisations) are *Yardbird Suite, Bird Lore, Anthropology,* and *Relaxin' at Camarillo.* His nickname, eventually abbreviated simply to "Bird," derived from his fondness for chicken, the "yardbird."

PARTCH, HARRY (1901–1974) Composer, theorist. Born in Oakland, Calif., June 24, 1901, Partch, whose parents had been missionaries in China, grew up in Arizona. He became interested in music at about the age of 6, when he taught himself to play several instruments. Partch had no formal musical training and learned musical theory by reading books in the local library. He began composing around the time he was 14, but later destroyed all of his juvenilia. Influenced by the musics of many cultures, Indian, Chinese, African, Jewish, etc., Partch began evolving his own musical theories in 1923 and designed and constructed the instruments to demonstrate them. As he explained, "I am not an instrument builder but a philosophic music-man seduced into carpentry." The beautifully fashioned instruments were a part of the performance, related to the unusual sounds they produced. Partch rejected the standard scale of Western music and divided the octave into 43 tones. Performance of a Partch work, in which musicians participated also as "actors," and in which vocalists and speakers spoke, intoned as well as sang, exemplified early efforts at what has since come to be called "multi-

media." Music is combined with speech, movement, drama, and lighting. To accomplish this revolutionary approach Partch (after a long period of earning his way at odd jobs) received aid from the Carnegie Corp., the Guggenheim Fund, and several universities. His works include *Seventeen Lyrics by Li Po* (1930), *By the Rivers of Babylon* (1930), *Inscriptions* (1932), *Y. D. Fantasy* (1941), *The Wayward,* "Barstow-eight hitchiker inscriptions from a highway railing," "The Letter," "San Francisco-newsboy cries," "U. S. Highball" (1941–43), *Dark Brother,* text by Thomas Wolfe (1943), *Two Psalms* (1943), *Two Excerpts from James Joyce* (1944), *Account of the Normandy Invasion* (1945), *Intrusions* (1950), *Oedipus* (1951), *Plectra and Percussion Dances* (1952), *The Bewitched* (1955), *Windsong,* film score (1958), *Rotate the Body in All Its Planes* (1961), *Water, Water* (1962), *And on the Seventh Day Petals Fell on Petaluma* (1964), and *Delusion of Fury* (1966). Partch published his book *Genesis of a Music* in 1949. He died in San Diego, Calif., Sept. 3, 1974.

PERSICHETTI, VINCENT (b. 1915) Composer, teacher, pianist, organist. Born in Philadelphia, Pa., June 6, 1915, Persichetti was a student of composition with Russell K. Miller, Paul Nordoff (q.v.), and Roy Harris. He studied piano with Olga Samaroff and Alberto Jonás, and conducting with Fritz Reiner. He is a graduate of Combs College of Music, the Curtis Institute, and the Philadelphia Conservatory, whose staff he joined in 1942. Since 1947 he has been on the staff of the Juilliard School of Music; in 1963 was appointed head of the Department of Composition. Persichetti is the recipient of many prizes, fellowships, and commissions. A prolific composer, his diversified works number well over 100. Among them are: *Suite for Chamber Orchestra* (1939), *String*

Quartet No. 1 (1939), *Piano Sonata No. 1* and *Piano Sonata No. 2* (1939), *Prelude* for solo dancer and piano (1940), *Magnificat* for chorus and piano (1940), *Quintet for Piano and Strings* (1940), *Sonatine No. 1* for piano (1940), *Sonata for Two Pianos* (1940), *Solo Violin Sonata* (1940), *Concertino* for piano and orchestra (1941), *Sonata for Violin and Piano* (1941), *Trio* for violin, cello, and piano (1941), *Symphony No. 1* and *Symphony No. 2* (1942), *Dance Overture* for orchestra (1942), *Pastoral* for flute, oboe, clarinet, horn, and bassoon (1943), *Fables* for narrator and orchestra (1943), *Piano Sonata No. 3* (1943), *String Quartet No. 2* (1944), *Then One Day,* for 3 dancers and piano (1944), *The Hollow Men* for trumpet and strings (1944), *Vocalise* for cello and piano (1945), *Symphony No. 3* (1947), *Dance Overture* (1948), *King Lear,* ballet (1949), *Divertimento* for band (1950), *Harmonium* for soprano and piano, text by Wallace Stevens (1951), *Symphony No. 4* (1951), *Pageant* for band (1953), *Symphony No. 5* (1953), *Piano Quintet No. 2* (1955), *Symphony No. 6* (1956), *String Quartet No. 3* (1959), *Symphony No. 7* (1959), *Mass* for chorus (1961), *Bagatelles* for band (1962), *Spring Cantata* for women's voices and piano (1964), *Stabat Mater* for chorus and orchestra (1964), *Te Deum* for chorus and orchestra (1964), *Introit* for strings (1965), *Winter Cantata* for women's chorus, flute, and marimba (1965), *Mascarade* for band (1965), *Symphony No. 8* (1967), *The Creation,* oratorio (1970), *Symphony No. 9* (1971), *Lincoln Address* for narrator and orchestra (1973), and *Concerto for English Horn and Strings* (1977). Persichetti has composed numerous *Serenades* for various instrumental combinations: No. 1 for 10 wind instruments dates from 1929 and No. 13, for 2 clarinets, from 1963. His 11th piano sonata was completed in 1965. There are several organ works, songs, and compositions for band. Persichetti is the author of *William Schuman,* with Flora Rheta (1954), *Twentieth-Century Harmony* (1961), and *Essays on Twentieth-Century Choral Music* (1963).

PHILLIPS, BURRILL (b. 1907) Composer, teacher. Born in Omaha, Neb., Nov. 9, 1907, Phillips was a student of Edwin Stringham (q.v.) at the Denver College of Music and of Edward Royce, Howard Hanson, and Bernard Rogers at the Eastman School of Music, Rochester, N.Y., from which he was graduated in 1933. He began teaching composition at the Eastman School the same year; he also taught at the University of Illinois, Urbana, and at the Juilliard School of Music, New York City. Phillips has been the recipient of a Guggenheim Fellowship (1942) and commissions from the League of Composers and the Koussevitzky Foundation. His works include *Grotesque Dance* for orchestra (1932), *Princess and Puppet,* ballet (1933), *Selections from McGuffey's Reader* (1934), *Courthouse Square* for orchestra (1935), *Symphony Concertante* (1936), *Concerto for Piano and Orchestra* (1937), *Trio for Trumpets* (1937), *Play Ball,* ballet (1938), *String Quartet No. 1* (1939), *Oh Angel* for a cappella chorus (1939), *Three Satiric Fragments,* ballet (1939), *Concert Piece* for bassoon and strings (1940), *Music for Strings* (1940), *Step Into My Parlor,* ballet (1941), *Piano Sonata,* "Nine by Nine" (1942), *Sonata for Violin and Piano* (1942), *Declaratives* for women's voices and chamber orchestra (1943), *Scherzo* for orchestra (1944), *Tom Paine* for orchestra (1944), *Sonata* for cello and piano (1946), *Go 'Way from My Window* for mezzo-soprano, baritone, and piano (1946), *Three Divertimentos* (1946), *Don't We All,* one-act opera (1948), *Cello Sonata* (1949),

Piano Sonata No. 2 (1949), *Four Figures in Time* for flute and piano (1953), *Triple Concerto* for viola, clarinet, piano, and orchestra (1953), *Piano Sonata No. 3* (1953), *The Return of Odysseus* for chorus and orchestra (1956), *String Quartet No. 2* (1958), *Piano Sonata No. 4* (1960), *La Piñata* for chamber orchestra (1960), *Perspectives in a Labyrinth* for triple string orchestra (1962), *Sonata da Camera* for organ (1964), *Soleriana* for orchestra (1965), *Sonata for Violin and Harpsichord* (1966), *That Time May Cease* for men's chorus and piano (1966), *Quartet* for oboe and strings (1967), and *Canzona III* for reader and chamber orchestra (1970).

"PIANO VARIATIONS" One of the peaks of American piano composition by Aaron Copland (q.v.). A work of stark, extraordinary economy (the performance requires about 10 minutes), the *Piano Variations* was written by Copland during 1930, beginning in January and completed in October–November. The first performance was given under the auspices of the League of Composers (q.v.), Jan. 4, 1931, at the Art Center (then at 65 East 65th Street, New York City) with the composer at the piano reading from a penciled manuscript. While some reviewers detected the influence of Schoenberg (the "serial" structure) and Bartók (the brittle, percussive piano sound), the *Piano Variations* is a highly original composition as Copland, in an unorthodox manner, (i.e., he introduces a variation of the theme first and then states the theme), takes his theme through 20 permutations. After the first performance the critical reception was not especially favorable. Jerome D. Bohm, of the New York *Herald Tribune,* noted that Copland "has in these variations sardonically thumbed his nose at all of those esthetic attributes which have hitherto

been considered essential to the creation of music." The *Variations* is important not only as a landmark in American music, but also in Copland's development. While there are elements of jazz that had appeared in his earlier works, such as the *Dance Symphony* (1925), *Music for the Theater* (1925, q.v.), and the *Piano Concerto* (1926), the treatment is abstract, intense, muscular, so to speak, pointing toward yet another "difficult" masterpiece, the *Short Symphony*. It took some time but Copland's *Piano Variations* is recognized as one of the major piano compositions of our time.

"PINS AND NEEDLES" A revue with lyrics and music by Harold Rome (q.v.) and sketches by Charles Friedman, Emanuel Eisenberg, Arthur Arent, Marc Blitzstein (q.v.), and Rome. *Pins and Needles* is unique in the history of the American musical theatre. It introduced composer Rome to not quite off-Broadway (Labor Stage, 106 West 39th Street, formally the Princess Theatre), it was produced by the International Ladies' Garment Workers' Union, and its cast consisted entirely of union members—all amateurs. The show ran only on weekends, when the cast was not stitching, cutting, or finishing. *Pins and Needles* was decidedly political: pro-labor, anti-Fascist (it opened in 1937), but with a charming, self-mocking undercurrent of humor. The idea for a topical revue for union members originated with Louis Schaffer, head of the union's theatrical activities. He, in turn, approached Rome, whose songs he had heard at a popular summer resort, Green Mansions, in the Adirondack Mountains of New York State. Having passed muster as songwriter, he was hired by Schaffer to be rehearsal pianist for the production to come. More than a year passed before the show was done, primarily because the cast found Rome's satirical though sunny songs not "serious" enough to match the spirit of the time. One song, "Sing Me a Song with Social Significance," would appear to lampoon that point of view as well as the typical Tin Pan Alley "ballad" (love song) of the time. Schaffer won over the union cast by staging a single runthrough in June 1936 with professionals, hired through the W.P.A. program, then arranging for work for actors. Rome officiated at one of the 2 pianos and Earl Robinson (q.v.) at the other. After a long period of rehearsal, *Pins and Needles* opened at the Labor Stage on Nov. 27, 1937. Running only weekends, ignored—at first—by the critics, the show attracted little but ILGWU audiences. But word got around and it became a hit and literally ran for years as new crises, national and international, inspired new skits and songs. The final edition was entitled *Pins and Needles 1940,* later *New Pins and Needles* (the first opening in September 1939). By this time the dangers that had been noted by the earlier versions of *Pins and Needles* had become realities. The total run reached more than 1,000 (the weekend run had also been expanded to full-time performances). Among the Rome songs written for the show: "One Big Union for Two," "Doin' the Reactionary," "Nobody Makes a Pass at Me," "Sunday in the Park" (which became popular), "Four Little Angels of Peace" (Hitler, Mussolini, Anthony Eden, and an unidentified Japanese), and "Not Cricket to Picket." Later editions included "It's Better with a Union Man" (added in 1939). By this time *Pins and Needles* had been transferred to the large Windsor Theatre. Rome would return to the proletarian theme in such shows as *Sing Out the News* (1938), the postwar *Call Me Mister* (1946), which drew upon his Army experiences, and the charming Catskill folk opera, *Wish You Were Here* (1952).

"THE PLOW THAT BROKE THE PLAINS" Score for a documentary film by Virgil Thomson (q.v.). Thomson was asked by film critic-turned-filmmaker Pare Lorentz, early in 1936, to compose the background music for a film he was preparing for the Farm Security Administration of the U. S. Department of Agriculture. *The Plow That Broke the Plains* attempted to show that the great drought in the Southwest could be blamed on man's abuse of the soil and greed as well as on nature, which then blew away the topsoil. Thomson, with some aid from musical secretary Henry Brant (q.v.), managed to complete the score—for an honorarium of $500—in about 2 weeks. The resulting film was one of the most powerful documentaries of the Depression—and the music contributed tremendously to its effect and importance. (Thomson and Lorentz collaborated on another outstanding documentary, *The River,* the next year.) In 1942 Thomson prepared a *The Plow That Broke the Plains* suite that consists of 6 sections: "Prelude," "Pastoral (Grass)," "Cattle," "Blues (Speculation)," "Drought," and "Devastation."

"PORGY AND BESS" Opera in 3 acts by George Gershwin (q.v.), libretto by DuBose Heyward and lyrics by Heyward and Ira Gershwin (q.v.). The idea to make an opera of Heyward's novel originated with Gershwin shortly after *Porgy* was published late in 1926. The project was postponed because Heyward's wife, Dorothy, had begun work on a dramatic version which became one of the great successes of the 1927 theatrical season. Gershwin came back to the idea in March 1932 and this time the way was clear and Heyward was happy with the idea. But Gershwin's commitments kept him occupied for nearly 2 years (he had shows to do, a radio program, and a nationwide concert tour). The work was almost postponed again when vaudevillian Al Jolson expressed an interest in doing *Porgy*—in blackface!—with songs by Jerome Kern and Oscar Hammerstein. That fell through and finally Gershwin actually began working on Heyward's libretto (which came from Charleston, S.C., via the mails) in February 1934. A great deal of the initial work was done in this fashion, although Gershwin visited Heyward on occasion and, during the summer of 1934, spent about 5 weeks at Folly Beach, S.C. From there Gershwin managed to visit Negro churches and to soak up local color—although he chose not to quote folk materials. Gershwin spent about 11 months composing the music and 9 on orchestration. His completed manuscript is marked "Finished August 23, 1935." *Porgy and Bess* tells the romanticized story of a cripple, Porgy, and his love for a quasi-prostitute, Bess. When the opera opens she is "Crown's woman," Crown being the tough, ill-tempered stevedore and the opera's major villain. The minor villain is the smooth-talking, narcotics-peddling dapper operator from New York, "Sportin' Life." The setting is "Catfish Row," which Heyward based on the Negro section of Charleston, inhabited by dock workers and fishermen. During a Saturday night crap game Crown kills Robbins in an argument and is forced to flee. The only one in Catfish Row who will give Bess sanctuary before the police arrive is Porgy. As time goes by Bess is accepted by the community and she and Porgy find temporary happiness. But one night Crown returns and Porgy kills him. Porgy is taken by the police, not as a suspect but to identify Crown. Sportin' Life assures Porgy and Bess that when Crown's murderer looks at him, Crown's wounds will begin to bleed again. With Porgy gone, Sportin' Life plies Bess with "Happy Dust," and then convinces her that she can live "the high life in New York" with him and they leave. Porgy returns from the jail with gifts for everyone only to find Bess gone. Calling for his goatcart, he sets out for New York as the curtain comes down. The original production of *Porgy and Bess* opened at the Alvin Theatre, Oct. 10, 1935, and starred Todd Duncan as "Porgy," Anne Brown as "Bess," John W. Bubbles (of the vaudeville team Buck and Bubbles) as "Sportin' Life," Warren Coleman as "Crown," and Ruby Elzy as "Serena." It closed after 124 performances, resulting in the loss of the total investment raised by the Theatre Guild, which produced it. After a tour of 2 months, *Porgy and Bess* was closed and never revived during Gershwin's lifetime. Its first major revival opened in New York City in January 1942 and was enthusiastically received—although it was no longer really Gershwin's opera but a watered-down version concentrating on the popular songs. This production was equally successful on its tour of the United States and Canada (1942–44). There were also many European productions. In 1952 it was revived again in a production directed by Robert Breen and, after a most successful New York run, made history in a tour of the world: Vienna, Paris, Egypt, Israel, Milan (at La Scala), and Moscow (1952–58). Although Breen restored some of the music that had been eliminated from the original production ("The Buzzard Song," "I Ain't Got No Shame," etc.), his *Porgy and Bess* continued to emphasize the succession of popular songs rather than the operatic aspect. The full restoration finally came in 1976 with the production by the Houston Grand Opera which opened in New York, Sept. 25. Gershwin finally came into his own as the composer of a major American opera. An unfortunate film version, produced by Samuel Goldwyn, was released in 1959. In her supplement to Isaac Goldberg's *George Gershwin*, Edith Garson, writing in 1958, observed that Gershwin, in *Porgy and Bess,* had "created a truly American masterpiece, bursting with energy, overflowing with life, filled with his best and characteristic melodies. It is brilliantly organized and orchestrated; in short, his finest work." Most critics and musicologists would now concur, but Garson made that statement in 1958.

"THE PRAIRIE" Cantata for soloists, chorus, and orchestra by Lukas Foss (q.v.). The composer was 19 when he read Carl Sandburg's *Prairie* (1918) and decided to set it to music. Foss, whose family had fled Nazi Germany in 1933, and who came to the United States 4 years later, was, by his own admission, "in love with America." *The Prairie* is his remarkable statement of that love. When someone suggested that before he went ahead with the composition of so complex a work he should acquire the proper permission to use the Sandburg poem, Foss wrote a "long, pleading letter" to the poet. Sandburg's answer was a short note to the publisher: "This young man has the right sporting approach; give him a break." Foss completed work on *The Prairie* late in 1943 (he was then all of 21). Its first full performance took place at New York's Town Hall, May 15, 1944, under Robert Shaw conducting his Collegiate Chorale. The next year it was performed by the New York Philharmonic, conducted by Artur Rodzinski and with a stellar cast of soloists: Dorothy Kirsten, Nan Merriman, William Hain, and Todd Duncan. *The Prairie* is a surprisingly idiomatic work, considering that its composer had been speaking American English for only a few years; the melodies and rhythms are fused with Sandburg's poetry. It is Americana unabashed, without apology, an expression of true love by a musician whose gifts matured early in his career.

RAINGER, RALPH (1901–1942) Composer, pianist. Born in New York City, Oct. 7, 1901, Rainger began to study the piano, along with several siblings, at the age of 6 (the teacher offered a special family rate). Although it was obvious that Rainger had a musical gift, his father, a merchant, discouraged it. While still in high school, Rainger won a musical scholarship at the Damrosch Institute of Musical Arts. Under the urging of his father and an uncle (the family financial adviser), Rainger reluctantly withdrew from the Institute and enrolled in the law school at Brown University. Graduating with honors Rainger began working in a law firm but, sometime in 1926, gave up to work as a pit pianist in the orchestra of the musical *Queen High.* After the show closed Rainger toured in vaudeville as accompanist for Clifton Webb and Mary Hay; the tour ended in Chicago, when Webb and Hay went their separate ways. Webb and Rainger returned to New York, where Webb joined the cast of the first *Little Show* (1929) and Rainger was hired as rehearsal pianist. Since Webb had no special song of his own, Rainger obliged with a melody and the show's prime lyricist, Howard Dietz, came up with lyrics. The song, "Moanin' Low," was interpolated into the score and became one of the show's major hits. Rainger was also employed as one of the duo pianists in the pit; the other was Adam Carroll. (Previously Rainger had formed a similar team with Edgar Fairchild for *Queen High* and the 1927 Irving Berlin–scored *Ziegfeld Follies.* Rainger made several piano rolls and phonograph recordings with, alternately, Fairchild and Carroll.) The success of "Moanin' Low" led to the then inevitable invitation from Hollywood in 1930, after which Rainger enjoyed a fruitful period of writing for musical films, especially for several starring Bing Crosby. With rare exception the songs had excellent lyrics by Leo Robin, another lawyer-turned-songwriter (q.v.). One of their first Crosby songs was "Please" from

The Big Broadcast (1932). They collaborated on many songs for a number of undistinguished Paramount film musicals before furnishing Crosby with another popular hit, "Love in Bloom" from *She Loves Me Not* (1935). That same year they also wrote "June in January" (*Here Is My Heart*). In 1935 Rainger collaborated with Dorothy Parker, poet and wit, on the romantic "I Wished on the Moon" which Crosby sang in *The Big Broadcast of 1936*. Other Rainger-Robin film songs include "Rendezvous with a Dream" (*Poppy*, 1936), "Blue Hawaii" (*Waikiki Wedding*, 1937), "Thanks for the Memory" (*The Big Broadcast of 1938*), "You're a Sweet Little Headache" (*Paris Honeymoon*, 1939), and "Faithful Forever" and "Bluebirds in the Moonlight" (*Gulliver's Travels*, 1939). In 1938 Rainger and Robin moved to 20th Century-Fox where they wrote songs for Betty Grable, among others, but without the success they had known writing for Crosby. Their last 2 scores were heard in *Coney Island* and *Riding High*, both released in 1943 after Rainger's death. He died in a plane crash near Palm Springs, Calif., Oct. 23, 1942.

READ, GARDNER (b. 1913) Composer, teacher. Born in Evanston, Ill., Jan. 2, 1913, Read studied at the Northwestern University School of Music, Evanston, the National Music Camp, Interlochen, Mich. (on a scholarship with Paul White), and completed work in composition and orchestration at the Eastman School of Music, Rochester, N.Y., with Bernard Rogers and Howard Hanson. He was graduated in 1937. Read also studied later with Ildebrando Pizzetti in Italy, Jean Sibelius in Finland, and with Aaron Copland at Tanglewood, Mass. On completing work with Copland, Read began teaching in 1941 at the St. Louis Institute of Music. He has also taught at the Kansas City Conservatory and the Cleveland Institute of Music. In 1948 he joined the staff of the College of Music, Boston University, where he remained until his retirement in 1978. In addition to teaching composition and theory, Read has lectured on American music on the radio and in Mexico during a State Department–sponsored tour in the late 1950s and early '60s. His works include *Mountain Sketches* for piano (1932), *The Lotus-Eaters* for orchestra (1932), *The Painted Desert* for orchestra (1933), *Sketches of the City* for orchestra (1933), *Four Nocturnes* for contralto and chamber orchestra (1934), *Sonata for Piano in A Minor* (1935), *Suite for String Quartet* (1935), *Fantasy for Violin and Orchestra* (1935), *From a Lute of Jade* for mezzo-soprano and chamber orchestra (1936), *Symphony No. 1* (New York Philharmonic Prize, 1936), *Where Corals Lie* for mixed chorus, 2 pianos (1937), *Prelude and Toccata* for orchestra (1937), *Passacaglia and Fugue* for orchestra (1938), *The Golden Journey to Samarkand* for soloists, chorus, and orchestra (1939), *To a Skylark* for mixed chorus, a cappella (1939), *Songs for a Rainy Night* for baritone and orchestra (1940), *Pan e Dafni* for orchestra (1940), *Petite Pastorale* for chamber orchestra (1940), *Three Satirical Sarcasms* for orchestra (1941), *American Circle* for small orchestra (1941), *Night Flight* for orchestra (1942), *Symphony No. 2* (1942), *First Overture* for orchestra (1943), *Dance of the Locomotives* (1944), *Sonata da Chiesa* for piano (1945), *Piano Quintet* (1945), *Concerto for Cello and Orchestra* (1945), *Music for Piano and Strings* (1946), *A Bell Overture* for orchestra (1946), *The Temptation of St. Anthony* for orchestra (1947), *Partita* for chamber orchestra (1947), *Pennsylvania Suite* for orchestra (1947), *Quiet Music* for strings (1948), *Symphony No. 3* (1948), *Sonata Brevis* for piano and violin (1948), *Suite for organ* (1949), *Sound Piece* for brass and percussion (1949), *Touch Piece* for piano (1949), *Nine by Six* for wind sextet (1950), *Jesous Ahatonhia* for chorus and organ (1950), *Eight Preludes on Old Southern Hymn Tunes* for organ (1950), *Arioso elegiaco* for strings (1951), *The Golden Harp* for chorus (1952), *Toccata Giocosa* for orchestra (1953), *Vernal Equinox* for orchestra (1955), *String Quartet No. 1* (1957), *Symphony No. 4* (1958), *Sonoric Fantasia No. 1* for harp, harpsichord, and celesta (1959), *Los Dioses Aztecas* for percussion (1959), *The Prophet,* oratorio (1960), *The Reveille* for chorus, winds, percussion, and organ (1962), *Sonoric Fantasy No. 2* for violin and orchestra (1965), *Villon,* 3-act opera (1967), *Sonoric Fantasia No. 3* for viola and small orchestra (1970), *Sonoric Fantasia No. 4* for organ and percussion (1976), and *Piano Concerto* (1978). Read is the author of *Thesaurus of Orchestra Devices* (1953), *Music Notation* (1964), and *Style and Orchestration* (1975).

REED, H. OWEN (b. 1910) Composer, teacher. Born in Odessa, Mo., June 17, 1910, Reed studied music at the University of Missouri (theory and composition) and Louisiana State University before moving on to the Eastman School of Music, Rochester, N.Y., where he completed his studies under Bernard Rogers and Howard Hanson. At the Berkshire Music Center, Mass., he studied with Aaron Copland, English conductor Stanley Chapple, and Czech composer Bohuslav Martinů; he also studied privately with Roy Harris in the late 1940s. Almost immediately upon his graduation from the Eastman School in 1939, Reed joined the music faculty of Michigan State University, East Lansing, where he taught until his retirement in 1976. Reed's compositions include a *Piano Sonata* (1934), *The Masque of Red Death,* ballet pantomime (1936),

String Quartet (1937), *A Psalm of Praise* for chorus, a cappella, or soprano and chamber group (1939), *Symphony No. 1* (1939), *Overture* for orchestra (1940), *Our Country* for chorus and orchestra (1942), *Symphonic Dance* for orchestra (1942); *The Passing of John Blackfeather* for voice and piano (1945), *Scherzo* for clarinet and piano (1945), *Three Nationalities* for piano (1947), *Cello Concerto* (1949), *La Fiesta Mexicana* for band (1949), *Nocturne* for piano (1953), *Symphonic Dance* for piano and woodwind quintet (1954), *Michigan Dream,* "folk opera" (1955), *Ripley Ferry* for women's voices and wind septet (1958), *Renascence* for band (1959), *Che-Ba-Kun-Ah* for string quartet (1959), *Earth Trapped,* opera-ballet (1960), *Overture for Strings* (1961), *A Tabernacle for the Sun,* oratorio (1963), *The Turning Mind* for orchestra (1968), and *Living Solid Face,* chamber opera (1976). Reed is the author of *A Workbook in the Fundamentals of Music* (1946), *Basic Music* (1954), *Basic Contrapuntal Technique* (with Paul Harder, 1964), and *Scoring for Percussion* (with J. T. Leach, 1969).

REVEL, HARRY (1905–1958) Popular composer, pianist. Born in London, Dec. 21, 1905, Revel was 24 when he arrived in the United States determined to pursue a musical career that had begun rather well in Europe. Revel began piano lessons at 9 and studied at the Guild Hall of Music in London. The death of his piano teacher led to his dropping out as a piano student; what Revel learned from then on he learned on his own. At 15 he joined what was billed as a "Hawaiian Band" in Paris; it was around this time that Revel began writing music. In 1922 he was the pianist in an orchestra that toured much of Europe. While in Berlin, Revel composed his first score for a German operetta, *Was Frauen Träumen*. He contributed songs to several European productions, including the *André Charlot's Revue* (1927). Determined to make his way in the great center of popular song of the time, Revel came to New York City in 1929—and found that his considerable European reputation meant little in Tin Pan Alley. Unable to place any of his music, Revel agreed to serve as accompanist for former boy soprano-turned-vaudeville singer-comedian Mack Gordon (1904–1959). Gordon, it turned out, was also a lyricist. Revel eventually coaxed Gordon to give up vaudeville and to concentrate on songwriting. One of their earliest efforts, "Underneath the Harlem Moon," led to their writing the songs for an all-black revue, *Fast and Furious* (1931). It lasted 7 performances. They also had a few songs in that year's *Ziegfeld Follies*. They collaborated on 2 scores in 1932, *Smiling Faces* and *Marching By* but without much success. They were then asked to come to Hollywood by the Paramount studios and their first film, *Sitting Pretty*, produced their first really significant song hit, "Did You Ever See a Dream Walking" (1933). From then until the late 1930s Revel and Gordon collaborated on numerous popular songs for musical films, several of which starred Bing Crosby. The first was *We're Not Dressing* (1934) from which came "Love Thy Neighbor" and "May I?" *Shoot the Works,* the same year, produced "With My Eyes Wide Open I'm Dreaming." They reached their peak in the mid '30s: "Take a Number from One to Ten" and "Stay as Sweet as You Are" (from *College Rhythm,* 1934), "Paris in the Spring" (*Paris in the Spring,* 1935), "But Definitely" and "When I'm with You" (*Poor Little Rich Girl,* 1936), "Good Night, My Love" (*Stowaway,* 1936), "Never in a Million Years," "Wake Up and Live," and "There's a Lull in My Life" (*Wake Up and Live,* 1937), and "Sweet Someone" (*Love and Kisses,* 1937). They

also wrote the songs for *Love Finds Andy Hardy* (1938) and *Thanks for Everything,* their last collaboration in 1939. Revel worked with other lyricists but did not enjoy the success he had had with Gordon (who went on to work with Harry Warren, q.v.). Revel returned to Broadway to do a successful show, *Are You with It?,* with lyrics by Arnold B. Horwitt. During World War II, Revel contributed much time and energy to wartime entertainment in military bases and hospitals; he edited a magazine, *At Ease,* for hospitalized veterans. After the war he became interested in musical therapy and composed such instrumental works as *Music Out of the Moon* and *Music for Peace of Mind.* He also composed a *Perfumes Set to Music* suite in the late 1940s. Revel was not very active in the '50s. He died in New York City, Nov. 3, 1958.

"ROBERTA" Musical with music by Jerome Kern (q.v.) and lyrics by Otto Harbach (q.v.). Harbach also adapted the book, *Gowns by Roberta* by Alice Duer Miller. The setting is the *couture* run by "Roberta" in Paris. She is, in fact, the Aunt Minnie of an American football star, "John Kent," who comes to Paris to recover from a broken romance. It seems, too, that, on her death, his aunt has left him her dress shop. John has another romance, this time with the shop's designer, "Stephanie." Together they decide they will continue in the tradition of Roberta. But John's U.S. sweetheart shows up in Paris to complicate matters, which are further complicated when it is revealed that Stephanie is, in fact, a *real* Russian princess! (In those days mere, even if wealthy, American football stars did not marry *real* Russian princesses.) Conditions in Russia in the '30s were such that it was highly unlikely that Stephanie would have been welcomed there by Stalin and company, so, once John has sent his American girl friend packing, he and Stephanie are free to marry, princess or not. When *Roberta* opened at the New Amsterdam Theatre, Nov. 18, 1933, it was critically drubbed for its inane story but went on for a respectable run despite the poor reviews— 295 performances in the depths of the Depression. The usual reason given by historians is the popularity of one song, "Smoke Gets in Your Eyes," as sung by Stephanie (Tamara, born Tamara Drasin in Russia) to her own guitar accompaniment. Other reasons were the opulent production afforded by producer Max Gordon and the climax, an onstage fashion show. The Kern-Harbach songs were also of high quality: "Yesterdays," "You're Devastating," "Let's Begin," "Something Had to Happen," "I'll Be Hard to Handle" (co-lyricist Bernard Dougall), and "The Touch of Your Hand." There were 2 film versions of *Roberta.* The first, which featured Irene Dunne and Fred Astaire and Ginger Rogers, also introduced additional songs, among them "I Won't Dance" and "Lovely to Look At," the first with lyrics by Harbach and Oscar Hammerstein II and the 2nd with lyrics by Dorothy Fields and Jimmy McHugh. The film was released in 1935. The 2nd filmed *Roberta,* entitled *Lovely to Look At,* was released in 1952. *Roberta* was one of those rare musicals that proved successful primarily on the strength of its fine score. The stars of the original 1933 production, besides Tamara, were Raymond —later Ray—Middleton as "John," the football hero, veteran Fay Templeton, who appeared as "Roberta–Aunt Minnie," and, in a small but his first major Broadway role, Bob Hope as "Huckleberry Haines."

ROBIN, LEO (b. 1900) Popular song lyricist. Born in Pittsburgh, Pa., Apr. 6, 1900, Robin studied law at the University of Pittsburgh, then switched to the Carnegie Tech School of Drama. He worked for a while as a newspaper reporter and in public relations before coming to New York in 1925, hoping to break into show business. He struggled for several months before he succeeded in placing songs in *By the Way,* a revue imported from Britain, which opened in 1925. With the same collaborator, Richard Myers (b. 1901), he had songs in *Bubbling Over* (1926), *Allez-Oop* (1927), and *Hello Yourself* (1928), without producing one true song hit. In 1927, however, Robin worked with Vincent Youmans (q.v.) and co-lyricist Clifford Grey on the musical *Hit the Deck,* out of which came such songs as "Why, Oh Why?" and "Hallelujah!" This success was followed by the call to Hollywood, then (1928–29) finding its singing voice. Robin's first film songs were written with Richard Whiting (q.v.) for *Close Harmony, The Dance of Life,* and *Innocents of Paris*—all released in 1929; from the last came the popular Maurice Chevalier song, "Louise." In 1930 Robin and Whiting wrote the songs for *Monte Carlo,* out of which came "Beyond the Blue Horizon" (co-composer was W. Franke Harling), and other films, mostly of little consequence, although *The Playboy of Paris* inspired the standard "My Ideal." In 1932, besides writing the popular title song for the film *One Hour with You* with Whiting, Robin began his most fruitful collaboration with Ralph Rainger (q.v.). They contributed a couple of songs—"Here Lies Love" and "Please"—to the score of *The Big Broadcast.* Other Robin film songs (music by Rainger unless otherwise noted): "Love in Bloom" (*She Loves Me Not,* 1934), "Love Is Just Around the Corner" (music by Lewis Gensler), "With Every Breath I Take" and "June in January" (all from *Here Is My Heart,* 1934), "I Can't Escape from You" (music by Richard Whiting, from *Rhythm on the Range,* 1936), "Blue Hawaii" and "Sweet Is the Word for You" (*Waikiki Wedding*, 1937), "Thanks for the Memory" (*Big Broadcast of 1938*), "You're a Sweet Little Headache" and "I Have Eyes" (*Paris Honeymoon*, 1939), "Faithful Forever" and "Bluebirds in the Moonlight" (*Gulliver's Travels*, 1939), "Journey to a Star" and "No Love, No Nothin'" (music by Harry Warren, from *The Gang's All Here*, 1943), "Up with the Lark" and "In Love in Vain" (music by Jerome Kern from *Centennial Summer*, 1946), "A Gal in Calico," "A Rainy Night in Rio," "Oh, But I Do," and "Through a Thousand Dreams" (music by Arthur Schwartz, from *The Time, the Place and the Girl*, 1946), "Hooray for Love," "It Was Written in the Stars," and "What's Good About Goodbye?" (music by Harold Arlen, from *Casbah*, 1948). The following year Robin returned to Broadway with an extremely popular musical, *Gentlemen Prefer Blondes*, with music by Jule Styne (q.v.). The show, starring Carol Channing, ran for more than 700 performances and was notable for several good songs: "Bye, Bye, Baby," "Diamond's Are a Girl's Best Friend," "A Little Girl from Little Rock," and "You Say You Care." Robin's film work slackened after 1949, along with the general slump in the production of film musicals. His last major work was done on yet another Broadway production, *The Girl in Pink Tights* (1954), Sigmund Romberg's last musical (the score was completed by composer-arranger Don Walker). The score produced at least one exceptional song, "Lost in Loveliness." *The Girl in Pink Tights* closed after 115 performances. Robin has been virtually inactive since.

ROBINSON, EARL (b. 1910) Composer, conductor, vocalist, teacher. Born in Seattle, Wash., July 2, 1910, Robinson earned his degree in music from the University of Washington; he also studied

with Aaron Copland (q.v.). Robinson began composing while still in college and conducted such early works as *Rhapsody in Brass* (1932) and *Symphonic Fragment* (1933) while a student. He was graduated in 1938 and traveled across the United States singing in concerts to his own guitar accompaniment. Robinson, in these travels, developed a deep interest in American folk music; many of the songs he learned on tour he eventually recorded for the Library of Congress. This dedication to the American ethos led to the writing of "The Ballad of Uncle Sam" to the lyrics of John Latouche (q.v.) for a W.P.A. production, *Sing for Your Supper*, in 1939. The cantata-like work attracted a good deal of attention (the show itself closed after 60 performances) which led to a radio performance with the great singer Paul Robeson singing the solo part. The broadcast of the work retitled *Ballad for Americans* (by Norman Corwin, whose show provided the outlet), led to greater popularity and a now classic recording. Robinson proceeded to write in the same vein, among them *In the Folded and Quiet Yesterdays* (1940), *Tower of Babel* (1941), *Battle Hymn* (1942), and another highly popular and moving work, *The Lonesome Train* (1943), to a text about the Lincoln funeral train by Millard Lampell. With Lampell, Robinson wrote the title song to a film set in wartime Italy, *A Walk in the Sun* (1940). In collaboration with lyricist E. Y. Harburg (q.v.), Robinson wrote the songs for a film musical, *California* (1946). With Harburg also he wrote the bitter social commentary song, "Free and Equal Blues." With Lewis Allan as lyricist Robinson composed the song "The House I Live In" for a short antidiscrimination film of the same title in 1945; it won the Academy Award in the short subject category that year. In the late 1950s Robinson became music director of the Elizabeth Irwin High School, New York City.

ROBISON, WILLARD (1894–1968) Songwriter, vocalist, performer. Born in Shelbina, Mo., Sept. 18, 1894, Robison had little formal musical education beyond a few piano lessons. He was attracted to the Negro music of his native South and to folk music in general. Around 1917 he formed an orchestra that eventually came to be called the "Deep River Orchestra." During the 1920s and '30s Robison made many recordings as vocalist-pianist as well as with his orchestra and others, most notably Nat Shilkret (q.v.). Robison was featured with his orchestra on national radio shows performing his "Deep River Music" and via a program called "Plantation Echoes." As a songwriter, Robison was admired by other songwriters, including another folk-poet, Johnny Mercer (q.v.), and by such singers who specialized in singing songs of unusual merit, but out of the mainstream of popular song. Among Robison's vocalist-admirers were Mildred Bailey, Anita Ellis, and Lee Wiley (who made a famous recording of "A Woman Alone with the Blues" with music and lyrics by Robison, written in 1955). Among the most admired songs by Robison are "Peaceful Valley" (1925), which was Paul Whiteman's theme before he switched to Gershwin's *Rhapsody in Blue,* "The Devil Is Afraid of Music" (1927), "A Cottage for Sale," lyrics by Larry Conley (1930), "Old Folks," lyrics by Dedette Lee Hill (1936), "Guess I'll Go Back Home This Summer," lyrics by Ray Mayer (1939), "Now We Know," lyrics by Mayer (1940), a song that was recorded by the then popular Artie Shaw band. Robison's songs went into eclipse during the 1950s but have continued to be sung by vocalists who appear in small clubs. One of Robison's most impressive songs, "Four

Walls (and One Dirty Window Blues)" has been frequently performed and twice recorded (the 2nd time in 1979) by Anita Ellis. Although he was best known for his folksy but almost urban songs, Robison composed some solo piano pieces, 2 of which were entitled *Rural Revelations* and *Six Studies in Modern Syncopation.* By the 1950s Robison, while he continued to write a song now and then, went into retirement. He died in Peekskill, N.Y., June 24, 1968.

ROGERS, BERNARD (1893–1968) Composer, teacher. Born in New York City, Feb. 4, 1893, Rogers studied with Percy Goetschius at the Institute of Musical Art, New York City, after abandoning the idea of becoming an architect. He also worked with Ernest Bloch (q.v.) at the Cleveland Institute. His other teachers include Arthur Farwell (q.v.), Nadia Boulanger (q.v.), and British composer Frank Bridge. He began teaching at the Eastman School, Rochester, N.Y., in 1929, and among his students were such composers as David Diamond, Burrill Phillips, and Gail Kubik. Besides composition Rogers taught orchestration, the mastery of which is evident in his works. Among them are *To the Fallen,* a dirge for orchestra (1915), *The Faithful* for orchestra (1918), *Soliloquy* for flute and strings (1922), *Japanese Landscapes* for orchestra (1925), *Adonais,* poem for orchestra (1927), *String Quartet* (1927), *Pastorale* for chamber orchestra (1928), *Prelude to Hamlet* for orchestra (1928), *The Raising of Lazarus* for soloists, chorus, and orchestra (1928), *Rhapsody Nocturne* for chamber orchestra (1928), *Symphony No. 2* (1929), *The Marriage of Aude,* opera (1931), *Two American Frescoes* for orchestra (1931), *The Exodus,* for soloists, chorus, and orchestra (1932), *Three Japanese Dances* for orchestra, with mezzo-soprano (1933), *Once Upon a Time* ("Five Fairy Tales") for orchestra (1934), *Symphony No. 3* (1936), *The Supper at Emmaus* for orchestra (1937), *Soliloquy* for bassoon and strings (1938), *Fantasy* for flute, viola, and orchestra (1938), *Dance of Salome* for orchestra (1939), *The Colours of War* for orchestra (1939), *The Song of the Nightingale* for orchestra (1939), *The Plains* for chamber orchestra (1940), *Sailors of Toulon* for orchestra (1940), *The Passion* for soloists, chorus, and orchestra (1943), *Invasion* for orchestra (1943), *Symphony No. 4* (1943), *Characters from Hans Christian Andersen* for chamber orchestra (1944), *Response to Silent Prayer* for chorus (1945), *Amphitryon*, overture for orchestra (1945), *The Warrior*, opera (1945), *In Memory of Franklin Delano Roosevelt* for orchestra (1946), *A Letter from Pete*, cantata to a text by Walt Whitman (1947), *The Silver World* for flute, oboe, and strings (1950), *The Prophet Isaiah*, cantata (1950), *The Veil*, opera (1950), *Leaves from the Tale of Pinocchio* for narrator and orchestra (1951), *Psalm 68* for baritone and orchestra (1952), *Portrait* for violin and orchestra (1952), *String Trio* (1953), *Dance Scenes* for orchestra (1953), *The Nightingale*, opera (1954), *The Musicians of Bremen* for narrator and chamber orchestra (1958), *Symphony No. 5*, "Africa" (1959), *Variations on a Song by Mussorgsky* for orchestra (1960), *Violin Sonata* (1962), *Apparitions* for orchestra (1967), *Dirge for Two Veterans* for chorus and piano (1967), and *Psalm 114* for chorus and piano (1968). Also a writer, Rogers was editor and critic for *Musical America* from 1913 to 1924 and the author of *The Art of Orchestration* (1951). He died in Rochester, N.Y., May 24, 1968.

ROME, HAROLD (b. 1908) Composer-lyricist. Born in Hartford, Conn., May 27, 1908, Rome was graduated from Yale's School of Architecture and spent 2 additional semesters studying law. He worked as a draftsman for a while during the Depression but when offered a job as pianist and composer-in-residence at Green Mansions, a summer resort in New York State's Adirondacks, he took it. (Rome, while at Yale, played piano in the orchestra and for local dancing classes.) Rome's urban folk songs eventually led to his being asked to write songs for a labor-sponsored musical, *Pins and Needles* (q.v.), which opened in New York City in 1937. His next score was written for a Broadway revue, *Sing Out the News* (1938), out of which came such songs as "My Heart Is Unemployed," "One of These Fine Days," and the popular "F. D. R. Jones." His other full scores include *Let Freedom Ring* (1942), which had a short run of 8 performances. *Call Me Mister* (1946) was an all-soldier show starring veterans of World War II; Rome himself had been in the U. S. Army during the war, attached to Special Services. During the stint he wrote the songs for *Stars and Gripes*. *Call Me Mister* was an enormous hit out of which came such songs as "The Face on the Dime" (about President Roosevelt), the bitingly satiric "Yuletide, Park Avenue," "Military Life (The Jerk Song)," "The Red Ball Express," "Little Surplus Me," and the show's hit, sung by Betty Garrett, "South America, Take It Away." *Bless You All* (1950) was successful also but produced no outstanding song. Rome wrote one of his finest scores for *Wish You Were Here* (1952), a musical set in the type of summer hotel, complete with social director to keep the adults entertained and occupied, at which Rome himself had spent 3 summers cutting his musical-lyrical teeth. Among the score's highlights are such songs as "Could Be," "Don Jose of Far Rockaway," "Ballad of a Social Director," "Tripping the Light Fantastic," "Wish You Were Here," and the haunting "Where Did the Night

Go?" *Fanny* (1954) was a change of pace and scene; the book, by S. N. Behrman and director Joshua Logan, was based on the Marcel Pagnol trilogy *Marius, César,* and *Fanny* (all successful French films). *Fanny,* starring Ezio Pinza and Walter Slezak, ran for some 880 performances. *Destry Rides Again* (1959) was also adapted from a popular film and ran for a year or so but produced no memorable songs. *I Can Get It for You Wholesale* (1962), a hard look at New York's competitive garment industry, was based on the book of the same title by Jerome Weidman. Rome's score fit the book, but the show's most remembered sequence was a song entitled "Miss Marmelstein," the lament of an overworked secretary which was sung by teenaged newcomer Barbra Streisand. Rome's next musical was another offbeat effort, *The Zulu and the Zayda* (1965), with an African setting—Johannesburg, not the exotic jungle. More a play-with-music, *The Zulu and the Zayda* (the last word is Yiddish for grandfather), the action centered on the relationship between the giant Zulu hired to be a companion to the grandfather of the Grossman family. For it Rome composed some interesting and original songs. In 1970 a musical entitled *Scarlet* opened in Tokyo —with a Japanese cast. It proved to be Rome's setting of Margaret Mitchell's *Gone With the Wind* (the book had been adapted by Horton Foote). An ambitious undertaking, to say the least, the musical has yet to appear in the United States. It had a London run under the full Mitchell title in 1972, however. Besides writing songs, Rome is also a painter of no little talent and a collector of African art. He has also composed instrumental music inspired by some of his original paintings; this was recorded under the title *Harold Rome's Gallery.*

RONELL, ANN (b. ca. 1910) Composer, lyricist, conductor. Born in Omaha, Neb., Dec. 25, ca. 1910, (she chooses not to release the year of her birth), Ronell was educated at Radcliffe College, Cambridge, Mass. For a while she taught music, coached singers, and began her career in popular music as a rehearsal pianist for Broadway shows. The success of one of her earliest songs, "Willow Weep for Me" (1932), led to an invitation from Hollywood. She worked for the Disney studios and for one of his cartoons, *Three Little Pigs* (1933), collaborated on one of the most popular songs of the 1930s, "Who's Afraid of the Big Bad Wolf?" A pioneer in film scoring, Ronell also did the background music for such films as *Champagne Waltz* (1937), *Algiers* (1938), *Commandos Strike at Dawn* (1942), *The Story of G.I. Joe* (1945), and others. She scored and collaborated with Kurt Weill on the film version of his Broadway show *One Touch of Venus* in 1948. She has written an opera, *Oh! Susanna,* and a ballet, *Magic of Spring.*

SANDERS, ROBERT (1906–1974) Composer, conductor, organist, teacher. Born in Chicago, Ill., July 2, 1906, Sanders was a musical prodigy who made his public debut before he was 4. By the time he was 19 he was graduated from the Bush Conservatory (later renamed the Chicago Conservatory of Music). Sanders went to Rome in 1925 on an American Academy fellowship to study composition with Ottorino Respighi. He later studied piano with Guy de Lioncourt in Paris. Upon his return to Chicago in 1929 Sanders studied conducting with Eric De Lamarter. He then joined the faculty of the Chicago Conservatory, where he was also conductor of the Conservatory Orchestra. Sanders had a deep interest in Protestant hymn tunes, studied them, lectured on them, and performed them as organist for the First Unitarian Church, Chicago. He eventually left the Chicago area to become dean of the School of Music, Indiana University, Bloomington (1938–47). His final post, professor of music, he held at Brooklyn College, New York City, from 1947. Sanders' works include *Trio in C-sharp Minor* for piano, violin, and cello (1926), *Two Songs* for soprano and orchestra (1926), *Psalm 23* for chorus, a cappella (1928), *Suite* for orchestra with piano (1928), *Sonata* for violin and piano (1928), *Mississippi,* suite for orchestra (1928), *Quartet in A Minor* (1929), *Sonata* for cello and piano (1932), *Recessional* for chorus and organ (1933), *Saturday Night: a Barn Dance* for orchestra (1933), *Concerto for Violin and Orchestra* (1935), *Scenes of Poverty and Toil* for orchestra (1935), *Little Symphony in G* (1937), *Chanson of the Bells of Oseney* for chorus, a cappella (1938), *The Mystic Trumpeter,* text by Walt Whitman, for narrator, baritone, chorus, and orchestra (1941), *Quintet in B for Brass Instruments* (1942), *Symphony in B Flat* for band (1943), *Twelve Two-Part Inventions* for piano (1943), *Movement for Woodwinds* (1943), *L'Ag'ya,* ballet (1944), *An American Psalm,* cantata for women's voices and organ (1945), *Sonata in Four Movements* for trombone and piano (1945), *Suite for Brass Quintet* (1949), *Little Symphony No. 2* (1953), *Symphony in A* (1955), *Variations on an Original Theme* for organ (1956), *Violin Sonata* (1961), *Little Symphony No. 3* (1963), and *Song of Myself,* cantata, text by Walt Whitman (1970). Sanders was the author of *Manual of Melody Writing* and co-editor of *A Dictionary of Hymn Tunes in the U.S.A.* He died in Delray Beach, Fla., Dec. 26, 1974.

SAPP, ALLEN DWIGHT (b. 1922) Composer, teacher. Born in Philadelphia, Pa., Dec. 10, 1922, Sapp began to study music in Philadelphia (piano with Robert Ellmore) before enrolling at Har-

vard, where he studied with Walter Piston (q.v.) and Edward B. Hill (q.v.). He also studied with Aaron Copland (q.v.) and Nadia Boulanger (q.v.). While still an undergraduate Sapp won a New York Philharmonic Society competition for his *Andante* for orchestra (1941). In 1943 Sapp entered the U. S. Army and served overseas in the Signal Corps. Besides working in the code-breaking section, Sapp also managed to compose a number of works for chamber groups that were performed in the various cities in which he was stationed during the war: London, Paris, Munich. In 1949 he joined the faculty of Harvard University, Cambridge, Mass. Sapp's compositions include a *Concertino for Piano and Small Orchestra* (1942), *Sonata for Violin and Piano* (1942), *Piano Sonatina* (1946), *Sonata for Piano,* 4 hands (1946), *The Double Image* for orchestra (1957), *Septagon* for orchestra (1957), *A Maiden's Complaint in Springtime* for women's chorus and chamber orchestra (1960), *Canticum Novum pro Pace* for male chorus and winds (1962), and *Colloquies* for piano and orchestra (1963).

SCHERTZINGER, VICTOR (1890–1941) Composer, violinist, conductor, film director. Born in Mahanoy City, Pa., Apr. 8, 1890, Schertzinger studied the violin as a child and made his debut at the age of 8 as soloist with the Victor Herbert Orchestra. He toured the United States and Europe while still in his teens and studied at the University of Brussels. He returned to the United States, conducted some Broadway musicals, and then went to Hollywood where he scored the silent film *Civilization* (1915), one of the first with a complete musical background (to be performed by an orchestra in the theatre). It is possible that "Marcheta," a song with words and music by Schertzinger which was very popular in 1913–14, led to this assignment. He chose to remain in Hollywood where he not only wrote songs but also directed many films—dramas as well as musicals. His film songs include "Dream Lover" and "Paris, Stay the Same" (lyrics by Clifford Grey, from *The Love Parade*, 1929), "One Night of Love" (lyrics by Gus Kahn, from *One Night of Love*, 1934), "Love Me Forever" (lyrics by Kahn, from *Love Me Forever*, 1935), "I Don't Want to Cry Anymore" (lyrics by Johnny Burke, from *Rhythm on the River*, 1940), "Sand in My Shoes" (lyrics by Frank Loesser, from *Kiss the Boys Goodbye*, 1941), "Tangerine," "I Remember You," "Not Mine," and "Arthur Murray Taught Me Dancing in a Hurry" (lyrics by Johnny Mercer, from *The Fleet's In*, released in 1942). Among the films Schertzinger directed are *The Return of Peter Grimm, Forgotten Faces, Nothing But the Truth, One Night of Love, The Music Goes Round, The Mikado, Road to Singapore, Rhythm on the River, Road to Zanzibar, Kiss the Boys Goodbye*, and others. Schertzinger died in Hollywood, Oct. 26, 1941.

SCHLEIN, IRVING (b. 1905) Composer, conductor, teacher. Born in New York City, Aug. 18, 1905, Schlein was graduated from Brooklyn College with a degree in pharmacy. He studied music at the Juilliard School as well as the New York College of Music and Columbia University. Among his teachers were Douglas Moore, Aaron Copland, Roger Sessions, Roy Harris, and Wallingford Riegger. Schlein worked as a pianist in Broadway musicals, as well as accompanist for Jan Peerce and Robert Merrill. He has taught music and English in New York public schools and lectured on music at Brooklyn College. Among his works are 11 symphonies (1936–43), a *Sinfonia Brevis* (1938), *Three Pieces for Woodwind Quintet* (1940), 150 *Piano Preludes* (1940–79), *Concertino for Piano and Orchestra* (1942), *Sonata for*

Oboe and Piano (1942), *Epic of Democracy*, text by Walt Whitman, for baritone, chorus, and orchestra (1942), *America* for piano (1943), *Ode to Victory* for orchestra (1943), *American Overture* for orchestra (1944), *Summer Piece* for band (1945), *Give Me the Splendid Silent Sun* for narrator and orchestra (1945), *Festive Overture* for band (1946), *The Aristocrats* for soloists, chorus, and 2 pianos (1946), *Dance Overture I* for orchestra (1947), *Sonatine* for viola d'amore and piano (1947), *Toccata* for piano and *Laughing Pianos* for 2 pianos (ca. 1950), *Dance Overture II* (1960), *Money*, one-act opera (1968), *Stackolee*, one-act opera (1968), *Blue Grass*, musical based on the story of Daniel Boone (1970), *A Children's Musical Calendar* for voice and piano (1978), *Johnny Merripranks*, one-act opera (1978), "Heave Away," "Let God's Chillun Come Home" and "Chariot Wheels Are Rollin'" for chorus (1975), *Salammbô*, opera after Flaubert (1979), *Testament to Freedom*, text by Louis Untermeyer for soloists, chorus, and orchestra (1979), *The Common School of Literature* for narrator, soloist, and piano (1979), *Strictly from the Birds*, based on the bird song collection of Schuyler Matthews, for piano (1979), and *My Heart's in the Highlands*, opera based on the life and work of Robert Burns (in progress: 1979). Schlein edited a revised edition of Allen, Ware, and Garrison's *Slave Songs of the United States* (1965).

SCHOENBERG, ARNOLD (1874–1951) Composer, theorist, pedagogue. Born in Vienna, Sept. 13, 1874, Schönberg (he changed the spelling after his arrival in America) had a considerable European musical reputation before the advent of Hitler and the Nazis necessitated his departure. Schoenberg's musical concept of a "method of composing with 12 tones" made him a controversial figure as early as 1914. He was the leader of what became known as the Second Viennese School, whose members numbered such students as Alban Berg and Anton Webern. Before leaving Germany in 1933 Schoenberg had already written such celebrated (or notorious) works as *Verklärte Nacht, Gurrelieder, Five Orchestra Pieces,* Op. 16, *Suite for Piano,* Op. 25, 3 of the numbered string quartets, *Pierrot Lunaire,* among others. In the United States, Schoenberg taught a master class in composition at the Malkin Conservatory in Boston but found the New England winter uncongenial. He then accepted a position at the University of Southern California, Los Angeles; then in 1935 he switched to the University of California, Los Angeles, where he taught for several years. Schoenberg's influence upon American music (especially strong after World War II) grew out of his teachings and lectures at the University of California; among his students were such innovators as John Cage, Lou Harrison, Gunther Schuller, Adolph Weiss, and Marc Blitzstein. Several American composers adapted the 12-tone method to their own style: Wallingford Riegger, Aaron Copland, George Perle, Ellis Kohs, Milton Babbitt, Ben Weber, Roger Sessions, even Virgil Thomson and Samuel Barber. Among Schoenberg's "American" works are the *Fourth String Quartet* (1936), *Violin Concerto* (1936), *Second Chamber Symphony* (1939), *Ode to Napoleon Buonaparte* for speaker, piano, and string quartet (1942), *Piano Concerto* (1942), *Trio* for violin, viola, and cello (1946), *A Survivor from Warsaw* for speaker, male chorus, and orchestra (1947), *De Profundis* for chorus, a cappella (1950), and *Modern Psalm* for speaker, chorus, and orchestra (unfinished, 1950). Schoenberg was the author of *Theory and Harmony* (originally published as *Harmonielehre,* 1911, in English,

1947), *Models for Beginners in Composition* (1942), and *Style and Idea* (1950). He died in Los Angeles, July 13, 1951.

SCHUMAN, WILLIAM (b. 1910) Composer, teacher, administrator. Born in New York City, Aug. 4, 1910, Schuman studied with Charles Haubiel (composition) and Max Persin (harmony) before he entered Columbia University (B.A., 1935). His early interest was in popular music, which encouraged him to form his own band, "Billy Schuman and his Alamo Society Orchestra," in which he served as banjoist and vocalist. He then moved into Tin Pan Alley to work as an arranger and staff composer. One of his songs, a collaborative effort with lyricist Frank Loesser (q.v.), was published in 1931 under the title of "In Love with a Memory of You." By the mid 1930s Schuman decided to go into music seriously; in 1935 he enrolled in the Mozarteum Academy, Salzburg, to study conducting. He returned to the United States to earn his master's at Columbia in 1937. Simultaneously during much of this time he was on the teaching staff of Sarah Lawrence College, Bronxville, N.Y., where he remained until 1945. Schuman, meanwhile, continued to study: between 1936 and 1938 he worked with Roy Harris (q.v.). In 1945 he was appointed president of the Juilliard School of Music, New York City, where he reorganized the teaching program with excellent, far-reaching results. Schuman's administrative abilities did not interfere with creative work, for he continued to write even while overseeing the details of running an efficient educational institution. In 1962 he left Juilliard to serve as president of Lincoln Center for the Performing Arts and remained at that post until 1969. Schuman is one of the few prolific American symphonists—although he withdrew his first 2 symphonies, composed in 1935 and

1937, respectively (also withdrawn: a *Prelude and Fugue* for orchestra and other pieces of the same period). Schuman first came into prominence following the introduction of his *American Festival Overture* in 1939 by the Boston Symphony under Koussevitzky. He has the distinction of being the first recipient of both the New York Critics Circle Award and the Pulitzer Prize. Schuman's major works include *Pioneers!* for chorus (1937), *String Quartet No. 2* (1937), *Choral Etude* for chorus, a cappella (1937), *String Quartet No. 3* (1939), *Prologue* for chorus and orchestra (1939), *Quartettino for Four Bassoons* (1939), *Prelude* for women's chorus, a cappella (1939), *This Is Our Time,* cantata for chorus and orchestra (1940), *Symphony No. 3* (1941, New York Critics Circle Award), *Symphony No. 4* (1941), *Newsreel in Five Shots* for band (1941), *A Free Song,* cantata for chorus and orchestra (1942, Pulitzer Prize), *Concerto for Piano and Orchestra* (1942), *Three Piano Moods* (1943), *Prayer in Time of War* for orchestra (1943), *Symphony (No. 5) for Strings* (1943), *Music for "Henry VIII": "Te Deum-Coronation Scene"* and *"Orpheus with His Lute"* (1944), *Circus Overture* for orchestra (1944), *Steeltown,* film score for an Office of War Information release (1944), *Three-Score Set* for piano (1945), *Undertow,* ballet (1945), *Violin Concerto* (1946), *Night Journey,* ballet (1947), *Symphony No. 6* (1948), *Judith,* ballet (1948), *String Quartet No. 4* (1950), *George Washington Bridge,* an impression for band (1950), *The Mighty Casey,* one-act opera (1953), *Voyage for a Theatre,* ballet (1953), *Credendum* for orchestra (1955), *New England Triptych* for orchestra (1956), *Carols of Death* for chorus (1958), *Symphony No. 7* (1960), *A Song of Orpheus,* fantasy for cello and orchestra (1961), *Symphony No. 8* (1962), *String Trio* (1964), *The Witch of Endor,*

ballet (1965), *To Thee Old Cause* for orchestra (1968), *Symphony No. 9* (1968), *In Praise of Shahn,* canticle for orchestra (1969), *Voyage,* orchestral version of pieces originally written for piano (1971), *Concerto on Old English Rounds* for viola, women's voices, and orchestra (1973), *The Young Dead Soldiers* for soprano, horn, and chamber orchestra of woodwinds and strings (text by Archibald MacLeish, 1976), *Symphony No. 10* (1976), *Three Colloquies* for horn and orchestra (1980), and *Time to the Old* for soprano and piano (1980).

SCHWARTZ, ARTHUR (b. 1900) Composer. Born in Brooklyn, N.Y., Nov. 25, 1900, Schwartz is a self-taught pianist who, initially, did not plan to go into music. The holder of several degrees, including that of Doctor of Jurisprudence (Columbia, '24), Schwartz taught high school English during the early 1920s and practiced law from 1924 to 1928. A natural gift for music enabled him, though not trained, to earn money while attending law school by playing the piano in movie houses. As early as 1923 Schwartz succeeded in getting a song published; with lyrics by Eli Dawson, it was entitled "Baltimore, M.D., You're the Only Doctor for Me." He also managed to place a few songs in a couple of revues in 1926. Eager to get out of his law office, Schwartz wrote to a young but already established lyricist, Howard Dietz, early in 1924, suggesting that they collaborate. Dietz rejected the offer, noting that he had already collaborated with a "well-established composer" (Jerome Kern) and suggested Schwartz do the same—and "then when we both get famous, we can collaborate with each other." Schwartz had already collaborated with Lorenz Hart on songs for a summer camp show, but Hart then was not "well-established" either. Schwartz persisted and finally—5 years later—

began a collaboration with Dietz, in 1929, when they wrote most of the songs for the first *Little Show*. Their best-known song was "I Guess I'll Have to Change My Plan." The show was so successful that a *Second Little Show* was produced the next year with songs by Schwartz and Dietz, among others; they did better with the songs for another revue produced that same year, *Three's a Crowd*, out of which came "Something to Remember You By." The collaboration "well-established," Schwartz worked with Dietz on *The Band Wagon* ("New Sun in the Sky," "I Love Louisa," and "Dancing in the Dark," 1931), *Flying Colors* ("Shine on Your Shoes," "Louisiana Hayride," and "Alone Together," 1932), *Revenge with Music* ("If There Is Someone Lovelier Than You" and "You and the Night and the Music," 1934), *At Home Abroad* ("Got a Bran' New Suit," "Farewell My Lovely," and "Love Is a Dancing Thing," 1935), *Between the Devil* ("By Myself," "Triplets," and "I See Your Face Before Me," 1937), *Inside U.S.A.* ("Haunted Heart," 1948), *The Gay Life* ("Magic Moment," "You're Not the Type," 1961), *Jennie* ("Where You Are" and "I Still Look at You That Way," 1963). During the years he worked with Dietz, Schwartz collaborated with other lyricists in both New York and London. His London shows include *Here Comes the Bride* (lyrics by Desmond Carter, 1930), *The Co-Optimists* (lyrics by Greatrex Newman, 1930), *Nice Goings On* (lyrics by Douglas Furber and Frank Eyton), and *Follow the Sun* (lyrics by Carter, 1936). Schwartz's non-Dietz productions include *Princess Charming* (lyrics by Arthur Swanstrom, 1930), *Virginia* ("Goodbye Jonah" and "You and I Know," lyrics by Albert Stillman, 1937), *Stars in Your Eyes* ("It's All Yours" and "This Is It," lyrics by Dorothy Fields, 1939), *American Jubilee* ("Tennessee Fish Fry" and

"How Can I Ever Be Alone?," lyrics by Oscar Hammerstein II, 1940), *Park Avenue* ("Don't Be a Woman If You Can," "Land of Opportunitee," "There's No Holding Me," and "The Dew Was on the Rose," lyrics by Ira Gershwin, 1946), *A Tree Grows in Brooklyn* ("Love Is the Reason," "I'll Buy You a Star," and "Make the Man Love Me," lyrics by Fields, 1951), and *By the Beautiful Sea* ("More Love Than Your Love" and "Alone Too Long," lyrics by Fields, 1954). Schwartz has written for radio, screen, and television. He and Dietz wrote songs for a weekly radio show, *The Gibson Family*, for 39 weeks in 1933. For this series they came up with about 90 songs (one of them, the theme of the show, "If There Is Someone Lovelier Than You," was reused in the score for *Revenge with Music*). Among Schwartz's most significant film scores are *Thank Your Lucky Stars* (1943), with lyrics by Frank Loesser: "Good Night, Neighbor," "How Sweet You Are," "Love Isn't Born," and "They're Either Too Young or Too Old." For *The Time, the Place and the Girl* (1946), Schwartz with lyricist Leo Robin created a good score: "Oh, But I Do," "A Gal in Calico," "A Rainy Night in Rio," and "Through a Thousand Dreams." The songs of Dietz and Schwartz were celebrated in the films *Dancing in the Dark* (1949) and *The Band Wagon*, which starred Fred Astaire and for which they wrote a new song, "That's Entertainment" (1953). Schwartz also scored television shows, *High Tor*, based on Maxwell Anderson's play, and *A Bell for Adano*, based on the novel by John Hersey; both were shown in 1956.

SERLY, TIBOR (1901–1978) Composer, theorist, teacher. Born in Losonc, Hungary, Nov. 25, 1901, Serly was brought to the United States when he was about 4. His father, Lajos, had been a prominent conductor-composer in Hungary; in the United States he taught music. Serly began violin lessons with his father, who had formed a Hungarian-German operetta company that toured in New Jersey and Pennsylvania. One of the younger Serly's first musical jobs was playing in the violin section of his father's orchestra. Serly began writing music at about the age of 11. At 15 he began to study with Abraham W. Lilienthal, a member of the Philharmonic's string section. After a brief fling in vaudeville accompanying the "Von Serly Sisters," Serly found work with several orchestras around New York. Offered a scholarship to study in Europe —he had the choice of the Paris Conservatoire or the Budapest Royal Academy —Serly chose the Budapest Academy. There he studied with Zoltán Kodály, with whom he formed a lifelong friendship; he also met Béla Bartók during his stay in Budapest and they too became close friends. Although he had studied composition and had many works already to his credit, Serly found work upon his return to the United States as violinist or violist with such orchestras as the Philadelphia Orchestra (under Stokowski) and the NBC Symphony, which had been formed for Toscanini. In 1938 Serly resigned from the NBC Symphony to devote his time to composition and teaching. He gave up the career of instrumentalist but continued to conduct. Serly became one of the most sought-after teachers (composition, theory, conducting) in New York. During his teaching sessions Serly evolved an approach to composition, which he taught to his students and called "Modus Lascivus." His own works from the early 1940s reflect this new manner of approaching the chromatic scale (Serly had little patience for the 12-tone school of composition). His original work was interrupted in 1945 when Serly was asked to salvage Bartók's last works. The Hungarian composer, in exile from his Nazi-held homeland, had died leaving a piano and viola concerto unfinished. The piano concerto, Bartók's *Third,* required the filling in of the final 17 bars, but the viola concerto consisted of several unnumbered manuscript pages of ideas— although the entire concerto was mapped out for anyone who could make sense of Bartók's musical shorthand. Serly could do this, but it took about 2 years, during which Serly did very little original work of his own. This action colored the rest of Serly's professional life, typing him as savior of Bartók's final works and a Bartók authority and not as Tibor Serly, composer. He was also constantly referred to as a "Hungarian-American" composer when he regarded himself as purely American. Few took into consideration that he had been an "American" from the age of 4, that most of his musical education was acquired in the United States, and that he had, in his early years, played in dance bands, theatre pit bands, "everything from bawdy houses to concert halls," as he put it. Among Serly's most important works are *Four Songs from "Chamber Music,"* text by James Joyce, for soprano and chamber orchestra (1926), *Strange Story,* text by Elinor Wylie, for soprano and orchestra (1927), *First Symphony* (ca. 1928), *Viola Concerto* (1929), *Six Dance Designs* for orchestra (1935), *Symphony No. 2* for woodwinds, brass, and percussion (1931), *Sonata Concertante* for strings (ca. 1930s), *American Fantasy of Quodlibets* (n.d., in the 1940s), *American Elegy* for orchestra (1945), *Lament for Strings* (1946), *Sonata in Modus Lascivus* for violin (1947), *Piano Sonata* (ca. 1947), *Medea,* incidental music (1947), *Rhapsody* for viola (1948), *Concerto for Two Pianos and Orchestra* (compl. 1958), *Concerto for Violin and Wind Symphony* (1958), *String Symphony in Four Cycles for Young People* (ca. 1965), *Forty Piano Preludes in Modus Lascivus* (1946–60),

Concertino 3 times 3 for piano and orchestra (1965), *Canonic Fugue* for 10 strings (1971), *Rondo Fantasy* for violin and harp (1971), *Cast Out,* ballet (1973), and *The Pleiades* for chorus and orchestra (1978). Other works include songs, arrangements of works by others, and "reconstructions" of works by Liszt, Schubert, orchestrations of pieces by Gesualdo, Bartók, and his father, Lajos Serly (the famous song "Kek Ne Felejts"—Forget Me Not). Serly is the author of *A Second Look at Harmony* (1964), *Modus Lascivus: A New Concept in Composition* (1975), and *The Rhetoric of Melody,* with Norman Newton (1978). Serly died in London, Oct. 8, 1978, after being struck by an automobile.

SHAPERO, HAROLD (b. 1920) Composer, teacher. Born in Lynn, Mass., Apr. 29, 1920, Shapero began piano studies at the age of 7; by the time he was in high school he was the leader-pianist in his own dance band. His major interest in music then was jazz. He was 16 when he decided that he needed to study musical theory and began to work with Nicolas Slonimsky in Boston. He spent a few months studying with Czech composer Ernst Krenek. At Harvard he worked under Walter Piston and occasionally met with Igor Stravinsky, then lecturing there. Shapero also studied at the Berkshire Music Center, Mass., during the summer with Paul Hindemith. Upon graduation from Harvard in 1941 he studied for 2 years with Nadia Boulanger (then in the United States) under Naumberg and Paine Fellowships. In 1952 Shapero joined the music staff of Brandeis University, Waltham, Mass., where he was chairman of the Music Department for several years. Shapero's works include *Three Pieces* for flute, clarinet, and bassoon (1938), *Trumpet Sonata* for trumpet and piano (1940), *Nine-Minute Overture* for orchestra (1940—awarded the Prix de Rome), *String Quartet* (1940), *Sonata for Piano,* 4 hands (1941), *Sonata for Violin and Piano* (1942), *Three Amateur Piano Sonatas* (1944), *Serenade in D* for strings (1945), *Symphony for Classical Orchestra* (1946), *The Travelers,* overture for orchestra (1948), *Piano Sonata in F Minor* (1948), *Concerto for Orchestra* (1950), *Credo* for orchestra (1955), *Hebrew Cantata* (1955), *On Green Mountain* (*Chaconne after Monteverdi*) "for 13 jazz players" (1957), *Partita* for piano and chamber orchestra (1960); *Partita* for piano and orchestra (1960), *Improvisations in B* for synthesizer and piano (1968), *Three Studies in C* for synthesizer and piano (1969), and *Four Pieces* for synthesizer and piano (1970).

SHAW, ARTIE (b. 1910) Bandleader, clarinetist, arranger, composer. Born Arthur Arshawsky in New York City, May 23, 1910, Shaw grew up in New Haven, Conn., where he first studied music and played saxophone in local bands while still in high school. At 16 he left home to play in a restaurant band in Cleveland (1926–29); he then moved to California to join the then well-known Irving Aaronson band. Shaw began writing arrangements about this time (1929), had switched to the clarinet and toured with the band. Shaw left the Aaronson group after it played New York in 1931 and began free-lancing with various local bands—Red Nichols, Vincent Lopez, Roger Wolfe Kahn, and others. In the mid 1930s he worked with several radio bands: Paul Whiteman, André Kostelanetz, Howard Barlow, and Richard Himber. During 1934–35 Shaw retired to a farm to write and to get away from the music business. He returned to New York in the summer of 1935 to perform at a jazz concert at the Imperial Theatre; accompanied by a string quartet, Shaw was the sensation of the concert. This led to formation of his first band, utilizing strings (no one associated jazz with strings) and one saxophone (his friend Tony Pastor), but the band was not a success. In the spring of 1937 Shaw organized a more conventional swing band, supplied it with well-wrought arrangements, and began to be heard via radio. A recording of Cole Porter's "Begin the Beguine," in an arrangement by Jerry Gray, became one of the hit records of 1938—in fact an All Time hit—which led to more recordings, radio and theatre and dance hall appearances. The grind led to another Shaw retreat in 1939, when he retired to Mexico. The next year Shaw returned with a new band, again featuring a string section and produced another best-selling recording, "Frenesi" (1940). By this time Shaw was considered the chief rival of "King of Swing" Benny Goodman. Shaw's arrangements were not especially jazzy, although several jazzmen made up his various orchestras. Shaw also played more popular songs and the better songs from films and Broadway shows. His jazzier (or swingier) efforts were assigned to the Gramercy Five, consisting of Billy Butterfield (trumpet), Shaw (clarinet), Jud De Naut (bass), Nick Fatool (drums) and—an unusual touch—Johnny Guarnieri on harpsichord. (The personnel of the Gramercy Five shifted over the years; this was the original group.) The band's great hit records during this period were "Star Dust" (1940) and "Moonglow" (1941). Shaw broke up the band again in 1942 to enlist in the U. S. Navy, for which he organized a star-studded band—Claude Thornhill, Max Kaminsky, Dave Tough, et al.—and toured the United States and the South Pacific. With the rank of chief petty officer, Shaw was given a medical discharge from the Navy in 1944, following the exhausting Pacific tour. He formed a new band later that year and continued in the band business until 1955, when he retired and moved to Spain (1955–59). Eventually he decided to stay out of music and went into theatrical and film production. Shaw's contempt for the music business was articulately presented in his autobiography, *The Trouble with Cinderella* (which also touched on his multiple marriages to film actresses and other beautiful women). His novel, *I Love You, I Hate You, Drop Dead!* was published in 1965. Among Shaw's composition-arrangements are *Back Bay Shuffle* (1938), *Nightmare*, the band's theme (1938), *One Night Stand* (1939), *Summit Ridge Drive* (1940), and *Concerto for Clarinet* (1940).

SIEGMEISTER, ELIE (b. 1909) Composer, teacher, conductor, author. Born in New York City, Jan. 15, 1909, Siegmeister studied piano as a youngster and followed that with work at Columbia University with Seth Bingham and Wallingford Riegger. He was graduated in 1927 and then went to Paris to study at the École Normale de Musique with Nadia Boulanger, completing his work there in 1931. From 1935 to 1938, on a Juilliard Graduate School Scholarship, Siegmeister studied conducting under Albert Stoessel. Even more important to Siegmeister's musical evolution was a chance meeting with folk singer Aunt Molly Jackson, who introduced him to the wide range of American folk music. Not only did this influence much of Siegmeister's composition during the late 1930s and the '40s, it also resulted in an admirable book, *The Treasury of American Song*, with Olin Downes (1940). He also formed his own singing group, the American Ballad Singers, which specialized in folk song. In addition he has taught at Brooklyn College, The New School for Social Research, New York City, and, since 1949, has been a member of the music faculty of Hofstra University, Hempstead, N.Y. His works include *Sonata No. 1 for Violin and Piano* (1931), *Theme and Variations for Piano No. 1* (1932), *Woodwind Quintet* (1932), *Strange Funeral in Braddock* for voice and orchestra (1933), *American Holiday* for orchestra (1933), *May Day* for orchestra (1933), *String Quartet No. 1* (1936), *Rhapsody for Orchestra* (1937), *Abraham Lincoln Walks at Midnight* for chorus and orchestra (1937), *Created Equal,* a musical (1938), *A Walt Whitman Overture* (1939), *Children's Games* for chorus, a cappella (1940), *Eight American Folksongs* for chorus, a cappella (1940), *Funnybone Alley,* song cycle (1941), *Nancy Hanks* for chorus and piano (1941), *Anne Rutledge* for chorus and piano (1941), *Paul Bunyan* for men's voices and piano (1941), *Doodle Dandy of the U.S.A.,* a musical (1942), *Freedom Train* for men's voices and piano (1943), *Ozark Set* for orchestra (1944), *Sing Out Sweet Land,* musical (1944), *American Sonata* for piano (1944), *Western Suite* for orchestra (1945), *Prairie Legend* for band (1945), *Wilderness Road* for orchestra (1945), *Sunday in Brooklyn* for orchestra (1946), *Symphony No. 1* (1948), *From My Window* for orchestra (1949), *Darling Corie,* opera (1951), *Symphony No. 2* (1952), *Three Cornered Suite* for band (1954), *Miranda and the Dark Young Man,* opera (1955), *Concerto for Clarinet and Orchestra* (1956), *Symphony No. 3* (1957), *The Mermaid in Lock No. 7,* opera (1958), *Cordura Suite* for orchestra drawn from a film score (1959), *Concerto for Flute and Orchestra* (1960), *String Quartet No. 2* (1960), *The Plough and the Stars,* opera (1963), *Sonata No. 2 for Piano* (1964), *Sextet for Brass and Percussion* (1965), *Sonata No. 3 for Violin and Piano* (1965), *In Our Time* for chorus (1965), *I Have a Dream,* cantata (1966), *Five Fantasies of the Theatre* for orchestra (1967), *The Face of War,* orchestral song cycle

(1968), *Symphony No. 4* (1970), *A Cycle of Cities* for orchestra and *Concerto for Piano and Orchestra* (1974). Siegmeister is the editor of *The Music Lover's Handbook* (1943, revised and reissued as *The New Music Lover's Handbook,* 1969), *Invitation to Music* (1959), and the 2-volume work *Harmony and Melody* (1965).

SINATRA, FRANK (b. 1915) Popular singer. Born in Hoboken, N.J., Dec. 12, 1915, Sinatra had no formal musical training when he began singing in New Jersey clubs. In the late 1930s he appeared on "Major Bowes and His Original Amateur Hour" and won a contract to tour with the Bowes group. While singing at the Rustic Cabin, Englewood, N.J., Sinatra was heard by bandleader Harry James who hired him in 1939. Although the famous Sinatra style had not yet formed, he was already appreciated for his way with song lyrics. A natural musicality and vocal equipment enabled him to phrase a song smoothly with remarkable intonation. Another bandleader, Tommy Dorsey, literally lured Sinatra away from James in 1940; it was while singing with the Dorsey band that Sinatra became the adored one of the bobby-soxers (the mothers of the groupies who went mad over the Beatles) in the '40s and during World War II. By January 1943, when Sinatra sang as a single at the mobbed Paramount Theatre, he had become one of the major vocalists in popular music. He made dozens—more!—of best-selling recordings, had his own radio show, sang for several years on "Your Hit Parade," and appeared in films. Initially not very successful as a film personality, Sinatra suffered professionally in the late 1940s and early '50s; he then won an Academy Award (1953) for a nonsinging role in the World War II drama *From Here to Eternity.* Since, he has appeared in more than 30 films of varying quality. Sinatra became a most successful nightclub attraction in the 1950s and '60s, appeared on television, and reinstated his successful recording career. He became popularly associated with the expensive, expense-accounty Las Vegas type of club as well as the swinging-single style of life. His 2 children, Nancy and Frank Jr., have enjoyed some success as vocalists. Sinatra has written song lyrics, most notably the 1941 success "This Love of Mine" (music by Sol Parker and Henry Sanicola). A man of many parts, Sinatra, out of enthusiasm for the chamber compositions of Alec Wilder (q.v.), actually recorded several of these pieces for Columbia Records in 1945. Sinatra conducted despite the fact that he did not really read music; he depended on his remarkable musical memory. A public personality of intimidating arrogance, Sinatra is also noted for private generosity and personal kindness. As late as 1979 he continued to make personal appearances and to record, despite several declarations of retirement.

SMITH, JULIA (b. 1911) Composer, pianist, teacher, author. Born in Denton, Tex., Jan. 25, 1911, Smith studied with Harold von Mickwitz at the Institute of Musical Art, Dallas, Tex. At North Texas State University, Denton, she earned her B.A. in music. She continued at the Juilliard School of Music, New York City, where she worked under Carl Friedberg, Rubin Goldmark (q.v.), Frederick Jacobi (q.v.), and Bernard Wagenaar (q.v.). She studied composition with Marion Bauer (q.v.) at New York University. She joined the music teaching staff of the Juilliard School in 1940 and was head of the Department of Music, Hartt College of Music, Hartford, Conn. (1941–46). Her compositions include *American Dance Suite* for orchestra (1936, rev. 1963), *Cynthia Parker*, 2-act opera (1938), *Piano Concerto* (1939), *Hellenic Suite* for orchestra

(1941), *The Gooseherd and the Goblin*, one-act opera (1946), *Sonatine in C* for piano (1944), *Folkways Symphony* (1948), *Characteristic Suite* for piano (1949), *Cockcrow*, one-act opera (1953), *Our Heritage* for chorus and piano, also for chorus and orchestra (1956), *String Quartet* (1964), *Remember the Alamo* for chorus, band, and narrator (1964), and *Sails Aloft*, overture for band, with Cecile Vashaw (1965). Her books include *Aaron Copland* (1955), *Master Pianist: the Career and Teaching of Carl Friedberg* (1963), and *A Directory of American Women Composers* (1970).

"SOUTH PACIFIC" Musical, music by Richard Rodgers (q.v.) and lyrics by Oscar Hammerstein II (q.v.). Hammerstein and director Josh Logan based the book on stories from James Michener's *Tales of the South Pacific*. There are 2 plots, both concerned with the subject of miscegenation. The major story tells of an American nurse, "Nellie Forbush," and her love for an older, more experienced French planter, "Emile de Becque," who has fathered children by a "native woman." This proves to be difficult to take for a young woman from Arkansas. The subplot tells of the love of a young lieutenant "Joe Cable" for "Liat," a Polynesian. Other characters, such as the beefy sailor "Luther Billis" and the sharp-dealing "Bloody Mary," provided the musical's lighter moments. Before the musical ends, the May-December romance of de Becque and Nellie is happily resolved and the problem of miscegenation is solved by the death of Lieutenant Cable, who had joined de Becque in a dangerous mission against the Japanese. Among the songs written for *South Pacific:* "Some Enchanted Evening," "There Is Nothing Like a Dame," "Bali Ha'i," "I'm Gonna Wash That Man Right Out of My Hair," "I'm in Love with a Wonderful Guy,"

"Younger Than Springtime," "Happy Talk," "You've Got to Be Taught," and "This Nearly Was Mine." *South Pacific* opened at the Majestic Theatre, New York, Apr. 7, 1949, and ran for 1,925 performances; it also had a good run in London in 1951. It was made into a musical film in 1958. In the original 1949 cast were Mary Martin ("Nellie"), Ezio Pinza ("Emile"), William Tabbert ("Joe Cable"), Betta St. John ("Liat"), Myron McCormick ("Luther Billis"), and Juanita Hall as "Bloody Mary."

"STAR DUST" Popular song, music by Hoagy Carmichael (q.v.) and lyrics by Mitchell Parish (q.v.). Carmichael originally composed the melody of what is now known as "Star Dust" ca. 1929 as an instrumental for piano in a rather quick tempo, with ragtime feeling. Some stories have Carmichael writing it in the Book Nook, near the University of Indiana campus, while he was still a student there (the most likely tale) and others date it to a brief period, after his graduation with a law degree, when he was working as a professional pianist for Mills Music. The instrumental version was published by Mills in 1929; it was recorded in 1931 by the Isham Jones orchestra and achieved some popularity. Arranger Jimmy Dale suggested that Carmichael slow down the song—ease the tempo and have words written. Lyricist Mitchell Parish, also a staff songwriter, fashioned the words and "Star Dust," with an added verse, was published in this form in 1931; it has been around ever since.

STEIN, LEON (b. 1910) Composer, conductor, teacher. Born in Chicago, Ill., Sept. 18, 1910, Stein began in music by studying the violin at the American Conservatory, Chicago; he later studied composition with John Becker (q.v.) and Leo Sowerby (q.v.), among others. He was also a student of conducting. He received his bachelor's degree in music

from De Paul University in 1931; in the same year he joined the music faculty of the university and remained there until 1976, when he retired as dean of the School of Music. During his tenure, Stein was conductor of the school's chamber orchestra and did much guest conducting in the Chicago area, including at the Great Lakes Training Center during World War II. Stein's compositions include a *Suite* for string quartet (1930), *Adagio* and *Dance* for violin, cello, and piano (1932), *Sonata for Violin and Piano* (1932), *String Quartet No. 1* (1934), *Prelude and Fugue* for orchestra (1935), *String Quartet No. 2* (1935), *Passacaglia* for orchestra (1936), *Sonatina for Two Violins* (1937), *Quintet for Winds* (1937), *Sinfonietta* for strings (1938), *Larghetto* for strings (1938), *Violin Concerto* (1939), *Exodus*, ballet, with piano accompaniment (1939), *Three Hassidic Dances* for orchestra (1940), *Doubt*, ballet, with piano accompaniment (1940), *Symphony No. 1* (1940), *Symphony No. 2* (1942), *Triptych* for orchestra (1943), *Sailor's Hornpipe* for orchestra (1944), *Great Lakes Suite* for chamber orchestra (1944), *Twelve Preludes* for violin and piano (1949), *Symphony No. 3* (1951), *Trio for Trumpets* (1953), *The Fisherman's Wife*, opera (1954), *Rhapsody* for flute, harp, and strings (1954), *Deidre*, opera (1956), *Adagio and Rondo Ebraico* for orchestra (1957), *Quintet for Saxophone and String Quartet* (1957), *Sonata for Solo Violin* (1960), *String Quartet No. 3* (1964), *String Quartet No. 4* (1965), *Saxophone Sonata* (1967), *String Quartet No. 5* (1967), *Sonata for Solo Flute* (1968), *Suite* for wind quintet (1970), *Then Shall Dust Return* for orchestra (1971), *Symphony No. 4* (1974), *Brass Quintet* (1975), and *Quintet for Harp and String Quartet* (1977). Stein is the author of *An Analytic Study of Brahms' Variations on a Theme by Haydn*

(1944), *Structure and Style* (1962), and *An Anthology of Musical Forms* (1962).

STEINER, MAX (1888–1971) Composer, conductor. Born in Vienna, Austria, May 10, 1888, Steiner came from a family of impresarios; both his grandfather and father were involved with the musical theatre of Vienna. Young Steiner attended the Imperial Academy of Music, where he studied with Felix Weingartner and Gustav Mahler. His first operetta, *The Beautiful Greek Girl*, for which Steiner wrote book, lyrics, and music, was produced when he was 14. The show ran for a year with Steiner as conductor. Although he composed a good deal at the time, Steiner was best known as a conductor; in that capacity he worked with the London Opera House, among other theatres, from 1904. He went to Paris in 1911 and came to the United States in 1914. Steiner found work in the musical theatre conducting, arranging, orchestrating shows for such composers as Victor Herbert, Jerome Kern, and George Gershwin. Steiner was conductor and orchestrator for the 1927 show *Rio Rita*, and when it was transformed into a screen musical in 1929 composer Harry Tierney suggested that Steiner do what he had done for the show for the film. Steiner arrived in Hollywood on Dec. 25, 1929, and remained to enjoy one of the most successful careers in composing for the movies. Not only did Steiner score several popular film musicals, as music director, he also turned out full background scores. He initially worked for RKO where he scored more than 100 films, among them Vincent Youmans' *Flying Down to Rio*, Cole Porter's *The Gay Divorcee*, Jerome Kern's *Roberta*, and Irving Berlin's *Top Hat*. As music director Steiner often assigned the actual scoring to other orchestrators. His first important background scoring was done for *King Kong*

(1933); he won his first Academy Award for *The Informer* (1935). Other significant Steiner scorings include *Four Daughters* (1938), for which he composed the romantic *Symphonie Moderne* for piano and orchestra, *Gone With the Wind* (1939), from which came the popular "Tara's Theme," *Now, Voyager* (1943), another Academy Award score, out of which came the popular song, "It Can't Be Wrong," lyrics by Kim Gannon, and *Since You Went Away* (1944), another Academy Award score. From *Saratoga Trunk* (1945) came another popular song, "As Long as I Live" (not to be confused with the Arlen-Koehler song of the same title), with lyrics by Charles Tobias. Steiner's last screen scoring was for *Youngblood Hawke* (1964). Although he was a pioneer in the art of composing for films, Steiner was no musical trail-blazer. He wrote in a direct, uncomplex manner and scored or had his music scored in the rich style of the 19th century. (Steiner's orchestrations were generally done by Hugo Friedhofer or Murray Cutter, working from the composer's full sketches.) Steiner's method was Wagnerian, in that he assigned leitmotivs to the different characters, even things, in the films he scored. This method, in its most extreme form, came to be called "Mickey Mouse music," after the practice of composers who wrote for cartoons and who, imitating Steiner, wrote music for not only the characters, but for every little action, from the wiggling of a tail to the lifting of an eyebrow. Steiner continued to conduct throughout his career as studio music director and composer and recorded several of his own works, including the *Gone With the Wind* score. He died in Hollywood, Dec. 28, 1971.

STEVENS, HALSEY (b. 1908) Composer, teacher, writer. Born in Scott, N.Y., Dec. 3, 1908, Stevens began to study the piano and music theory in

1917. He continued at Syracuse University, where he studied composition with William Berwald and piano with George Mulfinger. He also studied with Ernest Bloch at the University of California, Berkeley, in 1944. Stevens has taught at Dakota Wesleyan University, Syracuse University, the University of Redlands (Calif.), Bradley Polytechnic Institute, as professor of music, and in 1946 was appointed professor of music and chairman of the Composition Department at the University of Southern California, Los Angeles. Stevens has written and lectured extensively on music and for several years (1946–51) wrote the program annotations for the Los Angeles Philharmonic. His compositions include *String Quartet No. 1* (1931), *Concertino* for piano and orchestra (1936), *Sextet* (1936), *Trio* for violin, cello, and piano (1937), *Sonatina No. 1* for violin and piano (1937), *When I am Dead, My Dearest* for chorus, a cappella (1938), *Of the Heavenly Bodies* for chorus (1942), *Go, Lovely Rose* for chorus, a cappella (1942), *Sonatina* for flute and piano (1943), *Diversion on "Beau Chasseur de Lièvre"* for two violins, viola, and cello (1943), *String Quartet No. 2* (1944), *Sonatina No. 2* for violin and piano (1944), *Suite* for chamber orchestra (1945), *Symphony No. 1* (1945), *Trio No. 2* for violin, cello, and piano (1945), *Symphony No. 2* (1945), *Suite* for clarinet and piano (1945), *Quintet* for flute, violin, viola, cello, and piano (1945), *Symphony No. 3* (1946), *Quartet* for violin, viola, cello, and piano (1946), *Piano Sonata No. 3* (1948), *A Green Mountain Overture* for orchestra (1948), *String Quartet No. 3* (1949), *Viola Sonata* (1950), *Sonatina No. 3* for piano (1950), *Sonatina No. 4* for piano (1952), *Triskelion* for orchestra (1953), *Like as the Culver* for chorus (1954), *Psalm 98* for chorus (1955), *The Ballad of William Sycamore*, text by Stephen Vincent Benét, for chorus and orchestra

(1955), *Sonetto del Petrarca* for voice and piano (1956), *Sinfonia Breve* for orchestra (1957), *Symphonic Dances* for orchestra (1958), *Sonata for Solo Cello* (1958), *Five Pieces for Orchestra* (1958), *A Testament of Life* for chorus and orchestra (1959), *Sonatina No. 3* for violin and piano (1959), *Sonatina No. 6* for piano (1959), *Ritratti* for piano (1960), *Fantasia* for piano (1961), *Magnificat* for chorus and orchestra (1962), *Cello Concerto* (1964), *Cello Sonata* (1965), *Six Slovakian Folksongs* for harp (1966), *Campion Suite* for chorus (1967), *Four Duos* for double basses (1967), *Threnos* for orchestra (1968), and *Concerto for Clarinet and Strings* (1969). Stevens is the author of *The Life and Music of Béla Bartók* (1953).

"STORMY WEATHER" Popular song, music by Harold Arlen (q.v.) and lyrics by Ted Koehler (q.v.). "Stormy Weather" was written for the spring edition of the Cotton Club show *Cotton Club Parade* in 1933. Originally the show was to have starred Cab Calloway and his orchestra, so Arlen conceived the melody, particularly the opening ("the front shout," is Arlen's term), deliberately for the "hi-de-ho" singing style of Calloway. The song was casually written in about a half hour—words and music —and submitted as one of the songs for that year's *Parade*. Duke Ellington had, by then, replaced Calloway so the song was assigned to the singing star, Ethel Waters. Meanwhile, on Feb. 28, 1933, Arlen recorded "Stormy Weather" accompanied by the Leo Reisman band. By the time the *Cotton Club Parade* opened on Apr. 6, the recording was a best-seller and the audience expectant when Waters sang it; she stopped the show nightly. The song and its melancholy reflected some of the sadness of the Depression as well as the emotions of an abandoned woman. "Stormy Weather" is a characteristic Arlen song in that its structure does not fall into the standard 32-bar popular song form. It has no introductory verse, also a convention rarely overlooked. Koehler's lyrics are exemplary.

STRANG, GERALD (b. 1908) Composer, conductor, teacher. Born in Claresholm, Alberta, Canada, Feb. 13, 1908, Strang was graduated from Stanford University, Calif., in 1928 and continued in music at the University of California, Berkeley, and the University of Southern California, Los Angeles. Among his teachers were Charles Koechlin, Ernst Toch, and Arnold Schoenberg. Strang had a long association with Schoenberg, initially as a teaching assistant at USC and as an editorial assistant; this association lasted until a year before Schoenberg's death in 1951. Strang taught also at Long Beach College, San Fernando College, California State College, Long Beach, and lectured at the University of California, L.A. During World War II he was employed as an engineer at Douglas Aircraft. Strang's musical direction was "modernist" from the beginning and he became the founder and director of the New Music Workshops (1933) and was appointed director of the New Music Society of California (1936). From 1935 to 1940 he was managing editor of *New Music Editions* (q.v.). He has lectured on electronic music and is an authority on acoustics. His works include *Sonatina for Solo Clarinet* (1932), *Quintet* for clarinet and string quartet (1933), *Five Pieces* for flute and clarinet (1933), *Three Pieces* for flute, or oboe, and clarinet (1933), *String Quartet* (1934), *Intermezzo* for orchestra (1935), *Percussion Music* for 3 players (1935), *Vanzetti in the Death House* for baritone, chorus, and chamber orchestra (1937), *Canzonet* for strings (1942), *1943* for orchestra (1942), *Symphony No. 1* (1942), *Overland Trail*

for orchestra (1943), *Symphony No. 2* (1947), *Divertimento for Four Instruments* (1948), *Concerto for Cello* (1951), *Concerto Grosso* (1951), *Sonata for Solo Flute* (1953), *Variation for Four Instruments* (1956), and *Compusition*, computerized compositions on tape (1963–69).

STRAVINSKY, IGOR (1882–1971) Composer, conductor. Born in Oranienbaum, Russia, June 17, 1882, Stravinsky studied both law and composition (with Nicolai Rimsky-Korsakov) simultaneously. From a musical environment (his father sang bass with the Russian Imperial Opera), Stravinsky began piano at around the age of 9. He decided to give up law and to concentrate on music. His first symphony dates from 1908. Stravinsky made his musical impression with the ballet scores written for the Ballets Russes and its impresario, Serge Diaghilev: *The Firebird* (1910), *Petrouchka* (1911), and the revolutionary *Le Sacre du Printemps* (1913). Stravinsky spent World War I in Switzerland, then settled in Paris in 1917. He was a tremendous influence upon students who came to Paris to study, many of them pupils of Nadia Boulanger. During the between-the-wars period Stravinsky became an internationally famous composer whose works rarely failed to stir up controversy. He first visited the United States in 1925 as a guest of the New York Philharmonic as conductor of his own compositions. Stravinsky came to the United States again in 1939 to give the Charles Eliot Norton lectures at Harvard University (these were published as *Poetics of Music* in 1947). The outbreak of World War II no doubt contributed to Stravinsky's decision to remain in the United States in 1939 (he became a citizen in 1945) for the rest of his life (with several excursions to other countries, even to his former homeland, Soviet Russia, as conductor and honored musical personality). Stravinsky can hardly be claimed as an American composer (it is difficult to classify him as a Russian, for that matter), but as a musical father figure for a generation or 2 of American composers, his influence is outstanding. While he confuted his critics, even his followers, Stravinsky passed through his several phases—primitive folk Russian, "neoclassic," even 12-tone (despite a longtime aversion to it, which estranged him from his near neighbor in Hollywood, Schoenberg)—Stravinsky remained Stravinsky throughout. He was one of music's master orchestrators, a master of form, who composed in almost every genre, from a ballet "for a young elephant" to full-fledged symphonies. Among the works written in the United States are *Danses Concertantes,* ballet (1942), *Circus Polka* for orchestra (1942), *Four Norwegian Moods* for orchestra (1942), *Ode* for orchestra (1943), *Scènes de Ballet* (1944), *Sonata for Two Pianos* (1944), *Symphony in Three Movements* (1945), *Ebony Concerto* (q.v., 1945), *Concerto in D* for orchestra (1946), *Orpheus,* ballet (1947), *Mass* (1947), *The Rake's Progress,* opera (1951), *Cantata* for mezzo-soprano, tenor, chorus, and chamber orchestra (1952), *Canticum Sacrum* for tenor, baritone, chorus, and orchestra (1955), *Agon,* ballet (1957), *Threni* for soloists, chorus, and orchestra (1958), *Movements* for piano and orchestra (1959), *The Flood,* "A Musical Play" for speakers, soloists, chorus, and orchestra (1962), *Abraham and Isaac,* "a Sacred Ballad for baritone and orchestra" (1963), *Orchestra Variations* (1964), *Requiem Canticles* for soloists, chorus, and orchestra (1966). After years of poor health, Stravinsky died in New York, Apr. 6, 1971.

"STREET SCENE" A musical play, or opera—the designation is academic—with music by Kurt Weill (q.v.), lyrics by Langston Hughes (1902–1967), and a book by Elmer Rice (1892–1967), based on his successful 1929 play of the same name. A backdrop of brownstones is the setting of *Street Scene* against which the tragic story of love-starved "Anna Maurrant" and her affair with a milk salesman ends in the murder of both. Anna is neglected by her husband and ignored by her children, a young son and a grown daughter, "Rose." In love with Rose is the tenement's resident intellectual-dreamer, "Sam Kaplan." Other characters are a black janitor, an Italian music teacher, an expectant young father whose wife is only heard not seen, and various other residents, including children who sing folk-like street songs and a youthful, brash couple who come on for a song and a quite athletic dance. Weill composed—and orchestrated—a rich, full score, the only musical in which he felt he had achieved "a real blending of drama and music in which the singing continues naturally where the speaking stops and the spoken word, as well as the dramatic action, is embedded in the overall musical structure." From the opening music, brooding and pungent in its harmonies, it is obvious that *Street Scene* is not a musical comedy; there are lighter moments in such songs as the janitor's "I Got a Marble and a Star," the ensemble's "Ice Cream," the children's game song, and the brash couple's "Moon-Faced, Starry-Eyed," but these are counterbalanced by Anna's aria "Somehow I Never Could Believe," Sam's "Lonely House," Rose's "What Good Would the Moon Be?," and "Frank Maurrant's" (Rose's father and Anna's husband) "I Loved Her Too." *Street Scene* is a moving musical-lyrico experience. It opened at the Adelphi Theatre, New York, Jan. 9, 1947, and ran for a mere 148 performances, despite the general critical praises. It was revived by the New York City Opera in 1966 and, with great success, in 1979. In the original Broadway production the role of "Anna" was sung by Polyna Stoska, her husband "Frank" by Norman Cordon, her daughter "Rose" by Anne Jeffreys, and "Sam" by Brian Sullivan. Certain members of the 1979 cast deserve to be noted: Eileen Schauler ("Anna"), Catherine Malfitano ("Rose"), and Alan Kays ("Sam").

STYNE, JULE (b. 1905) Composer, pianist, arranger, producer. Born in London, Dec. 31, 1905, Styne and his family moved to the United States in 1913, settling in Chicago. A musical prodigy, Styne made his debut as a solo pianist with the Chicago Symphony at the age of 9. He won a scholarship to the Chicago College of Music and completed his education at Northwestern University. Despite his formal training in music, Styne was drawn to the popular music of the 1920s and soon formed his own dance band to work in the Chicago area. For his band he wrote arrangements and officiated from the piano. For a time he was associated with the Art Jarrett band in the mid 1930s, after which he went to New York City to work as a vocal coach and to write special songs for various performers. By the late '30s he had worked his way to Hollywood where he was employed as vocal coach (among his students were Alice Faye and Shirley Temple) and to do background scoring for films and to write a song now and then. Some of his first efforts were heard in insignificant films (*Hold That Co-ed, Kentucky Moonshine, Stop, Look and Love,* and *Barnyard Follies,* 1939–40). Among his lyricists was Frank Loesser (q.v.), with whom he wrote "I Don't Want to Walk Without You" for *Sweater Girl* (1942), Styne's first important hit song. The following year Styne was united with lyricist Sammy Cahn (q.v.) to add songs to the film version of Kurt

Weill's *Knickerbocker Holiday,* with little more than middling results. In 1944 they had a couple of songs in a typical wartime hodgepodge, *Follow the Boys,* and came up with the very popular "I'll Walk Alone." Over the next several years Styne and Cahn produced a good number of popular, profitable songs: "There Goes That Song Again" (*Carolina Blues,* 1944), "What Makes the Sun Set?" (*Anchors Aweigh,* 1945), "Love Is a Merry-Go-Round" (*Tars and Spars,* 1945), "Five Minutes More" (*Sweetheart of Sigma Chi,* 1946), "Time After Time" (*It Happened in Brooklyn,* 1947), and "It's Magic" (*Romance on the High Seas,* 1948). During the same period they collaborated on nonproduction songs that achieved popularity also (usually in recorded form by such singers as Bing Crosby, Jo Stafford, and Frank Sinatra and the bands of Harry James and Jimmy Dorsey): "It's Been a Long, Long Time" (1944), "Let It Snow, Let It Snow" (1945), "The Things We Did Last Summer" (1946), and "Saturday Night (Is the Loneliest Night of the Week)" (1946). The following year Styne and Cahn moved to Broadway for Styne's first important stage musical, the successful *High Button Shoes,* the first of 16 musicals Styne turned out between 1947 and 1972. (During this period he also produced shows to which he contributed no songs, among them the revival of Rodgers and Hart's *Pal Joey* in 1952.) Styne's most important Broadway scores are: *Gentlemen Prefer Blondes* (lyrics by Leo Robin, 1949: "You Say You Care," "A Little Girl from Little Rock," and "Diamonds Are a Girl's Best Friend"), *Bells Are Ringing* (lyrics by Comden and Green, 1956: "The Party's Over," "Long Before I Knew You," "Just in Time"), *Gypsy* (lyrics by Stephen Sondheim, 1959: "Let Me Entertain You," "Everything Is Coming Up Roses," "Some People," "Small World,"

"Rose's Turn," etc.), and *Funny Girl* (lyrics by Bob Merrill, 1964: "Don't Rain on My Parade," "People"). Styne's later Broadway shows were not as successful although they had their moments. He did *Hallelujah, Baby!* with Comden and Green in 1967, *Darling of the Day* with E. Y. Harburg in 1968, *Look to the Lilies* with Cahn in 1970, and *Sugar* (adapted from the movie *Some Like It Hot*) with Merrill in 1972. *Gentlemen Prefer Blondes,* with added songs, was revived as *Lorelei* in 1974. The show was constructed around the original "Lorelei" of *Blondes,* Carol Channing. It did not repeat the success of the original, which ran 740 performances.

SUESSE, DANA (b. 1911) Composer, pianist, author. Born in Kansas City, Mo., Dec. 3, 1911, Suesse was a musical prodigy who gave her first public piano recital at the age of 8. At the age of 10 she won an American Federation of Music prize for composition. She later came to New York City to study piano with Alexander Siloti, who had been a pupil of Liszt; she studied composition with Rubin Goldmark. Suesse worked for music publishers as an arranger in the late 1920s and began composing popular songs and small piano pieces. One of these, *Jazz Nocturne,* became the popular "My Silent Love" in 1932 when Edward Heyman added a lyric. That same year Suesse made her Carnegie Hall debut in a performance of her *Concerto in Three Rhythms* with the Paul Whiteman Orchestra. Whiteman also commissioned her *Symphonic Waltzes* for piano and orchestra (1933) and *Blue Moonlight* (1934). Gershwin-like, Suesse alternated between the popular and "classical" worlds of music. Besides "My Silent Love" she composed the music for other popular songs such as "You Oughta Be in Pictures" (lyrics by Heyman, 1934), "The Night Is Young and You're So Beautiful" (lyrics by Billy Rose and Irving Kahal, 1936), and "Yours for a Song" from her score for *Billy Rose's Aquacade* at the New York World's Fair (lyrics by Rose and Ted Fetter, 1939). Suesse deserted the pop field for a time and studied with Nadia Boulanger from 1947 to 1950. In the late 1930s and early '40s she composed many attractive piano miniatures with such titles as *Afternoon of a Black Faun, Berceuse, Swamp Bird, Scherzette,* and *Serenade to a Skyscraper.* Among her more ambitious compositions are *Suite for Harp and Orchestra,* "Young Man with a Harp" (1939), *American Nocturne* for orchestra (1939), *Three Cities,* suite for orchestra (ca. 1941), *Concerto in e* for 2 pianos and orchestra (1943), and *Jazz Concerto in D for Combo and Orchestra* (1955). In 1955 also Suesse scored the film *Seven Year Itch* whose theme song was entitled "The Girl Without a Name." Her compositions also include works for chorus, other piano and orchestral pieces, and the plays *Mrs. Mooney* and *It Takes Two.*

"SUMMERTIME" The lullaby which opens George Gershwin's (q.v.) opera, *Porgy and Bess* (q.v.). It is the first song heard in the opera immediately after a brief instrumental introduction and a piano solo, *Jazzbo Brown.* With lyrics by the librettist-poet DuBose Heyward, "Summertime" has become one of the most popular of American songs and has been performed on the concert stage as well as in jazz concerts. In the original 1935 production it was sung by Abbie Mitchell in the role of Clara and reprised later by Anne Brown as Bess. "Summertime," incidentally, was the first song completed by Gershwin for his opera; it was composed during a working vacation in Palm Beach, Fla., in December 1933.

SWANSON, HOWARD (1907–1978) Composer. Born in Atlanta, Ga., Aug.

18, 1907, Swanson moved to Cleveland when he was about 10. The death of his father 7 years later forced Swanson to abandon his wish to go to college. He worked as a "greaser" in a locomotive roundhouse; later he became a letter carrier for a couple of years until he graduated to an inside job in the Cleveland Post Office. Although he had begun to study music at the age of 12, Swanson was 20 before he became a systematic music student at the Cleveland Institute. He went to night school after he had finished work at the post office. When he won a Rosenwald Fellowship in 1938, his teacher, Herbert Elwell, persuaded Swanson to study with Nadia Boulanger. He remained in Paris until 1940, when the outbreak of World War II ended hopes for further study. Back in the United States, Swanson composed while he earned a living working for the Internal Revenue Service—a job he quit in 1945, when he began to gain recognition as a composer. Swanson's star began to shine when the great contralto Marian Anderson sang one of his songs, "The Negro Speaks of Rivers," to a text by Langston Hughes in January 1950. In November his *Short Symphony* (No. 2), composed in 1948, was performed by the New York Philharmonic under Dimıtrı Mıtropoulos; it won the Music Critics Circle Award the next year. After leaving the Treasury Department, Swanson lived simply on grants from the Academy of Arts and Letters, a Guggenheim Fellowship, commissions, and gifts from friends. From 1952 to 1966 Swanson lived in Paris but, because of the high cost of living there, returned to the United States. He settled in New York for the rest of his life. His works include *Symphony No. 1* (1945), *Suite for Cello and Piano* (1949), *Seven Songs* for soprano and piano (1950), *Night Music* for chamber orchestra (1950), *Music for Strings* (1952), *Sound Piece* for brass quintet (1952),

Concerto for Piano and Orchestra (1956), *Concerto for Orchestra* (1956), *Symphony No. 3* (1970), and *Trio* for flute, oboe, and piano (1976). Swanson also composed a *Piano Sonata,* a *Nocturne* for violin and piano, and many songs. He died in New York City, Nov. 12, 1978.

SWIFT, KAY (b. 1897) Composer, lyricist, pianist. Born in New York City, Apr. 19, 1897, Swift began music studies at the age of 7 with Bertha Tapper at the Juilliard School of Music, New York. She later studied at the New England Conservatory, Boston. Among her teachers were Heinrich Gebhard (piano), Arthur Johnstone (composition), Charles Martin Loeffler (composition), and Percy Goetschius (counterpoint and orchestration). After completing her musical studies, Swift taught for a while, served as accompanist for others, and toured with a trio. Her interest was only in what was regarded as "good music" in the early 1920s. She and her husband, James Paul Warburg, of the international banking family, met George Gershwin in the mid 1920s. Through familiarity with Gershwin's music, Swift realized "good music" could exist in the form of well-wrought songs. To learn more about the popular music world, she took a job as rehearsal pianist for Rodgers and Hart's *A Connecticut Yankee* (1927). Shortly after, she was asked to write the background music for a Marc Connelly play that was never produced; she then wrote a song—the music—for a proposed musical revue. Since it needed words, her husband, also in love with the Broadway musical theatre, wrote them, using "Paul James" as a pen name. The revue got no closer to Broadway than the Bronx, but Swift and James did place a song in the successful first *Little Show* (1929). The song was "Can't We Be Friends?," one of the most popular songs of the era.

Their next effort went into the unsuccessful *9:15 Revue* (1930) and was sung by Ruth Etting. Entitled "Up Among the Chimney Pots," it was a song much admired by others, including Gershwin and Harold Arlen. *Fine and Dandy,* for which Swift and her husband wrote all the songs, had a run of 255 performances after its opening in September 1930. Among the songs were the popular title tune, the ballad "Can This Be Love?," and "Let's Go Eat Worms in the Garden." By the early 1930s Warburg decided to concentrate on economics, political science, and government so the team of Swift and James was dissolved. Swift worked in radio, writing scripts; she also wrote one of the first regular magazine radio columns. She was musical director at the Radio City Music Hall for 2 years and served as chairman (that was the term then) of music for the New York World's Fair in 1939. It was for the Fair's musical program that Swift, working with Ira Gershwin (whose brother had died in 1937), edited 3 Gershwin song fragments into the Fair's theme song, "The Dawn of a New Day." In 1946 she and Ira Gershwin worked together again with unpublished and in some instances unfinished Gershwin songs to provide a full score for the film *The Shocking Miss Pilgrim.* Swift also set down many George Gershwin tunes that might otherwise have been lost—there are more than 100. Although she did some film work of her own, Swift was not happy in Hollywood. Her autobiographical book, *Never a Dull Moment,* was made into a film in 1950 and, while Swift could not recognize herself as portrayed by Irene Dunne, she did write such songs as "Once You Find Your Guy" and "Sagebrush Lullaby" for it. She made a successful return to Broadway with the songs and incidental music for *Paris '90* (1952). She has composed a great deal of music for special films ("industrials")

and other events, such as World Fairs. Her works include *Alma Mater,* ballet (1935), *Reaching for the Brass Ring,* a song cycle for soprano and orchestra (ca. 1950–55), *One Little Girl,* a musical commissioned to celebrate the 50th anniversary of the founding of the Camp Fire Girls, *Century 21,* orchestral suite composed for the Seattle World's Fair (1962), *Theme and Variations* for cello and piano (1960), *Man Have Pity on Man,* text by Ursula Vaughan Williams, for soloists, chorus, and orchestra (ca. 1970), *Two on a Bicycle,* and new music for the revised *Alma Mater* (1974). Other notable Swift songs (most with her own lyrics) are "In Between Age," "Now and Always," "Can't Win 'em All," and "Nobody Breaks My Heart."

SWING Popular dance music, tinctured with jazz, from around the mid 1930s until the late '40s. Swing is most closely associated with the Benny Goodman band but was also the staple of earlier, less publicized groups, such as the bands of Fletcher Henderson and Count Basie. Swing bands employed more than twice the number of men than did the early, classic jazz bands. There were generally 5 brasses, 4 reeds, and 4 percussion in the typical swing band. Unlike the jazz groups, swing bands could not perform without specially written arrangements (one of the early pioneers in this field was Don Redman, who did arrangements for Henderson, who, in turn, arranged for Goodman). Arrangements enabled the star soloists to play over the accompaniment by the brasses, reeds, and percussion. Ensemble playing was important and swing musicians, with rare exceptions, had to be able to read music. The jazzier swing bands—Goodman, the Dorseys, Duke Ellington, Woody Herman, others—also qualified as big bands, although these more pop-oriented bands were considered "commercial" by aficionados, not "hot." These included the bands of Artie Shaw, Glenn Miller, Will Bradley, et al. At the further extreme were the "sweet bands," whose arrangements provided quiet, sweetened (often with violins) dance music in ballrooms and hotels: Guy Lombardo, Wayne King (who specialized in waltzes in the swing era), Eddy Duchin, Sammy Kaye, and others. Swing musicians referred to their music as "Mickey Mouse," because of the simple, bland arrangements. They did not swing. Swing in character was smoother than jazz, syncopation was subtle, and while the brass and reeds alternated in playing (these short phrases were called "riffs" and such playing was called riffing), the star soloist—trumpet, sax, clarinet, sometimes piano—would hold forth. Vocalists sang with swing bands, but the real product was the instrumental that showed what the band could do and gave jitterbugs something to jitter to. Vestiges of the swing band sound were heard in the "progressive" big bands after the advent of "bop" (q.v.) played by the 1950s and '60s bands of Stan Kenton, Duke Ellington, the Herman Herds, and Boyd Raeburn, but with a marked difference in the "modern" sound. The old traditions were kept alive for a while in the revival of the sounds of such bands as Glenn Miller's and the Dorseys', often led by former members of the originals and drawing upon the old arrangements. Other notable swing bands of the 1935–45 era were led by Bob Crosby, Glen Gray (the Casa Loma Orchestra), Harry James, Paul Whiteman, and Claude Thornhill.

TALMA, LOUISE (b. 1906) Composer, teacher. Born in Arcachon, France, Oct. 31, 1906, Talma was educated and has taught in France and the United States. Her earliest formal musical training was taken at the Institute of Musical Art (now the Juilliard School of Music, New York City) and Columbia University; she also studied at the Fontainebleau School of Music. Talma's teachers were Howard Brockway (composition), Nadia Boulanger (organ, composition), and Isidor Philipp (piano). She taught at the Fontainebleau School, the Manhattan School of Music, and, since 1946, she has been on the faculty of Hunter College, where she was appointed full professor. She has twice been awarded Guggenheim Fellowships, as well as a Fulbright Research Grant, the Marjorie Peabody Waite Award, and the Sibelius Medal. Talma's works include a song cycle, *Terre de France* (1925), *Three Madrigals* for women's voices and string quartet (1929), *La Belle Dame sans Merci* for baritone, women's chorus, and organ (1929), *Five Sonnets from the Portuguese,* song cycle (1934), *In Principio Erat Verbum* for chorus and organ (1939), *Four Handed Fun* for piano, 4 hands (1941), *Carmina Mariana* for soprano duo and piano (1943), *Piano Sonata* (1943), *Toccata* for orchestra (1944), *Alleluia in Form of Toccata* for piano (1944), *Introduction and Rondo Giocoso* for orchestra (1946), *The Divine Flame,* oratorio (1948), *The Leaden Echo and the Golden Echo* for soprano, double chorus, and piano (1951), *Let's Touch the Sky* for chorus, flute, oboe, and clarinet (1952), *Six Etudes* for piano (1954), *String Quartet* (1954), *Piano Sonata No. 2* (1955), *La Corona* for chorus (1955), *The Alcestiad,* opera, libretto by Thornton Wilder (1958), *Passacaglia and Fugue* for piano (1962), *Violin Sonata* (1962), *Dialogues* for piano and orchestra (1964), *All the Days of My Life,* cantata for tenor and chamber group (1965), *A Time to Remember* for chorus and orchestra (1967), *Three Dialogues* for clarinet and piano (1968), *The Tolling Bell* for baritone and orchestra (1969), *Voices of Peace* for chorus and strings (1973),

Summer Sounds for clarinet and string quartet (1973), and *Textures* for piano (1978).

TATUM, ART (1910–1956) Pianist. Born in Toledo, Ohio, Oct. 13, 1910, Tatum began in music on the violin when he was 13, but switched to the piano. His teacher, Overton G. Rainey, tried to get Tatum, whose technique was phenomenal, to concentrate on "serious" music but Tatum preferred the kind of music he heard on the radio played by Lee Sims and Fats Waller (q.v.). Tatum attended the Cousino School for the Blind, Columbus (he was totally blind in one eye and had only limited vision in the other), and the Toledo School of Music. By the late 1920s he was playing solo piano around Toledo and broadcasting over its station, WSPD. Tatum, as accompanist for singer Adelaide Hall, came to New York City ca. 1932 to make his first recordings. In March 1933 he recorded his first piano solos; from that time on into the '50s Tatum won a great following among musicians and jazz aficionados as well as such pianists as Vladimir Horowitz and Leopold Godowsky. Tatum's style, which he admitted was greatly influenced by Waller, was characterized by brilliant piano technique (although he chose to ignore the rules of playing the piano "correctly") and a flow of striking musical ideas as he improvised on and around popular songs, jazz tunes, and his own original melodies. His great reputation was based on his solo piano work, although Tatum was a sensitive accompanist and band pianist; some of his best work was done with a trio consisting of himself, Tiny Grimes, later Everett Barksdale, on guitar, and Slam Stewart on bass in the early '40s. George Gershwin was an admirer of Tatum (and vice versa), but it was Fats Waller who best summed up the consensus when, upon Tatum's entrance into a club where Waller was

playing, he said, "Ladies and gentlemen, I play piano, but God is in the house tonight." Frequently overweight, an irregular but sometimes excessive eater, and a great consumer of alcohol (especially beer), Tatum suffered a health breakdown in the '50s. In the mid 1950s his poor health broke off his final concert tour. He died of uremia in Los Angeles, Nov. 5, 1956.

"THIS IS THE ARMY" An all-soldier revue, conceived and with songs by Irving Berlin (q.v.). A sequel to Berlin's World War I show, *Yip! Yip! Yaphank*, which also had an all-soldier cast (including Sergeant Irving Berlin), it was presented for the benefit of the Army Emergency Relief Fund. *This Is the Army* was to have had a limited run but proved so successful that its New York run was extended from 4 to 12 weeks, after which the show toured the United States, went to England in 1943, and then moved into various combat zones (the show's secondary purpose was to entertain the troops) in Europe and the Pacific. The skits and songs were written from the viewpoint of the civilian draftee and his concept of Army life. Characteristically, Berlin provided songs that saluted the other branches of the services: "American Eagles" (the Air Forces), "How About a Cheer for the Navy," "I Get Along with the Aussies," "My British Buddies," and "That Russian Winter." Berlin captured in song many of the sentiments and emotions of those who were away from their homes for the first time: "I'm Getting Tired So I Can Sleep," "I Left My Heart at the Stage Door Canteen," "Oh to Be Home Again," and "Poor Little Me I'm on K.P." Berlin himself appeared, dressed in a World War I doughboy uniform, to sing a song originally written for *Yip! Yip! Yaphank,* "Oh! How I Hate to Get Up in the Morning." *This Is the Army* opened at the Broadway Theatre, July 4,

1942, and ran for 113 performances before setting out on its cross-country and international tour. It opened in London in November 1943 (the money raised was donated to British War Charities), then went to Italy, Africa, New Guinea, and other points before the last performance in Honolulu, Oct. 22, 1945. *This Is the Army* had raised $10,000,000 for the Army Relief Fund. It had also been made into a popular film in 1943. Some of the members of the original 1942 cast (all in military service) were Ezra Stone (co-director with Joshua Logan), Gary Merrill, Julie Oshins, Zinn Arthur, and Burl Ives.

"TONIGHT WE LOVE" One of the most popular "adaptations" from a musical classic into pop song. The opening theme of the first movement of Tchaikovsky's *Piano Concerto in B-flat Minor* was arranged into song form by Ray Austin for bandleader Freddy Martin in 1941; the lyrics were written by Bobby Worth. As a song "Tonight We Love" became very popular (and since the music was in public domain, other versions—including a "Boogie de Concerto" —were quickly forthcoming). The great appeal of the melody led many a popular song lover to seek out the original Tchaikovsky concerto, which was one of the more positive aspects of the borrowing. Tin Pan Alley noted this practice with a song entitled "Everybody's Making Money but Tchaikovsky." "Tonight We Love" was not the first result of the raiding of the classics, often deplored by critics and "serious music" lovers. Composer Sigmund Romberg transformed the theme from Schubert's "Unfinished Symphony" into "Song of Love" for the 1921 musical *Blossom Time*. Bandleader Larry Clinton, Buddy Bernier, and Bob Emmerich borrowed a theme from Tchaikovsky's *Romeo and Juliet Overture* to produce the hit "Our Love" (1939); that

same year conductor André Kostelanetz, Mack David, and Mack Davis borrowed a theme from Tchaikovsky's *Symphony No. 5* and came up with "Moon Love," which was also very popular. Ravel got his chance with "The Lamp Is Low," concocted by Peter DeRose, Bert Shefter, and Mitchell Parish from the *Pavane pour une Infante Défunte,* undoubtedly one of the top hits of 1899—and 1939.

"TOP HAT" Film musical, with words and music by Irving Berlin (q.v.), released in the summer of 1935. This was the 4th Fred Astaire–Ginger Rogers song-and-dance comedy and the first of 3 with Berlin songs (the others: *Follow the Fleet* and *Carefree*). The plot was sheer gossamer: it had Rogers mistake Astaire for her good friend's philandering husband. Most of Berlin's songs were geared to the sprightly plot; they rank with his best. The songs include "No Strings," "Isn't This a Lovely Day?," "Top Hat, White Tie and Tails," "Cheek to Cheek," and the required big dance number of the period, "The Piccolino." An excellent song, "Get Thee Behind Me, Satan," was eliminated. Besides Astaire and Rogers the polished cast included Edward Everett Horton, Helen Broderick, Erik Rhodes, and Eric Blore. *Top Hat* is considered to be, in the words of Stanley Green, "the quintessential Fred Astaire–Ginger Rogers movie."

TORCH SONG A metropolitan blues, not necessarily structured in the 12-bar traditional folk blues form, nor even depending on blues harmonies. The torch song, at best, is a sophisticated lament usually written for a woman to sing. Arlen and Koehler's "Stormy Weather," while bluesy, is a torch song; so is the Gershwins' "Boy, What Love Has Done to Me!" and Rodgers and Hart's "Glad to Be Unhappy."

"TROUBLED ISLAND" Opera, music by William Grant Still (q.v.) and libretto by Langston Hughes (1902–1967). Produced by the New York City Opera Company in March 1949, *Troubled Island* has been regarded as one of the historic operas because it was the first written by a black composer and librettist to be presented by a major opera company. Based on Hughes's *Drums of Haiti, Troubled Island* is set in 18th-century Haiti at the time of the revolution led by Jean Jacques Dessalines. Ironically, all the leading roles were sung by whites in black face: Robert Weede, Helena Bliss, and Marie Powers.

VAN HEUSEN, JIMMY (b. 1913) Popular composer. Born in Syracuse, N.Y., Jan. 26, 1913, Van Heusen (who was actually born Edward Chester Babcock) was the son of a contractor who expected him one day to take over the family business. Van Heusen took piano lessons as a boy and by the age of 16 was performing as vocalist-pianist on a local radio station. At his father's insistence he enrolled in Syracuse University to prepare for the business world, but he also took courses in music. Although he studied a little, Van Heusen devoted more time to working on the college shows. One of his collaborators was another student, Jerry Arlen, brother of composer Harold Arlen (q.v.). In 1933 Van Heusen dropped out of Syracuse and left for New York. For a time he ran the freight elevator at the Park Central Hotel. He later worked as a staff pianist for a music publisher. It was not until 1938, when Van Heusen and bandleader Jimmy Dorsey collaborated on "It's the Dreamer in Me," which won some popularity, that Van Heusen began to come into his own. That same year he collaborated with Edgar DeLange (1904–1949) on a fine song, "Deep in a Dream." They collabo-

rated on several popular songs after that: "Heaven Can Wait," "Oh, You Crazy Moon," and "Imagination" (all 1939). They also did the songs for a Broadway production of *Swingin' the Dream* (1939), a jazzed-up version of *A Midsummer Night's Dream,* which starred Louis Armstrong, Maxine Sullivan, Benny Goodman and his sextette, and Bud Freeman's Summa Cum Laude band. The show ran only 13 performances and produced one song that became popular, "Darn That Dream." Van Heusen moved on to Hollywood in 1940 and enjoyed a most successful career writing songs for Bing Crosby (in collaboration with Johnny Burke) and Frank Sinatra (with Sammy Cahn). With Burke (1908–1964) he wrote "Moonlight Becomes You" (from *The Road to Morocco,* 1941), "Sunday, Monday or Always" (*Dixie,* 1943), "Suddenly It's Spring" (*Lady in the Dark,* 1944), "Swinging on a Star" (*Going My Way,* 1944), "It Could Happen to You" (*And the Angels Sing,* 1944), "Personality" (*Road to Utopia,* 1945), "Aren't You Glad You're You?" (*The Bells of St. Mary's,* 1946), and "But Beautiful" (*Road to Rio,* 1947). In 1946 Van Heusen and Burke wrote the songs for an unsuccessful Broadway show, *Nellie Bly.* They were no more fortunate with another Broadway try, *Carnival in Flanders* (1953), which barely lasted a week. By the mid 1950s Van Heusen formed a songwriting partnership with Sammy Cahn (q.v.), with whom he wrote several popular songs, often the title songs of films. Among their more popular songs were "Love and Marriage" (1955), "The Tender Trap" (from *The Tender Trap,* 1955), "All the Way" (*The Joker Is Wild,* 1957), "High Hopes" (*A Hole in the Head,* 1959), "Call Me Irresponsible" (*Papa's Delicate Condition,* 1963), and the title songs for *Thoroughly Modern Millie* (1967) and

Star! (1968). Van Heusen and Cahn collaborated on the scores for 2 Broadway shows, *Skyscraper* (1965) and *Walking Happy* (1966), neither of which ran for any length of time or inspired any song of lasting popularity. Obviously Van Heusen was more at home in Hollywood. It would be an unforgivable omission not to mention that during World War II Van Heusen served as a test pilot for Lockheed Aircraft; this was during the period when he and Burke were also writing songs for the Bing Crosby films. He has been the recipient of several Academy Awards for such songs as "Swinging on a Star" (1944), "All the Way" (1957), "High Hopes" (1959), and "Call Me Irresponsible" (1963). He was also awarded an Emmy and a Christopher Award for "Love and Marriage" from the television musical version of Thornton Wilder's *Our Town* in 1955.

VAN VACTOR, DAVID (b. 1906) Composer, conductor, flutist, teacher. Born in Plymouth, Ind., May 8, 1906, Van Vactor studied flute, theory, and composition at Northwestern University, Evanston, Ill. Upon graduation in 1928 he went to Vienna to study with Josef Niedermayr (flute), then to the Paris Conservatory to continue his flute studies with Marcel Moyse. In 1931 he enrolled at the École Normale to study composition with Paul Dukas. He returned to the United States that year and joined the Chicago Symphony as flutist; he remained until 1943, when he became flutist and assistant conductor of the Kansas City Philharmonic. Since 1947 he has been conductor of the Knoxville Symphony and active on the faculty of the University of Tennessee. In 1945 Van Vactor was invited by the government of Chile to conduct the Orquesta Sinfónica de Chile and to lecture at the University of Chile. His original works include a *Chaconne* for string orchestra

(1928), *Five Small Pieces for Large Orchestra* (1929), *Cristóbal Colón,* overture for orchestra (1930), *Concerto for Flute* and chamber orchestra (1931), *The Masque of the Red Death,* symphonic prelude for orchestra (1932), *Quintet for Flute,* 2 violins, viola, and cello (1932), *Suite for Two Flutes* (1933), *Passacaglia and Fugue in D Minor* for orchestra (1933), *The Play of Words,* ballet (1934), *Nachtlied* for soprano and string quartet (1935), *Overture to a Comedy* for orchestra (1935), *Concerto Grosso* for orchestra (1935), *O Haupt voll Blut und Wunden* for chorus and organ (1936), *Symphony No. 1* (1937), *Five Bagatelles for Strings* (1938), *Symphonic Suite* for orchestra (1938), *Divertimento* for chamber orchestra (1939), *String Quartet* (1940), *Concerto for Viola* (1940), *Gavotte* for woodwind quintet (1940), *Overture to a Comedy, No. 2* (1941), *Credo* for chorus and orchestra (1941), *Variazioni Solenne* for orchestra (1941), *Trio* for violin, viola, and cello (1942), *Fanfare,* "Salute to Russia," for orchestra (1943), *Music for the Marines,* "Ode," for orchestra (1943), *Sonata* for flute and piano (1945), *Recitative and Salterello* for orchestra (1946), *Introduction and Presto* for strings (1947), *Cantata* for high voices and orchestra (1947), *Pastoral and Dance* for flute and strings (1947), *String Quartet No. 2* (1949), *Violin Concerto* (1950), *Prelude and March* for orchestra (1950), *Eight Choruses* from Housman's *Shropshire Lad* for voices (1953), *The New Light,* cantata for Christmas (1954), *Fantasia, Chaconne and Allegro* for orchestra (1957), *Symphony No. 2* (1958), *Suite* for woodwind quintet (1959), *Suite on Chilean Folk Tunes,* ballet (1962), *Brass Octet* (1963), *Passacaglia, Chorale and Scamper* for band (1964), *Sinfonia Breve* (1964), *Economy Band No. 1* (1966), *Four Etudes* for winds and percussion (1968), *Econ-*

omy Band No. 2 (1969), Symphony No. 4, "Walden," for chorus and orchestra (1969), Symphony No. 5 (1976), Crucifixus, cantata (1976), and Episodes Jesus Christ (1977).

VERRALL, JOHN W. (b. 1908) Composer, teacher. Born in Britt, Iowa, June 17, 1908, Verrall studied cello and composition at various schools: Minneapolis College of Music, the Royal College of Music, London, the Liszt Conservatory, Budapest, and the University of Minnesota. Among his teachers were the Hungarian master Zoltán Kodály, Frank Merrick, and Donald Ferguson; Verrall also had briefer sessions with Aaron Copland, Roy Harris, and Frederick Jacobi. He himself has taught at Hamline University in Minnesota (piano and composition), Mount Holyoke College, Mass., the University of Washington, Seattle, from 1948 until 1973. From 1941 to 1945, Verrall served in the U. S. Army. His works include a Symphony No. 1 (1940), String Quartet No. 1 (1940), Concert Piece for horns and strings (1941), Portrait of Man for orchestra (1941), Sonata for horn and piano (1941), Sonata for viola and piano (1941), Serenade for clarinet, horn, and bassoon (1942), String Trio (1942), Symphony No. 2 (1943), String Quartet No. 2 (1943), Serenade for 5 wind instruments (1944), Six Variations for orchestra (1945), The Children, overture for orchestra (1945), Ah, Come, Sweet Death for chorus (1945), Violin Concerto (1946), Prelude and Allegro for string orchestra (1948), String Quartet No. 3 (1948), Symphony for Young Orchestras (1948), The Dark Night of St. John for chamber orchestra (1949), String Quartet No. 4 (1949), The Cowherd and the Sky Maiden, opera (1952), String Quartet No. 5 (1952), The Wedding Knell, opera (1952), Three Blind Mice, opera (1955), Portrait of St. Christopher for orchestra (1956), String Quartet No. 6 (1956), Suite for orchestra (1958), Nocturne for bass clarinet and piano (1958), Piano Concerto (1960), String Quartet No. 7 (1961), Sonata No. 2 for viola and piano (1964), Chamber Symphony (1967), Viola Concerto (1968), and Sonata for Flute (1972). Verrall is also the author of Elements of Harmony (1937), Form and Meaning in the Arts (1958), Fugue and Invention in Theory and Practice (1967), and Basic Theory of Music (1970).

"WALKING THE DOG" Brief instrumental piece written by George Gershwin (q.v.) for the film score of Shall We Dance (1937). The music accompanied a dog-walking sequence on a ship's promenade deck by the principals, Fred Astaire and Ginger Rogers, during one of the film's many moments of misunderstanding between them. Gershwin's music was charming and sprightly and the orchestration, probably by the film's musical director, Nat Shilkret, is spare, cleanly bringing out Gershwin's wit. Walking the Dog was published in solo piano form under the title Promenade in 1960. An orchestral version was prepared by André Kostelanetz but its overblown forces smother the humor and charm. In 1979 arranger Don Rose prepared a suite, Gershwin in Hollywood, which restores Walking the Dog to its original form. This piece and a few ballet sequences were Gershwin's last compositions in instrumental form.

WALLER, THOMAS "FATS" (1904–1943) Pianist, vocalist, composer, organist, bandleader. Born in New York City, May 21, 1904, Waller "took piano" as a youngster and was recognized as musically gifted. He played the organ in the church where his father was pastor— the Abyssinian Baptist Church in Harlem. It was the family plan that young Thomas would follow in his father's footsteps, but once he had learned to play the piano Waller's interest lay in music. He absorbed the Harlem "stride" style of performance—the firm, powerful left hand and the inventive, decorative right—and added his own distinctive touch to the art. His idol was James P. Johnson (q.v.). At 15 Waller won an amateur pianist's competition performing his variations on Johnson's *Carolina Shout*. Soon he was welcomed into the fraternity of Harlem pianists and learned much from Johnson himself. He also studied with Leopold Godowsky and Carl Bohm. Waller began playing professionally in Harlem clubs and played organ in the Lincoln Theatre. He performed with small bands, accompanied vocalists, among them the great blues singers Bessie Smith (q.v.) and Alberta Hunter. With his own band Waller toured the United States and Europe in the 1930s. Ca. 1931 Waller had his own radio show on Cincinnati's WLW, "Fats Waller's Rhythm Club." He formed a small band when back in New York in 1934 and began cutting some of his finest recordings. Waller actually started recording in the early '20s, when his teacher, James P. Johnson, got him work perforating piano rolls for QRS. Although best known as a pianist, Waller was an inventive improviser-composer (he composed virtually as fast as he could play)—although at times both of these gifts were overshadowed by his personality. Irrepressible, ebullient, satirical (especially in his attitude toward the conventional popular song), Waller was more often regarded as a comic singer than the musician he was. His breezy, sunny personality was believed by many to be a screen for the troubled soul inside him; Waller lost his mother when he was in his teens and was much affected by this loss. He drank and ate prodigiously, which greatly shortened his life. Since he recorded widely, much of Waller's important solo and band work

(as well as some performances on his favorite instrument—"God's box"—the organ) have been preserved. Among his own compositions are "Squeeze Me" (with Clarence Williams, 1925), "I've Got a Feeling I'm Falling" (with Harry Link, lyrics by Billy Rose, 1929), "Honeysuckle Rose" (lyrics by Andy Razaf, 1929), "Keeping Out of Mischief Now" (lyrics by Razaf, 1932). Waller wrote songs for 3 Broadway productions: *Keep Shufflin'* (1928), *Hot Chocolates* (lyrics by Razaf, 1929), and *Early to Bed* (lyrics by George Marion, Jr., 1943). In 1943, Waller's last year of life, he appeared in the musical film *Stormy Weather*. His many instrumental works include *Handful of Keys, Numb Fumblin', Valentine Stomp, Smashing Thirds* (all ca. 1929), *African Ripples, Clothes Line Ballet, Alligator Crawl* (all ca. 1934), *Russian Fantasy* and *E Flat Blues* (both ca. 1935). *The London Suite*—"Piccadilly," "Chelsea," "Soho," "Bond Street," "Limehouse," and "Whitechapel"—was composed in London in June 1939. A successful Broadway musical celebrating the songs and the song stylings of Fats Waller opened in 1978 titled after the hit song from *Hot Chocolates,* "Ain't Misbehavin'." During a 1943 tour of Army camps en route from Los Angeles, Waller died of pneumonia aboard the train as it pulled into Kansas City, Dec. 15, 1943, at the age of 39.

WARD, ROBERT (b. 1917) Composer, teacher. Born in Cleveland, Ohio, Sept. 13, 1917, Ward received his earliest musical education in Cleveland, then went on to the Eastman School, Rochester, N.Y., to study composition with Howard Hanson (q.v.) and Bernard Rogers (q.v.). Upon graduation in 1939 he earned his master's degree at the Juilliard School, New York City, under Frederick Jacobi (composition), Albert Stoessel (conducting), and Bernard Wagenaar (orchestration). He did further work in composition with Aaron Copland (q.v.) at the Berkshire Music Center, Tanglewood, Mass., in 1940. Ward was on the faculty of Queens College, New York City, before being inducted into the U. S. Army. He was a bandleader of the 7th Infantry Division and wrote the songs for an all-soldier show, *The Life of Riley* (1942). After the war, Ward joined the staffs of the Juilliard School and Columbia University. During this period he was also the director of the Third Street Settlement Music School (1952–55). He left teaching for about a decade (1956–67) for an executive post with the Galaxy Music Corporation. Since 1967 Ward has been associated with the North Carolina School of the Arts, Winston-Salem. His works include *Fatal Interview* for soprano and orchestra (1937), *Hush'd Be the Camps Today* for chorus and orchestra (1940), *Symphony No. 1* (1941), *Adagio and Allegro* for orchestra (1943), *Jubilation* for orchestra (1946), *Symphony No. 2* (1947), *Lamentation* for piano (1948), *Concert Music* for orchestra (1948), *Folk Dance* for piano (1949), *Sonata for Violin and Piano* (1950), *Symphony No. 3* (1950), *Sacred Songs for Pantheists* for soprano and orchestra (1951), *Euphony* for orchestra (1954), *He Who Gets Slapped*, 3-act opera (1956), *Fantasia for Brass Choir and Timpani* (1956), *Symphony No. 4* (1958), *Invocation and Toccata* for orchestra (1959), *Earth Shall Be Fair* for soprano, children's chorus, chorus, and orchestra (1960), *Divertimento* for strings (1960), *The Crucible*, 4-act opera (1961, Pulitzer Prize), *Music for a Celebration* for orchestra (1963), *Prairie Overture* for orchestra (1963), *The Lady from Colorado*, 2-act opera (1964), *String Quartet* (1965), *Sweet Freedom's Song*, cantata for narrator, vocalists, chorus, and orchestra (1965), *Festive Ode* for orchestra (1966), *Antiphony* for wind instruments (1967),

Concerto for Piano and Orchestra (1968), *Symphony No. 5* (1976), and *Claudia Legare*, opera based on Ibsen's *Hedda Gabler* (1978).

WAXMAN, FRANZ (1906–1967) Composer, conductor. Born in Königshütte, Germany (now Chorzów, Poland), Dec. 24, 1906, Waxman began to study the piano at the age of 6, although at the insistence of his businessman father, he was trained in banking. Waxman actually worked for more than 2 years as a bank teller. He quit that job when he had saved enough to study music in Dresden and then Berlin. He also earned money as pianist with what was probably regarded as a "jazz band," the Weintraub Syncopaters. Some of his arrangements for the Syncopaters led to Waxman's early work as an orchestrator for German films, his first being the classic *The Blue Angel* (1929), whose background music he also conducted. His first full score was for the Fritz Lang film *Liliom* (1933). Waxman then came to the United States in 1934 to score the film version of Jerome Kern's *Music in the Air*. Waxman was commissioned to write the score for *The Bride of Frankenstein* (1935), which resulted in his first film contract and a decision to remain in Hollywood. From 1935 to 1966's *Lost Command* Waxman composed and arranged for some 180 films. His best-known film scores were written for such movies as *Rebecca* (1940), *The Philadelphia Story* (1940), *Old Acquaintance* (1943), *Sunset Boulevard* (1950, Academy Award), *A Place in the Sun* (1951, Academy Award), *Peyton Place* (1957), *The Spirit of St. Louis* (1957), and *Taras Bulba* (1961). Waxman often reworked his background scores into concert works, i.e., *Rebecca Suite, Symphonic Fantasy on "A Mighty Fortress"* (from *The Edge of Darkness*, 1943), *Elegy for Strings* (from *Old Acquaintance*), and *Crime in the Streets* suite (1956). Waxman was the founder of the Los Angeles Music Festival in 1947; he was also conductor of the orchestra for 2 decades. The Festival introduced the works of contemporary composers to U.S. audiences. Other concert works by Waxman include a *Sinfonietta for Strings and Timpani* (1955), *Three Sketches* for orchestra (1955), and *Theme, Variations and Fugato* for orchestra (1956). His *Overture for Trumpet and Orchestra* was derived from the music written for the Jack Benny comedy *The Horn Blows at Midnight* (1944) and his *Carmen Fantasy* for violin and orchestra was frequently performed by Jascha Heifetz in the 1940s. Waxman died in Los Angeles, Feb. 24, 1967.

WEBB, WILLIAM "CHICK" (1907–1939) Drummer, bandleader. Born in Baltimore, Md., Feb. 10, 1907 (or 1909), Webb was a small man with a powerful driving drum style who greatly influenced the percussionists of the big band era, including Gene Krupa. Webb, who was deformed (he was hunchbacked) made his way in music despite this handicap. He began as a teenager as a drummer on the excursion boats out of Baltimore. He arrived in New York City in 1924 and by 1926 had his own band. The Webb band at first was known only in Harlem, but by 1934 it had won national prominence, when it began to feature the singer Ella Fitzgerald (q.v.). In the band were such fine musicians as Edgar Sampson, who played alto-saxophone and wrote many of the band's arrangements, Taft Jordan, trumpeter, and John Kirby, bass. Webb and Sampson collaborated on the popular big band instrumental "Stompin' at the Savoy" (named for the Savoy Club, where the band was frequently featured). The greatest hit recording made by Webb and Fitzgerald was their variation on a nursery song, "A-Tisket, A-Tasket" (1938). Webb was

afflicted with tuberculosis of the spine; an operation was attempted but he died not long after, in Baltimore, June 16, 1939, and Fitzgerald took over his band. She left it in 1942 to make her way as a single singer.

WEBSTER, PAUL FRANCIS (b. 1907) Popular song lyricist. Born in New York City, Dec. 20, 1907, Webster was graduated from Cornell University and New York University. Before turning to songwriting he was a sailor and a dance instructor. It was not until the early 1930s that he began publishing songs that gained popularity, one of the first being "Two Cigarettes in the Dark" with a melody by Lew Pollack that was used in the 1934 film *Kill That Story*. Webster left for Hollywood, where he teamed with Louis Alter (q.v.) to do the songs for *Rainbow on the River* (1937), starring boy singer Bobby Breen. In 1941 he and Duke Ellington (q.v.) wrote the songs for a revue produced in Los Angeles, *Jump for Joy*, among them "Rocks in My Bed" and "I Got It Bad and That Ain't Good." A collaboration with Hoagy Carmichael (q.v.) resulted in "Memphis in June" (from the film, *Johnny Angel*, 1945), "Baltimore Oriole" (1945), and "Doctor, Lawyer, Indian Chief" (from the film *Stork Club*, 1945). From the 1950s on, after the decline of large-scale film musicals, Webster frequently provided the lyrics for a title song: *Love Is a Many-Splendored Thing, Friendly Persuasion* (music by Dmitri Tiomkin), "The Song of Raintree County," *A Certain Smile* (music by Sammy Fain), etc. "Love Is a Many-Splendored Thing," with music by Sammy Fain, won an Academy Award in 1955. Webster and Fain wrote the songs for a Broadway show, *Christine* (1960), but it was not successful. One of Webster's most popular songs, "The Lamplighter's Serenade" (1942), was written with Hoagy Carmichael. A song written with Johnny Mandel for the film *The Sandpiper,* "The Shadow of Your Smile," won Webster another Academy Award in 1965.

WEILL, KURT (1900–1950) Composer. Born in Dessau, Germany, Mar. 2, 1900, Weill was one of the best-educated of all musicians who composed for Broadway. Although he began composing at the age of 14, he did not begin the study of composition and counterpoint until a year later. In 1918 he went to Berlin for further study; one of his teachers at the Hochschule für Musik was Engelbert Humperdinck. In 1919 Weill was appointed staff conductor of opera and operetta at the Civic Theatre in Ludenscheid; an early—presumably lost—opera was composed during this period. Weill's first serious composition was a string quartet (1920), written shortly before he was accepted as one of 6 students in Ferruccio Busoni's master class in composition. From 1921 until 1935, when Weill and his wife, Lotte Lenya, arrived in the United States, Weill composed several concert works as well as the stage works that marked him as a unique composer for the theatre. A symphony, much in the contemporary Viennese manner, dates from 1921; his *Concerto for Violin and Wind Instruments* was composed in 1925. His first major stage work was *Der Protagonist* (1926) with a libretto by George Kaiser. *Die Dreigroschenoper,* written in collaboration with Bertolt Brecht, was presented in Berlin in 1928. This sardonic work (with music to match) has become one of the classics of the musical theatre. As *The Threepenny Opera* in an English translation and with lyrics by Marc Blitzstein, it ran for more than 2,000 performances when revived in New York City in 1954. Other important Weill productions of this period are *Aufstieg und Fall der Stadt Mahagonny* (*The Rise and Fall of the City of Maha-*

gonny), again with Brecht (1930), *Der Jasager,* an opera for school children, libretto by Brecht (1930), and *Der Silbersee,* 3-act opera with lyrics and libretto by George Kaiser (1933). Since his operas contained political overtones that did not please the Nazis and because he was Jewish, the Weills were forced to flee from Berlin in March 1933. His compositions were banned in Germany and his scores were burned publicly in front of the Berlin Opera. Settling in Paris, Weill continued writing for the stage, plus songs and orchestral pieces: *The Seven Deadly Sins,* a ballet with songs (1933), the musical play *Marie Galante,* lyrics by Jacques Deval (1933), and *Symphony No. 2* (1934). Director Max Reinhardt, also a refugee from Nazi Germany, persuaded the Weills to come to the United States, which they did in September 1935. Weill never returned to Germany. At the invitation of George Gershwin the Weills attended a rehearsal of *Porgy and Bess.* "Listening for the first time to that score," Weill later recalled, "I discovered that the American theatre was already on the way to the more integrated form of musical that we had begun to attempt in Europe. That gave me courage to start working on a serious musical for the American stage—*Johnny Johnson.*" Although this fine antiwar musical was not particularly successful (68 performances), it contained poignant songs (the book and lyrics were by Paul Green), among them the haunting "Listen to My Song" (Johnny's Song). But in 1936 the theatregoing public was not prepared for an antiwar musical. Weill's next musical, *Knickerbocker Holiday* (1938), was notable for its political bite, a great performance by Walter Huston as the dictator, and "September Song." (Libretto and lyrics were by Maxwell Anderson.) Another fine song is "Nowhere to Go But Up." Between *Knickerbocker Holiday* and what was to be Weill's first major Broadway success, he wrote a "Folk Cantata," with text by Edward Hungerford, entitled *Railroads on Parade* (1939), for the New York World's Fair and a "school cantata," *The Ballad of Magna Carta* (1940), with Maxwell Anderson. Working with Moss Hart, (book) and Ira Gershwin (lyrics), Weill wrote the songs (actually several little operettas) for *Lady in the Dark* (1941). Other shows followed: *One Touch of Venus* (book by S. J. Perelman and lyrics by Ogden Nash, 1943), *The Firebrand of Florence* (book by Edwin Justus Mayer, lyrics by Gershwin, 1945), *Street Scene* (book by Elmer Rice, lyrics by Langston Hughes, 1947), the American folk opera for school presentation, *Down in the Valley* (book and lyrics by Arnold Sundgaard, 1947), *Love Life* (book and lyrics by Alan J. Lerner, 1947), and *Lost in the Stars* (book and lyrics by Maxwell Anderson, 1949). Weill contributed songs to 2 films, *You and Me* (1938) and *Where Do We Go from Here?* (lyrics by Gershwin, 1945). Among the songs for which Weill composed the music are "My Ship," "The Saga of Jenny," and "This Is New" (from *Lady in the Dark*), "Speak Low," "I'm a Stranger Here Myself," and "That's Him" (*One Touch of Venus*), "Sing Me Not a Ballad," "You're Far Too Near Me," "A Rhyme for Angela," and "The Cozy Nook Song" (*The Firebrand of Florence*), "If Love Remains," "All at Once," "The Song of the Rhineland," and "The Nina, the Pinta, the Santa Maria" (the film *Where Do We Go from Here?*), "Somehow I Never Could Believe," "What Good Would the Moon Be?," "Moon-Faced, Starry-Eyed," and "Lonely House" (*Street Scene*), "Green-Up Time," "Susan's Dream," and "Love Song" (*Love Life*), "Trouble Man," "Lost in the Stars" (originally written for *Knickerbocker Holiday*), and "Stay

Well" (*Lost in the Stars*). Weill was collaborating with Maxwell Anderson on a musical version of Mark Twain's *Huckleberry Finn* and had completed 5 songs when he suffered a heart attack; he died in New York City, Apr. 3, 1950.

WEISGALL, HUGO (b. 1912) Composer, teacher. Born in Ivančice, Czechoslovakia, Oct. 13, 1912, Weisgall and his family moved to the United States when he was about 8. They settled in Baltimore, where Weisgall had his schooling at the Peabody Conservatory and Johns Hopkins University. He also studied at the Curtis Institute, working under Rosario Scalero (composition) and Fritz Reiner (conducting). He studied privately with Roger Sessions. In 1942 Weisgall enlisted in the U. S. Army and served as a military attaché to governments in exile in London; he was cultural attaché to the American Embassy in Prague (1946–47). Weisgall has taught at the Baltimore Institute of Musical Arts and the Jewish Theological Seminary, the Juilliard School, and Queens College in New York City. The bulk of Weisgall's original output has been in opera. Among his works are *Quest*, ballet (1937), *One Thing Is Certain*, ballet (1939), *Hymn* for chorus and orchestra (1941), *Overture* for orchestra (1942), *Soldier Songs* for baritone and orchestra (1945), *Outpost*, ballet (1947), *The Tenor*, one-act opera (1950), *The Stronger*, one-act opera (1952), *Three Symphonic Songs* (1952), *A Garden Eastward*, cantata for voice and orchestra (1952), *Choral Etude* (1953), *Two Madrigals* for voice and piano (1955), *Six Characters in Search of an Author*, opera (1956), *Purgatory*, one-act opera (1958), *Athalia*, opera (1961), *Graven Images* for various chamber groupings (1966), *Nine Rivers from Jordan*, opera (1968), *Fancies and Inventions* for chamber orchestra (1970), *End of Summer,* 3 songs with instrumental interludes (1974), and *The Hundred Nights,* opera (1976).

"WHITE CHRISTMAS" Very popular song, words and music by Irving Berlin (q.v.). Written for *Holiday Inn* (1942), which starred Fred Astaire and Bing Crosby. "White Christmas" was introduced in the film by Crosby, who made one of the all-time best-selling recordings of it. Crosby also introduced the song on the air after *Holiday Inn* was released in the summer of 1942. Its direct, simple nostalgia struck a chord in those wartime days (each year of the war it was a jukebox perennial in military installations throughout the world). In its first 4 months "White Christmas" sold 4,000,000 copies of sheet music. Eventually Crosby's recordings sold more than 30,000,000 copies alone. In 1954 a film entitled *White Christmas,* again starring Crosby, with co-star comedian Danny Kaye, was released. The movie utilized several Berlin songs, including the title song as well as 2 fine new songs, "Love, You Didn't Do Right by Me" and "Count Your Blessings." "White Christmas" made "Your Hit Parade" for the first time Oct. 17, 1942, and eventually appeared some 38 weeks, 10 of them in the coveted first place (it was the longest running song in the history of the radio show). Around Christmas time it returned for the next several years, 1943–55 (skipping only 1953), to "Your Hit Parade."

"WHO'S AFRAID OF THE BIG BAD WOLF?" A popular Depression rallying song first heard in a Walt Disney cartoon, *The Three Little Pigs* (1933). Written by Disney's musical director, Frank E. Churchill (1901–1942), and Ann Ronell (q.v.). Who did what is not quite clear since "words and music" are attributed to Churchill and "additional lyrics" to Ronell, a composer.

While the original cartoon was aimed at the kiddie audience, the song became as popular, even more so, with their economically troubled parents. "Keeping the wolf from the door" was a way of life during the Depression and the sentiments of the song captured the somewhat defiant, hopeful mood of Americans in the mid 1930s.

WILDER, ALEC (1907–1980) Composer, arranger. Born in Rochester, N.Y., Feb. 17, 1907, Wilder studied at the Eastman School with Edward Royce (composition) and Herbert Inch (counterpoint). In the late 1930s Wilder settled in New York City and began writing arrangements and orchestrations for dance bands (Tommy Dorsey, Benny Goodman) and popular vocalists, among them Frank Sinatra and Judy Garland. He also composed many small charming works for unusual chamber groups, building usually around Wilder's favorite grouping, a woodwind quintet. In 1939–40 he had his own Octet with which he recorded several of his chamber pieces with such titles as *Seldom the Sun, Her Old Man Was Suspicious, Such a Tender Night,* etc. In 1945 Frank Sinatra (q.v.) conducted an orchestra of woodwinds, strings, and harpsichord in a number of Wilder compositions, among them *Theme and Variations, Air for Flute, Slow Dance,* and other *Airs* (bassoon, English horn, oboe). Wilder wrote his earliest known song, "All the King's Horses" (with Howard Dietz and Edward Brandt), for the Broadway show *Three's A Crowd* (1930). Wilder is the composer of many songs, among them "It's So Peaceful in the Country" (1941), "Who Can I Turn To?" (1942), "I'll Be Around" (1943), and "While We're Young" (1951). His other works include *Eight Songs* for voice and orchestra (1928), *Symphonic Piece* for orchestra (1929), *Juke Box,* ballet (1942),

Suite for clarinet and strings (1947), *Concerto for Oboe and Strings* (1950), *The Lowland Sea,* operetta (1951), *Sunday Excursion,* operetta (1952), *Beginner's Luck* for winds (1953), *Concerto for Horn and Chamber Orchestra* (1954), *The Long Way,* opera (1955), *Sonata for Flute* (1958), *Suite for Brass Quintet* (1959), *Saxophone Sonata* (1960), *An Entertainment* for winds (1961), *Sonata for Flute,* No. 2 (1962), *Suite* for string bass and piano (1965), *Suite* for trumpet and piano (1965), *Concerto for Saxophone and Chamber Orchestra* (1967), *Children's Plea for Peace* for narrator, chorus, and orchestra (1969), *Concerto for Euphonium and Winds* (1971), *Suite No. 2* for horn, tuba, and piano (1972), *Quintet No. 4* for brass (1973), *Quintet No. 5* for brass (1975), *Quintet No. 6* for brass (1977), etc. There are numerous sonatas, suites, etc. for small groups generally written on commission for specific musicians. Wilder is the author of *American Popular Song* (edited by James T. Maher, 1972). He died in Gainesville, Fla., Dec. 24, 1980.

WILLMAN, ALLAN ARTHUR (b. 1909) Composer, teacher. Born in Hinckley, Ill., May 11, 1909, Willman was awarded a scholarship when he was 16 to the Knox College Conservatory of Music, Galesburg, Ill. He continued at the Chicago Musical College and was graduated in 1930. His teachers included A. Albert Noelte, Thorvald Otterstroem, and Nadia Boulanger, with whom he studied in Paris in the mid 1930s. His symphonic poem *Solitude* won the Paderewski Award in 1935. A year later Willman joined the faculty of the University of Wyoming, Laramie, where he is chairman of the Music Division, College of Arts and Sciences. From 1943 to 1945 Willman served in the U. S. Army, chiefly in connection with broadcasting. Among his other works are a *Piano So-*

nata (1930), *Idyl* for orchestra (1930), *Symphonic Overture* for orchestra (1935), *A Ballade of the Night* for voice and string quartet (1936), *Suite for Violin and Piano* (1937), and *Quartet for Strings* (ca. 1946).

"THE WIZARD OF OZ" Classic film released in 1939. Based on the book by L. Frank Baum, with a screenplay by Noel Langley, Florence Ryerson, and Edgar Allan Wolf, *The Wizard of Oz* was graced with an outstanding score by Harold Arlen (music) and E. Y. Harburg (lyrics). It also had fine performances by Judy Garland, as "Dorothy," in her first major screen role, Frank Morgan as the "Wizard," Bert Lahr as the "Cowardly Lion," Ray Bolger as the "Scarecrow," Jack Haley as the "Tin Woodman," and Margaret Hamilton as the "Wicked Witch." The story is about a lonely girl in Kansas who is caught in a tornado and who dreams while unconscious of escaping to the beautifully tinctured land of Oz. Her adventures, accompanied by her dog and 3 oddly assorted companions, presented filmic opportunities in the use of color and for spotting musical sequences. The songs were woven into the plot, a quite innovational concept in screen musicals of the period. Among the songs were "We're Off to See the Wizard," "Ding-Dong! the Witch Is Dead," "If I Only Had a Brain (a Heart, the Nerve)," "If I Were King of the Forest," "The Merry Old Land of Oz," and the classic, Academy Award–winning "Over the Rainbow," which was cut from the film several times after early preview screenings because certain studio executives thought it impeded the flow of the movie. Assistant Director Arthur Freed (q.v.) insisted upon retaining the song and was proved right. Since its release in August 1939, *The Wizard of Oz* has proved to be an enduring classic in movie houses and its annual television broadcasts.

WOLPE, STEFAN (1902–1972) Composer, teacher. Born in Berlin, Germany, Aug. 25, 1902, Wolpe studied piano and theory, then continued his education at the Berlin Hochschule für Musik. Among his more informal musical mentors were Ferruccio Busoni, Anton von Webern, and the conductor-composer Hermann Scherchen. Wolpe's music of this period reflects the theories of the Second Viennese School, although he modified his compositional stance when interest in politics encouraged him to write in a more accessible style. His political views, plus the fact that he was a Jew, compelled Wolpe to leave Germany in 1933; the next year he emigrated to Palestine, where he taught composition and theory from 1934 until 1938, when he came to the United States. In his mid thirties, Wolpe could hardly be labeled an "American composer," but like so many of the gifted European-born-and-educated musicians his music and particularly his musical thinking were influential through his students. After arriving in the United States, Wolpe taught in New York City, Philadelphia, Pa., North Carolina, and from 1957 to 1968 was head of the Music Department at C. W. Post College, Long Island University. Wolpe also taught privately; among his students were Morton Feldman, Ralph Shapey, Ezra Laderman, and Elmer Bernstein (who made his mark as a composer of impressive film background scores). Among Wolpe's important works (among many, for he was most prolific) composed in the United States are *The Man from Midian,* ballet (1942), *Sonata for Violin and Piano* (1945), *Seven Pieces for Three Pianos* (1951), *Enactments* for 3 pianos (1953), *Symphony* (1956, rev. 1964), *String Quartet in Two Parts* (1969), and *Broken Sequences* for piano (1969). Afflicted with Parkinson's disease in 1964, Wolpe nonetheless continued to teach and to compose; he died in New York City, Apr. 4, 1972.

WOOD, JOSEPH (b. 1915) Composer, teacher. Born in Pittsburgh, Pa., May 12, 1915, Wood, after graduating from Bucknell University, enrolled in the Institute of Musical Art; he then was awarded a fellowship at the Juilliard School and studied with Bernard Wagenaar. His opera, *The Mother,* with a libretto by Hurd Hatfield, won him a Juilliard prize in 1942. Wood's association with the Chekov Theatre Studio resulted in the incidental music for their productions of *Twelfth Night* and *Cricket on the Hearth* (both 1940). In 1943 Wood went into the U. S. Army and served in the Special Services branch. After the war he received a fellowship and studied with Otto Luening at Columbia University. Upon receiving his M.A., Wood joined the faculty of the Oberlin (Ohio) Conservatory of Music in 1950. His works include a *Romanza* for strings (1937), *String Quartet No. 1* (1938), *Symphony No. 1* (1939), *String Quartet No. 2* (1941), *Land of Fame,* incidental music (1943), *Sonata for Violin* (1947), *Poem for Orchestra* (1950), *Symphony No. 2* (1952), *Piano Quintet* (1956), *Symphony No. 3* (1958), and *Divertimento* for piano and chamber orchestra (1959).

YARDUMIAN, RICHARD (b. 1917) Composer, teacher. Born in Philadelphia, Pa., Apr. 5, 1917, Yardumian did not study music formally until he was in his twenties—after he had already composed some works and around the time he had written one of his most performed compositions, the *Armenian Suite* (1937). He proceeded to study with several teachers, including George F. Boyle, William Happich, and Alexander Matthews; Yardumian also studied at L'École Monteux, Hancock, Maine. In his home city

Yardumian was long associated with the Philadelphia Youth Concerts and church music. During World War II he served in the Pacific with the U. S. Army Air Forces. For his musical materials Yardumian draws upon Armenian themes and contemporary techniques, including 12-tone writing. Many of his works were commissioned and performed by the Philadelphia Orchestra. His compositions include *Desolate City* for orchestra (1945), *Violin Concerto* (1951), *Cantus Animae et Cordis,* string quartet (1954), *Passacaglia, Recitatives and Fugue* for piano and orchestra (1957), *Symphony No. 1* (1961), *Symphony No. 2* for contralto and orchestra (1964), *Come, Creator Spirit,* mass for contralto, chorus, and orchestra (1966), and *Oratorio on the Story of Abraham* (1971). Other works include: *Prelude-Fugue* for piano, *Psalm 30* for tenor and orchestra, *Three Piano Preludes,* and *Monologues* for violin.

YOUNG, VICTOR (1900–1956) Composer, violinist, conductor, arranger. Born in Chicago, Ill., Aug. 8, 1900, Young was sent to Poland at the age of 10 to study the violin at the Warsaw Conservatory. He made his professional debut with the Warsaw Philharmonic. The outbreak of World War I forced him to return to the United States in 1914; he toured as a concert violinist before becoming concertmaster in the orchestra of the Chicago Theatre. Young began drifting into popular music—he made arrangements and played in Ted Fiorito's orchestra and was active in radio. In 1931 he came to New York City to work in radio; 3 years later he had his own show and conducted for popular entertainers, among them Al Jolson and Don Ameche. Young moved to California in 1935 to settle in and became a prolific composer for films; he worked on nearly 400 in one capacity or the other between 1937 and 1956. Be-

fore leaving for Hollywood, Young collaborated on a number of popular and lasting songs: "Sweet Sue, Just You" (lyrics by Will J. Harris, 1928), "A Ghost of a Chance" (lyrics by Ned Washington and Bing Crosby, 1933), and "A Hundred Years from Today" (lyrics by Washington, 1934). Working as a film musical director afforded Young little time for composing popular songs, but often a theme from one of his background scores was converted into a popular song, or a song was somehow worked into the plot. Among such efforts was "Love Letters" (from *Love Letters,* lyrics by Edward Heyman, 1946); that same year Young also collaborated with Washington on the popular "Stella by Starlight." "Golden Earrings" was the popular title song of a film; this was written in collaboration with Jay Livingston and Raymond Evans in 1947. Among the most important film scores composed by Young were *For Whom the Bell Tolls* (1943), *The Uninvited* (1944), *Bitter Victory* (1949), *The Quiet Man* and *The Greatest Show on Earth* (both 1952), *Shane* (1953), *Strategic Air Command* (1955), and *Around the World in 80 Days* (1956; posthumous Academy Award). Among Young's compositions are such orchestra works as an *Elegy to F.D.R.* (ca. 1945), a tone poem, *Walt Whitman,* and a *String Quartet* based on themes by Stephen Foster. Young died in Palm Springs, Calif., Nov. 11, 1956.

"YOUR HIT PARADE" A radio show, especially popular with the young in the mid and late 1930s. When introduced on July 20, 1935, "Your Hit Parade" was an hour-long show which presented guest stars and presented the 15 most popular songs of the week determined by a "nationwide survey." The implication was that sheet music sales, record sales, and performances were studied to see what songs were the favorites of the American public. During the initial run of the show no attempt was made to decide which were the top 3, 7 or, eventually, 10 songs of the week. When that format was adopted, the top 3 songs of the week were played at the close of the show as the excitement mounted. The top 3, especially, were announced as if these songs were masterpieces of high degree or, had they been human, conquering heroes. Whatever the accuracy and objectivity of the "nationwide survey," "Your Hit Parade" presented a cross section of American popular musical tastes via the radio from July 1935 until it went over to television in July 1950; the last televised show was seen on April 14, 1959. The song survey research was left to the advertising agency Batten, Barton, Durstine & Osborn, which, indeed, did canvas music stores and bandleaders. The sponsor was Lucky Strike Cigarettes, whose distinctive chanting of a tobacco auctioneer was the trademark of the show. Among the show's bandleaders were Lennie Hayton (the first), Al Goodman, Mark Warnow, Leo Reisman, and Peter Van Steeden, to name a few. Vocalists included Kay Thompson, Buddy Clark, Freda Gibson (later known as Georgia Gibbs), Lanny Ross, Bea Wain, Joan Edwards, Frank Sinatra, Lawrence Tibbett, Johnny Mercer, Dinah Shore, Ginny Simms, Dick Haymes, Doris Day, Snooky Lanson (remember him?), Dorothy Collins, Tommy Leonetti, and Johnny Desmond on the final television shows in 1959. The all-time run of any song was made by Irving Berlin's "White Christmas" (38 times, over a number of years, 10 of them in first place); "I Saw Mommy Kissing Santa Claus" appeared on the show once —in first place, no less—in 1953. The longest, consistently running song was Rodgers and Hammerstein's "People Will Say We're in Love" which remained on "Your Hit Parade" for 30 weeks between June 1943 and January 1944; the song was in first place 3 times. The song that held the top-tune position for the greatest number of plays was "Too Young," with music by Sid Lippman and lyrics by Sylvia Dee; during its 22 weeks on the show (in 1951), it was in first place 12 times. The demise of "Your Hit Parade" has been attributed by one of its historians, John R. Williams, to the change in American musical tastes represented by the advent of rock groups and to the sway of the radio disc jockey over the most popular songs of the moment (sometimes of the instant). The switch to television introduced the problem of presentation, particularly if a song was on "Your Hit Parade" for any length of time. One wonders how, week after week, human ingenuity managed to give a faithful audience a different visual presentation of, say, "Too Young."

ᕲᕲᕲᕲ VII ᕲᕲᕲᕲ

The Present
(1950–1981)

Today's music is not necessarily the music of tomorrow. This is true for art music and especially for popular music, with its high mortality rate. Last year's fad is this year's old hat.

The music industry flowered in the years following the Second World War; it literally became big business. By the mid 1950s, for example, the record industry was grossing more than the moviemakers. The development of the long-playing record, high fidelity, and tape recording revolutionized the record market and made it possible to preserve with remarkable accuracy uninterrupted performances of symphonic works or jazz concerts without the customary 3- or 4-minute time limit per side. The preoccupation with hardware and gadgetry ("components") sometimes put the sound of music second; but in the main, long-playing recordings opened new worlds of music to many who had never attended a concert.

Columbia Records in 1948 introduced the long-playing record, which had been developed by Peter Goldmark. While slower-speed recordings had been around for years (radio transcriptions revolved at 16 rpm's), one of Goldmark's contributions was to adopt a microgroove in cutting the disc, making it possible to record about 25 minutes per LP side (by the '70s even more recorded time per side was possible with minimal distortion).

The success of Columbia's LP, with the other major companies following—and they, in turn, by dozens of smaller companies—had a tremendous effect on music in the United States. In the concert field even symphonies and concertos, not to mention operas, made the best-seller charts; as for popular music, by the '50s and '60s its sales figures ran into the billions of dollars and superstars became millionaires literally overnight (and some disappeared almost as quickly).

The rise of television and the continuing popularity of music-dispersing radio stations provided further outlets for music, especially popular music. Some radio stations, in turn, depended heavily on phonograph records for their "product." FM (frequency modulation) radio stations often specialized in programming: the "good music" stations broadcast the classics, others concentrated on jazz, some on mood music—lush orchestral versions of popular music —and the really big-time stations had personalities, disc jockeys (DJ's) to instruct the youth market in the acquisition of the Top 40 hits. Activity in this field produced a new word, "payola," when it was learned that certain record companies were providing DJ's with all sorts of goods and services (money, drugs, women) to huckster their product into the Top 40.

In the more sedate precincts of music in the United States after the war, the affluence that followed encouraged the proliferation of schools and colleges teaching music and turning out composers—or musicians who had studied composition—and more music teachers in droves. By the mid '60s there were nearly 1,500 concert orchestras in the country and nearly 1,000 opera houses. While the field of "serious music" was dominated by the major big-name orchestras, led by big-name conductors, the lesser orchestras in the smaller cities and towns (often associated with schools) were more adventurous in the music they performed. With rare exceptions the New York Philharmonic, the Philadelphia Orchestra, the Chicago Symphony, et al., disseminated the same old repertory that pleases the big contributors. A little sprinkling of modernism, such as one of Bartók's more accessible works, say the *Concerto for Orchestra,* made for grumbling and even premature exits.

The contemporary composer, the living unknown or "difficult" experimentalist, is therefore up against it as far as the major status orchestras go. Here again, the long-playing record is (at times) a major factor that preserves and distributes a new work. In popular music, a recording is now regarded as more crucial than publication—in fact, is often the implied prerequisite.

Aaron Copland commented in 1959 on "the variety and complexity of our creative musical scene today." "There are so many composers active in so many parts of the country," he noted, "that no one observer can pretend to know them all." New York was no longer, as it had been in the '20s, the major music center of the nation, as far as creativity was concerned (it still remains the major outlet, the goal of most creators, however). Activity is not necessarily creatively productive; only time will decide which works of the great postwar outpouring will survive.

Copland was writing about his particular field, the world of the concert hall, of "serious" music. The members of Copland's generation, and the one that followed (Bernstein, Schuman, Barber) were now the "older men," even the Establishment. They continued to work and teach, but the younger generation sought its inspiration and influence elsewhere: in experiment and in the works and theories of the Second Viennese School—more so in the small body of works left by Anton von Webern rather than in those of his teacher Schoenberg (although Schoenberg's 12-tone system was adapted by many American composers, including Copland).

What might be called the established generation of composers in general

THE ENCYCLOPEDIA OF AMERICAN MUSIC

continued as before, producing works in an already fixed style. Walter Piston's symphonic series reached 8 by 1965; the indefatigable Roy Harris that same year composed an *Abraham Lincoln Symphony,* his 10th. His former pupil William Schuman's output totaled 10 by 1976. In the more conservative tradition, there were Douglas Moore's opera *The Ballad of Baby Doe* (1956) and Samuel Barber's *Vanessa* (1958) and *Antony and Cleopatra* (1966). While the Barber works have yet to find their niche, they represent the solid work being done by American composers in a time rife with experimentation and rapid changes. The steady output—particularly in the form of the symphonies already mentioned and those of Howard Hanson, the romantic traditionalist, whose 7th symphony, *A Sea Symphony,* was performed in 1977—revealed that the symphony was not dead, only ignored by the younger generation.

Of the older generation, Elliott Carter has emerged in the postwar years as one of the most admired and respected of American composers (even Stravinsky singled him out for praise). An original musical thinker, Carter has evolved a highly individual style that often perplexes the uninitiated but invariably impresses his fellow musicians.

The sound textures of Carter's work often conjure up the compositions inspired by the 12-tone school and heard in the later music of Wallingford Riegger, some of Copland, and George Perle, among others. Carter, however, is a unique figure, following his own concepts, and is not easily labeled with such convenient terms as "neoclassicism" (most regularly applied to Sessions, one of the most honored of the older generation) or "serialism."

Another solitary figure who emerged during this period is a former mathematician turned composer, Milton Babbitt, who applied his discipline to Schoenbergian principles. His findings led him and some of his students, among them Charles Wuorinen, into the realm of electronically produced music, composing with tape and to computerized composition.

Another branch of the contemporary avant-garde can be traced through the Henry Cowell–John Cage–Harry Partch innovations. Not only does unusual instrumentation characterize their work, but the influence of Eastern music has been most pronounced and has reached some kind of apogee in the process or minimal music of the young school of musician-philosophers grouped around Steve Reich and Philip Glass. The playing of the same chord for several minutes, changing imperceptibly, is to some listeners simple monotony in the concert hall. During a performance of Reich's *Four Organs* (1970), a work lasting more than 20 minutes, a member of the audience is supposed to have shouted from the balcony, "Stop! Stop! I confess."

There has been similar resistance to much electronically produced music, although some fascinating sounds have been invented and stitched together by Morton Subotnick in such pieces specially created for recordings as *Silver Apples of the Moon* (1967) and *The Wild Bull* (1968). Subotnick used an electronic synthesizer to produce the sounds he then selected and arranged for his work. A synthesizer produces certain desired sounds electronically and can even reproduce the sound of various orchestral instruments. The composer then becomes a one-man orchestra, to a greater or lesser degree. (It is reported that the earliest electronic music-producing gadget made in America was Thaddeus Cahill's telharmonium, dating to 1906. This monster required 2 boxcars for transport and weighed more than 6 tons. The telharmonium came close to sounding like a piano, which could, someone eventually realized, be transported in a small truck and lifted by 2 strong men. So back to the keyboard.)

Among the more outré of the avant-garde the production of "chance" music became the thing. The "composer" gave the performers a number of possible musical ideas and the musicians played what they wished to play. The manuscript for this kind of music looked more like an abstract drawing than the conventional printed score. Some musical performances became happenings or events, in which lighting or the very reaction of the audience determined the music. The average concertgoer would hardly recognize the setting and the product as music. To many, some of the very new music sounds like a catalog of effects that displays the musicians' technique rather than composition as it grew out of the 19th century, in which harmony and form were important determinants. Without these guidelines, to the average listener much of today's music is a music of estrangement, "broken-glass music," consisting of icy shards of sound.

This period has seen the return of the fusion of concert hall music and jazz, given the name of "Third Stream" by one of its more successful practitioners, Gunther Schuller. A younger contemporary, a former member of the Stan Kenton Orchestra, William Russo, completed *Three Pieces for Blues Band and Symphony Orchestra* (1968), which was performed by the San Francisco Symphony augmented by the Siegel-Schwall Band of harmonica, bass, percussion, and a jazzy solo violin. While Third Stream has not created a large body of works, as have the serialists and electronics composers, jazz elements abound in much work of the younger composers. But this has been going on since the days of Charles Ives.

The nonmetrical, improvisatory nature of jazz, plus the electronic materials and possibilities, not to mention such technically nonmusical constituents as mathematics and philosophy, enter into the work of the younger composers (born around or after 1930). Predictions of trends and what will last are pointless, but the work of such composers as Frederic Rzewski, Michael Colgrass, John Corigliano (who prefers the more traditional idioms, with modern flourishes), David Amram, and Lucia Dlugoszewski, to name only a few, are fascinating, often strangely beautiful, and at least worth hearing. So is the not easily categorized music of George Crumb (b. 1929), who draws upon aleatory, arrhythmic methods, Eastern music, electronics—even the voice of a whale—in his work.

One other phenomenon should be mentioned: the remarkable rediscovery of Gottschalk and Joplin in the early and mid '70s, followed by a renaissance of the music and a reevaluation of Gershwin's contribution, not to mention the final recognition of *Porgy and Bess* as true opera by most critics and musicologists. This coincided with the growth in the nostalgia market in the recording industry, old radio shows, sound tracks of the classic musical films (most of them bootlegged from prints of the films or from television broadcasts) and the reissuing of old jazz recordings. Was this merely gratification of the human desire for a simpler America or the gentler days of youth—or was it the recognition of a valuable body of creativity?

Nostalgic wishful thinking cannot endow a trashy piece of work—music, film, or musical performance—with value if it is not there from the beginning. Perhaps there is something in the fact that part of this rediscovery of our older music coincided with the most unpopular and pointless war ever fought by the United States. At the same time, much estranged, embittered music by many New Composers was written in opposition to the war in Vietnam.

Musical activity, then, in post–World War II United States eludes labeling, but it underscores Copland's view on the variety and complexity of the American musical scene: it is not neat, but it is lively.

This is especially true of the popular music scene (or market), which has been dominated since about the mid '50s by that frenetic phenomenon initially known as rock 'n' roll, but more familiarly called just rock, although there are many subdivisions within that simpler term: acid rock, hard rock, soft rock, and punk rock. Another popular, and profitable, musical manifestation, which first came to the attention primarily of the so-called Beautiful People, is called disco. The term "disco" is, of course, an abbreviation of the French "discothèque," meaning a dance hall whose music is supplied by an overamplified jukebox (again the importance of the phonograph recording is evident). By the '70s disco had become an enormous extramusical industry, ranging in products from makeup to drugs.

The advent of rock, in 1954, brought a tremendous change to the popular music scene. Its previous distinctly different markets—popular, country and western (C&W), rhythm and blues (R&B)—began to fuse, as elements from all 3 styles were adapted by each of the other styles. The popular music field was dominated by the large, well-established record companies who distributed the albums of such "artists" (as they came to be called) as Frank Sinatra, Andy Williams, Tony Bennett, Teresa Brewer, and Doris Day. These majors, as they were termed to differentiate them from the small independents ("indies"), also released the big-selling original cast albums of Broadway shows, film sound tracks, and most of the classical music albums.

The independents catered to the more specialized country and western and rhythm and blues markets; the former sold best in the South and West, and the latter reached the black record collector, primarily in the cities with substantial black populations. With the coming of rock, some of these independents challenged the majors in competing for ascendancy in the record marketplace as represented by the Top 40 listings, radio plays—and, of course, sales.

While the roots of rhythm and blues and country and western could be traced to folk forms, the crossovers that produced rock eventually placed them in the profit market once dominated by popular music. This mix disturbed the purists, although the "purer" forms of R&B could still be heard in its more traditional performances by various blues singers—Mississippi John Hurt, Muddy Waters, Big Bill Broonzy, and such younger vocalists as B. B. King. The blending of the blues, gospel music, and rock produced a popular offspring, "soul."

Rock came into American consciousness, and eventually the world's, in 1954 via a C&W group, Bill Haley and his Comets (formerly the Saddlemen). Their recording of "Rock Around the Clock," which featured a driving rhythm, an emphasis on the guitar, and a declaimed, rather than sung, lyric, caught the attention of the youth market. The sound alienated the older generation (too loud, was the initial objection; later, rock songs were labeled as smut because of their sex-oriented lyrics) and came to represent the youth rebellion of the '50s—the so-called generation gap. "Rock Around the Clock" became a best-selling country and western disc; when connected the next year to the film *The Blackboard Jungle* (about the frightful situation in a tough high school), the song made the top of the popular charts in the United States and Britain.

At the same time another C&W hopeful had begun to move; in 1956, when his first record release by a major company, "Heartbreak Hotel" (RCA), hit the market, a Mississippi-born resident of Memphis, Elvis Presley, arrived on the scene, to dominate it for nearly a decade. The Presley style drew upon the traditional blues, coupled with the driving beat and the vocalist's stage performance that the older generation found offensively carnal. Although eventually grouped with popular singers—for, besides his rock recordings, Presley returned to country and western songs as well as out-and-out popular music—he held on to a faithful following until his untimely death at the age of 42.

Although rock was based in black music, its first superstars were white. In this period, however, an important black artist was recognized (recognition being equated with a top-selling record); he was Chuck Berry, who wrote the songs he sang and accompanied himself on the guitar. Although he did not enjoy the glory and riches of the white rock stars, Berry undoubtedly influenced all of them.

Strangely, the major influence on rock music in the United States in the '60s originated in Britain with a group called the Beatles. Their first recording was released in the United States in 1964; within a year their albums and singles cornered the record market. Influenced themselves by the earlier work of Chuck Berry, Little Richard, and Buddy Holly, among others, the Beatles in turn dominated the rock market through the heyday of rock. English-born, they greatly affected their American audiences and musicians. Other important British rock groups followed, the most important being the Rolling Stones and The Who.

By the time the Beatles broke up in 1970, the rock scene had become rather static, repetitive, and perhaps not quite as profitable as the 1964–68 period of excitement, change, and the rise and fall of group after group and artist after artist (some of whom died after drug overdoses). A bizarre manifestation, punk rock, surfaced in the '70s. A kind of protest music, it was as much characterized by the strange dress, makeup, and jewelry (safety pins through the ears, for example) of its adherents as by any particular differences from the early rock.

Just as rock borrowed from rhythm and blues and country and western, so did these once very distinct forms borrow from rock and from each other. Popular folk singers did likewise. Among the most important were Bob Dylan, whose protest songs sang for a generation; Joan Baez, who retained the purity of folk song; and the group Peter, Paul and Mary. "Soul" reached a wide audience in the mid '60s and was no longer a product only for the black audience and record buyers. Many of its hits made the Top 40 charts of the popular market. James Brown, John Lee Hooker, Otis Redding, and, later, Jimi Hendrix had a tremendous impact on the popular music scene. More restrained but no less popular were Ray Charles and Stevie Wonder. Women also achieved recognition singing in the supercharged soul style: Nina Simone, Aretha Franklin, and the Supremes—all of whom owed much to the gospel singer Mahalia Jackson.

While soul is regarded as the province of black singers and performers, country and western is predominantly white, Charley Pride being a major exception. Since the end of the Second World War, country music—the term "hillbilly" having been generally dropped—has become big business via radio, recordings, and television. In addition, it no longer appeals merely to rural America. Its superstars are nearly as celebrated as rock and popular stars; Johnny Cash and Dolly Parton come to mind.

The sound of country music has changed since the '20s and is less folksy and more pop, what with the introduction of electric guitars. Still, the purists continue to favor the old Anglo-American instrumentation of fiddles, dulcimer, banjo—and the characteristic but seemingly anomalous Hawaiian steel guitar. Like rock music, country music has often crossed into the province of popular music.

Its major center continues to be Nashville, home of the Grand Ole Opry, publishing companies, and recording studios. An interesting development in country music since the '50s has been the rise of women star singers—Kitty Wells, Loretta Lynn, Tammy Wynette, Crystal Gayle, Patsy Cline, and, all too briefly, Bobbie Gentry with her "Ode to Billie Joe." Male stars in this period include Glen Campbell, Lefty Frizzell, Kris Kristofferson, Willie Nelson, Jerry Lee Lewis, Charlie Rich, Porter Wagoner, Merle Haggard, and Flatt and Scruggs, as well as such crossovers (from folk-pop) as John Denver. Some historians of country music view its rise as the end of rock, which has stagnated into imitations of imitations since the demise of the Beatles.

The trendiest popular music in the mid- and late '70s has been disco music. This is the music that is fed into a large dancing area populated by often startlingly dressed dancers (who really do not dance with each other, but around each other). Disco record producer Freddie Perren has explained it thus: "At discos people put themselves on display for strangers. Everyone has the potential to be a star, the center of attention. The music, therefore, is dramatic. There are more swirls of notes, more effects, more Syndrums [drum sounds produced by a synthesizer]. It's a more theatrical style of music." John Rockwell of the New York *Times* put it more succinctly: "Disco is the heavily amplified, steadily rhythmic dance music that has emerged as one of the dominant pop forms since 1975. . . ." Disco is most dependent on recordings—and is played back with the volume up and lights flashing in a darkened dance hall. It was the music featured in the popular film *Saturday Night Fever*. Though a new arrival on the American music scene, disco has begun to build its roster of stars (Gloria Gaynor and Donna Summer) and star groups (the Bee Gees). Even pop superstar Barbra Streisand crossed over into the disco scene in 1979.

Jazz, during this period—as always—has not fared well financially despite the frenzy of activity in the popular, rock, and quasi-folk fields. In a creative sense, however, jazz has continued to evolve: from "hot" to bop to "cool" to Third Stream and avant-garde.

By the early '50s bop, with its complex rhythms, "far-out," harmonies, and fragmented melodies had begun to lose its popular audience; bop musicians played for other musicians. They produced listening music whose erratic beat (to untutored ears) was not for dancing. Musicians performed without appearing to be aware of the audience; trumpeter Miles Davis was known to turn his back on the audience—he was cool. Cool jazz impressed the listener as a detached, somnolent, rambling kind of music. Tenor saxophonist Lester Young was one of the most influential of the cool pioneers. The Modern Jazz Quartet, formed around pianist-arranger John Lewis, was recognized as one of the finest exponents of modern jazz. The Gillespie-Parker school continued to be a major influence, but new stars appeared on the scene: Dave Brubeck, Lennie Tristano, Thelonious Monk, Charles Mingus, a bassist and composer, George Russell (who emphasized the importance of Afro-Cuban music in jazz), Gerry Mulligan, and others.

The more impassioned avant-garde jazz produced such figures as saxophonist-composer Ornette Coleman, and Albert Ayler.

The contemporary jazzmen were frequently conservatory-trained musicians, a far cry from the early jazzmen who could not (and did not want to) read music. Consequently much of the cool and avant-garde jazz since the '50s drew upon the devices of classical music (not a few of the early experiments reminded the listener of snatches of Bartók, Stravinsky, Milhaud, or Debussy). This was done intentionally, for to the jazz musician all was grist for his mill. In the more self-conscious practice, this came to be called Third Stream. It took at times the form of pitting a jazz group against a standard symphony orchestra, as in Gunther Schuller's *12 by 11* for chamber orchestra and jazz group; Schuller, incidentally, coined the term "Third Stream" and played French horn in a Miles Davis band in 1950.

Third Stream was performed by standard jazz (or big) bands such as those of Kenton (Pete Rugolo's *Mirage*), and *Egdon Heath* (by Bill Russo), George Russell (his own *Concerto for Billy the Kid*), Woody Herman (Ralph Burns's

Summer Sequence), and Duke Ellington in his own *The Clothed Woman*. While it lasted, the Modern Jazz Quartet moved into the Third Stream, as did Lennie Tristano, George Russell, and Charles Mingus. As in the world of rock, jazz between 1950 and 1980 bristled with great names and myriads of crossovers demanding new definitions for old words.

The Broadway musical scene was dominated well into the '50s by the successful team of Rodgers and Hammerstein, who began the new decade with the highly popular and frequently revived *The King and I* (1951). They faltered a bit with *Me and Juliet* (1953) and *Pipe Dream* (1955), but proved they had the touch with *The Sound of Music* (1959), their final collaboration before Hammerstein's death. The team of Alan Jay Lerner and Frederick Loewe might have gracefully moved into the gap left by the end of the Rodgers and Hammerstein partnership; beginning with *Paint Your Wagon* (1951), they produced several highly successful shows, reaching their peak with *My Fair Lady* in 1956. However, after their trouble-plagued *Camelot,* their collaboration ended in 1960, the year of Hammerstein's death.

Many of the older hands added to the musical scene: Irving Berlin wrote the score for an Ethel Merman musical, *Call Me Madam,* and Frank Loesser began the decade on a high note with his classic *Guys and Dolls* (both shows opened in 1950). Harold Rome's *Wish You Were Here* (1952) and *Fanny* (1954) enjoyed huge successes, as did Leonard Bernstein with *Wonderful Town* (1953) and especially with *West Side Story* (1957), which introduced a new name to the musical scene, lyricist Stephen Sondheim, of whom more later. Harold Arlen, after a long Hollywood stay, returned to Broadway with *House of Flowers* (1954), a beautifully scored show but not very successful financially. *Jamaica* (1957) made it, however, primarily because of the presence of Lena Horne and the fine Arlen-Harburg songs.

Jule Styne enjoyed a good few seasons on Broadway in the '50s and '60s, particularly with *Bells Are Ringing* (1956, lyrics by Comden and Green), *Gypsy* (1959, lyrics by Sondheim), and *Funny Girl* (1964, lyrics by Bob Merrill). Burton Lane, one of the younger old hands—and unfortunately not too prolific—composed a superior score with Alan Jay Lerner for *On a Clear Day You Can See Forever* in 1965, his first since *Finian's Rainbow* (1947) for Broadway. Richard Rodgers wrote both words and music for *No Strings* (1962), his first show since the death of Hammerstein. His collaborations since *No Strings* with Sondheim, Martin Charnin, and Sheldon Harnick did not prove very fruitful.

A new generation of Broadway composers and lyricists began to make their mark in this period. Richard Adler and Jerry Ross created the songs for the hit show *The Pajama Game* (1954) and followed that with another, *Damn Yankees,* the next year. Tragically, the partnership ended with Ross's death in 1955. Meredith Willson, better known as a radio conductor and sometime serious composer, enjoyed great success in his Broadway debut with an exercise in Americana-nostalgia, *The Music Man* (1957), followed by *The Unsinkable*

Molly Brown (1960). Composer Charles Strouse and lyricist Lee Adams built their score for a successful musical, *Bye Bye Birdie,* in 1960, around the generation gap and the Elvis Presley phenomenon; they had another long-running show in *Applause* (1970). Composer-lyricist Jerry Herman, who had written songs for revues and a mildly successful show, *Milk and Honey* (1961), came into prominence with the wildly successful *Hello, Dolly!* (1964). *Fiddler on the Roof* (1964) was an emphatic reminder that the team of Sheldon Harnick (lyrics) and Jerry Bock (music) had produced earlier scores of merit in *Fiorello!* (1959) and *She Loves Me* (1963). John Kander and Fred Ebb became active as a team in the '60s and proved most successful with *Cabaret* (1966) and *Chicago* (1970). Almost totally unknown was composer-lyricist Sherman Edwards, who wrote the songs for the successful *1776* (1969); a former dance band pianist and songwriter, Edwards has been silent ever since. An ex-New Yorker, Marvin Hamlisch, who had worked in Hollywood as an arranger (*The Sting*) and as composer of special material for various performers, wrote the music, and Edward Kleban the lyrics, for the long-running *A Chorus Line* (1975).

Most of these shows were in the traditional Broadway musical mold. *A Chorus Line* broke somewhat with the usual approach, telling the stories of show people as they struggle toward opening night. The music was not particularly innovative, though the form of the show itself ("book by James Kirkwood and Nicholas Dante, from a concept by Michael Bennett") was.

The shows that moved away from the tried and true Broadway musical were frequently presented off-Broadway, away from the Times Square area—*Hair,* aimed at the youth market and adult shock; *Godspell* (1971); *Jesus Christ, Superstar* (1971); *You're a Good Man, Charlie Brown* (1967); *The Fantasticks* (which has been running in a tiny theatre for nearly 2 decades, since 1960).

Most of these shows suggest a genre of musical that is designed to appeal more to a younger audience than the standard Broadway show. Another type that appeared during this period was fashioned for a black audience—and was very successful: *Ain't Supposed to Die a Natural Death* (Melvin Van Peebles, 1971), *Purlie* (music by Gary Geld, lyrics by Peter Udell; 1970), *Raisin* (though its composer and lyricist, Judd Woldin and Robert Brittan, are white; 1973), *Don't Bother Me, I Can't Cope* (Micki Grant, 1972), and the very popular shows inspired by the music of 2 great black musicians, Fats Waller (*Ain't Misbehavin',* 1978) and Eubie Blake (*Eubie,* 1979).

The subject of feminism has yet to be fully examined in a musical, although an interesting beginning has been made in *I'm Getting My Act Together and Taking It on the Road* (1978) with music by Nancy Ford and lyrics by Gretchen Cryer, a team whose earlier musical *The Last Sweet Days of Isaac* (1970) and its rock-inflected score received high praise.

The most consistently adventurous new figure in the American musical theatre is Stephen Sondheim, who first attracted attention with his lyrics to

Leonard Bernstein's music for *West Side Story* (1957), which was followed by even better work for *Gypsy* (1959), to the music of Jule Styne. In 1962 Sondheim fashioned both words and music for *A Funny Thing Happened on the Way to the Forum,* which revealed him to be the most gifted composer-lyricist since Cole Porter. Except for one more collaboration (with Richard Rodgers on *Do I Hear a Waltz?,* 1965), Sondheim has written both words and music for a series of unusual musicals. Although working within traditional musical theatre forms in general, Sondheim has written scores that serve the show rather than the hit song marketplace. The themes of his musicals vary and touch upon subjects that might seem alien to what was once termed "musical comedy": madness (*Anyone Can Whistle,* 1964), the failure of marriage among the affluent (*Company,* 1979), and mass murder and unconscious cannibalism (*Sweeney Todd,* 1979). To those who have decried the decline of the American musical, Sondheim has been the brightest ray of hope since the '50s began.

In the field of the musical film, the '50s opened with a trend setter for the next 2 decades or so: a filmed version of a Broadway musical. In 1950 it was Irving Berlin's *Annie Get Your Gun.* Some of the most profitable and well-wrought film musicals of the period were based on Broadway musicals: *Show Boat* (1951), *Kiss Me, Kate* (1953), *The Pajama Game* (1957), *South Pacific* (1958), a poorly screened *Porgy and Bess* (1959), and 3 of the most successful: *West Side Story* (1961), *My Fair Lady* (1964), and *The Sound of Music* (1965). And this continued into the late '70s with the release of such popular youth-oriented films as *Jesus Christ, Superstar; Godspell;* and *Hair.* The first 2 were hardly memorable, but the rewritten-for-films *Hair* (1979) was superior to the original.

The '50s also opened with a series of outstanding original film musicals, although many depended on already existing songs: *Three Little Words* (1950), a "biography" of songwriters Kalmar and Ruby; the stunning *An American in Paris* (1951), which drew upon the music of George and the songs of George and Ira Gershwin; *Singin' in the Rain* (1952), one of the best, utilizing the songs of Nacio Herb Brown and Arthur Freed in one of the sprightliest satires on early Hollywood ever filmed. New songs were written for the folk-style comedy *Seven Brides for Seven Brothers* by Gene DePaul and Johnny Mercer in 1954, and *Gigi* (1958) was graced with a wonderful score by Lerner and Loewe. One of the last of the fine originals was Judy Garland's *A Star Is Born* (1954) with songs by Harold Arlen and Ira Gershwin. (A 1976 remake, with a new score, starring Barbra Streisand, proved to be a dramatic and musical disaster.)

By the mid '50s Hollywood began feeling the television-induced slump and the effects of Europe's shrunken market for musicals (the translation of song lyrics was always a problem—especially when the lyricist was a master of American idioms, which could not be translated to begin with). Big musicals continued to be produced but not in great numbers, though a cluster of "blockbusters" was released in the '60s: *West Side Story* (1961), *My Fair Lady* and

Mary Poppins (both 1964), and *The Sound of Music* (1965). Only *Mary Poppins* was a Hollywood original; the others were all former solid Broadway hits.

In 1964 the Beatles made their film debut with the delightful *A Hard Day's Night,* which, although English-made, had its influence. Around this time a series of surfer films with pop scores began infiltrating the market. Elvis Presley had also initiated a series of films with *Love Me Tender* (1956), all of them centered on his persona and not many much else. Although the traditional background scores were used for the dramatic films—Henry Mancini, Elmer Bernstein, Leonard Rosenman, Ernest Gold, among others, were active during this period—others drew on rock music for contemporary ambiance. So-called compiled scores used the songs of the period for atmosphere. *Paper Moon* (1973) evoked the sounds and feel of the Depression with phonograph recordings by Paul Whiteman, Leo Reisman, Dick Powell, Bing Crosby, et al. *The Last Picture Show* (1971) drew upon the pop stars and performances of the '50s. *Easy Rider* (1969), no musical but a statement about youth in the America of the time, depended on a rock score; and the highly successful *Saturday Night Fever* (1978), also not a musical, provided John Travolta with disco music for escape from the realities of a humdrum life the rest of the week.

One of the most successful of the compiled scores (and also a best-selling record album) was inspired by a recording of the Don Rose *Gershwin Broadway Overtures.* Producer-star Woody Allen based the score of his film *Manhattan* (1979) on music in the album, adding more Gershwin music where needed.

Film music, like concert, popular, and jazz, might best be described as eclectic; whatever the composer, arranger, or performer thinks will work is used.

A technological development on the brink of maturity as the '80s began is the digital recording. Briefly described, digital recording electronically transforms sound waves into numbers rather than a magnetic pattern on tape, as has been the usual method. It is tantamount, to oversimplify, to recording on file cards. The result is a startlingly true, clear recording, free of surface noise and distortion and capable of handling the great differences in volume changes from fortissimo to pianissimo. Among the developments in this process is a system equipped with a laser (in place of the old-fashioned stylus, or "needle") which beams onto a small record—a full hour, by this method, can be put on one side of a 4½-inch disc. The musical possibilities of this new technology will be explored in the '80s.

Just over the horizon—and expected to be generally available by the mid or late '80s—are the revolutionary videodiscs and tapes. (Video cassette recorders have, of course, been around for some time and have been used in the home for the showing of films, or for copying from television—regular TV shows, films, the news. In this field, too, there are certain extramusical activities—the bootlegging of new and recent films not yet licensed for video cassette release and X-rated movies.)

The videodisc would provide both picture and sound via laser beam (the

MCA/Philips laser-optical system) or the RCA SelectaVision with its grooved disc and diamond stylus. Once on the general market these systems, and no doubt others competing with them, will permit further viewing of operas, ballets, concerts, and recitals in the home.

ADAMS, LEE (b. 1924) See Strouse, Charles.

ADLER, SAMUEL (b. 1928) Composer, teacher. Born in Mannheim, Germany, Mar. 4, 1928, Adler and his parents came to the United States in 1939. The family settled in Worcester, Mass., where Adler resumed the study of the viola and violin which he had begun in Germany before the advent of the Nazis. He studied composition with Herbert Fromm in 1943; in 1946 he enrolled in Boston University to study composition (Hugo Norden), violin (Wolfe Wolfinsohn), and musicology (Paul Pisk, Karl Geiringer). From 1948 to 1950 he studied at Harvard with Paul Hindemith, Walter Piston (q.v.), and Randall Thompson (q.v.). At Tanglewood around this same time he also studied composition with Aaron Copland (q.v.) and conducting with Serge Koussevitzky. From 1950 to 1952 Adler served in the U. S. Army. He organized the Seventh Army Symphony, which he led in Austria and Germany; during this period Adler was guest conductor of several European orchestras, as well as for ballet and opera. Upon his return to the United States he took the post of music director, Temple Emanu-El, Dallas, Texas. He combined this work with teaching composition at North Texas State University, organized and led the Dallas Chorale, and conducted the Dallas Chamber Opera. Since 1966 he has been professor of composition, Eastman School of Music, Rochester, N.Y. His works include *String Quartet No. 1* (1945), *Sonata for Horn and Piano* (1948), *String Quartet No. 2* (1950), *Symphony No. 1* (1953), *String Quartet No. 3* (1953), *Capriccio* for piano (1954), *Toccata* for orchestra (1954),

Sonata for Violin No. 2 (1956), *The Outcasts of Poker Flat,* one-act opera (1959), *Symphony No. 3* (1960), *Shir chadash,* synagogue service (1960), *Southwestern Sketches* for wind orchestra (1961), *Rhapsody* for violin and orchestra (1961), *The Vision of Isaiah,* cantata for bass, chorus, and orchestra (1962), *Sonata breve* for piano (1963), *String Quartet No. 4* (1963), *Requiescat in Pace* for orchestra (1963), *Trio* for violin, cello, and piano (1964), *Shiru ladonay,* synagogue service (1964), *Song and Dance* for viola and orchestra (1965), *Violin Sonata No. 3* (1965), *Symphony No. 4, "Geometrics"* (1967), *The Binding: A Biblical Oratorio* (1967), *Concerto* for winds, brass, and percussion (1968), *City by the Lake* for orchestra (1968), *From Out of Bondage,* cantata (1968), *String Quartet No. 5* (1969), *Concerto for Organ* (1970), *Sinfonietta* for orchestra (1971), *The Wrestler,* opera (1971), *Xenia, a Dialogue for Organ and Percussion* (1972), *Four Dialogues* for euphonium and marimba (1974), *Symphony No. 5* (1975), *String Quartet No. 6,* with mezzo-soprano (1975), and *Déjà vu* for recorder sextet (1975). In time for the Bicentennial, Adler reconstructed the music for Andrew Barton's (q.v.) ballad opera *The Disappointment,* for performances at the Library of Congress. Adler is also the author of the *Anthology for the Teaching of Choral Conducting* (1970).

ADLER AND ROSS A most promising songwriting team. Richard Adler (b. New York City, Aug. 3, 1921) and Jerry Ross (b. New York City, Mar. 9, 1926; d. New York City, Nov. 11, 1955) had begun an auspicious Broadway partnership with 2 successful shows in a row,

The Pajama Game (1954) and *Damn Yankees* (1955). They had also contributed songs to a revue, *John Murray Anderson's Almanac* (1953). Encouraged by songwriter Frank Loesser (q.v.), they produced such songs for their shows as "Hey There," "Steam Heat," and "Hernando's Hideaway" (*The Pajama Game*) and "Goodbye, Old Girl," "Heart," "Two Lost Souls," and "Whatever Lola Wants" (*Damn Yankees*). The collaboration was cut short by the untimely death of Ross. Adler later wrote words and music for an unsuccessful but more than interesting musical about a white-black love affair in West Africa, *Kwamina* (1961). He thereafter concentrated on writing commercials for television and radio and producing.

AITKEN, HUGH (b. 1924) Composer, teacher. Born in New York City, Sept. 7, 1924, Aitken came from a musical family. After service in the U. S. Army Air Forces in World War II, Aitken studied at the Juilliard School of Music, New York City, where he worked under Vincent Persichetti (q.v.) and Bernard Wagenaar (q.v.) in composition. Upon graduation, in 1950, he joined the teaching staff of Juilliard. He remained there until 1971, when he became associated with the College of Arts & Sciences, William Paterson College, Wayne, N.J. His works include *Cantata No. 1* for tenor, oboe, violin, viola, and cello (1958), *Cantata No. 3* for tenor, oboe, and viola (1960), *The Moirai*, ballet (1961), *Cantata No. 4* for soprano, flute, oboe, cello, and bass (1961), *Piano Fantasy* (1967), *Trumpet!* for solo trumpet (1974), *Fables*, chamber opera (1975), *Quintet* for oboe and strings (1975), *Quintet* for trumpet and strings (1976), and *Johannes: an Homage to Ockeghem for Five Players* (1977). Other works include a piano concerto, *Montages* for solo bassoon, and a *Suite for Solo Bass*.

ALBRIGHT, WILLIAM (b. 1944) Composer, organist, pianist, teacher. Born in Gary, Ind., Oct. 20, 1944, Albright enrolled in the Juilliard School of Music, New York City, in 1959, studied composition (Hugh Aitken, q.v.) and piano (Rosetta Goodkind), and graduated in 1962. From 1963 to 1970 he studied at the University of Michigan, Ann Arbor, with Leslie Bassett (q.v.), Ross Lee Finney (q.v., composition), and Marilyn Mason (organ). This was followed by a year in Paris (1968–69) where he studied at the Conservatory with Olivier Messiaen. In 1970 Albright joined the staff of the University of Michigan, where he is associate director of its Electronic Music Studio. He is also associated with the Michigan Contemporary Directions ensemble. Albright has performed widely as a pianist and organist. His works are decidedly in the modern idiom and include *Chorale-Partita in an Old Style* for organ (1963), *Foils* for winds (1964), *Salvos* for flute, clarinet, bassoon, violin, viola, cello, and percussion (1964), *Juba* for organ (1965), *Pneuma* for organ (1966), *Two Pieces for Nine Instruments* (1966), *Pianoagogo* for piano (1966), *Caroms* for septet (1966), *Organbook* (1967), *Tic* for soloists, 2 jazz-rock ensembles, film, and tape (1967), *Grand Sonata in Rag* for piano (1968), *Beulahland Rag* for narrator, jazz quartet, improvisation ensemble, tape, film, and slides (1969), *Brass Knuckles,* piano rag, with William Bolcom (q.v., 1969), *Alliance* for orchestra (1970), *Marginal Worlds* for winds, strings, piano, and percussion (1970), *Organbook II* for organ (1971), *Take That* for percussion (1972), *Concerto for Organ and Orchestra* (1972), *Gothic Suite* for organ, strings, and percussion (1973), *Chichester Mass* for mixed choir a cappella (1974), *Dream and Dance* for organ and percussion (1974), *Sweet Sixteenths* for piano

(1975), *Five Chromatic Dances* for piano (1976), *Shadows* for solo guitar (1977), *Organbook III,* Etudes (1977–78), *Halo* for organ and metal instruments (1978), *Four Fancies* for harpsichord (1979), and *The Birth of Jesus/Alleluia* (1979).

AMRAM, DAVID (b. 1930) Composer, pianist, trumpeter, French horn soloist, jazz performer, conductor. Born in Philadelphia, Pa., Nov. 17, 1930, Amram studied piano and trumpet as a youngster. He was graduated from George Washington University, Washington, D.C., with a degree in history in 1952; during this period he provided incidental music for productions at Ford's Theatre and formed a jazz band. From 1952 to 1955 Amram was in the U. S. Army and served, part of the time, in Germany as a member of the Seventh Army Symphony. After leaving the Army, Amram enrolled in the Manhattan School of Music, where he studied composition with Vittorio Giannini (q.v.) and French horn with Gunther Schuller, q.v. (1955–56). He became associated as music director with the N. Y. Shakespeare Festival, as well as the Lincoln Center Repertory Theatre and the Phoenix Theatre. Concurrently Amram was active as a jazz performer; among the bands in which he played were those led by Lionel Hampton, Sonny Rollins, and Charles Mingus (q.v.). Amram's original works are colored by his jazz experiences and by the music of the Middle East—all folk music, in fact. One of the dozens of instruments he plays, for example, is the Pakistani flute. Composer of more than 100 works, Amram has also been active as a goodwill ambassador for American music in Brazil, Cuba, Egypt, and Kenya. His works include the film score *Echo of an Era* (1958; winner of Brussels World Fair Prize), *Trio* for saxophone, horn, and bassoon (1958),

Overture and Allegro for solo flute (1959), *Discussion* for flute, cello, piano, and percussion (1960), *Piano Sonata* (1960), *Violin Sonata* (1960), *String Quartet* (1961), *Two Anthems* for chorus (1961), *Dirge and Variations* for violin, cello, and piano (1962), *Thou Shalt Love the Lord, Thy God* for chorus and organ (1962), *The Wind and the Rain* for viola and piano (1963), *A Year in Our Land,* cantata for voices and orchestra (1964), *Sonata for Solo Violin* (1964), *The Final Ingredient,* opera for television (1965), *By the Rivers of Babylon* for soprano solo and women's chorus (1966), *Fanfare and Processional* for brass quintet (1966), *King Lear Variations* for winds and percussion (1966), *Three Dances* for oboe and strings (1966), *Songs from Shakespeare* for voice and piano (1968), *Quintet for Winds* (1968), *Twelfth Night,* opera (1968), *Three Songs for America* for baritone and chamber group (1969), *Triptych* for solo viola (1969), *Triple Concerto* for woodwind, brass, jazz quintets, and orchestra (1970), *Elegy for Violin and Orchestra* (1971), *The Trail of Beauty* for mezzo-soprano, oboe, and orchestra (1976), *In Memory of Chano Pozo* for jazz group featuring percussion (1977), and *Harold and Maude,* songs and incidental music (1979). Amram has composed incidental music for chamber orchestra for 18 Shakespeare plays. He has composed a *Shakespearean Concerto* for oboe, 2 horns, and strings. His film scores include the music for *Splendor in the Grass* and *The Manchurian Candidate.* Amram is the author of *Vibrations: the Adventures and Musical Times of David Amram* (1968).

ANDERSON, THOMAS JEFFERSON (b. 1928) Composer, teacher. Born in Coatesville, Pa., Aug. 17, 1928, Anderson, whose parents were teachers (his mother was also a musician) earned a master's degree in music education at Pennsylvania State University in 1951. He received his doctorate in composition from the University of Iowa (1958); his teachers include Scott Huston (q.v.), Philip Bezanson, and Darius Milhaud (q.v.). Anderson has taught at West Virginia State College; Langston University, Okla.; Tennessee State University; and Morehouse College, Atlanta, Ga., where, under a grant from the Rockefeller Foundation, he was also composer-in-residence to the Atlanta Symphony. He has also served as chairman of the advisory board of the Black Music Center, at the University of Indiana. In 1972 he was appointed chairman of the Music Department, Tufts University, Medford, Mass. As a composer, Anderson draws upon his experience as a jazz performer as well as from contemporary advanced techniques. His works include *New Dances* for orchestra (1960), *Classical Symphony* (1961), *Six Pieces* for clarinet and chamber orchestra (1962), *Five Bagatelles* for violin, oboe, and harpsichord (1964), *Symphony in Three Movements* (1964), *Five Portraitures of Two People* for piano duo (1965), *Squares: An Essay for Orchestra* (1965), *Connections* for string quintet (1966), *Personals,* cantata for narrator, chorus, and brass (1966), *Rotations* for band (1967), *Chamber Symphony* (1968), *In Memoriam Zach Walker* for band (1968), *Variations on a Theme by M. B. Tolson* for voice and chamber orchestra (1969), *Intervals* for orchestra (1971), *Watermelon* for piano (1971), *Transitions* for chamber group (1971), *Swing Set* for clarinet and piano (1971), *Block Songs* for voice and toys (1972), *In Memoriam Malcolm X* for voice and orchestra (1974), *Horizons '76* for soprano and orchestra (1975), *Fanfare* for trumpet and winds (1976), and *The Shell Fairy,* operetta (1976). In 1972 Anderson prepared an orchestration of

Joplin's (q.v.) *Treemonisha* for its first performance in Atlanta.

ARGENTO, DOMINICK (b. 1927) Composer, teacher. Born in York, Pa., Oct. 27, 1927, Argento first became interested in music as a teenager upon reading a biography of George Gershwin. He then began reading other books on music from biographies to theory, composition, and harmony. He began teaching himself to play on the family piano (which happened to be in his father's restaurant). On his 16th birthday he received a piano and began taking lessons. He had barely gotten started when he was drafted into the U. S. Army (1945–47), in which he served as a cryptographer. Upon completion of military service, Argento enrolled at the Peabody Conservatory, Baltimore, where his teachers in composition were Nicolas Nabokov, Hugo Weisgall, and Henry Cowell (all q.v.). On a Fulbright Fellowship (1951–52) he went to Florence, Italy, where he studied with Luigi Dallapiccola. From 1955 to 1957 Argento studied at the Eastman School, Rochester, N.Y., under Howard Hanson, Alan Hovhaness, and Bernard Rogers (all q.v.). In 1958 he joined the faculty of the University of Minnesota, Minneapolis. There he helped found the Center (now Minnesota) Opera in 1964. Argento has also been associated with the Guthrie Theater, for whose productions he has composed much music. His prime interest has been in writing for the voice; many of his operas have been highly praised as well as popular. As Argento has observed, "The voice is not just another instrument. It's the instrument par excellence, the original instrument, a part of the performer rather than an adjunct to him." Argento's works include a *Polka* for flute and orchestra, composed while he was still in high school in York, Pa., *Songs About Spring* for soprano and chamber orchestra (1950), *Divertimento* for piano and strings (1954), *The Resurrection of Don Juan*, ballet (1955), *String Quartet* (1956), *The Boor*, opera (1957), *Ode to the West Wind* for soprano and orchestra (1957), *Six Elizabethan Songs* for voice and piano (1958), *Colonel Jonathan the Saint*, opera (1961), *Christopher Sly*, opera (1963), *The Masque of Angels*, opera (1964), *Royal Invitation, or Homage to the Queen of Tonga* for chamber orchestra (1964), *The Mask of Night* for orchestra (1965), *The Revelation of St. John the Divine* for tenor, men's chorus, brass, and percussion (1966), *The Shoemaker's Holiday*, opera (1967), *A Nation of Cowslips* for chorus (1968), *Letters from Composers* for tenor and guitar (1968), *Bravo Mozart!* for oboe, violin, horn, and orchestra (1969), *Tria Carmina Paschalia*, cantata for women's chorus (1970), *Postcard from Morocco*, opera (1971), *A Ring of Time* for orchestra (1972), *To Be Sung Upon the Water* for high voice, clarinet, and piano (1972), *Jonah and the Whale* for narrator, soloists, chorus, and chamber orchestra (1974), *A Waterbird Talk*, monodrama (1974), *From the Diary of Virginia Woolf* for high voice and piano (1974; Pulitzer Prize 1975), *The Voyage of Edgar Allan Poe*, opera (1976), *Praise of Music* for orchestra (1978), and *Miss Havisham's Fire*, opera (1979).

ASHLEY, ROBERT (b. 1930) Composer, theoretician. Born in Ann Arbor, Mich., Mar. 28, 1930, Ashley is a graduate of the University of Michigan, Ann Arbor (music, theory, acoustics), and the Manhattan School of Music, New York City (1954). His teachers were Ross Lee Finney (q.v.), Leslie Bassett (q.v.), Roberto Gerhard, and Wallingford Riegger (q.v.). Ashley, a leader of the Ann Arbor–based ONCE group, is an advocate of so-called action and gesture music, depending upon electronics, theatrics, and the interaction between audience and performer: in short, music as experience rather than traditional performance in the formal concert hall. The ONCE group has stated that its aim is "to consciously explore those performance elements which extend beyond the realm of 'pure music' and sound. . . . These performance elements can be included in the category of 'theatre,' and include *dance* (physical activity, human gesture, and movement of all sorts), *staging* (lighting, the juxtaposition and manipulation of stage properties), *natural sounds* (the artistic integration of stage-activity sounds and speech), and the *spatial disposition* of performance (the means of involvement of audience-spectator with the performance activities)." To explore this concept, Ashley has worked with electronic instruments and film. He has also worked as a research assistant in acoustics and has served as director of the Ann Arbor ONCE (the name implies that they are willing to perform any work in music —of whatever quality—once); in 1969 Ashley was appointed director at the Center for Contemporary Music, Mills College, Oakland, Calif. His "works" include *The Image in Time*, film score (1957), *Piano Sonata* (1959), *The Bottleman*, film score (1960), *The 4th of July*, tape composition (1960), *Maneuvers for Small Hands* for piano (1961), *Something* for clarinet, piano, and tape (1961), *Public Opinion Descends upon the Demonstrators*, for electronics playback and audience (1961), *Detroit Divided*, tape composition (1962), *Heat*, throat sounds and tape (1962), *Trios: White on White* for assorted instruments (1963), *In memoriam . . . Esteban Gomez* for 4 instruments (1963), *In memoriam . . . John Smith*, concerto for any instruments (1963), *Crazy*

Horse, a symphony (1963), *In memoriam . . . Kit Carson*, opera (1963), *Jenny and the Poet*, film score (1964), *The Wolfman*, tape composition (1964), *Kitty Hawk: An Antigravity Piece*, "electronic music theatre" (1964), *Combination Wedding and Funeral*, electronic music theatre (1964), *My May*, film score (1965), *Quartet* for any number of instruments (1965), *She Was a Visitor* for speaker and chorus (1967), *Overdrive*, film score (1968), *The Trial of Anne Opie Wehrer and Unknown Accomplices for Crimes Against Humanity*, electronic music theatre (1968), *Portraits, Self-Portraits, and Still Lifes*, film score (1969), *Illusion Models* for hypothetical computer (1970), *Battery Davis*, film score (1970), *Fancy Free or It's There* for voice and tape (1971), *String Quartet Describing the Motions of Large Real Bodies* for string quartet and electronics (1972), *Revised Finally (April 1961–April 1973)* for percussion (1973), *Night Sport* for voices and electronics (1975), *Title Withdrawn* videotape, voices with electronics (1976), *The Supermarket* for voices, piano, and orchestra (1977), *The Church* for voices, piano, and orchestra (1978), *Interiors Without Flash* on magnetic tape (1978), and *Perfect Lives (Private Parts)*, opera for singer-speakers, piano, organ, and tape (1977–79).

AUSTIN, LARRY (b. 1930) Composer, teacher. Born in Duncan, Okla., Sept. 12, 1930, Austin is a graduate of North Texas State College, Denton; the University of California, Berkeley; and Mills College, Oakland, Calif. Among his teachers were Andrew Imbrie (q.v.), Seymour Shifrin (q.v.), and Darius Milhaud. Austin also spent a few years as a jazz trumpeter and bassist. Upon completion of his musical training, he joined the faculty of the University of California. Berkeley; in 1958 he was appointed professor of music at the University of California, Davis. Austin became a member of the musical staff at the University of Florida, Tampa, in 1972. In 1963 he organized the New Music Ensemble for the performance of contemporary and improvised music. A fellowship, granted in 1964, afforded Austin the opportunity to spend a year in Rome. Austin was one of the founders, as well as editor, of the avant-garde publication *Source* (1967). His work draws upon electronics, Third Stream (q.v.) jazz, and all other avant-garde devices and practices. Among Austin's compositions are a *Woodwind Quartet* (1948), *Woodwind Quintet* (1949), *String Trio* (1952), *Concertino* for flute, trumpet, and strings (1952), *Prosody* for orchestra (1953), *Homecoming*, cantata for soprano and jazz quintet (1959), *Fantasy on a Theme by Berg* for jazz band (1960), *Triptych* for chorus and string quartet (1961), *Improvisations* for orchestra and jazz soloists (1961), *Collage* for chamber group (1963), *Continuum* for from 2 to 7 instruments (1964), *Piano Variations* (1964), *Quartet in Open Style* (1964), *In Memoriam J. F. Kennedy* for band (1964), *Open Style* for piano and orchestra (1965), *The Maze*, theatre piece for projections, tapes, and percussionists (1965), *Accidents* for electronically prepared piano, mirrors, and black lights (1967), *Cyclotron Stew* for cyclotron with tape montage (1967), *The Magicians* for children, tapes, black light, and film (1968), *Piano Set* (1968), *Agape* for soloists, dancers, rock band, tapes, and projections (1970), *Plastic Surgery* for electric piano, percussion, tape, and film (1970), *Heaven Music* for flutes (1975), and *Phantasmagoria* based on themes by Charles Ives for various instrumental combinations (1977).

BABBITT, MILTON (b. 1916) Composer, theoretician, teacher. Born in Philadelphia, Pa., May 10, 1916, Babbitt would seem to belong properly to the previous section. In fact, as a composer and musical thinker, Babbitt belongs to the present and first came into prominence in the 1950s. At about 4, Babbitt began to study the violin and clarinet in Jackson, Miss., where the family was then living. Besides a flair for music, Babbitt also revealed an early interest in mathematics (his father was a math teacher). His academic years were devoted to the study of music and mathematics; his music teachers at New York University were Marion Bauer (q.v.) and Philip James (q.v.). Following his graduation in 1935, Babbitt went to Princeton University, where he worked under Roger Sessions (q.v.). As a graduate student and after acquiring a master's degree, Babbitt taught both music theory and mathematics. Because the music of Schoenberg (q.v.) had made a deep impression on him in his early student days (while he was concentrating on mathematics and logic), Babbitt initially explored the musical paths of serialism and wrote a number of highly technical papers on the subject. The advent of tape recording and the synthesizer opened even more fascinating avenues to Babbitt's analytical mind. Since 1961 he has been one of the directors of the Columbia-Princeton Center for Electronic Music (the others are Otto Luening, Roger Sessions, and Vladimir Ussachevsky, all q.v.). In 1960 Babbitt was appointed professor of music at Princeton; he is also on the staff of the Juilliard School of Music. The author of such articles as "Twelve-Tone Invariants as Compositional Determinants" and "The Synthesis, Perception and Specification of Musical Time," Babbitt actually had a fling in the popular music field in the late '40s, writing and arranging a number of songs and even composing the score for a quite unknown musical, *Fabled Voyage* (1946). As a theorist and teacher, Babbitt is an impor-

tant figure in contemporary American music. Among his student disciples are Eric Salzman, Benjamin Boretz, and Donald Martino (all q.v.). Babbitt's works include *Music for a Mass* (1940), *Three Compositions for Piano* (1947), *Composition for Four Instruments* (1948), *Composition for Twelve Instruments* (1948), *Composition for Viola and Piano* (1948), *The Widow's Lament in Springtime* for soprano and piano (1950), *String Trio* (1951), *Du* for soprano and piano (1951), *Quartet* for flute, oboe, clarinet, and bassoon (1953), *String Quartet No. 1* (1954), *String Quartet No. 2* (1954), *Two Sonnets* for baritone, clarinet, viola, and cello (1955), *Semi-simple Variations* for piano (1956), *All Set,* octet for jazz ensemble (1957), *Partitions* for piano (1957), *Sounds and Words* for voice and piano (1958), *Composition for Tenor and Six Instruments* (1960), *Vision and Prayer* for soprano and tape (1961), *Composition for synthesizer* (1961), *Philomel* for soprano and synthesized tape (1964), *Ensemble* for synthesizer (1964), *Relata I* for orchestra (1965), *Post-Partitions* for piano (1966), *Sextets* for piano and violin (1966), *Correspondences* for strings and tape (1967), *Relata II* for orchestra (1968), *String Quartet No. 3* (1970), *Phonemena* for soprano and piano (1970), *Tableaux* for piano (1973), *Reflections* for piano and tape (1974), *Phonemena* for soprano and tape (1974), *Concerti* for violin, chamber orchestra, and tape (1976), *String Quartet No. 4* (1977), *My Ends Are My Beginnings* (1978), and *Images* for saxophone and tape (1980).

BACH, P. D. Q. See Peter Schickele.

BACHARACH, BURT (b. 1928) Composer, pianist, conductor. Born in Kansas City, Mo., May 12, 1928, Bacharach studied piano as a youngster and began in the music business as a nightclub pianist. He switched to "serious" music and studied with Henry Cowell (q.v.), Bohuslav Martinů, and Darius Milhaud (q.v.) at such schools as the New School for Social Research and the Mannes School of Music, New York City, and the Music Academy of the West, Santa Barbara, Calif. From 1950 to 1952 Bacharach served in the U. S. Army, after which he returned to music as arranger-conductor for popular singer-entertainers—the Ames Brothers, Vic Damone, and Marlene Dietrich. He was also associated with popular singer Dionne Warwick, who introduced and popularized many of his songs. A collaboration with lyricist Hal David (b. 1921) resulted in several popular songs, among them "What the World Needs Now Is Love," "Walk On By," and "Raindrops Keep Fallin' on My Head" (from the film *Butch Cassidy and the Sundance Kid,* 1969). Bacharach has composed several film scores (and title songs to match): *What's New Pussycat?* (1965), *Alfie* (1966), and *Lost Horizon* (1973). His broadway musical *Promises, Promises* (1968), with lyrics by David, ran for more than 1,000 performances in New York and more than 500 in London. One of his more ambitious compositions is entitled *Woman,* a work for piano and symphony orchestra.

BAKER, DAVID (b. 1931) Composer, teacher. Born in Indianapolis, Ind., Dec. 21, 1931, Baker began studying music while in high school, mastered the trombone, and then earned a B.A. and master's degree in music education at the University of Indiana. He taught in Indianapolis public schools before moving on to Indiana Central College, Indianapolis, Lincoln University, Jefferson City, Mo., and then Indiana University, Bloomington, where he was appointed chairman of the Department of Jazz Studies. While in college, Baker played in both jazz and concert orches-

tras. Among the jazz bands in which he played the trombone were those led by Stan Kenton (q.v.), Lionel Hampton, and Quincy Jones, with whom Baker toured Europe in 1961. An accident forced Baker to give up playing in bands in 1966, the year he joined the faculty of Indiana University. Baker's music is replete with the devices of modern jazz, the blues, serial music, and traditional Western symphonic practices. His works include *A Summer's Day in 1945* for jazz ensemble and tape, the cantata *Black America* (1968), *But I Am a Worm* for chorus, jazz ensemble, and strings, *Reflections* for jazz ensemble and orchestra, *The Beatitudes* for narrator, chorus, dancers, and orchestra, *Psalm 22: A Modern Jazz Oratorio, Sonatina for Tuba and String Quartet* (1971), *Sonata* for cello and piano (1974), *Le Chat qui pêche* for soprano, jazz quartet, and orchestra (1974), *Cello Concerto,* and *Contrasts* for piano trio (1976). Baker, a writer and lecturer, has contributed to such publications as *Black Music in Our Culture* (1970) and *Reflections on Afro-American Music.*

"THE BALLAD OF BABY DOE" Douglas Moore's (q.v.) most popular opera, with libretto by John Latouche (1917–1956). The story of the opera is based on true incidents and characters: Horace and Augusta Tabor and Mrs. Elizabeth Doe, the "Baby" of the opera's title. The settings are Leadville and Denver in the Colorado mining country in the late 19th century. Tabor, after years of struggle, has become wealthy through an investment in a silver mine. He has also become a successful banker; Augusta, his wife of many years, finds their affluence difficult to deal with and becomes dour and distant. Tabor spends a good deal of time with his friends in the saloon next to his opera house. Enter Baby Doe, who has left her unsuccessful husband in Central City to seek her fortune in Leadville. She is 30 years younger than Tabor, blond and beautiful. (The real-life Baby Doe was also most attractive and a strong personality; when her husband failed as a miner, she herself went into mining. She was the first woman miner on record in Colorado in the 1880s.) Baby Doe arranges to meet Tabor; they fall in love and eventually marry. Augusta Tabor, shocked (especially after a secretly arranged divorce), swears revenge. Tabor, having become a senator, marries Baby Doe in Washington, D.C., and although Washington society is scandalized by the marriage, their wedding is attended by President Arthur. Tabor's fortune is built on silver—the cause of his collapse after the election of 1896 and the defeat of William Jennings Bryan, the free-silver candidate. Although Augusta, after 10 years of smoldering, has warned Tabor of the coming of a gold standard, he stays with silver—and is wiped out financially. Tabor dies penniless and leaves Baby Doe nothing but the now not very profitable Matchless silver mine. The real Baby Doe lived out her final years as the town eccentric, wearing cast-off miner's clothing, her feet wrapped in gunnysacks, hoping to find investors in her worthless mine. (Her daughter by Tabor, Silver Dollar, had by then become an alcoholic prostitute.) In March 1935 Baby Doe was found frozen to death in her cabin near the mine. It was a news item about this that first interested Moore in writing an opera about Baby Doe. *The Ballad of Baby Doe* was commissioned in honor of the Columbia University Bicentennial by the Serge Koussevitzky Music Foundation in the Library of Congress. Its world premiere was given by the Central City Opera Association, Central City, Colo., July 7, 1956. The New York premiere, by the City Center Opera, occurred on Apr. 3, 1958. In the leading singing roles were Beverly Sills (Baby), Walter Cassel (Tabor), and Frances Bible (Augusta). The orchestra and chorus of the New York City Center Opera was conducted by Emerson Buckley. *The Ballad of Baby Doe* musically presents no problems; it is characterically lyrical and diatonic, as might be expected from Douglas Moore. It has often been called a "folk opera," in the mold of *Porgy and Bess* (q.v.). As such, it is a major contribution to musical Americana.

BARAB, SEYMOUR (b. 1921) Composer, pianist, cellist. Born in Chicago, Ill., Jan. 9, 1921, Barab began his musical career as a young pianist, accompanying vocalists, choral groups, and instrumentalists. At 13 he was the regular organist in a church. In high school he took up the cello and eventually took it up professionally, playing in chamber groups and several major symphony orchestras. Self-taught in composition, Barab has composed more than 200 songs, as well as many theatrical works and instrumental pieces. His compositions include *Chanticleer*, one-act opera (1957), *A Game of Chance*, one-act opera (1958), *Little Red Riding Hood*, for young audiences (1960), *The Pink Siamese*, for young performers (1961), *Fortune's Favorites*, one-act opera (1965), *Tales of Rhyme and Reason* for narrator and orchestra (1968), *Not a Spanish Kiss*, one-act opera (1970), *A Very Special Gift*, for young performers (1975), *String Quartet* (1977), *Little Stories in Tomorrow's Paper*, one-act opera (1977), *The Toy Shop*, for young audiences (1977), *Gage* for narrator and orchestra (1979), and *Quintet* for piano, flute, oboe, clarinet, and bassoon (1980).

BASSETT, LESLIE (b. 1923) Composer, teacher. Born in Hanford, Calif., Jan. 22, 1923, Bassett grew up in Fresno, where he attended the State College. He withdrew during World War II and served overseas with the 13th Armored Division Band as a trombonist. After the war he returned to Fresno State College to complete his education under Homer Keller (q.v.); he had further study in composition with Ross Lee Finney (q.v.) at the University of Michigan, Ann Arbor. He also studied (1950–51) in Paris with Arthur Honegger and Nadia Boulanger (q.v.). He also worked with the Swiss-Spanish composer, and student of Schoenberg, Roberto Gerhard, and with Mario Davidovsky in the field of electronic music. Bassett has been a member of the music faculty of the University of Michigan since 1952. His works include *Suite in G* for orchestra (1946), *Trio* for viola, clarinet, and piano (1953), *Five Pieces* for string quartet (1957), *To Music* for solo voice (1962), *Five Movements* for orchestra (1962), *Variations for Orchestra* (1963; Pulitzer Prize), *Designs, Images, and Textures* for band (1964), *Three Studies in Electronic Sounds* (1965), *Elaborations* for piano (1966), *Notes in Silence* for chorus and piano (1966), *Music for Cello and Piano* (1966), *Nonet* for piano and wind instruments (1967), *Colloquy* for orchestra (1968), *Music for Saxophone and Piano* (1968), *Collect* for choir and tape (1969), *Sextet* for piano and strings (1972), *Sounds Remembered* for violin and piano (1975), *Echoes from an Invisible World* for orchestra (1975), and *Wind Music* for 6 wind instruments (1976).

BAZELON, IRWIN (b. 1922) Composer. Born in Chicago, Ill., June 4, 1922, Bazelon graduated from DePaul University, Chicago, in 1945. He continued his study of music with Darius Milhaud (q.v.) at Mills College, Oakland, Calif., and Ernest Bloch (q.v.) at the University of California, Berkeley. In 1948 Bazelon settled in New York City to make a living as a composer; his work ranges from abstract concert and recital compositions to scores for documentary films and television. Among his compositions are *Suite* for clarinet, cello, and piano (1947), *Ballet Suite* (1949), *Concert Overture* for orchestra (1952), *Movimento da Camera* for flute, bassoon, horn, and harpsichord (1954), *Adagio and Fugue* for strings (1956), *Suite* for chamber orchestra (1956), *Chamber Symphony* for septet (1957), *Symphony No. 1* (1960), *Short Symphony: Testament to a Big City* (1962), *Symphony No. 3* (1963), *Duo* for viola and piano (1963), *Brass Quintet* (1963), *Symphony No. 4* (1965), *Fusions* for orchestra (1965), *Excursions* for orchestra (1966), *Symphony No. 5* (1967), *Chamber Concerto,* "Churchill Downs" (1970), *Symphony No. 6* (1970), *Propulsions* for percussion (1974), *Wind Quintet* (1975), *Sound Dreams* for flute, clarinet, viola, cello, bass, and percussion (1978), *Junctures* for orchestra (1979), *De-Tonations,* concerto for brass quintet and orchestra (1979), *Partnership* for 5 timpani, one player, and marimba (1980), and *Seventh Symphony,* ballet for orchestra (1980). Bazelon has also composed incidental music for the American Shakespeare Festival Theatre's productions of *The Merry Wives of Windsor* (1958) and *The Taming of the Shrew* (1959), at Stratford, Conn. He provided the score for the Jules Dassin documentary film *Survival 1967* and the television version of *What Makes Sammy Run?* (1959). Bazelon is the author of *Knowing the Score: Notes on Film Music* (1975).

THE BEATLES Phenomenally successful and influential British rock group: Paul McCartney (b. 1942), John Lennon (1940–1980), George Harrison (b. 1943), and Ringo Starr (b. 1940, real name Richard Starkey). All were born in Liverpool, England. After performing with other bands in Liverpool and Hamburg, Germany, in the late '50s, and under various group names, the Beatles were formed in 1960 (although Starr was not yet the drummer). The greatest influences on the Beatles were such white blues inspired performers as Bill Haley, whose recordings began appearing on British hit record charts ca. 1955 ("Shake, Rattle and Roll" and "Rock Around the Clock"), and Elvis Presley, whose "Heartbreak Hotel" was popular in Britain in 1956. Other influences were Buddy Holly and Bob Dylan. Eventually the Beatles evolved a distinctive style of their own and began composing their own songs, mostly by McCartney and Lennon. The Beatles began recording in England in 1962, but these recordings were not released in America at the time. By 1963 what came to be called "Beatlemania" was rife in Britain among the young. In February 1964 the Beatles came to the United States to promote the release of their first American-issued disc, "I Want to Hold Your Hand." Beatlemania soon came to the United States and their single recordings made the charts, their long-playing album *Meet the Beatles* became a best seller, and their remarkable, imaginative, film *A Hard Day's Night* was a critical as well as an audience success. From their first appearance on the American scene until their dissolution in 1970, the Beatles were a dominating force in American popular music; each successive album introduced new ideas and was unusually popular. Imitators sprung up —the television group the Monkees was an out-and-out clone job—and spread the youth hysteria in rock. Beatles songs represented the point of view of youth questioning the values of the older generations. The songs, many of them beautifully formed and with poetic, often trenchant lyrics ("Eleanor Rigby," for example) treated several controversial subjects: drugs, estrangement between children and parents, aging, war and peace, Eastern religion, and sex. Personal differences and separate ambitions led to the breakup of the Beatles (all of whom, by 1970, were financially comfortable) and each went his separate way. Although one or another recorded new albums, they did not equal individually what had been accomplished as a unit. But their impression on American and British popular music during the '60s was considerable.

BEESON, JACK (b. 1921) Composer, teacher. Born in Muncie, Ind., July 15, 1921, Beeson began studying music theory and piano at the University of Toronto at the age of 17. From 1939 to 1944 he was enrolled at the Eastman School of Music, Rochester, N.Y., where he studied under Howard Hanson (q.v.) and Bernard Rogers (q.v.). He also took courses in musicology at Columbia University, New York, where he met the Hungarian composer Béla Bartók, then working on the Milman Parry collection of Serbo-Croatian folk songs. Although Bartók refused to accept composition students, Beeson managed to study informally with him for the year preceding the Hungarian composer's death in 1945. Beeson joined Columbia's musical staff in 1945 and was appointed MacDowell Professor of Music. He has also worked with the Columbia Opera Workshop and has taught at the Juilliard School of Music, New York. Beeson's particular interest, since he was a boy, has been opera, although he has also composed several instrumental works, among them several piano sonatas (the 5th dates from 1946), songs, and choral pieces. His compositions include the opera *Jonah* (1950), *Hello, Out There,* opera (1953), *Two Diversions* for piano (1953), *The Sweet Bye and Bye,* opera (1956), *Sketches in Black and White* for piano (1958), *Symphony No. 1 in A* (1959), *Transformations* for orchestra (1959), *Commemoration* for band

(1960), *Fanfare* for brass, winds, and percussion (1963), *Lizzie Borden,* opera (1965), *My Heart's in the Highlands,* opera for television (1970), and *Captain Jinks of the Horse Marines* (1975).

BOCK, JERRY See Bock and Harnick.

BOCK AND HARNICK Successful Broadway songwriting team: Jerry Bock (b. New Haven, Conn., Nov. 23, 1928) and Sheldon Harnick (b. Chicago, Ill., Apr. 30, 1924). Bock and Harnick had been going their separate ways in the musical theatre during the mid '50s before they were united to do the songs for the 1958 musical *The Body Beautiful.* Harnick was around this time best known as the composer-lyricist of "The Boston Beguine," which had first been heard in *New Faces of 1952;* Bock, among other credits, had done a complete score, *Mr. Wonderful,* in 1956, in collaboration with Larry Holofcener and George Weiss. Upon the advice of E. Y. Harburg, the great lyricist, Harnick sought a composer, who turned out to be Bock; they were introduced in a bar by vocalist Jack Cassidy in the spring of 1956. Although *The Body Beautiful* had not been too well received, many of its songs were admired by influential theatre people, among them producer-director George Abbott. The result was the score for the second Bock-Harnick effort, *Fiorello!* (1959), which won a Pulitzer Prize for the new songwriting team. They collaborated on several musicals, almost all notable for a period flavor or a sense of place. *Fiorello!,* a musical celebrating the times and personality of a former mayor of New York City, Fiorello La Guardia, had songs such as " 'Til Tomorrow," and "When Did I Fall in Love?" that brought out the more innocent quality of pre–World War I New York. There was also pointed political commentary in "Little Tin Box" and "Politics and Poker." *Tenderloin* (1960), also a period musical with a New York

City setting, which centered on the antivice campaign of a crusading minister, did not do as well. *She Loves Me* (1963) was set in Budapest and is graced by one of the team's finest scores (the songs are truly integrated with plot), although its run of just over 300 performances eliminates it from the Broadway success category. A television production in 1979 underscored its charm and quality. Among its outstanding songs are "Tonight at Eight," "Ilona," "Ice Cream," "She Loves Me," "Romantic Atmosphere," and "Will He Like Me?" This operalike work was followed by Bock and Harnick's most successful musical, *Fiddler on the Roof* (1964): "Sunrise, Sunset," "Matchmaker, Matchmaker," "If I Were a Rich Man," etc. Again the time and place were a departure: czarist Russia and a Jewish village. *Fiddler on the Roof,* starring Zero Mostel during most of its first year, ran for more than 3,000 performances. Bock and Harnick followed that success with an experimental 3-part revuelike show, *The Apple Tree* (1966), a musical setting of 3 stories, Mark Twain's "Adam and Eve," Frank Stockton's "The Lady or the Tiger?" and Jules Feiffer's "Passionella." In 1970 Bock and Harnick took on the subject of banking in *The Rothschilds.* Harnick has also worked with composer David Baker on *Smiling the Boy Fell Dead* (1961), with Jack Beeson (q.v.) on *Captain Jinks of the Horse Marines* (1975), and with Richard Rodgers (q.v.) on *Rex* (1976).

BOLCOM, WILLIAM (b. 1938) Composer, pianist, teacher. Born in Seattle, Wash., May 26, 1938, Bolcom was 11 when he was enrolled in the University of Washington's School of Music. His teachers in composition were John Verrall (q.v.) and George Frederick McKay (q.v.); he studied piano with Berthe Jacobson. Further work was done under Darius Milhaud (q.v.) at Mills College, Oakland, Calif. He studied also with Milhaud in Paris, where he studied with Olivier Messiaen and Jean Rivier as well. Upon his return to the United States, Bolcom enrolled in Stanford University (Calif.) to study with Leland Smith. He was graduated from Stanford in 1964 with a doctorate in music. He has since taught at the University of Washington; Queens College, New York City; and the University of Michigan, Ann Arbor. Bolcom's musical materials range from the most advanced contemporary devices to popular song and ragtime. With his wife, Joan Morris, he has performed and recorded dozens of the songs of the "Gay Nineties" and from musicals of the '20s and '30s, as well as, on his own, the rags of Joplin and the piano works of Gershwin. His original compositions include several string quartets (No. 8 completed in 1965), *Décalage* for cello and piano (1962), *Octet* (1962), *Fantasy-Sonata* for piano (1962), *Dynamite Tonite*, opera (1963), *Twelve Etudes* (1966), *Session 2* for violin and viola (1966), *Fives* for violin, piano, and strings (1966), *Black Host* for organ and percussion (1967), *Session 4* for assorted instruments, including harp, piano, percussion, and tape (1967), *Dream Music No. 2* for percussion (1967), *Fourteen Piano Rags* (1970), *Dark Music* for cello and tympani (1970), *Commedia* (1971), *Whisper Moon* for chamber orchestra (1971), *Frescoes* for 2 pianos, harmonium, and harpsichord (1971), *Open House*, song cycle with chamber orchestra (1975), and *Seasons* for guitar (1976). Bolcom is co-author, with Robert Kimball, of *Reminiscing with Sissle and Blake* (1973).

BORETZ, BENJAMIN (b. 1934) Composer, critic, editor. Born in New York City, Oct. 3, 1934, Boretz was a student of Irving Fine (q.v.), Darius Milhaud (q.v.), Roger Sessions (q.v.), and Milton Babbitt (q.v.); he studied at Brooklyn College, New York, Brandeis University, Waltham, Mass., and Princeton University. As a composer, Boretz might be classified with the Babbitt-Princeton group, whose works are accompanied by recondite explanations, theories, and curious sounds. Boretz has taught at New York University and Columbia and has produced much critical writing, primarily as a reviewer for *The Nation*, and for the periodical *Perspectives of New Music* since 1962. Among his compositions are *Concerto Grosso* for chamber orchestra (1955), *Divertimento* for chamber orchestra (1955), *Partita* for piano (1955), *Violin Concerto* (1957), *String Quartet* (1958), *John Donne Songs* for soprano and piano (1961), *Brass Quintet* (1963), *Group Variations I* for chamber group (1967), and *Group Variations II* for computerized tape (1970). With Edward T. Cone (q.v.), Boretz is co-editor of *Perspectives on American Composers* and *Perspectives on Contemporary Music Theory*.

BROWN, EARLE (b. 1926) Composer, theorist, teacher. Born in Lunenburg, Mass., Dec. 26, 1926, Brown majored in engineering and mathematics at Northeastern University, Boston. In 1947 he switched to music and studied with Roslyn B. Henning at the Schillinger House School of Music, Boston; his subjects with her were composition and counterpoint. Brown took further work in composition and orchestration, still within the Schillinger techniques, with Kenneth McKillop (1946–50). From 1950 to 1952 he taught the Schillinger System of Musical Composition in Denver, after which he settled in New York City and became associated with John Cage (q.v.) and others in the avant-garde. Brown has also worked as an engineer with Capitol Records; he was the producer (1955–60) for Time Records' "Contemporary Sound Series" of advanced contemporary music. He has been composer-in-residence at the Peabody Conservatory (1968–70). Not only has Brown employed the Schillinger System in his work, he has also drawn upon 12-tone techniques and tape. He has been influenced by abstract art and sculpture and has devised musical works that are not conventionally notated. A complete "work" by Brown, such as his *December 1952*, appears on a single page as a number of horizontal and vertical lines of varying lengths, widths, and thicknesses (such a page has been compared by H. Wiley Hitchcock to a drawing by Mondrian). The musicians, who are instructed to approach the work from any one of its 4 sides, use the lines as a guide to their performance. This has been called "open form" composition. Another characteristic Brown composition, *Available Forms II*, calls for 2 conductors, leading 2 orchestras, neither of whom knows what portion of the work the other will select in what sequence. Brown has written that he was much influenced by the paintings of Jackson Pollock: "I was very much moved by the life, energy, and immediacy of his work, and thought that these qualities should be in music." The mobile sculptures of Alexander Calder, too, had much the same effect on the composer. Among Brown's compositions are *Three Pieces for Piano* (1951), *Perspectives* for piano (1952), *Music for Violin, Cello, and Piano* (1952), *Folio: November 1952, December 1952, December 1953* (1953), *25 Pages* for piano or pianos, up to 25 (1953), *Four Systems* for amplified cymbals (1954), *Pentathis* for 9 instruments (1957), *Available Forms I* for 18 musicians (1961), *Light Music* (1961), *Available Forms II* for 98 musicians, 2 conductors (1962), *Novara* for flute, bass clarinet, trumpet, piano, 2 violins, viola, and cello (1962),

From Here for an orchestra of 20 and 4 optional choruses (1963), *Corroboree* for 3 pianos (1964), *String Quartet* (1965), *Nine Rarebits* for one or 2 harpsichords (1965), *Event: Synergy II* for chamber orchestra (1968), *Syntagm III,* octet (1970), *New Piece* for orchestra (1971), *Time Spans* for orchestra (1972), *Sign Sounds* for chamber orchestra (1972), *Centering* for violin and chamber group (1973), and *Cross Sections and Color Fields* for orchestra (1975).

BRUBECK, DAVE (b. 1920) Pianist, bandleader. Born in Concord, Calif., Dec. 6, 1920, Brubeck was raised in a musical family. His mother was a pianist (his first teacher) and 2 brothers were music teachers. An older brother, Howard (b. 1916), is a composer and teacher. Brubeck learned the piano and cello as a boy and, by age 13, played in local bands. When he attended the University of the Pacific, Stockton, Calif., he led his own orchestra (1941–42). He also attended Mills College, Oakland, Calif., and studied with Darius Milhaud (q.v.). He also studied privately with Arnold Schoenberg (q.v.). During some of that period, Brubeck served in the U. S. Army. In 1944 he was leader of his own service band in Europe. After leaving the Army, Brubeck again took up studies with Milhaud and Fred Saatman (piano). In 1949 he formed an octet that performed avant-garde jazz, but with little success; it dwindled to a trio, but finally hit its stride with the formation of the Dave Brubeck Quartet in 1951. An outstanding member of that quartet was alto saxophonist Paul Desmond (b. 1924). The Brubeck Quartet enjoyed great popularity during the '50s, making numerous recordings and winning jazz publication (*Down Beat* and *Metronome*) polls. The Quartet's performance style combined improvisation with references to the classics flavored with modern jazz. The group flourished in the '50s and remained active in the '60s, although Desmond left from time to time—usually to be replaced by baritone saxophonist Gerry Mulligan (b. 1927). In the '60s the Quartet toured Europe with Brubeck serving as pianist-leader-lecturer. In the '70s the group consisted of Brubeck and his sons, Chris, Daniel, and Darius. Besides arranging, Brubeck has done some composing; one of his works, an oratorio, *Truth Has Fallen,* was written in 1971.

BUCCI, MARK (b. 1924) Composer. Born in New York City, Feb. 26, 1924, Bucci grew up in a family of musicians with a predisposition for the theatre. He began studying at St. John's University, Brooklyn, then studied privately with Tibor Serly (q.v.) from 1944 to 1946. At the Juilliard School his teachers were Frederick Jacobi (q.v.) and Vittorio Giannini (q.v.), 1947–51. He studied with Aaron Copland (q.v.) at Tanglewood, Mass., in the summer of 1949. Bucci has demonstrated a remarkable affinity for vocal music, although he has also written for instruments. His compositions include *The Boor,* one-act opera (1949), *The Thirteen Clocks,* musical (1952), *The Dress,* one-act opera (1953), *Sweet Betsy from Pike,* a horse opera (1953), *Tale for a Deaf Ear,* one-act opera (1957), *Concerto for a Singing Instrument* for any voice or instrument and chamber orchestra (1959; at the premiere hearing the singing instrument was a kazoo "played" by vocalist Anita Darian), *The Wondrous Kingdom* for chorus (1962), *The Hero,* one-act opera for television (1965), *A Time to Play,* film score (1967), *The Wondrous Kingdom* for chorus (1968), *The Mouse That Roared,* a musical (1969), *I Wish I Were a Trumpet,* musical play for mixed media (1969), *Echo of a Massacre,* film score (1972), *Second Coming,* rock musical with S. Akerman (1973), *Joining/Departures/Arrival,* 3 rock celebrations for chorus (1974), and *No Way Out,* film score (1980). Bucci has also written plays, among them *Days on End* (1960), and adaptations: *Two Angels on Duty* (L. Wibberley, 1967), *Diary of Adam and Eve* (Mark Twain, 1972), and *The Court of Stone Children* (1978). His screenplays include *Time and Again,* written with Donna Jones (1962), *The Fastest Curlin' Iron in the West,* with Rod Arrants (1970), and *Love Me Till Death* (1972).

CHAMBERS, STEPHEN A. (b. 1940) See Talib Rasul Hakim.

"CHANCE MUSIC" Compositions in which the composer provides suggestions and the performers decide which music they will play when. Also called "aleatory" music, from the Latin words for gambler and dice. Neither composer, instrumentalist, nor audience knows quite what the result will be. In other words, chance music is experimental in the sense that John Cage (q.v.), one of its leaders, has defined it: "An experimental action is one the outcome of which is unforeseen." "Indeterminacy" is another term applied. Among the practitioners of chance music, besides the pioneer Cage, are Morton Feldman, Christian Wolff, Earle Brown, and Robert Ashley (all q.v.). The general philosophy of chance music is that all sound and even silence are admissible ingredients of the performance, which in itself is chancy, improvisatory. A generally anti-Establishment movement, the chance-music philosophy engenders the idea that all music aesthetically is as valuable as any other; i.e., there are no masterpieces or classics in the traditional sense. The movement has also brought a revolution to the Western system of musical notation; chance-music notation ranges from instructions on cards or a page covered with various lines to verbal coaching before the "happening." The sight and sound of chance music presents a problem to the listener educated in the traditional music of the concert hall.

CHARNIN, MARTIN (b. 1934) Lyricist, director, television producer. Born in New York City, Nov. 24, 1934, Charnin first worked on Broadway, and off, in revues and musicals, most notably in the cast of *West Side Story* (q.v.) in the singing role of "Big Deal" in 1957. Soon after, he began contributing lyrics to songs interpolated into revues. His first major collaboration was with Mary Rodgers (the daughter of Richard) on the songs for *Hot Spot* (1963). The following year Charnin joined Harold Arlen (q.v.) to write the songs for a musical, *Softly,* for which some 2 dozen songs were completed, although the show itself never was. One song from that score has been performed a little; its title: "I Could Be Good for You." Arlen and Charnin collaborated on another song, "That's a Fine Kind o' Freedom," which was recorded by the composer for Columbia Records (1965). Before returning to Broadway, Charnin spent some time in television production; among the shows were tributes to Arlen and the Gershwins and the award-winning "Annie, the Women in the Life of a Man" starring Anne Bancroft in 1970. The same year saw the production of *Two by Two,* with music by Richard Rodgers. Charnin then joined composer Charles Strouse (q.v.) to do the songs for the hugely successful *Annie.* He and Rodgers produced the songs for the not successful *I Remember Mama* (1979).

CHIHARA, PAUL SEIKO (b. 1938) Composer, teacher. Born in Seattle, Wash., July 9, 1938, Chihara started in music as a boy on the violin. He is also a violist. Chihara majored in English literature and music and has degrees in both. His schools include the University of Washington, Seattle, and Cornell Univer-

sity, Ithaca, N.Y., where he was a student in composition with Robert Palmer (q.v.). Under a Fulbright Fellowship he studied with Nadia Boulanger (q.v.); he also worked with Ernst Pepping at the Berlin Hochschule für Musik. Upon his return to the United States in 1966, Chihara became a student of Gunther Schuller (q.v.) for 3 summers at Tanglewood, Mass. Chihara has taught at the California Institute of the Arts, Valencia, and at the University of California, Los Angeles. His compositions include *Viola Concerto* (1963), *Tree Music* for sextet of violas and trombones (1966), *Branches* for bassoons and percussion (1966), *Magnificat* for high voices (1966), *The 90th Psalm,* cantata (1966), *Nocturne* for chorus (1966), *Redwood* for viola and percussion (1967), *Willow, Willow* for flute, tuba, and percussion (1968), *Rain Music* for tape (1968), *Forest Music* for orchestra (1968), *Driftwood* for violin, 2 violas, and cello (1969), *Logs XVI* for string bass and tape (1970), *Ceremony I* for oboe, 2 cellos, contrabass, and percussion (1971), *Windsong* for cello and orchestra (1971), *Ceremony II* for flute, 2 cellos, and percussion (1972), *Grass* for double bass and orchestra (1972), *Ceremony III* for small orchestra (1973), *Ceremony IV* for large orchestra (1974), *Ceremony V: Symphony in Celebration* for orchestra (1975), *Missa Carminum,* "Folk Song Mass," for chorus (1976), and *String Quartet,* "Primavera" (1978).

CHILDS, BARNEY (b. 1926) Composer, teacher. Born in Spokane, Wash., Feb. 13, 1926, Childs, though fascinated by music from an early age, did not begin formal music study until he was in his mid twenties. His early education was in English literature, and he earned a master's degree as a Rhodes scholar at Oxford University, England (1955). At Stanford University, Calif., Childs studied both English and music. His first music teacher was Leonard Ratner, with whom he studied (1952–53). (Even before, however, Childs had begun composing on his own.) He also worked with Aaron Copland (q.v.), Carlos Chávez, and Elliott Carter (q.v.). Childs has taught English at the University of Arizona, Tucson, and English and music at Deep Springs College, Nev., where he was also dean (1965–69). From 1969 to 1971 he taught theory at the Wisconsin College Conservatory, Milwaukee. Childs's early compositions reflect the influence of his teacher Chávez and other modernists. In the '60s he began experimenting with the practice of indeterminacy, "chance music" (q.v.). His works include *Sonata* for clarinet (1951), *Trio* for flute, oboe, and clarinet (1952), *Sonata* for bassoon (1953), *Quartet* for clarinet and strings (1953), *Symphony No. 1* (1954), *Bass Quintet* (1954), *Four Involutions* for English horn (1955), *Five Considerations* for French horn (1955), *Seven Epigrams* for soprano and clarinet (1955), *Concerto for English Horn, Strings, Harp, and Percussion* (1955), *Symphony No. 2* (1956), *Sonata for Violin, No. 2* (1956), *Septet* for instruments and voices (1958), *Bassoon Quartet* (1958), *Trio* for brass (1959), *Flute Sonata* (1960), *Sonata* for solo trombone (1961), *Welcome to Whipperginny* for percussion (1961), *Interbalances IV* for trumpet and speaker (1962), *Music* for 2 flutes (1963), *Stances* for flute (1963), *Quartet* for flute, oboe, double bass, and percussion (1964), *Music for Double Bass and Friend* (1964), *Six Events* for band (1965), *Music* for piano and strings (1965), *Jack's New Bag* for 10 instruments (1966), *The Golden Bubble* for contrabass, sarrusophone, and percussion (1967), *The Bayonne Barrel and Drum Company* for solo wind and chamber group (1968), *Operation Flabby Sleep* for any instruments (1968), *Music* for 6 tubas (1969), *Keet Seel* for chorus (1970), *Clarinet Concerto* (1970), *When Lilacs Last in the Dooryard Bloom'd* for soloists, chorus, and band (1970), and *Trio* for clarinet, cello, and piano (1972).

CHOU WEN-CHUNG (b. 1923) Composer, teacher. Born in Chefoo, China, June 29, 1923, Chou came to the United States in 1946. He went to the New England Conservatory of Music, Boston, where he studied under Nicolas Slonimsky (q.v.) and Carl McKinley (q.v.); at Columbia University he was a student of Otto Luening (q.v.). Other musical mentors included Bohuslav Martinů and Edgard Varèse (q.v.). Chou was awarded a master's degree in music in 1954. He has taught at Brooklyn College and Hunter College, New York City, has been composer-in-residence at the University of Illinois, Urbana, and was the recipient of several awards, a Guggenheim Fellowship (1957–58), a Rockefeller Foundation Grant, and other honors. In his composition, Chou has drawn upon the theories of his teacher Varèse and the music of the land of his birth. Virgil Thomson has summarized Chou's work as "Impressionist music of strong Chinese flavor, imaginative, poetic and deliciously scored." His compositions include *Landscapes* for orchestra (1949), *Suite* for harp and wind quintet (1951), *Seven Poems of the T'ang Dynasty* for tenor, winds, piano, and percussion (1952), *All in the Spring Wind* for orchestra (1953), *And the Fallen Petals* for orchestra (1954), *Two Miniatures from the T'ang Dynasty* for chamber group (1957), *The Willows Are New* for piano (1957), *In the Mode of Shang* for chamber orchestra (1957), *To a Wayfarer* for clarinet and strings (1958), *Soliloquy of a Bhiksuni* for trumpet, brass, and percussion (1958), *Metaphors* for winds (1961), *Cursive* for flute and piano (1963), *Riding the*

Wind for wind orchestra (1964), *The Dark and the Light* for piano, strings, and percussion (1964), *Yu Ko* for chamber group (1965), *Pien* for piano, winds, and percussion (1966), and *Yun* for 2 pianos, winds, and percussion (1969).

COATES, GLORIA (b. 1938) Composer, vocalist, teacher, author. Born in Wausau, Wis., Oct. 10, 1938, Coates began composing at the age of 12. A student of art and theatre as well as music, she attended Columbia University and Cooper Union Art School, New York City, Louisiana State University, Baton Rouge, and the Mozarteum, Salzburg, Austria. Her teachers in composition included Alexander Tcherepnin, Otto Luening (q.v.), and Jack Beeson (q.v.). Dividing her time between the cities of Munich, London, and New York, she has had her compositions performed widely throughout the United States and Europe. Her works include *Five Abstractions* for piano (1962), *Mathematical Problems* for soprano and piano (1962), *Overture to "St. Joan"* for organ, timpani, and tape (1963), *Mass* for treble voices and organ (1964), *Trio for Three Flutes* (1966), *First String Quartet* (1967), *Five Poems of Emily Dickinson* for voice and piano (1972), *Eine Stimme ruft elektronische Klang auf* for live electronic, modulator, voice, and laser (1972), *Second String Quartet* (1972), *Structures* for piano (1972), *Natural Voice and Electronic Sound* for live electronics and voice (1973), *Voices of Women in Wartime* for soprano and chamber ensemble (1973), *Fantasy on "How Lovely Shines the Morning Star"* for organ and electronic viola (1973), *Variations on "Lo How a Rose"* for organ, viola, and violin (1973), *Music for Open Strings* for string orchestra (1973–74), *Planets* for orchestra (1974), *Five Abstractions from Poems of Emily Dickinson* for woodwind quar-

tet (1975), *Spring Morning at Grobholz* for 3 flutes and tape (1975), *Third String Quartet* (1976), *Fourth String Quartet* (1977), *We Have Ears and Hear Not* for string quartet and chamber soloists (1978), *Leonardo da Vinci,* oratorio for soloists, chorus, and orchestra (1979), *The Beatitudes* for 6-part chorus and organ (1979), and *Nonet* for flute, oboe, bassoon, 2 violins, viola, cello, and bass horn (1980).

COLEMAN, CY (b. 1929) Composer, pianist. Born in New York City, June 14, 1929, Coleman is a graduate of the High School of Music and Art, New York, and the New York College of Music. His major teachers in music were Adele Marcus and Rudolph Gruen. A prodigy, Coleman made his debut as a pianist at the age of 6. Initially, he was best known as a pianist, led his own trio, and made several recordings. He also composed a number of songs, including the popular "Witchcraft." Coleman made his Broadway debut with the score for *Wildcat* (1960), with lyrics by Carolyn Leigh (b. 1926). The show starred television queen Lucille Ball and had a good song in "Hey, Look Me Over." Coleman and Leigh collaborated again in 1962 on the songs for *Little Me,* among them "Real Live Girl" and "I've Got Your Number." Coleman then did 2 fine scores with lyricist Dorothy Fields: *Sweet Charity* (1966) and *Seesaw* (1973). Among the songs from the former were "Big Spender," "There's Gotta Be Something Better Than This," and the superb "Where Am I Going?" From *Seesaw* came "Welcome to the Holiday Inn," "He's Good for Me," and "We've Got It." Coleman teamed with librettist-lyricist Michael Stewart (b. 1929) on the award-winning *I Love My Wife* (1977), a musical about wife-swapping. The songs had such titles as "Married Couple Seeks Married Couple," "We're Still Friends," "Sexually

Free," and "Hey There, Good Times." Coleman's next successful project brought him together with Betty Comden and Adolph Green (q.v.) for the score of *On the Twentieth Century* (1978). The songs were finely woven into the zany tale of a far from honest producer and the young woman he had made into a star. Among the songs were "Stranded Again," "Veronique," "Our Private World," "Five Zeros," and "She's a Nut." Coleman has also composed film background scores: *The Troublemaker, The Art of Love,* and *Father Goose.* His musical *Barnum* (lyrics by Michael Stewart) was produced in 1980.

COLGRASS, MICHAEL (b. 1932) Composer, percussionist, conductor. Born in Chicago, Ill., Apr. 22, 1932, Colgrass was graduated from the University of Illinois in 1954. He studied composition with Eugene Weigel and percussion with Paul Price. He also studied with Lukas Foss (q.v.), Darius Milhaud (q.v.), Wallingford Riegger (q.v.), and Ben Weber (q.v.). In addition to composing and conducting, Colgrass has been active as a percussionist in virtually every type of band and orchestra from jazz to opera. He has also written scripts for the theatre and poetry. His compositions include *Three Brothers* for percussion (1950), *Percussion Music* (1953), *Chamber Music* for 4 drums and string quartet (1953), *Quintet for Percussion* (1954), *Inventions on a Motive* for percussion quartet (1955), *Variations* for viola and percussion quartet (1957), *Divertimento* for piano, strings, and percussion (1960), *Fantasy-Variations* for percussion (1961), *Wind Quintet* (1962), *Rhapsody* for clarinet, violin, and piano (1962), *Light Spirit* for flute, viola, guitar, and percussion (1963), *Rhapsodic Fantasy* for percussion (1965), *As Quiet As* for orchestra (1966), *Sea Shadow,* ballet, for orchestra (1965), *Virgil's Dream* for actor-singer and mime-musi-

cians (1967), *The Earth's a Baked Apple* for chorus and orchestra (1968), *New People* for mezzo-soprano, viola, and piano (1969), *Letter from Mozart* for piano and orchestra (1976), *Best Wishes* for soloists, double chorus, jazz band, and orchestra (1976), *Concertmasters* for 3 violins and orchestra (1976), and *Déjà vu* for 4 percussionists and orchestra (1978; Pulitzer Prize).

COMPUTER MUSIC Compositions devised by or for computer performance. In the former instance, the "composer" employs a computer to solve the problems of the composition; he feeds the machine a set of instructions (based on selected musical practices), and the computer prints out the resolution, determining the tones, their duration, and their combination. This resolution could then be notated and performed by a conventional musical group. An example of such a computer-composed work is Lejaren Hiller's (q.v.) *Illiac Suite* (1957). The computer selected the materials from Hiller's information and provided him with the stuff of his intended composition. This was then transcribed onto music paper and scored for a string quartet. It might be mentioned that the Illiac computer (from Illinois Accumulator) made a random selection of possibilities. Hiller did not edit, or change, the work of the computer, and the result may confuse the listener accustomed to standard musical fare. Hiller and others who followed him in this field have refined the process, as in his *Computer Cantata* for voice, instruments, and electronic tape (1963). Since work was begun in this field, also, computers that produce sound instead of merely data have evolved and serve as instruments; Hiller's *Cantata* draws upon computer-derived data and is performed in part by a sound-producing computer. Research in computer composition is continuing. With computers, it is possible to analyze musical practices of other times, even the style of an individual composer. Computers, too, are capable of producing rhythms far beyond the grasp of the most skilled virtuoso; computers can also produce microtones with absolute precision. Other American composers working with computers are Charles Dodge, Gerald Strang (q.v.), and a handful of others. Computer music is not the same as music composed electronically on tape or by synthesizer. A word frequently encountered in explanations of computer music is "stochastic." For example, in writing about Hiller's *Algorithms I* (1968), the annotator states: "The first movement of *Algorithms I* is stochastic music in which melodic lines become more dependent upon previous pitch and rhythm choices." The term has been borrowed from statistics and implies that any tone has an equal probability of being selected. Stochastic music merely means that the computer, having been given certain information, selects at random those elements that fulfill the "composer's" intentions according to his predetermined ideas.

COOL JAZZ Jazz performance that evolved out of the bebop (q.v.) school that came to the fore after World War II. Bop's masters, Charles "Yardbird" Parker (q.v.), Lester Young, and Dizzy Gillespie (q.v.), produced a music characterized by dissonance, polyrhythms, and choppy musical phrases. Although the beat was steady, the music that resulted was definitely not for dancing. The practitioners were extraordinarily skilled, but seemed to play for each other. Young, especially, performed on his saxophone in what sounded like a detached—cool—manner. The excitement, bustle, and clamor of "hot" jazz was supplanted by the offhand, quiet, subtle beat of cool jazz. In the late '40s a band lead by trumpeter Miles Davis (q.v.) specialized in cool jazz and made several now-classic recordings. He in turn influenced what came to be called the West Coast Jazz group, most of whose members were white: Shorty Rogers, Gerry Mulligan, Chet Baker, and Jimmy Giuffre. The movement pretty much ran its course by the mid '50s, when jazzmen, especially black jazzmen, turned away from the understated cool jazz and returned to the blues and spirituals for inspiration; this initiated the era of so-called hard bop and of "soul" jazz (with its roots in gospel song). Among the masters in this new wave were Thelonious Monk (q.v.), John Coltrane, and Cannonball Adderley.

COOLIDGE, PEGGY STUART (b. 1913) Composer, pianist. Born in Swampscott, Mass., July 19, 1913, as Peggy Stuart, Coolidge began piano lessons at the age of 5 and composed her first work, a song, at 9. She later studied piano with Heinrich Gebhard and composition with Raymond Robinson and Quincy Porter (q.v.). Most of her early compositions were written for the piano, and she herself considered a career as a concert pianist. In 1937 she was commissioned to write the score for a skating ballet, *Cracked Ice,* which was orchestrated by Ferde Grofé (q.v.). The work was performed by the Boston Pops Orchestra under Arthur Fiedler (q.v.), who commissioned Stuart (not yet Mrs. Coolidge) to compose pieces for the Pops. She proceeded to study orchestration and produced little orchestral pieces with such titles as *The Island, Night Froth, Smoke Drift,* and *Twilight City.* During World War II, Stuart conducted and served as pianist in the Women's Symphony, Boston; she also played for hospitalized servicemen and assisted soldiers and sailors visiting Boston to find housing, etc. After the war, a resident of New York City, Coolidge continued to work in the field of music therapy. Her works include the background score for the film *The Silken Affair* (1957), *Dublin Town*, orchestral suite (1963), *An Evening in New Orleans*, ballet (1965), *Rhapsody* for harp and orchestra (1965), *Spirituals in Sunshine and Shadow* (1969), *Pioneer Dances* for orchestra (1970), *New England Autumn* for orchestra (1971), *The Blue Planet*, with a text by Joseph R. Coolidge, for narrator and orchestra (1975), *American Mosaic* for winds (1978), *Lullaby in Blue* for harp quartet (1980), and *The Voice*, symphonic tone poem (1980). Coolidge has also produced several piano pieces, songs to the words of such poets as A. E. Housman, Emily Dickinson, and Edna St. Vincent Millay, a string quartet, and works for harp.

COOPER, PAUL (b. 1926) Composer, teacher. Born in Victoria, Ill., May 19, 1926, Cooper studied music at the University of Southern California, Los Angeles, with Roger Sessions (q.v.) and Ernest Kanitz. After graduation he went to Paris in 1953 to study with Nadia Boulanger (q.v.) for a year. He has taught at the University of Michigan, Ann Arbor, and has been composer-in-residence at the University of Cincinnati, Ohio, and at Rice University, Houston, Texas. His compositions include *Piano Sonata* (1949), *Sinfonia* for strings (1952), *String Quartet No. 1* (1953), *Symphony No. 1* (1954), *Missa Brevis* for chorus (1954), *String Quartet No. 2* (1954), *Symphony No. 2* (1956), *Mementos* for piano (1957), *Sinfonia* for winds (1958), *String Quartet No. 3* (1959), *Canonic Variations* for wind quintet (1960), *Sonata for Violin* (1961), *Concerto for Harpsichord and Organ* (1962), *Sonata* for flute and piano (1963), *Piano Sonata No. 2* (1963), *String Quartet No. 4* (1964), *Concert for Two* for cello and piano (1965), *Concert for Five* for wind quintet (1965), *Partimento* for piano (1967), *Concerto for Winds, Percussion,* and *Piano* (1968), *Cycles* for piano (1969), *Genesis II* for chorus (1969), *Symphony No. 3* for strings (1971), *Variants* for organ (1971–72), *Cantigas* for chorus and orchestra (1972), *Aegina Music* for violin, cello, and piano (1973), *String Quartet No. 5* (1975), *Symphony No. 4: "Landscape"* (1975), and *String Quartet No. 6* (1977). Cooper is also the author of *Perspectives in Music Theory* (1973).

CORIGLIANO, JOHN (b. 1938) Composer, teacher, writer, arranger. Born in New York City, Feb. 16, 1938, Corigliano grew up in a musical family (his father, John, Sr., was a violinist and for years concertmaster of the New York Philharmonic; his mother was a pianist). Corigliano studied at Columbia University with Otto Luening (q.v.) and at the Manhattan School of Music with Vittorio Giannini (q.v.). In 1959 he had private lessons with Paul Creston (q.v.). In the late '50s and early '60s Corigliano was associated with radio, for which he wrote scripts, and with television production. He taught at the National Cathedral College of Church Musicians, Washington, D.C. (1968–69). He has also written arrangements for rock groups and music for commercials. His compositions include *Kaleidoscope* for 2 pianos (1959), *Fern Hill* for mezzo-soprano, chorus, and orchestra (1961), *What I Expected Was* . . . for chorus, brass, and percussion (1962), *Sonata for Violin and Piano* (1963), *The Cloisters* for voice and orchestra (1965), *Elegy* for orchestra (1965), *Tournaments Overture* for orchestra (1967), *Piano Concerto* (1968), *Poem in October* for tenor and chamber ensemble (1970), *Oboe Concerto* (1975), *Poem on His Birthday* for baritone, chorus, and orchestra (1976), and *Clarinet Concerto* (1977).

CRUMB, GEORGE (b. 1929) Composer, teacher. Born in Charleston,

W.Va., Oct. 24, 1929, Crumb studied composition with Ross Lee Finney (q.v.) at the University of Michigan; he also studied with German composer Boris Blacher at the Berkshire Music Center, Mass., and the Berlin Hochschule für Musik (1955–56). Upon completion of his studies in 1959 Crumb began teaching at the University of Colorado, Boulder. From 1964 to 1965 Crumb was associated with the Center of the Creative and Performing Arts, Buffalo, N.Y. In 1965 he joined the staff of the University of Pennsylvania, Philadelphia, as teacher of composition. In his own original composition, Crumb has sought for new sonorities (many works are written for prepared instruments—or unusual instruments; e.g., a musical saw is heard in *Ancient Voices of Children*). Among his compositions are a *String Quartet* (1954), *Cello Sonata* (1955), *Variazioni* for orchestra (1959), *Five Pieces* for piano (1962), *Night Music I* for soprano, piano, and percussion (1963), *Four Nocturnes: Night Music II* for violin and piano (1964), *Madrigals, Book I*, for soprano, vibraphone, and bass (1965), *Madrigals, Book II*, for soprano, alto flute, and percussion (1965), *Echoes I*, "Eleven Echoes of Autumn 1965," for violin, clarinet, alto flute, and piano (1966), *Echoes II*, "Echoes of Time and the River," for orchestra (1967; Pulitzer Prize), *Songs, Drones, and Refrains of Death* for baritone, electric guitar, electric bass, electric piano, and percussion (1968), *Madrigals, Book III*, for soprano, harp, and percussion (1969), *Night of the Four Moons* for mezzo-soprano, banjo, alto flute, piccolo, cello, and percussion (1969), *Madrigals, Book IV*, for soprano, flute, harp, double bass, and percussion (1969), *Black Angels* for electric string quartet (1970), *Ancient Voices for Children* for mezzo-soprano, boy soprano, oboe, mandolin, harp, electric piano, and percussion (1970), *Voice of the Whale* for flute, piano, cello, and antique cymbals (1971), *Lux Eterna* for soprano, bass flute, sitar, and 2 percussionists (1971), *Makrokosmos I* for amplified piano (1972), *Makrokosmos II* for amplified piano (1973), *Makrokosmos III*, "Music for a Summer Evening," for 2 amplified pianos and percussion (1974), *Dream Sequence* for violin, cello, piano, percussion, plus crystal glasses offstage (1976), *Star-Child: A Parable* for soprano, antiphonal children's voices, bell ringers, and large orchestra (1977), and *Makrokosmos IV*, "Celestial Mechanics," for amplified piano (1979).

CRYER AND FORD Important songwriting team specializing in contemporary subjects, including the position of women in today's world. Gretchen Kiger Cryer (b. Dunreith, Ind., Oct. 17, 1935) and Nancy Ford (b. Kalamazoo, Mich., Oct. 1, 1935) met as students at DePauw University, Greencastle, Ind., where they began collaborating on songs. Their paths crossed again, and later, in New York City, where Cryer sang in the choruses of Broadway shows (*Little Me*, in 1962, for example) and Ford was pianist for the off-Broadway success, *Fantasticks* (q.v.). Reunited, they began collaborating again and produced the score for their first major off-Broadway musical, *Now Is the Time for All Good Men* (1967), for which Cryer also provided the book, a protest against the Vietnam War. Their next was the successful *The Last Sweet Days of Isaac* (1970), a satirical, affectionate look at contemporary life. Their first Broadway production, *Shelter* (1973), not too different in theme from *Isaac*, ran for a mere 31 performances. Cryer and Ford returned to the more comfortable precincts of off Broadway with the successful *I'm Getting My Act Together and Taking It on the Road* (1978, still running in early '81, as well as on the road). In the early phase of the run, Cryer starred in the role of a recently divorced, rapidly approaching 40, vocalist coping with life and show business. As with all previous Cryer-Ford musicals, Cryer wrote both book and lyrics.

CUNNINGHAM, ARTHUR (b. 1928) Composer, pianist, timpanist, bassist, conductor. Born in Nyack, N.Y., Nov. 11, 1928, Cunningham studied music at Fisk University, Nashville, Tenn., from which he was graduated in 1951. He also studied at Teachers College, Columbia University, New York City, and with Wallingford Riegger (q.v.) at the Metropolitan School of Music, New York City. As a teenager, Cunningham led his own jazz group, for which he composed original instrumentals and songs (his output consists of more than 400 songs and 100 piano pieces). Other compositions include *Adaglo* for strings and oboe (1954), *Patsy Patch and Susan's Dream,* children's musical (1963), *Ostrich Feathers,* rock musical for children (1964), *Concentrics* for orchestra (1968), *His Natural Grace,* one-act rock opera (1969), *Shango,* incidental music (1969), *Engrams* for piano (1969), *Lullabye for a Jazz Baby* for orchestra (1969), also a ballet for string quartet and jazz quartet.

CURTIS-SMITH, CURTIS O. B. (b. 1941) Composer, pianist, teacher. Born in Walla Walla, Wash., Sept. 9, 1941, Curtis-Smith studied composition with Alan Stout, Kenneth Gaburo (q.v.) at the University of Illinois, Urbana, and with Italian composer-conductor Bruno Maderna. He also studied piano with Gui Mombaerts, David Burge, and John Ringgold. He has been the recipient of several fellowships, grants, and awards. During 1976–77 he lectured on composition at the University of Michigan, Ann Arbor, and since 1977 has been associate professor of music at Western Michigan

University, Kalamazoo. His compositions include *Variations* for piano (1963), *Flute Sonata* for flute and piano (1963), *Six Movements for String Quartet* (1965), *Second String Quartet* (1965), *All Day I Hear* for 12 voices, a cappella (1965), *Quasi-Passacaglia* for piano (1966), *Third String Quartet,* "Elegies for String Quartet" (1967), *Yu Sareba,* "Rice Leaves" for orchestra (1968), *Trajectories* for piano (1968), *Quotation: Voices* for brass quintet (1970), *Passant. Un. Nous Passons. Deux. De Notre Somme Passons. Trois* for 19 solo voices, narrator, flute, harp, piano, cello, percussion, and electronic sounds (1970), *Canticum Novum/Desideria* for 6 sopranos, 4 tenors, and chamber group (1971), *Piece du Jour* for piano (1971), *Fanaffair for Fanny* for 9 trumpets and 4-channel tape (1971), *Electronic Study/ Gong Sounds* for 4-channel tape (1972), *Praeludium* for 13 instruments (1972), *Comedie* for 2 sopranos and chamber orchestra (1972; Koussevitzky Prize), *A Song of Degrees* for 2 pianos and percussion (1973), *Rhapsodies* for piano (1973), *Five Sonorous Inventions* for violin and piano (1973), *Winter Pieces,* modern dance for chamber orchestra (1974), (Bells) *Belle du Jour* for orchestra with piano soloist (1975), *Suite in Four Movements* for harpsichord (1975), *Tristana Variations* for piano (1976), *Music for Handbells* for 10 players (1976–77), *Three Pieces* for harp (1976), *Unisonics* for alto saxophone and piano (1976), *Partita* for flute, clarinet, piano, percussion, violin, viola, and cello (1977), *Ensembles/ Solos,* "composed in the 'Five and Seven' temperament," for chamber group (1977), *Gargoyles* for organ (1978), *Masquerades* for organ (1978), *Plays and Rimes* for brass quintet and piano (1979), *Sundry Dances* for chamber group (1979), *Prelude and Blues* for guitar (1979), *The Barbershop String*

Quartet (1980), and *Black and Blues* for brass quintet (1980).

DAVIS, MILES (b. 1926) Trumpeter, bandleader. Born in Alton, Ill., May 25, 1926, Davis was 13 and living in East St. Louis when his father, a dentist, presented him with a trumpet on his birthday. He played in the high school band and, at 15, in the band of Eddie Randall in East St. Louis. Upon finishing high school, Davis joined the Adam Lambert band in Chicago. In 1945 he came to New York City to study at the Juilliard School of Music. During this period he was befriended by jazz musicians Charlie Parker (q.v.) and Dizzy Gillespie (q.v.). Soon after, Davis joined the Parker band, playing on 52nd Street, then a major jazz center in New York. Davis left Juilliard that same year to work in the Benny Carter band in Los Angeles. By the late '40s he had begun forming his own jazz combinations and recording. Davis evolved a cool, detached style of performance and has been recognized as one of the finest of modern jazz trumpeters. In addition to recording with his own bands, Davis also recorded with the Charlie Parker band. He has toured extensively with his bands; in 1964 he played at the World Jazz Festival in Japan, and he toured Europe in 1971. Davis has had a long and successful musical friendship with arranger Gil Evans (b. 1912). Among their successful, and now historic, collaborations are the albums entitled *Miles Ahead* and *Porgy and Bess,* recorded by Columbia Records.

DEL TREDICI, DAVID (b. 1937) Composer, pianist, teacher. Born in Cloverdale, Calif., Mar. 16, 1937, Del Tredici studied piano with Bernhard Abramowitsch (1953–59). During much of the same period he was enrolled in the composition classes of Arnold Elston and Seymour Shifrin (q.v.) at the University of California, Berkeley. He had further study at Princeton University under Roger Sessions (q.v.) and Earl Kim (q.v.). Originally Del Tredici had planned on a career as a concert pianist, but he decided to compose seriously after attending Darius Milhaud's classes and being encouraged by him. He was a member of the Harvard University music faculty from 1966 until 1972. His compositions include *Six Songs* for voice and piano (1959), *String Trio* (1959), *Scherzo* for 2 pianos (1960), *I Hear an Army* for soprano and string quartet (1964), *Night Conjure-Verse* for soprano, countertenor, and chamber group (1965), *Syzygy* for soprano and chamber orchestra (1966), *The Last Gospel* for amplified soprano, rock group, chorus, and orchestra (1967), *Pop-Pourri* for amplified soprano, rock group, chorus, and orchestra (1968), *The Lobster Quadrille* for orchestra and *Vintage Alice* (1972), *Adventures Underground* (1973), *In Wonderland* (1975), *The Annotated Alice* and *The Final Alice* (1976)—all for soprano and various instrumental combinations.

DISCO A place and the music heard in that place. From the French "discothèque," dating from the early '60s. Discos featured music for dancing via the jukebox programmed by a disc jockey. By the mid '60s there were thousands of discos in the United States crowded with dancers moving to music at a high volume, flashing lights, and minimal light. The music now called "disco" is characterized by a heavy beat, even more pronounced than that of rock. In New York City such "in" clubs as Arthur, the Electric Circus, and Cheetah (alas, all gone the way of all flash) attracted crowds of youthful and not so youthful swingers. In the late '70s the place to go was the notorious Studio 54, which was frequented by the Beautiful People, such as Liza Minnelli and Andy Warhol—although the younger, perhaps less beautiful people preferred the Mudd Club in Soho (in lower Manhattan), where the music played was closer to rock and not disco. Disco music, besides the insistent beat, is generally repetitious and mechanical (in that the recordings are studio products). The major point of disco music is to serve as dance music and little else.

DLUGOSZEWSKI, LUCIA (b. 1931) Composer, poet, teacher. Born in Detroit, Mich., June 16, 1931, Dlugoszewski studied piano at the Detroit Conservatory as a child but majored in mathematics and physics at Wayne State University, Detroit (1946–49). In 1950, having decided to concentrate on music, she enrolled in the Mannes School of Music, New York City; she also studied privately with Grete Sultan (piano) and Felix Salzer and Edgard Varèse, q.v. (composition). Varèse was especially influential in shaping the direction of Dlugoszewski's work. Besides exploring the mathematical basis of music, she has sought out new sounds and has constructed dozens of instruments. She is definitely of the contemporary school. Her works include *Piano Sonata No. 1* (1949), *Melodic Sonata* for piano (1950), *Orchestra Structure for the Poetry of Everyday Sounds* (1952), *Openings of the Eye*, ballet for flute, timbre piano, and percussion (1952), *Desire,* "theatre structure" for voice and timbre piano (1952), *Moving Theatre Piece* for many players (1953), *Arithmetic Points* for orchestra (1955), *Instants in Form and Movement* for timbre piano and chamber orchestra (1957), *Music for the Left Ear* for piano (1958), *Eight Clear Places* for a 100-piece invented percussion orchestra, ballet (1961), *To Everyone Out There*, ballet for orchestra (1964), *Dazzle on a Knife's Edge*, ballet for timbre piano and orchestra (1966), *Hanging Bridges* for string quartet (1967), *Tight Rope*, ballet for chamber

orchestra (1968), *The Heidi Songs,* opera (1970), *Space Is a Diamond* for solo trumpet (1970), *A Zen in Ryoko-In*, film score for invented percussion orchestra (1971), *Angels of the Inmost Heaven* for brass (1975), *Fire Fragile Flight* for orchestra (1976), and *Tender Theatre Flight Nageire* for brass and percussion (1971–78). Dlugoszewski's volume of poetry, *A New Folder,* was published in 1969.

DRUCKMAN, JACOB (b. 1928) Composer, teacher. Born in Philadelphia, Pa., June 26, 1928, Druckman studied composition as a youngster in Philadelphia with Louis Gesensway. He also learned the trumpet. In 1949 he studied at the Juilliard School of Music, New York City, with Peter Mennin, Vincent Persichetti, and Bernard Wagenaar (all q.v.). He also studied with Aaron Copland (q.v.) at Tanglewood, Mass., and at the École Normale de Musique, Paris (1954–55), with Tony Aubin. Druckman has taught at Bard College, Annandale, N.Y., at Juilliard, and at the Columbia-Princeton Electronics Music Center, and was director of the Brooklyn College Electronic Music Studio. Since 1976 he has been professor of composition, director of the Electronic Music Studio, and chairman of the Composition Department, Yale University School of Music, New Haven, Conn. His works include *Duo* for violin and piano (1949), *Divertimento* for clarinet, horn, harp, violin, viola, and cello (1950), *Laude* for baritone, alto flute, viola, and cello (1952), *The Seven Deadly Sins* for piano (1955), *Four Madrigals* for mixed chorus a cappella (1958), *Dark Upon the Harp* for soprano, brass quintet, and percussion (1962), *Antiphonies I, II, and III* for 2 mixed choruses unaccompanied (1963), *The Sound of Time* for soprano and piano (1964; for soprano and orchestra, 1965), *Animus I* for trombone and tape (1966), *String Quar-*

tet No. 2 (1966), *Sabbath Eve Service* for tenor, chorus, and organ (1967), *Animus II* for soprano, percussion, and tape (1968), *Incenters* for 13 instruments (1968), *Valentine* for contrabass (1969), *Animus III* for clarinet and tape (1969), *Orison* for organ and tape (1970), *Synapse* for tape (1971), *Windows* for orchestra (1972; Pulitzer Prize), *Delizie Contente Che l'Alme Beate* for woodwind quintet and tape (1973), *Lamia* for soprano and orchestra (1974–75), *Mirage* for orchestra (1976), *Other Voices* for brass quintet (1976), *Chiaroscuro* for orchestra (1977), *Animus IV* for tenor, 6 instrumentalists, and tape (1977), *Concerto for Viola and Orchestra* (1978), *Aureole* for orchestra (1979), *Bō* for marimba, harp, bassoon, clarinet, and 3 women's voices (1979), and *Prism* for orchestra (1980).

DYLAN, BOB (b. 1941) Composer, singer, guitarist. Born, as Robert Zimmerman, in Duluth, Minn., May 24, 1941, Dylan grew up in Hibbing, Minn., where by the age of 10 he was performing on the guitar. At 12 he ran away from home for the first time and was returned to his parents. This continued for several years, until the wandering minstrel reached 18 and his parents gave up sending for him. Dylan's travels took him as far west as California and as far north as North Dakota. (The name Dylan, by the way, was borrowed from that of the poet Dylan Thomas.) In the fall of 1960 Dylan arrived in New York to see another hero of his, Woody Guthrie (q.v.), whose recordings he heard while he was a scholarship student at the University of Minnesota. Dropping out of college, Dylan headed for New York, where he began singing folk songs in Greenwich Village youth hangouts. In 1961 Dylan was noticed by a New York *Times* writer as he sang at Folk City, and the alert record producer

John Hammond, of Columbia Records, arranged for an album to be cut. Dylan's own folklike songs contained political allusions that appealed to a generation in revolt against the Establishment (which to them meant big business, the military, politicians—those in power). "Blowin' in the Wind" (1962) became very popular and was adopted by civil rights groups— and recorded by dozens of folk and pop vocalists. Dylan appeared at concerts, on television, and at folk festivals around the country. At the Monterey Folk Festival in 1963 he met another folkish singer, Joan Baez (b. 1941), and made frequent appearances with her in concert. Dylan recorded several successful albums, although he began to lose his folk following ca. 1965 when he began using electric guitars and amplification. His turning to rock (or "rockabilly," the country-flavored rock) alienated additional folk purists. A motorcycle accident in 1966 led to a year and a half of silence and rumor. (There were suggestions that Dylan had been so seriously injured that he would never perform again.) In 1968, not only did Dylan emerge from seclusion to sing at a Woody Guthrie Memorial Concert at Carnegie Hall, he also cut a new album, *John Wesley Harding*, which revealed a return to more folkish ways. He also appeared with yet another country-folk singer Johnny Cash (b. 1932). He moved further into the country field with his next album, *Nashville Skyline* (1969). Among his popular songs are "The Times They Are A-changin'" (1964), "Talking World War III Blues" (1964), "Don't Think Twice, It's All Right" (1966), and others tinctured with folk humor and penetrating social comment. Dylan continued making successful, best-selling albums well into the '70s. His *Blood on the Tracks* and *Desire* albums were in No. 1 spots on the *Billboard* charts in 1975 and 1976 respectively. One of Dylan's tours was filmed and released as *Don't Look Back,* in 1967, and was widely praised. Dylan published a novel, *Tarantula,* in 1971— then wisely returned to writing songs and singing.

EATON, JOHN (b. 1935) Composer, pianist. Born in Bryn Mawr, Pa., Mar. 30, 1935, Eaton studied at Princeton University with Milton Babbitt, Edward Cone, and Roger Sessions (all q.v.). He studied piano with Frank Sheridan and Eduard Steuermann. He has been the recipient of 3 Prix de Rome awards and 2 Guggenheim grants. In 1958 he toured the United States with his own jazz group and later (1962) toured with and was coleader of the American Jazz Ensemble. Eaton has composed several pieces for an instrument called the Syn-Ket, a synthesizer designed and built by Italian engineer Paul Ketoff. Another instrument built for Eaton by Edward Miller combines the Moog synthesizer with Miller's modifications; this is called the Syn-Mill. Both these sound-making devices are portable. Eaton's compositions include *Holy Sonnets of John Donne* for soprano and orchestra (1957), *Ma Barker,* opera (1957), *Piano Variations* (1958), *Trumpet Sonata* (1958), *String Quartet* (1959), *Concert Piece* jazz ensemble and tape (1962), *Songs for R.P.B.* (1964), *Prelude to Myshkin* (1965), *Microtonal Fantasy* (1965), *Piece for Solo Syn-Ket No. 3* (1966), *Thoughts on Rilke* for soprano, Syn-Ket, and Syn-Mill (1967), *Concert Piece* for Syn-Ket and orchestra (1967), *Blind Man's Cry* for soprano and ensemble of electronic synthesizers (1968), *Mass* for soprano, clarinet, ensemble of synthesizers, and tape (1970), *Concert Music for Solo Clarinet* (1971), and *The Cry of Clytaemnestra,* one-act opera and *Danton and Robespierre,* one-act opera (both 1980).

EBB, FRED (b. 1932) See Kander and Ebb.

ELECTRONIC MUSIC Music that is generally, but not always, produced by specially designed instruments called synthesizers, i.e., machines that can electrically reproduce a wide range of sounds, including those of conventional instruments. Pure electronic music is not intended for concert hall performance, for the elaborate synthesizer is not readily transportable. The synthesized composition is stored on tape; in this form it can be, and has been, combined with real instruments and vocalists for concert performance. One of the best-known synthesizers (although not the first) was developed by electric engineer Robert A. Moog; his device is called the Moog (q.v.) and garnered a degree of musical fame with the release of an album entitled *Switched-on Bach* in which excerpts from various works by Bach (including a complete *Brandenburg Concerto,* the 3rd) were "realized" on the Moog by Walter Carlos. Various electronic music centers have been established, mostly at universities, although some have been set up by individuals. Among these are the Columbia-Princeton Electronic Music Center, New York City, which uses an RCA-manufactured synthesizer; other centers are at Yale, Brandeis, the University of California, at Davis and San Diego, as well as in other countries. American composers who have worked in the electronic medium include Robert Ashley, Milton Babbitt, John Cage, Otto Luening, Gordon Mumma, Pauline Oliveros, Morton Subotnick, and Vladimir Ussachevsky (all q.v.). Composers working in the electronic music-making medium have devised methods of notating it that look more like charts and graphs than conventional music notation.

ERB, DONALD (b. 1927) Composer, teacher, trumpeter. Born in Youngstown, Ohio, Jan. 17, 1927, Erb studied composition with Harold Miles at Kent State

University, Ohio; with Marcel Dick at the Cleveland Institute of Music, and with Bernard Herdew at Indiana University, Bloomington. Erb also studied with Nadia Boulanger (q.v.) in Paris in 1952. He joined the music faculty of the Cleveland Institute of Music the following year; he has held teaching posts at Indiana University; Bowling Green State University, Ohio; and the Case Institute of Technology, Cleveland, among others. For a year (1968–69) Erb was composer-in-residence to the Dallas Symphony. His compositions include a *Dialogue* for violin and piano (1958), *Correlations* for piano (1959), *String Quartet No. 1* (1960), *Sonneries* for brass ensemble (1961), *Compendium* for band (1963), *Symphony of Overtures* (1964), *Fallout* for narrator, chorus, string quartet, and piano (1964), *Phantasma* for flute, oboe, double bass, and harpsichord (1965), *Diversion for Two (Other Than Sex)* for trumpet and percussion (1966), *String Trio* (1966), *Summermusic* for piano (1966), *Reconnaissance* for violin, double bass, piano, and 2 Moog synthesizers (1967), *Christmasmusic* for orchestra (1967), *Three Pieces* for brass quintet and piano (1968), *The Seventh Trumpet* for orchestra (1969), *Klangfarbenfunk* for rock band and electronic instruments (1970), *Harold's Trip to the Sky* for viola, piano, and percussion (1972), *Cello Concerto* (1976), and *Trombone Concerto* (1976).

"THE FANTASTICKS" Small-scale musical (1960) with music by Harvey Schmidt (b. 1929) and lyrics and book by Tom Jones (b. 1928). Based on Edmond Rostand's *Les Romanesques, The Fantasticks* tells of 2 fathers who attempt to bring their son and daughter together by expressing disapproval of the match and even staging a fake rape so that the young man can prove himself a hero. When the hoax is exposed, the young would-be lovers quarrel and the young man, Matt, leaves to suffer through a number of unpleasant adventures before he returns to his Luisa, a sadder, more mature young man. From this score comes the popular "Try to Remember" and a fine duet, "Soon It's Gonna Rain." *The Fantasticks* opened at the 150-seat Sullivan Street Playhouse, New York City, May 3, 1960, and was still running in 1980. In the original production, Matt was portrayed by Kenneth Nelson and Luisa by Rita Gardner; Jerry Orbach appeared in the pivotal role of El Gallo. A London production of *The Fantasticks* in 1961 ran only 44 performances.

FELDMAN, MORTON (b. 1926) Composer, theoretician. Born in New York City, Jan. 12, 1926, Feldman was a composition student of Wallingford Riegger (q.v.) and Stefan Wolpe (q.v.); his piano teacher was Vera-Maurina Press. Feldman's musical thinking was influenced by John Cage (q.v.) and his contemporaries Earle Brown (q.v.) and Christian Wolff (q.v.). In his composition, Feldman employs what has been called "predetermined indeterminancy," graphic notation (rather than standard musical notation), and instructions to the performer to use a great degree of free choice in what is played. Feldman graphs out a general idea of register: high, low, or in-between. Tempo is indicated at the beginning of the performance, and it is up to the instrumentalist to select the duration of the music in the register in which he or she has chosen, for that performance, to play. In much of his work, Feldman prefers slow tempos; the resulting music is quiet, characterized by floating harmonies of interesting color and a general static quality. His works include *Projection 1* for cello (1950), *Structures* for string quartet (1951), *Marginal Intersection* for orchestra (1951), *Projections* for chamber group (1951), *Extensions 1* for violin and piano (1951), *Projection IV* for violin and piano (1951), *Intersection III* for piano (1953), *Extensions IV* for 3 pianos (1953), *Two Pieces* for 2 pianos (1954), *Three Pieces* for string quartet (1954–56), *Piece* for 4 pianos (1957), *Atlantis* for chamber orchestra (1959), *The Swallows of Salangan* for wordless chorus and small orchestra (1961), *Durations* for chamber groups (1960–61), *Out of Last Pieces* for orchestra (1962), *King of Denmark* for percussion and electronic equipment (1964), *Four Instruments* (1965), *Chorus and Instruments II* for tuba, chimes, and chorus (1967), *First Principles* for orchestra (1966–67), *In Search of an Orchestration* for orchestra (1967), *Vertical Thoughts II* (1968), *The Viola in My Life* for viola and sextet (1970), *Rothko Chapel* for chorus, viola, and percussion (1972), and *For Frank O'Hara* for flute, clarinet, violin, cello, piano, and percussion (1973).

"FIDDLER ON THE ROOF" Highly successful musical set in czarist Russia around the turn of the century. The music is by Jerry Bock and lyrics by Sheldon Harnick (see Bock and Harnick). The book, by Joseph Stein, was based on stories of Sholem Aleichem and traced the ill fortunes of a Jewish dairyman and his problems with his marriageable daughters. The dairyman, Tevye contends not only with his daughters, but also with poverty. At the close of the musical a Russian pogrom destroys his village. This may appear to be unlikely stuff for a musical, but, under the direction of Jerome Robbins, *Fiddler on the Roof* proved to be one of the longest-running Broadway shows of its time: 3,242 performances. It opened at the Imperial Theatre, New York City, Sept. 22, 1964 (its long record was broken by another musical, *Grease*, in 1979). The London production, which opened in 1967, ran for more than 2,000 performances. A film version was released in 1971. In the original production, Tevye was protrayed by comedian Zero Mostel; he was the first of many, but is most associated with the part.

FLAGELLO, NICOLAS (b. 1928) Composer, pianist, conductor, teacher. Born in New York City, Mar. 15, 1928, Flagello mastered the piano as a youngster and began composing in his teens. He studied informally with Vittorio Giannini, q.v. (composition) and was graduated from the Manhattan School of Music in 1950. A Fulbright Fellowship enabled him to study at the Academy of Santa Cecilia, Rome, with Ildebrando Pizzetti. He also studied conducting with Dimitri Mitropoulos. Flagello toured extensively as a pianist and played various instruments in several orchestras; he became assistant conductor of the Chicago Lyric Opera (1960–61). He has also conducted the Orchestra da Camera di Roma in recordings of American music. Flagello has taught at the Manhattan School of Music and at the Curtis Institute, Philadelphia. His compositions include *Three Dances* for piano (1945), *Lyra* for brass sextet (1945), *Chorale and Episode* for brass (1948), *Beowulf* for orchestra (1949), *Piano Concerto* (1950), *Mirra*, opera (1950), *The Wig*, one-act opera (1953), *Concerto Antoniano* for flute and orchestra (1953), *Piano Concerto No. 2* (1955), *Violin Concerto* (1956), *Three Episodes* for piano (1957), *Rip Van Winkle*, opera for children (1957), *The Sisters*, one-act opera (1958), *Concerto for Strings* (1959), *The Judgment of St. Francis*, opera (1959), *Divertimento* for piano and percussion (1960), *Burlesca* for flute and guitar (1961), *Capriccio* for cello and orchestra (1962), *Piano Sonata* (1962), *Concertino* for piano, brass, and timpani (1963), *Piano Concerto No. 3* (1963), *Lautrec: Suite for Orchestra* (1965), *Symphony No. 1*

(1967), *Te Deum for Mankind* for chorus (1968), and *The Piper of Hamelin,* opera for children (1970). There are also several song cycles, instrumental pieces, and a 2nd symphony composed in the '70s.

FLANAGAN, WILLIAM (1923–1969) Composer, critic, author. Born in Detroit, Mich., Aug. 14, 1923, Flanagan studied composition with Burrill Phillips (q.v.) and Bernard Rogers (q.v.) at the Eastman School of Music, Rochester, N.Y. At the Berkshire Music Center, Tanglewood, Mass., he studied with Arthur Berger (q.v.), Aaron Copland (q.v.), and Arthur Honegger. He studied privately in New York City with David Diamond (q.v.). From 1957 to 1960 he wrote music criticism for the New York *Herald Tribune;* he also wrote regularly for the magazine *Stereo Review.* Flanagan's compositions include a *Passacaglia* for piano (1947), *Divertimento* for string quartet (1947), *Piano Sonata* (1950), *Song for a Winter Child* for voice and piano (1950), *A Concert Ode* for orchestra (1951), *Time's Long Ago,* 6 songs for soprano and piano (1951), *The Weeping Pleiades* for baritone, flute, clarinet, violin, cello, and piano (1953), *Bartleby,* one-act opera (1957), *The Lady of Tearful Regret* for coloratura soprano and chamber group (1958), *A Concert Overture* for orchestra (1959), *Notations* for orchestra (1960), *Moss,* songs for soprano and piano (1962), *Chapter from Ecclesiastes* for chorus and string quintet (1963), *A Narrative* for orchestra (1965), and *Another August* for soprano and orchestra (1967). Flanagan composed incidental music for several plays by Edward Albee, including *The Death of Bessie Smith* (1960) and *The Ballad of the Sad Café* (1963). Albee, many of whose poems Flanagan set to music, was commissioned to write an opera with Flanagan, but the work was never completed. Flanagan was found dead in his New York City apartment of a drug overdose on Aug. 31, 1969.

FLOYD, CARLISLE (b. 1926) Composer, teacher. Born in Latta, S.C., June 11, 1926, Floyd earned his master's degree in music as a student of Ernst Bacon (q.v.) from Syracuse University, N.Y. He also studied piano with Sidney Foster and Rudolf Firkusny. Since 1947 Floyd has taught piano and composition at Florida State University, Tallahassee. He is best known for his operas. His works include *Slow Dusk,* one-act opera (1949), *Fugitives,* musical drama (1951), *Lost Eden,* ballet for 2 pianos (1952), *Susannah,* 2-act opera (1955; New York Music Critics Circle Award 1956), *Pilgrimage,* cantata for voice and orchestra (1956), *Piano Sonata* (1957), *Wuthering Heights,* opera (1958), *The Mystery: Five Songs of Motherhood* for soprano and orchestra (1960), *The Passion of Jonathan Wade,* opera (1962), *The Sojourner and Mollie Sinclair,* one-act opera (1963), *Markheim,* one-act opera (1966), *Introduction, Aria, and Dance* for orchestra (1967), *Of Mice and Men,* opera (1969), *Bilby's Doll,* opera (1976), and *Willie Stark,* opera (1981).

FORD, NANCY   *See* Cryer and Ford.

"4'33'"   That is, *Four Minutes, Thirty-three Seconds,* a composition for pianist by John Cage (q.v.) "composed" in 1952. To perform this work the pianist makes his entrance onstage, closes the lid on the piano's keyboard, and sits—without playing a note—for 4'33" listening to the sounds generated by the audience. This demonstrates Cage's belief that even silence has musical content. Of course, even an uncrowded hall is not truly silent. The work, by the way, is divided into 3 movements and can be played by any number of instruments.

FUNKY When applied to jazz of the late '50s and later, the term connotes a rough, folklike music as compared with bop, cool, and other more refined types of jazz performance. Its earlier, and original, meaning was malodorous—the stench one often encountered in hallways of tenements of the poor. The popularity of latter-day funky renewed interest in the recordings of such folk stylists as Arthur "Big Boy" Crudup and a renewed night club career of octogenarian Alberta Hunter.

GABURO, KENNETH (b. 1926) Composer, teacher. Born in Somerville, N.J., July 5, 1926, Gaburo is a graduate of the Eastman School of Music, Rochester, N.Y., where he studied composition with Bernard Rogers (q.v.); he also studied with Goffredo Petrassi at the Accademia di Santa Cecilia, Rome, and with Burrill Phillips (q.v.) and Hubert Kessler at the University of Illinois, Urbana. He has taught at Kent State University, Ohio; McNeese State University, Lake Charles, La.; the University of Illinois, Urbana; and, since 1968, the University of California, San Diego. He is conductor of the New Music Choral Ensemble, which he formed in 1964. An experimentalist, Gaburo has written dodecaphonic music as well as for electronic instruments. His compositions include *Three Interludes* for strings (1949), *On a Quiet Theme* for orchestra (1951; Gershwin Memorial Award), *The Snow Queen,* opera (1952), *Four Inventions* for clarinet and piano (1953), *Music for Five Instruments* (1954), *Ideas and Transformations* for strings (1955), *String Quartet* (1956), *Elegy* for small orchestra (1956), *Tiger Rag,* incidental music for play (1957), *Bodies,* opera (1957), *Line Studies* for flute, clarinet, viola, and trombone (1957), *Ave Maria* for chorus (1957), *Viola Concerto* (1959), *The Widow,* one-act opera (1961), *Two* for

mezzo-soprano, alto flute, and double bass (1963), *Psalm* for chorus (1963), *For Harry* for electronic instrument (1964), *Lemon Drops,* electronic composition (1965), *Circumcision* for male chorus (1966), *Antiphony IV,* "Poised," for piccolo, trombone, string bass, and electronic instruments (1967), *Lingua II: Maledetto* (1968), *Antiphony V* for piano and electronic instruments (1969), *Inside,* quartet for bass solo (1969), and *Mouthpiece* for trumpet and projected slides (1970).

GLASS, PHILIP (b. 1937) Composer. Born in Baltimore, Md., Jan. 31, 1937, Glass began studying the flute at the Peabody Conservatory, Baltimore, in 1945 and was graduated in 1951. From 1952 to 1956 he was in Chicago, taking courses at the University. He came to New York City in 1957 to study composition at the Juilliard School of Music; his teacher there was Vincent Persichetti (q.v.). He later went to Paris to study with Nadia Boulanger (q.v.). In Paris he was impressed with the Indian sitarist Ravi Shankar and joined him to make a study of the music of the East. Glass eventually made several trips to India to study its music—which greatly influenced his original output since 1966. Glass can be grouped with the so-called minimalist composers who, as in Eastern music, write music that sounds repetitive to the uninitiated. For example, Glass in describing his piece *Two Pages* for organ and piano, writes: ". . . the music is written out as a sequence of figures (or measures). Each figure is repeated from six to sometimes as many as thirty times before the player(s) proceed to the next figure. The succeeding figure is the same with the addition (or subtraction) of one (or a group) of note(s). The music is heard then, as a slow and easily perceptible transformation of the original figure. In this period of my work the emphasis is on structural clarity and the gradual unfolding of the musical process." In his composition, Glass not only draws upon the musical materials of the East, but also uses such contemporary popular forms as rock. His works have such titles as *Music in Fifths, Music in Contrary Motions, Music in Similar Motion, Music with Changing Parts, Music in Eight Parts, Music in Twelve Parts,* and *Piece in the Shape of a Square*—all written between 1968 and 1975. Glass has had great success with what is loosely called an opera, written with Robert Wilson, *Einstein on the Beach* (1976), and *Satyagraha,* one-act opera (1980).

"THE GOLDEN APPLE" Operalike musical (1954) based on *The Odyssey* and *The Iliad* with music by Jerome Moross (q.v.) and book and lyrics by John Latouche. The latter changed the setting from Homer's Greece to a town in the state of Washington ca. 1900. Instead of a warrior, Paris is now a salesman. Ulysses returns home from the Spanish-American War to learn that the wife of his friend Menelaus has gone off with the salesman. He sets off in pursuit and finally, after 10 years of searching and fighting off temptations, finds Helen and Paris and challenges Paris to a fistfight. Ulysses wins, of course. *The Golden Apple* had virtually no dialogue, as one song led into the next. One song, "Lazy Afternoon," has been widely sung and recorded since the original production. It was sung by Kaye Ballard in the role of Helen. *The Golden Apple* opened at the off-Broadway Phoenix Theatre, New York City, Mar. 11, 1954, and ran for 125 performances. An attempt to capitalize on the show's success by bringing it uptown to Broadway's Alvin Theatre led to its closing in the summer of 1954. A 1962 off-Broadway revival proved reasonably successful, with a run of 112 performances. In the original production, Priscilla Gillette sang the role of Pe-

nelope, Ulysses' faithful wife; Stephen Douglass was the stalwart Ulysses; Jonathan Lucas was the salesman, Paris; and Dean Michener, Menelaus, the long-suffering husband of the wandering Helen (Kaye Ballard).

GOTTLIEB, JACK (b. 1930) Composer, conductor, teacher, author. Born in New Rochelle, N.Y., Oct. 12, 1930, Gottlieb studied with Karol Rathaus at Queens College, Long Island, N.Y., and with Irving Fine (q.v.) at Brandeis University, Waltham, Mass. Other teachers include Aaron Copland (q.v.), Boris Blacher, Robert Palmer, and Burrill Phillips (both q.v.). As a student at the University of Illinois, Urbana, Gottlieb conducted the chorus; later he was assistant to Leonard Bernstein (q.v.) for the New York Philharmonic (1958–66). He has taught at Loyola University, New Orleans, La., and at the Institute in Judaic Arts, Warwick, N.Y. From 1970 to 1973 he was music director at the Congregation Temple Israel, St. Louis, Mo. Since 1973 he has been composer-in-residence at Hebrew Union College, New York City. Gottlieb's works include a *Quartet* for clarinets (1952), *Hoofprints* for soprano and piano (1954), *String Quartet* (1954), *Piano Sonata* (1960), *Twilight Crane* for woodwind quintet (1961), *Songs of Loneliness* for baritone and piano (1962), *Pieces of Seven* for orchestra (1962), *Shirei Ahavah l'Shabbat* for cantor, chorus, organ, female speaker, and dancers (1965), *Articles of Faith* for voices and orchestra (1965), *The Silent Flickers* for piano, 4 hands (1967), *Haiku Souvenirs* for voice and piano, text by Leonard Bernstein (1967), *New Year's Service for Young People* for 2-part chorus and organ (1970), *Four Affirmations* for chorus and brass sextet (1976), *I Think Continually,* in memory of Felicia Montealegre Bernstein, for mezzo-soprano and piano (1980), and *Psalmistry* for soloists, chorus, and chamber group (1980).

GUTCHË, GENE (b. 1907) Composer. Born in Berlin, Germany, July 3, 1907, Gutchë was in his late '30s before he began to study music systematically. He was born into an affluent business family that provided him with the usual early musical training but in no way encouraged his interests. Despite the praises of composer Ferruccio Busoni, Gutchë's family urged him toward a business career with study at Heidelberg, Lausanne, and Padua. Having had enough, Gutchë one day set out on his own and eventually arrived at Galveston, Texas, in 1925. He worked his way east and northward (working at times as a migratory worker) until he settled in Minneapolis, Minn. He took up music again by studying with Donald N. Ferguson and, by 1925, had arrived in New York City, where he put some of his early training to use in the export and oil business. After several years as a successful businessman-musician, Gutchë returned to Minneapolis to study again with Ferguson, and also with James Aliferis, at the University of Minnesota, Minneapolis (1948–50); he studied with Philip Greeley Clapp at the University of Iowa, Iowa City. By the '50s Gutchë's music had begun to be known beyond Minneapolis and he was awarded Guggenheim Fellowships and obtained performances and recordings. Gutchë's compositions include *Symphony No. 1* (1950) and *String Quartet No. 3* (1950)—these 2 works earned his master's degree; *Symphony No. 2* (1950–54), *Symphony No. 3* (1952), *Rondo Capriccio* for chamber orchestra (1953), *Piano Concerto* (1955), *Holofernes* for orchestra (1958), *Concertino* for orchestra (1959), *Symphony No. 4* (1960), *String Quartet No. 4* (1960), *Timpani Concertante* for orchestra (1961), *Piano Sonata*, Op. 32, No. 2

(1962), *Symphony No. 5* for strings (1962), *Bongo Divertimento* for percussion (1962), *Violin Concerto* (1962), *Genghis Khan* for orchestra (1963), *Raquel* for orchestra (1963), *Rites in Tenochtitlán* for piano and orchestra (1965), *Gemini* for orchestra (1966), *Classic Concerto* for orchestra (1967), *Epimetheus U.S.A.* for orchestra (1969), and *Icarus* for orchestra.

HAILSTORK, ADOLPHUS C. (b. 1941) Composer, pianist, teacher. Born in Rochester, N.Y., Apr. 17, 1941, Hailstork studied composition with Mark Fax at Howard University, Washington, D.C. Upon graduation in 1963, he was awarded a Lucy E. Moten Fellowship to study in France with Nadia Boulanger (q.v.) at the American Institute, Fontainebleau. At the Manhattan School of Music, New York City, he studied with Ludmila Ulehla, Nicolas Flagello (q.v.), Vittorio Giannini (q.v.), and David Diamond (q.v.). During 1966–68 Hailstork served in the U. S. Army in Germany as a captain. He earned his Ph.D. in composition (1968–71) at Michigan State University, East Lansing, working under H. Owen Reed (q.v.). He was an assistant choral director while still a student at Howard University and was director of the male chorus and taught piano at Michigan State University; at Youngstown State University, Ohio, he taught theory, counterpoint, and composition; since 1976 he has served as associate professor of music and composer-in-residence at Norfolk State University, Virginia. Hailstork's compositions include *The Race for Space*, a musical (1963), *Phaedra*, tone poem for orchestra (1965), *Sonata for Horn and Piano* (1966), *Statement, Variations and Fugue* for orchestra (1966), *Pieces of Eight* for piano (1967–68), *In Memoriam: Langston Hughes* for chorus (1968), *Piano Rhapsody* (1968), *Suite for Organ* (1968), *A Charm at Parting* for mezzo-soprano and piano (1969), *Lament for the Children of Biafra* for mezzo-soprano and jazz band (1970), *Elegy and Dance* for clarinet and piano (1970), *Sextet for Strings* (1971), *From the Dark Side of the Sun* for orchestra (1971), *Sonata for Violin and Piano* (1971), *Sonatina* for flute and piano (1972), *My Name Is Toil* for chorus, brass, and timpani (1973), *Duo* for tuba and piano (1973), *Scherzo* for percussion solo and winds (1974), *Bagatelles for Brass* for 2 trumpets and 2 trombones (1974), *Pulse* for percussion ensemble (1974), *Out of the Depths* for band (1974), *Bellevue* for orchestra (1974), *Spiritual* for 4 trumpets and 4 trombones (1975), *Celebration* for orchestra (1975; J. C. Penney commission), *Ignis Fatuus* for piano (1976), *Concerto for Violin, Horn and Orchestra* (1976), *Five Friends* for piano (1977), *Guest Suite,* piano duet (1977), *Oracle of Tu Fu* for tenor solo, women's chorus and tape (1977), *American Landscape No. 1* for band (1977), *If We Must Die* for baritone and piano (1978), *American Landscape No. 2* for violin and cello (1978), *Canto Carcelera* for flute and guitar (1978), *Who Gazes at the Stars* (1978), *Piano Sonata* (1978), *Set Me as a Seal Upon Thine Heart* for chorus (1979), *A Romeo and Juliet Fantasy* for violin and cello (1979), *Suite* for violin and piano (1979), *Elegy* for cello and piano (1979), *Easter Music* for cello and piano (1979), *The Cloths of Heaven* for chorus (1979), and *Epitaph: For a Man Who Dreamed* (1979).

"HAIR" The self-styled "American Tribal Love-Rock Musical" celebrating "hippie" life in New York's East Village. A youthful protest musical, *Hair* was designed as an Establishment shocker in expressing the point of view of society's dropouts, their attitudes toward the Vietnam War, drugs, and sex. The first act concluded with the entire cast on stage totally nude. The book and lyrics were written by Gerome Ragni and James Rado, with music by Galt MacDermot. As a nightclub revue, *Hair* was first presented in a nightclub, Cheetah. It was then taken under the wing of Joseph Papp, who produced it, with revisions, at the Public Theater in October 1967. It was taken to Broadway in 1968, where it opened at the Biltmore Theatre on Apr. 29 and ran for 1,742 performances. In 1979 it was released as a film, which critics found superior to the original stage production. Its best-known song is "Aquarius."

HAKIM, TALIB RASUL (b. 1940) Composer, teacher. Born Stephen A. Chambers in Asheville, N.C., Feb. 8, 1940, Hakim studied music at the Manhattan School of Music, New York College of Music, and the New School for Social Research, New York City. Among his teachers were saxophonist Ornette Coleman, and Chou Wen-chung, Morton Feldman, Hall Overton, Robert Starer, William Sydeman, and Charles Whittenberg (all q.v.). He studied composition as well as piano and clarinet. Hakim has taught at Pace College, New York City, and at Adelphi University, Garden City, N.Y., since 1972. Hakim's music is extremely avant-garde and tinctured with touches of modern jazz. His compositions include *A Piano Piece* (1965), *Shapes* for orchestra (1965), *Contours* for oboe, bassoon, horn, trumpet, piano, and percussion (1966), *Sound-Gone* for piano (1967), *Elements* for strings, flutes, clarinets, piano, and chimes (1967), *Currents* for string quartet (1967), *Placements* for piano and percussion (1970), *Visions of Ishwara* for orchestra (1970), *Sketchy Blue-bop* for jazz band (1973), *Tone-Prayers* for chorus, piano, and percussion (1973), *Concepts* for orchestra (1976), and *Music* for soprano and chamber group (1977).

HAMLISCH, MARVIN (b. 1944) Composer, arranger. Born in New York City, June 2, 1944, Hamlisch first studied with his father, Max, an accordionist. He also studied piano at the Juilliard School of Music, New York City, and earned a B.A. in music from Queens College, City University of New York. Hamlisch began writing songs at around the age of 8 ("What Did You Give Santa Claus for Christmas?"). Following his graduation, he arranged songs for "The Bell Telephone Hour," worked in nightclubs, and wrote songs and arrangements for show people, among them Liza Minnelli (for whom he wrote "Travelin' Man") and Joel Grey. He was 18 when he was hired as an assistant vocal arranger for the successful show *Funny Girl*. At a party, Hamlisch was heard playing the piano by a movie producer who asked him to score a film. One of Hamlisch's early efforts was the theme music for *The Swimmer* (1967); he also wrote scores for the Woody Allen films *Take the Money and Run* (1969) and *Bananas* (1971). In 1974 Hamlisch received no less than 3 Academy Awards for his contribution to 2 films released the previous year: *The Way We Were* (the title song, with lyrics by Marilyn and Alan Bergman) and *The Sting*, for which he drew upon the music of Scott Joplin. The big hit from *The Sting* was, of course, Joplin's *The Entertainer*. Hamlisch's Broadway shows include *A Chorus Line* (1975), which won a Pulitzer Prize and an Antoinette Perry Award ("Tony") for best musical score of the season. The book for *A Chorus Line*, based on experiences of dancers in show business, is by James Kirkwood and Nicholas Dante, "from a concept by Michael Bennett," who also directed and choreographed. The lyrics are by Edward Kleban. Another Broadway success, though not as groundbreaking as *A Chorus Line*, is *They're*

Playing Our Song (1979); the lyrics are by Carole Bayer Sager.

HARBISON, JOHN (b. 1938) Composer, conductor, pianist, teacher. Born in Orange, N.J., Dec. 20, 1938, Harbison studied at Harvard, Princeton, and the Hochschule für Musik, Berlin. His teachers include Earl Kim (q.v.), Roger Sessions (q.v.), and Boris Blacher. Besides composing, Harbison is also active as a conductor. He has led the Cantata Singers of Boston (1969–73), as well as various orchestras. The recipient of several commissions and awards, Harbison was Rockefeller composer-in-residence, Reed College, Portland, Ore. (1968–69). Since 1969 he has served on the music faculty of the Massachusetts Institute of Technology. His compositions include *Sinfonia* for violin and orchestra (1963), *Confinement* for chamber orchestra (1965), *Shakespeare Series* for soprano and piano (1965), *Confinement* for 12 players (1965), *Serenade* for wind quintet and flute or piccolo (1968), *Parody Fantasia* for piano (1968), *Trio* for violin, cello, and piano (1969), *Die Kürze* for piano, flute clarinet/bass clarinet, violin, and cello (1970), *Bermuda Triangle* from "December Music" for amplified cello, tenor saxophone, and electric organ (1970), *Five Songs of Experience* for soloists, chorus, string quartet, and 2 percussionists (1971), *Incidental Music for The Merchant of Venice* for strings (1971), *Elegiac Songs*, texts by Emily Dickinson, for mezzo-soprano and chamber orchestra (1974), *The Winter's Tale*, opera after Shakespeare adapted by the composer (1974), *Moments of Vision* for soprano, tenor, lute recorders, and viola da gamba (1975), *Three Harp Songs* for tenor and harp (1975), *Book of Hours and Seasons* for mezzo-soprano or tenor, flute, cello, and piano (1975), *Diotima* for orchestra (1976), *The Flower-Fed Buffaloes* for baritone, chorus, and chamber group (1976), *Descant-Nocturne* on a lullaby by Seymour Shifrin for orchestra (1976), *Full Moon in March,* one-act opera (1977), *Samuel Chapter* from the King James Bible for soprano or tenor and chamber group (1978), *Quintet* for winds (1979), and *Piano Concerto* (1979).

HARMAN, CARTER (b. 1918) Composer, critic, author, record producer. Born in Brooklyn, N.Y., June 14, 1918, Harman studied composition with Roger Sessions (q.v.) at Princeton University. His musical studies were interrupted by World War II, during which (1942–45) he served as a helicopter pilot with the U. S. Army Air Forces. After the war, Harman returned to Columbia University for more musical studies with Otto Luening (q.v.). From 1947 until 1952 he wrote on music for the New York *Times;* in 1952 he became music editor for *Time* magazine. An interest in the technical side of musical reproduction led Harman into recording (he is an accomplished recording engineer). His work as an engineer and an executive has afforded Harman little time for composing. Since 1967 he has been associated with Composers Recordings, Inc., New York City, which specializes in issuing the music written in the 20th century, with special emphasis on American music. Among Harman's original compositions are the ballet *Blackface* (1947), *Circus at the Opera,* a children's opera (1951), *The Food of Love,* opera (1951), *Castles in the Sand,* children's opera (1952), *Hymn to the Virgin* for chorus a cappella (1952), and *You and I and Amyas,* round for vocal trio (1952). Harman is the author of *A Popular History of Music* (1952) and *Making Sense of Music* (1980).

HARNICK, SHELDON See Bock and Harnick.

HARRIS, DONALD (b. 1931) Composer, teacher. Born in St. Paul, Minn.,

Apr. 7, 1931, Harris was a student of Ross Lee Finney (q.v.) at the University of Michigan, Ann Arbor; in Paris he studied with André Jolivet and Nadia Boulanger (q.v.). Other teachers include Max Deutsch and Boris Blacher. During a 13-year stay in France, Harris was music consultant to the U. S. Information Service. Since 1967 he has been associated with the New England Conservatory of Music, Boston, and was appointed vice-president in 1971. Harris is a noted authority on the music and life of Alban Berg. His compositions include a *Piano Sonata* (1957), *Fantasy* for violin and piano (1957), *Symphony No. 1* (1961), *String Quartet* (1965), *Ludus* for 10 instruments (1966), *Ludus II* for quintet (1973), and *Charmes* for voice and orchestra (1976).

HERMAN, JERRY (b. 1933) Songwriter. Born in New York City, July 10, 1933, Herman is self-taught in music and plays the piano by ear. He studied drama at the University of Miami and was also a student at the Parsons School of Design, New York City. Before turning to songwriting, Herman wrote television scripts. He wrote words and music for a college revue, *I Feel Wonderful* (1954), which was brought to off-Broadway. A nightclub revue, *Nightcap,* followed. By 1960, when another Herman revue, *Parade,* was produced, Herman had established himself on the Broadway musical scene. He made his first major Broadway breakthrough with a musical set in Israel, *Milk and Honey* (1961); the same year saw production of the less-successful *Madame Aphrodite. Hello, Dolly!* (1964), despite early tryout problems, opened on Broadway and became one of the all-time long-running (2,844 performances) hits. Its best-known song was the popular title song (which songwriter Mack David claimed had been borrowed from his earlier tune "Sunflower"; the dispute was settled out of court for a quarter of a million dollars). Herman's next show was another success, *Mame* (1966), with 1,508 performances. Other Herman musicals: *Dear World* (1969), *Mack & Mabel* (1974), and *The Grand Tour* (1979).

HILLER, LEJAREN (b. 1924) Composer, teacher, chemist. Born in New York City, Feb. 23, 1924, Hiller took the usual piano lessons as a boy and even studied theory and composition with Milton Babbitt (q.v.) and Roger Sessions (q.v.) at Princeton—but earned a Ph.D. in chemistry. He spent 4 years working as a research chemist from 1947 until 1952, when he resigned to devote himself to music. During this period he continued to write music, although he spent time traveling in Europe and then joined the faculty at the University of Illinois, in the Chemistry Department, in 1953; in 1958 he moved to the Music Department. Hiller's scientific bent led him into electronic and computer music, among other aspects. Since 1968 Hiller has been in the Music Department of the State University of New York, Buffalo. His works include *Piano Sonata No. 1* (1949), *Piano Concerto* (1949), *Jesse James* for vocal quartet and piano (1950), *String Quartet No. 2* (1951), *Suite* for small orchestra (1951), *Symphony No. 1* (1953), *String Quartet No. 3* (1953), *Twelve-Tone Variations* for piano (1954), *Illiac Suite,* computerized for string quartet, with Leonard M. Isaacson (1957), *Five Appalachian Ballads* for voice and guitar (1958), *Piano Sonata No. 5* (1960), *String Quartet No. 4* (1962), *Computer Cantata* for soprano, chamber group, and tape, in collaboration with R. A. Baker (1963), *Machine Music* for piano, percussion, and tape (1964), *A Triptych for Hieronymus,* mixed-media theatre music piece (1965), *An Avalanche for Pitchman, Prima Donna, Player Piano, Percussion, and Prerecorded Playback* (1968), *HPSCHD*

for various combinations of harpsichords and tapes, with John Cage (1968), *Algorithms,* computerized compositions (1968), *Computer Music* for percussion and tape, with Allan O'Conner (1968), *Three Rituals* for 2 percussionists (1969), *Sonata No. 3* for violin and piano (1970), and *Ponteach* for narrator and piano (1978). Hiller is author of *Experimental Music,* with L. M. Isaacson (1950), and *Principles of Chemistry,* with R. H. Herber (1960).

HOIBY, LEE (b. 1926) Composer, pianist, teacher. Born in Madison, Wis., Feb. 17, 1926, Hoiby studied piano with Gunnar Johansen at the University of Wisconsin, Madison, and was graduated in 1947; he also studied with Egon Petri at Mills College, Oakland, Calif., and composition with Gian Carlo Menotti (q.v.) at the Curtis Institute, Philadelphia. After graduation in 1952 with a master's degree in music, Hoiby left for Europe on a Fulbright Grant to study and work in Salzburg and Rome. Returning to the United States the following year, he has since devoted his time to composition and teaching privately. His works include a *Toccata* for piano (1949), *Hearts, Meadows and Flags,* ballet for orchestra (1950), *Pastoral Dances* for flute and small orchestra (1950), *Sonata for Violin and Piano* (1951), *Five Preludes* for piano (1952), *Second Suite* for orchestra (1953), *Diversions* for woodwind quartet (1953), *The Scarf,* one-act opera (1955), *Three Songs for Men's Chorus,* to texts by W. H. Auden, Wilfred Owen, and Rudyard Kipling (1955), *Songs of the Fool* for chorus, texts by Shakespeare (1955), *Piano Concerto* (1958), *Beatrice,* 3-act opera (1959), *A Hymn to the Nativity* for soprano, baritone, chorus, and orchestra (1960), *The Tides of Sleep,* symphonic song for low voice and orchestra (1961), *Capriccio on Five Notes* for piano (1962), *Natalia Petrovna,* 2-act opera (1964), *Design for Strings*

(1965), *After Eden,* ballet, for orchestra (1966), *Landscape,* ballet, for orchestra (1968), *Inherit the Kingdom* for chorus and organ (1968), *Let This Mind Be in You* for chorus (1968), *Ascension* for chorus and organ, also in versions for chorus and orchestra and brass quintet and organ (1969), *Summer and Smoke,* 2-act opera (1970), *Glorious Hill March* for band, from *Summer and Smoke* (1970), *At the Round Earth's Imagined Corners* for chorus and organ, text by John Donne (1972), *Piano Quintet* for string quartet and piano (1974; also a *Sextet* for winds and piano), *Music for a Celebration* for orchestra (1975), *Galileo Galilei* for soloists, mixed chorus, and orchestra (1975), *A Christmas Carol* for chorus and piano (1977), *Something New for the Zoo,* opera (1979), *Noctambulation* for 2 pianos (1979), many songs and incidental music to plays ranging from *The Duchess of Malfi* (1956) to *Love's Labour's Lost* (1979).

HOLLY, BUDDY (1936–1959) Popular vocalist, guitarist. Born in Lubbock, Tex., Sept. 7, 1936, Holly made his first public appearance at the age of 5 singing in a local talent show. Encouraged by the $5 prize, he continued singing in the traditional country vein and, by the time he was a high school student, had formed a group called the Western and Bop Band. Ca. 1956 he began cutting country recordings, but with little success. He formed another group, the Crickets, and began about a year later to move from country to rock (sometimes called "rockabilly") and began making successful and influential recordings ("Peggy Sue," "Maybe Baby," "Here Comes the Sun," etc.), many written by himself. Holly's impression on the Beatles and the Beach Boys, among others, was important. His influence was great, but was cut short when he died in a plane crash near Clear Lake, Iowa, Feb. 3, 1959. Killed in the same accident were country rock stars Ritchie Valens and the Big Bopper (J. P. Richardson).

"HOUSE OF FLOWERS" Exquisitely scored musical (1954) with music by Harold Arlen and lyrics by Arlen and Truman Capote (b. 1924). Capote's book is based on one of his short stories set in the Caribbean, which tells the story of 2 competing madams and of 2 innocents in love. One of them, Ottilie, lives in Madame Fleur's brothel. She falls in love with a young fisherman, Royal. But Madame Fleur has other plans, hoping to marry off the virginal Ottilie to the wealthy Mr. Jamison. (Incidentally, all of Madame Fleur's employees are named for flowers, such as Tulip, and Pansy, with Ottilie in line for Violet.) The rich score is a sequence of fine moments, from the exotic music of a steel band to soaring, poetic, love songs. Among the outstanding songs are "Two Ladies in de Shade of de Banana Tree," "A Sleepin' Bee," "Don't Like Goodbyes," "Waitin'," and "I Never Has Seen Snow." *House of Flowers* opened at the Alvin Theatre, New York City, Dec. 30, 1954, and ran for only 165 performances. Although the songs (especially Arlen's music), the cast, and the sets and costumes by Oliver Messel were highly praised, the book came in for much criticism. An off-Broadway revival was attempted in 1968—with its story put back into its original form by Capote and with a few additional songs—but that did not run for very long either. In the original production on Broadway the role of Madame Fleur was taken by Pearl Bailey, Ottilie by Diahann Carroll, and Royal by Rawn Spearman. The important role of the Houngan (the witch doctor) was danced by Geoffrey Holder.

HOVEY, SERGE (b. 1920) Composer. Born in New York City, Mar. 10, 1920, Hovey went to California while still a youngster (his mother was the noted screenwriter Sonya Levien). Although primarily educated as an engineer, Hovey turned to music and was a student of Arnold Schoenberg (q.v.) and Hanns Eisler. His compositions include *Fable*, ballet (1948), *The Fiddle*, "a Sholem Aleichem story," for narrator, 2 violins, clarinet, cello, and piano (1948), *Dreams in Spades*, one-act opera (1949), *The Magic Hat*, score for short film (1952), *The World of Sholem Aleichem*, music for a play (1953), *Sholem Aleichem Suite* for orchestra and chorus (1954), *A Ballad of August Bond*, cantata for narrator, ballad singer, soloists, chorus, and chamber orchestra (1956), *Tevya and His Daughters*, music for a play (1957), *Robert Burns Rhapsody* for soloists, chorus, and orchestra (1958), *African Ballet Suite* for orchestra (1960), *Weekend—U.S.A.* for orchestra (1961), *Intermezzo* for piano and strings (1961), *A Little New York Music* for orchestra (1961), *Four Afro-American Variations* for clarinet, piano duet, and percussion (1965), *Symphony No. 1* for prepared tape (3rd movement), vocal solo (4th movement), and large orchestra (1967), *Freedom Variations* for orchestra (1969), *Hangman*, film score (1964), *Storm of Strangers*, film score (1969), *Denmark 43*, film score (1970–71), *The Robert Burns Song Book*, in 4 volumes: 323 songs (1970–73), *Piano Transformations* for 2 pianos and tape (1973), *Nine Pieces for Children* for 2 pianos (1973), *A Storm of Strangers: The Irish*, film score (1974), and *Dialogue with Europe*, 6 Jewish songs, for voice and 2 pianos (1975).

HUSA, KAREL (b. 1921) Composer, teacher, conductor. Born in Prague, Czechoslovakia, Aug. 7, 1921, Husa has studied engineering as well as painting. Among his teachers were Pavel Dědeček, Arthur Honegger, and Nadia Boulanger, q.v. (composition). He also studied conducting with Jean Fournet and André Cluytens. All of Husa's musical training was completed in Europe, where he was influenced by such ethnic specialists as Janáček and Bartók (q.v.) and such modernists as Stravinsky (q.v.) and Schoenberg (q.v.) and his followers. Husa moved to Paris in 1946 and to the United States in 1954. His influence on American music does not lie so much in his own fascinating compositions as in the impressions he made upon his students at Cornell University, on whose faculty he has been since his arrival in the United States. Husa's compositions include *Sonatina* for piano (1943), *Three Fresques* for orchestra (1947), *String Quartet No. 1* (1948), *Divertimento* for string orchestra (1948), *Concertino* for piano and orchestra (1949), *Évocations de Slovaquie* for clarinet, viola, and cello (1951), *Portrait* for strings (1953), *Symphony No. 1* (1952–53); *String Quartet No. 2* (1953), *Four Easy Pieces* for string orchestra (1955), *Eight Czech Duets* for piano, 4 hands (1955), *Fantasies* for orchestra (1956), *Elegie* for piano (1957), *Poem* for viola and chamber orchestra (1959), *Elegie and Rondeau* for saxophone and chamber orchestra (1961), *Mosaïques* for orchestra (1961), *Serenade* for wind quintet, with strings, harp, and xylophone (1963), *Concerto* for brass quintet and strings (1965), *Two Preludes* for flute, clarinet, and bassoon (1966), *Concerto* for alto saxophone and concert band (1967), *String Quartet No. 3* (1968), *Music for Prague* for orchestra (1968), *Divertimento* for brass quintet (1968), *Apotheosis of the Earth* for winds (1971), *Concerto* for percussion and winds (1971), *Sonata for Violin and Piano* (1972–73), *Trumpet Concerto* (1973), *The Steadfast Tin Soldier* for narrator and orchestra (1975), *Piano Sonata No. 2* (1975), *Monodrama*, ballet (1976), and *Landscapes* for brass quintet (1977).

HUSTON, SCOTT (b. 1916) Composer, teacher. Born in Tacoma, Wash., Oct. 10, 1916, Huston received his musical education at the Eastman School of Music, Rochester, N.Y., where he worked under Howard Hanson (q.v.), Burrill Phillips (q.v.), and Bernard Rogers (q.v.). Huston has been associated with the College-Conservatory of Music, University of Cincinnati, Ohio, since 1952. His compositions include an *Abstract* for orchestra (1954), *Trimurti* for 4 trombones (1957), *Piano Sonata* (1958), *The Eighth Word of Christ* for chorus and organ (1959), *Organ Sonata* (1960), *Three Biblical Songs* for alto and piano (1961), *Intensity* ♯*1* for winds (1962), *Trumpet Concerto* for string orchestra with harp and timpani (1963), *Suite for Solo Timpanist* (1963), *Suite of Three* for harp (1963), *Lamentations of Jeremiah* for chorus, a cappella (1964), *Four Phantasms for orchestra* (1964), *Toccata for Piano and Orchestra* (1964), *Four Conversations* for woodwind quintet (1965), *Mass in English* for chorus and organ (1965), *Pro Vita* for piano and brass quintet (1965), *Penta-Tholoi* for piano (1966), *Three Psalms* for chorus, a cappella (1966), *Violin Sonata*, "Venus and Mercury" (1967), *Phenomena*, "for Baroque quartet" (1967), *Ante Mortem* and *Post Mortem* for bass baritone and piano (1967), *Autumn Evening* and *Evening Ebb* for soprano and piano (1968), *Suite* for string bass and harpsichord (1968), *Idioms* for violin, clarinet, and French horn (1968), *Diorama* for organ (1968), *The Song of Deborah* for chorus, narrator, and orchestra (1969), *The Oratorio of Understanding* for soloists, chorus, and orchestra (1969), *Orthographics* for 4 trombones (1970), *A Game of Circles* for clarinet, piano, and celesta (1971), *Life-Styles I and II, III, and IV* for piano trio (1972), *Symphony No. IV for Strings* (1972), *Quintessences* for brass quintet (1973), *Tamar* for soprano and prepared piano (1973), *Eleatron* for viola and piano (1975), *Intensity* ♯*2* for winds (1975), *FanFare for the Two Hundredth* for orchestra (1975), *Quiet Movement, Kanon and Fantasy* for 2 marimbas (1975), *Symphony No. V* (1975), *Impressions from Life* for chamber group (1976), *Shadowy Waters* for clarinet, piano, and cello (1977), *Ecstacies of Janus*, song cycle for countertenor and chamber ensemble (1978), *Time Reflections*, "cantata enigmatica" for chorus and chamber orchestra (1978), *Fragments, Disputes, Mirrors* for 2 oboes (1978), and *Variables* for saxophone quartet (1979).

IMBRIE, ANDREW (b. 1921) Composer, teacher. Born in New York City, Apr. 6, 1921, Imbrie was a piano student of Leo Ornstein (q.v.) and a composition student of Roger Sessions (q.v.) at Princeton University and the University of California, Berkeley, from which he was graduated in 1947. Between the periods with Sessions, Imbrie served in the U. S. Army Signal Corps during World War II. He has been on the musical staff at the University of California at Berkeley since 1947 and professor of music since 1960. Imbrie's compositions include *String Quartet No. 1* (1942), *Piano Sonata* (1947), *Ballad in D* for orchestra (1947), *Divertimento* for sextet (1948), *On the Beach at Night* for chorus (1948), *Serenade* for flute, violin, and piano (1952), *String Quartet No. 2* (1953), *Violin Concerto* (1954), *Little Concerto* for piano, 4 hands (1956), *String Quartet No. 3* (1957), *Legend* for orchestra (1959), *Impromptu* for violin and piano (1960), *Christmas in Peeples Town*, opera (1960), *String Quartet No. 4* (1960), *Drum Taps*, cantata (1961), *Psalm 42* for male chorus and organ (1962), *Symphony No. 1* (1965), *Cello Sonata* (1966), *Three Sketches* for trombone and piano (1967), *Chamber Sym-*

phony (1968), *Symphony No. 2* (1969), *Symphony No. 3* (1970), *Cello Concerto* (1972), *Piano Concerto No. 1* (1973), *Piano Concerto No. 2* (1974), *Flute Concerto* (1974), and *Angle of Repose*, opera (1976).

JACKSON, MAHALIA (1911–1972) Gospel singer. Born in New Orleans, La., Oct. 26, 1911, Jackson learned singing from the early blues singers in her hometown. She rejected jazz and other popular-folk forms in favor of singing hymns—gospel music. In 1927 Jackson moved to Chicago, where she worked as a maid in a hotel and ran a beauty shop and a flower shop. She sang in Baptist churches in Chicago before she began making recordings in the mid '30s; her first success came, however, in 1954: "Move On Up a Little Higher." Many of the gospel songs Jackson sang and recorded were her own creations. She appeared at Carnegie Hall in the '50s, was acclaimed at the Newport Jazz Festival in 1957 and 1958, and sang at the inauguration of President John F. Kennedy in 1961. She was also most successful abroad, where her fervent, sincere gospel style endeared her to large numbers of Europeans. In the later phase of her career, Jackson unbent a little and sang popular songs provided she approved of their content and thought they were in good taste. During one of her European tours she was hospitalized in Munich with a heart condition and was forced to take time out during 1964–65. In 1971 she again went on a European tour, but it was cut short by another heart attack. Jackson died in Evergreen Park (a suburb of Chicago), Ill., Jan. 27, 1972. She has appeared in films, *St. Louis Blues* (1958) among them, and published her autobiography, *Movin' On,* in 1966.

JARRETT, KEITH (b. 1945) Composer, pianist, saxophonist. Born in Allentown, Pa., May 8, 1945, Jarrett began picking out melodies on the family upright when he was about 3. Around this same time he began taking piano lessons. By the time he was 7 he appeared in public performing the standard classics and his own compositions. Besides perfect pitch, Jarrett also has a gift for improvisation. He began professionally playing in a local Dixieland band and was heard by bandleader Fred Waring, who hired Jarrett as a pianist for his orchestra. Jarrett was offered a scholarship to study with Nadia Boulanger (q.v.), which he rejected, explaining, "There's some very fragile thing that can easily be destroyed by studying, and on the other hand there are other things you can learn by studying. But there are different ways of study. . . ." He then enrolled in the Berklee School of Music, Boston, but left after a year ("It's a trade school really") to try his luck in New York City. In ca. 1965 Jarrett was playing jazz piano rather than the standard repertory in the classic field. He eventually joined the orchestras of Art Blakey and Charles Lloyd; he also formed his own trio, with which he recorded. For a time (1970–71) Jarrett also played in the Miles Davis (q.v.) band. Jarrett soon achieved a following and a reputation for jazz improvisations as well as classical performances—especially in Europe. He frequently performed with his own group or presented solo piano recitals; his recorded output consists of jazz improvisations and original large-scale compositions. His compositions, most of them dating from the '70s, have such titles as *Pagan Hymn* for piano, *Fughata* for harpsichord, *Short Piece* for guitar and strings, *Crystal Moment* for cello quartet and 2 trombones, *Metamorphosis* for flute and strings, *In the Cave* and *In the Light* for orchestra, *Hymns/Spheres* for solo organ, and a *String Quartet* and a *Brass Quintet.* Unlike many of his contemporaries, Jarrett shuns electronic instruments. His other compositions/improvisations include *Coral, Gypsy Moth, Pardon My Rags, (If the) Misfits (Wear It), Still Life,* and *Mortgage on My Soul.* A unique talent, Jarrett simply does not fall into the usual musical categories.

JOHNSTON, BEN (b. 1926) Composer, pianist, teacher. Born in Macon, Ga., Mar. 15, 1926, Johnston studied composition with Mary Leighton at the Cincinnati Conservatory of Music. He also studied at Mills College, Oakland, Calif.; the University of California, Berkeley; the University of Illinois, Urbana; and the Columbia-Princeton Electronic Music Center, New York City. Among his teachers were Darius Milhaud (q.v.), Burrill Phillips (q.v.), Claire Richards, Robert Palmer (q.v.), John Powell (q.v.), John Cage (q.v.), and Harry Partch (q.v.). Johnston spent a couple of years as a pianist in a dance band. Since 1951 he has been on the music staff at the University of Illinois, Urbana. His work has been influenced by the experimentation of Cage and the use of unusual instruments, among which is the "microtonal piano" that Johnston devised with the aid of Arnold Brewe, a piano technician. His compositions include *Night* for baritone, women's chorus, and chamber group (1955), *Three Chinese Lyrics* for soprano and 2 violins (1955), *Gertrude, or Would She Be Pleased to Receive It?,* opera for soloists, chorus, and chamber ensemble (1956), *Gambit for Dancers and Orchestra,* ballet (1959), *Nine Variations* for string quartet (1959), *Five Fragments* for alto, oboe, cello, and bassoon (1960), *Ivesberg Revisited* for jazz band (1960), *A Sea Dirge* for mezzo-soprano, flute, violin, and oboe (1962), *Knocking Piece* for piano and percussion (1962), *Duo* for flute and string bass (1963), *String Quartet No. 2* (1964), *Sonata for Microtonal Piano* (1965), *Quintet for Groups* for orchestra (1966), *String Quartet No. 3* (1966), *Ci-gît Satie* for chorus (originally the Swingle Singers), double bass, and drums (1967), *Museum Piece,* film sound track (1969), *Carmilla,* opera (1970), *Mass* for chorus, 8 trombones, and rhythm (1972), *String Quartet No. 4* (1973), *In Memory, Harry Partch* for soprano, computer tape, tape, string quartet, and 8 percussionists (1975), and *String Quartet No. 5* (1975).

KANDER AND EBB Successful songwriting team: John Kander (b. Kansas City, Mo., Mar. 18, 1927) and Fred Ebb (b. New York City, Apr. 8, 1932). Composer Kander studied music at Oberlin College, Ohio, and at Columbia University, New York City. Upon graduation he began working in the musical theatre as a rehearsal pianist, conductor, and arranger. He wrote his first Broadway score with James and William Goldman for *A Family Affair* (1962), which was not very successful. Lyricist Ebb was educated at New York University and Columbia, then began contributing individual songs to revues. Kander and Ebb collaborated on their first songs in the early '60s: "My Coloring Book" (1962), which was written for Kaye Ballard, and "I Don't Care Much" (1963). The first was taken up by Barbra Streisand. The first Kander and Ebb musical was *Flora, the Red Menace* (1965). Their *Cabaret* (1966), set in Berlin just before the advent of Hitler, was a searing, unsentimental musical and a great success (1,165 performances). Other Kander and Ebb musicals include *The Happy Time* (1968), *Zorba* (1968), *70, Girls, 70* (1971), *Chicago* (1975), and *The Act,* written as a vehicle for Liza Minnelli (1977).

KIM, EARL (b. 1920) Composer, teacher. Born in Dinuba, Calif., Jan. 6, 1920, Kim was a composition student of Arnold Schoenberg (q.v.) and Roger Sessions (q.v.); he was graduated from the University of California at Berkeley in 1952. He then taught at Princeton University until 1967, when he moved to Harvard University, where he was appointed professor of music. His works include *Two Bagatelles* for piano (1948, 1950), *Dialogues* for piano and orchestra (1959), *They Are Far Out* for soprano, violin, cello, and percussion (1966), and *Gooseberries, She Said* for soprano, quintet, and percussion (1968). There are also a sonata for violin and piano, a sonata for cello and piano, the song *Letter Found Near a Suicide,* the song cycle *The Road* for baritone and piano, *Earthlight* for soprano, violin, and piano, a *Violin Concerto* (1979), and *Narratives* for narrator and chamber group (1979).

"THE KING AND I" Musical play (1951) with music by Richard Rodgers (q.v.) and lyrics and book by Oscar Hammerstein II (q.v.). Hammerstein based the book on the novel *Anna and the King of Siam* by Margaret Landon, which, in turn, had been drawn from *The English Governess at the Siamese Court,* the diaries of Anna Leonowens. Set in Siam in the 1860s, *The King and I* told the story of an English governess, Anna, who has been hired to be the teacher of the King's many children. The effect of Anna upon the King, his children, and the court is the stuff of the musical play; though of different backgrounds, Anna and the King eventually learn to respect each other's views. Unusually for a musical, the King dies before the end of the show. Although Anna had decided to leave, because of clashes with the King, she decides to remain with the children. *The King and I* proved to be one of Rodgers and Hammerstein's most successful musicals; it opened at the St. James Theatre, New York City, Mar. 29, 1951, and ran for 1,246 performances. It was also successful in London. There have been many revivals and a film version in 1956. The original King was portrayed by Yul Brynner and Anna by Gertrude Lawrence, who died during the run of the show; she was replaced by Constance Carpenter. Among the songs written for *The King and I* were "Hello, Young Lovers," "Shall We Dance?," "Getting to Know You," "A Puzzlement," "Something Wonderful," and the instrumental *March of the Siamese Children.*

KOHN, KARL (b. 1926) Composer, pianist, conductor, teacher. Born in Vienna, Austria, Aug. 1, 1926, Kohn was brought to the United States in 1938 after Nazi Germany annexed Austria. He studied at the New York College of Music (piano and conducting), 1940–44. In 1946 he entered Harvard to study with Walter Piston (q.v.), Edward Ballantine, Irving Fine (q.v.), and Randall Thompson (q.v.). Since 1950 Kohn has taught piano and theory at Pomona College, Claremont, Calif.; he has also taught at the Berkshire Music Center, Tanglewood, Mass. He has been active in the Monday Evening Concerts, Los Angeles. Kohn's compositions include *Sinfonia Concertante* for piano and orchestra (1951), *Fanfare* for brass and percussion (1952), *Motets* for horn octet (1953), *Overture* for strings (1956), *Concert Music* for winds (1956), *Three Descants* for chorus and piano (1957), *Quartet* for horns (1957), *Castles and Kings* for orchestra (1958), *Three Pieces* for flute and piano (1959), *Rhapsody No. 1* for piano (1960), *Three Scenes* for orchestra (1960), *Five Bagatelles* for piano (1961), *Sensus spei* for chorus and piano (1961), *Capriccio* for flute, clarinet, cello, harp, and piano (1962), *Concerto mutabile* for piano and orchestra (1962), *Serenade* for wind quintet and piano (1962), *Partita* for piano (1963), *Little Suite* for wind quintet (1963), *Interludes* for orchestra (1964), *Kaleidoscope* for string quartet

(1964), *Sonata da camera* for alto flute, clarinet, and piano (1964), *Encounters I* for flute, piccolo, and piano (1965), *Episodes* for piano and orchestra (1966), *Introduction and Parodies* for clarinet, bassoon, horn, string quartet, and piano (1967), *Encounters II* for horn and piano (1967), *Musical Pictures* for violin and piano (1967), *Recreations* for piano, 4 hands (1968), *Rhapsodies* for marimba, vibraphone, and percussion (1968), *Impromptus* for wind octet (1968), *Interlude I* for flute and strings (1969), *Interlude II* for piano and strings (1969), *Reflections* for clarinet and piano (1970), *Esdras* for chorus, flute, piano, and orchestra (1970), *Rhapsody No. 2* for piano (1971), *Encounters III* for violin and piano (1971), *Trio* for violin, horn, and piano (1972), *Centone per Orchestra* (1973), *Bits and Pieces* for piano (1973), *Paronyms* for flutes and piano (1974), *Concerto* for horn and piano (1974), *Innocent Psaltery* for orchestra (1976), *The Prophet Bird* for orchestra (1976), *Rhapsody No. 3* for piano (1977), and *Son of Prophet Bird* for harp (1977).

KOLB, BARBARA (b. 1939) Composer, conductor. Born in Hartford, Conn., Feb. 10, 1939, Kolb studied composition with Arnold Franchetti at the Hartt College of Music, Hartford, and with Gunther Schuller (q.v.) and Lukas Foss (q.v.) at Tanglewood, Mass. A Prix de Rome enabled her to spend a year at the American Academy (1969–70). Kolb's compositions include *Rebuttal* for 2 clarinets (1964), *Chansons Bas* for soprano, harp, and 2 percussionists (1966), *Figments* for flute and piano (1967), *Three Place Settings* for narrator, clarinet, violin, double bass, and percussion (1968), *Crosswinds* for alto saxophone and winds (1969), *Toccata* for harpsichord and tape (1971), *The Sentences* for voice and guitar, text

by Robert Pinsky (1976), *Spring River Flowers Moon Night* for 2 pianos, guitar, mandolin, and percussion ensemble (1976), and *Grisaille* for orchestra (1979).

KORTE, KARL (b. 1928) Composer, teacher. Born in Ossining, N.Y., June 23, 1928, Korte grew up in Englewood, N.J. Korte's earliest musical experience was in jazz and popular music. A graduate of the Juilliard School of Music, New York City, he has taught at Brevard Music Center, Spartanburg, S.C.; Arizona State University, Tempe; Harpur College, State University of New York, Binghamton, N.Y.; and the University of Texas, Austin, where he is professor of composition. Korte's works include *A Mass for Youth, Nocturne and March* for band, *Song and Dance* for string orchestra, 2 symphonies, *Remembrances* for flute and tape (1972), *Pale Is This Good Prince,* an oratorio, *Matrix* for woodwind quintet, *Concerto for Piano and Winds* (1976), and *Piano Trio* (1979).

KRAFT, LEO (b. 1922) Composer, pianist, teacher. Born in New York City, July 24, 1922, Kraft studied composition at Queens College, City University of New York, with Karol Rathaus, then with Randall Thompson (q.v.) at Princeton University. Upon graduation he joined the musical teaching staff of Queens College. During 1954–55 he studied with Nadia Boulanger (q.v.) in Paris. His compositions include a *Short Suite* for flute, clarinet and bassoon (1951), *Concerto No. 1* for flute, clarinet, trumpet, and strings (1951), *A Proverb of Solomon* for chorus and chamber orchestra (1953), *Let Me Laugh* for chorus and piano (1954), *Two's Company* for 2 clarinets (1957), *Variations* for orchestra (1958), *Partita No. 1* for piano (1958), *String Quartet No. 2* (1959), *When Israel Came Forth* for chorus (1961), *Partita No. 2* for violin and viola (1961), *English Love Songs* for voice and piano (1961), *Five Pieces* for clarinet and piano (1962), *Three Pieces* for orchestra (1963), *Partita No. 3* for wind quintet (1964), *Statements and Commentaries* for piano (1965), *Trios and Interludes* for flute, viola, and piano (1965), *Night Music* for orchestra (1965), *Concerto No. 3* for chamber orchestra (1966), *Short Sonata No. 1* for harpsichord (1968), *String Quartet No. 2* (1968), *Dialogues* for flute and tape (1968), *Spring in the Harbor* for soprano, flute, cello, and piano (1969), *Concerto No. 3* for cello, winds, and percussion (1969), *Dualities* for 2 trumpets (1970), *Short Sonata No. 2* for harpsichord (1970), *Pentagram* for alto saxophone (1971), *Line Drawings* for flute and percussion (1972), *Ten Short Pieces* for piano (1976), *Trios and Interludes* for flute, viola, and piano (1977), and *Diaphonies* for oboe and piano (1978). Kraft is the author of *A New Approach to Ear Training* (1967) and *Gradus: An Integrated Approach to Harmony, Counterpoint, and Analysis* (1976).

KRAFT, WILLIAM (b. 1923) Composer, teacher, percussionist. Born in Chicago, Ill., Sept. 6, 1923, Kraft grew up in New York City and attended Columbia University, where his teachers were Henry Cowell, Normand Lockwood, Otto Luening, Jack Beeson, Seth Bingham, and Vladimir Ussachevsky (all q.v.). He graduated in 1952. During much the same period he studied timpani techniques with Saul Goodman and percussion with Morris Goldenberg at the Juilliard School of Music. In 1948 he studied composition with Irving Fine (q.v.) and conducting with Leonard Bernstein (q.v.) at the Berkshire Music Center, Tanglewood, Mass. He also studied composition with Boris Orr, at Cambridge University, England. Since 1955 he has been the lead percussionist with the Los Angeles Philharmonic. Kraft's compositions include *Three Miniatures* for percussion and orchestra (1958), *Nonet* for brass (1959), *Variations on a Folksong* for orchestra (1960), *Symphony* for strings and percussion (1961), *Concerto Grosso* for flute, bassoon, violin, cello, and orchestra (1961–62), *Morris Dance* for percussion solo (1963), *Silent Boughs* for soprano and strings (1963), *Concerto* for 4 percussionists and orchestra (1964), *Derivations* for orchestra (1964), *Configurations* for 4 percussionists and jazz orchestra (1965), *Momentum* for 8 percussionists (1966), *Encounters II* for solo tuba (1966), *Contextures: Riots—Decade '60* for orchestra (1967), *Triangles,* concerto for percussion and 10 instruments (1968), *Games: Collage No. 1* for brass and percussion (1969), *Mobiles* for 10 instruments (1970), *Cadenze* for 7 instruments (1972), *Piano Concerto* (1973), *Requiescat* for Rhodes electric piano (1974), *Des Imagistes* for 2 readers and percussion (1974), and *Tuba Concerto* (1978).

KUPFERMAN, MEYER (b. 1926) Composer, teacher. Born in New York City, July 3, 1926, Kupferman was educated at the High School of Music and Art, New York City, and at Queens College, City University of New York. He also studied the clarinet. He is self-taught in composition. Since 1951 he has been on the staff of Sarah Lawrence College, Bronxville, N.Y., where he teaches composition and chamber music. His compositions, many drawing upon 12-tone techniques and Cage-like experimentation, include *Little Sonata* for piano (1948), *Divertimento* for orchestra (1948), *In a Garden,* one-act opera (1948), *Variations* for piano (1948), *Libretto* for orchestra (1949), *Chamber*

Symphony (1950), *Little Symphony* (1952), *Evocation* for cello and piano (1952), *Doctor Faustus Lights the Lights,* opera (1953), *Ostinato Burlesco* for orchestra (1954), *Chamber Concerto* for flute, piano, and quartet (1955), *Symphony No. 4* (1956), *Lyric Symphony* (1956), *The Curious Fern,* one-act opera (1957), *Voices for a Mirror,* one-act opera (1957), *String Quartet No. 4* (1958), *Sonata on Jazz Elements* for piano (1958), *Variations* for orchestra (1959), *Curtain Raiser* for flute, clarinet, horn, and piano (1960), *Jazz Infinities No. 1* for flute (1961), *Jazz Infinities No. 2* for saxophone, double bass, and drums (1961), *Concerto* for cello and jazz band (1962), *Jazz Infinities No. 12* for chamber orchestra (1964), *Three Ideas* (1967), *The Judgment,* opera (1967), *Moonchild and the Doomsday Trombone* for voice, oboe, jazz ensemble, and chamber orchestra (1968), *Persephone,* ballet (1968), *Tunnel of Love* for jazz group (1971), *Concerto* for cello, tape, and orchestra (1974), *Abracadabra Quartet* for piano and strings (1976), *The Red King's Throne* for clarinet, piano, cello, and percussion (1978), and *A Nietzsche Cycle* for soprano, piano, and horn (1979).

KURKA, ROBERT (1921–1957) Composer, violinist. Born in Cicero, Ill., Dec. 22, 1921, Kurka studied the violin before switching to composition, which he studied with Darius Milhaud (q.v.) and Otto Luening (q.v.). He was the recipient of 2 Guggenheim Fellowships (1951, 1952). Besides a number of chamber works, including 5 string quartets, Kurka during an all too brief lifespan produced several impressive compositions, among them the *Symphony No. 2* (1953), the *Serenade for Small Orchestra* (1954), and *The Good Soldier Schweik,* suite for orchestra (1956). Kurka's opera, expanded from the suite, was produced posthumously in New York City in 1958. Kurka died in New York City, of leukemia, Dec. 12, 1957.

LADERMAN, EZRA (b. 1924) Composer, teacher. Born in Brooklyn, N.Y., June 29, 1924, Laderman began composing while he was a student at the High School of Music and Art, New York City. He then served in the U. S. Army during World War II; during this time he composed his *Leipzig Symphony* (1945) during his off-duty time. After the war he attended Brooklyn College; he then went on to Columbia University, where he studied composition with Otto Luening (q.v.) and Douglas Moore (q.v.). He also studied privately with Stefan Wolpe (q.v.). Laderman has taught at Sarah Lawrence College, Bronxville, N.Y., and has served as composer-in-residence at the Bennington Composers' Conference. His compositions include *Theme, Variations, and Finale* for chamber group (1957), *Jacob and the Indians,* opera (1957), *Sarah,* one-act opera for television (1958), *String Quartet No. 1* (1959), *Violin Sonata* (1959), *Goodbye to the Clown,* opera (1960), *Stanzas* for chamber orchestra (1960), *The Eagle Stirred,* oratorio (1961), *The Hunting of the Snark,* children's opera (1961), *Violin Concerto* (1961), *Songs for Eve* for soprano and piano (1963), *The Black Fox,* film score (1963), *Nonette* for chamber group (1963), *Symphony No. 1* (1964), *String Quartet No. 2* (1965), *The Trials of Galileo,* oratorio (1967), *Magic Prison* for 2 narrators and orchestra (1967), *Satire: Concerto for Orchestra* (1968), *Symphony No. 2* (1968), *Shadows Among Us,* 2-act opera (1969), and *And David Wept,* cantata (1971). Laderman has also composed 2 piano sonatas, several works for chamber groups (*Double Helix, Duo for Violin and Piano, Octet for Winds,* etc.), the prize-winning score for the film *The Eleanor Roosevelt Story,* and *Concerto for String Quartet*

(1980). In 1979 he was appointed director of the Music Program, National Endowment for the Arts.

LA MONTAINE, JOHN (b. 1920) Composer, pianist. Born in Chicago, Ill., Mar. 17, 1920, La Montaine grew up in Oak Park, Ill., where, before the age of 5, he was determined to become a composer and had begun to study the piano. In 1931 he gave his first piano recital in Bloomington, Ind.; on the program was his first piano composition. In 1935 he entered the American Conservatory of Music, Chicago, to study theory with Stella Roberts. Three years later he attended the Eastman School of Music, Rochester, N.Y., where his principal teachers were Howard Hanson and Bernard Rogers (both q.v.). From 1942 to 1946 La Montaine served in the U. S. Navy; during this period he also studied with Rudolph Ganz at the Chicago Musical College. After leaving the Navy, he returned to music, studying with Bernard Wagenaar (q.v.) at the Juilliard School of Music, New York City, and with Nadia Boulanger (q.v.) at the American Conservatory, Fontainebleau, France. He has taught at the Eastman School of Music (1961) and was composer in residence at the American Academy, Rome (1962). La Montaine played the piano and celeste in the NBC Symphony under Arturo Toscanini (1950–54). His first major composition was *Songs of the Rose of Sharon* for soprano and orchestra (1948). Between 1950 and 1958 he composed a few smaller works—*A Child's Picture Book* for piano, a *Sonata for Violoncello and Piano*—while he worked on his *Concerto for Piano and Orchestra* (1958; Pulitzer Prize). His other compositions include *Fragments from The Song of Songs* for soprano and orchestra (1959), *String Quartet* (1960), *Novellis, Novellis,* opera (1960), *Overture: From Sea to Shining Sea* for orchestra (1961), *Birds of Para-*

dise for piano and orchestra (1964), *Mass of Nature* for narrator, chorus, and orchestra (1966), *The Shephardes Playe,* opera (1967), *Erode the Greate,* opera (1969), *Incantation for Jazz Band* (1971), *Six Sonnets of Shakespeare* for high voice and piano (1971), *Wilderness Journal,* symphony for bass-baritone, organ, and orchestra (1972), *Conversations* for any solo instrument and piano (1973), *Wonder Tidings* for soloists, chorus, harp, and percussion (1974), *Nine Lessons of Christmas* for chorus and orchestra (1975), *Be Glad Then America, A Decent Entertainment from the Thirteen Colonies,* opera (1976), *Twelve Studies* for 2 flutes (1979), *The Whittier Service* for chorus, optional solos, guitar, and organ (1979), *Canonic Variations* for flute and clarinet (1980), and *Concerto for Flute and Orchestra* (1980).

LANSKY, PAUL (b. 1944) Composer, teacher. Born in New York City, June 18, 1944, Lansky studied composition with Hugo Weisgall (q.v.) and George Perle (q.v.) at Queens College, City University of New York, New York and with Milton Babbitt (q.v.), Edward Cone (q.v.), and others at Princeton University. He has taught at Princeton since 1969. His works include *String Quartet* (1967), *Computer Piece* on tape (1968), *Piano Piece in Three Parts* (1968), *Two Studies* for wind quintet (1969), *Short Serenade* for piano (1970), *Modal Fantasy* for piano (1970), *Crossworks* for chamber group (1975), and *String Quartet* (1971, revised 1977).

LAYTON, BILLY JIM (b. 1924) Composer, arranger, clarinetist, saxophonist, teacher. Born in Corsicana, Tex., Nov. 14, 1924, Layton, after military service during World War II, studied music at the New England Conservatory, Boston, under Francis Cooke and

Carl McKinley (q.v.). At Yale University he worked under Quincy Porter (q.v.), and at Harvard, under Walter Piston (q.v.); he was graduated with a Ph.D. in 1960. Layton also majored in musicology, which he studied with Nino Pirrotta and Otto Gombosi. He has taught at the New England Conservatory and Harvard, and since 1966 he has been on the music teaching staff at the State University of New York, Stony Brook, where he is chairman of the Department of Music. His compositions include *Five Studies* for violin and piano (1952), *An American Portrait* for orchestra (1953), *Three Dylan Thomas Poems* for chorus and brass sextet (1956), *String Quartet in Two Movements* (1956), *Three Studies* for piano (1957), *Divertimento* for chamber orchestra (1960), and *Dance Fantasy* for orchestra (1964).

LEE, NOËL (b. 1924) Composer, pianist, teacher. Born in Nanking, China, Dec. 25, 1924, Lee began studying music in Indiana, to which his family had moved. He revealed a talent for composition around the age of 6. He studied at Harvard University with Irving Fine (q.v.) and Walter Piston (q.v.). He also studied at the New England Conservatory and with Nadia Boulanger (q.v.) in Paris. A fine pianist, Lee has performed in recital and has made several recordings of music by contemporary composers. His own compositions include *Ballet Music* for orchestra (1950), *Quintet* (1952), *Capriccio* for orchestra (1952), *Four Rhapsodies* for chorus and orchestra (1952), *Fantasy in Four Movements* (1953), *Paraboles* for tenor, chorus, and orchestra (1954), *Overture and Litanies* for strings (1954), *Five Songs on Poems by Federico García Lorca* for soprano, flute, and guitar (1955), *String Quartet* (1956), *Dialogues* for violin and piano (1958), *Profile* for orchestra (1958), *Variations*

for orchestra (1960), *Convergences* for flute and harpsichord (1972), and *Caprices on the Name of Schoenberg* for piano and orchestra (1975).

LEES, BENJAMIN (b. 1924) Composer, pianist, teacher. Born in Harbin, Manchuria, China, Jan. 8, 1924, Lees was an infant when brought to the United States, where his parents settled in California. As a child he studied piano. After service in the U. S. Army during World War II, Lees enrolled in the University of Southern California, Los Angeles, where he studied composition with Halsey Stevens (q.v.) and piano with Marguerite Bitter (1946–48). He also studied orchestration and composition with George Antheil (q.v.). Lees has been the recipient of Guggenheim (1955) and Fulbright (1956) fellowships. He has taught at the Peabody Conservatory of Music, Baltimore; Queens College, City University of New York; New York and the Manhattan School of Music. His compositions include a *Piano Sonata No. 1* (1949), *Piano Sonata No. 2* (1950), *Sonata for Two Pianos* (1951), *Piano Sonata No. 3* (1951), *String Quartet No. 1* (1952), *Profile* for orchestra (1952), *Declamations* for piano and strings (1953), *Toccata* for piano (1953), *Symphony No. 1* (1953), *Violin Sonata No. 1* (1954), *Three Variables* for piano and wind quartet (1955), *The Oracle*, drama with music (1955), *String Quartet No. 2* (1955), *Piano Concerto No. 1* (1955), *Divertimento Burlesca* for orchestra (1957), *Symphony No. 2* (1957), *Violin Concerto* (1958), *Concerto for Orchestra* (1959), *Epigrams* for piano (1960), *Vision of Poets*, cantata (1961), *Oboe Concerto* (1963), *Spectrum* for orchestra (1964), *Piano Sonata No. 4* (1964), *The Gilded Cage*, opera (1964), *Concerto* for string quartet and orchestra (1965), *Concerto for Chamber Orchestra* (1966), *Piano Concerto No. 2*

(1966), *Silhouettes* for winds and percussion (1967), *Symphony No. 3* (1968), *Odyssey* for piano (1970), *Sonata for Violin and Piano No. 2* (1973), *Etudes* for piano and orchestra (1974), *Labyrinths* for winds (1975), *Variations* for piano and orchestra (1976), *Passacaglia* for orchestra (1976), *Concerto* for woodwind quintet and orchestra (1976), and *Dialogue* for cello and piano (1977).

LEIGH, CAROLYN (b. 1926) Lyricist, writer. Born in New York City, Aug. 21, 1926, Leigh was educated at Queens College, Long Island, N.Y., and New York University, New York City. She began her professional writing career as a copywriter in an advertising agency and as writer of continuity for radio. At the same time she continued to write poems and lyrics which she had been doing since she was a child. A song written in 1953 with composer Johnny Richards, "Young at Heart," was taken up by Frank Sinatra (q.v.) and was her first success. That success led to her first major Broadway show, *Peter Pan* (1954). In collaboration with composer Morris (also known as Moose and Mark) Charlap she contributed additional songs to the show, among them "Tender Shepherd," "I'm Flying," "I've Gotta Crow," and "I Won't Grow Up." Her next 2, complete, shows were written with Cy Coleman (q.v.), *Wildcat* (1960), whose "Hey, Look Me Over" was successful, and *Little Me* (1962). The team of Leigh and Coleman broke up and she collaborated with Hollywood film composer Elmer Bernstein (b. 1922) on the songs for the Broadway production *How Now, Dow Jones* (1967). Leigh has also written lyrics for several nonproduction songs and for films.

LESSARD, JOHN (b. 1920) Composer, teacher. Born in San Francisco, Calif., July 3, 1920, Lessard was a student of Nadia Boulanger (q.v.). He has been on the music staff of the State University of New York, Stony Brook, since 1963. His works include a *Piano Sonata* (1940), *Violin Concerto* (1942), *Lullaby* for voice and piano (1944), *Box Hill Overture* for orchestra (1946), *Mask* for piano (1946), *Cantilena* for oboe and string orchestra (1947), *Little Concert* for orchestra (1947), *Three Movements* for violin and piano (1948), *Concerto* for wind instruments (1949), *Toccata in Four Movements* for harpsichord (1951), *Octet* for winds (1952), *Concerto* for winds and strings (1952), *Serenade* for string orchestra (1953), *Four Preludes* for piano (1954), *Don Quixote and the Sheep* for bass, baritone, and orchestra (1955), *Three Songs for St. Cecilia's Day* for voice and piano (1956), *Sonata* for cello and piano (1956), *Serenade* for orchestra (1957), *Four Songs About Love* for voice and piano (1957), *Trio* for flute, violin, and piano (1959), *Suite* for orchestra (1959), *Sinfonietta Concertante* for orchestra (1961), *Duo Sonata in Five Movements* for violin and piano (1962), *String Trio* (1963), *Concerto* for harp and orchestra (1963), *Twelve Songs from Mother Goose* for voice and string trio (1964), *Trio in Sei Parti* for violin, cello, and piano (1966), *Fragments from the Cantos of Ezra Pound* for baritone and chamber group (1969), *Wind Quintet II* (1970), *Twelve Sketches* for piano, 4 hands (1972), *Pastimes and Alleluia* for orchestra (1974), and *Movements* for trumpet and various instruments: I—trumpet and vibraphone (1976), II—trumpet and viola (1976), III—trumpet and violin (1976), IV—trumpet and percussion (1976), V—trumpet, violin, and cello (1977), VI—trumpet, viola, cello, and percussion (1978), VII—trumpet and cello (1978), VIII—trumpet, flute, harp, and 2 cellos (1979).

LEWIS, JOHN (b. 1920) Pianist, arranger, composer. Born in La Grange, Ill., May 3, 1920, Lewis grew up in Albuquerque, N.Mex., where he began piano lessons at the age of 7. He was a student at the University of New Mexico, majoring in music and anthropology, when he went into the U. S. Army in 1942. After the war he settled in New York City, where, besides attending classes at the Manhattan School of Music, he began writing arrangements for Dizzy Gillespie (q.v.). He also served as pianist-arranger with the bands of Illinois Jacquet, Miles Davis (q.v.), and Kenny Clarke, a friend from Lewis' army days. In 1952 he formed the Modern Jazz Quartet (Lewis: piano; Milt Jackson: vibraphone; Percy Heath: bass; Kenny Clarke, and later Connie Kay: drums). From that time until the group dissolved in the late '70s, the Modern Jazz Quartet was one of the most influential units in contemporary jazz. Lewis' arrangements fused classical performance with jazz performance (i.e., "Third Stream," q.v.). Besides the originals and arrangements Lewis created for Gillespie and the Modern Jazz Quartet, he has composed works of ambitious design, among them *Toccata for Trumpet and Orchestra* (written for Gillespie in 1947). For the Quartet he composed the highly praised *Django* (1954). He has written several screen scores, among them scores for the French film *Sait-on Jamais* (released in the United States as *No Sun in Venice* in 1957) and *Odds Against Tomorrow* (1959). His ballet, *Original Sin*, was performed by the San Francisco Ballet in 1961.

LEWIS, ROBERT HALL (b. 1926) Composer, trumpeter, teacher. Born in Portland, Ore., Apr. 22, 1926, Lewis has studied composition, conducting, and the trumpet. Among his teachers in composition were Bernard Rogers (q.v.), Ernst Krenek (at the Vienna Academy of

Music), and Nadia Boulanger (q.v.) in Paris (1952–53). He also worked under conductors Eugène Bigot and Pierre Monteux. His principal instructors in the trumpet were Harry Glantz and Nathan Prager. Lewis has played trumpet in the Oklahoma City Symphony and the Rochester (N.Y.) Philharmonic. He has taught at Goucher College, Towson, Md., and at Johns Hopkins University, Baltimore, Md. His compositions include *String Quartet No. 1* (1956), *Five Songs* for soprano, clarinet, horn, cello, and piano (1957), *Prelude and Finale* for chamber orchestra (1959), *Five Movements* for piano (1960), *String Quartet No. 2* (1962), *Toccata* for violin and percussion (1963), *Designs* for orchestra (1963), *Symphony No. 1* (1964), *Music for Twelve Players* (1965), *Three Pieces* for orchestra (1966), *Trio* for violin, clarinet, and piano (1966), *Monophony No. 1* for flute (1966), *Monophony No. 3* for clarinet (1966), *Music for Brass Quintet* (1966), *Concerto* for chamber orchestra (1967), *Monophony No. 4* for bassoon (1967), *Diptychon* for orchestra (1967), *Sonata for Violin* (1968), *Monophony No. 2* for oboe (1968), *Tangents* for brass (1968), *Divertimento* for sextet (1969), *Inflection No. 1* for double bass (1969), *Serenades* for piano (1970), *Inflection No. 2* for violin, cello, and piano (1970), *Symphony No. 2* (1971), and *Nuances II* for orchestra (1975).

LUKE, RAY (b. 1928) Composer, conductor, teacher. Born in Fort Worth, Tex., May 30, 1928, Luke was educated at Texas Christian University, Fort Worth, and at the Eastman School of Music, Rochester, N.Y. (Ph.D. in theory and composition, 1960). He has taught at Atlantic Christian College, Wilson, N.C.; East Texas State University, Commerce; and Oklahoma City University, where he is head of the Instrumental Music Department. He has served as musical director of the Oklahoma City Lyric Theatre and since 1968 has been associate conductor of the Oklahoma City Symphony. Luke's compositions include *Suite No. 1* for orchestra (1958), *Symphony No. 2* (1961), *Symphony No. 3* (1963), *Symphonic Dialogues* for violin, oboe, and orchestra (1965), *Concerto* for bassoon and orchestra (1965), *Suite No. 2* for orchestra (1967), and *Medea,* opera (1979).

LYBBERT, DONALD (b. 1923) Composer, teacher. Born in Cresco, Iowa, Feb. 19, 1923, Lybbert is a graduate of the University of Iowa, Iowa City; at the Juilliard School of Music, New York City, he was a student of Bernard Wagenaar (q.v.) and Robert Ward (q.v.). At Columbia University he studied with Elliott Carter (q.v.) and Otto Luening (q.v.). He also studied, at the Fontainebleau School in France, with Nadia Boulanger (q.v.). He has taught at Hunter College, New York City, where he was also associated with the Electronic Studio. Lybbert's compositions include *Monica,* opera (1952), the song cycle *From Harmonium* (1954), *Introduction and Toccata* for brass and piano (1955), *Trio* for clarinet, horn, and bassoon (1956), *Chamber Sonata* for viola, horn, and piano (1957), *Concert Overture* for orchestra (1958), *Leopardi Canti* for soprano and chamber group (1959), *Movement* for piano, 4 hands (1960), *Sonorities* for chamber orchestra (1960), *Austro Terris Influente* for chorus (1961), *Sonata Brevis* for piano (1962), *Praeludium* for brass and percussion (1963), *The Scarlet Letter,* opera (1967), *Lines for the Fallen* for soprano and 2 pianos (1967), *Variants* for wind quintet (1973), and *Octagon* for soprano and chamber group (1975). Lybbert is the author of *The Essentials of Counterpoint* (1969).

THE LYRICS AND LYRICISTS SERIES A unique program initiated in 1970 by Arthur Cantor of the Billy Rose Foundation and presented at the 92nd Street YM-YWHA, New York City, to spotlight the unsung hero of songwriting, the lyricist. The series opened with "An Evening with E. Y. 'Yip' Harburg" (q.v.) on Sunday, Dec. 13, 1970. The series was sponsored by the Billy Rose Foundation and the 92nd Street Y under the direction of the Y's Music Department's Mrs. Hadasah Markson, who asked the conductor Maurice Levine to serve as artistic director. The point was to bring in the lyricist himself to discuss the art of songwriting. An immediate success (sellouts often required a 2nd evening), *Lyrics and Lyricists* was still continuing after a decade. Among the lyricists appearing were Comden and Green, Sheldon Harnick, Alan Jay Lerner, Johnny Mercer, Dorothy Fields, Carolyn Leigh (all q.v.), and others. The songwriters sang their own songs and were joined by more polished singers, among them Bobbi Baird, Margaret Whiting, Margery Gray, and Sylvia Syms. The programs were also recorded to preserve the comments of the songwriters, as well as their inimitable vocalizing. Some of these "Evenings," slightly condensed, were issued on long-playing records on the Laureate Records label (the first set contains the Evenings with Johnny Mercer, Alan Jay Lerner, and Sheldon Harnick) by the ML Record Co., 15 West 72nd Street, New York, N.Y., 10023.

MANCINI, HENRY (b. 1924) Composer, arranger, conductor, pianist. Born in Cleveland, Ohio, Apr. 16, 1924, Mancini grew up in Aliquippa, Pa., a steel mill town, to which his family moved while he was still an infant. He began studying the flute at 8 but eventually switched to the piano. His first musical performing experience was through playing in several local bands, including the Pennsylvania All State Band. Meanwhile, he studied with an eminent Pittsburgh conductor-arranger, Max Adkins. On finishing high school in 1942 Mancini enrolled in the Juilliard School of Music, New York City, but his education was interrupted by World War II; from 1942 until 1945 Mancini was in the U. S. Army Air Forces. After the war he joined the Tex Beneke–Glenn Miller orchestra as pianist-arranger. After leaving the band, Mancini settled in Hollywood, where he began scoring films; in 1952 he joined the musical staff of Universal-International. Among the scores he prepared were those for *Abbott and Costello Lost in Alaska,* Orson Welles's *Touch of Evil,* and the one for which he received his first Academy Award nomination, *The Glenn Miller Story* (1954). Switching to television Mancini wrote the very popular themes for 2 successful shows, *Peter Gunn* (1959) and *Mr. Lucky* (1960). In 1961, working with lyricist Johnny Mercer (q.v.), Mancini produced his first Academy Award-winning song, "Moon River," for the film *Breakfast at Tiffany's.* This was followed the next year with the Award-winning title song to *Days of Wine and Roses.* On his own, Mancini composed the celebrated opening theme music for *The Pink Panther* (1964). A student of such musicians as Ernst Krenek, Alfred Sendrey, and Mario Castelnuovo-Tedesco, Mancini has written larger orchestral works, among them *Beaver Valley '37* (1978).

MANILOW, BARRY (b. 1946) Composer, arranger, pianist, popular entertainer. Born in Brooklyn, N.Y., June 17, 1946, Manilow was given an accordion at the age of 7 and, according to his mother, "played it beautifully." At 13 he acquired a piano and a stepfather, William Murphy, who introduced Manilow to Cool Jazz (in the form of a Gerry Mulligan concert) and to concert music. On completing high school, Manilow left home, moved into Manhattan and got a job in the mailroom at the Columbia Broadcasting System. Initially he was a student—in college—of advertising but left to study music nights at the New York College of Music and, later, the Juilliard School of Music. Still a mailroom employee at CBS, Manilow was approached by an off-Broadway producer to arrange the music for a musical version of *The Drunkard;* not only did Manilow assemble the traditional period songs, he also worked some of his own into the score. *The Drunkard* opened in 1964 and ran for 8 years. Encouraged, Manilow began to concentrate on music, working as an arranger and vocal coach. In 1967 he was working as music director of the television series *Callback!,* following that as conductor-arranger for "The Ed Sullivan Show." He also began writing commercial jingles for such products as McDonald's "Big Mac," Pepsi-Cola, Dr. Pepper, and Kentucky Fried Chicken. By 1972 Manilow set out on his own, beginning at the notorious nightclub, the Continental Baths, New York City, as accompanist for singer Bette Midler. Before he left Midler, in 1974, he had arranged and coproduced her best-selling album "The Divine Miss M" as well as a second, "Bette Midler." Encouraged again, Manilow began working up his own albums as both arranger and performer, as well as coproducer (with Ron Dante). He had the first of his Gold or Platinum discs (depending on the millions of sales) in 1975 with a recording of the song "Mandy" (written by others). He followed that the next year with 2 of his own songs, with lyrics by Marty Panzer, "It's a Miracle" and "Could It Be Magic," which the composer admits was lifted from Chopin. Since these successes, Manilow has had a lucrative career in recordings, concert tours, and television; his *The Barry Manilow Special* (1977) was nominated for no less than 3 Emmys; a 2nd (1978) was equally successful. His "I Write the Songs" won a Grammy Award nomination in 1976. Manilow's style has been called "Romantic Pop," but undoubtedly his showmanship and arrangements have contributed to his impressive popularity and success.

MARTINO, DONALD (b. 1931) Composer, teacher. Born in Plainfield, N.J., May 16, 1931, Martino learned to play the clarinet and other wind instruments from about the age of 9. At Syracuse University, N.Y., he studied with Ernst Bacon (q.v.); he did further work in music at Princeton University, N.J., with Milton Babbitt (q.v.). A Fulbright Fellowship enabled Martino to study with Luigi Dallapiccola in Italy (1954–56). He also studied with Roger Sessions (q.v.). Martino has taught at Princeton, Yale, and the New England Conservatory of Music, Boston. His compositions include *Set for Clarinet* (1954), *Quodlibets for Flute* (1954), *Anyone Lived in a Pretty How Town* for chorus and piano, 4 hands (1955), *Portraits* for soloists, chorus, and orchestra (1956), *Sette Canoni Enigmatici* for string quartet (or other instrumental combinations, 1956), *Contemplations* for orchestra (1957), *Piano Fantasy* (1958), *Trio* for violin, clarinet, and piano (1959), *Five Fragmenti* for oboe and double bass (1962), *Fantasy Variations* for violin (1962), *Concerto* for wind quintet (1964), *Piano Concerto* (1965), *B-a-b-b-i-t-t* for clarinet (1966), *Mosaic* for orchestra (1967), a piano sonata entitled *Pianissimo* (1970), *Seven Pious Pieces* for chorus (1971), *Notturno* for chamber group (1974), *Paradiso Choruses* for chorus, tape, and orchestra (1974), *Ritorno* for orchestra (1976), *Triple Concerto* for clarinet, bass clarinet, contrabass clarinet, and chamber orchestra (1977).

MARTIRANO, SALVATORE (b. 1927) Composer, teacher. Born in Yonkers, N.Y., Jan. 12, 1927, Martirano studied with Herbert Elwell (q.v.) at the Oberlin (Ohio) Conservatory and with Bernard Rogers (q.v.) at the Eastman School of Music, Rochester, N.Y. Martirano also studied with Luigi Dallapiccola in Florence, Italy. He served in the U. S. Marines as a clarinetist in the Marine Corps Band. He has been on the music faculty of the University of Illinois, Urbana, since the early 1960s. Martirano's works include *Sextet* for winds (1949), *Prelude* for orchestra (1950), *Variations* for flute and piano (1950), *String Quartet No. 1* (1951), *The Magic Stones,* chamber opera (1951), *Violin Sonata* (1952), *Contrasts* for orchestra (1954), *Chansons Innocentes* for soprano and piano (1957), *O, O, O, O, That Shakespeherian Rag* for mixed chorus and sextet (1958), *Mass* (1959), *Cocktail Music* for piano (1962), *Octet* (1963), *Three Electronic Dances,* tape (1963), *Underworld* for 4 actors, tenor saxophone, 2 double basses, 4 percussionists and tape (1965), *Ballad* for amplified nightclub vocalist and instrumental ensemble (1966), *L'sGA* for actor (who alters his voice by inhaling helium), tape, and film (the title is an abbreviation of Lincoln's Gettysburg Address, 1968), *The Proposal* for tape and slides (1968), *Election Night Diversion,* "an evening's entertainment" (1968), *Action Analysis* (1968), and *Selections* for alto flute, bass clarinet, viola, and cello (1970).

"THE MIGHTY CASEY" One-act opera with music by William Schuman (q.v.) based on the poem *Casey at the Bat* by Ernest L. Thayer. The libretto, which consists of the original poem, plus some additional lines, is by Jeremy Gury. The setting is Mudville, U.S.A., and the story builds up to the climax when, to the horror of all except Casey's sweetheart, "Merry" (who fears losing the great batter to the Big Leagues), "the mighty Casey strikes out." Schuman, an unabashed baseball devotee, composed an unpretentious opera of great charm. It was produced for the first time by the Julius Hartt Opera Guild, Hartford, Conn., May 4, 1953. A concert version—a cantata—was prepared by Schuman in 1976.

MINGUS, CHARLES (1922–1979) Bassist, pianist, composer. Born in Nogales, Ariz., Apr. 22, 1922, Mingus grew up and began his musical education in Los Angeles. Before he was 16 Mingus had learned to play the trombone, cello, and bass (of which he was a noted master). He began playing professionally while in high school; during the 1940s he played in bands in the Los Angeles and San Francisco areas, among them those led by Louis Armstrong (q.v.), Kid Ory, Alvino Rey, and Lionel Hampton. In the '50s Mingus played in the modern jazz groups led by Charlie Parker (q.v.), Stan Getz, and Duke Ellington (q.v.). By the mid '50s he branched out on his own and released many recordings on his own record label, Debut. He was an extraordinary musician. His style of backing up his group with a unique bass performance made him an influence as a performer, as well as leader and composer. Mingus' use of the bass has been described by Martin Williams: It "not only [maintains] the rhythmic lead but at the same time becomes an instrument of counterpoint, participating directly in the ensemble texture with a sometimes complex melodic role." Mingus devoted much of what turned out to be the close of his life to original composition, often of an experimental cast. His *Meditations on Integration* was first performed by his own group at the Monterey Jazz Festival in 1964. His ballet *Mingus Dances* was presented in New York City in 1971. His autobiography, *Beneath the Underdog,* was published in the same year.

Mingus was afflicted in 1977 with a terminal nerve disease which made it impossible for him to play; confined to a wheelchair he continued to write music. He died in Mexico, Jan. 6, 1979.

MINIMAL MUSIC The term applied to compositions characterized by a steady beat, repetitive structure, stable tonality, and subtle change, if any. This approach is much influenced by the music of the East, particularly the classical music of India; the listener concentrates on very minute details to perceive the musical process. The most successful writers of minimal music among American musicians are Philip Glass (q.v.) and Steve Reich (q.v.), whose *Music for 18 Musicians* (q.v.) seems to have conquered the enigma of monotony.

MOEVS, ROBERT (b. 1921) Composer, teacher. Born in La Crosse, Wis., Dec. 2, 1921, Moevs was a student of Walter Piston (q.v.) before and after serving in the U. S. Army Air Forces as a pilot during World War II. He studied also with Nadia Boulanger (q.v.) in Paris after the war. After several years of teaching at Harvard University, Moevs joined the staff of Rutgers, the State University of New Jersey, New Brunswick, in 1964, where he serves as chairman of the Department of Music. His compositions include a *Piano Sonata* (1950), *Fantasia Sopra un Motivo* for piano (1951), *Fourteen Variations* for orchestra (1952), *Cantata Sacra* for chorus (1952), *Duo* for oboe and English horn (1953), *Three Symphonic Pieces* for orchestra (1955), *Sonata for Solo Violin* (1956), *String Quartet* (1957), *Attis* for tenor, mixed chorus, percussion, and orchestra (1958), *Concerto for Piano, Orchestra and Percussion* (1960; revised 1968, 1970), *Variazioni Sopra una Melodia* for viola and cello (1961), *In Festivitate* for winds and percussion (1962), *Et Nunc, Reges* for women's chorus, flute, clarinet, and bass clarinet

(1963), *Ode to an Olympic Hero* for voice and orchestra (1963), *Et Occidentum Illustrata* for chorus and orchestra (1964), *Musica da Camera, I* for chamber ensemble (1965), *Fanfara Canonica* for 6 herald trumpets (1966), *A Brief Mass* for chorus, organ, vibraphone, guitar, and double bass (1968), *Piece for Synket*, electronics (1969), *Time* for mezzo-soprano and piano (1969), *Heptachronon* for solo cello (1969), *B-A-C-H, Es Ist Genung* for organ (1970), *Phoenix* for piano (1971), *Musica da Camera, II* for chamber ensemble (1972), *Main-Travelled Roads, Symphonic Piece No. 4*, for orchestra (1973), *The Aulos Players* for soprano, 2 choruses, and 2 organs (1975), *Ludi Praeteriti: Games of the Past* for 2 pianos (1976), *Una Collana Musicale* for piano (1977), *Epigram* for voice and piano (1978), and *Crystals* for solo flute (1979).

MONK, THELONIOUS (b. 1918) Pianist, composer, arranger, leader. Born in Rocky Mount, N.C., Oct. 10, ca. 1918 (other dates: 1917, 1920), Monk is a self-taught pianist who emerged as a major force in modern jazz after the death of Charlie Parker (q.v.). Monk was a member of the adventurous musicians who liked to gather at Minton's in Harlem and who contributed to the birth of bebop. Monk's distinctive, if untutored, piano stylings made him one of the most influential members of this handful of pioneers. Until he set out on his own, as soloist, or as the leader of small jazz groups, Monk played in the bands of Lucky Millinder and Coleman Hawkins. Widespread recognition came to Monk ca. the mid 1950s, when he led his quartet and made several recordings —"Smoke Gets in Your Eyes," "I Should Care,"—and jazz concert appearances in the United States and abroad, from Europe to Japan. His own compositions and performances of them are regarded as classic by jazz authorities: *Misterioso* (1948), *Evidence* (1948), *Criss-Cross* (1951), *'Round Midnight* (1957), *Five Spot Blues* (1962), and *Bolivar Blues* (1962).

MOOG SYNTHESIZER Electronic device capable of producing musical sounds of extraordinary colors and rhythmic pulses. The Moog, as it has come to be called, was developed by engineer Robert A. Moog (b. 1934) in the mid 1960s. His, incidentally, is not the only synthesizer, merely the best known —perhaps because of the popular album *Switched-on Bach*, released by Columbia Records with Moog virtuoso Walter Carlos at the module's keyboard. For those who might be interested, the inventor's name rhymes with *vogue*. See also Electronic Music.

MOORE, CARMAN (b. 1936) Composer, cellist, French horn player. Born in Lorain, Ohio, Oct. 8, 1936, Moore was graduated from Ohio State University, Columbus, in 1958. He then earned a master's degree from the Juilliard School of Music, New York City, where he studied with Vincent Persichetti; his other teachers in composition include Luciano Berio and Stefan Wolpe. His *Youth in a Merciful House* for chamber orchestra was composed while he was a student at Juilliard. Other works include *Drum Major*, written in memory of Dr. Martin Luther King (ca. 1969), *Wild Fires and Field Songs* for orchestra (1973), *Museum Piece* (1975), and *Jo Anne!* with a libretto by Ed Bullins (1978). Moore is one of the organizers of the Society of Black Composers.

MOSS, LAWRENCE (b. 1927) Composer, teacher. Born in Los Angeles, Calif., Nov. 18, 1927, Moss was graduated from Pomona College in 1947. He continued in music at the University of California, Los Angeles, the Eastman School, Rochester, N.Y., and the University of Southern California, Los Angeles, from which he received a Ph.D. in 1957. Moss's principal teachers were Ingolf Dahl and Leon Kirchner (q.v.). He has taught at Mills College, Oakland, Calif., Yale University, New Haven, Conn., and the University of Maryland, Baltimore. His compositions include a *Suite* for orchestra (1950), *Fantasia* for piano (1953), *Song of Myself* for baritone and chamber group (1957), *String Quartet No. 1* (1958), *Sonata for Violin* (1959), *The Brute,* one-act opera (1960), *Four Scenes* for piano (1961), *Scenes for Small Orchestra* (1961), *The Queen and the Rebels,* opera (1962), *Three Rilke Songs* for soprano and piano (1963), *Music for 5* for brass (1963), *Remembrances* for octet (1964), *Windows* for flute, clarinet, and double bass (1966), *Omaggio I* for piano, 4 hands (1966), *Patterns* for flute, clarinet, viola, and piano (1967), *Exchanges* for chamber group (1968), *Ariel* for soprano and orchestra (1969), *Elegy* for 2 violins and viola (1969), *Timepiece* for violin, piano, and percussion (1970), *Paths* for orchestra (1971), *Evocation and Song* for saxophone and electronic equipment (1972), *Fantasy* for piano (1973), *Unseen Leaves* for soprano, oboe, and tape (1975), *String Quartet No. 2* (1975), *Symphony* for brass quintet and chamber orchestra (1977), and *Omaggio II* for piano, 4 hands, and tape (1977).

MOTOWN The word derives from "Motor Town," Detroit, where the characteristic style of singing proliferated in the 1960s. This was primarily a popularization of "soul," sung by a group and lead singer. The movements of the backup singers were choreographed and the singing stylized. Typical of the Motown singing group was the Supremes, with Diana Ross leading; also Gladys Knight and the Pips. Motown was the name of the record label on which the so-called "Detroit Sound" was promul-

gated. The company was founded in 1957 by aspiring songwriter and auto worker Berry Gordy, Jr. Other Motown stars of the period were the Miracles, the Marvelettes, and the Temptations. Simply put, the Motown sound is a sophisticated, black commercial production and, for Berry Gordy and many of his stars, highly profitable.

MUCZYNSKI, ROBERT (b. 1929) Composer, pianist, teacher. Born in Chicago, Ill., Mar. 19, 1929, Muczynski studied the piano as a child. He then continued at DePaul University, Chicago, where he studied composition with Alexander Tcherepnin and piano with Walter Knupfer. He made his New York debut as a pianist in a program of his own works at Carnegie Recital Hall in 1958. Muczynski has held 2 Ford Fellowships and since the early 1960s he has been associated with the University of Arizona, Tucson, where he was appointed professor of music and composer-in-residence. His compositions include a *Divertimento* for piano and orchestra (1950), *Five Sketches* for piano (1952), *Six Preludes* for piano (1954), *Piano Concerto No. 1* (1955), *Piano Sonata No. 1* (1957), *Galena* for orchestra (1958), *Trio* for trumpets (1958), *Dovetail Overture* for orchestra (1959), *Three Designs* for timpani (1960), *Suite* for piano (1960), *Statements* for percussion (1961), *Three Preludes* for solo flute (1962), *Dance Movements* for orchestra (1963), *Piano Trio, No. 2* (1975), and *Serenade for Summer* for orchestra (1976). Other works include a symphony, *American Songs* for piano, and a piano *Sonatina.*

MUMMA, GORDON (b. 1935) Composer, engineer. Born in Framingham, Mass., Mar. 30, 1935, Mumma studied piano and French horn (1949–52) before enrolling in the University of Michigan, Ann Arbor, to study composition and theory. At Ann Arbor, Mumma was associated with the Cooperative Studio for Electronic Music and the so-called "Once" (q.v.) group. He has done research in acoustics and has lectured on electronics and avant-garde composition. He has used the term "cybersonics" to describe his compositional philosophy which combines computerized sounds and live performers. Mumma's work not only calls for musical performance but a kind of theatrical interrelationship between musician and audience. For example, in his *Meanwhile, A Twopiece* for piano, percussion, and tape, there is also provision for "another instrument on which one of the players is proficient." The notation for this part does not indicate musical tones, but the gestures the performer makes; the performers are also instructed to exchange instruments now and then. Mumma's works include *Vectors* for tape (1959), *Sinfonia* for chamber group and tape (1960), *Gestures II* for 2 pianos (1962), *Megaton for William Burroughs* for assorted electronic systems (1963), *A Quarter of Fourpiece* for 4 instruments (1963), *Mographs* for pianos (1964), *Music for the Venezia Space Theatre* for tape and electronics (1964), *The Dresden Interleaf 13 February 1945* for multichannel tape (1965), *Le Corbusier* for organ, cybersonic console, tape, and orchestra (1965), *Mesa* for cybersonic console and bandonion (1966), *Hornpipe* for horn and cybersonic console (1967), *Swarm* for violin, concertina, bowed saw (*sic*), and cybersonic system (1968), *Communication in a Noisy Environment* (1970), etc., etc., etc.

"MUSIC FOR 18 MUSICIANS" Composition by minimalist, avant-garde composer Steve Reich (q.v.). Among the musicians are a violin, a cello, 4 women's voices that do not sing words, various percussion instruments, pianos, and 2 clarinetists doubling on bass clarinet.

Music for 18 Musicians is a pulsating work in which there is little musical action in the traditional sense. Instead, a cycle of 7 chords is treated to subtle variations in color, rhythm, and instrumentation. It is an extraordinary and fascinating work. The composition was completed by Reich in March 1976; its first performance was given at Town Hall, New York City, in April.

"MY FAIR LADY" Musical with music by Frederick Loewe (q.v.) and lyrics and book by Alan Jay Lerner (q.v.). Lerner based his book on George Bernard Shaw's *Pygmalion,* in which "Professor Henry Higgins" transforms a Cockney flower-seller, "Eliza Doolittle," into a well-spoken English lady. The major change from Shaw's original is the suggestion of a happy ending (which he had authorized for a film version). Liza rebels against Higgins and his conceit, leaves him but returns in the end. In character to the last, and despite an ill-concealed joy, Higgins has the final word: "Where the devil are my slippers?" Literate, beautifully scored, and perfectly cast, *My Fair Lady* became one of the great long-running musicals and is frequently revived. Some of its songs: "I Could Have Danced All Night," "The Rain in Spain," "With a Little Bit of Luck," "On the Street Where You Live," "Get Me to the Church on Time," and "I've Grown Accustomed to Her Face." The musical opened at the Mark Hellinger Theatre on Mar. 15, 1956, and ran for 2,717 performances. A London production opened in April 1958 and ran for 2,281 performances. A film version was released in 1964. Rex Harrison portrayed Higgins in the original production (also in the film) and Julie Andrews, Liza. Stanley Holloway appeared as Liza's conniving father, "Alfred," and Robert Coote as Higgins' friend "Colonel Pickering."

NANCARROW, CONLON (b. 1912) Composer. Born in Texarkana, Ark., Oct. 27, 1912, Nancarrow has been described by musicologist Charles Hamm as "a mysterious, shadowy player in the drama of twentieth-century music." His birthdate and his music would rightly place him in the 1930s, but he has remained virtually unrecognized until the '60s, when Columbia Records issued an album of his compositions. Nancarrow learned to play the trumpet and moved around the country playing in bands. While in Cincinnati, Ohio, he studied at the Conservatory of Music. He later moved on to Boston where he studied with Roger Sessions (q.v.), Nicolas Slonimsky (q.v.), and Walter Piston (q.v.). Stirred by the outbreak of civil war in Spain, Nancarrow enlisted in the Abraham Lincoln Brigade (composed of Americans against Franco and fascism). Upon his return, in 1939, Nancarrow learned that his politics made him an undesirable citizen and his passport was revoked (this was before the United States turned antifascist). In 1940 Nancarrow left the country and settled in Mexico City. His compositions are unique in that Nancarrow composes on piano rolls to be played through his specially prepared player pianos. He perforates the rolls by hand after having charted out the composition. His output is small, some 50 or 60 pieces entitled *Studies for Player Piano,* the first of which was set down in 1948. Some are simply numbered and some have names—i.e., "Canon." By ca. 1960 Nancarrow had completed some 30 pieces. John Cage arranged 6 *Studies* into a score for the Merce Cunningham Dance Company, entitling it *Crises* (1960). It was this production that brought Nancarrow attention.

NASHVILLE SOUND Catchall term for the brand of popular country music played and especially recorded in "Music City, U.S.A.," Nashville, Tenn. Besides being the site of the Grand Ole Opry, Nashville also is the headquarters for a large publishing industry as well as a great recording center. It is also the home base for the Country Music Association and its Country Music Hall of Fame. The Nashville sound is generally attributed to country musicians who back up popular country singers. The relaxed Southern atmosphere, the friendliness of the musicians, most longtime friends and colleagues, all contribute to the general easygoing, highly professional performances. Among the pioneers of the Nashville sound was Chet Atkins, a country singer-guitarist, who helped to establish Nashville as a major recording center. In the late 1950s Atkins supervised recordings by Jim Reeves, Hank Snow, and Elvis Presley. Another leader in the Nashville-oriented record industry was Owen Bradley (Decca Records); still another, Don Law of Columbia Records. They helped to transform country music into big business, i.e., crossing over from pure country to impure pop. The acoustic guitar gives the Nashville sound its characteristic tone, while the lead lines behind the vocalist are uncluttered and simple. The musicians, though most are readers, tend to improvise, basing their accompaniment on simple chord changes. Vocalists are not overwhelmed by the band and the performance retains some of the original folk qualities of directness and simplicity.

NELSON, OLIVER (1932–1975) Composer, saxophonist, arranger. Born in St. Louis, Mo., June 4, 1932, Nelson studied piano and saxophone. He studied privately with Elliott Carter (q.v.) and with Canadian-American composer George Tremblay. During the 1950s he played saxophone in several jazz bands, among them those led by Wild Bill Davis, Count Basie, and Louis Bellson.

In the late '60s Nelson moved to Hollywood, where he concentrated on composing, arranging and, on occasion, writing themes for television shows (*Ironside, It Takes a Thief*). His works include *Woodwind Quintet* (1960), *Song Cycle* for contralto and piano (1961), *Divertimento* for woodwinds (1962), *Dirge* for chamber orchestra (1962), *Soundpiece* for string quartet and contralto (1963), *Soundpiece for Jazz Orchestra* (1964), *Patterns* for orchestra (1965), *A Study in 5/4* for winds (1966), *Concerto Xylophone, Marimba and Vibraharp* (1967), and *The Kennedy Dream Suite* for jazz band (1967). Nelson died in Los Angeles, Calif., Oct. 27, 1975.

NELSON, RON (b. 1929) Composer, organist, teacher. Born in Joliet, Ill., Dec. 14, 1929, Nelson, who began composing at the age of 6, studied at the Eastman School of Music, Rochester, N.Y., with Howard Hanson (q.v.) and Bernard Rogers (q.v.). Afterward he studied, on a Fulbright Fellowship, at the École Normale de Musique, Paris, with Tony Aubin. He also worked with Arthur Honegger. Since 1963 he has been teaching at Brown University, Providence, R.I., and serves as chairman of the Music Department. He has also been organist and choir director at the Central Baptist Church in Providence. His works include *Savannah River Holiday* for orchestra (1952), the opera *The Birthday of the Infanta* (1956), *The Christmas Story*, cantata (1959), *Fanfare for a Festival* for chorus, brass, organ, and timpani (1960), *Triumphal Te Deum* for chorus, brass, and percussion (1962), *This Is the Orchestra* for orchestra (1963), *Jubilee* for orchestra (1963), *Sarabande: For Katherine in April* for orchestra (1964), *What Is Man?*, oratorio (1964), *Vocalise* for women's chorus (1965), *God, Show Thy Sword* for chorus, organ, and

percussion (1968), *Trilogy: JFK-MLK-RFK* for orchestra (1969), *Rocky Point Holiday* for band (1969), *Meditation on the Syllable Om* for men's chorus (1970), and *Alleluia, July 20, 1969* for chorus (1970). Nelson has also written a ballet entitled *Dance in Ruins* and an *Overture for Latecomers* for orchestra.

NEWMAN, RANDY (b. 1943) Songwriter, pianist, arranger, entertainer. Born in Los Angeles, Calif., Nov. 28, 1943, Newman began music study on the piano at around the age of 6; at 13 he was working on theory, harmony, and counterpoint, in preparation for following in the musical footsteps of his uncles, the successful film composers Alfred and Lionel Newman. Newman's first important piano teacher was Herbert Donaldson; he studied orchestration with Italian composer Mario Castelnuovo-Tedesco. He continued this study with George Tremblay at the University of California, Los Angeles, but dropped out just short of graduation. By this time Newman had begun writing songs and was playing the piano professionally. He worked with such entertainers as Leon Russell and Glen Campbell in Los Angeles sound studios and eventually began making recordings himself. His first album, *Randy Newman Creates Something New Under the Sun* (1968), was a critical, if not a commercial, success. It featured a songwriter with an acerbic social point of view, a musical "black humorist," in the classification of the New York *Times* critic John Rockwell. Newman then embarked on successful concert tours, singing primarily his own songs and introducing them with caustic, often self-effacing commentary. Since 1968 Newman has produced, sporadically, several best-selling albums and achieved a special notoriety with the release of *Little Criminals* (1977) with its controversial, seriocomic commentary on such unlikely song subjects as death

("Texas Girl at the Funeral of Her Father"), an excursion into iconoclasm ("Sigmund Freud's Impersonation of Einstein in America"), and, the most incendiary of all, the antibigotry song "Short People."

NIXON, ROGER (b. 1921) Composer, teacher. Born in Tulare, Calif., Aug. 8, 1921, Nixon started out in music studying the clarinet with Frank Mancini, who had been in the band of John Philip Sousa. He began studying music at the University of California, Berkeley, but this was interrupted when Nixon went into the U. S. Army during World War II. He returned to Berkeley after the war and studied under Roger Sessions (q.v.); he received a Ph.D. in music in 1952. Nixon also studied under British composer Arthur Bliss, as well as Charles Cushing, Ernest Bloch, and Arnold Schoenberg. He is professor of music, San Francisco State University. His compositions include a *String Quartet* (1949), *Air* for strings (1952), *Violin Concerto* (1956), *The Wine of Astonishment,* cantata (1960), *Elegy and Fanfare-March* for band (1961), *Reflections* for band (1962), *Elegiac Rhapsody* for viola and orchestra (1962), *Three Dances* for orchestra (1963), *Nocturne* for band (1965), *The Bride Comes to Yellow Sky,* opera (1968), *Viola Concerto* (1970), *A Solemn Processional* for band (1971), and *Music for a Civic Celebration* for band (1975). Nixon has also composed song cycles under the titles of *Six Moods of Love* and *Chinese Seasons;* his *Fiesta del Pacifico* for band was commissioned by the city of San Diego.

OLIVEROS, PAULINE (b. 1932) Composer, teacher. Born in Houston, Tex., May 30, 1932, Oliveros studied at the University of Houston and San Francisco State College, from which she was graduated in 1956. Her major teacher was Robert Erickson. Like him Oliveros composes electronic music, group improvisation, and mixed media musical performances. She has been associated with the San Francisco Tape Center, the Tape Music Center, Mills College, Oakland, Calif. Since 1967 she has been instructor in electronic music at the University of California, San Diego. Oliveros' works include *Sound Patterns* for chorus (1961), *Trio* for flute, piano, and page turner (*sic,* 1961), *Outline* for flute, percussion, and string bass (1963), *Duo* for accordion and bandonion with optional mynah bird obbligato (1964), *Pieces of Eight* for woodwinds and tape (1965), *George Washington Slept Here,* mixed media, including amplified violin, tape, projections, film (1965), *Rock Symphony* on tape (1965), *I of IV* on tape (1966), *Big Mother Is Watching You* on tape (1966), *Participle Dangling in Honor of Gertrude Stein* for tape, mobile, and work crew (1966), *Engineer's Delight* for piccolo and 7 conductors (1967), *Beautiful Soop* on tape (1967), *Night Jar* for viola d'amore, tape, film, and mime (1968), *The Wheel of Fortune,* improvisation based on tarot (1969), *To Valerie Solanas and Marilyn Monroe in Recognition of Their Desperation* for chorus, orchestra, and electronic device (1970; Valerie Solanas was the woman who shot Andy Warhol), *Meditations on the Points of the Compass* for chorus (1970), *Horse Sings from Clouds* for voice and accordion (1977), and *Fwynnghn,* "a funky fairy tale" for theatre (with Gordon Mumma, 1980).

"ONCE" GROUP See Robert Ashley.

OVERTON, HALL (1920–1972) Composer, teacher. Born in Bangor, Mich., Feb. 23, 1920, Overton studied at the Chicago Musical College (1940–42) before serving in the U. S. Army's 3rd Armored Division until 1945. He then enrolled in the Juilliard School of Music, New York City, where he studied composition with Vincent Persichetti (q.v.). Overton also studied privately with Wallingford Riegger and Darius Milhaud (both q.v.). In the 1940s he was a pianist-arranger for dance bands. He taught at the New School for Social Research, New York City, and the Juilliard School of Music. Overton's compositions include *The Enchanted Pear Tree,* opera (1949), *String Quartet No. 1* (1950), *Symphonic Movement* for orchestra (1950), *Three Elizabethan Songs* for soprano and piano (1953), *String Quartet No. 2* (1954), *Symphony for Strings* (1955), *Trio* for strings (1957), *Polarities* for piano (1959), *Viola Sonata* (1960), *Sonata for Viola and Piano* (1960), *Sonata for Cello and Piano* (1960), *Symphony No. 2* (1962), *Pietro's Petard,* opera (1963), *Dialogue* for chamber orchestra (1963), *Sonorities* for orchestra (1964), *String Quartet No. 3* (1966), and *Pulsations* for chamber group (1972). Overton died in New York City, Nov. 24, 1972.

PASATIERI, THOMAS (b. 1945) Composer. Born in New York City, Oct. 20, 1945, Pasatieri is a musical autodidact, who taught himself to play the piano and to compose, which he began while still in his early teens. He became a composition student of Vincent Persichetti (q.v.) and Vittorio Giannini (q.v.) at the Juilliard School of Music, New York City, in 1961. He also studied with Darius Milhaud at Aspen, Colo. The composer of hundreds of songs, Pasatieri has proved to be a most successful composer of popular operas, his first was *The Women,* which was staged in 1965 (the composer was then 19). Some of his works—all operas unless otherwise indicated—are *La Divina* (1966), *Padrevia* (1967), *Héloïse and Abelard* for soprano, baritone, and piano (1971), *Calvary* (1971), *The Trial of Mary Lincoln* (1972), *Black Widow* (1972), *Rites de Passage* for voice and

strings (1974), *The Seagull* (1974), *Three Poems of James Agee* for voice and piano (1974), *Signor Deluso* (1974), *The Penitentes* (1974), *Inés de Castro* (1976), *Washington Square* (1976), *Day of Love* for chorus (1979), *Three Sisters* (1979), and *Before Breakfast,* one-act opera (1980).

PERLE, GEORGE (b. 1915) Composer, theorist. Born in Bayonne, N.J., May 6, 1915, Perle was a student of Wesley La Violette (DePaul University, Chicago) and Ernst Krenek. He has taught at Yale University, New Haven, Conn., the University of California, Davis, the State University of New York, Buffalo; since 1961 he has been on the music faculty of Queens College, New York City. His compositions include *Two Rilke Songs* for voice and piano (1941), *Three Sonatas* for clarinet (1943), *Hebrew Melodies* for cello (1945), *Six Preludes* for piano (1946), *Solemn Procession* for band (1947), *Piano Sonata* (1950), *Rhapsody for Orchestra* (1954), *String Quintet* (1958), *Solo Violin Sonata* (1959), *Quintet for Winds* (1959), *Monody No. 1* for flute (1960), *Quintet for Winds No. 2* (1960), *Three Movements* for orchestra (1960), *Monody No. 2* for double bass (1962), *Serenade No. 1* for viola and chamber orchestra (1962), *Three Inventions* for bassoon (1963), *Short Sonata* for piano (1964), *Solo Partita* for viola and violin (1965), *Cello Concerto* (1966), *Quintet for Winds No. 3* (1967), *String Quartet No. 5* (1967), *Serenade No. 2* for chamber ensemble (1968), *String Quartet No. 6* (1969), *Toccata* for piano (1969), *Suite in C* for piano (1970), *String Quartet No. 7* (1973), *Songs of Praise and Lamentation* for chorus (1975), and *Thirteen Dickinson Songs* for voice and piano (1978). Perle is the author of *Serial Composition and Atonality* (1962).

PERRY, JULIA (b. 1925) Composer, conductor, teacher. Born in Lexington,

Ky., Mar. 25, 1925, Perry studied composition, piano, and voice at Westminster Choir College, Princeton, N.J. She later studied with Luigi Dallapiccola at Tanglewood, Mass., and in Italy. She studied counterpoint with Nadia Boulanger (q.v.) at Fontainebleau, France, in the summer of 1952. She has taught at Florida Agricultural and Mechanical University, Tallahassee, and the Atlanta (Ga.) Colleges Center. Perry has also lectured under the auspices of the U. S. Information Services in Europe, where she also conducted several concerts. Her works include the *Stabat Mater* for contralto and strings (1951), *A Short Piece for Orchestra* (1952), *The Cask of Amontillado*, opera (1954), *Symphony No. 1* (1959), *Homunculus* for percussion (1960), *Symphony No. 3* (1962), *Violin Concerto* (1963), *Symphony No. 4* (1964), *The Selfish Giant*, opera-ballet (1964), *Piano Concerto* (1965), *Symphony No. 6* (1966), *Symphony U.S.A.* for chorus and small orchestra (1967), *Symphony No. 8* (1969), and *Symphony No. 9* (1970).

"PIANO FANTASY" Solo piano work by Aaron Copland (q.v.). It was commissioned by the Juilliard School of Music for the celebration of the school's 50th anniversary which occurred in 1957. Of this impressive composition (which plays for close to 30 minutes) Copland has written: "Sketches for an extended piano solo work are to be found in my notebooks as far back as the early fifties. Consecutive work on the *Fantasy* was carried on during 1955 and 1956 in southern France, the MacDowell Colony in New Hampshire, and at my home in the Hudson Valley. Like my two previous extended works for solo piano, the *Piano Variations* (1930) [q.v.] and the *Piano Sonata* (1939–40), the new *Fantasy* belongs in the category of absolute music. It makes no use whatever of folk or popular music materials

. . . The musical framework of the entire piece is based upon a sequence of ten different tones of the chromatic scale. To these are joined, subsequently, the two unused tones of the scale, treated throughout as a kind of cadential interval. Thus, inherent in the materials are elements able to be associated with the twelve-tone method and with music tonally conceived. The *Piano Fantasy* is by no means rigorously controlled twelve-tone music, but it does make liberal uses of devices associated with that technique." The *Piano Fantasy* was completed by Copland on Jan. 19, 1957. Dedicated to the memory of pianist William Kapell (who died in a plane crash), the work was premiered at the Juilliard Concert Hall, New York City, in a performance by William Masselos on Oct. 25, 1957.

PRESLEY, ELVIS (1935–1977) Popular singer, entertainer. Born in Tupelo, Miss., Jan. 8, 1935. As a child Presley sang in a trio composed of his parents and himself performing at revival meetings and at church functions. When he was a little older he learned to play the guitar and accompanied himself. When he was 13 the family moved to Memphis, where Presley sang at his high school assemblies, dances, and church socials. Upon graduation from high school in 1953, however, he took a job as a $35-a-week truck driver. He combined truck driving with singing and playing with local country groups. He paid for a studio-made recording of one of his own tunes in mid-1953, which brought him more local work and a recording contract with Sun Records. This recording, although no hit, led to Presley's appearance on the radio show "Louisiana Hayride" in October 1954. He was heard by a certain "Colonel" Tom Parker, who took him under his promotional wing and sent him on a tour of the South as "The Hillbilly Cat." By

1955 Presley records appeared in the "top 10" category, with "Baby, Let's Play House" and "Mystery Train." Soon after RCA Victor bought out his Sun Record contract (at the urging of Parker). The release of Presley's first major album, *Heartbreak Hotel,* literally shot Presley to stardom in the country & western/rhythm & blues market. Presley's performance style fused country with the blues and, with the advent of rock 'n' roll, he adapted that to an exciting act. His was a physical performance, as he pummeled his guitar, gyrated, and sang to the ecstatic delight of his devoted fans, most of them teenaged girls. Having borrowed much from black singing and song, Presley went a step further and added hip movements to his act that could best be described as a phallic dance. This outraged parents but mesmerized the young. Soon Presley made appearances on important television shows (when he appeared on "The Ed Sullivan Show," he was shown to the viewing audience only from the waist up), signed a most lucrative long-term film contract and, of course, turned out one hit album after another. His films were lashed by critics but overwhelmingly attended by his devotees. His recordings—"Hound Dog," "Love Me Tender," "Hard Headed Woman," "All Shook Up"—sold in the millions. In 1958 Presley was drafted and served in West Germany with the U. S. Army for 2 years. After this stint, he made fewer public appearances and rarely was seen on television. By the 1970s he began making nightclub dates and sang in Las Vegas on occasion. By this time, he traveled with a group called the "Memphis Mafia" as companions, aides, and bodyguards. Presley's record sales slipped with the coming of the Beatles (q.v.), who admitted his influence. Presley symbolized the acme of the rock 'n' roll "artist." He influenced other performers and was adored by a generation of young fans. By the mid 1970s his appearances lessened and he isolated himself in his million-dollar home in Memphis. He was only 42 when he died in that house on Aug. 16, 1977, of what was termed "respiratory failure." It was obvious that Presley had been dependent on medication to keep him going; the hint that he may have died of a drug problem was not proved true.

PRINCETON SCHOOL The name applied to a group of composers associated with (many initially as students) electronics composer Milton Babbitt (q.v.). Besides teaching at Princeton University, N.J., Babbitt is also associated with Columbia-Princeton Electronics Music Center. Among his students were Eric Salzman (q.v.), Donald Martino (q.v.), Benjamin Boretz (q.v.), and others.

RANDALL, JAMES K. (b. 1929) Composer, teacher. Born in Cleveland, Ohio, June 16, 1929, Randall studied at Columbia University, New York City, Harvard University, Cambridge, Mass., and at Princeton University, N.J., where he was a student of Milton Babbitt (q.v.). Since 1957 Randall has taught at Princeton. His music shows the influence of Randall's fascination with mathematics and electronics. His compositions include *Slow Movement* for piano (1959), *Improvisation on a Poem of E. E. Cummings* (1960), *Pitch-derived Rhythm: Five Demonstrations* (1961), *Improvisation* for soprano and chamber ensemble (1961), *VI* (1963), *VII* (1964), *Mudgett: Monologues of a Mass Murderer* on tape (1965), and *Lyric Variations* for violin and computer (1968).

REICH, STEVE (b. 1936) Composer, pianist, conductor. Born in New York City, Oct. 3, 1936, Reich majored in philosophy (Cornell University, 1957) before he turned to music. He studied with Hall Overton (q.v.), then entered the Juilliard School of Music, New York City, in 1958. He also studied music at Mills College, Oakland, Calif., where he worked under Darius Milhaud and Luciano Berio. During 1964–65 Reich was associated with the Tape Music Center, San Francisco; he returned to New York in 1965 and formed his own group, Steve Reich and Musicians, the following year. An interest in the music of other cultures led to grants which enabled Reich to study drumming with the master drummer of a Ewe tribe at the Institute for African Studies, Ghana. He has also made a study of the Balinese Gamelan at the University of Washington, Seattle, under the auspices of the American Society of Eastern Arts. Another interest is in the traditional chanting of the Hebrew service. Many of Reich's compositions illustrate his philosophy of very gradual change in the musical development of a theme: a "musical process happening so gradually that listening to it resembles watching the minute hand of a watch—you perceive it moving after you stay with it a little while." The resulting work may sound static to the uninitiated. Reich's works include *Pitch Charts* for various instrumental combinations (1963), *Music* for pianos and tape (1964), *It's Gonna Rain* on tape (1965), *Livelihood,* tape (1965), *Come Out,* tape (1966), *Melodica,* tape (1966), *Reed Phase* for reed instrument and tape (1966), *Piano Phase* for 2 pianos (1967), *My Name Is* for performers, tape, and audience participation (1967), *Violin Phase* for violin and tape (1967), *Pendulum Music* for performers, microphone, etc. (1968), *Pulse Music* for phase shifting pulse gate, an electronic device created by the composer (1969), *Four Organs* for 4 electric organs and maracas (1970), *Phase Patterns* for 4 electric organs (1970), Drumming for various per-

cussion instruments and mixed voices (1971), *Clapping Music* for 2 performers (1972), *Music for Pieces of Wood* (1973), *Music for Mallet Instruments, Voices and Organ* (1973), *Music for 18 Musicians* (q.v., 1976), *Music for Large Ensemble* (1978), *Octet* (1979), and *Variations* for winds, strings, and keyboards (1979).

REYNOLDS, ROGER (b. 1934) Composer, pianist, teacher. Born in Detroit, Mich., July 18, 1934, Reynolds was a student of Ross Lee Finney (q.v.) and Roberto Gerhard at the University of Michigan, Ann Arbor (1952–61). Initially, however, he was an engineering student and exhibited an early interest in electronically devised music. He has organized concerts of contemporary music in Paris and Tokyo; he was one of the founders of the "Once" Group in Ann Arbor, Mich. Since 1970 he has taught at the University of California, San Diego. Reynolds' works include *Epigram and Evolution* for piano (1959), *Sky* for soprano, alto flute, bassoon, and harp (1960), *Wedge* for chamber orchestra (1961), *Acquaintances* for flute, double bass, and piano (1961), *Mosaic* for flute and piano (1962), *The Emperor of Ice Cream,* theatre piece for 8 vocalists, piano, percussion, and double bass (1962), *A Portrait of Vanzetti* for narrator, winds, percussion, and tape (1963), *Graffiti* for orchestra (1964), *Fantasy for Pianists* (1964), *Gathering* for wind quintet (1964), *Quick Are the Mouths of Earth* for chamber group (1965), *Masks* for chorus and orchestra (1965), *Ambages* for flute (1965), *Blind Men* for chorus and chamber group (1966), *Threshold* for orchestra (1967), *Ping* for piano, flute, harmonium, percussion, and electronics (1968), *Traces* for piano, flute, cello, and electronics (1969), *Again* for two sopranos, chamber group, and tape (1970), *I/O* for women's voices, mimes, chamber group, projections, electronics (1971), *Compass* for cello, double bass, tapes, and projections (1973), *Promises of Darkness* for chamber group (1976), and *Fiery Winds* for orchestra (1978).

RHODES, PHILLIP (b. 1940) Composer, teacher. Born in Forest City, N.C., June 6, 1940, Rhodes attended Duke University, where he studied with Iain Hamilton; at Yale he studied with Donald Martino (q.v.) and Mel Powell (composition). He also worked under George Perle (q.v.) and Gunther Schuller (q.v.). Rhodes has taught at Amherst (Mass.) College and at the University of Louisville, Ky. During 1966–68 Rhodes was composer-in-residence in Louisville, Ky., and composer-in-residence at Carleton College, Northfield, Minn. His compositions include *Four Movements* for chamber orchestra (1962), *Three Scenes* for voice and piano (1965), *Three Pieces* for cello solo (1966), *Kyrie* for women's voices (1966), *Remembrance* for band (1967), *Three Pieces* for band (1967), *Duo* for violin and cello (1968), *Autumn Setting* for soprano and string quartet (1969), *The Lament of Michael* for soprano and orchestra (1970), *Divertimento for Small Orchestra* (1971), *Museum Pieces* for string quartet (1973), *On the Morning of Christ's Nativity*, cantata (1976), and *Mountain Songs* for soprano and piano (1976).

RHYTHM AND BLUES A term applied to the popular music of the Negro, especially, but not always, in recorded form. What had been known as "race records" (q.v.) in the 1920s and '30s, during the '40s came to be called rhythm and blues, a less offensive term. The profitable (to record companies particularly) popularity of such emerging blues singer-instrumentalists of the '40s as Muddy Waters (McKinley Morganfield), Aaron "T-Bone" Walker, Arthur "Big Boy" Crudup, and others led to the dropping of the race record category and initiated the rhythm and blues charts in the music trade papers. White musicians and record collectors found excitement in the new performers, who often used electric guitars and bass accompaniment. The white adaptation and borrowing eventually led to the evolution of rock and roll (q.v.). Crudup has been called by his record company "the father of rock and roll." He recorded "Rock Me Mamma" in December 1944; it became the source of a hit recording by B. B. King in the '60s. Rhythm and blues performers had a profound influence on such country and western singers as Elvis Presley (q.v.) before he graduated into the pop charts with rock and roll. Although rhythm and blues recordings continue to be designed specifically for the black record-buying public, there has been some crossover into the white (rock 'n' roll) market by such singers as King, "Fats" Domino, James Brown, Edward "Chuck" Berry, and others.

RILEY, TERRY (b. 1935) Composer, saxophonist, pianist. Born in Colfax, Calif., June 24, 1935, Riley was a student of Robert Erickson at the University of California, Berkeley, from which he was graduated in 1961. Before becoming known as a composer, he earned his way playing the saxophone in France and Sweden. He has been deeply influenced by the music of India as well as contemporary practices and devices. His works include *Spectra* for sextet (1959), *Trio* for strings (1961), *In C* for orchestra (1964), *Dorian Reeds* for soprano saxophone, tape, feedback, and time lag (1966), *Untitled Organ* for amplified reed organ (1966), *Poppy Nogood and the Phantom Band* for soprano saxophone, tape, feedback, and time lag (1968), *A Rainbow in Curved Air* for electronic keyboard instruments (1969), and *Genesis '70,* ballet (1970). Riley has also composed a series of works for electronic keyboard instruments entitled *Keyboard Studies*.

ROCHBERG, GEORGE (b. 1918) Composer, teacher. Born in Paterson, N.J., July 5, 1918, Rochberg is a graduate of Montclair State Teachers College. He studied music (1939–42) at the Mannes School of Music, New York City, with Hans Weisse, George Szell, and Leopold Mannes. From 1942 until 1945 Rochberg served in the U. S. Army as a lieutenant in the infantry; some of this time was spent in Europe. "The war years were much more than an interruption of my musical studies," Rochberg has said. "They taught me what art really meant . . . The war shaped my psyche and precipitated my internal development. I came to grips with my own time." Upon his release from the Army, Rochberg enrolled in the Curtis Institute, Philadelphia, where he studied composition with Rosario Scalero and Gian Carlo Menotti (q.v.). A Fulbright Fellowship enabled him to spend a year (1950) at the American Academy, Rome. Rochberg has taught at the Curtis Institute (1948–60); he was appointed acting chairman of the Music Department, University of Pennsylvania, Philadelphia, in 1960. He later became chairman. Since 1967 Rochberg has given up administrative work; he continues to teach at the University of Pennsylvania and composes. His works include *Capriccio* for 2 pianos (1949), *Night Music* for orchestra (1949), *Symphony No. 1* (1949/57), *String Quartet No. 1* (1952), *Chamber Symphony* (1953), *Three Psalms* for chorus (1954), *David the Psalmist*, cantata (1954), *Duo Concertante* for violin and cello (1955), *Symphony No. 2* (1956), *Dialogues* for clarinet and piano (1957), *Cheltenham Concerto* for orchestra (1958), *La Bocca della Verità* for oboe and piano (1959), *Time-Span* for orchestra

(1960), *String Quartet No. 2*, with soprano (1961), *Blake Songs* for soprano and ensemble (1961), *Piano Trio* (1963), *Apocalyptica* for band (1964), *Contra Mortem et Tempus* for chamber group (1965), *Music for the Magic Theatre* for orchestra (1965), *Black Sounds* for winds (1965), *Nach Bach* for harpsichord (1966), *Tableaux* for soprano and chamber group (1968), *Symphony No. 3* for 4 solo voices, chorus, and orchestra (1968), *Songs in Praise of Krishna* for soprano and piano (1970), *Carnival Music* for piano (1970), *Ricordanza* for piano and cello (1972), *String Quartet No. 3* (1972), *Violin Concerto* (1974), and *Piano Quintet* (1975). Rochberg is the author of *The Hexachord and Its Relation to the Twelve-tone Row* (1955).

ROCK Abbreviation of rock 'n' roll, a form of popular music that began to be noticed ca. the mid 50s. This occurred when white country and western singers began borrowing ideas from black rhythm and blues performers. One of the early C&W vocalists who did this was Bill Haley, whose recording of "Rock Around the Clock" was released in 1954. Another ex-country singer, Buddy Holly (q.v.), was in the forefront of the rock movement when it first surfaced. The culmination came with the arrival of Elvis Presley and the release of his recording of "Heartbreak Hotel," which sold well in all 3 markets, popular, rhythm and blues, and country and western. The production of rock recordings and the staging of rock concerts became a great industry by the 1960s, during which rock 'n' roll music was less folk and more pop. New names, new groups came and went. No longer predominantly an American music style, rock produced its international idols. One of the longest lasting, and most inventive, was the English group, the Beatles (q.v.). Some historians suggest that after the Beatles, rock music petered out and was supplanted to some degree by disco and a revival of rhythm and blues. Since rock was essentially the music of the young, the generation for whom it was produced may have merely reached that critical age of "over 30," and a new generation sought its own form of popular expression. Rock songs, it might be noted, touched upon subjects that conventional popular songwriters would consider taboo: rebellion, sex, drugs, mysticism, estrangement, homosexuality—with language, at times, to match. It was during the 1950s and '60s proliferation of rock that the expression "generation gap" was widely used. Little so well symbolized the gap between the generations as the music of the big band era and rock 'n' roll.

ROREM, NED (b. 1923) Composer, author, teacher. Born in Richmond, Ind., Oct. 23, 1923, Rorem grew up in Chicago and began composing songs at the age of 9. His first love was poetry (he is an accomplished writer), which inspired the composition of some 400 songs and 7 operas. Rorem began to study composition and harmony with Leo Sowerby (q.v.) at the American Conservatory, Chicago, in 1938; further study was taken at Northwestern University, Evanston, Ill., the Curtis Institute, Philadelphia, Pa., and at the Juilliard School of Music, New York City. He also studied privately in New York City with Aaron Copland (q.v.) and Virgil Thomson (q.v.). On a Fulbright Fellowship (1951) Rorem studied in Paris with Arthur Honegger. Rorem was still a music student at Juilliard when one of his early songs, "The Lordly Hudson" (1947), was pronounced the "best published song of the year" by the Music Library Association. Around this time Rorem earned a living as accompanist for the vocal teaching classes given by Eva Gauthier (q.v.), who encouraged

and helped the young composer. Rorem left New York in 1949 to work in Morocco for about 2 years; in 1951 he moved to Paris to work with Honegger. These were musically prolific years. In 1957 he returned to the United States where he has continued writing and has held several composer-in-residence positions at Yaddo, Saratoga Springs, N.Y., the University of Buffalo, N.Y., and the University of Utah, Salt Lake City. Rorem's compositions include *Alleluia* for voice and piano (1946), *Concertino da Camera* (1946), *Four Madrigals* for chorus (1946), *Three Incantations for a Marionette Play* (1948), *Piano Sonata No. 1* (1948), *Death of the Black Knight,* ballet (1948), *Violin Sonata* (1949), *Barcarolles* for piano (1949), *Six Irish Poems* for voice and orchestra (1950), *Piano Sonata No. 2* (1950), *Piano Concerto No. 2* (1950), *String Quartet No. 2* (1950), *Symphony No. 1* (1950), *Cycle of Holy Songs* for voice and piano (1951), *A Childhood Miracle,* opera (1952), *Poems pour la Paix,* song cycle for voice and piano (1953), *Design* for orchestra (1953), *Piano Sonata No. 3* (1954), *Six Songs* for high voice and orchestra (1954), *Symphony No. 2* (1955), *The Poets' Requiem* for soprano, chorus, and orchestra (1956), *Sinfonia* for *Fifteen Wind Instruments* (1957), *Symphony No. 3* (1957), *Eagles* for orchestra (1958), *The Last Day,* opera (1959), *Trio* for flute, cello, and piano (1960), *Eleven Studies for Eleven Players* (1962), *Lions* for orchestra (1963), *Poems of Love and the Rain,* song cycle for voice and piano (1963), *Lovers* for harpsichord, oboe, cello, and percussion (1964), *Miss Julie,* opera (1965), *Letters from Paris* for chorus and orchestra (1966), *Sun* for voice and orchestra (1966), *Water Music* for violin, clarinet, and chamber orchestra (1967), *Spiders* for harpsichord (1968), *Bertha,* opera (1969), *War Scenes* for voice and piano (1969),

Three Sisters Who are Not Sisters, opera (1969), *Piano Concerto No. 3 in Six Movements* (1970), *Ariel* for soprano, clarinet, and piano (1971), *Day Music* for violin and piano (1971), *Night Music* for violin and piano (1972), *Air Music* for orchestra (1974), *Sky Music* for harp (1976), *Eight Etudes* for piano (1976), *Women's Voices,* song cycle (1976), *A Quaker Reader* for organ (1977), *Romeo and Juliet* for flute and guitar (1977), *Book of Hours* for flute and harp (1978), *Nantucket Songs* (1979), and *Santa Fe Songs* for baritone, piano, violin, viola, and cello (1980). Rorem is the author of *The Paris Diary of Ned Rorem* (1966), *The New York Diary* (1967), *Music from Inside Out* (1967), *Music and People* (1968), *Critical Affairs* (1970), *Pure Contraption* (1974), and *The Final Diary: 1961–1972* (1974).

ROSS, JERRY (1926–1955)   See Adler and Ross.

RUSSO, WILLIAM (b. 1928) Composer, arranger, trombonist, teacher. Born in Chicago, Ill., June 25, 1928, Russo initially studied for the law (his father was a prominent Chicago attorney), although he played the trombone as a youngster. As a teenager he worked as a trombonist in several professional bands, among them those led by Billie Rogers (1943), Orrin Tucker (1944), and Clyde McCoy (1945). Russo studied informally for several years with pianist Lennie Tristano. He began writing arrangements for the Johnny "Scat" Davis band in 1945, then left to form his "Experiment in Jazz" group which recorded and performed in the Chicago area (1948–49). From 1950 to 1955 he was arranger and trombonist with the Stan Kenton Orchestra. During the period with Kenton, Russo studied music privately with John J. Becker (q.v.) and later with Karel Jirak. As Bill Russo, he provided the Kenton band with some of its most "progressive" arrangements, fusing techniques of classical music with the new jazz of the '50s. He formed his own orchestra in 1950, then formed the London Jazz Orchestra in 1962. Since 1965 Russo has been associated with the Chicago Jazz Ensemble, Center of New Music, Columbia College, Chicago. In 1968 he took over the direction of the Free Theatre which is part of Columbia College. Since ca. 1970, Russo has been active in San Francisco. His works include *The English Suite* for jazz orchestra (1955), *Les Deux Errants,* ballet (1955), *Symphony No. 1* (1955), *Symphony No. 2* (1957), *Concerto Grosso* for band (1960), *John Hooton,* opera (1961), *Variations on an American Theme* for orchestra (1961), *Cello Concerto* (1962), *The English Concerto* for violin and orchestra (1963), *The Island* for soloists and jazz orchestra (1963), *In Memoriam* for 2 soloists, chorus, and orchestra (1966), *America 1966* for jazz orchestra (1966), *Antigone,* chamber opera (1967), *The Civil War,* rock cantata (1968), *Three Pieces for Blues Band and Symphony Orchestra* (1968), *David,* rock cantata (1969), *Aesop's Fables,* opera (1971), *Songs of Celebration* for soloists, chorus, and orchestra (1971), *Song of Songs* for soloists, chorus, and orchestra (1972), *Isabella's Fortune,* opera (1974), *Carousel Suite* for narrator, dancers, and orchestra (1975), *Street Music,* "A Blues Concerto" for harmonica, piano, and orchestra (1975), *Paris Lights,* songs and incidental music (1979), and *Paris Lights: The All-Star Literary Genius Expatriate Revue* (1980). Russo is the author of *Composing for the Jazz Orchestra* (1961) and *Jazz: Composition and Orchestration* (1968).

RZEWSKI, FREDERIC (b. 1938) Composer, pianist, teacher. Born in Westfield, Mass., Apr. 13, 1938, Rzewski began his study of music there with

Charles Mackey and then went on to Harvard and Princeton. His major instructors were Claudio Spies, Randall Thompson (q.v.), Walter Piston (q.v.), and Milton Babbitt (q.v.). Upon graduation from Princeton in 1960, Rzewski traveled to Rome on a Fulbright Fellowship; there he helped to found Musica Elettronica Viva, a group devoted to the production of experimental composition for conventional instruments as well as electronics. After a stay in Berlin on a Ford Foundation grant Rzewski returned to the United States. While in Europe he lectured on music and composition in Cologne. He has taught at the Art Institute, Chicago, and, in 1977, was appointed professor of composition, Royal Conservatory of Music, Liège, Belgium. His works include *Preludes* for piano (1957), *Poem* for piano (1959), *Sonata* for 2 pianos (1960), *Dreams* for piano (1961), *Octet* (1962), *For Violin* for solo violin (1962), *Composition for 2* for any 2 instruments (1964), *Speculum Dianae* for any 8 instruments (1964), *Self-portrait* for one person (1964), *Nature morte* chamber group and percussion (1965), *Zoologischer Garten,* tape (1965), *Spacecraft* (1967), *Requiem* for chorus and chamber group (1967), *Portrait* for actor, tapes, film, slides, etc. (1967), *Work Songs* (1969), *Last Judgement* for trombone (1969), *Monuments* for voice and piano (1970), *Music for Children,* tape (1971), *Falling Music* for piano and tape (1971), *Coming Together* for narrator and chamber group (1972), *Variations on "No Place to Go But Around"* for piano (1974), *The People Will Never Be Defeated!* (36 variations of a Chilean Song) for piano (1975), *Song and Dance* for chamber group (1977), *Thirteen Studies for Instruments* (1977), and *Down by the Riverside* for piano (1979).

SALZMAN, ERIC (b. 1933) Composer, teacher, writer. Born in New York City, Sept. 8, 1933, Salzman studied at Columbia University and at Princeton; his teachers were Otto Luening (q.v.), Vladimir Ussachevsky (q.v.), Milton Babbitt (q.v.), and Roger Sessions (q.v.). In Rome (1956–58) Salzman studied with Goffredo Petrassi on a Fulbright Fellowship; he also studied with Karlheinz Stockhausen in Darmstadt, West Germany. Upon his return to the United States, Salzman became a music critic for the New York *Times* and later (1963–66) for the New York *Herald Tribune.* Since 1962 he has been a contributing editor on the staff of the music/recordings monthly *Stereo Review,* specializing in contemporary avant-garde music. Salzman has taught at Queens College (he is also an erudite musicologist); he has also organized a series of "New Images of Sounds" concerts at Hunter College, New York City. For several seasons he was music director of the progressive New York radio station WBAI. Salzman's compositions include *Cummings Set* for voice and orchestra (1953), *String Quartet* (1955), *Flute Sonata* (1956), *Partita* for solo violin (1958), *Inventions* for orchestra (1959), *In Praise of the Owl and the Cuckoo* for voice, guitar, and chamber ensemble (1964), *Verses and Cantos* for 4 voices, chamber ensemble, electronics (1967), *Larynx Music* for voice and tape (1967), *The Peloponnesian War,* dance-theatre piece on tape (1968), *Feedback,* electronics and visuals (1968), *The Nude Paper Sermon* for actor, Renaissance consort, chorus, and electronics (1969), *Can Man Survive?,* multimedia work on tape for exhibition at the American Museum of Natural History, New York City (1969), *Strophe/Antistrophe* for harpsichord and tape (1971), *The Conjurer,* multimedia work (1975), and *Noah,* theatre work (1978). Salzman is the author of *Twentieth Century Music: An Introduction* (1967).

SCHICKELE, PETER (b. 1935) Composer, pianist, humorist, teacher. Born in Ames, Iowa, July 17, 1935, Schickele (a.k.a. "P. D. Q. Bach"), exhibited an early theatrical bent as a boy but turned to music in his teens under the influence of his parents' record collection, his brother's violin lessons, and his own collection of Spike Jones recordings. He first began to study theory with Sigvald Thompson in Fargo, N.D., where his family was living at the time. Schickele also studied with Roy Harris (q.v.); he completed his studies at the Juilliard School of Music, New York City, where his principal teacher was Vincent Persichetti (q.v.). Later Schickele taught at Juilliard as well as Swarthmore College, Pa., and at Aspen, Colo. Besides arranging for dance bands and rock groups, he is a prolific composer, although he is best known in the guise of his alter ego, P. D. Q. Bach and such outrageously titled—and performed—works as *Art of the Ground Round, Echo Sonata for Two Unfriendly Groups of Instruments, Fanfare for the Common Cold, The Stoned Guest,* and *Concerto for Piano vs. Orchestra* (the dates of these works will add nothing to your musical knowledge). Schickele's original compositions include *Two Pleasant Songs* for flute and piano (1954), *Three Folk Settings* for piano (1955), *The Household Moose* for piano (1956), *First Sonatina* for piano (1957), *Fantasy* for strings (1958), *Invention* for orchestra (1958), *Second Sonatina* for piano (1958), *Requiem* for strings (1958), *Songs* for baritone, bassoon, and trombone (1958), *The Boston Wonder* for flute and piano (1959), *String Trio* (1960), *Three Choruses from Cummings* (1960), *Celebration with Bells* for orchestra (1960), *Canzona* for organ (1960), *Pavilion Piece* for band (1961), *A Small World* for 2 flutes (1962), *Diversions* for oboe, clarinet, and bassoon (1963), *The Flow of Memory* for mezzo-soprano and chamber group (1963), *Third Sonatina* for piano (1964), *Three Scenes for Five Instruments* (1965), *The Last Supper* for chorus (1965), *Bellshadows* for cello and piano (1966), *In My Nine Lives* for piano (1967), *Gardens* for oboe and piano (1968), *The Fantastic Garden* for rock group, electric organ, electric piano, vocalists, and orchestra (1968), *A Zoo Called Earth* for narrator and orchestra (1970), *Three Girls, Three Women* for chorus and orchestra (1972), *Things to Try on a Summer Day* for unison choir and piano (1972), *The Lowest Trees Have Tops,* cantata (1974), *The Knight of the Burning Pestle,* comic opera (1974), *American Birthday Card* for narrator and orchestra (1976), *The Chenoo Who Stayed to Dinner,* legend for narrator and orchestra (1977), *Five of a Kind,* concerto for brass quintet and orchestra (1978), *Piano Concerto No. 2, "Ole!,"* (1978), *Three Meditations* for chorus (1978), and *Epitaphs* for piano (1979). Schickele has also composed for films and television, among them the music for *Where the Garbage Goes* for television's "Sesame Street" (1969) and the film *Silent Running* (1971).

SCHMIDT, WILLIAM (b. 1926) Composer. Born in Chicago, Ill., Mar. 6, 1926, Schmidt was a student of Ingolf Dahl (q.v.) and Halsey Stevens (q.v.) at the University of Southern California, Los Angeles. Besides composing he is a music publisher and is president of Western International Music, Los Angeles, which specializes in chamber music, especially for brass groupings. His compositions include *Rhapsody No. 1* for clarinet and piano (1955), *Septigrams* for flute, piano, and percussion (1956), *Concerto Breve for Brass and Band* (1957), *Serenade* for tuba and piano (1957), *Rondino* for trombone and piano (1959), *Woodwind Quintet*

(1959), *Variations on a Negro Folk Song* for brass quintet (1959), *Seven Variations on a Hexachord* for brass quintet (1963), *Suite No. 1* for brass quintet (1967), *Vendor's Call* for piano and clarinet choir (1968), *Suite No. 2, "Folksongs"* for brass quintet (1968), *Music for Scrimshaws* for harp and brass quintet (1969), *Ludos Americanus* for narrator and percussion (1971), *Short'nin' Bread Variations* for harp, brass, percussion (1972), and *Sonatina* for contrabass clarinet and piano (1977).

SCHULLER, GUNTHER (b. 1925) Composer, conductor, teacher, author. Born in New York City, Nov. 22, 1925, Schuller, whose father was a violinist in the New York Philharmonic, studied at the St. Thomas Choir School and the Manhattan School of Music. An exceptional French horn player, he played that instrument with the Cincinnati Symphony and the Metropolitan Opera, as well as with such jazz groups as the Miles Davis Orchestra and the Modern Jazz Quartet. Schuller taught at the Manhattan School of Music, Yale University, and the New England Conservatory of Music. Also active as a conductor, Schuller founded the New England Conservatory Ragtime Ensemble to perform ragtime and other jazz-like American music in authentic orchestrations. He orchestrated and conducted the successful 1975 production of Scott Joplin's *Treemonisha*. Schuller has been a proponent of what he calls "Third Stream" (q.v.) composition, in which contemporary jazz and contemporary concert music are joined in a single work. His compositions include a *Concerto for Horn and Orchestra* (1944), *Cello Concerto* (1945), *Suite* for woodwind quintet (1945), *Cello Sonata* (1946), *Fantasia Concertante* for 3 oboes and piano (1947), *Quartet* for 4 double basses (1947), *Trio* for oboe, horn, and viola (1948), *Quintet* for 4

horns and bassoon (1949), *Symphony* for brass and percussion (1950), *Dramatic Overture* for orchestra (1951), *Fantasy* for solo cello (1951), *Five Pieces* for horns (1952), *Recitative and Rondo* for violin and piano (1953), *12 by 11* for chamber group (1955), *Contours* for chamber orchestra (1956), *String Quartet No. 1* (1957), *Music* for violin, piano, and percussion (1957), *Woodwind Quintet* (1958), *Fantasy-Quartet* for brass (1958), *Concertino* for jazz quartet and orchestra (1958), *Seven Studies on Themes of Paul Klee* for orchestra (1959), *Spectra* for orchestra (1960), *Capriccio* for tuba and orchestra (1960), *Variants* for jazz orchestra, ballet (1960), *Music for brass quintet* (1961), *Contrasts* for woodwind quintet and orchestra (1961), *Piano Concerto* (1962), *Densities No. 1* for chamber group (1962), *Night Music* for jazz chamber group (1962), *Symphony* (1965), *Triptych: Three Studies in Texture* for orchestra (1965), *String Quartets Nos. 1 and 2* (1965), *Concerto for Orchestra* (1965), *The Visitation,* opera (1966), *Colloquy* for 2 pianos and orchestra (1966), *Triplum* for orchestra (1967), *Vertige d'Eros* for orchestra (1967), *Concerto* for double bass and orchestra (1968), *Shapes and Designs* for orchestra (1968), *Museum Piece* for ancient instruments (1970), *The Fisherman and His Wife,* opera for young people (1970), *Tre Invenzione* for chamber ensemble (1972), *Five Moods* for tuba quartet (1972), *Concerto for Violin* (1976), and *Octet* (1979). Schuller is the author of *Horn Technique* (1972) and *Jazz: Its Roots and Musical Development* (1968).

SCHWARTZ, ELLIOTT (b. 1936) Composer, pianist, teacher, author. Born in Brooklyn, N.Y., Jan. 19, 1936, Schwartz studied with Jack Beeson (q.v.) and Otto Luening (q.v.) at Columbia University; he also studied privately with them as well as with Paul Creston (q.v.). He studied piano with Thomas Richner and Alton Jones. He has taught at the University of Massachusetts, Amherst, and Bowdoin College, Maine. He has lectured at Trinity College of Music, London, and at the University of California, Santa Barbara. Schwartz's compositions include *Interruptions* for woodwind quintet (1964), *Concert Piece* for 10 players (1965), *Texture* for strings, winds, and brass (1966), *Dialogue* for double bass (1967), *Signals* for trombone and double bass (1968), *Magic Music* for piano and orchestra (1968), *Music for Prince Albert* for piano and tapes (1969), *Music for Napoleon and Beethoven* for trumpet, piano, and tapes (1969), *Septet* for voice, piano, and any other 5 instruments (1969), *Music for Soloists and Audience* for assorted instruments and audience which, divided into 4 sections, provides certain sounds; with 4 conductors, of course (1970), *Island* for orchestra (1970), *Eclipse I* for chamber group (1971), *Dream Overture* for orchestra and tape (1972), and *The Harmony of Maine* for synthesizer and orchestra (1975). Schwartz is the author of *The Symphonies of Ralph Vaughan Williams* (1965), co-editor, with Barney Childs, of *Contemporary Composers on Contemporary Music* (1967), and editor of *Electronic Music: A Listener's Guide* (1973).

SEEGER, PETE (b. 1919) Composer, singer, banjoist, guitarist. Born in New York City, May 3, 1919, Seeger came from a musical family. His father was the musician-ethnologist Charles Seeger (q.v.) and his mother, Constance de Clyver Edson, was a teacher and violinist. He exhibited little interest in music as a youngster. He was about 16 when he accompanied his father to a folk music festival, which planted a seed. Seeger, however, enrolled in Harvard as a sociology major. He dropped out after 2 years, in 1938, to travel around the United States and to collect folk songs. His travels enabled him to meet and to come under the influence of such folk figures (and singers) as Woody Guthrie, Leadbelly, and the composer Earl Robinson. He was associated, as an assistant, with John Lomax, curator of the Archive of the American Folk Song, in Washington, D.C. In 1940 Seeger formed the Almanac Singers, one of the earliest popular folk singing groups. This career was interrupted when 2 years later Seeger was drafted into the U. S. Army; after more than 3 years, during which he spent time in the Pacific, Seeger was discharged and returned to working with folk songs and folk singers. His material was very political—antifascist, prolabor, protest songs—which eventually led to a confrontation with the Un-American Activities Committee. In 1945 Seeger formed People's Songs, Inc., a union of folk singers and songwriters. In 1948 he became a member of another popular group that specialized in folk song, the Weavers (the others: Lee Hays, Ronnie Gilbert, and Fred Hellerman). Off and on, the group remained active from 1949 to 1952 and from 1955 to 1957. The House Un-American Activities Committee found the protest songs, and Seeger particularly, offensive during one of its publicity-seeking witch hunts. In 1956, when he refused to answer the questions put to him by the committee, Seeger was cited on 10 counts for contempt of Congress; he was officially convicted in 1961—and the conviction was overturned in the U. S. Court of Appeals the following year. Even while this was going on, Seeger remained active in the folk song movement, was instrumental in the revival of the Newport Folk Festival, and continued to protest injustices. One of his songs, "Where Have All the Flowers Gone?," is a powerful antiwar statement; Seeger is also co-lyricist of another protest song, "We Shall Overcome." As the 1970s ended and the '80s began Seeger continued to raise his voice against man's stupidities. He is also a dedicated environmentalist.

SHAPEY, RALPH (b. 1921) Composer, conductor, teacher. Born in Philadelphia, Pa., Mar. 12, 1921, Shapey was a violin student of Emanuel Zetlin and studied composition with Stefan Wolpe. He has been the recipient of several awards and grants, including 3 years spent working at the MacDowell Colony; also, the Brandeis Creative Arts Award, the Copley Foundations Award, etc. During World War II, Shapey served in the U. S. Army Air Forces. Since 1964 he has been on the faculty of the University of Chicago, where he is also the director of the Contemporary Chamber Players. Shapey's compositions include a *Piano Quintet* (1946), *String Quartet No. 1* (1946), *Piano Sonata No. 1* (1946), *String Quartet No. 2* (1949), *String Quartet No. 3* (1951), *Fantasy* for orchestra (Gershwin Memorial Award winner, 1951), *Symphony No. 1* (1952), *String Quartet No. 4* (1953), *Concerto* for clarinet and chamber ensemble (1954), *Challenge: The Family of Man* for orchestra (1955), *Mutations* for piano (1956), *Duo* for viola and piano (1957), *String Quartet No. 5, with voice* (1957), *Ontogeny* for orchestra (1958), *Form* for piano (1959), *Rituals* for orchestra (1959), *Evocation* for violin, piano, and percussion (1959), *Soliloquy* for narrator, string quartet, and percussion (1959), *Dimensions* for soprano and 23 instruments (1960), *Five* for violin and piano (1960), *Incantations* for soprano and chamber group (1961), *Discourse* for flute, clarinet, violin, and piano (1961), *Convocation* for chamber ensemble (1962), *Birthday Piece* for piano (1962), *Seven* for piano, 4 hands (1963), *Brass Quintet* (1963),

String Quartet No. 6 (1963), *Sonance* for carillon (1964), *String Trio* (1965), *Partita* for solo violin (1966), *Mutations No. 2* for piano (1966), *Partita* for violin and chamber group (1966), *Songs of Ecstasy* for soprano, piano, percussion, and tape (1967), *Reyem* for flute, violin and piano (1967), *Praise,* oratorio for bass-baritone, chorus, and chamber orchestra (1971), *String Quartet No. 7* (1972), *31 Variations* for piano (1973), *Songs of Eros* for soprano, orchestra, and tape (1975), *The Covenant* for soprano, 16 players, and tape (1977), *21 Variations* for piano (1978), *Song of Songs #1* for soprano, 14 players, and tape (1979), and *Evocations II* for cello, piano, and percussion (1979).

SHIFRIN, SEYMOUR (1926–1979) Composer, teacher. Born in Brooklyn, N.Y., Feb. 28, 1926, Shifrin began studying music at the age of 6. When he was a student at the High School of Music and Art he was awarded a 2-year scholarship to study with William Schuman (q.v.). At Columbia University he was a student of Otto Luening (q.v.). A Fulbright Scholarship took him to Paris for further study with Darius Milhaud. After his return to the United States, Shifrin was appointed in 1952 to the music faculty of the University of California, Berkeley; he left in 1966 to teach at Brandeis University, Waltham, Mass. He was especially noted for his chamber compositions. Shifrin's works include a *Cello Sonata* (1948), *String Quartet No. 1* (1949), *Fantasy* for piano (1950), *Chamber Symphony* (1954), *Serenade for Five Instruments* (1954), *Three Pieces for Orchestra* (1958), *String Quartet No. 2* (1962), *Odes of Shang* for chorus, piano, and percussion (1963), *Satires of Circumstance* for soprano and chamber group (1964), *String Quartet No. 3* (1966), *String Quartet No. 4* (1967), *In Elus Memorium* for chamber group (1968), *Duo* for violin and piano (1969), and *Chronicles* for vocalists and orchestra (1970). Shifrin completed a 5th string quartet before his death. He died in Boston, Mass., Sept. 26, 1979.

"SILVER APPLES OF THE MOON" A composition by Morton Subotnick (q.v.) for electronic synthesizer (the title comes from a poem by William Butler Yeats). Commissioned by Nonesuch Records—the idea, no doubt, of the creative direction of producer Teresa Sterne—*Silver Apples of the Moon* was "composed and realized" by Subotnick on a modular electronic music system built by Donald Buchla. The work, as the composer points out, was not intended for concert hall performance but created specifically for home listening. Despite the electronically generated sounds, the composition has form and development and makes fascinating listening. The success of the album led to another Subotnick electronic work, *The Wild Bull. Silver Apples of the Moon* was composed in 1967.

SMITH, GREGG (b. 1931) Composer, conductor, teacher. Born in Chicago, Ill., Aug. 4, 1931, Smith studied at the University of California, Los Angeles, with Fritz Zweig and Leonard Stein. After teaching at the university for several years, during which period he did much choral conducting, Smith formed the excellent Gregg Smith Singers in 1955. In addition to the standard repertory, the Smith Singers have made a specialty of contemporary and American music. Several of Stravinsky's choral pieces under the composer's direction were recorded by the Gregg Smith Singers. The American repertory ranges from the music of William Billings through Charles Ives, Gershwin, Irving Fine, and virtually the complete American choral literature from the Pilgrims to Barbara Kolb. Smith has made numerous arrangements for his group—American folk songs,

Christmas songs, and sacred songs. His own works include *Four Concord Chorales, Bible Songs for Young Voices* (1964), *Beware of the Soldier,* cantata (1969), *Steps* for voice and guitar (1975), *Jazz Mass for St. Peter's* (1978), and *Eleven Palindromes* for chorus and piano (1980).

SMITH, HALE (b. 1925) Composer, arranger, teacher. Born in Cleveland, Ohio, June 29, 1925, Smith earned his degree in music at the Cleveland Institute of Music in 1950; among his teachers were Dorothy Price (piano) and Marcel Dick (composition). In the late 1950s Smith came to New York City to work as an editor for a music publisher. He has taught at C. W. Post College, Long Island University, N.Y., and the University of Connecticut, Storrs. Smith has also written arrangements for several major jazz figures, among them Quincy Jones, Ahmad Jamahl, and Dizzy Gillespie. His own original work utilizes jazz devices and serial techniques. His compositions include *In Memoriam—Beryl Rubinstein* for choir and chamber orchestra (1953), *Duo* for violin and piano (1953), *Blood Wedding,* opera (1953), *Valley Wind* for soprano and piano (1955), *Cello Sonata* (1955), *Epicedial Variations* for violin and piano (1956), *Five Songs* for voice and piano (1956), *Two Love Songs of John Donne* for soprano and chamber group (1958), *Three Brevities* for flute (1960), *Contours* for orchestra (1962), *Orchestra Set* (1962), *By Yearning and By Beautiful* for strings (1964), *Evocation* for piano (1966), *Expansions* for wind ensemble (1967), *Music for Harp and Orchestra* (1967), *Faces of Jazz* for piano (1968), *Anticipations, Introspections and Reflections* for piano (1971), *Comes Tomorrow,* jazz cantata (1972), *Ritual and Incantations* for orchestra (1974), *Introductions, Cadenzas and Interludes,* octet

(1974), *Variations* for sextet (1975), *Innerflexions* for orchestra (1977), and *Toussaint L'Ouverture 1803* for chorus and piano (1977).

SMITH, RUSSELL (b. 1927) Composer, teacher. Born in Tuscaloosa, Ala., Apr. 23, 1927, Smith grew up in northern Virginia and studied at the Eastman School of Music, Rochester, N.Y., and at Columbia University, New York City, where he was a student of Douglas Moore (q.v.) and Otto Luening (q.v.). He also studied, in the summer of 1947, with Aaron Copland (q.v.) at the Berkshire Music Center, Tanglewood, Mass. The recipient of Rockefeller Foundation grants, Smith has been composer in residence, the Cleveland Orchestra (1966–67) and the New Orleans Philharmonic (1969–70). He has taught at Queens College and Hunter College, New York City, and the University of Alabama, Tuscaloosa. He has written numerous articles on music for *Stereo Review, High Fidelity,* and *Harper's Magazine.* His compositions include *Songs of Innocence* (1949), *Eclogue* for violin and piano (1949), *Duo and Fugue* for woodwind quintet (1949), *Antigone,* ballet (1949), *Piano Concerto No. 1* (1953), *Service in G* for chorus (1954), *The Unicorn in the Garden,* opera (1956), *Palatine Songs* for voice and chamber orchestra (1956), *Piano Concerto No. 2* (1957), *Tetrameron* for orchestra (1957), *Three Chorale Preludes* for organ (1957), *Can-Can* and *Waltz* for orchestra (1958), *Divertimento* for orchestra (1958), *Preludes* for piano (1962), and *Nocturne* for strings (1967).

SMITH, WILLIAM O. (b. 1926) Composer, clarinetist, teacher. Born in Sacramento, Calif., Sept. 22, 1926, Smith began in music as a clarinet student; he studied composition with Darius Milhaud (q.v.) at Mills College, Oakland, Calif., and with Roger Sessions

(q.v.) at the University of California, Berkeley. Besides composing, Smith also teaches the clarinet. His compositions include a *Serenade* for flute, violin, trumpet, and clarinet (1947), *Clarinet Sonata* (1948), *Quintet* for clarinet and strings (1950), *String Quartet* (1952), *Divertimento* for jazz orchestra (1956), *Concerto for Jazz Clarinet and Orchestra* (1957), *Quartet* for clarinet, violin, cello, and piano (1958), *Five Pieces* for solo clarinet (1959), *Fancies* for solo clarinet (1969), *Quadrogram* for clarinet, trombone, piano, and percussion, dance piece with film (1970), *Theona* for orchestra (1975), *Elegia* for clarinet and strings (1976), and *Five* for brass quintet (1977).

SOLLBERGER, HARVEY (b. 1938) Composer, flutist, conductor, teacher. Born in Cedar Rapids, Iowa, May 11, 1938, Sollberger studied flute with Betty Mather and Samuel Baron. A graduate of the University of Iowa, Iowa City, where he studied composition with Philip Bezanson, and Columbia University, New York City, where he studied under Jack Beeson and Otto Luening (M.A., 1964). He taught at Columbia (1965–71) and was a director of its Group for Contemporary Music. Sollberger has been the recipient of many awards and commissions from the Walter W. Naumberg Foundation, the Martha B. Rockefeller Fund for Music, and the Guggenheim Foundation. His compositions include *Two Pieces for Two Flutes* (1958), *Trio* for flute, cello, and piano (1961), *Grand Quartet* for flutes (1962), *Solos for Violin and Five Instruments* (1962), *Two Oboes Troping* (1963), *Chamber Variations* for chamber orchestra (1964), *Musical Transalpina* for soprano, baritone, and sextet (1965), *Music for Sophocles Antigone* for narrator and tape (1968), *For No Clear Reason* for soprano and piano (1969), *Divertimento* for flute, cello, and piano (1970), *As Things Are and Become* for string trio (1971), *Riding the Wind I* for flute and chamber orchestra (1974), *Sunflowers* for flute and vibraphone (1976), and *Met Him Pike Roses* for flute and violin (1980).

SONDHEIM, STEPHEN (b. 1930) Composer, lyricist. Born in New York City, Mar. 22, 1930, Sondheim grew up in Doylestown, Pa., to which he was taken at the age of 10 after the divorce of his parents. He was considered a brilliant child; he read early and was precocious in school. His musical education was spotted, for he studied piano (and for a shorter time, the organ) off and on —and briefly—from the age of 7 until he was 19. During that period he accumulated about 4 years of keyboard study. A friendship with James Hammerstein, son of Oscar Hammerstein II (q.v.), led to Sondheim's coming under the wing of the lyricist. At 15 Sondheim made his first attempt at a musical at the school he attended in Bucks County, Pa. He showed it to Hammerstein, who vigorously criticized it and then began instructing Sondheim in the art of writing for the musical theatre. His interest sparked, Sondheim began to study music systematically. He studied with Robert Barrow at Williams College, Williamstown, Mass. He then won a scholarship to study with Milton Babbitt (q.v.) privately in New York City. Before he made his first try in the musical theatre, Sondheim wrote scripts, and collaborated on scripts with George Oppenheimer, for the television series *Topper*. His first musical was to have been entitled *Saturday Night,* but its producer's death canceled the project (it was announced for production later, in 1959, after Sondheim had done other shows, but he decided not to do it). The quality of the songs, particularly the lyrics, led to his assignment as lyricist for *West Side Story* (q.v.), with music by Leonard Bernstein

(q.v.). The show, a variation on the Romeo and Juliet story (with ethnic overtones), was most successful and established Sondheim as one of the most skilled lyricists in the theatre. He next collaborated with Jule Styne (q.v.) on another success, *Gypsy,* for which Sondheim's lyrics were even more polished and incisive. He then set out on his own with words and music for *A Funny Thing Happened on the Way to the Forum* (1962). Each show that followed revealed a richly gifted songwriter with a predilection for offbeat themes in the books for his musicals. His next solo venture, *Anyone Can Whistle* (1964), was set in a small town in which the only sane people were patients in a motel for mental misfits. (Among its impressive songs are the title song and "A Parade in Town.") The next year Sondheim joined Richard Rodgers (q.v.) to provide the lyrics for *Do I Hear a Waltz?* He followed that with a series of remarkably scored shows. *Company* (1970) touched on contemporary marriage problems among the trendy affluent, with such trenchant songs as "You Can Drive a Person Crazy," "Barcelona," and "Another Hundred People." *Follies* (1971) had a bitter show-business setting and such songs as "I'm Still Here," "Too Many Mornings," "Losing My Mind," and "Could I Leave You?" *A Little Night Music* (1973), adapted from the Ingmar Bergman film *Smiles of a Summer Night,* took a jaundiced look at love among the wealthy with such songs as "Liaisons," "Every Day a Little Death," "You Must Meet My Wife," "A Weekend in the Country," "The Miller's Son," and "Send in the Clowns." *Pacific Overtures* (1976) essayed a negative sociological view of the devastating effect of the impact of Western civilization on the culture of Japan following the visit by American Commodore Matthew Perry. Not as successful as other Sondheim shows, *Pacific*

Overtures was innovative and adventurous. Some of its songs: "There Is No Other Way," "Four Black Dragons," "Chrysanthemum Tea," "Poems," "Someone in a Tree," "Pretty Lady," and "Next." *Sweeney Todd, the Demon Barber of Fleet Street* (1979), whose theme is man's inhumanity to man, is a brilliant opera-like successful experiment. While the subject matter is undeniably repellent—a revenge-maddened barber who slashes his customers' throats, then delivers them to his accomplice to bake into meat pies—*Sweeney Todd* is an outstanding achievement. Its songs, integrated seamlessly, do not lend themselves to popularity in the Tin Pan Alley marketplace. They include "The Ballad of Sweeney Todd," "My Friends," "Wait," and "By the Sea." To match these there is the orchestration by Jonathan Tunick. Sondheim has also written a screenplay, in collaboration with actor Anthony Perkins, a mystery entitled *The Last of Sheila* (1973), a musical setting of Aristophanes' *The Frogs* (1974), which was "staged" in the Yale University swimming pool, and the background score for the film *Stavisky* (1975). His television musical *Evening Primrose* was produced in 1966. Sondheim himself acted in a television production of the Ring Lardner–George S. Kaufman comedy *June Moon* in 1974.

THE SONGWRITERS' HALL OF FAME Nonprofit organization, situated in New York's Times Square, which functions as a storehouse and exhibition center for the memorabilia of American popular song. Besides a library and archive, the Hall of Fame stores films, videotapes, and sheet music. Such items as the pianos of Duke Ellington and Fats Waller, George Gershwin's desk (which he designed and had built), and sheet music may be seen. Special exhibits and programs are scheduled regularly. The library contains an extensive collection of volumes devoted to popular song. Admission to the Hall of Fame is free. The full name and address is The Songwriters' Hall of Fame and Museum, One Times Square, New York, N.Y., 10036.

SOUL A term first widely applied in the mid 1960s to a style of singing and performance based on gospel singing, but more emotionally charged. Most simply, the urgency and impetus of rhythm and blues were applied to gospel music by such popular R&B singers as Otis Redding, Aretha Franklin, and B. B. King. Based in black music, soul cannot be performed by white singers, it is generally averred. Characteristic of soul is the energetic, virtually shouted singing of the performer. Emotional, protesting, this has soul. To perform properly, one must have suffered. Some critics have suggested that soul as taken up by many popular groups is little more than a commercialization of gospel music. Rock and roll (q.v.) had its roots in soul music.

STARER, ROBERT (b. 1924) Composer, pianist, teacher. Born in Vienna, Austria, Jan. 8, 1924, Starer studied at the State Academy before his family moved to Jerusalem after the Nazi takeover of Austria in 1938. He studied composition at the Jerusalem Conservatory with Joseph Tal and Ödöen Partos. He worked for a time as a pianist for a Jerusalem radio station. Starer served in the Royal Air Force during World War II. He came to the United States in 1947 and studied at the Juilliard School of Music, New York City, with Frederick Jacobi (q.v.). Starer himself has taught at the Juilliard School and the New York College of Music, and has been at Brooklyn College since 1963. His works include a *String Quartet* (1947), *Piano Concerto No. 1* (1947), *Miniatures* for woodwinds (1948), *Prelude and Dance* for orchestra (1949), *Piano Sonata No. 1* (1949), *Symphony No. 1* (1950), *Symphony No. 2* (1951), *Kohelet* for soprano, baritone, chorus, and orchestra (1952), *Prelude and Rondo Giocoso* for orchestra (1953), *Piano Concerto No. 2* (1953), *Concerto a Tre* for clarinet, trumpet, trombone, and strings (1954), *Ballade* for violin and orchestra (1955), *The Intruder,* one-act opera (1956), *Viola Concerto* (1958), *Ariel* for soprano, baritone, chorus, and orchestra (1959), *Fantasia Concertante* for piano, 4 hands (1959), *The Dybbuk,* ballet (1960), *Samson Agonistes,* ballet (1961), *Phaedra,* ballet (1962), *Sketches in Color* for piano (1963), *Trio* for clarinet, cello, and piano (1964), *Mutabili* for orchestra (1965), *Piano Sonata No. 2* (1965), *Joseph and His Brothers* for narrator, soloists, chorus, and orchestra (1966), *Concerto* for violin, cello, and orchestra (1967), *Sabbath Eve Service* (1967), *On the Nature of Things* for chorus (1968), *The Lady of the House of Sleep,* ballet (1968), *Symphony No. 3* (1969), *Piano Concerto No. 3* (1972), *Heptahedron* for harpsichord (1972), *Profiles in Brass* for 4 brass (1974), *Holy Jungle,* ballet (1974), *The Last Lover,* opera (1975), *Evanescents* for piano (1975), and *Quartet* for piano and strings (1977).

STROUSE, CHARLES (b. 1928) Composer, songwriter. Born in New York City, June 7, 1928, Strouse is a graduate of the Eastman School of Music, Rochester, N.Y. He also studied at Tanglewood, Mass. with Aaron Copland (q.v.). He later studied also with Nadia Boulanger. In spite of his "classical" training, Strouse is best known for his show scores, usually with lyrics by Lee Adams (b. 1924). He has composed a string quartet and a symphonic work entitled *What Have We to Sing About?* (1976); his shows include *Bye Bye Birdie* (1960), *All American* (1962),

Golden Boy (1964), *It's a Bird . . . It's a Plane . . . It's Superman* (1966), *Applause* (1970), *Six* (1971), *A Broadway Musical* (1978), and *Bring Back Birdie* (1981). Strouse and Adams also did the score for a London production, *I and Albert* (1972). Strouse and Adams' songs include "Put on a Happy Face," "One Boy," "A Lot of Livin' to Do," "Kids," and "The Telephone Hour," all from *Bye Bye Birdie,* a successful spoof of the Elvis Presley (q.v.) adulation that swept the young in the late 1950s. Other songs: "Once Upon a Time" (*All American*), "Night Song," "I Want to Be with You," and "Lorna's Here" (*Golden Boy*), "One of a Kind," "Fasten Your Seat Belts," and "Think How It's Gonna Be" (*Applause*). Strouse, in collaboration with Martin Charnin (lyrics), did the score for *Annie* (1977) and collaborated with David Rogers (book and lyrics) on *Charlie and Algernon* (1980).

SUBOTNICK, MORTON (b. 1933) Composer, teacher. Born in Los Angeles, Calif., Apr. 14, 1933, Subotnick studied the clarinet but graduated from the University of Denver, Colorado, with a B.A. in English literature. He received an M.A. in music from Mills College, Oakland, Calif. in 1959; his teachers were Leon Kirchner (q.v.) and Darius Milhaud. As a clarinetist Subotnick worked with the Denver and San Francisco symphonies. He has taught at Mills College and has taught at, or been associated with, New York University, the University of Maryland, the University of Pittsburgh, and the California Institute of the Arts, Valencia. Subotnick composes in the electronic medium. His works include *Serenade 1* for flute, clarinet, vibraphone, cello, piano, and mandolin (1959), *Mandolin* for viola, tape, and film (1960), *Play! 1* for woodwind quintet, piano, and tape (1962), *Music to "The Caucasian Chalk Circle"* for narrator, soloists, mandolin, and percussion (1963), *Play! 2* for orchestra and tape (1963), *Play! 3* for tape, film, and mime (1965), *The Tarot* for chamber group and tape (1965), *Prelude 4* for piano and electronics (1966), *Play! 4* for assorted assemblage (1967), *Silver Apples of the Moon* (q.v.) for synthesizer (1967), *The Wild Bull* for synthesizer (1968), *Ritual Electronic Chamber Music* (1968), *Touch* on tape (1969), *Misfortunes of the Immortals: A Concert* for winds, tape, film (1969), *Lamination* for synthesizer (1969), *Sidewinder* for synthesizer (1970), *Until Spring* for synthesizer (1976), *Before the Butterfly* for orchestra (1976), *Liquid Strata* for piano and electronics (1977), *A Sky of Cloudless Sulphur,* for electronics (1978), and *After the Butterfly* for trumpet, "ghost electronics," and 7 players (1979).

SUDERBURG, ROBERT (b. 1936) Composer, pianist, conductor, teacher. Born in Spencer, Iowa, Jan. 28, 1936, Suderburg was educated at the University of Minnesota, Minneapolis, the Yale School of Music (composition and piano), New Haven, Conn., and the University of Pennsylvania, Philadelphia (Ph.D., 1966). He has taught at Bryn Mawr College, Pa., the University of Pennsylvania, the Philadelphia Musical Academy, and the University of Washington, Seattle. Since 1974 he has been chancellor of the North Carolina School of Arts, Winston-Salem. The recipient of many grants and awards (among them a Rockefeller Grant in 1967, a Naumberg Award in 1971, 2 Guggenheim Fellowships and a National Endowment for the Arts Grant in 1974). A co-founder of the Contemporary Group of the University of Washington, Suderburg has been an active proponent of contemporary and American music. He has frequently accompanied his wife, Elizabeth, who also programs unusual recitals featuring

contemporary American composers, as well as Stephen Foster, Charles Ives, and Charles T. Griffes (all q.v.). Although Suderburg has written in many forms—choral, chamber, orchestral, for voice—he is best known for his piano concerto, *Within the Mirror of Time* (1974). Other works include *Chamber Music IV* for percussion (1976) and *Chamber Music V* for voice, percussion, and tape (1976).

SWADOS, ELIZABETH (b. 1951) Composer, author, performer. Born in Buffalo, N.Y., Feb. 5, 1951, Swados studied with Henry Brant (q.v.) at Bennington College, Vt., Frank Baker, and mezzo-soprano Jan De Gaetani. Most of Swados' work has been done for the offbeat theatre as presented at the La-MaMa Experimental Theatre Club, Lennox Art Center, and the New York Shakespeare Festival, all New York City. Combining popular, classical, and just about any form that suits her fancy, Swados has written such theatre pieces (always with her music and often adapted or written by her) as *The Greek Trilogy* (1973), *The Good Woman of Setzuan* (1975), *Nightclub Cantata* (1975), *Agamemnon* (1976), *Runaways* (1978), *Wonderland in Concert* (1978), *Dispatches* (1979), *The Incredible Feeling Show* (1979), *As You Like It* (1980), *The Haggadah,* oratorio (1980), *Lullabye and Goodnight* (1980), *New York Gypsy Suite* (1980), and *Alice* (1980). She has composed music for several television productions, among them: *Step by Step* (1978), *Sky Dance* (1979), *Too Far to Go* (1978), and *Barn Burning* (1979). Her ballet, *Truth and Variations,* was performed by the National Theatre of Canada, Toronto, in 1979. Her published books include *The Girl with the Incredible Feeling* (1976), *Runaways* (1979), *Lullaby* (1980), and *For All Our Children* (1980).

SYDEMAN, WILLIAM (b. 1928) Composer, teacher. Born in New York City, May 8, 1928, Sydeman studied music at the Mannes College of Music, New York City, with Roy Travis and Felix Salzer. He also studied with Roger Sessions (q.v.) at Tanglewood, Mass. He has been on the teaching staff at Mannes since 1959. His works include a *String Quartet* (1955), *Woodwind Quintet No. 1* (1955), *Quartet* for clarinet, violin, trumpet, and double bass (1955), *Divertimento* for octet (1956), *"For Double Bass Alone"* (1957), *Orchestral Abstractions* (1958), *Concerto da Camera for Violin* and players (1959), *Concerto da Camera No. 2 for Violin* and 4 players (1960), *Wind Quintet No. 2* (1961), *Piano Sonata* (1961), *Chamber Concerto* for piano, 2 flutes, and string quartet (1961), *Quartet* for oboe and strings (1961), *Homage to "L'Histoire du Soldat"* for chamber group and percussion (1962), *Music* for flute, viola, guitar, percussion (1962), *Quartet* for flute, violin, clarinet, and piano (1963), *Duo* for viola and harpsichord (1963), *Duo* for violin and piano (1963), *The Lament for Elektra* for alto, chorus, and chamber orchestra (1964), *Oecumenicus* for orchestra (1964), *The Affections* for trumpet and piano (1965), *Study for Orchestra No. 3* (1965), *Concerto da Camera No. 3* for chamber group (1965), *Fantasy Piece* for harpsichord (1965), *In Memoriam John Kennedy* for narrator and orchestra (1966), *Music* for viola, winds, and percussion (1966), *Texture Studies* for wind quintet (1966), *Concerto* for piano, 4 hands, and chamber orchestra or tape (1967), *Projections No. 1* for violin, tape, and slides (1968), *Texture Studies* for orchestra (1969), *Trio* for bassoon, bass clarinet, and piano (1969), and *Maledictions* for tenor, actor, string quartet, and tape (1971).

SYNTHESIZER An instrument or machine—depending on the point of view —capable of producing more or less— depending on the point of view—musical sounds. This is accomplished with a keyboard of sorts and batteries of knobs and switches and an electronic circuitry. What is now termed electronic music— i.e., presynthesizer—dates back to the late 1940s, when *musique concrète* surfaced in France, the brainchild of radio engineer Pierre Schaeffer. His "studies" used natural, everyday sounds to form his works. This method was taken up by such eminent composers as Karlheinz Stockhausen and Pierre Boulez in their work but with greater sophistication. The advent of tape recorders, around the same time, provided the more adventurous composers with yet another means of making music or tampering with sound—depending on the point of view. Conventional instruments, or the human voice, could be recorded and then played back at faster speeds, backward, etc., to achieve highly unusual effects. Around 1960, synthesizers, equipped with the new electronic technology, including solid state circuitry (i.e., no old-fashioned tubes), came into being and composers had yet another means of duplicating the sounds of various instruments via one synthesizer. The best known of these were the Moog in the United States and the Syn-Ket in Italy. Others: the Buchla and some produced by such specialists as RCA and Bell Laboratories. Centers for the production of electronic and synthesizer generated music were established: the Columbia-Princeton Electronic Music Center, New York City, for example, as well as others at Yale University, Brandeis University, Mills College, the University of California at Davis and San Diego. Also, many private studios were set up. Among the most successful composers producing synthesizer music in the United States are Morton Subotnick (q.v.), Milton Babbitt (q.v.), and Charles Wuorinen (q.v.).

THIRD STREAM Coined by composer-conductor Gunther Schuller (q.v.), "third stream," in his usage, refers to the combination of the conventional concert (symphony orchestra) with a jazz band or orchestra in the same work. This is not quite the same as Paul Whiteman's "symphonic jazz," in which his usual dance orchestra was expanded and the jazzier soloists provided an occasional jazz lick now and then. Schuller's third stream would combine 2 units, the symphony orchestra and the jazz group, to perform individually and in ensemble. He himself accomplished this in the "Kleiner Blauteufel" section of *Seven Studies of Paul Klee*. Another third stream work by Schuller is *Transformation* (1957). William Russo (q.v.) also works in the third stream vein: *Three Pieces for Blues Band and Orchestra* and *Street Music*.

THOMAS, EDWARD (b. 1924) Composer, arranger. Born in Chisholm, Minn., Oct. 1, 1924, Thomas' early musical education was directed toward popular music. He was an accomplished guitarist when World War II interrupted his musical career. Thomas served in the U. S. Army in Europe. After the war he settled in New York City and found work as a guitarist in radio, television, and recording studio orchestras. In the late 1950s, having decided to expand his musical horizons, Thomas approached Tibor Serly (q.v.) for further musical study. No easy taskmaster, Serly taught theory, composition, and conducting. He taught Thomas his revolutionary concept of harmony which he called "modus lascivus." Under Serly's guidance Thomas began writing in the larger musical forms (simultaneously he composed music for films and television). His works include a *Woodwind Suite, Impressions for Orchestra, String Quartet* (1967), and *Concerto for Clarinet*. His opera, a setting of Eugene O'Neill's *Desire Under the Elms*, was completed in 1980.

"TIME CYCLE" Important transitional work by Lukas Foss (q.v.). *Time Cycle* was commissioned by the Ford Foundation's Humanities and Arts Program for soprano Adele Addison. It was sung by her accompanied by the New York Philharmonic under Leonard Bernstein (q.v.) on Oct. 21, 1960 (the following year it was awarded the New York Music Critics Award). In its original, full orchestral, version (it exists also in a reduced chamber version) *Time Cycle* consisted of 4 songs with interludes. These interludes were filled by the Improvisation Chamber Ensemble (clarinet, piano, cello, percussion) with improvisations (the chamber version dispenses with the interludes). The *Time Cycle* texts are W. H. Auden's "We're Late," A. E. Housman's "When the Bells Justle," "Sechzehnter Januar" ("January 16") from Franz Kafka's *Diaries*, and Friedrich Nietzsche's "O Mensch! Gib acht!" from *Thus Spake Zarathustra*. "O Man! Take Heed!" and "January 16" are sung in the original German. *Time Cycle* was Foss's first major excursion into improvisational composition. It greatly influenced the new direction of his work and had an effect on other American composers. Such works as *Echoi* (1963), *Elytres* (1964), *Baroque Variations* (1967), and *Paradigm* (1968) followed.

USSACHEVSKY, VLADIMIR (b. 1911) Composer, teacher, theorist. Born in Hailar, Manchuria, Oct. 21, 1911, or Nov. 3, 1911, depending on whether you favor the Julian or the Gregorian calendar, of Russian parents, Ussachevsky belongs in a section devoted to recent music by virtue of his work in the field of electronic and computer music. Ussachevsky came to the United States in 1930 and, after study at Pomona College, Calif., enrolled in the Eastman School of Music, Rochester, N.Y., where he worked under Bernard Rogers (q.v.) and Howard Hanson (q.v.). He was graduated in 1939 and moved on to Columbia University, where he studied with Otto Luening (q.v.). Since 1947 Ussachevsky has taught at Columbia; ca. 1951 he began experimenting with tapes and has collaborated with Luening on several compositions. With Luening, Roger Sessions (q.v.), and Milton Babbitt (q.v.) he founded the Columbia-Princeton Electronic Music Center. Ussachevsky has lectured widely in the United States, the Soviet Union, and in Latin America. He was composer-in-residence at the University of Utah, Salt Lake City, during 1970–71. His compositions include *Theme and Variations* for orchestra (1935), *Jubilee Cantata* for narrator, baritone, chorus, and orchestra (1938), *Miniatures for a Curious Child* for orchestra (1950), *Piano Concerto* (1951), *Sonic Contours* for tape and instruments (1951), *Experimental Composition No. 1* for tape recorder (1952), *Piano Sonata* (1952), *Incantation* for tape, with Otto Luening (1953), *A Poem in Cycles and Bells* for tape recorder and orchestra, with Otto Luening (1954), *Rhapsodic Variations* for tape recorder and orchestra (1954), *Piece for Tape Recorder* (1955), *Studies in Sound* for tape recorder (1955), *Linear Contrasts* for tape recorder (1957), *Metamorphoses* on tape (1957), *Experiment 4711* (1958), *Wireless Fantasy* on tape (1960), *Three Scenes from the Creation* for chorus and electronics (1961), *No Exit*, taped score for film (1962), *Of Wood and Brass* for tape (1965), *Line of Apogee*, taped film score (1967), *An Incredible Voyage*, taped score for television production, with Luening (1967), *Suicide Music* for *Mourning Becomes Electra*, opera by Marvin Levy (1967), *Music for Films*, suite on tape (1967), *Four Miniatures* for electronics (1968), *Two Images of a Computer Piece*, taped film score (1969), *Two Sketches for a Computer*

Piece on tape (1971), *Missa Brevis* for soprano and chorus (1972), *Colloquy* for symphony orchestra, tape recorder, and various chairs (1976), *Celebration* for strings and electronic valve instrument (1980), and *Pentagram* for oboe and tape (1980).

WALKER, GEORGE THEOPHILUS (b. 1922) Composer, pianist, teacher. Born in Washington, D.C., June 27, 1922, Walker was educated at the Oberlin (Ohio) College Conservatory of Music, the Curtis Institute of Music, Philadelphia, and the Eastman School of Music, Rochester, N.Y. His teachers include Rosario Scalero, Gian Carlo Menotti (q.v.), Rudolf Serkin, Robert Casadesus, Gregor Piatigorsky, William Primrose, and Clifford Curzon. Walker also studied with Nadia Boulanger (q.v.) at the American Conservatory, Fontainebleau, France, in 1947. Two years before, Walker had made his New York debut as a pianist at Town Hall. Since that first recital he appeared as piano soloist throughout the United States and in Europe. Walker has taught composition and piano at Dillard University, New Orleans, the New School for Social Research, New York City, and the University of Colorado, Boulder; since 1970 he has been professor of music, Rutgers University, Newark, N.J. He is also on the music staff of the Peabody Conservatory of Music, Baltimore. Walker's compositions include a *Lyric for Strings* (1941), *String Quartet No. 1* (1946), *Piano Sonata No. 1* (1953), *Concerto for Trombone* (1957), *Cello Sonata* (1957), *Piano Sonata No. 2* (1957), *Three Lyrics* for chorus (1958), *Sonata for Violin* (1958), *Address* for orchestra (1959), *Symphony* (1961), *Perimeters* for clarinet and piano (1966), *String Quartet No. 2* (1967), *Antiphonies* for chamber orchestra (1968), *Music for Three* for violin, cello, and piano (1970), *Varia-*

tions for orchestra (1971), *Spirituals* for orchestra (1974), *Five Fancys* for clarinet and piano, 4 hands (1974), *Sacred and Profane* for brass (1975), *Piano Concerto* (1975), *Mass* for chorus and orchestra (1975), *Three Spirituals* for voice and piano (1975), *Piano Sonata No. 3* (1976), and *Dialogues* for cello and orchestra (1976).

WAXMAN, DONALD (b. 1925) Composer, conductor, teacher. Born in Steubenville, Ohio, Oct. 29, 1925, Waxman grew up in Baltimore, Md., where he enrolled at an early age at the Peabody Conservatory. He also studied at the Juilliard School of Music, New York City; his principal teachers were Bernard Wagenaar (q.v.) and Elliott Carter (q.v.). Waxman's works fall mainly into the chamber grouping: a *String Quartet*, a *Suite* for piano, 4 hands, a *Duo* for viola and harp, and a *Trio for Oboe, Clarinet and Bassoon* (1960).

WEBER, BEN (1916–1979) Composer, teacher. Born in St. Louis, Mo., July 23, 1916, Weber dropped out of premedical school at the University of Illinois to enroll in music courses at DePaul University, Chicago. He studied voice, piano, and theory but was self-taught in composition. He was encouraged by Arnold Schoenberg (q.v.) and pianist Artur Schnabel. After leaving Chicago, where he was co-director of the New Music Group, Weber settled in New York City in the early 1940s and taught music privately. He was one of the first American composers to work with 12-tone materials. His compositions include *Five Pieces* for cello and piano (1941), *String Quartet No. 1* (1942), *Trio for Strings No. 1* (1943), *Trio for Strings No. 2* (1946), *Second Piano Suite* (1948), *Concert Aria after Solomon* for soprano and chamber orchestra (1949), *Episodes* for piano (1950), *Sonata da Camera* for violin and piano (1950), *Symphony on Poems of William*

Blake for baritone and orchestra (1951), *String Quartet No. 2* (1951), *Serenade* for harpsichord, flute, oboe, and cello (1953), *Violin Concerto* (1954), *Prelude and Passacaglia* for orchestra (1954), *Concertino* for flute, oboe, clarinet, and string quartet (1955), *Serenade* for strings (1956), *Rapsodie Concertante* for viola and orchestra (1957), *Chamber Fantasy* for orchestra (1959), *Piano Concerto* (1961), *Nocturne* for flute, cello, and celesta (1962), *The Ways* for soprano and piano (1964), *Suite for Piano*, 4 hands (1964), *Dolmen: An Elegy* for winds and strings (1964), *The Enchanted Midnight* for orchestra (1967), *Concert Poem* for violin and orchestra (1970), *Sinfonia Clarion* for orchestra (1973), *Consort of Winds* (1974), and *Capriccio* for cello and piano (1975). Weber died of a heart attack in New York City, May 9, 1979.

WERNICK, RICHARD (b. 1934) Composer, conductor, teacher. Born in Boston, Mass., Jan. 16, 1934, Wernick was a student of Irving Fine (q.v.) and Harold Shapero (q.v.) at Brandeis University, Waltham, Mass. He also studied with Leon Kirchner at Mills College, Oakland, Calif. and with Ernst Toch, Boris Blacher, and Aaron Copland (q.v.) at Tanglewood, Mass. Wernick was a conducting student of Leonard Bernstein (q.v.). For a year (1957–58) Wernick was composer-in-residence for the Royal Winnipeg Ballet in Canada. He has taught at the State University of New York, Buffalo, the University of Chicago, and was chairman of the Music Department, University of Pennsylvania, Philadelphia (1969–74). His compositions include *Music* for viola d'amore (1963), *Aevia* for orchestra (1965), *Stretti* for violin, clarinet, viola, and guitar (1965), *Lyrics from 1x1* for soprano, string bass, vibraphone, and marimba (1966), *Haiku of Basho* for soprano, chamber group, and tape

(1967), *Cadenzas and Variations* for viola and piano (1968), *Moonsongs from the Japanese* for soprano(s) and tape (1969), *Cadenzas and Variations II* for violin (1969), *Hexagrams* for orchestra (1971), *A Prayer for Jerusalem* for mezzo-soprano and percussion (1971), *Kaddish-Requiem: A Secular Service for the Victims of Indochina* for mezzo-soprano, cantor, chamber group, and tape (1971), and *Visions of Terror and Wonder* for mezzo-soprano and orchestra (1976; Pulitzer Prize, 1977).

WESTERGAARD, PETER (b. 1931) Composer, teacher, theorist. Born in Champaign, Ill., May 28, 1931, Westergaard studied with Walter Piston (composition) and Otto Gombosi (musicology) at Harvard University, Cambridge, Mass.; he worked with Milton Babbitt and Roger Sessions at Princeton University, N.J. Other teachers include Darius Milhaud and Wolfgang Fortner. Westergaard has taught at Columbia University, New York City, Amherst College, Mass., and Princeton University, where he was appointed chairman of the Music Department in 1974. His compositions include the chamber opera *Charivari* (1953), *Symphonic Movement* for orchestra (1954), *Invention* for flute and piano (1955), *The Plot Against the Giant,* cantata for women's chorus, clarinet, cello, and harp (1956), *A Refusal to Mourn the Death, by Fire, of a Child in London,* cantata, text by Dylan Thomas, for bass and chamber orchestra (1958), *Five Movements* for small orchestra (1958), *Quartet* for violin, vibraphone, clarinet, and cello (1960), *Spring and Fall: To a Young Child* for voice and piano (1960), *Leda and the Swan,* cantata for mezzo-soprano and chamber group (1961), *Trio* for flute, cello, and piano (1962), *Variations* for flute, clarinet, violin, cello, piano, and percussion (1963), *Mr. and Mrs. Discobbolos,* chamber opera (1965), *Divertimento on*

Discobolic Fragments for flute and piano (1967), *Noises, Sounds and Sweet Airs* for chamber orchestra (1968), *Tuckets and Sennets* for band (1969), and *Moto Perpetuo* for wind sextet (1976). Westergaard is the author of *Introduction to Tonal Theory* (1975).

"WEST SIDE STORY" Musical tragedy based on *Romeo and Juliet* (the idea of choreographer Jerome Robbins), with book by Arthur Laurents, music by Leonard Bernstein (q.v.), and lyrics by Stephen Sondheim (q.v.). Set in New York of the early 1950s when gang rumbles led to injuries and even death, *West Side Story* transformed the feuding Montagues and Capulets of the Shakespeare play into the rival street gangs, the Jets and the Sharks, one consisting of newly arrived Puerto Ricans and the other native-born white New Yorkers. The tightly choreographed plot tells the story of the love of Maria, a Puerto Rican, for Tony, who, while attempting to stop a street fight, kills her brother and is eventually killed himself. Bernstein's score is one of his most brilliant and Sondheim, making his major Broadway debut, revealed a remarkable talent for writing lyrics that has since bloomed in his own work. Among the songs are "Gee, Officer Krupke," "Tonight," "Maria," "America," and "I Feel Pretty." It should be mentioned that Robbins' choreography added greatly to the effectiveness of *West Side Story*. It opened at the Winter Garden Theatre, New York City, Sept. 26, 1957, ran for 734 performances, toured for 10 months, then returned to the Winter Garden for an additional 246 performances. A London production, which opened in 1958, ran for more than 1,000 performances. A film version was released in 1961. A successful New York revival opened in February 1980. In the original 1957 production Carol Lawrence portrayed "Maria," Larry Kert, "Tony," Chita Rivera,

"Anita," and songwriter-to-be Martin Charnin, "Big Deal."

WHITTENBERG, CHARLES (b. 1927) Composer, teacher. Born in St. Louis, Mo., July 6, 1927, Whittenberg is a graduate (1948) of the Eastman School of Music, Rochester, N.Y., where he studied with Bernard Rogers (q.v.) and Burrill Phillips (q.v.). He has taught theory and composition at the University of Connecticut, Storrs, since 1967. Some of his work has been accomplished at the Columbia-Princeton Electronic Music Center, New York City, and at Yale's Electronic Studio, New Haven, Conn. Whittenberg's compositions include a *Dialogue and Aria* for flute and piano (1956), an *Electronic Study* for cello and tape (1960), *Structures* for 2 pianos (1961), *Fantasy* for wind quintet (1962), *Electronic Study II* for double bass and tape (1962), *Triptych* for brass quintet (1962), *Three Pieces for Clarinet Alone* (1963), *Identities and Variations* for piano (1963), *Event* for small orchestra (1963), *Chamber Concerto* for violin and chamber group (1963), *Vocalise* for soprano, viola, and percussion (1963), *Duo-Divertimento* for flute and double bass (1963), *Variations for 9 Players* (1965), *Quartet for Strings in One Movement* (1965), *Polyphony for Solo Trumpet* (1965), *Four Forms and an Epilogue* for harpsichord (1965), *Three Compositions for Piano* (1967), *Conversations* for double bass (1967), *Sextet* (1967), *Games of Five* for woodwind quintet (1968), *Iambi* for 2 oboes (1968), *Concerto* for brass quintet (1969), *A Due* for flute and percussion (1969), *Correlations* for orchestra (1969), and *From John Donne: A Sacred Triptych* for vocal octet (1971).

WIGGLESWORTH, FRANK (b. 1918) Composer, teacher. Born in Boston, Mass., Mar. 3, 1918, Wigglesworth was a student of Otto Luening (q.v.) and Henry Cowell (q.v.). After a tour of duty during World War II in the U. S. Army Air Forces, he returned to the United States to teach at Columbia University, Queens College, and the New School for Social Research, New York City. Wigglesworth's compositions include *Creation* for chorus and orchestra (1940), *New England Concerto* for violin and strings (1941), *The Plunger* for soprano, flute, viola, cello, and piano (1941), *Trio* for flute, banjo, and harp (1942), *Jeremiah* for baritone, chorus, and orchestra (1942), *Lake Music* for solo flute (1947), *Sleep Becalmed* for chorus and orchestra (1948), *Three Movements* for strings (1949), *Telesis* for chamber orchestra and percussion (1949), *Serenade* for flute, viola, and guitar (1952), *Symphony No. 1* (1955), *Brass Quintet* (1957), *Symphony No. 2* (1958), *Duo* for cellos (1959), *Sonata for Viola and Piano* (1969), *Exodus*, ballet for chamber orchestra (1960), *Trios* for 3 flutes (1960), *Wood Wind Quintet* (1960), *Brass Quintet* (1961), *Short Mass* for chorus (1962), *Super Flumina Babilonis* for chorus (1964), *Sonata for Violin and Piano* (1965), *Moderato for Strings* (1966), *March* for chamber group (1967), *Symphony No. 3*, "Three Portraits for String Orchestra" (1969), *Willowdale Handcar*, opera with libretto by Edward Gorey (1969), *Overton Mass* for chorus (1970), *Viola Concertino* for small orchestra (1970), *New Mass* for chorus (1973), *Psalm 148* for chorus, 3 flutes, and 2 trombones (1974), *Woodwind Quintet* (1975), *String Trio I* for violin, viola, and cello (1975), *String Trio II* for violin, viola, and cello (1976), *Fanfare* for chamber orchestra (1977), *Song Cycle* for mezzo-soprano and clarinet (1978), *Suite for String Orchestra* (1979), *Brass Quartet*, "The Four Winds" (1979), and *Sonata* for solo viola (1979).

WILLIAMS, JOHN (b. 1932) Composer, conductor. Born in Queens, N.Y., Feb. 8, 1932, Williams, whose father was a timpanist, studied music in Los Angeles and New York City. His piano teacher at the Juilliard School of Music was Rosina Lhévinne. A resident of Los Angeles since 1948, Williams is most noted for his film scores, among them *Jaws* (which won an Academy Award in 1975), *Close Encounters of the Third Kind, Superman, 1941* (the ultimate disaster film), *Towering Inferno, Star Wars,* and *The Empire Strikes Back,* among dozens of others. Williams has also composed works for the concert hall such as an *Essay for Strings* (1966) and a *Violin Concerto.* In January 1980 he was appointed conductor of the Boston Pops Orchestra, as successor to Arthur Fiedler (q.v.).

WILSON, DONALD M. (b. 1937) Composer, teacher. Born in Chicago, Ill., June 30, 1937, Wilson studied oboe with Ray Still of the Chicago Symphony. He graduated from the University of Chicago (1959) with a B.A. in Humanities (Music Theory and Analysis). At the Juilliard School of Music, New York City, Wilson studied composition with Vittorio Giannini (q.v.); at Cornell University, Ithaca, N.Y., he worked under Karel Husa and Robert Palmer (both q.v.) and was awarded a doctorate in Musical Arts in 1965. He later studied composition with Gunther Schuller (q.v.) and electronic music with William Albright (q.v.). Since 1967 Wilson has been in the Department of Composition and History, College of Musical Arts, Bowling Green University, Ohio. His works include *Dedication* for string orchestra (1960), *Psalm 23* for mixed chorus and organ, or piano (1960), *Suite in Threes and Sevens* for 2 oboes (1961), *Quintet* for clarinet and string quartet (1961, revised 1962), *Sonata* for English horn and piano (1962), *Con-*

certo for piano and wind orchestra (1962–63), *Five Haiku* for tenor and sextet (1962), *Sett* for 3 low instruments and one to 3 optional voices (1962–63), *Lissa,* musical comedy (1963, revised 1973), *Adam,* incidental music for a French Mystery Play (1964), *Doubles,* a game-piece for 2 woodwinds vs. 2 strings (1964), *Stabile I* for 2 pianos (1965), *Stabile II* for 5 or more players (1965), *Stabile III,* "Ave Maria" for triple chorus and percussion (1966, revised 1972), *Stabile IV* for string quartet (1965–68), *Seventeen Views* for one or 2 violins with slides and/or narrator (1966–67), *Tic-Tac-Toe* piano, 2 hands or 2 players (1968), *Prisms* for organ, also for orchestra (1968), *Visions* for mixed chorus and symphonic band (1969–70), *Space-Out,* a rock cantata for soprano, jazz band, tape, and visuals (1970–71), *Electronic Wedding,* 2 pieces for tape with or without dancers (1971–72), *Accidents Will Happen,* an improvisation for musicians, dancers, and audience (1971–72, revised 1975), *Six International Etudes* for viola (1976–77), and *Decisions, Decisions!* for harp with or without tape-delay apparatus (1968; 1977).

WILSON, OLLY (b. 1937) Composer, pianist, bassist, teacher. Born in St. Louis, Mo., Sept. 9, 1937, Wilson learned to play the clarinet while in high school. His playing won him a music scholarship at Washington University, St. Louis. He continued in graduate work at the University of Illinois and the University of Iowa, Iowa City, where he received his Ph.D. in music in 1964. As an undergraduate Wilson earned extra money as a bassist in jazz bands; he has also played double bass in symphony orchestras in St. Louis and Cedar Rapids, Iowa. Wilson has taught at Florida Agricultural and Mechanical University, Tallahassee, West Virginia University, Morgantown, Indiana University, Bloomington, Oberlin College, Ohio, and the University of California, Berkeley. Wilson has made a study of electronic music, which has influenced the direction of his work; he has also done research in the music of West Africa. His compositions include *Prelude and Line Study* for woodwind quartet (1959), *Trio* for flute, cello, and piano (1959), *String Quartet* (1960), *Violin Sonata* (1961), *Wry Fragments* for tenor and percussion (1961), *Dance Suite* for winds (1962), *Soliloquy* for bass viol (1962), *Sextet* for orchestra (1963), *And Death Shall Have No Dominion* for tenor and percussion (1963), *Three Movements* for orchestra (1964), *Chanson Innocent* for contralto and 2 bassoons (1965), *Piece for Four* for flute, trumpet, double bass, and piano (1966), *Cetus* for electronics (1967), *In Memoriam Martin Luther King* for chorus and tape (1968), *Voices* for orchestra (1970), *The Eighteen Hands of Jerome Harris,* ballet (1971), *Akwan* for piano, electric piano, amplified strings, and orchestra (1972), *Black Martyrs* for electronics (1972), *Spirit Song* for soprano, double chorus, and orchestra (1973), *Echoes* for clarinet and tape (1975), *Sometimes* for tenor and tape (1976), and *Piano Trio* (1977).

WILSON, RICHARD (b. 1941) Composer, teacher. Born in Cleveland, Ohio, May 15, 1941, Wilson studied both piano and cello before he enrolled in Harvard University where he studied with Randall Thompson (q.v.), Robert Moevs (q.v.), and G. W. Woodworth. He earned his M.A. in music at Rutgers University in 1966, then joined the faculty of Vassar College, Poughkeepsie, N.Y. Wilson's compositions include a *Suite for Five Players* (1963), *Trio* for oboe, violin, and cello (1964), *Concert Piece* for violin and piano (1967), *A Dissolve* for women's voices (1968), *String Quartet* (1968), *Quartet* for flutes, double bass, and harpsichord (1969), *Music* for violin and cello (1969), *Initiation* for orchestra (1970), *Music* for solo cello (1971), *Music* for solo flute (1972), *Wind Quintet* (1974), and *String Quartet No. 2* (1977).

"WISH YOU WERE HERE" Charming folk-musical, words and music by Harold Rome (q.v.). Based on a play by Arthur Kober (*Having Wonderful Time,* 1936), who collaborated on the book with director and co-producer Joshua Logan, *Wish You Were Here* was set in Camp Karefree, an adult summer camp in the New York Catskill Mountain area. The young and the lonely toilers in the great city's offices go to Camp Karefree for 2 weeks of rest—and, if lucky, romance. When *Wish You Were Here* opened it was devastated by the newspaper critics, which should have closed the show, but Logan refused to accept those opinions. He rewrote the script, then consulted with Kober and Rome (the show did not have the customary out-of-town tryout shakedown because Logan had insisted on an onstage swimming pool, which made travel impossible). The 3 produced a virtually rewritten book, new songs, and many surprises for a generally demoralized cast. *Wish You Were Here,* despite the critics, then went on to become one of the season's hit musicals. The story of the romance between the pretty secretary, "Teddy Stern," and one of the college-boy waiters, "Chick," is simply plotted. The romance nearly flounders on a misunderstanding (Chick is led to believe that Teddy has spent the night with the camp's professional lady killer, "Pinky"). But all is cleared up by the end of the show. Rome's score is replete with wistful, amusing Jewish-inflected songs: "Ballad of the Social Director," "Shopping Around," the lovely waltz "Could Be," "Tripping the Light Fantastic" with its Brooklyn-like exchange— Boy: "You dancin'?"/ Girl: "You askin'?"/ Boy, "I'm askin'."/ Girl: "I'm dancin'." The title song became a great hit via a recording by then vocal star Eddie Fisher. Perhaps the loveliest song in the score is the haunting "Where Did the Night Go?" *Wish You Were Here* opened at the Imperial Theatre, New York City, June 25, 1952, and ran for 598 performances. In the original production Teddy was portrayed by Patricia Marand, Chick by Jack Cassidy, and Pinky by Paul Valentine.

WOLFF, CHRISTIAN (b. 1934) Composer, teacher. Born in Nice, France, Mar. 8, 1934, Wolff came to the United States in 1941. Although influenced by the music of John Cage (q.v.), he was a student of the classics and comparative literature at Harvard University. He earned a Ph.D. in this field in 1963 and has been a member of the faculty of Harvard since 1962. Although Wolff has worked under John Cage and Morton Feldman (q.v.), he is largely self-taught in composition. In his work Wolff has used arithmetical progressions to determine rhythms and has also written works in which the performers are granted free play with the composition, basing their playing on the audience's reaction and their own intuition. Wolff's compositions include *For Prepared Piano* (1951), *Trio* for flute, trumpet, and cello (1951), *Nine* for flute, clarinet, horn, trumpet, 2 cellos, celesta, and piano (1951), *For Magnetic Tape* (1952), *For Piano I* (1952), *Chance,* ballet (1952), *For Piano II* (1953), *Suite* for prepared piano (1954), *Duo for Pianists I* (1957), *Duo for Pianists II* (1958), *For Pianist* (1959), *For Six or Seven Players* (1959), *Rune,* ballet (1959), *Duet I* for piano, 4 hands (1960), *Summer* for string quartet (1961), *Duet II* for piano and horn (1961), *Trio II* for piano, 4 hands and percussion (1961), *Duo for Violinist and Pianist* (1961), *For Five*

or *Ten Players* (1962), *In Between Pieces* for 3 players (1963), *For One, Two or Three People* (1964), *Septet* for any instruments (1964), *Electric Spring 1* for recorders, horn, trombone, violin, double bass, electric double bass, and electric guitar (1966), *Pairs* for 2, 4, 6, or 8 musicians on any instruments (1968), *Edges* for any instrument or instruments (1968), *Prose Collection* for various combinations of musicians and instruments (1969), *Tilbury* for keyboard or other instruments (1969), *Tread,* ballet (1970), *Snowdrop* for harpsichord (1970), *You Blew It* for chorus (1971), and *Lines* for quartet (1972).

WOODSTOCK The official, businesslike name for this remarkable youth rock music "love and peace" fest was the Woodstock Music and Art Fair. The brainchild of 4 sharp promoters, it promised 3 days, beginning on Aug. 16, 1969, of some of the greatest superstars in rock music. Tickets for the event went for $18 and the youth of the nation swarmed in from all directions. The promoters had rented 600 acres of alfalfa grazing meadowland and made ready to receive the 60,000 they expected; nearly 500,000 (it has been estimated) gathered in Max Yagur's alfalfa meadow and for 3 days listened to The Who, Jimi Hendrix, the Jefferson Airplane, Joan Baez, Janis Joplin, and others (all handsomely paid), took drugs, shocked the locals swimming in the nude, made love publicly—but managed to go through 3 trying days (there were few amenities and it rained, turning the meadow into a mudhole) peaceably. Meanwhile the promoters filmed the concert and the loving groups of youngsters—who came to be called "the Woodstock Nation"—and recorded the superstars. They claimed to have lost money on the festival (the crowd was so large that taking tickets became impossible), but the film *Woodstock* was released in 1970 and 2 record albums were released and all made money. Woodstock proved that the youth of the nation could assemble without violence (except for illnesses and drug overdoses), unlike their elders, who believed in war. But, as they learned later, they had been used. The promoters, who claimed a loss of a million dollars, instead made more than that on the film and albums. An attempt to repeat Woodstock was announced in 1979 but was blocked; it had never happened before and would not happen again. Besides, the original Woodstock Nation had been absorbed into the society they had so beautifully defied when they were 10 years younger, and perhaps wiser.

WUORINEN, CHARLES (b. 1938) Composer, teacher, pianist, conductor. Born in New York City, June 9, 1938, Wuorinen studied at Columbia University with Jack Beeson (q.v.), Otto Luening (q.v.), and Vladimir Ussachevsky (q.v.). He has taught at Columbia, Princeton University, N.J., the New England Conservatory, Boston, Mass., and the Manhattan School of Music, New York City. His works include *Symphony No. 3* (1959), *Concertone* for brass quintet and orchestra (1960), *Turetzky Pieces* for flute, clarinet, and double bass (1960), *Eight Variations* for harpsichord (1960), *Trio No. 1* for flute, cello, and piano (1961), *Symphonia Sacra* for male trio, 2 oboes, 2 violins, double bass, and organ (1961), *Evolutio Transcripta* for chamber orchestra (1961), *Invention* for percussion quintet (1962), *Octet* (1962), *Duuiensela* for cello and piano (1962), *Bearbeitungen über das Glogauer Liederbuch* for chamber orchestra (1962), *The Prayer of Jonah* for chorus and strings (1962), *Trio No. 2* for flute, violin, and piano (1962), *Chamber Concerto* for cello and 10 players (1963), *Piano Variations* (1963), *Flute Variations* (1963), *Composition* for violin and

10 instruments (1964), *Chamber Concerto* for flute and 10 players (1964), *Orchestral and Electronic Exchanges* (1965), *Composition* for oboe and piano (1965), *Chamber Concerto* for oboe and 10 players (1965), *Piano Concerto* (1966), *Janissary Music* for percussion (1966), *Harpsichord Divisions* (1966), *Making Ends Meet* for piano, 4 hands (1966), *Duo* for violin and piano (1966), *The Politics of Harmony* (1967), *Flute Variations* (1968), *String Trio* (1968), *Time's Encomium* for synthesized and processed synthesized sound (1969, Pulitzer Prize, 1970), *Adapting to the Times* for cello and piano (1969), *Contrafactum* for orchestra (1969), *The Long and the Short* for violin (1969), *Piano Sonata* (1969), *1851: A Message to Denmark Hill* for baritone, flute, cello, and piano (1970), *Ringing Changes* for percussion ensemble (1970), *Chamber Concerto* for tuba, winds, and percussion (1970), *A Song to the Lute in Musicke* for voice and piano (1970), *Cello Variations* (1970), *String Quartet* (1971), *Concerto for Amplified Violin and Orchestra* (1972), *Variations* for bassoon, harp, and timpani (1972), *Piano Concerto No. 2* for amplified piano and orchestra (1974), *The Waters of Babylon,* opera (1975), *Hyperion* for 12 instruments (1976), *Piano Sonata No. 2* (1976), *Percussion Symphony* (1976), *The Winds* (1977), and *Two-Part Symphony* (1978).

WYNER, YEHUDI (b. 1929) Composer, pianist, teacher, conductor. Born in Calgary, Canada, June 1, 1929, Wyner was brought up in New York City, where his parents settled while he was a boy. His father Lazar Weiner (b. 1897) became a prominent musician in New York's Jewish community. Wyner studied at the Yale School of Music (composition with Richard Donovan and Paul Hindemith; piano with Bruce Simonds). At Harvard University his teachers in composition were Walter Piston (q.v.) and Randall Thompson (q.v.). Wyner has taught composition at Yale University (where he was named chairman of the Music Department in 1969) and has been the pianist for the Bach Aria Group for several years. His compositions include *Partita* for piano (1952), *Psalm 143* for chorus (1952), *Dance Variations* for wind octet (1953), *Piano Sonata* (1954), *Seven Songs* for voice and piano (1950–55), *Concert Duo* for violin and piano (1956), *Serenade for Seven Instruments* (1958), *Passover Offering* for flute, clarinet, cello, and trombone (1959), *Three Informal Pieces* for violin and piano (1961), *Friday Evening Service* for cantor, chorus, and organ (1963), *Short Fantasy No. 1* for piano (1963), *Torah Service* for chorus, brass quartet, and double bass (1966), *Short Fantasy No. 2* for piano (1966), *Da Camera*, piano concerto (1967), *Cadenza* for clarinet and harpsichord (1970), *De Novo* for cello and chamber group (1971), *Short Fantasy No. 3* for piano (1971), *Canto Cantabile* for soprano and band (1972), *Intermedio, Lyric Ballet for Soprano and Strings* (1974), and *Dances of Atonement* for violin and piano (1976).

YOUNG, LA MONTE (b. 1935) Composer, teacher, theorist. Born in Bern, Idaho, Oct. 14, 1935, Young studied the saxophone and the clarinet, as well as ethnomusicology, counterpoint, and composition. His composition teachers include Leonard Stein and Karlheinz Stockhausen. The music of John Cage (q.v.) has greatly influenced Young; so has Indian philosophy and music and electronics. Young is one of the leaders of contemporary avant-garde and has produced some puzzling work: his *Composition 1960 #7* consists of a single chord with instructions "to be held for a long time." This "work" was, indeed, performed by a string trio which held the chord for a performance lasting more than a half hour. Young's *Composition 1960 #10* consists of a single sentence: "Draw a straight line and follow it." *Composition 1990* calls for a fire on the concert stage and the release of a bevy of butterflies in the hall. Young's other works include *Poem for Chairs, Tables and Benches* (1960), *The Second Dream of the High-Tension Line Stepdown Transformer* (1962), and *The Tortoise, His Dreams and Journeys*, theatre piece for voices, strings, electronics, and projections. Young was editor of *An Anthology* (of art, music, and poetry, 1963).

ZWILICH, ELLEN TAAFFE (b. 1939) Composer, violinist. Born in Miami, Fla., Apr. 30, 1939, Zwilich began studying music seriously at Florida State University, Tallahassee, with John Boda; she continued at the Juilliard School of Music, New York City, with Roger Sessions and Elliott Carter (both q.v.). She also studied violin with Richard Burgin and Ivan Galamian and has played professionally, principally in New York City, and for a time was a member of the American Symphony Orchestra under Leopold Stokowski. She has received grants and awards from the National Endowment for the Arts, the Martha Baird Rockefeller Fund for Music, others. Her works include *Einsame Nacht* for baritone and piano (1971), *Im Nebel* for contralto and piano (1972), *Symposium for Orchestra* (1973), *Sonata in Three Movements* for violin and piano (1974), *Trompeten* for soprano and piano (1974), *Allison* for chamber group (1974), *String Quartet 1974, Clarino Quartet* for piccolo and 3 trumpets (1977), *Concerto for Violin and Orchestra* (1978), *Emlékezet* for soprano and piano (1978), and *Chamber Symphony*.

Appendix

American Music on Records

When I started work on this volume some years ago, I also began an exhaustive discography that, before long, got out of hand. It was tedious, time-consuming, and would have added pages to an already thickish book. It was also rather frustrating. Because of the long time span, some of the recordings listed in the discography one year were out of print the next.

The intent was to make the reader aware of the richness of American music available on recordings, since hearing the music is even more important than reading about it. Not everyone who has a genuine interest in our music has access to concert halls (which rarely ring to the sounds of our native music anyhow), but the ubiquitous phonograph is within almost everyone's reach. Some libraries, too, lend recordings. So the discography had to remain, but in a less unwieldy form.

My first suggestion to the interested reader, then, is to consult the Schwann catalogs (both 1 and 2; the latter lists the older recordings) which list in-print recordings under the composer's name. Not that they catalog every possible recording—the releases of smaller record companies are not always listed, nor are some imports or offbeat labels. But there is plenty to find in the Schwanns.

Since the concentration is on the major labels I might point out certain valuable recordings that can be found on such imprints as Angel, Columbia, and RCA. Columbia, especially, was in the vanguard of American music with its coverage of the music of Charles Ives (most notably in the 4-record set *Charles Ives—The 100th Anniversary,* Columbia M4-32504), Aaron Copland conducting his own works. Many of the older, mono recordings dating back to the enlightened times of Goddard Lieberson are still available through its division called Special Service Records, CBS Records, 51 West 52nd Street, New York, N.Y., 10019. The record business being what it is in 1981 might mean the end of this service which made it possible to obtain recordings of Virgil Thomson's *Cello Concerto* and *The Mother of Us All Suite* (CML-4468), Lukas Foss's *A Parable of Death* (CML-4859), and Roy Harris' *Symphony 1933* (his first) and *Symphony No. 7* (CML-5095).

Columbia's lower-priced Odyssey label functions as a kind of reprint source —there is even a "Modern American Music Series" (or was in 1976) which brought back the recording of William Schuman's *Symphony No. 8* coupled with Robert Suderburg's *Piano Concerto* (Y-34140). Other releases are devoted to the music of Elliott Carter, Gunther Schuller, and others.

Columbia's excellent and highly commendable (but, alas, not too well supported) "Black Composers Series" resulted in recordings of much American music all too rarely heard, much of it by younger composers—Adolphus Hailstork, Hale Smith, Olly Wilson, and David Baker as well as the men of an earlier generation such as William Grant Still, George Walker, and Ulysses Simpson Kay. The series resulted in at least 9 volumes of well performed and recorded music, but it appears to have ended there and the records are going out of print. Volume 2 contained a fine performance of Still's *Afro-American Symphony* and other works (M-32782) and Volume 9 George Walker's *Piano Concerto,* Hale Smith's *Ritual and Incantation,* and Hailstork's *Celebration!* (M-34556). For a time it was almost as if Goddard Lieberson had returned. A most worthy series.

Nor should Columbia's excellent library of original, or re-created, cast albums of Broadway shows be overlooked. These too are a part of the Lieberson legacy and range from the original cast album of the Burton Lane–E. Y. Harburg score for *Finian's Rainbow* (CS-2080E) through Cole Porter's *Kiss Me, Kate* (S-32609), Harold Arlen's *House of Flowers* (COS-2320), a re-creation of Harold Rome's *Pins and Needles* (OL-5810), reissues from another label (the defunct Decca) of Irving Berlin's *This Is the Army* coupled with Rome's *Call Me Mister* by their original casts (X-14877) to Stephen Sondheim's *Anyone Can Whistle* (CSP As-32608). Others: *Goldilocks, Lady in the Dark, The Boys from Syracuse, Miss Liberty,* and *The Pajama Game.*

RCA (formerly RCA Victor) has been less generous to American music but has released some impressive recordings. Its complete recording of Gershwin's *Porgy and Bess* (ARL3-2109) is a stunning accomplishment, as are its cast album recordings of Stephen Sondheim's *Pacific Overtures* (ARL1-1367) and *Sweeney Todd* (CBL2-3379). The impressiveness of these releases owes much to producer Thomas Z. Shepard, a graduate of the Lieberson school of transcribing stage productions to disc.

Worth mentioning is a 5-record set of all of Scott Joplin's piano compositions appositely played by Dick Hyman (CRL5-1106). RCA's Victrola America series of historic reissues restored several fine recorded performances to the catalogs at a reasonable price. Among these are Koussevitzky's pioneering recordings of Copland's *Appalachian Spring, A Lincoln Portrait,* and *El Salón México* (AVM1-1739) and Paul Robeson's singing of Robinson and Latouche's *Ballad for Americans* coupled with John Charles Thomas' rendition of Kleinsinger's Whitman setting, *I Hear America Singing* (AVM1-1736). A delightful disc makes the first (acoustic) recording of Gershwin's *Rhapsody in Blue,* with the composer at the piano, available again, along with a sparkling performance of *An American in Paris* and several Gershwin piano solos: the *Three Preludes* and songs (AVM1-1740).

European-based major record companies have issued some fine musical Americana. Angel, which is a subsidiary of Britain's Electrical Music Industries (via Capitol Records), has a number of worthy records, among them a couple devoted to the piano music of Gottschalk played by Leonard Pennario (S-36077 and S-36090); of even greater interest are those releases of Roy Harris' *Folk-Song Symphony* (S-36091), Virgil Thomson's *The Plow That Broke the Plains/The River* and *Autumn* for harp, strings, and percussion (S-37300) and to Randall Thompson's *The Testament of Freedom* and *Symphony No. 1* (S-37315).

Germany's Deutsche Grammophon has many a surprise, including a complete recording, by the original American cast, of Joplin's "opera" *Treemonisha* (2-DG 2707 083). There is a superb performance, conducted by the youthful Michael Tilson Thomas of Piston's *Symphony No. 2* coupled with Schuman's *Violin Concerto* (2530-103). Under Leonard Bernstein's baton the Israel Philharmonic has recorded virtually all of Bernstein's orchestral music, including the *Symphony No. 1,* "Jeremiah," coupled with *Chichester Psalms* (2530-968), a marvelous rendering of *Symphony No. 2,* "The Age of Anxiety," with composer Lukas Foss doing wonders at the keyboard (2530-969), and a first recording of a fairly recent (1977) work, *Songfest* (2531-044). Bernstein's *Symphonic Dances* from *West Side Story* are well done by the San Francisco Symphony under Seiji Ozawa, but the more interesting work is William Russo's "third stream" composition *Three Pieces for Blues Band and Orchestra* (2530-309). Deutsche Grammophon has also reissued Douglas Moore's *The Ballad of Baby Doe* in the version starring Beverly Sills (3-DG 2709 061).

And speaking of American opera, also issued by a foreign-based label, London Records, is a finely performed complete recording of Gershwin's *Porgy and Bess* (3-London 13116). Not as dramatic as RCA's recording, perhaps, but a most musicianly one and very well done.

Philips, a Netherlands company, has revived the old Mercury label and has begun to reissue the excellent American Music series by Howard Hanson (mostly) and the Eastman Rochester Orchestra. Among the notable reissues are Hanson's *Symphony No. 1* and *No. 3* (Mercury SRI-75112), Hanson's *Symphony No. 2* and *Lament for Beowulf* (SRI-75007), Piston's *Symphony No. 3* and Hanson's *Fourth* (SRI-75107), MacDowell's *Indian Suite* (SRI-75026), Thomson's *Symphony on a Hymn Tune/Feast of Love* and Hanson's *Four Psalms* (SRI-75063), an album devoted to music by Griffes and Loeffler (SRI-75090), Corigliano's *Piano Concerto* (SRI-75118), and a fascinating album devoted to Colin McPhee's *Tabu-Tabuhan,* Gunther Schuller's *Seven Studies on Themes of Paul Klee,* with a bonus of Ernest Bloch's *Sinfonia Breve* (SRI-75116). Other reissues of the Hanson-Eastman Orchestra will be noted under the entry for Eastman Rochester Archives, further along in these commentaries.

All of these labels are reasonably available in record shops, and most likely listed in the Schwann catalog. I will now list a number of record companies whose distribution may be no threat to the major firms, but most of which specialize in or have large portions of their catalogs devoted to American music.

CMS RECORDS, 14 Warren Street, New York, N.Y., 10007, issues a large selection of American music on its Desto label (many of which, in turn, were available only by mail order from the no longer existing American Recording Society). It would be impossible to reproduce the entire catalog, but some of the highlights might be pointed out: John Alden Carpenter's *Skyscrapers* (Desto DC-6407), Jerome Moross' *Frankie and Johnny* (DC-6408), Horatio Parker's *Hora Novissima* (DC-6413/14), *Anthology of American Piano Music* (DC-6445/47), Douglas Moore's *The Devil and Daniel Webster* (DC-6450), Lou Harrison's *Pacifika Rondo,* etc. (DC-6478), *The Black Composer in America* (DC-7107), *Women Composers* (DC-7117), and Irving Fine's *Symphony 1962,* etc. (DC-7167).

COMPOSERS RECORDINGS, INC. (CRI), 170 West 74th Street, New York, N.Y., 10023, issues recordings supervised, performed, and often conducted by the composer. One of its happiest claims is that none of its by now (after 25 years) 300 discs ever go out of circulation. This doesn't mean that they are easy to get at your local record shop. CRI issues a catalog and takes mail orders. Another excellent policy of CRI is to reissue recordings that other companies have let go out of print (i.e., a collection of Virgil Thomson's orchestral and vocal music once available on Columbia; likewise Wallingford Riegger's *Symphony No. 3* and Harold Shapero's *Symphony for Classical Orchestra*). The emphasis of the CRI catalog is on contemporary (or recent contemporary) music; the music ranges from the conservatism of Douglas Moore and Samuel Barber to the adventures of Henry Cowell and John J. Becker through the avant-gardeism of Lucia Dlugoszewski. Nor is electronic music ignored—for example, the work of Luening and Ussachevsky. Undoubtedly CRI's catalog is one of the most valuable around.

CONNOISSEUR SOCIETY / IN SYNC LABORATORIES, 390 West End Avenue, New York, N.Y., 10024, has been issuing splendid piano recordings and only recently began exploring the American repertory, beginning, fittingly, with Gershwin. The duo piano team of Veri and Jamanis made the first recording of Gershwin's original 2-piano version of *Rhapsody in Blue* (CSQ-2054). This was followed by another set of "firsts": Gershwin's own transcriptions for 2 pianos of the *"I Got Rhythm" Variations, Second Rhapsody,* and the *Cuban Overture* for one piano, 4 hands. Veri and Jamanis will eventually record Gershwin's 2-piano version of the *Concerto in F*. Connoisseur will further explore other avenues of the American repertoire.

CRYSTAL RECORDS, 2235 Willida Lane, Sedro Wooley, Wash., 98284, issues much American music along with other contemporary as well as older music.

The emphasis, generally, is on the works of the younger composers: Donald Erb, William Kraft, William Schmidt, William O. Smith, et al. Much chamber music. Crystal fills a void and is worth looking into.

DELOS RECORDS, 855 Via de la Paz, Pacific Palisades, Calif., 90272, does not specialize in American music but does release interesting records of works by such composers as Donald Harris, William Kraft, and Ellen Taaffe Zwilich.

DRG RECORDS, INC., 200 West 57th Street, New York, N.Y., 10019, concentrates on personalities, sound tracks, and reissues of show albums as well as originals. Among this catalog's highlights are *The Act* starring Liza Minnelli (DRG-6101), a reissue of the charming *Leave It to Jane* revival on DRG's *Stet* label (Stet DS-15002), and the fine *She Loves Me* (Stet DS 2 15008). Also notable: *A Party with Comden and Green* (DRG S21-5177), *Judy Garland: the Beginning* (DRG S1-5187), and an album of ballet by Harold Arlen, Richard Rodgers, and Cole Porter played by British composer-pianist Richard Rodney Bennett. The latter album contains Arlen's Civil War ballet from *Bloomer Girl,* Rodgers' *Ghost Town,* and Porter's early (1923) jazzy *Within the Quota.* The title is *Special Occasions* (DRG-6102). *Very Good Eddie* (DRG-6100) is another charmer by Jerome Kern.

EASTMAN ROCHESTER ARCHIVES, Institute of American Music, 560 University Avenue, Rochester, N.Y., 14607, is reissuing some of the American music series once available on Mercury Records (others, as has already been noted, are being released by Philips on its Mercury label). Highlights: *Americana* for solo winds and string orchestra with music by Copland, Kennan, Keller, Barlow, Rogers, and Hanson (ERA-1001), *Fantasy Variations on a Theme of Youth* by Hanson/*The Bright Land* by Harold Triggs and *Leaves from the Tale of Pinocchio* by Bernard Rogers (ERA-1002), Works by Kennan, Rogers, and William Bergsma (ERA-1004), *Merry Mount Suite* by Hanson (ERA-1005), Hanson's *Piano Concerto* and *Mosaics* with La Montaine's *Bird of Paradise* (ERA-1006), Hanson's *Drum Taps*/Randall Thompson's *Testament of Freedom* (ERA-1007), Deems Taylor's *Through the Looking Glass* (ERA-1008), John Alden Carpenter's *Adventures in a Perambulator*/Burrill Phillips' *McGuffey's Reader* (ERA-1009), Hanson's *Song of Democracy* and *Elegy*/Richard Lane's *Four Songs* (ERA-1010), Charles Martin Loeffler's *Deux Rapsodies*/Barlow's *Night Song* (ERA-1011), *American Portraits,* works by Robert McBride, Charles Vardell, and Lyndol Mitchell (ERA-1012), Hanson's Excerpts from *Merry Mount*/George Templeton Strong's *Chorale on a Theme of Leo Hassler* and Horatio Parker's *Prelude to Mona* (ERA-1013), and Hanson's *Symphony No. 5* and *The Cherubic Hymn*/Victor Herbert's *Cello Concerto No. 2* (ERA-1014).

ENTRE'ACTE RECORDING SOCIETY, 845 California Street, San Francisco, Calif., specializes in film scores primarily, although it issues non-sound-track albums also. Of interest in the film-score category are Franz Waxman's *Crime in the Streets* coupled with *Music for Jazz Orchestra, Three Sketches,* and

Theme, Variations and Fugato for jazz orchestra, all conducted by the composer (ERM-6001), Max Steiner's *King Kong* (ERS-6504), Johnny Green's *Raintree County* (2-ERS-6503), Waxman's *Spirit of St. Louis* (ERS-6507), Bernard Herrmann's *Sisters* (ERQ-7001), and Hugo Friedhofer's *The Best Years of Our Lives* (EDP-8101). Other discs of interest: Halsey Stevens' *Chamber Music from USC* (ERS-6505) and 2 projected albums of piano music (on a digital disc) with music by Samuel Barber, Leonard Bernstein, Carl Ruggles, Louise Talma, Ross Lee Finney, Andrew Imbrie, Benjamin Lees, and Walter Piston.

FOLKWAYS RECORDS & SERVICE CORP., 43 West 61st Street, New York, N.Y., 10023, has released dozens of albums devoted to the folk music of the world, including that of the United States (also: Indian music). Folkways' jazz catalog is extensive and should be explored. Other items of interest: *Music for the Colonial Band* (FTS-32378), *The Cradle of Harmony*, fiddle music by William Sidney Mount (FTS-32379), *Music for the Colonial Orchestra* (FTS-32380), *The New England Harmony*, early American choral music (FA-2377), and 4 albums devoted to *New American Music* (FTS-33901, 33902, 33903, and 33904). Fascinating but perhaps difficult listening (for some). Also: *Joseph Lamb: A Study in Classic Ragtime* (FG-3562), *Zez Confrey*, piano music (RF-28), and James P. Johnson's *Yamekraw* performed by the composer (FJ-2842).

GOLDEN CREST RECORDS, 220 Broadway, Huntington Station, N.Y., 11746, has a varied catalog. Such composers as the oft-recorded Copland may be found among the lesser-known Donald Martino, William Kraft, and the too-neglected Arthur Foote. An album of piano music, recorded by Grant Johannesen, collects pieces by Roy Harris, Copland, Norman Dello Joio, and William Bergsma. Golden Crest has announced an "Authenticated Composers Series," which will feature composer-led or supervised recordings. A fascinating, but not all-American album, is *From Rags to Jazz* (CRS-31042) in which the New England Conservatory Ragtime Ensemble, led by Gunther Schuller, performs a good number of rags by all the great ragtime composers from Joplin to Artie Matthews (his beautiful *Pastime Rag No. 4*) as well as small works by Stravinsky and Satie.

GRENADILLA RECORDS, 345 Park Avenue South, New York, N.Y., 10010, releases a lot of American music. An especially worthy album couples Roy Harris' *Concerto for Piano, Clarinet and String Quartet* with David Diamond's 1950 *Quintet* (GS-1007). Other contemporaries featured on Grenadilla are Ned Rorem, Vincent Persichetti, Irwin Bazelon, Michael Colgrass, and Andrew Imbrie, among others.

HNH RECORDS, INC., P. O. Box 222, Evanston, Ill., 60204, has its own label and is also the American distributor of the English Unicorn Records. An excellent HNH release is devoted to the *Trios* by Charles Ives and Roy Harris (HNH-4070). There are some fine Samuel Barber performances by the London Symphony of the *Symphony in One Movement,* the 2 *Essays* for orchestra and *Night Flight,* a section from Barber's now-discarded *Second Symphony* (RHS-342). Unicorn has also recorded much music by Bernard Herrmann in composer-conducted performances. These include *The Devil and Daniel Webster / Welles Raises Kane,* from film scores (UNS-237), the cantata *Moby Dick* (UNS-255), *Symphony* (RHS-331), and the opera *Wuthering Heights* (UNB-400).

IN SYNC LABORATORIES, 2211 Broadway, New York, N.Y., 10024. See Connoisseur Society.

LIBRARY OF CONGRESS, RECORDING LABORATORY, Washington, D.C., 20540, is one of the finest sources for authentic American folk music recordings. An important series, among many, is entitled *Folk Music in America* and runs to 15 volumes. There are others devoted to Anglo-American folk song, Afro-American folk song, jazz, etc. The Library issues a catalog that details the content of the recordings. A valuable series is called *The Ballad Hunter,* a gathering of 10 radio lectures by the great folklorist John A. Lomax, complete with illustrations from the Library's vast folk-song collection. The recordings run from record number AAFS L49 through AAFS L53.

LOUISVILLE FIRST EDITION, Louisville Orchestra, 333 West Broadway, Louisville, Ky., features a rich collection of American as well as other contemporary music. Virtually every kind of American music is represented in the catalog. A few examples will illustrate the flavor: Elliott Carter's *Variations for Orchestra*/Everett Helm's *Piano Concerto No. 2* (L-583), Roger Goeb's *Concertino for Orchestra II*/Gail Kubik's *Symphony No. 2* (L-585), Robert Kurka's *Symphony No. 2* (L-616), Walter Piston's *Symphony No. 5*/William Kraft's *Concerto Grosso* (L-653), George Crumb's *Echoes of Time and the River* (L-711), Ned Rorem's *Piano Concerto in Six Movements* (L-733), and a complete (as opposed to the suite) version of Walter Piston's ballet *The Incredible Flutist* (LS-755). Piston's *Symphony No. 1* is coupled with Harris' zestful *When Johnny Comes Marching Home Overture* on LS-766.

MARK56 RECORDS, P. O. Box 1, Anaheim, Calif., 92805, has been releasing vintage radio shows but also has issued many treasurable collections of music. *Gershwin by Gershwin* (641, a 2-record set) collects assorted Gershwiniana such as Gershwin's piano roll performance of the *Rhapsody in Blue,* excerpts from the *Concerto in F* with Gershwin at the piano, 2 complete broadcasts of Gershwin's radio show from 1934, a rehearsal of the *Second Rhapsody* with Gershwin at the piano and conducting, and an inimitable rendition of a little-known Gershwin song, "Hi-Ho," by Ira Gershwin accompanied by Harold Arlen. *Gershwin Conducts Excerpts from "Porgy and Bess"* (667) features Gershwin conducting an informal rehearsal of his opera with members of the original 1935 cast. The record also contains some early Gershwin piano rolls and an appearance on the Rudy Vallee show, "The Fleischmann Hour," on which he performs songs and the *Second Piano Prelude. Gershwin . . . From*

Tin Pan Alley to Broadway (680, 2-record set) features 20 Gershwin piano rolls cut by Gershwin between about 1916 and 1925. There are songs by Irving Berlin, Jerome Kern—and 8 by Gershwin. *Harold Arlen Sings* (683, 2-record set) brings together a number of Harold Arlen vocal-piano performances of his songs (there are also some orchestral accompaniments led by Peter Matz). Two sides are devoted to a demonstration disc of songs from the musical *Jamaica,* sung by Arlen with Matz at one of the pianos. *"Fine and Dandy":* *The Music of Kay Swift* (700, 2-record set) brings together songs ("Can't We Be Friends?," "Fine and Dandy," "Can This Be Love?," etc.), orchestral pieces, including *Reaching for the Brass Ring,* a cycle of songs sung by Louise Carlyle, and instrumentals with the composer at the piano. Other worthy Mark56 albums to look into feature W. C. Handy reminiscing, singing, and playing; another gives us the irrepressible Louis Armstrong talking about life and art; Victor Herbert may be heard on discs transcribed from old Edison records (there is a fine series of Edison restorations, some featuring early show business and vaudeville personalities).

MONMOUTH-EVERGREEN RECORDS, 1697 Broadway, New York, N.Y., 10019, has many an interesting, and often rare, item in its catalog. Among the highlights is *Jerome Kern/All the Things You Are* (MES-6808) featuring songs from the composer's later years, including a half dozen gems from the unsuccessful *Very Warm for May. Through the Years with Vincent Youmans* (MES-6401/2, a 2-record set) brings together nearly 40 songs by this too neglected popular composer. *Lee Wiley Sings Rodgers & Hart and Harold Arlen* is a reissue of a couple of fine albums from the 1940s (MES-6807); classic performances by a remarkable stylist with sensitive jazz band backings. Monmouth-Evergreen has also reissued a number of original cast albums of London productions of American musicals. *George Gershwin: An American in London* (MES-7071) is a collection of songs from Gershwin's first London success, *Primrose,* as well as several piano solos by the composer. Other albums in this series: Kern's *Sally* (MES-7053) and Gershwin's *Lady, Be Good* (MES-7036) with Fred and Adele Astaire and Gershwin at the piano in some selections. Also: Gershwin's *Tip-Toes* (MES-7052), Gershwin's *Oh, Kay!* (MES-7043) with the original "Kay," Gertrude Lawrence, Gershwin's *Funny Face* (MES-7037) with the Astaires and a side devoted to Gershwin in piano solos. Not to be missed is *For George and Ira* (MES-7060) an album of Gershwin songs sung by the Gershwins' sister, Frances Godowsky.

MUSICAL HERITAGE SOCIETY, 14 Park Road, Tinton Falls, N.J., 07724, is a mail-order "classical music" specialty house which releases a great number of offbeat albums at most reasonable prices. A smattering of this company's Americana is quite fascinating: 3 volumes of American organ music from the *Eighteenth Century* (MHS 262K), *Nineteenth Century* (MHS 263F), and the *Twentieth Century* (MHS 264Z), orchestral pieces by Robert Ward (MHS-1600), chamber works of Daniel Gregory Mason (MHS-3143), *String Quartet No. 4* and other chamber works of William Bergsma (MHS-3533), *The Flute in American Music* from Benjamin Carr to Aaron Copland (MHS-3578), Francis Hopkinson's *The Temple of Minerva* (MHS-3684), Daniel Bayley's *A New Royal Harmony* (MHS-3686), Arthur Farwell's *Piano Quintet, Op. 103* (MHS-3827), *Harp of Joy,* a collection of Quaker hymns (MHS-4070), and several albums devoted to the music of Tibor Serly, from songs to chamber and orchestral works: MHS-3306, MHS-3337, MHS-3360, MHS-3447, and MHS-3590.

MUSIC MASTERS, 25 West 43rd Street, New York, N.Y., 10036, is a record shop dealing in often rare records as well as privately printed reissues of long-gone recordings, sound tracks, and composer performances. Catalogs are issued. A sampling of Music Masters wares: *Johnny Mercer Sings, Harold Arlen in Hollywood, Jerome Kern in Hollywood* (2 2-record sets), *The Gershwins in Hollywood, Rodgers and Hart in Hollywood,* etc. Most of the material is taken from the original sound tracks. The records are not cheap (the last price I heard was $12 per disc—and most are 2-record sets).

NEW WORLD RECORDS, Recorded Anthology of American Music, Inc., 231 East 51st Street, New York, N.Y., 10022, has issued over 100 albums of American music of great variety ranging from popular song to avant-garde; also included are the music of the American Indian, bluegrass, jazz (from traditional to modern), gospel, period songs (Civil War, Depression, World War II), etc. Among the choice albums: *White Spirituals from The Sacred Harp* (NW 205), *The Music of Arthur Farwell, Preston Ware Orem and Charles Cadman* (NW 213), *Songs by Samuel Barber and Ned Rorem* (NW 229), *The Vintage Irving Berlin* (NW 238), *American Opera* (NW 241), *Music for the Dance,* ballets by William Schuman and Morton Gould (NW 253), *Cuttin' the Boogie* (NW 259), John Knowles Paine's *Mass in D* (NW 262/263), *Composers of the New Music Edition,* John Becker, Henry Cowell, Ruth Crawford Seeger, and Wallingford Riegger (NW 285), works by *Charles T. Griffes* (NW 273), Virgil Thomson's opera *The Mother of Us All* (NW 288/289), Roger Sessions' *When Lilacs Last in the Dooryard Bloom'd* (NW 296), *Twentieth Century Song,* Charles Ives, Norman Dello Joio, Irving Fine, Robert Ward, Theodore Chanler (NW 300), and many more.

NONESUCH RECORDS, 665 Fifth Avenue, New York, N.Y., 10022, was one of the most adventurous of all record companies; "was" because of an upper level shakeup early in 1980 which led to the unceremonious dumping (no more graceful word will do) of Teresa Sterne, whose gift for imaginative, exploratory work in the artist and repertory field was remarkably creative. But record companies are more interested in profits (large ones, that is) and perhaps the innovative releases produced under the aegis of Ms. Sterne did not turn a large return. It would be impossible to list all of the Americana that was issued during her long stay (Nonesuch's best years), but here is a sampling: *Rivers of Delight,* American Folk Hymns from the Sacred Harp Tradition (H-71360), *Early American Vocal Music,* New England Anthems and Southern Folk

Hymns (H-71276), *After the Ball,* A Treasury of Turn-of-the-Century Popular Songs, sung by Joan Morris accompanied by William Bolcom (H-71304), *Vaudeville Songs of the Great Ladies of the Musical Stage,* Morris and Bolcom again (H-71330), *19th-Century Ballroom Music* (H-71313), *Who Shall Rule This American Nation?,* Songs of the Civil War Era by Henry Clay Work (H-71317), Charles Ives's *Piano Sonata No. 2,* the "Concord," performed by Gilbert Kalish (H-71337), *Charles Ives Songs,* beautifully sung by Jan De Gaetani (H-71325), and Charles Ives's *Four Violin and Piano Sonatas* played by Paul Zukofsky (violin and Kalish [HB-73025]). The wide range of practically up-to-the-moment composition would also require pages, but here are a few, at random: George Rochberg's *Spring Quartet No. 3* (H-71283), George Crumb's *Ancient Voices of Children* (H-71255), Morton Subotnick's *Silver Apples of the Moon* for synthesizer, a Nonesuch—i.e., T. Sterne—commission (H-71174), Charles Wuorinen's *Time's Ecomium* (H-71225), a collection of works by Milton Babbitt, T. J. Anderson, and Richard Wernick (H-71303), and Frederic Rzewski's *Song and Dance*/John Harbison's *The Flower-Fed Buffaloes* (H-71366). Not to be overlooked is Nonesuch's ragtime collection, much of it devoted to the works of Scott Joplin. Some of the works by the lesser-known ragtime composers may be found, performed by William Bolcom, in *Heliotrope Bouquet* (H-71257); *Pastimes and Piano Rags,* also by Bolcom, collects several rags by Artie Matthews and James Scott (H-71299).

ORION MASTER RECORDINGS, INC., 5840 Busch Drive, Malibu, Calif., 90265, a relatively new company, has an impressive catalog, varied and wide-ranging. Among its American releases are several albums devoted to the music of David Van Vactor (6910, 7024, 7025/2, 7029). William Grant Still is represented by albums of chamber works (7152, 7278), and Elie Siegmeister has an album of chamber works (7284) and orchestral music, one work being the evocative, Gershwin-like *Sunday in Brooklyn* (73116). Also: The *Complete Works of George Antheil for Violin and Piano* (73119), Dane Rudhyar's *Syntony* and *Third Pentagram* for piano (7285), pianist Leon Bates playing MacDowell's *Piano Sonata No. 4,* Samuel Barber's *Excursions* and George Walker's *Sonata No. 3* (76237), an attractive piano and violin sonata album of works by Arthur Foote and John Alden Carpenter (76243), Phillip Rhodes's cantata, *The Morning of Christ's Nativity/Five Mountain Songs* (77276), Leo Ornstein's *Biography Sonata* for piano (78285), an album by vocalist Anita Ellis, accompanied by pianist Ellis Larkins, in a program of American popular song, *A Legend Sings* (79358), and the historic first recordings, conducted by Nicolas Slonimsky, of works by Edgard Varèse, Charles Ives, and Carl Ruggles. Varèse's *Ionization* is especially interesting because the recording itself was supervised by Roy Harris; Carlos Salzedo, Henry Cowell, Paul Creston, Wallingford Riegger, William Schuman, and Varèse performed on the various percussion instruments in the orchestra (Orion 7150).

THE SMITHSONIAN COLLECTION, Division of the Performing Arts, Smithsonian Institution, Washington, D.C., 20560, issues, and reissues, well-recorded albums at reasonable prices. Among the prizes are *The Smithsonian Collection of Classic Jazz,* from Scott Joplin's piano roll of *Maple Leaf Rag* to Ornette Coleman's *Lonely Woman* (6 long-playing records, No. 2100), and *Music of Victor Herbert,* with Herbert conducting many sides and performing a cello solo and many vintage soloists in Herbert songs (3-record set, No. 2017). There are many excellent reconstructions of American musicals by, mainly, their original casts. In no special order these include *Ziegfeld Follies of 1919* (No. 2009), *Souvenirs of Hot Chocolates* (No. 2012), Gershwin's *Lady, Be Good!* (No. 2008) and *Oh, Kay!* (No. 2011), Cole Porter's *Anything Goes* (No. 2007) and *Let's Face It* and other shows (No. 2016), and the mixed score of Walter Donaldson's *Whoopee* (No. 2014). There are also reissues of rare Duke Ellington records (Nos. 2003, 2010, 2015, all 2-record sets), *Dizzy Gillespie* (2-record set, No. 2004), *John Kirby* (2-record set, No. 2013), *King Oliver* (2-record set, No. 2001), *Louis Armstrong and Earl Hines/1928* (2-record set, No. 2002), *Teddy Wilson* (No. 2005), *Fletcher Henderson* (2-record set, No. 2006), and reconstructions of Jelly Roll Morton's piano performances (No. 1003) and groups (No. 1006). There is also a charming album entitled *Classic Rags and Ragtime Songs* conducted by composer T. J. Anderson (No. 1001). An album entitled *There's a Good Time Coming* collects a number of the songs by the Hutchinson Family of the pre-Civil War period (No. 1020). Of interest also: *Music from the Age of Jefferson,* performed on instruments of the time (No. 1002).

SOCIETY FOR THE PRESERVATION OF THE AMERICAN MUSICAL HERITAGE, P. O. Box 4244, Grand Central Station, New York, N.Y., 10017, concentrates on neglected American music, with emphasis on the 19th century. However, several albums are devoted to early music: *Catholic Mission Music in California* (MIA-96), *Ballads in Colonial America* (MIA-97), Raynor Taylor's *Six Sonatas* for cello and piano (MIA-108), Benjamin Franklin's *String Quartet* (MIA-117), and an album of piano music by Alexander Reinagle, Raynor Taylor, and James Hewitt (MIA-126). From the 19th century there are symphonies by George Frederick Bristow (MIA-135, 143, 144), works for flute by poet-composer Sidney Lanier (MIA-117), *Symphonies 1* and *2* by John Knowles Paine (MIA-103, 120), Arthur Foote's *Suite in D Minor for Orchestra* (MIA-122) and piano music (MIA-123), George Whitefield Chadwick's *Second* and *Third Symphonies* (MIA-134, 140), Horatio Parker's *A Northern Ballad* (MIA-132), Mrs. H. H. A. Beach's *Symphony in E Minor* (MIA-139), and much orchestral MacDowell. From the early 20th century the Society has issued music by Griffes (MIA-104, 117, 129), and Leroy Robertson is represented by a *String Quartet* (MIA-115) and excerpts from his oratorio from *The Book of Mormon* (MIA-111).

TURNABOUT / VOX, Moss Music Group, 211 East 43rd Street, New York, N.Y., 10017, has produced a number of comprehensive (and inexpensive) boxed sets of musical Americana. Among the most impressive albums are those made by the Gregg Smith Singers that cover nearly 200 years of vocal composition. The survey begins with *America Sings: The Founding Years* (*1620–1800*) in album SVBX 5350, a 3-record set. There are songs from early psalters, the Bay Psalm Book, music of the Moravians and songs by William Billings, James Lyon, and Francis Hopkinson. Another volume is subtitled *The Great Sentimental Age* (SVBX-5304, 3-record set) and runs the vocal gamut from Stephen Foster to Charles Ives, with contributions also from George F. Root, Walter Kittredge, and others. *America Sings: 1920–1950* (SVBX-5353, 3-record set) collects songs and choral works by Ives, Irving Fine (a beautiful work entitled *The Choral New Yorker*), William Schuman, Louise Talma, George Gershwin (two madrigal spoofs), Aaron Copland, Lukas Foss, others. *American Choral Music After 1950* (SVBX-5354, 3-record set) brings on the moderns: Elliott Carter, Andrew Imbrie, Paul Chihara, Ned Rorem, Jacob Druckman, and Gregg Smith in the role of composer. Other boxed collections worth investigating are *Homespun America* (SVBX-5309) featuring "Marches, Waltzes, Polkas & Serenades" by the Manchester Cornet Band, "Music for the Social Orchestra" by the Manchester Quadrille Orchestra, and "Songs of 19th Century Patriotism, Temperance & Abolition & Popular Sentimental Tunes of the Hutchinson Family Singers." A survey of American piano music is presented in 2 3-record sets. *Piano Music in America: 19th Century Concert & Parlor Music* (SVBX-5302) ranges from Anonymous through Louis Moreau Gottschalk, Anthony Philip Heinrich, and George Bristow. The 2nd volume, *1900–1945* (SVBX-5303), is a compilation of such composers as Edward MacDowell, Roy Harris, Charles Ives, Aaron Copland, 16 composers in all. *The Early String Quartet in the U.S.A.* (SVBX-5301) contains Benjamin Franklin's (?) *String Quartet,* Charlers T. Griffes' fine *Two Indian Sketches,* and works by Daniel Gregory Mason, Arthur Foote, George W. Chadwick, Henry Hadley (actually a quintet, with piano), and Charles Martin Loeffler. *American String Quartets: 1900–1950* (SVBX-5305) is a collection of pieces by Aaron Copland, Charles Ives, Howard Hanson, Virgil Thomson, William Schuman, Walter Piston, Roger Sessions, and Peter Mennin. A collection devoted to more recent quartets by Lejaren Hiller, John Cage, Morton Feldman, Leon Kirchner, George Crumb, and others is also a 3-record set: SVBX-5306. Vox has also issued in an admirable *Contemporary Composer in the U.S.A.* series some quite unusual works. Only a few can be noted here: Morton Subotnick's *Lamination* for orchestra/John Eaton's *Concert Piece for Syn-Ket and Symphony Orchestra*/William Bergsma's *Violin Concerto* (Turnabout TV-S-34428), William Schuman's *Symphony No. 7*/Ned Rorem's *Third Symphony* (TV-S-34447), George Rochberg's *Tableux*/Shulamit Ran's *O the Chimneys* (TV-S-34492), George Rochberg's *String Quartet No. 2*/Robert Suderburg's *Chamber Music II* (TV-S-34524), Lejaren Hiller's *Twelve-tone Variations* for piano, *Machine Music for Piano, Percussion and Tape,* and *Sonata No. 3* for violin and piano (TV-S-34536), Paul Chihara's *Grass* for double bass and orchestra and *Ceremony I* and *Ceremony II* for orchestra (QTV-S-34572), Meyer

Kupferman's *Concerto for Cello, Tape and Orchestra*/ Lou Harrison's *Concerto for Violin and Percussion Orchestra* (QTV-S-34653), Michael Colgrass's *Concertmasters* for 3 violins and orchestra/Karl Korte's *Concerto for Piano and Winds* (TV-34704), Gene Gutchë's *Icarus* for orchestra/Vincent Persichetti's *The Hollow Men* for trumpet and chamber orchestra (TV-34705), and Benjamin Lees's *Violin Concerto*/Robert Starer's *Concerto for Viola, Strings and Percussion* (TV-34692). An album of much charm is devoted to the works of Peggy Coolidge, *American Reflections* (QTV-S-34635), and features her *Rhapsody for Harp and Orchestra, New England Autumn, Pioneer Dances,* and *Spirituals in Sunshine and Shadow.*

VANGUARD RECORDING SOCIETY, 71 West 23rd Street, New York, N.Y., 10010, has released a good number of folk song collections by Joan Baez, jazz (an especially important album, *From Spirituals to Swing* on VSD-47/48, a 2-record set, is devoted to the Carnegie Hall jazz concerts produced by John Hammond in 1938–39), and other musical Americana. An especially endearing album is the recording of Ernest Bloch's "Epic Rhapsody" *America* (SRV-346-SD) conducted by Leopold Stokowski. Bloch himself opens the recording with a delightful commentary on his work and what he intended to say in it. An important recent release by Vanguard is Frederic Rzewski's *The People United Will Never Be Defeated,* 36 variations on a Chilean song for piano, perfectly played by Ursula Oppens (VSD-71248). Works by Peter Schickele— Songs from *The Knight of the Burning Pestle, Elegies* for clarinet and piano, and *Summer Trio* for flute, cello, and piano—are collected on Vanguard VSD-71269. The other side of Schickele can be heard in *The Wurst of P. D. Q. Bach* (Vanguard 719/20, a 2-record set).

VARESE SARABANDE RECORDS, 1801 Avenue of the Stars, Suite 640, Los Angeles, Calif., 90067, is an enterprising, rather recent firm that produces both new recordings and nicely cleaned up (often an improvement on the originals) reissues. Among the latter are William Levi Dawson's *Negro Folk Symphony* (VC-81056) and Leonard Bernstein's *Fancy Free* in the first recording conducted by the composer (VC-81055), coupled with music by the Mexican composer Carlos Chávez. Franz Waxman conducts his *Sinfonietta for Strings and Timpani*/Lukas Foss plays the solo part in his *Piano Concerto No. 2* (VC-81052). Another album collects Don Gillis' *Tulsa: A Symphonic Portrait in Oil,* Peggy Glanville-Hicks's *Three Gymnopedies,* Dane Rudhyar's *Sinfonietta,* and John Freeman's *String Quartet* (VC-81046). Varese Sarabande has begun releasing recordings from the Roy Harris Archive: Harris conducting his *Concerto for Amplified Piano, Brass, String Basses and Percussion;* side 2 contains works for organ, brass, and (in one work) timpani (VC-81085). Another release, also conducted by the composer, features his *Concerto for Piano and Strings,* the *Symphony for Band,* "West Point," and the symphonic overture *Cimarron* (VC-81100). Varese Sarabande has also released recordings in the stunning digital process. One is devoted to works by Morton Gould, who conducts the Latin-American Symphonette in the *Philharmonic Waltzes, Festive Music,* the *Cotillion* from *Fall River Legend,* and *Quickstep* from the *Symphony on Marching Tunes* (VCDM-1000.10).

WESTERN INTERNATIONAL MUSIC, INC., 2859 Holt Avenue, Los Angeles, Calif., 90034 publishes music as well as issues recordings. Among its releases are albums devoted to the music of William Schmidt, *Folksongs in Brass* (WIMR-6), Raynor Brown, *Clarinet Symphony, Concerto* for 2 pianos, brass choir, and percussion (WIMR-8), and *Music of Boris Pillin* (WIMR-11). There is an album entitled *Sharon Davis: Pianist/Composer* (WIMR-13) in which she performs works, with various groups, by Schmidt, Brown, and her own *Though Men Call Us Free* for soprano, clarinet, and piano. More music by Schmidt is recorded on *Songs of Early America: Sacred and Profane* (WIMR-15).

A brief afterword: I should like to make note of FLYING FISH RECORDS, INC., 1304 West Schubert, Chicago, Ill., 60614, which releases recordings of works by David Amram. Flying Fish GRO-751 contains his *Triple Concerto* for woodwind, brass, jazz quintets, and orchestra coupled with *Elegy* for violin and orchestra.

POSEIDON RECORDS, 888 Seventh Avenue, New York, N.Y., 10019, is engaged in making new recordings and reissuing the compositions of Alan Hovhaness. Several symphonies have been released; of special interest is his *Magnificat* for 4 solo voices, chorus, and orchestra (Poseidon 1018).

And, finally, Steve Reich's *Music for 18 Musicians* has been released on ECM Records and is distributed by Warner Bros. Records, 3 East 54th Street, New York, N.Y., 10022. The number of the album is ECM-1-1129.

Index

Boldface figures refer to the main biographical entry in the text.